# Colour
# Oxford
# Thesaurus

**THIRD EDITION**

*Edited by*
Maurice Waite

OXFORD
UNIVERSITY PRESS

# OXFORD
UNIVERSITY PRESS

Great Clarendon Street, Oxford OX2 6DP

Oxford University Press is a department of the University of Oxford.
It furthers the University's objective of excellence in research, scholarship,
and education by publishing worldwide in

Oxford  New York

Auckland  Cape Town  Dar es Salaam  Hong Kong  Karachi
Kuala Lumpur  Madrid  Melbourne  Mexico City  Nairobi
New Delhi  Shanghai  Taipei  Toronto

With offices in

Argentina  Austria  Brazil  Chile  Czech Republic  France  Greece
Guatemala  Hungary  Italy  Japan  Poland  Portugal  Singapore
South Korea  Switzerland  Thailand  Turkey  Ukraine  Vietnam

Oxford is a registered trade mark of Oxford University Press
in the UK and in certain other countries

Published in the United States
by Oxford University Press Inc., New York

© Oxford University Press 2002, 2006

Database right Oxford University Press (makers)

First edition, entitled *Oxford Colour Thesaurus*, 1995
Second edition 2002
Third edition 2006

British Library Cataloguing in Publication Data

Data available

Library of Congress Cataloging in Publication Data

Data available

ISBN 978-0-19-861451-7   0-19-861451-9
ISBN 978-0-19-861450-0   0-19-861450-0 (US edn)

10 9 8 7 6 5 4 3

Typeset in Frutiger and Parable
by Interactive Sciences Ltd, Gloucester
Printed in Germany by Clausen & Bosse

# Contents

# Preface

Everyone occasionally finds that the right word will not come to them, and that is when a good thesaurus is essential.

You may have a word in mind but you know that it is not the right word because it does not accurately express what you want to say. In short, you want to find out how you can express something better.

Or perhaps you need to find alternatives when you wish to avoid using the same word again and again when speaking or writing.

Or you might be looking for a more modern or more formal equivalent that would be better suited to your audience and purpose.

The word *thesaurus* comes from Greek, meaning 'storehouse' or 'treasure'. A thesaurus will open up to you the vast riches of the English language by giving you lists of words with similar meaning (called 'synonyms'), providing an array of choices as well as ways of pinpointing the right word.

This thesaurus will be particularly useful for secondary school students, especially at Key Stages 3 and 4 of the UK National Curriculum. It includes a brand-new guide called 'How to use a thesaurus' in the blue-edged central section to help you get the most out of the thesaurus and make your English more effective.

In a tough, take-anywhere binding and with a clear, two-colour layout, this book is a perfect companion for all your writing needs, whether for schoolwork, crosswords and puzzle-solving, or just everyday quick reference.

# Guide to the thesaurus entry

For more help, see 'How to use a thesaurus' in the central section of the book.

example of use, to help distinguish different senses

headword

**cheerful adjective 1** *he arrived looking cheerful:* happy, jolly, merry, bright, sunny, joyful, in good/high spirits, buoyant, cheery, animated, smiling, good-humoured; informal chipper, chirpy, full of beans. **2** *a cheerful room:* pleasant, attractive, agreeable, bright, sunny, friendly, welcoming.
OPPOSITES sad, gloomy.

words meaning the opposite of the headword; most have entries of their own, where a wider choice will be found

numbered sense of the headword

core synonym— the closest synonym to the headword

part of speech of the headword

**everywhere adverb** all over, all around, in every nook and cranny, far and wide, near and far, high and low, {here, there, and everywhere}, the world over, worldwide; informal all over the place; Brit. informal all over the shop; N. Amer. informal all over the map.
OPPOSITES nowhere.

brackets around a phrase, to avoid confusion

**infant noun** baby, newborn, young child, tiny tot, little one; Medicine neonate; Scottish & N. English bairn, wean; informal tiny, sprog.

label indicating the specialist field in which the following synonym is used

label indicating the level or style of English in which the following synonyms are used (*see opposite for explanations*)

label indicating the region of the world in which the following synonyms are used (*see opposite for abbreviations*)

# Guide to the thesaurus entry

**root** noun **1** *the root of the problem:* source, origin, cause, reason, basis, foundation, bottom, seat. **2** (roots) origins, beginnings, family, birth, heritage.

*form of the headword for which synonyms are given*

**verb** *he rooted around in the cupboard:* rummage, hunt, search, rifle, delve, forage, dig, nose, poke.

*phrase for which synonyms are given*

■ **root something out** eradicate, eliminate, weed out, destroy, wipe out, stamp out, abolish, end, put a stop to.

**seldom** adverb rarely, infrequently, hardly (ever), scarcely (ever); informal once in a blue moon.
OPPOSITES often.

*brackets to show more than one possibility: hardly and hardly ever*

Most of the synonyms are part of standard English, but some are used only in certain styles or situations. These are grouped at the end of their sense and have labels in front of them:

informal, e.g. *swig*: normally only used in speech or informal writing.

formal, e.g. *dwelling*: normally only used in writing, such as official documents.

literary, e.g. *wondrous*.

historical, e.g. *serfdom*: only used today to refer to things that are no longer part of modern life.

archaic, e.g. *apothecary*: not in use today except for old-fashioned effect.

Synonyms are also labelled if they are exclusively or mainly British (abbreviated to Brit.), Northern English (N. English), Scottish, North American (N. Amer.), Australian (Austral.), or New Zealand (NZ).

## Note on trademarks and proprietary status

This thesaurus includes some words which have, or are asserted to have, proprietary status as trademarks or otherwise. Their inclusion does not imply that they have acquired for legal purposes a non-proprietary or general significance, nor any other judgement concerning their legal status. In cases where the editorial staff have some evidence that a word has proprietary status this is indicated by the label trademark, but no judgement concerning the legal status of such words is made or implied thereby.

**abandon** verb **1** *he abandoned his wife:* desert, leave, turn one's back on, cast aside, finish with, jilt, throw over; informal walk/run out on, dump, ditch; literary forsake. **2** *she had abandoned painting:* give up, stop, have done with; informal pack in, quit; Brit. informal jack in. **3** *they abandoned the car:* leave (behind), vacate, dump, quit, evacuate, discard, jettison. **4** *the party abandoned those policies:* renounce, relinquish, dispense with, discard, give up, drop; informal ditch, scrap, junk; formal forswear.
OPPOSITES keep, continue, retain.
noun *with reckless abandon:* uninhibitedness, recklessness, lack of restraint, lack of inhibition.
OPPOSITES self-control.

**abate** verb *the storm had abated:* subside, die down/away/out, lessen, ease (off), let up, decrease, diminish, fade, weaken.
OPPOSITES intensify.

**abatement** noun **1** *the storm still rages with no sign of abatement:* subsiding, dying down/away/out, lessening, easing (off), let-up. **2** *noise abatement:* reduction, control.

**abbreviate** verb shorten, reduce, cut, contract, condense, compress, abridge.
OPPOSITES lengthen, expand.

**abbreviation** noun short form, contraction, acronym, initialism.

**abdicate** verb resign, retire, stand down, step down, renounce the throne.

**abdomen** noun stomach, belly, gut, middle; informal tummy, guts; Austral. informal bingy.

**abdominal** adjective gastric, intestinal, stomach, duodenal, visceral, coeliac, ventral.

**abduct** verb kidnap, carry off, seize, capture, run away/off with; informal snatch.

**aberration** noun anomaly, deviation, abnormality, irregularity, variation, freak, oddity, peculiarity, curiosity, mistake.

**abhor** verb hate, detest, loathe, despise, regard with disgust, shudder at; formal abominate.
OPPOSITES love, admire.

**abhorrent** adjective hateful, detestable, loathsome, abominable, repellent, repugnant, repulsive, revolting, disgusting, horrible, horrid, horrifying, awful, heinous.
OPPOSITES admirable.

**abide** verb **1** (informal) *I can't abide smoke:* stand, bear; Brit. informal stick. **2** *one memory will abide:* continue, remain, survive, last, persist, live on.
■ **abide by** comply with, obey, observe, follow, keep to, adhere to, stick to, go along with, heed, accept.

**abiding** adjective enduring, lasting, everlasting, perpetual, eternal, unending, permanent.
OPPOSITES short-lived, ephemeral.

**ability** noun **1** *the ability to read:* capacity, capability, power,

faculty, facility, wherewithal, means. **2** *leadership ability:* talent, skill, aptitude, expertise, savoir faire, prowess, accomplishment, competence, proficiency, flair, gift, knack, genius; informal know-how.
OPPOSITES inability.

**able** adjective **1** *able to resume his duties:* capable of, competent to, up to, fit to, in a position to, allowed to, free to. **2** *an able student:* intelligent, clever, talented, skilful, skilled, accomplished, gifted, proficient, apt, adroit, adept, capable, competent.
OPPOSITES incompetent, incapable.

**abnormal** adjective unusual, uncommon, atypical, untypical, unrepresentative, irregular, anomalous, deviant, aberrant, freak, strange, odd, peculiar, bizarre, weird, unnatural, perverted, twisted, warped; informal funny, freaky, kinky.
OPPOSITES normal, typical, common.

**abnormality** noun oddity, strangeness, irregularity, anomaly, deviation, aberration, deformity, defect, malformation.
OPPOSITES normality.

**abolish** verb put an end to, get rid of, scrap, cancel, end, remove, dissolve, stop, ban; informal do away with, ditch.
OPPOSITES retain, create.

**abolition** noun scrapping, ending, cancellation, dissolution, removal.
OPPOSITES retention, creation.

**abominable** adjective loathsome, detestable, hateful, obnoxious, despicable, contemptible, disgusting, revolting, repellent, repulsive, repugnant, abhorrent, reprehensible, atrocious, foul, vile, wretched, horrible, awful, dreadful, appalling, nauseating; informal terrible, shocking, God-awful; Brit. informal beastly.
OPPOSITES good, admirable.

**abort** verb **1** miscarry, have a miscarriage, terminate. **2** *the crew aborted the take-off:* halt, stop, end, call off, abandon, discontinue, terminate, arrest; informal pull the plug on.

**abortion** noun termination, miscarriage.

**abortive** adjective unsuccessful, failed, vain, ineffective, ineffectual, unproductive.
OPPOSITES successful, fruitful.

**abound** verb **1** *cafes abound in the narrow streets:* be plentiful, be abundant, be numerous, be thick on the ground; informal grow on trees, be two/ten a penny. **2** *a stream which abounded with trout:* be full of, overflow with, teem with, be packed with, be crowded with; informal be stuffed with, be chock-a-block with.

**about** preposition *a book about Greece:* regarding, concerning, referring to, with regard to, with respect to, relating to, on, touching on, dealing with, on the subject of.
adverb **1** *there were babies crawling about:* around, here and there, to and fro, back and forth, in all directions. **2** *he was about somewhere:* near, nearby, around, hereabouts, in the vicinity, in the neighbourhood. **3** *about £15,000:* approximately, roughly, around, in the region of, circa, of the order of, or so, or thereabouts, more or less; Brit. getting on for; N. Amer. informal in

the ballpark of.

**above** preposition **1** over, higher (up) than, on top of, on. **2** *those above the Colonel:* superior to, senior to, over, higher (up) than, more powerful than, in charge of, commanding.
OPPOSITES below.
adverb overhead, on/at the top, high up, on high, up above, (up) in the sky.
■ **above all** most importantly, most of all, chiefly, primarily, first and foremost, essentially, in essence, at bottom; informal at the end of the day, when all is said and done.

**abrasion** noun **1** *he had abrasions to his forehead:* graze, cut, scrape, scratch, gash, laceration. **2** *the metal is resistant to abrasion:* erosion, wearing away/down.

**abrasive** adjective **1** *abrasive kitchen cleaners:* rough, coarse, harsh, scratchy. **2** *her abrasive manner:* curt, brusque, sharp, harsh, rough.
OPPOSITES gentle, friendly.

**abridge** verb shorten, cut (down), edit, abbreviate, condense, compress, truncate, prune, summarize, precis; (**abridged**) concise.
OPPOSITES extend.

**abroad** adverb overseas, out of the country, to/in foreign parts, to/in a foreign country/land.

**abrupt** adjective **1** *an abrupt halt:* sudden, rapid, quick, unexpected, unanticipated, unforeseen, precipitate. **2** *an abrupt manner:* curt, brusque, blunt, short, rude, sharp, terse, brisk, unceremonious.
OPPOSITES gradual, gentle.

**absence** noun **1** *his absence from the office:* non-attendance, absenteeism, truancy, leave, holiday, vacation, sabbatical. **2** *the absence of activity:* lack, want, non-existence, unavailability, scarcity, shortage, dearth.
OPPOSITES presence.

**absent** adjective **1** *she was absent from work:* away, off, out, elsewhere, off duty, on holiday, on leave; informal AWOL. **2** *symptoms were absent:* non-existent, lacking, missing. **3** *an absent look:* distracted, preoccupied, inattentive, vague, absorbed, dreamy, faraway, blank, empty, vacant.
OPPOSITES present, attentive, alert.
■ **absent oneself** stay away, be absent, go away, leave, withdraw.

**absent-minded** adjective forgetful, distracted, scatterbrained, preoccupied, inattentive; informal with a mind/ memory like a sieve.

**absolute** adjective **1** *absolute silence | an absolute disgrace:* complete, total, utter, out-and-out, outright, perfect, pure, thorough, unqualified, unreserved, downright, unmitigated, sheer. **2** *absolute power:* unlimited, unrestricted, unrestrained, infinite, total, supreme, unconditional. **3** *an absolute ruler:* autocratic, dictatorial, all-powerful, omnipotent, supreme.
OPPOSITES partial, qualified, limited, democratic.

**absolutely** adverb completely, totally, utterly, perfectly, entirely, wholly, fully, quite, thoroughly, unreservedly, definitely, certainly, unquestionably, undoubtedly, without (a) doubt, without question, in every way/respect,

one hundred per cent.
OPPOSITES partially.

**absorb** verb **1** *a material which absorbs water:* soak up, suck up, draw up/in, take up/in, mop up. **2** *she was absorbed in her book:* engross, captivate, occupy, preoccupy, engage, rivet, grip, hold, immerse, involve, enthral, spellbind, fascinate.

**absorbent** adjective spongy, sponge-like, porous, permeable.

**absorbing** adjective fascinating, interesting, captivating, gripping, engrossing, compelling, compulsive, enthralling, riveting, spellbinding; informal unputdownable.
OPPOSITES boring.

**absorption** noun **1** *the absorption of water:* soaking up, sucking up. **2** *her total absorption in the music:* involvement, immersion, raptness, preoccupation, captivation, fascination, enthralment.

**abstain** verb **1** *he abstained from wine:* refrain, desist, forbear, give up, renounce, avoid, eschew, forgo, go/do without, refuse, decline; informal cut out. **2** *one member abstained:* not vote, decline to vote.

**abstemious** adjective moderate, restrained, temperate, self-disciplined, self-restrained, sober, austere, ascetic, puritanical, spartan.
OPPOSITES self-indulgent.

**abstinence** noun self-denial, self-restraint, teetotalism, temperance, sobriety, abstemiousness.

**abstract** adjective *abstract concepts:* theoretical, conceptual, intellectual, metaphysical, philosophical, academic.
OPPOSITES actual, concrete.
noun *an abstract of her speech:* summary, synopsis, precis, résumé, outline; N. Amer. wrap-up.

**abstruse** adjective obscure, arcane, esoteric, rarefied, recondite, difficult, hard, cryptic, over/above one's head, incomprehensible, unfathomable, impenetrable.

**absurd** adjective irrational, illogical, inappropriate, ridiculous, ludicrous, farcical, comical, stupid, foolish, silly, pointless, senseless, preposterous; informal crazy, cockeyed; Brit. informal barmy, daft.
OPPOSITES reasonable, sensible.

**abundance** noun plenty, plethora, profusion, exuberance, riot, superabundance.
OPPOSITES lack, scarcity.

**abundant** adjective plentiful, copious, ample, profuse, large, huge, great, bumper, prolific, overflowing, teeming, superabundant; informal galore.
OPPOSITES scarce, sparse.

**abuse** verb **1** *the judge abused his power:* misuse, exploit, take advantage of. **2** *he was accused of abusing women:* mistreat, maltreat, ill-treat, molest, beat, sexually abuse, interfere with. **3** *the referee was abused by players:* insult, be rude to, swear at, shout at.
noun **1** *the abuse of power:* misuse, exploitation. **2** *the abuse of women:* mistreatment, maltreatment, ill-treatment, molestation, beating, sexual abuse. **3** *torrents of abuse:*

insults, expletives, swear words, swearing, name-calling, invective.

**abusive** adjective **1** *abusive language:* insulting, rude, offensive, derogatory, slanderous, libellous. **2** *an abusive husband:* violent, brutal, cruel, harsh, oppressive. OPPOSITES polite, kind.

**abysmal** adjective (informal) terrible, dreadful, awful, frightful, atrocious, disgraceful, lamentable; informal rotten, appalling, pathetic, pitiful, woeful, useless, lousy, dire, poxy, the pits; Brit. informal chronic, shocking.

**academic** adjective **1** *an academic institution:* educational, scholastic. **2** *his academic turn of mind:* scholarly, learned, literary, intellectual, bookish, studious. **3** *only of academic interest:* theoretical, hypothetical, notional, speculative, conjectural, irrelevant, beside the point.
noun *a group of academics:* scholar, intellectual, don, professor, man/woman of letters, thinker; informal egghead; Brit. informal boffin.

**academy** noun educational institution, school, college, university, institute.

**accelerate** verb **1** *the car accelerated:* speed up, go faster, gain momentum, increase speed, pick up speed, gather speed. **2** *sunlight accelerates growth:* hasten, quicken, speed up, further, advance, expedite; informal crank up.
OPPOSITES decelerate, delay.

**acceleration** noun speeding up, quickening, hastening.

**accent** noun **1** *a Scottish accent:*

pronunciation, intonation, enunciation, articulation, inflection. **2** *the accent is on comfort:* emphasis, stress, priority, importance, prominence.

**accept** verb **1** *he accepted a pen as a present:* receive, take, get, obtain, acquire, pick up. **2** *just accept what you're told:* go along with, believe, respect, abide by, defer to, put up with, give in to, resign oneself to; informal buy, swallow.
OPPOSITES refuse, reject.

**acceptable** adjective satisfactory, adequate, reasonable, fair, good enough, sufficient, tolerable, passable.
OPPOSITES unacceptable.

**acceptance** noun **1** *the acceptance of an award:* receipt, receiving, taking. **2** *his acceptance of her ideas:* respect, acknowledgement, belief, toleration, consent, agreement, assent, compliance, acquiescence.

**accepted** adjective recognized, acknowledged, established, traditional, orthodox, agreed, approved, customary, normal, standard.
OPPOSITES unorthodox.

**access** noun **1** *the building has a side access:* entrance, entry, approach, path, drive, way in. **2** *they were denied access to the stadium:* admission, admittance, entry.

**accessible** adjective approachable, attainable, reachable, obtainable, available, understandable, comprehensible, intelligible; informal get-at-able.

**accessory** noun **1** *a car accessory:* extra, add-on, addition, supplement,

a

attachment. **2** *an accessory to murder:* accomplice, abetter, collaborator, co-conspirator, henchman, associate.

**accident** noun **1** *an accident at work:* mishap, misadventure, disaster, tragedy, catastrophe, calamity. **2** *a road accident:* crash, collision, smash, bump, derailment; N. Amer. wreck; informal smash-up, pile-up; Brit. informal shunt. **3** *we met by accident:* chance, fate, fortune, luck, good luck, fluke, coincidence.

**accidental** adjective **1** *accidental death:* chance, coincidental, unexpected, incidental, fortuitous, serendipitous. **2** *accidental damage:* unintentional, unintended, unplanned, inadvertent, unwitting.
OPPOSITES predictable, intentional.

**acclaim** verb *the booklet has been acclaimed by teachers:* praise, applaud, cheer, commend, approve, welcome, hail.
OPPOSITES criticize.
noun *she has won widespread acclaim:* praise, applause, tributes, approval, admiration, congratulations, commendation.
OPPOSITES criticism.

**acclimatize** verb adjust, adapt, get used, familiarize oneself, find one's feet, get one's bearings; N. Amer. acclimate.

**accommodate** verb **1** *refugees were accommodated in army camps:* lodge, house, put up, billet, board. **2** *the cottages accommodate six people:* hold, take, have room for, sleep, seat. **3** *we tried to accommodate her:* help, assist, oblige, cater for, fit

in with, satisfy.

**accommodating** adjective obliging, cooperative, helpful, amenable, hospitable, flexible.

**accommodation** noun housing, homes, lodging(s), (living) quarters, rooms, billet, shelter, a roof over one's head; informal digs, pad; formal residence, dwelling.

**accompaniment** noun **1** *a musical accompaniment:* backing, support, background, soundtrack. **2** *the wine makes a superb accompaniment to cheese:* complement, addition, adjunct, accessory, companion.

**accompany** verb **1** *the driver accompanied her to the door:* go with, travel with, keep someone company, partner, escort, show, see, usher, conduct. **2** *an illness accompanied by nausea:* go along with, occur with, go together with, attend, be linked with. **3** *he accompanied the choir on the piano:* back, play along with, support.

**accomplice** noun partner in crime, abetter, accessory, collaborator, co-conspirator, henchman, associate.

**accomplish** verb achieve, succeed in, realize, attain, manage, bring off, carry through, execute, effect, perform, complete.

**accomplished** adjective expert, skilled, skilful, masterly, virtuoso, master, consummate, talented, gifted, able, capable; informal mean, nifty, crack, ace.

**accomplishment** noun **1** *a remarkable accomplishment:* achievement, success, act, deed, exploit, effort, feat, coup. **2** *her many accomplishments:* talent, skill, gift, ability.

**accord** verb **1** *the national assembly accorded him more power*: give, grant, present, award, confer on, bestow on. **2** *his views accorded with mine*: correspond, agree, tally, match, concur, be in harmony, be in tune.
OPPOSITES withhold, disagree, differ.
noun **1** *a peace accord*: pact, treaty, agreement, settlement, deal, entente, protocol. **2** *the two sides failed to reach accord*: agreement, consensus, unanimity, harmony.
OPPOSITES disagreement.
■ **of one's own accord** voluntarily, of one's own free will, of one's own volition, by choice, willingly, freely, readily.

**account** noun **1** *his account of the incident*: description, report, version, story, statement, explanation, tale, chronicle, history, record, log. **2** *the firm's accounts*: financial record, ledger, balance sheet, financial statement; (**accounts**) books. **3** *his background is of no account*: importance, import, significance, consequence, value.
■ **account for 1** *they must account for the delay*: explain, answer for, give reasons for, justify. **2** *excise duties account for over half the price*: constitute, make up, comprise, represent, be responsible for, produce.

**accountability** noun responsibility, liability, answerability.

**accountable** adjective responsible, liable, answerable, to blame.

**accumulate** verb gather, collect, amass, stockpile, pile up, build up, store (up), hoard, lay in/up, increase, accrue, run up.
OPPOSITES disperse.

**accumulation** noun mass, build-up, pile, collection, stock, store, stockpile, hoard.

**accuracy** noun correctness, precision, exactness, fidelity, truth, truthfulness, authenticity, realism.

**accurate** adjective **1** *accurate information*: correct, precise, exact, right, factual, literal, faithful, true, truthful, on the mark, authentic, realistic; Brit. informal spot on, bang on; N. Amer. informal on the money, on the button. **2** *an accurate shot*: well aimed, on target, unerring, deadly, true.

**accusation** noun allegation, charge, indictment, impeachment, claim, assertion, imputation.

**accuse** verb **1** *four people were accused of assault*: charge with, indict for, impeach for. **2** *you accused the companies of causing job losses*: blame for, hold responsible for, condemn for, criticize for, denounce for; informal point the finger at.
OPPOSITES absolve, exonerate.

**accustom** verb adapt, adjust, acclimatize, habituate, familiarize, become reconciled, get used to, come to terms with, learn to live with; N. Amer. acclimate.

**accustomed** adjective customary, established, habitual, usual, normal, regular, routine.

**ache** noun pain, twinge, pang, soreness, tenderness, irritation, discomfort, burning, cramp.
verb *my legs were aching*: hurt, be sore, be painful, be tender,

**a**
**b**
**c**
**d**
**e**
**f**
**g**
**h**
**i**
**j**
**k**
**l**
**m**
**n**
**o**
**p**
**q**
**r**
**s**
**t**
**u**
**v**
**w**
**x**
**y**
**z**

burn, be in pain.

**achieve** verb attain, reach, realize, bring off, pull off, accomplish, carry through, fulfil, complete; informal wrap up, swing.

**achievement** noun **1** *the achievement of high growth:* attainment, realization, accomplishment, fulfilment, implementation, completion. **2** *they were proud of their achievement:* feat, exploit, triumph, coup, accomplishment, act, action, deed, effort, work, handiwork.

**acid** adjective **1** *an acid flavour:* sour, acidic, tart, sharp, vinegary. **2** *acid remarks:* sharp, sharp-tongued, sarcastic, scathing, cutting, biting, stinging, caustic; informal bitchy, catty.
OPPOSITES alkali, sweet, kind.

**acknowledge** verb **1** *he acknowledges his unfitness for the role:* admit, accept, grant, allow, concede, confess, recognize. **2** *he did not acknowledge Colin:* greet, salute, address, nod to, wave to, say hello to. **3** *few people acknowledged my letters:* answer, reply to, respond to.
OPPOSITES reject, deny, ignore.

**acquaint** verb familiarize, make aware of, inform of, advise of; informal fill in on, clue in on.

**acquaintance** noun **1** *a business acquaintance:* contact, associate, colleague. **2** *my acquaintance with George:* association, relationship. **3** *some acquaintance with the language:* familiarity with, knowledge of, experience of, awareness of, understanding of, grasp of.

**acquire** verb get, obtain, come by, receive, collect, gain, buy, earn, win, come into, secure, pick up; informal get one's hands on, get hold of, land, bag, score.
OPPOSITES lose.

**acquisition** noun **1** *a new acquisition:* purchase, addition, investment, possession; informal buy. **2** *the acquisition of funds:* obtaining, collection, gaining, earning, winning, securing.

**acquit** verb **1** *the jury acquitted her:* clear, exonerate, find innocent, absolve, discharge, free, release; informal let off (the hook). **2** *the boys acquitted themselves well:* behave, conduct oneself, perform, act.
OPPOSITES convict.

**act** verb **1** *the Government must act:* take action, take steps, take measures, move. **2** *Alison began to act oddly:* behave, conduct oneself, react. **3** *I'll act as lookout:* function, work, serve, operate. **4** *he acted in a film:* perform, play, appear.
noun **1** *acts of kindness:* deed, action, gesture, feat, exploit. **2** *the act will raise taxes:* law, decree, statute, bill, edict, ruling, order. **3** *a comedy act:* performance, turn, routine, number, sketch. **4** *it was all an act:* pretence, show, front, facade, masquerade, charade, pose; informal a put-on.

**acting** adjective temporary, interim, caretaker, pro tem, provisional, stopgap; N. Amer. informal pinch-hitting.
OPPOSITES permanent.

**action** noun **1** *their actions are inexcusable:* deed, act, undertaking, exploit, behaviour, conduct, activity. **2** *the need for local action:* measures, steps, activism, campaigning, pressure. **3** *the action of hormones:* operation, working, effect, influence, process, power. **4** *he died in action:* battle, combat, hostilities, fighting, active service. **5** *a civil action:* lawsuit, suit, case, prosecution, litigation, proceedings.

**activate** verb start (up), switch on, turn on, set going, trigger (off), set off, energize.
OPPOSITES switch off.

**active** adjective **1** *she kept active:* busy, mobile, lively, vigorous; informal on the go, full of beans. **2** *an active member of the union:* hard-working, industrious, tireless, energetic. **3** *the watermill was active until 1960:* working, operative, functioning, operational, in action, in operation, in force; informal (up and) running.
OPPOSITES listless, inactive.

**activity** noun **1** *there was a lot of activity:* action, bustle, movement, life; informal toing and froing, comings and goings. **2** *a leisure activity:* pursuit, occupation, hobby, pastime, recreation, diversion, venture, undertaking, enterprise, project, scheme.
OPPOSITES inactivity.

**actor, actress** noun performer, player, thespian, star, starlet; Brit. informal luvvy.

**actual** adjective real, true, genuine, authentic, confirmed, definite, hard, concrete; informal real live.
OPPOSITES imaginary.

**actually** adverb really, in (actual) fact, in point of fact, as a matter of fact, in reality, in truth, if truth be told, to tell the truth.

**acute** adjective **1** *acute food shortages:* severe, dire, terrible, grave, serious, desperate. **2** *acute pain:* excruciating, sharp, severe, stabbing, agonizing, racking, searing. **3** *his acute mind:* quick, astute, shrewd, sharp, keen, penetrating, razor-sharp, quick-witted, agile, nimble, intelligent, canny, discerning, perceptive.
OPPOSITES mild, dull.

**adamant** adjective unshakeable, unwavering, unswerving, immovable, resolute, resolved, determined, firm, dead set.

**adapt** verb **1** *the policy can be adapted:* modify, alter, change, adjust, remodel, reorganize, customize, tailor; informal tweak. **2** *he adapts well to new surroundings:* adjust, conform, acclimatize, accommodate.

**add** verb **1** *the porch was added later:* attach, append, tack on, join on. **2** *they added the figures up:* total, count (up), reckon up, tally; Brit. tot up.
OPPOSITES subtract.
■ **add to** increase, augment, magnify, amplify, enhance, intensify, heighten, deepen, exacerbate, aggravate, compound, reinforce. ■ **add up to** amount to, come to, run to, make, total, equal, number.

**addict** noun **1** *a heroin addict:* abuser; informal junkie, druggy, -head, freak; N. Amer. informal hophead. **2** (informal) *skiing addicts:* enthusiast, fan, lover, devotee, aficionado; informal buff, freak, nut, fanatic.

**addicted** adjective dependent, obsessed, fixated, fanatical, passionate, a slave to; informal hooked.

**addiction** noun dependency, dependence, habit, obsession,

**a**
**b**
**c**
**d**
**e**
**f**
**g**
**h**
**i**
**j**
**k**
**l**
**m**
**n**
**o**
**p**
**q**
**r**
**s**
**t**
**u**
**v**
**w**
**x**
**y**
**z**

infatuation, passion, love, mania, enslavement.

**addictive** adjective
habit-forming, compulsive; Brit. informal moreish.

**addition** noun **1** *the addition of extra rooms:* adding, inclusion, incorporation, introduction. **2** *a useful addition:* add-on, extra, adjunct, appendage, supplement, rider.
OPPOSITES subtraction, removal, essential.
■ **in addition.** See **ADDITIONALLY**.

**additional** adjective extra, added, supplementary, further, more, spare, other, new, fresh.

**additionally** adverb also, in addition, besides, too, as well, on top (of that), furthermore, moreover, into the bargain, to boot, to say nothing of.

**address** noun **1** *officers called at the address:* house, flat, apartment, home; formal residence, dwelling. **2** *his address to Parliament:* speech, lecture, talk, presentation, dissertation, sermon.
verb *he addressed his audience:* speak to, talk to, give a talk to, make a speech to, hold forth to.

**adept** adjective expert, proficient, accomplished, skilful, practised, masterly, consummate.
OPPOSITES inept.

**adequate** adjective **1** *adequate financial resources:* sufficient, enough. **2** *an adequate service:* satisfactory, acceptable, passable, reasonable, tolerable, fair, average, not bad, all right, middling; informal OK.
OPPOSITES insufficient, inadequate.

**adhere** verb stick, cling, bond, hold.
■ **adhere to** abide by, stick to, hold to, comply with, conform to, follow, obey, heed, observe, respect, uphold, fulfil.

**adjacent** adjective adjoining, neighbouring, next-door, abutting.
■ **adjacent to** next to, by the side of, bordering on, beside, alongside, touching.

**adjoining** adjective connecting, connected, interconnecting, bordering, abutting, attached, adjacent, neighbouring, next-door.

**adjourn** verb **1** *the hearing was adjourned:* suspend, break off, discontinue, interrupt, recess. **2** *sentencing was adjourned until June 9:* postpone, put off/back, defer, delay, hold over.

**adjust** verb **1** *he adjusted the brakes:* modify, alter, regulate, tune, fine-tune, balance, tailor, customize, rearrange, change, reshape; informal tweak. **2** *Kate had adjusted to her new life:* adapt, become accustomed, get used, accommodate, acclimatize, habituate oneself, assimilate, come to terms with, blend in with, fit in with; N. Amer. acclimate.

**adjustable** adjective alterable, adaptable, modifiable, variable, multiway, versatile.

**administer** verb **1** *the union is administered by an executive:* manage, direct, control, operate, regulate, coordinate, conduct, handle, run, organize, govern, steer. **2** *the crew administered first aid:* dispense, issue, give out, provide, apply, offer, distribute, deliver, hand out, deal out, dole out.

**administration** noun **1** *the administration of the company:* management, direction, control, conduct, operation, running, coordination, governance, supervision, regulation. **2** *the Labour administration:* government, regime, executive, cabinet, authority, directorate, council, leadership, management, term of office, incumbency.

**administrative** adjective managerial, executive, operational, organizational, supervisory, directorial, governmental, regulatory.

**administrator** noun manager, director, executive, controller, official, coordinator, supervisor.

**admirable** adjective commendable, praiseworthy, laudable, creditable, exemplary, worthy, deserving, respectable, worthwhile, good, sterling, fine.
OPPOSITES deplorable.

**admiration** noun respect, approval, appreciation, (high) regard, esteem, recognition.
OPPOSITES scorn.

**admire** verb **1** *I admire your courage:* respect, think highly of, hold in high regard, rate highly, esteem, prize, approve of. **2** *Simon had admired her for a long time:* adore, love, worship, be taken with, be attracted to; informal carry a torch for, have a thing about.
OPPOSITES despise.

**admirer** noun fan, devotee, enthusiast, aficionado, supporter, adherent, follower, disciple.

**admission** noun **1** *an admission of liability:* confession, acknowledgement, acceptance, concession, disclosure, divulgence. **2** *free admission:* admittance, entry, entrance, access, entrée, acceptance, initiation.

**admit** verb **1** *Paul admitted that he was angry:* confess, acknowledge, concede, grant, accept, allow, reveal, disclose, divulge. **2** *he admitted the offence:* confess (to), plead guilty to, own up to. **3** *he was admitted to the college:* let in, accept, receive, initiate, take on.
OPPOSITES deny, exclude.

**admittance** noun entry, admission, entrance, access, entrée.
OPPOSITES exclusion.

**adolescence** noun teenage years, teens, youth, later childhood.

**adolescent** noun teenager, youth, juvenile; informal teen, teeny-bopper.
adjective teenage, young, immature, childish, juvenile, infantile, puerile; informal teen.
OPPOSITES mature.

**adopt** verb take on, embrace, take up, espouse, assume, follow, choose, endorse, approve.
OPPOSITES abandon.

**adore** verb love, be devoted to, dote on, cherish, treasure, prize, think the world of, admire, look up to, revere, worship.
OPPOSITES hate.

**adorn** verb decorate, embellish, array, ornament, enhance.
OPPOSITES disfigure.

**adrift** adjective **1** *adrift in a strange country:* lost, off course, drifting, disorientated, confused, (all) at sea, rootless, unsettled. **2** (informal) *the hook has come adrift:* loose, free, detached, unsecured, unfastened.

**adult** adjective **1** *an adult woman:* mature, grown-up,

**a**

fully grown, fully developed, of age. **2** *an adult movie:* (sexually) explicit, pornographic, obscene, dirty, erotic, sexy; informal porn, porno, naughty, blue, X-rated.

**advance** verb **1** *the battalion advanced rapidly:* move forward, press on, push on, attack, make progress, make headway, gain ground. **2** *the move advanced his career:* promote, further, forward, help, aid, assist, boost. **3** *technology has advanced:* progress, develop, evolve, make strides, move forward (in leaps and bounds), move on. **4** *a relative advanced him some money:* lend, loan, put up, come up with; Brit. informal sub.
OPPOSITES retreat, hinder, regress.
▶ noun **1** *the army's advance:* progress, (forward) movement, attack. **2** *a significant medical advance:* breakthrough, development, step forward, (quantum) leap.
▶ adjective *advance warning:* early, prior.
■ **in advance** beforehand, before, ahead of time, earlier, previously, in readiness.

**advanced** adjective **1** *advanced manufacturing techniques:* state-of-the-art, modern, up to date, up to the minute, cutting-edge, new, the latest, pioneering, innovative, sophisticated. **2** *an advanced course:* higher-level, higher, tertiary.
OPPOSITES primitive, elementary.

**advantage** noun **1** *they have the advantage:* upper hand, edge, lead, sway, whip hand, superiority, dominance, supremacy. **2** *the advantage of* *belonging to a union:* benefit, value, good/strong point, asset, plus, bonus, boon, blessing, virtue, profit, good.
OPPOSITES disadvantage.

**advantageous** adjective **1** *an advantageous position:* superior, dominant, powerful, fortunate, lucky, favourable. **2** *the arrangement is advantageous to both sides:* beneficial, of benefit, helpful, of assistance, useful, of value, profitable, in someone's interests.
OPPOSITES disadvantageous.

**adventure** noun **1** *her adventures in Italy:* exploit, escapade, undertaking, experience, incident. **2** *in search of adventure:* excitement, thrills, action, stimulation, risk, danger.

**adventurous** adjective **1** *an adventurous traveller:* daring, intrepid, bold, fearless, brave; informal gutsy. **2** *adventurous activities:* risky, dangerous, perilous, hazardous, exciting.
OPPOSITES cautious, safe, predictable.

**adversary** noun opponent, rival, enemy, antagonist, challenger, contender, competitor, opposition, competition; literary foe.
OPPOSITES ally, supporter.

**adverse** adjective **1** *adverse weather:* unfavourable, inclement, bad, poor, untoward. **2** *the drug's adverse side effects:* harmful, dangerous, injurious, detrimental. **3** *an adverse response:* hostile, unfavourable, antagonistic, unfriendly, negative.
OPPOSITES favourable, auspicious, beneficial.

**advertise** verb publicize, make

public, announce, broadcast, proclaim, trumpet, promote; informal push, plug, hype; N. Amer. informal ballyhoo, flack.

**advertisement** noun announcement, commercial, promotion, blurb, write-up; informal ad, push, plug, puff; Brit. informal advert.

**advice** noun guidance, counselling, counsel, help, direction, recommendations, guidelines, suggestions, hints, tips, pointers.

**advise** verb **1** *her grandmother advised her about marriage:* counsel, give guidance, guide, offer suggestions, give hints/ tips/pointers. **2** *he advised caution:* recommend, advocate, suggest, urge. **3** *you will be advised of our decision:* inform, notify, give notice, apprise, warn.

**adviser** noun counsellor, aide, mentor, guide, consultant, confidant, confidante, guru.

**advocate** noun champion, upholder, supporter, backer, promoter, proponent, campaigner, lobbyist; N. Amer. booster.
OPPOSITES critic.
verb recommend, champion, uphold, support, back, promote, campaign for, urge, subscribe to, speak for, argue for, lobby for.
OPPOSITES oppose, advise against.

**affair** noun **1** *it was a strange affair:* event, incident, episode, case, matter, business. **2** *what you do is your affair:* business, concern, matter, responsibility; Brit. informal lookout. **3** (**affairs**) *financial affairs:* transactions, activities, dealings, undertakings, ventures,

business. **4** *his affair with Anthea was over:* relationship, romance, fling, dalliance, liaison, involvement, amour; informal hanky-panky; Brit. informal carry-on.

**affect**[1] verb **1** *this affected our decision:* influence, have an effect on, have an impact on, act on, change, alter, modify. **2** *he was visibly affected by the experience:* move, touch, hit (hard), make an impression on, upset, trouble, distress, disturb, shake (up).

**affect**[2] verb *he affected an air of boredom:* put on, assume, take on, adopt, feign.

**affectation** noun pretension, pretentiousness, affectedness, artificiality, posturing, airs (and graces); Brit. informal side.

**affection** noun fondness, love, liking, tenderness, warmth, devotion, caring, attachment, friendship.

**affectionate** adjective fond, loving, adoring, devoted, caring, tender, warm, friendly, demonstrative; informal touchy-feely, lovey-dovey.
OPPOSITES cold.

**affiliate** verb associate, unite, combine, join (up), join forces, link up, ally, align, amalgamate, merge.

**affinity** noun empathy, rapport, sympathy, accord, harmony, similarity, relationship, bond, closeness, understanding; informal chemistry.
OPPOSITES aversion, dislike, dissimilarity.

**affirm** verb declare, state, assert, proclaim, pronounce, attest, swear.
OPPOSITES deny.

**affirmative** adjective positive, assenting, consenting,

approving, favourable.
OPPOSITES negative.

**afflict** verb trouble, burden, distress, beset, harass, worry, oppress, torment, plague.

**affluent** adjective wealthy, rich, prosperous, well off, well-to-do, of means; informal well heeled, rolling in it, made of money, loaded.
OPPOSITES poor.

**afford** verb 1 *I can't afford a new car:* pay for, find the money for, run to, stretch to, stand, manage. 2 *can you afford the time?* spare, allow oneself. 3 *the terrace affords beautiful views:* give, offer, supply, provide, furnish, yield.

**afraid** adjective 1 *they ran away because they were afraid:* frightened, scared, terrified, fearful, nervous, petrified, intimidated, cowardly, faint-hearted; informal scared stiff; N. Amer. informal spooked. 2 *don't be afraid to ask awkward questions:* reluctant, hesitant, unwilling, slow, shy. 3 *I'm afraid I'm late:* sorry.
OPPOSITES brave, confident, glad.

**after** preposition following, subsequent to, at the end of, in the wake of.

**aftermath** noun consequences, after-effects, results, repercussions, upshot.

**afterwards** adverb later, later on, subsequently, then, next, after this/that, in due course.

**again** adverb once more, another time, afresh, anew.

**against** preposition 1 *most delegates were against the motion:* opposed to, in opposition to, hostile to, antagonistic towards, unsympathetic to, at odds with, in disagreement with; informal anti, agin. 2 *swimming against the tide:* counter to, contrary to, in the opposite direction to, resisting. 3 *she leaned against the wall:* touching, in contact with, up against, abutting, on.
OPPOSITES in favour of, with.

**age** noun 1 *her hearing deteriorated with age:* old age, maturity, advancing years, elderliness, seniority. 2 *the Elizabethan age:* era, epoch, period, time.
verb 1 *Cabernet Sauvignon ages well:* mature, mellow, ripen, soften, season, weather. 2 *the experience has aged her:* make old, wear out, weather. 3 *she has aged a lot:* grow old, decline, wither, fade.

**agency** noun business, organization, company, firm, office, bureau.

**agenda** noun programme, schedule, to-do list, timetable, plan.

**agent** noun 1 *the sale was arranged through an agent:* representative, intermediary, negotiator, go-between, proxy, broker, emissary, envoy, spokesperson; informal rep. 2 *a CIA agent:* spy, secret agent, operative, mole; N. Amer. informal spook, G-man.

**aggravate** verb 1 *the new law could aggravate the situation:* worsen, make worse, exacerbate, inflame, compound. 2 (informal) *you'll only aggravate him!* annoy, antagonize, irritate, exasperate, nettle, provoke, get on someone's nerves; Brit. rub up the wrong way; informal needle, hack off, get someone's goat, get up someone's nose; Brit. informal wind up; N. Amer. informal tick off.

OPPOSITES alleviate, improve, placate.

**aggregate** noun total, sum, grand total, combined score.

**aggression** noun **1** *an act of aggression*: hostility, belligerence, force, violence, attack. **2** *he played with unceasing aggression*: confidence, self-confidence, boldness, determination, forcefulness, vigour, energy, dynamism, commitment.

**aggressive** adjective
**1** *aggressive behaviour*: violent, confrontational, antagonistic, pugnacious. **2** *aggressive foreign policy*: warmongering, warlike, warring, belligerent, bellicose, hawkish, militaristic, expansionist; informal gung-ho.
**3** *an aggressive promotional drive*: assertive, forceful, vigorous, energetic, dynamic, audacious; informal in-your-face, feisty.
OPPOSITES peaceable, peaceful, laid-back.

**agile** adjective **1** *she was as agile as a monkey*: nimble, lithe, supple, acrobatic. **2** *an agile mind*: alert, sharp, acute, shrewd, astute, perceptive, quick.
OPPOSITES stiff, clumsy, dull.

**agitate** verb **1** *any mention of Clare agitates my grandmother*: upset, fluster, ruffle, disconcert, unnerve, disquiet, disturb, distress, unsettle; informal rattle, faze. **2** *agitate the solution*: shake, whisk, beat, stir.

**agonizing** adjective excruciating, painful, acute, harrowing, torturous.

**agony** noun suffering, torture, pain, torment, anguish.

**agree** verb **1** *I agree with you*: concur, see eye to eye, be in sympathy, be as one, be unanimous. **2** *they agreed to a ceasefire*: consent, assent, acquiesce; formal accede. **3** *the plan and the drawing do not agree*: match (up), correspond, conform, coincide, fit, tally, be consistent; informal square. **4** *they agreed a price*: settle, decide on, arrive at, negotiate, shake hands on.
OPPOSITES differ, reject, contradict.

**agreeable** adjective **1** *an agreeable atmosphere*: pleasant, pleasing, enjoyable, pleasurable, nice, appealing, relaxing, friendly, congenial. **2** *an agreeable man*: likeable, amiable, affable, pleasant, nice, friendly, good-natured, sociable, genial. **3** *we should get together, if you're agreeable*: willing, amenable, in agreement.
OPPOSITES unpleasant.

**agreement** noun **1** *all heads nodded in agreement*: accord, concurrence, consensus, assent, acceptance, consent, acquiescence. **2** *an agreement on imports*: contract, treaty, pact, accord, settlement, understanding, bargain. **3** *there is some agreement between the two datasets*: correspondence, consistency, compatibility, accord, similarity, resemblance, likeness.
OPPOSITES discord, dissimilarity.

**agricultural** adjective farm, farming, agrarian, rural, rustic, countryside.
OPPOSITES urban.

**agriculture** noun farming, cultivation, husbandry, agribusiness, agronomy.

**aid** noun **1** *with the aid of his*

a
b
c
d
e
f
g
h
i
j
k
l
m
n
o
p
q
r
s
t
u
v
w
x
y
z

*colleagues:* assistance, support, help, backing, cooperation.
**2** *humanitarian aid:* relief, assistance, support, subsidy, funding, donations, grants; historical alms.
OPPOSITES hindrance.
verb help, assist, support, encourage, further, boost, promote, facilitate.
OPPOSITES hinder.

**aide** noun assistant, helper, adviser, supporter, right-hand man/woman, adjutant, deputy, second (in command), lieutenant.

**ailing** adjective **1** *his ailing mother:* ill, sick, sickly, poorly, weak, in poor/bad health, infirm. **2** *the country's ailing economy:* failing, weak, poor, tottering, fragile, unstable.
OPPOSITES healthy.

**ailment** noun illness, disease, disorder, affliction, malady, complaint, infirmity; informal bug, virus.

**aim** verb **1** *he aimed the rifle:* point, direct, train, sight, line up. **2** *she aimed at the target:* take aim, fix on, zero in on, draw a bead on. **3** *this food is aimed at children:* target, intend, direct, design, tailor, market, pitch. **4** *we aim to give you good service:* intend, mean, hope, want, plan, propose.
noun *our aim is to develop top gymnasts:* objective, object, goal, end, target, design, desire, intention, intent, plan, purpose, ambition, aspiration, wish, dream, hope.

**aimless** adjective purposeless, directionless, undirected, random.
OPPOSITES purposeful.

**air** noun **1** breeze, draught, wind, gust/puff of wind. **2** *an air of*

*defiance:* look, appearance, impression, aspect, manner, tone, feel, atmosphere, mood.
verb **1** *a chance to air your views:* express, voice, make public, articulate, state, declare. **2** *the room needs airing:* ventilate, freshen, refresh, cool.

**airless** adjective stuffy, close, stifling, suffocating, oppressive, unventilated.
OPPOSITES airy.

**airy** adjective spacious, uncluttered, light, bright, well ventilated, fresh.
OPPOSITES poky, stuffy.

**aisle** noun passage, passageway, lane, path, gangway, walkway.

**akin** adjective similar, related, close, near, comparable, equivalent, connected, alike, analogous.
OPPOSITES unlike.

**alarm** noun **1** *the girl spun round in alarm:* fear, anxiety, apprehension, distress, agitation, consternation, fright, panic. **2** *a fire alarm:* warning, danger signal, siren, bell, detector, sensor.
OPPOSITES calmness, composure.
verb *the news alarmed her:* frighten, scare, panic, unnerve, distress, agitate, upset, disconcert, shock, disturb; informal rattle, spook; Brit. informal put the wind up.
OPPOSITES reassure.

**alarming** adjective frightening, unnerving, shocking, worrying, upsetting, disconcerting, disturbing; informal scary.
OPPOSITES reassuring.

**alcoholic** adjective intoxicating, strong, hard, stiff, fermented, brewed, distilled.
noun drunkard, dipsomaniac, drunk, heavy drinker, problem

drinker, alcohol-abuser; informal boozer, alky, dipso, soak, wino; Austral./NZ informal hophead.

**alert** adjective **1** *an alert sentry:* vigilant, watchful, attentive, observant, wide awake, on the lookout, on one's guard/toes; informal keeping one's eyes open/peeled. **2** *mentally alert:* quick-witted, sharp, bright, quick, perceptive, on one's toes; informal on the ball, quick on the uptake, all there, with it.
OPPOSITES inattentive, dull.
noun **1** *a state of alert:* vigilance, watchfulness, attentiveness, alertness. **2** *a flood alert:* warning, notification, notice, siren, alarm, signal.
verb *police were alerted:* warn, notify, forewarn, put on one's guard; informal tip off.

**alien** adjective foreign, unfamiliar, unknown, peculiar, exotic, strange.
OPPOSITES native, familiar.
noun **1** *an illegal alien:* foreigner, non-native, immigrant, émigré, stranger. **2** *the alien's spaceship crashed:* extraterrestrial, ET; informal little green man.

**alienate** verb isolate, distance, estrange, cut off, turn away, drive apart, set at variance/odds, drive a wedge between.

**alienation** noun isolation, detachment, estrangement, separation.

**alight** adjective *the stable was alight:* burning, ablaze, on fire, in flames, blazing.

**align** verb **1** *the desks are aligned with the wall:* line up, straighten, even up, arrange, coordinate. **2** *he aligned himself with the workers:* ally, affiliate, associate, side, join forces, team up, band together, throw in

one's lot.

**alike** adjective *all the doors looked alike:* similar, (much) the same, indistinguishable, identical, uniform, interchangeable; informal much of a muchness.
OPPOSITES different.
adverb *great minds think alike:* similarly, the same, correspondingly, analogously, identically.
OPPOSITES differently.

**alive** adjective **1** *the synagogue has kept the Jewish faith alive:* active, in existence, functioning, in operation, operative, on the map. **2** *teachers need to be alive to their pupils' needs:* alert, awake, aware, conscious, mindful, heedful, sensitive, familiar.
OPPOSITES dead, unaware.

**allay** verb reduce, diminish, decrease, lessen, alleviate, ease, relieve, soothe, soften, calm.
OPPOSITES increase, intensify.

**allegation** noun claim, assertion, charge, accusation, contention.

**allege** verb claim, assert, charge, accuse, contend.

**alleged** adjective reported, supposed, so-called, claimed, professed, purported, ostensible, unproven.
OPPOSITES confirmed.

**allegiance** noun loyalty, faithfulness, fidelity, obedience, adherence, devotion.
OPPOSITES disloyalty, treachery.

**alleviate** verb ease, relieve, take the edge off, deaden, dull, lessen, reduce, moderate, allay, soothe, help, soften.
OPPOSITES aggravate.

**alley** noun passage, passageway, alleyway, backstreet, lane, path,

**a**

pathway, walk.

**alliance** noun association, union, league, confederation, federation, coalition, marriage, cooperation.

**allied** adjective associated, united, related, connected, interconnected, linked, cooperating, in league, affiliated, combined, coupled, married.
OPPOSITES unrelated, independent.

**allocate** verb allot, assign, set aside, earmark, consign, distribute, apportion, share out, dole out, give out.

**allocation** noun 1 *the efficient allocation of resources:* allotment, assignment, distribution, sharing out, doling out, giving out. 2 *our annual allocation of funds:* allowance, allotment, consignment, quota, share, ration; informal cut; Brit. informal whack.

**allow** verb 1 *the police allowed him to go home:* permit, let, enable, authorize, give leave, license, entitle, consent to, assent to, acquiesce in, agree to, approve; informal give the go-ahead to, give the thumbs up to, OK, give the green light to; formal accede to. 2 *allow an hour or so for driving:* set aside, allocate, allot, earmark, designate, reserve.
OPPOSITES prevent, forbid.

**allowance** noun 1 *your baggage allowance:* allocation, allotment, quota, share, ration, grant, limit. 2 *her father gave her an allowance:* payment, pocket money, contribution, grant, handout, subsidy, maintenance.

**all right** adjective 1 *the tea was all right:* satisfactory, acceptable, adequate, passable, reasonable; informal so-so, OK. 2 *are you all right?* unhurt, uninjured, unharmed, in one piece, safe (and sound), alive and well; informal OK. 3 *it's all right for you to go:* permissible, permitted, allowed, acceptable, legal, lawful, authorized, approved, in order; informal OK, legit, cool.
OPPOSITES unsatisfactory, hurt, forbidden.
adverb *the system works all right:* satisfactorily, adequately, fairly well, passably, acceptably, reasonably, well, fine; informal OK.
OPPOSITES unsatisfactorily.

**ally** noun *a political ally:* associate, colleague, friend, confederate, partner, supporter.
OPPOSITES enemy, opponent.
verb *the Catholic powers allied with Philip II:* unite, combine, join (up), join forces, band together, team up, collaborate, side, align oneself.
OPPOSITES split.

**almost** adverb nearly, (just) about, practically, virtually, all but, as good as, close to, not quite; informal pretty nearly/much/well; literary well-nigh, nigh on.

**alone** adjective & adverb 1 *she was alone in the house:* by oneself, on one's own, apart, solitary, single, solo; Brit. informal on one's tod. 2 *she felt terribly alone:* lonely, isolated, deserted, abandoned, friendless.
OPPOSITES accompanied, loved.
adverb *he travelled alone:* by oneself, on one's own, solo, singly, independently, unaccompanied, without help.
OPPOSITES in company.

**also** adverb too, as well, besides, in addition, additionally, furthermore, further, moreover, into the bargain, on top (of that), what's more, to boot.

**alter** verb **1** *Eliot was persuaded to alter the passage:* change, adjust, adapt, amend, modify, revise, rework, redo, transform; informal tweak. **2** *the situation has altered:* change, become different, undergo a (sea) change, evolve, move on.
OPPOSITES preserve, stay the same.

**alternate** verb **1** *rows of trees alternate with dense shrub:* be interspersed, follow one another, take turns, take it in turns, oscillate, see-saw. **2** *we could alternate the two groups:* rotate, swap, exchange, interchange.
adjective **1** *she attended on alternate days:* every other, every second, alternating. **2** (N. Amer.) *an alternate plan.* See **ALTERNATIVE** adjective sense 1.

**alternative** adjective **1** *an alternative route:* different, other, second, substitute, replacement, standby, emergency, reserve, backup, auxiliary, fallback; N. Amer. alternate. **2** *an alternative lifestyle:* unorthodox, unconventional, nonconformist, radical, revolutionary, avant-garde; informal offbeat, way-out.
noun *we have no alternative:* (other) option, (other) choice, substitute, replacement.

**altogether** adverb **1** *he wasn't altogether happy:* completely, totally, entirely, absolutely, wholly, fully, thoroughly, utterly, perfectly, one hundred per cent, in all respects. **2** *we have five offices altogether:* in all, all told, in total.

**always** adverb **1** *he's always late:* every time, all the time, without fail, consistently, invariably, regularly, habitually, unfailingly. **2** *she's always complaining:* continually, continuously, constantly, forever, all the time, day and night; informal 24-7. **3** *the place will always be dear to me:* forever, for good, for evermore, for ever and ever, until the end of time, eternally.
OPPOSITES never, seldom, sometimes.

**amalgamate** verb combine, merge, unite, join, fuse, blend, meld.
OPPOSITES separate.

**amass** verb gather, collect, assemble, accumulate, stockpile, hoard.
OPPOSITES disperse.

**amateur** noun **1** *the crew were all amateurs:* non-professional, non-specialist, layman, layperson, dilettante, dabbler. **2** *what a bunch of amateurs:* incompetent, bungler; Brit. informal bodger, cowboy, clown.
OPPOSITES professional, expert.
adjective non-professional, unpaid, non-specialist, lay, dilettante.

**amateurish** adjective incompetent, inept, inexpert, amateur, clumsy, bumbling; Brit. informal bodged.

**amaze** verb astonish, astound, surprise, stun, stagger, nonplus, shock, startle, stop someone in their tracks, leave open-mouthed, dumbfound; informal bowl over, flabbergast; Brit. informal knock for six; (**amazed**) thunderstruck, at a loss for words, speechless; Brit. informal

a

gobsmacked.

**amazement** noun astonishment, surprise, shock, speechlessness, awe, wonder.

**amazing** adjective astonishing, astounding, surprising, stunning, staggering, breathtaking, awesome, awe-inspiring, sensational, remarkable, spectacular, stupendous, phenomenal, extraordinary, incredible, unbelievable; informal mind-blowing; literary wondrous.

**ambassador** noun envoy, emissary, representative, diplomat, minister, consul, attaché.

**ambiguous** adjective vague, unclear, ambivalent, equivocal, inconclusive, enigmatic, cryptic. OPPOSITES clear.

**ambition** noun 1 *young people with ambition*: drive, determination, enterprise, initiative, eagerness, motivation, a sense of purpose; informal get-up-and-go. 2 *her ambition was to become a model*: aspiration, desire, dream, intention, goal, aim, objective, plan.

**ambitious** adjective 1 *an ambitious politician*: aspiring, determined, motivated, energetic, committed, purposeful, power-hungry; informal go-ahead, go-getting. 2 *an ambitious task*: challenging, exacting, demanding, formidable, difficult, hard, tough. OPPOSITES laid-back, easy.

**ambush** verb surprise, waylay, trap, ensnare, attack, jump on, pounce on; N. Amer. bushwhack.

**amend** verb revise, alter, change, modify, adapt, adjust,

edit, rewrite, redraft, rephrase, reword.

**amends**
■ **make amends for** make up for, atone for, make good.
■ **make amends to** compensate, recompense, indemnify, make it up to.

**amenity** noun facility, service, resource, convenience, comfort.

**amnesty** noun pardon, reprieve, forgiveness, release, discharge; informal let-off.

**amount** noun quantity, number, total, aggregate, sum, quota, size, mass, weight, volume.
■ **amount to** 1 *the bill amounted to £50*: add up to, come to, run to; Brit. tot up to. 2 *their actions amounted to conspiracy*: constitute, comprise, be tantamount to.

**ample** adjective 1 *there is ample time for discussion*: enough, sufficient, adequate, plenty of, more than enough. 2 *an ample supply of wine*: plentiful, abundant, copious, profuse, lavish, liberal, generous; informal galore. 3 *his ample tunic*: spacious, full, capacious, roomy, voluminous, loose-fitting, baggy, sloppy. OPPOSITES insufficient, meagre, tight.

**amuse** verb 1 *her annoyance simply amused him*: make someone laugh, entertain, delight, divert, cheer (up), please, charm, tickle; informal crack up; Brit. informal crease up. 2 *he amused himself by writing poetry*: occupy, engage, busy, absorb, engross, entertain. OPPOSITES bore.

**amusement** noun 1 *the cause of much amusement*: mirth, merriment, hilarity, glee, delight. 2 *I read the book for*

b
c
d
e
f
g
h
i
j
k
l
m
n
o
p
q
r
s
t
u
v
w
x
y
z

*amusement:* entertainment, pleasure, leisure, relaxation, fun, enjoyment, interest. **3** *a range of amusements:* activity, entertainment, diversion, pastime, recreation, game, sport.

**amusing** adjective funny, comical, humorous, light-hearted, jocular, witty, droll, entertaining, diverting; informal rib-tickling.
OPPOSITES solemn, boring.

**analogy** noun similarity, parallel, correspondence, likeness, resemblance, correlation, relation, comparison.
OPPOSITES dissimilarity.

**analyse** verb examine, inspect, survey, study, scrutinize, investigate, probe, explore, evaluate.

**analysis** noun examination, inspection, study, scrutiny, investigation, exploration, evaluation.

**analytical, analytic** adjective systematic, logical, scientific, methodical, precise, meticulous, rigorous, investigative, enquiring.
OPPOSITES unsystematic.

**anarchy** noun lawlessness, disorder, chaos, pandemonium, riot, revolution.
OPPOSITES government, order.

**anatomy** noun structure, make-up, composition, constitution, form, body, physique.

**ancestor** noun forefather, forebear, predecessor, antecedent, progenitor, parent, grandparent.
OPPOSITES descendant.

**ancient** adjective **1** *ancient civilizations:* early, prehistoric, primeval, primordial, primitive. **2** *an ancient custom:* old, age-

old, archaic, antediluvian, time-honoured. **3** *I feel positively ancient:* antiquated, decrepit, antediluvian, geriatric; informal out of the ark; Brit. informal past its/one's sell-by date.
OPPOSITES recent, contemporary, young.

**anecdote** noun story, tale, urban myth, narrative, reminiscence; informal yarn.

**angelic** adjective innocent, pure, virtuous, saintly, cherubic, adorable.

**anger** noun annoyance, vexation, temper, indignation, rage, fury, wrath, outrage.
OPPOSITES pleasure, good humour.
verb annoy, irk, vex, enrage, incense, infuriate, rile, outrage.
OPPOSITES pacify, placate.

**angle** noun **1** *an angle of 33°:* gradient, slope, slant, inclination. **2** *right in the angle of the roof:* corner, point, fork, nook, crook, edge. **3** *consider the problem from a different angle:* perspective, point of view, viewpoint, standpoint, position, aspect, slant, direction, approach, tack.
verb *Anna angled her camera upwards:* tilt, slant, twist, swivel, lean, tip, turn.

**angry** adjective furious, irate, vexed, irked, enraged, seething, infuriated, in a temper, fuming, outraged, cross; informal (hopping) mad, up in arms, foaming at the mouth, steamed up, in a paddy; Brit. informal shirty; N. Amer. informal sore, teed off, ticked off; Austral./NZ informal ropeable, snaky.
OPPOSITES pleased, good-humoured.
■ **get angry** lose one's temper, go berserk, flare up; informal go

mad/crazy/wild, go bananas, hit the roof, go through the roof, go up the wall, see red, go off the deep end, fly off the handle, blow one's top, blow a fuse/gasket, lose one's rag, flip (one's lid), have a fit, foam at the mouth, explode, go ballistic; Brit. informal go spare, do one's nut; N. Amer. informal flip one's wig, blow one's lid/stack.

**anguish** noun agony, pain, torment, torture, suffering, distress, woe, misery, sorrow, heartache.
OPPOSITES happiness.

**animal** noun 1 creature, beast, (living) thing; (**animals**) wildlife, fauna. 2 *the man was an animal*: beast, brute, monster, devil, fiend; informal swine, bastard, pig.

**animate** verb *the forces animating community life*: enliven, energize, invigorate, liven up, inspire, fire, rouse, excite, move.
OPPOSITES depress.
adjective *an animate being*: living, alive, live, breathing, sentient.
OPPOSITES inanimate.

**animated** adjective lively, spirited, energetic, full of life, excited, enthusiastic, eager, alive, vigorous, vibrant, vivacious, exuberant, ebullient, bouncy, bubbly, perky; informal bright-eyed and bushy-tailed, full of beans, bright and breezy, chirpy, chipper.
OPPOSITES lethargic, lifeless.

**animosity** noun hostility, antipathy, antagonism, enmity, resentment, ill feeling/will, bad blood.
OPPOSITES goodwill, friendship.

**annihilate** verb destroy, obliterate, eradicate, wipe out,

wipe off the face of the earth; informal rub out, snuff out.
OPPOSITES create.

**announce** verb make public, make known, report, declare, state, give out, publicize, broadcast, publish, advertise, circulate, proclaim, release.

**announcement** noun 1 *an announcement by the Minister*: statement, declaration, proclamation, pronouncement, bulletin, communiqué; N. Amer. advisory. 2 *the announcement of the decision*: declaration, notification, reporting, publishing, broadcasting.

**annoy** verb irritate, bother, vex, make cross, exasperate, irk, anger, antagonize, nettle; Brit. rub up the wrong way; informal aggravate, peeve, miff, rile, needle, get (to), bug, hack off; Brit. informal wind up, nark, get on someone's wick; N. Amer. informal tee off, tick off, burn up, rankle, gravel.
OPPOSITES please, gratify.

**annoyance** noun irritation, exasperation, vexation, indignation, anger, displeasure, chagrin.

**annual** adjective yearly, once-a-year, year-long, twelve-month.

**annually** adverb yearly, once a year, each year, per annum.

**annul** verb declare invalid, declare null and void, nullify, invalidate, void, repeal, revoke.
OPPOSITES restore, enact.

**anomaly** noun oddity, peculiarity, abnormality, irregularity, inconsistency, aberration, quirk.

**anonymous** adjective 1 *an anonymous donor*: unnamed, nameless, unidentified, unknown, incognito. 2 *an anonymous letter*: unsigned,

unattributed.
OPPOSITES known.

**answer** noun 1 *her answer was unequivocal:* reply, response, rejoinder, reaction, retort, riposte; informal comeback. 2 *the answer to this problem:* solution, remedy, way out, explanation.
OPPOSITES question.
verb *Steve was about to answer:* reply, respond, rejoin, retort, riposte.
■ answer for *he will answer for his crime:* pay for, be punished for, suffer for, make amends for.

**antagonistic** adjective hostile, opposed, antipathetic, ill-disposed, resistant, in disagreement; informal anti.
OPPOSITES pro.

**antagonize** verb provoke, intimidate, alienate, anger, annoy.
OPPOSITES pacify, disarm.

**anthem** noun hymn, song, chorale, chant, psalm, canticle.

**anticipate** verb 1 *the police did not anticipate trouble:* expect, foresee, predict, be prepared for, bargain on, reckon on; N. Amer. informal figure on. 2 *we eagerly anticipated his arrival:* look forward to, await, long for, can't wait for.

**anticipation** noun expectation, expectancy, prediction, hope, excitement, suspense.

**anticlimax** noun let-down, disappointment, comedown, non-event, disillusionment; Brit. damp squib; informal washout.

**antics** plural noun capers, pranks, larks, high jinks, skylarking, horseplay, clowning; Brit. informal monkey tricks.

**antidote** noun remedy, cure, solution, countermeasure,

corrective.

**antipathy** noun hostility, antagonism, animosity, aversion, animus, distaste, hatred, abhorrence, loathing.
OPPOSITES affinity, liking.

**antiquated** adjective outdated, outmoded, outworn, behind the times, old-fashioned, anachronistic; informal out of the ark; N. Amer. informal horse-and-buggy, clunky.
OPPOSITES modern, up to date.

**antique** noun collector's item, museum piece, period piece, bygone, antiquity.
adjective *antique furniture:* antiquarian, old, collectable, vintage, classic.
OPPOSITES modern.

**antisocial** adjective 1 *antisocial behaviour:* objectionable, offensive, unacceptable, disruptive, rowdy. 2 *I'm feeling a bit antisocial:* unsociable, unfriendly, uncommunicative, reclusive.
OPPOSITES acceptable, sociable.

**anxiety** noun worry, concern, apprehension, unease, fear, disquiet, doubts, nervousness, nerves; informal butterflies (in one's stomach), the jitters, collywobbles.
OPPOSITES confidence.

**anxious** adjective 1 *I'm anxious about her:* worried, concerned, apprehensive, fearful, uneasy, disturbed, fretful, agitated, nervous, on edge, worked up, jumpy; informal uptight, with butterflies in one's stomach, jittery, twitchy; N. Amer. informal antsy, squirrelly, in a twit; Austral./NZ informal toey. 2 *she was anxious for news:* eager, keen, itching, impatient.
OPPOSITES confident, unconcerned.

**apart**
■ **apart from** except for, but for, aside from, with the exception of, excepting, excluding, bar, barring, besides, other than; informal outside of.

**apartment** noun **1** *a rented apartment:* flat, suite, penthouse; Austral. home unit; N. Amer. informal crib. **2** *the royal apartments:* suite (of rooms), rooms, quarters, accommodation.

**apathetic** adjective uninterested, indifferent, unconcerned, unmoved, uninvolved, unemotional, lukewarm, lethargic; informal couldn't-care-less.
OPPOSITES interested, enthusiastic, involved.

**apathy** noun indifference, lack of interest, lack of enthusiasm, lack of concern, lack of involvement, unconcern, lethargy.
OPPOSITES enthusiasm, interest, concern.

**aperture** noun opening, hole, gap, slit, slot, vent, crevice, chink, crack; technical orifice.

**apologetic** adjective sorry, regretful, contrite, remorseful, penitent, repentant.
OPPOSITES unrepentant.

**apologize** verb say sorry, express regret, ask forgiveness, ask for pardon, eat humble pie.

**apology** noun regrets, expression of regret.
■ **apology for** travesty of, poor imitation of, poor substitute for, pale shadow of; informal excuse for.

**appal** verb horrify, shock, dismay, distress, outrage, scandalize, disgust, revolt, sicken, nauseate, offend, make someone's blood run cold.

**appalling** adjective **1** *an appalling crime:* horrific, shocking, horrible, terrible, awful, dreadful, ghastly, hideous, horrendous, frightful, atrocious, abominable, outrageous. **2** (informal) *your schoolwork is appalling:* dreadful, terrible, atrocious, deplorable, hopeless, lamentable; informal rotten, crummy, woeful, useless, lousy, abysmal, dire; Brit. informal chronic, shocking.

**apparatus** noun **1** *laboratory apparatus:* equipment, gear, tackle, mechanism, appliance, device. **2** *the apparatus of government:* system, machinery, framework, structure, organization.

**apparent** adjective **1** *their relief was all too apparent:* evident, plain, obvious, clear, manifest, visible, discernible, unmistakable. **2** *his apparent lack of concern:* seeming, ostensible, outward, superficial.
OPPOSITES unclear, real.

**apparently** adverb seemingly, evidently, ostensibly, outwardly.

**appeal** verb ask, request, call, plead, entreat, beg, implore.
■ **appeal to** attract, interest, fascinate, please, tempt, lure, draw; informal float someone's boat.
noun **1** *an appeal for help:* plea, request, entreaty, cry, call. **2** *the cultural appeal of the island:* attraction, allure, charm, fascination, magnetism, pull.

**appealing** adjective attractive, engaging, alluring, enchanting, captivating, bewitching, fascinating, tempting, enticing, irresistible, charming; Brit. informal tasty.

OPPOSITES disagreeable, off-putting.

**appear** verb **1** become visible, come into view/sight, materialize. **2** *differences were beginning to appear:* be revealed, emerge, surface, manifest itself, become apparent/evident, come to light, arrive, arise, crop up, show up. **3** *they appeared completely devoted:* seem, look, give the impression of being, come across as, strike someone as.
OPPOSITES vanish.

**appearance** noun **1** *her dishevelled appearance:* look, air, aspect, looks, mien, expression, behaviour. **2** *an appearance of respectability:* impression, air, (outward) show, semblance, illusion, facade, front, pretence. **3** *the appearance of these symptoms:* occurrence, manifestation, emergence, arrival, development, materialization.

**appease** verb placate, conciliate, pacify, mollify, reconcile, win over; informal sweeten.
OPPOSITES provoke, inflame.

**appendix** noun supplement, addendum, postscript, codicil, coda, epilogue, afterword, tailpiece.

**appetite** noun **1** hunger, taste, palate. **2** *my appetite for learning:* desire, liking, hunger, thirst, longing, yearning, passion, enthusiasm, keenness, eagerness; informal yen.

**applaud** verb **1** *the audience applauded:* clap, give a standing ovation, put one's hands together; informal give someone a big hand. **2** *police have applauded the decision:* praise,

commend, salute, welcome, celebrate, approve of.
OPPOSITES boo, criticize.

**applause** noun clapping, (standing) ovation, cheering.

**appliance** noun device, machine, instrument, gadget, contraption, apparatus, mechanism, contrivance, labour-saving device; informal gizmo.

**applicable** adjective relevant, appropriate, pertinent, apposite, material, fitting, suitable, apt.
OPPOSITES inappropriate, irrelevant.

**applicant** noun candidate, interviewee, contender, entrant, claimant, petitioner, prospective student/employee, job-seeker.

**application** noun **1** *an application for an overdraft:* request, appeal, petition, approach, claim, demand. **2** *the application of anti-inflation policies:* implementation, use, exercise, employment, execution, enactment. **3** *the job requires a great deal of application:* hard work, diligence, industry, effort, commitment, dedication, devotion, perseverance, persistence, concentration.

**apply** verb **1** *300 people applied for the job:* bid, put in, try, audition, seek, solicit, claim, request, ask, petition. **2** *the Act did not apply to Scotland:* be relevant, pertain, relate, concern, affect, involve, cover, touch, deal with, have a bearing on. **3** *countries apply their own national rules:* implement, put into practice, introduce. **4** *she applied some ointment:* put on, rub in/on, work in, spread,

a
b
c
d
e
f
g
h
i
j
k
l
m
n
o
p
q
r
s
t
u
v
w
x
y
z

a
b
c
d
e
f
g
h
i
j
k
l
m
n
o
p
q
r
s
t
u
v
w
x
y
z

smear on, slap on. **5** *steady pressure should be applied:* **exert**, administer, use, exercise, employ, utilize, bring to bear.

■ **apply oneself** work hard, exert oneself, make an effort, be industrious, show dedication, buckle down, persevere, persist, concentrate; informal put one's back in it, knuckle down, get stuck in.

**appoint** verb **nominate**, name, designate, install, commission, engage, co-opt, select, choose, elect, vote in.
OPPOSITES reject.

**appointed** adjective **1** *at the appointed time:* **scheduled**, arranged, prearranged, specified, agreed, designated, allotted, set, fixed. **2** *a well appointed room:* **furnished**, decorated, fitted out, supplied.

**appointment** noun **1** *a six o'clock appointment:* **meeting**, engagement, interview, consultation, session. **2** *the appointment of directors:* **nomination**, naming, designation, installation, commissioning, engagement, co-option, selection, choosing, election. **3** *he held an appointment at the university:* **job**, post, position, situation, place, office.

**appraisal** noun **assessment**, evaluation, estimation, judgement, summing-up, consideration.

**appreciate** verb **1** *I'm not appreciated here:* **value**, admire, respect, think highly of, think much of, be grateful for, be glad of. **2** *we appreciate the problems:* **recognize**, realize, know, be aware of, be conscious of, be sensitive to, understand, sympathize with. **3** *a home will*

*appreciate in value:* **increase**, gain, grow, rise, go up, soar.
OPPOSITES disparage, depreciate, decrease.

**appreciation** noun **1** *her appreciation of literature:* **knowledge**, awareness, enjoyment, love, feeling, discrimination, sensitivity. **2** *he showed his appreciation:* **gratitude**, thanks, gratefulness. **3** *an appreciation of the value of teamwork:* **acknowledgement**, recognition, realization, knowledge, awareness, consciousness, understanding. **4** *an appreciation of the professor's work:* **review**, critique, criticism, analysis, assessment, evaluation, judgement; Brit. informal crit. **5** *the appreciation of the euro against the pound:* **increase**, gain, growth, rise, inflation, escalation.
OPPOSITES ingratitude, unawareness, depreciation, decrease.

**appreciative** adjective **1** *we are appreciative of all your efforts:* **grateful**, thankful, obliged, indebted. **2** *an appreciative audience:* **admiring**, enthusiastic, approving, complimentary.
OPPOSITES ungrateful, disparaging.

**apprehension** noun **1** *he was filled with apprehension:* **anxiety**, worry, unease, nervousness, nerves, misgivings, disquiet, concern, trepidation. **2** *the apprehension of a criminal:* **arrest**, capture, seizure, detention.
OPPOSITES confidence.

**apprehensive** adjective **anxious**, worried, uneasy, nervous, concerned, agitated.

OPPOSITES confident.

**apprentice** noun trainee, learner, probationer, novice, beginner, starter, pupil, student; N. Amer. tenderfoot; informal rookie; N. Amer. informal greenhorn.
OPPOSITES veteran, master, expert.

**approach** verb 1 *she approached the altar:* move towards, near, come near, close in on, close with, gain on. 2 *she approached him for a pay rise:* speak to, talk to, sound out, make a proposal to, proposition. 3 *he approached the problem in the best way:* tackle, address, manage, set about, go about, start work on.
OPPOSITES leave.
noun 1 *the traditional British approach:* method, procedure, technique, modus operandi, style, way, strategy, tactic, system, means, line of action. 2 *he considered an approach to the High Court:* proposal, submission, application, appeal, plea, request. 3 *the dog barked at the approach of any intruder:* advance, arrival, appearance. 4 *the approach to the castle:* driveway, drive, road, path, entry, way.

**approachable** adjective 1 *students found the staff approachable:* friendly, welcoming, pleasant, agreeable, sympathetic, congenial. 2 *the island is approachable by boat:* accessible, reachable, attainable; informal get-at-able.
OPPOSITES aloof, inaccessible.

**appropriate** adjective *this isn't the appropriate time:* suitable, proper, fitting, apt, right, convenient, opportune, relevant, apposite.
OPPOSITES inappropriate.
verb *the barons appropriated church lands:* seize, commandeer, expropriate, usurp, take over, hijack, steal; informal swipe, rip off, nab; Brit. informal pinch, nick.

**approval** noun 1 *their proposals went to the ministry for approval:* acceptance, agreement, consent, assent, permission, rubber stamp, sanction, blessing, endorsement, ratification, authorization; informal the go-ahead, the green light, the OK, the thumbs up. 2 *Lily looked at him with approval:* favour, liking, appreciation, admiration, regard, esteem, respect.
OPPOSITES refusal, disapproval.

**approve** verb agree to, accept, consent to, assent to, give one's blessing to, bless, ratify, sanction, endorse, authorize, validate, pass; informal give the go-ahead, give the green light to, give the OK to, give the thumbs-up to.
OPPOSITES refuse.
■ approve of agree with, hold with, endorse, support, be in favour of, favour, think well of, like, take kindly to, admire.

**approximate** adjective estimated, rough, imprecise, inexact, broad, loose; N. Amer. informal ballpark.
OPPOSITES precise.
■ approximate to roughly equal, come near/close to, approach, border on, verge on, resemble, be similar to.

**approximately** adverb roughly, about, around, circa, round about, more or less, nearly, almost, approaching; Brit. getting on for; informal pushing;

N. Amer. informal **in the ballpark of.**
OPPOSITES **spot on.**

**apt** adjective **1** *a very apt description:* suitable, fitting, appropriate, relevant, apposite; Brit. informal **spot on. 2** *they are apt to be a bit slipshod:* inclined, given, likely, liable, prone. **3** *an apt pupil:* bright, quick, clever, sharp, smart, able, gifted, talented.
OPPOSITES inappropriate, unlikely, slow.

**arbitrary** adjective random, unpredictable, capricious, subjective, whimsical, wanton, motiveless, irrational, groundless, unjustified.
OPPOSITES reasoned, democratic.

**arbitration** noun adjudication, judgement, mediation, conciliation, intervention.

**arbitrator** noun adjudicator, arbiter, judge, referee, umpire, mediator, go-between.

**arc** noun curve, arch, bow, curl, crescent, semicircle, half-moon.

**arch** noun *a stone arch:* archway, vault, span.
verb *she arched her eyebrows:* curve, arc, bend, bow, crook, hunch.

**architect** noun designer, planner, originator, author, creator, founder, inventor.

**architecture** noun **1** *modern architecture:* building, planning, design, construction. **2** *computer architecture:* structure, construction, organization, layout, design, build, make-up; informal set-up.

**archive** noun **1** *the family archives:* records, papers, documents, files, annals, chronicles, history. **2** *the National Sound Archive:* record office, registry, repository, museum, library.

verb *the videos are archived for future use:* file, log, catalogue, document, record, register, store.

**ardent** adjective passionate, fervent, zealous, wholehearted, intense, enthusiastic, keen, eager, avid, committed, dedicated.
OPPOSITES apathetic.

**arduous** adjective tough, difficult, hard, heavy, laborious, onerous, taxing, strenuous, back-breaking, demanding, challenging, punishing, gruelling; informal killing; Brit. informal knackering.
OPPOSITES easy.

**area** noun **1** *an inner-city area:* district, zone, region, sector, quarter, locality, neighbourhood; informal neck of the woods; Brit. informal manor; N. Amer. informal turf. **2** *the dining area:* space, section, part, place, room. **3** *specific areas of knowledge:* field, sphere, realm, domain, sector, province, territory.

**arena** noun **1** *an ice-hockey arena:* stadium, amphitheatre, ground, field, ring, rink, pitch, court; N. Amer. bowl, park. **2** *the political arena:* scene, sphere, realm, province, domain, forum, territory, world.

**argue** verb **1** *they argued that the government was to blame:* claim, maintain, insist, contend, assert, hold, reason, allege. **2** *the children are always arguing:* quarrel, disagree, dispute, row, squabble, bicker, have words, cross swords.

**argument** noun **1** *he had an argument with Tony:* quarrel, disagreement, squabble, dispute, altercation; informal slanging match; Brit. informal row, barney. **2** *an argument for the existence of God:* reasoning, justification, explanation, case, defence, vindication, evidence, reasons, grounds.

**arise** verb **1** *many problems arose:* come about, happen, occur, come into being, emerge, crop up, come to light, become apparent, appear, turn up, surface, spring up. **2** *injuries arising from defective products:* result, stem, originate, proceed, follow, ensue, be caused by.

**aristocrat** noun nobleman, noblewoman, lord, lady, peer (of the realm), patrician; informal aristo; Brit. informal toff, nob.
OPPOSITES commoner.

**aristocratic** adjective noble, titled, upper-class, blue-blooded, high-born; informal upper crust, top drawer; Brit. informal posh.
OPPOSITES common.

**arm** verb equip, provide, supply, furnish, issue, fit out.

**armaments** plural noun arms, weapons, weaponry, firearms, guns, ordnance, artillery, munitions, materiel.

**armoured** adjective armour-plated, steel-plated, ironclad, bulletproof, bombproof, reinforced, toughened.

**arms** plural noun weapons, weaponry, firearms, guns, ordnance, artillery, armaments, munitions.

**army** noun **1** armed force, military force, land force(s), military, soldiery, infantry, militia, troops, soldiers. **2** *an army of tourists:* crowd, swarm, horde, mob, gang, throng, mass, flock, herd, pack.

**aroma** noun smell, odour, fragrance, scent, perfume, bouquet, nose.

**aromatic** adjective fragrant, scented, perfumed, fragranced.

**around** preposition **1** *the hills around the city:* surrounding, enclosing, on all sides of. **2** *around three miles:* approximately, about, round about, circa, roughly, more or less, nearly, almost, approaching; Brit. getting on for; N. Amer. informal in the ballpark of.
OPPOSITES precisely.

**arouse** verb **1** *they had aroused suspicion:* provoke, trigger, stir up, kindle, engender, cause. **2** *his ability to arouse the masses:* stir up, whip up, rouse, galvanize, electrify, stimulate, inspire, fire up, inflame, agitate, incite. **3** *she was aroused from sleep:* wake (up), awaken, bring to/round, rouse.
OPPOSITES allay, pacify.

**arrange** verb **1** *she arranged the flowers in a vase:* set out, order, lay out, position, present, display, exhibit, group, sort, organize. **2** *they hoped to arrange a meeting:* organize, fix (up), plan, schedule, contrive, determine, agree. **3** *he arranged the piece for a full orchestra:* adapt, set, score, orchestrate.

**arrangement** noun **1** *the arrangement of the furniture:* positioning, presentation, grouping, organization, alignment. **2** *the arrangements for my trip:* preparation, plan, provision, planning. **3** *we had an arrangement:* agreement, deal, understanding, bargain, settlement, pact. **4** *an arrangement of Beethoven's symphonies:* adaptation, orchestration, scoring, interpretation.

**array** noun range, collection,

selection, assortment, variety, arrangement, line-up, display, exhibition.
**verb** arrange, assemble, group, order, range, place, position, set out, lay out, spread out, display, exhibit.

**arrest** verb 1 *police arrested him for murder:* detain, apprehend, seize, capture, take into custody; informal pick up, pull in, collar; Brit. informal nick. 2 *the spread of the disease can be arrested:* stop, halt, check, block, curb, prevent, obstruct.
OPPOSITES release, start.
**noun** detention, apprehension, seizure, capture.

**arresting** adjective striking, eye-catching, conspicuous, impressive, imposing, spectacular, dramatic, breathtaking, stunning, awe-inspiring.
OPPOSITES inconspicuous.

**arrival** noun 1 *they awaited Ruth's arrival:* coming, appearance, entrance, entry, approach. 2 *the arrival of democracy:* emergence, appearance, advent, coming, dawn, onset.
OPPOSITES departure, end.

**arrive** verb 1 *more police arrived:* come, turn up, get here/there, make it, appear; informal show (up), roll in/up, blow in. 2 *virtual reality had arrived:* emerge, appear, surface, dawn, be born, come into being, arise.
OPPOSITES depart, leave.

**arrogant** adjective haughty, conceited, self-important, cocky, supercilious, condescending, full of oneself, overbearing, proud; informal high and mighty, too big for one's boots.

OPPOSITES modest.

**art** noun 1 *he studied art:* fine art, design, artwork, aesthetics. 2 *the art of writing:* skill, craft, technique, knack, aptitude, talent, flair, mastery, expertise.

**article** noun 1 *household articles:* object, thing, item, piece, artefact, device, implement. 2 *an article in The Times:* report, account, story, essay, feature, item, piece (of writing), column, commentary. 3 *the crucial article of the treaty:* clause, section, paragraph, head, point, item.

**articulate** adjective *an articulate speaker:* eloquent, fluent, effective, persuasive, lucid, expressive, silver-tongued.
OPPOSITES unintelligible.
**verb** *they were unable to articulate their emotions:* express, voice, vocalize, put in words, communicate, state.

**artificial** adjective 1 *artificial flowers:* synthetic, fake, imitation, mock, ersatz, man-made, manufactured, plastic; informal pretend. 2 *an artificial smile:* insincere, feigned, false, unnatural, contrived, put-on, forced, laboured, hollow; informal pretend, phoney.
OPPOSITES natural, genuine.

**artistic** adjective 1 *he's very artistic:* creative, imaginative, inventive, expressive, sensitive, perceptive, discerning. 2 *artistic dances:* aesthetic, beautiful, stylish, ornamental, graceful, subtle, expressive.
OPPOSITES unimaginative.

**ascent** noun 1 *the ascent of the Matterhorn:* climbing, scaling, conquest. 2 *the ascent grew steeper:* slope, incline, gradient.
OPPOSITES descent, drop.

**ascertain** verb find out,

discover, get to know, work out, make out, fathom (out), learn, deduce, divine, establish, determine; informal figure out.

**ashamed** adjective **1** *she felt ashamed that she had hit him:* sorry, shamefaced, sheepish, guilty, contrite, remorseful, regretful, mortified, humiliated. **2** *he was ashamed to admit it:* reluctant, loath, unwilling, afraid, embarrassed.
OPPOSITES proud, pleased.

**ask** verb **1** *he asked what time we opened:* enquire, want to know, question, interrogate, quiz. **2** *they'll ask a few questions:* put (forward), pose, raise, submit. **3** *do ask for advice:* request, demand, seek, solicit, apply, petition, call, appeal.
OPPOSITES answer.

**asleep** adjective sleeping, napping, dozing, drowsing; informal snoozing, dead to the world; humorous in the land of Nod.
OPPOSITES awake.

**aspect** noun **1** *every aspect of life:* feature, facet, side, characteristic, particular, detail. **2** *from every aspect:* point of view, position, standpoint, viewpoint, perspective, angle, slant. **3** *his face had a sinister aspect:* appearance, look, air, mien, demeanour, expression.

**aspiration** noun desire, hope, dream, wish, longing, yearning, aim, ambition, expectation, goal, target.

**aspire**
■ aspire to desire, aim for, hope for, dream of, long for, yearn for, set one's heart on, wish for, want, seek, set one's sights on.

**aspiring** adjective would-be, hopeful, budding, potential, prospective; informal wannabe.

**assassin** noun murderer, killer, gunman, executioner; informal hit man.

**assassinate** verb murder, kill, eliminate, liquidate, execute; N. Amer. terminate; informal hit.

**assault** verb *he assaulted a police officer:* attack, hit, strike, beat up, thump; informal wallop, belt, clobber, lay into, rough up; Austral. informal quilt.
noun **1** *he was charged with assault:* violence, battery; Brit. grievous bodily harm, GBH, actual bodily harm, ABH. **2** *an assault on the city:* attack, strike, onslaught, offensive, charge, push, thrust, raid.

**assemble** verb **1** *a crowd had assembled:* gather, collect, get together, congregate, convene, meet, muster, rally. **2** *he assembled the suspects:* bring/call together, gather, collect, round up, marshal, muster. **3** *how to assemble the kite:* construct, build, erect, set up, put together, connect.
OPPOSITES disperse, dismantle.

**assembly** noun **1** *an assembly of dockers:* gathering, meeting, congregation, convention, council, rally, group, crowd; informal get-together. **2** *car assembly:* construction, manufacture, building, fabrication, erection.

**assert** verb **1** *she asserts that hysteria is universal:* declare, maintain, contend, argue, claim, insist. **2** *you should assert your rights:* insist on, stand up for, uphold, defend, press/push for.

**assertion** noun declaration, contention, statement, claim, opinion, protestation.

**assertive** adjective confident, self-confident, bold, decisive,

a
b
c
d
e
f
g
h
i
j
k
l
m
n
o
p
q
r
s
t
u
v
w
x
y
z

**a**
**b**
**c**
**d**
**e**
**f**
**g**
**h**
**i**
**j**
**k**
**l**
**m**
**n**
**o**
**p**
**q**
**r**
**s**
**t**
**u**
**v**
**w**
**x**
**y**
**z**

forceful, insistent, determined, commanding, pushy; informal feisty.
OPPOSITES timid.

**assess** verb 1 *the committee's power is hard to assess:* evaluate, judge, gauge, rate, estimate, appraise, weigh up; informal size up. 2 *the damage was assessed at £5 billion:* value, calculate, work out, determine, cost, price, estimate.

**assessment** noun 1 *a teacher's assessment of the pupil's abilities:* evaluation, judgement, rating, estimation, appraisal, opinion. 2 *some assessments valued the estate at £2 million:* valuation, calculation, costing, pricing, estimate.

**asset** noun 1 benefit, advantage, blessing, good/strong point, strength, forte, virtue, recommendation, attraction, resource. 2 (**assets**) property, resources, estate, holdings, funds, valuables, possessions, effects, belongings.
OPPOSITES liability.

**assign** verb 1 *a young doctor was assigned the task:* allocate, allot, give, set, charge with, entrust with. 2 *she was assigned to a new post:* appoint, promote, delegate, nominate, commission, post, co-opt; Military detail. 3 *we assign large sums of money to travel budgets:* earmark, designate, set aside, reserve, appropriate, allot, allocate.

**assignation** noun rendezvous, date, appointment, meeting.

**assignment** noun task, job, duty, mission, errand, undertaking, exercise, project, homework.

**assist** verb 1 help, aid, lend a (helping) hand to, support, back (up), work with. 2 *the aim was to assist cashflow:* facilitate, aid, ease, promote, boost, speed, benefit, encourage, further.
OPPOSITES hinder.

**assistance** noun help, aid, a (helping) hand, support, backing, reinforcement.
OPPOSITES hindrance.

**assistant** noun helper, aide, deputy, second (in command), number two, right-hand man/woman, PA, mate, auxiliary, attendant; informal sidekick, gofer; Brit. informal dogsbody, skivvy.

**associate** verb 1 *the colours that we associate with fire:* link, connect, relate, bracket, identify, equate. 2 *I was forced to associate with them:* mix, keep company, mingle, socialize, go around, have dealings; informal hobnob, hang out/around/round.
OPPOSITES avoid.
noun *a business associate:* partner, colleague, co-worker, workmate, collaborator, comrade, ally; informal crony.

**associated** adjective related, connected, linked, similar, corresponding, attendant, accompanying, incidental.
OPPOSITES unrelated.

**association** noun 1 *a trade association:* alliance, consortium, coalition, union, league, guild, syndicate, federation, confederation, cooperative, partnership. 2 *the association between man and environment:* relationship, relation, interrelation, connection, interconnection, link, bond, interdependence.

# assorted → astute

**assorted** adjective various, miscellaneous, mixed, varied, diverse, different, sundry.
OPPOSITES uniform.

**assortment** noun variety, mixture, array, mix, miscellany, selection, medley.

**assume** verb **1** *I assumed he wanted me to keep the book:* presume, suppose, take it (as given), take for granted, take as read, conclude, infer, think, fancy, believe, understand, gather; N. Amer. figure. **2** *he assumed a Southern accent:* affect, adopt, put on. **3** *they are to assume more responsibility:* accept, shoulder, bear, undertake, take on/up. **4** *he assumed control of their finances:* seize, take (over), appropriate, wrest, usurp.
OPPOSITES know, drop, give up.

**assumed** adjective false, fictitious, fake, bogus, invented, made-up; informal pretend, phoney.
OPPOSITES genuine.

**assumption** noun presumption, supposition, inference, conjecture, belief.
OPPOSITES knowledge.

**assurance** noun **1** *you have my assurance:* promise, word (of honour), pledge, vow, oath, undertaking, guarantee, commitment. **2** *her calm assurance:* confidence, self-confidence, self-assurance, self-possession, nerve, poise; informal cool. **3** *life assurance:* insurance, indemnity, protection, security, cover.
OPPOSITES self-doubt, nervousness.

**assure** verb **1** *we must assure him of our loyal support:* reassure, convince, satisfy, persuade. **2** *I assure you all is well:* promise, guarantee, swear, confirm, certify, vow. **3** *he wants to assure a favourable vote:* ensure, secure, guarantee, seal, clinch; informal sew up.
OPPOSITES avoid.

**assured** adjective **1** *an assured performance:* confident, self-confident, self-assured, self-possessed, poised, composed, imperturbable, unruffled; informal unflappable, together. **2** *an assured supply of weapons:* guaranteed, certain, sure, secure, reliable, dependable; informal sure-fire.
OPPOSITES nervous, uncertain.

**astonish** verb amaze, astound, stagger, startle, stun, confound, dumbfound, nonplus, take aback, leave open-mouthed; informal flabbergast, bowl over; Brit. informal knock for six.

**astonishing** adjective amazing, astounding, staggering, surprising, breathtaking, remarkable, extraordinary, incredible, unbelievable, phenomenal; informal mind-boggling.
OPPOSITES unremarkable.

**astound** verb amaze, astonish, stagger, surprise, startle, stun, confound, dumbfound, take aback, leave open-mouthed; informal flabbergast, bowl over; Brit. informal knock for six.

**astounding** adjective amazing, astonishing, staggering, surprising, breathtaking, remarkable, extraordinary, incredible, unbelievable, phenomenal; informal mind-boggling.
OPPOSITES unremarkable.

**astute** adjective shrewd, sharp, acute, quick, clever, intelligent, bright, smart, canny,

a b c d e f g h i j k l m n o p q r s t u v w x y z

perceptive; informal quick on the uptake.
OPPOSITES stupid.

**asylum** noun *political asylum:* **refuge**, sanctuary, shelter, protection, immunity, a safe haven.

**athletic** adjective **muscular**, fit, strapping, well built, strong, sturdy, powerful, brawny, burly.
OPPOSITES puny.

**atmosphere** noun **1** air, sky; literary the heavens. **2** *a relaxed atmosphere:* **spirit**, ambience, air, mood, feel, feeling, character, tone, aura, quality; informal vibe.

**atrocious** adjective **1** *atrocious cruelties:* **wicked**, cruel, brutal, barbaric, vicious, monstrous, vile, inhuman, fiendish. **2** *the weather was atrocious:* **appalling**, dreadful, terrible, miserable; informal abysmal, dire, rotten, lousy; Brit. informal shocking.
OPPOSITES admirable, superb.

**atrocity** noun **1** *a number of atrocities:* **outrage**, horror, violation, abuse, massacre. **2** *scenes of hardship and atrocity:* **wickedness**, cruelty, brutality, barbarity, viciousness, savagery, inhumanity.
OPPOSITES humanity.

**attach** verb **1** *a weight is attached to the cord:* **fasten**, fix, join, secure, stick. **2** *they attach importance to research:* **ascribe**, assign, attribute, accredit, impute. **3** *the medical officer attached to HQ:* **assign**, appoint, allocate, second.
OPPOSITES detach.

**attached**
■ **attached to** fond of, devoted to, keen on; informal mad about.

**attachment** noun **1** *a strong attachment to his mother:* **bond**, closeness, devotion, loyalty, fondness for, love for, affection for, feeling for, sympathy for. **2** *the shower had a massage attachment:* **accessory**, fitting, extension, add-on.

**attack** verb **1** *Chris was brutally attacked:* **assault**, beat up, set upon, mug; N. Amer. beat up on; informal work over, rough up; Brit. informal duff up. **2** *the French attacked the fort:* **strike at**, assault, charge, pounce on, raid, storm. **3** *the clergy attacked government policies:* **criticize**, censure, condemn, disparage; informal knock, slam, lay into; Brit. informal slate, slag off, rubbish.
OPPOSITES defend, praise.
noun **1** *an attack on their home:* **assault**, onslaught, offensive, strike, blitz, raid, charge, invasion. **2** *an attack on his leadership:* **criticism**, censure, condemnation, disparagement; Brit. informal slating. **3** *an asthmatic attack:* **fit**, seizure, spasm, convulsion, paroxysm, bout, episode.
OPPOSITES defence, praise.

**attacker** noun **assailant**, assaulter, mugger, aggressor, raider, invader.
OPPOSITES defender, victim.

**attain** verb **achieve**, accomplish, reach, obtain, gain, secure, get, win, earn, realize, fulfil; informal clinch, bag, wrap up.

**attempt** verb *I attempted to answer the question:* **try**, strive, aim, venture, endeavour, seek, have a go.
noun *an attempt to reach the summit:* **try**, effort, endeavour, venture, bid, go; informal crack, shot, stab.

**attend** verb **1** *they attended a carol service:* **be present at**, sit in on, take part in, appear at, turn up at, visit, go to; informal show up at. 2 *the children were not attending:* pay attention, listen, be attentive, concentrate.

OPPOSITES miss, take no notice.

■ **attend to something** deal with, see to, look after, manage, organize, sort out, handle, take care of, tackle. ■ **attend to someone** care for, look after, minister to, see to, tend, treat, help.

**attendance** noun 1 *you requested the attendance of a doctor:* presence, appearance, attention. 2 *their gig attendances grew:* audience, turnout, house, gate, crowd; Austral. informal muster.

OPPOSITES absence.

**attendant** noun *a royal attendant:* assistant, aide, companion, steward, equerry, escort, servant, retainer, valet, maid.

adjective *new discoveries and the attendant excitement:* accompanying, associated, related, connected, resulting, consequent.

**attention** noun 1 *the issue needs further attention:* consideration, contemplation, deliberation, thought, study, observation, mind, investigation, action. 2 *he tried to attract the attention of a policeman:* awareness, notice, scrutiny, eye, gaze. 3 *medical attention:* care, treatment, relief, aid, assistance.

**attentive** adjective 1 *an attentive pupil:* alert, perceptive, observant, acute, aware, heedful, focused, studious, diligent, conscientious, earnest. 2 *the most attentive of husbands:* considerate, conscientious, thoughtful, kind, caring, solicitous, understanding, sympathetic.

OPPOSITES inattentive.

**attic** noun loft, roof space, garret.

**attitude** noun 1 *you seem ambivalent in your attitude:* view, viewpoint, outlook, perspective, stance, standpoint, position, approach, opinion. 2 *an attitude of prayer:* position, posture, pose, stance.

**attract** verb 1 *he was attracted by her smile:* entice, appeal to, tempt, lure, allure, charm, win, woo, captivate; informal turn on. 2 *electrical equipment attracts dust:* draw, pull, suck.

OPPOSITES repel, put off.

**attraction** noun 1 *she had lost her attraction:* appeal, attractiveness, pull, desirability, fascination, allure, charisma, charm. 2 *the town's attractions:* entertainment, activity, diversion, amenity, service. 3 *magnetic attraction:* pull, draw, force.

OPPOSITES repulsion.

**attractive** adjective

1 good-looking, beautiful, pretty, handsome, lovely, stunning, striking, arresting, gorgeous, prepossessing, fetching; Scottish & N. English bonny; informal drop-dead gorgeous; Brit. informal fit; N. Amer. informal cute; Austral./NZ informal spunky. 2 *an attractive career:* appealing, inviting, tempting, pleasing, interesting.

OPPOSITES unattractive, ugly, uninviting.

**attribute** verb *they attributed their success to him:* ascribe, assign, accredit, credit, put down, chalk up, pin on.

a
b
c
d
e
f
g
h
i
j
k
l
m
n
o
p
q
r
s
t
u
v
w
x
y
z

**a**

noun *the attributes of a top player:* quality, characteristic, trait, feature, element, aspect, property, sign, hallmark, mark.

**audible** adjective perceptible, discernible, detectable, clear, distinct.
OPPOSITES inaudible, faint.

**audience** noun 1 *the audience applauded:* spectators, listeners, viewers, onlookers, crowd, throng, gallery, congregation, turnout. 2 *an audience with the Pope:* meeting, interview, consultation, conference, hearing, reception.

**augment** verb increase, add to, supplement, enhance, build up, raise, up, hike up, enlarge, swell, expand, extend; informal jack up.
OPPOSITES decrease, reduce.

**august** adjective distinguished, respected, eminent, venerable, illustrious, prestigious, renowned, celebrated, honoured, acclaimed, esteemed.
OPPOSITES lowly, obscure, disreputable.

**aura** noun atmosphere, ambience, air, quality, character, mood, feeling; informal vibe.

**auspicious** adjective favourable, promising, encouraging, fortunate, opportune, timely, advantageous, good.
OPPOSITES inauspicious, unfavourable.

**austere** adjective 1 *an austere man:* severe, stern, strict, harsh, dour, grim, cold, frosty, unfriendly. 2 *an austere life:* spartan, frugal, ascetic, puritanical, abstemious, strict, simple, hard. 3 *an austere building:* plain, simple, basic, functional, unadorned, bleak, bare, clinical.
OPPOSITES easy-going, friendly, luxurious, extravagant, ornate.

**authentic** adjective 1 *an authentic document:* genuine, real, bona fide, true, legitimate; informal pukka, kosher; Austral./NZ informal dinkum. 2 *an authentic depiction of the situation:* accurate, factual, true, truthful, reliable, trustworthy, honest, faithful.
OPPOSITES fake, inaccurate, unreliable.

**authenticate** verb verify, validate, prove, substantiate, corroborate, confirm, support, back up.
OPPOSITES disprove.

**author** noun 1 *modern Canadian authors:* writer, novelist, poet, playwright, columnist, reporter, wordsmith; informal scribe, scribbler. 2 *the author of the peace plan:* creator, originator, founder, father, architect, designer, producer.

**authoritarian** adjective strict, autocratic, dictatorial, despotic, tyrannical, domineering, imperious, illiberal, undemocratic; informal bossy.
OPPOSITES democratic, liberal.
noun disciplinarian, autocrat, dictator, despot, tyrant.
OPPOSITES democrat, liberal.

**authoritative** adjective 1 *authoritative information:* reliable, dependable, trustworthy, accurate, authentic, valid. 2 *the authoritative edition:* definitive, most reliable, best, authorized, approved. 3 *his authoritative manner:* commanding, masterful, assertive, self-assured, self-confident.
OPPOSITES unreliable, timid.

**authority** noun **1** *a rebellion against those in authority:* power, command, control, charge, dominance, jurisdiction, rule; informal clout. **2** *the authority to arrest drug traffickers:* right, authorization, power, mandate, prerogative, licence. **3** *the money was spent without parliamentary authority:* permission, authorization, consent, sanction, assent, agreement, approval, clearance; informal the go-ahead. **4** *the authorities:* officials, officialdom, government, administration, establishment, police; informal the powers that be. **5** *an authority on coins:* expert, specialist, professional, master, connoisseur, pundit, doyen(ne), guru.
OPPOSITES amateur, ignoramus.

**authorize** verb **1** *they authorized further action:* permit, sanction, allow, approve, consent to, assent to; informal give the go-ahead to, OK. **2** *the troops were authorized to fire:* empower, give authority, mandate, commission, entitle.
OPPOSITES forbid.

**authorized** adjective approved, sanctioned, accredited, recognized, licensed, certified, official, legal, legitimate.
OPPOSITES unauthorized, unofficial.

**automatic** adjective **1** *automatic garage doors:* mechanized, powered, mechanical, automated, computerized, electronic, robotic. **2** *an automatic reaction:* instinctive, involuntary, unconscious, reflex, knee-jerk, subconscious, spontaneous, impulsive, unthinking, mechanical; informal gut. **3** *the automatic choice:* inevitable, unavoidable, inescapable, only possible.
OPPOSITES manual, conscious, deliberate.

**autonomous** adjective self-governing, independent, sovereign, free.
OPPOSITES dependent, repressed.

**autonomy** noun self-government, self-rule, home rule, self-determination, independence, sovereignty, freedom.
OPPOSITES dependence, repression.

**auxiliary** adjective additional, supplementary, extra, reserve, backup, emergency, fallback, second.
OPPOSITES primary, regular.

**available** adjective **1** *refreshments will be available:* obtainable, accessible, to/at hand, to be had, on sale, untaken, unsold; informal up for grabs, on tap. **2** *I'll see if he's available:* free, unoccupied, on duty, contactable.
OPPOSITES unavailable, taken, busy.

**avalanche** noun *an avalanche of enquiries:* barrage, flood, deluge, torrent, wave.
OPPOSITES trickle.

**avant-garde** adjective experimental, modern, cutting-edge, progressive, unorthodox, unconventional; informal edgy, offbeat, way-out.
OPPOSITES conservative, established.

**avarice** noun greed, acquisitiveness, covetousness, materialism.
OPPOSITES generosity.

**average** noun *the national average:* mean, median, mode, norm, standard, rule, par.

a
b
c
d
e
f
g
h
i
j
k
l
m
n
o
p
q
r
s
t
u
v
w
x
y
z

**a**

adjective 1 *the average temperature:* mean, median, modal. 2 *a woman of average height:* ordinary, standard, normal, typical, regular.
OPPOSITES abnormal, unusual.
■ on average normally, usually, ordinarily, generally, typically, for the most part, as a rule, by and large, overall, on the whole.

**averse** adjective opposed, hostile, antagonistic, resistant, disinclined, reluctant, loath; informal anti.
OPPOSITES keen.

**aversion** noun dislike, hatred, loathing, abhorrence, distaste, antipathy, hostility, reluctance, disinclination.
OPPOSITES liking.

**avert** verb 1 *she averted her gaze:* turn aside, turn away, shift, redirect. 2 *an attempt to avert political chaos:* prevent, avoid, stave off, ward off, head off, forestall.
OPPOSITES bring about, allow.

**avid** adjective keen, eager, enthusiastic, ardent, passionate, zealous, devoted.
OPPOSITES apathetic.

**avoid** verb 1 *I avoid situations that cause me stress:* keep away from, steer clear of, give a wide berth to. 2 *he avoids responsibility:* evade, dodge, sidestep, escape, run away from; informal duck, wriggle out of, get out of. 3 *book early to avoid disappointment:* prevent, preclude, stave off, forestall, head off, ward off. 4 *he should avoid drinking alcohol:* refrain from, abstain from, desist from, steer clear of.
OPPOSITES confront, face up to, seek out, cause, allow, continue, insist on.

**await** verb 1 *Peter was awaiting news:* wait for, expect, look forward to, anticipate. 2 *many dangers await them:* be in store for, lie ahead of, lie in wait for, be waiting for, be round the corner.

**awake** verb *she awoke early:* wake up, wake, awaken, waken, stir, come to, come round, rouse, call.
adjective 1 *she was still awake:* sleepless, wide awake, restless, insomniac. 2 *too few are awake to the dangers:* aware of, conscious of, mindful of, alert to.
OPPOSITES asleep, oblivious.

**awaken** verb 1 See AWAKE verb. 2 *he had awakened strong emotions in her:* arouse, bring out, trigger, stir up, stimulate, kindle, revive.
OPPOSITES suppress.

**award** verb *the society awarded him a medal:* give, grant, accord, confer on, bestow on, present to, decorate with.
noun 1 *an award for long service:* prize, trophy, medal, decoration, reward; informal gong. 2 *an award of £1,500:* grant, scholarship, endowment; Brit. bursary.

**aware** adjective 1 *she is aware of the dangers:* conscious of, mindful of, informed about, acquainted with, familiar with, alive to, alert to; informal wise to, in the know about.
2 *environmentally aware:* sensitive, enlightened, knowledgeable, (well) informed; informal clued up; Brit. informal switched-on.
OPPOSITES unaware, ignorant.

**awareness** noun consciousness, recognition, realization, perception, understanding, grasp, appreciation, knowledge, familiarity.

**away** adverb *we'll be away for two weeks:* elsewhere, abroad, gone, off, out, absent, on holiday, on vacation.

**awe** noun wonder, wonderment, admiration, reverence, respect, fear, dread.

**awesome** adjective breathtaking, awe-inspiring, magnificent, amazing, stunning, staggering, imposing, formidable, intimidating; informal mind-boggling, mind-blowing, brilliant.
OPPOSITES unimpressive.

**awful** adjective **1** *the place smelled awful:* disgusting, terrible, dreadful, ghastly, horrible, vile, foul, revolting, repulsive, repugnant, sickening, nauseating; informal gross; Brit. informal beastly. **2** *an awful book:* dreadful, terrible, frightful, atrocious, lamentable; informal crummy, pathetic, rotten, woeful, lousy, appalling, abysmal, dismal, dire; Brit. informal rubbish. **3** *an awful accident:* serious, bad, terrible, dreadful, shocking. **4** *I feel awful:* ill, unwell, sick, nauseous; Brit. off colour, poorly; Brit. informal grotty, ropy; Scottish informal wabbit, peely-wally; Austral./NZ informal crook.
OPPOSITES delightful, excellent, well.

**awfully** adverb **1** (informal) *an awfully nice man:* very, extremely, really, immensely, exceedingly, thoroughly, dreadfully, terrifically, terribly, exceptionally, remarkably, extraordinarily; N. English right; informal seriously, majorly; Brit. informal jolly, dead, well; N. Amer. informal real, mighty, awful;

informal, dated frightfully. **2** *we played awfully:* terribly, dreadfully, atrociously, appallingly; informal abysmally, pitifully, diabolically.

**awkward** adjective **1** *the box was awkward to carry:* difficult, tricky, cumbersome, unwieldy; Brit. informal fiddly. **2** *you're being really awkward:* unreasonable, uncooperative, unhelpful, difficult, obstructive, contrary, obstinate; Brit. informal bloody-minded, bolshie; N. Amer. informal balky. **3** *an awkward time:* inconvenient, inappropriate, inopportune, untimely. **4** *he put her in a very awkward position:* embarrassing, uncomfortable, unenviable, delicate, tricky, problematic, troublesome, humiliating, compromising; informal sticky. **5** *she felt awkward when alone with him:* uncomfortable, uneasy, tense, nervous, edgy, self-conscious, embarrassed. **6** *his awkward movements:* clumsy, ungainly, uncoordinated, graceless, inelegant, gauche, gawky, stiff, unskilful, inept, blundering; informal ham-fisted, cack-handed; Brit. informal all (fingers and) thumbs.
OPPOSITES easy, amenable, convenient, at ease, graceful, dexterous.

**axe** noun hatchet, chopper, cleaver, adze.
verb **1** *the show was axed:* cancel, withdraw, drop, scrap, cut, discontinue, end; informal ditch, dump, pull the plug on. **2** *500 staff were axed:* dismiss, make redundant, lay off, get rid of; informal sack, fire.
OPPOSITES start, launch, recruit.

**axle** noun shaft, spindle, rod.

# Bb

**babble** verb prattle, rattle on, gabble, chatter, jabber, twitter, burble, blather; informal yatter, blabber, jaw, gas, shoot one's mouth off; Brit. informal witter, rabbit, chunter, natter, waffle.

**baby** noun infant, newborn, child; Scottish & N. English bairn; technical neonate; informal sprog, tot; literary babe.
adjective *baby carrots:* miniature, mini, little, toy, pocket, midget, dwarf; Scottish wee; N. Amer. vest-pocket; informal teeny, teensy, tiddly, bite-sized; Brit. informal titchy; N. Amer. informal little-bitty.
OPPOSITES large.

**babyish** adjective childish, infantile, juvenile, puerile, immature.
OPPOSITES mature.

**back** noun 1 spine, backbone, spinal column, vertebral column. 2 *the back of the house:* rear; Nautical stern. 3 *the back of the queue:* end, tail end, rear end; N. Amer. tag end. 4 *the back of a postcard:* reverse, other side, underside; informal flip side.
OPPOSITES front, bow, head, face.
adverb 1 *he pushed his chair back:* backwards, behind one, to one's rear, rearwards, away. 2 *a few months back:* ago, earlier, previously, before.
OPPOSITES forward, ahead.
verb 1 *companies backed the scheme generously:* sponsor, finance, fund, subsidize, underwrite; informal pick up the bill for. 2 *most people backed the idea:* support, endorse, sanction, approve of, give one's

blessing to, smile on, favour, advocate, promote, champion; informal throw one's weight behind. 3 *he backed the horse at 33–1:* bet on, gamble on, stake money on. 4 *he backed away:* reverse, draw back, step back, pull back, retreat, withdraw.
OPPOSITES oppose, advance.
adjective 1 *the back seats:* rear, rearmost, hind, hindmost, posterior. 2 *a back copy:* past, old, previous, earlier.
OPPOSITES front, future.
■ **back down** give in, concede defeat, surrender, yield, submit, climb down. ■ **back out of** renege on, withdraw from, pull out of, fail to honour.
■ **back something up** substantiate, corroborate, confirm, support, bear out, endorse, lend weight to. ■ **back someone up** support, stand by, side with, take someone's part.

**backer** noun 1 *our financial backers:* sponsor, investor, underwriter, financier, patron, benefactor; informal angel. 2 *the backers of the proposition:* supporter, defender, advocate, promoter; N. Amer. booster.

**backfire** verb *Bernard's plan backfired on him:* rebound, boomerang, come back, fail; informal blow up in someone's face.

**background** noun 1 *a background of trees:* backdrop, backcloth, surrounding(s), setting, scene. 2 *students from different backgrounds:* social circumstances, family circumstances, environment,

class, culture, tradition. **3** *her nursing background:* experience, record, history, past, training, education.
OPPOSITES foreground.

**backing** noun **1** *he has the backing of his colleagues:* support, endorsement, approval, blessing. **2** *financial backing:* sponsorship, finance, funding, subsidy, patronage.

**backlash** noun adverse reaction, counterblast, repercussion, comeback, retaliation, reprisal.

**backup** noun *troops will provide backup:* help, support, assistance, aid, reserve, reinforcements.
adjective *a backup supply:* reserve, spare, substitute, replacement, standby, fallback, emergency.

**backward** adjective **1** *a backward look:* rearward, towards the rear, behind one, reverse. **2** *the decision was a backward step:* retrograde, regressive, for the worse, in the wrong direction, downhill, negative. **3** *economically backward:* underdeveloped, undeveloped, primitive. **4** *he was not backward in displaying his talents:* hesitant, reticent, reluctant, shy, diffident, timid.
OPPOSITES forward, progressive, advanced, confident.

**backwards** adverb towards the rear, rearwards, behind one.
OPPOSITES forwards.

**bad** adjective **1** *bad workmanship:* unsatisfactory, substandard, poor, inferior, second-rate, second-class, inadequate, deficient, imperfect, defective, faulty, shoddy, negligent; informal crummy, rotten, pathetic, useless, woeful, lousy; Brit. informal duff, rubbish. **2** *the alcohol had a bad effect:* harmful, damaging, detrimental, injurious, hurtful, destructive. **3** *the bad guys:* wicked, evil, sinful, criminal, immoral, corrupt; informal crooked, bent. **4** *you bad girl!* naughty, badly behaved, disobedient, wayward, wilful, defiant, unruly, undisciplined. **5** *bad news:* unpleasant, disagreeable, unwelcome, unfavourable, unfortunate, grim, distressing, gloomy. **6** *a bad time to arrive:* unfavourable, inauspicious, inopportune, unfortunate, disadvantageous, inappropriate, unsuitable. **7** *a bad accident:* serious, severe, grave, critical, acute. **8** *the meat's bad:* rotten, off, decayed, putrid, rancid, curdled, sour, mouldy. **9** *a bad knee:* injured, wounded, diseased; Brit. informal gammy, knackered; Austral./NZ informal crook.
OPPOSITES good, quality, beneficial, virtuous, well behaved, welcome, favourable, slight, fresh, healthy.

**badge** noun **1** brooch, pin, emblem, crest, insignia; N. Amer. button. **2** *a badge of success:* sign, symbol, indication, signal, mark, hallmark, trademark.

**badger** verb pester, harass, hound, harry, nag, bother, go on at; informal hassle, bug.

**badly** adverb **1** *the job had been badly done:* poorly, unsatisfactorily, inadequately, incorrectly, faultily, defectively, shoddily, amateurishly, carelessly, negligently, incompetently, inexpertly. **2** *try not to think badly of me:* unfavourably, ill, critically,

disapprovingly. **3** *stop behaving badly:* **naughtily**, disobediently, wilfully, mischievously. **4** *he had been badly treated:* **cruelly**, wickedly, unkindly, harshly, shamefully, unfairly, unjustly, wrongly. **5** *it turned out badly:* **unfavourably**, unsuccessfully, adversely, unfortunately. **6** *some of the victims are badly hurt:* **severely**, seriously, gravely, acutely, critically.
OPPOSITES well, properly, humanely, fairly, favourably, slightly.

**bad-tempered** adjective **irritable**, irascible, tetchy, testy, grumpy, grouchy, crotchety, in a (bad) mood, cantankerous, curmudgeonly, ill-tempered, ill-humoured, peevish, cross, fractious, pettish, crabby; informal **snappish**, on a short fuse; Brit. informal **shirty**, stroppy, ratty; N. Amer. informal **cranky**, ornery; Austral./NZ informal **snaky**.
OPPOSITES good-humoured, affable.

**baffle** verb **puzzle**, perplex, bewilder, mystify, confuse; informal **flummox**, stump, beat, fox.
OPPOSITES enlighten.

**bag** noun **suitcase**, case, valise, holdall, grip.
verb **1** *locals bagged the most fish:* **catch**, land, capture, trap, net, snare. **2** *he bagged seven medals:* **get**, secure, obtain, acquire, pick up, win, achieve; informal **land**, net.

**baggage** noun **luggage**, suitcases, cases, bags.

**baggy** adjective **loose**, roomy, generously cut, sloppy, full, voluminous.
OPPOSITES tight.

**bail** noun *he was released on bail:* **surety**, security, indemnity,

bond, guarantee, pledge.
■ **bail out** *the pilot bailed out:* **eject**, parachute to safety. ■ **bail someone/something out** **rescue**, save, relieve, finance, help (out), aid.

**bait** noun *was she the bait to lure him into a trap?* **enticement**, lure, decoy, snare, trap, inducement, siren, carrot, attraction; informal **come-on**.
verb *he was baited at school:* **taunt**, tease, goad, pick on, torment, persecute; informal **needle**; Brit. informal **wind up**.

**balance** noun **1** *I tripped and lost my balance:* **stability**, equilibrium, steadiness, footing. **2** *political balance in broadcasting:* **fairness**, justice, impartiality, parity, equity, evenness, uniformity, comparability. **3** *the balance of the rent:* **remainder**, outstanding amount, rest, residue, difference.
OPPOSITES instability, bias.
verb **1** *she balanced the book on her head:* **steady**, stabilize, poise, level. **2** *he balanced his radical remarks with more familiar declarations:* **counterbalance**, balance out, offset, counteract, compensate for, make up for. **3** *their income and expenditure do not balance:* **correspond**, agree, tally, match up, coincide. **4** *you need to balance cost against benefit:* **weigh (up)**, compare, evaluate, consider, assess.

**bald** adjective **1** *a bald head:* **hairless**, smooth, shaven, depilated. **2** *a bald statement:* **plain**, simple, direct, blunt, unadorned, unvarnished; informal **upfront**.
OPPOSITES hairy, vague.

**ball** noun **sphere**, globe, orb,

globule, spheroid.

**ballot** noun vote, poll, election, referendum, show of hands, plebiscite.

**ban** verb 1 *smoking was banned:* prohibit, forbid, veto, proscribe, outlaw, make illegal, bar. 2 *Gary was banned from the playground:* exclude, bar, banish, expel, eject, evict, drive out, force out; informal kick out.
OPPOSITES permit, admit.
noun 1 *a ban on smoking:* prohibition, veto, bar, proscription, moratorium, injunction. 2 *a ban from league football:* exclusion, bar, banishment, expulsion, ejection, eviction.
OPPOSITES permission, admission.

**banal** adjective unoriginal, unimaginative, trite, hackneyed, clichéd, commonplace, stereotyped, overused, stale, boring, obvious; informal corny.
OPPOSITES original.

**band¹** noun *a band round his wrist:* loop, wristband, headband, ring, hoop, circlet, belt, sash, girdle, strap, strip, tape, circle.

**band²** noun 1 *a band of robbers:* gang, group, mob, pack, troop, troupe, company, set, party, crew, body, team; informal bunch. 2 *the band played on:* group, pop group, ensemble, orchestra; informal combo.

**bandage** noun dressing, covering, plaster, compress, gauze, lint.
verb *she bandaged my knee:* bind, dress, cover, strap (up).

**bandit** noun robber, thief, raider, mugger, pirate, outlaw, hijacker, looter, gangster; literary brigand; historical rustler, highwayman.

**bang** noun 1 *the door slammed with a bang:* thud, thump, bump, crack, crash, smack, boom, blast, clap, report, explosion. 2 *a bang on the head:* blow, knock, thump, bump, hit, smack, crack; informal bash, whack.
verb 1 *he banged the table with his fist:* hit, strike, beat, thump, hammer, knock, rap, pound, thud, punch, bump, smack, crack, slap, slam; informal bash, whack, clobber, clout, wallop. 2 *fireworks banged in the air:* thud, thump, bump, crack, crash, boom, pound, explode, detonate, burst, blow up.

**banish** verb 1 *he was banished for his crime:* exile, expel, deport, eject, repatriate, transport, extradite, evict, throw out, exclude, shut out, ban. 2 *he tried to banish his fear:* dispel, dismiss, disperse, scatter, dissipate, drive away, chase away, shut out.
OPPOSITES admit, cause, induce.

**bank¹** noun 1 *the banks of Lake Michigan:* edge, shore, side, embankment, levee, margin, verge, brink. 2 *a grassy bank:* slope, rise, incline, gradient, ramp, mound, pile, heap, ridge, hillock, knoll, bar, shoal, mass, drift. 3 *a bank of switches:* array, row, line, tier, group, series.
verb 1 *they banked up the earth:* pile up, heap up, stack up, amass. 2 *the aircraft banked:* tilt, lean, tip, slant, incline, angle, list, camber, pitch.
OPPOSITES level, spread out, level out.

**bank²** noun store, reserve, stock, stockpile, supply, pool, fund, cache, hoard, deposit.

**verb** *I banked the money:* deposit, pay in, save.
OPPOSITES withdraw.

**bankrupt** adjective insolvent, ruined; Brit. in administration, in receivership; informal bust, broke, belly up, wiped out.
OPPOSITES solvent.

**banner** noun 1 *students waved banners:* placard, sign, poster, notice. 2 *banners fluttered above the troops:* flag, standard, ensign, colour(s), pennant, banderole.

**banquet** noun feast, dinner; informal spread, blowout; Brit. informal nosh-up, slap-up meal.
OPPOSITES snack.

**baptize** verb 1 *he was baptized as a baby:* christen. 2 *they were baptized into the church:* admit, initiate, enrol, recruit. 3 *he was baptized Enoch:* name, call, dub.

**bar** noun 1 *an iron bar:* rod, stick, pole, batten, shaft, rail, spar, strut, crosspiece, beam. 2 *a bar of chocolate:* block, slab, cake, tablet, wedge, ingot. 3 *your drinks are on the bar:* counter, table, buffet. 4 *she had a drink in a bar:* inn, tavern, hostelry; Brit. pub, public house; Brit. informal local, boozer. 5 *a bar to promotion:* obstacle, impediment, hindrance, obstruction, block, hurdle, barrier.
OPPOSITES aid.
**verb** 1 *they have barred the door:* bolt, lock, fasten, secure, block, barricade, obstruct. 2 *I was barred from entering:* prohibit, debar, preclude, forbid, ban, exclude, obstruct, prevent, hinder, block.
OPPOSITES open, admit, allow.

**barbarian** noun 1 *the city was besieged by barbarians:* savage, heathen. 2 *you arrogant barbarian!* brute, beast, philistine, boor, yahoo, oaf, lout; Brit. informal yob.

**barbaric** adjective 1 *barbaric crimes:* cruel, brutal, barbarous, brutish, savage, vicious, wicked, ruthless, vile, inhuman. 2 *barbaric cultures:* uncultured, uncivilized, barbarian, philistine, boorish, loutish; Brit. informal yobbish.
OPPOSITES civilized.

**bare** adjective 1 *he was bare to the waist:* naked, unclothed, undressed, uncovered, stripped, with nothing on, nude; informal without a stitch on, in the altogether; Brit. informal starkers; Scottish informal in the scud; N. Amer. informal buck naked. 2 *the room was bare:* empty, unfurnished, clear, undecorated, unadorned. 3 *the bare facts:* basic, essential, fundamental, plain, straightforward, simple, unembellished, pure, stark, bald, cold, hard.
OPPOSITES dressed, furnished, decorated, embellished.

**barely** adverb hardly, scarcely, only just, narrowly, by the skin of one's teeth, by a hair's breadth; informal by a whisker; Brit. informal at a push.
OPPOSITES easily.

**bargain** noun 1 *I'll make a bargain with you:* agreement, arrangement, understanding, deal, contract, pact. 2 *this binder is a bargain at £1.98:* good value; informal good buy, cheap buy, snip, steal, giveaway.
OPPOSITES rip-off.
**verb** haggle, negotiate, discuss terms, deal, barter.
■ **bargain for/on** expect, anticipate, be prepared for, allow for, plan for, reckon with, envisage, foresee, predict,

count on, reckon on; N. Amer. informal figure on. ■ into the bargain in addition, as well, also, besides, on top, to boot, for good measure.

**bark**[1] verb **1** *the dog barked:* woof, yap. **2** *'Okay, outside!' he barked:* shout, snap, bawl, yell, roar, bellow, thunder; informal holler.
OPPOSITES whisper.

**bark**[2] noun *the bark of a tree:* rind, skin, peel, covering.

**barracks** plural noun garrison, camp, encampment, depot, billet, quarters, fort, cantonment.

**barrage** noun **1** *an artillery barrage:* bombardment, gunfire, shelling, salvo, volley, fusillade; historical broadside. **2** *a barrage of criticism:* deluge, stream, storm, torrent, onslaught, flood, spate, tide, avalanche, hail, blaze. **3** *a barrage across the river:* dam, barrier, weir, dyke, embankment, wall.

**barrel** noun cask, keg, butt, vat, tun, drum, hogshead, firkin.

**barren** adjective unproductive, infertile, unfruitful, sterile, arid, desert.
OPPOSITES fertile.

**barricade** noun *a barricade across the street:* barrier, roadblock, blockade, obstacle, obstruction.
verb *they barricaded the building:* seal up, close up, block off, shut off/up, defend, protect, fortify, occupy.

**barrier** noun **1** fence, railing, barricade, hurdle, bar, blockade, roadblock. **2** *a barrier to international trade:* obstacle, obstruction, hurdle, stumbling block, bar, impediment, hindrance, curb.

**barter** verb **1** *they bartered grain for salt:* trade, swap, exchange, sell. **2** *you can barter for souvenirs:* haggle, bargain, negotiate, deal.

**base**[1] noun **1** *the base of the tower:* foundation, bottom, foot, support, stand, pedestal, plinth. **2** *the system uses existing technology as its base:* basis, foundation, bedrock, starting point, source, origin, root(s), core, key component. **3** *the troops returned to their base:* headquarters, camp, site, station, settlement, post, centre.
OPPOSITES top.
verb **1** *he based his idea on a movie:* found, build, construct, form, ground; (be based on) derive from, spring from, stem from, depend on. **2** *the company was based in London:* locate, situate, position, install, station, site.

**base**[2] adjective *base motives:* sordid, ignoble, low, mean, immoral, unscrupulous, unprincipled, dishonest, dishonourable, shameful.
OPPOSITES noble.

**bashful** adjective shy, reserved, diffident, inhibited, retiring, reticent, reluctant, shrinking, timid, nervous.
OPPOSITES bold, confident.

**basic** adjective **1** *basic human rights:* fundamental, essential, vital, primary, principal, cardinal, elementary, intrinsic, central, pivotal, critical, key, focal. **2** *basic cooking facilities:* plain, simple, unsophisticated, straightforward, adequate, spartan, stark, severe, austere, limited, meagre, rudimentary, patchy, sketchy, minimal, crude, makeshift; informal bog-standard.

**basically** adverb fundamentally, essentially, first and foremost, primarily, at heart, at bottom, intrinsically, inherently, principally, chiefly, above all, mostly, mainly, on the whole, by and large; informal at the end of the day.

OPPOSITES secondary, unimportant, elaborate.

**basics** plural noun fundamentals, essentials, first principles, foundations, preliminaries, groundwork, essence, basis, core; informal nitty-gritty, brass tacks, nuts and bolts, ABC.

**basin** noun bowl, dish, pan.

**basis** noun 1 *the basis of his method:* foundation, support, base, reasoning, rationale, defence, reason, grounds, justification. 2 *the basis of discussion:* starting point, base, point of departure, beginning, premise, fundamental point/principle, cornerstone, core, heart. 3 *on a part-time basis:* footing, condition, status, position, arrangement.

**bask** verb laze, lie, lounge, relax, sprawl, loll.

**bass** adjective low, deep, resonant, sonorous, rumbling, booming, resounding.

OPPOSITES high.

**batch** noun group, quantity, lot, bunch, cluster, raft, set, collection, bundle, pack, consignment, shipment.

**bathe** verb 1 *I bathed in the pool:* swim, take a dip. 2 *they bathed his wounds:* clean, wash, rinse, wet, soak. 3 *the room was bathed in light:* flood, cover, envelop, fill, wash, pervade, suffuse.

**baton** noun 1 *the conductor's baton:* stick, rod, staff, wand. 2 *police batons:* truncheon, club, cudgel, stick, mace, shillelagh; N. Amer. nightstick, blackjack; Brit. informal cosh.

**batter** verb beat up, hit repeatedly, pummel, pound, rain blows on, buffet, belabour, thrash; informal knock about/around, lay into, do over.

**battle** noun 1 *he was killed in the battle:* fight, engagement, armed conflict, clash, struggle, skirmish, fray, war, campaign, crusade, warfare, combat, action, hostilities; informal scrap, dogfight, shoot-out. 2 *a legal battle:* conflict, clash, struggle, disagreement, argument, dispute.

OPPOSITES peace.

verb fight, combat, contend with, resist, withstand, stand up to, confront, war, feud, struggle, strive, work.

**battlefield** noun battleground, field of battle, field of operations, combat zone, lines, front, theatre of war.

**bawl** verb 1 *'Come on!' he bawled:* shout, yell, roar, bellow, screech, scream, shriek, bark, thunder; informal yammer, holler. 2 *the children continued to bawl:* cry, sob, weep, wail, whine, howl; Scottish informal greet.

OPPOSITES whisper.

**bay**[1] noun *ships were anchored in the bay:* cove, inlet, gulf, sound, bight, basin, fjord.

**bay**[2] noun *there was a bay let into the wall:* alcove, recess, niche, nook, opening, inglenook.

**bazaar** noun 1 *a Turkish bazaar:* market, marketplace, souk, mart. 2 *the church bazaar:* fête, fair, fund-raiser, charity event; Brit. jumble sale, bring-and-buy sale, car boot sale; N. Amer. tag sale.

**beach** noun sands, seaside, seashore, coast; literary strand.
verb *they beached the boat:* land, ground, strand, run ashore.

**beacon** noun signal, light, fire, danger signal, bonfire, lighthouse.

**bead** noun 1 *a string of beads:* ball, pellet, pill, globule, sphere, spheroid, orb, round; (**beads**) necklace, rosary, chaplet. 2 *beads of sweat:* droplet, drop, drip, blob, pearl, dot.

**beaker** noun cup, tumbler, glass, mug, drinking vessel.

**beam** noun 1 *an oak beam:* plank, timber, joist, rafter, lintel, spar, girder, support. 2 *a beam of light:* ray, shaft, stream, streak, flash, gleam, glint. 3 *the beam on her face:* grin, smile.
OPPOSITES frown.
verb 1 *the signal is beamed out:* broadcast, transmit, relay, disseminate, direct, send, aim. 2 *the sun beamed down:* shine, radiate, glare, gleam. 3 *he beamed broadly:* grin, smile, smirk.
OPPOSITES frown.

**bear** verb 1 *she was bearing a box:* carry, bring, transport, move, convey, take, fetch; informal tote. 2 *the bag bore my name:* display, be marked with, show, carry, exhibit. 3 *will it bear his weight?* support, withstand, sustain, stand, take, carry, hold up, cope with, handle. 4 *she bore no grudge:* harbour, foster, entertain, cherish, nurse. 5 *I can't bear sport:* endure, tolerate, put up with, stand, abide, countenance, stomach; informal

hack, swallow; Brit. informal stick, wear, be doing with; formal brook. 6 *she bore a son:* give birth to, bring forth, deliver, have, produce, spawn. 7 *a shrub that bears berries:* produce, yield, give, provide, supply.
■ bear fruit yield results, succeed, be effective, be profitable, work; informal pay off, do the trick. ■ bear something out confirm, corroborate, substantiate, endorse, vindicate, give credence to, support, justify, prove. ■ bear up remain cheerful, cope, manage, get by, muddle through. ■ bear with be patient with, make allowances for, tolerate, put up with, endure.

**bearer** noun 1 *a lantern-bearer:* carrier, porter. 2 *the bearer of bad news:* bringer, messenger, agent, conveyor, emissary.

**bearing** noun 1 *a man of military bearing:* posture, stance, carriage, gait; Brit. deportment. 2 *a rather regal bearing:* demeanour, manner, air, aspect, attitude, style. 3 *this has no bearing on the matter:* relevance, pertinence, connection, import, significance. 4 *a bearing of 015°:* direction, orientation, course, trajectory, heading, tack, path. 5 (**bearings**) orientation, sense of direction, whereabouts, location, position.
OPPOSITES irrelevance.

**beast** noun 1 *the beasts of the forest:* animal, creature, brute; N. Amer. informal critter. 2 *he is a cruel beast:* monster, brute, savage, barbarian, animal, swine, ogre, fiend, sadist, demon, devil.

**beat** verb 1 hit, strike, batter, thump, bang, hammer, punch,

a
**b**
c
d
e
f
g
h
i
j
k
l
m
n
o
p
q
r
s
t
u
v
w
x
y
z

knock, thrash, pound, pummel, slap, rain blows on, assault; informal wallop, belt, bash, whack, clout, clobber. **2** *her heart was still beating:* throb, pulse, pulsate, pump, palpitate, pound, thump, thud, hammer, drum. **3** *the eagle beat its wings:* flap, flutter, thrash, wave, vibrate. **4** *beat the cream into the mixture:* whisk, mix, blend, whip. **5** *the team they need to beat:* defeat, conquer, vanquish, trounce, rout, overpower, overcome; informal lick, thrash, whip. **6** *he beat the record:* exceed, surpass, better, improve on, eclipse, transcend, top, trump, cap.

noun **1** *the song has a good beat:* rhythm, pulse, metre, time, measure, cadence, stress, accent. **2** *the beat of hooves:* pounding, banging, thumping, thudding, hammering, crashing. **3** *the beat of her heart:* pulse, pulsation, vibration, throb, palpitation, reverberation, pounding, thump, thud, hammering, drumming. **4** *a policeman on his beat:* circuit, round, route, path.

■ **beat someone/something off** repel, fight off, fend off, stave off, repulse, drive away/back, push back. ■ **beat someone up** assault, attack, mug; informal knock about/around, do over, work over, rough up; Brit. informal duff someone up; N. Amer. informal beat up on.

**beautiful** adjective attractive, pretty, handsome, good-looking, fetching, lovely, charming, graceful, elegant, appealing, winsome, ravishing, gorgeous, stunning, glamorous; Scottish & N. English bonny; informal tasty, knockout, drop-dead gorgeous; Brit. informal smashing; N. Amer. informal cute, foxy; Austral./NZ informal beaut, spunky.
OPPOSITES ugly.

**beauty** noun **1** attractiveness, prettiness, good looks, loveliness, appeal, winsomeness, charm, grace, elegance, exquisiteness, glamour; Scottish & N. English bonniness. **2** *she is a beauty:* belle, vision, goddess, picture, Venus; informal babe, looker, lovely, stunner, knockout, bombshell, bit of all right.
OPPOSITES ugliness, hag, boot.

**because** conjunction since, as, seeing that, in view of the fact that, in that. ■ **because of** on account of, as a result of, as a consequence of, owing to, due to, thanks to, by virtue of; formal by reason of.

**beckon** verb **1** *the guard beckoned to Benny:* gesture, signal, wave, gesticulate, motion. **2** *the countryside beckons you:* entice, invite, tempt, lure, charm, attract, draw, call.

**become** verb **1** *she became rich:* grow, get, turn, come to be, get to be. **2** *he became a tyrant:* turn into, change into, transform into, be converted into. **3** *he became Foreign Secretary:* be appointed, be assigned as, be nominated, be elected. **4** *the dress becomes her:* suit, flatter, look good on, set off; informal do something for. ■ **become of** happen to, be the fate of, be the lot of, overtake.

**becoming** adjective flattering, fetching, attractive, pretty, elegant, handsome, well-chosen, stylish, fashionable, tasteful.

**bed** noun **1** couch, berth, billet, cot; informal the sack. **2** *a flower*

*bed:* patch, plot, border, strip.
**3** *built on a bed of stones:* base,
foundation, footing, support,
basis.

**verb** *the tiles are bedded in
mortar:* embed, set, fix, insert,
inlay, implant, bury, plant.
■ **go to bed** retire; informal hit
the sack, hit the hay, turn in.

**bedraggled** adjective
dishevelled, disordered, untidy,
unkempt, tousled; N. Amer. informal
mussed.
OPPOSITES neat.

**before** preposition **1** *he dressed
up before going out:* prior to,
previous to, earlier than,
preparatory to, in advance of,
ahead of, pre-.... **2** *he appeared
before the judge:* in front of, in
the presence of. **3** *death before
dishonour:* in preference to,
rather than, sooner than.
OPPOSITES after.

**adverb** previously, before now/
then, until now/then, up to
now/then, earlier, formerly,
hitherto, in the past.
OPPOSITES afterwards, later.

**beforehand** adverb in advance,
in readiness, ahead of time,
before, before now/then,
earlier (on), previously, already,
sooner.
OPPOSITES afterwards.

**beg** verb **1** *he begged on the
streets:* ask for money, seek
charity; informal sponge, cadge,
scrounge, bum. **2** *we begged for
mercy:* plead for, request, ask
for, appeal for, call for, sue for,
solicit, seek. **3** *he begged her not
to go:* implore, entreat, plead
with, appeal to, pray to, call on,
petition; literary beseech.

**beggar** noun tramp, vagrant,
vagabond, mendicant; N. Amer.
hobo; informal scrounger,
sponger, cadger, freeloader; Brit.

informal **dosser**; N. Amer. informal
bum; Austral./NZ informal bagman.

**begin** verb **1** *we began work:*
start, commence, set about, go
about, embark on, launch into,
get down to, take up, initiate,
set in motion, get going, get off
the ground, lead off, institute,
inaugurate, open; informal get
cracking on, kick off. **2** *when
did the illness begin?* appear,
arise, become apparent, spring
up, crop up, turn up, come into
existence, originate, start,
commence, develop.
OPPOSITES finish, end, disappear.

**beginner** noun novice, learner,
starter, (raw) recruit,
newcomer, tyro, fresher,
probationer; N. Amer. tenderfoot;
informal rookie, new kid (on the
block), newie; N. Amer. informal
greenhorn.
OPPOSITES expert, veteran.

**beginning** noun **1** *the beginning
of socialism:* start,
commencement, creation, birth,
inception, conception,
origination, origin, genesis,
emergence, rise, dawn, launch,
onset, outset, day one; informal
kick-off. **2** *the beginning of the
article:* opening, start,
commencement, first part,
introduction, preamble.
OPPOSITES end, conclusion.

**behalf**
■ **on behalf of/on someone's
behalf 1** *I am writing on behalf
of my client:* as a representative
of, as a spokesperson for, for, in
the name of, in place of, on the
authority of. **2** *a campaign on
behalf of cycling:* in the
interests of, in support of, for,
for the benefit of, for the good
of, for the sake of.

**behave** verb **1** *she behaved
badly:* act, conduct oneself,

a
**b**
c
d
e
f
g
h
i
j
k
l
m
n
o
p
q
r
s
t
u
v
w
x
y
z

acquit oneself. **2** *the children behaved themselves:* act correctly, be good, be well behaved, conduct oneself well. OPPOSITES misbehave.

**behaviour** noun **1** *his behaviour was inexcusable:* conduct, actions, doings, manners, ways, deportment, bearing, etiquette. **2** *the behaviour of these organisms:* functioning, action, performance, operation, working, reaction, response.

**behind** preposition **1** *he hid behind a tree:* at the back/rear of, beyond, on the far/other side of; N. Amer. in back of. **2** *a guard ran behind him:* after, following, at the back/rear of, hard on the heels of, in the wake of. **3** *you are behind the rest of the class:* less advanced than, slower than, weaker than. **4** *he was behind the bombings:* responsible for, at the bottom of, the cause of, the perpetrator of, the organizer of, to blame for, guilty of. **5** *they have the nation behind them:* supporting, backing, for, on the side of, in agreement with; informal rooting for. OPPOSITES in front of, ahead of, against.

adverb **1** *a man followed behind:* after, afterwards, at the back/end, in the rear. **2** *I looked behind:* over one's shoulder, towards the back/rear, backwards. **3** *we're behind, so don't stop:* running late, behind schedule, behindhand, not on time. **4** *he was behind with his subscription:* in arrears, overdue, late, unpunctual, behindhand. OPPOSITES in front, ahead, in advance.

**being** noun **1** *she is warmed by his very being:* existence, living, life, reality, lifeblood, vital force. **2** *God is alive in the being of man:* soul, spirit, nature, essence, psyche, heart, bosom, breast. **3** *an enlightened being:* creature, life form, organism, living thing, individual, person, human.

**belated** adjective late, overdue, behindhand, delayed, tardy, unpunctual. OPPOSITES early, punctual.

**beleaguered** adjective **1** *the beleaguered garrison:* besieged, blockaded, surrounded, encircled, hemmed in, under attack. **2** *a beleaguered government:* troubled, harassed, hard-pressed, in difficulties, under pressure, in a tight corner; informal up against it.

**belief** noun **1** *it's my belief that age is irrelevant:* opinion, view, conviction, judgement, thinking, idea, theory. **2** *belief in God:* faith, trust, reliance, confidence, credence. **3** *traditional beliefs:* ideology, principle, ethic, tenet, doctrine, teaching, dogma, creed, credo. OPPOSITES disbelief, doubt.

**believe** verb **1** *I don't believe you:* trust, have confidence in, consider honest, consider truthful. **2** *do you believe that story?* accept, be convinced by, give credence to, credit, trust, put confidence in; informal swallow, buy, go for. **3** *I believe he worked for you:* think, be of the opinion that, have an idea that, imagine, assume, presume, take it, understand, gather; informal reckon, figure. OPPOSITES doubt.

■ **believe in** have faith in, trust in, have every confidence in, cling to, set (great) store by, value, be convinced by, be persuaded by; informal swear by, rate.

**believer** noun disciple, follower, supporter, adherent, devotee, upholder, worshipper.
OPPOSITES infidel, sceptic.

**belittle** verb disparage, denigrate, run down, deprecate, play down, trivialize, minimize; informal do down, pooh-pooh.
OPPOSITES praise, magnify.

**belligerent** adjective 1 *a belligerent stare:* hostile, aggressive, threatening, antagonistic, pugnacious, bellicose, truculent, confrontational, contentious, militant, combative; informal spoiling for a fight; Brit. informal stroppy, bolshie; N. Amer. informal scrappy. 2 *the belligerent states:* warring, combatant, fighting, battling.
OPPOSITES peaceable, neutral.

**bellow** verb roar, shout, bawl, thunder, boom, bark, yell, shriek, howl, scream; informal holler.
OPPOSITES whisper.

**belly** noun stomach, abdomen, paunch, middle, midriff, girth; informal tummy, gut, insides.

**belong** verb 1 *the house belongs to his mother:* be owned by, be the property of, be held by, be in the hands of. 2 *I belong to a union:* be a member of, be in, be affiliated to, be allied to, be associated with. 3 *the garden belongs to the flat:* be part of, be attached to, go with. 4 *she doesn't belong here:* fit in, be suited to; informal go, click.

**belongings** plural noun possessions, effects, worldly goods, chattels, property; informal gear, tackle, kit, things, stuff,

bits and pieces; Brit. informal clobber.

**beloved** adjective *her beloved brother:* darling, dear, precious, adored, cherished, treasured, prized, valued, idolized.
OPPOSITES hated.
noun *he watched his beloved:* sweetheart, love, darling, dearest, lover, girlfriend, boyfriend; informal steady, baby, angel, honey, pet.

**below** preposition 1 *the water rushed below them:* beneath, under, underneath, lower than. 2 *the sum is below average:* less than, lower than, under, not as much as, smaller than. 3 *a captain is below a major:* lower than, under, inferior to, subordinate to.
OPPOSITES above, over, more than.
adverb 1 *I could see what was happening below:* further down, lower down, underneath, beneath. 2 *the statements below:* underneath, following, further on, at a later point.
OPPOSITES above.

**belt** noun 1 sash, girdle, band, strap, cummerbund. 2 *the commuter belt:* region, strip, stretch, zone, area, district, sector, territory.

**bemused** adjective bewildered, confused, puzzled, perplexed, baffled, mystified, nonplussed, dumbfounded, at sea, at a loss; informal flummoxed, bamboozled, fazed.

**bench** noun 1 *he sat on a bench:* seat, form, pew, stall, settle. 2 *a laboratory bench:* workbench, worktop, counter.

**benchmark** noun standard, point of reference, guide, guideline, norm, touchstone,

a
**b**
c
d
e
f
g
h
i
j
k
l
m
n
o
p
q
r
s
t
u
v
w
x
y
z

yardstick, barometer, model, gauge, criterion, specification.

**bend** verb **1** *the frames can be bent to fit your face:* curve, crook, flex, angle, hook, bow, arch, buckle, warp, contort, distort, deform, twist. **2** *the highway bent to the left:* turn, curve, incline, swing, veer, fork, change course, curl, loop. **3** *he bent down to tie his shoe:* stoop, bow, crouch, hunch, lean down/over.
OPPOSITES straighten.
noun *a bend in the road:* curve, turn, corner, kink, angle, arc, twist.
OPPOSITES straight.

**beneath** preposition **1** *we sat beneath the trees:* under, underneath, below, at the foot of, at the bottom of, lower than. **2** *the rank beneath theirs:* inferior to, below, lower than, subordinate to. **3** *such an attitude was beneath her:* unworthy of, unbecoming to, degrading to.
OPPOSITES above.
adverb *sand with rock beneath:* underneath, below, further down, lower down.
OPPOSITES above.

**benefactor** noun patron, supporter, backer, sponsor, donor, contributor, subscriber; informal angel.

**beneficial** adjective advantageous, favourable, helpful, useful, of assistance, valuable, profitable, rewarding, gainful.
OPPOSITES disadvantageous.

**beneficiary** noun recipient, payee, heir, heiress, inheritor.

**benefit** noun **1** *for the benefit of others:* good, sake, welfare, well-being, advantage, comfort, ease, convenience, help, aid,

assistance, service. **2** *the benefits of working for a large firm:* advantage, profit, plus point, boon, blessing, reward; informal perk. **3** *state benefit:* social security payment, welfare, charity; informal the dole; Scottish informal the broo.
OPPOSITES detriment, disadvantage.
verb **1** *the deal benefited them both:* be advantageous to, be beneficial to, profit, do good to, be of service to, serve, be useful to, be helpful to, aid. **2** *they may benefit from drugs:* profit, gain, reap reward, make the most of, exploit, turn to one's advantage, put to good use.
OPPOSITES disadvantage, harm, suffer.

**benevolent** adjective kind, kindly, kind-hearted, good-natured, compassionate, caring, altruistic, humanitarian, philanthropic.
OPPOSITES unkind.

**benign** adjective **1** *a benign grandfatherly role:* kindly, kind, warm-hearted, good-natured, friendly, genial, tender-hearted, gentle, sympathetic, compassionate, caring, well disposed, benevolent. **2** *a benign climate:* mild, temperate, gentle, balmy, soft, pleasant, favourable, healthy. **3** (Medicine) *a benign tumour:* harmless, non-malignant, non-cancerous.
OPPOSITES unkind, unhealthy, hostile, malignant.

**bent** adjective **1** twisted, crooked, warped, contorted, deformed, misshapen, out of shape, bowed, arched, curved, angled, hooked, kinked; N. Amer. informal pretzeled. **2** *a mob bent*

*on violence:* intent, determined, set, insistent, resolved.
OPPOSITES straight.

noun *an artistic bent:* inclination, leaning, tendency, talent, gift, flair, aptitude, facility, skill.

**bequeath** verb leave, will, hand down, pass on, entrust, make over, grant, transfer, give, bestow on, confer on.

**bequest** noun legacy, estate, inheritance, endowment, settlement.

**bereavement** noun death in the family, loss, passing (away), demise.

**berserk** adjective mad, crazy, insane, out of one's mind, hysterical, frenzied, crazed, demented, maniacal, manic, frantic, raving, wild, out of control, amok, on the rampage; informal off one's head, off the deep end, ape, bananas, bonkers; Brit. informal spare; N. Amer. informal postal.

**berth** noun 1 *a 4-berth cabin:* bunk, bed, cot, couch, hammock. 2 *the vessel left its berth:* mooring, dock, pier, jetty, quay.
verb *the ship berthed in London:* dock, moor, land, tie up, make fast.

**beside** preposition alongside, by/ at the side of, next to, parallel to, abreast of, adjacent to, next door to, neighbouring.
■ **beside oneself** distraught, overcome, out of one's mind, frantic, desperate, distracted, at one's wits' end, frenzied, hysterical.

**besides** preposition *who did you ask besides Mary?* in addition to, as well as, over and above, on top of, apart from, other than, aside from, not counting,

excluding, leaving aside; N. Amer. informal outside of.
adverb 1 *there's a lot more besides:* in addition, as well, too, also, into the bargain, on top of that, to boot. 2 *besides, he's a man:* furthermore, moreover, further; informal what's more.

**besiege** verb 1 *the army besieged Leith:* lay siege to, beleaguer, blockade. 2 *he was besieged by fans:* surround, mob, harass, pester, badger. 3 *we were besieged with requests:* overwhelm, bombard, inundate, deluge, flood, swamp, snow under.

**best** adjective 1 *the best hotel in Paris:* finest, premier, greatest, top, foremost, leading, pre-eminent, supreme, superlative, unrivalled, second to none, without equal, unsurpassed, unparalleled, unbeatable, optimum, ultimate, incomparable, record-breaking; informal star, number-one, a cut above the rest, top-drawer. 2 *do whatever you think best:* most advantageous, most useful, most suitable, most fitting, most appropriate, most advisable.
OPPOSITES worst.
adverb 1 *the best-dressed man:* to the highest standard, in the best way. 2 *the food he liked best:* most, to the highest/ greatest degree. 3 *this is best done at home:* most appropriately, most suitably, most fittingly, most usefully, most advantageously, most sensibly, most prudently, most wisely.
OPPOSITES worst, least.
noun *only the best will do:* finest, choicest, top, cream, choice, prime, elite, crème de la

crème, flower, jewel in the crown; informal tops, pick of the bunch.
OPPOSITES worst.

**bestow** verb confer on, grant, accord, afford, endow someone with, present, award, give, donate, entrust with, vouchsafe.

**bet** verb **1** *he bet £10 on the favourite:* wager, gamble, stake, risk, venture, hazard, chance; Brit. informal punt, have a flutter. **2** (informal) *I bet it was your idea:* be certain, be sure, be convinced, be confident, expect, predict, guess.
noun **1** *a £20 bet:* wager, gamble, stake, ante; Brit. informal punt, flutter. **2** (informal) *your best bet is to go early:* option, choice, alternative, course of action, plan.

**betray** verb **1** *he betrayed his own brother:* be disloyal to, be unfaithful to, break faith with, play someone false, inform on/against, give away, denounce, sell out, stab in the back; informal split on, rat on, stitch up, do the dirty on, sell down the river; Brit. informal grass on, shop, sneak on; N. Amer. informal rat out, drop a/the dime on, finger; Austral./NZ informal dob in, point the bone at. **2** *he betrayed a secret:* reveal, disclose, divulge, tell, give away, leak, bring out into the open.
OPPOSITES be loyal to, keep.

**betrayal** noun disloyalty, treachery, bad faith, breach of faith, breach of trust, faithlessness, duplicity, deception, double-dealing, stab in the back, double-cross, sell-out.
OPPOSITES loyalty.

**better** adjective **1** *better*

*facilities:* superior, finer, of higher quality, preferable; informal a cut above, streets ahead, head and shoulders above, ahead of the pack/field. **2** *there couldn't be a better time:* more advantageous, more suitable, more fitting, more appropriate, more useful, more valuable, more desirable. **3** *are you better?* healthier, fitter, stronger, well again, cured, healed, recovered, recovering, on the road to recovery, on the mend.
OPPOSITES worse, inferior.
adverb **1** *I played better today:* to a higher standard, in a superior way, more effectively. **2** *this may suit you better:* more, to a greater degree/extent. **3** *the money could be better spent:* more wisely, more sensibly, more suitably, more fittingly, more advantageously, more usefully.
verb **1** *he bettered the record:* surpass, improve on, beat, exceed, top, cap, trump, eclipse. **2** *refugees who want to better their lot:* improve, ameliorate, raise, advance, further, lift, upgrade, enhance.
OPPOSITES worsen.

**between** preposition **1** *Philip stood between his parents:* in the middle of, with one on either side, among; archaic betwixt. **2** *the bond between her and her mother:* connecting, linking, joining, uniting, allying.

**beware** verb watch out, look out, mind out, be alert, keep your eyes open/peeled, keep an eye out, take care, be careful, be cautious, watch your step, guard against.

**bewilder** verb baffle, mystify,

bemuse, perplex, puzzle, confuse; informal flummox, faze, stump, beat.
OPPOSITES enlighten.

**beyond** preposition **1** *beyond the trees:* on the far side of, on the other side of, further away than, behind, past, after. **2** *beyond six o'clock:* later than, past, after. **3** *inflation beyond 10 per cent:* greater than, more than, exceeding, in excess of, above, upwards of. **4** *little beyond food was provided:* apart from, except, other than, besides; informal outside of; formal save.

**bias** noun *he accused the media of bias:* prejudice, partiality, favouritism, unfairness, one-sidedness, discrimination, leaning, tendency, inclination.
OPPOSITES impartiality.
verb *this may have biased the result:* prejudice, influence, colour, sway, predispose, distort, skew, slant.

**biased** adjective prejudiced, partial, partisan, one-sided, bigoted, discriminatory, distorted, warped, twisted, skewed.
OPPOSITES impartial.

**bid** verb *United bid £1 million for the striker:* offer, put up, tender, proffer, propose.
noun **1** *a bid of £3,000:* offer, tender, proposal. **2** *a bid to cut crime:* attempt, effort, endeavour, try; informal crack, go, shot, stab.

**bidding** noun command, order, direction, instruction, decree, injunction, demand, beck and call.

**big** adjective **1** *a big building:* large, sizeable, substantial, great, huge, immense, enormous, extensive, colossal, massive, vast, gigantic, giant, spacious; informal jumbo, whopping, thumping, bumper, mega; Brit. informal whacking, ginormous; formal commodious. **2** *a big man:* well built, sturdy, brawny, burly, broad-shouldered, muscular, bulky, hulking, strapping, hefty, tall, huge, fat, stout; informal hunky, beefy. **3** *my big brother:* grown-up, adult, mature, grown, elder, older. **4** *a big decision:* important, significant, major, momentous, weighty, far-reaching, key, vital, crucial. **5** *that was big of you:* generous, kind, kindly, caring, compassionate, loving.
OPPOSITES small, little, younger, minor, mean.

**bigoted** adjective prejudiced, biased, partial, one-sided, sectarian, discriminatory, opinionated, dogmatic, intolerant, narrow-minded, blinkered, illiberal.
OPPOSITES open-minded.

**bill** noun **1** *a bill for £6:* invoice, account, statement, list of charges; humorous the damage; N. Amer. check; N. Amer. informal tab. **2** *a parliamentary bill:* draft law, proposal, measure. **3** *she was top of the bill:* programme, line-up; N. Amer. playbill. **4** (N. Amer.) *a $10 bill:* banknote, note; US informal greenback. **5** *he had been posting bills:* poster, advertisement, notice, announcement, flyer, leaflet, handbill; informal ad; Brit. informal advert.
verb **1** *please bill me for the work:* invoice, charge, debit. **2** *the concert went ahead as billed:* advertise, announce, schedule, programme, timetable; N. Amer. slate. **3** *he was billed as the new Sean*

*Connery:* describe, call, style, label, dub; informal hype, promote, talk up; informal hype.

**billow** noun *billows of smoke:* cloud, mass.

verb 1 *her dress billowed around her:* puff up/out, balloon (out), swell, fill (out). 2 *smoke billowed from the chimney:* swirl, spiral, roll, undulate, eddy, pour, flow.

**bind** verb 1 *they bound her hands:* tie up, fasten together, secure, make fast, attach, rope, lash, tether. 2 *Shelley bound up the wound:* bandage, dress, cover, wrap, strap up, tape up. 3 *the edges are bound in a contrasting colour:* trim, hem, edge, border, fringe. See also **BOUND**[1].

OPPOSITES untie.

**binding** adjective irrevocable, unalterable, inescapable, unbreakable, contractual, compulsory, obligatory, mandatory, incumbent.

**binge** noun (informal) bout, spell, fling, spree, orgy, drinking bout; informal bender, session; Scottish informal skite; N. Amer. informal jag, toot.

**birth** noun 1 childbirth, delivery, nativity. 2 *the birth of science:* beginning(s), emergence, genesis, dawn, dawning, rise, start. 3 *he is of noble birth:* ancestry, lineage, blood, descent, parentage, family, extraction, origin, stock.

OPPOSITES death, end.

■ **give birth to** have, bear, produce, be delivered of, bring into the world; N. Amer. birth; informal drop.

**bit** noun piece, portion, section, part, chunk, lump, hunk, fragment, scrap, shred, crumb, grain, speck, spot, drop, pinch, dash, morsel, mouthful, bite, sample, iota, jot, whit, atom, particle, trace, touch, suggestion, hint, tinge; informal smidgen, tad.

OPPOSITES lot.

**bite** verb 1 chew, sink one's teeth into, munch, crunch, champ. 2 *my boots failed to bite:* grip, hold, get a purchase. 3 *the measures begin to bite:* take effect, work, act, have results.

noun 1 *he took a bite at his sandwich:* chew, munch, nibble, gnaw, nip, snap. 2 *he ate it in two bites:* mouthful, piece, bit, morsel. 3 *the appetizer had a fiery bite:* piquancy, pungency, spiciness, tang, zest; informal kick, punch, zing.

**biting** adjective 1 *biting comments:* vicious, harsh, cruel, savage, cutting, sharp, bitter, scathing, caustic, acid, acrimonious, spiteful, venomous; informal bitchy, catty. 2 *the biting wind:* freezing, icy, arctic, bitter, piercing, penetrating, raw.

OPPOSITES mild, pleasant, warm.

**bitter** adjective 1 *bitter coffee:* sharp, acid, acrid, tart, sour, vinegary. 2 *a bitter row:* acrimonious, hostile, angry, rancorous, spiteful, vicious, vitriolic, savage, ferocious, nasty. 3 *a bitter woman:* resentful, embittered, aggrieved, spiteful, jaundiced, sullen, sour. 4 *a bitter wind:* freezing, icy, arctic, biting, piercing, penetrating, raw.

OPPOSITES pleasant, sweet, amicable, magnanimous, content, mild, warm.

**bitterness** noun 1 *the bitterness of the medicine:* sharpness, acidity, tartness, sourness. 2 *there was no bitterness*

*between them*: acrimony, hostility, anger, antipathy, antagonism, enmity, animus, friction, rancour, vitriol, venom, nastiness, bad blood. **3** *his bitterness grew*: resentment, rancour, indignation, grudge, spite, sullenness, sourness, pique.
OPPOSITES sweetness, pleasantness, goodwill, magnanimity, contentment.

**bizarre** adjective strange, peculiar, odd, funny, fantastic, curious, outlandish, eccentric, unconventional, unorthodox; informal weird, wacky, oddball, way out, freaky; N. Amer. informal wacko.
OPPOSITES normal.

**black** adjective **1** *a black horse*: dark, pitch-black, jet-black, ebony, inky. **2** *the blackest day of the war*: tragic, dark, disastrous, calamitous, catastrophic, cataclysmic, fateful. **3** *Mary was in a black mood*: miserable, unhappy, sad, wretched, heartbroken, grief-stricken, sorrowful, anguished, desolate, despairing, disconsolate, downcast, dejected, gloomy; informal blue. **4** *black humour*: macabre, cynical, unhealthy, ghoulish, weird, morbid, gruesome; informal sick.
OPPOSITES white, bright, happy.
■ **black out** faint, lose consciousness, pass out, swoon.

**blacklist** verb boycott, ostracize, avoid, embargo, ignore, refuse to employ.

**blackmail** noun *he was accused of blackmail*: extortion, demanding money with menaces, threats, intimidation.
verb **1** *he was blackmailing the murderer*: extort money from, threaten, hold to ransom, intimidate. **2** *she blackmailed me into working for her*: coerce, pressure, force, dragoon; informal lean on, twist someone's arm.

**blame** verb **1** *he always blames others*: hold responsible, hold accountable, condemn, accuse, find/consider guilty. **2** *they blame youth crime on unemployment*: attribute to, ascribe to, impute to, lay at the door of, put down to; informal pin.
OPPOSITES absolve.
noun *he was cleared of all blame*: responsibility, guilt, accountability, liability, culpability, fault.

**blameless** adjective innocent, guiltless, above reproach, unimpeachable, in the clear, exemplary; informal squeaky clean.
OPPOSITES blameworthy.

**bland** adjective **1** *a bland film*: uninteresting, dull, boring, tedious, monotonous, ordinary, run-of-the-mill, drab, dreary, unexciting, lacklustre, flat, stale, trite. **2** *bland food*: tasteless, flavourless, plain, insipid, weak, watery, thin, wishy-washy.
OPPOSITES interesting, tangy.

**blank** adjective **1** *a blank sheet of paper*: empty, unmarked, unused, clear, free, bare, clean, plain. **2** *a blank face*: expressionless, deadpan, wooden, stony, impassive, glazed, fixed, lifeless, inscrutable.
OPPOSITES full, marked, expressive.
noun *fill in the blanks*: space, gap.

**blanket** noun *a blanket of cloud*: covering, layer, coating, carpet,

a b c d e f g h i j k l m n o p q r s t u v w x y z

cloak, mantle, veil, pall, shroud.
verb *snow blanketed the mountains:* **cover**, coat, carpet, cloak, shroud, swathe, envelop.

**blast** noun 1 *the blast from the bomb:* **shock wave**, pressure wave. 2 *Friday's blast killed two people:* **explosion**, detonation, discharge, burst. 3 *a blast of cold air:* **gust**, rush, gale, squall, flurry. 4 *the shrill blast of the trumpets:* **blare**, wail, roar, screech, shriek, hoot, honk, beep.
verb 1 *bombers were blasting airfields:* **blow up**, bomb, blow (to pieces), dynamite, explode. 2 *guns were blasting away:* **fire**, shoot, blaze, let fly, discharge. 3 *he blasted his horn:* **honk**, beep, toot, sound. 4 *radios blasting out pop music:* **blare**, boom, roar, thunder, bellow, pump, shriek, screech.

**blatant** adjective **flagrant**, glaring, obvious, undisguised, open, shameless, barefaced, unashamed, brazen.
OPPOSITES inconspicuous, shamefaced.

**blaze** noun 1 **fire**, flames, conflagration, inferno, holocaust. 2 *a blaze of light:* **glare**, flash, burst, flare, streak, radiance, brilliance, beam, glitter.
verb 1 *the fire blazed merrily:* **burn**, be alight, be on fire, be in flames. 2 *headlights blazed:* **shine**, flash, flare, glare, gleam, glitter, glisten. 3 *soldiers blazed away:* **fire**, shoot, blast, let fly.

**bleach** verb **turn white**, whiten, turn pale, blanch, lighten, fade.
OPPOSITES darken.

**bleak** adjective 1 *a bleak landscape:* **bare**, exposed, desolate, stark, desert, lunar, open, empty, windswept. 2 *the future is bleak:* **unpromising**, unfavourable, dim, gloomy, black, grim, discouraging, disheartening, depressing.
OPPOSITES lush, promising.

**bleary** adjective **blurry**, unfocused, fogged, clouded, misty, watery.
OPPOSITES clear.

**blend** verb 1 *blend the ingredients until smooth:* **mix**, mingle, combine, merge, amalgamate, stir, whisk, fold in. 2 *the new buildings blend with the older ones:* **harmonize**, go (well), fit (in), be in tune, be compatible, coordinate, match, complement, suit.
noun *a blend of bananas and ginger:* **mixture**, mix, combination, compound, amalgam, fusion, alloy.

**bless** verb 1 *the Cardinal blessed the memorial plaque:* **consecrate**, sanctify, dedicate to God, make holy; formal **hallow**. 2 *the gods blessed us with magical voices:* **endow**, bestow, furnish, give, favour, confer on. 3 *the government refused to bless the undertaking:* **sanction**, consent to, endorse, agree to, approve, back, support; informal give the green light to, OK.
OPPOSITES curse, trouble, oppose.

**blessed** adjective **holy**, sacred, hallowed, consecrated, sanctified, ordained, canonized, beatified.
OPPOSITES cursed.

**blessing** noun 1 *a blessing from the priest:* **benediction**, dedication, consecration, grace, invocation, intercession. 2 *she gave the plan her blessing:* **sanction**, endorsement, approval, consent, assent, agreement, backing, support;

informal the green light, OK. **3** *it was a blessing they didn't have far to go:* advantage, godsend, boon, benefit, help, bonus, plus, stroke of luck, windfall.
OPPOSITES condemnation, affliction.

**blight** noun **1** *potato blight:* disease, canker, infestation, fungus, mildew, mould. **2** *the blight of aircraft noise:* curse, scourge, affliction, plague, menace, misfortune, bane, trouble, nuisance, pest.
OPPOSITES blessing.
verb *scandal blighted his career:* ruin, wreck, spoil, mar, frustrate, disrupt, undo, scotch, destroy, shatter, devastate, demolish; informal mess up, foul up, put paid to, put the kibosh on, stymie; Brit. informal scupper.

**blind** adjective **1** sightless, unsighted, visually impaired, unseeing. **2** *blind acceptance of conventional opinion:* uncritical, unreasoned, unthinking, unquestioning, mindless, undiscerning, indiscriminate. **3** *she was blind to the realities of her position:* unaware of, oblivious to, ignorant of, unmindful of, heedless of, insensible to, indifferent to.
OPPOSITES sighted, discerning, mindful.
noun *a window blind:* screen, shade, sunshade, curtain, awning, canopy, louvre, jalousie, shutter.

**blindly** adverb **1** *he ran blindly upstairs:* impetuously, impulsively, recklessly, heedlessly. **2** *they blindly followed US policy:* uncritically, unquestioningly, unthinkingly, mindlessly, indiscriminately.
OPPOSITES cautiously, critically,
selectively.

**bliss** noun joy, happiness, pleasure, delight, ecstasy, elation, rapture, euphoria.
OPPOSITES misery.

**blitz** noun bombing, air raid, air strike, bombardment, barrage, attack, assault.

**bloated** adjective swollen, distended, bulging, inflated, dilated.
OPPOSITES shrunken.

**blob** noun **1** *a blob of cold gravy:* drop, droplet, globule, bead, bubble. **2** *a blob of ink:* spot, dab, blotch, blot, dot, smudge; informal splodge.

**bloc** noun group, alliance, coalition, federation, confederation, league, union, axis, association.

**block** noun **1** *a block of cheese:* chunk, hunk, lump, wedge, cube, brick, slab, piece. **2** *an apartment block:* building, complex, structure, development. **3** *a block to development:* obstacle, bar, barrier, impediment, hindrance, check, hurdle.
OPPOSITES aid.
verb **1** *weeds can block ditches:* clog, stop up, choke, plug, bung up, obstruct, gum up, dam up, congest, jam. **2** *picket lines blocked access to the factory:* hinder, hamper, obstruct, impede, inhibit, halt, stop, bar, check, prevent, fend off, hold off, repel.
OPPOSITES clear, aid, allow.
■ **block something out** keep out, exclude, stop, conceal, blot out, obliterate.

**blockage** noun obstruction, stoppage, block, jam, congestion.

**blonde, blond** adjective fair, light, yellow, flaxen, golden.

OPPOSITES dark.

**blood** noun **1** lifeblood, gore, vital fluid. **2** *a woman of noble blood:* ancestry, lineage, descent, parentage, family, birth, extraction, origin, stock.

**bloodshed** noun slaughter, massacre, killing, wounding, carnage, butchery, bloodletting, bloodbath.

**bloodthirsty** adjective murderous, homicidal, violent, vicious, barbarous, barbaric, savage, brutal, cut-throat.

**bloody** adjective **1** *his hands were all bloody:* bloodstained, blood-soaked, gory, bleeding. **2** *a bloody civil war:* vicious, ferocious, savage, fierce, brutal, cruel, murderous, gory. OPPOSITES clean, bloodless.

**bloom** verb **1** *the geraniums bloomed:* flower, blossom, open, mature. **2** *the children bloomed in the Devonshire air:* flourish, thrive, prosper, progress, burgeon; informal be in the pink. OPPOSITES wither, fade, decline.

**blossom** noun *pink blossoms:* flower, bloom, bud.
verb **1** *the snowdrops have blossomed:* bloom, flower, open, mature. **2** *the whole region had blossomed:* develop, grow, mature, progress, evolve, burgeon, flourish, thrive, prosper, bloom. OPPOSITES wither, fade, decline.

**blot** noun **1** *an ink blot:* patch, dab, smudge, blotch, mark, dot, spot; Brit. informal splodge. **2** *the only blot on a clean campaign:* blemish, taint, stain, blight, flaw, fault. **3** *a blot on the landscape:* eyesore, monstrosity, carbuncle, mess; informal sight.
■ **blot something out 1** *clouds were starting to blot out the stars:* conceal, hide, obscure, exclude, obliterate, shadow, eclipse. **2** *he urged her to blot out the memory:* erase, blank out, wipe out, eradicate.

**blow¹** verb **1** *the icy wind blew around us:* gust, puff, flurry, blast, roar, bluster, rush, storm. **2** *his ship was blown on to the rocks:* sweep, carry, toss, drive, push, force. **3** *leaves blew across the road:* drift, flutter, waft, float, glide, whirl, move. **4** *he blew a smoke ring:* exhale, puff. **5** *he blew a trumpet:* sound, blast, toot, play, pipe, trumpet.
■ **blow something out** extinguish, put out, snuff, douse, quench, smother. ■ **blow up** *a lorryload of shells blew up:* explode, detonate, go off, ignite, erupt. ■ **blow something up 1** *they blew the plane up:* explode, detonate, bomb, blast, destroy. **2** *blow up the balloons:* inflate, pump up, fill up, puff up, swell, expand.

**blow²** noun **1** *a blow on the head:* knock, bang, hit, punch, thump, smack, crack, rap; informal whack, bash, clout, wallop. **2** *losing his wife must have been a blow:* upset, disaster, setback, misfortune, disappointment, calamity, catastrophe, thunderbolt, bombshell, shock, surprise, jolt.

**blue** adjective sky-blue, azure, cobalt, sapphire, navy, ultramarine, aquamarine, cyan.

**blueprint** noun **1** *blueprints of the aircraft:* plan, design, diagram, drawing, sketch, layout. **2** *a blueprint for similar measures in other countries:* model, plan, template, pattern, example, guide, prototype, pilot.

**bluff¹** noun *this offer was*

*denounced as a bluff:* trick, deception, fraud, ruse, pretence, sham, fake, hoax, charade; informal put-on.

**verb 1** *they are bluffing to hide their guilt:* pretend, sham, fake, feign, lie, hoax, pose. **2** *I managed to bluff the board into believing me:* deceive, delude, mislead, trick, fool, hoodwink, dupe, hoax; informal con, kid, have on.

**bluff²** adjective *a bluff man:* plain-spoken, straightforward, blunt, direct, no-nonsense, frank, open, candid, forthright, unequivocal; informal upfront.
OPPOSITES guarded, secretive.

**blunder** noun *he shook his head at his blunder:* mistake, error, gaffe, slip, oversight, faux pas; informal slip-up, boo-boo; Brit. informal clanger, boob; N. Amer. informal blooper.

**verb 1** *the government admitted it had blundered:* make a mistake, err, miscalculate, bungle, trip up; informal slip up, screw up, blow it, goof; Brit. informal boob. **2** *she blundered down the steps:* stumble, lurch, stagger, flounder, grope.

**blunt** adjective **1** *a blunt knife:* dull, worn. **2** *the leaf is broad with a blunt tip:* rounded, flat, stubby. **3** *a blunt message:* straightforward, frank, plain-spoken, candid, direct, bluff, forthright, unequivocal, brusque, abrupt, curt, bald, brutal, harsh, stark; informal upfront.
OPPOSITES sharp, pointed, subtle.

**verb** *age hasn't blunted my passion for life:* dull, deaden, dampen, numb, take the edge off, weaken, allay, diminish, lessen.
OPPOSITES intensify.

**blur** verb **1** *she felt tears blur her vision:* cloud, fog, obscure, dim, make hazy, make fuzzy, soften, dull, numb, deaden, mute. **2** *the digits on the screen blurred:* become fuzzy, become dim, become hazy, become vague.
OPPOSITES sharpen, focus.

**noun** *a blur on the horizon:* indistinct shape, smudge, haze, cloud, mist.

**blurred** adjective indistinct, fuzzy, hazy, misty, foggy, faint, unclear, vague, indefinite, unfocused.
OPPOSITES sharp, clear.

**blurt**
■ **blurt something out** burst out with, exclaim, call out, divulge, disclose, reveal, betray, let slip, give away; informal blab, let on, spill the beans.

**blush** verb *Joan blushed at the compliment:* redden, go pink, go red, flush, colour, burn up.
**noun** *the darkness hid her blush:* flush, rosiness, redness, pinkness, bloom, high colour, glow.

**blustery** adjective stormy, gusty, blowy, windy, squally, wild.
OPPOSITES calm.

**board** noun **1** *a wooden board:* plank, beam, panel, slat, batten, timber. **2** *the board of directors:* committee, council, panel, directorate, commission.
**verb 1** *he boarded the aircraft:* get on, go aboard, enter, mount, ascend, embark, catch. **2** *a number of students boarded with them:* lodge, live, reside, stay, be housed; N. Amer. room; informal put up.

**boast** verb **1** *his mother had been boasting about him:* brag, crow, swagger, swank, gloat, show off; informal talk big, lay it on thick; Austral./NZ informal skite.

a
**b**
c
d
e
f
g
h
i
j
k
l
m
n
o
p
q
r
s
t
u
v
w
x
y
z

**2** *the hotel boasts a fine restaurant*: have, possess, own, enjoy, pride oneself/itself on, offer.
OPPOSITES hush up.
noun **1** *the government's main boast seemed undone*: brag, exaggeration, overstatement; informal swank; Austral./NZ informal skite. **2** *the hall is the boast of the county*: pride, joy, pride and joy, apple of someone's eye, wonder, delight.

**boastful** adjective bragging, swaggering, bumptious, puffed up, full of oneself, cocky, conceited, arrogant; informal swanky, big-headed.
OPPOSITES modest.

**bob** verb move up and down, bounce, toss, skip, dance, wobble, jiggle, joggle, jolt, jerk.

**bodily** adjective *bodily sensations*: physical, corporeal, corporal, mortal, material, tangible, concrete, real, actual.
OPPOSITES spiritual, mental.
adverb *he hauled her bodily from the van*: forcefully, forcibly, violently, completely, entirely.

**body** noun **1** *the human body*: figure, frame, form, physique, anatomy, skeleton. **2** *he was hit by shrapnel in the head and body*: torso, trunk. **3** *the bodies were put in the fire*: corpse, carcass, skeleton, remains; informal stiff; Medicine cadaver. **4** *the body of the article*: main part, core, heart, hub. **5** *the representative body of the employers*: association, organization, assembly, delegation, committee, executive, company, society, corporation, group.

**bog** noun marsh, swamp, mire, quagmire, morass, slough, fen, wetland.

■ **bog someone/something down** mire, stick, entangle, ensnare, embroil, hamper, hinder, impede, obstruct, swamp, overwhelm.

**bogus** adjective fake, spurious, false, fraudulent, sham, counterfeit, forged, feigned; informal phoney, pretend.
OPPOSITES genuine.

**boil¹** verb *the soup is boiling*: simmer, bubble, stew, seethe, froth, foam.

**boil²** noun *a boil on her neck*: swelling, spot, pimple, blister, gathering, pustule, carbuncle, abscess.

**boisterous** adjective lively, animated, exuberant, spirited, noisy, loud, rowdy, unruly, wild, uproarious, unrestrained, uninhibited, uncontrolled, rough, disorderly, riotous; informal rumbustious.
OPPOSITES restrained.

**bold** adjective **1** *bold adventurers*: daring, intrepid, brave, courageous, valiant, fearless, dauntless, audacious, daredevil, adventurous, heroic, plucky; informal gutsy, spunky. **2** *a bold pattern*: striking, vivid, bright, strong, eye-catching, prominent, gaudy, lurid, garish.
OPPOSITES timid, pale, faint.

**bolster** verb strengthen, reinforce, boost, fortify, support, buoy up, shore up, maintain, help, augment, increase.
OPPOSITES undermine.

**bolt** noun **1** *the bolt on the door*: bar, lock, catch, latch, fastener. **2** *nuts and bolts*: pin, rivet, peg, screw.
verb **1** *he bolted the door*: lock, bar, latch, fasten, secure. **2** *the lid was bolted down*: pin, rivet, peg, screw, fasten, fix. **3** *Anna*

bolted from the room: **dash,** dart, run, sprint, hurtle, rush, fly, shoot; informal tear, scoot, leg it. **4** he bolted his breakfast: **gobble,** gulp, wolf, guzzle, devour; informal demolish, polish off, shovel down; N. Amer. informal scarf, snarf.

**bomb** noun **explosive,** incendiary (device), missile, projectile.
**verb** their headquarters were bombed: **blow up,** blast, shell, blitz, strafe, pound, bombard, attack, assault, destroy, demolish.

**bombard** verb **1** gun batteries bombarded the islands: **shell,** pound, blitz, strafe, bomb, batter, blast, pelt. **2** we were bombarded with information: **swamp,** inundate, flood, deluge, snow under, overwhelm.

**bonanza** noun **windfall,** godsend, blessing, bonus, stroke of luck; informal jackpot.

**bond** noun **1** the women forged a close bond: **friendship,** relationship, fellowship, partnership, association, affiliation, alliance, attachment. **2** I've broken my bond: **promise,** pledge, vow, oath, word (of honour), guarantee, assurance, agreement, contract, pact, deal.
**verb** the extensions are bonded to your hair: **join,** fasten, fix, affix, attach, secure, bind, stick, fuse.

**bonus** noun **1** the extra work's a real bonus: **extra,** plus, benefit, advantage, boon, blessing, godsend, stroke of luck, attraction. **2** she's on a good salary and she gets a bonus: **gratuity,** handout, gift, present, reward, prize, incentive; informal perk, sweetener.
OPPOSITES disadvantage.

**bony** adjective **skinny,** thin, lean, gaunt, spare, skin and bone, skeletal, emaciated, underweight.
OPPOSITES plump.

**book** noun **1** he published his first book in 1610: **volume,** tome, publication, title, novel, treatise, manual. **2** he scribbled in his book: **notepad,** notebook, pad, exercise book, logbook, ledger, journal, diary; Brit. jotter, pocketbook; N. Amer. scratch pad.
**verb 1** she booked a table at the restaurant: **reserve,** prearrange, order; informal bag. **2** we booked a number of events in the Festival: **arrange,** programme, schedule, timetable, line up, lay on; N. Amer. slate.
■ **book in register,** check in, enrol.

**booklet** noun **pamphlet,** brochure, leaflet, tract; N. Amer. folder, mailer.

**boom** noun **1** the boom of the waves on the rocks: **roar,** rumble, thunder, crashing, drumming, pounding, echoing, resonance, reverberation. **2** an unprecedented boom in sales: **increase,** growth, advance, boost, escalation, improvement, upsurge, upturn.
OPPOSITES slump.
**verb 1** thunder boomed overhead: **roar,** rumble, thunder, crash, roll, clap, explode, bang, resound, blare, echo, resonate, reverberate. **2** a voice boomed at her: **shout,** yell, bellow, roar, thunder, bawl; informal holler. **3** the market continued to boom: **flourish,** thrive, prosper, burgeon, progress, improve, pick up, expand.
OPPOSITES whisper, slump.

**boorish** adjective **coarse,**

uncouth, rude, vulgar,
uncivilized, unrefined, rough,
thuggish, loutish, Neanderthal;
Brit. informal yobbish; Austral. informal
ocker.
OPPOSITES refined.

**boost** verb *they used advertising
to boost sales:* increase, raise,
escalate, improve, strengthen,
inflate, push up, promote,
advance, foster, stimulate,
encourage, facilitate, help,
assist, aid; informal hike, bump
up.
OPPOSITES decrease.
noun **1** *a boost to one's morale:*
uplift, lift, spur,
encouragement, help,
inspiration, stimulus, fillip;
informal shot in the arm. **2** *a
boost in sales:* increase,
expansion, upturn, upsurge,
rise, escalation, improvement,
advance, growth, boom; informal
hike.
OPPOSITES decrease.

**boot** verb kick, punt, tap, propel,
drive, knock.

**booth** noun **1** *booths for
different traders:* stall, stand,
kiosk. **2** *a phone booth:* cubicle,
kiosk, box, enclosure, cabin.

**booty** noun loot, plunder, haul,
spoils, ill-gotten gains, pickings;
informal swag.

**border** noun **1** *the border of a
medieval manuscript:* edge,
margin, perimeter,
circumference, periphery, rim,
fringe, verge, sides. **2** *the
French border:* frontier,
boundary, borderline,
perimeter.
verb **1** *the fields were bordered
by hedges:* surround, enclose,
encircle, edge, fringe, bound,
flank. **2** *the straps are bordered
with gold braid:* edge, fringe,
hem, trim, pipe, finish. **3** *the

forest bordered Broadmoor:*
adjoin, abut, be next to, be
adjacent to, touch.
■ **border on** verge on, approach,
come close to, be comparable
to, approximate to, be
tantamount to.

**bore**[1] verb *bore a hole:* drill,
pierce, perforate, puncture,
punch, tunnel, burrow, mine,
dig, gouge, sink.

**bore**[2] verb *the television news
bored Philip:* weary, pall on,
tire, fatigue, send to sleep,
leave cold; informal turn off.
OPPOSITES interest.
noun *you can be such a bore:*
tedious person/thing, tiresome
person/thing, bother, nuisance,
pest, annoyance, trial, thorn in
one's flesh/side; informal drag,
pain (in the neck), headache,
hassle.

**boredom** noun tedium, ennui,
apathy, weariness, dullness,
monotony, repetitiveness,
flatness, dreariness.
OPPOSITES interest, excitement.

**boring** adjective tedious, dull,
dreary, monotonous, repetitive,
uneventful, unimaginative,
characterless, featureless,
colourless, lifeless,
uninteresting, unexciting,
lacklustre, humdrum, mind-
numbing, soul-destroying,
wearisome, tiresome; informal
deadly; Brit. informal samey; N. Amer.
informal dullsville.
OPPOSITES interesting, exciting.

**borrow** verb **1** *we borrowed a
lot of money:* loan, lease, hire;
informal cadge, scrounge, bum,
touch someone for; N. Amer.
informal mooch; Austral./NZ informal
bludge. **2** *adventurous chefs
borrow foreign techniques:*
adopt, take on, acquire,
embrace.

OPPOSITES lend.

**boss** (informal) noun *the boss of a large company:* head, chief, principal, director, president, chief executive, chair, manager, supervisor, foreman, overseer, controller, employer, owner, proprietor; Brit. informal **gaffer, governor;** N. Amer. informal **head honcho.**

verb *you have no right to boss me about:* order about/around, dictate to, bully, push around/about, call the shots, lay down the law; informal **bulldoze, walk all over, railroad.**

**bossy** adjective (informal) domineering, pushy, overbearing, imperious, officious, authoritarian, dictatorial; informal **high and mighty.**

OPPOSITES submissive.

**bother** verb **1** *no one bothered her:* disturb, trouble, inconvenience, pester, badger, harass, molest, plague; informal **hassle, bug;** N. English informal **mither;** N. Amer. informal **ride. 2** *the incident was too small to bother about:* mind, care, worry, concern oneself, trouble oneself. **3** *there was something bothering him:* worry, trouble, concern, perturb, disturb, disquiet; informal **rattle.**

noun **1** *I don't want to put you to any bother:* trouble, effort, exertion, inconvenience, fuss, pains; informal **hassle. 2** *the food was such a bother to cook:* nuisance, pest, palaver, rigmarole, job, trial, bind, bore, drag, inconvenience, trouble; informal **hassle, headache, pain (in the neck). 3** *a spot of bother in the public bar:* disorder, fighting, trouble, disturbance, commotion, uproar; informal **hoo-ha, aggro, argy-bargy, kerfuffle.**

**bottom** noun **1** *the bottom of the stairs:* foot, lowest part, base, foundation. **2** *the bottom of the car:* underside, underneath, undersurface, underbelly. **3** *the bottom of Lake Ontario:* floor, bed, depths. **4** *the bottom of his garden:* farthest point, far end, extremity. **5** (Brit.) *I've got a tattoo on my bottom:* buttocks, rear (end), rump, seat; informal **behind, backside;** Brit. informal **bum, botty, jacksie;** N. Amer. informal **butt, fanny;** humorous **posterior.**

OPPOSITES top, surface.

adjective *she sat on the bottom step:* lowest, last, bottommost.

OPPOSITES top.

**bounce** verb **1** *the ball bounced:* rebound, spring back, ricochet; N. Amer. **carom. 2** *William bounced down the stairs:* bound, leap, jump, spring, bob, hop, skip, gambol, trip, prance.

noun **1** *the pitch's uneven bounce:* springiness, resilience, elasticity, give. **2** *she had lost her bounce:* vitality, vigour, energy, vivacity, liveliness, animation, sparkle, verve, spirit; informal **get-up-and-go, pep, zing.**

**bound**[1] adjective **1** *he raised his bound ankles:* tied, restrained, fixed, fastened, secured. **2** *she seemed bound to win:* certain, sure, very likely, destined. **3** *bound by the Official Secrets Act:* constrained, obliged, compelled, required, obligated. **4** *religion and morality are bound up with one another:* connected, linked, tied, united, allied, interdependent.

OPPOSITES free, unlikely, independent.

**bound**[2] verb *Louis came*

a
**b**
c
d
e
f
g
h
i
j
k
l
m
n
o
p
q
r
s
t
u
v
w
x
y
z

*bounding down the stairs:* **leap,** jump, spring, vault, bounce, hop, skip, dance, prance, gambol, gallop.

**bound³** verb **1** *corporate freedom is bounded by law:* **limit,** restrict, confine, circumscribe, demarcate, delimit. **2** *the heath is bounded by a hedge:* **enclose,** surround, encircle, circle, border, close in/off, hem in. **3** *the garden was bounded by Mill Lane:* **border,** adjoin, abut, be next to, be adjacent to.

**boundary** noun **1** *the boundary between Israel and Jordan:* **border,** frontier, borderline, partition. **2** *the boundary between art and advertising:* **dividing line,** division, borderline, cut-off point. **3** *the boundary of his estate:* **limits,** confines, bounds, margins, edges, fringes, border, periphery, perimeter.

**bouquet** noun **1** *her bridal bouquet:* **posy,** nosegay, spray, corsage, buttonhole, garland, wreath, arrangement. **2** *the Chardonnay has a fine bouquet:* **aroma,** nose, smell, fragrance, perfume, scent, odour.

**bourgeois** adjective **middle-class,** conservative, conformist, conventional, propertied, provincial, suburban, small-town. OPPOSITES proletarian.

**bout** noun **1** *a bout of exercise:* **spell,** period, stretch, stint, session, burst, flurry, spurt. **2** *a coughing bout:* **attack,** fit, spasm. **3** *he is fighting only his fifth bout:* **contest,** fight, match, round, competition, meeting, encounter.

**bow¹** verb **1** *the officers bowed:* **nod,** bend, stoop, bob, curtsy,

kneel, genuflect. **2** *the mast quivered and bowed:* **bend,** buckle, curve, flex, deform. **3** *the government bowed to foreign pressure:* **give in,** submit, yield, surrender, succumb, capitulate.
noun *a perfunctory bow:* **nod,** bob, obeisance, curtsy, genuflection.

**bow²** noun *the bow of the tanker:* **prow,** front, stem, nose, head.

**bowels** plural noun **1** *a disorder of the bowels:* **intestines,** entrails, viscera, innards, digestive system; Medicine gut; informal guts, insides. **2** *the bowels of the ship:* **interior,** inside, core, belly, depths, recesses; informal innards.

**bowl¹** verb *he bowled a hundred or so balls:* **throw,** pitch, hurl, toss, lob, fling, roll, launch, propel; informal chuck, sling, bung.

**bowl²** noun **dish,** basin, pot, crock, vessel, receptacle.

**box¹** noun **1** *carton,* pack, packet, case, crate, chest, coffer, casket. **2** *a telephone box:* **booth,** cubicle, compartment, kiosk, cabin, hut.
verb *Muriel boxed up his clothes:* **pack,** package, parcel, encase, bundle, crate.

**box²** verb *he began boxing professionally:* **fight,** prizefight, spar, battle, brawl; informal scrap.

**boxer** noun **fighter,** pugilist, prizefighter; informal bruiser, scrapper.

**boy** noun **lad,** youth, young man, stripling; Scottish & N. English laddie; derogatory brat. See also CHILD.

**boycott** verb *they boycotted the election:* **shun,** snub, spurn, avoid, abstain from, reject, veto.

OPPOSITES support.

**noun** *a boycott on the use of tropical timbers:* ban, veto, embargo, prohibition, sanction, restriction, avoidance, rejection.

**boyfriend noun** lover, sweetheart, beloved, darling, partner; informal fella, flame, fancy man; N. Amer. informal squeeze.

**brace noun** *the aquarium is supported by wooden braces:* prop, strut, stay, support, bracket.
**verb 1** *the plane's wing is braced by rods:* support, shore up, prop up, hold up, buttress, reinforce. **2** *he braced his hand on the railing:* steady, secure, stabilize, poise, fix. **3** *brace yourself for disappointment:* prepare, get ready, gear up, nerve, steel, fortify; informal psych oneself up.

**bracing adjective** invigorating, refreshing, stimulating, energizing, exhilarating, restorative, rejuvenating.

**bracket noun 1** *each speaker is fixed on a bracket:* support, prop, stay, batten, rest, mounting, rack, frame. **2** *a higher tax bracket:* group, category, grade, classification, division.

**brag verb** boast, crow, swagger, swank, bluster, gloat, show off, blow one's own trumpet, sing one's own praises; informal talk big.

**brain noun** intelligence, intellect, brainpower, cleverness, wit(s), reasoning, wisdom, judgement, understanding, sense; informal nous, grey matter; N. Amer. informal smarts.

**brake noun** curb, check,

restraint, constraint, control, limit.
OPPOSITES accelerator.
**verb** slow (down), decelerate, reduce speed.
OPPOSITES accelerate.

**branch noun 1** *the branches of a tree:* bough, limb, arm, offshoot, twig. **2** *the judicial branch of government:* division, subdivision, section, subsection, department, unit, sector, wing. **3** *the corporation's New York branch:* office, bureau, agency, subsidiary.
**verb 1** *the place where the road branches:* fork, divide, split, bifurcate. **2** *narrow paths branched off the road:* diverge, deviate, split off, fan out, radiate.

**brand noun 1** *a new brand of margarine:* make, line, label, marque, trade name, trademark, proprietary name. **2** *her particular brand of humour:* type, kind, sort, variety, class, category, genre, style, ilk; N. Amer. stripe.
**verb 1** *the letter M was branded on each animal:* mark, stamp, burn, sear. **2** *the scene was branded on her brain:* engrave, stamp, etch, imprint. **3** *the media branded us as communists:* stigmatize, mark out, denounce, discredit, vilify, label.

**brandish verb** flourish, wave, shake, wield, swing, swish.

**brash adjective 1** *a brash man:* self-assertive, pushy, cocky, self-confident, arrogant, bold, audacious, brazen. **2** *brash colours:* garish, gaudy, loud, flamboyant, showy, tasteless; informal flashy, tacky.
OPPOSITES meek, subdued.

**brave adjective** courageous,

intrepid, bold, plucky, heroic, fearless, daring, audacious, dauntless, valiant; informal game, gutsy.
OPPOSITES cowardly.
verb *fans braved freezing temperatures:* endure, put up with, bear, withstand, weather, suffer, face, confront, defy.
OPPOSITES succumb to.

**bravery** noun courage, boldness, heroism, intrepidity, nerve, daring, fearlessness, audacity, pluck, valour; informal guts; Brit. informal bottle; N. Amer. informal moxie.

**brawl** noun fight, skirmish, scuffle, tussle, fray, melee, fracas, fisticuffs; informal scrap, set-to; Brit. informal punch-up.

**brawny** adjective strong, muscular, muscly, well built, powerful, strapping, burly, sturdy; informal beefy, hulking.
OPPOSITES puny, weak.

**breach** noun 1 *a breach of the regulations:* contravention, violation, infringement, infraction, transgression. 2 *a breach in the sea wall:* break, rupture, split, crack, fracture, opening, gap, hole, fissure.
OPPOSITES observance.
verb 1 *the river breached its banks:* break (through), burst, rupture. 2 *the changes breached union rules:* break, contravene, violate, infringe, defy, disobey, flout.

**breadth** noun 1 *a breadth of 100 metres:* width, broadness, thickness, span, diameter. 2 *the breadth of his knowledge:* range, extent, scope, depth, reach, compass, scale.

**break** verb 1 shatter, smash, crack, snap, fracture, fragment, splinter, split, burst; informal bust. 2 *the coffee machine has*

broken: stop working, break down, give out, go wrong, malfunction, crash; informal go kaput, conk out; Brit. informal pack up. 3 *traders who break the law:* violate, contravene, infringe, breach, defy, flout, disobey. 4 *the film broke box-office records:* beat, surpass, exceed, better, cap, top, outdo, outstrip. 5 *he tried to break the news gently:* reveal, disclose, divulge, impart, tell, announce, release.
OPPOSITES repair, obey.
noun 1 *the magazine has been published without a break since 1950:* stop, interruption, interval, gap, disruption, stoppage, cessation. 2 *let's have a break:* rest, respite, recess, pause, interval, intermission; informal breather, time out. 3 *a break in the wall:* gap, opening, space, hole, breach, chink, crack, fracture, fissure, tear, split.
■ **break down** 1 *his van broke down.* See **BREAK** verb sense 2. 2 *pay negotiations broke down:* fail, collapse, founder, fall through. 3 *Vicky broke down, sobbing loudly:* burst into tears, lose control, be overcome, go to pieces; informal crack up, lose it.
■ **break something down** 1 *police broke the door down:* knock down, kick down, smash in, pull down, tear down, demolish. 2 *the information can be broken down:* analyse, categorize, classify, sort, itemize, organize, divide, separate, split. ■ **break something off** 1 *I broke off a branch from the tree:* snap off, pull off, sever, detach. 2 *they threatened to break off diplomatic relations:* end, terminate, stop, cease, call a halt to, suspend, discontinue;

informal pull the plug on. ■ **break out 1** *he broke out of the detention centre*: escape, abscond, flee, get free. **2** *fighting broke out*: flare up, start suddenly, erupt, burst out. ■ **break up 1** *the meeting broke up*: end, finish, stop, terminate, adjourn; N. Amer. recess. **2** *the crowd began to break up*: disperse, scatter, disband, part company. **3** *Danny and I broke up last year*: split up, separate, part (company), divorce. ■ **break something up 1** *police tried to break up the crowd*: disperse, scatter, disband. **2** *I'm not going to let you break up my marriage*: wreck, ruin, destroy.

**breakdown** noun **1** *the breakdown of the negotiations*: failure, collapse, disintegration, foundering. **2** *she suffered a breakdown*: nervous breakdown, collapse. **3** *a breakdown of the computer system*: malfunction, failure, crash. **4** *a breakdown of the figures*: analysis, itemization, classification, examination, investigation, explanation.

**break-in** noun burglary, robbery, theft, raid, breaking and entering; informal smash-and-grab.

**breakthrough** noun advance, development, step forward, success, improvement, discovery, innovation, revolution.
OPPOSITES setback.

**breast** noun **1** *the curve of her breasts*: bosom(s), bust; informal boobs, knockers. **2** *her heart was hammering in her breast*: chest, bosom, front.

**breath** noun inhalation, gulp of air, puff, gasp, exhalation; Medicine respiration.

**breathe** verb **1** *she breathed deeply*: inhale, exhale, respire, draw breath, puff, pant, blow, gasp, wheeze; Medicine inspire, expire. **2** *'Together at last,' she breathed*: whisper, murmur, purr, sigh.

**breathless** adjective **1** *Will arrived breathless*: out of breath, panting, puffing, gasping, wheezing, winded; informal out of puff. **2** *the crowd were breathless with anticipation*: eager, agog, open-mouthed, excited, on the edge of one's seat, on tenterhooks.

**breathtaking** adjective spectacular, magnificent, awe-inspiring, awesome, astonishing, amazing, stunning, thrilling; informal sensational, out of this world.
OPPOSITES run-of-the-mill.

**breed** verb **1** *elephants breed readily in captivity*: reproduce, produce offspring, procreate, multiply, mate. **2** *she was born and bred in the village*: bring up, rear, raise, nurture. **3** *the political system bred discontent*: cause, produce, bring about, give rise to, arouse, stir up, generate, foster.
OPPOSITES stifle.
noun **1** *a breed of cow*: variety, stock, strain, race, species. **2** *a new breed of journalist*: type, kind, sort, variety, class, genre, generation.

**breeding** noun (good) manners, gentility, refinement, cultivation, polish, urbanity; informal class.

**breeze** noun gentle wind, puff of air, gust, draught; literary zephyr.

**breezy** adjective **1** *a breezy day*: windy, fresh, brisk, blowy, blustery, gusty. **2** *his breezy* *manner:* jaunty, cheerful, cheery, brisk, carefree, easy, casual, relaxed, informal, light-hearted; informal upbeat.

**brew** verb 1 *this beer is brewed in Frankfurt:* ferment, make. 2 *I'll brew some tea:* prepare, infuse, make; Brit. informal mash. 3 *there's trouble brewing:* develop, loom, be imminent, be on the horizon, be in the offing, be just around the corner.
noun 1 *home brew:* beer, ale. 2 *a hot reviving brew:* drink, beverage. 3 *a rich brew of myths and distortion:* mixture, mix, blend, combination, amalgam, cocktail.

**bribe** verb *they tried to bribe the police:* buy off, pay off, suborn; informal grease someone's palm, keep someone sweet, square; Brit. informal nobble.
noun *he accepted a bribe:* inducement; informal backhander, pay-off, kickback, sweetener.

**bribery** noun corruption; N. Amer. payola; informal palm-greasing, graft, hush money.

**brief** adjective 1 *a brief account:* concise, succinct, short, pithy, compact, thumbnail, potted. 2 *a brief visit:* short, flying, fleeting, hasty, hurried, quick, cursory, perfunctory, temporary, short-lived.
OPPOSITES lengthy.
noun 1 *my brief is to reorganize the project:* instructions, directions, directive, remit, mandate. 2 *a barrister's brief:* case, summary, argument, contention, dossier.
verb *employees were briefed about the decision:* inform, tell, update, notify, advise, prepare, prime, instruct; informal fill in, put in the picture.

**briefing** noun 1 *a press briefing:* conference, meeting, interview. 2 *this briefing explains the systems:* information, rundown, guidance, instructions, directions, guidelines.

**briefly** adverb 1 *tell me as briefly as you can:* concisely, succinctly. 2 *Henry paused briefly:* momentarily, temporarily, fleetingly. 3 *briefly, the plot is as follows:* in short, in brief, in a word, in a nutshell, in essence.

**briefs** plural noun underpants, pants, knickers, bikini briefs; N. Amer. shorts; informal panties; Brit. informal kecks.

**brigade** noun squad, team, group, band, party, crew, force, outfit.

**bright** adjective 1 *the bright surface of the metal:* shining, brilliant, dazzling, glaring, sparkling, flashing, glittering, gleaming, glowing, luminous, shiny, glossy. 2 *a bright morning:* sunny, cloudless, clear, fair, fine. 3 *bright colours:* vivid, brilliant, intense, strong, vibrant, bold, gaudy, lurid, garish. 4 *a bright young graduate:* clever, intelligent, quick-witted, smart, canny, astute, perceptive, ingenious; informal brainy.
OPPOSITES dull, cloudy, dark, stupid.

**brighten** verb 1 *sunshine brightened the room:* illuminate, light up, lighten. 2 *the sky brightened:* become lighter, grow brighter, lighten. 3 *Sarah brightened up:* cheer up, perk up, rally, feel heartened; informal buck up.

**brilliance** noun 1 *the brilliance of the sunshine:* brightness, vividness, intensity, sparkle, glitter, blaze, luminosity, radiance. **2** *a philosopher of great brilliance:* genius, intelligence, talent, ability, prowess, skill, expertise, aptitude, flair, wisdom, intellect. **3** *the brilliance of Paris:* splendour, magnificence, grandeur, resplendence, glory. OPPOSITES dullness, stupidity, simplicity, lowliness.

**brilliant** adjective **1** *a shaft of brilliant light:* bright, shining, blazing, dazzling, vivid, intense, glaring, luminous, radiant. **2** *a brilliant student:* clever, bright, intelligent, smart, able, talented, gifted, skilful, astute; informal brainy. **3** *his brilliant career:* superb, glorious, illustrious, impressive, remarkable, exceptional. OPPOSITES dim, stupid, undistinguished.

**bring** verb **1** *he brought over a tray:* fetch, carry, bear, take, convey, transport, shift. **2** *Philip brought his bride to his mansion:* escort, conduct, guide, lead. **3** *the wind brought rain:* cause, produce, create, generate, precipitate, occasion, provoke, lead to, give rise to, result in.
■ **bring something about/on.** See **BRING** sense 3. ■ **bring something in** introduce, launch, inaugurate, initiate, institute.
■ **bring something off** achieve, accomplish, bring about, succeed in, pull off, carry off, manage. ■ **bring something out** launch, establish, begin, start, found, set up, market, publish, issue. ■ **bring someone up** rear, raise, nurture, look after.
■ **bring something up** mention, raise, broach, introduce, air, suggest.

**brink** noun **1** *the brink of the crater:* edge, verge, margin, rim, lip, border, boundary. **2** *two countries on the brink of war:* verge, threshold, point, edge.

**brisk** adjective **1** *a brisk pace:* quick, rapid, fast, swift, speedy, hurried, energetic, lively; informal nippy. **2** *his tone became brisk:* no-nonsense, businesslike, decisive, brusque, abrupt, short, sharp, curt, blunt, terse; informal snappy. OPPOSITES leisurely.

**bristle** noun **1** *the bristles on his chin:* hair, whisker; (bristles) stubble, five o'clock shadow. **2** *a hedgehog's bristles:* spine, prickle, quill, barb.
verb **1** *the hair on the back of his neck bristled:* rise, stand up, stand on end. **2** *she bristled at his tone:* take offence, bridle, take umbrage, be offended. **3** *the roof bristled with antennae:* be crowded, be full, be packed, be jammed, be covered, overflow; informal be thick, be chock-full.

**brittle** adjective breakable, fragile, crisp, crumbly, delicate. OPPOSITES flexible, solid.

**broach** verb bring up, raise, introduce, mention, touch on, air.

**broad** adjective **1** *a broad expanse of prairie:* wide, extensive, vast, immense, great, spacious, expansive, sweeping. **2** *a broad range of opportunities:* comprehensive, inclusive, extensive, wide, all-embracing, unlimited. **3** *this report gives a broad outline:* general, non-specific, rough, approximate, basic, loose, vague. OPPOSITES narrow, limited, detailed.

**broadcast** verb 1 *the show will be broadcast worldwide:* transmit, relay, air, beam, show, televise, screen. 2 *the result was broadcast far and wide:* report, announce, publicize, advertise, make public, proclaim, spread, circulate.
noun *a live broadcast:* transmission, programme, show, telecast, production, screening.

**broaden** verb 1 *her smile broadened:* widen, expand, stretch (out), spread. 2 *the government tried to broaden its political base:* expand, enlarge, extend, widen, swell, increase, add to, develop.
OPPOSITES narrow, restrict.

**broad-minded** adjective liberal, tolerant, freethinking, indulgent, progressive, permissive, unshockable, unprejudiced, unbiased.
OPPOSITES intolerant.

**brochure** noun booklet, prospectus, catalogue, pamphlet, leaflet, circular, mailshot; N. Amer. folder.

**broken** adjective 1 smashed, shattered, fragmented, splintered, crushed, snapped, in bits, in pieces, cracked, split, fractured; informal in smithereens. 2 *his video's broken:* faulty, damaged, defective, not working, malfunctioning, out of order, broken down, down; informal kaput, bust, acting up; Brit. informal knackered. 3 *a night of broken sleep:* interrupted, disturbed, fitful, disrupted, discontinuous, intermittent. 4 *she spoke in broken English:* halting, hesitating, disjointed,

faltering, imperfect.
OPPOSITES whole, working, uninterrupted, fluent, perfect.

**broker** noun dealer, agent, middleman, intermediary, mediator, factor, liaison, stockbroker.
verb arrange, organize, orchestrate, work out, settle, clinch, negotiate, mediate.

**brood** noun *she looked after her brood well:* offspring, young, family, litter, clutch, progeny.
verb *he does brood a lot:* think, ponder, contemplate, meditate, ruminate, muse, worry, fret, agonize.

**brook** noun stream, rill; N. English beck; Scottish & N. English burn; N. Amer. & Austral./NZ creek.

**brotherly** adjective fraternal, friendly, comradely, affectionate, amicable, kind, devoted, loyal.

**brow** noun 1 forehead, temple. 2 *the brow of the hill:* summit, peak, top, crest, crown, head, pinnacle, apex.

**brown** adjective 1 *brown eyes:* hazel, chocolate, coffee, brunette, sepia, mahogany, tan, café au lait, caramel, chestnut. 2 *his face was brown from the sun:* tanned, suntanned, bronzed.
verb *the grill browns food evenly:* grill, toast, singe, sear, barbecue, sauté.

**browse** verb look round/over, scan, skim, glance, peruse, thumb, leaf, flick, dip into.

**bruise** noun *a bruise on her forehead:* contusion, bump, swelling, lump, mark, injury, welt.
verb 1 *her face was badly bruised:* contuse, injure, mark, discolour, make black and blue. 2 *every one of the apples is*

a
**b**
c
d
e
f
g
h
i
j
k
l
m
n
o
p
q
r
s
t
u
v
w
x
y
z

*bruised:* mark, discolour, blemish, damage, spoil.

**brush**[1] noun **1** *a dustpan and brush:* broom, sweeper, besom, whisk. **2** *he gave the seat a brush with his hand:* clean, sweep, wipe, dust. **3** *a brush with the law:* encounter, clash, confrontation, conflict, altercation, incident; informal run-in, to-do; Brit. informal spot of bother.
verb **1** *he spent his day brushing the floors:* sweep, clean, buff, polish, scrub. **2** *she brushed her hair:* groom, comb, neaten, tidy, smooth, arrange, curry. **3** *she felt his lips brush her cheek:* touch, stroke, caress, skim, sweep, graze, contact, kiss.
■ **brush something aside** disregard, ignore, dismiss, shrug off, wave aside, reject, spurn, laugh off, make light of; informal pooh-pooh. ■ **brush up (on)** revise, read up, go over, improve, polish up, enhance, hone, perfect; informal bone up on; Brit. informal swot up (on).

**brush**[2] noun undergrowth, scrub, brushwood, shrubs, bushes; N. Amer. underbrush, chaparral.

**brusque** adjective curt, abrupt, blunt, short, sharp, brisk, peremptory, gruff.
OPPOSITES polite.

**brutal** adjective **1** *a brutal attack:* savage, cruel, vicious, ferocious, barbaric, wicked, murderous, bloodthirsty, cold-blooded, callous, heartless, merciless, sadistic. **2** *brutal honesty:* harsh, unforgiving, pitiless, frank, blunt, tough, hard, bleak, disagreeable.
OPPOSITES gentle, kind.

**bubbly** adjective **1** *bubbly water:*
fizzy, sparkling, effervescent, gassy, aerated, carbonated, frothy, foamy. **2** *she was bubbly and full of life:* vivacious, animated, ebullient, lively, high-spirited, bouncy, merry, happy, cheerful, sunny; informal chirpy.
OPPOSITES still, listless.

**buckle** noun *a belt buckle:* clasp, clip, catch, hasp, fastener.
verb **1** *he buckled the belt round his waist:* fasten, do up, hook, secure, clasp, clip. **2** *the front axle buckled:* bend, warp, twist, distort, contort, deform, crumple, collapse, give way.
OPPOSITES unbuckle, straighten.

**budding** adjective promising, up-and-coming, rising, in the making, aspiring, future, fledgling, developing.

**budge** verb **1** *the horses wouldn't budge:* move, shift, stir, go. **2** *I couldn't budge the door:* dislodge, shift, move, stir, reposition.

**budget** noun **1** *your budget for the week:* financial plan, forecast. **2** *the defence budget:* allowance, allocation, quota, funds, resources, capital.
verb *we have to budget £7,000 for the work:* allocate, allot, allow, earmark, designate, set aside.

**buff**[1] verb *he buffed the glass:* polish, burnish, shine, smooth, rub.

**buff**[2] noun (informal) *a film buff:* enthusiast, fan, devotee, lover, admirer, expert, aficionado, authority; informal freak, nut, addict.

**buffer** noun cushion, bulwark, shield, barrier, guard, safeguard.

**buffet**[1] noun **1** *a sumptuous buffet:* cold table, self-service meal, smorgasbord. **2** *a station buffet:* **cafe**, cafeteria, snack bar, canteen, restaurant.

**buffet**[2] verb *rough seas buffeted the coast:* **batter**, pound, lash, strike, hit.

**bug** noun **1** (informal) *a stomach bug:* **illness**, disease, sickness, disorder, upset, ailment, infection, virus; Brit. informal lurgy. **2** *bugs were crawling everywhere:* **insect**, minibeast; informal creepy-crawly, beastie. **3** *the bug planted on his phone:* **listening device**, hidden microphone, wire, wiretap, tap. **4** *the program developed a bug:* **fault**, error, defect, flaw, virus; informal glitch, gremlin.
verb *her conversations were bugged:* **eavesdrop on**, spy on, tap, monitor.

**build** verb **construct**, erect, put up, assemble, make, create, fashion, model, shape.
OPPOSITES demolish, dismantle.
noun *a man of slim build:* **physique**, frame, body, figure, form, shape, stature, proportions; informal vital statistics.
■ **build up increase**, grow, mount up, intensify, strengthen. ■ **build something up 1** *he built up his stamina:* **boost**, strengthen, increase, improve, augment, raise, enhance, swell. **2** *I have built up a collection of prints:* **accumulate**, amass, collect, gather.

**building** noun **structure**, construction, edifice, erection, property, premises, establishment.

**build-up** noun **increase**, growth, expansion, enlargement, escalation, accumulation, development.

**bulbous** adjective **bulging**, round, fat, rotund, swollen, distended, bloated.

**bulge** noun *a bulge under his jacket:* **swelling**, bump, lump, hump, protrusion.
verb *the veins in his neck bulged:* **swell**, stick out, project, protrude, stand out, puff out, balloon (out), fill out, distend.

**bulk** noun **1** *the sheer bulk of the bags:* **size**, volume, dimensions, proportions, mass, scale. **2** *the bulk of entrants were British:* **majority**, mass, generality, main part, lion's share, preponderance.
OPPOSITES minority.

**bulky** adjective **unwieldy**, cumbersome, unmanageable, awkward, ponderous, outsize, oversized; informal hulking.
OPPOSITES manageable, handy.

**bullet** noun **ball**, shot, pellet; informal slug; (**bullets**) lead.

**bulletin** noun **1** *a news bulletin:* **report**, dispatch, story, flash, statement, announcement, message, communication, communiqué. **2** *the society's monthly bulletin:* **newsletter**, news-sheet, proceedings, newspaper, magazine, gazette, review.

**bully** noun *the school bully:* **persecutor**, oppressor, tyrant, tormentor, intimidator, bully boy, thug.
verb **1** *the others bully him:* **persecute**, oppress, tyrannize, browbeat, intimidate, dominate; informal push around/about. **2** *she was bullied into helping:* **coerce**, pressure, press, push, prod, browbeat, dragoon, strong-arm; informal bulldoze, railroad, lean on.

**bump** noun **1** *I landed with a bump:* **jolt**, crash, smash,

smack, crack, bang, thud, thump; informal whack, wallop. **2** *I was woken by a bump:* bang, crack, boom, clang, knock, thud, thump, clunk, crash, smash. **3** *a bump in the road:* hump, lump, ridge, bulge, knob. **4** *a bump on his head:* swelling, lump, bulge, injury, contusion.
**verb 1** *cars bumped into each other:* hit, crash, smash, slam, bang, knock, run, plough, ram, collide with, strike; N. Amer. impact. **2** *a cart bumping along the road:* bounce, jolt, jerk, rattle, shake.

**bumper** adjective exceptional, large, abundant, rich, bountiful, good, plentiful, record, successful; informal whopping.
OPPOSITES meagre.

**bumpy** adjective **1** *a bumpy road:* uneven, rough, rutted, pitted, potholed, lumpy, rocky. **2** *a bumpy ride:* bouncy, rough, uncomfortable, jolting, lurching, jerky, jarring, bone-shaking.
OPPOSITES smooth.

**bunch** noun **1** *a bunch of flowers:* bouquet, posy, nosegay, spray, wreath, garland. **2** *a bunch of keys:* cluster, clump, knot, group.
**verb** *the runners bunched up behind him:* cluster, huddle, gather, congregate, collect, amass, group, crowd.
OPPOSITES scatter.

**bundle** noun *a bundle of clothes:* bunch, roll, clump, wad, parcel, sheaf, bale, pile, stack, heap, mass; informal load, wodge.
**verb 1** *she bundled up her things:* tie, pack, parcel, wrap, swathe, roll, fold, bind.
**2** (informal) *he was bundled into a van:* push, shove, thrust, throw, propel, jostle, manhandle.

**bungle** verb mishandle, mismanage, mess up, spoil, ruin; informal blow, botch, fluff, make a hash of, screw up; Brit. informal make a pig's ear of, cock up; N. Amer. informal goof up.
OPPOSITES carry off.

**bungling** adjective incompetent, blundering, amateurish, inept, unskilful, clumsy, awkward, bumbling; informal ham-fisted, cack-handed.
OPPOSITES competent.

**buoy** noun float, marker, beacon.

**buoyant** adjective **1** *a buoyant substance:* floating, floatable. **2** *a buoyant mood:* cheerful, cheery, happy, light-hearted, carefree, joyful, bubbly, bouncy, sunny; informal upbeat.
OPPOSITES gloomy.

**burden** noun *a financial burden:* responsibility, onus, obligation, liability, trouble, care, problem, worry, strain.
**verb** *avoid burdening them with guilt:* oppress, trouble, worry, weigh down, harass, upset, distress, haunt, afflict.

**bureau** noun **1** *an oak bureau:* desk, writing table, secretaire. **2** *the intelligence bureau:* department, agency, office, division, branch, section, station, unit.

**bureaucracy** noun **1** *the ranks of the bureaucracy:* civil service, government, administration, establishment, system, powers that be, authorities. **2** *unnecessary bureaucracy:* red tape, rules and regulations, protocol, officialdom, paperwork.

**burgeon** verb grow, increase, rocket, mushroom, expand, escalate, swell, boom, flourish, thrive, prosper.

a **b** c d e f g h i j k l m n o p q r s t u v w x y z

a
**b**
c
d
e
f
g
h
i
j
k
l
m
n
o
p
q
r
s
t
u
v
w
x
y
z

**burglar** noun housebreaker, robber, thief, raider, looter, cat burglar.

**burglary** noun 1 *a sentence for burglary:* housebreaking, breaking and entering, theft, stealing, robbery, larceny, looting, pillaging. 2 *a series of burglaries:* break-in, theft, robbery, raid; informal smash-and-grab; N. Amer. informal heist.

**burgle** verb rob, loot, steal from, pillage.

**burial** noun funeral, interment, committal, inhumation, entombment.
OPPOSITES exhumation.

**burly** adjective strapping, well built, strong, muscular, muscly, hefty, sturdy, brawny; informal hunky, beefy.
OPPOSITES puny.

**burn** verb 1 *the coal was burning:* be on fire, be alight, blaze, go up (in smoke), be in flames, smoulder, glow. 2 *he burned the letters:* set fire to, set alight, set light to, kindle, ignite, touch off, incinerate, cremate; informal torch. 3 *I burned my dress with the iron:* scorch, singe, sear, char, blacken, brand.

**burning** adjective 1 *burning coals:* on fire, blazing, flaming, fiery, glowing, red-hot, smouldering. 2 *a burning desire:* intense, passionate, deep-seated, profound, strong, ardent, fervent, urgent, fierce, consuming. 3 *burning issues:* important, crucial, critical, vital, essential, pivotal, urgent, pressing, compelling.

**burrow** noun *a rabbit's burrow:* warren, tunnel, hole, dugout, lair, set, den, earth.
verb *rabbits burrowed among the roots:* tunnel, dig, excavate, mine, bore, channel.

**burst** verb 1 *one balloon burst:* split (open), rupture, break, tear. 2 *a shell burst:* explode, blow up, detonate, go off. 3 *smoke burst through the hole:* gush, erupt, surge, rush, stream, flow, pour, spurt, jet. 4 *he burst into the room:* charge, plunge, barge, plough, hurtle, career, rush, dash, tear.
noun 1 *a burst in the tyre:* rupture, puncture, breach, split, blowout. 2 *mortar bursts:* explosion, detonation, blast, eruption, bang. 3 *a burst of gunfire:* volley, salvo, barrage, hail, rain. 4 *a burst of activity:* outbreak, eruption, flare-up, blaze, attack, fit, rush, storm, surge, spurt.

**bury** verb 1 *the dead were buried:* inter, lay to rest, entomb. 2 *she buried her face in her hands:* hide, conceal, cover, enfold, cup, sink. 3 *the bullet buried itself in the wood:* embed, sink, implant, submerge, lodge.
OPPOSITES exhume.

**bush** noun 1 *a rose bush:* shrub, thicket; (bushes) undergrowth, shrubbery. 2 *the bush:* wilds, wilderness, backwoods; N. Amer. backcountry; Austral./NZ outback, backblocks; N. Amer. informal boondocks.

**bushy** adjective thick, shaggy, curly, fuzzy, bristly, fluffy, woolly.
OPPOSITES sleek, wispy.

**business** noun 1 *she has to smile in her business:* work, occupation, profession, career, employment, job, position. 2 *who do you do business with?* trade, commerce, dealing, traffic, dealings, transactions, negotiations. 3 *her own*

*business:* firm, company, concern, enterprise, venture, organization, operation, undertaking; informal outfit.
**4** *none of your business:* concern, affair, responsibility, duty. **5** *an odd business:* affair, matter, case, circumstance, situation, event, incident.

**businessman, businesswoman** noun
executive, entrepreneur, industrialist, merchant, dealer, trader, manufacturer, tycoon, employer, broker, buyer, seller, tradesman, retailer, supplier.

**bust** noun **1** *her large bust:* bosom, breasts, chest; informal boobs, knockers; N. Amer. informal bazooms. **2** *a bust of Caesar:* sculpture, carving, effigy, statue, head and shoulders.

**bustle** verb *people bustled about:* rush, dash, hurry, scurry, scuttle, scamper, scramble; informal scoot, beetle, buzz.
noun *the bustle of the market:* activity, action, liveliness, excitement, tumult, commotion, hubbub, whirl; informal toing and froing.

**bustling** adjective busy, crowded, swarming, teeming, humming, buzzing, hectic, lively.
OPPOSITES leisurely, deserted.

**busy** adjective **1** *they are very busy at the moment:* hard at work, involved, rushed off one's feet, hard-pressed, on the job; informal on the go, hard at it; Brit. informal on the hop. **2** *I'm sorry, she is busy:* unavailable, engaged, occupied, absorbed, engrossed, immersed, preoccupied, working; informal tied up. **3** *a busy day:* hectic, active, lively, full, eventful, energetic, tiring.

OPPOSITES idle, free, quiet.
verb *he busied himself with paperwork:* occupy, involve, engage, concern, absorb, engross, immerse, distract, divert.

**but** conjunction **1** *he stumbled but didn't fall:* however, nevertheless, nonetheless, even so, yet, still. **2** *I am clean but you aren't:* whereas, conversely.
preposition *everyone but him:* except (for), apart from, other than, besides, aside from, with the exception of, bar.
■ **but for** except for, if it were not for, barring, notwithstanding.

**butt**[1] verb *she butted him:* ram, headbutt, bump, poke, prod, push, shove, thrust.
■ **butt in** interrupt, intrude, break in, cut in, interfere, put one's oar in; informal poke one's nose in; Brit. informal chip in.

**butt**[2] noun *the butt of a joke:* target, victim, object, dupe, laughing stock.

**butt**[3] noun **1** *the butt of a gun:* stock, end, handle, hilt, haft. **2** *a cigarette butt:* stub, end, stump; informal fag end, dog end.
verb *the shop butts up against the house:* adjoin, abut, be next to, be adjacent to, border (on), neighbour.

**buttocks** plural noun bottom, rear (end), rump, seat; informal behind, backside; Brit. informal bum, botty, jacksie; N. Amer. informal butt, fanny; humorous posterior.

**buy** verb *they bought a new house:* purchase, acquire, obtain, get, pick up, snap up, invest in; informal get hold of, score.
OPPOSITES sell.
noun (informal) *a good buy:*

a

**b**

**c**

d
e
f
g
h
i
j
k
l
m
n
o
p
q
r
s
t
u
v
w
x
y
z

purchase, deal, bargain, investment, acquisition.

**buzz** noun 1 *the buzz of the bees:* hum, murmur, drone. 2 *an insistent buzz from her control panel:* tone, purr, ring, warble, note, beep, alarm, warning.

**by** preposition 1 *I broke it by forcing the lid:* through, as a result of, because of, by dint of, by means of, with the help of, by virtue of. 2 *be there by midday:* no later than, in good time for, before. 3 *a house by the lake:* next to, beside, alongside, by/at the side of, adjacent to.

adverb *people hurried by:* past, on, along.

**bypass** noun ring road, detour, diversion, alternative route; Brit. relief road.

verb 1 *bypass the farm:* go round, go past, make a detour round, avoid. 2 *the system had been bypassed:* ignore, sidestep, avoid, evade, escape, elude, skirt, dodge, circumvent, get round, go over the head of, pass over; informal short-circuit, duck.

**bystander** noun onlooker, passer-by, observer, spectator, eyewitness.

# Cc

**cab** noun taxi, taxi cab; Brit. minicab, hackney carriage; N. Amer. hack.

**cabin** noun 1 *a ship's cabin:* berth, stateroom, compartment. 2 *a cabin by the lake:* hut, log cabin, shanty, shack, chalet; Scottish bothy; N. Amer. cabana.

**cabinet** noun cupboard, bureau, chest of drawers.

**cable** noun 1 *a thick cable moored the ship:* rope, cord, line; Nautical hawser; N. Amer. choker. 2 *electric cables:* wire, lead, cord, power line; Brit. flex.

**cache** noun hoard, store, stockpile, stock, supply, reserve, arsenal; informal stash.

**cafe** noun snack bar, cafeteria, coffee bar/shop, tea room/shop, bistro, brasserie; N. Amer. diner, lunchroom.

**cafeteria** noun self-service restaurant, canteen, cafe,

buffet, refectory, mess hall.

**cage** noun *the lion's cage:* enclosure, pen, pound, coop, hutch, birdcage, aviary.
verb *they were caged up like animals:* confine, shut in/up, pen, coop up, enclose.

**cagey** adjective (informal) secretive, guarded, tight-lipped, reticent, evasive; informal playing one's cards close to one's chest.
OPPOSITES open.

**cajole** verb persuade, wheedle, coax, talk into, prevail on; informal sweet-talk, soft-soap.

**cake** noun 1 *cream cakes:* bun, pastry, gateau, slice. 2 *a cake of soap:* bar, tablet, block, slab, lump, wedge.
verb *boots caked with mud:* coat, encrust, plaster, cover.

**calculate** verb 1 *the interest is calculated daily:* compute, work out, reckon, figure, add up/together, count up, tally, total;

Brit. **tot up**. **2** *his words were calculated to wound her:* **intend**, mean, design.

**calculated** adjective **deliberate**, premeditated, planned, pre-planned, preconceived, intentional, intended.
OPPOSITES unintentional, rash.

**calculating** adjective **cunning**, crafty, wily, sly, scheming, devious, disingenuous.
OPPOSITES ingenuous, innocent.

**calculation** noun **1** *the calculation of the overall cost:* **computation**, reckoning, adding up, counting up, working out, figuring; Brit. totting up. **2** *political calculations:* **assessment**, judgement, forecast, projection, prediction.

**calendar** noun *my social calendar:* **schedule**, programme, diary, timetable, agenda.

**calibre** noun **1** *a man of his calibre:* **quality**, merit, distinction, stature, excellence, ability, expertise, talent, capability. **2** *rugby of this calibre:* **standard**, level, quality. **3** *the calibre of a gun:* **bore**, diameter, gauge.

**call** verb **1** *'Wait for me!' she called:* **cry out**, shout, yell, sing out, chant, exclaim; informal holler. **2** *Mum called me in the morning:* **wake (up)**, awaken, rouse; Brit. informal knock up. **3** *I'll call you tomorrow:* **phone**, telephone, give someone a call; Brit. ring (up); informal call up; Brit. informal give someone a bell, get someone on the blower; N. Amer. informal get someone on the horn. **4** *Rose called a taxi:* **summon**, send for, order. **5** *he called at Ashgrove Cottage:* **pay a visit to**, visit, call/drop/look

in on, drop/stop by, pop into, nip over to. **6** *the prime minister called a meeting:* **convene**, summon, assemble. **7** *they called their daughter Hannah:* **name**, christen, baptize, designate, style, term, dub. **8** *I would call him a friend:* **describe as**, regard as, look on as, think of as, consider to be.

noun **1** *I heard calls from the auditorium:* **cry**, shout, yell, chant, exclamation; informal holler. **2** *the call of the barn owl:* **cry**, song. **3** *I'll give you a call tomorrow:* **phone call**, telephone call; Brit. ring; informal buzz; Brit. informal bell. **4** *a call for party unity:* **appeal**, request, plea. **5** *there's no call for that kind of language:* **need**, necessity, reason, justification, excuse. **6** *there's no call for expensive wine here:* **demand**, desire, market. **7** *the call of the Cairngorms:* **attraction**, appeal, lure, allure, pull, draw.
■ **call for 1** *this calls for a celebration:* **require**, need, necessitate, make necessary, demand, be grounds for, justify, warrant. **2** *he called for an enquiry:* **ask for**, request, seek, apply for, appeal for, demand, insist on, order. ■ **call something off** cancel, abandon, scrap, drop, axe; informal scrub; N. Amer. informal redline. ■ **call someone up 1** (informal) *Roland called me up.* See CALL verb sense 3. **2** *they called up the reservists:* **enlist**, recruit, conscript; US draft.

**calling** noun **profession**, occupation, vocation, career.

**callous** adjective **heartless**, unfeeling, uncaring, cold, cold-hearted, hard, as hard as nails, hard-hearted, insensitive,

unsympathetic.
OPPOSITES kind, compassionate.

**calm** adjective **1** *she seemed very calm:* relaxed, serene, tranquil, unruffled, unperturbed, unflustered, untroubled, unexcitable, unemotional, phlegmatic, composed; informal unflappable, laid-back. **2** *the night was calm:* windless, still, quiet, tranquil, smooth.
OPPOSITES excited, nervous, stormy.

noun **1** *his usual calm deserted him:* composure, coolness, calmness, self-possession, sangfroid, serenity, tranquillity; informal cool, unflappability. **2** *calm prevailed:* tranquillity, stillness, quiet, peace.
■ **calm down 1** *I tried to calm him down:* soothe, pacify, placate, mollify; Brit. quieten (down); Austral. square off. **2** *she forced herself to calm down:* compose oneself, recover/regain one's composure, control oneself, pull oneself together, simmer down, cool down/off, take it easy; Brit. quieten down; informal get a grip, keep one's shirt on; N. Amer. informal decompress.

**camouflage** noun *the stripes act as camouflage:* disguise, mask, screen, cover, cloak, front, facade, blind, concealment, subterfuge.
verb *I used cement to camouflage the hole:* disguise, hide, conceal, mask, screen, cover (up).

**camp** noun **1** *an army camp:* campsite, encampment, camping ground, bivouac, base, settlement. **2** *the liberal and conservative camps:* faction, wing, group, lobby, caucus, bloc.

**campaign** noun **1** *Napoleon's Russian campaign:* operation(s), manoeuvre(s), offensive, attack, war, battle, crusade. **2** *the campaign to reduce vehicle emissions:* effort, drive, push, struggle, movement, crusade, operation, strategy.
verb *they are campaigning for political reform:* fight, battle, push, press, strive, struggle, lobby, agitate.

**cancel** verb **1** *the match was cancelled:* call off, abandon, scrap, drop, axe; informal scrub; N. Amer. informal redline. **2** *his visa has been cancelled:* annul, invalidate, declare null and void, void, revoke, rescind, retract, withdraw.
■ **cancel out** neutralize, negate, nullify, wipe out, balance (out), make up for, compensate for, offset.
OPPOSITES arrange, confirm, reinstate, validate.

**cancer** noun (malignant) growth, tumour.

**candid** adjective frank, forthright, direct, blunt, open, honest, truthful, sincere; informal upfront; N. Amer. informal on the up and up.
OPPOSITES guarded.

**candidate** noun applicant, contender, competitor, entrant, claimant, nominee, interviewee, examinee, possible; Brit. informal runner.

**canny** adjective shrewd, astute, smart, sharp, discerning, discriminating, perceptive.
OPPOSITES foolish.

**canopy** noun awning, shade, sunshade, covering.

**canvass** verb **1** *he's canvassing for the Green Party:* campaign, electioneer. **2** *they promised to* *canvass all members:* poll, question, survey, interview, consult.

**canyon** noun ravine, gorge, gully, chasm, abyss, gulf; N. Amer. gulch, coulee.

**cap** noun **1** *a white plastic cap:* lid, top, stopper, cork, bung; N. Amer. stopple. **2** *a cap on spending:* limit, ceiling, curb, check.
verb **1** *mountains capped with snow:* top, crown, cover, coat, tip. **2** *budgets will be capped:* limit, restrict, curb, control, peg.

**capability** noun ability, capacity, power, potential, competence, aptitude, faculty, skill, talent, flair; informal know-how.
OPPOSITES inability.

**capable** adjective able, competent, effective, proficient, accomplished, experienced, skilful, talented, gifted; informal useful.
OPPOSITES incompetent.

**capacity** noun **1** *the capacity of the freezer:* volume, size, dimensions, measurements, proportions. **2** *his capacity to inspire trust.* See CAPABILITY. **3** *in his capacity as Commander-in-Chief:* role, function, position, post, job, office.

**cape**¹ noun *a woollen cape:* cloak, mantle, poncho.

**cape**² noun *the ship rounded the cape:* headland, promontory, point, head, horn, mull, peninsula.

**capital** noun money, finance(s), funds, cash, wherewithal, means, assets, wealth, resources.

**capitalism** noun private enterprise, free enterprise, the free market, private ownership.

OPPOSITES communism.

**capitalize**
■ capitalize on take advantage of, profit from, make the most of, exploit, develop; informal cash in on.

**capitulate** verb surrender, give in, yield, concede defeat, give up (the struggle), submit, lay down one's arms, throw in the towel/sponge.
OPPOSITES resist, hold out.

**capricious** adjective fickle, volatile, unpredictable, temperamental, erratic, wayward, whimsical, flighty, faddish.
OPPOSITES consistent.

**capsule** noun **1** *he swallowed a capsule:* pill, tablet, lozenge, pastille; informal tab. **2** *a space capsule:* module, craft, probe.

**captain** noun **1** *the ship's captain:* commander, master; informal skipper. **2** *the team captain:* leader, head, chief; informal boss, skipper.

**caption** noun title, heading, legend, description.

**captivate** verb enthral, charm, enchant, bewitch, fascinate, beguile, entrance, delight, attract, allure.
OPPOSITES repel, bore.

**captive** noun prisoner, convict, detainee, hostage, prisoner of war, internee.
adjective confined, caged, incarcerated, locked up, jailed, imprisoned, interned, detained.
OPPOSITES free.

**captivity** noun imprisonment, incarceration, confinement, detention, internment.
OPPOSITES freedom.

**capture** verb **1** *Mark Dawes was captured in Moscow:* catch, apprehend, seize, arrest. **2** *guerrillas have captured*

a b **c** d e f g h i j k l m n o p q r s t u v w x y z

several towns: **occupy, invade, conquer, seize, take.**
OPPOSITES release, abandon, liberate.
noun _he tried to avoid capture:_ **arrest,** seizure.

**car** noun **1** _he drove up in his car:_ **motor,** motor car, automobile; informal **wheels;** N. Amer. informal auto. **2** _the dining car:_ **carriage,** coach; Brit. **saloon.**

**carcass** noun **corpse,** dead body, remains; Medicine **cadaver;** informal **stiff.**

**care** noun **1** _the care of the child:_ **safe keeping,** supervision, custody, charge, protection, responsibility, guardianship.
**2** _she chose her words with care:_ **discretion,** caution, sensitivity, thought, regard, consideration.
**3** _the cares of the day:_ **worry,** anxiety, trouble, concern, stress, pressure, strain.
OPPOSITES neglect, carelessness.
verb _the teachers didn't care about our work:_ **be concerned,** worry (oneself), trouble/ concern oneself, bother, mind, be interested; informal **give a damn/hoot.**
■ **care for 1** _he cares for his children:_ **love,** be fond of, be devoted to, treasure, adore, dote on, think the world of, worship. **2** _the hospice cares for the terminally ill:_ **look after,** take care of, tend, attend to, minister to, nurse.

**career** noun _a business career:_ **profession,** occupation, vocation, calling, life's work, employment.
verb _they careered down the hill:_ **hurtle,** rush, shoot, race, speed, charge, hare, fly; informal **belt, tear;** Brit. informal **bucket.**

**carefree** adjective **unworried,** untroubled, blithe, nonchalant,

happy-go-lucky, free and easy, easy-going, relaxed; informal **laid-back.**
OPPOSITES troubled.

**careful** adjective **1** _be careful when you go up the stairs:_ **cautious,** alert, attentive, watchful, vigilant, wary, on one's guard, circumspect.
**2** _careful with money:_ **prudent,** thrifty, economical, sparing, frugal. **3** _careful consideration of the facts:_ **attentive,** conscientious, painstaking, meticulous, diligent, assiduous, scrupulous, methodical.
OPPOSITES careless, extravagant, casual.

**careless** adjective **1** _careless motorists:_ **inattentive,** negligent, heedless, irresponsible, impetuous, reckless. **2** _careless work:_ **shoddy,** slapdash, slipshod, scrappy, slovenly, sloppy, negligent, lax, slack, disorganized, hasty, hurried.
**3** _a careless remark:_ **thoughtless,** insensitive, indiscreet, unguarded, incautious, inadvertent.
OPPOSITES careful, attentive, meticulous, deliberate, calculated.

**caress** verb **stroke,** touch, fondle, brush, feel, skim.

**caretaker** noun **janitor,** attendant, porter, custodian, concierge; N. Amer. **superintendent.**
adjective _the caretaker manager:_ **temporary,** acting, provisional, substitute, interim, stand-in, fill-in, stopgap; N. Amer. informal **pinch-hitting.**
OPPOSITES permanent.

**cargo** noun **freight,** load, haul, consignment, delivery, shipment, goods, merchandise.

**carnage** noun slaughter, massacre, murder, butchery, bloodbath, bloodletting, holocaust.

**carnival** noun festival, fiesta, fête, fair, gala, Mardi Gras.

**carp** verb complain, find fault, quibble, grumble, grouse, whine; informal nit-pick, gripe, moan, bitch, whinge.
OPPOSITES praise.

**carpenter** noun woodworker, joiner, cabinetmaker; Brit. informal chippy.

**carriage** noun 1 *a railway carriage:* coach, car; Brit. saloon. 2 *a horse and carriage:* wagon, coach. 3 *an erect carriage:* posture, bearing, gait; Brit. deportment.

**carry** verb 1 *she carried the box into the kitchen:* convey, transfer, transport, move, take, bring, bear, fetch; informal cart, hump, lug. 2 *satellites carry the signal over the Atlantic:* transmit, conduct, relay, communicate, convey, beam, send. 3 *a resolution was carried:* approve, pass, accept, endorse, ratify. 4 *his voice carried across the quay:* be audible, travel, reach, be heard.
OPPOSITES reject.
■ carry on continue, keep (on), go on, persist in; informal stick with/at. ■ carry something out 1 *they carried out an operation:* conduct, perform, execute, implement. 2 *I carried out my promise:* keep, honour, fulfil, observe, abide by, comply with, adhere to, stick to.

**carton** noun box, package, cardboard box, case, container, pack, packet.

**cartoon** noun 1 *a cartoon of the Prime Minister:* caricature, parody, lampoon, satire; informal take-off, send-up. 2 *he was reading cartoons:* comic strip, comic, graphic novel. 3 *we watched Yogi Bear cartoons:* cartoon film, animated film, animation.

**cartridge** noun cassette, magazine, canister, case, container.

**carve** verb 1 *he carved horn handles:* sculpt, cut, hew, whittle, chisel, shape, fashion. 2 *I carved my initials on the tree:* engrave, incise, score, cut. 3 *he carved the roast chicken:* slice, cut up, chop.
■ carve something up divide, break up, partition, apportion, subdivide, split up, share out.

**case**¹ noun 1 *a classic case of overreaction:* instance, example, occurrence, occasion, demonstration, illustration. 2 *is that the case?* situation, position, state of affairs, circumstances, conditions, facts; Brit. state of play; informal score. 3 *the officers on the case:* assignment, job, project, investigation, exercise. 4 *he lost his case:* lawsuit, legal action, trial, legal proceedings, litigation. 5 *the case against animal testing:* argument, defence, justification, vindication, exposition, thesis.

**case**² noun 1 *a cigarette case:* container, box, canister, holder. 2 *a seed case:* casing, cover, sheath, envelope, sleeve, jacket, shell. 3 (Brit.) *she threw some clothes into a case:* suitcase, travel bag, valise; (cases) luggage, baggage. 4 *a glass display case:* cabinet, cupboard.

**cash** noun 1 *a wallet stuffed with cash:* money, currency, bank notes, coins, change; N. Amer. bills; informal dough, loot; Brit.

informal **dosh**, **brass**; N. Amer. informal **dinero**. **2** *a lack of cash:* **finance**, money, resources, funds, assets, means, wherewithal.

**cashier** noun **clerk**, teller, banker, treasurer, bursar, purser.

**cast** verb **1** *he cast the stone into the stream:* **throw**, toss, fling, pitch, hurl, lob; informal chuck, sling, bung. **2** *she cast a fearful glance over her shoulder:* **direct**, shoot, throw, fling, send. **3** *each citizen cast a vote:* **register**, record, enter, file. **4** *the fire cast a soft light:* **emit**, give off, throw, send out, radiate. **5** *printing type was cast by hand:* **mould**, fashion, form, shape, forge.
noun **1** *a cast of his hand:* **mould**, die, matrix, shape, casting, model. **2** *the cast of 'Hamlet':* **actors**, performers, players, company, troupe, dramatis personae, characters.

**caste** noun **class**, rank, level, order, stratum, echelon, status.

**castle** noun **fortress**, fort, stronghold, fortification, keep, citadel, palace, chateau, tower.

**casual** adjective **1** *a casual attitude to life:* **unconcerned**, uncaring, indifferent, lackadaisical, nonchalant, offhand, flippant, easy-going, free and easy, blithe, carefree, devil-may-care; informal laid-back. **2** *a casual remark:* **offhand**, spontaneous, unthinking, unconsidered, impromptu, throwaway, unguarded; informal off-the-cuff. **3** *a casual glance:* **cursory**, perfunctory, superficial, passing, fleeting. **4** *a casual acquaintance:* **slight**, superficial. **5** *casual work:* **temporary**, freelance, irregular,

occasional. **6** *a casual meeting changed his life:* **chance**, accidental, unplanned, unintended, unexpected, unforeseen. **7** *a casual shirt:* **informal**, leisure, everyday; informal sporty. **8** *the inn's casual atmosphere:* **relaxed**, friendly, informal, easy-going, free and easy; informal laid-back.
OPPOSITES serious, premeditated, careful, good, permanent, planned, formal.

**casualty** noun **victim**, sufferer, fatality, death, loss, wounded person, injured person.

**cat** noun **feline**, tomcat, tom, kitten; informal pussy (cat), puss, kitty; Brit. informal moggie, mog.

**catalogue** noun *a library catalogue:* **directory**, register, index, list, listing, record, schedule, archive, inventory.
verb *the collection is fully catalogued:* **classify**, categorize, index, list, archive, record, itemize.

**catastrophe** noun **disaster**, calamity, cataclysm, ruin, tragedy, fiasco, debacle.

**catch** verb **1** *he caught the ball:* **seize**, grab, snatch, grasp, grip, clutch, intercept, trap, receive, get. **2** *we've caught the thief:* **capture**, seize, apprehend, arrest, take prisoner, trap, snare, net; informal nab, collar; Brit. informal nick. **3** *her heel caught in a hole:* **become trapped**, become entangled, snag, jam, wedge, lodge, get stuck. **4** *they were caught siphoning petrol:* **discover**, find, come across, stumble on, chance on, surprise. **5** *he caught malaria:* **contract**, go/come down with, be taken ill with, develop, pick up.
OPPOSITES drop, miss, release.

**noun 1** *he inspected the catch:* haul, net, bag, yield. **2** *he slipped the catch:* latch, lock, fastener, clasp, hasp. **3** *there must be a catch:* snag, disadvantage, drawback, stumbling block, hitch, complication, problem, trap, trick.

■ **catch on** (informal) **1** *radio soon caught on:* become popular, take off, boom, flourish, thrive. **2** *I caught on fast:* understand, comprehend, learn, see the light; informal cotton on, latch on.

**catching** adjective (informal) infectious, contagious, communicable; dated infective. OPPOSITES non-infectious.

**catchy** adjective memorable, unforgettable, haunting, appealing, popular. OPPOSITES forgettable.

**categorical** adjective unqualified, unconditional, unequivocal, absolute, explicit, unambiguous, definite, direct, emphatic, positive, out-and-out. OPPOSITES qualified, equivocal.

**category** noun class, classification, group, grouping, bracket, heading, set, type, sort, kind, grade, order, rank.

**cater**
■ **cater for 1** *we cater for vegetarians:* provide (food) for, feed, serve, cook for. **2** *a resort catering for older holidaymakers:* serve, provide for, meet the needs/wants of, accommodate. **3** *he seemed to cater for all tastes:* take into account/consideration, allow for, consider, bear in mind, make provision for, have regard for.

**cattle** plural noun cows, oxen, herd, livestock.

**cause** noun **1** *the cause of the*
*fire:* source, root, origin, beginning(s), starting point, originator, author, creator, agent. **2** *there is no cause for alarm:* reason, grounds, justification, call, need, necessity, occasion, excuse. **3** *the cause of human rights | a good cause:* principle, ideal, belief, conviction, object, aim, objective, purpose, charity. verb *this disease can cause blindness:* bring about, give rise to, lead to, result in, create, produce, generate, engender, spawn, bring on, precipitate, prompt, provoke, trigger, make happen, induce, inspire, promote, foster.

**caution** noun **1** *proceed with caution:* care, attention, alertness, circumspection, discretion, prudence. **2** *a first offender may receive a caution:* warning, admonishment, injunction, reprimand, rebuke; informal telling-off, dressing-down; Brit. informal ticking-off. verb **1** *advisers cautioned against tax increases:* advise, warn, counsel, urge. **2** *he was cautioned by the police:* warn, admonish, reprimand; informal tell off; Brit. informal tick off.

**cautious** adjective careful, attentive, alert, judicious, circumspect, prudent, tentative, guarded. OPPOSITES reckless.

**cave** noun cavern, grotto, pothole, chamber, gallery, hollow.

**cavity** noun space, chamber, hollow, hole, pocket, gap, crater, pit.

**cease** verb come/bring to an end, come/bring to a halt, end, halt, stop, conclude, terminate, finish, wind up, discontinue,

a b c d e f g h i j k l m n o p q r s t u v w x y z

a
b
**c**
d
e
f
g
h
i
j
k
l
m
n
o
p
q
r
s
t
u
v
w
x
y
z

suspend, break off.
OPPOSITES start, continue.

**celebrate** verb **1** *they were celebrating their wedding anniversary:* commemorate, observe, mark, keep, honour, remember. **2** *let's all celebrate!* enjoy oneself, make merry, have fun, have a good time, have a party; N. Amer. step out; informal party, whoop it up, have a ball. **3** *the priest celebrated mass:* perform, observe, officiate at, preside at.

**celebrated** adjective acclaimed, admired, highly rated, esteemed, exalted, vaunted, eminent, great, distinguished, prestigious, illustrious, notable.
OPPOSITES unsung.

**celebration** noun **1** *the celebration of his 50th birthday:* commemoration, observance, marking, keeping. **2** *a cause for celebration:* merrymaking, jollification, revelry, revels, festivities; informal partying. **3** *a birthday celebration:* party, function, gathering, festivities, festival, fête, carnival, jamboree; informal do, bash, rave; Brit. informal rave-up. **4** *the celebration of the Eucharist:* performance, observance, officiation, solemnization.

**celebrity** noun **1** *his celebrity grew:* fame, prominence, renown, stardom, popularity, distinction, prestige, stature, repute, reputation. **2** *a sporting celebrity:* famous person, VIP, personality, big name, household name, star, superstar; informal celeb, megastar.
OPPOSITES obscurity, nonentity.

**cell** noun **1** *a prison cell:* room, cubicle, chamber, dungeon, compartment, lock-up.

**2** *terrorist cells:* unit, squad, detachment, group.

**cellar** noun basement, vault, crypt.

**cement** noun adhesive, glue, fixative, gum, paste; N. Amer. mucilage; N. Amer. informal stickum.

**cemetery** noun graveyard, churchyard, burial ground, necropolis, garden of remembrance, mass grave; Scottish kirkyard.

**censor** verb *letters home were censored:* cut, edit, expurgate, sanitize, clean up, ban, delete.

**censure** verb *he was censured for his conduct:* condemn, criticize, attack, reprimand, rebuke, admonish, upbraid, reproach.
OPPOSITES defend, praise.
noun *a note of censure:* condemnation, criticism, attack, reprimand, rebuke, admonishment, reproof, disapproval, reproach.
OPPOSITES approval, praise.

**central** adjective **1** *occupying a central position:* middle, centre, halfway, midway, mid. **2** *central London:* inner, innermost, middle, mid. **3** *their central campaign issue:* main, chief, principal, primary, foremost, key, crucial, vital, essential, basic, fundamental, core; informal number-one.
OPPOSITES side, extreme, outer, subordinate.

**centralize** verb concentrate, consolidate, amalgamate, condense, unify, focus.
OPPOSITES devolve.

**centre** noun *the centre of the town:* middle, nucleus, heart, core, hub.
OPPOSITES edge.
verb *the story centres on a*

*doctor:* **focus**, concentrate, pivot, revolve, be based.

**ceremonial** adjective **formal**, official, state, public, ritual, ritualistic, stately, solemn.
OPPOSITES informal.

**ceremony** noun **1** *a wedding ceremony:* **rite**, ritual, observance, service, event, function, formality. **2** *the new Queen was proclaimed with due ceremony:* **pomp**, protocol, formalities, niceties, decorum, etiquette.

**certain** adjective **1** *I'm certain he's guilty:* **sure**, confident, positive, convinced, in no doubt, satisfied. **2** *it is certain that more changes are in the offing:* **unquestionable**, sure, definite, beyond question, indubitable, undeniable, indisputable. **3** *they are certain to win:* **sure**, bound, destined. **4** *certain defeat:* **inevitable**, assured, unavoidable, inescapable, inexorable. **5** *there is no certain cure for this:* **reliable**, dependable, foolproof, guaranteed, sure, infallible; informal sure-fire.
OPPOSITES doubtful, unlikely, possible.

**certainly** adverb **definitely**, surely, assuredly, unquestionably, beyond/without question, undoubtedly, without doubt, indubitably, undeniably, irrefutably, indisputably.
OPPOSITES possibly.

**certainty** noun **1** *she knew with certainty that it was true:* **confidence**, sureness, conviction, assurance. **2** *he accepted defeat as a certainty:* **inevitability**, foregone conclusion; informal sure thing; Brit. informal (dead) cert.

OPPOSITES doubt, possibility.

**certificate** noun **guarantee**, document, authorization, authentication, accreditation, credentials, testimonial.

**certify** verb **1** *the aircraft was certified as airworthy:* **verify**, guarantee, attest, validate, confirm, endorse. **2** *a certified hospital:* **accredit**, recognize, license, authorize, approve.

**cessation** noun **end**, termination, halt, finish, stoppage, conclusion, winding up, pause, suspension.
OPPOSITES start, resumption.

**chain** noun **1** *he was held in chains:* **fetters**, shackles, irons, manacles, handcuffs; informal cuffs, bracelets. **2** *a chain of events:* **series**, succession, string, sequence, train, course.
verb *she chained her bicycle to the railings:* **secure**, fasten, tie, tether, hitch, restrain, shackle, fetter, manacle, handcuff.

**chairman, chairwoman** noun **chair**, chairperson, president, chief executive, leader, master of ceremonies, MC.

**challenge** noun **1** *he accepted the challenge:* **dare**, provocation, offer. **2** *a challenge to his leadership:* **opposition**, confrontation, stand, dispute, test. **3** *it was proving quite a challenge:* **problem**, difficult task, test, trial.
OPPOSITES cinch.
verb **1** *we challenged their statistics:* **question**, dispute, take issue with, call into question. **2** *he challenged me to deny it:* **dare**, defy, invite, throw down the gauntlet to. **3** *changes that would challenge them:* **test**, tax, strain, make demands on, stretch.

**challenging** adjective

demanding, testing, taxing, exacting.
OPPOSITES easy.

**champion** noun **1** *the world champion:* winner, title-holder, gold medallist, prizewinner; informal champ, number one. **2** *a champion of change:* advocate, proponent, promoter, supporter, defender, upholder, backer; N. Amer. booster.
verb *championing the rights of tribal peoples:* advocate, promote, defend, uphold, support, espouse, stand up for, campaign for, lobby for, fight for.
OPPOSITES oppose.

**chance** noun **1** *there was a chance he might be released:* possibility, prospect, probability, likelihood, risk, threat, danger. **2** *I gave her a chance to answer:* opportunity, opening, occasion, window; N. Amer. & Austral./NZ show; Brit. informal look-in. **3** *Nigel took an awful chance:* risk, gamble, leap in the dark. **4** *pure chance:* accident, coincidence, fate, destiny, providence, happenstance, good fortune, luck, fluke.
OPPOSITES certainty.
adjective *a chance discovery:* accidental, fortuitous, fluky, coincidental.
OPPOSITES planned.
■ **by chance** by accident, fortuitously, accidentally, coincidentally, unintentionally, inadvertently.

**change** verb **1** *this could change Britain | things have changed:* alter, make/become different, adjust, adapt, amend, modify, revise, vary, transform, metamorphose, evolve. **2** *he's changed his job:* exchange,

substitute, swap, switch, replace, alternate.
OPPOSITES preserve, keep.
noun **1** *a change of plan:* alteration, modification, variation, revision, amendment, adjustment, adaptation, metamorphosis, transformation, evolution. **2** *a change of government:* replacement, exchange, substitution, swap, switch.

**channel** noun **1** *the English Channel:* strait(s), sound, narrows, passage. **2** *the water ran down a channel:* duct, gutter, conduit, trough, sluice, drain. **3** *a channel of communication:* means, medium, instrument, mechanism, agency, vehicle, route, avenue.
verb *many countries channel their aid through charities:* convey, transmit, conduct, direct, relay, pass on, transfer.

**chant** noun shout, cry, call, slogan, chorus, refrain.
verb shout, chorus, repeat, call.

**chaos** noun disorder, disorganization, confusion, mayhem, bedlam, pandemonium, havoc, turmoil, anarchy, lawlessness; Brit. a shambles; informal all hell broken loose.
OPPOSITES order.

**chaotic** adjective disorderly, disorganized, in confusion, in turmoil, topsy-turvy, anarchic, lawless; Brit. informal shambolic.

**chap** noun (Brit.) man, boy, individual, character; informal fellow, guy, geezer; Brit. informal bloke, lad; N. Amer. informal dude, hombre.

**chapter** noun **1** *the first chapter of the book:* section, part, division, topic, stage, episode.

**2** *a new chapter in our history:* period, phase, page, stage, epoch, era.

**character** noun **1** *a forceful character* | *the character of a town:* personality, nature, quality, disposition, temperament, mentality, make-up, spirit, identity, tone, feel. **2** *a woman of character:* integrity, honour, moral strength/fibre, strength, backbone, resolve, grit, will power; informal guts; Brit. informal bottle. **3** *a stain on his character:* reputation, (good) name, standing, position, status. **4** (informal) *a bit of a character:* eccentric, oddity, crank, original, individualist, madcap, nonconformist; informal oddball. **5** *a boorish character:* person, man, woman, soul, creature, individual, customer; informal cookie; Brit. informal bod, guy. **6** *written in Cyrillic characters:* letter, figure, symbol, mark, device, sign, hieroglyph.

**characteristic** noun *interesting characteristics:* attribute, feature, quality, property, trait, aspect, idiosyncrasy, peculiarity, quirk.
adjective *his characteristic eloquence:* typical, usual, normal, distinctive, representative, particular, special, peculiar, idiosyncratic. OPPOSITES abnormal.

**characterize** verb **1** *the period was characterized by scientific advancement:* distinguish, mark, typify, set apart. **2** *the women are characterized as prophets of doom:* portray, depict, present, represent, describe, categorize, class, brand.

**charade** noun pretence, act, masquerade, show, facade, pantomime, farce, travesty, mockery, parody.

**charge** verb **1** *he didn't charge much:* ask, demand, bill, invoice. **2** *two men were charged with murder:* accuse, indict, arraign, prosecute, try, put on trial; N. Amer. impeach. **3** *they charged him with reforming the system:* entrust, burden, encumber, saddle, tax. **4** *the cavalry charged the tanks:* attack, storm, assault, assail, descend on; informal lay into, tear into. **5** *we charged into the crowd:* rush, storm, stampede, push, plough, launch oneself, go headlong; informal steam; N. Amer. informal barrel. **6** *charge your glasses!* fill (up), top up, load (up), arm.
noun **1** *all customers pay a charge:* fee, payment, price, rate, tariff, fare, levy. **2** *he pleaded guilty to the charge:* accusation, allegation, indictment, arraignment; N. Amer. impeachment. **3** *an infantry charge:* attack, assault, offensive, onslaught, drive, push. **4** *the child was in her charge:* care, protection, safe keeping, control, custody, hands.

**charisma** noun charm, presence, (force of) personality, strength of character, (animal) magnetism, appeal, allure.

**charismatic** adjective charming, magnetic, compelling, inspiring, captivating, mesmerizing, appealing, alluring, glamorous.

**charitable** adjective **1** *charitable activities:* philanthropic, humanitarian, altruistic, benevolent, non-profit-making.

a
b
**c**
d
e
f
g
h
i
j
k
l
m
n
o
p
q
r
s
t
u
v
w
x
y
z

**2** *charitable people:* **generous,** open-handed, munificent. **3** *he was charitable in his judgements:* **magnanimous,** generous, liberal, tolerant, sympathetic, understanding, lenient, indulgent, forgiving. OPPOSITES commercial, mean, harsh.

**charity** noun **1** *an AIDS charity:* **voluntary organization,** charitable institution, fund, trust, foundation. **2** *we don't need charity:* **aid,** financial assistance, welfare, relief, donations, handouts, gifts, largesse; historical alms. **3** *his actions are motivated by charity:* **philanthropy,** humanitarianism, altruism, public-spiritedness, social conscience, benevolence. **4** *show a bit of charity:* **goodwill,** compassion, consideration, concern, kindness, sympathy, indulgence, tolerance, leniency. OPPOSITES business, misanthropy, intolerance.

**charm** noun **1** *people were captivated by her charm:* **appeal,** attraction, fascination, beauty, loveliness, allure, seductiveness, magnetism, charisma; informal pulling power. **2** *magical charms:* **spell,** incantation, formula; N. Amer. mojo, hex. **3** *a lucky charm:* **talisman,** trinket, amulet, mascot, fetish. verb **1** *he charmed them with his singing:* **delight,** please, win (over), attract, captivate, lure, fascinate, enchant, beguile. **2** *he charmed his mother into agreeing:* **coax,** cajole, wheedle; informal sweet-talk, soft-soap.

**charming** adjective **delightful,** pleasing, endearing, lovely, adorable, appealing, attractive, good-looking, alluring, winning, fetching, captivating, enchanting, entrancing. OPPOSITES repulsive.

**chart** noun *check your ideal weight on the chart:* **graph,** table, diagram, plan, map; Computing graphic. verb **1** *the changes were charted accurately:* **plot,** tabulate, graph, record, register, represent. **2** *the book charted his progress:* **follow,** trace, outline, describe, detail, record, document.

**charter** noun **1** *a Royal charter:* **authority,** authorization, sanction, dispensation, permit, licence, warrant. **2** *the UN Charter:* **constitution,** code, principles. verb *they chartered a bus:* **hire,** lease, rent, book.

**chase** verb **1** *the dogs chased the fox:* **pursue,** run after, follow, hunt, track, trail; informal tail. **2** *she chased away the donkeys:* **drive,** send, scare; informal send packing. **3** *she chased away all thoughts of him:* **dispel,** banish, dismiss, drive away, shut out, put out of one's mind. noun *they gave up the chase:* **pursuit,** hunt, trail.

**chat** noun *I popped in for a chat:* **talk,** conversation, gossip; informal jaw, gas, confab; Brit. informal natter, chinwag. verb *they chatted with the guests:* **talk,** gossip; informal gas, jaw, chew the rag/fat; Brit. informal natter, have a chinwag; N. Amer. informal shoot the breeze/bull; Austral./NZ informal mag.

**chatter** verb *they chattered excitedly:* **prattle,** chat, gossip, jabber, babble; informal yatter; Brit.

informal natter, chunter, rabbit on.

**noun** *she tired him with her chatter:* prattle, chat, gossip, patter, jabber, babble; informal chit-chat, yattering; Brit. informal nattering, chuntering, rabbiting on.

**chatty** adjective talkative, communicative, effusive, gossipy, loquacious, voluble; informal mouthy, gabby.
OPPOSITES taciturn.

**cheap** adjective **1** *cheap tickets:* inexpensive, low-priced, low-cost, economical, competitive, affordable, reasonable, budget, economy, bargain, cut-price, reduced, discounted; informal dirt cheap. **2** *plain without looking cheap:* poor-quality, second-rate, substandard, inferior, vulgar, shoddy, trashy, tawdry, cheap and nasty; informal rubbishy, cheapo, junky, tacky, kitsch; Brit. informal naff, duff, ropy, grotty; N. Amer. informal two-bit, dime-store. **3** *a cheap remark:* despicable, contemptible, immoral, unscrupulous, unprincipled, cynical.
OPPOSITES expensive, superior, kind.

**cheat** verb swindle, defraud, deceive, trick, dupe, hoodwink, double-cross, gull; informal diddle, rip off, con, pull a fast one on; N. Amer. informal sucker, goldbrick; Austral. informal rort.
**noun** swindler, fraudster, confidence trickster, double-dealer, double-crosser, fraud, fake, charlatan; informal con artist; N. Amer. informal bunco artist, gold brick; Austral. informal shicer.

**check** verb **1** *troops checked all vehicles:* examine, inspect, look at/over, scrutinize, study, investigate, probe, look into, enquire into; informal check out, give something a/the once-over. **2** *he checked that the gun was cocked:* make sure, confirm, verify. **3** *two defeats checked their progress:* halt, stop, arrest, bar, obstruct, foil, thwart, curb, block.
**noun 1** *a check of the records:* examination, inspection, scrutiny, perusal, study, investigation, test, check-up; informal once-over. **2** *a check on the abuse of authority:* control, restraint, constraint, curb, limitation.
■ **check in** register, book in, report. ■ **check out** pay the bill, settle up, leave.

**cheek** noun impudence, impertinence, insolence, rudeness, disrespect; informal brass neck, lip, mouth, chutzpah; Brit. informal backchat; N. Amer. informal sass, nerviness, back talk.
OPPOSITES respect, politeness.

**cheeky** adjective impudent, impertinent, insolent, rude, disrespectful; informal brass-necked, lippy, mouthy, fresh; N. Amer. informal sassy, nervy.
OPPOSITES respectful, polite.

**cheer** verb **1** *they cheered their team:* applaud, hail, salute, shout for, clap, put one's hands together for; informal holler for, give someone a big hand; N. Amer. informal ballyhoo. **2** *the bad weather did little to cheer me:* raise/lift someone's spirits, brighten, buoy up, hearten, gladden, perk up, encourage; informal buck up.
OPPOSITES boo, depress.
**noun** *the cheers of the crowd:* hurrah, hurray, whoop, bravo,

a
b
**c**
d
e
f
g
h
i
j
k
l
m
n
o
p
q
r
s
t
u
v
w
x
y
z

shout; (**cheers**) acclaim, applause, ovation.
OPPOSITES boo.

■ **cheer up** perk up, brighten up, rally, revive, bounce back, take heart; informal buck up.

■ **cheer someone up** See CHEER verb sense 2.

**cheerful** adjective **1** *he arrived looking cheerful:* happy, jolly, merry, bright, sunny, joyful, in good/high spirits, buoyant, cheery, animated, smiling, good-humoured; informal chipper, chirpy, full of beans. **2** *a cheerful room:* pleasant, attractive, agreeable, bright, sunny, friendly, welcoming.
OPPOSITES sad, gloomy.

**chemist** noun pharmacist, dispenser; N. Amer. druggist; archaic apothecary.

**cherish** verb **1** *a woman he could cherish:* adore, love, dote on, be devoted to, revere, think the world of, care for, look after, protect, keep safe. **2** *I cherish her letters:* treasure, prize, hold dear. **3** *they cherished dreams of glory:* harbour, entertain, nurse, cling to, foster.
OPPOSITES hate, disdain.

**chest** noun **1** *a wound in the chest:* breast, upper body, torso, trunk, front. **2** *an oak chest:* box, case, casket, crate, trunk, coffer, strongbox.

**chew** verb munch, champ, chomp, crunch, gnaw, bite, masticate.

**chic** adjective stylish, smart, elegant, sophisticated, fashionable; informal trendy; Brit. informal swish; N. Amer. informal kicky, tony.
OPPOSITES unfashionable.

**chief** noun **1** *a Highland chief:* leader, chieftain, head, ruler, master, commander. **2** *the chief*

*of the central bank:* head, chief executive, chief executive officer, president, chairman, chairwoman, principal, governor, director, manager; informal boss, (head) honcho; Brit. informal gaffer, guv'nor.
adjective **1** *the chief rabbi:* head, leading, principal, premier, highest, supreme, arch. **2** *their chief aim:* main, principal, primary, prime, first, cardinal, central, key, crucial, essential; informal number-one.
OPPOSITES subordinate, minor.

**chiefly** adverb mainly, in the main, primarily, principally, predominantly, mostly, for the most part, usually, typically, commonly, generally, on the whole, largely.

**child** noun youngster, baby, infant, toddler, minor, juvenile, junior, descendant; Scottish & N. English bairn; informal kid, kiddie, nipper, tiny, tot; derogatory brat.

**childbirth** noun labour, delivery, birthing; archaic confinement.

**childhood** noun youth, early years/life, infancy, babyhood, boyhood, girlhood, minority.
OPPOSITES adulthood.

**childish** adjective *childish behaviour:* immature, babyish, infantile, juvenile, puerile, silly.
OPPOSITES mature.

**childlike** adjective *childlike curiosity:* youthful, innocent, unsophisticated, naive, trusting, artless, unaffected, uninhibited, natural, spontaneous.
OPPOSITES adult.

**chill** noun **1** *a chill in the air:* coldness, chilliness, coolness, nip. **2** *he had a chill:* cold, dose of flu, fever. **3** *a chill ran down my spine:* shiver, frisson.

OPPOSITES warmth.

**verb** *his quiet tone chilled Ruth:* scare, frighten, petrify, terrify, alarm, make someone's blood run cold; informal scare the pants off; Brit. informal put the wind up.
OPPOSITES warm.

**adjective** *a chill wind:* cold, chilly, cool, fresh, wintry, frosty, icy, arctic, bitter, freezing; informal nippy; Brit. informal parky.

**chilly** adjective **1** *the weather had turned chilly:* cold, cool, crisp, fresh, wintry, frosty, icy; informal nippy; Brit. informal parky. **2** *a chilly reception:* unfriendly, unwelcoming, cold, cool, frosty; informal stand-offish.
OPPOSITES warm.

**china** noun crockery, dishes, plates, cups and saucers, tableware, porcelain, dinnerware, dinner service, tea service.

**chink** noun *a chink in the curtains:* gap, crack, space, hole, aperture, fissure, cranny, cleft, split, slit.

**chip** noun **1** *wood chips:* fragment, sliver, splinter, shaving, shard, flake. **2** *a chip in the glass:* nick, crack, scratch. **3** *gambling chips:* counter, token; N. Amer. check.
**verb** **1** *the teacup was chipped:* nick, crack, scratch. **2** *chip off the old plaster:* cut, hack, chisel, carve, hew, whittle.

**choice** noun **1** *freedom of choice:* selection, choosing, picking, pick, preference, decision, say, vote. **2** *you have no other choice:* option, alternative, course of action. **3** *an extensive choice:* range, variety, selection, assortment.
**adjective** *choice plums:* superior, first-class, first-rate, prime,

premier, grade A, best, finest, select, quality, top, top-quality, high-grade, prize; informal A1, top-notch.
OPPOSITES inferior.

**choke** verb **1** *Christopher started to choke:* gag, retch, cough, fight for breath. **2** *she had been choked to death:* suffocate, asphyxiate, smother, stifle, strangle, throttle; informal strangulate. **3** *the guttering was choked with leaves:* clog (up), bung up, stop up, block, obstruct.

**choose** verb **1** *we chose a quiet country hotel:* select, pick (out), opt for, plump for, settle on, prefer, decide on, fix on, elect, adopt. **2** *I'll stay as long as I choose:* wish, want, desire, please, like.

**chop** verb cut (up), cube, dice, hew, split, fell; N. Amer. hash.
■ **chop something off** cut off, sever, lop, shear.

**chore** noun task, job, duty, errand, burden; informal hassle.

**christen** verb **1** *she was christened Sara:* baptize, name, give the name of, call. **2** *a group who were christened 'The Magic Circle':* call, name, dub, style, term, label, nickname.

**chronicle** noun *a chronicle of the region's past:* record, account, history, annals, archive(s), log, diary, journal.
**verb** *the events have been chronicled:* record, write down, set down, document, report.

**chubby** adjective plump, tubby, flabby, rotund, portly, chunky; Brit. informal podgy; N. Amer. informal zaftig, corn-fed.
OPPOSITES skinny.

**chuck** verb (informal) **1** *he chucked the letter on to the table:* throw, toss, fling, hurl, pitch, cast, lob;

a
b
**c**
d
e
f
g
h
i
j
k
l
m
n
o
p
q
r
s
t
u
v
w
x
y
z

informal sling, bung; Austral. informal hoy; NZ informal bish. **2** *I chucked the rubbish:* throw away/out, discard, dispose of, get rid of, dump, bin, jettison; informal ditch, junk; N. Amer. informal trash. **3** *I've chucked my job:* give up, leave, resign from; informal quit, pack in; Brit. informal jack in. **4** *Mary chucked him for another guy:* leave, finish with, break off with, jilt; informal dump, ditch, give someone the elbow; Brit. informal give someone the push.

**chuckle** verb laugh, chortle, giggle, titter, snigger.

**chum** noun (informal) friend, companion, playmate, classmate, schoolmate, workmate; informal pal, crony; Brit. informal mate; N. Amer. informal buddy.
OPPOSITES enemy, stranger.

**chunk** noun lump, hunk, wedge, block, slab, square, nugget, brick, cube; informal wodge; N. Amer. informal gob.

**churlish** adjective rude, ill-mannered, discourteous, impolite, inconsiderate, surly, sullen.
OPPOSITES polite.

**churn** verb disturb, stir up, agitate, beat.

**cinema** noun **1** *the local cinema:* the movies, the pictures; N. Amer. movie theatre/house; informal the flicks. **2** *British cinema:* films, film, movies, pictures, motion pictures.

**circa** preposition approximately, (round) about, around, in the region of, roughly, something like, or so, or thereabouts, more or less; informal as near as dammit; N. Amer. informal in the ballpark of.
OPPOSITES exactly.

**circle** noun **1** *a circle of gold stars:* ring, band, hoop, circlet, halo, disc. **2** *her circle of friends:* group, set, crowd, band, company, clique, coterie, club, society; informal gang, bunch.
verb **1** *seagulls circled above:* wheel, revolve, rotate, whirl, spiral. **2** *satellites circling the earth:* go round, travel round, circumnavigate, orbit. **3** *the abbey was circled by a wall:* surround, encircle, ring, enclose.

**circuit** noun **1** *two circuits of the track:* lap, turn, round, circle. **2** (Brit.) *a racing circuit:* track, racetrack, course, route, stadium.

**circular** adjective *a circular room:* round, ring-shaped.
noun leaflet, pamphlet, handbill, flyer, advertisement, notice.

**circulate** verb **1** *the news was widely circulated:* spread, communicate, disseminate, make known, make public, broadcast, publicize, distribute. **2** *they circulated among the guests:* socialize, mingle, mix, wander, stroll.

**circumstances** plural noun situation, conditions, state of affairs, position, the lie of the land, (turn of) events, factors, facts, background, environment, context.

**cite** verb **1** *cite the passage in full:* quote, reproduce, excerpt. **2** *he cited the case of Leigh v. Gladstone:* refer to, allude to, instance, specify, mention, name.

**citizen** noun **1** *a British citizen:* subject, national, passport holder. **2** *the citizens of Edinburgh:* inhabitant, resident, native, townsman, townswoman, taxpayer, people; formal denizen.

**city** noun town, municipality, metropolis, conurbation, urban area; Scottish burgh; informal big smoke; N. Amer. informal burg.

**civic** adjective municipal, city, town, urban, metropolitan, public, community.

**civil** adjective 1 *a civil marriage:* secular, non-religious, lay. 2 *civil aviation:* non-military, civilian. 3 *he behaved in a civil manner:* polite, courteous, well mannered, gentlemanly, chivalrous, ladylike.
OPPOSITES religious, military, rude.

**civilization** noun 1 *a higher stage of civilization:* human development, advancement, progress, enlightenment, culture, refinement, sophistication. 2 *ancient civilizations:* culture, society, nation, people.

**civilize** verb enlighten, improve, educate, instruct, refine, cultivate, socialize.

**civilized** adjective 1 *civilized society:* advanced, developed, sophisticated, enlightened, educated, cultured, cultivated. 2 *civilized behaviour:* polite, courteous, well mannered, civil, refined, polished.
OPPOSITES unsophisticated, rude.

**claim** verb 1 *he claimed that she was lying:* assert, declare, profess, protest, maintain, insist, contend, allege. 2 *you can claim compensation:* request, ask for, apply for, demand.
noun 1 *her claim that she was robbed:* assertion, declaration, profession, protestation, insistence, contention, allegation. 2 *a claim for damages:* application, request, demand.

**clamour** noun noise, din, racket, rumpus, uproar, shouting, commotion, hubbub; informal hullaballoo; Brit. informal row.

**clamp** verb fasten, secure, fix, attach, clench, grip, hold, press, clasp, screw, bolt.

**clan** noun family, house, dynasty, tribe.

**clap** verb *the audience clapped:* applaud, give someone a round of applause, put one's hands together; informal give someone a (big) hand; N. Amer. informal give it up.
noun 1 *everybody gave him a clap:* round of applause, handclap; informal hand. 2 *a clap of thunder:* crack, peal, crash, bang, boom.

**clarify** verb make clear, shed/throw light on, illuminate, elucidate, explain, interpret, spell out, clear up.
OPPOSITES confuse.

**clarity** noun 1 *the clarity of his explanation:* lucidity, precision, coherence, transparency, simplicity. 2 *the clarity of the image:* sharpness, clearness, crispness, definition. 3 *the clarity of the water:* transparency, clearness, limpidity, translucence.
OPPOSITES vagueness, blurriness, cloudiness.

**clash** noun 1 *clashes between armed gangs:* fight, battle, confrontation, skirmish, engagement, encounter, conflict. 2 *clashes in parliament:* argument, altercation, confrontation, quarrel, disagreement, dispute; informal run-in, slanging match. 3 *the clash of cymbals:* crash, clang, bang.

**verb 1** *protesters clashed with police:* fight, battle, confront, skirmish, contend, come to blows. **2** *the prime minister clashed with union leaders:* disagree, differ, wrangle, dispute, cross swords, lock horns, be at loggerheads. **3** *the dates clash:* conflict, coincide, overlap. **4** *she clashed the cymbals together:* bang, strike, clang, crash.

**clasp** verb *Ruth clasped him to her:* grasp, grip, clutch, hold, squeeze, seize, grab, embrace, hug.
noun **1** *a gold clasp:* fastener, catch, clip, pin, buckle. **2** *his tight clasp:* grasp, grip, squeeze, embrace, hug.

**class** noun **1** *a new class of drug:* kind, sort, type, variety, genre, category, grade, rating, classification. **2** *mixing with people of her own class:* group, grouping, rank, stratum, level, echelon, status, caste.
verb *the 12-seater is classed as a commercial vehicle:* classify, categorize, group, grade, order, rate, bracket, designate, label, rank.

**classic** adjective **1** *the classic work on the subject:* definitive, authoritative, outstanding, first-rate, first-class, best, finest, excellent, superior, masterly. **2** *a classic example of Norman design:* typical, archetypal, quintessential, model, representative, perfect, prime, textbook. **3** *a classic look:* timeless, traditional, simple, elegant, understated.
OPPOSITES insignificant, second-rate, atypical, ephemeral.
noun *a classic of the genre:* definitive example, model, epitome, paradigm, exemplar, masterpiece.

**classification** noun categorization, classifying, grouping, grading, ranking, organization, sorting, codification.

**classify** verb categorize, group, grade, rank, order, organize, sort, type, codify, bracket.

**classy** adjective (informal) stylish, high-class, superior, exclusive, chic, elegant, smart, sophisticated; Brit. upmarket; N. Amer. high-toned; informal posh, ritzy, plush, swanky; Brit. informal swish.

**clause** noun section, paragraph, article, passage, subsection, chapter, condition, proviso, rider.

**claw** noun **1** *a bird's claw:* talon, nail. **2** *a crab's claw:* pincer, nipper.
verb *her fingers clawed his shoulders:* scratch, lacerate, tear, rip, scrape, dig into.

**clean** adjective **1** *keep the wound clean:* washed, scrubbed, cleansed, cleaned, laundered, spotless, unstained, unsullied, unblemished, immaculate, pristine, disinfected, sterilized, sterile, aseptic, decontaminated. **2** *a clean sheet of paper:* blank, empty, clear, plain, unused, new, pristine, fresh, unmarked. **3** *clean air:* pure, clear, fresh, unpolluted, uncontaminated.
OPPOSITES dirty, polluted, used.
verb *Dad cleaned the windows:* wash, cleanse, wipe, sponge, scrub, mop, rinse, scour, swab, shampoo, launder, dry-clean.
OPPOSITES dirty.

**cleanse** verb **1** *the wound was cleansed:* clean (up), wash, bathe, rinse, disinfect. **2** *cleansing the environment of* *traces of lead:* rid, clear, free, purify, purge.

**clear** adjective **1** *clear instructions:* understandable, comprehensible, intelligible, plain, uncomplicated, explicit, lucid, coherent, simple, straightforward, unambiguous, clear-cut. **2** *a clear case of harassment:* obvious, evident, plain, sure, definite, unmistakable, manifest, indisputable, unambiguous, patent, incontrovertible, visible, conspicuous, overt, blatant, glaring. **3** *clear water:* transparent, limpid, translucent, crystal clear. **4** *a clear sky:* bright, cloudless, unclouded, blue, sunny, starry. **5** *the road was clear:* unobstructed, passable, open, unrestricted, unhindered. OPPOSITES vague, disputed, cloudy, obstructed.
verb **1** *the smoke had cleared:* disappear, go away, stop, die away, fade, wear off, lift, settle, evaporate, dissipate, decrease, lessen, shift. **2** *they cleared the table:* empty, unload, strip. **3** *clearing drains:* unblock, unstop. **4** *staff cleared the building:* evacuate, empty, leave. **5** *Karen cleared the dirty plates:* remove, take away, carry away, tidy away/up. **6** *I cleared the bar at my first attempt:* go over, pass over, sail over, jump (over), vault (over), leap (over). **7** *he was cleared by the court:* acquit, declare innocent, find not guilty, absolve, exonerate; informal let off (the hook).

■ **clear something up 1** *clear up the garden:* tidy (up), put in order, straighten up, clean up, fix. **2** *we've cleared up the problem:* solve, resolve,

straighten out, find an/the answer to, get to the bottom of, explain; informal crack, figure out, suss out.

**clearance** noun **1** *slum clearance:* removal, clearing, demolition. **2** *you must have Home Office clearance:* authorization, permission, consent, approval, leave, sanction, licence, dispensation; informal the go-ahead. **3** *there is plenty of clearance:* space, room (to spare), headroom, margin, leeway.

**clear-cut** adjective definite, distinct, precise, specific, explicit, unambiguous, unequivocal, black and white. OPPOSITES vague.

**clearly** adverb **1** *write clearly:* intelligibly, plainly, distinctly, comprehensibly, legibly, audibly. **2** *clearly, substantial changes are needed:* obviously, evidently, patently, unquestionably, undoubtedly, without doubt, plainly, undeniably.

**cleft** noun split, crack, fissure, crevice.

**clench** verb grip, grasp, grab, clutch, clasp, clamp, hold tightly, seize, squeeze.

**clergyman, clergywoman** noun priest, cleric, minister, preacher, chaplain, padre, father, pastor, vicar, rector, parson, curate; Scottish kirkman.

**clever** adjective **1** intelligent, bright, smart, astute, quick-witted, shrewd, talented, gifted, capable, able, competent; informal brainy. **2** *a clever scheme:* ingenious, canny, cunning, crafty, artful, slick, neat. **3** *she was clever with her hands:* skilful, dexterous, adroit, adept, deft,

nimble, handy, skilled, talented, gifted.
OPPOSITES stupid.

**cliché** noun **platitude**, hackneyed phrase, commonplace, banality, truism, stock phrase; informal old chestnut.

**client** noun **customer**, buyer, purchaser, shopper, patient, patron; Brit. informal punter.

**cliff** noun **precipice**, rock face, crag, bluff, ridge, escarpment, scar, scarp.

**climate** noun **1** *a mild climate:* (weather) conditions, weather. **2** *the political climate:* atmosphere, mood, spirit, ethos, feeling, ambience, environment.

**climax** noun *the climax of his career:* peak, pinnacle, height, high point, top, zenith, culmination.
OPPOSITES anticlimax, nadir.

**climb** verb **1** *we climbed the hill:* ascend, mount, scale, scramble up, clamber up, shin up, conquer. **2** *the plane climbed:* rise, ascend, go up, gain height, soar, rocket. **3** *the road climbs steeply:* slope (upwards), rise, go uphill, incline.
OPPOSITES descend.
■ climb down back down, retreat, give in, backtrack, eat one's words, eat humble pie, do a U-turn; N. Amer. informal eat crow.

**clinch** verb **1** *he clinched the deal:* secure, settle, conclude, close, confirm, seal, finalize; informal sew up. **2** *these findings clinched the matter:* settle, decide, determine, resolve. **3** *they clinched the title:* win, secure.
OPPOSITES lose.

**cling** verb *rice grains cling together:* stick, adhere, hold.
■ cling (on) to hold on, clutch, grip, grasp, clasp, hang on, embrace, hug.

**clinical** adjective **1** *he seemed so clinical:* detached, impersonal, dispassionate, indifferent, uninvolved, distant, remote, aloof, cold. **2** *the room was very clinical:* plain, stark, austere, spartan, bleak, bare, functional, basic, institutional.
OPPOSITES emotional, luxurious.

**clip¹** noun *the clip on his briefcase:* fastener, clasp, hasp, catch, hook, buckle, lock.
verb *he clipped the pages together:* fasten, attach, fix, join, pin, staple, tack.

**clip²** verb **1** *I clipped the hedge:* trim, prune, cut, snip, crop, shear, lop. **2** *his lorry clipped a van:* hit, strike, graze, glance off, nudge, scrape.
noun **1** *a film clip:* extract, excerpt, snippet, fragment, trailer. **2** *I gave the dog a clip:* trim, cut, crop, haircut, clout.

**cloak** noun **1** *the cloak over his shoulders:* cape, robe, wrap, mantle. **2** *a cloak of secrecy:* cover, veil, mantle, shroud, screen, blanket.
verb *a peak cloaked in mist:* conceal, hide, cover, veil, shroud, mask, obscure, cloud, envelop, swathe, surround.

**clog** verb block, obstruct, congest, jam, choke, bung up, plug, stop up.

**close¹** adjective **1** *the town is close to Leeds:* near, nearby, adjacent, neighbouring, adjoining, abutting, at hand. **2** *a very close match:* even, neck and neck. **3** *close friends:* intimate, dear, bosom, close-knit, inseparable, devoted, faithful, special, firm. **4** *a close*

*resemblance:* noticeable, marked, distinct, pronounced, strong. **5** *a close examination:* careful, detailed, thorough, minute, searching, painstaking, meticulous, rigorous. **6** *the weather was close:* humid, muggy, stuffy, airless, heavy, sticky, sultry, stifling.
OPPOSITES far, distant, one-sided, slight, cursory, fresh.

**close²** verb **1** *she closed the door:* shut, pull to, push to, slam. **2** *close the hole:* block, stop up, plug, seal, bung up, clog up, choke, obstruct. **3** *he closed the meeting:* end, conclude, finish, terminate, wind up. **4** *the factory is to close:* shut down, close down, cease production, cease trading, be wound up, go out of business; informal fold, go to the wall, go bust. **5** *he closed a deal:* clinch, settle, secure, seal, confirm, pull off, conclude, finalize; informal wrap up.
OPPOSITES open, start.
noun *the close of the talks:* end, finish, conclusion.
OPPOSITES beginning.

**cloth** noun **1** *a maker of cloth:* fabric, material, textile(s). **2** *a cloth to wipe the table:* rag, wipe, duster, flannel; Austral. washer.

**clothe** verb dress, attire, robe, garb, costume, swathe, deck (out), turn out, fit out, rig (out); informal get up.

**clothes** plural noun clothing, garments, attire, garb, dress, wear, costume, wardrobe; informal gear, togs; Brit. informal clobber; N. Amer. informal threads.

**clothing** noun. See CLOTHES.

**cloud** noun *a cloud of exhaust smoke:* mass, billow, pall, mantle, blanket.

verb *anger clouded my judgement:* confuse, muddle, obscure.

**cloudy** adjective **1** *a cloudy sky:* overcast, dark, grey, black, leaden, murky, gloomy, sunless, starless. **2** *cloudy water:* murky, muddy, milky, dirty, turbid.
OPPOSITES clear, sunny.

**clown** noun **1** *the class clown:* joker, comedian, comic, wag, wit, jester, buffoon. **2** *bureaucratic clowns:* fool, idiot, dolt, ass, ignoramus; informal moron, numbskull, halfwit, fathead; Brit. informal prat, berk, twit, twerp.
verb *Harvey clowned around:* fool around/about, play the fool, play about/around, monkey about/around, joke; informal mess about/around, lark (about/around); Brit. informal muck about/around.

**club¹** noun **1** *a canoeing club:* society, association, group, circle, league, guild, union. **2** *the city has great clubs:* nightclub, bar; informal disco. **3** *the top club in the league:* team, squad, side.

**club²** noun *a wooden club:* stick, cudgel, truncheon, bludgeon, baton, mace, bat; N. Amer. blackjack, nightstick; Brit. informal cosh.
verb *he was clubbed with an iron bar:* hit, beat, strike, cudgel, bludgeon, batter; informal clout, clobber; Brit. informal cosh.

**clue** noun hint, indication, sign, signal, pointer, lead, tip, evidence.

**clump** noun **1** *a clump of trees:* cluster, thicket, group, bunch. **2** *a clump of earth:* lump, clod, mass, chunk.

**clumsy** adjective **1** *she was terribly clumsy:* awkward,

uncoordinated, ungainly, graceless, lumbering, inelegant, inept, unskilful, accident-prone, all fingers and thumbs; informal cack-handed, ham-fisted, butterfingered; N. Amer. informal klutzy. **2** *a clumsy contraption:* unwieldy, cumbersome, bulky, awkward.
OPPOSITES graceful, handy.

**cluster** noun *clusters of berries:* bunch, clump, mass, knot, group, clutch, huddle, crowd.
verb *they clustered around the television:* congregate, gather, collect, group, assemble, huddle, crowd.

**clutch** verb grip, grasp, clasp, cling to, hang on to, clench, hold, grab, snatch.

**clutter** noun disorder, chaos, disarray, untidiness, mess, confusion, litter, rubbish, junk.
verb litter, mess up, be strewn, be scattered, cover, bury.

**coach**[1] noun **1** *a journey by coach:* bus. **2** *a railway coach:* carriage, wagon; N. Amer. car.

**coach**[2] noun *a football coach:* instructor, trainer, teacher, tutor, mentor, guru.
verb *he coached Richard in maths:* instruct, teach, tutor, school, educate, drill, train.

**coalition** noun alliance, union, partnership, bloc, federation, league, association, confederation, consortium, syndicate, amalgamation, merger.

**coarse** adjective **1** *coarse blankets:* rough, scratchy, prickly, wiry, harsh. **2** *coarse manners:* uncouth, oafish, loutish, boorish, rude, impolite, ill-mannered, vulgar, common, rough. **3** *a coarse remark:* vulgar, crude, rude, off colour, lewd, smutty, indelicate.

OPPOSITES soft, refined, polite.

**coast** noun *the west coast:* shore, coastline, seashore, seaboard, shoreline, seaside.
verb *the car coasted down a hill:* freewheel, cruise, taxi, drift, glide, sail.

**coat** noun **1** *a dog's coat:* fur, hair, wool, fleece, hide, pelt, skin. **2** *a coat of paint:* layer, covering, coating, skin, film, deposit.
verb *the tube was coated with wax:* cover, surface, plate, spread, daub, smear, plaster.

**coax** verb persuade, wheedle, cajole, get round, inveigle, manoeuvre; informal sweet-talk, soft-soap, twist someone's arm.

**cocky** adjective arrogant, conceited, overconfident, swollen-headed, self-important, egotistical, presumptuous, boastful.
OPPOSITES modest.

**code** noun **1** *a secret code:* cipher. **2** *a strict social code:* convention, etiquette, protocol, ethic. **3** *the penal code:* law(s), rules, regulations, constitution, system.

**coerce** verb pressure, press, push, constrain, force, compel, oblige, browbeat, bully, threaten, intimidate, dragoon, twist someone's arm; informal railroad, steamroller, lean on.

**coherent** adjective logical, reasoned, rational, sound, cogent, consistent, lucid, articulate, intelligible.
OPPOSITES muddled.

**coil** verb wind, loop, twist, curl, spiral, twine, wrap.

**coin** verb invent, create, make up, conceive, originate, think up, dream up.

**coincide** verb **1** *the events coincided:* occur

simultaneously, happen together, co-occur, coexist. **2** *their interests do not always coincide:* **tally,** correspond, agree, accord, match up, be compatible, dovetail, mesh; informal square.
OPPOSITES differ.

**coincidence** noun accident, chance, providence, happenstance, fate, luck, fortune, fluke.

**coincidental** adjective accidental, chance, fluky, random, fortuitous.

**cold** adjective **1** *a cold day:* chilly, chill, cool, freezing, icy, wintry, frosty, bitter, raw; informal nippy; Brit. informal parky. **2** *a cold reception:* unfriendly, inhospitable, unwelcoming, cool, frigid, frosty, distant, formal, stiff.
OPPOSITES hot, warm.

**collaborate** verb **1** *they collaborated on the project:* **cooperate,** join forces, work together, combine, pool resources, club together. **2** *they collaborated with the enemy:* **fraternize,** conspire, collude, cooperate, consort.

**collaborator** noun **1** *his collaborator on the book:* **co-worker,** partner, associate, colleague, confederate, assistant. **2** *a wartime collaborator:* **sympathizer,** traitor, quisling, fifth columnist.

**collapse** verb **1** *the roof collapsed:* **cave in,** fall in, subside, fall down, give (way), crumple, crumble, disintegrate. **2** *he collapsed last night:* **faint,** pass out, black out, lose consciousness. **3** *she collapsed in tears:* **break down,** go to pieces, be overcome; informal

crack up. **4** *peace talks collapsed:* **break down,** fail, fall through, fold, founder; informal flop, fizzle out.
noun **1** *the collapse of the roof:* **cave-in,** disintegration. **2** *the collapse of the talks:* **breakdown,** failure.

**colleague** noun co-worker, fellow worker, workmate, teammate, associate, partner, collaborator, ally, confederate.

**collect** verb **1** *he collected up the rubbish:* **gather,** accumulate, assemble, amass, stockpile, pile up, heap up, store (up), hoard, save. **2** *a crowd soon collected:* **gather,** assemble, meet, muster, congregate, convene, converge. **3** *I must collect the children:* **fetch,** pick up, go/come and get, call for, meet.
OPPOSITES distribute, disperse, deliver.

**collected** adjective calm, cool, self-possessed, self-controlled, composed, poised, serene, tranquil, relaxed; informal laid-back.
OPPOSITES excited, hysterical.

**collection** noun **1** *a collection of stolen items:* **hoard,** pile, heap, stock, store, stockpile, accumulation, reserve, supply, bank, pool, fund; informal stash. **2** *a collection of shoppers:* **group,** crowd, body, gathering, knot, cluster. **3** *a collection of short stories:* **anthology,** selection, compendium, compilation, miscellany. **4** *a collection for famine relief:* **appeal;** informal whip-round.

**collective** adjective common, shared, joint, combined, mutual, communal, pooled, united, allied, cooperative, collaborative.
OPPOSITES individual.

**collide** verb crash, hit, strike, run into, bump into.

**collision** noun crash, accident, smash; N. Amer. wreck; informal pile-up; Brit. informal shunt.

**colloquial** adjective informal, conversational, everyday, familiar, popular, casual, idiomatic, slangy, vernacular.
OPPOSITES formal.

**colonize** verb settle (in), people, populate, occupy, take over, invade.

**colony** noun territory, dependency, protectorate, satellite, settlement, outpost, province.

**colossal** adjective huge, massive, enormous, gigantic, giant, mammoth, vast, immense, monumental, mountainous; informal monster, whopping, humongous; Brit. informal ginormous.
OPPOSITES tiny.

**colour** noun 1 *the lights changed colour:* hue, shade, tint, tone, coloration. 2 *oil colour:* paint, pigment, colourant, dye, stain. verb 1 *the wood was coloured blue:* tint, dye, stain, tinge. 2 *the experience coloured her outlook:* influence, affect, taint, warp, skew, distort.

**colourful** adjective 1 *a colourful picture:* brightly coloured, vivid, vibrant, brilliant, radiant, gaudy, garish, multicoloured; informal jazzy. 2 *a colourful account:* vivid, graphic, lively, animated, dramatic, fascinating, interesting, stimulating, scintillating, evocative.
OPPOSITES drab, plain, boring.

**column** noun 1 *arches supported by massive columns:* pillar, post, support, upright, pier, pile. 2 *a column in the paper:* article, piece, feature. 3 *we walked in a column:* line, file, queue, procession, convoy; informal crocodile.

**comb** verb 1 *she combed her hair:* groom, brush, untangle, smooth, straighten, neaten, tidy, arrange. 2 *police combed the area:* search, scour, explore, sweep.

**combat** noun *he was killed in combat:* battle, fighting, action, hostilities, conflict, war, warfare.
verb *they tried to combat the disease:* fight, battle, tackle, attack, counter, resist.

**combination** noun mixture, mix, blend, fusion, amalgamation, amalgam, merger, marriage, synthesis.

**combine** verb 1 *he combines comedy with tragedy:* mix, blend, fuse, amalgamate, integrate, merge, marry. 2 *teachers combined to tackle the problem:* unite, collaborate, join forces, get together, team up.

**come** verb 1 *come and listen:* approach, advance, draw close/ closer, draw near/nearer. 2 *they came last night:* arrive, get here/there, make it, appear, turn up, materialize; informal show (up), roll up. 3 *they came to a stream:* reach, arrive at, get to, come across, run across, happen on, chance on, come upon, stumble on, end up at; informal wind up at. 4 *she comes from Belgium:* be from, be a native of, hail from, live in, reside in. 5 *attacks came without warning:* happen, occur, take place, come about, fall, crop up.
OPPOSITES go, leave.

■ **come about** happen, occur, take place, transpire, fall, arise.

■ **come across** meet, run into, run across, come upon, chance on, stumble on, happen on, discover, encounter, find; informal bump into. ■ **come on** progress, develop, shape up, take shape, come along, turn out, improve.

**comeback** noun return, recovery, resurgence, rally, upturn; Brit. fightback.

**comedian** noun 1 *a famous comedian:* comic, comedienne, funny man/woman, humorist, stand-up; N. Amer. tummler. 2 *Dad was such a comedian:* joker, wit, wag, comic, clown; informal laugh, hoot.

**comedy** noun *the comedy in their work:* humour, fun, hilarity, funny side, laughs, jokes.
OPPOSITES tragedy.

**comfort** noun 1 *travel in comfort:* ease, repose, luxury, prosperity. 2 *words of comfort:* consolation, condolence, sympathy, commiseration, support, reassurance, cheer.
OPPOSITES discomfort.
verb *a friend tried to comfort her:* console, support, reassure, soothe, calm, cheer, hearten.
OPPOSITES distress, depress.

**comfortable** adjective 1 *a comfortable lifestyle:* pleasant, affluent, well-to-do, luxurious, opulent. 2 *a comfortable room:* cosy, snug, warm, pleasant, agreeable, homely; informal comfy. 3 *comfortable clothes:* loose, casual; informal comfy.
OPPOSITES hard, spartan, restricting.

**comforting** adjective soothing, reassuring, calming, heartening, cheering.
OPPOSITES upsetting.

**comic** adjective humorous, funny, amusing, hilarious, comical, zany, witty.
OPPOSITES serious.
noun comedian, comedienne, funny man/woman, humorist, wit, joker.

**comical** adjective 1 *he could be quite comical:* funny, humorous, droll, witty, amusing, entertaining; informal wacky. 2 *they look comical in those suits:* silly, absurd, ridiculous, laughable, ludicrous, preposterous, foolish; informal crazy.
OPPOSITES serious, sensible.

**coming** adjective *the coming election:* forthcoming, imminent, impending, approaching.
noun *the coming of spring:* approach, advance, advent, arrival, appearance, emergence.

**command** verb 1 *he commanded his men to retreat:* order, tell, direct, instruct, call on, require. 2 *Jones commanded a tank squadron:* be in charge of, be in command of, head, lead, control, direct, manage, supervise, oversee; informal head up.
noun 1 *officers shouted commands:* order, instruction, direction. 2 *he had 160 men under his command:* authority, control, charge, power, direction, dominion, guidance, leadership, rule, government, management, supervision, jurisdiction. 3 *a brilliant command of English:* knowledge, mastery, grasp, comprehension, understanding.

**commander** noun leader, head, chief, overseer, director, controller; informal boss, skipper, head honcho; Brit. informal gaffer, guv'nor.

**commanding** adjective

a
b
**c**
d
e
f
g
h
i
j
k
l
m
n
o
p
q
r
s
t
u
v
w
x
y
z

dominant, controlling, superior, powerful, advantageous, favourable.
OPPOSITES disadvantageous, weak.

**commemorate** verb celebrate, remember, recognize, acknowledge, observe, mark, pay tribute to, pay homage to, honour, salute.

**commence** verb begin, inaugurate, start, initiate, launch into, open, get the ball rolling, get going, get under way, get off the ground, set about, embark on; informal kick off.
OPPOSITES conclude.

**commend** verb 1 *we should commend him*: praise, compliment, congratulate, applaud, salute, honour, sing the praises of, pay tribute to. 2 *I commend her to you without reservation*: recommend, endorse, vouch for, speak for, support, back.
OPPOSITES criticize.

**commendable** adjective admirable, praiseworthy, creditable, laudable, meritorious, exemplary, honourable, respectable.
OPPOSITES reprehensible.

**comment** noun 1 *their comments on her appearance*: remark, observation, statement, pronouncement, judgement, reflection, opinion, view. 2 *a great deal of comment*: discussion, debate, interest. 3 *a comment in the margin*: note, annotation, commentary, footnote, gloss, explanation.
verb 1 *they commented on the food*: remark on, speak about, talk about, discuss, mention. 2 *'It will soon be night,' he commented*: remark, observe,

say, state, note, point out.

**commentary** noun 1 *the test match commentary*: narration, description, report, review, voice-over. 2 *textual commentary*: explanation, elucidation, interpretation, analysis, assessment, review, criticism, notes, comments.

**commentator** noun 1 *a sports commentator*: reporter, narrator, journalist, newscaster. 2 *a political commentator*: analyst, pundit, critic, columnist, leader-writer, opinion-former, monitor, observer.

**commerce** noun trade, trading, business, dealing, buying and selling, traffic, trafficking.

**commercial** adjective 1 *a vessel built for commercial purposes*: trade, trading, business, mercantile, sales. 2 *a commercial organization*: profit-making, materialistic, mercenary.
OPPOSITES non-profit-making.

**commission** noun 1 *the dealer's commission*: percentage, share, premium, fee, bonus, royalty; informal cut, rake-off, slice; Brit. informal whack. 2 *a commission to design a monument*: contract, engagement, assignment, booking, job. 3 *an independent commission*: committee, board, council, panel, body.
verb 1 *he was commissioned to paint a portrait*: engage, contract, book, employ, hire, recruit, take on, retain, appoint. 2 *they commissioned a sculpture*: order.

**commit** verb 1 *he committed a murder*: carry out, do, perpetrate, engage in, execute, accomplish, be responsible for; informal pull off. 2 *she was* committed to their care: entrust, consign, assign, deliver, hand over. **3** *the judge committed him to prison:* consign, send, confine.

**commitment** noun **1** *the pressure of his commitments:* responsibility, obligation, duty, liability, engagement, tie. **2** *her commitment to her students:* dedication, devotion, allegiance, loyalty. **3** *he made a commitment:* promise, vow, pledge, undertaking.

**committed** adjective devoted, dedicated, staunch, loyal, faithful, devout, firm, steadfast, unwavering, passionate, ardent, sworn.
OPPOSITES apathetic.

**common** adjective **1** *a common occurrence:* frequent, regular, everyday, normal, usual, ordinary, familiar, standard, commonplace. **2** *a common belief:* widespread, general, universal, popular, mainstream, prevalent, rife, established, conventional, accepted. **3** *the common people:* ordinary, normal, average, unexceptional, typical, simple. **4** *the common good:* collective, communal, shared, community, public, popular, general. **5** *she's so common:* uncouth, vulgar, coarse, rough, uncivilized, unsophisticated, unrefined, inferior, plebeian; informal plebby.
OPPOSITES unusual, rare, individual, refined.

**commonplace** adjective. See **COMMON** sense 1.

**common sense** noun good sense, native wit, good judgement, level-headedness, prudence, wisdom; informal horse sense, nous; Brit. informal

common; N. Amer. informal smarts.
OPPOSITES stupidity.

**commotion** noun disturbance, uproar, disorder, confusion, rumpus, fuss, furore, hue and cry, stir, storm, chaos, havoc, pandemonium.

**communal** adjective **1** *a communal kitchen:* shared, joint, common. **2** *they farm on a communal basis:* collective, cooperative, community.
OPPOSITES private, individual.

**communicate** verb **1** *they communicate daily:* liaise, be in touch, be in contact, have dealings, talk, speak. **2** *he communicated the news to his boss:* convey, tell, relay, transmit, impart, pass on, report, recount, relate. **3** *the disease is communicated easily:* transmit, spread, transfer, pass on.

**communication** noun **1** *there was no communication between them:* contact, dealings, relations, connection, correspondence, dialogue, conversation. **2** *an official communication:* message, statement, announcement, report, dispatch, bulletin, disclosure, communiqué, letter, correspondence.

**communicative** adjective forthcoming, expansive, expressive, unreserved, vocal, outgoing, frank, open, candid, talkative, chatty.
OPPOSITES uncommunicative.

**communist** noun & adjective collectivist, Bolshevik, Marxist, Maoist, Soviet; informal, derogatory Commie, red.

**community** noun society, population, populace, people, public, residents, inhabitants, citizens.

a b c d e f g h i j k l m n o p q r s t u v w x y z

a
b
**c**
d
e
f
g
h
i
j
k
l
m
n
o
p
q
r
s
t
u
v
w
x
y
z

**compact**[1] adjective **1** *extremely compact rugs:* dense, tightly packed, compressed, thick, tight, firm, solid. **2** *a very compact phone:* neat, small, handy, petite. **3** *her tale is compact and readable:* concise, succinct, condensed, brief, pithy, to the point, short and sweet; informal snappy.
OPPOSITES loose, bulky, lengthy.
verb *the rubbish is then compacted:* compress, condense, pack down, tamp (down), flatten.

**compact**[2] noun *the warring states signed a compact:* treaty, pact, accord, agreement, contract, bargain, deal, settlement.

**companion** noun comrade, fellow ..., partner, associate, escort, compatriot, confederate, friend; informal pal, chum, crony; Brit. informal mate; N. Amer. informal buddy.

**company** noun **1** *an oil company:* firm, business, corporation, establishment, agency, office, house, institution, concern, enterprise, consortium, syndicate; informal outfit. **2** *I enjoy his company:* companionship, fellowship, society, fellowship, presence. **3** *a company of infantry:* unit, section, detachment, corps, squad, platoon.

**comparable** adjective **1** *comparable incomes:* similar, close, near, approximate, equivalent, proportional. **2** *nobody is comparable with him:* equal to, as good as, in the same league as, on a level with, a match for.
OPPOSITES incomparable.

**compare** verb **1** *we compared the two portraits:* contrast,

balance, set against, weigh up. **2** *he was compared to Wagner:* liken, equate, class with, bracket with. **3** *the porcelain compares with Dresden china:* be as good as, be comparable to, bear comparison with, be the equal of, match up to, be on a par with, be in the same league as, come close to, rival.

**comparison** noun *there's no comparison between them:* resemblance, likeness, similarity, correspondence.

**compartment** noun bay, locker, recess, alcove, cell, cubicle, pod, pigeonhole, cubbyhole.

**compass** noun scope, range, extent, reach, span, breadth, ambit, limits, parameters, bounds.

**compassion** noun sympathy, empathy, understanding, fellow feeling, pity, care, concern, sensitivity, kindness.
OPPOSITES indifference, cruelty.

**compassionate** adjective sympathetic, understanding, pitying, caring, sensitive, warm, loving, kind.
OPPOSITES unsympathetic, uncaring.

**compatible** adjective well matched, (well) suited, like-minded, in tune, in harmony, in keeping, consistent, consonant; informal on the same wavelength.
OPPOSITES incompatible.

**compel** verb force, pressure, coerce, dragoon, press, push, oblige, require, make; informal lean on, railroad, put the screws on.

**compelling** adjective **1** *a compelling performance:* enthralling, captivating, gripping, riveting, spellbinding, mesmerizing, absorbing. **2** *a compelling argument:*

**convincing**, persuasive, cogent, irresistible, powerful, strong.
OPPOSITES boring, weak.

**compensate** verb **1** *we agreed to compensate him for his loss:* recompense, repay, pay back, reimburse, remunerate, indemnify. **2** *his flair compensated for his faults:* balance (out), counterbalance, counteract, offset, make up for, cancel out.

**compensation** noun recompense, repayment, reimbursement, remuneration, redress, amends, damages; N. Amer. informal comp.

**compete** verb **1** *they competed in a tennis tournament:* take part, participate, be a contestant, play, enter, go in for. **2** *they had to compete with other firms:* contend, vie, battle, jockey, go head to head, pit oneself against, challenge, take on.

**competence** noun **1** *my technical competence:* ability, capability, proficiency, accomplishment, expertise, skill, prowess; informal know-how. **2** *the competence of the system:* adequacy, suitability, fitness.
OPPOSITES incompetence.

**competent** adjective **1** *a competent carpenter:* able, capable, proficient, adept, accomplished, skilful, skilled, expert. **2** *the court was not competent to hear the case:* fit, suitable, suited, appropriate, qualified, empowered, authorized.
OPPOSITES incompetent, unfit.

**competition** noun **1** *Stephanie won the competition:* contest, tournament, championship. **2** *I'm not interested in competition:* rivalry, competitiveness, conflict; informal keeping up with the Joneses. **3** *we must stay ahead of the competition:* opposition, rivals, other side, field, enemy; informal other guy.

**competitive** adjective **1** *a competitive player:* ambitious, zealous, keen, combative, aggressive; informal go-ahead. **2** *a highly competitive industry:* ruthless, aggressive, fierce, cut-throat; informal dog-eat-dog. **3** *competitive prices:* reasonable, moderate, keen, low, cheap, budget, bargain, rock-bottom, bargain-basement.
OPPOSITES apathetic, exorbitant.

**competitor** noun **1** *the competitors in the race:* contestant, contender, challenger, participant, entrant, player. **2** *our European competitors:* rival, challenger, opponent, competition, opposition.
OPPOSITES partner, teammate, ally.

**compile** verb assemble, put together, make up, collate, compose, organize, arrange, gather, collect.

**complacency** noun smugness, self-satisfaction, self-congratulation, self-regard.

**complacent** adjective smug, self-satisfied, self-congratulatory, resting on one's laurels.

**complain** verb protest, grumble, whine, bleat, carp, cavil, grouse, make a fuss, object, find fault; informal whinge, gripe, moan, bitch.

**complaint** noun **1** *they lodged a complaint:* protest, objection, grievance, grouse, grumble, criticism; informal gripe, whinge.

a
b
c
d
e
f
g
h
i
j
k
l
m
n
o
p
q
r
s
t
u
v
w
x
y
z

**2** *a kidney complaint*: disorder, disease, illness, sickness, ailment, infection, condition, problem, upset, trouble.

**complement** noun **1** *the perfect complement to the food*: accompaniment, companion, addition, supplement, accessory, finishing touch. **2** *a full complement of lifeboats*: amount, contingent, capacity, allowance, quota.
OPPOSITES contrast.
verb *this sauce complements the dessert*: accompany, go with, round off, set off, suit, harmonize with, enhance, complete.
OPPOSITES contrast with.

**complementary** adjective harmonious, compatible, corresponding, matching, reciprocal.
OPPOSITES incompatible.

**complete** adjective **1** *the complete text*: entire, whole, full, total, uncut, unabridged, unexpurgated. **2** *their research was complete*: finished, ended, concluded, completed; informal wrapped up, sewn up. **3** *a complete fool*: absolute, utter, out-and-out, total, downright, prize, perfect, unqualified, unmitigated, sheer; N. Amer. full-bore.
OPPOSITES partial, unfinished.
verb **1** *he had to complete his training*: finish, end, conclude, finalize, wind up; informal wrap up. **2** *the outfit was completed with a veil*: finish off, round off, top off, crown, cap. **3** *complete the application form*: fill in/out, answer.

**completely** adverb totally, entirely, wholly, thoroughly, fully, utterly, absolutely, perfectly, downright.

**complex** adjective **1** *a complex structure*: compound, composite, multiplex. **2** *a complex situation*: complicated, involved, intricate, convoluted, elaborate, difficult; Brit. informal fiddly.
OPPOSITES simple.
noun **1** *a complex of roads*: network, system, nexus, web. **2** (informal) *he had a complex about losing his hair*: obsession, fixation, preoccupation, neurosis; informal hang-up, thing.

**complexion** noun **1** *a pale complexion*: skin, skin colour/tone, colouring. **2** *governments of all complexions*: kind, nature, character, colour, persuasion, outlook.

**complicate** verb make (more) difficult, make complicated, mix up, confuse, muddle, compound.
OPPOSITES simplify.

**complicated** adjective **1** *a complicated stereo system*: compound, composite, multiplex. **2** *a long and complicated saga*: involved, intricate, complex, convoluted, elaborate, difficult; Brit. informal fiddly.
OPPOSITES simple, straightforward.

**complication** noun difficulty, problem, obstacle, hurdle, stumbling block, snag, catch, hitch; Brit. spanner in the works; informal headache.

**compliment** noun *an unexpected compliment*: tribute, accolade, commendation, pat on the back; (**compliments**) praise, acclaim, admiration, flattery, congratulations.
OPPOSITES criticism, insult.
verb *they complimented him on*

*his performance:* praise, pay tribute to, flatter, commend, acclaim, applaud, salute, congratulate.
OPPOSITES criticize.

**complimentary** adjective
**1** *complimentary remarks:* flattering, appreciative, congratulatory, admiring, approving, favourable, glowing.
**2** *complimentary tickets:* free (of charge), gratis, donated, courtesy; informal on the house.
OPPOSITES critical.

**comply** verb obey, observe, abide by, adhere to, conform to, follow, respect, go along with.
OPPOSITES disobey.

**component** noun part, piece, bit, element, constituent, ingredient, unit, module.

**compose** verb **1** *a poem composed by Shelley:* write, devise, make up, think up, produce, invent, pen, author.
**2** *how to compose a photograph:* organize, arrange, construct, set out. **3** *the congress is composed of ten senators:* make up, constitute, form, comprise.
■ compose oneself calm down, control oneself, regain one's composure, pull oneself together, steady oneself; informal get a grip.

**composed** adjective calm, collected, cool (as a cucumber), self-possessed, poised, serene, relaxed, at ease, unruffled, unperturbed; informal unflappable, together, laid-back.
OPPOSITES excited.

**composition** noun **1** *the composition of the council:* make-up, constitution, configuration, structure, formation, anatomy, organization. **2** *a literary*

*composition:* work (of art), creation, opus, piece. **3** *the composition of a poem:* writing, creation, formulation, compilation. **4** *a school composition:* essay, paper, study, piece of writing; N. Amer. theme. **5** *the composition of the painting:* arrangement, layout, proportions, balance, symmetry.

**compound** noun *a compound of two materials:* amalgam, blend, mixture, mix, alloy.
adjective *a compound substance:* composite, complex, multiple.
OPPOSITES simple.
verb **1** *soap compounded with disinfectant:* mix, combine, blend. **2** *his illness compounds their problems:* aggravate, exacerbate, worsen, add to, augment, intensify, heighten, increase.
OPPOSITES separate, alleviate.

**comprehend** verb understand, grasp, see, take in, follow, make sense of, fathom; informal work out, figure out, get.

**comprehensible** adjective intelligible, understandable, accessible, self-explanatory, clear, plain, straightforward.
OPPOSITES opaque.

**comprehension** noun understanding, grasp, mastery, conception, knowledge, awareness.
OPPOSITES ignorance.

**comprehensive** adjective inclusive, all-inclusive, complete, thorough, full, extensive, all-embracing, blanket, exhaustive, detailed, sweeping, wholesale, broad, wide-ranging.
OPPOSITES limited.

**compress** verb **1** *it is coconut compressed into a slab:* squeeze, press, squash, crush, compact.

a b **c** d e f g h i j k l m n o p q r s t u v w x y z

a
b
**c**
d
e
f
g
h
i
j
k
l
m
n
o
p
q
r
s
t
u
v
w
x
y
z

**2** *the material has been compressed into 17 pages:* shorten, abridge, condense, abbreviate, contract, telescope, summarize, precis.
OPPOSITES expand, pad out.

**comprise** verb **1** *the country comprises twenty states:* consist of, be made up of, be composed of, contain. **2** *this breed comprises half the herd:* make up, constitute, form, account for.

**compromise** noun *they reached a compromise:* agreement, understanding, settlement, terms, deal, trade-off, bargain, middle ground.
OPPOSITES intransigence.
verb **1** *we compromised:* meet each other halfway, come to an understanding, make a deal, make concessions, find a happy medium, strike a balance. **2** *his actions could compromise his reputation:* undermine, weaken, damage, harm, jeopardize, prejudice.

**compulsion** noun **1** *he is under no compulsion to go:* obligation, pressure, coercion. **2** *a compulsion to tell the truth:* urge, impulse, need, desire, drive, obsession, fixation, addiction.

**compulsive** adjective **1** *a compulsive desire:* irresistible, uncontrollable, compelling, overwhelming. **2** *compulsive eating:* obsessive, obsessional, addictive, uncontrollable. **3** *a compulsive liar:* inveterate, chronic, incorrigible, incurable, hopeless, persistent, habitual; informal pathological. **4** *it's compulsive viewing:* fascinating, compelling, gripping, riveting, engrossing, enthralling, captivating.

**compulsory** adjective obligatory, mandatory, required, requisite, necessary, binding, enforced, prescribed.
OPPOSITES optional.

**compute** verb calculate, work out, reckon, determine, evaluate, add up, total.

**comrade** noun companion, friend, colleague, associate, partner, ally; Brit. informal mate; N. Amer. informal buddy.

**conceal** verb **1** *clouds concealed the sun:* hide, screen, cover, obscure, block out, blot out, mask. **2** *he concealed his true feelings:* keep secret, hide, disguise, mask, veil, bottle up; informal keep a/the lid on.
OPPOSITES reveal, confess.

**concede** verb **1** *I had to concede that I'd overreacted:* admit, acknowledge, accept, allow, grant, recognize, own, confess, agree. **2** *he eventually conceded the title:* surrender, yield, give up, relinquish, hand over.
OPPOSITES deny, retain.

**conceit** noun vanity, pride, arrogance, egotism, self-importance, narcissism, self-admiration.
OPPOSITES humility.

**conceited** adjective vain, proud, egotistic, self-satisfied, self-important, narcissistic, full of oneself; informal big-headed, stuck-up.

**conceive** verb **1** *the project was conceived in 1977:* think up, think of, dream up, devise, formulate, design, create, develop. **2** *I could hardly conceive what it must be like:* imagine, envisage, visualize, picture, grasp, appreciate.

**concentrate** verb **1** *the government concentrated its efforts on staying in power:*

focus, direct, centre. **2** *she concentrated on the film:* focus on, pay attention to, keep one's mind on, be absorbed in, be engrossed in, be immersed in. **3** *troops concentrated on the horizon:* collect, gather, congregate, converge, mass, rally.
OPPOSITES disperse.

**concentrated** adjective **1** *a concentrated effort:* strenuous, concerted, intensive, all-out, intense. **2** *a concentrated solution:* condensed, reduced, undiluted, strong.
OPPOSITES half-hearted, diluted.

**concentration** noun close attention, attentiveness, application, single-mindedness, absorption.
OPPOSITES inattention.

**concept** noun idea, notion, conception, abstraction, theory, hypothesis.

**conception** noun **1** *the fertility treatment resulted in conception:* pregnancy, fertilization, impregnation, insemination. **2** *the product's conception:* inception, genesis, origination, creation, invention, beginning, origin. **3** *his original conception:* plan, idea, notion, scheme, project, proposal, intention, aim.

**concern** verb **1** *the report concerns the war:* be about, deal with, cover, relate to, pertain to. **2** *that doesn't concern you:* affect, involve, be relevant to, apply to, have a bearing on, impact on. **3** *one thing still concerns me:* worry, disturb, trouble, bother, perturb, unsettle.
noun **1** *a voice full of concern:* anxiety, worry, disquiet, apprehensiveness, unease,

misgiving. **2** *his concern for others:* care, consideration, solicitude, sympathy. **3** *housing is the concern of the council:* responsibility, business, affair, duty, job; informal bailiwick; Brit. informal lookout. **4** *issues of concern to women:* interest, importance, relevance, significance. **5** *a publishing concern:* firm, business, company, enterprise, operation, corporation; informal outfit.
OPPOSITES indifference.

**concerned** adjective **1** *her mother looked concerned:* worried, anxious, upset, troubled, uneasy, bothered. **2** *all concerned parties:* interested, involved, affected, implicated.
OPPOSITES unconcerned.

**concerning** preposition about, regarding, relating to, with reference to, referring to, with regard to, as regards, touching, in connection with, re, apropos.

**concession** noun **1** *the government made several concessions:* compromise, accommodation, trade-off, sop. **2** *tax concessions:* reduction, cut, discount, deduction, rebate; informal break. **3** *a logging concession:* right, privilege, licence, permit, franchise, warrant.

**concise** adjective succinct, pithy, brief, abridged, condensed, abbreviated, compact, potted.
OPPOSITES lengthy.

**conclude** verb **1** *the meeting concluded at ten:* finish, end, draw to a close, stop, cease. **2** *he concluded the press conference:* bring to an end, close, wind up, terminate; informal wrap up. **3** *an attempt to conclude a deal:* settle, clinch,

a
b
**c**
d
e
f
g
h
i
j
k
l
m
n
o
p
q
r
s
t
u
v
w
x
y
z

finalize, tie up. **4** *I concluded that he was rather unpleasant*: deduce, infer, gather, judge, decide, surmise; N. Amer. figure.
OPPOSITES begin.

**conclusion** noun **1** *the conclusion of his speech*: end, ending, finish, close. **2** *the conclusion of a trade agreement*: settlement, clinching, completion, arrangement. **3** *his conclusions have been verified*: deduction, inference, interpretation, judgement, verdict.
OPPOSITES beginning.

**concrete** adjective **1** *concrete objects*: solid, material, real, physical, tangible. **2** *concrete proof*: definite, specific, firm, positive, conclusive, precise.
OPPOSITES abstract, imaginary.

**condemn** verb **1** *he condemned the suspended players*: censure, criticize, denounce; informal slam; Brit. informal slate, slag off. **2** *his illness condemned him to a lonely life*: doom, destine, damn, sentence.
OPPOSITES praise.

**condemnation** noun censure, criticism, denunciation; informal flak, a bad press.

**condense** verb abridge, compress, summarize, shorten, cut, abbreviate, edit.
OPPOSITES expand.

**condition** noun **1** *check the condition of your wiring*: state, shape, order; Brit. informal nick. **2** *they lived in appalling conditions*: circumstances, surroundings, environment, situation. **3** *she was in tip-top condition*: fitness, health, form, shape. **4** *a liver condition*: disorder, problem, complaint, illness, disease. **5** *a condition of employment*: stipulation,

constraint, prerequisite, precondition, requirement, term, proviso.
verb *our minds are conditioned by habit*: train, teach, educate, guide, accustom, adapt, habituate, mould.

**conditional** adjective qualified, dependent, contingent, with reservations, limited, provisional, provisory.

**condone** verb disregard, accept, allow, let pass, turn a blind eye to, overlook, forget, forgive, pardon, excuse.
OPPOSITES condemn.

**conduct** noun **1** *they complained about her conduct*: behaviour, actions, deeds, doings, exploits. **2** *the conduct of the elections*: management, running, direction, control, supervision, regulation, administration, organization, coordination, handling.
verb **1** *the election was conducted lawfully*: manage, direct, run, administer, organize, coordinate, orchestrate, handle, carry out/on. **2** *he was conducted through the corridors*: escort, guide, lead, usher, steer. **3** *aluminium conducts heat*: transmit, convey, carry, channel.
■ conduct oneself behave, act, acquit oneself, bear oneself.

**confer** verb **1** *she conferred a knighthood on him*: bestow on, present to, grant to, award to, decorate with. **2** *she went to confer with her colleagues*: consult, talk, speak, converse, have a chat, deliberate.

**conference** noun meeting, congress, convention, seminar, discussion, council, forum, summit.

**confess** verb **1** *he confessed that*

*he had done it:* admit, acknowledge, reveal, disclose, divulge, own up; informal come clean. **2** *they could not make him confess:* own up, plead guilty, accept the blame; informal come clean. **3** *I confess I don't know:* acknowledge, admit, concede, grant, allow, own.
OPPOSITES deny.

**confide** verb reveal, disclose, divulge, impart, declare, vouchsafe, tell, confess.

**confidence** noun **1** *I have little confidence in these figures:* trust, belief, faith, credence. **2** *she's brimming with confidence:* self-assurance, self-confidence, self-possession, assertiveness, self-belief, conviction.
OPPOSITES distrust, doubt.

**confident** adjective **1** *we are confident that business will improve:* sure, certain, positive, convinced, in no doubt, satisfied. **2** *a confident girl:* self-assured, assured, self-confident, positive, assertive, self-possessed.

**confidential** adjective private, personal, intimate, quiet, secret, sensitive, classified, restricted; informal hush-hush.

**confine** verb **1** *they were confined in the house:* enclose, incarcerate, imprison, intern, hold captive, cage, lock up, coop up. **2** *he confined his remarks to the weather:* restrict, limit.

**confirm** verb **1** *records confirm the latest evidence:* corroborate, verify, prove, substantiate, justify, vindicate, bear out. **2** *he confirmed that help was on the way:* affirm, reaffirm, assert, assure someone, repeat. **3** *his*

*appointment was confirmed by the President:* ratify, approve, endorse, validate, sanction, authorize.
OPPOSITES contradict, deny.

**confiscate** verb impound, seize, commandeer, requisition, appropriate, expropriate, sequester.
OPPOSITES return.

**conflict** noun **1** *industrial conflicts:* dispute, quarrel, squabble, disagreement, clash, feud, discord, friction, strife, antagonism, hostility. **2** *the Vietnam conflict:* war, campaign, fighting, engagement, struggle, hostilities, warfare, combat. **3** *a conflict between work and home life:* clash, incompatibility, friction, mismatch, variance, contradiction.
OPPOSITES agreement, peace, harmony.
verb *their interests sometimes conflict:* clash, be incompatible, be at odds, differ, diverge, disagree, collide.

**conflicting** adjective contradictory, incompatible, inconsistent, irreconcilable, contrary, opposite, opposing, clashing.

**conform** verb **1** *visitors have to conform to our rules:* comply with, abide by, obey, observe, follow, keep to, stick to, adhere to, uphold, heed, accept, go along with. **2** *they refuse to conform:* fit in, behave (oneself), toe the line, obey the rules, informal play by the rules.
OPPOSITES flout, rebel.

**confound** verb baffle, bewilder, mystify, bemuse, perplex, puzzle, confuse, dumbfound, throw; informal flabbergast, flummox.

**confront** verb 1 *Martin confronted the burglar:* challenge, square up to, face (up to), come face to face with, meet, accost, stand up to, tackle. 2 *the problems that confront us:* face, plague, bother, trouble, beset, threaten. 3 *they must confront these issues:* tackle, address, face, get to grips with, grapple with. 4 *she confronted him with the evidence:* present, face.
OPPOSITES evade.

**confrontation** noun conflict, clash, fight, battle, encounter, head-to-head; informal set-to, run-in, dust-up, showdown.

**confuse** verb 1 *don't confuse students with too much detail:* bewilder, baffle, mystify, bemuse, perplex, puzzle, nonplus; informal flummox, faze. 2 *the authors have confused the issue:* complicate, muddle, blur, obscure, cloud. 3 *some confuse strokes with heart attacks:* mix up, muddle, mistake for.
OPPOSITES enlighten, simplify.

**confused** adjective 1 *they are confused about what is going on:* puzzled, bemused, bewildered, perplexed, baffled, mystified; informal flummoxed. 2 *her confused elderly mother:* disorientated, bewildered, muddled, addled, befuddled, demented, senile. 3 *a confused recollection:* vague, unclear, indistinct, imprecise, blurred, hazy, dim. 4 *a confused mass of bones:* disorderly, disorganized, untidy, jumbled, mixed up, chaotic, topsy-turvy, tangled; informal higgledy-piggledy; Brit. informal shambolic.
OPPOSITES clear, lucid, precise, neat.

**confusing** adjective puzzling, baffling, perplexing, bewildering, mystifying, ambiguous, misleading, inconsistent, contradictory.

**confusion** noun 1 *there is confusion about the new system:* uncertainty, doubt, ignorance. 2 *she stared in confusion:* bewilderment, bafflement, perplexity, puzzlement, befuddlement. 3 *her life was in utter confusion:* disorder, disarray, chaos, mayhem, turmoil, muddle, mess; informal shambles.
OPPOSITES certainty, order.

**congenial** adjective 1 *very congenial people:* sociable, convivial, hospitable, genial, personable, agreeable, friendly, amiable. 2 *a congenial environment:* pleasant, agreeable, enjoyable, pleasurable, relaxing, welcoming, hospitable, favourable.
OPPOSITES unsociable, unpleasant.

**congested** adjective blocked, clogged, choked, jammed, obstructed, crowded, overcrowded, overflowing, packed; informal snarled up, gridlocked.
OPPOSITES clear.

**congratulate** verb compliment, wish someone happiness, pay tribute to, pat on the back, take one's hat off to, praise, applaud, salute, honour.
OPPOSITES criticize.

**congratulations** plural noun best wishes, compliments, greetings, felicitations.

**congregate** verb assemble, gather, collect, come together, convene, rally, muster, meet, cluster, group.

OPPOSITES disperse.

**conjure** verb **1** *he conjured a cigarette out of the air:* produce, magic, summon. **2** *the picture that his words conjured up:* bring to mind, call to mind, evoke, summon up, suggest.

**connect** verb **1** *electrodes were connected to the device:* attach, join, fasten, fix, link, hook (up), secure, hitch, stick. **2** *customs connected with Easter:* associate, link, couple, identify, relate to.
OPPOSITES detach.

**connection** noun **1** *the connection between commerce and art:* link, relationship, relation, interconnection, interdependence, association, bond, tie, tie-in, correspondence. **2** *he has the right connections:* contact, friend, acquaintance, ally, colleague, associate, relation.

**conquer** verb **1** *the Franks conquered the Visigoths:* defeat, beat, vanquish, triumph over, overcome, overwhelm, overpower, overthrow, subdue, subjugate. **2** *Peru was conquered by Spain:* seize, take (over), appropriate, capture, occupy, invade, annex, overrun. **3** *the first men to conquer Mount Everest:* climb, ascend, scale. **4** *the way to conquer fear:* overcome, get the better of, control, master, deal with, cope with, rise above; informal lick.
OPPOSITES lose to, lose, give in to.

**conquest** noun **1** *the conquest of the Aztecs:* defeat, overthrow, subjugation. **2** *their conquest of the territory:* seizure, takeover, capture, occupation, invasion, annexation. **3** *the conquest of Everest:* ascent, climbing.

**conscience** noun sense of right and wrong, morals, standards, values, principles, ethics, beliefs, scruples, qualms.

**conscientious** adjective diligent, industrious, punctilious, painstaking, dedicated, careful, meticulous, thorough, attentive, hard-working, rigorous, scrupulous, religious.
OPPOSITES casual.

**conscious** adjective **1** *the patient was conscious:* aware, awake; informal with us. **2** *a conscious decision:* deliberate, purposeful, knowing, considered, calculated, wilful, premeditated.
OPPOSITES unaware, unconscious.

**consecutive** adjective successive, succeeding, in succession, running, in a row, straight; informal on the trot.

**consensus** noun **1** *there was consensus among delegates:* agreement, unanimity, harmony, accord, unity, solidarity. **2** *the consensus was that they should act:* general opinion, common view.
OPPOSITES disagreement.

**consent** noun *the consent of all members:* agreement, assent, acceptance, approval, permission, authorization, sanction; informal go-ahead, green light, OK.
OPPOSITES dissent.
verb *she consented to surgery:* agree, assent, submit, allow, sanction, approve, go along with.
OPPOSITES forbid, refuse.

**consequence** noun **1** *a consequence of inflation:* result, upshot, outcome, effect, repercussion, ramification,

a
b
**c**
d
e
f
g
h
i
j
k
l
m
n
o
p
q
r
s
t
u
v
w
x
y
z

product, end result. **2** *the past is of no consequence:* importance, import, significance, account, value, concern.
OPPOSITES cause.

**consequently** adverb as a result, as a consequence, so, thus, therefore, accordingly, hence, for this/that reason, because of this/that.

**conservation** noun preservation, protection, safe keeping, husbandry, upkeep, maintenance, repair, restoration.

**conservative** adjective **1** *the conservative wing of the party:* right-wing, reactionary, traditionalist. **2** *the conservative trade-union movement:* traditionalist, old-fashioned, dyed-in-the-wool, hidebound, unadventurous, reactionary, set in one's ways; informal stick in the mud. **3** *a conservative suit:* conventional, sober, modest, sensible, restrained; informal square.
OPPOSITES socialist, radical, ostentatious.

**conserve** verb *fossil fuel should be conserved:* preserve, protect, save, safeguard, keep, look after, sustain, husband.
OPPOSITES squander.

**consider** verb **1** *Isabel considered her choices:* think about, contemplate, reflect on, mull over, ponder, deliberate on, chew over, meditate on, ruminate on, evaluate, weigh up, appraise, take account of, bear in mind; informal size up. **2** *I consider him irresponsible:* deem, think, believe, judge, rate, count, find, regard as, hold to be, reckon to be, view as, see as. **3** *he considered the painting:*

look at, contemplate, observe, regard, survey, examine, inspect.

**considerable** adjective sizeable, substantial, appreciable, significant, plentiful, goodly; informal tidy.
OPPOSITES paltry.

**considerably** adverb greatly, (very) much, a great deal, a lot, lots, significantly, substantially, appreciably, markedly, noticeably; informal plenty.

**considerate** adjective attentive, thoughtful, solicitous, kind, unselfish, caring, polite, sensitive.

**consideration** noun **1** *your case needs careful consideration:* thought, deliberation, reflection, contemplation, examination, inspection, scrutiny, analysis, discussion, attention. **2** *his health is the prime consideration:* factor, issue, matter, concern, aspect, feature. **3** *firms should show more consideration:* attentiveness, concern, care, thoughtfulness, solicitude, understanding, respect, sensitivity.

**considering** preposition bearing in mind, taking into consideration, taking into account, in view of, in the light of.

**consist**
■ consist of be composed of, be made up of, be formed of, comprise, include, contain.

**consistent** adjective **1** *consistent opinion-poll evidence:* constant, regular, uniform, steady, stable, even, unchanging. **2** *her injuries were consistent with a knife attack:* compatible, in tune, in line, corresponding to, conforming to.

OPPOSITES irregular, incompatible.

**consolation** noun comfort, solace, sympathy, pity, commiseration, relief, encouragement, reassurance.

**console** verb comfort, sympathize with, commiserate with, show compassion for, help, support, cheer (up), hearten, encourage, reassure, soothe.
OPPOSITES upset.

**consolidate** verb 1 *we consolidated our position in the market:* strengthen, secure, stabilize, reinforce, fortify. 2 *consolidate the results into an action plan:* combine, unite, merge, integrate, amalgamate, fuse, synthesize.

**conspicuous** adjective obvious, evident, apparent, visible, noticeable, clear, plain, marked, patent, blatant.
OPPOSITES inconspicuous.

**conspiracy** noun plot, scheme, intrigue, plan, collusion, ploy.

**conspire** verb 1 *they admitted conspiring to steal cars:* plot, scheme, intrigue, manoeuvre, plan. 2 *circumstances conspired against them:* combine, unite, join forces, work together.

**constant** adjective 1 *constant noise:* continuous, persistent, sustained, ceaseless, unceasing, perpetual, incessant, never-ending, eternal, endless, non-stop. 2 *a constant speed:* consistent, regular, steady, uniform, even, invariable, unvarying, unchanging. 3 *a constant friend:* faithful, loyal, devoted, true, fast, firm, unswerving.
OPPOSITES intermittent, variable, fickle.

**constitute** verb 1 *farmers constituted 10 per cent of the population:* comprise, make up, form, account for. 2 *this constitutes a breach of copyright:* amount to, be tantamount to, be equivalent to, represent. 3 *the courts were constituted in 1875:* establish, inaugurate, found, create, set up.

**constitution** noun 1 *the chemical constitution of the dye:* composition, make-up, structure, construction, arrangement, configuration, formation, anatomy. 2 *she has the constitution of an ox:* health, condition, strength, stamina, build, physique.

**constraint** noun 1 *financial constraints:* restriction, limitation, curb, check, restraint, control. 2 *they were able to talk without constraint:* inhibition, uneasiness, embarrassment, self-consciousness, awkwardness.
OPPOSITES freedom, ease.

**constrict** verb narrow, tighten, compress, contract, squeeze, strangle.
OPPOSITES expand, dilate.

**construct** verb 1 *a bridge constructed by the army:* build, erect, put up, set up, assemble, fabricate. 2 *he constructed a faultless argument:* create, formulate, form, put together, devise, compose, work out, frame.
OPPOSITES demolish.

**construction** noun 1 *the station was a spectacular construction:* structure, building, edifice, work. 2 *you put such a sordid construction on it:* interpretation, explanation, analysis, reading, meaning; informal take.

a
b
**c**
d
e
f
g
h
i
j
k
l
m
n
o
p
q
r
s
t
u
v
w
x
y
z

**constructive** adjective useful, helpful, productive, positive, practical, valuable, profitable, worthwhile.
OPPOSITES unhelpful.

**consult** verb 1 *you need to consult a solicitor:* seek advice from, ask, call (on), turn to; informal pick someone's brains. 2 *the government must consult with interested parties:* confer, talk things over, communicate, deliberate, compare notes. 3 *she consulted her diary:* refer to, look at, check.

**consultant** noun adviser, expert, specialist, authority.

**consultation** noun 1 *the need for further consultation with industry:* discussion, dialogue, debate, negotiation, deliberation. 2 *a 30-minute consultation:* meeting, talk, discussion, interview, examination, audience, hearing.

**consume** verb 1 *vast amounts of food and drink were consumed:* eat, devour, swallow, gobble up, wolf down, guzzle, drink. 2 *natural resources are being consumed at an alarming rate:* use (up), expend, deplete, exhaust, spend. 3 *the fire consumed fifty houses:* destroy, demolish, lay waste, raze, devastate, gut, ruin, wreck. 4 *Carolyn was consumed with guilt:* eat up, devour, grip, overwhelm, absorb, obsess, preoccupy.

**consumer** noun buyer, purchaser, customer, shopper, user.

**contact** noun 1 *have you had any contact with him?* communication, correspondence, connection, relations, dealings, touch. 2 *he had many contacts in Germany:* connection, link, acquaintance, associate, friend.
verb *he should contact the police:* get in touch with, communicate with, approach, notify, speak to, write to, come forward; informal get hold of.

**contain** verb 1 *the boat contained four people:* hold, carry, enclose, accommodate. 2 *the archive contains much unpublished material:* include, comprise, incorporate, involve, consist of, be made up of, be composed of. 3 *he must contain his anger:* restrain, control, curb, rein in, suppress, stifle, swallow, bottle up, keep in check.
OPPOSITES vent.

**container** noun receptacle, vessel, holder, repository.

**contaminate** verb pollute, taint, poison, stain, adulterate, defile, debase, corrupt.
OPPOSITES purify.

**contemplate** verb 1 *she contemplated her image in the mirror:* look at, gaze at, stare at, view, regard, examine, inspect, observe, survey, study, eye. 2 *he contemplated his fate:* think about, ponder, reflect on, consider, mull over, muse on, dwell on, deliberate over, meditate on, ruminate on, chew over. 3 *he was contemplating legal action:* consider, think about, have in mind, intend, plan, propose.

**contemporary** adjective 1 *contemporary sources:* of the time, contemporaneous, concurrent, coexisting. 2 *contemporary society:* modern, present-day, present, current. 3 *a very contemporary design:* modern, up to date, up to the minute, fashionable,

recent; informal trendy.
OPPOSITES older, newer, former, old-fashioned.

**contempt** noun scorn, disdain, derision, disgust, disrespect.
OPPOSITES respect.

**contemptuous** adjective scornful, disdainful, derisive, mocking, sneering, scoffing, condescending, dismissive.
OPPOSITES respectful.

**contend** verb 1 *three groups were contending for power:* compete, vie, battle, tussle, struggle, jostle, strive. 2 *he contends that the judge was wrong:* assert, maintain, hold, claim, argue, insist, allege.
■ **contend with** cope with, struggle with, grapple with, deal with, take on, handle.

**content**[1] adjective *she seemed content with life:* satisfied, contented, pleased, fulfilled, happy, glad, at ease.
OPPOSITES dissatisfied.
verb *her reply seemed to content him:* satisfy, comfort, gratify, gladden, please, soothe, placate, appease, mollify.

**content**[2] noun 1 *foods with a high fibre content:* amount, proportion, level. 2 (**contents**) *the contents of a vegetarian sausage:* constituents, ingredients, components. 3 *the content of the essay:* subject matter, theme, argument, thesis, message, substance, material, ideas.

**contented** adjective. See **CONTENT**[1] adjective.

**contentious** adjective 1 *a contentious issue:* controversial, debatable, disputed, open to debate, moot, vexed. 2 *contentious people:* quarrelsome, argumentative,

confrontational; Brit. informal stroppy.

**contest** noun 1 *a boxing contest:* competition, match, tournament, game, bout. 2 *the contest for the party leadership:* fight, battle, tussle, struggle, competition, race.
verb 1 *he intended to contest the seat:* compete for, contend for, vie for, fight for. 2 *a system where parties contest elections:* compete in, take part in, fight, enter. 3 *we contested the decision:* oppose, challenge, take issue with, question, call into question, object to.
OPPOSITES accept.

**contestant** noun competitor, participant, player, contender, candidate, entrant.

**context** noun circumstances, conditions, frame of reference, factors, state of affairs, situation, background, scene, setting.

**contingency** noun eventuality, possibility, chance event, incident, occurrence, accident, emergency.

**continual** adjective 1 *continual breakdowns:* frequent, repeated, constant, recurrent, recurring, regular. 2 *continual pain:* constant, continuous, unremitting, unrelenting, chronic, uninterrupted, unbroken.
OPPOSITES occasional, temporary.

**continue** verb 1 *he was unable to continue with his job:* carry on, proceed, pursue, go on, keep on, persist, persevere, keep at; informal stick at. 2 *discussions continued throughout the year:* go on, carry on, last, extend, run on, drag on. 3 *we are keen to continue this relationship:*

maintain, keep up, sustain, keep going, keep alive, preserve. **4** *his willingness to continue in office:* remain, stay, carry on, keep going. **5** *we continued our conversation after supper:* resume, pick up, take up, carry on with, return to, revisit.

OPPOSITES stop, break off, leave.

**continuous** adjective continual, persistent, sustained, ceaseless, unceasing, perpetual, incessant, never-ending, eternal, endless, non-stop.

OPPOSITES intermittent.

**contort** verb twist, bend out of shape, distort, misshape, warp, buckle, deform.

**contract** noun *a legally binding contract:* agreement, arrangement, commitment, settlement, understanding, compact, covenant, deal, bargain.
verb **1** *the market began to contract:* shrink, diminish, reduce, decrease, dwindle, decline. **2** *her stomach muscles contracted:* tighten, tense, flex, constrict, draw in. **3** *the company was contracted to build the stadium:* engage, take on, hire, commission, employ. **4** *she contracted German measles:* catch, pick up, come/ go down with, develop.

OPPOSITES expand, relax, lengthen.

**contraction** noun **1** *the contraction of the industry:* shrinking, shrinkage, decline, decrease, diminution, dwindling. **2** *the contraction of muscles:* tightening, tensing, flexing. **3** *'goodbye' is a contraction of 'God be with you':* abbreviation, short form, shortening.

OPPOSITES expansion, relaxation, lengthening.

**contradict** verb **1** *he contradicted the government's account:* deny, refute, rebut, dispute, challenge, counter. **2** *nobody dared contradict him:* argue with, go against, challenge, oppose.

OPPOSITES confirm, agree with.

**contradiction** noun **1** *the contradiction between his faith and his lifestyle:* conflict, clash, disagreement, inconsistency, mismatch. **2** *a contradiction of his statement:* denial, refutation, rebuttal, countering.

OPPOSITES agreement, confirmation.

**contradictory** adjective inconsistent, incompatible, irreconcilable, opposed, opposite, contrary, conflicting, at variance.

**contrary** adjective **1** *contrary views:* opposite, opposing, contradictory, clashing, conflicting, antithetical, incompatible, irreconcilable. **2** *she was sulky and contrary:* perverse, awkward, difficult, uncooperative, obstinate, pig-headed, intractable; Brit. informal bloody-minded, stroppy; N. Amer. informal balky.

OPPOSITES compatible, accommodating.
noun *in fact, the contrary is true:* opposite, reverse, converse, antithesis.

**contrast** noun **1** *the contrast between rural and urban trends:* difference, dissimilarity, disparity, divergence, variance, distinction, comparison. **2** *Jane was a complete contrast to Sarah:* opposite, antithesis, foil, complement.

OPPOSITES similarity.

**verb 1** *a view which contrasts with his earlier opinion:* differ, be at variance, be contrary, conflict, be at odds, disagree, clash. **2** *people contrasted her with her sister:* compare, juxtapose, measure, distinguish, differentiate.

OPPOSITES resemble, liken.

**contribute verb** give, donate, put up, grant, provide, supply; informal chip in; Brit. informal stump up.

■ contribute to play a part in, be instrumental in, have a hand in, be conducive to, make for.

**contribution noun** gift, donation, offering, present, handout, grant, subsidy.

**contributor noun** donor, benefactor, supporter, backer, patron, sponsor.

**contrive verb 1** *they contrived a plan:* create, engineer, manufacture, devise, concoct, construct, fabricate, hatch. **2** *Lomax contrived to bump into him:* manage, find a way, engineer a way, arrange, succeed in.

OPPOSITES fail.

**contrived adjective** forced, strained, laboured, overdone, unnatural, artificial, false, affected.

OPPOSITES natural.

**control noun 1** *China retained control over the region:* power, authority, command, dominance, sway, management, direction, leadership, rule, government, sovereignty, supremacy. **2** *strict import controls:* limit, limitation, restriction, restraint, check, curb, regulation. **3** *her control deserted her:* self-control, self-

restraint, composure, calm; informal cool.

**verb 1** *one family controlled the company:* run, manage, direct, preside over, supervise, command, rule, govern, lead, dominate. **2** *she struggled to control her temper:* restrain, keep in check, curb, hold back, suppress, repress. **3** *public spending was controlled:* limit, restrict, curb, cap.

**controversial adjective** disputed, contentious, moot, debatable, arguable, vexed.

**controversy noun** dispute, disagreement, argument, debate, contention, quarrel, war of words, storm; Brit. informal row.

**convene verb 1** *he convened a secret meeting:* summon, call, order. **2** *the committee convened for its final session:* assemble, gather, meet, come together; formal foregather.

OPPOSITES disperse.

**convenience noun 1** *the convenience of the arrangement:* advantage, benefit, expedience, suitability. **2** *for convenience, the handset is wall-mounted:* ease of use, usefulness, utility, accessibility, availability.

OPPOSITES inconvenience.

**convenient adjective 1** *a convenient time:* suitable, favourable, advantageous, appropriate, opportune, timely, expedient. **2** *a convenient shop:* nearby, handy, well situated, practical, useful, accessible.

OPPOSITES inconvenient.

**convention noun 1** *social conventions:* custom, usage, practice, tradition, etiquette, protocol. **2** *a convention signed by 74 countries:* agreement, accord, protocol, pact, treaty. **3** *the party's biennial*

**convention:** conference, meeting, congress, assembly, gathering.

**conventional** adjective
**1** *conventional wisdom:* orthodox, traditional, established, accepted, received, prevailing. **2** *a conventional railway:* normal, standard, regular, ordinary, usual, traditional, typical. **3** *a very conventional woman:* conservative, traditional, conformist, old-fashioned; informal square, stick-in-the-mud. **4** *a conventional piece of work:* unoriginal, formulaic, predictable, unadventurous.
OPPOSITES unorthodox, unconventional, original.

**converge** verb *here the lines converge:* meet, intersect, cross, connect, link up, join, merge.
OPPOSITES diverge.
■ **converge on** meet at, arrive at, close in on, bear down on, descend on, approach, move towards.

**conversation** noun discussion, talk, chat, gossip, tête-à-tête, exchange, dialogue; Brit. informal chinwag, natter.

**conversion** noun **1** *the conversion of waste into energy:* change, transformation, metamorphosis. **2** *the conversion of the building:* adaptation, alteration, modification, redevelopment.

**convert** verb **1** *plants convert the sun's energy into chemical energy:* change, turn, transform, metamorphose. **2** *the factory was converted into flats:* adapt, turn, change, alter, modify, redevelop. **3** *they sought to convert sinners:* win over, claim, redeem, save, reform, re-educate, proselytize,

evangelize.

**convey** verb **1** *taxis conveyed guests to the station:* transport, carry, bring, take, fetch, move. **2** *he conveyed the information to me:* communicate, pass on, impart, relate, relay, transmit, send. **3** *it's impossible to convey how I felt:* express, communicate, get across/over, put across/over, indicate.

**convict** verb find guilty, sentence.
OPPOSITES acquit.
noun prisoner, inmate, criminal, offender, felon; informal jailbird, con, (old) lag.

**conviction** noun **1** *his political convictions:* beliefs, opinions, views, persuasion, ideals, position, stance, values. **2** *she spoke with conviction:* assurance, confidence, certainty.
OPPOSITES diffidence.

**convince** verb **1** *he convinced me that I was wrong:* assure, persuade, satisfy, prove to. **2** *I convinced her to marry me:* persuade, induce, prevail on, talk into, talk round, win over, coax, cajole, inveigle.

**convincing** adjective **1** *a convincing argument:* persuasive, powerful, strong, forceful, compelling, cogent, plausible, irresistible, telling. **2** *a convincing 5–0 win:* resounding, emphatic, decisive, conclusive.
OPPOSITES unconvincing, narrow.

**cool** adjective **1** *a cool breeze:* chilly, chill, cold, bracing, brisk, crisp, fresh; informal nippy; Brit. informal parky. **2** *a cool response to the suggestion:* unenthusiastic, lukewarm, tepid, indifferent, uninterested, apathetic. **3** *David seemed*

*distinctly cool:* unfriendly, distant, remote, aloof, cold, chilly, frosty, unwelcoming; informal stand-offish. **4** *his ability to keep cool in a crisis:* calm, collected, composed, self-possessed, poised, serene, relaxed, at ease, unruffled, unperturbed; informal unflappable, together, laid-back.
OPPOSITES warm, enthusiastic, friendly, excited.
noun **1** *the cool of the evening:* chill, chilliness, coldness, coolness. **2** (informal) *Ken lost his cool:* self-control, control, composure, self-possession, calmness, aplomb, poise.
OPPOSITES warmth.
verb *cool the sauce in the fridge:* chill, refrigerate, freeze.
OPPOSITES warm.

**cooperate** verb **1** *police and social services cooperated:* collaborate, work together, pull together, join forces, team up, unite, combine, pool resources. **2** *he was happy to cooperate:* assist, help, lend a hand, be of service, do one's bit; informal play ball.

**cooperation** noun
**1** *cooperation between management and workers:* collaboration, joint action, combined effort, teamwork, give and take, compromise. **2** *thank you for your cooperation:* assistance, help.

**cooperative** adjective **1** *a cooperative effort:* collaborative, collective, combined, joint, shared, united, concerted. **2** *pleasant and cooperative staff:* helpful, eager to help, obliging, accommodating, willing.

**coordinate** verb organize,

arrange, order, synchronize, bring together, orchestrate.

**cope** verb **1** *she couldn't cope on her own:* manage, survive, look after oneself, fend for oneself, shift for oneself, get by/through, hold one's own. **2** *his inability to cope with the situation:* deal with, handle, manage, address, face (up to), confront, tackle, get to grips with.

**copy** noun **1** *a copy of the report:* duplicate, facsimile, photocopy; trademark Xerox. **2** *a copy of a sketch by Leonardo da Vinci:* replica, reproduction, imitation, likeness, forgery, fake, counterfeit.
verb **1** *each form had to be copied:* duplicate, photocopy, xerox, photostat, reproduce. **2** *portraits copied from originals:* reproduce, replicate, forge, fake, counterfeit. **3** *their sound was copied by a lot of jazz players:* imitate, reproduce, emulate, mimic; informal rip off.

**cord** noun string, thread, line, rope, cable, wire, twine, yarn.

**cordon** noun barrier, line, chain, ring, circle.
■ cordon something off close off, seal off, fence off, separate off, isolate, enclose, encircle, surround.

**core** noun **1** *the earth's core:* centre, interior, middle, nucleus. **2** *the core of the argument:* heart, nucleus, nub, kernel, meat, essence, crux, pith, substance; informal nitty-gritty.
OPPOSITES edge, periphery.

**corner** noun **1** *the cart lurched round the corner:* bend, curve, turn, junction; Brit. hairpin bend. **2** *a charming corner of*

a
b
**c**
d
e
f
g
h
i
j
k
l
m
n
o
p
q
r
s
t
u
v
w
x
y
z

*Italy:* district, region, area, quarter; informal neck of the woods.

**verb 1** *he was eventually cornered by police dogs:* surround, trap, hem in, pen in, cut off. **2** *crime syndicates have cornered the stolen car market:* gain control of, take over, dominate, monopolize, capture; informal sew up.

**corporation** noun company, firm, business, concern, operation, conglomerate, group, chain, multinational.

**corpse** noun dead body, carcass, remains; informal stiff; Medicine cadaver.

**correct** adjective **1** *the correct answer:* right, accurate, exact, true, perfect. **2** *correct behaviour:* proper, right, decent, respectable, decorous, suitable, appropriate, accepted. OPPOSITES wrong, improper.
**verb** *correct any mistakes:* rectify, right, put right, set right, amend, remedy, repair, reform, cure.

**correction** noun rectification, righting, amendment, repair, remedy, cure.

**correctly** adverb **1** *the questions were answered correctly:* accurately, right, perfectly, exactly, precisely. **2** *she behaved correctly at all times:* properly, decorously, with decorum, decently, fittingly, appropriately, well.
OPPOSITES wrongly, improperly.

**correspond** verb **1** *the setting corresponds with the number on the dial:* be consistent, correlate, agree, accord, coincide, tally, tie in, match; informal square. **2** *a rank corresponding to a British sergeant:* be equivalent, be analogous, be comparable, equate. **3** *Debbie and I corresponded for years:* exchange letters, write, communicate.

**correspondence** noun **1** *there is some correspondence between the two variables:* parallel, correlation, agreement, consistency, conformity, similarity, resemblance, comparability. **2** *his private correspondence:* letters, messages, mail, post, communication.

**correspondent** noun reporter, journalist, columnist, writer, contributor, commentator.

**corresponding** adjective equivalent, related, parallel, matching, comparable, analogous.

**corrupt** adjective **1** *a corrupt official | corrupt practices:* dishonest, unscrupulous, criminal, fraudulent, illegal, unlawful; informal crooked; Brit. informal bent. **2** *he is utterly corrupt:* immoral, depraved, degenerate, debauched, vice-ridden, perverted, dissolute. OPPOSITES honest, ethical, pure.
**verb** deprave, pervert, lead astray, debauch, defile, pollute, sully.

**corruption** noun **1** *political corruption:* dishonesty, unscrupulousness, double-dealing, fraud, misconduct, bribery, venality; N. Amer. payola; informal graft, sleaze. **2** *his fall into corruption:* immorality, depravity, vice, degeneracy, perversion, debauchery, wickedness, evil, sin.
OPPOSITES honesty, morality, purity.

**cosmetic** adjective superficial, surface, skin-deep, outward,

external.
OPPOSITES fundamental.

**cosmopolitan** adjective **1** *the student body has a cosmopolitan character:* multicultural, multiracial, international, worldwide, global. **2** *a very cosmopolitan chap:* sophisticated, cultivated, cultured, worldly, suave, urbane.

**cost** noun **1** *the cost of the equipment:* price, fee, tariff, fare, toll, levy, charge, payment, value, rate, outlay; humorous damage. **2** *the human cost of the conflict:* sacrifice, loss, toll, harm, damage, price. **3** (**costs**) *we need to cover our costs:* expenses, outgoings, overheads, expenditure, spend, outlay.
verb **1** *the chair costs £186:* be priced at, sell for, be valued at, fetch, come to, amount to; informal set someone back, go for. **2** *the proposal has not yet been costed:* price, value, put a price/value/figure on.

**costly** adjective **1** *costly machinery:* expensive, dear, high-cost, overpriced; informal steep, pricey. **2** *a costly mistake:* catastrophic, disastrous, calamitous, ruinous, damaging, harmful, deleterious.
OPPOSITES cheap.

**costume** noun clothes, garments, outfit, ensemble, dress, clothing, attire, garb, uniform, livery; formal apparel.

**cosy** adjective **1** *a cosy country cottage:* snug, comfortable, warm, homely, welcoming, safe, sheltered, secure; informal comfy. **2** *a cosy chat:* intimate, relaxed, informal, friendly.

**cottage** noun lodge, chalet, cabin, shack, shanty; (in Russia)

dacha; Scottish bothy; Austral. informal weekender.

**cough** verb *he coughed loudly:* hack, hawk, bark, clear one's throat.
noun *a loud cough:* bark, hack; informal frog in one's throat.

**council** noun **1** *the town council:* authority, government, administration, executive, chamber, assembly; Brit. corporation. **2** *the Schools Council:* committee, board, commission, assembly, panel, synod.

**counsel** noun **1** *his wise counsel:* advice, guidance, counselling, recommendations, suggestions, direction. **2** *the counsel for the defence:* barrister, lawyer; Scottish advocate; N. Amer. attorney, counselor(-at-law).
verb *he counselled the team to withdraw:* advise, recommend, advocate, warn, caution, guide.

**count** verb **1** *she counted the money again:* add up, reckon up, total, tally, calculate, compute; Brit. tot up. **2** *250 employees, not counting overseas staff:* include, take into account/consideration, take account of, allow for. **3** *I count it a privilege to be asked:* consider, think, feel, regard, look on as, view as, hold to be, judge, deem. **4** *it's your mother's feelings that count:* matter, be important, be of consequence, be significant, signify, carry weight, rate.
■ **count on/upon** rely on, depend on, bank on, be sure of, have confidence in, believe in, put one's faith in, take for granted, take as read.

**counter** verb **1** *workers countered accusations of*

dishonesty with claims of oppression: respond to, parry, hit back at, answer. **2** *the second argument is more difficult to counter:* oppose, dispute, argue against/with, contradict, challenge, contest.
OPPOSITES support.

■ **counter to** against, in opposition to, contrary to, at variance with, in defiance of, in conflict with, at odds with.

**counterpart** noun equivalent, opposite number, peer, equal, parallel, complement, analogue, match, twin, mate, fellow.

**countless** adjective innumerable, numerous, untold, legion, numberless, limitless, incalculable; informal umpteen; N. Amer. informal gazillions of.
OPPOSITES few.

**country** noun **1** *foreign countries:* nation, state, kingdom, realm, land, territory, province. **2** *the country took to the streets:* people, public, population, populace, citizens, nation; Brit. informal Joe Public. **3** *thickly forested country:* terrain, land, territory, landscape, countryside, scenery, surroundings, environment. **4** *she hated living in the country:* countryside, provinces, rural areas, backwoods, hinterland; Austral./NZ outback, bush, back country; informal sticks.

**countryside** noun. See **COUNTRY** senses 3, 4.

**county** noun shire, province, territory, region, district, area.

**coup** noun **1** *a violent military coup:* takeover, coup d'état, overthrow, palace revolution, rebellion, uprising. **2** *a major publishing coup:* success,

triumph, feat, masterstroke, accomplishment, achievement, scoop.

**couple** noun **1** *a couple of girls:* pair, duo, twosome, two, brace. **2** *a honeymoon couple:* husband and wife, twosome, partners, lovers; informal item.
verb **1** *hope is coupled with a sense of loss:* combine, accompany, mix, incorporate, ally, add to. **2** *a cable is coupled to one of the wheels:* connect, attach, join, fasten, fix, link, secure, hook (up).
OPPOSITES detach.

**coupon** noun voucher, token, ticket, slip; N. Amer. informal rain check.

**courage** noun bravery, pluck, valour, fearlessness, nerve, daring, audacity, boldness, grit, heroism, gallantry; informal guts; Brit. informal bottle.
OPPOSITES cowardice.

**courageous** adjective brave, plucky, fearless, intrepid, valiant, heroic, undaunted, dauntless; informal gutsy, have-a-go.
OPPOSITES cowardly.

**course** noun **1** *the island was not far off our course:* route, way, track, path, line, trail, trajectory, bearing, heading. **2** *the best course to adopt:* procedure, plan (of action), course of action, practice, approach, technique, policy, strategy, tactic. **3** *a waterlogged course:* racecourse, racetrack, track. **4** *a French course:* programme/course of study, curriculum, syllabus, classes, lectures, studies. **5** *a course of antibiotics:* programme, series, sequence, system, schedule, regime.
verb *tears coursed down her*

*cheeks:* flow, pour, stream, run, rush, gush, cascade, flood, roll.
■ of course naturally, as you would expect, needless to say, as a matter of course, obviously, it goes without saying.

**court** noun **1** *the court found him guilty:* court of law, law court, bench, bar, tribunal, assizes. **2** *the King's court:* household, retinue, entourage, train, courtiers, attendants.
verb **1** *he was courting a girl from the village:* woo, go out with, date, go steady with. **2** *an editor who was courted by politicians:* cultivate, flatter, curry favour with, wine and dine; informal butter up. **3** *he was courting public attention:* seek, pursue, go after, strive for, solicit. **4** *he's often courted controversy:* risk, invite, attract, bring on oneself.

**courteous** adjective polite, well mannered, civil, respectful, well behaved, gracious, obliging, considerate.
OPPOSITES rude.

**courtesy** noun politeness, good manners, civility, respect, grace, consideration, thought.

**cove** noun bay, inlet, fjord.

**cover** verb **1** *she covered her face with a towel:* protect, shield, shelter, hide, conceal, mask. **2** *his car was covered in mud:* cake, coat, encrust, plaster, smother. **3** *snow covered the fields:* blanket, carpet, coat, shroud, smother. **4** *a course covering all aspects of the business:* deal with, consider, take in, include, involve, incorporate, embrace.
OPPOSITES reveal.
noun **1** *a protective cover:* covering, sleeve, wrapping, wrapper, envelope, sheath, housing, jacket, casing, cowling, canopy. **2** *a manhole cover:* lid, top, cap. **3** *a book cover:* binding, jacket, dust jacket, dust cover, wrapper. **4** *a thick cover of snow:* coating, coat, covering, layer, carpet, blanket, film, sheet, veneer, crust, skin, cloak, mantle, veil, pall, shroud. **5** *panicking onlookers ran for cover:* shelter, protection, refuge, sanctuary.

**coward** noun mouse, baby; informal chicken, scaredy-cat, yellow-belly, sissy; Brit. informal big girl's blouse; N. Amer. informal pantywaist, pussy; Austral./NZ informal sook.
OPPOSITES hero.

**cowardly** adjective faint-hearted, lily-livered, spineless, craven, timid, timorous, fearful; informal yellow, chicken, gutless, yellow-bellied.
OPPOSITES brave.

**cower** verb cringe, shrink, flinch, crouch, blench.

**coy** adjective demure, shy, modest, bashful, diffident, self-effacing, shrinking.
OPPOSITES brazen.

**crack** noun **1** *a crack in the glass:* split, break, chip, fracture, rupture. **2** *a crack between two rocks:* space, gap, crevice, fissure, cleft, cranny, chink. **3** *the crack of a rifle:* bang, report, explosion, detonation, clap, crash. **4** *a crack on the head:* blow, bang, hit, knock, rap, bump, smack, slap; informal bash, whack, clout.
verb **1** *the glass cracked in the heat:* break, split, fracture, rupture, snap. **2** *he finally cracked:* break down, give way, cave in, go to pieces, give in, yield, succumb. **3** *she cracked*

a
b
**c**
d
e
f
g
h
i
j
k
l
m
n
o
p
q
r
s
t
u
v
w
x
y
z

a
b
**c**
d
e
f
g
h
i
j
k
l
m
n
o
p
q
r
s
t
u
v
w
x
y
z

*him across the forehead:* hit, strike, smack, slap, beat, thump, knock, rap; informal bash, whack, clobber, clout, clip. **4** (informal) *the code proved hard to crack:* decipher, interpret, decode, break, solve.

**cradle** noun **1** *the baby's cradle:* crib, Moses basket, cot, carrycot. **2** *the cradle of democracy:* birthplace, fount, fountainhead, source, spring, origin.
verb *she cradled his head in her arms:* hold, support, cushion, pillow, nurse, rest.

**craft** noun **1** *the historian's craft:* activity, occupation, trade, profession, work, line of work, job. **2** *he used craft and diplomacy:* cunning, craftiness, guile, wiliness, artfulness, deviousness, slyness, trickery, duplicity, dishonesty, deceit, deceitfulness, deception, intrigue, subterfuge, wiles, ploys, ruses, schemes, tricks. **3** *a sailing craft:* vessel, ship, boat, aircraft, spacecraft.

**craftsman, craftswoman** noun artisan, artist, skilled worker, technician, expert, master.

**crafty** adjective cunning, wily, sly, artful, devious, tricky, scheming, calculating, shrewd, canny, dishonest, deceitful.
OPPOSITES open, honest.

**cram** verb **1** *wardrobes crammed with clothes:* fill, stuff, pack, jam, fill to overflowing, overload, crowd, throng. **2** *they all crammed into the car:* crowd, pack, pile, squash. **3** *he crammed his clothes into a suitcase:* push, thrust, shove, force, ram, jam, stuff, pack, pile, squash, squeeze. **4** *most of the students are cramming for*

*exams:* revise; informal swot, mug up, bone up.

**cramp** noun *stomach cramps:* spasm, pain, shooting pain, twinge, pang, convulsion.
verb *tighter rules will cramp economic growth:* hinder, impede, inhibit, hamper, constrain, hamstring, interfere with, restrict, limit, slow.

**cramped** adjective **1** *cramped accommodation:* poky, uncomfortable, confined, restricted, constricted, small, tiny, narrow, crowded, congested. **2** *cramped handwriting:* small, crabbed, illegible, unreadable, indecipherable.
OPPOSITES spacious, flamboyant.

**crash** verb **1** *the car crashed into a tree:* smash into, collide with, be in collision with, hit, strike, ram, cannon into, plough into, meet head-on; N. Amer. impact. **2** *he crashed his car:* smash, wreck; Brit. write off; N. Amer. informal total. **3** *a tree crashed to the ground:* fall, drop, plummet, plunge, sink, dive, tumble. **4** (informal) *his company crashed:* collapse, fold, fail, go under, go bankrupt; informal go bust, go to the wall.
noun **1** *a crash on the motorway:* accident, collision, smash; N. Amer. wreck; informal pile-up; Brit. informal shunt. **2** *a loud crash:* bang, smash, smack, crack, bump, thud. **3** *the crash of her company:* collapse, failure, liquidation, bankruptcy.

**crate** noun packing case, chest, tea chest, box, container.

**crater** noun hollow, bowl, basin, hole, cavity, depression, dip; Geology caldera.

**crave** verb long for, yearn for, hanker after, desire, want, hunger for, thirst for, pine for; informal be dying for.

**craving** noun longing, yearning, desire, hankering, hunger, thirst, appetite.

**crawl 1** *they crawled under the table:* creep, worm one's way, go on all fours, wriggle, slither, squirm. **2** (informal) *I'm not crawling to him:* grovel, kowtow, pander, toady, bow and scrape, fawn; informal suck up, lick someone's boots.

**craze** noun fad, fashion, trend, vogue, enthusiasm, mania, passion, rage; informal thing.

**crazy** adjective (informal) **1** *a crazy old man:* mad, insane, out of one's mind, deranged, demented, crazed, lunatic, unbalanced, unhinged; informal mental, off one's head, round the bend; Brit. informal barmy, crackers, barking (mad), potty, round the twist. **2** *a crazy idea:* stupid, foolish, idiotic, silly, absurd, ludicrous, preposterous; informal cockeyed; Brit. informal barmy, daft. **3** *he's crazy about her:* passionate, very keen, enamoured, infatuated, smitten, enthusiastic, fanatical; informal wild, mad, nuts; Brit. informal potty.
OPPOSITES sane, sensible, apathetic.

**cream** noun **1** *skin cream:* lotion, ointment, moisturizer, cosmetic, salve, rub. **2** *the cream of the world's photographers:* best, finest, pick, flower, crème de la crème, elite.
OPPOSITES dregs.
adjective *a cream dress:* off-white, creamy, ivory.

**creamy** adjective smooth, thick, velvety, rich, buttery.

OPPOSITES lumpy.

**crease** noun **1** *trousers with creases:* fold, line, ridge, furrow, groove, corrugation. **2** *creases at the corners of her eyes:* wrinkle, line, crinkle, pucker, crow's foot.
verb *her skirt was creased:* crumple, wrinkle, crinkle, line, scrunch up, rumple.

**create** verb **1** *she has created a work of stunning originality:* produce, generate, bring into being, make, fashion, build, construct. **2** *regular socializing creates a good team spirit:* bring about, give rise to, lead to, result in, cause, breed, generate, engender, produce. **3** *the governments planned to create a free-trade zone:* establish, found, initiate, institute, constitute, inaugurate, launch, set up. **4** *she was created a life peer:* appoint, make.
OPPOSITES destroy, abolish.

**creation** noun **1** *the creation of a government:* establishment, formation, foundation, initiation, institution, constitution, setting up. **2** *the whole of creation:* the world, the universe, the cosmos, nature, the natural world. **3** *Dickens's literary creations:* work, work of art, production, opus, achievement, concoction, invention; informal brainchild.
OPPOSITES abolition, destruction.

**creative** adjective inventive, imaginative, innovative, experimental, original, artistic, inspired, visionary.
OPPOSITES unimaginative.

**creativity** noun inventiveness, imagination, innovation,

a b c d e f g h i j k l m n o p q r s t u v w x y z

a
b
**c**
d
e
f
g
h
i
j
k
l
m
n
o
p
q
r
s
t
u
v
w
x
y
z

originality, artistry, inspiration, vision.

**creator** noun maker, producer, author, designer, deviser, originator, inventor, architect.

**creature** noun animal, beast, brute, living thing, living being; N. Amer. informal critter.

**credentials** plural noun 1 *a biologist with impeccable credentials:* suitability, eligibility, attributes, qualifications, record, experience, background. 2 *examine the credentials of all callers:* documents, identity papers, ID, passport, testimonial, reference, certification.

**credibility** noun plausibility, believability, credence, trustworthiness, reliability, dependability, integrity.

**credible** adjective believable, plausible, conceivable, persuasive, convincing, tenable, probable, possible, feasible, reasonable.

**credit** noun *he got the credit for the work:* praise, commendation, acclaim, acknowledgement, recognition, kudos, glory, respect, appreciation.
verb (Brit.) *you wouldn't credit it!* believe, accept, give credence to, trust, have faith in.
■ **credit someone with something** ascribe something to someone, attribute something to someone.

**creed** noun 1 *people of many creeds:* faith, religion, belief, religious persuasion. 2 *his political creed:* beliefs, principles, articles of faith, ideology, credo.

**creek** noun inlet, bay, estuary, fjord; Scottish firth.

**creep** verb tiptoe, steal, sneak, slink, edge, inch, skulk, prowl.

**creepy** adjective (informal) frightening, eerie, disturbing, sinister, weird, menacing, threatening; informal spooky, scary.

**crest** noun 1 *the bird's crest:* tuft, comb, plume, crown. 2 *the crest of the hill:* summit, peak, top, ridge, pinnacle, brow, crown, apex. 3 *the Duke's crest:* insignia, emblem, coat of arms, arms, badge, device, regalia.

**crevice** noun crack, fissure, cleft, chink, cranny, slit, split.

**crew** noun 1 *the ship's crew:* company, complement, sailors, hands. 2 *a film crew:* team, squad, company, unit, party, gang.

**crime** noun 1 *kidnapping is a serious crime:* offence, unlawful act, illegal act, felony, violation, misdemeanour. 2 *the increase in crime:* lawbreaking, delinquency, wrongdoing, criminality, misconduct, illegality, villainy, vice.

**criminal** noun *a convicted criminal:* lawbreaker, offender, villain, delinquent, felon, culprit; informal crook; Austral./NZ informal crim.
adjective 1 *criminal conduct:* unlawful, illegal, illicit, lawless, delinquent, corrupt; informal crooked; Brit. informal bent. 2 (informal) *a criminal waste of money:* deplorable, shameful, reprehensible, disgraceful, inexcusable, outrageous, scandalous.
OPPOSITES lawful, reasonable.

**cripple** verb 1 *the accident crippled her:* disable, paralyse, immobilize, incapacitate, handicap. 2 *the company had been crippled by the recession:*

damage, weaken, hamper, paralyse, ruin, destroy, wipe out, bring to a standstill, put out of action, put out of business.
OPPOSITES assist.

**crippled** adjective disabled, paralysed, incapacitated, (physically) handicapped, lame, immobilized, bedridden, confined to a wheelchair; euphemistic physically challenged.

**crisis** noun 1 *the current economic crisis*: emergency, disaster, catastrophe, calamity, meltdown, predicament, plight, dire straits. 2 *the situation had reached a crisis*: critical point, turning point, crossroads, head, moment of truth; informal crunch.

**crisp** adjective 1 *crisp bacon*: crunchy, crispy, brittle, breakable, dry. 2 *a crisp autumn day*: invigorating, brisk, fresh, refreshing, exhilarating. 3 *crisp white bedlinen*: smooth, fresh, ironed, starched.
OPPOSITES soft, sultry, crumpled.

**criterion** noun standard, measure, gauge, test, benchmark, yardstick, touchstone, barometer.

**critic** noun 1 *a literary critic*: reviewer, commentator, analyst, judge, pundit, expert. 2 *critics of the government*: detractor, attacker, fault-finder; informal knocker.

**critical** adjective 1 *a highly critical report*: disapproving, disparaging, scathing, fault-finding, judgemental, negative, unfavourable, censorious; informal nit-picking, picky. 2 *the situation is critical*: serious, grave, precarious, touch-and-go, in the balance, desperate, dire,

acute, life-and-death. 3 *the choice of materials is critical*: crucial, vital, essential, all-important, paramount, fundamental, key, pivotal.
OPPOSITES complimentary, safe, unimportant.

**criticism** noun 1 *she was stung by his criticism*: fault-finding, censure, condemnation, disapproval, disparagement; informal flak, a bad press, panning; Brit. informal stick. 2 *literary criticism*: evaluation, assessment, appraisal, appreciation, analysis, critique, judgement, commentary.
OPPOSITES praise.

**criticize** verb find fault with, censure, condemn, attack, disparage, denigrate, run down; informal knock, pan, pull to pieces; Brit. informal slag off, slate, rubbish; N. Amer. informal pummel, trash; Austral./NZ informal bag.
OPPOSITES praise.

**crook** noun (informal). See **CRIMINAL** noun.

**crooked** adjective 1 *narrow, crooked streets*: winding, twisting, zigzag, meandering, tortuous, serpentine. 2 *a crooked spine*: bent, twisted, misshapen, deformed, malformed, contorted, warped, bowed, distorted. 3 *the picture over the bed looked crooked*: lopsided, askew, awry, off-centre, out of true, at an angle, slanting, squint; Scottish agley; Brit. informal skew-whiff, wonky. 4 (informal) *a crooked deal*: dishonest, criminal, illegal, unlawful, nefarious, fraudulent, corrupt; informal shady; Brit. informal bent.
OPPOSITES straight, legal, honest.

**crop** noun *some farmers lost their entire crop*: harvest, yield,

a
b
c
d
e
f
g
h
i
j
k
l
m
n
o
p
q
r
s
t
u
v
w
x
y
z

fruits, produce, vintage.
verb 1 *she's had her hair cropped:* cut, clip, trim, shear, shave, lop off, chop off, hack off, dock. 2 *a flock of sheep were cropping the turf:* graze on, browse on, feed on, nibble, eat.
■ crop up happen, occur, arise, turn up, pop up, emerge, materialize, surface, appear, come to light.

**cross** noun 1 *we all have our crosses to bear:* burden, trouble, worry, trial, affliction, curse, misfortune, woe; informal hassle, headache. 2 *a cross between a yak and a cow:* mixture, blend, combination, amalgam, hybrid, cross-breed, mongrel.
verb 1 *they crossed the hills on foot:* travel across, traverse, negotiate, navigate, cover. 2 *the two roads cross:* intersect, meet, join, connect. 3 *no one dared cross him:* oppose, resist, defy, obstruct, contradict, argue with, stand up to. 4 *the breed was crossed with Friesian:* hybridize, cross-breed, interbreed, cross-fertilize, cross-pollinate.
adjective *Jane was getting cross:* angry, annoyed, irate, irritated, in a bad mood, put out; informal hot under the collar, peeved; Brit. informal shirty, ratty; N. Amer. informal sore, ticked off; Austral./NZ informal ropeable, snaky.
OPPOSITES pleased.
■ cross something out delete, strike out, score out, cancel, obliterate.

**crouch** verb squat, bend (down), hunker down, hunch over, stoop, duck, cower.

**crow** verb boast, brag, blow one's own trumpet, swagger, swank, gloat.

**crowd** noun 1 *a crowd gathered:* throng, horde, mass, multitude, host, army, swarm, mob, rabble; informal gaggle. 2 *they're a nice crowd:* group, set, circle, clique; informal gang, bunch, crew, lot. 3 *the final attracted a capacity crowd:* audience, spectators, listeners, viewers, house, turnout, attendance, gate, congregation.
verb 1 *reporters crowded round her:* cluster, flock, swarm, mill, throng, huddle, gather, assemble, congregate, converge. 2 *the guests crowded into the dining room:* surge, throng, push, jostle, elbow one's way, squeeze, pile, cram. 3 *the quayside was crowded:* throng, pack, jam, cram, fill.

**crowded** adjective packed, full, filled to capacity, full to bursting, congested, overflowing, teeming, swarming, thronged, populous, overpopulated, busy; informal jam-packed, stuffed, chock-a-block, chock-full, bursting at the seams, full to the gunwales, wall-to-wall, mobbed; Austral./NZ informal chocker.
OPPOSITES deserted.

**crown** noun 1 *the royal crown:* coronet, diadem, tiara, circlet. 2 *loyal servants of the Crown:* monarch, sovereign, king, queen, emperor, empress, monarchy, royalty. 3 *the crown of the hill:* top, crest, summit, peak, pinnacle, tip, brow, apex.
verb 1 *the building is crowned by a balustrade:* top, cap, tip, head, surmount. 2 *a teaching post at Harvard crowned his career:* round off, cap, be the climax of, be the culmination of, top off, complete.

**crucial** adjective 1 *negotiations*

*were at a crucial stage:* pivotal, critical, key, decisive, life-and-death. **2** *confidentiality is crucial:* all-important, of the utmost importance, of the essence, critical, paramount, essential, vital.
OPPOSITES insignificant, unimportant.

**crude** adjective **1** *crude oil:* unrefined, unpurified, unprocessed, untreated, coarse, raw, natural. **2** *a crude barricade:* primitive, simple, basic, homespun, rudimentary, rough and ready, improvised. **3** *crude jokes:* vulgar, rude, dirty, naughty, smutty, indecent, obscene, coarse; informal blue.
OPPOSITES refined, sophisticated, clean.

**cruel** adjective **1** *a cruel man:* brutal, savage, inhuman, barbaric, vicious, sadistic, monstrous, callous, ruthless, merciless, heartless, unkind, inhumane. **2** *her death was a cruel blow:* harsh, severe, bitter, heartbreaking, heart-rending, painful, agonizing, traumatic.
OPPOSITES compassionate.

**cruelty** noun brutality, savagery, inhumanity, barbarity, viciousness, sadism, callousness, ruthlessness.

**cruise** noun *a cruise down the Nile:* (boat) trip, voyage, sail. verb **1** *she cruised across the Atlantic:* sail, voyage. **2** *a taxi cruised past:* drive slowly, drift, sail; informal mosey, tootle; Brit. informal pootle.

**crumb** noun fragment, bit, morsel, particle, speck, scrap, shred, atom, trace, mite, jot, ounce; informal smidgen, tad.

**crumble** verb **1** *the plaster was crumbling:* disintegrate, fall apart, fall to pieces, collapse, decompose, break up, decay, become dilapidated. **2** *crumble the cheese with your fingers:* break up, crush, fragment. **3** *party unity began to crumble:* collapse, deteriorate, degenerate, fail.

**crumple** verb **1** *she crumpled the note in her fist:* crush, scrunch up, screw up, squash, squeeze. **2** *his trousers were dirty and crumpled:* crease, wrinkle, crinkle, rumple. **3** *her resistance crumpled:* collapse, give way, cave in, go to pieces, break down, crumble.
OPPOSITES flatten out, iron, hold.

**crunch** verb munch, chomp, champ, bite into, crush, grind, break, smash.

**crusade** noun *a crusade against crime:* campaign, drive, push, movement, effort, struggle, battle, war, offensive. verb *he has crusaded for hopeless causes:* campaign, fight, battle, strive, struggle, agitate, lobby.

**crush** verb **1** *essential oils are released when the herbs are crushed:* squash, squeeze, press, pulp, mash, mangle, pulverize. **2** *your dress will get crushed:* crease, crumple, rumple, wrinkle, scrunch up. **3** *crush the biscuits with a rolling pin:* pulverize, pound, grind, break up, smash, crumble. **4** *the new regime crushed all opposition:* suppress, put down, quell, stamp out, repress, subdue, extinguish. **5** *Alan was crushed by her words:* demoralize, deflate, flatten, squash, devastate, shatter, mortify, humiliate.
OPPOSITES allow, promote,

a
b
**c**
d
e
f
g
h
i
j
k
l
m
n
o
p
q
r
s
t
u
v
w
x
y
z

encourage.

noun *the crush of people:* crowd, throng, horde, swarm, press, mob.

**crust** noun covering, layer, coating, surface, topping, sheet, film, skin, shell, scab.

**cry** verb 1 *Mandy started to cry:* weep, shed tears, sob, wail, snivel, whimper; Scottish greet; informal blub, blubber; Brit. informal grizzle. 2 *'Wait!' he cried:* call, shout, exclaim, sing out, yell, bawl, bellow, roar; informal holler.
OPPOSITES laugh, whisper.

noun call, shout, exclamation, yell, bawl, bellow, roar; informal holler.

■ **cry off** (informal) back out, pull out, cancel, withdraw, change one's mind; informal get cold feet, cop out.

**cuddle** verb 1 *she picked up the baby and cuddled her:* hug, embrace, clasp, hold in one's arms. 2 *the pair were kissing and cuddling:* embrace, hug, caress, pet, fondle; informal canoodle, smooch. 3 *I cuddled up to him:* snuggle, nestle, curl, nuzzle.

**cudgel** noun club, truncheon, bludgeon, baton, shillelagh, mace; N. Amer. blackjack, nightstick; Brit. informal cosh.
verb club, bludgeon, beat, batter, bash; Brit. informal cosh.

**cue** noun signal, sign, indication, prompt, reminder.

**culminate** verb come to a climax, come to a head, climax, end, finish, conclude, build up to, lead up to.

**culpable** adjective to blame, guilty, at fault, in the wrong, answerable, accountable, responsible.
OPPOSITES innocent.

**culprit** noun guilty party,

offender, wrongdoer, miscreant, criminal, lawbreaker, felon, delinquent; informal baddy, crook.

**cult** noun 1 *a religious cult:* sect, group, movement. 2 *the cult of youth in Hollywood:* obsession, fixation, idolization, devotion, worship, veneration.

**cultivate** verb 1 *the peasants cultivated the land:* farm, work, till, plough, dig. 2 *they cultivated basic food crops:* grow, raise, rear, tend, plant, sow. 3 *Tessa tried to cultivate her:* woo, court, curry favour with, ingratiate oneself with; informal get in someone's good books. 4 *he wants to cultivate his mind:* improve, better, refine, educate, develop, enrich.

**cultivated** adjective. See CULTURED.

**cultural** adjective 1 *cultural differences:* social, lifestyle, sociological, anthropological, racial, ethnic. 2 *cultural achievements:* aesthetic, artistic, intellectual, educational, civilizing.

**culture** noun 1 *a lover of culture:* the arts, high art. 2 *a man of culture:* education, cultivation, enlightenment, discernment, discrimination, taste, refinement, sophistication. 3 *Afro-Caribbean culture:* civilization, society, way of life, lifestyle, customs, traditions, heritage, values. 4 *a corporate culture of greed and envy:* philosophy, ethic, outlook, approach, rationale.

**cultured** adjective cultivated, artistic, enlightened, civilized, educated, well read, learned, discerning, discriminating, refined, sophisticated; informal arty.

OPPOSITES ignorant.

**cunning** adjective **1** *a cunning scheme:* crafty, wily, artful, devious, sly, scheming, canny, dishonest, deceitful. **2** *a cunning plan:* clever, ingenious, imaginative, enterprising, inventive, creative, original, inspired, brilliant.
OPPOSITES open, honest, stupid.
noun **1** *his political cunning:* guile, craftiness, deviousness, trickery, duplicity. **2** *it took cunning just to survive:* ingenuity, imagination, inventiveness, enterprise, creativity, brilliance.

**curator** noun custodian, keeper, conservator, guardian, caretaker.

**curb** noun *a curb on imports:* restraint, restriction, check, brake, rein, control, limit.
verb *a plan to curb consumer spending:* restrain, hold back, keep in check, control, rein in, contain; informal keep a lid on.

**cure** verb **1** *he was cured of the disease:* heal, restore to health, make well/better. **2** *economic equality cannot cure all social ills:* rectify, remedy, put/set right, right, fix, mend, repair, solve, sort out, eliminate, end. **3** *some farmers cured their own bacon:* preserve, smoke, salt, dry, pickle.
noun *a cure for cancer:* remedy, medicine, medication, antidote, treatment, therapy.

**curiosity** noun **1** *his evasiveness roused my curiosity:* interest, inquisitiveness, attention, prying; informal nosiness. **2** *the shop is full of curiosities:* oddity, curio, novelty, rarity.

**curious** adjective **1** *she was curious to know what had happened:* intrigued,
interested, eager, inquisitive. **2** *her curious behaviour:* strange, odd, peculiar, funny, unusual, bizarre, weird, eccentric, extraordinary, abnormal, anomalous.
OPPOSITES uninterested, normal.

**curl** verb **1** *smoke curled up from his cigarette:* spiral, coil, wreathe, twirl, swirl, wind, curve, twist (and turn), snake, corkscrew. **2** *Ruth curled her arms around his neck:* wind, twine, entwine, wrap.
noun **1** *the tangled curls of her hair:* ringlet, corkscrew, kink, lock. **2** *a curl of smoke:* spiral, coil, twirl, swirl, twist, corkscrew.

**curly** adjective wavy, curling, curled, frizzy, kinky, corkscrew.
OPPOSITES straight.

**currency** noun **1** *foreign currency:* money, legal tender, cash, banknotes, notes, coins; N. Amer. bills. **2** *a term which has gained new currency:* popularity, circulation, exposure, acceptance, prevalence.

**current** adjective **1** *current events:* contemporary, present-day, modern, topical, live, burning. **2** *the idea is still current:* prevalent, common, accepted, in circulation, popular, widespread. **3** *a current driving licence:* valid, usable, up to date. **4** *the current prime minister:* incumbent, present, in office, in power, reigning.
OPPOSITES past, out of date, former.
noun **1** *a current of air:* flow, stream, draught, jet, tide. **2** *the current of human life:* course, progress, progression, flow, tide, movement.

**curse** noun **1** *she'd put a curse on him:* jinx; N. Amer. hex. **2** *the curse of unemployment:* affliction, burden, misery, ordeal, evil, scourge. **3** *muffled curses:* swear word, expletive, oath, profanity, four-letter word, dirty word, obscenity; informal cuss word.
verb **1** *she was cursed with feelings of inadequacy:* afflict, trouble, plague, bedevil. **2** *he cursed loudly:* swear, take the Lord's name in vain; informal cuss, turn the air blue, eff and blind.

**cursed** adjective damned, doomed, ill-fated, ill-starred; informal jinxed.

**cursory** adjective brief, hasty, hurried, rapid, passing, perfunctory, desultory, casual.
OPPOSITES thorough.

**curt** adjective terse, brusque, abrupt, clipped, blunt, short, sharp.
OPPOSITES expansive.

**curtail** verb **1** *policies designed to curtail spending:* reduce, cut, cut down, decrease, trim, restrict, limit, curb, rein in/back; informal slash. **2** *his visit was curtailed:* shorten, cut short, truncate.
OPPOSITES increase, extend.

**curve** noun *the curves of the river:* bend, turn, loop, arc, arch, bow, curvature.
verb *the road curved back on itself:* bend, turn, loop, wind, meander, snake, arc, arch.

**curved** adjective bent, arched, bowed, rounded, crescent.
OPPOSITES straight.

**cushion** noun *a cushion against inflation:* protection, buffer, shield, defence, bulwark.
verb **1** *residents are cushioned from the outside world:* protect, shield, shelter, cocoon. **2** *to cushion the blow, pensions were increased:* soften, lessen, diminish, mitigate, alleviate, take the edge off, dull, deaden.

**custody** noun *custody of the child:* care, guardianship, charge, supervision, safe keeping, responsibility, protection.
■ in custody in prison, in jail, imprisoned, incarcerated, under lock and key, on remand; informal behind bars, doing time, inside; Brit. informal banged up.

**custom** noun **1** *his unfamiliarity with local customs:* tradition, practice, usage, way, convention, formality, ritual, mores. **2** *it was his custom to sleep in a chair:* habit, practice, routine, way; formal wont.

**customary** adjective usual, traditional, normal, conventional, habitual, familiar, accepted, accustomed, routine, established, time-honoured, prevailing.
OPPOSITES unusual.

**customer** noun consumer, buyer, purchaser, patron, client, shopper; Brit. informal punter.

**cut** verb **1** *he cut his finger:* gash, slash, lacerate, slit, wound, scratch, graze, nick. **2** *cut the pepper into small pieces:* slice, chop, dice, cube, carve; N. Amer. hash. **3** *the name had been cut into the stone:* carve, engrave, incise, etch, score, chisel, whittle. **4** *the government will cut expenditure:* reduce, cut back/down on, decrease, lessen, mark down, discount, lower; informal slash. **5** *the text has been substantially cut:* shorten, abridge, condense, abbreviate, truncate, edit, censor. **6** *you need to cut ten lines per page:*

delete, remove, take out, excise.
**noun 1** *a cut on his jaw:* gash, slash, laceration, incision, wound, scratch, graze, nick. **2** *a cut of beef:* piece, joint, fillet, section. **3** (informal) *they want their cut:* share, portion, quota, percentage; informal slice (of the cake). **4** *a cut in interest rates:* reduction, cutback, decrease, lessening; N. Amer. rollback. **5** *the cut of his jacket:* style, design, line, fit.

**cutback noun** reduction, cut, decrease, economy, saving; N. Amer. rollback.
OPPOSITES increase.

**cute adjective** endearing, adorable, lovable, sweet, lovely, appealing, engaging, delightful, dear; informal twee; Brit. informal dinky.
OPPOSITES hateful, ugly.

**cutting noun** *a newspaper cutting:* clipping, article, piece, column, paragraph.
**adjective** *a cutting remark:* hurtful, wounding, barbed, scathing, caustic, sarcastic, snide, spiteful, malicious, cruel; informal bitchy; Brit. informal sarky; N. Amer. informal snarky.
OPPOSITES friendly, warm.

**cycle noun 1** *the cycle of birth, death, and rebirth:* circle, round, pattern, rhythm, loop. **2** *a cycle of three plays:* series, set, sequence, succession, run.

**cynic noun** sceptic, doubter, doubting Thomas, pessimist, prophet of doom.
OPPOSITES idealist, optimist.

**cynical adjective** sceptical, doubtful, distrustful, suspicious, disbelieving, pessimistic, negative, world-weary, disillusioned, disenchanted, jaundiced.
OPPOSITES idealistic, optimistic.

# Dd

**dab verb** *she dabbed disinfectant on the cut:* pat, press, touch, swab, daub, wipe.
**noun** *a dab of glue:* drop, spot, smear, splash, bit.

**dabble verb** toy with, dip into, flirt with, tinker with, play with.

**daft adjective** (Brit. informal) **1** *a daft idea:* absurd, preposterous, ridiculous, ludicrous, idiotic, stupid, foolish; informal crazy; Brit. informal barmy. **2** *he's really daft:* stupid, idiotic, empty-headed, unhinged, insane, mad; informal thick, dim, dopey; Brit. informal barmy, crackers. **3** *she's daft about him:* infatuated, smitten, besotted; informal crazy, mad, nuts; Brit. informal potty.
OPPOSITES sensible, sane.

**daily adjective** *a daily event:* everyday, day-to-day.
**adverb** *the museum is open daily:* every day, once a day, day after day.

**dainty adjective 1** *a dainty china cup:* delicate, fine, elegant, exquisite. **2** *a dainty eater:* fastidious, fussy, particular; informal choosy, picky; Brit. informal faddy.
OPPOSITES unwieldy, undiscriminating.

**dam noun** barrage, barrier, wall, embankment, barricade,

obstruction.

**verb** block (up), obstruct, bung up, close, hold back.

**damage** noun **1** *did the thieves do any damage?* harm, destruction, vandalism, injury, ruin, devastation. **2** (**damages**) compensation, recompense, restitution, redress, reparation(s); N. Amer. informal comp.

**verb** *the parcel had been damaged:* harm, injure, deface, spoil, impair, vandalize, ruin, destroy, wreck; N. Amer. informal trash.

OPPOSITES repair.

**damaging** adjective harmful, detrimental, injurious, hurtful, destructive, ruinous, deleterious.

OPPOSITES beneficial.

**damn** verb condemn, censure, criticize, attack, denounce.

OPPOSITES bless, praise.

**damning** adjective incriminating, implicating, damaging, condemnatory, conclusive, irrefutable.

**damp** adjective *her hair was damp:* moist, humid, muggy, clammy, sweaty, dank, wet, rainy, drizzly, showery, misty, foggy, dewy.

OPPOSITES dry.

**noun** *the damp in the air:* moisture, liquid, wet, wetness, dampness, humidity.

OPPOSITES dryness.

**dampen** verb **1** *the rain dampened her face:* moisten, damp, wet, soak. **2** *nothing could dampen her enthusiasm:* lessen, decrease, diminish, reduce, moderate, cool, suppress, stifle, inhibit.

OPPOSITES dry, heighten.

**dance** verb **1** *he danced with her:* trip, sway, twirl, whirl,

pirouette, gyrate; informal bop, trip the light fantastic; N. Amer. informal get down. **2** *the girls danced round me:* caper, cavort, frolic, skip, prance, gambol, leap, bop, bounce.

**noun** *the school dance:* ball; N. Amer. prom, hoedown; informal disco, rave, hop, bop.

**danger** noun **1** *an element of danger:* peril, hazard, risk, jeopardy. **2** *he is a danger to society:* menace, hazard, threat, risk. **3** *a serious danger of fire:* possibility, chance, risk, probability, likelihood.

OPPOSITES safety.

**dangerous** adjective **1** *a dangerous animal:* menacing, threatening, treacherous. **2** *dangerous wiring:* hazardous, perilous, risky, unsafe, unpredictable, precarious, insecure; informal dicey, hairy; Brit. informal dodgy.

OPPOSITES harmless, safe.

**dangle** verb **1** *a chain dangled from his belt:* hang, swing, droop, wave, trail, stream. **2** *he dangled the keys:* wave, swing, jiggle, brandish, flourish.

**dank** adjective damp, musty, chilly, clammy.

OPPOSITES dry.

**dapper** adjective smart, spruce, trim, debonair, neat, well dressed, elegant; informal snappy, natty; N. Amer. informal spiffy, fly.

OPPOSITES scruffy.

**dare** verb **1** *nobody dared to say a word:* be brave enough, have the courage, venture, have the nerve, risk, take the liberty of; N. Amer. take a flyer; informal stick one's neck out. **2** *she dared him to go:* challenge, defy, invite, bid, provoke, goad.

**noun** *she accepted the dare:*

challenge, invitation, wager, bet.

**daring** adjective *a daring attack*: bold, audacious, intrepid, fearless, brave, heroic, dashing; informal gutsy.
OPPOSITES cowardly, timid.
noun *his sheer daring*: boldness, audacity, temerity, fearlessness, bravery, courage, pluck; informal nerve, guts; Brit. informal bottle; N. Amer. informal moxie.
OPPOSITES cowardice.

**dark** adjective **1** *a dark night*: dingy, gloomy, shadowy, murky, poorly lit, grey, inky, black. **2** *dark hair*: brunette, dark brown, sable, jet-black, ebony. **3** *dark skin*: swarthy, dusky, olive, black, ebony. **4** *dark thoughts*: gloomy, dismal, negative, downbeat, bleak, grim, fatalistic, black. **5** *a dark look*: angry, forbidding, threatening, ominous, moody, brooding, sullen, scowling, glowering. **6** *dark deeds*: evil, wicked, sinful, bad, iniquitous, ungodly, vile, foul, monstrous; informal dirty, crooked, shady.
OPPOSITES bright, light, blonde, pale, white, happy, friendly, good.
noun *walking in the dark*: night, night-time, darkness, nightfall, blackout.
OPPOSITES light, day.

**darken** verb grow dark, make dark, blacken, grow dim, cloud over, lour.
OPPOSITES lighten.

**darkness** noun **1** *lights shone in the darkness*: dark, blackness, gloom, dimness, murk, shadow, shade. **2** *darkness fell*: night, night-time, dark. **3** *the forces of darkness*: evil, wickedness, sin, ungodliness, the Devil.

**darling** noun **1** *good night, darling*: dear, dearest, love, sweetheart, beloved; informal honey, angel, pet, sweetie, baby, poppet. **2** *the darling of the media*: favourite, idol, hero, heroine; Brit. informal blue-eyed boy/girl.
OPPOSITES bugbear, villain.
adjective **1** *his darling wife*: dear, dearest, precious, beloved. **2** *a darling little hat*: adorable, charming, cute, sweet, enchanting, dear, delightful; Scottish & N. English bonny.
OPPOSITES ugly.

**dart** verb **1** *Karl darted across the road*: dash, rush, tear, shoot, sprint, bound, scurry, scamper; informal scoot, whip. **2** *he darted a glance at her*: direct, cast, throw, shoot, send, flash.

**dash** verb **1** *he dashed home*: rush, race, run, sprint, career, charge, shoot, hurtle, hare, fly, speed, zoom; informal tear, belt; Brit. informal bomb; N. Amer. informal barrel. **2** *he dashed the glass to the ground*: hurl, smash, fling, slam, throw, toss, cast; informal chuck, sling; N. Amer. informal peg. **3** *her hopes were dashed*: shatter, destroy, wreck, ruin, demolish, scotch, frustrate, thwart; informal put paid to; Brit. informal scupper.
OPPOSITES dawdle, raise.
noun **1** *a dash for the door*: rush, race, run, sprint, bolt, dart, leap, charge, bound. **2** *a dash of salt*: pinch, touch, sprinkle, taste, spot, drop, dab, splash; informal smidgen, tad. **3** *he led off with such dash*: verve, style, flamboyance, gusto, zest, elan, flair, vigour, panache; informal pizzazz, oomph.

**dashing** adjective **1** *a dashing pilot*: debonair, devil-may-care, raffish, flamboyant, swashbuckling. **2** *he looked very dashing:* stylish, smart, elegant, dapper, spruce, trim, debonair; informal **natty;** N. Amer. informal **spiffy.**

**data** noun facts, figures, statistics, details, particulars, information.

**date** noun **1** *at a later date:* day, occasion, time, year, age, period, era, epoch. **2** *a lunch date:* appointment, meeting, engagement, rendezvous, commitment. **3** (informal) *a date for tonight:* partner, escort, girlfriend, boyfriend.
verb **1** *the best films don't date:* age, grow old, become dated, show its age, be of its time. **2** assign a date to, put a date on. **3** (informal) *he's dating Jill:* go out with, take out, go with, see; informal go steady with.
■ **date from** be from, originate in, come from, belong to, go back to.

**dated** adjective old-fashioned, outdated, outmoded, unfashionable, passé, behind the times, archaic, obsolete, antiquated; informal old hat, out of the ark.
OPPOSITES modern.

**daunting** adjective intimidating, forbidding, challenging, formidable, unnerving, disconcerting, discouraging, disheartening, demoralizing, dismaying, scary, frightening, alarming.
OPPOSITES inviting, reassuring.

**dawdle** verb **1** *they dawdled over breakfast:* linger, take one's time, be slow, waste time, dally; informal dilly-dally. **2** *Ruth dawdled home:* amble, stroll, trail, dally, move at a snail's pace; informal mosey, tootle; Brit.

informal **pootle.**
OPPOSITES hurry.

**dawn** noun **1** *we got up at dawn:* daybreak, sunrise, first light, daylight, cockcrow, first thing; N. Amer. **sunup. 2** *the dawn of civilization:* beginning, start, birth, inception, genesis, emergence, advent, appearance, arrival, rise, origin.
OPPOSITES dusk, end.
verb **1** *Thursday dawned crisp and sunny:* begin, break, arrive, emerge. **2** *a bright new future has dawned:* begin, start, commence, be born, appear, arrive, emerge, arise, rise, unfold, develop. **3** *the reality dawned on him:* become evident, register, cross someone's mind, suggest itself, occur, come, strike, hit.
OPPOSITES end.

**day** noun **1** *I stayed for a day:* twenty-four hours. **2** *enjoy the beach during the day:* daytime, daylight, waking hours. **3** *the leading architect of the day:* period, time, date, age, era, generation.
OPPOSITES night.

**daze** verb *she was dazed by the revelations:* dumbfound, stupefy, stun, shock, stagger, bewilder, take aback, nonplus; informal flabbergast; Brit. informal knock for six.
noun *she is in a daze:* stupor, trance, haze, spin, whirl, muddle, jumble.

**dazzle** verb **1** *she was dazzled by the headlights:* blind, confuse, disorient. **2** *I was dazzled by the exhibition:* overwhelm, overcome, impress, move, stir, touch, awe, overawe; informal bowl over, blow away, knock out.

**dead** adjective **1** *my parents are*

*dead:* passed on/away, departed, late, lost, perished, fallen, killed, lifeless, extinct; informal six feet under, pushing up daisies; formal deceased. **2** *a dead issue/language:* obsolete, extinct, defunct, disused, abandoned, superseded, vanished, archaic, ancient. **3** *the phone was dead:* not working, out of order, inoperative, inactive, broken, defective; informal kaput, conked out, on the blink, bust; Brit. informal knackered. **4** *a dead town:* boring, uninteresting, unexciting, uninspiring, dull, flat, quiet, sleepy, slow, lifeless; informal one-horse; N. Amer. informal dullsville.
OPPOSITES alive, live, living, working, lively.
adverb **1** *he was dead serious:* completely, absolutely, totally, utterly, deadly, perfectly, entirely, quite, thoroughly. **2** *flares were seen dead ahead:* directly, exactly, precisely, immediately, right, straight, due.

**deadline** noun time limit, finishing date, target date, cut-off point.

**deadlock** noun stalemate, impasse, checkmate, stand-off, standstill, gridlock.

**deadly** adjective **1** *these drugs can be deadly:* fatal, lethal, mortal, life-threatening, noxious, toxic, poisonous. **2** *deadly enemies:* mortal, irreconcilable, implacable, bitter, sworn. **3** *his aim is deadly:* unerring, unfailing, perfect, true, accurate; Brit. informal spot on.
OPPOSITES harmless, inaccurate.

**deafening** adjective ear-splitting, thunderous,

crashing, uproarious, almighty, booming.
OPPOSITES low, soft.

**deal** noun *completion of the deal:* agreement, understanding, pact, bargain, covenant, contract, treaty, arrangement, compromise, settlement, terms.
verb **1** *how to deal with difficult children:* cope with, handle, manage, treat, take care of, take charge of, take in hand, sort out, tackle, take on, control. **2** *the article deals with advances in biochemistry:* concern, be about, have to do with, discuss, consider, cover, tackle, explore, investigate, examine. **3** *the company deals in high-tech goods:* trade in, buy and sell, purvey, supply, market, traffic in. **4** *the cards were dealt:* distribute, give out, share out, divide out, hand out, pass out, pass round, dispense, allocate.

**dealer** noun trader, merchant, salesman/woman, seller, vendor, purveyor, pedlar, distributor, supplier, shopkeeper, retailer, wholesaler, tradesman, tradesperson; Brit. stockist.

**dear** adjective **1** *a dear friend:* beloved, precious, close, intimate, bosom. **2** *her pictures were too dear to part with:* precious, treasured, valued, prized, cherished, special. **3** *such a dear man:* endearing, adorable, lovable, appealing, engaging, charming, captivating, lovely, delightful, sweet, darling. **4** *rather dear meals:* expensive, costly, high-priced, overpriced, exorbitant, extortionate; Brit. over the odds; informal pricey.
OPPOSITES disagreeable, cheap.

**noun** *don't worry, my dear:*
darling, dearest, love, beloved,
sweetheart, precious; informal
sweetie, sugar, honey, baby, pet,
poppet.

**dearly** adverb *I love him dearly:*
very much, a great deal,
greatly, deeply, profoundly.

**dearth** noun lack, scarcity,
shortage, shortfall, deficiency,
insufficiency, inadequacy,
absence.
OPPOSITES surfeit.

**death** noun 1 *her father's death:*
dying, demise, end, passing,
loss of life; formal decease. 2 *the
death of their dream:* end,
finish, termination, extinction,
extinguishing, collapse,
destruction.
OPPOSITES life, birth, start.

**deathly** adjective deathlike,
ghostly, ghastly, ashen, white,
pale, pallid.

**debacle** noun fiasco, failure,
catastrophe, disaster.

**debate** noun *a debate on the
reforms:* discussion, argument,
dispute, talks.
verb 1 *MPs will debate our
future:* discuss, talk over/
through, talk about, thrash out,
argue, dispute. 2 *he debated
whether to call her:* consider,
think over/about, chew over,
mull over, weigh up, ponder,
deliberate.

**debris** noun ruins, remains,
rubble, wreckage, detritus,
refuse, rubbish, waste, scrap,
flotsam and jetsam.

**debt** noun 1 *he couldn't pay his
debts:* bill, account, dues,
arrears, charges. 2 *his debt to
the author:* indebtedness,
obligation, gratitude,
appreciation.

**decay** verb 1 *the corpses had
decayed:* decompose, rot,

putrefy, go bad, go off, spoil,
fester, perish. 2 *the cities
continue to decay:* deteriorate,
degenerate, decline, go
downhill, slump, slide, go to
rack and ruin, go to seed; informal
go to the dogs.
noun 1 *signs of decay:*
decomposition, putrefaction,
rot. 2 *the decay of American
values:* deterioration,
degeneration, decline,
weakening, crumbling,
disintegration, collapse.

**deceit** noun deception,
deceitfulness, duplicity, double-
dealing, lies, fraud, cheating,
trickery.
OPPOSITES honesty.

**deceitful** adjective dishonest,
untruthful, insincere, false,
disingenuous, untrustworthy,
unscrupulous, unprincipled,
two-faced, duplicitous,
fraudulent, double-dealing;
informal sneaky, tricky, crooked;
Brit. informal bent.
OPPOSITES honest.

**deceive** verb trick, cheat,
defraud, swindle, hoodwink,
hoax, dupe, take in, mislead,
delude, fool; informal con, pull
the wool over someone's eyes;
N. Amer. informal sucker, goldbrick;
Austral. informal rort.

**decency** noun 1 *standards of
taste and decency:* propriety,
decorum, good taste,
respectability, morality, virtue,
modesty. 2 *he didn't have the
decency to tell me:* courtesy,
politeness, good manners,
civility, consideration,
thoughtfulness.

**decent** adjective 1 *a decent
burial:* proper, correct, right,
appropriate, suitable,
respectable, decorous, modest,
seemly, accepted; informal pukka.

**2** *a job with decent pay:* satisfactory, reasonable, fair, acceptable, adequate, sufficient, not bad, all right, tolerable, passable, suitable; informal OK. **3** (Brit. informal) *a very decent chap:* kind, generous, thoughtful, considerate, obliging, courteous, polite, well mannered, neighbourly, hospitable, pleasant, agreeable, amiable.
OPPOSITES indecent, unsatisfactory, unpleasant.

**deception** noun **1** *they obtained money by deception:* deceit, duplicity, double-dealing, fraud, cheating, trickery, guile, bluff, lying, pretence, treachery. **2** *it was all a deception:* trick, sham, fraud, pretence, hoax, ruse, scheme, dodge, cheat, swindle; informal con, set-up, scam.

**deceptive** adjective misleading, confusing, illusory, distorted, ambiguous.

**decide** verb **1** *she decided to become a writer:* resolve, determine, make up one's mind, choose, opt, plan, aim, intend, have in mind, set one's sights on. **2** *research to decide a variety of questions:* settle, resolve, determine, work out, answer; informal sort out. **3** *the court is to decide the case:* adjudicate, arbitrate, judge, pronounce on, give a verdict on, rule on.

**decidedly** adverb distinctly, clearly, markedly, obviously, noticeably, unmistakably, patently, manifestly, definitely, positively.

**decision** noun **1** *they came to a decision:* resolution, conclusion, settlement, choice, option, selection. **2** *the judge's decision:* verdict, finding, ruling, judgement, adjudication, sentence.

**decisive** adjective **1** *a decisive man:* resolute, firm, strong-minded, strong-willed, determined, purposeful. **2** *the decisive factor:* deciding, conclusive, determining, key, pivotal, critical, crucial.
OPPOSITES indecisive.

**declaration** noun **1** *they issued a declaration:* announcement, statement, communication, pronouncement, proclamation; N. Amer. advisory. **2** *a declaration of faith:* assertion, profession, affirmation, acknowledgement, revelation, disclosure, confirmation, testimony, avowal, protestation.

**declare** verb **1** *she declared her political principles:* announce, proclaim, state, reveal, air, voice, articulate, express, vent, set forth, publicize, broadcast. **2** *he declared that they were guilty:* assert, profess, affirm, maintain, state, contend, argue, insist.

**decline** verb **1** *she declined all invitations:* turn down, reject, brush aside, refuse, rebuff, spurn, repulse, dismiss, pass up, say no; informal give something a miss. **2** *the number of traders has declined:* decrease, reduce, lessen, diminish, dwindle, contract, shrink, fall off, tail off, drop, fall, go down. **3** *standards steadily declined:* deteriorate, degenerate, decay, crumble, collapse, slump, slip, slide, go downhill, worsen; informal go to the dogs.
OPPOSITES accept, increase, rise, improve.
noun **1** *a decline in profits:* reduction, decrease, downturn, downswing, diminution, ebb,

a
b
c
**d**
e
f
g
h
i
j
k
l
m
n
o
p
q
r
s
t
u
v
w
x
y
z

drop, slump, plunge. **2** *habitat decline:* deterioration, degeneration, degradation, shrinkage, erosion.
OPPOSITES rise, improvement.

**decor** noun decoration, furnishing, colour scheme.

**decorate** verb **1** *the door was decorated with a wreath:* ornament, adorn, trim, embellish, garnish, furnish, enhance. **2** *he started to decorate his home:* paint, wallpaper, paper, refurbish, renovate, redecorate; informal do up, give something a facelift, give something a makeover.
**3** *he was decorated for courage:* give a medal to, honour, cite, reward.

**decoration** noun **1** *a ceiling with rich decoration:* ornamentation, adornment, trimming, embellishment, beautification. **2** *a Christmas tree decoration:* ornament, bauble, trinket, knick-knack. **3** *a decoration won on the battlefield:* medal, award, prize; Brit. informal gong.

**decorative** adjective ornamental, fancy, ornate, attractive, pretty, showy.
OPPOSITES functional.

**decrease** verb **1** *pollution levels decreased:* lessen, reduce, drop, diminish, decline, dwindle, fall off, plummet, plunge.
**2** *decrease the amount of fat in your body:* reduce, lessen, lower, cut, deplete, minimize; informal slash.
OPPOSITES increase.
noun *a decrease in crime:* reduction, drop, decline, downturn, cut, cutback, diminution.
OPPOSITES increase.

**decree** noun **1** *a presidential*

*decree:* order, command, commandment, edict, proclamation, law, statute, act.
**2** *a court decree:* judgement, verdict, adjudication, finding, ruling, decision.
verb *he decreed that a stadium should be built:* order, direct, command, rule, dictate, pronounce, proclaim, ordain.

**dedicate** verb **1** *she dedicated her life to the sick:* devote, commit, pledge, give (up), sacrifice, set aside. **2** *the book is dedicated to his wife:* inscribe, address, offer. **3** *a chapel dedicated to St Jude:* devote, assign, bless, consecrate, sanctify.

**dedicated** adjective **1** *a dedicated supporter:* committed, devoted, staunch, firm, steadfast, loyal, faithful. **2** *a dedicated rail link:* specialized, custom-built, customized, purpose-built, exclusive.
OPPOSITES half-hearted, general-purpose.

**dedication** noun **1** *sport requires dedication:* commitment, devotion, loyalty, allegiance, application, resolve, conscientiousness, perseverance, persistence. **2** *the book has a dedication to his wife:* inscription, message.
OPPOSITES apathy.

**deduct** verb subtract, take away, take off, debit, dock, stop; informal knock off.
OPPOSITES add.

**deduction** noun **1** *the deduction of tax:* subtraction, removal, debit. **2** *gross pay, before deductions:* stoppage, tax, expenses, rebate, discount, concession. **3** *she was right in her deduction:* conclusion, inference, supposition, hypothesis, assumption, presumption, suspicion.

**deed** noun **1** *heroic deeds*: act, action, feat, exploit, achievement, accomplishment, endeavour. **2** *mortgage deeds*: document, contract, instrument.

**deep** adjective **1** *a deep ravine*: cavernous, yawning, gaping, huge, extensive, bottomless, fathomless. **2** *deep affection*: intense, heartfelt, wholehearted, deep-seated, sincere, genuine, earnest, enthusiastic, great. **3** *a deep sleep*: sound, heavy. **4** *a deep thinker*: profound, serious, intelligent, intellectual, learned, wise, scholarly. **5** *he was deep in concentration*: rapt, absorbed, engrossed, preoccupied, immersed, lost, gripped. **6** *a deep mystery*: obscure, complex, mysterious, unfathomable, opaque, abstruse, esoteric, enigmatic. **7** *his deep voice*: low-pitched, low, bass, rich, resonant, booming, sonorous. **8** *a deep red*: dark, intense, rich, strong, vivid.
OPPOSITES shallow, superficial, light, high, shrill.

**deepen** verb **1** *his love for her had deepened*: grow, increase, intensify, strengthen; informal step up. **2** *they deepened the hole*: dig out, dig deeper, excavate.

**deeply** adverb profoundly, greatly, enormously, extremely, strongly, intensely, keenly, acutely, thoroughly, completely, entirely, seriously, gravely; informal majorly.

**defeat** verb **1** *the army which defeated the Scots*: beat, conquer, win against, triumph over, get the better of, vanquish, rout, trounce, overcome, overpower; informal lick, thrash. **2** *this defeats the original point of the plan*: thwart, frustrate, foil, ruin, scotch, derail; informal put paid to, stymie; Brit. informal scupper.
noun *a crippling defeat*: loss, conquest, rout; informal thrashing, hiding, drubbing, licking.
OPPOSITES victory.

**defect** noun *he spotted a defect in my work*: fault, flaw, imperfection, deficiency, deformity, blemish, mistake, error.

**defective** adjective faulty, flawed, imperfect, unsound, inoperative, malfunctioning, out of order, broken; informal on the blink; Brit. informal duff.
OPPOSITES perfect, working, intact.

**defence** noun **1** *the defence of the fortress*: protection, guarding, security, fortification, resistance. **2** *more spending on defence*: armaments, weapons, weaponry, arms, the military, the armed forces. **3** *the prisoner's defence*: justification, vindication, explanation, mitigation, excuse, alibi, denial, rebuttal, plea, pleading, argument, case.
OPPOSITES attack, prosecution.

**defend** verb **1** *a fort built to defend Ireland*: protect, guard, safeguard, secure, shield, fortify, watch over. **2** *he defended his policy*: justify, vindicate, explain, argue for, support, back, stand by, make a case for, stick up for.
OPPOSITES attack, criticize.

**defender** noun **1** *defenders of*

*the environment:* protector, guardian, guard, custodian. **2** *a defender of colonialism:* supporter, upholder, backer, champion, advocate, apologist.

**defensive** adjective **1** *troops in defensive positions:* defending, protective, guarding. **2** *a defensive response:* self-justifying, oversensitive, prickly, paranoid, neurotic; informal twitchy.

**defer** verb postpone, put off, delay, hold over/off, put back, shelve, suspend; N. Amer. table; informal put on ice, put on the back burner.

**defiance** noun resistance, opposition, non-compliance, disobedience, insubordination, rebellion, disregard, contempt, insolence.
OPPOSITES obedience.

**defiant** adjective disobedient, resistant, obstinate, uncooperative, non-compliant, recalcitrant, insubordinate; Brit. informal stroppy, bolshie.
OPPOSITES cooperative.

**deficiency** noun **1** *a vitamin deficiency:* lack, insufficiency, shortage, inadequacy, deficit, shortfall, scarcity, dearth. **2** *the team's big deficiency:* defect, fault, flaw, failing, weakness, shortcoming, limitation.
OPPOSITES surplus, sufficiency, strength.

**deficit** noun shortfall, deficiency, shortage, debt, arrears, loss.
OPPOSITES surplus.

**definite** adjective specific, explicit, express, precise, exact, clear, clear-cut, unambiguous, certain, sure, positive, conclusive, decisive, firm, unequivocal, unmistakable, proven, decided, marked,

distinct, identifiable.
OPPOSITES vague, ambiguous, indeterminate.

**definitely** adverb certainly, surely, for sure, unquestionably, without doubt, undoubtedly, undeniably, clearly, positively, absolutely, unmistakably.

**definition** noun **1** *the definition of 'intelligence':* meaning, sense, interpretation, explanation, description. **2** *the definition of the picture:* clarity, sharpness, focus, crispness, resolution.

**definitive** adjective **1** *a definitive decision:* conclusive, final, unqualified, absolute, categorical, positive, definite. **2** *the definitive guide:* authoritative, best, ultimate, classic, standard, recognized, accepted, exhaustive.
OPPOSITES provisional, average.

**deflect** verb divert, turn away, draw away, distract, fend off, parry, stave off.

**defraud** verb swindle, cheat, rob, deceive, dupe, hoodwink, double-cross, trick; informal con, do, sting, diddle, rip off, shaft, pull a fast one on, put one over on, sell a pup to; N. Amer. informal sucker, snooker, stiff; Austral. informal pull a swifty on.

**defy** verb disobey, flout, disregard, ignore, break, violate, contravene, breach, challenge, confront.
OPPOSITES obey.

**degenerate** adjective *her degenerate brother:* corrupt, perverted, decadent, dissolute, dissipated, debauched, immoral, unprincipled, disreputable.
OPPOSITES upright, pure.
verb *their quality of life had*

*degenerated:* deteriorate, decline, slip, slide, go downhill; informal go to the dogs.
OPPOSITES improve.

**degrade** verb demean, debase, humiliate, humble, belittle, mortify, dehumanize, brutalize.
OPPOSITES dignify.

**degree** noun level, standard, grade, stage, mark, amount, extent, measure, intensity, strength, proportion.

**dejected** adjective downcast, downhearted, despondent, disconsolate, dispirited, crestfallen, disheartened, depressed; informal down in the mouth, down in the dumps.
OPPOSITES cheerful.

**delay** verb 1 *we were delayed by the traffic:* detain, hold up, make late, slow up/down, bog down, hinder, hamper, impede, obstruct. 2 *don't delay:* linger, drag one's feet, hold back, dawdle, waste time, stall, hesitate, dither, shilly-shally; informal dilly-dally. 3 *he may delay the cut in interest rates:* postpone, put off, defer, hold over, adjourn, reschedule.
OPPOSITES assist, hurry, advance.
noun 1 *drivers will face lengthy delays:* hold-up, wait, interruption, stoppage. 2 *the delay of his trial:* postponement, deferral, adjournment.

**delegate** noun *trade union delegates:* representative, envoy, emissary, commissioner, agent, deputy.
verb *she must delegate routine tasks:* assign, entrust, pass on, hand on/over, turn over, devolve.

**delegation** noun 1 *the delegation from South Africa:* deputation, mission,

commission, contingent, legation. 2 *the delegation of tasks to others:* assignment, entrusting, devolution.

**delete** verb remove, cut (out), take out, edit out, excise, cancel, cross out, strike out, obliterate, rub out, erase.
OPPOSITES add.

**deliberate** adjective 1 *a deliberate attempt to provoke him:* intentional, calculated, conscious, intended, planned, wilful, premeditated. 2 *small, deliberate steps:* careful, cautious, measured, regular, even, steady. 3 *a deliberate worker:* methodical, systematic, careful, painstaking, meticulous, thorough.
OPPOSITES accidental, hasty, careless.
verb *she deliberated on his words:* think about/over, ponder, consider, contemplate, reflect on, muse on, meditate on, ruminate on, mull over; N. Amer. think on.

**deliberately** adverb 1 *he deliberately hurt me:* intentionally, on purpose, purposely, by design, knowingly, wittingly, consciously, wilfully. 2 *he walked deliberately down the aisle:* carefully, cautiously, slowly, steadily, evenly.

**deliberation** noun thought, consideration, reflection, contemplation, discussion.

**delicacy** noun 1 *the delicacy of the fabric:* fineness, delicateness, fragility, thinness, lightness, flimsiness. 2 *the delicacy of the situation:* difficulty, trickiness, sensitivity, ticklishness, awkwardness. 3 *treat this matter with delicacy:* care,

a
b
c
**d**
e
f
g
h
i
j
k
l
m
n
o
p
q
r
s
t
u
v
w
x
y
z

a
b
c
**d**
e
f
g
h
i
j
k
l
m
n
o
p
q
r
s
t
u
v
w
x
y
z

sensitivity, tact, discretion, diplomacy, subtlety. **4** *an Australian delicacy*: treat, luxury, speciality.

**delicate** adjective **1** *delicate embroidery*: fine, intricate, dainty. **2** *a delicate shade of blue*: subtle, soft, muted, pastel, pale, light. **3** *delicate china cups*: fragile, frail. **4** *his wife is very delicate*: sickly, unhealthy, frail, feeble, weak. **5** *a delicate issue*: difficult, tricky, sensitive, ticklish, awkward, touchy, embarrassing; informal sticky, dicey. **6** *the matter required delicate handling*: careful, sensitive, tactful, diplomatic, discreet, kid-glove, subtle. **7** *a delicate mechanism*: sensitive, light, precision.
OPPOSITES coarse, lurid, strong, robust, clumsy, crude.

**delicious** adjective delectable, mouth-watering, appetizing, tasty, flavoursome; informal scrumptious; N. Amer. informal nummy.
OPPOSITES unpalatable.

**delight** verb *her manners delighted him*: charm, enchant, captivate, entrance, thrill, entertain, amuse, divert; informal send, tickle pink, bowl over.
OPPOSITES dismay, disgust.
noun *she squealed with delight*: pleasure, happiness, joy, glee, excitement, amusement, bliss.
OPPOSITES displeasure.
■ **delight in** love, relish, savour, adore, lap up, take pleasure in, enjoy, revel in.

**delighted** adjective pleased, glad, happy, thrilled, overjoyed, ecstatic, elated, on cloud nine, walking on air, in seventh heaven, jumping for joy; enchanted, charmed; amused;

diverted; gleeful, cock-a-hoop; informal over the moon, tickled pink, as pleased as Punch, on top of the world, as happy as Larry; Brit. informal chuffed; N. English informal made up; Austral. informal wrapped.

**delightful** adjective **1** *a delightful evening*: lovely, enjoyable, amusing, entertaining. **2** *the delightful Sally*: charming, enchanting, captivating, bewitching, appealing, sweet, endearing, cute.

**deliver** verb **1** *the parcel was delivered to his house*: bring, take, convey, carry, transport, send, distribute, dispatch, ship. **2** *the court delivered its verdict*: state, utter, give, read, broadcast, pronounce, announce, declare, proclaim, hand down, return. **3** *she delivered a blow to his head*: administer, deal, inflict, give; informal land.

**delivery** noun **1** *the delivery of the goods*: conveyance, carriage, transportation, transport, distribution, dispatch, shipping. **2** *we get several deliveries a day*: consignment, load, shipment. **3** *her delivery was stilted*: speech, pronunciation, enunciation, articulation, elocution.

**delusion** noun misapprehension, misconception, false impression, misunderstanding, mistake, error, misconstruction, illusion, fantasy, fancy.

**demand** noun **1** *I gave in to her demands*: request, call, command, order, dictate. **2** *the demands of a young family*: requirement, need, claim, commitment, imposition. **3** *the* *big demand for such toys:* market, call, appetite, desire. verb 1 *workers demanded wage increases:* call for, ask for, request, push for, seek, claim. 2 *Harvey demanded that I tell him the truth:* order, command, enjoin, require, insist. 3 *'Where is she?' he demanded:* ask, enquire. 4 *an activity demanding detailed knowledge:* require, need, necessitate, call for, involve, entail. 5 *they demanded complete anonymity:* insist on, stipulate, expect, look for.

**demanding** adjective 1 *a demanding task:* difficult, challenging, taxing, exacting, tough, hard, onerous, formidable, arduous, gruelling, back-breaking, punishing. 2 *a demanding child:* nagging, trying, tiresome, hard to please. OPPOSITES easy.

**demeaning** adjective degrading, humiliating, shameful, undignified, menial; informal infra dig.

**demise** noun 1 *her tragic demise:* death, dying, passing, end. 2 *the demise of the Ottoman Empire:* end, break-up, disintegration, fall, downfall, collapse, overthrow. OPPOSITES birth.

**democratic** adjective elected, representative, parliamentary, popular, egalitarian, self-governing.

**demolish** verb 1 *they demolished a block of flats:* knock down, pull down, tear down, destroy, flatten, raze to the ground, dismantle, level, bulldoze, blow up. 2 *he demolished her credibility:* destroy, ruin, wreck, overturn, explode, drive a coach and

horses through; informal shoot full of holes. OPPOSITES build, strengthen.

**demonstrate** verb 1 *his findings demonstrate that boys commit more crimes:* show, indicate, establish, prove, confirm, verify. 2 *she demonstrated various drawing techniques:* show, display, present, illustrate, exemplify. 3 *his work demonstrated an analytical ability:* reveal, manifest, indicate, signify, signal, denote, show, display, exhibit. 4 *they demonstrated against the Government:* protest, march, parade, picket, strike.

**demonstration** noun 1 *a demonstration of carving:* exhibition, presentation, display. 2 *his paintings are a demonstration of his talent:* manifestation, indication, sign, mark, proof, testimony. 3 *an anti-racism demonstration:* protest, march, rally, mass lobby, sit-in, sit-down strike; informal demo.

**demoralized** adjective dispirited, disheartened, downhearted, dejected, downcast, low, depressed, dismayed, daunted, discouraged.

**demure** adjective modest, reserved, shy, unassuming, decorous, decent, proper. OPPOSITES brazen.

**den** noun 1 *the wolves' den:* lair, burrow, hole, shelter, hiding place, hideout. 2 *sulking in his den:* study, studio, workshop, retreat, sanctuary, hideaway; informal hidey-hole.

**denial** noun 1 *the reports met with a denial:* contradiction, rebuttal, repudiation, refutation, disclaimer. **2** *the denial of insurance to certain people:* refusal, withholding.

**denomination** noun **1** *a Christian denomination:* religious group, sect, cult, movement, persuasion, order, creed, school, church. **2** *banknotes in a number of denominations:* value, unit, size.

**denote** verb indicate, be a mark of, signify, signal, designate, symbolize, represent.

**denounce** verb **1** *the pope denounced his critics:* condemn, attack, censure, decry, stigmatize, deprecate, disparage, revile, damn. **2** *he was denounced as a traitor:* expose, betray, inform on, incriminate, implicate, cite, accuse.
OPPOSITES praise.

**dense** adjective **1** *a dense forest:* thick, crowded, compact, solid, tight, overgrown, impenetrable, impassable. **2** *dense smoke:* thick, heavy, opaque, murky. **3** (informal) *they were dense enough to believe me:* stupid, brainless, foolish, slow, simple-minded, empty-headed, idiotic; informal thick, dim; Brit. informal daft.
OPPOSITES sparse, thin, clever.

**dent** noun *a dent in his car:* knock, indentation, dint, depression, hollow, crater, pit; N. Amer. informal ding.
verb *Jamie dented his car:* knock, dint, mark; N. Amer. informal ding.

**deny** verb **1** *the report was denied by witnesses:* contradict, rebut, repudiate, refute, challenge, contest. **2** *he denied the request:* refuse, turn down, reject, rebuff, decline, veto,

dismiss; informal give the thumbs down to.
OPPOSITES confirm, allow, accept.

**depart** verb **1** *James departed after lunch:* leave, go away, withdraw, absent oneself, quit, exit, decamp, retreat, retire, make off; informal make tracks, take off, split; Brit. informal sling one's hook. **2** *the budget departed from the norm:* deviate, diverge, digress, stray, veer, differ, vary.
OPPOSITES arrive, stick to.

**department** noun division, section, sector, unit, branch, wing, office, bureau, agency, ministry.

**departure** noun **1** *he tried to delay her departure:* leaving, going, leave-taking, withdrawal, exit. **2** *a departure from normality:* deviation, divergence, digression, shift, variation. **3** *an exciting departure for film-makers:* change, innovation, novelty.

**depend** verb **1** *her career depends on this reference:* be dependent on, hinge on, hang on, rest on, rely on. **2** *my family depends on me:* rely on, lean on, count on, bank on, trust (in), pin one's hopes on.

**dependent** adjective **1** *she is dependent on drugs:* addicted, reliant; informal hooked. **2** *he is ill and dependent:* reliant, needy, helpless, infirm, invalid, incapable, debilitated, disabled.
OPPOSITES independent.
■ **dependent on 1** conditional on, contingent on, based on, subject to, determined by, influenced by. **2** reliant on, relying on, counting on, sustained by.

**depict** verb **1** *the painting depicts the Last Supper:*

portray, show, represent, picture, illustrate, reproduce, render. **2** *the process depicted by Darwin's theory*: describe, detail, relate, present, set forth, set out, outline.

**deplete** verb reduce, decrease, diminish, exhaust, use up, consume, expend, drain, empty.
OPPOSITES augment.

**deplore** verb **1** *we deplore violence*: abhor, find unacceptable, frown on, disapprove of, take a dim view of, take exception to, condemn, denounce. **2** *he deplored their lack of flair*: regret, lament, mourn, bemoan, bewail, complain about, grieve over, sigh over.
OPPOSITES applaud, rejoice at.

**deploy** verb **1** *forces were deployed at strategic points*: position, station, post, place, install, locate, base. **2** *she deployed all her skills*: use, utilize, employ, take advantage of, exploit, call on.

**deport** verb expel, banish, extradite, repatriate.
OPPOSITES admit.

**depose** verb overthrow, unseat, dethrone, topple, remove, supplant, displace, oust.

**deposit** noun **1** *a thick deposit of ash*: layer, covering, coating, blanket, accumulation, sediment. **2** *a copper deposit*: seam, vein, lode, layer, stratum, bed. **3** *they paid a deposit*: down payment, advance payment, prepayment, instalment, retainer, security.
verb **1** *she deposited her books on the table*: put down, place, set down, unload, rest, drop; informal dump, park, plonk; N. Amer. informal plunk. **2** *the silt deposited by flood water*: leave

(behind), precipitate, dump, wash up, cast up. **3** *the gold was deposited at the bank*: lodge, bank, house, store, stow.

**depot** noun **1** *the bus depot*: terminal, terminus, station, garage, headquarters, base. **2** *an arms depot*: storehouse, warehouse, store, repository, depository, cache, arsenal, armoury, dump.

**depress** verb **1** *the news depressed him*: sadden, dispirit, cast down, get down, dishearten, demoralize, crush, weigh down on. **2** *new economic policies depressed sales*: slow down, weaken, impair, inhibit, restrict. **3** *imports will depress farm prices*: reduce, lower, cut, cheapen, discount, deflate, diminish, depreciate, devalue. **4** *depress each key in turn*: press, push, hold down, tap.
OPPOSITES cheer, boost, raise, lift.

**depressed** adjective **1** *he felt lonely and depressed*: sad, unhappy, miserable, gloomy, dejected, downhearted, downcast, down, despondent, dispirited, low, morose, dismal, desolate; informal blue, down in the dumps, down in the mouth. **2** *a depressed economy*: weak, inactive, flat, slow, slack, sluggish, stagnant. **3** *a depressed area*: poverty-stricken, poor, disadvantaged, deprived, needy, distressed, run down.
OPPOSITES cheerful, strong, prosperous.

**depressing** adjective dismal, sad, unhappy, sombre, gloomy, grave, bleak, black, melancholy, dreary, grim, cheerless.

**depression** noun **1** *she ate to*

a b c **d** e f g h i j k l m n o p q r s t u v w x y z

*ease her depression:*
unhappiness, sadness,
melancholy, melancholia,
misery, sorrow, gloom,
despondency, low spirits. **2** *an
economic depression:* recession,
slump, decline, downturn. **3** *a
depression in the ground:*
hollow, indentation, dent,
cavity, dip, pit, crater, basin,
bowl.

**deprivation** noun
**1** *unemployment and
deprivation:* poverty,
impoverishment, privation,
hardship, destitution, need,
want. **2** *deprivation of political
rights:* dispossession,
withholding, withdrawal,
removal, seizure.
OPPOSITES prosperity, granting.

**deprive** verb dispossess, strip,
divest, relieve, rob, cheat out
of.

**deprived** adjective
disadvantaged,
underprivileged, poverty-
stricken, impoverished, poor,
destitute, needy.
OPPOSITES privileged.

**depth** noun **1** *the depth of the
caves:* deepness, drop, height.
**2** *the depth of his knowledge:*
extent, range, scope, breadth,
width. **3** *her lack of depth:*
profundity, wisdom,
understanding, intelligence,
discernment, penetration,
insight, awareness. **4** *depth of
colour:* intensity, richness,
vividness, strength, brilliance.
OPPOSITES triviality.

**deputy** noun second in
command, number two,
assistant, aide, proxy, stand-in,
replacement, substitute,
representative, reserve.

**derelict** adjective *a derelict
building:* dilapidated,

ramshackle, run down,
tumbledown, in ruins, falling
down, disused, abandoned,
deserted.
noun *the derelicts who survive
on the streets:* tramp, vagrant,
down and out, homeless
person, drifter, beggar, outcast;
informal dosser, bag lady.

**derision** noun mockery,
ridicule, jeers, sneers, taunts,
disdain, disparagement,
denigration, insults.

**derogatory** adjective
disparaging, disrespectful,
demeaning, critical, pejorative,
negative, unfavourable,
uncomplimentary, unflattering,
insulting, defamatory,
slanderous, libellous.
OPPOSITES complimentary.

**descend** verb **1** *the plane started
descending:* go down, come
down, drop, fall, sink, dive,
plummet, plunge, nosedive.
**2** *she descended the stairs:*
climb down, go down, come
down, shin down, slide down.
**3** *the road descends to a village:*
slope, dip, slant, go down, fall
away. **4** *she saw Leo descend
from the bus:* alight, disembark,
get down, get off, dismount.
OPPOSITES climb, board.
■ **descend on** flock to, besiege,
surround, take over, invade,
swoop on, occupy.

**descent** noun **1** *the plane began
its descent:* dive, drop, fall,
plunge, nosedive. **2** *a steep
descent:* slope, incline, dip,
drop, gradient. **3** *his descent
into alcoholism:* decline, slide,
fall, degeneration,
deterioration. **4** *she is of Italian
descent:* ancestry, parentage,
ancestors, family, extraction,
origin, derivation, birth,

lineage, stock, blood, roots, origins.

**describe** verb **1** *he described his experiences:* report, recount, relate, narrate, tell of, set out, detail, give a rundown of. **2** *she described him as a pathetic figure:* portray, depict, paint, define, characterize, call, label, class, brand. **3** *the pen described a circle:* mark out, delineate, outline, trace, draw.

**description** noun **1** *a description of my travels:* account, report, narrative, story, portrayal, portrait, sketch, details. **2** *the description of oil as 'black gold':* designation, labelling, naming, dubbing, characterization, definition, classification, branding. **3** *vehicles of every description:* sort, variety, kind, type.

**desert**[1] verb **1** *his wife deserted him:* abandon, leave, jilt, leave high and dry, leave in the lurch, leave behind, strand, maroon; informal walk/run out on, dump, ditch; literary forsake. **2** *soldiers deserted in droves:* abscond, defect, run away, decamp, flee, turn tail, take French leave; Military go AWOL.

**desert**[2] noun *an African desert:* wasteland, wastes, wilderness, dust bowl.

**deserted** adjective **1** *a deserted wife:* abandoned, jilted, cast aside, neglected, stranded, marooned, forlorn; literary forsaken. **2** *a deserted village:* empty, uninhabited, unoccupied, abandoned, evacuated, desolate, lonely, godforsaken.
OPPOSITES cherished, populous.

**deserve** verb merit, earn, warrant, rate, justify, be worthy of, be entitled to.

**deserved** adjective well earned, merited, warranted, justified, rightful, due, fitting, just, proper.

**deserving** adjective *a deserving cause:* worthy, commendable, praiseworthy, admirable, estimable, creditable.

**design** noun **1** *a design for the offices:* plan, blueprint, drawing, sketch, outline, map, plot, diagram, draft. **2** *a Celtic design:* pattern, motif, device, style, theme, layout.
verb **1** *they designed a new engine:* invent, create, think up, come up with, devise, formulate, conceive; informal dream up. **2** *this paper is designed to provoke discussion:* intend, aim, mean.

**designate** verb **1** *some firms designate a press officer:* appoint, nominate, delegate, select, choose, pick, elect, name, identify, assign. **2** *the rivers are designated 'Sites of Special Scientific Interest':* classify, class, label, tag, name, call, term, dub.

**desirable** adjective **1** *a desirable location:* attractive, sought-after, in demand, popular, enviable; informal to die for, must-have. **2** *it is desirable that they should meet:* advantageous, advisable, wise, sensible, recommended, beneficial, preferable. **3** *a very desirable woman:* (sexually) attractive, beautiful, pretty, appealing, seductive, alluring, irresistible; informal sexy.
OPPOSITES unattractive, unwise, ugly.

**desire** noun **1** *a desire to see the world:* wish, want, aspiration, yearning, longing, craving,

hankering, hunger; informal yen, itch. **2** *his eyes glittered with desire:* lust, passion, sensuality, sexuality, libido, lasciviousness, lechery.
verb *they desired peace:* want, wish for, long for, yearn for, crave, hanker after, be desperate for, be bent on, covet, aspire to.

**desolate** adjective **1** *desolate moorlands:* bleak, stark, bare, dismal, grim, wild, inhospitable, deserted, uninhabited, godforsaken, abandoned, empty, isolated, remote. **2** *she is desolate:* miserable, despondent, depressed, disconsolate, devastated, despairing, inconsolable.
OPPOSITES populous, joyful.

**despair** noun desperation, anguish, unhappiness, despondency, depression, misery, wretchedness, hopelessness.
OPPOSITES hope, joy.
verb lose hope, give up, lose heart, be discouraged, be despondent, be demoralized.

**despatch** verb & noun. See DISPATCH.

**desperate** adjective **1** *a desperate look:* despairing, hopeless, anguished, distressed, wretched, desolate, forlorn, distraught, at one's wits' end, at the end of one's tether. **2** *a desperate attempt to escape:* last-ditch, last-gasp, eleventh-hour, do-or-die, final, frantic, frenzied, wild. **3** *a desperate shortage of teachers:* grave, serious, critical, acute, urgent, pressing, drastic, extreme.

**desperation** noun hopelessness, despair, distress,

anguish, agony, torment, misery.

**despise** verb detest, hate, loathe, abhor, deplore, scorn, disdain, deride, sneer at, revile, spurn, shun.
OPPOSITES adore, respect.

**despite** preposition in spite of, notwithstanding, regardless of, in the face of, in the teeth of, undeterred by, for all, even with.

**destined** adjective **1** *he is destined to lead a troubled life:* fated, ordained, predestined, doomed, meant, intended. **2** *computers destined for Pakistan:* heading, bound, en route, scheduled, headed.

**destiny** noun **1** *master of his own destiny:* future, fate, fortune, doom, lot. **2** *she was sent by destiny:* fate, providence, God, the stars, luck, fortune, chance, karma.

**destroy** verb **1** *their offices were destroyed by bombing:* demolish, knock down, level, raze to the ground, fell, blow up. **2** *traffic would destroy the conservation area:* spoil, ruin, wreck, blight, devastate, wreak havoc on. **3** *the horse had to be destroyed:* kill, put down, put to sleep, slaughter, cull. **4** *we had to destroy the enemy:* annihilate, wipe out, obliterate, eliminate, eradicate, liquidate, exterminate; informal take out; N. Amer. informal waste.
OPPOSITES build, preserve, spare.

**destruction** noun **1** *the destruction caused by allied bombers:* devastation, carnage, ruin, chaos, wreckage. **2** *the destruction of the countryside:* wrecking, ruining, annihilation, obliteration, elimination, eradication, devastation. **3** *the destruction of cattle:* killing, slaughter, putting down, extermination, culling.

OPPOSITES preservation.

**destructive** adjective
devastating, ruinous, damaging, harmful, detrimental, injurious, hurtful, deleterious.

**detach** verb disconnect, separate, unfasten, disengage, uncouple, isolate, remove, loose, unhitch, unhook, free, pull off, cut off, break off, split off, sever.

OPPOSITES attach, join.

**detached** adjective **1** *a detached collar:* disconnected, separated, separate, unfastened, disengaged, uncoupled, isolated, loosened, unhitched, unhooked, free, severed, cut off. **2** *a detached observer:* dispassionate, disinterested, objective, outside, neutral, unbiased, impartial.

**detachment** noun **1** *she looked on with detachment:* objectivity, dispassion, disinterest, neutrality, impartiality. **2** *a detachment of soldiers:* unit, squad, detail, troop, contingent, task force, party, platoon.

**detail** noun **1** *the picture is correct in every detail:* particular, respect, feature, characteristic, specific, aspect, fact, point, element. **2** *that's just a detail:* triviality, technicality, nicety, fine point. **3** *a guard detail:* unit, detachment, squad, troop, contingent, outfit, task force, party, platoon.
verb *the report details our objections:* describe, relate, catalogue, list, spell out, itemize, identify, specify.

**detailed** adjective
comprehensive, full, complete, thorough, exhaustive, all-inclusive, elaborate, minute, precise, itemized, blow-by-blow.

OPPOSITES general.

**detain** verb **1** *they were detained for questioning:* hold, take into custody, confine, imprison, intern, arrest, apprehend, seize; informal pick up; Brit. informal nick. **2** *don't let me detain you:* delay, hold up, make late, keep, slow up/down, hinder.

OPPOSITES release.

**detect** verb **1** *I detected a note of urgency in her voice:* notice, perceive, discern, become aware of, note, make out, spot, recognize, identify, catch, sense. **2** *they are responsible for detecting fraud:* discover, uncover, turn up, unearth, dig up, root out, expose. **3** *the hackers were detected:* catch, hunt down, track down, find out, expose, reveal, unmask, smoke out.

**detective** noun investigator, police officer; informal private eye, sleuth; N. Amer. informal gumshoe.

**detention** noun custody, imprisonment, incarceration, internment, captivity, remand, arrest, quarantine.

OPPOSITES release.

**deter** verb **1** *the high cost deterred many:* discourage, dissuade, put off, scare off, dishearten, demoralize, daunt, intimidate. **2** *the presence of a caretaker deters crime:* prevent, stop, avert, stave off, ward off.

OPPOSITES encourage.

**deteriorate** verb worsen, decline, degenerate, fail, go downhill, wane.

OPPOSITES improve.

**determination** noun
resolution, resolve, will power,
strength of character,
dedication, single-mindedness,
perseverance, persistence,
tenacity, staying power,
doggedness; informal guts.

**determine** verb 1 *chromosomes
determine the sex of the embryo:*
control, decide, regulate,
direct, dictate, govern. 2 *he
determined to sell up:* resolve,
decide, make up one's mind,
choose, elect, opt. 3 *the rent
shall be determined by an
accountant:* specify, set, fix,
decide on, settle, establish,
ordain, prescribe, decree.
4 *determine the composition of
the fibres:* ascertain, find out,
discover, learn, establish,
calculate, work out; informal
figure out.

**determined** adjective resolute,
purposeful, adamant, single-
minded, unswerving,
unwavering, persevering,
persistent, tenacious,
dedicated, dogged.
OPPOSITES irresolute.

**deterrent** noun disincentive,
discouragement, damper, curb,
check, restraint, inhibition.
OPPOSITES incentive.

**detest** verb hate, abhor, loathe,
regard with disgust, be unable
to bear, have an aversion to,
find intolerable, disdain,
despise.
OPPOSITES love.

**devastate** verb 1 *the city was
devastated by an earthquake:*
destroy, ruin, wreck, lay waste,
ravage, demolish, raze to the
ground, level, flatten. 2 *he was
devastated by the news:* shatter,
shock, stun, daze, dumbfound,
traumatize, distress; informal
knock sideways; Brit. informal
knock for six.

**devastation** noun destruction,
ruin, desolation, wreckage,
ruins.

**develop** verb 1 *the industry
developed rapidly:* grow,
expand, spread, advance,
progress, evolve, mature. 2 *a
plan was developed:* initiate,
instigate, set in motion,
originate, invent, form.
3 *children should develop their
talents:* expand, augment,
broaden, supplement, reinforce,
enhance, refine, improve,
polish, perfect. 4 *a row
developed:* start, begin, emerge,
erupt, break out, arise, break,
unfold.
OPPOSITES shrink, regress.

**development** noun 1 *the
development of the firm:*
evolution, growth, expansion,
enlargement, spread, progress.
2 *there have been a number of
developments:* event, change,
circumstance, incident,
occurrence. 3 *a housing
development:* estate, complex,
site.

**deviate** verb diverge, digress,
drift, stray, veer, swerve, get
sidetracked, branch off, differ,
vary.

**device** noun 1 *a device for
measuring pressure:*
implement, gadget, utensil,
tool, appliance, apparatus,
instrument, machine,
mechanism, contrivance,
contraption; informal gizmo. 2 *an
ingenious legal device:* ploy,
tactic, move, stratagem,
scheme, plot, trick, ruse,
manoeuvre.

**devil** noun 1 *God and the Devil:*
Satan, Beelzebub, Lucifer, the
Prince of Darkness; informal Old

Nick. **2** *they drove out the devils:* evil spirit, demon, fiend. **3** *he was a devil:* brute, beast, monster, fiend, villain, sadist, barbarian, ogre.

**devious** adjective **1** *the devious ways in which they bent the rules:* underhand, dishonest, crafty, cunning, conniving, scheming, sneaky, furtive; informal crooked, shady; Brit. informal dodgy. **2** *a devious route:* circuitous, roundabout, indirect, meandering, tortuous. OPPOSITES open, honest, direct.

**devise** verb conceive, think up, dream up, work out, formulate, concoct, hatch, contrive, design, invent, coin; informal cook up.

**devoid**
■ **devoid of** empty of, free of, bereft of, lacking, deficient in, without, wanting in; informal minus.

**devote** verb dedicate, allocate, assign, allot, commit, give (over), consign, pledge, set aside, earmark, reserve.

**devoted** adjective dedicated, committed, devout, loyal, faithful, true, staunch, steadfast, fond, loving.

**devotee** noun enthusiast, fan, lover, aficionado, admirer, supporter, disciple; informal buff, freak, nut, fanatic.

**devotion** noun **1** *wifely devotion:* loyalty, fidelity, commitment, allegiance, dedication, fondness, love, care. **2** *a life of devotion:* piety, spirituality, godliness, holiness, sanctity.

**devour** verb **1** *he devoured his meal:* gobble, guzzle, gulp down, bolt, wolf; informal polish off; Brit. informal scoff. **2** *flames devoured the house:* consume, engulf, envelop.

**devout** adjective dedicated, devoted, committed, loyal, sincere, fervent, pious, reverent, God-fearing, dutiful, churchgoing.

**diagnose** verb identify, determine, distinguish, recognize, interpret, detect, pinpoint.

**diagnosis** noun **1** *the diagnosis of coeliac disease:* identification, detection, recognition, determination, discovery, pinpointing. **2** *the results confirmed his diagnosis:* opinion, judgement, verdict, conclusion.

**diagonal** adjective crosswise, crossways, slanting, slanted, oblique, angled, cornerways, cornerwise.

**diagram** noun drawing, representation, plan, outline, figure, chart, graph.

**dialogue** noun conversation, talk, discussion, chat, tête-à-tête, exchange, debate, conference, consultation; informal confab.

**diary** noun **1** *he put the date in his diary:* appointment book, engagement book, personal organizer; trademark Filofax. **2** *her World War II diaries:* journal, memoir, chronicle, log, logbook, history, annal, record; N. Amer. daybook.

**dictate** verb **1** *his attempts to dictate policy:* prescribe, lay down, impose, set down, order, command, decree, ordain, direct. **2** *choice is often dictated by availability:* determine, control, govern, decide, influence, affect.
■ **dictate to** give orders to, order about/around, lord it over; informal boss about/around, push about/around.

a
b
c
**d**
e
f
g
h
i
j
k
l
m
n
o
p
q
r
s
t
u
v
w
x
y
z

**dictator** noun autocrat, despot, tyrant, absolute ruler.
OPPOSITES democrat.

**dictatorial** adjective domineering, autocratic, authoritarian, oppressive, imperious, overweening, overbearing, peremptory; informal bossy, high-handed.

**dictionary** noun lexicon, glossary, vocabulary.

**die** verb 1 *her father died last year:* pass away, pass on, perish; informal give up the ghost, kick the bucket, croak; Brit. informal snuff it, peg out; N. Amer. informal buy the farm. 2 *the wind had died:* lessen, subside, drop, ease (off), let up, moderate, abate, fade, peter out, wane, ebb. 3 (informal) *the engine died:* fail, cut out, give out, break down, stop; informal conk out, go kaput; Brit. informal pack up.
OPPOSITES live, intensify.

**diet** noun 1 *a healthy diet:* food, nutrition, eating habits. 2 *she's on a diet:* dietary regime, regimen, restricted diet, fast, abstinence.
OPPOSITES binge.
verb *I began dieting again:* be on a diet, slim, lose weight, watch one's weight; N. Amer. reduce; N. Amer. informal slenderize.
OPPOSITES binge.

**differ** verb 1 *the second set of data differed from the first:* contrast with, be different to, vary from, deviate from, conflict with, run counter to, be at odds with, contradict. 2 *the two sides differed over this issue:* disagree, conflict, be at variance/odds, be in dispute, not see eye to eye.
OPPOSITES resemble, agree.

**difference** noun 1 *the difference*

between the two sets of data: dissimilarity, contrast, distinction, differentiation, variance, variation, divergence, disparity, contradiction. 2 *we've had our differences:* disagreement, difference of opinion, dispute, argument, quarrel; Brit. informal row. 3 *I'll pay the difference:* balance, remainder, rest.
OPPOSITES similarity.

**different** adjective 1 *people with different lifestyles:* dissimilar, unlike, contrasting, differing, varying, disparate, poles apart, incompatible, mismatched; informal like chalk and cheese. 2 *suddenly everything in her life was different:* changed, altered, transformed, new, unfamiliar, unknown, strange. 3 *two different occasions:* distinct, separate, individual, independent. 4 (informal) *try something different:* unusual, out of the ordinary, unfamiliar, novel, new, fresh, original, unconventional, exotic.
OPPOSITES similar, normal, related, ordinary.

**difficult** adjective 1 *a very difficult job:* laborious, strenuous, arduous, hard, tough, demanding, punishing, gruelling, back-breaking, exhausting, tiring; informal hellish, killing, no picnic. 2 *a difficult problem:* hard, complicated, beyond one, puzzling, baffling, problematic, thorny, ticklish. 3 *a difficult child:* troublesome, tiresome, trying, exasperating, awkward, demanding, contrary, uncooperative, fussy.
OPPOSITES easy, simple, cooperative, accommodating.

**difficulty** noun 1 *the difficulty*

*of balancing motherhood with a career:* **strain, trouble, problems, struggle, laboriousness, arduousness;** informal **hassle, stress. 2** *practical difficulties:* **problem, complication, snag, hitch, obstacle, hurdle, stumbling block;** Brit. **spanner in the works;** informal **headache. 3** *Charles got into difficulties:* **trouble, predicament, plight, hard times.**
OPPOSITES **ease.**

**dig** verb **1** *she began to dig the soil:* **turn over, work, break up. 2** *he dug a hole:* **excavate, dig out, quarry, hollow out, scoop out, bore, burrow, mine. 3** *Winnie dug her elbow into his ribs:* **poke, prod, jab, stab, shove, ram, push, thrust, drive, stick. 4** *he'd been digging into my past:* **delve, probe, search, enquire, look, investigate, research.**
noun **1** *a dig in the ribs:* **poke, prod, jab, stab, shove, push. 2** (informal) *they're always making digs at each other:* **snide remark, cutting remark, jibe, taunt, sneer, insult;** informal **wisecrack, put-down.**
■ **dig something up** exhume, disinter, unearth.

**digest** verb *Liz digested this information:* **assimilate, absorb, take in, understand, comprehend, grasp.**
noun *a digest of their findings:* **summary, synopsis, abstract, precis, résumé, summation.**

**dignified** adjective **stately, noble, majestic, distinguished, regal, imposing, impressive, grand, solemn, formal, ceremonious, decorous, sedate.**

**dignity** noun **1** *the dignity of the Crown:* **stateliness, nobility,** majesty, impressiveness, grandeur, magnificence, ceremoniousness, formality, decorum, propriety, respectability, worthiness, integrity, solemnity, gravitas. **2** *little regard for human dignity:* **self-respect, pride, self-esteem, self-worth.**
OPPOSITES **informality.**

**dilemma** noun **quandary, predicament, catch-22, vicious circle, plight, conflict;** informal **fix, tight spot/corner; (in a dilemma) between the devil and the deep blue sea, between a rock and a hard place.**

**dilute** verb **1** *strong bleach can be diluted with water:* **make weaker, water down, thin, doctor, adulterate;** informal **cut. 2** *the original plans have been diluted:* **weaken, moderate, tone down, water down, compromise.**
OPPOSITES **concentrate, beef up.**

**dim** adjective **1** *the dim light:* **faint, weak, feeble, soft, pale, dull, subdued, muted. 2** *long dim corridors:* **dark, badly lit, dingy, dismal, gloomy, murky. 3** *a dim figure:* **indistinct, ill-defined, vague, shadowy, nebulous, blurred, fuzzy. 4** *dim memories:* **vague, imprecise, imperfect, unclear, indistinct, sketchy, hazy. 5** (informal) *I'm awfully dim.* See **STUPID.**
OPPOSITES **bright, distinct, clear.**
verb **1** *the lights were dimmed:* **turn down, lower, soften, subdue. 2** *memories have dimmed:* **fade, dwindle, dull.**
OPPOSITES **brighten.**

**dimension** noun **1** *the dimensions of the room:* **size, measurements, proportions, extent, length, width, breadth, depth. 2** *the cultural*

a b c **d** e f g h i j k l m n o p q r s t u v w x y z

*dimensions of the problem:* aspect, feature, element, angle, facet, side.

**diminish** verb **1** *the pain will gradually diminish:* decrease, lessen, decline, reduce, subside, dwindle, fade, slacken off, let up. **2** *new legislation diminished the courts' authority:* reduce, decrease, lessen, curtail, cut, limit, curb.
OPPOSITES increase.

**din** noun noise, racket, rumpus, cacophony, hubbub, uproar, commotion, clangour, clatter, clamour; informal hullabaloo; Brit. informal row.
OPPOSITES silence.

**dine** verb eat, have dinner, have lunch; dated sup.

**dinner** noun main meal, lunch, evening meal, supper, feast, banquet; Brit. tea.

**dip** verb **1** *he dipped a rag in the water:* immerse, submerge, plunge, dunk, bathe, sink. **2** *the sun dipped below the horizon:* sink, set, drop, fall, descend. **3** *the president's popularity has dipped:* decrease, fall, drop, fall off, decline, diminish, dwindle, slump, plummet, plunge. **4** *the road dipped:* slope down, descend, go down, drop (away), fall away.
OPPOSITES rise, increase.
noun **1** *a dip in the pool:* swim, bathe, paddle. **2** *the hedge at the bottom of the dip:* slope, incline, decline, descent, hollow, depression, basin. **3** *a dip in sales:* decrease, fall, drop, downturn, decline, falling-off, slump, reduction.
■ **dip into 1** draw on, use, spend. **2** browse through, skim through, look through, flick through.

**diplomacy** noun **1** *diplomacy failed to win them independence:* statesmanship, statecraft, negotiation(s), discussion(s), talks. **2** *Jack's quiet diplomacy:* tact, tactfulness, sensitivity, discretion.

**diplomat** noun ambassador, attaché, consul, chargé d'affaires, envoy, emissary.

**diplomatic** adjective tactful, sensitive, subtle, delicate, polite, discreet, judicious, politic.
OPPOSITES tactless.

**dire** adjective terrible, dreadful, appalling, frightful, awful, grim, sore, alarming, acute, grave, serious, urgent, pressing, wretched, desperate, parlous.

**direct** adjective **1** *the most direct route:* straight, short, quick. **2** *a direct flight:* non-stop, through, unbroken, uninterrupted. **3** *he is very direct:* frank, candid, straightforward, open, blunt, plain-spoken, outspoken, forthright, no-nonsense, matter-of-fact; informal upfront.
verb **1** *an economic elite directed the nation's affairs:* manage, govern, run, administer, control, conduct, handle, be in charge of, preside over, lead, head, rule. **2** *was that remark directed at me?* aim, target, address to, intend for, mean for, design for. **3** *a man in uniform directed them to the hall:* give directions, show the way, point someone in the direction of. **4** *the judge directed the jury to return a not guilty verdict:* instruct, tell, command, order, require.

**direction** noun **1** *a northerly direction:* way, route, course, line, bearing, orientation. **2** *his direction of the project:*

running, management, administration, conduct, handling, supervision, superintendence, command, rule, leadership. **3** *explicit directions about nursing care:* instruction, order, command, rule, regulation, requirement.

**directive** noun instruction, direction, command, order, injunction, decree, dictum, edict.

**directly** adverb **1** *they flew directly to New York:* straight, as the crow flies. **2** *directly after breakfast:* immediately, right (away), straight (away), without delay, promptly. **3** *the houses directly opposite:* exactly, right, immediately, diametrically; informal bang. **4** *she spoke simply and directly:* frankly, candidly, openly, bluntly, forthrightly, without beating around the bush.

**director** noun manager, head, chief, principal, leader, governor, president, chair, chief executive; informal boss, gaffer.

**dirt** noun **1** *his face was streaked with dirt:* grime, filth, muck, dust, mud; Brit. informal gunge. **2** *a dirt road:* earth, soil, clay, ground.

**dirty** adjective **1** *a dirty sweatshirt | dirty water:* soiled, grimy, grubby, filthy, mucky, stained, unwashed, greasy, muddy, dusty, polluted, contaminated, foul, unhygienic; Brit. informal manky, grotty. **2** *a dirty joke:* obscene, indecent, rude, naughty, vulgar, smutty, coarse, crude, filthy, off colour, pornographic, explicit, X-rated; informal blue; euphemistic adult. **3** *a dirty look:* malevolent, hostile, black, angry, disapproving. OPPOSITES clean, friendly.

verb *the dog had dirtied her dress:* soil, stain, muddy, blacken, mess (up), mark, spatter, smudge, smear, splatter, sully, pollute, foul. OPPOSITES clean.

**disability** noun handicap, incapacity, impairment, infirmity, defect, abnormality, condition, disorder, affliction.

**disable** verb **1** *an injury that could disable somebody for life:* incapacitate, put out of action, debilitate, handicap, cripple, lame, maim, immobilize, paralyse. **2** *the bomb squad disabled the device:* deactivate, defuse, disarm, make safe.

**disabled** adjective handicapped, incapacitated, infirm, crippled, lame, paralysed, immobilized, bedridden; euphemistic physically challenged, differently abled. OPPOSITES able-bodied.

**disadvantage** noun **1** *that's the disadvantage of this scheme:* drawback, snag, downside, fly in the ointment, catch, nuisance, handicap, trouble, informal minus. **2** *she did nothing to his disadvantage:* detriment, prejudice, harm, loss, hurt. OPPOSITES advantage.

**disagree** verb **1** *no one disagreed with him:* be of a different opinion, not see eye to eye, take issue, challenge, contradict, differ, dissent, be in dispute, clash. **2** *their accounts disagree:* differ, be dissimilar, be different, be at variance/odds, vary, contradict each other, conflict. **3** *the spicy food disagreed with her:* make ill, make unwell, sicken, upset. OPPOSITES agree.

**disagreement** noun dissent, difference of opinion, controversy, discord, division,

dispute, quarrel.
OPPOSITES agreement.

**disappear** verb 1 *the mist had disappeared:* vanish, be lost to view/sight, recede, fade away, melt away, clear. 2 *this way of life has disappeared:* die out, cease to exist, end, go, pass away, pass into oblivion, perish, vanish.
OPPOSITES materialize, arise.

**disappoint** verb let down, fail, dissatisfy, upset, dismay, sadden, disenchant, disillusion, shatter someone's illusions.
OPPOSITES delight.

**disappointed** adjective upset, saddened, let down, displeased, dissatisfied, disheartened, downhearted, discouraged, crestfallen, disenchanted, disillusioned; informal choked, cut up; Brit. informal gutted, as sick as a parrot.
OPPOSITES delighted.

**disappointment** noun 1 *she tried to hide her disappointment:* sadness, sorrow, regret, dismay, displeasure, dissatisfaction, disenchantment, disillusionment. 2 *the trip was a disappointment:* let-down, non-event, anticlimax; Brit. damp squib; informal washout.
OPPOSITES delight, pleasant surprise.

**disapproval** noun disfavour, objection, dislike, dissatisfaction, distaste, displeasure, criticism, censure, condemnation, denunciation.
OPPOSITES approval.

**disapprove**
■ disapprove of object to, have a poor opinion of, take exception to, dislike, take a dim view of, look askance at, frown on, be against, not believe in, deplore,

censure, condemn, denounce.

**disarm** verb 1 *the militia refused to disarm:* lay down one's arms, demobilize, disband, demilitarize. 2 *police disarmed the bomb:* defuse, disable, deactivate, make safe. 3 *the warmth in his voice disarmed her:* win over, charm, persuade, soothe, mollify, appease, placate.
OPPOSITES arm, antagonize.

**disarmament** noun demilitarization, demobilization, disbandment, decommissioning, arms reduction, arms limitation.
OPPOSITES arming.

**disarming** adjective winning, charming, irresistible, persuasive, soothing, conciliatory, mollifying.
OPPOSITES infuriating.

**disarray** noun disorder, confusion, chaos, untidiness, disorganization, a mess, a muddle, a shambles.
OPPOSITES tidiness.

**disaster** noun 1 *a railway disaster:* catastrophe, calamity, cataclysm, tragedy, act of God, accident. 2 *a string of personal disasters:* misfortune, mishap, misadventure, setback, reversal, stroke of bad luck, blow. 3 (informal) *the film was a disaster:* failure, fiasco, catastrophe; informal flop, washout, dead loss.
OPPOSITES success.

**disastrous** adjective catastrophic, calamitous, cataclysmic, tragic, devastating, ruinous, terrible, awful.

**disbelief** noun incredulity, incredulousness, scepticism, doubt, cynicism, suspicion, distrust, mistrust.
OPPOSITES belief.

**discard** verb dispose of, throw away/out, get rid of, toss out, jettison, dispense with, scrap, reject, drop; informal ditch, bin, junk; Brit. informal get shot of; N. Amer. informal trash.
OPPOSITES keep.

**discharge** verb 1 *he was discharged from service:* dismiss, eject, expel, throw out, make redundant, release, let go; Military cashier; informal sack, fire. 2 *he was discharged from prison:* release, free, let out. 3 *oil is routinely discharged from ships:* release, eject, let out, pour out, give off, dump. 4 *he accidentally discharged a pistol:* fire, shoot, let off, set off, loose off, trigger, launch. 5 *the ferry was discharging passengers:* unload, offload, put off, remove. 6 *they discharged their duties efficiently:* carry out, perform, execute, conduct, fulfil, complete.
OPPOSITES recruit, imprison, take on.
noun 1 *his discharge from the service:* dismissal, release, removal, ejection, expulsion; Military cashiering; informal the sack, the boot. 2 *her discharge from prison:* release. 3 *a discharge of diesel oil into the river:* leak, leakage, emission, release, outflow. 4 *a watery discharge from the eyes:* emission, secretion, excretion, suppuration, pus. 5 *the discharge of their duties:* carrying out, performance, execution, conduct, fulfilment, accomplishment, completion.

**disciple** noun follower, adherent, believer, admirer, devotee, acolyte, apostle, supporter, advocate.

**discipline** noun 1 *parental discipline:* control, regulation, direction, order, authority, strictness. 2 *he maintained discipline among his men:* good behaviour, order, control, obedience. 3 *sociology is a fairly new discipline:* field (of study), branch of knowledge, subject, area, speciality.
verb 1 *she had disciplined herself to ignore the pain:* train, drill, teach, school, coach. 2 *he was disciplined by the management:* punish, penalize, bring to book, reprimand, rebuke; Brit. informal carpet.

**disclose** verb 1 *the information must not be disclosed:* reveal, make known, divulge, tell, impart, communicate, pass on, release, make public, broadcast, publish. 2 *surgery disclosed a growth:* uncover, reveal, show, bring to light.
OPPOSITES keep secret, conceal.

**discomfort** noun 1 *discomfort caused by indigestion:* pain, aches and pains, soreness, aching, twinge, pang, throb, cramp. 2 *the discomforts of life at sea:* inconvenience, difficulty, problem, trial, tribulation, hardship. 3 *Thomas noticed her discomfort:* embarrassment, discomfiture, unease, awkwardness, discomposure, confusion, nervousness, distress, anxiety.

**discontent** noun dissatisfaction, disaffection, grievances, unhappiness, displeasure, resentment, envy, restlessness, unrest, unease.
OPPOSITES satisfaction.

**discontented** adjective dissatisfied, disgruntled, disaffected, unhappy, aggrieved, displeased, resentful, envious, restless,

frustrated; informal fed up.
OPPOSITES satisfied.

**discount** noun *a 10 per cent discount:* reduction, deduction, markdown, price cut, concession, rebate.
verb 1 *I discounted the rumours:* disregard, pay no attention to, take no notice of, dismiss, ignore, overlook; informal pooh-pooh. 2 *the price is heavily discounted:* reduce, mark down, cut, lower; informal knock down.
OPPOSITES believe, increase.

**discourage** verb 1 *we want to discourage children from smoking:* dissuade, deter, put off, talk out of. 2 *she was discouraged by his hostile tone:* dishearten, dispirit, demoralize, disappoint, put off, unnerve, daunt, intimidate. 3 *he sought to discourage further speculation:* prevent, deter, stop, avert, inhibit, curb.
OPPOSITES encourage.

**discover** verb 1 *firemen discovered a body:* find, locate, come across/upon, stumble on, chance on, uncover, unearth, turn up. 2 *I discovered the truth:* find out, learn, realize, ascertain, work out, recognize; informal figure out; Brit. informal twig.

**discovery** noun 1 *the discovery of the body:* finding, location, uncovering, unearthing. 2 *the discovery that she was pregnant:* realization, recognition, revelation, disclosure. 3 *he failed to take out a patent on his discoveries:* find, finding, breakthrough, innovation.

**discredit** verb 1 *an attempt to discredit him:* bring into disrepute, disgrace, dishonour, blacken the name of, put/show in a bad light, compromise, smear, tarnish; N. Amer. slur. 2 *that theory has been discredited:* disprove, invalidate, explode, refute; informal debunk.
OPPOSITES honour, prove.
noun *to his discredit:* dishonour, disgrace, shame, humiliation, ignominy.
OPPOSITES honour, glory.

**discreet** adjective tactful, circumspect, diplomatic, judicious, sensitive, careful, cautious, strategic.

**discrepancy** noun difference, disparity, variation, deviation, divergence, disagreement, inconsistency, mismatch, conflict.
OPPOSITES correspondence.

**discretion** noun 1 *you can rely on his discretion:* tact, diplomacy, delicacy, sensitivity, good sense, prudence, circumspection. 2 *at the discretion of the council:* choice, option, preference, disposition, pleasure, will, inclination.
OPPOSITES tactlessness.

**discriminate** verb 1 *he cannot discriminate between fact and opinion:* differentiate, distinguish, draw a distinction, tell the difference, tell apart, separate. 2 *policies that discriminate against women:* be biased, be prejudiced, treat differently, treat unfairly, put at a disadvantage, victimize, pick on.

**discriminating** adjective discerning, perceptive, judicious, selective, tasteful, refined, sensitive, cultivated, cultured.
OPPOSITES indiscriminate.

**discrimination** noun 1 *racial discrimination:* prejudice, bias, bigotry, intolerance,

favouritism, partisanship. **2** *a man with no discrimination:* discernment, judgement, perceptiveness, (good) taste, refinement, sensitivity, cultivation.
OPPOSITES impartiality.

**discuss** verb **1** *I discussed the matter with my wife:* talk over, talk about, talk through, debate, confer about. **2** *chapter three discusses this topic:* examine, explore, study, analyse, go into, deal with, consider, tackle.

**discussion** noun **1** *a long discussion with her husband:* conversation, talk, dialogue, conference, debate, exchange of views, consultation, deliberation; informal confab. **2** *see Chapter 7 for a detailed discussion:* examination, exploration, study, analysis, treatment, consideration.

**disdain** noun *she looked at him with disdain:* contempt, scorn, derision, disrespect, condescension, superciliousness, hauteur, haughtiness.
OPPOSITES respect.
verb *she disdained exhibitionism:* scorn, deride, regard with contempt, sneer at, look down one's nose at, look down on, despise.
OPPOSITES value.

**disease** noun illness, sickness, ill health, infection, ailment, malady, disorder, condition, problem; informal bug, virus; Brit. informal lurgy.
OPPOSITES health.

**diseased** adjective unhealthy, ill, sick, unwell, ailing, infected, septic, rotten, bad.

**disgrace** noun **1** *he brought disgrace on the family:* dishonour, shame, discredit, ignominy, disrepute, infamy, scandal, stigma, humiliation, loss of face. **2** *the unemployment figures are a disgrace:* scandal, discredit, reproach, stain, blemish, blot, outrage, affront.
OPPOSITES honour, credit.
verb *you have disgraced the family name:* shame, bring shame on, dishonour, discredit, stigmatize, taint, sully, tarnish, stain, blacken.
OPPOSITES honour.

**disgraceful** adjective shameful, scandalous, contemptible, dishonourable, discreditable, disreputable, reprehensible, blameworthy, unworthy, ignoble.
OPPOSITES admirable.

**disgruntled** adjective dissatisfied, discontented, aggrieved, resentful, displeased, unhappy, disappointed, annoyed; informal hacked off, browned off; Brit. informal cheesed off, narked; N. Amer. informal sore, ticked off.
OPPOSITES contented.

**disguise** verb camouflage, conceal, hide, cover up, mask, screen, veil, paper over.
OPPOSITES expose.

**disgust** noun **1** *the sight filled her with disgust:* revulsion, repugnance, aversion, distaste, abhorrence, loathing, hatred. **2** *the audience walked out in disgust:* disapproval, displeasure, indignation, annoyance, anger, fury, outrage, contempt, resentment.
OPPOSITES delight.
verb **1** *they were disgusted by the violence:* revolt, repel, repulse, sicken, horrify, appal, turn someone's stomach; N. Amer.

a
b
c
**d**
e
f
g
h
i
j
k
l
m
n
o
p
q
r
s
t
u
v
w
x
y
z

informal **gross out. 2** *Toby's behaviour disgusted her:* displease, dissatisfy, arouse the disapproval of, annoy, anger, outrage, scandalize, offend, affront, dismay.
OPPOSITES delight.

**disgusting** adjective **1** *the food was disgusting:* revolting, repulsive, sickening, nauseating, stomach-turning, off-putting; N. Amer. vomitous; informal sick-making. **2** *I find racism disgusting:* outrageous, objectionable, abhorrent, repellent, loathsome, offensive, appalling, shocking, horrifying, scandalous, monstrous, detestable; informal gross, sick.
OPPOSITES delightful.

**dish** noun **1** *a china dish:* bowl, plate, platter, salver, pot. **2** *vegetarian dishes:* recipe, meal, course, fare.
■ **dish something out** distribute, dispense, issue, hand out/round, give out, pass round, deal out, dole out, allocate.

**dishonest** adjective fraudulent, cheating, underhand, devious, treacherous, unfair, dirty, criminal, illegal, unlawful, false, untruthful, deceitful, lying; informal crooked, shady, sharp; Brit. informal bent; Austral./NZ informal shonky.
OPPOSITES honest.

**disintegrate** verb break up, crumble, break apart, fall apart, fall to pieces, collapse, fragment, shatter, splinter.

**disinterested** adjective *disinterested advice:* unbiased, unprejudiced, impartial, neutral, detached, objective, dispassionate.

**dislike** verb *a man she had always disliked:* find distasteful, regard with distaste, be averse to, have an aversion to, hate, disapprove of, object to, take exception to.
OPPOSITES like.
noun *she viewed the other woman with dislike:* distaste, aversion, disfavour, antipathy, disgust, abhorrence, hatred.
OPPOSITES liking.

**dismal** adjective **1** *a dismal look:* gloomy, glum, melancholy, morose, doleful, woebegone, forlorn, dejected, downcast. **2** *dismal weather:* dim, dingy, dark, gloomy, dreary, drab, dull.
OPPOSITES cheerful, bright.

**dismantle** verb take apart, take to pieces/bits, pull to pieces, disassemble, break up, strip (down).
OPPOSITES build.

**dismay** noun *to his dismay:* alarm, distress, concern, surprise, consternation, disquiet.
OPPOSITES pleasure, relief.
verb *he was dismayed by the answer:* concern, distress, disturb, worry, alarm, disconcert, take aback, unnerve, unsettle.
OPPOSITES encourage, please.

**dismiss** verb **1** *the president dismissed five ministers:* give someone their notice, discharge, lay off, make redundant; informal sack, fire. **2** *the guards were dismissed:* send away, let go, release. **3** *don't dismiss the idea so lightly:* reject, deny, repudiate, spurn. **4** *she dismissed the thought:* banish, set aside, put out of one's mind.
OPPOSITES appoint, keep on, entertain, dwell on.

**disobedient** adjective naughty, insubordinate, defiant, unruly, wayward, badly behaved,

delinquent, rebellious, mutinous, troublesome, wilful.
OPPOSITES obedient.

**disobey** verb defy, go against, flout, contravene, infringe, transgress, violate, disregard, ignore, pay no heed to.

**disorder** noun 1 *he hates disorder:* untidiness, mess, disarray, chaos, confusion, clutter, jumble, a muddle, a shambles. 2 *incidents of public disorder:* unrest, disturbance, turmoil, mayhem, violence, fighting, fracas, rioting, lawlessness, anarchy, breach of the peace. 3 *a blood disorder:* disease, infection, complaint, condition, affliction, malady, sickness, illness, ailment.
OPPOSITES order, tidiness, peace.

**disorderly** adjective 1 *a disorderly desk:* untidy, disorganized, messy, cluttered, in disarray; informal like a bomb's hit it, higgledy-piggledy; Brit. informal shambolic. 2 *disorderly behaviour:* unruly, riotous, disruptive, troublesome, lawless.
OPPOSITES tidy, peaceful.

**dispatch** verb 1 *all the messages were dispatched:* send (off), post, mail, forward. 2 *the business was dispatched in the morning:* deal with, finish, conclude, settle, discharge, perform. 3 *the good guy dispatched a host of villains:* kill, put to death, massacre, wipe out, exterminate, eliminate, murder, assassinate, execute.
noun *the latest dispatch from the front:* message, report, communication, communiqué, bulletin, statement, letter, news, intelligence.

**dispel** verb banish, drive away/ off, chase away, scatter, eliminate, dismiss, allay, ease, quell.
OPPOSITES form, give rise to.

**dispense** verb 1 *servants dispensed the drinks:* distribute, pass round, hand out, dole out, dish out, share out. 2 *the soldiers dispensed summary justice:* administer, deliver, issue, deal out, mete out. 3 *dispensing medicines:* prepare, make up, supply, provide.
■ **dispense with** 1 *let's dispense with the formalities:* waive, omit, drop, leave out, forgo, do away with; informal give something a miss. 2 *he dispensed with his crutches:* get rid of, throw away/out, dispose of, discard; informal ditch, scrap, dump, chuck out/away; Brit. informal get shot of.

**disperse** verb 1 *the crowd began to disperse | police dispersed the demonstrators:* break up, split up, disband, scatter, leave, go their separate ways, drive away/off, chase away. 2 *the fog finally dispersed:* dissipate, dissolve, melt away, fade away, clear, lift. 3 *the seeds are dispersed by birds:* scatter, distribute, spread, disseminate.
OPPOSITES assemble, form, gather.

**displace** verb 1 *roof tiles were displaced by gales:* dislodge, dislocate, move out of place/ position, shift. 2 *English displaced the local language:* replace, take the place of, supplant, supersede.
OPPOSITES replace.

**display** verb 1 *the Crown Jewels are displayed in London:* exhibit, show, arrange, array, present, lay out, set out. 2 *the*

a
b
c
**d**
e
f
g
h
i
j
k
l
m
n
o
p
q
r
s
t
u
v
w
x
y
z

play displays his many theatrical talents: show off, parade, highlight, reveal, showcase. **3** *she displayed a vein of sharp humour:* manifest, show evidence of, reveal, demonstrate, show.
OPPOSITES conceal.

noun **1** *a display of dolls:* exhibition, exposition, array, arrangement, presentation, demonstration, spectacle, show, parade. **2** *his display of concern:* manifestation, expression, show, proof, demonstration, evidence.

**displease** verb annoy, irritate, anger, incense, irk, vex, nettle, put out, upset, exasperate.

**dispose**
■ dispose of throw away/out, get rid of, discard, jettison, scrap; informal dump, junk, ditch, chuck (out/away); Brit. informal get shot of; N. Amer. informal trash.

**disposition** noun **1** *a nervous disposition:* temperament, nature, character, constitution, make-up, mentality. **2** *the disposition of the troops:* arrangement, positioning, placement, configuration, set-up, line-up, layout.

**disprove** verb refute, prove false, rebut, debunk, give the lie to, demolish; informal shoot full of holes, blow out of the water.

**dispute** noun **1** *a subject of dispute:* debate, discussion, argument, controversy, disagreement, dissent, conflict. **2** *they have settled their dispute:* quarrel, argument, altercation, squabble, falling-out, disagreement, difference of opinion, clash; Brit. informal row.
OPPOSITES agreement.

verb **1** *George disputed with him:* debate, discuss, exchange views, quarrel, argue, disagree, clash, fall out, wrangle, bicker, squabble. **2** *they disputed his proposals:* challenge, contest, question, call into question, quibble over, contradict, argue about, disagree with, take issue with.
OPPOSITES accept.

**disregard** verb *Annie disregarded the remark:* ignore, take no notice of, pay no attention to, discount, overlook, turn a blind eye to, shut one's eyes to, gloss over, brush off/aside, shrug off.
OPPOSITES heed.

noun *blithe disregard for the rules:* indifference, non-observance, inattention, heedlessness, neglect, contempt.
OPPOSITES attention.

**disrupt** verb interrupt, disturb, interfere with, play havoc with, upset, unsettle, obstruct, impede, hold up, delay.

**disruptive** adjective troublesome, disturbing, upsetting, unsettling, unruly, badly behaved, rowdy, disorderly, undisciplined, unmanageable, uncontrollable, uncooperative.
OPPOSITES well behaved.

**dissatisfaction** noun discontent, disaffection, disquiet, unhappiness, disappointment, disgruntlement, displeasure, vexation, annoyance, irritation.

**dissatisfied** adjective discontented, disappointed, disaffected, displeased, disgruntled, aggrieved, unhappy.
OPPOSITES contented.

**dissent** verb disagree, differ, demur, be at variance/odds, take issue, protest, object.
OPPOSITES agree, conform.
noun disagreement, difference of opinion, argument, dispute, resistance, objection, protest, opposition.
OPPOSITES agreement, conformity.

**dissident** noun dissenter, objector, protester, rebel, revolutionary, subversive, agitator, refusenik.
OPPOSITES conformist.
adjective dissenting, opposing, objecting, protesting, rebellious, revolutionary, subversive, nonconformist.
OPPOSITES conformist.

**dissociate** verb separate, detach, disconnect, sever, cut off, divorce, isolate, alienate.
OPPOSITES relate.

**dissolve** verb 1 *sugar dissolves in water*: break down, liquefy, melt, deliquesce, disintegrate. 2 *the crowd dissolved*: disperse, disband, break up, scatter. 3 *the assembly was dissolved*: disband, bring to an end, end, terminate, discontinue, close down, wind up/down, suspend, adjourn. 4 *their marriage was dissolved*: annul, nullify, void, invalidate, revoke.

**dissuade** verb discourage, deter, prevent, divert, stop, talk out of, persuade against, advise against, argue out of.
OPPOSITES encourage.

**distance** noun 1 *they measured the distance*: interval, space, span, gap, extent, length, range, reach. 2 *a mix of warmth and distance*: aloofness, remoteness, detachment, unfriendliness, reserve, reticence, formality; informal stand-offishness.
OPPOSITES proximity, friendliness.

**distant** adjective 1 *distant parts of the world*: faraway, far-off, far-flung, remote, out of the way, outlying. 2 *the distant past*: remote, bygone, ancient, prehistoric. 3 *a distant memory*: vague, faint, dim, indistinct, sketchy, hazy. 4 *father was always very distant*: aloof, reserved, remote, detached, unapproachable, unfriendly; informal stand-offish. 5 *a distant look in his eyes*: distracted, absent, faraway, detached, vague.
OPPOSITES near, recent, clear, close, friendly, alert.

**distinct** adjective 1 *two distinct categories*: discrete, separate, different, unconnected, distinctive, contrasting. 2 *the tail has distinct black tips*: clear, well defined, unmistakable, easily distinguishable, recognizable, visible, obvious, pronounced, prominent, striking.
OPPOSITES overlapping, similar, indefinite.

**distinction** noun 1 *distinctions that we observed*: difference, contrast, variation, division, differentiation, discrepancy. 2 *a painter of distinction*: merit, worth, greatness, excellence, quality, repute, renown. 3 *he had served with distinction*: honour, credit, excellence, merit.
OPPOSITES similarity, mediocrity, dishonour.

**distinctive** adjective distinguishing, characteristic, typical, individual, particular, peculiar, unique, exclusive, special.

a
b
c
**d**
e
f
g
h
i
j
k
l
m
n
o
p
q
r
s
t
u
v
w
x
y
z

OPPOSITES common.

**distinctly** adverb **1** *there's something distinctly odd about him:* decidedly, markedly, definitely, unmistakably, manifestly, patently. **2** *Laura spoke quite distinctly:* clearly, plainly, intelligibly, audibly.

**distinguish** verb **1** *he can distinguish reality from fantasy:* differentiate, tell apart, discriminate between, tell the difference between. **2** *he could distinguish shapes in the dark:* discern, see, perceive, make out, detect, recognize, identify. **3** *this is what distinguishes history from other disciplines:* separate, set apart, make distinctive, make different, single out, mark off.

**distinguished** adjective eminent, famous, renowned, prominent, well known, esteemed, respected, illustrious, acclaimed, celebrated.
OPPOSITES unknown, obscure.

**distorted** adjective **1** *a distorted face:* twisted, warped, contorted, buckled, deformed, malformed, misshapen, disfigured, crooked, out of shape. **2** *a distorted version:* misrepresented, perverted, twisted, falsified, misreported, misstated, garbled, inaccurate, biased, prejudiced.
OPPOSITES normal, straight, honest.

**distract** verb divert, sidetrack, draw away, lead astray, disturb, put off.

**distracted** adjective preoccupied, inattentive, vague, abstracted, absent-minded, faraway, in a world of one's own, troubled, harassed, worried; informal miles away, not with it.
OPPOSITES attentive.

**distraction** noun **1** *a distraction from the real issues:* diversion, interruption, disturbance, interference. **2** *frivolous distractions:* amusement, entertainment, diversion, recreation, pastime, leisure pursuit.

**distraught** adjective distressed, frantic, fraught, overcome, overwrought, beside oneself, out of one's mind, desperate, hysterical, worked up, at one's wits' end; informal in a state.
OPPOSITES calm.

**distress** noun **1** *she concealed her distress:* anguish, suffering, pain, agony, torment, heartache, heartbreak, sorrow, sadness, unhappiness. **2** *a ship in distress:* danger, peril, difficulty, trouble, jeopardy, risk.
OPPOSITES happiness, safety.
verb *he was distressed by the trial:* upset, pain, trouble, worry, perturb, disturb, disquiet, agitate, torment.
OPPOSITES comfort.

**distribute** verb **1** *the proceeds were distributed among his creditors:* give out, deal out, dole out, dish out, hand out/round, share out, divide out/up, parcel out. **2** *the newsletter is distributed free:* circulate, issue, deliver, disseminate, publish.
OPPOSITES gather in, pool.

**distribution** noun **1** *the distribution of aid:* giving out, dealing out, doling out, handing out/round, issuing, allocation, sharing out, dividing up/out, parcelling out. **2** *centres of food distribution:* supply,

delivery, dispersal, transportation.
OPPOSITES gathering in, pooling, collection.

**district** noun area, region, quarter, sector, zone, territory, locality, neighbourhood, community.

**distrust** noun *distrust of Soviet intentions:* mistrust, suspicion, wariness, chariness, scepticism, doubt, cynicism, misgivings, qualms.
OPPOSITES trust.
verb *the Army distrusted the peace process:* mistrust, be suspicious of, be wary of, be chary of, regard with suspicion, suspect, be sceptical of, doubt, be unsure of/about, have misgivings about.
OPPOSITES trust.

**disturb** verb 1 *somewhere where we won't be disturbed:* interrupt, intrude on, butt in on, barge in on, distract, disrupt, bother, trouble, pester, harass. 2 *don't disturb his papers:* move, rearrange, mix up, interfere with, mess up, muddle. 3 *he wasn't disturbed by the allegations:* perturb, trouble, concern, worry, upset, fluster, disconcert, dismay, alarm, distress, unsettle.
OPPOSITES calm, reassure.

**disturbance** noun 1 *a disturbance to local residents:* disruption, distraction, interference, inconvenience, upset, annoyance, irritation, intrusion. 2 *disturbances in the town centre:* riot, fracas, brawl, street fight, free-for-all, commotion, disorder.
OPPOSITES order.

**disturbed** adjective 1 *disturbed sleep:* disrupted, interrupted, fitful, intermittent, broken.

2 *disturbed children:* troubled, distressed, upset, distraught, unbalanced, unstable, disordered, dysfunctional, maladjusted, neurotic, unhinged; informal screwed up.
OPPOSITES uninterrupted, well adjusted, sane.

**ditch** noun trench, trough, channel, dyke, drain, gutter, gully, watercourse.

**dive** verb 1 *they dived into the clear water | the plane was diving towards the ground:* plunge, nosedive, jump, plummet, fall, drop, pitch. 2 *they dived for cover:* leap, jump, lunge, throw/fling oneself, go headlong, duck.
noun 1 *a dive into the pool:* plunge, nosedive, jump, fall, drop, swoop. 2 *a sideways dive:* lunge, spring, jump, leap.

**diverge** verb 1 *the two roads diverged:* separate, part, fork, divide, split, bifurcate, go in different directions. 2 *areas where our views diverge:* differ, be different, be dissimilar, disagree, be at variance/odds, conflict, clash.
OPPOSITES converge, agree.

**diverse** adjective various, sundry, varied, varying, miscellaneous, assorted, mixed, diversified, divergent, different, differing, distinct, unlike, dissimilar.
OPPOSITES similar.

**diversion** noun 1 *the diversion of the river:* re-routing, redirection, deflection, deviation, divergence. 2 *traffic diversions:* detour, deviation, alternative route. 3 *the noise created a diversion:* distraction, disturbance, smokescreen; informal red herring. 4 *a city full of diversions:* entertainment,

a b c **d** e f g h i j k l m n o p q r s t u v w x y z

amusement, pastime, delight, fun, recreation, pleasure.

**diversity** noun variety, miscellany, assortment, mixture, mix, range, array, multiplicity, variation, diverseness, difference.
OPPOSITES uniformity.

**divert** verb 1 *a plan to divert Siberia's rivers:* re-route, redirect, change the course of, deflect, channel. 2 *he diverted her from her studies:* distract, sidetrack, disturb, draw away, put off. 3 *the story diverted them:* amuse, entertain, distract, delight, enchant, interest, fascinate, absorb, engross, rivet, grip.

**divide** verb 1 *he divided his kingdom into four:* split (up), cut up, carve up, dissect, bisect, halve, quarter. 2 *a curtain divided her cabin from the galley:* separate, segregate, partition, screen off, section off, split off. 3 *the stairs divide at the mezzanine:* diverge, separate, part, branch (off), fork, split (in two). 4 *Jack divided the cash:* share out, ration out, parcel out, deal out, dole out, dish out, distribute. 5 *he aimed to divide his opponents:* disunite, drive apart, drive a wedge between, break up, split (up), separate, isolate, alienate.
OPPOSITES unify, converge, collect, unite.

**divine**[1] adjective 1 *a divine being:* godly, angelic, heavenly, celestial, holy. 2 *divine worship:* religious, holy, sacred, sanctified, consecrated, blessed, devotional.
OPPOSITES mortal, infernal.

**divine**[2] verb *Fergus divined how afraid she was:* guess, surmise, deduce, infer, discern, discover, perceive; informal figure (out); Brit. informal suss.

**division** noun 1 *the division of the island | cell division:* dividing (up), breaking up, break-up, carving up, splitting, dissection, partitioning, separation, segregation. 2 *the division of his estates:* sharing out, dividing up, parcelling out, dishing out, allocation, allotment, splitting up, carving up. 3 *the division between nomadic and urban cultures:* dividing line, divide, boundary, border, demarcation line, gap, gulf. 4 *each class is split into nine divisions:* section, subsection, subdivision, category, class, group, grouping, set. 5 *an independent division of the executive:* department, branch, arm, wing. 6 *the causes of social division:* disunity, disunion, conflict, discord, disagreement, alienation, isolation.
OPPOSITES unification, unity.

**divorce** noun 1 *she wants a divorce:* dissolution, annulment, decree nisi, separation. 2 *a growing divorce between the church and people:* separation, division, split, disunity, alienation, schism, gulf.
OPPOSITES unity.
verb 1 *her parents have divorced:* split up, get a divorce, separate, end one's marriage. 2 *religion cannot be divorced from morality:* separate, divide, detach, isolate, alienate, set apart, cut off.

**divulge** verb disclose, reveal, tell, communicate, pass on, publish, give away, let slip.
OPPOSITES conceal.

**dizzy** adjective giddy, light-headed, faint, unsteady, shaky, muzzy, wobbly; informal woozy.

**do** verb **1** *she does most of the work:* carry out, undertake, discharge, execute, perform, accomplish, achieve, bring about, engineer; informal pull off. **2** *they can do as they please:* act, behave, conduct oneself. **3** *regular coffee will do:* suffice, be adequate, be satisfactory, fill/fit the bill, serve. **4** *a portrait I am doing:* make, create, produce, work on, design, manufacture.
■ **do away with** *they want to do away with the old customs:* abolish, get rid of, eliminate, discontinue, stop, end, terminate, drop, abandon, give up; informal scrap. ■ **do without** forgo, dispense with, abstain from, refrain from, eschew, give up, cut out, renounce, manage without.

**dock**[1] noun *his boat was moored at the dock:* harbour, marina, port, wharf, quay, pier, jetty, landing stage.
verb *the ship docked:* moor, berth, put in, tie up, anchor.

**dock**[2] verb **1** *they docked the money from my salary:* deduct, subtract, remove, debit, take off/away; informal knock off. **2** *workers had their pay docked:* reduce, cut, decrease. **3** *the dog's tail was docked:* cut off, cut short, shorten, crop, lop.

**doctor** noun physician, medical practitioner, general practitioner, GP, clinician, consultant; informal doc, medic.
verb **1** *he doctored Stephen's drink:* adulterate, tamper with, lace; informal spike. **2** *the reports have been doctored:* falsify, tamper with, interfere with, alter, change, forge, fake; Brit. informal fiddle.

**doctrine** noun creed, credo, dogma, belief, teaching, ideology, tenet, maxim, canon, principle.

**document** noun *a legal document:* paper, certificate, deed, form, contract, agreement, report, record.
verb *its history is well documented:* record, register, report, log, chronicle, authenticate, verify.

**dodge** verb **1** *he could easily dodge the two coppers:* elude, evade, avoid, escape, run away from, lose, shake (off); informal give someone the slip. **2** *the minister tried to dodge the debate:* avoid, evade, get out of, back out of, sidestep; informal duck, wriggle out of. **3** *she dodged into a telephone booth:* dart, bolt, dive, slip.
noun *a clever dodge | a tax dodge:* ruse, ploy, scheme, tactic, stratagem, subterfuge, trick, hoax, cheat, deception, fraud; informal scam; Brit. informal wheeze; Austral. informal lurk, rort.

**dog** noun hound, canine, man's best friend; informal pooch, mutt; Austral. informal bitzer.
verb *the scheme was dogged by bad weather:* plague, beset, bedevil, blight, trouble.

**dogged** adjective tenacious, determined, resolute, stubborn, obstinate, purposeful, persistent, persevering, single-minded, tireless.
OPPOSITES half-hearted, tentative.

**dogmatic** adjective opinionated, assertive, insistent, emphatic, adamant, doctrinaire, authoritarian, imperious, dictatorial, uncompromising.

a b c **d** e f g h i j k l m n o p q r s t u v w x y z

a
b
c
**d**
e
f
g
h
i
j
k
l
m
n
o
p
q
r
s
t
u
v
w
x
y
z

**dole**
■ **dole something out** deal out, share out, divide up, allocate, distribute, dispense, hand out, give out, dish out.

**domain** noun **1** *they extended their domain:* realm, kingdom, empire, dominion, province, territory, land. **2** *the domain of art:* field, area, sphere, discipline, province, world.

**domestic** adjective **1** *domestic commitments:* family, home, household. **2** *she was not at all domestic:* domesticated, homely, home-loving. **3** *small domestic animals:* tame, pet, domesticated, household. **4** *the domestic car industry:* national, state, home, internal.

**dominant** adjective **1** *the dominant classes:* ruling, governing, controlling, presiding, commanding. **2** *he has a dominant personality:* assertive, authoritative, forceful, domineering, commanding, controlling, pushy. **3** *the dominant issues in psychology:* main, principal, prime, chief, primary, central, key, crucial, core.
OPPOSITES subservient, subsidiary.

**dominate** verb **1** *the Russians dominated Iran in the nineteenth century:* control, influence, command, be in charge of, rule, govern, direct. **2** *the village is dominated by the viaduct:* overlook, command, tower above/over, loom over.

**domination** noun control, power, command, authority, dominion, rule, supremacy, superiority, ascendancy, sway.

**don** verb put on, get dressed in, dress (oneself) in, get into, slip into/on, change into.

**donate** verb give, contribute, gift, subscribe, grant, present, endow.

**donation** noun gift, contribution, subscription, present, handout, grant, offering.

**donor** noun giver, contributor, benefactor, benefactress, subscriber, supporter, backer, patron, sponsor.
OPPOSITES beneficiary.

**doom** noun *prepare to meet your doom:* destruction, downfall, ruin, extinction, annihilation, death, nemesis.
verb *they were doomed to die:* destine, fate, predestine, preordain, mean, condemn, sentence.

**doomed** adjective ill-fated, ill-starred, cursed, jinxed, damned.

**dope** verb **1** *the horse was doped:* drug, tamper with, interfere with, sedate; Brit. informal nobble. **2** *they doped his drink:* add drugs to, tamper with, adulterate, lace; informal spike, doctor.

**dose** noun *a dose of medicine:* measure, portion, draught, dosage.
verb *he dosed himself with vitamins:* drug, fill (up), pump, prime, load, stuff, cram.

**dot** noun *a pattern of dots:* spot, speck, fleck, speckle, full stop, decimal point.
verb **1** *spots of rain dotted his shirt:* spot, fleck, mark, spatter. **2** *restaurants are dotted around the site:* scatter, pepper, sprinkle, strew, spread.

**dote**
■ **dote on** adore, love dearly, be devoted to, idolize, treasure, cherish, worship.

**double** adjective *a double garage:* dual, duplex, twin, binary,

duplicate, coupled, matching, twofold, in pairs.
OPPOSITES single.
noun *it must be her double:* lookalike, twin, clone, duplicate, exact likeness, replica, copy, facsimile, Doppelgänger; informal spitting image, dead ringer.

**doubt** noun 1 *there was some doubt as to the caller's identity:* uncertainty, confusion, controversy. 2 *a weak leader racked by doubt:* indecision, hesitation, uncertainty, insecurity, hesitancy, vacillation. 3 *there is doubt about their motives:* scepticism, distrust, mistrust, suspicion, cynicism, wariness, reservations, misgivings, suspicions.
OPPOSITES certainty, conviction, trust.
verb *they doubted my story:* disbelieve, distrust, mistrust, suspect, be suspicious of, have misgivings about.
OPPOSITES trust.
■ **in doubt 1** *the outcome is in doubt:* doubtful, uncertain, unconfirmed, unknown, undecided, unresolved, in the balance, up in the air; informal iffy. 2 *if you are in doubt, ask for advice:* irresolute, hesitant, doubtful, unsure, uncertain, in two minds, undecided, in a quandary/dilemma. ■ **no doubt** doubtless, undoubtedly, indubitably, without (a) doubt, unquestionably, undeniably, clearly, plainly, obviously, patently.

**doubtful** adjective 1 *I was doubtful about going:* hesitant, in doubt, unsure, uncertain, in two minds, in a quandary, in a dilemma. 2 *it is doubtful whether he will come:* in doubt, uncertain, open to question, unsure, debatable, up in the air. 3 *the whole trip is looking rather doubtful:* unlikely, improbable. 4 *they are doubtful of the methods used:* distrustful, mistrustful, suspicious, wary, chary, leery, sceptical. 5 *this decision is of doubtful validity:* questionable, arguable, debatable, controversial, contentious.
OPPOSITES confident, certain, probable, trusting.

**doubtless** adverb undoubtedly, no doubt, unquestionably, indisputably, undeniably, certainly, surely, of course.

**douse** verb 1 *a mob doused the thieves with petrol:* drench, soak, saturate, wet. 2 *a guard doused the flames:* extinguish, put out, quench, smother.

**downfall** noun ruin, ruination, undoing, defeat, overthrow, destruction, annihilation, end, collapse, fall, crash, failure.
OPPOSITES rise.

**downgrade** verb demote, reduce, relegate.
OPPOSITES promote.

**downright** adjective *downright lies:* complete, total, absolute, utter, thorough, out-and-out, outright, sheer, arrant, pure.
adverb *that's downright dangerous:* thoroughly, utterly, positively, profoundly, really, completely, totally, entirely.

**drab** adjective 1 *a drab interior:* colourless, grey, dull, washed out, dingy, dreary, dismal, cheerless, gloomy, sombre. 2 *a drab existence:* uninteresting, dull, boring, tedious, monotonous, dry, dreary.
OPPOSITES bright, cheerful, interesting.

**draft** noun 1 *the first draft of his*

*speech:* version, sketch, attempt, effort, outline, plan. **2** *a banker's draft:* cheque, order, money order, bill of exchange.

**drag** verb *she dragged the chair backwards:* haul, pull, tug, heave, lug, draw, trail.
noun **1** *the drag from the parachute:* pull, resistance, tug. **2** (informal) *work can be a drag:* bore, nuisance, bother, trouble, pest, annoyance, trial; informal pain (in the neck), bind, headache, hassle.

**drain** verb **1** *a valve for draining the tank:* empty (out), void, clear (out), evacuate, unload. **2** *drain off any surplus liquid:* draw off, extract, siphon off, pour out, pour off, bleed, tap, filter, discharge. **3** *the water drained away to the sea:* flow, pour, trickle, stream, run, rush, gush, flood, surge, leak, ooze, seep, dribble. **4** *more people would just drain our resources:* use up, exhaust, deplete, consume, expend, get through, sap, milk, bleed. **5** *he drained his drink:* drink (up/down), gulp (down), guzzle, quaff, swallow, finish off, toss off; informal sink, down, swig, swill (down), knock back.
OPPOSITES fill.
noun **1** *the drain filled with water:* sewer, channel, ditch, culvert, duct, pipe, gutter. **2** *a drain on the battery:* strain, pressure, burden, load, demand.

**drama** noun **1** *a television drama:* play, show, piece, theatrical work, stage show, dramatization. **2** *he is studying drama:* acting, the theatre, the stage, dramatic art, stagecraft, dramaturgy. **3** *she liked to create a drama:* incident, scene, spectacle, crisis, disturbance, row, commotion, excitement, thrill, sensation, dramatics, theatrics, histrionics.

**dramatic** adjective **1** *dramatic art:* theatrical, thespian, stage, dramaturgical. **2** *a dramatic increase:* considerable, substantial, significant, remarkable, extraordinary, exceptional, phenomenal. **3** *there were dramatic scenes in the city:* exciting, stirring, action-packed, sensational, spectacular, startling, unexpected, tense, gripping, riveting, thrilling, hair-raising, lively. **4** *dramatic headlands:* striking, impressive, imposing, spectacular, breathtaking, dazzling, sensational, awesome, awe-inspiring, remarkable. **5** *a dramatic gesture:* exaggerated, theatrical, ostentatious, actressy, stagy, showy, melodramatic.
OPPOSITES insignificant, boring, unremarkable, unimposing, restrained.

**dramatize** verb **1** *the novel was dramatized for television:* turn into a play/film, adapt (for the stage/screen). **2** *the tabloids dramatized the event:* exaggerate, overdo, overstate, hyperbolize, magnify, amplify, inflate, sensationalize, embroider, colour, aggrandize, embellish, elaborate; informal blow up (out of all proportion).

**drape** verb wrap, cover, envelop, shroud, wind, swathe, festoon, hang.

**drastic** adjective extreme, serious, desperate, radical, far-reaching, momentous, substantial.
OPPOSITES moderate.

**draught** noun **1** *the draught made Robin shiver:* current of air, wind, breeze, gust, puff, waft. **2** *a draught of beer:* gulp, drink, swallow, mouthful; informal swig.

**draw** verb **1** *he drew the house:* sketch, outline, rough out, illustrate, render, represent, trace, portray, depict. **2** *she drew her chair in to the table:* pull, haul, drag, tug, heave, lug, tow; informal yank. **3** *the train drew into the station:* move, go, come, proceed, progress, pass, drive, inch, roll, glide, cruise, sweep. **4** *he drew his gun:* pull out, take out, produce, fish out, extract, withdraw, unsheathe. **5** *she drew huge audiences:* attract, win, capture, catch, engage, lure, entice, bring in.
noun **1** *she won the Christmas draw:* raffle, lottery, sweepstake, sweep, tombola, ballot. **2** *the match ended in a draw:* tie, dead heat, stalemate. **3** *the draw of central London:* attraction, lure, allure, pull, appeal, temptation, charm, fascination.
■ **draw on** call on, have recourse to, turn to, look to, exploit, use, employ, utilize, bring into play. ■ **draw something out** prolong, protract, drag out, spin out, string out, extend, lengthen.
■ **draw something up** compose, formulate, frame, write down, draft, prepare, think up, devise, work out, create, invent, design.

**drawback** noun disadvantage, snag, downside, stumbling block, catch, hitch, pitfall, fly in the ointment, weak spot/point, weakness, imperfection; informal minus.
OPPOSITES benefit.

**drawing** noun sketch, picture, illustration, representation, portrayal, depiction, diagram, outline.

**dread** verb *I used to dread going to school:* fear, be afraid of, worry about, be anxious about, shudder at the thought of.
OPPOSITES look forward to.
noun *she was filled with dread:* fear, apprehension, trepidation, anxiety, panic, alarm, terror, disquiet, unease.
OPPOSITES confidence.

**dreadful** adjective **1** *a dreadful accident:* terrible, frightful, horrible, grim, awful, horrifying, shocking, distressing, appalling, harrowing, ghastly, fearful, horrendous, tragic. **2** *a dreadful meal:* very bad, frightful, shocking, awful, abysmal, atrocious, disgraceful, deplorable; informal woeful, rotten, lousy, ropy; Brit. informal duff, rubbish. **3** *you're a dreadful flirt:* outrageous, shocking, real, awful, terrible, inordinate, incorrigible, quite a.
OPPOSITES pleasant, wonderful, excellent, no.

**dream** noun **1** *she went around in a dream:* daydream, reverie, trance, daze, stupor. **2** *he realized his childhood dream:* ambition, aspiration, hope, goal, aim, objective, intention, desire, wish, daydream, fantasy. **3** *he's an absolute dream:* delight, joy, marvel, wonder, gem, treasure, beauty, vision.
OPPOSITES alertness, nightmare, horror.
verb **1** *I dreamed of making the Olympic team:* fantasize, daydream, wish, hope, long, yearn, hanker. **2** *she's always dreaming:* daydream, be in a

a
b
c
**d**
e
f
g
h
i
j
k
l
m
n
o
p
q
r
s
t
u
v
w
x
y
z

trance, be lost in thought, be preoccupied, be abstracted, stare into space, be in cloud cuckoo land.

■ **dream something up** think up, invent, concoct, devise, hatch, come up with.

**dreary** adjective dull, uninteresting, tedious, boring, unexciting, unstimulating, uninspiring, soul-destroying, monotonous, uneventful.
OPPOSITES exciting.

**drench** verb soak, saturate, wet through, douse, steep, flood, drown.

**dress** verb 1 *he dressed quickly:* put on clothes, clothe oneself, get dressed. **2** *she was dressed in a suit:* clothe, attire, deck out; informal get up. **3** *she enjoyed dressing the tree:* decorate, trim, adorn, arrange, prepare. **4** *they dressed his wounds:* bandage, cover, bind, wrap.
OPPOSITES undress.
noun 1 *a long blue dress:* frock, gown, robe, shift. **2** *full evening dress:* clothes, clothing, garments, attire, costume, outfit; informal get-up; Brit. informal clobber.

**dribble** verb 1 *the baby started to dribble:* drool, slaver, slobber. **2** *rainwater dribbled down her face:* trickle, drip, roll, run, drizzle, ooze, seep, leak.

**drift** verb 1 *his raft drifted down the river:* be carried, be borne, float, bob, glide, coast, waft. **2** *the guests drifted away:* wander, meander, stray, stroll, dawdle, float, roam. **3** *don't allow your attention to drift:* stray, digress, wander, deviate, be diverted. **4** *snow drifted over the path:* pile up, bank up, heap up, accumulate, gather, amass.
noun 1 *a drift from the country to urban areas:* movement, shift, flow, transfer, gravitation. **2** *he caught the drift of her thoughts:* gist, meaning, sense, significance, thrust, import, tenor, intention, direction. **3** *a drift of deep snow:* pile, heap, bank, mound, mass, accumulation.

**drill** noun 1 *military drill:* training, instruction, coaching, teaching, (physical) exercises; informal square-bashing. **2** *Estelle knew the drill:* procedure, routine, practice, programme, schedule, method, system.
verb 1 *drill the piece of wood:* bore, pierce, puncture, perforate. **2** *a sergeant drilling new recruits:* train, instruct, coach, teach, discipline, exercise.

**drink** verb 1 *she drank her coffee:* swallow, gulp (down), quaff, guzzle, imbibe, sip, drain; informal swig, down, knock back. **2** *he never drank:* drink alcohol, tipple, indulge, carouse; informal hit the bottle, booze; Brit. informal bevvy.
noun 1 *cocoa is a nice drink:* beverage, liquid refreshment; Brit. informal bevvy. **2** *she turned to drink:* alcohol, intoxicating liquor, spirits; informal booze, the hard stuff, the bottle, grog. **3** *she took a drink of wine:* swallow, gulp, mouthful, draught, sip; informal swig, slug.

**drip** verb 1 *there was a tap dripping:* dribble, leak. **2** *sweat dripped from his chin:* drop, dribble, trickle, run, splash, sprinkle, leak.
noun *a bucket caught the drips:* drop, dribble, spot, trickle, splash.

**drive** verb 1 *I can't drive a car:*

operate, handle, manage, pilot, steer, work. **2** *he drove to the police station:* go by car, motor. **3** *I'll drive you to the airport:* run, chauffeur, give someone a lift, take, ferry, transport, convey. **4** *the engine drives the front wheels:* power, propel, move, push. **5** *he drove a nail into the boot:* hammer, screw, ram, sink, plunge, thrust, knock. **6** *she was driven to crime:* force, compel, prompt, precipitate, oblige, coerce, pressure, spur, prod.
noun **1** *an afternoon drive:* excursion, outing, trip, jaunt, tour, ride, run, journey; informal spin. **2** *she lacked the drive to succeed:* motivation, ambition, single-mindedness, willpower, dedication, doggedness, tenacity, enthusiasm, zeal, commitment, energy, vigour; informal get-up-and-go. **3** *an anti-corruption drive:* campaign, crusade, movement, effort, push, initiative.

**droop** verb hang down, wilt, dangle, sag, flop, sink, slump, drop.

**drop** verb **1** *Eric dropped the box:* let fall, let go of, lose one's grip on, release. **2** *a plane dropped out of the sky:* fall, descend, plunge, plummet, dive, sink, dip, tumble. **3** *the exchange rate dropped:* decrease, lessen, reduce, fall, decline, dwindle, sink, slump. **4** *let's drop this pretence:* abandon, give up, discontinue, finish with, renounce, reject, forgo, relinquish, dispense with, leave out; informal dump, pack in, quit.
OPPOSITES rise, increase, keep.
noun **1** *a drop of water:* droplet, blob, globule, bead. **2** *it needs a drop of oil:* small amount,

little, bit, dash, spot, dribble, sprinkle, trickle, splash, mouthful; informal smidgen, tad. **3** *a small drop in profits:* decrease, reduction, decline, fall-off, downturn, slump. **4** *I walked to the edge of the drop:* cliff, precipice, slope, descent, incline.
OPPOSITES flood, increase.
■ **drop off** fall asleep, doze (off), nap, drowse; informal nod off, drift off, snooze, take forty winks. ■ **drop out** leave, give up, withdraw, retire, pull out, abandon something, fall by the wayside; informal quit, pack something in, jack something in.

**drug** noun **1** *drugs prescribed by doctors:* medicine, medication, remedy, cure, antidote. **2** *she was under the influence of drugs:* narcotic, stimulant, hallucinogen; informal dope, gear.
verb **1** *he was drugged:* anaesthetize, poison, knock out; informal dope. **2** *she drugged his coffee:* tamper with, lace, poison; informal dope, spike, doctor.

**drum** noun *a drum of radioactive waste:* canister, barrel, cylinder, tank, bin, can.
verb **1** *she drummed her fingers on the desk:* tap, beat, rap, thud, thump, tattoo, thrum. **2** *the rules were drummed into us at school:* instil, drive, din, hammer, drill, implant, ingrain, inculcate.
■ **drum something up** round up, gather, collect, summon, attract, canvass, solicit, petition.

**drunk** adjective intoxicated, inebriated, drunken, tipsy, under the influence; informal tight, merry, plastered, sloshed,

pickled, tanked (up), ratted; Brit. informal legless, paralytic, Brahms and Liszt, trolleyed, tiddly; N. Amer. informal loaded, trashed, sauced.
OPPOSITES sober.
noun drunkard, inebriate; informal boozer, soak, wino, alky.
OPPOSITES teetotaller.

**dry** adjective **1** the dry desert: arid, parched, waterless, dehydrated, desiccated, withered, shrivelled, wizened. **2** a dry debate: dull, uninteresting, boring, unexciting, tedious, dreary, monotonous, unimaginative, sterile; informal deadly. **3** a dry sense of humour: wry, subtle, laconic, ironic, sardonic, sarcastic, cynical.
OPPOSITES wet, moist, interesting, lively, broad.
verb **1** the sun dried the ground: parch, scorch, bake, sear, dehydrate, desiccate, wither, shrivel. **2** he dried the dishes: wipe, towel, rub dry, drain.
OPPOSITES wet, moisten.

**dual** adjective double, twofold, duplex, binary, twin, matching, paired, coupled.
OPPOSITES single.

**dub** verb name, call, nickname, label, christen, term, tag.

**dubious** adjective **1** I was rather dubious about the idea: doubtful, uncertain, unsure, hesitant, sceptical, suspicious; informal iffy. **2** a dubious businessman: suspicious, suspect, untrustworthy, unreliable, questionable; informal shady; Brit. informal dodgy.
OPPOSITES certain, trustworthy.

**duck** verb **1** he ducked behind the wall: bob down, bend down, stoop, crouch, squat, hunch down, hunker down. **2** (informal)

they cannot duck the issue forever: shirk, dodge, evade, avoid, elude, escape, sidestep.

**duct** noun tube, channel, canal, vessel, conduit, pipe, outlet, inlet, flue, shaft, vent.

**due** adjective **1** their fees were due: owing, owed, payable, outstanding, overdue, unpaid, unsettled. **2** the chancellor's statement is due today: expected, anticipated, scheduled for, awaited, required. **3** a little respect is due: deserved, merited, warranted, justified, owing, appropriate, fitting, right, rightful, proper. **4** he drove without due care: proper, correct, suitable, appropriate, adequate, sufficient.
noun members have paid their dues: fee, subscription, charge, payment, contribution, levy.
adverb due north: directly, straight, exactly, precisely, dead.
■ **due to 1** her death was due to an infection: attributable to, caused by, because of, down to. **2** the train was cancelled due to staff shortages: because of, owing to, on account of, as a consequence of, as a result of, thanks to.

**duel** noun **1** he was killed in a duel: single combat, fight, confrontation, head-to-head; informal shoot-out. **2** a snooker duel: contest, match, game, meet, encounter, clash.

**dull** adjective **1** a dull novel: uninteresting, boring, tedious, monotonous, unimaginative, uneventful, characterless, featureless, colourless, lifeless, unexciting, uninspiring, flat, bland, stodgy, dreary; informal deadly; N. Amer. informal dullsville.

**2** *a dull morning*: overcast, cloudy, gloomy, dark, dismal, dreary, sombre, grey, murky, sunless. **3** *dull colours*: drab, dreary, sombre, dark, subdued, muted. **4** *a dull sound*: muffled, muted, quiet, soft, faint, indistinct, stifled. **5** *the chisel became dull*: blunt, worn. **6** *a rather dull child*: unintelligent, stupid, slow, brainless, mindless, foolish, idiotic; informal dense, dim, half-witted, thick.
OPPOSITES interesting, bright, resonant, sharp, clever.
verb *the pain was dulled by drugs*: lessen, decrease, diminish, reduce, dampen, blunt, deaden, allay, ease.
OPPOSITES intensify.

**duly** adverb **1** *the document was duly signed*: properly, correctly, appropriately, suitably, fittingly. **2** *he duly arrived to collect Alice*: at the right time, on time, punctually.

**dumb** adjective **1** *she stood dumb while he shouted*: mute, speechless, tongue-tied, silent, at a loss for words. **2** (informal) *he is not as dumb as you'd think*: stupid, unintelligent, ignorant, dense, brainless, foolish, slow, dull, simple; informal thick, dim; Brit. informal daft.
OPPOSITES talkative, clever.

**dummy** noun *a shop-window dummy*: mannequin, model, figure.
adjective *a dummy attack*: simulated, practice, trial, mock, make-believe; informal pretend.
OPPOSITES real.

**dump** noun **1** *take the rubbish to the dump*: tip, rubbish dump, dumping ground, recycling centre. **2** (informal) *the house is a dump*: hovel, slum; informal hole, pigsty.

verb **1** *he dumped his bag on the table*: put down, set down, deposit, place, shove, unload, drop, throw down; informal stick, park, plonk; Brit. informal bung. **2** *they will dump asbestos at the site*: dispose of, get rid of, throw away/out, discard, bin, jettison; informal ditch, junk.

**dune** noun bank, mound, hillock, hummock, knoll, ridge, heap, drift.

**duplicate** noun *a duplicate of the invoice*: copy, photocopy, facsimile, reprint, replica, reproduction, clone; trademark Xerox, photostat.
adjective *duplicate keys*: matching, identical, twin, corresponding, equivalent.
verb **1** *she will duplicate the newsletter*: copy, photocopy, photostat, xerox, reproduce, replicate, reprint, run off. **2** *a feat difficult to duplicate*: repeat, do again, redo, replicate.

**durable** adjective **1** *durable carpets*: hard-wearing, wear-resistant, heavy-duty, tough, long-lasting, strong, sturdy, robust. **2** *a durable peace*: lasting, long-lasting, long-term, enduring, persistent, abiding, permanent, undying, everlasting.
OPPOSITES delicate, short-lived.

**duration** noun length, time, period, term, span, extent, stretch.

**dusk** noun twilight, nightfall, sunset, sundown, evening, close of day, semi-darkness, gloom; literary gloaming.
OPPOSITES dawn.

**dust** noun *the desk was covered in dust*: dirt, grime, grit, powder, particles.
verb **1** *she dusted her*

*mantelpiece:* wipe, clean, brush, sweep. **2** *dust the cake with icing sugar:* sprinkle, scatter, powder, dredge, sift, cover.

**dusty** adjective **1** *the floor was dusty:* dirty, grimy, grubby, mucky, unswept. **2** *dusty sandstone:* powdery, crumbly, chalky, granular, soft, gritty.
OPPOSITES clean, hard, smooth.

**duty** noun **1** *a misguided sense of duty:* responsibility, obligation, commitment, allegiance, loyalty. **2** *it was his duty to attend the king:* job, task, assignment, mission, function, role. **3** *the duty was raised on alcohol:* tax, levy, tariff, excise, toll, rate.

**dwarf** noun **1** small person, person of restricted growth, midget, pygmy. **2** *the wizard captured the dwarf:* gnome, goblin, hobgoblin, troll, imp, elf, brownie, leprechaun.
adjective *dwarf conifers:* miniature, toy, pocket, baby, pygmy; informal mini.
OPPOSITES giant.
verb **1** *the buildings dwarf the trees:* dominate, tower over, loom over, overshadow. **2** *her*

*progress was dwarfed by her sister's success:* overshadow, outshine, surpass, exceed, outclass, outstrip, outdo, top.

**dwindle** verb diminish, decrease, reduce, lessen, shrink, wane.
OPPOSITES increase.

**dye** noun *a blue dye:* colouring, dyestuff, pigment, tint, stain, wash.
verb *the gloves were dyed:* colour, tint, pigment, stain, wash.

**dying** adjective **1** *his dying aunt:* terminally ill, at death's door, on one's deathbed, fading fast, not long for this world. **2** *a dying art form:* declining, vanishing, fading, waning; informal on the way out. **3** *her dying words:* final, last.
OPPOSITES thriving, first.

**dynamic** adjective energetic, spirited, active, lively, vigorous, forceful, high-powered, aggressive, enterprising; informal go-getting, go-ahead.
OPPOSITES lackadaisical.

**dynasty** noun family, house, line, lineage, regime, empire.

# Ee

**each** adverb *they gave a tenner each:* apiece, per person, per head, per capita.

**eager** adjective **1** *small eager faces:* keen, enthusiastic, avid, ardent, highly motivated, committed, earnest. **2** *we were eager for news:* anxious, impatient, longing, yearning, wishing, hoping; informal itching, dying.

OPPOSITES apathetic.

**early** adjective **1** *early copies of the book:* advance, initial, preliminary, first. **2** *an early death:* untimely, premature, unseasonable. **3** *early man:* primitive, ancient, prehistoric, primeval. **4** *an early response:* prompt, timely, quick, speedy.
OPPOSITES late, timely, modern.
adverb **1** *get your application in*

*early:* in advance, in good time, ahead of schedule, with time to spare, before the last moment. **2** *she was widowed very early:* prematurely, before the usual time, too soon, ahead of schedule.
OPPOSITES late.

**earmark** verb set aside, keep (back), reserve, designate, assign, allocate.

**earn** verb **1** *they earned £20,000:* be paid, take home, gross, receive, get, make, collect, bring in; informal pocket, bank. **2** *he has earned their trust:* deserve, merit, warrant, justify, be worthy of, gain, win, secure, obtain.
OPPOSITES lose.

**earnest** adjective **1** *he is dreadfully earnest:* serious, solemn, grave, sober, humourless, staid, intense. **2** *earnest prayer:* devout, heartfelt, wholehearted, sincere, impassioned, fervent, intense.
OPPOSITES frivolous, half-hearted.

**earnings** plural noun income, pay, wages, salary, stipend, remuneration, fees, revenue, yield, profit, takings, proceeds.

**earth** noun **1** *the moon orbits the earth:* world, globe, planet. **2** *a trembling of the earth:* land, ground, terra firma, floor. **3** *he ploughed the earth:* soil, clay, dust, dirt, loam, ground, turf.

**earthly** adjective worldly, temporal, mortal, human, material, carnal, fleshly, bodily, physical, corporeal, sensual.
OPPOSITES extraterrestrial, heavenly.

**ease** noun **1** *he defeated them all with ease:* effortlessness, no trouble, simplicity. **2** *his ease of*

*manner:* naturalness, casualness, informality, composure, nonchalance, insouciance. **3** *a life of ease:* affluence, wealth, prosperity, luxury, plenty, comfort, enjoyment, well-being.
OPPOSITES difficulty, formality, hardship.
verb **1** *the alcohol eased his pain:* relieve, alleviate, soothe, moderate, dull, deaden, numb. **2** *the rain eased off:* let up, abate, subside, die down, slacken off, diminish, lessen. **3** *work helped to ease her mind:* calm, quieten, pacify, soothe, comfort, console. **4** *he eased out the cork:* slide, slip, squeeze, guide, manoeuvre, inch, edge.
OPPOSITES aggravate, intensify, unsettle.

**easily** adverb effortlessly, comfortably, simply, without difficulty, readily, without a hitch.

**easy** adjective **1** *the task was very easy:* uncomplicated, undemanding, effortless, painless, trouble-free, simple, straightforward, elementary, plain sailing; informal a piece of cake, child's play, a cinch. **2** *an easy target:* vulnerable, susceptible, defenceless, naive, gullible, trusting. **3** *Vic's easy manner:* natural, casual, informal, unceremonious, unreserved, unaffected, easy-going, amiable, affable, genial, good-humoured, carefree, nonchalant, unconcerned; informal laid-back. **4** *an easy life:* quiet, tranquil, serene, peaceful, untroubled, contented, relaxed, comfortable, secure, safe; informal cushy. **5** *an easy pace:* leisurely, unhurried, comfortable, undemanding,

easy-going, gentle, sedate, moderate, steady.
OPPOSITES difficult, formal, hard, demanding.

**eat** verb 1 *we ate a hearty breakfast:* consume, devour, swallow, partake of, munch, chomp; informal tuck into, put away. 2 *we ate at a local restaurant:* have a meal, feed, snack, breakfast, lunch, dine; informal graze.

**ebb** verb 1 *the tide ebbed:* recede, go out, retreat. 2 *his courage began to ebb:* diminish, dwindle, wane, fade (away), peter out, decline, flag.
OPPOSITES flow, increase.

**eccentric** adjective *eccentric behaviour:* unconventional, abnormal, anomalous, odd, strange, peculiar, weird, bizarre, outlandish, idiosyncratic, quirky; informal oddball, kooky, cranky.
OPPOSITES conventional.
noun *he was something of an eccentric:* oddity, free spirit, misfit; informal oddball, weirdo.

**echo** noun *a faint echo of my shout:* reverberation, reflection, ringing, repetition, repeat.
verb 1 *his laughter echoed round the room:* reverberate, resonate, resound, reflect, ring, vibrate. 2 *Bill echoed Rex's words:* repeat, restate, reiterate, imitate, parrot, mimic, reproduce, recite.

**eclipse** verb outshine, overshadow, surpass, exceed, outclass, outstrip, outdo, transcend.

**economic** adjective 1 *economic reform:* financial, monetary, budgetary, fiscal, commercial. 2 *the firm cannot remain economic:* profitable,

moneymaking, lucrative, remunerative, fruitful, productive.
OPPOSITES unprofitable.

**economical** adjective 1 *an economical car:* cheap, inexpensive, low-cost, budget, economy, cut-price, bargain. 2 *a very economical shopper:* thrifty, provident, prudent, sensible, frugal.
OPPOSITES expensive, spendthrift.

**economize** verb save (money), cut costs, cut back, make cutbacks, retrench, scrimp.

**economy** noun 1 *the nation's economy:* wealth, financial resources, financial system, financial management. 2 *one can combine good living with economy:* thrift, thriftiness, prudence, careful budgeting, saving, restraint, frugality.
OPPOSITES extravagance.

**ecstasy** noun rapture, bliss, joy, elation, euphoria, rhapsodies.
OPPOSITES misery.

**ecstatic** adjective enraptured, elated, euphoric, rapturous, joyful, overjoyed, blissful; informal over the moon, on top of the world.

**eddy** noun *eddies at the river's edge:* swirl, whirlpool, vortex.
verb *the snow eddied around her:* swirl, whirl, spiral, wind, twist.

**edge** noun 1 *the edge of the lake:* border, boundary, extremity, fringe, margin, side, lip, rim, brim, brink, verge, perimeter. 2 *she had an edge in her voice:* sharpness, severity, bite, sting, sarcasm, malice, spite, venom. 3 *they have an edge over their rivals:* advantage, lead, head start, the whip hand, the upper hand, dominance.

OPPOSITES middle, kindness, disadvantage.

**verb 1** *poplars edged the orchard:* border, fringe, skirt, surround, enclose, encircle, bound. **2** *a frock edged with lace:* trim, decorate, finish, border, fringe. **3** *he edged closer to the fire:* creep, inch, work one's way, ease oneself, sidle, steal.
OPPOSITES stride.

**edit** verb correct, check, copy-edit, improve, polish, modify, adapt, revise, rewrite, reword, shorten, condense, cut, abridge.

**edition** noun issue, number, volume, printing, impression, publication, programme, version.

**educate** verb teach, school, tutor, instruct, coach, train, inform, enlighten.

**educated** adjective informed, literate, schooled, tutored, well read, learned, knowledgeable, enlightened, intellectual, academic, erudite, scholarly, cultivated, cultured.
OPPOSITES uneducated.

**education** noun **1** *the education of young children:* teaching, schooling, tuition, tutoring, instruction, coaching, training, guidance, enlightenment. **2** *a woman of some education:* learning, knowledge, literacy, scholarship, enlightenment.

**educational** adjective **1** *an educational establishment:* academic, scholastic, learning, teaching, pedagogic. **2** *an educational experience:* instructive, instructional, educative, informative, illuminating, enlightening; formal edifying.

**eerie** adjective uncanny, sinister, ghostly, unnatural, unearthly, supernatural, other-worldly, strange, abnormal, weird, freakish; informal creepy, scary, spooky.

**effect** noun **1** *the effect of these changes:* result, consequence, upshot, outcome, repercussions, end result, aftermath. **2** *the effect of the drug:* impact, action, effectiveness, power, potency, strength, success. **3** *the dead man's effects:* belongings, possessions, worldly goods, chattels, property; informal things, stuff; Brit. informal clobber.
OPPOSITES cause.

**verb** *they effected many changes:* achieve, accomplish, carry out, manage, bring off, execute, conduct, engineer, perform, do, cause, bring about, produce.

**effective** adjective **1** *an effective treatment:* successful, effectual, potent, powerful, helpful, beneficial, advantageous, valuable, useful. **2** *an effective argument:* convincing, compelling, strong, forceful, persuasive, plausible, credible, logical, reasonable, cogent. **3** *the new law will be effective from next week:* operative, in force, in effect, valid, official, legal, binding. **4** *Korea was under effective Japanese control:* virtual, practical, essential, actual.
OPPOSITES ineffective, weak, invalid, theoretical.

**efficiency** noun **1** *we need reforms to bring efficiency:* economy, productivity, cost-effectiveness, organization, order, orderliness, regulation. **2** *I compliment you on your efficiency:* competence, capability, ability, proficiency, expertise, skill, effectiveness.
OPPOSITES inefficiency, incompetence.

a b c d e f g h i j k l m n o p q r s t u v w x y z

a
b
c
d
**e**
f
g
h
i
j
k
l
m
n
o
p
q
r
s
t
u
v
w
x
y
z

**efficient** adjective **1** *efficient techniques*: economic, productive, effective, cost-effective, streamlined, organized, methodical, systematic, orderly. **2** *an efficient secretary*: competent, capable, able, proficient, skilful, skilled, effective, productive, organized, businesslike.
OPPOSITES inefficient, incompetent.

**effort** noun **1** *an effort to work together*: attempt, try, endeavour; informal shot, stab, bash. **2** *a fine effort*: achievement, accomplishment, feat, undertaking, enterprise, work, result, outcome. **3** *the job requires little effort*: exertion, energy, work, application; informal elbow grease; Brit. informal graft.

**eject** verb **1** *the volcano ejected ash*: emit, spew out, discharge, give off, send out, belch, vent. **2** *the pilot had time to eject*: bail out, escape. **3** *they were ejected from the hall*: expel, throw out, remove, oust, evict, banish; informal kick out.
OPPOSITES admit.

**elaborate** adjective **1** *an elaborate plan*: complicated, complex, intricate, involved, detailed. **2** *an elaborate plasterwork ceiling*: ornate, decorated, embellished, adorned, ornamented, fancy, fussy, busy.
OPPOSITES simple, plain.
verb *both sides refused to elaborate on their reasons*: expand on, enlarge on, add to, flesh out, develop, fill out, amplify.

**elastic** adjective **1** *elastic material*: stretchy, elasticated, springy, flexible, pliable, supple. **2** *an elastic concept of nationality*: adaptable, flexible, adjustable, accommodating, variable, fluid, versatile.
OPPOSITES rigid.

**elder** adjective *his elder brother*: older, senior, big.
noun *the church elders*: leader, patriarch, father.

**elderly** adjective aged, old, ageing, long in the tooth, grey-haired, in one's dotage; informal getting on, over the hill.
OPPOSITES youthful.

**elect** verb **1** *a new president was elected*: vote in, vote for, return, cast one's vote for, choose, pick, select. **2** *she elected to stay behind*: choose, decide, opt, prefer, vote.

**election** noun ballot, vote, poll; Brit. by-election; US primary.

**electric** adjective *the atmosphere was electric*: exciting, charged, electrifying, thrilling, dramatic, dynamic, stimulating, galvanizing.

**electrify** verb excite, thrill, stimulate, arouse, rouse, inspire, stir (up), exhilarate, galvanize, fire (with enthusiasm), fire someone's imagination, invigorate, animate; N. Amer. light a fire under.

**elegance** noun **1** *he was attracted by her elegance*: style, grace, taste, sophistication, refinement, dignity, poise. **2** *the elegance of the idea*: neatness, simplicity.

**elegant** adjective **1** *an elegant black outfit*: stylish, graceful, tasteful, sophisticated, classic, chic, smart, poised, cultivated, polished, cultured. **2** *an elegant solution*: neat, simple.
OPPOSITES inelegant.

**element** noun **1** *an essential*

*element of the local community:* component, constituent, part, section, portion, piece, segment, aspect, factor, feature, facet, ingredient, strand, detail, member. **2** *there is an element of truth in this stereotype:* trace, touch, hint, smattering, soupçon. **3** (**elements**) *I braved the elements:* weather, climate, weather conditions.

**elementary** adjective **1** *an elementary astronomy course:* basic, rudimentary, preparatory, introductory. **2** *a lot of the work is elementary:* easy, simple, straightforward, uncomplicated, undemanding, painless, child's play, plain sailing; informal a piece of cake.
OPPOSITES advanced, difficult.

**elevate** verb **1** *we need a breeze to elevate the kite:* raise, lift (up), raise up/aloft, hoist, hike up, haul up. **2** *he was elevated to Secretary of State:* promote, upgrade, move up, raise; informal kick upstairs.
OPPOSITES lower, demote.

**elevated** adjective **1** *an elevated motorway:* raised, overhead, in the air, high up. **2** *elevated language:* lofty, grand, exalted, fine, sublime, inflated, pompous, bombastic. **3** *his elevated status:* high, high-ranking, lofty, exalted, grand, noble.
OPPOSITES sunken, everyday, lowly.

**elicit** verb obtain, draw out, extract, bring out, evoke, induce, prompt, generate, trigger, provoke.

**eligible** adjective **1** *those eligible to vote:* entitled, permitted, allowed, qualified, able. **2** *an eligible bachelor:* desirable, suitable, available, single,
unmarried, unattached.

**eliminate** verb **1** *a policy that would eliminate inflation:* remove, get rid of, put an end to, do away with, end, stop, eradicate, destroy, stamp out. **2** *he was eliminated from the title race:* knock out, exclude, rule out, disqualify.

**elite** noun best, pick, cream, crème de la crème, flower, high society, beautiful people, aristocracy, ruling class.
OPPOSITES dregs.

**eloquent** adjective articulate, fluent, expressive, persuasive, well expressed, effective, lucid, vivid.
OPPOSITES inarticulate.

**elusive** adjective **1** *her elusive husband:* difficult to find, slippery. **2** *an elusive quality:* indefinable, intangible, impalpable, fugitive, fleeting, transitory, ambiguous.

**embargo** noun *an embargo on oil sales:* ban, bar, prohibition, stoppage, veto, moratorium, restriction, block, boycott.
verb *arms sales were embargoed:* ban, bar, prohibit, stop, outlaw, blacklist, restrict, block, boycott.
OPPOSITES allow.

**embark** verb board (ship), go on board, go aboard; informal hop on, jump on.
OPPOSITES disembark.
■ **embark on** begin, start, undertake, set out on, take up, turn one's hand to, get down to, enter into, venture into, launch into, plunge into, engage in.

**embarrass** verb humiliate, shame, put someone to shame, abash, mortify, fluster, discomfit; informal show up.

**embarrassed** adjective

a
b
c
d
e
f
g
h
i
j
k
l
m
n
o
p
q
r
s
t
u
v
w
x
y
z

a
b
c
d
**e**
f
g
h
i
j
k
l
m
n
o
p
q
r
s
t
u
v
w
x
y
z

humiliated, mortified, red-faced, blushing, abashed, shamed, ashamed, shamefaced, self-conscious, uncomfortable, discomfited, disconcerted, flustered; informal with egg on one's face.

**embarrassing** adjective humiliating, shameful, mortifying, ignominious, awkward, uncomfortable, compromising; discomfiting; informal cringeworthy, cringe-making, toe-curling.

**embarrassment** noun 1 *he was scarlet with embarrassment:* humiliation, mortification, shame, shamefacedness, awkwardness, self-consciousness, discomfort, discomfiture. 2 *his current financial embarrassment:* difficulty, predicament, plight, problem, mess; informal bind, pickle, fix.

**emblem** noun symbol, representation, token, image, figure, mark, sign, crest, badge, device, insignia, coat of arms, shield, logo, trademark.

**embody** verb 1 *Gradgrind embodies the spirit of industrial capitalism:* personify, manifest, symbolize, represent, express, epitomize, stand for, typify, exemplify. 2 *the changes embodied in the Act:* incorporate, include, contain.

**embrace** verb 1 *he embraced her warmly:* hug, take/hold in one's arms, hold, cuddle, clasp to one's bosom, squeeze, clutch, enfold. 2 *most western European countries have embraced the concept:* welcome, welcome with open arms, accept, take on board, take up, take to one's heart, adopt, espouse. 3 *the faculty embraces*

*a wide range of disciplines:* include, take in, comprise, contain, incorporate, encompass, cover, subsume. noun *a fond embrace:* hug, cuddle, squeeze, clinch, caress.

**emerge** verb 1 *a policeman emerged from the alley:* come out, appear, come into view, become visible, surface, materialize, issue, come forth. 2 *several unexpected facts emerged:* become known, become apparent, be revealed, come to light, come out, turn up, transpire, unfold, turn out, prove to be the case.

**emergence** noun appearance, arrival, coming, materialization, advent, inception, dawn, birth, origination, start, development.

**emergency** noun *a military emergency:* crisis, disaster, catastrophe, calamity, plight; informal panic stations. adjective 1 *an emergency meeting:* urgent, crisis, extraordinary. 2 *emergency supplies:* reserve, standby, backup, fallback.

**emigrate** verb move abroad, move overseas, leave one's country, migrate, relocate, resettle. OPPOSITES immigrate.

**eminent** adjective illustrious, distinguished, renowned, esteemed, pre-eminent, notable, noted, noteworthy, great, prestigious, important, outstanding, celebrated, prominent, well known, acclaimed, exalted. OPPOSITES unknown.

**emission** noun discharge, release, outpouring, outflow, outrush, leak.

**emit** verb 1 *hydrocarbons emitted from vehicle exhausts:*

discharge, release, give out/off, pour out, radiate, leak, ooze, disgorge, eject, belch, spew out, exude. **2** *he emitted a loud cry:* utter, voice, let out, produce, give vent to, come out with.
OPPOSITES absorb, stifle.

**emotion** noun **1** *she was good at hiding her emotions:* feeling, sentiment, reaction, response, instinct, intuition, heart. **2** *overcome by emotion, she turned away:* passion, strength of feeling.

**emotional** adjective **1** *an emotional young man:* passionate, hot-blooded, ardent, fervent, excitable, temperamental, demonstrative. **2** *he paid an emotional tribute to his wife:* poignant, moving, touching, affecting, powerful, stirring, emotive, impassioned, dramatic; *informal* tear-jerking.
OPPOSITES cold, clinical.

**emphasis** noun **1** *the curriculum gave more emphasis to reading and writing:* prominence, importance, significance, value, stress, weight, accent, attention, priority. **2** *the emphasis is on the word 'little':* stress, accent, weight, beat.

**emphasize** verb stress, underline, highlight, focus attention on, point up, lay stress on, draw attention to, spotlight, foreground.
OPPOSITES understate.

**emphatic** adjective forceful, firm, vehement, wholehearted, energetic, vigorous, direct, insistent, certain, definite, out-and-out, decided, categorical, unqualified, unconditional, unequivocal, unambiguous, absolute, explicit, downright, outright, clear.
OPPOSITES hesitant.

**empire** noun **1** *the Ottoman Empire:* kingdom, realm, domain, territory, commonwealth, power. **2** *a worldwide shipping empire:* business, firm, company, corporation, multinational, conglomerate, group, consortium, operation.

**employ** verb **1** *she employed a chauffeur:* hire, engage, recruit, take on, sign up, appoint, retain. **2** *Sam was employed in carving a stone figure:* occupy, engage, involve, keep busy, tie up. **3** *the team employed subtle psychological tactics:* use, utilize, make use of, apply, exercise, practise, put into practice, exert, bring into play, bring to bear, draw on, resort to, turn to, have recourse to.
OPPOSITES dismiss.

**employed** adjective working, in work, in employment, holding down a job, earning, salaried, waged.
OPPOSITES unemployed.

**employee** noun worker, member of staff, blue-collar worker, white-collar worker, workman, labourer, (hired) hand; (**employees**) personnel, staff, workforce.

**employment** noun work, labour, service, job, post, position, situation, occupation, profession, trade, business, line of work.

**empower** verb **1** *the act empowered Henry to punish heretics:* authorize, entitle, permit, allow, license, enable. **2** *movements to empower the poor:* emancipate, unshackle, set free, liberate, enfranchise.
OPPOSITES forbid.

**empty** adjective **1** *an empty*

a
b
c
d
e
f
g
h
i
j
k
l
m
n
o
p
q
r
s
t
u
v
w
x
y
z

a
b
c
d
**e**
f
g
h
i
j
k
l
m
n
o
p
q
r
s
t
u
v
w
x
y
z

*house:* vacant, unoccupied, uninhabited, bare, clear, free. **2** *an empty threat:* meaningless, hollow, idle, vain, futile, worthless, useless, ineffectual. **3** *without her my life is empty:* futile, pointless, purposeless, worthless, meaningless, valueless, of no value, aimless, senseless.
OPPOSITES full, occupied, serious, worthwhile.
verb **1** *I emptied the dishwasher:* unload, unpack, clear, evacuate, drain. **2** *he emptied out the contents of the case:* remove, take out, extract, tip out, pour out.
OPPOSITES fill, replace.

**emulate** verb imitate, copy, mirror, echo, follow, model oneself on, take a leaf out of someone's book.

**enable** verb allow, permit, let, equip, empower, make able, fit, authorize, entitle, qualify.
OPPOSITES prevent.

**enact** verb **1** *the government enacted an environmental protection bill:* make law, pass, approve, ratify, validate, sanction, authorize. **2** *they are to enact a nativity play:* act out, perform, appear in, stage, mount, put on, present.
OPPOSITES repeal.

**enchanting** adjective captivating, charming, delightful, adorable, lovely, attractive, appealing, engaging, fetching, irresistible, fascinating.

**enclose** verb **1** *tall trees enclosed the garden:* surround, circle, ring, encircle, bound, close in, wall in. **2** *please enclose a stamped addressed envelope:* include, insert, put in, send.

**enclosure** noun compound, pen, fold, stockade, ring, paddock, yard, run, coop; N. Amer. corral.

**encompass** verb include, cover, embrace, incorporate, take in, contain, comprise, involve, deal with.

**encounter** verb **1** *we encountered a slight problem:* experience, run into, meet, come up against, face, be faced with, confront, suffer. **2** *I encountered a girl I used to know:* meet, run into, come across/upon, stumble across/on, chance on, happen on; informal bump into.
noun **1** *an unexpected encounter:* meeting, chance meeting. **2** *a violent encounter between police and demonstrators:* battle, fight, clash, scuffle, confrontation, struggle; informal run-in, scrap.

**encourage** verb **1** *the players were encouraged by the crowd:* hearten, cheer, buoy up, uplift, inspire, motivate, spur on, stir, fire up, stimulate, embolden; informal buck up. **2** *she encouraged him to go:* persuade, coax, urge, press, push, pressure, prod. **3** *the Government was keen to encourage local businesses:* support, back, promote, further, foster, nurture, cultivate, strengthen, stimulate.
OPPOSITES discourage, dissuade, hinder.

**encouragement** noun **1** *she needed a bit of encouragement:* support, cheering up, inspiration, motivation, stimulation, morale-boosting. **2** *they required no encouragement to get back to work:* persuasion, coaxing, urging, prodding, prompting,

**end** noun 1 *the end of the novel:* conclusion, termination, ending, finish, close, resolution, climax, finale, culmination, denouement. 2 *the end of the road:* extremity, limit, edge, border, boundary, periphery, point, tip, head, top, bottom. 3 *wealth is not an end in itself:* aim, goal, purpose, objective, object, target, intention, aspiration, wish, desire, ambition.
OPPOSITES beginning, means.
verb 1 *the show ended with a wedding scene:* finish, conclude, terminate, close, stop, cease, culminate, climax. 2 *she ended their relationship:* break off, call off, bring to an end, put an end to, stop, finish, terminate, discontinue, cancel.
OPPOSITES begin.

**endanger** verb jeopardize, risk, put at risk, put in danger, be a danger to, threaten, compromise, imperil.
OPPOSITES safeguard.

**endearing** adjective charming, appealing, attractive, engaging, winning, captivating, enchanting, cute, sweet, delightful, lovely.

**endeavour** verb *the company endeavoured to expand:* try, attempt, seek, strive, struggle, labour, toil, work.
noun 1 *an endeavour to build a more buoyant economy:* attempt, try, bid, effort. 2 *an extremely unwise endeavour:* undertaking, enterprise, venture, exercise, activity, exploit, deed, act, action, move.

**ending** noun end, finish, close, conclusion, resolution, summing-up, denouement, finale.
OPPOSITES beginning.

**endless** adjective 1 *a woman with endless energy:* unlimited, limitless, infinite, inexhaustible, boundless, unbounded, ceaseless, unending, everlasting, constant, continuous, interminable, unfailing, perpetual, eternal. 2 *we played endless games:* countless, innumerable, numerous, a multitude of; informal umpteen, no end of; literary myriad.
OPPOSITES limited, few.

**endorse** verb support, back, agree with, approve (of), favour, subscribe to, recommend, champion, uphold, sanction.
OPPOSITES oppose.

**endorsement** noun support, backing, approval, seal of approval, agreement, recommendation, patronage, sanction.

**endow** verb 1 *Henry II endowed the hospital:* finance, fund, pay for, subsidize, sponsor. 2 *he was endowed with great strength:* provide, supply, furnish, equip, favour, bless, grace.

**endowment** noun gift, present, grant, funding, award, donation, contribution, subsidy, sponsorship, bequest, legacy.

**endurance** noun 1 *she pushed him beyond endurance:* toleration, tolerance, forbearance, patience, acceptance, resignation, stoicism. 2 *an endurance test:* resistance, durability, permanence, longevity,

a
b
c
d
**e**
f
g
h
i
j
k
l
m
n
o
p
q
r
s
t
u
v
w
x
y
z

strength, toughness, stamina, staying power, fortitude.

**endure** verb **1** *he endured much pain*: undergo, go through, live through, experience, cope with, deal with, face, suffer, tolerate, put up with, brave, bear, withstand. **2** *our love will endure*: last, live, live on, go on, survive, abide, continue, persist, remain.
OPPOSITES fade.

**enemy** noun opponent, adversary, rival, antagonist, combatant, challenger, competitor, opposition, competition, the other side; literary foe.
OPPOSITES friend, ally.

**energetic** adjective **1** *an energetic woman*: active, lively, dynamic, spirited, animated, bouncy, bubbly, sprightly, tireless, indefatigable, enthusiastic; informal full of beans. **2** *energetic exercises*: vigorous, strenuous, brisk, hard, arduous, demanding, taxing, tough, rigorous. **3** *an energetic advertising campaign*: forceful, vigorous, aggressive, hard-hitting, high-powered, all-out, determined, bold, intensive; informal in-your-face.
OPPOSITES lethargic, gentle, half-hearted.

**energy** noun vitality, vigour, strength, stamina, animation, spirit, verve, enthusiasm, zest, exuberance, dynamism, drive; informal punch, bounce, oomph, go, get-up-and-go.

**enforce** verb **1** *the sheriff enforced the law*: impose, apply, administer, carry out, implement, bring to bear, put into effect. **2** *they cannot enforce cooperation*: force, compel, coerce, exact.

**engage** verb **1** *tasks which engage children's interest*: capture, catch, arrest, grab, draw, attract, gain, hold, grip, absorb, occupy. **2** *he engaged a secretary*: employ, hire, recruit, take on, enrol, appoint. **3** *the chance to engage in a wide range of pursuits*: participate in, join in, take part in, partake in/of, enter into, embark on. **4** *infantry units engaged the enemy*: attack, fall on, take on, clash with, encounter, meet, fight, do battle with.
OPPOSITES lose, dismiss.

**engagement** noun **1** *a business engagement*: appointment, meeting, arrangement, commitment, date, assignation, rendezvous. **2** *Britain's engagement in open trading*: participation, involvement. **3** *the first engagement of the war*: battle, fight, clash, confrontation, encounter, conflict, skirmish, action, hostilities.

**engaging** adjective charming, attractive, appealing, pleasing, pleasant, agreeable, likeable, lovable, sweet, winning, fetching; Scottish & N. English bonny.
OPPOSITES unappealing.

**engine** noun motor, generator, machine, turbine.

**engineer** noun **1** *a structural engineer*: designer, planner, builder. **2** *a repair engineer*: mechanic, repairer, technician, maintenance man, operator, driver, controller.
verb *he engineered a takeover deal*: bring about, arrange, pull off, bring off, contrive, manoeuvre, negotiate, organize, plan, mastermind.

**engraving** noun etching, print,

plate, picture, illustration, inscription.

**engulf** verb swamp, inundate, flood, deluge, immerse, swallow up, submerge, bury, envelop, overwhelm.

**enhance** verb improve, add to, strengthen, boost, increase, intensify, heighten, magnify, amplify, inflate, build up, supplement, augment.
OPPOSITES diminish.

**enjoy** verb 1 *he enjoys playing the piano:* like, be fond of, take pleasure in, be keen on, delight in, relish, revel in, adore, lap up, savour, luxuriate in, bask in; informal get a thrill out of.
2 *she had always enjoyed good health:* benefit from, be blessed with, be favoured with, be endowed with, possess, own, boast.
OPPOSITES dislike, lack.
■ **enjoy oneself** have fun, have a good time, make merry, celebrate, revel; informal party, have a whale of a time, let one's hair down.

**enjoyable** adjective entertaining, amusing, delightful, pleasant, congenial, convivial, agreeable, pleasurable, satisfying.
OPPOSITES disagreeable.

**enjoyment** noun pleasure, fun, entertainment, amusement, recreation, relaxation, happiness, merriment, joy, satisfaction, liking.

**enlarge** verb 1 *they enlarged the scope of their research:* extend, expand, grow, add to, amplify, augment, magnify, build up, stretch, widen, broaden, lengthen, elongate, deepen, thicken. 2 *the lymph glands had enlarged:* swell, distend, bloat, bulge, dilate, blow up, puff up.

OPPOSITES reduce, shrink.
■ **enlarge on** elaborate on, expand on, add to, flesh out, add detail to, develop, fill out, embellish, embroider.

**enlighten** verb inform, tell, make aware, open someone's eyes, illuminate; informal put someone in the picture.

**enlightened** adjective informed, aware, sophisticated, liberal, open-minded, broad-minded, educated, knowledgeable, civilized, refined, cultured.
OPPOSITES benighted.

**enlightenment** noun insight, understanding, awareness, education, learning, knowledge, illumination, awakening, instruction, teaching, open-mindedness, broad-mindedness, culture, refinement, cultivation, civilization.

**enlist** verb 1 *he enlisted in the Royal Engineers:* join up, enrol, sign up, volunteer, register.
2 *he was enlisted in the army:* recruit, call up, enrol, sign up, conscript, mobilize; US draft.
3 *he enlisted the help of a friend:* obtain, engage, secure, win, get.
OPPOSITES discharge, demobilize.

**enormity** noun 1 *the enormity of his crimes:* wickedness, vileness, heinousness, baseness, depravity, outrageousness.
2 *the enormity of the task:* immensity, hugeness, size, extent, magnitude.

**enormous** adjective huge, vast, immense, gigantic, giant, massive, colossal, mammoth, tremendous, extensive, mighty, monumental, mountainous; informal mega, monster, whopping; Brit. informal ginormous.

a
b
c
d
e
f
g
h
i
j
k
l
m
n
o
p
q
r
s
t
u
v
w
x
y
z

a
b
c
d
**e**
f
g
h
i
j
k
l
m
n
o
p
q
r
s
t
u
v
w
x
y
z

OPPOSITES tiny.

**enough** determiner *they had enough food:* sufficient, adequate, ample, abundant, the necessary; informal plenty of.
OPPOSITES insufficient.
pronoun *there's enough for everyone:* sufficient, plenty, an adequate amount, as much as necessary, a sufficiency, an ample supply, one's fill.

**enquire, inquire** verb 1 *I enquired about training courses:* ask, make enquiries. 2 *the commission is to enquire into the payments:* investigate, probe, look into, research, examine, explore, delve into; informal check out.

**enquiry, inquiry** noun
1 *telephone enquiries:* question, query. 2 *an enquiry into alleged security leaks:* investigation, probe, examination, inquest, hearing.

**enrage** verb anger, infuriate, incense, madden, inflame, antagonize, provoke; informal drive mad/crazy, make someone see red, make someone's blood boil.
OPPOSITES placate.

**enraged** adjective furious, infuriated, irate, incensed, raging, incandescent, fuming, seething, beside oneself; informal mad, livid, foaming at the mouth.
OPPOSITES calm.

**enrich** verb enhance, improve, better, add to, augment, supplement, complement, refine.
OPPOSITES spoil.

**enrol** verb 1 *they both enrolled for the course:* register, sign on/up, put one's name down, apply, volunteer, enter, join.
2 *280 new members were*

*enrolled:* accept, admit, take on, sign on/up, recruit, engage.

**ensemble** noun 1 *a Bulgarian folk ensemble:* group, band, company, troupe, cast, chorus, corps; informal combo. 2 *the buildings present a charming provincial ensemble:* whole, unit, body, set, collection, combination, composite, package. 3 *a pink and black ensemble:* outfit, costume, suit; informal get-up.

**ensue** verb result, follow, develop, succeed, emerge, arise, proceed, stem.

**ensure** verb 1 *ensure that the surface is completely clean:* make sure, make certain, see to it, check, confirm, establish, verify. 2 *legislation to ensure equal opportunities for all:* secure, guarantee, assure, certify.

**entail** verb involve, necessitate, require, need, demand, call for, mean, imply, cause, give rise to, occasion.

**enter** verb 1 *police entered the house:* go into, come into, get into, set foot in, gain access to. 2 *a bullet entered his chest:* penetrate, pierce, puncture, perforate. 3 *they entered the Army at eighteen:* join, enrol in/for, enlist in, volunteer for, sign up for. 4 *she entered a cookery competition:* go in for, register for, enrol for, sign on/ up for, compete in, take part in, participate in. 5 *the cashier entered the details in a ledger:* record, write, put down, take down, note, jot down, register, log. 6 *please enter your password:* key (in), type (in), tap in.
OPPOSITES leave.

**enterprise** noun 1 *a joint*

*enterprise:* undertaking, endeavour, venture, exercise, activity, operation, task, business, project, scheme. **2** *a woman with enterprise:* initiative, resourcefulness, imagination, ingenuity, inventiveness, originality, creativity. **3** *a profit-making enterprise:* business, company, firm, venture, organization, operation, concern, establishment; informal outfit.

**enterprising** adjective resourceful, entrepreneurial, imaginative, ingenious, inventive, creative, adventurous; informal go-ahead.
OPPOSITES unimaginative.

**entertain** verb **1** *he wrote stories to entertain them:* amuse, please, charm, cheer, interest, engage, occupy. **2** *he entertains foreign visitors:* receive, play host/hostess to, invite (round/over), throw a party for, wine and dine, feed. **3** *I would never entertain such an idea:* consider, contemplate, think of, hear of, countenance.
OPPOSITES bore, reject.

**entertainment** noun amusement, pleasure, leisure, recreation, relaxation, fun, enjoyment, interest.

**enthusiasm** noun keenness, eagerness, passion, fervour, zeal, zest, gusto, energy, vigour, fire, spirit, interest, commitment, devotion; informal get-up-and-go.
OPPOSITES apathy.

**enthusiast** noun fan, devotee, supporter, follower, aficionado, lover, admirer; informal buff.

**enthusiastic** adjective keen, eager, avid, ardent, fervent, passionate, zealous, excited, wholehearted, committed,

devoted, fanatical, earnest.
OPPOSITES apathetic.

**entice** verb tempt, lure, attract, appeal to, invite, persuade, beguile, coax, woo, lead on, seduce; informal sweet-talk.

**entire** adjective whole, complete, total, full.

**entirely** adverb **1** *that's entirely out of the question:* absolutely, completely, totally, wholly, utterly, quite, altogether, thoroughly. **2** *a gift entirely for charitable purposes:* solely, only, exclusively, purely, merely, just, alone.

**entitle** verb **1** *this pass entitles you to visit the museum:* qualify, make eligible, authorize, allow, permit, enable, empower. **2** *a chapter entitled 'Comedy and Tragedy':* name, title, call, label, designate, dub.

**entity** noun being, creature, individual, organism, life form, body, object, article, thing.

**entrance**[1] noun **1** *the main entrance:* entry, way in, access, approach, door, portal, gate, opening, mouth, foyer, lobby, porch; N. Amer. entryway. **2** *the entrance of Mrs Knight:* appearance, arrival, entry, coming. **3** *he was refused entrance:* admission, admittance, (right of) entry, entrée, access.
OPPOSITES exit, departure.

**entrance**[2] verb *I was entranced by her beauty:* enchant, bewitch, beguile, captivate, mesmerize, hypnotize, spellbind, transfix, enthral, engross, absorb, fascinate, stun, electrify, charm, delight; informal bowl over, knock out.

**entrant** noun competitor, contestant, contender,

a
b
c
d
**e**
f
g
h
i
j
k
l
m
n
o
p
q
r
s
t
u
v
w
x
y
z

participant, candidate, applicant.

**entrust** verb 1 *he was entrusted with the task:* charge, give someone the responsibility for, present. 2 *the powers entrusted to the Home Secretary:* assign, confer on, bestow on, vest in, delegate, give, grant, vouchsafe.

**entry** noun 1 *my moment of entry:* appearance, arrival, entrance, coming. 2 *the entry to the flats:* entrance, way in, access, approach, door, portal, gate, entrance hall, foyer, lobby; N. Amer. entryway. 3 *he was refused entry:* admission, admittance, entrance, access. 4 *entries in the cash book:* item, record, note, memo, memorandum. 5 *data entry:* recording, archiving, logging, documentation, capture. 6 *we must pick a winner from the entries:* submission, entry form, application.
OPPOSITES departure, exit.

**envelop** verb surround, cover, enfold, engulf, encircle, cocoon, sheathe, swathe, enclose, cloak, veil, shroud.

**environment** noun 1 *the hospital environment:* situation, setting, milieu, background, backdrop, context, conditions, ambience, atmosphere. 2 *the impact of pesticides on the environment:* the natural world, nature, the earth, the ecosystem, the biosphere, Mother Nature, wildlife, flora and fauna, the countryside.

**environmentalist** noun conservationist, ecologist, nature-lover, green; informal eco-warrior, tree-hugger.

**envisage** verb 1 *it was envisaged that the hospital would open soon:* foresee, predict, forecast, anticipate, expect, think likely. 2 *I cannot envisage what the future holds:* imagine, contemplate, picture, conceive of, think of.

**envoy** noun ambassador, emissary, diplomat, representative, delegate, spokesperson, agent, intermediary, mediator; informal go-between.

**envy** noun *feelings of envy:* jealousy, covetousness, resentment, bitterness.
verb 1 *I admired and envied her:* be envious of, be jealous of, be resentful of. 2 *we envied her lifestyle:* covet, desire, aspire to, wish for, want, long for, yearn for, hanker after, crave.

**epidemic** noun 1 *an epidemic of typhoid:* outbreak, plague, pandemic. 2 *a joyriding epidemic:* spate, rash, wave, eruption, plague, outbreak, craze, upsurge.

**episode** noun 1 *the best episode of his career:* incident, event, occurrence, chapter, experience, occasion, interlude, adventure, exploit. 2 *the final episode of the series:* instalment, chapter, passage, part, portion, section, programme, show. 3 *an episode of illness:* period, spell, bout, attack, phase; informal dose.

**equal** adjective 1 *lines of equal length:* identical, uniform, alike, like, the same, matching, equivalent, corresponding. 2 *equal treatment before the law:* impartial, non-partisan, fair, just, equitable, unprejudiced, non-discriminatory. 3 *an equal contest:* evenly matched, even, balanced, level; informal level pegging, neck and neck.

OPPOSITES different, discriminatory.

noun *they did not treat him as their equal:* equivalent, peer, fellow, like, counterpart, match, parallel.

verb **1** *two plus two equals four:* be equal to, be equivalent to, be the same as, come to, amount to, make, total, add up to. **2** *he equalled the world record:* match, reach, parallel, be level with.

**equality** noun fairness, equal rights, equal opportunities, impartiality, even-handedness, justice.

**equate** verb **1** *he equates criticism with treachery:* identify, compare, bracket, class, associate, connect, link, relate. **2** *moves to equate supply and demand:* equalize, balance, even out/up, level, square, tally, match.

**equilibrium** noun balance, stability, poise, symmetry, harmony.
OPPOSITES imbalance.

**equip** verb **1** *the boat was equipped with a flare gun:* provide, furnish, supply, issue, kit out, stock, provision, arm. **2** *the course will equip them for the workplace:* prepare, qualify, ready, suit, train.

**equipment** noun apparatus, paraphernalia, tools, utensils, implements, hardware, gadgetry, things; informal stuff, gear.

**equivalent** adjective *a degree or equivalent qualification:* comparable, corresponding, commensurate, similar, parallel, analogous.

noun *Denmark's equivalent of the Daily Mirror:* counterpart, parallel, alternative, analogue,

twin, opposite number.

**era** noun age, epoch, period, time, date, day, generation.

**eradicate** verb eliminate, get rid of, remove, obliterate, extinguish, exterminate, destroy, annihilate, kill, wipe out.

**erase** verb **1** *they erased his name:* delete, rub out, wipe off, blank out, expunge, excise, remove, obliterate. **2** *the data had been erased:* wipe, kill, delete, record over, format.

**erect** adjective upright, straight, vertical, perpendicular, standing (on end), bristling, stiff.
OPPOSITES bent, flat.
verb build, construct, put up, assemble, put together, fabricate, raise.
OPPOSITES demolish, dismantle, lower.

**erode** verb wear away/down, abrade, grind down, crumble, weather, undermine, weaken, deteriorate, destroy.

**erosion** noun wearing away, abrasion, attrition, weathering, dissolution, deterioration, disintegration, destruction.

**erotic** adjective sexually arousing, sexually stimulating, titillating, suggestive, pornographic, sexually explicit; informal blue, X-rated; euphemistic adult.

**errand** noun task, job, chore, assignment, mission.

**erratic** adjective unpredictable, inconsistent, changeable, variable, inconstant, irregular, fitful, unstable, varying, fluctuating, unreliable.
OPPOSITES consistent.

**error** noun mistake, inaccuracy, miscalculation, blunder, slip, oversight, misconception,

a b c d e f g h i j k l m n o p q r s t u v w x y z

delusion, misprint; Brit. informal boob.

**erupt** verb **1** *the volcano erupted:* give out lava, become active, explode. **2** *fighting erupted:* break out, flare up, start.

**eruption** noun **1** *a volcanic eruption:* discharge, explosion, lava flow, pyroclastic flow. **2** *an eruption of violence:* outbreak, flare-up, upsurge, outburst, explosion, wave, spate.

**escalate** verb **1** *prices have escalated:* increase rapidly, soar, rocket, shoot up, spiral; informal go through the roof. **2** *the dispute escalated:* grow, develop, mushroom, increase, heighten, intensify, accelerate.
OPPOSITES plunge, subside.

**escape** verb **1** *he escaped from prison:* run away/off, get out, break out, break free, bolt, make one's getaway, slip away; Brit. informal do a runner. **2** *he escaped his pursuers:* get away from, elude, avoid, dodge, shake off; informal give someone the slip. **3** *they escaped injury:* avoid, evade, elude, cheat, sidestep, circumvent, steer clear of, shirk. **4** *lethal gas escaped:* leak (out), spill (out), seep (out), discharge, flow (out), pour (out).
noun **1** *his escape from prison:* getaway, breakout, flight. **2** *a gas escape:* leak, spill, seepage, discharge, outflow, outpouring.

**escort** noun *a police escort:* guard, bodyguard, protector, minder, attendant, chaperone, entourage, retinue, protection, convoy.
verb **1** *he was escorted home by the police:* conduct, accompany, guide, usher, shepherd, take. **2** *he escorted her in to dinner:*

accompany, partner, take, bring.

**especially** adverb **1** *work poured in, especially from Kent:* mainly, mostly, chiefly, particularly, principally, largely, primarily. **2** *a committee formed especially for the purpose:* expressly, specially, specifically, exclusively, just, particularly, explicitly. **3** *he is especially talented:* exceptionally, particularly, specially, unusually, extraordinarily, uncommonly, uniquely, remarkably, outstandingly; informal seriously, majorly.

**essay** noun article, composition, paper, dissertation, thesis, discourse, study, assignment, treatise, piece, feature; N. Amer. theme.

**essence** noun **1** *the very essence of economics:* nature, heart, core, substance, basis, principle, quintessence, soul, spirit, reality; informal nitty-gritty. **2** *essence of ginger:* extract, concentrate, elixir, juice, oil.

**essential** adjective **1** *it is essential to remove the paint:* crucial, key, vital, indispensable, all-important, critical, imperative. **2** *the essential simplicity of his style:* basic, inherent, fundamental, quintessential, intrinsic, underlying, characteristic, innate, primary.
OPPOSITES unimportant, incidental.
noun **1** *an essential for broadcasters:* necessity, prerequisite; informal must. **2** *the essentials of the job:* fundamentals, basics, rudiments, first principles, foundations, essence, basis, core, kernel, crux; informal nitty-

gritty, nuts and bolts.

**establish** verb **1** *they established an office in Moscow:* set up, start, initiate, institute, found, create, inaugurate. **2** *evidence to establish his guilt:* prove, demonstrate, show, indicate, determine, confirm.

**establishment** noun **1** *the establishment of a democracy:* foundation, institution, formation, inception, creation, installation, inauguration. **2** *a dressmaking establishment:* business, firm, company, concern, enterprise, venture, organization, operation; informal outfit. **3** *educational establishments:* institution, place, premises, institute. **4** *they dare to poke fun at the Establishment:* the authorities, the powers that be, the system, the ruling class.

**estate** noun **1** *the Balmoral estate:* property, grounds, garden(s), park, parkland, land(s), territory. **2** *a housing estate:* area, development, complex; Scottish scheme. **3** *a coffee estate:* plantation, farm, holding, forest, vineyard; N. Amer. ranch. **4** *he left an estate worth £610,000:* assets, capital, wealth, riches, holdings, fortune, property, effects, possessions, belongings.

**esteem** noun *she was held in high esteem:* respect, admiration, acclaim, appreciation, recognition, honour, reverence, estimation, regard.
verb *such ceramics are highly esteemed:* respect, admire, value, regard, appreciate, like, prize, treasure, revere.

**estimate** verb **1** *estimate the cost:* calculate roughly, approximate, guess, evaluate, judge. **2** *we estimate it to be worth £50,000:* consider, believe, reckon, deem, judge, rate.
noun *an estimate of the cost:* rough calculation, approximation, estimation, guess, costing, quotation, valuation, evaluation; informal guesstimate.

**etch** verb engrave, carve, inscribe, incise, score, mark, scratch, scrape.

**etching** noun engraving, print, plate.

**eternal** adjective **1** *eternal happiness:* everlasting, never-ending, endless, perpetual, undying, immortal, abiding, permanent, enduring. **2** *eternal vigilance:* constant, continual, continuous, perpetual, sustained, uninterrupted, unbroken, non-stop, round-the-clock.
OPPOSITES transient, intermittent.

**eternity** noun **1** *the memory will remain for eternity:* ever, all time, perpetuity. **2** (informal) *I waited an eternity for you:* a long time, an age, ages, a lifetime, hours, years, forever.

**ethical** adjective **1** *an ethical dilemma:* moral. **2** *ethical investment:* morally correct, right-minded, principled, good, moral, just, honourable, fair.
OPPOSITES unethical.

**ethics** plural noun morals, morality, values, principles, ideals, standards (of behaviour).

**ethnic** adjective racial, race-related, national, cultural, folk, tribal, ethnological.

**euphoria** noun elation, happiness, joy, delight, glee,

a
b
c
d
e
f
g
h
i
j
k
l
m
n
o
p
q
r
s
t
u
v
w
x
y
z

excitement, exhilaration, jubilation, exultation, ecstasy, bliss, rapture.
OPPOSITES misery.

**evacuate** verb 1 *local residents were evacuated:* remove, move out, take away. 2 *they evacuated the building:* leave, vacate, abandon, move out of, quit, withdraw from, retreat from, flee. 3 *police evacuated the area:* clear, empty.

**evade** verb 1 *they evaded the guards:* elude, avoid, dodge, escape (from), steer clear of, sidestep, lose, leave behind, shake off; informal give someone the slip. 2 *he evaded the question:* avoid, dodge, sidestep, bypass, skirt round; informal duck.
OPPOSITES confront.

**evaluate** verb assess, judge, gauge, rate, estimate, appraise, weigh up; informal size up.

**evaporate** verb 1 *the water evaporated:* vaporize, dry up. 2 *the feeling has evaporated:* end, pass (away), fizzle out, peter out, wear off, vanish, fade, disappear, melt away.
OPPOSITES condense, materialize.

**evasive** adjective equivocal, prevaricating, elusive, ambiguous, non-committal, vague, unclear, oblique.

**even** adjective 1 *an even surface:* flat, smooth, uniform, level, plane. 2 *an even temperature:* uniform, constant, steady, stable, consistent, unvarying, unchanging, regular. 3 *the score was even:* level, drawn, tied, all square, neck and neck; Brit. level pegging; informal even-steven(s).
OPPOSITES bumpy, irregular, unequal.

**evening** noun dusk, twilight,
nightfall, sunset, sundown, night.

**event** noun 1 *an annual event:* occurrence, happening, incident, affair, occasion, phenomenon, function, gathering; informal do. 2 *a team event:* competition, contest, tournament, match, fixture, race, game, sport, discipline.

**eventful** adjective busy, action-packed, full, lively, active, hectic.
OPPOSITES dull.

**eventual** adjective final, ultimate, resulting, ensuing, consequent, subsequent.

**eventually** adverb in the end, in due course, by and by, in time, after a time, finally, at last, ultimately, in the long run, at the end of the day, one day, some day, sometime, sooner or later.

**ever** adverb 1 *the best I've ever done:* at any time, at any point, on any occasion, under any circumstances, on any account, until now. 2 *he was ever the optimist:* always, forever, eternally. 3 *an ever increasing rate of crime:* continually, constantly, always, endlessly, perpetually, incessantly.

**everlasting** adjective eternal, endless, never-ending, perpetual, undying, abiding, enduring, infinite.
OPPOSITES transient, occasional.

**every** determiner 1 *he exercised every day:* each, each and every, every single. 2 *we make every effort to satisfy our clients:* all possible, the utmost.
OPPOSITES no.

**everybody** pronoun everyone, every person, each person, all, one and all, all and sundry, the whole world, the public.

OPPOSITES nobody.

**everyday** adjective **1** *the everyday demands of a baby:* daily, day-to-day, ongoing. **2** *everyday drugs like aspirin:* commonplace, ordinary, common, usual, regular, familiar, conventional, routine, run-of-the-mill, standard, stock, household, domestic; Brit. common or garden.
OPPOSITES unusual.

**everyone** pronoun. See **EVERYBODY.**

**everything** pronoun every single thing, each thing, the (whole) lot, all; informal the works.
OPPOSITES nothing.

**everywhere** adverb all over, all around, in every nook and cranny, far and wide, near and far, high and low, {here, there, and everywhere}, the world over, worldwide; informal all over the place; Brit. informal all over the shop; N. Amer. informal all over the map.
OPPOSITES nowhere.

**evidence** noun **1** *evidence of his infidelity:* proof, confirmation, verification, substantiation, corroboration. **2** *the court accepted her evidence:* testimony, witness statement, declaration, submission; Law deposition, affidavit. **3** *evidence of a struggle:* signs, indications, marks, traces, suggestions, hints.

**evident** adjective obvious, apparent, noticeable, conspicuous, visible, discernible, clear, plain, manifest, patent; informal as clear as day.

**evidently** adverb **1** *he was evidently upset:* obviously, clearly, plainly, unmistakably,

manifestly, patently. **2** *evidently, she believed him:* seemingly, apparently, as far as one can tell, from all appearances, on the face of it, it seems, it appears.

**evil** adjective **1** *an evil deed:* wicked, bad, wrong, immoral, sinful, vile, iniquitous, villainous, vicious, malicious, malevolent, demonic, diabolical, fiendish, dark, monstrous. **2** *an evil spirit:* harmful, bad, malign. **3** *evil weather:* unpleasant, disagreeable, nasty, horrible, foul, filthy, vile.
OPPOSITES good, benign, pleasant.
noun **1** *the evil in our midst:* wickedness, badness, wrongdoing, sin, sinfulness, immorality, vice, iniquity, corruption, villainy. **2** *nothing but evil will result:* harm, pain, misery, sorrow, suffering, trouble, disaster, misfortune, woe.
OPPOSITES good.

**evoke** verb bring to mind, put one in mind of, conjure up, summon (up), invoke, elicit, induce, kindle, awaken, arouse.

**evolution** noun **1** *the evolution of Bolshevism:* development, progress, rise, expansion, growth. **2** *his interest in evolution:* natural selection, Darwinism, adaptation, development.

**evolve** verb develop, progress, advance, grow, expand, spread.

**exact** adjective **1** *an exact description:* precise, accurate, correct, faithful, close, true, literal, strict, perfect. **2** *an exact record keeper:* careful, meticulous, painstaking, punctilious, conscientious,

a b c d e f g h i j k l m n o p q r s t u v w x y z

scrupulous.
OPPOSITES inaccurate, careless.
**verb 1** *he exacted certain promises:* demand, require, impose, extract, compel, force, wring. **2** *they exacted a terrible vengeance on him:* inflict, impose, administer, mete out, wreak.

**exacting** adjective demanding, stringent, testing, challenging, arduous, laborious, taxing, gruelling, punishing, hard, tough.
OPPOSITES easy, easy-going.

**exactly** adverb **1** *it's exactly as I expected:* precisely, entirely, absolutely, completely, totally, just, quite, in every respect. **2** *write it out exactly:* accurately, precisely, unerringly, faultlessly, perfectly, faithfully.

**exaggerate** verb overstate, overemphasize, overestimate, inflate, embellish, embroider, elaborate, overplay, dramatize; Brit. informal blow out of all proportion.
OPPOSITES understate.

**examination** noun **1** *artefacts spread out for examination:* scrutiny, inspection, perusal, study, investigation, consideration, analysis. **2** *a medical examination:* inspection, check-up, assessment, appraisal, test, scan. **3** *a school examination:* test, exam, assessment; N. Amer. quiz.

**examine** verb **1** *they examined the bank records:* inspect, scrutinize, investigate, look at, study, appraise, analyse, review, survey; informal check out. **2** *students were examined after a year:* test, quiz, question, assess, appraise.

**example** noun **1** *a fine example of Chinese porcelain:* specimen, sample, instance, case, illustration. **2** *we must follow their example:* precedent, lead, model, pattern, ideal, standard. **3** *he was hanged as an example to others:* warning, lesson, deterrent, disincentive.

**excavate** verb unearth, dig up, uncover, reveal, disinter, exhume, dig out, quarry, mine.

**exceed** verb be more than, be greater than, be over, go beyond, top, surpass.

**excel** verb shine, be excellent, be outstanding, be skilful, be talented, stand out, be second to none.

**excellence** noun distinction, quality, superiority, brilliance, greatness, calibre, eminence.

**excellent** adjective very good, superb, outstanding, exceptional, marvellous, wonderful, splendid; informal terrific, fantastic.
OPPOSITES inferior.

**except** preposition excluding, not including, excepting, except for, omitting, not counting, but, besides, apart from, aside from, barring, bar, other than; informal outside of.
OPPOSITES including.

**exception** noun anomaly, irregularity, deviation, special case, peculiarity, abnormality, oddity.

**exceptional** adjective **1** *the drought was exceptional:* unusual, abnormal, atypical, out of the ordinary, rare, unprecedented, unexpected, surprising. **2** *her exceptional ability:* outstanding, extraordinary, remarkable, special, phenomenal, prodigious.

OPPOSITES normal, average.

**excerpt** noun extract, part, section, piece, portion, snippet, clip, citation, quotation, quote, line, passage, fragment.

**excess** noun 1 *an excess of calcium:* surplus, surfeit, over-abundance, superabundance, superfluity, glut. 2 *the excess is turned into fat:* extra, surplus, remainder, rest, residue. 3 *a life of excess:* overindulgence, intemperance, immoderation, profligacy, extravagance, self-indulgence.
OPPOSITES lack, restraint.
adjective *excess oil:* surplus, superfluous, redundant, unwanted, unneeded, excessive, extra.

**excessive** adjective 1 *excessive alcohol consumption:* immoderate, intemperate, overindulgent, unrestrained, uncontrolled, extravagant. 2 *the cost is excessive:* exorbitant, extortionate, unreasonable, outrageous, uncalled for, inordinate, unwarranted, disproportionate; informal over the top.

**exchange** noun 1 *the exchange of ideas:* interchange, trade, trading, swapping, traffic, trafficking. 2 *a brief exchange:* conversation, dialogue, chat, talk, discussion.
verb *we exchanged shirts:* trade, swap, switch, change.

**excite** verb 1 *the prospect of a holiday excited me:* thrill, exhilarate, animate, enliven, rouse, stir, stimulate, galvanize. 2 *his clothes excited envy:* provoke, stir up, rouse, arouse, kindle, trigger, spark off, incite, cause.
OPPOSITES bore.

**excitement** noun 1 *the*

*excitement of seeing a leopard in the wild:* thrill, pleasure, delight, joy; informal buzz. 2 *excitement in her eyes:* exhilaration, elation, animation, enthusiasm, eagerness, anticipation.

**exciting** adjective thrilling, exhilarating, stirring, rousing, stimulating, intoxicating, electrifying, invigorating, gripping, compelling, powerful, dramatic.

**exclaim** verb cry out, declare, proclaim, blurt out, call out, shout, yell.

**exclude** verb 1 *women were excluded from the club:* keep out, deny access to, shut out, bar, ban, prohibit. 2 *the clause excluded any judicial review:* rule out, preclude. 3 *the price excludes postage:* be exclusive of, not include.
OPPOSITES admit, include, allow for.

**exclusive** adjective 1 *an exclusive club:* select, chic, high-class, elite, fashionable, stylish, elegant, premier; Brit. upmarket; informal posh, classy; Brit. informal swish. 2 *a room for your exclusive use:* sole, unshared, unique, individual, personal, private. 3 *prices exclusive of VAT:* not including, excluding, leaving out, omitting, excepting.
OPPOSITES shared, inclusive.

**excursion** noun outing, trip, jaunt, expedition, journey, tour, day trip, day out, drive, run; informal spin.

**excuse** verb 1 *please excuse me:* forgive, pardon. 2 *such conduct cannot be excused:* justify, defend, condone, forgive, overlook, disregard, ignore, tolerate, explain, mitigate. 3 *she*

a
b
c
d
**e**
f
g
h
i
j
k
l
m
n
o
p
q
r
s
t
u
v
w
x
y
z

*was excused from her duties:* let off, release, relieve, exempt, absolve, free.
OPPOSITES punish, blame, condemn.
noun **1** *that's no excuse for stealing:* justification, defence, reason, explanation, mitigating circumstances, mitigation. **2** *an excuse to get away:* pretext, pretence; Brit. get-out; informal story, alibi.

**execute** verb **1** *he executed a series of financial deals:* carry out, accomplish, bring off/about, implement, achieve, complete, engineer; informal pull off. **2** *he was finally executed:* put to death, kill, hang, behead, electrocute, shoot.

**execution** noun **1** *the execution of the plan:* implementation, carrying out, performance, accomplishment, bringing off/about, attainment, realization. **2** *public execution:* killing, capital punishment, the death penalty.

**executive** adjective *executive powers:* administrative, managerial, decision-making, law-making, governing, controlling.
noun **1** *the company's chief executive:* director, manager, senior official, administrator; informal boss, exec, suit. **2** *the future role of the executive:* administration, management, directorate, government, authority.

**exemplary** adjective perfect, ideal, model, faultless, flawless, impeccable, irreproachable.
OPPOSITES deplorable.

**exemplify** verb typify, epitomize, be an example of, be representative of, symbolize, illustrate, demonstrate.

**exempt** adjective **1** free, not liable, not subject, immune, excepted, excused, absolved.
OPPOSITES subject to.
verb excuse, free, release, exclude, grant immunity, spare, absolve; informal let off.
OPPOSITES oblige.

**exemption** noun immunity, exception, dispensation, indemnity, exclusion, freedom, release, relief, absolution.

**exercise** noun **1** *exercise improves your heart:* physical activity, a workout, working out, movement, training. **2** *translation exercises:* task, piece of work, problem, assignment, practice. **3** *a military exercise:* manoeuvre, operation, deployment.
verb **1** *she exercised every day:* work out, do exercises, train. **2** *he must learn to exercise patience:* use, employ, make use of, utilize, practise, apply. **3** *the problem continued to exercise him:* concern, occupy, worry, trouble, bother, disturb, prey on someone's mind.

**exert** verb bring to bear, apply, use, utilize, deploy.
■ **exert oneself** work hard, labour, toil, make an effort, endeavour, slog away, push oneself.

**exhaust** verb **1** *the effort had exhausted him:* tire out, wear out, overtire, fatigue, weary, drain; informal take it out of one, shatter; Brit. informal knacker; N. Amer. informal poop, tucker out. **2** *the country has exhausted its reserves:* use up, get through, consume, finish, deplete, spend, empty, drain; informal blow.
OPPOSITES invigorate, replenish.

**exhaustion** noun tiredness, overtiredness, fatigue,

weariness.

**exhibit** verb 1 *the paintings were exhibited in Glasgow:* display, show, put on display, unveil, present. 2 *Luke exhibited signs of jealousy:* show, reveal, display, manifest, indicate, demonstrate, express. noun *an exhibit at the British Museum:* item, piece, artefact, display, collection.

**exhibition** noun 1 *a photography exhibition:* display, show, showing, presentation, exposition. 2 *a convincing exhibition of concern:* display, show, demonstration, manifestation, expression.

**exhilarating** adjective thrilling, exciting, invigorating, stimulating, intoxicating, electrifying.

**exile** noun 1 *his exile from his homeland:* banishment, expulsion, deportation, eviction, isolation. 2 *political exiles:* expatriate, émigré, deportee, displaced person, refugee.

**exist** verb 1 *animals that existed long ago:* live, be alive, be, be present. 2 *the liberal climate that now exists:* prevail, occur, be found, be in existence, be the case. 3 *she had to exist on a low income:* survive, subsist, live, support oneself, manage, make do, get by, scrape by, make ends meet.

**existence** noun 1 *the industry's continued existence:* survival, continuation. 2 *her suburban existence:* way of life, life, lifestyle, situation.
■ **in existence** existing, alive, surviving, remaining, extant, existent, in circulation, current.

**exit** noun 1 *a fire exit:* way out, door, escape route, egress.

2 *take the second exit:* turning, turn-off, junction. 3 *his sudden exit:* departure, leaving, withdrawal, going, retreat, flight, exodus, escape.
OPPOSITES entrance, arrival.
verb *the doctor had just exited:* leave, go out, depart, withdraw, retreat.
OPPOSITES enter.

**exotic** adjective 1 *exotic birds:* foreign, non-native, alien, tropical. 2 *exotic places:* foreign, faraway, far-off, far-flung, distant. 3 *Linda's exotic appearance:* striking, colourful, eye-catching, unusual, unconventional, extravagant, outlandish.
OPPOSITES native, nearby, conventional.

**expand** verb 1 *metals expand when heated:* enlarge, increase in size, swell, lengthen, stretch, spread, thicken, fill out. 2 *the company is expanding:* grow, enlarge, increase in size, extend, augment, broaden, widen, develop, diversify, build up, branch out, spread.
OPPOSITES contract.
■ **expand on** elaborate on, enlarge on, go into detail about, flesh out, develop.

**expansion** noun 1 *expansion and contraction:* enlargement, swelling, lengthening, elongation, stretching, thickening. 2 *the expansion of the company:* growth, increase in size, enlargement, extension, development, diversification, spread.
OPPOSITES contraction.

**expect** verb 1 *I expect she'll be late:* suppose, presume, imagine, assume, surmise; informal guess, reckon; N. Amer. informal figure. 2 *a 10 per cent*

a
b
c
d
e
f
g
h
i
j
k
l
m
n
o
p
q
r
s
t
u
v
w
x
y
z

*rise was expected:* anticipate, envisage, await, look for, hope for, look forward to, contemplate, bargain for/on, predict, forecast. **3** *we expect total loyalty:* require, ask for, call for, want, insist on, demand.

**expectation** noun **1** *her expectations were unrealistic:* supposition, assumption, presumption, conjecture, calculation, prediction, hope. **2** *tense with expectation:* anticipation, expectancy, eagerness, excitement, suspense.

**expedition** noun journey, voyage, tour, safari, trek, mission, quest, hike, trip.

**expel** verb throw out, bar, ban, debar, drum out, banish, exile, deport, evict; informal chuck out.
OPPOSITES admit.

**expense** noun cost, expenditure, spending, outlay, outgoings, payment, price, charge, fees, overheads, tariff, bill.
OPPOSITES income, profit.

**expensive** adjective costly, dear, high-priced, overpriced, exorbitant, extortionate; informal steep, stiff, pricey.
OPPOSITES cheap.

**experience** noun
**1** *qualifications and experience:* skill, practical knowledge, understanding, background, track record, history; informal know-how. **2** *an enjoyable experience:* incident, occurrence, event, happening, episode, adventure. **3** *his first experience of business:* involvement in, participation in, contact with, acquaintance with, exposure to.
verb *they experience daily harassment:* undergo, go

through, encounter, face, meet, come across, come up against.

**experienced** adjective knowledgeable, skilful, skilled, expert, proficient, trained, competent, capable, seasoned, practised, mature, veteran.
OPPOSITES inexperienced.

**experiment** noun *the calculations were confirmed by experiment:* test, investigation, trial, examination, observation, research, assessment, evaluation, appraisal, analysis, study.
verb *they experimented with new ideas:* carry out experiments, test, trial, try out, assess, appraise, evaluate.

**experimental** adjective **1** *the experimental stage:* exploratory, investigational, trial, test, pilot, speculative, tentative, preliminary. **2** *experimental music:* new, innovative, creative, radical, avant-garde, alternative, unorthodox, unconventional, cutting-edge.

**expert** noun specialist, authority, pundit, maestro, virtuoso, master, wizard, connoisseur, aficionado; informal ace, pro, hotshot; Brit. informal dab hand; N. Amer. informal maven.
OPPOSITES amateur.
adjective skilful, skilled, adept, accomplished, experienced, practised, knowledgeable, talented, masterly, virtuoso; informal ace, crack, mean.
OPPOSITES incompetent.

**expertise** noun skill, prowess, proficiency, competence, knowledge, ability, aptitude, capability; informal know-how.

**expire** verb **1** *my contract has expired:* run out, become invalid, become void, lapse, end, finish, stop, terminate.

**2** *the spot where he expired:* die, pass away, breathe one's last; informal kick the bucket, croak; Brit. informal snuff it, peg out; N. Amer. informal buy the farm.

**explain** verb **1** *he explained the procedure:* describe, make clear, spell out, put into words, define, elucidate, expound, clarify, throw light on. **2** *that could explain his behaviour:* account for, give a reason for, excuse.

**explanation** noun **1** *an explanation of his theory:* clarification, description, statement, interpretation, definition, commentary. **2** *I owe you an explanation:* account, reason, justification, answer, excuse, defence, vindication.

**explicit** adjective **1** *explicit instructions:* clear, plain, straightforward, crystal clear, precise, exact, specific, unequivocal, unambiguous, detailed. **2** *sexually explicit material:* graphic, candid, full-frontal, uncensored. OPPOSITES vague, tasteful, decent.

**explode** verb **1** *a bomb has exploded:* blow up, detonate, go off, burst, erupt. **2** *exploding an atomic device:* detonate, set off, let off, discharge. **3** *he just exploded:* lose one's temper, blow up; informal fly off the handle, hit the roof, blow one's top; Brit. informal go spare; N. Amer. informal blow one's lid/stack. **4** *the city's exploding population:* increase rapidly, mushroom, snowball, escalate, burgeon, rocket. **5** *exploding the myths about men:* disprove, refute, rebut, repudiate, debunk, give the lie to; informal shoot full of holes, blow out of the water. OPPOSITES shrink.

**exploit** verb **1** *we should exploit this opportunity:* utilize, make use of, turn/put to good use, make the most of, capitalize on, benefit from; informal cash in on. **2** *exploiting the workers:* take advantage of, abuse, impose on, treat unfairly, misuse, ill-treat; informal walk (all) over. noun *his exploits brought him notoriety:* feat, deed, act, adventure, stunt, escapade, achievement.

**exploitation** noun taking advantage, abuse, misuse, ill-treatment, unfair treatment, oppression.

**exploration** noun investigation, study, survey, research, inspection, examination, scrutiny, observation.

**explore** verb **1** *exploring Iceland:* travel through, tour, survey, scout, reconnoitre. **2** *they explored the possibilities:* investigate, look into, consider, examine, research, survey, scrutinize, study, review; informal check out.

**explosion** noun **1** *Ed heard the explosion:* detonation, eruption, bang, blast, boom. **2** *an explosion of anger:* outburst, flare-up, outbreak, eruption, storm, rush, surge, fit, paroxysm. **3** *a population explosion:* sudden increase, mushrooming, snowballing, escalation, multiplication, burgeoning, rocketing.

**explosive** adjective **1** *explosive gases:* volatile, inflammable, flammable, combustible, incendiary. **2** *Marco's explosive temper:* fiery, stormy, violent, volatile, passionate,

tempestuous, turbulent, touchy, irascible. **3** *an explosive situation:* tense, highly charged, overwrought, dangerous, perilous, hazardous, sensitive, delicate, unstable, volatile.
OPPOSITES inert, cool, stable.
noun *stocks of explosives:* bomb, charge, incendiary (device).

**expose** verb **1** *at low tide the rocks are exposed:* reveal, uncover, lay bare. **2** *he was exposed to radiation:* lay open, subject, put at risk of, put in jeopardy of, leave unprotected from. **3** *they were exposed to new ideas:* introduce to, bring into contact with, make aware of, familiarize with, acquaint with. **4** *he was exposed as a liar:* uncover, reveal, unveil, unmask, detect, find out, denounce, condemn; informal blow the whistle on.
OPPOSITES cover, protect from, insulate from, protect.

**exposure** noun **1** *suffering from exposure:* frostbite, cold, hypothermia. **2** *the exposure of a banking fraud:* uncovering, revelation, disclosure, unveiling, unmasking, discovery, detection. **3** *we're getting a lot of exposure:* publicity, advertising, public attention, media interest; informal hype.

**express**[1] verb communicate, convey, indicate, show, demonstrate, reveal, put across/over, get across/over, articulate, put into words, voice, give voice to, state, air, give vent to.
■ **express oneself** communicate one's thoughts/opinions/views, put thoughts into words, speak one's mind, say what's on one's mind.

**express**[2] adjective rapid, swift, fast, high-speed, non-stop, direct.
OPPOSITES slow.

**express**[3] adjective **1** *it was his express wish:* explicit, clear, direct, plain, distinct, unambiguous, categorical. **2** *his express purpose was to do aid work:* sole, specific, particular, special, specified.
OPPOSITES vague, implied.

**expression** noun **1** *the free expression of their views:* utterance, uttering, voicing, declaration, articulation. **2** *an expression of sympathy:* indication, demonstration, show, exhibition, token, communication, illustration. **3** *a sad expression:* look, appearance, air, manner, countenance. **4** *a well-known expression:* idiom, phrase, term, proverb, saying, adage, maxim. **5** *put more expression into it:* emotion, feeling, spirit, passion, intensity, style.

**expressive** adjective **1** *an expressive shrug:* eloquent, meaningful, demonstrative, suggestive. **2** *an expressive song:* emotional, passionate, poignant, moving, stirring, emotionally charged.
OPPOSITES undemonstrative, inexpressive.

**expulsion** noun **1** *expulsion from the party:* removal, debarment, dismissal, exclusion, ejection, banishment, eviction. **2** *the expulsion of waste:* discharge, ejection, excretion, voiding, evacuation, elimination, passing.
OPPOSITES admission.

**exquisite** adjective **1** *exquisite antiques:* beautiful, lovely, elegant, fine, delicate, fragile, dainty, subtle. **2** *exquisite taste:* discriminating, discerning, sensitive, fastidious, refined.

**extend** verb **1** *we've extended the kitchen:* expand, enlarge, increase, lengthen, widen, broaden. **2** *the garden extends to the road:* continue, carry on, stretch, reach. **3** *we have extended our range:* widen, expand, broaden, augment, supplement, increase, add to, enhance, develop. **4** *extending the life of parliament:* prolong, lengthen, increase, stretch out, protract, spin out, string out. **5** *he extended a hand:* hold out, reach out, hold forth, stretch out, offer, give, proffer. **6** *we wish to extend our thanks:* offer, proffer, give, accord. OPPOSITES reduce, shorten, withdraw.
■ extend to include, take in, incorporate, encompass.

**extension** noun **1** *they are planning an extension:* addition, add-on, adjunct, annex, wing. **2** *an extension of our knowledge:* expansion, increase, enlargement, widening, broadening, deepening, augmentation, enhancement, development, growth. **3** *an extension of opening hours:* prolongation, lengthening, increase. OPPOSITES restriction, shortening.

**extensive** adjective **1** *extensive grounds:* large, sizeable, substantial, considerable, ample, great, vast. **2** *extensive knowledge:* comprehensive, thorough, exhaustive, broad, wide, wide-ranging, catholic.

**extent** noun **1** *two acres in extent:* area, size, expanse, length, proportions,

dimensions. **2** *the full extent of her illness:* degree, scale, level, magnitude, scope, size, reach, range.

**exterior** adjective *the exterior surface:* outer, outside, outermost, outward, external. OPPOSITES interior.
noun *a beautiful exterior:* outside, external surface, outward appearance, facade. OPPOSITES interior.

**external** adjective **1** *an external wall:* outer, outside, outermost, outward, exterior. **2** *an external examiner:* outside, independent, visiting. OPPOSITES internal.

**extinct** adjective **1** *an extinct species:* vanished, lost, gone, died out, wiped out, destroyed. **2** *an extinct volcano:* inactive. OPPOSITES living, dormant.

**extinction** noun dying out, disappearance, vanishing, extermination, destruction, elimination, eradication, annihilation.

**extra** adjective additional, more, added, supplementary, further, auxiliary, ancillary, subsidiary, secondary.
adverb exceptionally, particularly, specially, especially, extremely.
noun addition, supplement, bonus, adjunct, addendum, add-on.

**extract** verb **1** *he extracted the cassette:* take out, draw out, pull out, remove, withdraw, release, extricate. **2** *they extracted a confession:* wrest, exact, wring, screw, squeeze, obtain by force, extort. **3** *the roots are crushed to extract the juice:* squeeze out, press out, obtain. OPPOSITES insert.

a b c d e f g h i j k l m n o p q r s t u v w x y z

a
b
c
d
**e**
**f**
g
h
i
j
k
l
m
n
o
p
q
r
s
t
u
v
w
x
y
z

noun **1** *an extract from his article*: excerpt, passage, citation, quotation. **2** *an extract of ginseng*: distillation, distillate, concentrate, essence, juice.

**extraordinary** adjective **1** *an extraordinary coincidence*: remarkable, exceptional, amazing, astonishing, astounding, sensational, stunning, incredible, unbelievable, phenomenal; informal fantastic. **2** *extraordinary speed*: very great, tremendous, enormous, immense, prodigious, stupendous, monumental.
OPPOSITES unremarkable, tiny.

**extravagant** adjective **1** *an extravagant lifestyle*: spendthrift, profligate, wasteful, prodigal, lavish. **2** *extravagant praise*: excessive, immoderate, exaggerated, gushing, unrestrained, effusive, fulsome. **3** *decorated in an extravagant style*: ornate, elaborate, fancy, over-elaborate, ostentatious, exaggerated; informal flashy.
OPPOSITES thrifty, moderate, plain.

**extreme** adjective **1** *extreme danger*: utmost, (very) great, greatest (possible), maximum, great, acute, enormous, severe,

serious. **2** *extreme measures*: drastic, serious, desperate, dire, radical, far-reaching, draconian; Brit. swingeing. **3** *extreme views*: radical, extremist, immoderate, fanatical, revolutionary, subversive, militant. **4** *extreme sports*: dangerous, hazardous, risky, high-risk, adventurous; informal white-knuckle. **5** *the extreme north-west*: furthest, farthest, utmost, remotest, ultra-.
OPPOSITES slight, moderate, safe, near.

noun *the two extremes*: opposite, antithesis, side of the coin, (opposite) pole, limit, extremity, contrast.

**extremely** adverb very, exceptionally, especially, extraordinarily, tremendously, immensely, hugely, supremely, highly, mightily; informal awfully, terribly, seriously; Brit. informal jolly; N. Amer. informal mighty.
OPPOSITES slightly.

**extremist** noun fanatic, radical, zealot, fundamentalist, hardliner, militant, activist.
OPPOSITES moderate.

**eye** verb look at, observe, view, gaze at, stare at, regard, contemplate, survey, scrutinize, consider, glance at, watch; informal check out, size up; N. Amer. informal eyeball.

# Ff

**fable** noun parable, allegory, myth, legend, story.

**fabric** noun **1** *the finest fabrics*: cloth, material, textile. **2** *the fabric of society*: structure, construction, make-up,

organization, framework, essence.

**fabulous** adjective **1** *fabulous salaries*: stupendous, prodigious, phenomenal, exceptional, fantastic, breathtaking, staggering, unthinkable, unimaginable, incredible, undreamed of. **2** (informal) *we had a fabulous time.* See **EXCELLENT**.

**facade** noun **1** *a half-timbered facade:* front, frontage, face, elevation, exterior, outside. **2** *a facade of bonhomie:* show, front, appearance, pretence, simulation, affectation, act, charade, mask, veneer.

**face** noun **1** *a beautiful face:* countenance, physiognomy, features, profile. **2** *her face grew sad:* expression, look, appearance, countenance. **3** *he made a face:* grimace, scowl, wince, frown, pout. **4** *a cube has six faces:* side, aspect, surface, plane, facet, wall, elevation.
verb **1** *the hotel faces the sea:* look out on, front on to, look towards, look over/across, overlook, be opposite (to). **2** *you'll have to face the truth:* accept, get used to, adjust to, learn to live with, cope with, deal with, come to terms with, become resigned to. **3** *the problems facing our police force:* beset, worry, trouble, confront, torment, plague, bedevil. **4** *he faced the challenge:* brave, face up to, encounter, meet (head-on), confront. **5** *a wall faced with flint:* cover, clad, veneer, surface, dress, laminate, coat, line.

**facelift** noun renovation, redecoration, refurbishment, revamp, makeover.

**facet** noun aspect, feature, side, dimension, strand, component, element.

**facilitate** verb make easy/easier, ease, make possible, smooth the way for, enable,

assist, help (along), aid, promote, hasten, speed up. OPPOSITES impede.

**facility** noun **1** *car-parking facilities:* provision, space, means, equipment. **2** *the camera has a zoom facility:* feature, setting, mode, option. **3** *a wealth of local facilities:* amenity, resource, service. **4** *a medical facility:* establishment, centre, station, location, premises, site, post, base.

**fact** noun **1** *a fact we cannot ignore:* reality, actuality, certainty, truth, verity, gospel. **2** *every fact was double-checked:* detail, particular, finding, point, factor, feature, characteristic, aspect; (**facts**) information, data. OPPOSITES lie, fiction.

**faction** noun **1** *a faction of the Liberal Party:* clique, coterie, caucus, bloc, camp, group, grouping, splinter group. **2** *the council was split by faction:* infighting, dissent, dispute, discord, strife, conflict, friction, argument, disagreement, disunity, schism. OPPOSITES agreement, unity.

**factor** noun element, part, component, ingredient, strand, constituent, feature, facet, aspect, characteristic, consideration, influence, circumstance.

**factory** noun works, plant, yard, mill, facility, workshop, shop.

**factual** adjective truthful, true, accurate, authentic, historical, genuine, true-to-life, correct, exact. OPPOSITES fictitious.

**faculty** noun **1** *the faculty of speech:* power, capability, capacity, facility; (**faculties**) senses, wits, reason,

a b c d e f g h i j k l m n o p q r s t u v w x y z

intelligence. **2** *the arts faculty:* department, school.

**fad** noun craze, vogue, trend, fashion, mode, mania, rage.

**fade** verb **1** *the paintwork has faded:* become pale, become bleached, become washed out, lose colour, discolour. **2** *sunlight had faded the picture:* bleach, wash out, make pale, blanch. **3** *the afternoon light began to fade:* (grow) dim, grow faint, fail, dwindle, die away, wane, disappear, vanish, decline, melt away. **4** *Communism was fading away:* decline, die out, diminish, decay, crumble, collapse, fail. OPPOSITES brighten, grow.

**fail** verb **1** *the scheme had failed:* be unsuccessful, fall through, fall flat, collapse, founder, backfire, miscarry, come unstuck; informal flop, bomb. **2** *he failed his examination:* be unsuccessful in, not make the grade; informal flunk. **3** *his friends had failed him:* let down, disappoint, desert, abandon, betray, be disloyal to. **4** *the ventilation system has failed:* break (down), stop working, cut out, crash, malfunction, go wrong; informal conk out; Brit. informal pack up. **5** *Ceri's health was failing:* deteriorate, degenerate, decline, fade. **6** *900 businesses are failing a week:* collapse, crash, go under, go bankrupt, cease trading, be wound up; informal fold, go bust. OPPOSITES succeed, pass, work, improve, thrive.

**failing** noun fault, shortcoming, weakness, imperfection, deficiency, defect, flaw, frailty. OPPOSITES strength.

**failure** noun **1** *the failure of the escape attempt:* lack of success, defeat, collapse, foundering. **2** *the scheme had been a failure:* fiasco, debacle, catastrophe, disaster; informal flop, washout, dead loss. **3** *she was a failure:* loser, underachiever, ne'er-do-well, disappointment; informal no-hoper. **4** *a failure on my part:* negligence, dereliction, omission, oversight. **5** *the failure of the heating system:* breaking down, breakdown, malfunction, crash. **6** *company failures:* collapse, crash, bankruptcy, insolvency, liquidation, closure. OPPOSITES success.

**faint** adjective **1** *a faint mark:* indistinct, vague, unclear, indefinite, ill-defined, imperceptible, pale, light, faded. **2** *a faint cry:* quiet, muted, muffled, stifled, feeble, weak, low, soft, gentle. **3** *a faint possibility:* slight, slender, slim, small, tiny, remote, vague. **4** *I suddenly felt faint:* dizzy, giddy, light-headed, unsteady; informal woozy. OPPOSITES clear, loud, strong. verb *he nearly fainted:* pass out, lose consciousness, black out, keel over, swoon. noun *a dead faint:* blackout, fainting fit, loss of consciousness, coma, swoon.

**faintly** adverb **1** *Maria called his name faintly:* indistinctly, softly, gently, weakly, in a whisper. **2** *he looked faintly bewildered:* slightly, vaguely, somewhat, quite, fairly, rather, a little, a bit, a touch, a shade. OPPOSITES loudly, extremely.

**fair**[1] adjective **1** *the courts were generally fair:* just, equitable, honest, impartial, unbiased, unprejudiced, neutral, even-

handed. **2** *fair weather:* fine,
dry, bright, clear, sunny,
cloudless. **3** *fair hair:* blond(e),
yellow, golden, flaxen, light.
**4** *fair skin:* pale, light, pink,
white, creamy. **5** *a fair
achievement:* reasonable,
passable, tolerable, satisfactory,
acceptable, respectable, decent,
all right, good enough, pretty
good.
OPPOSITES unfair, inclement,
dark, poor.

**fair²** noun **1** *a country fair:* fête,
gala, festival, carnival. **2** *an
antiques fair:* market, bazaar,
exchange, sale. **3** *an art fair:*
exhibition, display, show,
exposition.

**fairly** adverb **1** *we were treated
fairly:* justly, equitably,
impartially, without bias,
without prejudice, even-
handedly, equally. **2** *in fairly
good condition:* reasonably,
passably, tolerably, adequately,
moderately, quite, relatively,
comparatively; informal pretty.
**3** *he fairly hauled her along the
street:* positively, really, simply,
actually, absolutely.
OPPOSITES unfairly.

**fairy** noun sprite, pixie, elf, imp,
brownie, puck, leprechaun.

**faith** noun **1** *our faith in him:*
trust, belief, confidence,
conviction, reliance. **2** *she died
for her faith:* religion, belief,
creed, church, persuasion,
ideology, doctrine.
OPPOSITES mistrust.

**faithful** adjective **1** *his faithful
assistant:* loyal, constant, true,
devoted, staunch, steadfast,
dedicated, committed, trusty,
dependable, reliable. **2** *a
faithful copy:* accurate, precise,
exact, true, strict, realistic,
authentic.
OPPOSITES disloyal, inaccurate.

**fake** noun **1** *the sculpture was a
fake:* forgery, counterfeit, copy,
pirated copy, sham, fraud, hoax,
imitation; informal phoney, rip-
off. **2** *that doctor is a fake:*
charlatan, quack, sham, fraud,
impostor; informal phoney.
adjective **1** *fake banknotes:*
counterfeit, forged, fraudulent,
sham, pirated, false, bogus;
informal phoney, dud. **2** *fake
diamonds:* imitation, artificial,
synthetic, simulated,
reproduction, replica, ersatz,
man-made, dummy, false, mock;
informal pretend. **3** *a fake accent:*
feigned, faked, put-on,
assumed, invented, affected.
OPPOSITES genuine, real,
authentic.
verb **1** *the certificate was faked:*
forge, counterfeit, falsify, copy,
pirate. **2** *he faked a yawn:*
feign, pretend, simulate, put
on, affect.

**fall** verb **1** *bombs began to fall:*
drop, descend, plummet,
plunge, sink, dive, tumble,
cascade. **2** *he tripped and fell:*
topple over, tumble over, fall
down/over, collapse. **3** *the
water level began to fall:*
subside, recede, drop, retreat,
fall away, go down, sink.
**4** *inflation will fall:* decrease,
decline, diminish, fall off, drop
off, lessen, dwindle, plummet,
plunge, slump, sink. **5** *those
who fell in the war:* die, perish,
lose one's life, be killed, be
slain, be lost; informal bite the
dust, buy it. **6** *the town fell to
the barbarians:* surrender,
yield, submit, give in,
capitulate, succumb, be taken,
be overwhelmed. **7** *Easter falls
on 23rd April:* occur, take place,
happen, come about.
OPPOSITES rise.

noun **1** *an accidental fall:* tumble, trip, spill, topple. **2** *a fall in sales:* decline, fall-off, drop, decrease, cut, dip, reduction, slump; informal crash. **3** *the fall of the Roman Empire:* downfall, collapse, failure, decline, destruction, overthrow, demise. **4** *the fall of Berlin:* surrender, capitulation, yielding, submission, defeat. **5** *a steep fall down to the ocean:* descent, slope, slant.
OPPOSITES rise.
■ **fall back** retreat, withdraw, back off, draw back, pull back, move away. ■ **fall back on** resort to, turn to, look to, call on, have recourse to. ■ **fall for** (informal) **1** *she fell for John:* fall in love with, take a fancy to, be smitten by, be attracted to. **2** *she won't fall for that trick:* be deceived by, be duped by, be fooled by, be taken in by; informal go for, buy, swallow. ■ **fall out** quarrel, argue, row, fight, squabble, bicker. ■ **fall through** fail, be unsuccessful, come to nothing, miscarry, go awry, collapse, founder, come to grief.

**false** adjective **1** *a false report:* incorrect, untrue, wrong, inaccurate, untruthful, fictitious, fabricated, invented, made up, trumped up, counterfeit, forged, fraudulent. **2** *a false friend:* disloyal, faithless, unfaithful, untrue, inconstant, treacherous, double-crossing, deceitful, dishonest, duplicitous. **3** *false pearls:* fake, artificial, imitation, synthetic, simulated, reproduction, replica, ersatz, man-made, dummy, mock; informal pretend.
OPPOSITES correct, faithful, genuine.

**falter** verb hesitate, delay, drag one's feet, stall, waver, vacillate, be indecisive, be irresolute; Brit. hum and haw; informal sit on the fence.

**fame** noun renown, celebrity, stardom, popularity, prominence, distinction, esteem, eminence, repute.
OPPOSITES obscurity.

**familiar** adjective **1** *a familiar task:* well known, recognized, accustomed, everyday, day-to-day, habitual, customary, routine. **2** *are you familiar with the subject?* acquainted, conversant, versed, knowledgeable, well informed, au fait; informal well up on. **3** *he is too familiar with the teachers:* overfamiliar, presumptuous, disrespectful, forward, bold, impudent, impertinent.
OPPOSITES unfamiliar, formal.

**familiarity** noun **1** *a familiarity with politics:* acquaintance with, awareness of, knowledge of, experience of, insight into, understanding of, comprehension of. **2** *she was affronted by his familiarity:* overfamiliarity, presumption, forwardness, boldness, cheek, impudence, impertinence, disrespect. **3** *our familiarity allows us to tease each other:* closeness, intimacy, friendliness, friendship.

**family** noun **1** *I met his family:* relatives, relations, (next of) kin, clan, tribe; informal folks. **2** *she is married with a family:* children, little ones, youngsters; informal kids. **3** *the cat family:* species, order, class, genus, phylum.

**famine** noun **1** *a nation threatened by famine:* food

shortage, hunger, starvation, malnutrition. **2** *the cotton famine:* shortage, scarcity, lack, dearth, deficiency, insufficiency, shortfall, drought.
OPPOSITES plenty.

**famous** adjective well known, prominent, famed, popular, renowned, noted, eminent, distinguished, celebrated.
OPPOSITES unknown.

**fan** noun enthusiast, devotee, admirer, lover, supporter, follower, disciple, adherent; informal buff.

**fanatic** noun extremist, militant, dogmatist, bigot, zealot, radical, diehard; informal maniac.

**fancy** verb **1** (Brit. informal) *I fancied a change of scene:* wish for, want, desire, long for, yearn for, crave, thirst for, hanker after, dream of, covet. **2** (Brit. informal) *she fancied him:* be attracted to, find attractive, be infatuated with, be taken with; informal have a crush on, carry a torch for. **3** *I fancied I could see lights:* imagine, believe, think, be under the impression; informal reckon.
adjective *fancy clothes:* elaborate, ornate, ornamental, decorative, embellished, intricate, ostentatious, showy, flamboyant, lavish, expensive; informal flashy, snazzy, posh, classy; Brit. informal swish.
OPPOSITES plain.
noun **1** *a passing fancy:* whim, foible, urge, whimsy, fascination, fad, craze, enthusiasm, passion, caprice. **2** *a flight of fancy:* fantasy, dreaming, imagination, delusion, creativity.

**fantastic** adjective **1** *a fantastic notion:* fanciful, extravagant, extraordinary, irrational, wild, absurd, far-fetched, unthinkable, implausible, improbable, unlikely; informal crazy. **2** *fantastic shapes:* strange, weird, bizarre, outlandish, grotesque, surreal, exotic. **3** (informal) *a fantastic car:* marvellous, wonderful, sensational, outstanding, superb, excellent; informal terrific, fabulous; Brit. informal brilliant; Austral./NZ informal bonzer.
OPPOSITES rational, ordinary, indifferent.

**fantasy** noun **1** *a mix of fantasy and realism:* imagination, fancy, invention, make-believe, creativity, vision, daydreaming, reverie. **2** *his fantasy about being famous:* dream, daydream, pipe dream, fanciful notion, wish, fond hope, delusion; informal pie in the sky.
OPPOSITES realism.

**far** adverb **1** *far from the palace:* a long way, a great distance, a good way, afar. **2** *her charm far outweighs any flaws:* much, considerably, markedly, greatly, significantly, substantially, appreciably, by a long way, by a mile, easily.
OPPOSITES near, barely.
adjective **1** *far places:* distant, faraway, far-off, remote, out of the way, far-flung, outlying. **2** *the far side:* further, opposite.
OPPOSITES near.

**farce** noun mockery, travesty, parody, sham, pretence, charade, joke; informal shambles.
OPPOSITES tragedy.

**fare** noun **1** *we paid the fare:* price, cost, charge, fee, toll, tariff. **2** *they eat simple fare:* food, meals, cooking, cuisine.

a
b
c
d
e
**f**
g
h
i
j
k
l
m
n
o
p
q
r
s
t
u
v
w
x
y
z

a
b
c
d
e
**f**
g
h
i
j
k
l
m
n
o
p
q
r
s
t
u
v
w
x
y
z

verb *how are you faring?* get on, get along, cope, manage, do, survive; informal make out.

**farewell** exclamation *farewell, Patrick!* goodbye, so long, adieu, au revoir, ciao; informal bye, cheerio, see you (later); Brit. informal ta-ta, cheers.
noun *an emotional farewell:* goodbye, adieu, leave-taking, parting, departure, send-off.

**farming** noun agriculture, cultivation, husbandry; Brit. crofting.

**fascinating** adjective interesting, captivating, engrossing, absorbing, enchanting, enthralling, spellbinding, riveting, engaging, compelling, compulsive, gripping, charming, attractive, intriguing, diverting, entertaining.

**fascination** noun interest, preoccupation, passion, obsession, compulsion, allure, lure, charm, attraction, appeal, pull, draw.

**fashion** noun **1** *the fashion for tight clothes:* vogue, trend, craze, rage, mania, fad, style, look, convention; informal thing. **2** *the world of fashion:* clothes, clothing design, couture; informal the rag trade. **3** *in a sensible fashion:* manner, way, method, style, approach.
verb *fashioned from clay:* construct, build, make, manufacture, cast, shape, form, mould, sculpt, forge, hew, carve.

**fashionable** adjective in vogue, in fashion, popular, up to date, up to the minute, modern, all the rage, trendsetting, stylish, chic; informal trendy, classy, cool; N. Amer. informal tony.
OPPOSITES unfashionable.

**fast**[1] adjective **1** *a fast pace:* speedy, quick, swift, rapid, high-speed, accelerated, express, blistering, breakneck, hasty, hurried; informal nippy, scorching, supersonic; Brit. informal cracking. **2** *make the rope fast:* secure, fastened, tight, firm, closed, shut, immovable. **3** *fast friends:* loyal, devoted, faithful, firm, steadfast, staunch, true, boon, bosom, inseparable.
OPPOSITES slow, loose, temporary.
adverb **1** *she drove fast:* quickly, rapidly, swiftly, speedily, briskly, at full tilt, hastily, hurriedly, in a hurry; informal double quick, nippily; N. Amer. informal lickety-split. **2** *his wheels were stuck fast:* securely, firmly, tight. **3** *he's fast asleep:* deeply, sound, completely.
OPPOSITES slowly, loosely, lightly.

**fast**[2] verb *we must fast and pray:* eat nothing, refrain from eating, go without food, go hungry, starve oneself, go on hunger strike.
OPPOSITES eat.
noun *a five-day fast:* period of fasting, period of abstinence, hunger strike, diet.
OPPOSITES feast.

**fasten** verb **1** *he fastened the door:* bolt, lock, secure, make fast, chain, seal. **2** *they fastened splints to his leg:* attach, fix, affix, clip, pin, tack, stick, join. **3** *he fastened his horse to a tree:* tie (up), tether, hitch, truss, fetter, lash, anchor, strap, rope.
OPPOSITES unlock, remove, untie.

**fat** adjective **1** *a fat man:* obese, overweight, plump, stout, chubby, portly, flabby, paunchy,

pot-bellied, corpulent; informal tubby; Brit. informal podgy. **2** *fat bacon:* fatty, greasy, oily. **3** *a fat book:* thick, big, chunky, substantial, long.
OPPOSITES thin, slim, lean.
noun **1** *whale fat:* blubber, fatty tissue, adipose tissue, cellulite. **2** *eggs in sizzling fat:* oil, grease, lard, suet, butter, margarine.

**fatal** adjective **1** *a fatal disease:* deadly, lethal, mortal, death-dealing, terminal, incurable, untreatable, inoperable. **2** *a fatal mistake:* disastrous, devastating, ruinous, catastrophic, calamitous, dire.
OPPOSITES harmless, beneficial.

**fate** noun **1** *what has fate in store for me?* destiny, providence, the stars, chance, luck, serendipity, fortune. **2** *my fate was in their hands:* future, destiny, outcome, end, lot. **3** *a similar fate would befall Harris:* death, demise, end, sentence.
verb *she was fated to face the same problem:* predestine, preordain, destine, mean, doom.

**father** noun **1** informal dad, daddy, pop, pa, old man. **2** *the father of democracy:* originator, initiator, founder, inventor, creator, author, architect.
verb sire, spawn, breed, give life to.

**fatigue** noun tiredness, weariness, exhaustion.
OPPOSITES energy.
verb tire out, exhaust, wear out, drain, weary, overtire; informal knock out, take it out of; Brit. informal knacker.
OPPOSITES invigorate.

**fatty** adjective greasy, fat, oily, creamy, rich.
OPPOSITES lean.

**fault** noun **1** *he has his faults:* defect, failing, imperfection, flaw, blemish, shortcoming, weakness, vice. **2** *engineers have located the fault:* defect, flaw, imperfection, bug, error, mistake, inaccuracy; informal glitch. **3** *it was not my fault:* responsibility, liability, culpability, guilt.
OPPOSITES strength.
verb *you can't fault their commitment:* find fault with, criticize, attack, condemn; informal knock; Brit. informal slag off.
■ **at fault** to blame, blameworthy, culpable, responsible, guilty, in the wrong.

**faulty** adjective **1** *a faulty electric blanket:* malfunctioning, broken, damaged, defective, not working, out of order; informal on the blink, acting up; Brit. informal playing up. **2** *her logic is faulty:* defective, flawed, unsound, inaccurate, incorrect, erroneous, wrong.
OPPOSITES working, sound.

**favour** noun **1** *will you do me a favour?* good turn, service, good deed, act of kindness, courtesy. **2** *she looked on him with favour:* approval, approbation, goodwill, kindness, benevolence.
OPPOSITES disservice, disapproval.
verb **1** *the party favours electoral reform:* advocate, recommend, approve of, be in favour of, support, back, champion, campaign for, press for, lobby for, promote; informal push for. **2** *Robyn favours loose clothes:* prefer, go for, choose, opt for, select, pick, plump for. **3** *Father always favoured George:* prefer, be biased

towards, indulge, like more/ better. **4** *the conditions favoured the other team*: **benefit**, be to the advantage of, help, assist, aid, be of service to.
OPPOSITES oppose, dislike, hinder.
■ **in favour of** on the side of, pro, for, giving support to, approving of, sympathetic to.

**favourable** adjective **1** *a favourable review*: **approving**, positive, complimentary, full of praise, flattering, glowing, enthusiastic, kind, good; informal rave. **2** *conditions are favourable*: **advantageous**, beneficial, in one's favour, good, right, suitable, appropriate, auspicious, promising, encouraging. **3** *a favourable reply*: **positive**, affirmative, assenting, approving, encouraging, reassuring.
OPPOSITES critical, disadvantageous, negative.

**favourite** adjective **favoured**, preferred, chosen, choice, best-loved, dearest, pet.
noun **first choice**, pick, preference, pet, darling, the apple of one's eye; informal golden boy, teacher's pet; Brit. informal blue-eyed boy/girl; N. Amer. informal fair-haired boy/girl.

**fear** noun **1** *she felt fear at entering the house*: **terror**, fright, fearfulness, horror, alarm, panic, trepidation, dread, anxiety, angst, apprehension, nervousness. **2** *a fear of heights*: **phobia**, aversion, antipathy, dread, nightmare, horror, terror; informal hang-up.
verb **1** *she feared her husband*: **be afraid of**, be fearful of, be scared of, be apprehensive of, dread, live in fear of, be terrified of. **2** *I fear you may be right*: **suspect**, be afraid, have a sneaking suspicion, be inclined to think, have a hunch.
■ **fear for** worry about, feel anxious about, feel concerned about, have anxieties about.

**fearful** adjective **1** *they are fearful of being overheard*: **afraid**, scared, frightened, scared stiff, scared to death, terrified, petrified, nervous, apprehensive, uneasy, anxious, timid; informal jittery. **2** *a fearful accident*: **terrible**, dreadful, awful, appalling, frightful, ghastly, horrific, horrible, shocking, gruesome.
OPPOSITES unafraid.

**fearless** adjective **brave**, courageous, bold, audacious, intrepid, valiant, plucky, heroic, daring, unafraid; informal gutsy.
OPPOSITES timid, cowardly.

**feasible** adjective **practicable**, practical, workable, achievable, attainable, realizable, viable, realistic, possible; informal doable.
OPPOSITES impracticable.

**feast** noun *a wedding feast*: **banquet**, dinner, treat; informal spread; Brit. informal beanfeast, slap-up meal.
verb *they feasted on lobster*: **gorge**, dine, binge; (**feast on**) devour, consume, partake of, eat one's fill of; informal stuff one's face with, pig out.

**feat** noun **achievement**, accomplishment, coup, triumph, undertaking, enterprise, venture, exploit, operation, exercise, endeavour, effort.

**feather** noun **plume**, quill; (**feathers**) plumage, down.

**feature** noun **1** *a feature of*

*Indian music:* characteristic, attribute, quality, property, trait, hallmark, aspect, facet, factor, ingredient, component, element. **2** *her delicate features:* face, countenance, physiognomy; informal mug; Brit. informal mush, phizog. **3** *she made a feature of her sculptures:* centrepiece, special attraction, highlight, focal point, focus, conversation piece. **4** *a series of short features:* article, piece, item, report, story, column.
verb **1** *Radio 3 is featuring a week of live concerts:* present, promote, make a feature of, spotlight, highlight, showcase, foreground. **2** *she is to feature in a new movie:* star, appear, participate.

**federation** noun
confederation, confederacy, association, league, alliance, coalition, union, syndicate, guild, consortium.

**fee** noun payment, wage, salary, price, charge, bill, tariff, rate; (**fees**) remuneration, dues, earnings, pay; formal emolument.

**feeble** adjective **1** *old and feeble:* weak, weakened, debilitated, enfeebled, frail, decrepit, infirm, delicate, sickly, ailing, unwell, poorly. **2** *a feeble argument:* ineffective, unconvincing, implausible, unsatisfactory, poor, weak, flimsy, lame. **3** *he's too feeble to stand up to her:* cowardly, faint-hearted, spineless, timid, timorous, fearful, unassertive, weak, ineffectual; informal sissy, chicken; Brit. informal wet. **4** *a feeble light:* faint, dim, weak, pale, soft, subdued, muted.
OPPOSITES strong, well, brave.

**feed** verb **1** *a large family to*
*feed:* cater for, provide for, cook for, dine, nourish. **2** *cows feeding:* eat, graze, browse, crop. **3** *she fed secrets to the Russians:* supply, provide, give, deliver, furnish, issue, leak.
noun *animal feed:* fodder, food, provender.

**feel** verb **1** *she felt the fabric:* touch, stroke, caress, fondle, finger, paw, handle. **2** *she felt a breeze on her back:* perceive, sense, detect, discern, notice, be aware of, be conscious of. **3** *he will not feel any pain:* experience, undergo, go through, bear, endure, suffer. **4** *he felt his way towards the door:* grope, fumble, scrabble. **5** *he feels that he should go:* believe, think, consider it right, be of the opinion, hold, maintain, judge; informal reckon, figure.
noun **1** *the feel of the paper:* texture, finish, touch, consistency. **2** *the feel of the house:* atmosphere, ambience, aura, mood, feeling, air, impression, spirit; informal vibes. **3** *a feel for languages:* aptitude, knack, flair, bent, talent, gift, ability.

**feeling** noun **1** *a feeling of nausea:* sensation, sense. **2** *I had a feeling I would win:* (sneaking) suspicion, notion, inkling, hunch, intuition, funny feeling, fancy, idea. **3** *the strength of her feeling:* love, affection, fondness, tenderness, warmth, emotion, passion, desire. **4** *public feeling:* mood, (tide of) opinion, attitude, sentiment, emotion, belief, views, consensus. **5** *show some feeling:* compassion, sympathy, empathy, fellow feeling, concern, pity, sorrow, commiseration. **6** *he had hurt*

a
b
c
d
e
f
g
h
i
j
k
l
m
n
o
p
q
r
s
t
u
v
w
x
y
z

a
b
c
d
e
**f**
g
h
i
j
k
l
m
n
o
p
q
r
s
t
u
v
w
x
y
z

*her feelings:* sensibilities, sensitivities, self-esteem, pride. **7** *my feeling is that it is true:* opinion, belief, view, impression, intuition, instinct, hunch, estimation, guess. **8** *a feeling of peace:* atmosphere, ambience, aura, air, mood, impression, spirit; informal vibes. **9** *a remarkable feeling for language:* aptitude, knack, flair, bent, talent, feel, gift, ability.

**fell** verb **1** *the dead trees had to be felled:* cut down, chop down, hack down, saw down, clear. **2** *she felled him with one punch:* knock down, knock to the ground, floor, strike down, knock out; informal deck, flatten, lay out.

**fellow** noun **1** (informal) *he's a decent sort of fellow:* man, boy, person, individual, character; informal guy, lad; Brit. informal chap, bloke; N. Amer. informal dude. **2** *he exchanged glances with his fellows:* companion, friend, comrade, partner, associate, co-worker, colleague; informal pal, buddy; Brit. informal mate.

**fellowship** noun **1** *a community bound together in fellowship:* companionship, comradeship, camaraderie, friendship, sociability, solidarity. **2** *the church fellowship:* association, organization, society, club, league, union, guild, alliance, fraternity, brotherhood.

**feminine** adjective womanly, ladylike, soft, gentle, tender, delicate, pretty.
OPPOSITES masculine.

**fence** noun barrier, paling, railing, enclosure, barricade, stockade.
verb **1** *they fenced off the meadow:* enclose, surround, encircle. **2** *he fenced in his*

*chickens:* confine, pen in, coop up, shut in/up, enclose, surround; N. Amer. corral.

**fend**
■ **fend someone/something off** ward off, head off, stave off, hold off, repel, repulse, resist, fight off. ■ **fend for oneself** take care of oneself, look after oneself, shift for oneself, cope alone, stand on one's own two feet.

**ferocious** adjective **1** *ferocious animals:* fierce, savage, wild, predatory, ravening, aggressive, dangerous. **2** *a ferocious attack:* brutal, vicious, violent, bloody, barbaric, savage, frenzied.
OPPOSITES gentle, mild.

**ferry** verb transport, convey, carry, run, ship, shuttle.

**fertile** adjective **1** *the soil is fertile:* productive, fruitful, fecund, rich, lush. **2** *a fertile imagination:* creative, inventive, innovative, visionary, original, ingenious, prolific.
OPPOSITES barren, uncreative.

**fertilizer** noun plant food, dressing, manure, muck, compost.

**festival** noun celebration, festivity, fête, fair, gala, carnival, fiesta, jamboree, feast day, holiday, holy day.

**festive** adjective jolly, merry, joyous, joyful, happy, jovial, light-hearted, cheerful, jubilant, celebratory, holiday, carnival.

**fetch** verb **1** *he went to fetch a doctor:* go and get, go for, call for, summon, pick up, collect, bring, carry, convey, transport. **2** *the land could fetch millions:* sell for, bring in, raise, realize, yield, make, command; informal go for.

**fetching** adjective attractive,

appealing, sweet, pretty, lovely, delightful, charming, captivating, enchanting; Scottish & N. English bonny; Brit. informal fit.

**feud** noun *a long-standing feud:* vendetta, conflict, quarrel, row, rivalry, hostility, strife.
verb *feuding families:* quarrel, fight, clash, argue, squabble, dispute.

**fever** noun **1** *he developed fever:* feverishness, high temperature; Medicine pyrexia; informal temperature. **2** *World Cup fever:* excitement, mania, frenzy, agitation, passion.

**few** determiner *police are revealing few details:* not many, hardly any, scarcely any, a small number of, a couple of, one or two.
OPPOSITES many.
adjective *comforts here are few:* scarce, scant, meagre, sparse, in short supply, thin on the ground, few and far between.
OPPOSITES plentiful.

**fiasco** noun failure, disaster, catastrophe, debacle, farce, mess; informal flop, washout, shambles; Brit. informal cock-up; N. Amer. informal snafu; Austral./NZ informal fizzer.
OPPOSITES success.

**fibre** noun thread, strand, filament, wisp, yarn.

**fickle** adjective capricious, flighty, giddy, changeable, volatile, mercurial, erratic, unpredictable, unreliable, unsteady.
OPPOSITES constant.

**fiction** noun **1** *the traditions of British fiction:* novels, stories, literature, creative writing. **2** *this is an absolute fiction:* fabrication, invention, lie, fib, tall story, untruth, falsehood, fantasy, nonsense.
OPPOSITES non-fiction, fact.

**fictitious** adjective false, fake, fabricated, bogus, spurious, assumed, affected, adopted, invented, made up; informal pretend, phoney.
OPPOSITES genuine.

**fiddle** (informal) noun *a VAT fiddle:* fraud, swindle, confidence trick; informal racket, scam.
verb **1** *he fiddled with a beer mat:* fidget, play, toy, finger, handle. **2** *he fiddled with the dials:* adjust, tinker, play about/ around, fool about/around, meddle, interfere, tamper; informal tweak, mess about/ around; Brit. informal muck about/ around. **3** *fiddling the figures:* falsify, manipulate, massage, rig, distort, misrepresent, doctor, tamper with, interfere with; informal fix, cook (the books).

**fidelity** noun **1** *fidelity to her husband:* faithfulness, loyalty, constancy, allegiance, commitment, devotion. **2** *the fidelity of the reproduction:* accuracy, exactness, precision, correctness, strictness, closeness, authenticity.
OPPOSITES disloyalty, inaccuracy.

**field** noun **1** *a large ploughed field:* meadow, pasture, paddock, grassland. **2** *a football field:* pitch, ground; Brit. informal park. **3** *the field of biotechnology:* area, sphere, discipline, province, department, domain, territory, branch, subject. **4** *your field of vision:* scope, range, sweep, reach, extent. **5** *she is well ahead of the field:* competitors, entrants, competition, applicants, candidates, runners.
verb **1** *she fielded the ball:* catch, stop, retrieve, return, throw

back. **2** *fielding a great team:* send out, play, put up, assemble, offer. **3** *he fielded some awkward questions:* deal with, handle, cope with, answer, reply to, respond to.

**fierce** adjective **1** *a fierce black mastiff:* ferocious, savage, vicious, aggressive. **2** *fierce competition:* aggressive, cut-throat, keen, intense, strong, relentless. **3** *fierce jealousy:* intense, powerful, vehement, passionate, impassioned, fervent, ardent. **4** *a fierce wind:* powerful, strong, violent, forceful, stormy, howling, raging, tempestuous.
OPPOSITES gentle, mild.

**fiery** adjective **1** *a fiery blast:* burning, blazing, flaming, on fire, ablaze. **2** *a fiery red:* bright, brilliant, vivid, intense, rich. **3** *her fiery spirit:* passionate, impassioned, excitable, spirited, quick-tempered, volatile, explosive, impetuous.

**fight** verb **1** *two men were fighting:* brawl, exchange blows, scuffle, grapple, wrestle; informal scrap; Brit. informal have a punch-up; N. Amer. informal rough-house; Austral./NZ informal stoush. **2** *he fought in Vietnam:* do battle, serve one's country, go to war, take up arms, engage, meet, clash, skirmish. **3** *a war fought for freedom:* wage, engage in, conduct, prosecute, undertake. **4** *they are always fighting:* quarrel, argue, row, bicker, squabble, fall out; informal scrap. **5** *fighting against injustice:* campaign, strive, battle, struggle, contend, crusade, agitate, lobby, push, press. **6** *they will fight the decision:* oppose, contest,

confront, challenge, appeal against, combat, dispute. **7** *Don fought the urge to cry:* repress, restrain, suppress, stifle, smother, hold back, fight back, keep in check, curb, choke back; informal keep the lid on, cork up.
noun **1** *a fight outside a club:* brawl, scuffle, disturbance, fisticuffs, fracas, melee, skirmish, clash; informal scrap, dust-up; Brit. informal punch-up; N. Amer. informal rough house; Austral./NZ informal stoush. **2** *a heavyweight fight:* boxing match, bout, match, contest. **3** *the fight against terrorism:* battle, engagement, conflict, struggle, war, campaign, crusade, action, hostilities. **4** *a fight with my girlfriend:* argument, quarrel, squabble, row, wrangle, disagreement, falling-out, dispute; informal tiff, spat, scrap; Brit. informal barney, ding-dong. **5** *their fight for control of the company:* struggle, battle, campaign, push, effort. **6** *she had no fight left in her:* will, resistance, spirit, pluck, grit, strength, backbone, determination, resolution, resolve.

**fighter** noun **1** *a guerrilla fighter:* soldier, fighting man/woman, warrior, combatant, serviceman, servicewoman; (**fighters**) troops, personnel, militia. **2** *the fighter was knocked to the ground:* boxer, pugilist, prizefighter, wrestler.

**figure** noun **1** *the figure for April:* statistic, number, quantity, amount, level, total, sum; (**figures**) data, statistics, information. **2** *the second figure was 9:* digit, numeral, character, symbol. **3** *he can't put a figure on it:* price, cost, amount, value, valuation. **4** *her petite figure:* shape, outline, form, silhouette, proportions, physique, build, frame. **5** *a figure of authority:* person, personage, individual, character, personality, celebrity. **6** *geometrical figures:* shape, pattern, design, motif. **7** *figure 1 shows an ignition circuit:* diagram, illustration, drawing, picture, plate.

verb *he figures in many myths:* feature, appear, be featured, be mentioned, be referred to.

■ **figure something out** (informal) work out, fathom, puzzle out, decipher, make sense of, think through, get to the bottom of, understand, comprehend, see, grasp, get the hang of; informal twig, crack; Brit. informal suss out.

**file¹** noun **1** *he opened the file:* folder, portfolio, binder. **2** *we have files on all of you:* dossier, document, record, report, data, information, documentation, archives.

verb **1** *file the documents correctly:* categorize, classify, organize, put in order, order, arrange, catalogue, store, archive. **2** *two women have filed a civil suit:* bring, press, lodge.

**file²** noun *a file of boys:* line, column, row, queue, string, chain, procession; Brit. informal crocodile.

verb *we filed out into the park:* walk in a line, queue, march, parade, troop.

**file³** verb *she filed her nails:* smooth, buff, rub down, polish, shape, scrape, abrade, rasp, manicure.

**fill** verb **1** *he filled a bowl:* fill up, top up, charge. **2** *guests filled the room:* crowd into, throng, pack (into), occupy, squeeze

into, cram (into). **3** *he began filling his shelves:* stock, pack, load, supply, replenish. **4** *fill all the holes with putty:* block up, stop (up), plug, seal, caulk. **5** *the perfume filled the room:* pervade, permeate, suffuse, penetrate, infuse. **6** *the person who fills this vacancy:* occupy, hold, take up.

OPPOSITES empty, clear, leave.

**filling** noun *filling for cushions:* stuffing, padding, wadding, filler, contents.

adjective *a filling meal:* substantial, hearty, ample, satisfying, square, heavy, stodgy.

**film** noun **1** *a film of sweat:* layer, coat, coating, covering, cover, skin, patina, tissue. **2** *Emma was watching a film:* movie, picture, feature film, motion picture, video, DVD. **3** *she would like to work in film:* cinema, movies, the pictures, films, the silver screen, the big screen.

verb **1** *he filmed the next scene:* photograph, record on film, shoot, capture on film, video. **2** *his eyes had filmed over:* cloud, mist, haze, blur.

**filter** noun *a carbon filter:* strainer, sifter, sieve, gauze, mesh, net.

verb **1** *the farmers filter the water:* sieve, strain, sift, clarify, purify, refine, treat. **2** *the rain had filtered through her jacket:* seep, percolate, leak, trickle, ooze, leach.

**filthy** adjective **1** *the room was filthy:* dirty, mucky, grimy, foul, squalid, sordid, soiled, stained, polluted, contaminated, unwashed. **2** *filthy jokes:* obscene, rude, vulgar, dirty, smutty, improper, coarse,

a
b
c
d
e
**f**
g
h
i
j
k
l
m
n
o
p
q
r
s
t
u
v
w
x
y
z

bawdy, lewd; informal blue. **3** *he was in a filthy mood:* bad, foul, irritable, grumpy, grouchy, cross; informal snappy; Brit. informal shirty, stroppy; N. Amer. informal cranky, ornery.
OPPOSITES clean, pleasant.

**final** adjective **1** *the final year of study:* last, closing, concluding, finishing, end, ultimate, eventual. **2** *their decisions are final:* irrevocable, unalterable, absolute, conclusive, irrefutable, incontrovertible, indisputable, unchallengeable, binding.
OPPOSITES first, provisional.

**finale** noun climax, culmination, end, ending, finish, close, conclusion, termination, denouement.
OPPOSITES opening.

**finally** adverb **1** *she finally got married:* eventually, ultimately, in the end, after a long time, at (long) last, in the long run, in the fullness of time. **2** *finally, attach the ribbon:* lastly, last, in conclusion. **3** *this should finally dispel that myth:* conclusively, irrevocably, decisively, definitively, for ever, for good, once and for all.

**finance** noun **1** *he knows about finance:* financial affairs, money matters, economics, commerce, business, investment. **2** *short-term finance:* funds, money, capital, cash, resources, assets, reserves, funding.
verb *a project financed by grants:* fund, pay for, back, capitalize, endow, subsidize, invest in, sponsor; N. Amer. informal bankroll.

**financial** adjective monetary, money, economic, pecuniary, fiscal, banking, commercial, business, investment.

**find** verb **1** *I found the book I wanted:* locate, spot, pinpoint, unearth, obtain, search out, track down, root out, come across/upon, run across/into, chance on, happen on, stumble on, encounter; informal bump into. **2** *they found a cure for rabies:* discover, invent, come up with, hit on. **3** *you'll find that it's a lively area:* discover, become aware, realize, observe, notice, note, learn. **4** *I find this strange:* consider, think, feel to be, look on as, view as, see as, judge, deem, regard as. **5** *he was found guilty:* judge, deem, rule, declare, pronounce.
OPPOSITES lose.
noun **1** *an archaeological find:* discovery, acquisition. **2** *this table is a real find:* bargain, godsend, boon, catch, asset; informal good buy.

■ **find something out** discover, become aware of, learn, detect, discern, observe, note, get/come to know, realize, bring to light; informal figure out, cotton on, tumble; Brit. informal twig, suss.

**fine**[1] adjective **1** *fine wines:* good, choice, select, prime, quality, special, superior, of distinction, premium, classic, vintage. **2** *a fine piece of work:* excellent, first-class, first-rate, great, exceptional, outstanding, splendid, magnificent, exquisite, superb, wonderful, superlative; informal A1, top-notch. **3** *a fine fellow:* worthy, admirable, praiseworthy, laudable, upright, upstanding, respectable. **4** *that's fine, but it's not enough:* all right, acceptable, suitable, good (enough), passable, satisfactory, adequate, reasonable, tolerable;

informal OK. **5** *I feel fine:* good, well, healthy, all right, (fighting) fit, blooming, thriving, in good shape/ condition; informal OK, great, in the pink. **6** *a fine day:* fair, dry, bright, clear, sunny, cloudless. **7** *fine clothes:* elegant, stylish, expensive, smart, chic, fashionable, fancy, sumptuous, lavish, opulent; informal flashy. **8** *a fine mind:* keen, quick, alert, sharp, bright, brilliant, astute, clever, intelligent. **9** *fine china:* delicate, dainty, thin, light, fragile. **10** *fine hair:* thin, light, delicate, wispy, flyaway. **11** *a fine point:* sharp, keen, acute, razor-sharp. **12** *fine material:* sheer, light, lightweight, thin, flimsy, diaphanous, filmy, see-through. **13** *fine sand:* fine-grained, powdery, dusty, ground, crushed. **14** *fine details:* intricate, delicate, detailed, elaborate, meticulous. **15** *a fine distinction:* subtle, ultra-fine, nice, hair-splitting.
OPPOSITES everyday, poor, contemptible, ill, dull, wet, coarse.

**fine²** noun *heavy fines:* financial penalty, forfeit, damages, sanction, fee, excess charge.

**finger** noun digit.
verb *she fingered her brooch:* touch, feel, handle, stroke, rub, caress, fondle, toy with, play (about/around) with, fiddle with.

**finish** verb **1** *Pam finished her work:* complete, end, conclude, terminate, wind up, round off; informal wrap up, sew up, polish off. **2** *Hitch finished his dinner:* consume, eat, devour, drink, finish off, polish off, gulp (down), use (up), exhaust,

empty, drain, get through; informal down. **3** *the programme has finished:* end, come to an end, stop, conclude, come to a close, cease. **4** *finished in a black lacquer:* coat, surface, texture.
OPPOSITES start.
noun **1** *the finish of filming:* end, ending, completion, conclusion, close, termination, finale, denouement. **2** *a shiny finish:* surface, texture, coating, covering, lacquer, glaze, veneer, gloss, patina, sheen, lustre.
OPPOSITES start.
■ **finish someone/something off** **1** *the hunters finished them off:* kill, execute, terminate, exterminate, liquidate, get rid of; informal wipe out, bump off, dispose of; N. Amer. informal waste. **2** *financial difficulties finished us off:* overwhelm, overcome, defeat, get the better of, bring down; informal drive to the wall.

**fire** noun **1** *a fire broke out:* blaze, conflagration, inferno, flames, burning, combustion. **2** *he lacked fire:* dynamism, energy, vigour, animation, vitality, exuberance, zest, elan, passion, zeal, spirit, verve, vivacity, enthusiasm; informal go, get-up-and-go, oomph. **3** *machine-gun fire:* gunfire, firing, shooting, bombardment, shelling, volley, salvo, hail.
verb **1** *howitzers firing shells:* launch, shoot, discharge, let fly with. **2** *someone fired a gun:* shoot, discharge, let off, set off. **3** (informal) *he was fired:* dismiss, discharge, give someone their notice, lay off, let go; informal sack. **4** *the story fired my imagination:* stimulate, stir up, excite, awaken, rouse, inflame, animate, inspire, motivate.
■ **catch fire** ignite, catch light,

a b c d e **f** g h i j k l m n o p q r s t u v w x y z

a
b
c
d
e
**f**
g
h
i
j
k
l
m
n
o
p
q
r
s
t
u
v
w
x
y
z

burst into flames, go up in flames. ∎ **set on fire** ignite, light, set fire to, set alight.

**firm**[1] adjective **1** *the ground is fairly firm:* **hard**, solid, unyielding, resistant, compacted, compressed, dense, stiff, rigid, set. **2** *firm foundations:* **secure**, stable, steady, strong, fixed, fast, tight, immovable, rooted, stationary, motionless. **3** *I was very firm | a firm supporter:* **resolute**, determined, decided, resolved, steadfast, adamant, emphatic, insistent, single-minded, wholehearted, unfaltering, unwavering, unflinching, unswerving, unbending, committed. **4** *firm friends:* **close**, good, boon, intimate, inseparable, dear, special, constant, devoted, loving, faithful, long-standing, steady, steadfast. **5** *firm plans:* **definite**, fixed, settled, decided, cut-and-dried, established, confirmed, agreed.
OPPOSITES soft, unstable, irresolute, indefinite.

**firm**[2] noun *an accountancy firm:* **business**, company, concern, enterprise, organization, corporation, conglomerate, office, bureau, agency, consortium; informal outfit, operation.

**first** adjective **1** *the first chapter:* **earliest**, initial, opening, introductory. **2** *first principles:* **fundamental**, basic, rudimentary, primary, key, cardinal, central, chief, vital, essential. **3** *our first priority:* **foremost**, principal, highest, greatest, paramount, top, main, overriding, central, core; informal number-one. **4** *first prize:* **top**, best, prime, premier, winner's,

winning.
OPPOSITES last.
adverb **1** *the room they had first entered:* **at first**, to begin with, first of all, at the outset, initially. **2** *I'd like to eat first:* **before anything else**, now. **3** *she wouldn't go—she'd die first!* **rather**, sooner, in preference.
OPPOSITES last, later.
noun *that's a first:* **novelty**, innovation, departure, break with tradition.

**fish** verb **1** *some people were fishing in the lake:* **go fishing**, angle, trawl. **2** *she fished for her purse:* **search**, delve, look, hunt, grope, fumble, ferret, rummage.
∎ **fish someone/something out** pull out, haul out, remove, extricate, extract, retrieve, rescue, save.

**fit**[1] adjective **1** *a fit subject for a book:* **suitable**, appropriate, suited, apposite, fitting, good enough, apt, -worthy. **2** *not fit to look after children:* **competent**, able, capable, ready, prepared, equipped. **3** *tanned and fit:* **healthy**, well, in good health, in (good) shape, in trim, in good condition, fighting fit, athletic, muscular, strapping, strong, robust, hale and hearty.
OPPOSITES unsuitable, incapable, unfit.
verb **1** *having carpets fitted:* **lay**, install, put in, position, place, fix, arrange. **2** *cameras fitted with autofocus:* **equip**, provide, supply, fit out, furnish. **3** *they fitted the slabs together:* **join**, connect, piece together, attach, unite, link. **4** *a sentence that fits his crime:* **be appropriate to**, suit, match, correspond to, tally with, go with, accord with.

**5** *an MSc fits you for a scientific career:* qualify, prepare, make ready, train.

■ **fit in** conform, be in harmony, blend in, be in line, be assimilated.

**fit²** noun **1** *an epileptic fit:* convulsion, spasm, paroxysm, seizure, attack. **2** *a fit of the giggles:* outbreak, outburst, attack, bout, spell. **3** *mum would have a fit:* tantrum, frenzy; informal paddy, heart attack; N. Amer. informal blowout.

**fitness** noun **1** *polo requires tremendous fitness:* good health, strength, robustness, vigour, athleticism, toughness, stamina. **2** *his fitness for active service:* suitability, capability, competence, ability, aptitude, readiness, preparedness.

**fitting** noun **1** *a light fitting:* attachment, part, piece, component, accessory, apparatus. **2** *bathroom fittings:* furnishings, furniture, fixtures, fitments, equipment.
adjective *a fitting conclusion:* apt, appropriate, suitable, apposite, fit, proper, right, seemly, correct.
OPPOSITES unsuitable.

**fix** verb **1** *signs were fixed to lamp posts:* fasten, attach, affix, secure, connect, couple, link, install, stick, glue, pin, nail, screw, bolt, clamp, clip. **2** *his words are fixed in my memory:* stick, lodge, embed. **3** *his eyes were fixed on the ground:* focus, direct, level, point, train. **4** *he fixed my car:* repair, mend, put right, get working, restore.
**5** *Jim fixed it for us to see the show:* arrange, organize, contrive, manage, engineer; informal swing, wangle. **6** (informal) *Laura was fixing her hair:*

arrange, put in order, adjust, style, groom, comb, brush; informal do. **7** (informal) *I'll fix supper:* prepare, cook, make, get; informal rustle up; Brit. informal knock up. **8** *let's fix a date:* decide on, select, choose, settle, set, arrange, establish, allot, designate, name, appoint, specify. **9** (informal) *the fight was fixed:* rig, tamper with, skew, influence; informal fiddle.
OPPOSITES remove.
noun (informal) **1** *they are in a bit of a fix:* predicament, plight, difficulty, awkward situation, corner, tight spot, mess; informal pickle, jam, hole, scrape, bind. **2** *the result was a fix:* fraud, swindle, trick, charade, sham; informal set-up, fiddle.

**fixed** adjective predetermined, set, established, arranged, specified, decided, agreed, determined, confirmed, prescribed, definite, defined, explicit, precise.

**fizz** verb *the mixture fizzed like mad:* bubble, sparkle, effervesce, froth.
noun **1** *the fizz in champagne:* bubbles, sparkle, fizziness, effervescence, gassiness, froth. **2** *the fizz of the static:* crackle, buzz, hiss, white noise.

**fizzy** adjective sparkling, effervescent, carbonated, gassy, bubbly, frothy.
OPPOSITES still, flat.

**flag¹** noun *the Irish flag:* banner, standard, ensign, pennant, streamer, colours; Brit. pendant.
verb *flag the misspelt words:* indicate, identify, point out, mark, label, tag, highlight.
■ **flag someone/something down** hail, wave down, stop, halt.

**flag²** verb **1** *they were flagging towards the finish:* tire, grow

a
b
c
d
e
**f**
g
h
i
j
k
l
m
n
o
p
q
r
s
t
u
v
w
x
y
z

tired, weaken, grow weak, wilt, droop. **2** *my energy flags in the afternoon:* fade, decline, wane, ebb, diminish, decrease, lessen, dwindle.
OPPOSITES revive.

**flagrant** adjective blatant, glaring, obvious, conspicuous, barefaced, shameless, brazen, undisguised.

**flair** noun **1** *a flair for publicity:* aptitude, talent, gift, instinct, ability, facility, knack, skill. **2** *she dressed with flair:* style, elegance, panache, dash, elan, poise, taste; informal class.

**flake** noun *a flake of paint:* sliver, wafer, shaving, paring, chip, fragment, scrap, shred.
verb *the paint was flaking off:* peel (off), chip, blister, come off.

**flamboyant** adjective **1** *her flamboyant personality:* ostentatious, exuberant, confident, lively, animated, vibrant, vivacious. **2** *a flamboyant cravat:* colourful, bright, vibrant, vivid, dazzling, bold, showy, gaudy, garish, loud; informal jazzy, flashy.
OPPOSITES restrained.

**flame** noun **1** *a sheet of flames:* fire, blaze, conflagration, inferno. **2** (informal) *an old flame:* sweetheart, boyfriend, girlfriend, lover, partner.
■ **in flames** on fire, burning, alight, flaming, blazing.

**flank** noun **1** *the horse's flanks:* side, haunch, quarter, thigh. **2** *the southern flank of the Eighth Army:* side, wing, sector, face, aspect.
verb *the garden is flanked by two rivers:* edge, bound, line, border, fringe.

**flap** verb **1** *the mallards flapped their wings:* beat, flutter, agitate, vibrate, wag, thrash, flail. **2** *the flag flapped in the breeze:* flutter, wave, fly, blow, swing, ripple, stir.
noun **1** *a few flaps of its wing:* beat, stroke, flutter, movement. **2** (informal) *in a flap:* panic, fluster; informal state, stew, tizzy; N. Amer. informal twit.

**flare** noun **1** *the flare of the match:* blaze, flame, flash, burst, flicker. **2** *a flare set off by the crew:* signal, beacon, rocket, light, torch, maroon.
verb **1** *the match flared:* blaze, flash, flare up, flame, burn, flicker. **2** *her nostrils flared:* spread, splay, broaden, widen, dilate.

**flash** verb **1** *a torch flashed:* shine, flare, blaze, gleam, glint, sparkle, burn, blink, wink, flicker, shimmer, twinkle, glimmer, glisten. **2** (informal) *flashing his money about:* show off, flaunt, flourish, display, parade. **3** *racing cars flashed past:* zoom, streak, tear, shoot, dash, dart, fly, whistle, hurtle, rush, bolt, race, speed, career; informal belt, zap; Brit. informal bomb, bucket; N. Amer. informal barrel.
noun *a flash of light:* flare, blaze, burst, gleam, glint, sparkle, flicker, shimmer, twinkle, glimmer.

**flashy** adjective (informal) ostentatious, flamboyant, showy, conspicuous, extravagant, expensive, vulgar, tasteless, brash, garish, loud, gaudy; informal snazzy, fancy, swanky, flash, glitzy.
OPPOSITES understated.

**flat¹** adjective **1** *a flat roof:* level, horizontal. **2** *the sea was flat:* calm, still, glassy, smooth, placid, like a millpond. **3** *plane*

*the wood completely flat:* smooth, even, plane. **4** *a flat wooden box:* shallow, low, low-sided. **5** *his voice was flat:* monotonous, toneless, droning, boring, dull, tedious, uninteresting, unexciting. **6** *the market was flat:* slow, inactive, sluggish, slack, quiet, depressed. **7** (Brit.) *a flat battery:* run down, dead, used up, expired. **8** *a flat tyre:* deflated, punctured, burst, blown. **9** *a flat fee:* fixed, set, invariable, regular, constant. **10** *a flat denial:* outright, direct, absolute, definite, positive, straight, plain, explicit.
OPPOSITES sloping, vertical, rough, uneven, curved, tall, animated, lively, charged, new, inflated, variable, equivocal.
adverb *she lay flat on the floor:* stretched out, outstretched, spreadeagled, sprawling, prone, prostrate.

**flat²** noun *a two-bedroom flat:* apartment, suite, penthouse, rooms.

**flatten** verb **1** *Tom flattened the crumpled paper:* make/become flat, even out, smooth out, level. **2** *the cows flattened the grass:* squash, compress, press down, crush, compact, trample. **3** *tornadoes can flatten buildings in seconds:* demolish, raze (to the ground), tear down, knock down, destroy, wreck, devastate.
OPPOSITES crumple, raise, build.

**flatter** verb **1** *it amused him to flatter her:* compliment, praise, express admiration for, fawn on, humour, wheedle, blarney; informal sweet-talk, soft-soap, butter up, play up to. **2** *I was flattered to be asked:* honour, gratify, please, delight; informal

tickle pink. **3** *a hairstyle that flattered her:* suit, become, look good on, go well with; informal do something for.
OPPOSITES insult, offend.

**flattering** adjective **1** *flattering remarks:* complimentary, praising, favourable, admiring, appreciative, fulsome, honeyed, obsequious, ingratiating, sycophantic. **2** *it was very flattering to be nominated:* pleasing, gratifying, an honour. **3** *her most flattering dress:* becoming, enhancing.
OPPOSITES unflattering.

**flattery** noun praise, adulation, compliments, blandishments, honeyed words, fawning, blarney; informal sweet talk, soft soap, buttering up, toadying.

**flaunt** verb show off, display, make a great show of, put on show/display, parade, draw attention to, brag about, crow about, vaunt; informal flash.

**flavour** noun **1** *the flavour of basil:* taste, savour, tang, smack. **2** *salami can give extra flavour:* flavouring, seasoning, taste, tang, relish, bite, piquancy, spice. **3** *a strong international flavour:* character, quality, feel, feeling, ambience, atmosphere, air, mood, tone, spirit. **4** *this excerpt will give you a flavour of the report:* impression, suggestion, hint, taste.
verb *spices for flavouring food:* season, spice (up), add piquancy to, ginger up, enrich, infuse.

**flaw** noun defect, blemish, fault, imperfection, deficiency, weakness, weak spot/point, failing; Computing bug; informal glitch.
OPPOSITES strength.

**flawed** adjective **1** *a flawed mirror:* faulty, defective, unsound, imperfect, blemished, broken, cracked, scratched; Brit. informal duff. **2** *the findings were flawed:* unsound, distorted, inaccurate, incorrect, erroneous, fallacious.
OPPOSITES flawless.

**flee** verb run (away/off), run for it, make off, take off, take to one's heels, make a break for it, bolt, beat a (hasty) retreat, make a quick exit, escape; informal beat it, clear off/out, skedaddle, scram; Brit. informal scarper; N. Amer. informal light out; Austral./NZ informal shoot through.

**fleet** noun navy, naval force, (naval) task force, armada, flotilla, squadron, convoy.

**fleeting** adjective brief, short-lived, quick, momentary, cursory, transient, ephemeral, passing, transitory.
OPPOSITES lasting.

**flesh** noun **1** *his smooth, white flesh:* tissue, skin, body, muscle, fat. **2** *strip the flesh from the bone:* meat, muscle. **3** *a fruit with juicy flesh:* pulp, marrow, meat. **4** *the pleasures of the flesh:* the body, human nature, physicality, sensuality, sexuality.

**flexibility** noun **1** *the flexibility of wood:* pliability, suppleness, elasticity, stretchiness, springiness, spring, resilience, bounce; informal give. **2** *the flexibility of an endowment loan:* adaptability, adjustability, versatility, open-endedness, freedom, latitude. **3** *the flexibility shown by the local authority:* willingness to compromise, accommodation, give and take, amenability, cooperation, tolerance.

OPPOSITES rigidity, inflexibility, intransigence.

**flexible** adjective **1** *flexible tubing:* bendy, pliable, supple, pliant, plastic, elastic, stretchy, springy, resilient, bouncy. **2** *a flexible arrangement:* adaptable, adjustable, variable, versatile, open-ended, open. **3** *the need to be flexible towards tenants:* accommodating, amenable, willing to compromise, cooperative, tolerant.
OPPOSITES rigid, inflexible, intransigent.

**flick** noun *a flick of the wrist:* jerk, snap, flip, whisk.
verb **1** *he flicked the switch:* click, snap, flip, jerk, throw. **2** *the horse flicked its tail:* swish, twitch, wave, wag, waggle, shake.
■ **flick through** thumb (through), leaf through, flip through, skim, scan, look through, browse through, dip into, glance at/through.

**flicker** verb **1** *the lights flickered:* glimmer, flare, dance, gutter, twinkle, sparkle, wink, flash. **2** *his eyelids flickered:* flutter, quiver, tremble, shiver, shudder, jerk, twitch.

**flight** noun **1** *the history of flight:* aviation, flying, air transport, aeronautics. **2** *a flight to Rome:* plane trip/journey, air trip/journey, service. **3** *the flight of the ball:* trajectory, path (through the air), track, orbit. **4** *a flight of birds:* flock, swarm, cloud, throng. **5** *his headlong flight from home:* escape, getaway, hasty departure, exit, exodus, breakout, bolt, disappearance; Brit. informal flit.

**flimsy** adjective **1** *a flimsy*

*building:* **insubstantial**, fragile, frail, rickety, ramshackle, makeshift, jerry-built, shoddy. **2** *a flimsy dress:* **thin**, light, fine, filmy, floaty, diaphanous, sheer, delicate, gossamer, gauzy. **3** *flimsy evidence:* **weak**, feeble, poor, inadequate, insufficient, thin, unsubstantial, unconvincing, implausible.
OPPOSITES sturdy, thick, sound.

**flinch** verb **1** *he flinched at the noise:* **wince**, start, shudder, quiver, jerk. **2** *he never flinched from his duty:* **shrink from**, recoil from, shy away from, dodge, evade, avoid, duck, baulk at.

**fling** verb *he flung the axe into the river:* **throw**, hurl, toss, sling, launch, pitch, lob; informal chuck, heave.
noun **1** *a birthday fling:* **good time**, party, spree, fun and games; informal binge, bash, night on the town. **2** *she had a brief fling with him:* **affair**, love affair, relationship, romance, liaison, entanglement, involvement.

**flippant** adjective **frivolous**, facetious, tongue-in-cheek, disrespectful, irreverent, cheeky; informal flip, saucy; N. Amer. informal sassy.
OPPOSITES serious, respectful.

**flirt** noun *Anna was quite a flirt:* **tease**, coquette, heartbreaker.
■ **flirt with 1** *he liked to flirt with her:* **tease**, lead on, toy with. **2** *those who flirt with fascism:* **dabble in**, toy with, trifle with, play with, tinker with, dip into, scratch the surface of.

**float** verb **1** *oil floats on water:* **stay afloat**, stay on the surface, be buoyant, be buoyed up. **2** *the*

*balloon floated in the air:* **hover**, levitate, be suspended, hang, defy gravity. **3** *a cloud floated across the moon:* **drift**, glide, sail, slip, slide, waft. **4** *the company was floated on the Stock Exchange:* **launch**, offer, sell, introduce.
OPPOSITES sink, drop, rush, take private.

**floating** adjective **1** *floating voters:* **uncommitted**, undecided, undeclared, wavering; informal sitting on the fence. **2** *a floating population:* **unsettled**, transient, temporary, migrant, wandering, nomadic, migratory, itinerant.
OPPOSITES committed, decided, settled.

**flock** noun **1** *a flock of sheep:* **herd**, drove. **2** *a flock of birds:* **flight**, swarm, cloud, gaggle, skein.
verb **1** *people flocked around her:* **gather**, collect, congregate, assemble, converge, mass, crowd, throng, cluster, swarm. **2** *tourists flock to the place:* **stream**, go in large numbers, swarm, crowd, troop.

**flog** verb **whip**, thrash, lash, scourge, birch, cane, beat.

**flood** noun **1** *a severe flood:* **inundation**, deluge, torrent, overflow, flash flood; Brit. spate. **2** *a flood of tears:* **gush**, outpouring, torrent, rush, stream, surge, cascade. **3** *a flood of complaints:* **succession**, series, string, barrage, volley, battery, avalanche, torrent, stream, storm.
OPPOSITES trickle.
verb **1** *the town was flooded:* **inundate**, swamp, deluge, immerse, submerge, drown, engulf. **2** *the river could flood:* **overflow**, burst its banks, brim

over, run over. **3** *cheap goods flooding the market:* glut, swamp, saturate. **4** *refugees flooded in:* pour, stream, flow, surge, swarm, pile, crowd.
OPPOSITES drain, starve, trickle.

**floor** noun **1** *he sat on the floor:* ground, flooring. **2** *the second floor:* storey, level, deck, tier, stage.
verb **1** *he floored his attacker:* knock down, knock over, fell; informal deck, lay out. **2** (informal) *the question floored him:* baffle, defeat, confound, perplex, puzzle, disconcert; informal throw, beat, stump; N. Amer. informal buffalo.

**flop** verb **1** *he flopped into a chair:* collapse, slump, crumple, sink, drop. **2** *his hair flopped over his eyes:* hang (down), dangle, droop, sag, loll. **3** (informal) *the play flopped:* be unsuccessful, fail, fall flat, founder; informal bomb; N. Amer. informal tank.
OPPOSITES spring, succeed.
noun (informal) *the play was a flop:* failure, disaster, fiasco, debacle, catastrophe; Brit. damp squib; informal washout, also-ran; N. Amer. informal clinker.
OPPOSITES success.

**floppy** adjective limp, flaccid, slack, flabby, relaxed, drooping, droopy, loose, flowing.
OPPOSITES erect, stiff.

**flounder** verb **1** *floundering in the water:* struggle, thrash, flail, twist and turn, splash, stagger, stumble, reel, lurch, blunder. **2** *she floundered, not knowing what to say:* struggle, be out of one's depth, be confused; informal scratch one's head, be flummoxed, be fazed, be floored.

**flourish** verb **1** *ferns flourish in the shade:* grow, thrive, prosper, do well, burgeon, bloom, increase, multiply, proliferate, run riot. **2** *the arts flourished:* thrive, prosper, bloom, be in good health, be vigorous, be in its heyday, make progress, advance, expand; informal go places. **3** *he flourished a sword:* brandish, wave, shake, wield, swing, display, show off.
OPPOSITES die, wither, decline.

**flout** verb defy, refuse to obey, disobey, break, violate, fail to comply with, fail to observe, contravene, infringe, breach, commit a breach of, transgress against, ignore, disregard; informal cock a snook at.
OPPOSITES observe.

**flow** verb **1** *the water flowed down the channel:* pour, run, course, circulate, stream, swirl, surge, sweep, gush, cascade, roll, rush, trickle, seep, ooze, dribble. **2** *many questions flow from today's announcement:* result, proceed, arise, follow, ensue, stem, originate, emanate, spring.
noun *a good flow of water:* movement, motion, current, circulation, stream, swirl, surge, gush, rush, spate, tide, trickle, ooze.

**flower** noun & verb bloom, blossom.

**fluctuate** verb vary, change, shift, alter, waver, swing, oscillate, alternate, rise and fall.

**fluent** adjective articulate, eloquent, silver-tongued, communicative, natural, effortless.
OPPOSITES inarticulate.

**fluid** noun *the fluid seeps up the tube:* liquid, solution, liquor, gas, vapour.

OPPOSITES solid.

**adjective 1** *a fluid substance:*
free-flowing, runny, liquid,
liquefied, melted, molten,
gaseous. **2** *he stood up in one
fluid movement:* smooth,
fluent, flowing, effortless, easy,
continuous, graceful, elegant.
OPPOSITES solid, jerky.

**flurry noun 1** *a flurry of snow:*
swirl, whirl, eddy, shower,
gust. **2** *a flurry of activity:*
burst, outbreak, spurt, fit,
spell, bout, rash, eruption.
OPPOSITES dearth.

**flush verb 1** *she flushed in
embarrassment:* blush, redden,
go pink, go red, go crimson, go
scarlet, colour (up). **2** *flushing
toxins from the body:* rinse,
wash, sluice, swill, cleanse,
clean; Brit. informal sloosh. **3** *they
flushed out the snipers:* drive,
chase, force, dislodge, expel.
OPPOSITES pale.

**noun** *a flush crept over her face:*
blush, colour, rosiness,
pinkness, ruddiness, bloom.
OPPOSITES pallor.

**flutter verb 1** *butterflies
fluttered around:* flit, hover,
dance. **2** *a tern was fluttering
its wings:* flap, beat, quiver,
agitate, vibrate. **3** *she fluttered
her eyelashes:* flicker, bat.
**4** *flags fluttered:* flap, wave,
ripple, undulate, quiver, fly.
**5** *her heart fluttered:* beat
irregularly, palpitate, miss/skip
a beat, quiver.

**fly verb 1** *a bird flew overhead:*
wing, glide, soar, wheel, take
wing, take to the air. **2** *they
flew to Paris:* travel by plane/
air, jet. **3** *we flew in supplies:*
transport (by plane/air),
airlift, lift, jet, drop, parachute.
**4** *he can fly a plane:* pilot,
operate, control, manoeuvre,

steer. **5** *the ship was flying a
French flag:* display, show,
exhibit. **6** *flags flew in the town:*
flutter, flap, wave. **7** *doesn't
time fly?* go quickly, fly by/past,
pass swiftly, rush past.

**foam noun** *the foam on the
waves:* froth, spume, surf,
spray, fizz, effervescence,
bubbles, head, lather, suds.
**verb** *the water foamed:* froth,
fizz, effervesce, bubble, lather,
ferment, boil, seethe.

**focus noun 1** *a focus of
community life:* centre, focal
point, central point, centre of
attention, hub, pivot, nucleus,
heart, cornerstone, linchpin.
**2** *the main focus of this chapter:*
subject, theme, concern,
subject matter, topic, point,
essence, gist.
**verb** *he focused his binoculars on
the tower:* bring into focus,
aim, point, turn.
■ **focus on** concentrate, centre,
zero in, zoom in, address
oneself to, pay attention to,
pinpoint, revolve around.

**fog noun** mist, smog, murk,
haze; informal pea-souper.

**foil[1] verb** *the escape attempt was
foiled:* thwart, frustrate, stop,
defeat, block, prevent, obstruct,
hinder, snooker, scotch; informal
put paid to; Brit. informal scupper.
OPPOSITES assist.

**foil[2] noun** *the wine was a perfect
foil to pasta:* contrast,
complement, antithesis.

**fold verb 1** *I folded the cloth:*
double, crease, turn, bend,
tuck, pleat. **2** *the firm folded
last year:* fail, collapse, founder,
go bankrupt, cease trading, be
wound up, be shut (down);
informal crash, go bust, go under,
go to the wall, go belly up.
**noun** *there was a fold in the*

*paper:* crease, knife-edge, wrinkle, crinkle, pucker, furrow, pleat.

**folk** noun (informal) **1** *the local folk:* people, individuals, {men, women, and children}, (living) souls, citizenry, inhabitants, residents, populace, population. **2** *my folks live in Hull:* relatives, relations, family, people; informal peeps.

**follow** verb **1** *we'll let the others follow:* come behind, come after, go behind, go after, walk behind. **2** *people who follow the band around:* accompany, go along with, go around with, travel with, escort, attend; informal tag along with. **3** *the police followed her everywhere:* shadow, trail, stalk, track; informal tail. **4** *follow the instructions:* obey, comply with, conform to, adhere to, stick to, keep to, act in accordance with, abide by, observe. **5** *I couldn't follow what he said:* understand, comprehend, take in, grasp, fathom, see; informal make head or tail of, figure out; Brit. informal suss out. **6** *he follows Manchester United:* be a fan of, be a supporter of, support, watch, keep up with.
OPPOSITES lead, flout, misunderstand.

**follower** noun **1** *a follower of Christ:* disciple, apostle, defender, champion, believer, worshipper. **2** *followers of Scottish football:* fan, enthusiast, admirer, devotee, lover, supporter, adherent.
OPPOSITES leader, opponent.

**following** noun *his devoted following:* admirers, supporters, backers, fans, adherents, devotees, public, audience.

OPPOSITES opposition.
adjective **1** *the following day:* next, ensuing, succeeding, subsequent. **2** *the following questions:* below, underneath, these.
OPPOSITES preceding, above.

**folly** noun foolishness, foolhardiness, stupidity, idiocy, lunacy, madness, rashness, recklessness, irresponsibility.
OPPOSITES wisdom.

**fond** adjective **1** *she was fond of dancing:* keen on, partial to, enthusiastic about, attached to, attracted to; informal into. **2** *his fond father:* adoring, devoted, doting, loving, caring, affectionate. **3** *a fond hope:* unrealistic, naive, foolish, over-optimistic, absurd, vain.
OPPOSITES indifferent, uncaring, realistic.

**fondle** verb caress, stroke, pat, pet, finger, tickle, play with.

**food** noun nourishment, sustenance, nutriment, fare, cooking, cuisine, foodstuffs, refreshments, meals, provisions, rations; informal eats, grub.

**fool** noun **1** *acting like a fool:* idiot, ass, halfwit, blockhead, dunce, simpleton; informal nincompoop, clod, dimwit, dummy, fathead, numbskull; Brit. informal nitwit, twit, clot, berk, prat, pillock, wally, dork, twerp, charlie; Scottish informal nyaff, balloon; N. Amer. informal schmuck, turkey; Austral./NZ informal drongo, nong, galah, boofhead. **2** *she made a fool of me:* laughing stock, dupe, gull; informal stooge, sucker, mug, fall guy; N. Amer. informal sap.
OPPOSITES genius.
verb **1** *he'd been fooled:* deceive, trick, hoax, dupe, take in,

mislead, delude, hoodwink, bluff, gull; informal bamboozle, take for a ride, have on; N. Amer. informal sucker; Austral. informal pull a swifty on. **2** *I'm not fooling, I promise:* pretend, make believe, put on an act, act, sham, fake, joke, jest; informal kid; Brit. informal have someone on.

**foolish** adjective stupid, idiotic, mindless, unintelligent, thoughtless, imprudent, unwise, ill-advised, rash, reckless, foolhardy; informal dumb, dim, dim-witted, half-witted, thick, hare-brained; Brit. informal barmy, daft; Scottish & N. English informal glaikit; N. Amer. informal dumb-ass, chowderheaded.
OPPOSITES sensible, wise.

**footing** noun **1** *a solid financial footing:* basis, base, foundation. **2** *on an equal footing:* standing, status, position, condition, arrangement, basis, relationship, terms.

**forbid** verb prohibit, ban, outlaw, make illegal, veto, proscribe, embargo, bar, debar, rule out.
OPPOSITES permit.

**forbidding** adjective threatening, ominous, menacing, sinister, brooding, daunting.
OPPOSITES inviting.

**force** noun **1** *he pushed with all his force:* strength, power, energy, might, effort. **2** *they used force to achieve their aims:* coercion, compulsion, constraint, duress, pressure, oppression, harassment, intimidation, violence; informal arm-twisting. **3** *the force of the argument:* power, weight, effectiveness, validity, strength, significance, influence,

authority; informal punch. **4** *a peacekeeping force:* body, group, outfit, party, team, detachment, unit, squad.
verb **1** *he was forced to pay:* compel, coerce, make, constrain, oblige, impel, drive, pressure, press-gang, bully; informal lean on, twist someone's arm. **2** *the door had to be forced:* break open, knock/smash/break down, kick in. **3** *water was forced through a hole:* propel, push, thrust, shove, drive, press, pump.
■ in force **1** *the law is now in force:* effective, in operation, operative, valid, current, binding. **2** *her fans were out in force:* in great numbers, in hordes/droves, in their hundreds/thousands.

**forced** adjective **1** *forced repatriation:* enforced, compulsory, obligatory, mandatory, involuntary, imposed, required. **2** *a forced smile:* strained, unnatural, artificial, false, feigned, simulated, contrived, laboured, affected, hollow; informal phoney, pretend, put on.
OPPOSITES voluntary, natural.

**forceful** adjective **1** *a forceful personality:* dynamic, energetic, assertive, authoritative, vigorous, powerful, strong, pushy; informal in-your-face, go-ahead, feisty. **2** *a forceful argument:* convincing, cogent, compelling, strong, powerful, persuasive, coherent.
OPPOSITES weak, submissive, unconvincing.

**forecast** verb *they forecast record profits:* predict, prophesy, foretell, foresee.
noun *a gloomy forecast:* prediction, prophecy,

prognostication, prognosis.

**foreign** adjective alien, overseas, non-native, imported, distant, external, far-off, exotic, strange. OPPOSITES domestic, native.

**foreigner** noun alien, non-native, stranger, outsider, immigrant, settler, newcomer, incomer.
OPPOSITES native, national.

**foremost** adjective leading, principal, premier, prime, top, greatest, best, supreme, pre-eminent, outstanding, most important, most notable; N. Amer. ranking; informal number-one.
OPPOSITES minor.

**foresee** verb anticipate, expect, envisage, predict, forecast, foretell, prophesy.

**foretell** verb predict, forecast, prophesy, foresee, anticipate, envisage, warn of.

**forever** adverb 1 *their love would last forever:* for always, evermore, for ever and ever, for good, for all time, until the end of time, eternally; N. Amer. forevermore; informal until the cows come home. 2 *he was forever banging into things:* always, continually, constantly, perpetually, incessantly, endlessly, persistently, repeatedly, regularly; informal 24-7.
OPPOSITES never, occasionally.

**forfeit** verb lose, be deprived of, surrender, relinquish, sacrifice, give up, renounce, forgo.
OPPOSITES retain.
noun penalty, sanction, punishment, penance, fine, confiscation, loss, forfeiture, surrender.

**forge** verb 1 *he forged a huge sword:* hammer out, beat out, fashion. 2 *they forged a partnership:* build, construct, form, create, establish, set up. 3 *he forged her signature:* fake, falsify, counterfeit, copy, imitate; informal pirate.

**forged** adjective fake, false, counterfeit, imitation, copied, pirate, bogus; informal phoney, dud.
OPPOSITES genuine.

**forgery** noun fake, counterfeit, fraud, imitation, replica, copy, pirate copy; informal phoney.

**forget** verb 1 *he forgot where he was:* fail to remember, be unable to remember. 2 *I never forget my briefcase:* leave behind, fail to take/bring, travel/leave home without. 3 *I forgot to close the door:* neglect, fail, omit.
OPPOSITES remember.

**forgive** verb 1 *she would not forgive him:* pardon, excuse, exonerate, absolve. 2 *you must forgive his rude conduct:* excuse, overlook, disregard, ignore, make allowances for, turn a blind eye to, condone, indulge, tolerate.
OPPOSITES blame, resent.

**forgiveness** noun pardon, absolution, exoneration, indulgence, clemency, mercy, reprieve, amnesty; informal let-off.
OPPOSITES mercilessness, punishment.

**fork** verb split, branch, divide, separate, part, diverge, go in different directions, bifurcate.

**form** noun 1 *the form of the landscape:* shape, configuration, formation, structure, construction, arrangement, appearance, exterior, outline, format, layout, design. 2 *the human form:* body, shape, figure, frame, physique, anatomy; informal vital statistics.

**3** *the infection takes different forms:* manifestation, appearance, embodiment, incarnation, semblance, shape, guise. **4** *sponsorship is a form of advertising:* kind, sort, type, class, category, variety, genre, brand, style. **5** *you have to fill in a form:* questionnaire, document, coupon, slip. **6** *what form is your daughter in?* class, year; N. Amer. grade. **7** *in good form:* condition, fettle, shape, health; Brit. informal nick.
▶ verb **1** *formed from mild steel:* make, construct, build, manufacture, fabricate, assemble, put together, create, fashion, shape. **2** *he formed a plan:* formulate, devise, conceive, work out, think up, lay, draw up, put together, produce, fashion, concoct, forge, hatch; informal dream up. **3** *they formed a company:* set up, establish, found, launch, create, institute, start, inaugurate. **4** *a mist was forming:* materialize, come into being/existence, emerge, develop, take shape, gather, accumulate, collect, amass. **5** *his men formed themselves into a line:* arrange, draw up, line up, assemble, organize, sort, order. **6** *these parts form an integrated whole:* comprise, make, make up, constitute, compose, add up to.
OPPOSITES dissolve, disappear.

**formal** adjective **1** *a formal dinner:* ceremonial, ritualistic, ritual, conventional, traditional, stately, solemn, elaborate. **2** *a very formal manner:* aloof, reserved, remote, detached, unapproachable, stiff, stuffy, ceremonious, correct, proper; informal stand-offish. **3** *formal permission:* official, legal,

authorized, approved, certified, endorsed, sanctioned, licensed, recognized.
OPPOSITES informal, friendly, casual, colloquial, unofficial.

**formality** noun **1** *the formality of the occasion:* ceremony, ritual, protocol, decorum, solemnity. **2** *his formality was off-putting:* aloofness, reserve, remoteness, detachment, unapproachability, stiffness, stuffiness, correctness; informal stand-offishness. **3** *we keep the formalities to a minimum:* official procedure, bureaucracy, red tape, paperwork. **4** *the interview is just a formality:* routine, routine practice, normal procedure.
OPPOSITES informality, friendliness.

**format** noun design, style, appearance, look, form, shape, size, arrangement, plan, structure, scheme, composition, configuration.

**formation** noun **1** *the formation of the island:* emergence, genesis, development, evolution, shaping, origin. **2** *the formation of a new government:* establishment, setting up, institution, foundation, creation, inauguration. **3** *fighters flying in a V formation:* configuration, arrangement, grouping, pattern, array, alignment, order.
OPPOSITES destruction, disappearance, dissolution.

**former** adjective **1** *the former bishop:* one-time, erstwhile, sometime, ex-, previous, preceding, earlier, prior, last. **2** *in former times:* earlier, old, past, bygone, olden, long ago, gone by, long past, of old. **3** *the*

a b c d e f g h i j k l m n o p q r s t u v w x y z

a
b
c
d
e
**f**
g
h
i
j
k
l
m
n
o
p
q
r
s
t
u
v
w
x
y
z

*former view:* first-mentioned, first.
OPPOSITES future, current, latter.

**formerly** adverb previously, earlier, before, until now/then, once, once upon a time, at one time, in the past.

**formidable** adjective 1 *a formidable beast:* intimidating, forbidding, alarming, frightening, awesome, fearsome, threatening. 2 *a formidable pianist:* accomplished, masterly, virtuoso, expert, impressive, powerful, terrific, superb; informal tremendous, nifty, crack, ace, wizard, magic, mean, wicked, deadly.
OPPOSITES pleasant-looking, comforting, poor.

**formula** noun 1 *a legal formula:* form of words, set expression, phrase, saying. 2 *a peace formula:* recipe, prescription, blueprint, plan, policy, method, procedure.

**formulate** verb 1 *the miners formulated a plan:* devise, conceive, work out, think up, lay, draw up, form, concoct, contrive, forge, hatch, prepare, develop. 2 *how Marx formulated his question:* express, phrase, word, define, specify, put into words, frame, couch, put, articulate, say.

**fort** noun fortress, castle, citadel, bunker, stronghold, fortification, bastion.

**forte** noun strength, strong point, speciality, strong suit, talent, skill, gift; informal thing.
OPPOSITES weakness.

**forthcoming** adjective
1 *forthcoming events:* coming, upcoming, approaching, imminent, impending, future.
2 *no reply was forthcoming:* available, on offer, offered.
3 *he was not very forthcoming:* communicative, talkative, chatty, expansive, expressive, frank, open, candid.
OPPOSITES past, current, unavailable, uncommunicative.

**fortify** verb 1 *measures to fortify the building:* strengthen, secure, barricade, protect. 2 *I'll have a drink to fortify me:* invigorate, strengthen, energize, enliven, animate, vitalize; informal pep up, buck up.
OPPOSITES weaken, sedate, subdue.

**fortitude** noun courage, bravery, endurance, resilience, mettle, strength of character, backbone, grit; informal guts; Brit. informal bottle.
OPPOSITES faint-heartedness.

**fortress** noun fort, castle, citadel, bunker, stronghold, fortification.

**fortunate** adjective 1 *he was fortunate enough to survive:* lucky, favoured, blessed, blessed with good luck, in luck; Brit. informal jammy. 2 *in a fortunate position:* favourable, advantageous, happy.
OPPOSITES unfortunate, unfavourable.

**fortunately** adverb luckily, by good luck, by good fortune, as luck would have it, happily, mercifully, thankfully.

**fortune** noun 1 *fortune favoured him:* chance, accident, coincidence, serendipity, destiny, providence; N. Amer. happenstance. 2 *a change of fortune:* luck, fate, destiny, predestination, the stars, karma, lot. 3 *an upswing in Sheffield's fortunes:* circumstances, state of affairs, condition, position, situation.

**4** *he made his fortune in steel:* wealth, money, riches, assets, resources, means, possessions, property, estate.

**forum** noun meeting, assembly, gathering, rally, conference, seminar, convention, symposium.

**forward** adverb **1** *the traffic moved forward:* ahead, forwards, onwards, onward, on, further. **2** *the winner stepped forward:* towards the front, out, forth, into view, up. **3** *from that day forward:* onward, onwards, on, forth, for ever. OPPOSITES backwards, back.
adjective **1** *a forward movement:* onward, advancing. **2** *the Red Army's forward bridgehead:* front, advance, foremost, leading. **3** *forward planning:* future, forward-looking, for the future, anticipatory. **4** *the girls were very forward:* bold, brazen, cheeky, shameless, familiar, overfamiliar, presumptuous; informal fresh. OPPOSITES backward, rear, shy.
verb **1** *my mother forwarded your letter:* send on, post on, redirect, readdress, pass on. **2** *the goods were forwarded by sea:* send, dispatch, transmit, carry, convey, deliver, ship.

**foster** verb **1** *he fostered the arts:* encourage, promote, further, nurture, help, aid, assist, support, back. **2** *they fostered two children:* bring up, rear, raise, care for, take care of, look after, provide for. OPPOSITES suppress, neglect.

**foul** adjective **1** *a foul smell:* disgusting, revolting, repulsive, repugnant, abhorrent, loathsome, offensive, sickening, nauseating; informal ghastly, gruesome, gross. **2** *foul drinking water:* contaminated, polluted, infected, tainted, impure, filthy, dirty, unclean. **3** *foul language:* vulgar, crude, coarse, filthy, dirty, obscene, indecent, naughty, offensive; informal blue. OPPOSITES pleasant, clean.
verb **1** *the river had been fouled:* dirty, pollute, contaminate, poison, taint. **2** *the trawler had fouled its nets:* tangle up, entangle, snarl, catch, entwine. OPPOSITES clean up, disentangle.

**found** verb establish, set up, start, begin, get going, institute, inaugurate, launch. OPPOSITES dissolve.

**foundation** noun **1** *the foundations of the wall:* footing, foot, base, substructure, underpinning. **2** *there was no foundation for the claim:* justification, grounds, evidence, basis. **3** *an educational foundation:* endowed institution, charitable body, funding agency.

**founder**[1] noun *the founder of modern physics:* originator, creator, (founding) father, architect, developer, pioneer, author, inventor, mastermind.

**founder**[2] verb **1** *the ship foundered:* sink, go to the bottom, go down, be lost at sea. **2** *the scheme foundered:* fail, be unsuccessful, fall flat, fall through, collapse, backfire, meet with disaster; informal flop, bomb. OPPOSITES be raised, succeed.

**fountain** noun **1** *a fountain of water:* jet, spray, spout, spurt, cascade, water feature. **2** *a fountain of knowledge:* source, fount, well, reservoir, fund, mine.

**foyer** noun entrance hall, hallway, entry, porch, reception area, atrium, concourse, lobby, anteroom; N. Amer. entryway.

**fraction** noun 1 *a fraction of the population:* tiny part, fragment, snippet, snatch. 2 *he moved a fraction closer:* tiny amount, little, bit, touch, soupçon, trifle, mite, shade, jot; informal smidgen, tad.
OPPOSITES whole.

**fracture** noun break, crack, split, rupture, fissure.
verb break, crack, split, rupture, snap, shatter, fragment, splinter.

**fragile** adjective 1 *fragile vases:* breakable, delicate, brittle, flimsy, dainty, fine. 2 *the fragile ceasefire:* tenuous, shaky, insecure, vulnerable, flimsy. 3 *she is still very fragile:* weak, delicate, frail, debilitated, ill, unwell, poorly, sickly.
OPPOSITES sturdy, durable, robust.

**fragment** noun 1 *meteorite fragments:* piece, bit, particle, speck, chip, shard, sliver, splinter, flake. 2 *a fragment of conversation:* snatch, snippet, scrap, bit.
verb *explosions caused the chalk to fragment:* break up, crack open, shatter, splinter, fracture, disintegrate, fall to pieces, fall apart.

**fragrance** noun 1 *the fragrance of spring flowers:* sweet smell, scent, perfume, bouquet, aroma, nose. 2 *a daring new fragrance:* perfume, scent, eau de toilette.

**fragrant** adjective sweet-scented, sweet-smelling, scented, perfumed, aromatic.
OPPOSITES smelly.

**frail** adjective 1 *a frail old lady:* weak, delicate, feeble, infirm, ill, unwell, sickly, poorly. 2 *a frail structure:* fragile, easily damaged, delicate, flimsy, insubstantial, unsteady, unstable, rickety.
OPPOSITES strong, robust.

**frame** noun 1 *a tubular metal frame:* framework, structure, substructure, skeleton, casing, chassis, shell. 2 *his tall, slender frame:* body, figure, form, shape, physique, anatomy, build.
verb 1 *he had the picture framed:* mount, set in a frame. 2 *those who frame the regulations:* formulate, draw up, draft, shape, compose, put together, form, devise.
■ frame of mind mood, state of mind, humour, temper, disposition.

**framework** noun 1 *a metal framework:* frame, structure, skeleton, chassis, support, scaffolding. 2 *the framework of society:* structure, shape, fabric, order, scheme, system, organization, anatomy; informal make-up.

**frank** adjective 1 *he was quite frank with me:* candid, direct, forthright, plain, straight, to the point, matter-of-fact, open, honest; informal upfront. 2 *she looked at Sam with frank admiration:* open, undisguised, unconcealed, naked, unmistakable, clear, obvious, transparent, patent, evident.
OPPOSITES evasive, disguised.

**frankly** adverb 1 *frankly, I'm not interested:* to be frank, to be honest, to tell the truth, in all honesty. 2 *he stated the case quite frankly:* candidly, directly, plainly, straightforwardly, forthrightly, openly, honestly, without beating about the bush, bluntly.

**frantic** adjective panic-stricken, panicky, beside oneself, at one's wits' end, distraught, overwrought, worked up, frenzied, frenetic, fraught, feverish, desperate; informal in a state, tearing one's hair out; Brit. informal having kittens, in a flat spin.

OPPOSITES calm.

**fraternity** noun 1 *a spirit of fraternity:* brotherhood, fellowship, kinship, friendship, mutual support, solidarity, community. 2 *the teaching fraternity:* profession, community, trade, set, circle. 3 (N. Amer.) *a college fraternity:* society, club, association, group.

**fraud** noun 1 *he was arrested for fraud:* deception, sharp practice, cheating, swindling, trickery, embezzlement, deceit, double-dealing, chicanery. 2 *social security frauds:* swindle, racket, deception, trick, cheat, hoax; informal scam, con, rip-off, sting, fiddle; N. Amer. informal hustle. 3 *they exposed him as a fraud:* impostor, fake, sham, charlatan, swindler, fraudster, confidence trickster; informal phoney.

**fraudulent** adjective dishonest, cheating, swindling, corrupt, criminal, deceitful, double-dealing, duplicitous; informal crooked, shady, dirty; Brit. informal bent, dodgy; Austral./NZ informal shonky.

OPPOSITES honest.

**frayed** adjective 1 *a frayed collar:* worn, threadbare, tattered, ragged, the worse for wear; informal tatty; N. Amer. informal raggedy. 2 *his frayed nerves:* strained, fraught, tense, edgy, stressed.

**freak** noun 1 *a genetically engineered freak:* aberration, abnormality, oddity, monster, monstrosity, mutant, chimera. 2 *the accident was a freak:* anomaly, aberration, rarity, oddity, one-off, fluke, twist of fate. 3 (informal) *a bunch of freaks:* oddity, eccentric, misfit, crank; informal oddball, weirdo, nut; Brit. informal nutter; N. Amer. informal wacko, kook. 4 (informal) *a fitness freak:* enthusiast, fan, devotee, lover, aficionado; informal nut, fanatic, addict, maniac.
adjective *a freak storm:* unusual, anomalous, aberrant, atypical, unrepresentative, irregular, exceptional, isolated.

OPPOSITES normal.

**free** adjective 1 *admission is free:* free of charge, without charge, for nothing, complimentary, gratis; informal for free, on the house. 2 *free of any pressures:* without, unencumbered by, unaffected by, clear of, rid of, exempt from, not liable to, safe from, immune to, excused. 3 *I'm free this afternoon:* unoccupied, not busy, available, off duty, off work, on holiday, on leave, at leisure, with time to spare. 4 *bathroom's free:* vacant, empty, available, unoccupied, not in use. 5 *a free nation:* independent, self-governing, self-determining, sovereign, autonomous, democratic. 6 *the killer is still free:* on the loose, at liberty, at large, loose, unrestrained. 7 *you are free to leave:* able, in a position, allowed, permitted. 8 *the free flow of water:* unobstructed, unimpeded, unrestricted, unhampered, clear, open. **9** *she was free with her money:* generous, liberal, open-handed, unstinting.

OPPOSITES chargeable, busy, occupied, captive, confined, obstructed, mean.

**verb 1** *the hostages were freed:* release, set free, let go, liberate, set loose, untie. **2** *victims were freed by firefighters:* extricate, release, get out, cut free, pull free, rescue.

OPPOSITES confine, trap.

**freedom** noun **1** *a desperate bid for freedom:* liberty, liberation, release, deliverance. **2** *the fight for freedom:* independence, self-government, self-determination, self-rule, home rule, sovereignty, autonomy, democracy. **3** *freedom from political accountability:* exemption, immunity, dispensation, impunity. **4** *patients have more freedom to choose who treats them:* right, entitlement, privilege, prerogative, discretion, latitude, elbow room, licence, free rein, a free hand, carte blanche.

OPPOSITES captivity, subjection, liability, obligation.

**freely** adverb **1** *may I speak freely?* openly, candidly, frankly, directly, without beating about the bush, without mincing one's words. **2** *they gave their time and labour freely:* voluntarily, willingly, readily, of one's own accord, of one's own free will, without being told to.

**freeze** verb **1** *the stream had frozen:* ice over, ice up, solidify. **2** *she froze in horror:* stop dead in one's tracks, stand (stock)

still, go rigid, become motionless, become paralysed. **3** *the prices of basic foodstuffs were frozen:* fix, hold, peg, set, limit, restrict, cap.

OPPOSITES thaw.

**freezing** adjective **1** *a freezing wind:* icy, bitter, chill, frosty, glacial, arctic, wintry, sub-zero, raw, biting. **2** *you must be freezing:* frozen, numb with cold, chilled to the bone/marrow.

OPPOSITES balmy, hot.

**freight** noun goods, cargo, merchandise.

**frenzied** adjective frantic, wild, frenetic, hectic, feverish, fevered, mad, crazed, manic, furious, uncontrolled.

OPPOSITES calm.

**frenzy** noun hysteria, madness, mania, delirium, wild excitement, fever, lather, passion, panic, fury, rage.

**frequent** adjective *frequent complaints:* recurrent, recurring, repeated, periodic, continual, habitual, regular, successive, numerous, several.

OPPOSITES occasional.

**verb** *he frequented chic clubs:* visit, patronize, spend time in, visit regularly, haunt; informal hang out at.

OPPOSITES avoid.

**frequently** adverb often, all the time, habitually, regularly, customarily, routinely, again and again, repeatedly, recurrently, continually; N. Amer. oftentimes.

OPPOSITES infrequently.

**fresh** adjective **1** *a fresh approach:* new, modern, original, novel, different, innovative. **2** *fresh food:* recently made, just picked, crisp, raw, natural, unprocessed.

**3** *feeling fresh after a sleep:* refreshed, rested, restored, energetic, vigorous, invigorated, lively, sprightly, bright, alert, bouncing, perky; informal full of beans, bright-eyed and bushy-tailed. **4** *a fresh breeze:* strong, brisk, bracing, invigorating, chilly, cool; informal nippy; Brit. informal parky. **5** *the night air was fresh:* cool, crisp, refreshing, invigorating, pure, clean, clear. **6** (informal) *he's getting too fresh:* impudent, impertinent, insolent, presumptuous, forward, cheeky, disrespectful, rude; informal mouthy, saucy, lippy; N. Amer. informal sassy.

OPPOSITES stale, old, used, cooked, preserved, processed, tired, light, warm, sultry, respectful.

**fret** verb worry, be anxious, distress oneself, upset oneself, concern oneself, agonize, lose sleep.

**friction** noun **1** *lubrication reduces friction:* rubbing, chafing, grating, rasping, scraping, resistance, drag, abrasion. **2** *friction between father and son:* discord, disagreement, dissension, dispute, conflict, hostility, animosity, antipathy, antagonism, resentment, acrimony, bitterness, bad feeling.

OPPOSITES harmony.

**friend** noun companion, comrade, confidant, confidante, familiar, intimate, soul mate, playmate, playfellow, ally, associate; informal pal, chum; Brit. informal mate; N. Amer. informal buddy, amigo, compadre, homeboy.

OPPOSITES enemy.

**friendly** adjective **1** *a friendly woman:* amiable, companionable, sociable, gregarious, comradely, neighbourly, hospitable, easy to get on with, affable, genial, cordial, warm, affectionate, convivial; Scottish couthy; informal chummy, pally; Brit. informal matey; N. Amer. informal buddy-buddy. **2** *friendly conversation:* amicable, cordial, pleasant, easy, relaxed, casual, informal, unceremonious, close, intimate, familiar.

OPPOSITES unfriendly, hostile.

**friendship** noun **1** *lasting friendships:* relationship, attachment, association, bond, tie, link, union. **2** *ties of friendship:* friendliness, affection, camaraderie, comradeship, companionship, fellowship, closeness, affinity, unity, intimacy.

OPPOSITES hostility.

**fright** noun **1** *she was paralysed with fright:* fear, terror, horror, alarm, panic, dread, trepidation, dismay, nervousness. **2** *the experience gave everyone a fright:* scare, shock, surprise, turn, jolt, start.

OPPOSITES pleasant surprise.

**frighten** verb scare, startle, alarm, terrify, petrify, shock, chill, panic, unnerve, intimidate; informal spook; Brit. informal put the wind up.

OPPOSITES reassure.

**frightful** adjective horrible, horrific, ghastly, horrendous, awful, dreadful, terrible, nasty; informal horrid.

**fringe** noun **1** *the city's northern fringe:* edge, border, margin, extremity, perimeter, periphery, rim, limits, outskirts. **2** *blue curtains with a yellow fringe:*

a
b
c
d
e
**f**
g
h
i
j
k
l
m
n
o
p
q
r
s
t
u
v
w
x
y
z

edging, border, trimming, frill, flounce, ruffle.
OPPOSITES middle.
adjective *fringe theatre:* alternative, avant-garde, experimental, innovative, left-field, radical, off-Broadway.
OPPOSITES mainstream.

**frivolous** adjective flippant, glib, facetious, joking, jokey, light-hearted, fatuous, inane; informal flip.
OPPOSITES serious.

**front** noun 1 *the front of the boat:* fore, foremost part, forepart, nose, head, bow, prow, foreground. 2 *a shop front:* frontage, face, facing, facade, window. 3 *the front of the queue:* head, beginning, start, top, lead. 4 *a brave front:* appearance, air, face, manner, exterior, veneer, (outward) show, act, pretence. 5 *the shop was a front for his real business:* cover, blind, disguise, facade, mask, cloak, screen, smokescreen, camouflage.
OPPOSITES back.
adjective leading, lead, first, foremost.
OPPOSITES back, last.
■ in front ahead, to/at the fore, at the head, up ahead, in the lead, leading, coming first, at the head of the queue; informal up front.

**frontier** noun border, boundary, borderline, dividing line, perimeter, limit, edge.

**frosty** adjective 1 *a frosty morning:* cold, freezing, frozen, icy, bitter, chill, wintry, arctic; informal nippy; Brit. informal parky. 2 *a frosty reception:* unfriendly, cold, frigid, icy, glacial, inhospitable, unwelcoming, forbidding, hostile, stony.
OPPOSITES warm, friendly.

**frown** verb scowl, glower, glare, lour, make a face, look daggers, give someone a black look, knit one's brows; informal give someone a dirty look.
OPPOSITES smile.
■ frown on disapprove of, take a dim view of, take exception to, object to, look askance at, not take kindly to.

**fruitful** adjective productive, constructive, useful, worthwhile, helpful, beneficial, valuable, rewarding, profitable, advantageous.
OPPOSITES barren, futile.

**frustrate** verb 1 *his plans were frustrated:* thwart, defeat, foil, block, stop, counter, spoil, check, forestall, scotch, derail, snooker; informal stymie; Brit. informal scupper. 2 *the delays frustrated him:* exasperate, infuriate, discourage, dishearten, disappoint.
OPPOSITES further, satisfy.

**frustration** noun 1 *he clenched his fists in frustration:* exasperation, annoyance, anger, vexation, irritation, disappointment, dissatisfaction. 2 *the frustration of his plans:* thwarting, defeat, prevention, foiling, blocking, spoiling, forestalling, derailment, obstruction.

**fudge** verb evade, avoid, dodge, skirt, duck, gloss over, cloud, hedge, beat about the bush, equivocate.

**fuel** verb 1 *power stations fuelled by coal:* power, fire, drive, run. 2 *the rumours fuelled people's anxiety:* fan, feed, stoke up, inflame, intensify, stimulate, encourage, provoke, incite, sustain.

**fugitive** noun escapee, runaway, deserter, absconder, refugee.

**fulfil** verb **1** *he fulfilled a lifelong ambition:* achieve, attain, realize, make happen, succeed in, bring to completion, bring to fruition, satisfy. **2** *she failed to fulfil her duties:* carry out, perform, accomplish, execute, do, discharge, conduct. **3** *they fulfilled the criteria:* meet, satisfy, comply with, conform to, fill, answer.

**fulfilled** adjective satisfied, content, contented, happy, pleased, at peace.
OPPOSITES discontented.

**full** adjective **1** *her glass was full:* filled, brimming, brimful, packed, loaded, crammed, crowded, bursting, overflowing, congested; informal jam-packed, wall-to-wall, chock-a-block, chock-full, awash. **2** *I'm full:* replete, full up, satisfied, sated, satiated; informal stuffed. **3** *a full life:* eventful, interesting, exciting, lively, action-packed, busy, active. **4** *a full list of facilities:* comprehensive, thorough, exhaustive, all-inclusive, all-encompassing, all-embracing, in-depth, complete, entire, whole, unabridged, uncut. **5** *at full speed:* maximum, top. **6** *a full figure:* plump, rounded, buxom, shapely, ample, curvaceous, voluptuous; informal busty, curvy, well endowed; N. Amer. informal zaftig. **7** *a full skirt:* loose-fitting, loose, baggy, voluminous, roomy, capacious, billowing.
OPPOSITES empty, hungry, uneventful, selective, low, thin, tight.

**fully** adverb completely, entirely, wholly, totally, perfectly, quite, altogether, thoroughly, in all respects, (up) to the hilt.

OPPOSITES partly, nearly.

**fumble** verb grope, fish, scrabble, feel.

**fume** noun *toxic fumes:* smoke, vapour, gas, exhaust, pollution.
verb *Ella was fuming at his arrogance:* be furious, seethe, be livid, be incensed, boil, be beside oneself, spit; informal foam at the mouth, see red.

**fumigate** verb disinfect, purify, sterilize, sanitize, decontaminate, cleanse, clean out.
OPPOSITES soil.

**fun** noun **1** *I joined in with the fun:* enjoyment, entertainment, amusement, pleasure, jollification, merrymaking, recreation, leisure, relaxation, a good time; informal living it up, a ball. **2** *she's full of fun:* merriment, cheerfulness, jollity, joviality, high spirits, mirth, laughter, hilarity, light-heartedness, levity. **3** *he became a figure of fun:* ridicule, derision, mockery, scorn, contempt.
OPPOSITES boredom, misery, respect.
adjective (informal) *a fun evening:* enjoyable, entertaining, amusing, pleasurable, pleasant, agreeable, convivial.
■ **make fun of** tease, poke fun at, ridicule, mock, laugh at, parody, caricature, satirize; informal take the mickey out of, send up; N. Amer. informal goof on.

**function** noun **1** *the main function of the machine:* purpose, task, use, role. **2** *my function was to train the recruits:* responsibility, duty, role, province, activity, assignment, task, job, mission. **3** *a function attended by local dignitaries:* social event, party, social occasion, affair, gathering, reception, soirée; N. Amer. levee; informal do, bash.

**verb 1** *the system had ceased to function:* work, go, run, be in working/running order, operate. **2** *the museum functions as an education centre:* act, serve, operate, perform, do duty.

**functional** adjective **1** *a small functional kitchen:* practical, useful, utilitarian, workaday, serviceable, no-frills. **2** *the machine is now fully functional:* working, in working order, functioning, in service, in use, going, running, operative; informal up and running.

**fund** noun **1** *an emergency fund:* collection, kitty, reserve, pool, purse, savings, coffers. **2** *short of funds:* money, cash, wealth, means, assets, resources, savings, capital, reserves, the wherewithal; informal dosh; Brit. informal lolly.

**verb** *we were funded by the Treasury:* finance, pay for, back, capitalize, subsidize, endow, invest in, sponsor; N. Amer. informal bankroll.

**fundamental** adjective basic, underlying, core, rudimentary, root, primary, prime, cardinal, principal, chief, key, central, vital, essential.
OPPOSITES secondary, incidental.

**fundamentally** adverb essentially, in essence, basically, at heart, at bottom, deep down, profoundly, primarily, above all.

**funeral** noun burial, interment, entombment, committal, laying to rest, cremation.

**funny** adjective **1** *a very funny film:* amusing, humorous, witty, comic, comical, hilarious, hysterical, riotous, uproarious, farcical; informal rib-tickling, priceless. **2** *a funny coincidence:* strange, peculiar, odd, weird, bizarre, curious, freakish, quirky, unusual. **3** *there's something funny about him:* suspicious, suspect, dubious, untrustworthy, questionable; informal fishy; Brit. informal dodgy.
OPPOSITES unfunny, serious, unsurprising, trustworthy.

**furious** adjective **1** *he was furious when we told him:* very angry, enraged, infuriated, irate, incensed, fuming, ranting, raving, seething, beside oneself, outraged; informal hopping mad, wild, livid. **2** *a furious debate:* fierce, heated, passionate, fiery, tumultuous, turbulent, tempestuous, violent, stormy, acrimonious.
OPPOSITES pleased, calm.

**furnish** verb **1** *the bedrooms are elegantly furnished:* fit out, appoint, equip; Brit. informal do out. **2** *they furnished us with waterproofs:* supply, provide, equip, issue, kit out; informal fix up.

**furore** noun commotion, uproar, outcry, fuss, upset, brouhaha, stir; informal to-do, hoo-ha, hullabaloo.

**further** adverb *further, it gave him an alibi.* See **FURTHERMORE**.
**adjective** *further information:* additional, more, extra, supplementary, new, fresh.
OPPOSITES existing.
**verb** *attempts to further his career:* promote, advance, forward, develop, facilitate, aid, assist, help, boost, encourage.
OPPOSITES impede.

**furthermore** adverb moreover, further, what's more, also, additionally, in addition, besides, as well, too, on top of that, into the bargain.

**furthest** adjective most distant, remotest, farthest, furthermost, farthermost, outer, outermost, extreme.
OPPOSITES nearest.

**furtive** adjective surreptitious, secretive, secret, clandestine, hidden, covert, conspiratorial, cloak-and-dagger, sneaky; informal shifty.
OPPOSITES open.

**fury** noun 1 *she exploded with fury:* rage, anger, wrath, outrage. 2 *the fury of the storm:* ferocity, violence, turbulence, tempestuousness, savagery, severity, intensity, vehemence, force.
OPPOSITES pleasure.

**fuss** noun 1 *what's all the fuss about?* commotion, excitement, stir, confusion, disturbance, brouhaha, uproar, furore, storm in a teacup; informal hoo-ha, to-do, song and dance, performance. 2 *he didn't put up too much of a fuss:* protest, complaint, objection, argument, row. 3 *they settled in with very little fuss:* trouble, bother, inconvenience, effort, exertion, labour; informal hassle.
verb *he was still fussing about his clothes:* worry, fret, be agitated, be worked up, make a big thing out of, make a

mountain out of a molehill; informal flap, be in a tizzy.

**fussy** adjective 1 *he's very fussy about what he eats:* particular, finicky, fastidious, hard to please, faddish; informal pernickety, choosy, picky; Brit. informal faddy; N. Amer. informal persnickety. 2 *a fussy bridal gown:* over-elaborate, ornate, fancy, busy, cluttered.

**futile** adjective fruitless, vain, pointless, useless, ineffectual, forlorn, hopeless.
OPPOSITES useful.

**future** noun 1 *plans for the future:* time to come, what lies ahead. 2 *her future lay in acting:* destiny, fate, fortune, prospects, chances.
OPPOSITES past.
adjective 1 *a future date:* later, to come, following, ensuing, succeeding, subsequent, coming. 2 *his future wife:* to be, destined, intended, planned, prospective.
OPPOSITES previous, past.

**fuzzy** adjective 1 *her fuzzy hair:* frizzy, fluffy, woolly, downy. 2 *a fuzzy picture:* blurred, indistinct, unclear, out of focus, misty. 3 *a fuzzy concept:* unclear, imprecise, unfocused, nebulous, vague, hazy, loose, woolly.
OPPOSITES straight, smooth, sharp, clear.

a
b
c
d
e
**f**
g
h
i
j
k
l
m
n
o
p
q
r
s
t
u
v
w
x
y
z

# Gg

**gadget** noun device, appliance, apparatus, instrument, implement, tool, utensil, contrivance, contraption, machine, mechanism, invention; informal gizmo.

**gag**[1] verb 1 *the government tried to gag its critics:* silence, muzzle, suppress, stifle, censor, curb, restrain. 2 *the stench made her gag:* retch, heave.

**gag**[2] noun (informal) *he told a few gags:* joke, quip, jest, witticism; informal crack, wisecrack, one-liner.

**gain** verb 1 *he gained a scholarship:* obtain, get, secure, acquire, come by, procure, attain, achieve, earn, win, capture; informal land. 2 *they stood to gain from the deal:* profit, make money, benefit, do well out of. 3 *she gained weight:* put on, increase in, build up. 4 *they were gaining on us:* catch up (with), catch, reduce someone's lead, narrow the gap.
OPPOSITES lose, fall behind.
noun 1 *his gain from the deal:* profit, earnings, income, yield, return, reward, advantage, benefit; informal take. 2 *weight gain:* increase, addition, rise, increment, advance.
OPPOSITES loss.

**gala** noun festival, fair, fête, carnival, pageant, jubilee, jamboree, celebration.

**gale** noun 1 *a howling gale:* high wind, blast, squall, storm, tempest, hurricane, tornado, cyclone, whirlwind, typhoon. 2 *gales of laughter:* peal, howl, hoot, shriek, scream, roar, fit, paroxysm.

**gamble** verb 1 *he started to gamble:* bet, place a bet, wager, hazard; Brit. informal punt, have a flutter. 2 *investors are gambling that the pound will fall:* take a chance, take a risk; N. Amer. take a flyer; informal stick one's neck out; Brit. informal chance one's arm.
noun *I took a gamble:* risk, chance, leap in the dark, speculation, lottery, pot luck.

**game** noun 1 *the children invented a new game:* pastime, diversion, entertainment, amusement, distraction, recreation, sport, activity. 2 *we lost the game:* match, contest, fixture, meeting, tie, clash.
adjective *are you game?* willing, prepared, ready, disposed, interested, eager, keen, enthusiastic.

**gang** noun 1 *a gang of teenagers:* band, group, crowd, pack, horde, throng, mob, herd, swarm, troop; informal bunch, gaggle, load. 2 *a gang of workmen:* crew, team, group, squad, shift, detachment, unit.

**gangster** noun hoodlum, racketeer, thug, villain, criminal, Mafioso; informal mobster, crook, tough; N. Amer. informal hood.

**gaol** noun. See JAIL.

**gap** noun 1 *a gap in the shutters:* opening, aperture, space, breach, chink, slit, crack, crevice, cleft, cavity, hole. 2 *a gap between meetings:* pause, intermission, interval, interlude, break, breathing space, breather, respite; N. Amer. recess. **3** *a gap in our records:* omission, blank. **4** *the gap between rich and poor:* chasm, gulf, separation, contrast, difference, disparity, divergence, imbalance.

**gape** verb **1** *she gaped at him in astonishment:* stare, stare open-mouthed, goggle, gaze, ogle; informal rubberneck; Brit. informal gawp. **2** *a jacket which gaped at every seam:* open, yawn, part, split.

**gaping** adjective wide, broad, vast, wide open, yawning, cavernous.

**garish** adjective gaudy, lurid, loud, harsh, showy, glittering, brash, tasteless, vulgar; informal flashy.
OPPOSITES drab, subdued, tasteful.

**garment** noun item/article of clothing; (**garments**) clothes, clothing, dress, garb, wardrobe, costume; N. Amer. attire; Brit. informal clobber; N. Amer. informal threads.

**garnish** verb decorate, adorn, ornament, trim, dress, embellish.
noun decoration, adornment, ornament, embellishment, enhancement, finishing touch.

**garrison** noun **1** *the English garrison had left:* troops, forces, militia, soldiers, force, detachment, unit. **2** *forces from three garrisons:* base, camp, station, barracks, fort, command post.
verb *troops were garrisoned in York:* station, post, deploy, base, site, place, billet.

**gash** noun cut, laceration, slash, slit, split, wound, injury.
verb cut, lacerate, slash, slit, split, wound, injure.

**gasp** verb **1** *I gasped in surprise:*

catch/draw in one's breath, gulp. **2** *he fell on the ground, gasping:* pant, puff, puff and blow, wheeze, breathe hard/heavily, choke, fight for breath.
noun *he could speak only between gasps:* gulp, pant, puff.

**gate** noun barrier, turnstile, gateway, doorway, entrance, exit, door, portal; N. Amer. entryway.

**gather** verb **1** *we gathered in the hotel lobby:* congregate, assemble, meet, collect, get together, convene, muster, rally, converge. **2** *he gathered his family:* summon, call together, bring together, assemble, convene, rally, round up, muster, marshal. **3** *they gathered the crops:* harvest, reap, crop, pick, pluck, collect. **4** *I gather he's a footballer:* understand, believe, be led to believe, conclude, infer, assume, take it, surmise, hear, learn, discover. **5** *her dress was gathered at the waist:* pleat, pucker, tuck, fold, ruffle.
OPPOSITES disperse.

**gathering** noun assembly, meeting, convention, rally, council, congress, congregation, audience, crowd, group, throng, mass; informal get-together.

**gaudy** adjective garish, lurid, loud, glaring, harsh, showy, glittering, ostentatious, tasteless; informal flashy, tacky.
OPPOSITES drab, tasteful.

**gauge** noun *the temperature gauge:* meter, measure, indicator, dial, scale, display.
verb **1** *astronomers can gauge the star's brightness:* measure, calculate, compute, work out, determine, ascertain, count, weigh, quantify, put a figure on. **2** *it is hard to gauge how*

a b c d e f **g** h i j k l m n o p q r s t u v w x y z

a
b
c
d
e
f
**g**
h
i
j
k
l
m
n
o
p
q
r
s
t
u
v
w
x
y
z

*effective the ban was:* assess, evaluate, determine, estimate, form an opinion of, appraise, weigh up, judge, guess; informal size up.

**gay** adjective homosexual, lesbian; informal queer, pink.
OPPOSITES heterosexual.

**gaze** verb stare, gape, look fixedly, goggle, eye, scrutinize, ogle; informal rubberneck; Brit. informal gawp; N. Amer. informal eyeball.
noun stare, gape, fixed look, regard, scrutiny.

**gear** noun 1 *fishing gear:* equipment, apparatus, paraphernalia, tools, utensils, implements, instruments, rig, tackle; Brit. informal clobber. 2 (informal) *I'll pick up my gear from my hotel:* belongings, possessions, effects, paraphernalia, bits and pieces; informal things, stuff, kit; Brit. informal clobber, gubbins. 3 (informal) *the best designer gear:* clothes, clothing, garments, outfits, attire, garb, wardrobe; informal togs; Brit. informal clobber, kit; N. Amer. informal threads.

**gem** noun 1 *rubies and other gems:* jewel, precious stone, semi-precious stone; informal rock. 2 *a musical gem:* masterpiece, classic, treasure, prize, find; informal one in a million, the bee's knees.

**general** adjective 1 *suitable for general use:* widespread, common, extensive, universal, wide, popular, public, mainstream. 2 *a general pay increase:* comprehensive, overall, across the board, blanket, global, universal, mass, wholesale. 3 *the general practice:* usual, customary, habitual, traditional, normal,

conventional, typical, standard, regular, accepted, prevailing, routine, established, everyday. 4 *a general description:* broad, rough, loose, approximate, unspecific, vague, imprecise, inexact.
OPPOSITES restricted, localized, exceptional, detailed.

**generally** adverb 1 *summers were generally hot:* normally, in general, as a rule, by and large, mainly, mostly, for the most part, predominantly, on the whole, usually. 2 *the idea was generally accepted:* widely, commonly, extensively, universally, popularly.

**generate** verb create, make, produce, engender, spawn, precipitate, prompt, provoke, trigger, spark off, stir up, induce.

**generation** noun 1 *people of the same generation:* age, age group, peer group. 2 *the next generation of computers:* crop, batch, wave, range.

**generosity** noun liberality, lavishness, magnanimity, bounty, munificence, open-handedness, largesse, unselfishness, altruism, charity.
OPPOSITES meanness, selfishness.

**generous** adjective 1 *she is generous with money:* liberal, lavish, magnanimous, giving, open-handed, bountiful, unselfish, ungrudging, free. 2 *a generous amount of fabric:* plentiful, copious, ample, liberal, large, abundant.
OPPOSITES mean, selfish, meagre.

**genesis** noun origin, source, root, beginning, start.

**genius** noun 1 *the world knew of his genius:* brilliance, intelligence, intellect, ability, cleverness, brains. 2 *he has a* *genius for organization:* talent, gift, flair, aptitude, facility, knack, ability, expertise, capacity, faculty. **3** *he is a genius:* brilliant person, gifted person, mastermind, Einstein, intellectual, brain, prodigy; informal **egghead, bright spark;** Brit. informal **brainbox, clever clogs;** N. Amer. informal **brainiac.** OPPOSITES stupidity, dunce.

**genre** noun category, class, classification, group, set, type, sort, kind, variety.

**gentle** adjective **1** *his manner was gentle:* kind, tender, sympathetic, considerate, understanding, compassionate, humane, mild, placid, serene. **2** *a gentle breeze | gentle music:* light, soft, quiet, low, slow. **3** *a gentle slope:* gradual, slight, easy, slow, imperceptible. OPPOSITES brutal, strong, loud, steep.

**genuine** adjective **1** *a genuine Picasso:* authentic, real, actual, original, bona fide, true; informal **pukka, the real McCoy, the real thing, kosher;** Austral./NZ informal **dinkum. 2** *a very genuine person:* sincere, honest, truthful, straightforward, direct, frank, candid, open, natural; informal **straight, upfront.** OPPOSITES bogus, insincere.

**germ** noun **1** *this detergent kills germs:* microbe, micro-organism, bacillus, bacterium, virus; informal **bug. 2** *the germ of an idea:* start, beginnings, seed, embryo, bud, root, origin, source.

**gesture** noun **1** *a gesture of surrender:* signal, sign, motion, indication, gesticulation. **2** *a symbolic gesture:* action, act, deed, move.

verb *he gestured to her:* signal, motion, gesticulate, wave, indicate, give a sign.

**get** verb **1** *where did you get that hat?* obtain, acquire, come by, receive, gain, earn, win, be given; informal **get hold of, score. 2** *your tea's getting cold:* become, grow, turn, go. **3** *get the children from school:* fetch, collect, go/come for, call for, pick up, bring, deliver, convey. **4** *did the police get him?* capture, catch, arrest, apprehend, seize; informal **collar, grab, pick up;** Brit. informal **nick. 5** *she got flu:* contract, develop, go down with, catch, fall ill with. **6** *I didn't get what he said:* hear, catch, make out, follow, take in. **7** *I don't get the joke:* understand, comprehend, grasp, see, fathom, follow. **8** *we got there early:* arrive, reach, make it, turn up, appear, present oneself, come along; informal **show up. 9** *we got her to agree:* persuade, induce, prevail on, influence, talk into. **10** *I'll get supper:* prepare, get ready, cook, make; informal **fix, rustle up;** Brit. informal **knock up.** OPPOSITES give, shake off.

■ **get something across** communicate, get over, impart, convey, transmit, make clear, express. ■ **get along** be friendly, be compatible, get on, agree, see eye to eye; informal **hit it off.** ■ **get away** escape, run away/off, break free, bolt, flee, make off, take off, decamp; informal **skedaddle, scarper;** Brit. informal **do a bunk, do a runner.** ■ **get by** manage, cope, survive, exist, subsist, muddle through/along, scrape by, make ends meet, make do; informal **make out.** ■ **get out of** evade, dodge, shirk, avoid, escape, sidestep; informal wriggle out of. ■ **get round someone** cajole, persuade, wheedle, coax, prevail on, win over, bring round, sway, inveigle; informal sweet-talk, butter up. ■ **get up** get out of bed, rise, stir, rouse oneself; informal surface.

**ghastly** adjective **1** *a ghastly murder*: **terrible**, frightful, horrible, grim, awful, horrifying, shocking, appalling, horrendous, monstrous.
**2** (informal) *a ghastly building*: **unpleasant**, objectionable, disagreeable, distasteful, awful, terrible, dreadful, frightful, detestable, vile; informal horrible, horrid.
OPPOSITES pleasant.

**ghost** noun **spectre**, phantom, wraith, spirit, presence, apparition; informal spook.

**ghostly** adjective **supernatural**, unearthly, spectral, phantom, unnatural, eerie, weird, uncanny; informal spooky.

**giant** noun **colossus**, mammoth, monster, leviathan, ogre.
OPPOSITES dwarf.
adjective **huge**, colossal, massive, enormous, gigantic, mammoth, vast, immense, monumental, mountainous, titanic, towering, gargantuan; informal mega, monster, whopping; Brit. informal ginormous.
OPPOSITES miniature.

**giddy** adjective **1** *she felt giddy*: **dizzy**, light-headed, faint, unsteady, wobbly, reeling; informal woozy. **2** *she was young and giddy*: **flighty**, silly, frivolous, skittish, irresponsible, scatty; informal dizzy.
OPPOSITES steady, sensible.

**gift** noun **1** *he gave the staff a gift*: **present**, handout,

donation, offering, bonus, award, endowment; informal prezzie. **2** *a gift for music*: **talent**, flair, aptitude, facility, knack, bent, ability, skill, capacity, faculty.

**gifted** adjective **talented**, skilled, accomplished, expert, able, proficient, intelligent, clever, bright, brilliant, precocious; informal crack, ace.
OPPOSITES inept.

**gigantic** adjective **huge**, enormous, vast, giant, massive, colossal, mammoth, immense, monumental, mountainous, gargantuan; informal mega, monster, whopping, humongous; Brit. informal ginormous.
OPPOSITES tiny.

**giggle** verb & noun **titter**, snigger, chuckle, chortle, laugh.

**girl** noun **young woman**, young lady, miss; Scottish & N. English lass, lassie; Irish colleen; informal chick; Brit. informal bird; N. Amer. informal gal, broad, dame, babe; Austral./NZ informal sheila.

**girlfriend** noun **sweetheart**, lover, partner, significant other, girl, woman; informal steady; Brit. informal bird; N. Amer. informal squeeze.

**give** verb **1** *he gave them £2,000*: **donate**, contribute, present with, award, grant, bestow, hand (over). **2** *can I give him a message?* **convey**, pass on, impart, communicate, transmit, send, deliver, relay. **3** *he gave his life for them*: **sacrifice**, give up, relinquish, devote, dedicate. **4** *he gave a party*: **organize**, arrange, lay on, throw, host, hold, have. **5** *Dominic gave a bow*: **perform**, execute, make, do. **6** *she gave a shout*: **utter**, let out, emit, produce, make.

OPPOSITES receive, take.

■ **give someone away** betray, inform on; informal split on, rat on; Brit. informal grass on, shop; N. Amer. informal finger; Austral./NZ informal dob in. ■ **give in/up** capitulate, concede defeat, admit defeat, give up, surrender, yield, submit. ■ **give something off** emit, produce, send out, throw out, discharge, release. ■ **give something up** stop, cease, discontinue, desist from, abstain from, cut out, renounce, forgo; informal quit; Brit. informal jack in.

**glad** adjective **1** *I'm really glad you're coming:* pleased, happy, delighted, thrilled; informal over the moon; Brit. informal chuffed; N. English informal made up. **2** *I'd be glad to help:* willing, eager, happy, pleased, delighted, ready, prepared.
OPPOSITES dismayed, reluctant.

**gladly** adverb with pleasure, happily, cheerfully, willingly, readily, eagerly, freely, ungrudgingly.

**glamorous** adjective **1** *a glamorous woman:* beautiful, elegant, chic, stylish, fashionable. **2** *a glamorous lifestyle:* exciting, glittering, glossy, colourful, exotic; informal glitzy, jet-setting.
OPPOSITES dowdy, dull.

**glamour** noun **1** *she had undeniable glamour:* beauty, allure, elegance, chic, style, charisma, charm, magnetism. **2** *the glamour of TV:* allure, attraction, fascination, charm, magic, romance, excitement, thrill; informal glitz, glam.

**glance** verb **1** *Rachel glanced at him:* look briefly, look quickly, peek, peep. **2** *I glanced through the report:* read quickly, scan,
skim, leaf, flick, flip, thumb, browse.
OPPOSITES study.
noun *a glance at his watch:* peek, peep, brief look, quick look.

**glare** verb *she glared at him:* scowl, glower, look daggers, frown, lour; informal give someone a dirty look.
noun **1** *a cold glare:* scowl, glower, angry stare, frown, black look; informal dirty look. **2** *the glare of the lights:* blaze, dazzle, shine, beam, brilliance.

**glaring** adjective **1** *glaring lights:* dazzling, blinding, blazing, strong, harsh. **2** *a glaring omission:* obvious, conspicuous, unmistakable, inescapable, unmissable, striking, flagrant, blatant.
OPPOSITES soft, inconspicuous.

**glaze** verb *pastry glazed with caramel:* cover, coat, varnish, lacquer, polish.
noun *a cake with an apricot glaze:* coating, topping, varnish, lacquer, polish.

**gleam** verb *a light gleamed:* shine, glint, glitter, shimmer, glimmer, sparkle, twinkle, flicker, wink, glisten, flash.
noun *a gleam of light:* flash, glimmer, glint, shimmer, twinkle, sparkle, flicker, beam, ray, shaft.

**glide** verb **1** *a gondola glided past:* slide, slip, sail, float, drift, flow. **2** *seagulls gliding over the waves:* soar, wheel, plane, fly.

**glimpse** noun *a glimpse of her face:* brief/quick look, glance, sight, sighting, peek, peep.
verb *he glimpsed a figure:* catch sight of, sight, spot, notice, discern, spy, pick out, make out.

**glitter** verb *crystal glittered in*

*the candlelight:* sparkle, twinkle, glint, shimmer, glimmer, wink, flash, shine. **noun** *the glitter of light on the water:* sparkle, twinkle, glint, shimmer, glimmer, flicker, flash.

**global** adjective **1** *the global economy:* worldwide, international, world, intercontinental, universal. **2** *a global view of the problem:* comprehensive, overall, general, all-inclusive, all-encompassing, universal, broad.

**gloom** noun **1** *she peered into the gloom:* darkness, dark, murk, shadows, shade. **2** *his gloom deepened:* despondency, depression, dejection, melancholy, unhappiness, sadness, misery, woe, despair. OPPOSITES light, happiness.

**gloomy** adjective **1** *a gloomy room:* dark, shadowy, murky, sunless, dim, dingy. **2** *Joanna looked gloomy:* despondent, depressed, downcast, downhearted, dejected, dispirited, disheartened, demoralized, crestfallen, glum, melancholy; informal down in the mouth, down in the dumps. **3** *gloomy forecasts about the economy:* pessimistic, depressing, downbeat, disheartening, disappointing, unfavourable, bleak, black. OPPOSITES bright, cheerful, optimistic.

**glorious** adjective wonderful, marvellous, magnificent, superb, sublime, spectacular, lovely, fine, delightful; informal stunning, fantastic, terrific, tremendous, sensational, heavenly, divine, gorgeous, fabulous, awesome.

OPPOSITES undistinguished, horrid.

**glory** noun **1** *a sport that won him glory:* honour, distinction, prestige, fame, renown, kudos, eminence, acclaim, praise, celebrity, recognition. **2** *a house restored to its former glory:* magnificence, splendour, grandeur, majesty, greatness, nobility, opulence, beauty, elegance. OPPOSITES shame, obscurity, modesty. **verb** *we gloried in our independence:* delight, triumph, revel, rejoice, exult, relish, savour, be proud of; informal get a kick out of.

**gloss** noun *the gloss of her hair:* shine, sheen, lustre, gleam, patina, polish, brilliance, shimmer.
■ **gloss over** conceal, cover up, hide, disguise, mask, veil, play down, minimize, understate.

**glossy** adjective shiny, gleaming, lustrous, brilliant, glistening, glassy, polished, lacquered, glazed. OPPOSITES dull.

**glow** verb **1** *lights glowed in the windows:* shine, gleam, glimmer, flicker, flare. **2** *a fire glowed in the hearth:* smoulder, burn. **noun** *the glow of the fire:* radiance, light, gleam, glimmer.

**glowing** adjective **1** *glowing coals:* bright, radiant, incandescent, luminous, smouldering. **2** *his glowing cheeks:* rosy, pink, red, ruddy, flushed, blushing, burning. **3** *glowing colours:* vivid, vibrant, bright, brilliant, rich, intense, radiant. **4** *a glowing report:* complimentary,

favourable, enthusiastic, admiring, rapturous, fulsome; informal rave.
OPPOSITES dead, pale, drab, damning.

**glue** noun *a tube of glue*: adhesive, gum, paste, cement; N. Amer. mucilage; N. Amer. informal stickum.
verb *the planks were glued together*: stick, gum, paste, fix, seal, cement.

**glum** adjective gloomy, downcast, dejected, despondent, crestfallen, disheartened, depressed, doleful, miserable; informal fed up, down in the dumps.
OPPOSITES cheerful.

**go** verb **1** *he's gone into town*: travel, move, proceed, make one's way, journey, advance, progress, pass. **2** *the road goes to London*: lead, stretch, reach, extend. **3** *it's time to go*: leave, depart, take oneself off, go away, withdraw, absent oneself, exit, set off, start out, get under way, be on one's way; Brit. make a move; informal make tracks. **4** *all our money had gone*: be used up, be spent, be exhausted, be consumed. **5** *his hair had gone grey*: become, get, turn, grow. **6** *everything went well*: turn out, work out, develop, progress, result, end (up); informal pan out. **7** *those colours don't go*: match, harmonize, blend, be complementary, coordinate, be compatible. **8** *my car won't go*: function, work, run, operate.
OPPOSITES arrive, come, return, clash, malfunction.
noun (informal) **1** *here, have a go*: try, attempt, effort, bid; informal shot, stab, crack. **2** *whose go is it?*: turn, opportunity, chance,

stint, spell, time.
■ **go down 1** *the ship went down*: sink, founder. **2** *interest rates are going down*: decrease, get lower, fall, drop, decline, plummet, plunge, slump. ■ **go in for** take part in, participate in, engage in, get involved in, join in, enter into, undertake, practise, pursue, espouse, adopt, embrace. ■ **go into** investigate, examine, enquire into, look into, research, probe, explore, delve into, consider, review, analyse. ■ **go off 1** *the bomb went off*: explode, detonate, blow up. **2** (Brit.) *the milk's gone off*: go bad, go stale, go sour, turn, spoil, go rancid. ■ **go on 1** *the lecture went on for hours*: last, continue, carry on, run on, proceed, endure, persist, take. **2** *she went on about the sea*: talk at length, ramble, rattle on, chatter, prattle; Brit. informal witter, rabbit. **3** *I'm not sure what went on*: happen, take place, occur, transpire; N. Amer. informal go down. ■ **go out 1** *the lights went out*: be turned off, be extinguished, stop burning. **2** *he's going out with Kate*: see, take out, be someone's boyfriend/girlfriend, be in a relationship with; informal date, go with. ■ **go over**. See **GO THROUGH 3**. ■ **go through 1** *the terrible things she has gone through*: undergo, experience, face, suffer, live through, endure. **2** *he went through Susie's bag*: search, look, hunt, rummage, rifle. **3** *I went through the report*: examine, study, scrutinize, inspect, look over, scan, check.

**goal** noun objective, aim, end, target, intention, plan, purpose, ambition, aspiration.

a b c d e f g h i j k l m n o p q r s t u v w x y z

**gobble** verb guzzle, bolt, gulp, devour, wolf; informal tuck into, put away, demolish; Brit. informal scoff; N. Amer. informal scarf (down/up).

**god** noun deity, goddess, divine being, divinity, immortal.

**golden** adjective blonde, yellow, fair, flaxen.
OPPOSITES dark.

**gone** adjective 1 *I wasn't gone long:* away, absent, off, out, missing. 2 *those days are gone:* past, over (and done with), no more, done, finished, ended, forgotten. 3 *the milk's all gone:* used up, consumed, finished, spent, depleted.
OPPOSITES present, here.

**good** adjective 1 *a good product:* fine, superior, excellent, superb, outstanding, magnificent, exceptional, marvellous, wonderful, first-rate, first-class, quality; informal great, ace, terrific, fantastic, fabulous, class, awesome, wicked; Brit. informal brilliant. 2 *a good person:* virtuous, righteous, upright, upstanding, moral, ethical, principled, law-abiding, blameless, honourable, decent, respectable, trustworthy; informal squeaky clean. 3 *the children are good at school:* well behaved, obedient, dutiful, polite, courteous, respectful. 4 *a good driver:* capable, able, proficient, adept, adroit, accomplished, skilful, talented, masterly, expert; informal mean, wicked, nifty; N. Amer. informal crackerjack. 5 *a good friend:* close, intimate, dear, bosom, special, best, firm, loyal. 6 *we had a good time:* enjoyable, pleasant, agreeable, pleasurable, delightful, lovely, amusing. 7 *it was good of you to come:* kind, generous, charitable, gracious, noble, altruistic, unselfish. 8 *a good time to call:* convenient, suitable, appropriate, fitting, fit, opportune, timely, favourable. 9 *milk is good for you:* wholesome, healthy, nourishing, nutritious, beneficial. 10 *good food:* tasty, appetizing, flavoursome, palatable, succulent; informal scrumptious, scrummy, yummy; Brit. informal moreish; N. Amer. informal nummy. 11 *a good reason:* valid, genuine, authentic, legitimate, sound, bona fide, convincing, compelling. 12 *good weather:* fine, fair, dry, bright, clear, sunny, cloudless, calm, warm, mild.
OPPOSITES bad, wicked, naughty, unenjoyable, mean, inconvenient, disgusting.
noun 1 *issues of good and evil:* virtue, righteousness, goodness, morality, integrity, honesty, truth, honour. 2 *it's for your own good:* benefit, advantage, profit, gain, interest, welfare, well-being.
OPPOSITES wickedness, disadvantage.
■ **for good** forever, permanently, for always, (for) evermore, for ever and ever; N. Amer. forevermore; informal for keeps.

**goodbye** exclamation farewell, adieu, au revoir, ciao, adios; Austral./NZ hooray; informal bye, bye-bye, so long, see you (later); Brit. informal cheerio, cheers, ta-ta.

**goodness** noun 1 *he had some goodness in him:* virtue, good, righteousness, morality, integrity, rectitude, honesty, honour, decency, respectability, nobility, worth, merit. **2** *his goodness towards us:* kindness, humanity, benevolence, tenderness, warmth, affection, love, goodwill, sympathy, compassion, care, concern, understanding, generosity, charity.

**goods** plural noun merchandise, wares, stock, commodities, produce, products, articles.

**goodwill** noun kindness, compassion, goodness, benevolence, consideration, charity, decency, neighbourliness.
OPPOSITES hostility.

**gorge** noun ravine, canyon, gully, defile, couloir, chasm, gulf; S. English chine; N. English gill; N. Amer. gulch, coulee.
■ **gorge oneself** stuff oneself, guzzle, overindulge; informal pig oneself, stuff one's face.

**gorgeous** adjective **1** *a gorgeous girl:* good-looking, attractive, beautiful, pretty, handsome, lovely, stunning; Scottish & N. English bonny; informal fanciable, tasty, hot; Brit. informal fit; N. Amer. informal cute, foxy. **2** *a gorgeous view:* spectacular, splendid, superb, wonderful, grand, impressive, awe-inspiring, awesome, stunning, breathtaking; informal sensational, fabulous, fantastic. **3** *gorgeous uniforms:* resplendent, magnificent, sumptuous, luxurious, elegant, dazzling, brilliant.
OPPOSITES ugly, dreary, drab.

**gossip** noun **1** *tell me all the gossip:* news, rumours, scandal, hearsay; informal dirt, buzz; Brit. informal goss; N. Amer. informal scuttlebutt. **2** *they went for a gossip:* chat, talk, conversation, chatter, heart-to-heart, tête-à-tête; informal jaw, gas; Brit. informal natter, chinwag; N. Amer. informal gabfest; Austral./NZ informal yarn. **3** *she's such a gossip:* gossip-monger, busybody, scandalmonger, rumour-monger, muckraker.
verb **1** *she gossiped about his wife:* talk, whisper, tell tales; informal dish the dirt. **2** *people sat around gossiping:* chat, talk, converse, discuss things; informal gas, chew the fat, jaw; Brit. informal natter, chinwag; N. Amer. informal shoot the breeze.

**gourmet** noun gastronome, epicure, epicurean, connoisseur; informal foodie.

**govern** verb **1** *he governs the province:* rule, preside over, control, be in charge of, command, run, head, manage, oversee, supervise. **2** *the rules governing social behaviour:* determine, decide, control, constrain, regulate, direct, rule, dictate, shape, affect.

**government** noun administration, executive, regime, authority, council, powers that be, cabinet, ministry.

**governor** noun leader, ruler, chief, head, administrator, principal, director, chairman, chairwoman, chair, superintendent, commissioner, controller; informal boss.

**gown** noun dress, frock, robe, habit, costume.

**grab** verb seize, grasp, snatch, take hold of, grip, clasp, clutch, catch.

**grace** noun **1** *the grace of a ballerina:* elegance, poise, finesse, polish, fluency, suppleness. **2** *he had the grace to apologize:* courtesy, decency, (good) manners, politeness,

a
b
c
d
e
f
**g**
h
i
j
k
l
m
n
o
p
q
r
s
t
u
v
w
x
y
z

respect, tact. **3** *he fell from grace:* **favour**, approval, approbation, acceptance, esteem, regard, respect.
OPPOSITES awkwardness, effrontery, disfavour.
verb *a mosaic graced the floor:* **adorn**, embellish, decorate, ornament, enhance.

**graceful** adjective **elegant**, fluid, fluent, easy, polished, supple.

**gracious** adjective **courteous**, polite, civil, well-mannered, tactful, diplomatic, kind, considerate, thoughtful, obliging, accommodating, hospitable.
OPPOSITES ungracious.

**grade** noun **1** *hotels within the same grade:* **category**, class, classification, ranking, quality, grouping, group, bracket. **2** *his job is of the lowest grade:* **rank**, level, standing, position, class, status, order, echelon. **3** (N. Amer.) *the best grades in the school:* **mark**, score, assessment, evaluation, appraisal. **4** (N. Amer.) *the fifth grade:* **year**, form, class.
verb *eggs are graded by size:* **classify**, class, categorize, bracket, sort, group, arrange, pigeonhole, rank, evaluate, rate, value.

**gradient** noun **slope**, incline, hill, rise, ramp, bank; N. Amer. grade.

**gradual** adjective **1** *a gradual transition:* **slow**, steady, measured, unhurried, cautious, piecemeal, step-by-step, bit-by-bit, progressive, continuous. **2** *a gradual slope:* **gentle**, moderate, slight, easy.
OPPOSITES abrupt, steep.

**gradually** adverb **slowly**, steadily, slowly but surely, cautiously, gently, gingerly,

piecemeal, bit by bit, by degrees, progressively, systematically.
OPPOSITES abruptly.

**graft** noun *a skin graft:* **transplant**, implant.
verb **1** *graft a bud onto the stem:* **splice**, join, insert, fix. **2** *tissue is grafted on to the cornea:* **transplant**, implant.

**grain** noun **1** *fields of grain:* **cereal**. **2** *a grain of corn:* **kernel**, seed. **3** *grains of sand:* **granule**, particle, speck, bit, scrap, crumb, fragment, morsel. **4** *a grain of truth:* **trace**, hint, tinge, suggestion, shadow, soupçon, ounce, iota, jot, scrap, shred; informal smidgen. **5** *the grain in paper:* **texture**, weave, pattern.

**grand** adjective **1** *a grand hotel:* **magnificent**, imposing, impressive, awe-inspiring, splendid, resplendent, majestic, monumental, palatial, stately; Brit. upmarket; N. Amer. upscale; informal fancy, posh; Brit. informal swish. **2** *a grand scheme:* **ambitious**, bold, epic, big, extravagant. **3** *a grand old lady:* **august**, distinguished, illustrious, eminent, venerable, dignified, proud. **4** (informal) *you're doing a grand job:* **excellent**, marvellous, splendid, first-class, first-rate, wonderful, outstanding; informal superb, terrific, great, super; Brit. informal brilliant.
OPPOSITES humble, small-scale, poor.

**grandeur** noun **splendour**, magnificence, glory, resplendence, majesty, greatness, stateliness, pomp, ceremony.

**grant** verb **1** *he granted them leave of absence:* **allow**, permit,

accord, afford. **2** *he granted them £20,000:* give, award, bestow on, confer on, present with, endow with. **3** *I grant that the difference is slight:* admit, accept, concede, allow, appreciate, recognize, acknowledge, confess.
OPPOSITES refuse, deny.
noun *a grant from the council:* award, bursary, endowment, scholarship, allowance, subsidy, contribution, handout, donation, gift.

**graphic** adjective **1** *a graphic representation:* visual, pictorial, illustrative, diagrammatic. **2** *a graphic account:* vivid, explicit, detailed, realistic, descriptive, powerful, colourful, lurid, shocking.
OPPOSITES vague.

**grapple** verb **1** *the police grappled with him:* wrestle, struggle, tussle, scuffle, battle. **2** *grappling with addiction:* deal, cope, get to grips, tackle, confront, face.

**grasp** verb **1** *she grasped his hand:* grip, clutch, clasp, clench, squeeze, catch, seize, grab, snatch. **2** *he grasped the important points:* understand, comprehend, take in, see, apprehend, assimilate, absorb; informal get, take on board; Brit. informal twig.
OPPOSITES release, overlook.
noun **1** *his grasp on her hand:* grip, hold, squeeze. **2** *a prize lay within their grasp:* reach, scope, power, range, sights. **3** *a grasp of history:* understanding, comprehension, awareness, grip, knowledge, mastery, command.

**grasping** adjective greedy, acquisitive, avaricious, rapacious, mercenary, materialistic; informal tight-fisted, tight, money-grubbing; N. Amer. informal grabby.

**grate** verb **1** *grate the cheese:* shred, pulverize, mince, grind, crush, crumble. **2** *her bones grated together:* grind, rub, rasp, scrape, jar, creak.

**grateful** adjective thankful, appreciative, indebted, obliged, in someone's debt, beholden.

**gratitude** noun thanks, gratefulness, thankfulness, appreciation, indebtedness, recognition, acknowledgement.

**grave**[1] noun *an unmarked grave:* tomb, burial place, last resting place, vault, mausoleum, sepulchre.

**grave**[2] adjective **1** *a grave matter:* serious, important, weighty, profound, significant, momentous, critical, urgent, pressing, dire, terrible, dreadful. **2** *Jackie looked grave:* solemn, serious, sober, unsmiling, grim, sombre, dour.
OPPOSITES trivial, light-hearted.

**graveyard** noun cemetery, churchyard, burial ground, necropolis, garden of remembrance; Scottish kirkyard.

**gravity** noun **1** *the gravity of the situation:* seriousness, importance, significance, weight, consequence, magnitude, acuteness, urgency, dreadfulness. **2** *the gravity of his demeanour:* solemnity, seriousness, sobriety, severity, grimness, sombreness, dourness.
OPPOSITES triviality, light-heartedness.

**graze**[1] verb *the deer grazed:* feed, eat, crop, nibble, browse.

**graze**[2] verb **1** *he grazed his arm:* scrape, skin, scratch, chafe,

scuff, rasp. **2** *his shot grazed the bar:* touch, brush, shave, skim, kiss, scrape, clip, glance off.
noun *grazes on the skin:* scratch, scrape, abrasion.

**grease** noun oil, fat, lubricant.

**greasy** adjective oily, fatty, buttery, slippery, slick, slimy, slithery; informal slippy.
OPPOSITES fat-free, clean, dry.

**great** adjective **1** *they showed great interest:* considerable, substantial, significant, serious, exceptional, extraordinary. **2** *a great expanse of water:* large, big, extensive, expansive, broad, wide, vast, immense, huge, enormous, massive; informal humongous, whopping; Brit. informal ginormous. **3** *great writers:* prominent, eminent, distinguished, illustrious, celebrated, acclaimed, admired, esteemed, renowned, notable, famous, well known, leading, top, major. **4** *a great castle:* magnificent, imposing, impressive, awe-inspiring, grand, splendid, majestic. **5** *a great sportsman:* expert, skilful, skilled, adept, accomplished, talented, fine, masterly, master, brilliant, virtuoso, marvellous, outstanding, first-class, superb; informal crack, class. **6** *a great fan of rugby:* keen, eager, enthusiastic, devoted, ardent, fanatical, passionate, dedicated, committed. **7** *we had a great time:* enjoyable, delightful, lovely, excellent, marvellous, wonderful, fine, splendid; informal terrific, fantastic, fabulous, super, cool; Brit. informal brilliant.
OPPOSITES little, small, minor, modest, poor, apathetic, half-hearted, miserable.

**greatly** adverb very much,

extremely, considerably, substantially, significantly, markedly, seriously, materially, enormously, vastly, immensely, tremendously, mightily; informal majorly.
OPPOSITES slightly.

**greatness** noun **1** *a woman destined for greatness:* eminence, distinction, celebrity, fame, prominence, renown, importance. **2** *his greatness as a writer:* brilliance, genius, prowess, talent, expertise, mastery, artistry, skill, proficiency, flair.

**greed, greediness** noun **1** *human greed:* avarice, acquisitiveness, covetousness, materialism, mercenariness; informal money-grubbing. **2** *her mouth watered with greed:* gluttony, hunger, voracity, self-indulgence; informal piggishness. **3** *their greed for power:* desire, appetite, hunger, thirst, craving, longing, yearning, hankering; informal itch.
OPPOSITES generosity, temperance, indifference.

**greedy** adjective **1** *a greedy eater:* gluttonous, ravenous, voracious; informal piggish, piggy. **2** *his greedy manager:* avaricious, acquisitive, covetous, grasping, materialistic, mercenary; informal money-grubbing; N. Amer. informal grabby.

**green** adjective **1** olive green, pea green, emerald green, lime green, avocado, pistachio, bottle green, Lincoln green, jade, sea green. **2** *a green island:* verdant, grassy, leafy. **3** *Green issues:* environmental, ecological, conservation, eco-. **4** *a green alternative to diesel:* environmentally friendly, eco-

friendly. **5** *the new supervisor was very green:* inexperienced, callow, raw, unseasoned, untried, naive, innocent, unworldly; informal wet behind the ears.
OPPOSITES barren, experienced.

**greet** verb **1** *she greeted Hank cheerily:* say hello to, address, salute, hail, welcome, meet, receive. **2** *the decision was greeted with outrage:* receive, respond to, react to, take.

**greeting** noun **1** *he shouted a greeting:* hello, salutation, welcome, reception. **2** *birthday greetings:* best wishes, good wishes, congratulations, compliments, regards, respects.
OPPOSITES farewell.

**grey** adjective **1** silvery, gunmetal, slate, charcoal, smoky. **2** *a grey day:* cloudy, overcast, dull, sunless, murky. **3** *her face looked grey:* pale, wan, ashen, pasty, pallid, colourless. **4** *his grey existence:* characterless, colourless, nondescript, flat, bland, dull, boring, tedious, monotonous. **5** *a grey area:* ambiguous, doubtful, unclear, uncertain, indefinite, debatable.
OPPOSITES sunny, ruddy, exciting, certain.

**grief** noun sorrow, misery, sadness, anguish, pain, distress, heartache, heartbreak, agony, woe, desolation.
OPPOSITES joy.

**grievance** noun complaint, objection, grumble, grouse, ill feeling, bad feeling, resentment; informal gripe.

**grieve** verb **1** *she grieved for her father:* mourn, sorrow, cry, sob, weep. **2** *it grieved me to leave her:* sadden, upset, distress, pain, hurt, wound, break

someone's heart.
OPPOSITES rejoice, please.

**grim** adjective **1** *his grim expression:* stern, forbidding, uninviting, unsmiling, dour, formidable. **2** *grim secrets:* dreadful, ghastly, horrible, terrible, awful, appalling, frightful, shocking, grisly, gruesome, depressing, distressing, upsetting. **3** *a grim hovel:* bleak, dismal, dingy, wretched, miserable, depressing, cheerless, joyless, gloomy, uninviting.
OPPOSITES amiable, pleasant, cheerful.

**grin** verb & noun smile, beam, smirk.
OPPOSITES frown, scowl.

**grind** verb **1** *the ore is ground into powder:* crush, pound, pulverize, mill, crumble. **2** *one stone grinds against another:* rub, grate, scrape. **3** *the edge of the knife is then ground:* sharpen, whet, hone, put an edge on, mill, machine, polish, smooth.
noun *the daily grind:* drudgery, toil, labour, donkey work, exertion, chores, slog.

**grip** verb **1** *she gripped the edge of the table:* grasp, clutch, clasp, take hold of, clench, cling to, grab, seize, squeeze. **2** *we were gripped by the drama:* engross, enthral, absorb, rivet, spellbind, fascinate, mesmerize.
OPPOSITES release.
noun **1** *a tight grip:* grasp, hold. **2** *the wheels lost their grip on the road:* traction, purchase, friction, adhesion. **3** *in the grip of an obsession:* control, power, hold, stranglehold, clutches, influence.

**gripping** adjective engrossing, enthralling, absorbing, riveting,

a b c d e f g h i j k l m n o p q r s t u v w x y z

**groan** verb **1** *she groaned and rubbed her stomach:* moan, cry. **2** *they groan about everything:* complain, grumble, moan, mutter; informal grouse, bellyache, bitch, whinge. **3** *the tree groaned:* creak, grate, rasp.
noun **1** *a groan of anguish:* moan, cry. **2** *she listens to all their moans and groans:* complaint, grumble, grievance, moan, muttering; informal grouse, gripe, whinge. **3** *the groan of the timbers:* creaking, creak, grating, grinding.

**groom** verb **1** *she groomed her pony:* curry, brush, clean, rub down. **2** *his hair was carefully groomed:* brush, comb, arrange, do; informal fix. **3** *groomed for stardom:* prepare, prime, condition, coach, train, drill, teach, school.
noun *the bride and groom:* bridegroom.

**groove** noun furrow, channel, trench, trough, rut, gutter, canal, hollow, indentation.

**grope** verb fumble, scrabble, fish, ferret, rummage, feel, search, hunt.

**gross** adjective **1** (informal) *the place smelled gross:* disgusting, repulsive, revolting, foul, nasty, obnoxious, sickening, nauseating, stomach-churning. **2** *a gross distortion of the truth:* thorough, complete, utter, out and out, shameful, serious, unacceptable, flagrant, blatant, obvious, barefaced, shameless, brazen. **3** *gross income:* total, full, overall, combined, before deductions, before tax.
OPPOSITES pleasant, slight, acceptable, net.
verb *he grosses over a million a year:* earn, make, bring in, take, get, receive; informal rake in.

**grotesque** adjective **1** *a grotesque creature:* misshapen, deformed, distorted, twisted, monstrous, hideous, freakish, unnatural, abnormal, strange; informal weird. **2** *a grotesque exaggeration:* outrageous, monstrous, shocking, appalling, preposterous, ridiculous, ludicrous, unbelievable, incredible.
OPPOSITES normal, sensible.

**ground** noun **1** *she collapsed on the ground:* floor, earth, terra firma; informal deck. **2** *soggy ground:* earth, soil, turf, land, terrain. **3** *the team's home ground:* stadium, pitch, field, arena, track; Brit. informal park. **4** *the mansion's grounds:* estate, gardens, park, land, property, surroundings, territory. **5** *grounds for dismissal:* reason, cause, basis, foundation, justification, rationale, argument, occasion, excuse, pretext.
verb **1** *the religious life must be grounded on the law:* base, found, establish, root, build, form. **2** *she was well grounded in the classics:* teach, instruct, coach, tutor, educate, school, train, drill.

**group** noun **1** *the exhibits are in three groups:* category, class, classification, grouping, cluster, set, batch, type, sort, kind, variety, family. **2** *a group of tourists:* crowd, party, body, band, company, gathering, congregation, assembly, collection, cluster, clump, knot, flock, pack, troop, gang; informal

bunch. **3** *a folk group:* band, ensemble, act; informal line-up, combo, outfit.
verb **1** *patients were grouped according to age:* categorize, classify, class, catalogue, sort, bracket, pigeonhole. **2** *chairs were grouped in fours:* assemble, collect, organize, place, arrange, range, line up, lay out.

**grow** verb **1** enlarge, get bigger, get larger, get taller, expand, increase in size, extend, spread, swell, multiply, snowball, mushroom, balloon, build up, mount up, pile up. **2** *flowers grew among the rocks:* sprout, germinate, spring up, develop, bud, bloom, flourish, thrive, run riot. **3** *he grew vegetables:* cultivate, produce, propagate, raise, rear, farm. **4** *Leonora grew bored:* become, get, turn, begin to be.
OPPOSITES shrink, decline.

**grown-up** adjective *she has two grown-up daughters:* adult, mature, of age, fully grown, independent.
OPPOSITES under age.
noun *she wanted to be treated like a grown-up:* adult, woman, man, grown man/woman.
OPPOSITES child.

**growth** noun **1** *population growth:* enlargement, increase in size, expansion, extension, swelling, multiplication, mushrooming, snowballing, rise, escalation, build-up, development. **2** *a growth on his jaw:* tumour, malignancy, cancer, lump, swelling.
OPPOSITES shrinkage, decline.

**grubby** adjective dirty, grimy, filthy, mucky, unwashed, stained, soiled; informal cruddy, yucky; Brit. informal manky; Austral./

NZ informal scungy.
OPPOSITES clean.

**grudge** noun grievance, resentment, bitterness, rancour, ill will, animosity, antipathy, antagonism; informal a chip on one's shoulder.

**gruelling** adjective exhausting, tiring, taxing, draining, demanding, exacting, difficult, arduous, strenuous, back-breaking, punishing, crippling; informal murderous; Brit. informal knackering.

**gruesome** adjective grisly, ghastly, frightful, horrid, horrifying, hideous, horrible, grim, awful, dreadful, terrible, horrific; informal sick, sick-making, gross.
OPPOSITES pleasant.

**grumble** verb complain, grouse, whine, mutter, carp, make a fuss; informal moan, bellyache, bitch, whinge; N. English informal mither.
noun complaint, grouse, grievance, protest; informal grouch, moan, whinge, beef, gripe.

**grumpy** adjective bad-tempered, crabby, tetchy, touchy, irascible, cantankerous, curmudgeonly, surly, fractious; informal grouchy; Brit. informal ratty; N. Amer. informal cranky, ornery.
OPPOSITES good-humoured.

**guarantee** noun **1** *a one-year guarantee:* warranty. **2** *a guarantee that the hospital will stay open:* promise, assurance, word (of honour), pledge, vow, oath, commitment. **3** *a guarantee for loans:* collateral, security, surety, bond.
verb **1** *I guarantee he will accept:* promise, swear, pledge, vow, give one's word, give an assurance, give an undertaking.

a
b
c
d
e
f
**g**
h
i
j
k
l
m
n
o
p
q
r
s
t
u
v
w
x
y
z

**2** *he agreed to guarantee the loan:* underwrite, stand surety.

**guard** verb *troops guarded the bridge:* protect, defend, shield, secure, cover, mind, stand guard over, watch, keep an eye on.
noun **1** *border guards:* sentry, sentinel, nightwatchman, protector, defender, guardian, lookout, watch. **2** *a prison guard:* warder, warden, keeper, jailer; informal screw. **3** *a metal guard:* cover, shield, screen, fender, bumper, buffer.

**guarded** adjective cautious, careful, circumspect, wary, chary, reluctant, non-committal; informal cagey.

**guardian** noun protector, defender, preserver, custodian, warden, guard, keeper, curator, caretaker, steward, trustee.

**guerrilla** noun rebel, irregular, partisan, freedom fighter, revolutionary, terrorist.

**guess** verb **1** *he guessed that she was about 40:* estimate, reckon, judge, speculate, conjecture, hypothesize, surmise. **2** (informal) *I guess I owe you an apology:* suppose, think, imagine, expect, suspect, dare say; informal reckon.
noun *my guess was right:* hypothesis, theory, conjecture, surmise, estimate, belief, opinion, supposition, speculation, suspicion, impression, feeling.

**guest** noun **1** *we have guests:* visitor, caller, company. **2** *hotel guests:* client, customer, resident, boarder, lodger, patron, diner, holidaymaker, tourist.
OPPOSITES host, staff.

**guidance** noun **1** *she looked to him for guidance:* advice,

counsel, instruction, suggestions, tips, hints, pointers, guidelines. **2** *under the guidance of an expert:* direction, control, leadership, management, supervision.

**guide** noun **1** *our guide took us back to the hotel:* escort, attendant, courier, leader, usher. **2** *the techniques given serve as a guide:* outline, template, example, exemplar, model, pattern, guideline, yardstick, precedent. **3** *a guide to Paris:* guidebook, travel guide, companion, handbook, manual, directory, A to Z, instructions, directions; informal bible.
verb **1** *he guided her to her seat:* lead, conduct, show, usher, shepherd, direct, steer, pilot, escort. **2** *the chairman guides the meeting:* direct, steer, manage, conduct, run, be in charge of, govern, preside over, supervise, oversee. **3** *he was always there to guide me:* advise, counsel, direct.

**guild** noun association, society, union, league, organization, company, fellowship, club, order, lodge.

**guilt** noun **1** *the proof of his guilt:* culpability, blameworthiness, responsibility. **2** *a terrible feeling of guilt:* remorse, shame, regret, contrition, self-reproach, a guilty conscience.
OPPOSITES innocence, shamelessness.

**guilty** adjective **1** *the guilty party:* culpable, to blame, at fault, in the wrong. **2** *I still feel guilty about it:* ashamed, guilt-ridden, conscience-stricken, remorseful, sorry, contrite, repentant, penitent, regretful,

rueful, shamefaced.
OPPOSITES innocent,
unrepentant.

**gulf** noun 1 *our ship sailed into the gulf:* bay, inlet, cove, bight, fjord, estuary, sound; Scottish firth. 2 *a gulf between rich and poor:* gap, divide, separation, difference, contrast.

**gulp** verb 1 *she gulped her juice:* swallow, quaff, swill down; informal swig, down, knock back. 2 *he gulped down the rest of his meal:* gobble, guzzle, devour, bolt, wolf; informal shovel down; Brit. informal scoff. 3 *Jenny gulped back her tears:* choke back, fight/hold back, suppress, stifle, smother.
OPPOSITES sip, nibble, let out.
noun *a gulp of cold beer:* mouthful, swallow, draught; informal swig.

**gum** noun *stuck down with gum:* glue, adhesive, paste, cement; N. Amer. mucilage; N. Amer. informal stickum.
verb *the receipts were gummed in:* stick, glue, paste, cement, attach.

**gun** noun firearm, side arm, handgun, weapon; informal shooter; N. Amer. informal piece, shooting iron.

**gunman** noun armed criminal, assassin, sniper, terrorist, gunfighter; informal hit man, gunslinger; N. Amer. informal shootist.

**guru** noun 1 *a Hindu guru and mystic:* spiritual teacher, tutor, sage, mentor, spiritual leader, master. 2 *a management guru:* expert, authority, pundit, leading light, master, specialist.
OPPOSITES disciple.

**gush** verb surge, stream, spout, spurt, jet, rush, pour, spill, cascade, flood; Brit. informal sloosh.
noun surge, stream, spout, spurt, jet, rush, outpouring, spill, outflow, cascade, flood, torrent.

**gushing, gushy** adjective effusive, overenthusiastic, extravagant, fulsome, lavish; informal over the top.
OPPOSITES restrained.

**gust** noun flurry, blast, puff, blow, rush, squall.

**gut** noun 1 *an ache in his gut:* stomach, belly, abdomen, paunch, intestines; informal tummy, insides, innards. 2 (informal) *Nicola has a lot of guts:* courage, bravery, backbone, nerve, pluck, spirit, daring, grit, fearlessness, determination; Brit. informal bottle; N. Amer. informal moxie.
adjective (informal) *a gut feeling:* instinctive, intuitive, deep-seated, involuntary, spontaneous, unthinking.
verb 1 *gut the sardines:* clean (out), disembowel, draw. 2 *builders had gutted the old place:* strip, empty, devastate, lay waste, ravage, ruin, wreck.

**gutter** noun drain, trough, trench, ditch, sluice, sewer, channel, conduit, pipe.

**guy** noun (informal) man, fellow; informal lad; Brit. informal chap, bloke; N. Amer. informal dude, hombre.

**guzzle** verb 1 *he guzzled his burger:* gobble, bolt, wolf, devour; informal tuck into, shovel down; Brit. informal scoff; N. Amer. informal scarf. 2 *she guzzled down the orange juice:* gulp down, quaff, swill; informal knock back, swig, down.

a
b
c
d
e
f
g
**h**
i
j
k
l
m
n
o
p
q
r
s
t
u
v
w
x
y
z

# Hh

**habit** noun **1** custom, practice, routine, way. **2** (informal) *his cocaine habit*: addiction, dependence, craving, fixation.

**hack** verb cut, chop, hew, lop, saw, slash.

**haggle** verb barter, bargain, negotiate, wrangle.

**hail**[1] noun *a hail of bullets*: barrage, volley, shower, stream, salvo.

**hail**[2] verb **1** *a friend hailed him*: call out to, shout to, address, greet, say hello to, salute. **2** *he hailed a cab*: flag down, wave down. **3** *critics hailed the film as a masterpiece*: acclaim, praise, applaud. **4** *Rick hails from Australia*: come, be, be a native of.

**hair** noun **1** head of hair, shock of hair, mane, mop, locks, tresses, curls. **2** hairstyle, haircut; informal hairdo. **3** fur, wool, coat, fleece, mane.

**hairdresser** noun hairstylist, coiffeur, coiffeuse, barber.

**hairy** adjective **1** *animals with hairy coats*: shaggy, bushy, long-haired, woolly, furry, fleecy. **2** *his hairy face*: bearded, unshaven, stubbly, bristly; formal hirsute. **3** (informal) *a hairy situation*: risky, dangerous, perilous, hazardous, tricky; informal dicey; Brit. informal dodgy.
OPPOSITES short-haired, smooth-haired, shaven, safe.

**halfway** adjective *the halfway point*: midway, middle, mid, central, centre, intermediate. adverb *halfway down the passage*: midway, in the middle, in the centre, part of the way.

**hall** noun **1** entrance hall, hallway, entry, entrance, lobby, foyer, vestibule. **2** *the village hall*: assembly room, meeting room, chamber, auditorium, theatre, house.

**halt** verb **1** *halt at the barrier*: stop, come to a halt, come to a stop, come to a standstill, pull up, draw up. **2** *a strike has halted production*: stop, bring to a stop, put a stop to, suspend, arrest, check, curb, stem, staunch, block, stall.
OPPOSITES start, continue, restart.
noun **1** *a bus screeched to a halt*: stop, standstill. **2** *a halt in production*: stoppage, break, pause, interval, interruption.
OPPOSITES start, resumption.

**halting** adjective hesitant, faltering, hesitating, stumbling, stammering, stuttering, broken, imperfect.
OPPOSITES fluent.

**hammer** verb **1** *hammered metal*: beat, forge, shape, form, mould, fashion. **2** *he hammered the nail in*: batter, bang, pummel, pound, knock, thump.

**hamper** verb hinder, obstruct, impede, inhibit, delay, slow down, hold up, interfere with, handicap, hamstring.
OPPOSITES help.

**hand** noun **1** fist, palm; informal paw, mitt. **2** *written in his own hand*: handwriting, writing, script. **3** *a factory hand*: worker, employee, workman, labourer, operative, craftsman, roustabout.

**verb** *hand me a spanner:* pass, give, present, let someone have.

**handbook** noun manual, instructions, ABC, A to Z, companion, guide, guidebook.

**handcuff** verb *he was handcuffed:* manacle, shackle, clap/put someone in irons; informal cuff.

noun (**handcuffs**) manacles, shackles, irons; informal cuffs, bracelets.

**handful** noun few, small number, small amount, small quantity, sprinkling, smattering, one or two, some, not many.
OPPOSITES lot.

**handicap** noun 1 disability, infirmity, defect, impairment, affliction. 2 *a handicap to industrial competitiveness:* impediment, hindrance, obstacle, barrier, constraint, disadvantage, stumbling block.
OPPOSITES benefit, advantage.
verb *handicapped by lack of funding:* hamper, impede, hinder, impair, hamstring, restrict, constrain.
OPPOSITES help.

**handle** verb 1 *handle the vase carefully:* hold, pick up, grasp, grip, lift, finger. 2 *a car which is easy to handle:* control, drive, steer, operate, manoeuvre. 3 *she handled the job well:* deal with, manage, tackle, take care of, look after, take charge of, attend to, see to, sort out. 4 *the traders handled imported goods:* trade in, deal in, buy, sell, supply, peddle, traffic in.
noun *a knife handle:* grip, haft, hilt, stock, shaft.

**handsome** adjective 1 *a handsome man:* good-looking, attractive, striking; informal

hunky, dishy, tasty, fanciable; Brit. informal fit; N. Amer. informal cute. 2 *a handsome woman:* striking, imposing, prepossessing, good-looking, attractive. 3 *a handsome profit:* substantial, considerable, sizeable, princely, generous, lavish, ample, bumper; informal tidy, whopping; Brit. informal ginormous.
OPPOSITES ugly, meagre.

**handy** adjective 1 *a handy gadget:* useful, convenient, practical, neat, easy to use, user-friendly, helpful. 2 *keep your credit card handy:* ready, to hand, within reach, accessible, readily available, nearby, at the ready. 3 *he's handy with a needle:* skilful, skilled, dexterous, deft, adept, proficient.
OPPOSITES useless, unwieldy, inconvenient, inept.

**hang** verb 1 *lights hung from the trees:* be suspended, dangle, swing, sway, hover, float. 2 *hang the picture at eye level:* suspend, put up, pin up, display. 3 *the room was hung with streamers:* decorate, adorn, drape, festoon, deck out. 4 *he was hanged for murder:* send to the gallows, execute, lynch; informal string up.

**hanker** verb yearn, long, wish, hunger, thirst, lust, ache; informal itch.

**happen** verb 1 *remember what happened last time:* occur, take place, come about, develop, result, transpire; N. Amer. informal go down. 2 *they happened to be in London:* chance, have the good/bad luck.

**happening** noun occurrence, event, incident, episode, affair.

**happily** adverb 1 cheerfully,

a
b
c
d
e
f
g
**h**
i
j
k
l
m
n
o
p
q
r
s
t
u
v
w
x
y
z

contentedly, cheerily, merrily, joyfully. **2** *I will happily do as you ask:* gladly, willingly, readily, freely. **3** *happily, we arrived just in time:* fortunately, luckily, thankfully, mercifully, as luck would have it.
OPPOSITES unhappily.

**happiness** noun pleasure, contentment, satisfaction, cheerfulness, merriment, joy, well-being.
OPPOSITES unhappiness.

**happy** adjective **1** cheerful, cheery, merry, joyful, jovial, jolly, carefree, in good spirits, in a good mood, pleased, contented, content, satisfied. **2** *we will be happy to advise you:* glad, pleased, delighted, more than willing. **3** *a happy coincidence:* fortunate, lucky, timely, convenient.
OPPOSITES unhappy, unwilling, unfortunate.

**harass** verb persecute, intimidate, hound, pester, bother; informal hassle, bug; N. Amer. informal ride.

**harassed** adjective stressed, hard-pressed, careworn, worried, troubled; informal hassled.
OPPOSITES carefree.

**harassment** noun persecution, intimidation, victimization, trouble, bother; informal hassle.

**harbour** noun port, dock, haven, marina, mooring, wharf, anchorage, waterfront.
verb **1** *he is harbouring a dangerous criminal:* shelter, conceal, hide, shield, protect, give asylum to. **2** *Rose harboured a grudge against him:* bear, hold, nurse, foster.

**hard** adjective **1** *hard ground:* firm, solid, rigid, stiff, unbreakable, unyielding, compacted, tough, strong. **2** *hard physical work:* arduous, strenuous, tiring, exhausting, back-breaking, gruelling, heavy, laborious, demanding; Brit. informal knackering. **3** *hard workers:* industrious, diligent, assiduous, conscientious, energetic, keen, enthusiastic, indefatigable. **4** *a hard problem:* difficult, puzzling, complicated, intricate, thorny, problematic. **5** *times are hard:* harsh, grim, austere, difficult, bad, bleak, tough. **6** *a hard blow:* forceful, heavy, strong, sharp, violent, powerful.
OPPOSITES soft, easy, lazy, gentle.
adverb **1** *George pushed her hard:* forcefully, roughly, heavily, sharply, violently. **2** *they worked hard:* diligently, industriously, assiduously, conscientiously, energetically, doggedly; informal like mad, like crazy. **3** *she looked hard at me:* closely, intently, critically, carefully, searchingly.
OPPOSITES gently, lazily, casually.

**harden** verb **1** *this glue hardens in four hours:* solidify, set, stiffen, thicken. **2** *their suffering had hardened them:* toughen, desensitize, inure, season, train, numb.
OPPOSITES soften.

**hardened** adjective *a hardened criminal:* inveterate, seasoned, habitual, chronic, compulsive, confirmed, incorrigible.

**hardly** adverb scarcely, barely, only just, just.
OPPOSITES fully, easily.

**hardship** noun difficulty, privation, destitution, poverty, austerity, need, distress, suffering, adversity.
OPPOSITES prosperity, ease.

**hardware** noun equipment, apparatus, gear, paraphernalia, tackle, kit, machinery.

**hardy** adjective robust, healthy, fit, strong, sturdy, tough, rugged.
OPPOSITES delicate.

**harm** noun *it won't do you any harm:* injury, damage, mischief.
OPPOSITES good.
verb **1** *he's never harmed anybody:* hurt, injure, lay a finger on, mistreat, ill-treat. **2** *this could harm his prospects:* damage, spoil, affect, undermine, ruin.
OPPOSITES heal, help.

**harmful** adjective damaging, injurious, detrimental, dangerous, unhealthy, unwholesome, hurtful, destructive, hazardous.
OPPOSITES beneficial.

**harmless** adjective **1** *a harmless substance:* safe, innocuous, gentle, mild, non-toxic. **2** *he seems harmless enough:* inoffensive, innocuous, gentle.
OPPOSITES harmful, objectionable.

**harmony** noun **1** *musical harmony:* tunefulness, euphony, melodiousness, unison. **2** *the villagers live together in harmony:* accord, agreement, peace, friendship, fellowship, cooperation, understanding, rapport, unity.
OPPOSITES dissonance, disagreement.

**harrowing** adjective distressing, traumatic, upsetting, shocking, disturbing, painful, agonizing.

**harry** verb harass, hound, torment, pester, worry, badger, nag, plague; informal hassle, bug.

**harsh** adjective **1** *a harsh voice:* grating, rasping, strident, raucous, discordant. **2** *harsh colours:* glaring, loud, garish, gaudy, lurid. **3** *his harsh treatment of captives:* cruel, savage, barbarous, merciless, inhumane, ruthless. **4** *they took harsh measures to end the crisis:* severe, stringent, firm, stiff, stern, rigorous. **5** *harsh words:* rude, discourteous, unfriendly, sharp, bitter, unkind, critical, disparaging. **6** *harsh conditions:* austere, grim, spartan, hard, inhospitable. **7** *a harsh winter:* cold, freezing, icy, bitter, hard, severe, bleak.
OPPOSITES soft, subdued, kind, mild, friendly, comfortable.

**harvest** noun *a poor harvest:* crop, yield, vintage, produce.
verb *he harvested the wheat:* gather, bring in, reap, pick, collect.

**hassle** (informal) noun *parking is such a hassle:* inconvenience, bother, nuisance, trouble, annoyance, irritation, fuss; informal aggravation, headache, pain in the neck.
verb *don't hassle me!* harass, pester, be on at, badger, hound, bother, nag, torment; informal bug; N. English informal mither.

**hasten** verb **1** *we hastened back:* hurry, rush, dash, race, fly, speed; informal zip; N. Amer. informal hightail. **2** *chemicals can hasten ageing:* speed up, bring on, precipitate, advance.
OPPOSITES dawdle, delay.

**hasty** adjective hurried, rash, impetuous, impulsive, reckless, precipitate, spur-of-the-moment.
OPPOSITES considered.

**hate** verb **1** *they hate each other:* loathe, detest, despise, dislike, abhor, shrink from, be unable to bear/stand. **2** *I hate to bother*

*you:* be sorry, be reluctant, be loath.
OPPOSITES love.
**noun** *feelings of hate:* hatred, loathing, abhorrence, abomination, aversion, disgust.
OPPOSITES love.

**hatred** noun. See **HATE** noun.

**haul** verb *she hauled the basket upstairs:* drag, pull, heave, lug, hump.
**noun** *the thieves' haul:* booty, loot, plunder, spoils, stolen goods; informal swag.

**haunt** verb *the sight haunted me:* torment, disturb, trouble, worry, plague, prey on.
**noun** *a favourite haunt of artists:* meeting place, stamping ground, spot, venue; informal hang-out; N. Amer. stomping ground.

**haunted** adjective 1 *the church is haunted:* possessed, cursed, jinxed, eerie. 2 *his haunted eyes:* tormented, anguished, tortured, obsessed, troubled, worried.

**haunting** adjective evocative, affecting, stirring, powerful, poignant, memorable.

**have** verb 1 *he had a new car:* own, be in possession of, be blessed with, boast, enjoy. 2 *the flat has five rooms:* comprise, consist of, contain, include, incorporate, be composed of, be made up of. 3 *they had tea:* eat, drink, take. 4 *let's have a party:* organize, hold, give, throw, put on, lay on. 5 *I have to get up at six:* must, be obliged to, be required to, be compelled to, be forced to, be bound to.
■ **have someone on** (Brit. informal) play a trick on, play a joke on, pull someone's leg; Brit. informal wind someone up; N. Amer. informal put someone on. ■ **have**

something on be wearing, be dressed in, be clothed in, be decked out in.

**haven** noun refuge, retreat, shelter, sanctuary, oasis.

**havoc** noun chaos, mayhem, bedlam, pandemonium, a shambles.

**hazard** noun danger, risk, peril, menace, jeopardy, threat.

**hazardous** adjective risky, dangerous, unsafe, perilous, fraught with danger, high-risk; informal dicey; Brit. informal dodgy.
OPPOSITES safe, certain.

**haze** noun mist, fog, cloud, vapour.

**head** noun 1 *her head hit the wall:* skull, cranium; informal nut. 2 *he had to use his head:* brain(s), brainpower, intellect, intelligence, grey matter; Brit. informal loaf; N. Amer. informal smarts. 3 *she had a head for business:* aptitude, talent, gift, capacity. 4 *the head of the church:* leader, chief, controller, governor, superintendent, commander, captain, director, manager, principal, president; informal boss; Brit. informal gaffer, guv'nor. 5 *the head of the queue:* front, beginning, start, top.
OPPOSITES back.
**adjective** *the head waiter:* chief, principal, leading, main, first, top, highest.
**verb** *a team headed by a manager:* command, control, lead, manage, direct, supervise, superintend, oversee, preside over.
■ **head someone/something off** 1 *he went to head off the visitors:* intercept, divert, redirect, re-route, turn away. 2 *they headed off an argument:* forestall, avert, stave off, nip in

the bud, prevent, avoid, stop.

**headache** noun **1** *I've got a headache*: sore head, migraine, hangover. **2** (informal) *it was a real headache*: problem, worry, hassle, pain in the neck, bind.

**heading** noun title, caption, legend, rubric, headline.

**heady** adjective **1** *heady wine*: potent, intoxicating, strong. **2** *the heady days of my youth*: exhilarating, exciting, stimulating, thrilling, intoxicating.
OPPOSITES weak, boring.

**heal** verb **1** *he heals the sick*: cure, make better, restore to health, treat. **2** *his knee had healed*: get better, be cured, recover, mend. **3** *we tried to heal the rift*: put right, repair, resolve, settle; informal patch up.
OPPOSITES worsen, aggravate.

**health** noun **1** *he was restored to health*: well-being, fitness, good condition, strength, robustness, vigour. **2** *poor health*: condition, physical shape, constitution.
OPPOSITES illness.

**healthy** adjective **1** *a healthy baby*: well, fit, in good shape, in fine fettle, in tip-top condition, strong, fighting fit. **2** *a healthy diet*: wholesome, good for one, health-giving, nutritious, nourishing, invigorating, sanitary, hygienic.
OPPOSITES unhealthy.

**heap** noun *a heap of boxes*: pile, stack, mound, mountain.
verb *she heaped logs on the fire*: pile (up), stack (up), make a mound of.

**hear** verb **1** *she could hear voices*: make out, catch, get, perceive, overhear. **2** *they heard that I had moved*: learn, find out, discover, gather, glean. **3** *a jury heard the case*: try, judge, adjudicate on.

**hearing** noun **1** *she moved out of hearing*: earshot, hearing distance. **2** *I had a fair hearing*: chance to speak, opportunity to be heard. **3** *he gave evidence at the hearing*: trial, court case, enquiry, inquest, tribunal.

**heart** noun **1** *he poured out his heart*: emotions, feelings, sentiments, soul, mind. **2** *he has no heart*: compassion, sympathy, humanity, feeling(s), empathy, understanding, soul, goodwill. **3** *they lost heart*: enthusiasm, spirit, determination, resolve, nerve; Brit. informal bottle. **4** *the heart of the city*: centre, middle, hub, core. **5** *the heart of the matter*: essence, crux, core, nub, root, meat, substance, kernel; informal nitty-gritty.
OPPOSITES edge.
■ **at heart** deep down, basically, fundamentally, essentially, in essence, intrinsically. ■ **by heart** from memory, off pat, word for word, verbatim, parrot-fashion, word-perfect. ■ **take heart** be encouraged, be heartened, be comforted, be consoled.

**heartily** adverb **1** *we heartily welcome the changes*: wholeheartedly, warmly, profoundly, eagerly, enthusiastically. **2** *they were heartily sick of her*: thoroughly, completely, absolutely, exceedingly, downright; N. Amer. quite; informal seriously; Brit. informal jolly; N. Amer. informal real, mighty.

**hearty** adjective **1** *a hearty character*: exuberant, jovial, ebullient, cheerful, lively, loud, animated, vivacious, energetic, spirited. **2** *hearty*

**heat** *congratulations:* wholehearted, heartfelt, sincere, genuine, real. **3** *a hearty woman of sixty-five:* robust, healthy, hardy, fit, vigorous, sturdy, strong. **4** *a hearty meal:* substantial, large, ample, satisfying, filling, generous.
OPPOSITES introverted, half-hearted, frail, light.

**heat** noun **1** *a plant sensitive to heat:* warmth, hotness, high temperature. **2** *he took the heat out of the dispute:* passion, intensity, vehemence, fervour, excitement, agitation, anger.
OPPOSITES cold, apathy.
verb **1** *the food was heated:* warm (up), reheat, cook, keep warm. **2** *the pipes expand as they heat up:* get hot, get warm, warm up; Brit. informal hot up.
OPPOSITES cool.

**heated** adjective **1** *a heated argument:* vehement, passionate, impassioned, animated, lively, acrimonious, angry, bitter, furious, fierce. **2** *Robert grew heated as he spoke:* excited, animated, worked up, wound up, keyed up; informal het up.

**heaven** noun **1** *the good will have a place in heaven:* paradise, the hereafter, the next world, the afterworld, nirvana, Zion, Elysium. **2** *a good book is my idea of heaven:* bliss, ecstasy, rapture, contentment, happiness, delight, joy, paradise.
OPPOSITES hell, misery.

**heavenly** adjective **1** *heavenly choirs:* divine, holy, celestial, angelic. **2** *a heavenly body:* celestial, cosmic, stellar, sidereal. **3** (informal) *a heavenly morning:* delightful, wonderful, glorious, sublime, exquisite,

beautiful, lovely, gorgeous, enchanting; informal divine, super, fantastic, fabulous.
OPPOSITES mortal, infernal, terrestrial, dreadful.

**heavily** adverb **1** *Dad walked heavily:* laboriously, slowly, ponderously, awkwardly, clumsily. **2** *we were heavily defeated:* decisively, conclusively, roundly, soundly, utterly, completely, thoroughly. **3** *he drank heavily:* excessively, immoderately, copiously, intemperately. **4** *the area is heavily planted with trees:* densely, closely, thickly. **5** *I became heavily involved:* deeply, extremely, greatly, exceedingly, tremendously, profoundly.
OPPOSITES easily, narrowly, moderately, thinly, slightly.

**heavy** adjective **1** *a heavy box:* weighty, hefty, substantial, ponderous, solid, dense. **2** *a heavy blow to the head:* forceful, hard, strong, violent, powerful, mighty, sharp, severe. **3** *heavy work:* strenuous, hard, physical, difficult, arduous, demanding, back-breaking, gruelling. **4** *heavy fighting:* intense, fierce, relentless, severe, serious. **5** *a heavy meal:* substantial, filling, stodgy, rich, big.
OPPOSITES light.

**hectic** adjective frantic, frenetic, frenzied, feverish, manic, busy, active, fast and furious.
OPPOSITES leisurely.

**heed** verb *heed the warnings:* pay attention to, take notice of, take note of, listen to, consider, take to heart, take into account, obey, adhere to, abide by, observe.
OPPOSITES disregard.

noun *he paid no heed:* attention, notice, note, regard, thought.

**hefty** adjective **1** *a hefty young man:* burly, sturdy, strapping, bulky, strong, muscular, big, solid, well built; informal hulking, beefy. **2** *a hefty kick:* powerful, violent, hard, forceful. **3** *a hefty fine:* substantial, sizeable, considerable, stiff, large, heavy; informal whopping.
OPPOSITES slight, feeble, light, small.

**height** noun **1** *the height of the wall:* tallness, stature, elevation, altitude. **2** *mountain heights:* summit, top, peak, crest, crown, tip, cap, pinnacle. **3** *the height of their fame:* highest point, peak, zenith, pinnacle, climax.
OPPOSITES width, depth, nadir.

**heighten** verb intensify, increase, enhance, add to, augment, boost, strengthen, deepen, magnify, reinforce.
OPPOSITES reduce.

**heir, heiress** noun successor, next in line, inheritor, beneficiary, legatee.

**hell** noun **1** the underworld, the netherworld, eternal damnation, perdition, hellfire, fire and brimstone, the Inferno, Hades. **2** *he made her life hell:* misery, torture, agony, purgatory, torment, a nightmare.
OPPOSITES heaven, bliss.

**help** verb **1** assist, aid, abet, lend a hand (to), give assistance to, come to the aid of, be of service to, do someone a favour, do someone a service, do someone a good turn, rally round, pitch in. **2** *this credit card helps cancer research:* support, contribute to, give money to, donate to, promote, boost, back. **3** *sore throats are helped by lozenges:* relieve, soothe, ease, alleviate, improve, lessen. **4** *he could not help laughing:* resist, avoid, refrain from, keep from, stop.
OPPOSITES hinder, impede, worsen.

noun **1** *this could be of help:* assistance, aid, support, succour, benefit, use, advantage, service. **2** *help for his eczema:* relief, alleviation, improvement, healing.
OPPOSITES hindrance, aggravation.

**helper** noun assistant, aide, deputy, auxiliary, supporter, second, mate, right-hand man/woman, attendant.

**helpful** adjective **1** *the staff are very helpful:* obliging, of assistance, supportive, accommodating, cooperative, eager to please. **2** *we found your comments helpful:* useful, beneficial, valuable, constructive, informative, instructive. **3** *a helpful new tool:* handy, useful, convenient, practical, easy-to-use, serviceable; informal neat, nifty.
OPPOSITES unhelpful, useless.

**helping** noun portion, serving, piece, slice, share, plateful; informal dollop.

**helpless** adjective dependent, incapable, powerless, paralysed, defenceless, vulnerable, exposed, unprotected.
OPPOSITES independent.

**hence** adverb consequently, as a consequence, for this reason, therefore, so, accordingly, as a result, that being so.

**herd** noun drove, flock, pack, fold, swarm, mass, crowd, horde.

**hereditary** adjective **1** *a*

a
b
c
d
e
f
g
**h**
i
j
k
l
m
n
o
p
q
r
s
t
u
v
w
x
y
z

*hereditary right:* inherited, bequeathed, handed down, passed down, family, ancestral. **2** *a hereditary disease:* genetic, inborn, inherited, inbred, innate, in the family, in the blood, in the genes.
OPPOSITES acquired, infectious.

**heritage** noun **1** *Europe's cultural heritage:* tradition, history, past, background, culture, customs. **2** *his Greek heritage:* ancestry, lineage, descent, extraction, parentage, roots, heredity.

**hero** noun **1** *a sporting hero:* star, superstar, megastar, idol, celebrity, favourite, darling; informal celeb. **2** *the hero of the film:* main character, starring role, male protagonist, (male) lead, leading man; informal good guy.
OPPOSITES loser, supporting role, villain.

**heroic** adjective brave, courageous, valiant, intrepid, bold, fearless, daring; informal gutsy, spunky.
OPPOSITES cowardly.

**heroine** noun **1** *a sporting heroine:* star, superstar, megastar, idol, celebrity, favourite, darling; informal celeb. **2** *the film's heroine:* main character, female protagonist, lead, leading lady, prima donna, diva.
OPPOSITES loser, supporting role.

**heroism** noun bravery, courage, valour, daring, fearlessness, pluck; informal guts, spunk; Brit. informal bottle; N. Amer. informal moxie.
OPPOSITES cowardice.

**hesitant** adjective **1** *she is hesitant about buying:* uncertain, undecided, unsure, doubtful, dubious, nervous,

ambivalent, in two minds; Brit. havering, humming and hawing; informal iffy. **2** *a hesitant child:* timid, diffident, shy, bashful, insecure.
OPPOSITES certain, decisive, confident.

**hesitate** verb **1** *she hesitated, unsure of what to say:* pause, delay, wait, stall, be uncertain, be unsure, be doubtful, be indecisive, vacillate, waver; Brit. haver; informal dilly-dally. **2** *don't hesitate to ask:* be reluctant, be unwilling, be disinclined, scruple, have misgivings about, have qualms about, think twice about.
OPPOSITES plunge in.

**hidden** adjective **1** *a hidden camera:* concealed, secret, invisible, unseen, camouflaged. **2** *a hidden meaning:* obscure, unclear, concealed, cryptic, mysterious, secret, covert, abstruse, deep.
OPPOSITES visible, obvious.

**hide** verb **1** *he hid the money:* conceal, secrete, put out of sight, cache; informal stash. **2** *they hid in an air vent:* conceal oneself, secrete oneself, take cover, lie low, go to ground; informal hole up. **3** *clouds hid the moon:* obscure, block out, blot out, obstruct, cloud, shroud, veil, eclipse. **4** *he could not hide his dislike:* conceal, keep secret, cover up, keep quiet about, bottle up, suppress, disguise, mask; informal keep a/the lid on.
OPPOSITES flaunt, reveal, emerge, betray.

**hideaway** noun retreat, refuge, hiding place, hideout, safe house, den, bolt-hole; informal hidey-hole.

**hideous** adjective **1** *a hideous face:* ugly, repulsive, repellent,

unsightly, revolting, grotesque.
**2** *hideous cases of torture:*
horrific, terrible, appalling,
awful, dreadful, frightful,
horrible, horrendous,
horrifying, shocking, sickening,
gruesome, ghastly.
OPPOSITES beautiful, pleasant.

**hiding** noun (informal) beating,
thrashing, whipping, drubbing;
informal licking, belting, pasting,
walloping.

**hierarchy** noun ranking, order,
pecking order, grading, ladder,
scale.

**high** adjective **1** *a high mountain:*
tall, lofty, towering, giant, big,
multi-storey, high-rise,
elevated. **2** *a high position in
the government:* high-ranking,
leading, top, prominent, senior,
influential, powerful,
important, exalted; N. Amer.
ranking. **3** *high prices:* inflated,
excessive, unreasonable,
expensive, exorbitant,
extortionate, informal steep, stiff.
**4** *a high voice:* high-pitched,
shrill, piercing, squeaky,
penetrating, soprano, treble,
falsetto. **5** (informal) *high on
drugs:* intoxicated, befuddled,
delirious, hallucinating; informal
high as a kite, stoned, wrecked,
off one's head.
OPPOSITES low, short, lowly,
deep.
adverb *a jet flew high overhead:*
at a great height, high up, way
up, at altitude, in the sky, aloft,
overhead, to a great height.
OPPOSITES low.

**highlight** noun *the highlight of
his career:* high point, climax,
peak, pinnacle, height, zenith,
summit, focus, feature.
OPPOSITES low point.
verb *he has highlighted
shortcomings in the plan:*

spotlight, call attention to,
focus on, underline, show up,
bring out, accentuate, accent,
stress, emphasize.
OPPOSITES play down.

**highly** adverb very, extremely,
immensely, thoroughly,
decidedly, exceptionally,
extraordinarily; N. English right;
informal awfully, terribly,
seriously; Brit. informal dead, jolly;
N. Amer. informal real, mighty,
awful.
OPPOSITES slightly.

**hijack** verb commandeer, seize,
take over, appropriate,
expropriate.

**hike** noun **1** *a hike across
country:* walk, trek, tramp,
trudge, slog, march, ramble. **2** *a
price hike:* increase, advance,
boom.
OPPOSITES reduction.
verb **1** *they hiked across Europe:*
walk, trek, tramp, trudge, slog,
march, ramble, backpack. **2** *they
hiked the price:* increase, raise,
up, put up, push up; informal jack
up, bump up.
OPPOSITES reduce.

**hilarious** adjective very funny,
hysterical, uproarious, rib-
tickling; informal side-splitting,
priceless, a scream, a hoot.
OPPOSITES unfunny, serious.

**hill** noun high ground, hillock,
hillside, rise, mound, knoll,
hummock, fell, mountain;
Scottish brae.

**hinder** verb hamper, impede,
inhibit, thwart, foil, delay,
interfere with, slow down, hold
back, hold up, restrict,
handicap, hamstring.
OPPOSITES ease.

**hint** noun **1** *a hint that he would
leave:* clue, inkling, suggestion,
indication, sign, signal,
intimation. **2** *handy hints about*

a
b
c
d
e
f
g
**h**
i
j
k
l
m
n
o
p
q
r
s
t
u
v
w
x
y
z

a
b
c
d
e
f
g
**h**
i
j
k
l
m
n
o
p
q
r
s
t
u
v
w
x
y
z

*painting:* **tip**, suggestion, pointer, guideline, recommendation. **3** *a hint of garlic:* **trace**, touch, suspicion, suggestion, dash, soupçon; informal **smidgen**, tad.
**verb** *what are you hinting?* **imply**, insinuate, intimate, suggest, refer to, drive at, mean; informal **get at**.

**hire verb 1** *we hired a car:* **rent**, lease, charter. **2** *they hire workers locally:* **employ**, engage, recruit, appoint, take on, sign up.
OPPOSITES dismiss.

**hiss verb 1** *the escaping gas hissed:* **fizz**, whistle, wheeze. **2** *the audience hissed:* **jeer**, catcall, whistle, hoot.
OPPOSITES cheer.
**noun 1** *the hiss of steam:* **fizz**, whistle, wheeze. **2** *the speaker received hisses:* **jeer**, catcall, whistle, abuse, derision.
OPPOSITES cheer.

**historic adjective** **significant**, notable, important, momentous, memorable, groundbreaking; informal **earth-shattering**.
OPPOSITES insignificant.

**historical adjective 1** *historical evidence:* **documented**, recorded, chronicled, authentic, factual, actual. **2** *historical figures:* **past**, bygone, ancient, old, former.
OPPOSITES anecdotal, contemporary.

**history noun 1** *my interest in history:* **the past**, former times, the olden days, yesterday, antiquity. **2** *a history of the Civil War:* **chronicle**, archive, record, report, narrative, account, study. **3** *she gave details of her history:* **background**, past, life story,

experiences, record.

**hit verb 1** **strike**, beat, punch, thump, thrash; informal **whack**, wallop, bash, clout, belt; Brit. informal **stick one on**; N. Amer. informal **slug**; Austral./NZ informal **dong**, quilt. **2** *a car hit the barrier:* **crash into**, run into, smash into, knock into, bump into, plough into, collide with, meet head-on. **3** *the tragedy hit her hard:* **devastate**, affect badly, upset, shatter, crush, traumatize; informal **knock sideways**; Brit. informal **knock for six**.
**noun 1** **blow**, thump, punch, knock, bang; informal **whack**, wallop, bash, clout, belt; N. Amer. informal **slug**; Austral./NZ **king-hit**. **2** *he directed many big hits:* **success**, sell-out, winner, triumph, sensation, best-seller; informal **smash hit**, chart-topper, crowd-puller.
OPPOSITES failure.
■ **hit back** retaliate, respond, reply, react, counter. ■ **hit it off** (informal) get on (well), get along, be compatible, be on the same wavelength, see eye to eye, take to each other; informal **click**.
■ **hit on/upon** discover, come up with, think of, conceive of, dream up, invent, devise.

**hitch verb 1** *she hitched the blanket around her:* **pull**, lift, raise; informal **yank**. **2** *Tom hitched the pony to his cart:* **harness**, yoke, couple, fasten, connect, attach.
**noun** *it went without a hitch:* **problem**, difficulty, snag, setback, obstacle, complication; informal **glitch**, hiccup.

**hoard noun** *a secret hoard:* **cache**, stockpile, store, collection, supply, reserve; informal **stash**.

**verb** *they hoarded their rations:* stockpile, store up, put aside, put by, lay by, set aside, cache, save, squirrel away; informal salt away.
OPPOSITES squander.

**hoax** noun practical joke, prank, trick, deception, fraud; informal con, spoof, wind-up, scam.

**hobby** noun pastime, leisure activity, sideline, diversion, relaxation, recreation, amusement.

**hoist** verb *we hoisted the mainsail:* raise, lift, haul up, heave up, winch up, pull up, elevate.
OPPOSITES lower.
**noun** *a mechanical hoist:* crane, winch, pulley, windlass.

**hold** verb **1** *she held a suitcase:* clasp, clutch, grasp, grip, clench, cling to, hold on to, embrace, hug, squeeze. **2** *he was being held by police:* detain, imprison, lock up, keep behind bars, confine, intern. **3** *the tank held 250 gallons:* take, contain, accommodate, fit, have room for. **4** *the court held that there was no evidence:* maintain, consider, take the view, believe, think, feel, deem, be of the opinion, rule, decide; informal reckon. **5** *they held a meeting:* convene, call, summon, conduct, organize, run.
OPPOSITES release.
**noun 1** *she kept a hold on my hand:* grip, grasp, clasp, clutch. **2** *Tom had a hold over his father:* influence, power, control, dominance, authority, sway. **3** *the military tightened their hold on the capital:* control, grip, power, stranglehold.

**holder** noun **1** *the licence holder:* bearer, owner, possessor,

keeper. **2** *a knife holder:* container, receptacle, case, cover, housing, sheath.

**hold-up** noun **1** *a hold-up in production:* delay, setback, hitch, snag, difficulty, problem, glitch, hiccup, traffic jam, tailback; informal snarl-up. **2** *a bank hold-up:* robbery, raid, armed robbery, mugging; informal stick-up; N. Amer. informal heist.

**hole** noun **1** *a hole in the roof:* opening, aperture, gap, space, vent, chink, breach, crack, rupture, puncture. **2** *a hole in the ground:* pit, crater, depression, hollow, cavern, cave, chamber. **3** *the badger's hole:* burrow, lair, den, earth, sett.

**holiday** noun vacation, break, rest, recess, time off, leave, day off, festival, feast day.

**hollow** adjective **1** *a hollow tube:* empty, hollowed out, void. **2** *hollow cheeks:* sunken, deep-set, concave, depressed, recessed. **3** *a hollow promise:* insincere, hypocritical, feigned.
OPPOSITES solid, chubby, convex, sincere.
**noun 1** *a hollow under the tree:* hole, pit, cavity, crater, trough, depression, indentation, dip. **2** *the village lay in a hollow:* valley, vale, dale, dell.
OPPOSITES rise.
**verb** *hollowed out of rock:* gouge, scoop, dig, cut, excavate, channel.

**holy** adjective **1** *holy men:* saintly, godly, pious, religious, devout, God-fearing, spiritual. **2** *a holy place:* sacred, consecrated, hallowed, sanctified, venerated, revered.
OPPOSITES sinful, irreligious, cursed.

**homage** noun respect, honour,

a
b
c
d
e
f
g
**h**
i
j
k
l
m
n
o
p
q
r
s
t
u
v
w
x
y
z

reverence, worship, admiration, esteem, adulation, tribute. OPPOSITES contempt.

**home** noun 1 *they fled their homes:* residence, house, accommodation, property, quarters, lodgings, address, place; informal pad; formal abode, dwelling. 2 *I am far from my home:* homeland, native land, home town, birthplace, roots, fatherland, mother country, motherland. 3 *a home for the elderly:* institution, hospice, shelter, refuge, retreat, asylum, hostel.
adjective *the UK home market:* domestic, internal, local, national.
OPPOSITES foreign, international.

**homeless** adjective of no fixed abode, without a roof over one's head, on the streets, vagrant, sleeping rough, destitute.

**homely** adjective 1 (Brit.) *a homely atmosphere:* cosy, comfortable, snug, welcoming, friendly; informal comfy. 2 (N. Amer.) *she's rather homely:* unattractive, plain, unprepossessing, ugly; Brit. informal no oil painting.
OPPOSITES uncomfortable, attractive.

**homicide** noun murder, manslaughter, killing, slaughter, butchery, assassination.

**honest** adjective 1 *an honest man:* upright, honourable, principled, virtuous, decent, law-abiding, trustworthy, scrupulous. 2 *I haven't been honest with you:* truthful, sincere, candid, frank, open, forthright, straight; informal upfront.
OPPOSITES dishonest.

**honestly** adverb 1 *he earned the money honestly:* fairly, lawfully, legally, legitimately, honourably, decently, ethically; informal on the level. 2 *we honestly believe this:* sincerely, genuinely, truthfully, truly, wholeheartedly, to be honest, to be frank, in all honesty, in all sincerity.
OPPOSITES dishonestly.

**honesty** noun 1 *I can attest to his honesty:* integrity, uprightness, honour, righteousness, virtue, goodness, probity, trustworthiness. 2 *they spoke with honesty about their fears:* sincerity, candour, frankness, directness, truthfulness, truth, openness, straightforwardness.
OPPOSITES dishonesty, insincerity.

**honorary** adjective 1 *an honorary doctorate:* titular, nominal, in name only, unofficial, token. 2 (Brit.) *an honorary treasurer:* unpaid, unsalaried, voluntary, volunteer.
OPPOSITES paid.

**honour** noun 1 *a man of honour:* integrity, honesty, uprightness, morality, principles, high-mindedness, decency, probity, scrupulousness, fairness, justness. 2 *a mark of honour:* distinction, privilege, glory, kudos, cachet, prestige. 3 *our honour is at stake:* reputation, good name, character, repute, image, standing, status. 4 *the honour of meeting the Queen:* privilege, pleasure, compliment.
OPPOSITES unscrupulousness, shame.
verb 1 *we should honour our parents:* respect, esteem, admire, look up to, value,

cherish, revere, venerate. **2** *they were honoured at a special ceremony:* applaud, acclaim, praise, salute, recognize, celebrate, pay tribute to. **3** *he honoured the contract:* fulfil, observe, keep, obey, heed, follow, carry out, keep to, abide by, adhere to, comply with, conform to, be true to.
OPPOSITES scorn, disgrace, disobey, break.

**honourable** adjective **1** *an honourable man:* honest, moral, principled, righteous, decent, respectable, virtuous, good, upstanding, upright, noble, fair, trustworthy, law-abiding. **2** *an honourable career:* illustrious, distinguished, eminent, great, glorious, prestigious.
OPPOSITES crooked, deplorable.

**hook** noun **1** *she hung her jacket on the hook:* peg, nail. **2** *the dress has six hooks:* fastener, clasp, hasp, clip.
verb **1** *they hooked baskets onto the ladder:* attach, hitch, fasten, fix, secure, hang, clasp. **2** *he hooked a large pike:* catch, land, net, take, bag.

**hooked** adjective **1** *a hooked nose:* curved, hook-shaped, aquiline, angular, bent.
**2** (informal) *hooked on cocaine:* addicted to, dependent on.
**3** (informal) *he is hooked on crosswords:* keen on, enthusiastic about, addicted to, obsessed with, fanatical about; informal mad about.
OPPOSITES straight.

**hooligan** noun lout, thug, tearaway, vandal, ruffian, troublemaker; Austral. larrikin; informal tough, bruiser; Brit. informal yob, yobbo, lager lout; Scottish informal ned.

**hoop** noun ring, band, circle, wheel, circlet, loop.

**hop** verb & noun jump, bound, spring, bounce, skip, leap, prance, caper.

**hope** noun **1** *I had high hopes:* aspiration, desire, wish, expectation, ambition, aim, plan, dream. **2** *a life filled with hope:* optimism, expectation, confidence, faith, belief.
OPPOSITES pessimism.
verb **1** *he's hoping for a medal:* expect, anticipate, look for, be hopeful of, dream of. **2** *we're hoping to address this issue:* aim, intend, be looking, have the intention, have in mind, plan.

**hopeful** adjective **1** *he remained hopeful:* optimistic, full of hope, confident, positive, buoyant, bullish. **2** *hopeful signs:* promising, encouraging, heartening, reassuring, favourable, optimistic.
OPPOSITES pessimistic, discouraging.

**hopefully** adverb **1** *he rode on hopefully:* optimistically, full of hope, confidently, buoyantly, expectantly. **2** *hopefully it should finish soon:* all being well, if all goes well, God willing, with luck, touch wood, fingers crossed.

**hopeless** adjective **1** *a hopeless case:* forlorn, beyond hope, lost, irreparable, irreversible, incurable, impossible, futile.
**2** *hopeless at maths:* bad, poor, awful, terrible, dreadful, appalling, atrocious, incompetent; informal pathetic, useless, lousy, rotten; Brit. informal rubbish.
OPPOSITES competent.

**hopelessly** adverb utterly, completely, irretrievably, impossibly, extremely, totally.

a
b
c
d
e
f
g
**h**
i
j
k
l
m
n
o
p
q
r
s
t
u
v
w
x
y
z

**horde** noun crowd, mob, pack, gang, troop, army, swarm, mass, throng.

**horizontal** adjective level, flat, parallel.
OPPOSITES vertical.

**horrible** adjective 1 *a horrible murder:* dreadful, awful, terrible, shocking, appalling, horrifying, horrific, horrendous, grisly, ghastly, gruesome, harrowing, unspeakable. 2 (informal) *a horrible little man:* nasty, horrid, disagreeable, obnoxious, hateful, odious, objectionable, insufferable.
OPPOSITES pleasant, agreeable.

**horrific** adjective dreadful, horrendous, horrible, terrible, atrocious, horrifying, shocking, appalling, harrowing, hideous, grisly, ghastly, sickening.

**horrify** verb shock, appal, outrage, scandalize, offend, disgust, revolt, nauseate, sicken.

**horror** noun 1 *children screamed in horror:* terror, fear, fright, alarm, panic. 2 *to her horror she found herself alone:* dismay, consternation, alarm, distress, disgust, shock.
OPPOSITES delight, satisfaction.

**horse** noun mount, charger, cob, nag, hack, colt, stallion, mare, filly; N. Amer. bronco; Austral./NZ moke, yarraman; informal gee-gee.

**hospitable** adjective welcoming, friendly, sociable, cordial, gracious, accommodating, warm.
OPPOSITES inhospitable.

**hospitality** noun friendliness, neighbourliness, sociability, welcome, warmth, kindness, cordiality, generosity.

**host** noun *the host of a TV series:* presenter, compère, anchor, anchorman, anchorwoman, announcer.
OPPOSITES guest.
verb *the show is hosted by Angus:* present, introduce, compère, front, anchor.

**hostage** noun captive, prisoner, detainee, internee.

**hostile** adjective 1 *a hostile attitude:* unfriendly, unkind, unsympathetic, antagonistic, aggressive, confrontational, belligerent. 2 *hostile conditions:* unfavourable, adverse, bad, harsh, grim, inhospitable, forbidding. 3 *they are hostile to the idea:* opposed, averse, antagonistic, ill-disposed, unsympathetic, antipathetic, against; informal anti.
OPPOSITES friendly, favourable, in favour.

**hostility** noun 1 *he glared at her with hostility:* antagonism, unfriendliness, malevolence, venom, hatred, aggression, belligerence. 2 *their hostility to the present regime:* opposition, antagonism, animosity, antipathy. 3 *a cessation of hostilities:* fighting, armed conflict, combat, warfare, war, bloodshed, violence.

**hot** adjective 1 *hot food:* heated, piping, sizzling, roasting, boiling, scorching, scalding, red-hot. 2 *a hot day:* very warm, balmy, summery, tropical, scorching, searing, blistering, sweltering; informal boiling, baking, roasting. 3 *a hot chilli:* spicy, peppery, fiery, strong, piquant, powerful. 4 *the competition was hot:* fierce, intense, keen, competitive, cut-throat, ruthless, aggressive, strong. 5 (informal) *she is hot on local history:* knowledgeable

**about**, well informed about, au fait with, up on, well versed in; informal clued up about.
OPPOSITES cold, mild, weak.

**hotel** noun inn, motel, boarding house, guest house, bed and breakfast, B & B, hostel.

**hotly** adverb vehemently, vigorously, strenuously, fiercely, heatedly.
OPPOSITES calmly.

**hound** verb pursue, chase, stalk, harry, harass, pester, badger, torment.

**house** noun 1 residence, home; formal dwelling. 2 *the house of Stewart:* family, clan, tribe, dynasty, line, bloodline, lineage. 3 *a printing house:* firm, business, company, corporation, enterprise, establishment, institution, concern, organization, operation; informal outfit. 4 *the country's upper house:* assembly, legislative body, chamber, council, parliament, congress, senate.
verb 1 *we can house twelve adults:* accommodate, give someone a roof over their head, lodge, quarter, board, billet, take in, sleep, put up. 2 *this panel houses the main switch:* contain, hold, store, cover, protect, enclose.

**household** noun *the household was asleep:* family, house, occupants, clan, tribe; informal brood.
adjective *household goods:* domestic, family, everyday, workaday.

**housing** noun 1 *a housing development:* houses, homes, residences, accommodation, living quarters; formal dwellings. 2 *the housing for the equipment:* casing, covering, case, cover, holder, fairing, sleeve.

**hovel** noun shack, slum, shanty, hut; informal dump, hole.

**hover** verb 1 *helicopters hovered overhead:* hang, be poised, be suspended, float, fly, drift. 2 *a servant hovered nearby:* wait, linger, loiter.

**however** adverb nevertheless, nonetheless, even so, but, for all that, despite that, in spite of that.

**howl** noun 1 *the howl of a wolf:* baying, cry, bark, yelp. 2 *a howl of anguish:* wail, cry, yell, yelp, bellow, roar, shout, shriek, scream, screech.
verb 1 *dogs howled in the distance:* bay, cry, bark, yelp. 2 *a baby started to howl:* wail, cry, yell, bawl, bellow, shriek, scream, screech, caterwaul; informal holler.

**hub** noun centre, core, heart, focus, focal point, nucleus, kernel, nerve centre.
OPPOSITES periphery.

**huddle** verb 1 *they huddled together:* crowd, cluster, gather, bunch, throng, flock, collect, group, congregate. 2 *he huddled beneath the sheets:* curl up, snuggle, nestle, hunch up.
OPPOSITES disperse.
noun *a huddle of passengers:* group, cluster, bunch, collection; informal gaggle.

**hue** noun colour, shade, tone, tint, tinge.

**hug** verb *they hugged each other:* embrace, cuddle, squeeze, clasp, clutch, hold tight.
noun *there were hugs as we left:* embrace, cuddle, squeeze, bear hug.

**huge** adjective enormous, vast, immense, massive, colossal, prodigious, gigantic,

a b c d e f g h i j k l m n o p q r s t u v w x y z

gargantuan, mammoth, monumental, giant, towering, mountainous; informal mega, monster, astronomical; Brit. informal ginormous.
OPPOSITES tiny.

**hugely** adverb extremely, very, tremendously, exceptionally, immensely, extraordinarily, vastly; informal terrifically, awfully, terribly, seriously; Brit. informal dead, jolly; N. Amer. informal real, mighty, awful.

**hull** noun *the ship's hull:* framework, body, shell, frame, skeleton, structure.

**hum** verb 1 *the engine was humming:* purr, drone, murmur, buzz, whirr, throb. 2 *the workshops are humming:* be busy, be active, be lively, buzz, bustle, be a hive of activity, throb.
noun *a low hum of conversation:* murmur, drone, purr, buzz.

**human** adjective 1 *they're only human:* mortal, flesh and blood, fallible, weak, frail, imperfect, vulnerable, physical, bodily, fleshly. 2 *his human side:* compassionate, humane, kind, considerate, understanding, sympathetic.
OPPOSITES infallible, inhuman.
noun *the link between humans and animals:* person, human being, Homo sapiens, man, woman, individual, mortal, (living) soul, earthling; (humans) the human race, humanity, humankind, mankind, man, people.

**humane** adjective compassionate, kind, considerate, understanding, sympathetic, tolerant, forbearing, forgiving, merciful, humanitarian, charitable.
OPPOSITES cruel.

**humanitarian** adjective 1 *a humanitarian act:* compassionate, humane, unselfish, altruistic, generous. 2 *a humanitarian organization:* charitable, philanthropic, public-spirited, socially concerned, welfare, aid.
OPPOSITES selfish, commercial.
noun philanthropist, altruist, benefactor, social reformer, good Samaritan, do-gooder.

**humanity** noun 1 *humanity evolved from the apes:* humankind, mankind, man, people, the human race, Homo sapiens. 2 *he praised them for their humanity:* compassion, brotherly love, fellow feeling, humaneness, kindness, consideration, understanding, sympathy, tolerance.

**humble** adjective 1 *she was very humble:* meek, deferential, respectful, submissive, self-effacing, unassertive, modest, unassuming, self-deprecating; Scottish mim. 2 *a humble background:* lowly, poor, undistinguished, mean, common, ordinary, simple. 3 *my humble abode:* modest, plain, simple, ordinary, little.
OPPOSITES proud, illustrious, grand.
verb *it humbled him to ask for help:* humiliate, demean, lower, degrade, debase, mortify, shame.

**humid** adjective muggy, close, sultry, sticky, steamy, clammy, heavy.
OPPOSITES dry, fresh.

**humiliate** verb embarrass, mortify, humble, shame, disgrace, chasten, deflate, crush, squash, demean, take down a peg or two; informal show

up, put down, cut down to size;
N. Amer. informal make someone
eat crow.
OPPOSITES dignify.

**humiliating** adjective
embarrassing, mortifying,
humbling, ignominious,
inglorious, shaming,
undignified, chastening,
demeaning, degrading,
deflating.

**humiliation** noun
embarrassment, mortification,
shame, indignity, ignominy,
disgrace, dishonour,
degradation, discredit, loss of
face, blow to one's pride.
OPPOSITES honour.

**humility** noun modesty,
humbleness, meekness, respect,
deference, diffidence,
unassertiveness.
OPPOSITES pride.

**humorous** adjective amusing,
funny, comic, comical,
entertaining, diverting, witty,
jocular, light-hearted, hilarious,
uproarious, riotous, farcical.
OPPOSITES serious.

**humour** noun 1 *the humour of
the situation:* comedy, funny
side, hilarity, absurdity,
ludicrousness, satire, irony.
2 *the stories are spiced up with
humour:* jokes, jests, quips,
witticisms, funny remarks, wit,
comedy; informal gags,
wisecracks. 3 *his good humour
was infectious:* mood, temper,
disposition, spirits.
OPPOSITES seriousness.
verb *she was always humouring
him:* indulge, accommodate,
pander to, cater to, give in to,
go along with, flatter, mollify,
placate.
OPPOSITES stand up to.

**hunch** noun feeling, guess,

suspicion, impression, inkling,
idea, notion, fancy, intuition;
informal gut feeling.

**hunger** noun 1 *she was faint
with hunger:* lack of food,
starvation, malnutrition,
undernourishment. 2 *a hunger
for news:* desire, craving,
longing, yearning, hankering,
appetite, thirst; informal itch.
■ hunger after/for desire, crave,
long for, yearn for, pine for,
ache for, hanker after, thirst
for, lust for; informal itch for, be
dying for, be gagging for.

**hungry** adjective 1 *I was really
hungry:* ravenous, starving,
starved, famished,
malnourished, undernourished,
underfed; informal peckish. 2 *they
are hungry for success:* eager,
keen, avid, longing, yearning,
aching, greedy, craving,
desirous of, hankering after;
informal itching, dying, gagging.
OPPOSITES full.

**hunk** noun chunk, wedge, block,
slab, lump, square, gobbet; Brit.
informal wodge.

**hunt** verb 1 *they hunted deer:*
chase, stalk, pursue, course,
track, trail. 2 *police are hunting
for her:* search, seek, look high
and low, scour the area.
noun 1 *the thrill of the hunt:*
chase, pursuit. 2 *a police hunt:*
search, quest.

**hurdle** noun obstacle, difficulty,
problem, barrier, bar, snag,
stumbling block, impediment,
obstruction, complication,
hindrance.

**hurl** verb throw, toss, fling,
launch, pitch, cast, lob; informal
chuck, bung.

**hurricane** noun cyclone,
typhoon, tornado, storm,
windstorm, whirlwind, gale,

tempest; Austral. willy-willy; N. Amer. informal twister.

**hurried** adjective 1 *hurried glances*: quick, fast, swift, rapid, speedy, brisk, cursory, perfunctory, brief, short, fleeting. 2 *a hurried decision*: hasty, rushed, precipitate, spur-of-the-moment.
OPPOSITES slow, considered.

**hurry** verb 1 *hurry or you'll be late*: be quick, hurry up, hasten, speed up, run, dash, rush, race, scurry, scramble, scuttle, sprint; informal get a move on; Brit. informal get one's skates on; N. Amer. informal get a wiggle on. 2 *she hurried him out*: hustle, hasten, push, urge, usher.
OPPOSITES dawdle, delay.
noun *in all the hurry, we forgot*: rush, haste, speed, urgency, hustle and bustle.
OPPOSITES ease.

**hurt** verb 1 *my back hurts*: be painful, ache, be sore, be tender, smart, sting, burn, throb; informal be agony. 2 *Dad hurt his leg*: injure, wound, damage, disable, bruise, cut, gash, graze, scrape, scratch. 3 *his words hurt her*: distress, pain, wound, sting, upset, sadden, devastate, grieve, mortify.
OPPOSITES comfort.
noun *all the hurt he had caused*: distress, pain, suffering, grief, misery, anguish, upset, sadness, sorrow.
OPPOSITES joy.
adjective 1 *my hurt hand*: injured, wounded, bruised, grazed, cut, gashed, sore, painful, aching. 2 *Anne's hurt expression*: pained, aggrieved, offended, distressed, upset, sad, mortified; informal miffed.
OPPOSITES unhurt, pleased.

**hurtful** adjective upsetting, distressing, wounding, unkind, cruel, nasty, mean, malicious, spiteful.

**hush** verb *he tried to hush her*: silence, quieten (down), shush, gag, muzzle; informal shut up.
noun *a hush descended*: silence, quiet, stillness, peace, calm, tranquillity.
OPPOSITES noise.
■ hush something up keep secret, conceal, hide, suppress, cover up, keep quiet about, sweep under the carpet.

**hut** noun shack, shanty, cabin, shelter, shed, lean-to, hovel; Scottish bothy; N. Amer. cabana.

**hybrid** noun *a hybrid of a goose and a swan*: cross, cross-breed, mixture, blend, combination, composite, fusion, amalgam.
adjective *hybrid roses*: composite, cross-bred, interbred, mixed, blended, compound.

**hygiene** noun cleanliness, sanitation, sterility, purity, disinfection.

**hygienic** adjective sanitary, clean, germ-free, disinfected, sterilized, sterile, antiseptic, aseptic.
OPPOSITES insanitary.

**hypocritical** adjective sanctimonious, pious, self-righteous, holier-than-thou, superior, insincere, two-faced.

**hysteria** noun frenzy, feverishness, hysterics, agitation, mania, panic, alarm, distress.
OPPOSITES calm.

**hysterical** adjective 1 *Janet became hysterical*: overwrought, overemotional, out of control, frenzied, frantic, wild, beside oneself, manic,

delirious; informal in a state.
2 *the film was hysterical:*
(informal) **very funny,** hilarious,
uproarious, rib-tickling; informal

side-splitting, priceless, a
scream, a hoot.
opposites calm, unfunny,
serious.

# Ii

**icy** adjective 1 *icy roads:* iced
(over), frozen, frosty, slippery,
treacherous; literary rimy. 2 *an
icy wind:* freezing, chill, biting,
bitter, raw, arctic. 3 *an icy
voice:* unfriendly, hostile,
forbidding, cold, chilly, frosty,
stern.

**idea** noun 1 *the idea of death:*
concept, notion, conception,
thought. 2 *our idea is to open a
new shop:* plan, scheme, design,
proposal, proposition,
suggestion, aim, intention,
objective, goal. 3 *Liz had
various ideas on the subject:*
thought, theory, view, opinion,
feeling, belief. 4 *I had an idea
this might happen:* sense,
feeling, suspicion, fancy,
inkling, hunch, notion. 5 *an
idea of the cost:* estimate,
approximation, guess,
conjecture; informal guesstimate.

**ideal** adjective *ideal flying
weather:* perfect, faultless,
exemplary, classic, model,
ultimate, theoretical, utopian.
opposites bad, real.
noun 1 *an ideal to aim at:*
model, pattern, exemplar,
example, perfection, epitome,
last word. 2 *liberal ideals:*
principle, standard, value,
belief, conviction.

**identical** adjective (exactly) the
same, indistinguishable, twin,
duplicate, interchangeable,
alike, matching.

opposites different.

**identification** noun 1 *the
identification of the suspect:*
recognition, singling out,
pinpointing, naming. 2 *early
identification of problems:*
determination, establishment,
ascertainment, discovery,
diagnosis. 3 *may I see your
identification?* ID, papers,
documents, credentials, card,
pass, badge.

**identify** verb 1 *Gail identified
her attacker:* recognize, pick
out, spot, point out, pinpoint,
put one's finger on, name. 2 *I
identified four problem areas:*
determine, establish, ascertain,
make out, discern, distinguish.
3 *we identify sport with
glamour:* associate, link,
connect, relate. 4 *Peter
identifies with the team
captain:* empathize,
sympathize, understand, relate
to, feel for.

**identity** noun individuality,
self, personality, character,
originality, distinctiveness,
uniqueness.

**idiot** noun fool, ass, halfwit,
blockhead, dunce, simpleton;
informal nincompoop, clod,
dimwit, dummy, fathead,
numbskull; Brit. informal nitwit,
twit, clot, berk, prat, pillock,
wally, dork, twerp, charlie;
Scottish informal nyaff, balloon; N.
Amer. informal schmuck, turkey;

a
b
c
d
e
f
g
h
**i**
j
k
l
m
n
o
p
q
r
s
t
u
v
w
x
y
z

Austral./NZ informal drongo, nong, galah, boofhead.
OPPOSITES genius.

**idle** adjective 1 *an idle fellow:* lazy, indolent, slothful, work-shy. 2 *I was bored with being idle:* unemployed, jobless, out of work, redundant, unoccupied; Brit. informal on the dole. 3 *their idle hours:* unoccupied, spare, empty, unfilled. 4 *idle remarks:* frivolous, trivial, trifling, minor, insignificant, unimportant, empty, meaningless, vain.
OPPOSITES industrious, employed, busy, serious.

**idol** noun 1 *an idol in a shrine:* icon, effigy, statue, figurine, totem. 2 *the pop world's latest idol:* hero, heroine, star, superstar, icon, celebrity, darling; informal pin-up, heart throb.

**if** conjunction 1 *if the weather is fine, we can walk:* provided, providing, on condition that, presuming, supposing, assuming, as long as, in the event that. 2 *if I go out she gets nasty:* whenever, every time. 3 *I wonder if he noticed:* whether, whether or not.
OPPOSITES unless.

**ignite** verb 1 *moments before the petrol ignited:* catch fire, burst into flames, explode. 2 *a cigarette ignited the fumes:* light, set fire to, set alight, kindle.
OPPOSITES go out, extinguish.

**ignorance** noun 1 *their attitudes are based on ignorance:* lack of knowledge, lack of education, unenlightenment. 2 *his ignorance of economics:* unfamiliarity with,

incomprehension, inexperience, innocence.
OPPOSITES education, knowledge.

**ignorant** adjective 1 *an ignorant country girl:* uneducated, unschooled, illiterate, uninformed, unenlightened, inexperienced, unsophisticated. 2 *ignorant of working-class life:* unaware, unconscious, unfamiliar, unacquainted, uninformed.
OPPOSITES educated, knowledgeable.

**ignore** verb 1 *he ignored her:* take no notice of, pay no attention to, snub, look right through, cold-shoulder. 2 *doctors ignored her instructions:* disregard, take no account of, fail to observe, disobey, defy, overlook, brush aside.
OPPOSITES acknowledge, obey.

**ill** adjective 1 *she was feeling rather ill:* unwell, sick, poorly; informal under the weather, rough; Brit. informal grotty; Austral./NZ informal crook. 2 *the ill effects of smoking:* harmful, damaging, detrimental, deleterious, adverse, injurious, destructive, dangerous.
OPPOSITES well, beneficial.
noun *the ills of society:* problem, trouble, difficulty, misfortune, trial, tribulation; informal headache, hassle.
adverb 1 *he can ill afford the loss:* barely, scarcely, hardly, only just. 2 *we are ill prepared:* inadequately, insufficiently, poorly, badly.
OPPOSITES easily, well.

**illegal** adjective unlawful, illicit, illegitimate, criminal, fraudulent, corrupt, dishonest, outlawed, banned, forbidden,

prohibited, proscribed, unlicensed, unauthorized; informal crooked, shady; Brit. informal bent, dodgy.
OPPOSITES legal.

**illegible** adjective unreadable, indecipherable, unintelligible.

**illicit** adjective illegal, unlawful, criminal, outlawed, banned, forbidden, prohibited, proscribed, unlicensed, unauthorized, improper, disapproved of.
OPPOSITES legal, approved.

**illness** noun sickness, poor health, disease, ailment, disorder, complaint, malady, affliction, infection; informal bug, virus.
OPPOSITES health.

**illuminating** adjective informative, enlightening, revealing, explanatory, instructive, helpful, educational.
OPPOSITES confusing.

**illumination** noun light, lighting, radiance, gleam, glow, glare.

**illusion** noun 1 *I had no illusions*: delusion, misapprehension, misconception, false impression, mistaken impression, fantasy, dream, fancy. 2 *the illusion of depth*: appearance, impression, semblance. 3 *it's just an illusion*: mirage, hallucination, apparition, figment of the imagination, trick of the light.

**illustrate** verb 1 *the photographs that illustrate the text*: decorate, ornament, accompany, support, explain, elucidate, clarify; informal get across/over. 2 *this can be illustrated through a brief example*: demonstrate, show,

exemplify, bring home.

**illustration** noun 1 *the illustrations in children's books*: picture, drawing, sketch, figure, plate, image, print. 2 *an illustration of such a dilemma*: example, sample, case, instance, exemplification, demonstration.

**image** noun 1 *images of the Queen*: likeness, depiction, portrayal, representation, painting, picture, portrait, drawing, photograph. 2 *the image of this country as a democracy*: conception, impression, idea, perception, notion. 3 *his public image*: persona, profile, face.

**imaginary** adjective unreal, non-existent, fictional, pretend, make-believe, invented, made-up, illusory.
OPPOSITES real.

**imagination** noun 1 *in your imagination*: mind's eye, fancy. 2 *she lacked imagination*: creativity, vision, inventiveness, resourcefulness, ingenuity, originality.

**imaginative** adjective creative, visionary, inventive, resourceful, ingenious, original, innovative.

**imagine** verb 1 *you can imagine the scene*: visualize, envisage, picture, see in the mind's eye, dream up, think up/of, conceive. 2 *I imagine he was at home*: assume, presume, expect, take it (as read), suppose.

**imitate** verb 1 *other artists have imitated his style*: copy, emulate, follow, echo, ape, parrot; informal rip off. 2 *he could imitate Winston Churchill*: mimic, do an impression of, impersonate; informal take someone off.

a
b
c
d
e
f
g
h
i
j
k
l
m
n
o
p
q
r
s
t
u
v
w
x
y
z

**imitation** noun 1 *an imitation of a sailor's hat:* copy, simulation, reproduction, replica, forgery. 2 *learning by imitation:* emulation, copying. 3 *a perfect imitation of Francis:* impersonation, impression, caricature; informal take-off, spoof.
▸ adjective *imitation ivory:* artificial, synthetic, mock, fake, simulated, man-made, manufactured, ersatz, substitute.
OPPOSITES real.

**immaculate** adjective 1 *an immaculate white shirt:* clean, spotless, shining, shiny, gleaming. 2 *immaculate condition:* perfect, pristine, mint, flawless, faultless, unblemished; informal tip-top, A1. 3 *his immaculate record:* unblemished, spotless, impeccable, unsullied, untarnished; informal squeaky clean.
OPPOSITES dirty, damaged, sullied.

**immediate** adjective 1 *the UN called for immediate action:* instant, instantaneous, prompt, swift, speedy, rapid, quick. 2 *their immediate concerns:* current, present, urgent, pressing. 3 *our immediate neighbours:* nearest, close, next-door, adjacent, adjoining.
OPPOSITES delayed.

**immediately** adverb 1 *you must decide immediately:* straight away, at once, right away, instantly, now, directly, forthwith, there and then. 2 *I sat immediately behind him:* directly, right, exactly, precisely, squarely, just, dead; informal slap bang; N. Amer. informal smack dab.

OPPOSITES sometime, later, somewhere.

**immense** adjective huge, vast, massive, enormous, gigantic, colossal, monumental, towering, giant, mammoth; informal monster, whopping (great); Brit. informal ginormous.
OPPOSITES tiny.

**immerse** verb 1 *the metal was immersed in acid:* dip, submerge, dunk, duck, sink. 2 *Elliot was immersed in his work:* absorb, engross, occupy, engage, involve, bury, preoccupy; informal lose.

**immigrant** noun newcomer, settler, incomer, migrant, non-native, foreigner, alien.
OPPOSITES native.

**imminent** adjective near, close (at hand), impending, approaching, coming, forthcoming, on the way, expected, looming.
OPPOSITES distant.

**immoral** adjective wicked, bad, wrong, unethical, unprincipled, unscrupulous, dishonest, corrupt, sinful, impure.
OPPOSITES ethical, pure.

**immortal** adjective 1 *our immortal souls:* undying, deathless, eternal, everlasting, imperishable, indestructible. 2 *an immortal children's story:* timeless, perennial, classic, time-honoured, enduring, evergreen.
OPPOSITES mortal, ephemeral.

**immune** adjective resistant, not subject, not liable, not vulnerable, protected from, safe from, secure against.
OPPOSITES susceptible, liable.

**immunity** noun 1 *immunity to malaria:* resistance, protection, defence. 2 *immunity from prosecution:* exemption,

exception, freedom.
**3** *diplomatic immunity:* indemnity, privilege, prerogative, licence, exemption, impunity, protection.
OPPOSITES susceptibility, liability.

**impact** noun **1** *the force of the impact:* collision, crash, smash, bump, knock. **2** *the job losses will have a major impact:* effect, influence, consequences, repercussions, ramifications.
verb **1** *an asteroid impacted the earth:* crash into, smash into, collide with, hit, strike, smack into, bang into. **2** *interest rates have impacted on spending:* affect, influence, hit, have an effect, make an impression.

**impair** verb weaken, damage, harm, have a negative effect on, undermine, diminish, reduce, lessen, decrease.
OPPOSITES improve, enhance.

**impart** verb communicate, pass on, convey, transmit, relay, relate, tell, make known, report, announce.

**impartial** adjective unbiased, unprejudiced, neutral, non-partisan, disinterested, detached, dispassionate, objective.
OPPOSITES biased, partisan.

**impasse** noun deadlock, dead end, stalemate, stand-off, standstill.

**impatient** adjective **1** *Melissa grew impatient:* restless, agitated, nervous, anxious. **2** *they are impatient to get back home:* anxious, eager, keen; informal itching, dying. **3** *an impatient gesture:* irritated, annoyed, angry, tetchy, snappy, cross, curt, brusque.
OPPOSITES patient, reluctant, calm.

**impeccable** adjective flawless, faultless, unblemished, spotless, stainless, perfect, exemplary, irreproachable; informal squeaky clean.
OPPOSITES imperfect.

**impede** verb hinder, obstruct, hamper, hold back/up, delay, interfere with, disrupt, retard, slow (down).
OPPOSITES facilitate.

**imperative** adjective vital, crucial, critical, essential, pressing, urgent.
OPPOSITES unimportant.

**imperfect** adjective faulty, flawed, defective, inferior, second-rate, substandard, damaged, blemished, torn, broken, cracked, scratched; Brit. informal duff.
OPPOSITES perfect.

**impertinent** adjective rude, insolent, impolite, ill-mannered, disrespectful, impudent, cheeky, presumptuous, forward.
OPPOSITES polite, respectful.

**impetuous** adjective impulsive, rash, hasty, reckless, foolhardy, imprudent, ill-considered, spontaneous, impromptu, spur-of-the-moment.
OPPOSITES considered, cautious.

**implant** verb **1** *the collagen is implanted under the skin:* insert, embed, bury, inject, transplant, graft. **2** *he implanted the idea in my mind:* instil, inculcate, introduce, plant, sow.
OPPOSITES excise, banish.

**implement** noun *garden implements:* tool, utensil, instrument, device, apparatus, gadget, contraption, appliance; informal gizmo.
verb *the cost of implementing the new law:* execute, apply,

a
b
c
d
e
f
g
h
**i**
j
k
l
m
n
o
p
q
r
s
t
u
v
w
x
y
z

a
b
c
d
e
f
g
h
**i**
j
k
l
m
n
o
p
q
r
s
t
u
v
w
x
y
z

put into effect/action, put into practice, carry out/through, perform, enact, fulfil.
OPPOSITES abolish, cancel.

**implicate** verb 1 *he had been implicated in a financial scandal:* incriminate, involve, connect, embroil, enmesh. 2 *viruses are implicated in the development of cancer:* involve in, concern with, associate with, connect with.

**implication** noun 1 *he was smarting at their implication:* suggestion, inference, insinuation, innuendo, intimation, imputation. 2 *important political implications:* consequence, result, ramification, repercussion, reverberation, effect. 3 *his implication in the murder:* incrimination, involvement, connection, entanglement, association.
OPPOSITES exoneration.

**implore** verb plead with, beg, entreat, appeal to, ask, request, call on, exhort, urge.

**imply** verb 1 *are you implying he is mad?* insinuate, suggest, infer, hint, intimate, give someone to understand, make out. 2 *the forecast traffic increase implies more roads:* involve, entail, mean, point to, signify, indicate, presuppose.

**impolite** adjective rude, bad-mannered, ill-mannered, discourteous, uncivil, disrespectful, insolent, impudent, impertinent, cheeky; informal lippy.
OPPOSITES polite.

**import** verb *the UK imports iron ore:* bring in, buy in, ship in.
OPPOSITES export.
noun 1 *a matter of great import:* importance, significance,

consequence, momentousness, magnitude, substance, weight, note, gravity, seriousness. 2 *the full import of her words:* meaning, sense, essence, gist, drift, message, thrust, substance, implication.
OPPOSITES insignificance.

**importance** noun 1 *an event of immense importance:* significance, momentousness, moment, import, consequence, note, weight, seriousness, gravity. 2 *she had an exaggerated sense of her own importance:* status, eminence, prestige, worth, influence, power, authority.
OPPOSITES insignificance.

**important** adjective 1 *an important meeting:* significant, consequential, momentous, of great import, major, valuable, necessary, crucial, vital, essential, pivotal, decisive, far-reaching, historic. 2 *he was an important man:* powerful, influential, well-connected, high-ranking, prominent, eminent, notable, distinguished, esteemed, respected, prestigious.
OPPOSITES unimportant, insignificant.

**impose** verb 1 *he imposed his ideas on everyone:* foist, force, inflict, press, saddle someone with. 2 *new taxes will be imposed:* levy, charge, apply, enforce, set, establish, institute, introduce, bring into effect.
OPPOSITES abolish.
■ **impose on** take advantage of, exploit, take liberties with, bother, trouble, disturb, inconvenience, put out, put to trouble.

**imposing** adjective impressive, striking, dramatic, spectacular,

commanding, arresting, awesome, formidable, splendid, grand, majestic.
OPPOSITES modest.

**imposition** noun **1** *the imposition of an alien culture:* imposing, foisting, forcing, inflicting. **2** *the imposition of VAT:* levying, charging, application, enforcement, enforcing, setting, establishment, introduction. **3** *it would be no imposition:* burden, encumbrance, liberty, bother, worry; informal hassle.
OPPOSITES abolition.

**impossible** adjective **1** *the winds made fishing impossible:* out of the question, impracticable, non-viable, unworkable. **2** *an impossible dream:* unattainable, unachievable, unobtainable, hopeless, impracticable, unworkable. **3** *food shortages made life impossible:* unbearable, intolerable, unendurable. **4** (informal) *an impossible woman:* unreasonable, difficult, awkward, intolerable, unbearable, exasperating, maddening, infuriating.
OPPOSITES possible, attainable, bearable, reasonable.

**impound** verb confiscate, appropriate, take possession of, seize, commandeer, expropriate, requisition, take over.
OPPOSITES release.

**impress** verb *Hazel had impressed him mightily:* make an impression on, have an impact on, influence, affect, move, stir, rouse, excite, inspire, dazzle, awe.
OPPOSITES disappoint.

■ **impress something upon someone** emphasize to, stress to, bring home to, instil in, inculcate into, drum into.

**impression** noun **1** *he got the impression she was hiding something:* feeling, sense, fancy, (sneaking) suspicion, inkling, intuition, hunch, notion, idea. **2** *a favourable impression:* opinion, view, image, picture, perception, reaction, judgement, verdict, estimation. **3** *school made a profound impression on me:* impact, effect, influence. **4** *the lid had left a circular impression:* indentation, dent, mark, outline, imprint. **5** *he did a good impression of their science teacher:* impersonation, imitation, caricature; informal take-off.

**impressive** adjective magnificent, majestic, imposing, splendid, spectacular, grand, awe-inspiring, stunning, breathtaking.
OPPOSITES unimpressive.

**imprint** verb *patterns can be imprinted in the clay:* stamp, print, impress, mark, emboss.
noun *her feet left imprints on the floor:* impression, print, mark, stamp, indentation.

**imprison** verb incarcerate, send to prison, jail, lock up, put away, intern, detain, hold prisoner, hold captive; informal send down; Brit. informal bang up.
OPPOSITES release.

**improbable** adjective **1** *it seemed improbable that the hot weather would continue:* unlikely, doubtful, dubious, debatable, questionable, uncertain. **2** *an improbable exaggeration:* unconvincing, unbelievable, implausible, unlikely.
OPPOSITES probable, believable.

a
b
c
d
e
f
g
h
i
j
k
l
m
n
o
p
q
r
s
t
u
v
w
x
y
z

a
b
c
d
e
f
g
h
**i**
j
k
l
m
n
o
p
q
r
s
t
u
v
w
x
y
z

**improper** adjective **1** *it is improper for police to accept gifts:* unacceptable, unprofessional, irregular, unethical, dishonest. **2** *it was improper for young ladies to drive a young man home:* unseemly, unfitting, unbecoming, unladylike, ungentlemanly, inappropriate, indelicate, indecent, immodest, indecorous, immoral. **3** *an extremely improper poem:* indecent, risqué, suggestive, naughty, dirty, filthy, vulgar, crude, rude, obscene, lewd; informal blue, raunchy, steamy.
OPPOSITES acceptable, decent, clean.

**improve** verb **1** *ways to improve the service:* make better, ameliorate, upgrade, refine, enhance, boost, build on, raise. **2** *communications improved:* get better, advance, progress, develop, make headway, make progress, pick up, look up, move forward. **3** *the patient is improving:* recover, get better, recuperate, rally, revive, be on the mend.
OPPOSITES worsen, deteriorate.

**improvement** noun advance, development, upgrade, refinement, enhancement, betterment, amelioration, boost, augmentation, rally, recovery, upswing.

**improvise** verb **1** *she was improvising in front of the cameras:* extemporize, ad-lib; informal speak off the cuff, play it by ear, busk it, wing it. **2** *she improvised a sandpit:* contrive, devise, throw together, cobble together, rig up; informal whip up, rustle up; Brit. informal knock up.

**impulse** noun **1** *she had an*

*impulse to hide:* urge, instinct, drive, compulsion, itch, whim, desire, fancy, notion. **2** *a man of impulse:* spontaneity, impetuosity, recklessness, rashness.
OPPOSITES forethought.

**impulsive** adjective **1** *he had an impulsive nature:* impetuous, spontaneous, hasty, passionate, emotional. **2** *an impulsive decision:* impromptu, snap, spontaneous, unpremeditated, spur-of-the-moment.
OPPOSITES cautious, premeditated.

**inaccurate** adjective inexact, imprecise, incorrect, wrong, erroneous, faulty, imperfect, defective, unreliable, false, mistaken, untrue; Brit. informal adrift.
OPPOSITES accurate.

**inactivity** noun inaction, inertia, idleness, non-intervention, negligence, apathy, indolence, laziness, slothfulness.
OPPOSITES action.

**inadequate** adjective **1** *inadequate water supplies:* insufficient, deficient, poor, scant, scarce, sparse, in short supply, paltry, meagre. **2** *he's a bit inadequate:* incapable, incompetent, immature; informal not up to scratch.
OPPOSITES adequate.

**inadvertently** adverb accidentally, by accident, unintentionally, by mistake, mistakenly, unwittingly.
OPPOSITES intentionally.

**inappropriate** adjective unsuitable, unfitting, unseemly, unbecoming, improper, out of place/keeping, inapposite; informal out of order.
OPPOSITES appropriate.

**inaudible** adjective unclear, indistinct, faint, muted, soft, low, muffled, whispered, muttered, murmured, mumbled.

**inaugurate** verb 1 *he inaugurated a new policy:* initiate, begin, start, institute, launch, get going, get under way, establish, bring in, usher in; informal kick off. 2 *the new President will be inaugurated:* install, instate, swear in, invest, ordain, crown.
OPPOSITES terminate, abolish, dismiss.

**incapable** adjective incompetent, inept, inadequate, ineffective, ineffectual, unfit, unqualified, unequal to the task; informal not up to it.
OPPOSITES competent.

**incense** verb enrage, infuriate, anger, madden, outrage, exasperate, antagonize, provoke; informal make someone see red; N. Amer. informal burn someone up.
OPPOSITES placate, please.

**incensed** adjective enraged, furious, infuriated, irate, raging, incandescent, fuming, seething, beside oneself, outraged; informal mad, hopping mad, wild, livid.
OPPOSITES pleased.

**incentive** noun inducement, motivation, motive, reason, stimulus, spur, impetus, encouragement, carrot; informal sweetener.
OPPOSITES deterrent.

**incident** noun 1 *incidents in his youth:* event, occurrence, episode, happening, affair, business, adventure, exploit, escapade. 2 *police are investigating another incident:* disturbance, commotion, clash, confrontation, accident, shooting, explosion, scene, situation. 3 *the journey was not without incident:* excitement, adventure, drama, crisis, danger.

**incidental** adjective 1 *incidental details:* secondary, subsidiary, minor, peripheral, background, by-the-by, unimportant, insignificant, tangential. 2 *an incidental discovery:* chance, accidental, random, fluky, fortuitous, serendipitous, coincidental, unlooked-for.
OPPOSITES essential.

**incidentally** adverb 1 *incidentally, I haven't had a reply yet:* by the way, by the by, in passing, speaking of which; informal as it happens. 2 *the infection was discovered incidentally:* by chance, by accident, accidentally, fortuitously, by a fluke, by happenstance.

**incite** verb 1 *he was arrested for inciting racial hatred:* stir up, whip up, encourage, stoke up, fuel, kindle, inflame, instigate, provoke, excite, trigger, spark off. 2 *she incited him to commit murder:* provoke, encourage, urge, goad, spur on, egg on, drive, prod, prompt; informal put up to.
OPPOSITES discourage, deter.

**inclination** noun tendency, propensity, leaning, predisposition, predilection, impulse, bent, liking, taste, penchant, preference.
OPPOSITES aversion.

**incline** verb 1 *his prejudice inclines him to overlook obvious facts:* predispose, lead, make, dispose, prejudice, prompt, induce. 2 *I incline to the*

a
b
c
d
e
f
g
h
i
j
k
l
m
n
o
p
q
r
s
t
u
v
w
x
y
z

*opposite view:* tend, lean, swing, veer, gravitate, be drawn, prefer, favour, go for. **3** *he inclined his head:* bend, bow, nod, bob, lower, dip.

**noun** *a steep incline:* slope, gradient, pitch, ramp, bank, ascent, rise, hill, dip, descent; N. Amer. grade.

**inclined** adjective **1** *I'm inclined to believe her:* disposed, minded, of a mind. **2** *she's inclined to gossip:* prone, given, in the habit of, liable, apt.

**include** verb **1** *activities include drama and music:* incorporate, comprise, encompass, cover, embrace, take in, number, contain. **2** *include the cost of repairs:* allow for, count, take into account, take into consideration. **3** *include your address:* add, insert, put in, append, enter.
OPPOSITES exclude, leave out.

**inclusive** adjective all-in, comprehensive, overall, full, all-round, umbrella, catch-all, all-encompassing.
OPPOSITES exclusive, limited.

**income** noun earnings, salary, wages, pay, remuneration, revenue, receipts, takings, profits, proceeds, yield, dividend; N. Amer. take.
OPPOSITES expenditure, outgoings.

**incoming** adjective **1** *incoming flights:* arriving, approaching, inbound, inward, returning, homeward. **2** *the incoming president:* new, next, future, ... elect, ... designate.
OPPOSITES outward, outgoing.

**incompatible** adjective mismatched, unsuited, poles apart, irreconcilable, inconsistent, conflicting, opposed, opposite, contradictory, at odds, at variance.
OPPOSITES well matched, harmonious, consistent.

**incompetent** adjective inept, unskilled, inexpert, amateurish, unprofessional, bungling, blundering, clumsy; informal useless, not up to it.
OPPOSITES competent.

**incomplete** adjective **1** *the manuscript is still incomplete:* unfinished, uncompleted, partial, half-finished. **2** *incomplete information:* deficient, insufficient, partial, sketchy, fragmentary, scrappy, bitty.
OPPOSITES completed, full.

**incomprehensible** adjective unintelligible, impenetrable, unclear, indecipherable, unfathomable, abstruse, difficult, involved; Brit. informal double Dutch.
OPPOSITES intelligible, clear.

**inconsistent** adjective **1** *inconsistent behaviour:* erratic, changeable, unpredictable, variable, unstable, fickle, unreliable, volatile; informal up and down. **2** *he had done nothing inconsistent with his morality:* incompatible, conflicting, at odds, at variance, irreconcilable, out of keeping, contrary to.
OPPOSITES consistent.

**inconvenience** noun **1** *we apologize for any inconvenience caused:* trouble, bother, problems, disruption, difficulty, disturbance; informal aggravation, hassle. **2** *his early arrival was clearly an inconvenience:* nuisance, trouble, bother, problem; informal headache, pain, pain in the neck, hassle.

**verb** *I don't want to inconvenience you:* trouble, bother, put out, put to any trouble, disturb, impose on.

**inconvenient adjective** awkward, difficult, inopportune, badly timed, unsuitable, inappropriate, unfortunate.
OPPOSITES convenient.

**incorporate verb 1** *the region was incorporated into Moldavian territory:* absorb, include, subsume, assimilate, integrate, swallow up. **2** *the model incorporates advanced features:* include, contain, embrace, build in, offer, boast. **3** *incorporate the salt and the butter:* blend, mix, combine, fold in, stir in.
OPPOSITES partition, separate.

**incorrect adjective 1** *an incorrect answer:* wrong, erroneous, mistaken, untrue, false. **2** *incorrect behaviour:* inappropriate, unsuitable, unacceptable, improper, unseemly; informal out of order.
OPPOSITES correct.

**increase verb 1** *demand is likely to increase:* grow, get bigger, get larger, enlarge, expand, swell, rise, climb, mount, intensify, strengthen, extend, spread, widen. **2** *higher expectations will increase user demand:* add to, make larger, make bigger, augment, supplement, top up, build up, extend, raise, swell, inflate, intensify, heighten; informal up, bump up.
OPPOSITES decrease, reduce.
**noun** *the increase in size* | *an increase in demand:* growth, rise, enlargement, expansion, extension, increment, gain, addition, augmentation, surge; informal hike.
OPPOSITES decrease.

**incredible adjective 1** *I find his story incredible:* unbelievable, unconvincing, far-fetched, implausible, improbable, inconceivable, unimaginable. **2** *an incredible feat of engineering:* wonderful, marvellous, spectacular, remarkable, phenomenal, prodigious, breathtaking; informal fantastic, terrific.
OPPOSITES believable, unremarkable.

**incur verb** bring upon oneself, expose oneself to, lay oneself open to, run up, earn, sustain, experience.

**indecent adjective 1** *indecent photographs:* obscene, dirty, filthy, rude, naughty, vulgar, smutty, pornographic; informal blue; euphemistic adult. **2** *indecent haste:* unseemly, improper, unbecoming, inappropriate.

**independence noun 1** *the struggle for American independence:* self-government, self-rule, home rule, self-determination, sovereignty, autonomy. **2** *the adviser's independence:* impartiality, neutrality, disinterestedness, detachment, objectivity.
OPPOSITES dependence, partiality.

**independent adjective 1** *an independent country:* self-governing, self-ruling, self-determining, sovereign, autonomous, non-aligned. **2** *two independent groups verified the results:* separate, different, unconnected, unrelated, discrete. **3** *an independent school:* private, non-state-run, private-sector, fee-paying, privatized,

a
b
c
d
e
f
g
h
i
j
k
l
m
n
o
p
q
r
s
,t
u
v
w
x
y
z

deregulated, denationalized.
**4** *independent advice:*
impartial, unbiased,
unprejudiced, neutral,
disinterested, uninvolved,
detached, dispassionate,
objective, non-partisan, with no
axe to grind.
OPPOSITES dependent, related,
state, public, biased.

**independently** adverb alone,
on one's own, separately,
individually, unaccompanied,
solo, unaided, unassisted,
without help, by one's own
efforts, under one's own steam,
single-handedly.

**index** noun list, listing,
inventory, catalogue, register,
directory, database.

**indicate** verb **1** *sales indicate a*
*growing market:* point to, be a
sign of, be evidence of,
demonstrate, show, testify to,
be symptomatic of, denote,
mark, signal, reflect, signify,
suggest, imply. **2** *the president*
*indicated his willingness to use*
*force:* state, declare, make
known, communicate,
announce, put on record.
**3** *please indicate your choice of*
*prize on the form:* specify,
designate, stipulate, show.

**indication** noun sign, signal,
indicator, symptom, mark,
demonstration, pointer, guide,
hint, clue, omen, warning.

**indicator** noun measure, gauge,
meter, barometer, guide, index,
mark, sign, signal.

**indictment** noun charge,
accusation, arraignment,
prosecution, citation, summons;
N. Amer. impeachment.

**indifference** noun detachment,
lack of concern, disinterest,
lack of interest, nonchalance,
boredom, unresponsiveness,

impassivity, coolness.
OPPOSITES concern.

**indifferent** adjective **1** *an*
*indifferent shrug:* detached,
unconcerned, uninterested,
uncaring, casual, nonchalant,
offhand, unenthusiastic,
unimpressed, unmoved,
impassive, cool. **2** *an indifferent*
*performance:* mediocre,
ordinary, average, middle-of-
the-road, uninspired,
undistinguished, unexceptional,
pedestrian, forgettable,
amateurish; informal no great
shakes, not up to much.
OPPOSITES enthusiastic, brilliant.

**indignant** adjective aggrieved,
affronted, displeased, resentful,
angry, annoyed, offended,
exasperated; informal peeved,
irked, put out; Brit. informal
narked; N. Amer. informal sore.
OPPOSITES content.

**indirect** adjective **1** *an indirect*
*effect:* incidental, secondary,
subordinate, ancillary,
collateral, concomitant,
contingent. **2** *an indirect route:*
roundabout, circuitous,
meandering, winding, tortuous.
**3** *an indirect attack:* oblique,
implicit, implied.
OPPOSITES direct.

**individual** adjective
**1** *exhibitions devoted to*
*individual artists:* single,
separate, discrete, independent,
lone. **2** *he had his own*
*individual style of music:*
unique, characteristic,
distinctive, distinct, particular,
idiosyncratic, peculiar,
personal, special. **3** *a highly*
*individual apartment:* original,
exclusive, different, unusual,
novel, unorthodox, out of the
ordinary.
OPPOSITES multiple, shared,

ordinary.

**noun** *a rather stuffy individual:* person, human being, soul, creature, character; informal type, sort, customer.

**individually** adverb separately, singly, one by one, one at a time, independently.
OPPOSITES together.

**induce** verb 1 *the pickets induced many workers to stay away:* persuade, convince, prevail upon, get, make, prompt, encourage, cajole into, talk into. 2 *these activities induce a feeling of togetherness:* bring about, cause, produce, create, give rise to, generate, engender.
OPPOSITES dissuade, prevent.

**indulge** verb 1 *Sally indulged her passion for chocolate:* satisfy, gratify, fulfil, feed, yield to, give in to. 2 *she did not like her children to be indulged:* pamper, spoil, overindulge, coddle, mollycoddle, cosset, pander to, wait on hand and foot.
■ indulge in carry out, become involved in, participate in, commit, yield to. ■ indulge oneself treat oneself, splash out; informal go to town, splurge.

**indulgence** noun 1 *the indulgence of all his desires:* satisfaction, gratification, fulfilment. 2 *indulgence contributed to his ill-health:* self-gratification, self-indulgence, overindulgence, intemperance, excess, lack of restraint, extravagance, hedonism. 3 *they viewed holidays as an indulgence:* extravagance, luxury, treat, non-essential, extra, frill. 4 *her indulgence left him spoilt:* pampering, coddling,

mollycoddling, cosseting. 5 *his parents view his lapses with indulgence:* tolerance, forbearance, understanding, compassion, sympathy, leniency.
OPPOSITES asceticism, intolerance.

**indulgent** adjective generous, permissive, easy-going, liberal, tolerant, forgiving, forbearing, lenient, kind, kindly, soft-hearted.
OPPOSITES strict.

**industrialist** noun manufacturer, factory owner, captain of industry, magnate, tycoon.

**industry** noun 1 *British industry:* manufacturing, production, construction, trade, commerce. 2 *the publishing industry:* business, trade, field, line of business, profession. 3 *the kitchen was a hive of industry:* activity, energy, effort, endeavour, hard work, industriousness, diligence, application.

**ineffective** adjective 1 *an ineffective scheme:* unsuccessful, unproductive, unprofitable, ineffectual. 2 *an ineffective president:* ineffectual, inefficient, inadequate, incompetent, incapable, unfit, inept; informal useless, hopeless.
OPPOSITES effective.

**inefficient** adjective 1 *an inefficient worker:* ineffective, ineffectual, incompetent, inept, disorganized, unprepared. 2 *inefficient processes:* uneconomical, wasteful, unproductive, time-wasting, slow, unsystematic.
OPPOSITES efficient.

**inequality** noun imbalance,

inequity, inconsistency, disparity, discrepancy, dissimilarity, difference, bias, prejudice, discrimination, unfairness.
OPPOSITES equality.

**inevitable** adjective unavoidable, inescapable, inexorable, assured, certain, sure.
OPPOSITES avoidable.

**inevitably** adverb unavoidably, necessarily, automatically, naturally, as a matter of course, of necessity, inescapably, certainly, surely; informal like it or not.

**inexpensive** adjective cheap, affordable, low-cost, economical, competitive, reasonable, budget, economy, bargain, cut-price, reduced.
OPPOSITES expensive.

**inexperienced** adjective inexpert, untrained, unqualified, unskilled, unseasoned, naive, new, callow, immature; informal wet behind the ears, wide-eyed.
OPPOSITES experienced.

**infamous** adjective notorious, disreputable, scandalous.
OPPOSITES reputable.

**infancy** noun beginnings, early days, early stages, emergence, dawn, outset, birth, inception.
OPPOSITES end.

**infant** noun baby, newborn, young child, tiny tot, little one; Medicine neonate; Scottish & N. English bairn, wean; informal tiny, sprog.

**infect** verb 1 they can infect their children: pass infection to, contaminate. 2 nitrates were infecting rivers: contaminate, pollute, taint, foul, poison.

**infection** noun 1 a kidney infection: disease, virus, illness, ailment, disorder, sickness; informal bug. 2 the infection in his wounds: contamination, poison, inflammation, germs; Medicine sepsis.

**infectious** adjective 1 infectious diseases: communicable, contagious, transmittable, transmissible, transferable; informal catching. 2 her laughter is infectious: irresistible, compelling, contagious; informal catching.

**inferior** adjective 1 she regards him as inferior: second-class, lower-ranking, subordinate, junior, minor, lowly, humble, menial, beneath one. 2 inferior accommodation: second-rate, substandard, low-grade, unsatisfactory, shoddy, poor; informal crummy, lousy.
OPPOSITES superior, luxury.
noun how dare she treat him as an inferior? subordinate, junior, underling, minion.
OPPOSITES superior.

**infertility** noun barrenness, sterility, childlessness.
OPPOSITES fertility.

**infested** adjective overrun, swarming, teeming, crawling, alive, plagued.

**infiltrate** verb penetrate, insinuate oneself into, worm one's way into, sneak into, slip into, creep into, invade.

**infiltrator** noun spy, secret agent, plant, intruder, interloper, subversive, informer, mole, fifth columnist; N. Amer. informal spook.

**infinite** adjective 1 the universe is infinite: boundless, unbounded, unlimited, limitless, never-ending, incalculable, untold. 2 in infinite combinations: countless, uncountable, innumerable, numberless,

immeasurable.
OPPOSITES finite, limited.

**inflame** verb 1 *his opinions inflamed his rival:* enrage, incense, anger, madden, infuriate, exasperate, provoke, antagonize; informal make someone see red. 2 *he inflamed a sensitive situation:* aggravate, exacerbate, intensify, worsen, compound.
OPPOSITES placate, calm.

**inflamed** adjective swollen, red, hot, burning, itchy, sore, painful, tender, infected.

**inflate** verb 1 *inflate the balloon:* blow up, pump up, fill, puff up/out, dilate, distend, swell, bloat. 2 *the demand inflated prices:* increase, raise, boost, escalate, put up; informal hike up, jack up.
OPPOSITES deflate, lower.

**inflated** adjective 1 *inflated prices:* high, sky-high, excessive, unreasonable, outrageous, exorbitant, extortionate; Brit. over the odds; informal steep. 2 *an inflated opinion of himself:* exaggerated, immoderate, overblown, overstated.
OPPOSITES low, modest.

**inflict** verb 1 *he inflicted an injury on Frank:* give, administer, deal out, mete out, cause someone something, exact, wreak. 2 *I won't inflict my views on my children:* impose, force, thrust, foist.
OPPOSITES spare.

**influence** noun 1 *the influence of parents on their children:* effect, impact, control, spell, hold, magic. 2 *a bad influence on young girls:* example to, role model for, inspiration to. 3 *political influence:* power, authority, sway, leverage, weight, pull; informal clout.
verb 1 *bosses can influence our careers:* affect, have an impact on, determine, guide, control, shape, govern, decide, change, alter. 2 *an attempt to influence the jury:* sway, bias, prejudice, suborn, pressurize, coerce, intimidate; informal lean on; Brit. informal nobble.

**influential** adjective powerful, controlling, important, authoritative, leading, significant, instrumental, guiding.

**inform** verb 1 *she informed him that she was ill:* tell, notify, apprise, advise, impart to, communicate to, let someone know, brief, enlighten, send word to. 2 *he informed on two colleagues:* betray, give away, denounce, incriminate, report; informal rat, squeal, split, tell, blow the whistle, snitch; Brit. informal grass, shop; N. Amer. informal finger; Austral./NZ informal dob in.

**informal** adjective 1 *an informal discussion:* unofficial, casual, relaxed, easy-going, low-key. 2 *informal language:* colloquial, vernacular, idiomatic, popular, familiar, everyday; informal slangy, chatty. 3 *informal clothes:* casual, relaxed, comfortable, everyday, sloppy, leisure; informal comfy.
OPPOSITES formal, official, literary, smart.

**information** noun facts, particulars, details, figures, statistics, data, knowledge, intelligence; informal info, gen.

**informative** adjective instructive, illuminating, enlightening, revealing, explanatory, factual, educational, edifying.

**informed** adjective

knowledgeable, enlightened, educated, briefed, up to date, up to speed, in the picture, in the know, au fait; informal clued up.
OPPOSITES ignorant.

**infuriate** verb enrage, incense, provoke, anger, madden, exasperate; informal make someone see red; Brit. informal wind up.
OPPOSITES please.

**ingenious** adjective inventive, creative, imaginative, original, innovative, pioneering, resourceful, enterprising, inspired, clever.
OPPOSITES unimaginative.

**ingredient** noun constituent, component, element, item, part, strand, unit, feature, aspect, attribute.

**inhabit** verb live in, occupy, settle, people, populate, colonize.

**inhabitant** noun resident, occupant, occupier, settler, local, native; (**inhabitants**) population, populace, people, public, community, citizenry, townsfolk, townspeople.

**inhale** verb breathe in, draw in, suck in, sniff in, drink in, gasp.
OPPOSITES exhale.

**inherit** verb 1 *she inherited the farm:* be left, be bequeathed, be willed, come into. 2 *Richard inherited the title:* succeed to, assume, take over.
OPPOSITES leave.

**inheritance** noun legacy, bequest, endowment, birthright, heritage, patrimony.

**inhibit** verb impede, hinder, hamper, hold back, discourage, interfere with, obstruct, slow down, retard.
OPPOSITES assist, allow.

**inhibited** adjective reserved,

reticent, guarded, self-conscious, insecure, withdrawn, repressed, undemonstrative, shy, diffident, bashful; informal uptight.
OPPOSITES uninhibited.

**initial** adjective beginning, opening, commencing, starting, first, earliest, primary, preliminary, preparatory, introductory, inaugural.
OPPOSITES final.

**initially** adverb at first, at the start, at the outset, in/at the beginning, to begin with, to start with, originally.

**initiate** verb 1 *the government initiated the scheme:* begin, start (off), commence, institute, inaugurate, launch, instigate, establish, set up. 2 *he was initiated into a religious cult:* introduce, admit, induct, install, swear in, ordain, invest.
OPPOSITES finish, expel.

**initiative** noun 1 *employers are looking for initiative:* enterprise, resourcefulness, inventiveness, imagination, ingenuity, originality, creativity. 2 *he has lost the initiative:* advantage, upper hand, edge, lead, start. 3 *a recent initiative on recycling:* scheme, plan, strategy, measure, proposal, step, action.
OPPOSITES apathy.

**inject** verb 1 *he injected the codeine:* administer, take; informal shoot (up), mainline, fix. 2 *troops were injected with the vaccine:* inoculate, vaccinate. 3 *a pump injects air into the valve:* insert, introduce, feed, push, force, shoot. 4 *he injected new life into the team:* introduce, instil, infuse, imbue, breathe.

**injection** noun 1 *injections*

*against diphtheria:* inoculation, vaccination, immunization, booster; informal jab, shot. **2** *a cash injection:* addition, introduction, investment, dose, infusion, insertion.

**injunction** noun order, ruling, direction, directive, command, instruction, mandate.

**injure** verb **1** *he injured his foot:* hurt, wound, damage, harm, disable, break; Medicine traumatize; Brit. informal knacker. **2** *a libel injured her reputation:* damage, mar, spoil, ruin, blight, blemish, tarnish, blacken.
OPPOSITES boost.

**injured** adjective **1** *his injured arm:* hurt, wounded, damaged, sore, bruised, broken, fractured; Medicine traumatized; Brit. informal gammy. **2** *an injured tone:* upset, hurt, wounded, offended, reproachful, pained, aggrieved.
OPPOSITES healthy.

**injury** noun **1** *minor injuries:* wound, bruise, cut, gash, scratch, graze; Medicine trauma, lesion. **2** *they escaped without injury:* harm, hurt, damage, pain, suffering. **3** *injury to his feelings:* offence, abuse, injustice, disservice, affront, insult.

**injustice** noun **1** *the injustice of the world:* unfairness, one-sidedness, inequity, bias, prejudice, discrimination, intolerance, exploitation, corruption. **2** *his sacking was an injustice:* wrong, offence, crime, sin, outrage, scandal, disgrace, affront.
OPPOSITES justice, just deserts.

**inland** adjective interior, inshore, internal, upcountry.
OPPOSITES coastal.

**inlet** noun **1** *a rocky inlet:* cove, bay, bight, creek, estuary, fjord, sound; Scottish firth. **2** *an air inlet:* vent, flue, shaft, duct, channel, pipe.

**inmate** noun **1** *the inmates of the hospital:* patient, inpatient, resident, occupant. **2** *prison inmates:* prisoner, convict, captive, detainee, internee.

**inner** adjective **1** *inner London:* central, downtown, innermost. **2** *the inner gates:* internal, interior, inside, innermost. **3** *the inner meaning:* hidden, secret, deep, underlying, veiled, esoteric.
OPPOSITES outer, apparent.

**innocence** noun **1** *he protested his innocence:* guiltlessness, blamelessness. **2** *she took advantage of his innocence:* naivety, credulity, inexperience, gullibility, ingenuousness.

**innocent** adjective **1** *he was entirely innocent:* guiltless, blameless, clean, irreproachable, honest, upright, law-abiding. **2** *innocent fun:* harmless, innocuous, safe, inoffensive. **3** *innocent foreign students:* naive, ingenuous, trusting, credulous, impressionable, easily led, inexperienced, unsophisticated, artless.
OPPOSITES guilty, dangerous, worldly.

**innovation** noun change, alteration, upheaval, reorganization, restructuring, novelty, departure.

**innovative** adjective original, new, novel, fresh, unusual, experimental, inventive, ingenious, pioneering, groundbreaking, revolutionary, radical.

a
b
c
d
e
f
g
h
i
j
k
l
m
n
o
p
q
r
s
t
u
v
w
x
y
z

**inquest** noun enquiry, investigation, probe, examination, review, hearing.

**inquire, inquiry** See ENQUIRE, ENQUIRY.

**insane** adjective 1 *she was declared insane*: mad, of unsound mind, certifiable, psychotic, schizophrenic, unhinged; informal crazy, (stark) raving mad, bonkers, loony, round the bend; Brit. informal crackers, off one's trolley; N. Amer. informal nutso, out of one's tree; Austral./NZ informal bushed. 2 *an insane suggestion*: stupid, idiotic, nonsensical, absurd, ridiculous, ludicrous, preposterous; informal crazy, mad; Brit. informal daft, barmy.
OPPOSITES sane, sensible.

**insect** noun bug; informal creepy-crawly; Brit. informal minibeast.

**insecure** adjective 1 *an insecure young man*: unconfident, uncertain, unsure, doubtful, diffident, hesitant, self-conscious, anxious, fearful. 2 *insecure windows*: unprotected, unguarded, vulnerable, unsecured. 3 *an insecure footbridge*: unstable, rickety, wobbly, shaky, unsteady, precarious.
OPPOSITES confident, secure, stable.

**insecurity** noun lack of confidence, uncertainty, self-doubt, diffidence, hesitancy, nervousness, self-consciousness, anxiety, worry, unease.

**insert** verb put, place, push, thrust, slide, slip, load, fit, slot, install; informal pop, stick, bung.
OPPOSITES extract, remove.

**inside** noun 1 *the inside of the volcano*: interior, centre, core, middle, heart, bowels. 2 (informal) *my insides are out of order*: stomach, gut, bowels, intestines; informal tummy, belly, guts.
OPPOSITES outside.
adjective 1 *his inside pocket*: inner, interior, internal, innermost. 2 *inside information*: confidential, classified, restricted, privileged, private, secret, exclusive; informal hush-hush.
OPPOSITES outside, public.
adverb *she ushered me inside*: indoors, within, in.
OPPOSITES outside.

**insight** noun 1 *your insight has been invaluable*: intuition, perception, understanding, comprehension, appreciation, judgement, vision, imagination; informal nous, savvy. 2 *an insight into the government*: understanding of, appreciation of, introduction to; informal eye-opener.
OPPOSITES stupidity.

**insignificant** adjective unimportant, trivial, trifling, negligible, inconsequential, of no account, paltry, petty, insubstantial; informal piddling.
OPPOSITES significant.

**insincere** adjective false, fake, hollow, artificial, feigned, pretended, put-on, disingenuous, hypocritical, cynical; informal phoney, pretend.
OPPOSITES sincere.

**insist** verb 1 *be prepared to insist*: stand firm, stand one's ground, be resolute, be determined, hold out, persist, be emphatic, lay down the law, not take no for an answer; informal stick to one's guns, put one's foot down. 2 *she insisted that they pay up*: demand, command, order, require. 3 *he* *insisted that he knew nothing:* maintain, assert, protest, swear, declare, repeat.

**insistent** adjective **1** *Tony's insistent questioning:* persistent, determined, tenacious, unyielding, dogged, unrelenting, inexorable. **2** *an insistent buzzing:* incessant, constant, unremitting.

**inspect** verb examine, check, scrutinize, investigate, vet, test, monitor, survey, study, look over; informal check out, give something a/the once-over.

**inspection** noun examination, check-up, survey, scrutiny, exploration, investigation; informal once-over, going-over.

**inspector** noun examiner, scrutineer, investigator, surveyor, assessor, supervisor, monitor, watchdog, ombudsman, auditor.

**inspiration** noun **1** *she's an inspiration to others:* stimulus, motivation, encouragement, influence, spur. **2** *his work lacks inspiration:* creativity, invention, innovation, ingenuity, imagination, originality, insight, vision. **3** *she had a sudden inspiration:* bright idea, revelation; informal brainwave; N. Amer. informal brainstorm.

**inspire** verb **1** *the landscape inspired him to write:* stimulate, motivate, encourage, influence, move, spur, energize, galvanize. **2** *the film inspired a musical:* give rise to, lead to, bring about, prompt, spawn, engender. **3** *Charles inspired awe in her:* arouse, awaken, prompt, induce, ignite, trigger, kindle, produce, bring out.

**inspired** adjective outstanding, wonderful, marvellous, excellent, magnificent, exceptional, first-class, virtuoso, superlative; informal tremendous, superb, awesome, out of this world; Brit. informal brilliant. OPPOSITES uninspired.

**inspiring** adjective inspirational, encouraging, heartening, uplifting, stirring, rousing, electrifying, moving. OPPOSITES uninspiring.

**instability** noun **1** *the instability of political life:* unreliability, uncertainty, unpredictability, insecurity, volatility, capriciousness, changeability, mutability. **2** *emotional instability:* volatility, unpredictability, variability, inconsistency. OPPOSITES steadiness.

**install** verb **1** *a photocopier was installed in the office:* put, place, station, site, insert. **2** *they installed a new president:* swear in, induct, inaugurate, invest, appoint, ordain, consecrate, anoint, enthrone, crown. **3** *she installed herself behind the table:* ensconce, position, settle, seat, plant, sit (down); informal plonk, park. OPPOSITES remove.

**instalment** noun **1** *they paid by monthly instalments:* payment, tranche, repayment, part payment, planned payment, regular payment. **2** *the book was published in instalments:* part, episode, chapter, issue, programme, section, volume.

**instance** noun example, occasion, occurrence, case, illustration, sample.

**instant** adjective **1** *instant access to your money:* immediate, instantaneous, on-the-spot, prompt, swift, speedy, rapid, quick; informal snappy. **2** *instant*

a b c d e f g h i j k l m n o p q r s t u v w x y z

*meals:* prepared, pre-cooked, microwaveable, convenience. OPPOSITES delayed.

**noun 1** *come here this instant!* moment, minute, second. **2** *it all happened in an instant:* flash, trice, moment, minute, (split) second, twinkling of an eye, no time (at all); informal jiffy.

**instantly** adverb immediately, at once, straight away, right away, instantaneously, forthwith, there and then, here and now, this/that minute, this/that second.

**instead** adverb as an alternative, in lieu, alternatively, rather, on second thoughts; N. Amer. alternately. OPPOSITES as well.

■ **instead of** as an alternative to, as a substitute for, as a replacement for, in place of, in lieu of, in preference to, rather than.

**instinct** noun **1** *some instinct told me to be careful:* inclination, urge, drive, compulsion, intuition, feeling, sixth sense, nose. **2** *a good instinct for acting:* talent, gift, ability, aptitude, skill, flair, feel, knack.

**instinctive** adjective intuitive, natural, instinctual, innate, inborn, inherent, unconscious, subconscious, automatic, reflex, knee-jerk; informal gut. OPPOSITES learned.

**institute** noun organization, establishment, institution, foundation, centre, academy, school, college, university, society, association, federation, body.
**verb** set up, inaugurate, found, establish, organize, initiate, set in motion, get under way, get off the ground, start, launch. OPPOSITES abolish, end.

**institution** noun **1** *an academic institution:* establishment, organization, institute, foundation, centre, academy, school, college, university, society, association, body. **2** *they spent their lives in institutions:* (residential) home, hospital, asylum, prison. **3** *the institution of marriage:* practice, custom, convention, tradition.

**institutional** adjective organized, established, bureaucratic, conventional, procedural, formal, formalized, systematic, systematized, structured, regulated. OPPOSITES free and easy.

**instruct** verb **1** *the union instructed them to strike:* order, direct, command, tell, mandate. **2** *nobody instructed him in how to operate it:* teach, coach, train, educate, tutor, guide, school, show.

**instruction** noun **1** *obey my instructions:* order, command, directive, direction, decree, injunction, mandate, commandment. **2** *read the instructions:* directions, handbook, manual, guide, advice, guidance. **3** *he gave instruction in self defence:* tuition, teaching, coaching, schooling, lessons, classes, lectures, training, drill, guidance.

**instructor** noun trainer, coach, teacher, tutor, adviser, counsellor, guide.

**instrument** noun **1** *a wound made with a sharp instrument:* implement, tool, utensil, device, apparatus, gadget. **2** *cockpit instruments:* gauge,

meter, indicator, dial, display.
**3** *an instrument of learning:*
agent, agency, cause, channel,
medium, means, vehicle.

**instrumental**
■ be instrumental in play a part
in, contribute to, be a factor in,
have a hand in, promote,
advance, further.

**insufficient** adjective
inadequate, deficient, poor,
scant, scanty, not enough, too
little, too few.

**insulate** verb **1** *pipes must be
insulated:* wrap, sheathe, cover,
encase, enclose, lag,
soundproof. **2** *they were
insulated from the impact of the
war:* protect, save, shield,
shelter, screen, cushion,
cocoon.

**insult** verb abuse, be rude to,
call someone names, slight,
disparage, discredit, malign,
defame, denigrate, offend, hurt,
humiliate; informal bad-mouth;
Brit. informal slag off.
OPPOSITES compliment.
noun jibe, affront, slight, slur,
barb, indignity, abuse,
aspersions; informal dig, put-
down.

**insulting** adjective abusive,
rude, offensive, disparaging,
belittling, derogatory,
deprecating, disrespectful,
uncomplimentary; informal
bitchy, catty.

**insurance** noun indemnity,
assurance, protection, security,
cover, safeguard, warranty.

**insure** verb provide insurance
for, indemnify, cover, assure,
protect, underwrite, warrant.

**intact** adjective whole, entire,
complete, unbroken,
undamaged, unscathed,
unblemished, unmarked, in one
piece.

OPPOSITES damaged.

**integral** adjective **1** *an integral
part of human behaviour:*
essential, fundamental,
component, basic, intrinsic,
inherent, vital, necessary. **2** *the
dryer has an integral heat
sensor:* built-in, inbuilt,
integrated, inboard, fitted. **3** *an
integral approach to learning:*
unified, integrated,
comprehensive, holistic, joined-
up, all-embracing.
OPPOSITES peripheral,
supplementary, fragmented.

**integrate** verb combine,
amalgamate, merge, unite, fuse,
blend, consolidate, meld, mix,
incorporate, assimilate,
homogenize, desegregate.
OPPOSITES separate.

**integrity** noun **1** *I never doubted
his integrity:* honesty, probity,
rectitude, honour, sincerity,
truthfulness, trustworthiness.
**2** *the integrity of the federation:*
unity, coherence, cohesion,
solidity. **3** *the structural
integrity of the aircraft:*
soundness, strength,
sturdiness, solidity, durability,
stability, rigidity.
OPPOSITES dishonesty, division,
fragility.

**intellect** noun mind, brain(s),
intelligence, reason, judgement,
grey matter, brain cells.

**intellectual** adjective **1** *his
intellectual capacity:* mental,
rational, conceptual,
theoretical, analytical, logical.
**2** *an intellectual man:* learned,
cerebral, academic, erudite,
bookish, highbrow, scholarly.
OPPOSITES physical, stupid.

**intelligence** noun *a man of
great intelligence:* cleverness,
intellect, brainpower,
judgement, reasoning, acumen,

a b c d e f g h i j k l m n o p q r s t u v w x y z

wit, insight, perception.
**2** *intelligence from our agents:* information, facts, details, particulars, data, knowledge; informal info.

**intelligent** adjective **1** *an intelligent woman:* clever, bright, quick-witted, smart, astute, insightful, perceptive; informal brainy. **2** *intelligent machines:* self-regulating, capable of learning, smart.
OPPOSITES unintelligent, dumb.

**intelligible** adjective comprehensible, understandable, accessible, digestible, user-friendly, clear, coherent, plain, unambiguous.

**intend** verb plan, mean, have in mind, aim, propose, hope, expect, envisage.

**intense** adjective **1** *intense heat:* extreme, great, acute, fierce, severe, high, exceptional, extraordinary, harsh, strong, powerful; informal serious. **2** *a very intense young man:* passionate, impassioned, zealous, vehement, earnest, eager, committed.
OPPOSITES mild, apathetic.

**intensify** verb escalate, increase, step up, raise, strengthen, reinforce, pick up, build up, heighten, deepen, extend, expand, amplify, magnify, aggravate, exacerbate, worsen, inflame, compound.
OPPOSITES abate.

**intensity** noun **1** *the intensity of the sun:* strength, power, force, severity, ferocity, fierceness, harshness. **2** *his eyes had a glowing intensity:* passion, ardour, fervour, vehemence, fire, emotion, eagerness.

**intensive** adjective thorough, thoroughgoing, in-depth, rigorous, exhaustive, vigorous, detailed, minute, meticulous, painstaking, methodical, extensive.
OPPOSITES cursory.

**intent** noun *he tried to divine his father's intent:* aim, intention, purpose, objective, goal.
adjective **1** *he was intent on proving his point:* bent, set, determined, insistent, resolved, hell-bent, keen, committed to, determined to. **2** *an intent expression:* attentive, absorbed, engrossed, fascinated, enthralled, rapt, focused, preoccupied.
OPPOSITES distracted.

**intention** noun aim, purpose, intent, objective, goal.

**intentional** adjective deliberate, done on purpose, wilful, calculated, conscious, intended, planned, meant, knowing.

**inter** verb bury, lay to rest, consign to the grave, entomb.
OPPOSITES exhume.

**intercept** verb stop, head off, cut off, catch, seize, block, interrupt.

**intercourse** noun **1** *social intercourse:* dealings, relations, relationships, contact, interchange, communication. **2** *she did not consent to intercourse:* sexual intercourse, sex, sexual relations, mating, coupling, copulation.

**interdict** noun prohibition, ban, bar, veto, embargo, moratorium, injunction.
OPPOSITES permission.

**interest** noun **1** *we listened with interest:* attentiveness, attention, regard, notice, curiosity, enjoyment, delight. **2** *this will be of interest:* concern, consequence, importance, import,

significance, note, relevance, value. **3** *her interests include reading:* hobby, pastime, leisure pursuit, amusement, recreation, diversion, passion. **4** *a financial interest in the firm:* stake, share, claim, investment, involvement, concern.
OPPOSITES boredom.
**verb** *a topic that interests you:* appeal to, be of interest to, attract, intrigue, amuse, divert, entertain, arouse someone's curiosity, whet someone's appetite; informal tickle someone's fancy.
OPPOSITES put off.

**interested** adjective **1** *an interested crowd:* attentive, fascinated, riveted, gripped, captivated, agog, intrigued, curious, keen, eager. **2** *the government consulted with interested bodies:* concerned, involved, affected.

**interesting** adjective absorbing, engrossing, fascinating, riveting, gripping, compelling, captivating, engaging, enthralling, appealing, amusing, entertaining, stimulating, diverting, intriguing.

**interfere** verb *she tried not to interfere:* butt in, barge in, intrude, meddle, tamper, encroach; informal poke one's nose in, stick one's oar in.
■ **interfere with** impede, obstruct, stand in the way of, hinder, inhibit, restrict, constrain, hamper, handicap, disturb, disrupt, influence, affect, confuse.

**interference** noun **1** *they resent state interference:* intrusion, intervention, involvement, meddling, prying. **2** *radio interference:* disruption,

disturbance, static, noise.

**interior** adjective **1** *the house has interior panelling:* inside, inner, internal. **2** *the interior deserts of the US:* inland, upcountry, inner, central. **3** *the country's interior affairs:* internal, home, domestic, national, state, civil, local. **4** *an interior monologue:* inner, mental, spiritual, psychological, private, personal, secret.
OPPOSITES exterior, border, coastal, foreign.
**noun 1** *the interior of the castle:* inside, depths, recesses, bowels, belly, heart. **2** *the country's interior:* centre, heartland.
OPPOSITES exterior, borders, coast.

**intermediary** noun mediator, go-between, negotiator, arbitrator, peacemaker, middleman, broker.

**intermediate** adjective halfway, in-between, middle, mid, midway, intervening, transitional.

**intermittent** adjective sporadic, irregular, fitful, spasmodic, discontinuous, isolated, random, patchy, scattered, occasional, periodic.
OPPOSITES continuous.

**internal** adjective **1** *an internal courtyard:* inner, interior, inside, central. **2** *the state's internal affairs:* domestic, home, interior, civil, local, national, state.
OPPOSITES external, foreign.

**international** adjective global, worldwide, world, intercontinental, universal, cosmopolitan, multiracial, multinational.
OPPOSITES national, local.

**interpret** verb **1** *the rabbis*

a
b
c
d
e
f
g
h
**i**
j
k
l
m
n
o
p
q
r
s
t
u
v
w
x
y
z

*interpret the Jewish law:* explain, elucidate, expound, clarify. **2** *the remark was interpreted as an invitation:* understand, construe, take (to mean), see, regard. **3** *the symbols are difficult to interpret:* decipher, decode, translate, understand.

**interpretation** noun **1** *the interpretation of the Bible's teachings:* explanation, elucidation, exposition, clarification, analysis. **2** *she did not care what interpretation he put on her haste:* meaning, understanding, explanation, inference. **3** *his interpretation of Mozart:* rendition, execution, presentation, performance, reading, playing, singing.

**interrupt** verb **1** *she opened her mouth to interrupt:* cut in (on), break in (on), barge in (on), intrude, intervene; informal butt in (on), chime in (on); Brit. informal chip in (on). **2** *the band had to interrupt their tour:* suspend, adjourn, break off, stop, halt; informal put on ice.

**interruption** noun **1** *he was not pleased at her interruption:* cutting in, barging in, interference, intervention, intrusion; informal butting in. **2** *an interruption of the power supply:* suspension, breaking off, cutting.

**interval** noun intermission, interlude, break, recess, time out.

**intervene** verb intercede, involve oneself, get involved, step in, interfere, intrude.

**interview** noun *all applicants will be called for an interview:* meeting, discussion, interrogation, cross-

examination, debriefing, audience, talk, chat; informal grilling.
verb *we interviewed seventy subjects for the survey:* talk to, question, quiz, interrogate, cross-examine, debrief, poll, canvass, sound out; informal grill, pump.

**interviewer** noun questioner, interrogator, examiner, assessor, journalist, reporter, inquisitor.

**intimacy** noun closeness, togetherness, rapport, attachment, familiarity, friendliness, affection, warmth.
OPPOSITES formality.

**intimate**[1] adjective **1** *an intimate friend:* close, bosom, dear, cherished, fast, firm. **2** *an intimate atmosphere:* friendly, warm, welcoming, hospitable, relaxed, informal, cosy, comfortable. **3** *intimate thoughts:* personal, private, confidential, secret, inward. **4** *an intimate knowledge:* detailed, thorough, exhaustive, deep, in-depth, profound.
OPPOSITES distant, formal, cold, public, sketchy.

**intimate**[2] verb **1** *he intimated his decision:* announce, state, proclaim, make known, make public, disclose, reveal, divulge. **2** *her feelings were subtly intimated:* imply, suggest, hint at, indicate.

**intimidate** verb frighten, menace, scare, terrorize, threaten, browbeat, bully, harass, hound; informal lean on.

**intricate** adjective complex, complicated, convoluted, tangled, elaborate, ornate, detailed.
OPPOSITES simple.

**intrigue** verb *her answer*

*intrigued him:* interest, fascinate, arouse someone's curiosity, attract, engage.
noun *the cabinet was a nest of intrigue:* plotting, conniving, scheming, machination, double-dealing, subterfuge.

**intriguing** adjective interesting, fascinating, absorbing, engaging.

**introduce** verb 1 *he has introduced a new system:* institute, initiate, launch, inaugurate, establish, found, bring in, set in motion, start, begin, get going. 2 *she introduced Lindsey to the young man:* present, make known, acquaint with. 3 *introducing nitrogen into canned beer:* insert, inject, put, force, shoot, feed. 4 *she introduced a note of seriousness:* instil, infuse, inject, add.
OPPOSITES end, remove.

**introduction** noun 1 *the introduction of democratic reforms:* institution, establishment, initiation, launch, inauguration, foundation. 2 *an introduction to the king:* presentation, meeting, audience. 3 *the introduction to the book:* foreword, preface, preamble, prologue, prelude; informal intro.
OPPOSITES ending, epilogue.

**introductory** adjective 1 *the introductory chapter:* opening, initial, starting, initiatory, first, preliminary. 2 *an introductory course:* elementary, basic, rudimentary, entry-level.
OPPOSITES final, advanced.

**intrude** verb encroach, impinge, trespass, infringe, invade, violate, disturb, disrupt.

**intruder** noun trespasser, interloper, invader, infiltrator, burglar, housebreaker; informal gatecrasher.

**intuition** noun 1 *he works by intuition:* instinct, feeling, insight, sixth sense. 2 *this confirms an intuition I had:* hunch, feeling in one's bones, inkling, sneaking suspicion, premonition; informal gut feeling.

**intuitive** adjective instinctive, innate, inborn, inherent, natural, unconscious, subconscious; informal gut.

**invade** verb 1 *the island was invaded:* occupy, conquer, capture, seize, take (over), annex, overrun, storm. 2 *someone had invaded our privacy:* intrude on, violate, encroach on, infringe on, trespass on, disturb, disrupt.
OPPOSITES leave, liberate.

**invader** noun attacker, raider, marauder, occupier, conqueror, intruder, trespasser.

**invalid**[1] adjective *her invalid husband:* ill, sick, ailing, infirm, incapacitated, bedridden, frail, sickly, poorly.
OPPOSITES healthy.
verb *an officer invalided by a chest wound:* disable, incapacitate, hospitalize, put out of action, lay up.

**invalid**[2] adjective 1 *the law was invalid:* void, null and void, not binding, illegitimate, inapplicable. 2 *the whole theory is invalid:* false, fallacious, spurious, unsound, wrong, untenable.
OPPOSITES binding, in force, true.

**invaluable** adjective indispensable, irreplaceable, all-important, crucial, vital, worth its weight in gold.
OPPOSITES dispensable.

**invariably** adverb always, at all

a
b
c
d
e
f
g
h
i
j
k
l
m
n
o
p
q
r
s
t
u
v
w
x
y
z

a
b
c
d
e
f
g
h
i
j
k
l
m
n
o
p
q
r
s
t
u
v
w
x
y
z

times, without fail, without exception, consistently, habitually, unfailingly.
OPPOSITES sometimes, never.

**invasion** noun 1 *the invasion of the islands:* occupation, conquering, capture, seizure, annexation, takeover. 2 *an invasion of my privacy:* violation, infringement, interruption, encroachment, disturbance, disruption, breach.
OPPOSITES withdrawal, liberation.

**invent** verb 1 *he invented television:* originate, create, design, devise, contrive, develop. 2 *they invented the story:* make up, fabricate, concoct, hatch, dream up; informal cook up.

**invention** noun 1 *the invention of the telescope:* origination, creation, development, design, discovery. 2 *medieval inventions:* innovation, creation, contraption, contrivance, device, gadget. 3 *a journalistic invention:* fabrication, concoction, (piece of) fiction, story, tale, lie, untruth, falsehood, fib.

**inventive** adjective 1 *the most inventive composer of his time:* creative, original, innovative, imaginative, resourceful. 2 *a fresh, inventive comedy:* original, innovative, unusual, fresh, novel, new, groundbreaking, unorthodox, unconventional.
OPPOSITES unimaginative, hackneyed.

**inventor** noun originator, creator, designer, deviser, developer, author, architect, father.

**inventory** noun list, listing, catalogue, record, register, checklist, log, archive.

**invest** verb *they invested £18 million:* put in, plough in, put up, advance, expend, spend; informal lay out.
■ invest in put money into, sink money into, plough money into, fund, back, finance, underwrite.

**investigate** verb enquire into, look into, go into, probe, explore, scrutinize, analyse, study, examine; informal check out, suss out.

**investigation** noun examination, enquiry, study, inspection, exploration, analysis, research, scrutiny, probe, review.

**investigator** noun researcher, examiner, analyst, inspector, scrutineer, detective.

**investment** noun 1 *investment in industry:* investing, speculation, outlay, funding, backing, financing, underwriting, buying shares. 2 *an investment of £305,000:* stake, payment, outlay, venture, proposition.

**invisible** adjective unseen, imperceptible, undetectable, inconspicuous, unnoticed, unobserved, hidden, out of sight.
OPPOSITES visible.

**invitation** noun request, call, summons; informal invite.

**invite** verb 1 *they invited us to lunch:* ask, summon, have someone over/round. 2 *applications are invited for the post:* ask for, request, call for, appeal for, solicit, seek. 3 *airing such views invites trouble:* cause, induce, provoke, ask for, encourage, lead to, bring on oneself, arouse.

**inviting** adjective tempting,

enticing, alluring, attractive, appealing, appetizing, mouth-watering, intriguing, seductive. OPPOSITES repellent.

**involve** verb 1 *the inspection involved a lot of work:* entail, require, necessitate, demand, call for. 2 *I try to involve everyone in key decisions:* include, bring in, consult. OPPOSITES preclude, exclude.

**involved** adjective 1 *social workers involved in the case:* associated, connected, concerned. 2 *he had been involved in burglaries:* implicated, caught up, mixed up. 3 *a long and involved story:* complicated, intricate, complex, convoluted. 4 *they were totally involved in their work:* engrossed, absorbed, immersed, caught up, preoccupied, intent. OPPOSITES unconnected, straightforward.

**involvement** noun 1 *his involvement in the plot:* participation, collaboration, collusion, complicity, association, connection, entanglement. 2 *emotional involvement:* attachment, friendship, intimacy, commitment.

**inwards** adverb inside, towards the inside, into the interior, inward, within.

**iron** adjective 1 *an iron bar:* ferric, ferrous. 2 *an iron will:* uncompromising, unrelenting, unyielding, unbending, rigid, steely. OPPOSITES flexible.

■ **iron something out** 1 *John had ironed out all the minor snags:* resolve, straighten out, sort out, clear up, put right, solve, rectify; informal fix. 2 *ironing out*

differences in national systems: eliminate, eradicate, reconcile, resolve.

**ironic** adjective 1 *Edward's tone was ironic:* sarcastic, sardonic, dry, caustic, scathing, acerbic, bitter, trenchant, mocking, derisive, scornful; Brit. informal sarky. 2 *it's ironic that I've ended up writing:* paradoxical, funny, strange; informal typical. OPPOSITES sincere.

**irony** noun 1 *that note of irony in her voice:* sarcasm, bitterness, mockery, ridicule, derision, scorn; Brit. informal sarkiness. 2 *the irony of the situation:* paradox. OPPOSITES sincerity.

**irrational** adjective unreasonable, illogical, groundless, baseless, unfounded, unjustifiable. OPPOSITES logical.

**irregular** adjective 1 *an irregular coastline:* uneven, crooked, misshapen, lopsided, asymmetrical, twisted. 2 *irregular surfaces:* rough, bumpy, uneven, pitted, rutted, lumpy, knobbly, gnarled. 3 *an irregular heartbeat:* inconsistent, unsteady, uneven, fitful, patchy, variable, varying, changeable, inconstant, erratic, unstable, spasmodic, intermittent. 4 *irregular financial dealings:* improper, illegitimate, unethical, unprofessional; informal shady, dodgy. 5 *an irregular army:* guerrilla, underground, paramilitary, partisan, mercenary, terrorist. OPPOSITES regular, above board. noun *gun-toting irregulars:* guerrilla, paramilitary, resistance fighter, partisan, mercenary, terrorist.

OPPOSITES regular.

**irrelevant** adjective beside the point, immaterial, unconnected, unrelated, peripheral, extraneous.

**irresistible** adjective **1** *her irresistible smile:* captivating, enticing, alluring, enchanting. **2** *an irresistible impulse:* uncontrollable, overwhelming, overpowering, ungovernable.

**irresponsible** adjective reckless, rash, careless, unwise, imprudent, ill-advised, injudicious, hasty, impetuous, foolhardy, foolish, unreliable, undependable, untrustworthy.
OPPOSITES responsible.

**irritable** adjective bad-tempered, short-tempered, irascible, tetchy, testy, grumpy, grouchy.
OPPOSITES good-humoured.

**irritate** verb **1** *his tone irritated her:* annoy, bother, vex, make cross, exasperate, infuriate, anger, madden; Brit. rub up the wrong way; informal aggravate, peeve, rile, needle, get (to), bug, hack off; Brit. informal nark, get on someone's wick; N. Amer. informal tee off, tick off, burn up. **2** *some sand irritated my eyes:* inflame, hurt, chafe, scratch, scrape, rub.
OPPOSITES delight, soothe.

**irritation** noun annoyance, exasperation, vexation, indignation, anger, displeasure, chagrin.
OPPOSITES delight.

**island** noun isle, islet, atoll; Brit. holm; (**islands**) archipelago.

**isolate** verb separate, segregate, detach, cut off, shut away, alienate, distance, cloister, seclude, cordon off, seal off, close off, fence off.

OPPOSITES integrate.

**isolated** adjective **1** *isolated communities:* remote, out of the way, outlying, off the beaten track, in the back of beyond, godforsaken, inaccessible, cut-off; informal in the middle of nowhere, in the sticks; N. Amer. informal jerkwater, in the tall timbers; Austral./NZ informal beyond the black stump. **2** *he lived a very isolated existence:* solitary, lonely, secluded, reclusive, hermit-like; N. Amer. lonesome. **3** *an isolated incident:* unique, lone, solitary, unusual, exceptional, untypical, freak; informal one-off.
OPPOSITES accessible, sociable, common.

**isolation** noun **1** *their feeling of isolation:* solitariness, loneliness, friendlessness. **2** *the isolation of some mental hospitals:* remoteness, inaccessibility.
OPPOSITES contact.

**issue** noun **1** *the committee discussed the issue:* matter, question, point at issue, affair, case, subject, topic, problem, situation. **2** *the latest issue of our magazine:* edition, number, instalment, copy. **3** *the issue of a special stamp:* issuing, release, publication.
verb **1** *the minister issued a statement:* release, put out, deliver, publish, broadcast, circulate, distribute. **2** *the captain issued the crew with guns:* supply, provide, furnish, arm, equip, fit out, rig out, kit out; informal fix up.
OPPOSITES withdraw, collect in.
■ take issue with someone/ something disagree with, challenge, dispute, (call into) question.

**itch** noun **1** *I have an itch on my back:* tingling, irritation, itchiness, prickle. **2** (informal) *the itch to travel:* longing, yearning, craving, ache, hunger, thirst, urge, hankering.
**verb 1** *my chilblains really itch:* tingle, be irritated, be itchy, sting, hurt, be sore. **2** (informal) *he itched to do something to help:* long, yearn, ache, burn, crave, hanker for/after, hunger, thirst, be eager, be desperate; informal be dying, be gagging.

**item** noun **1** *an item of farm equipment:* thing, article, object, piece, element, constituent, component, ingredient. **2** *the meeting discussed the item:* issue, matter, affair, case, subject, topic, question, point. **3** *a news item:* report, story, article, piece, write-up, bulletin, feature, review.

**itinerary** noun route, plan, schedule, timetable, programme.

# Jj

**jab** verb & noun poke, prod, dig, nudge, thrust, stab, push.

**jacket** noun wrapping, wrapper, sleeve, coat, cover, covering, sheath.

**jagged** adjective spiky, barbed, ragged, rough, uneven, irregular, serrated.
OPPOSITES smooth.

**jail** noun *he was thrown into jail:* prison, lock-up, detention centre; N. Amer. penitentiary, jailhouse, correctional facility; informal clink, cooler, the slammer, inside; Brit. informal nick; N. Amer. informal can, pen, slam, pokey.
**verb** *she was jailed for killing her husband:* send to prison/jail, put in prison/jail, imprison, incarcerate, lock up, put away, detain; informal send down, put behind bars, put inside; Brit. informal bang up.
OPPOSITES acquit, release.

**jam** verb **1** *he jammed a finger in each ear:* stuff, shove, force, ram, thrust, press, push, stick, cram. **2** *hundreds of people jammed into the hall:* crowd, pack, pile, press, squeeze, cram, throng, mob, fill, block, clog, congest. **3** *the rudder had jammed:* stick, become stuck, catch, seize (up). **4** *dust can jam the mechanism:* immobilize, paralyse, disable, clog, block; informal bung up.
**noun** *a traffic jam:* tailback, hold-up, queue, congestion, bottleneck; N. Amer. gridlock; informal snarl-up.

**jar¹** noun *a jar of honey:* pot, container, crock.

**jar²** verb **1** *each step jarred my whole body:* jolt, jerk, shake, vibrate. **2** *her shrill voice jarred on him:* grate, set someone's teeth on edge, irritate, annoy, get on someone's nerves. **3** *the verse jars with the words that follow:* clash, conflict, contrast, be incompatible, be at variance, be at odds, be inconsistent.

**jargon** noun slang, idiom, cant, argot, patter, gobbledegook; informal lingo, -speak, -ese.

**jaws** plural noun mouth, maw,

a
b
c
d
e
f
g
h
i
j
k
l
m
n
o
p
q
r
s
t
u
v
w
x
y
z

muzzle; informal chops.

**jealous** adjective **1** *jealous of his brother:* envious, covetous, resentful, grudging, green with envy. **2** *a jealous lover:* suspicious, distrustful, possessive, proprietorial, overprotective. **3** *jealous of their rights:* protective, vigilant, watchful, mindful, careful.
OPPOSITES proud, trusting, careless.

**jealousy** noun envy, resentment, bitterness.

**jeer** verb *the demonstrators jeered the police:* taunt, mock, scoff at, ridicule, sneer at, deride, insult, abuse, heckle, catcall (at), boo (at), whistle at; Brit. barrack.
OPPOSITES applaud, cheer.
noun *the jeers of the crowd:* taunt, sneer, insult, shout, jibe, boo, catcall, derision, teasing, scoffing, abuse, scorn, heckling, catcalling; Brit. barracking.
OPPOSITES applause, cheer.

**jeopardize** verb threaten, endanger, imperil, risk, put in danger/jeopardy, compromise, prejudice.
OPPOSITES safeguard.

**jeopardy** noun danger, peril, risk.

**jerk** noun **1** *she gave the reins a jerk:* yank, tug, pull, wrench. **2** *he let the clutch in with a jerk:* jolt, lurch, bump, judder, jump, bounce, shake.
verb **1** *she jerked her arm free:* yank, tug, pull, wrench, wrest, drag, snatch. **2** *the car jerked along:* jolt, lurch, bump, judder, bounce.

**jet** noun **1** *a jet of water:* stream, spurt, spray, spout, gush, surge, burst. **2** *carburettor jets:* nozzle, head, spout.

**jettison** verb dump, drop, ditch, throw out, get rid of, discard, dispose of, scrap.
OPPOSITES retain.

**jewel** noun **1** *priceless jewels:* gem, gemstone, (precious) stone; informal sparkler, rock. **2** *the jewel of his collection:* showpiece, pride (and joy), cream, crème de la crème, jewel in the crown, prize, pick.

**jewellery** noun jewels, gems, gemstones, precious stones, regalia, finery, ornaments, trinkets.

**jibe** noun *cruel jibes:* snide remark, taunt, sneer, jeer, insult, barb; informal dig, put-down.

**jilt** verb leave, walk out on, throw over, finish with, break up with, stand up, leave standing at the altar; informal chuck, ditch, dump, drop, run out on, give someone the push/ elbow, give someone the big E.

**jingle** noun & verb clink, chink, tinkle, jangle, ring.

**jinx** noun *the jinx struck six days later:* curse, spell, the evil eye, black magic, voodoo, bad luck; N. Amer. hex.
verb *the family is jinxed:* curse, cast a spell on, put the evil eye on; Austral. point the bone at; N. Amer. hex.

**job** noun **1** *my job involves a lot of travelling:* position, post, situation, appointment, occupation, profession, trade, career, work, vocation, calling. **2** *this job will take three months:* task, piece of work, assignment, project, chore, undertaking, venture, operation. **3** *it's your job to protect her:* responsibility, duty, charge, task, role, function, mission; informal department.

**jobless** adjective unemployed, out of work, out of a job, unwaged, redundant, laid off; Brit. informal on the dole, resting; Austral./NZ informal on the wallaby track.

OPPOSITES employed.

**jog** verb 1 *he jogged along the road:* run, trot, lope. 2 *a hand jogged his elbow:* nudge, prod, poke, push, bump, jar.

noun *he set off at a jog:* run, trot, lope.

**join** verb 1 *the two parts of the mould are joined with clay:* connect, unite, couple, fix, affix, attach, fasten, stick, glue, fuse, weld, amalgamate, bond, link, merge, secure, make fast, tie, bind. 2 *here the path joins a major road:* meet, touch, reach. 3 *I'm off to join the search party:* help in, participate in, get involved in, contribute to, enlist in, join up, sign up, band together, get together, team up.

OPPOSITES separate, leave.

**joint** noun *a leaky joint:* join, junction, intersection, link, connection, weld, seam.

adjective *a joint effort:* common, shared, communal, collective, mutual, cooperative, collaborative, concerted, combined, united.

OPPOSITES separate.

**jointly** adverb together, in partnership, in cooperation, cooperatively, in conjunction, in combination, mutually.

OPPOSITES separately.

**joke** noun 1 *telling jokes:* funny story, jest, witticism, quip, pun; informal gag, wisecrack, crack, funny, one-liner; N. Amer. informal boffola. 2 *playing stupid jokes:* trick, prank, stunt, hoax, jape; informal leg-pull, spoof, wind-up.

3 (informal) *he soon became a joke:* laughing stock, figure of fun, object of ridicule. 4 (informal) *the present system is a joke:* farce, travesty, waste of time; informal shambles; N. Amer. informal shuck.

verb *she joked with the guests:* tell jokes, jest, banter, quip; informal wisecrack, josh.

**joker** noun comedian, comedienne, comic, humorist, wit, jester, prankster, practical joker, clown.

**jolly** adjective cheerful, happy, cheery, good-humoured, jovial, merry, sunny, joyful, light-hearted, in high spirits, bubbly, genial; informal chipper, chirpy, perky, bright-eyed and bushy-tailed.

OPPOSITES miserable.

**jolt** verb 1 *the train jolted the passengers to one side:* push, thrust, jar, bump, knock, bang, shake, jog. 2 *the car jolted along:* bump, bounce, jerk, rattle, lurch, shudder, judder. 3 *she was jolted out of her reverie:* startle, surprise, shock, stun, shake; informal rock, knock sideways.

noun 1 *a series of sickening jolts:* bump, bounce, shake, jerk, lurch. 2 *he woke up with a jolt:* start, jerk, jump. 3 *the sight of the dagger gave him a jolt:* fright, shock, scare, surprise; informal turn.

**jostle** verb 1 *she was jostled by noisy students:* push, shove, elbow, barge. 2 *people jostled for the best position:* struggle, vie, jockey, scramble, fight.

**journal** noun 1 *a medical journal:* periodical, magazine, gazette, review, newsletter, news-sheet, bulletin, newspaper, paper, daily, weekly, monthly, quarterly. 2 *he keeps a*

a
b
c
d
e
f
g
h
i
**j**
k
l
m
n
o
p
q
r
s
t
u
v
w
x
y
z

*journal:* diary, log, logbook, chronicle, history, yearbook; N. Amer. daybook.

**journalist** noun reporter, correspondent, newspaperman, newspaperwoman, newsman, newswoman, columnist; informal news hound, hack, hackette, stringer, journo; N. Amer. informal newsie.

**journey** noun *his journey round the world:* trip, expedition, tour, trek, voyage, cruise, ride, drive, crossing, passage, flight, odyssey, pilgrimage.
verb *they journeyed south:* travel, go, voyage, sail, cruise, fly, hike, trek, ride, drive, make one's way.

**jovial** adjective cheerful, jolly, happy, cheery, good-humoured, convivial, genial, good-natured, affable, outgoing, smiling, merry, sunny.
OPPOSITES miserable.

**joy** noun delight, pleasure, jubilation, triumph, exultation, rejoicing, happiness, gladness, elation, euphoria, bliss, ecstasy, rapture.
OPPOSITES misery.

**joyful** adjective **1** *his joyful mood:* cheerful, happy, jolly, merry, sunny, joyous, cheery, smiling, mirthful, jubilant, gleeful, jovial. **2** *joyful news:* pleasing, happy, good, cheering, gladdening, welcome, heart-warming.
OPPOSITES sad.

**jubilant** adjective overjoyed, exultant, triumphant, joyful, cock-a-hoop, elated, thrilled, gleeful, euphoric, ecstatic; informal over the moon.
OPPOSITES despondent.

**jubilee** noun anniversary, commemoration, celebration, festival.

**judge** noun **1** *the judge sentenced him to five years:* justice, magistrate, recorder, sheriff, His/Her/Your Honour; N. Amer. jurist; Brit. informal beak. **2** *a panel of judges will select the winner:* adjudicator, referee, umpire, arbiter, assessor, examiner, moderator, scrutineer.
verb **1** *I judged that she was exhausted:* conclude, decide, consider, believe, think, deduce, infer, gauge, estimate, guess, surmise, conjecture, regard as, rate as, class as; informal reckon, figure. **2** *she was judged innocent:* pronounce, decree, rule, find. **3** *the competition will be judged by Alan Amey:* adjudicate, arbitrate, moderate, referee, umpire. **4** *entries were judged by a panel of experts:* assess, appraise, evaluate, examine, review.

**judgement** noun **1** *an error of judgement:* sense, discernment, perception, discrimination, understanding, powers of reasoning, reason, logic. **2** *his beliefs affect his judgement of Milton:* opinion, view, estimate, appraisal, conclusion, diagnosis, assessment, impression, conviction, perception, thinking. **3** *a court judgement:* verdict, decision, adjudication, ruling, pronouncement, decree, finding, sentence.

**judicious** adjective wise, sensible, prudent, shrewd, astute, canny, discerning.
OPPOSITES ill-advised.

**jug** noun pitcher, ewer, crock, jar, urn, carafe, flask, flagon, decanter; N. Amer. creamer.

**juice** noun liquid, fluid, sap, milk, gum, extract, concentrate, essence.

**juicy** adjective succulent, tender, moist, ripe.
OPPOSITES dry.

**jumble** noun *the books were in a jumble:* heap, muddle, mess, tangle, confusion, disarray, chaos, hotchpotch; N. Amer. hodgepodge; informal shambles.
verb *the photographs are all jumbled up:* mix up, muddle up, disorganize, disorder, tangle.

**jump** verb 1 *the cat jumped off his lap:* leap, spring, bound, hop, skip, caper, dance, prance, frolic, cavort. 2 *he jumped the fence:* vault (over), leap over, clear, sail over, hop over. 3 *pre-tax profits jumped:* rise, go up, shoot up, soar, surge, climb, increase; informal skyrocket. 4 *the noise made her jump:* start, jolt, flinch, recoil, shudder.
noun 1 *the short jump across the gully:* leap, spring, bound, hop, skip. 2 *a jump in profits:* rise, leap, increase, upsurge, upswing; informal hike. 3 *I woke up with a jump:* start, jerk, spasm, shudder.

**jumper** noun (Brit.) sweater, pullover, jersey; informal woolly.

**junction** noun crossroads, intersection, interchange, T-junction, turn, turn-off, exit; Brit. roundabout; N. Amer. turnout, cloverleaf.

**junior** adjective 1 *the junior members of the family:* younger, youngest. 2 *a junior minister:* minor, subordinate, lower, lesser, low-ranking, secondary.
OPPOSITES senior, older.

**junk** noun (informal) rubbish, clutter, odds and ends, bits and pieces, bric-a-brac, refuse, litter, scrap, waste, debris; N. Amer. trash; Austral./NZ mullock.

**just** adjective 1 *a just society:* fair, fair-minded, equitable, even-handed, impartial, unbiased, objective, neutral, disinterested, unprejudiced, honourable, upright, decent, principled. 2 *a just reward:* deserved, well deserved, well earned, merited, rightful, due, proper, fitting, appropriate.
OPPOSITES unfair, undeserved.
adverb 1 *I just saw him:* a moment ago, a short time ago, very recently, not long ago. 2 *she's just right for him:* exactly, precisely, absolutely, completely, totally, entirely, perfectly, utterly, thoroughly; informal dead. 3 *we just made it:* narrowly, only just, by a hair's breadth, by the skin of one's teeth, barely, scarcely, hardly; informal by a whisker. 4 *she's just a child:* only, merely, simply, (nothing) but, no more than.
OPPOSITES hardly, easily.

**justice** noun 1 *I appealed to his sense of justice:* fairness, justness, fair play, fair-mindedness, equity, right, even-handedness, honesty, morality. 2 *the justice of his case:* validity, justification, soundness, well-foundedness, legitimacy. 3 judge, magistrate, recorder, sheriff; N. Amer. jurist.

**justifiable** adjective valid, legitimate, warranted, well founded, justified, just, reasonable, defensible.
OPPOSITES unjustifiable.

**justification** noun grounds, reason, basis, rationale, premise, vindication, explanation, defence, argument, case.

**justify** verb 1 *directors must justify the expenditure:* give grounds for, give reasons for,

a
b
c
d
e
f
g
h
i
**j**
**k**
l
m
n
o
p
q
r
s
t
u
v
w
x
y
z

explain, account for, defend, vindicate, excuse, exonerate. **2** *the situation justified further investigation:* warrant, be good reason for, be a justification for.

**juvenile** adjective **1** *juvenile offenders:* young, teenage, adolescent, junior, pubescent.

**2** *juvenile behaviour:* childish, immature, puerile, infantile, babyish.
OPPOSITES adult, mature.
noun *many victims are juveniles:* young person, youngster, child, teenager, adolescent, minor, junior; informal kid.
OPPOSITES adult.

# Kk

**keen** adjective **1** *his publishers were keen to capitalize on his success:* eager, anxious, intent, impatient, determined; informal raring, itching, dying. **2** *a keen birdwatcher:* enthusiastic, avid, eager, ardent, fervent, conscientious, committed, dedicated. **3** *a girl he was keen on:* attracted to, passionate about, interested in, fond of, taken with, smitten with, enamoured of, infatuated with; informal struck on, gone on, mad about. **4** *a keen cutting edge:* sharp, well-honed, razor-sharp. **5** *a keen mind:* acute, penetrating, astute, incisive, sharp, perceptive, piercing, razor-sharp, shrewd, discerning, clever, intelligent, brilliant, bright, smart, wise, insightful. **6** *a keen sense of duty:* intense, acute, fierce, passionate, burning, fervent, ardent, strong, powerful.
OPPOSITES reluctant, unenthusiastic, dull.

**keep** verb **1** *you should keep all the old forms:* retain (possession of), hold on to, not part with, save, store, put by/aside, set aside; N. Amer. set by; informal hang on to. **2** *I tried to*

*keep calm:* remain, stay, carry on being. **3** *he keeps going on about the murder:* persist in, keep on, carry on, continue, insist on. **4** *I shan't keep you long:* detain, keep waiting, delay, hold up, slow down. **5** *most people kept the rules:* comply with, obey, observe, conform to, abide by, adhere to, stick to, heed, follow, carry out, act on, make good, honour, keep to, stand by. **6** *keeping the old traditions:* preserve, keep alive/up, keep going, carry on, perpetuate, maintain, uphold. **7** *where is her umbrella kept?* store, house, stow, put (away), place, deposit. **8** *he stole to keep his family:* provide for, support, feed, maintain, sustain, take care of, look after. **9** *she keeps rabbits:* breed, rear, raise, farm, own. **10** *his parents kept a shop:* manage, run, own, operate.
OPPOSITES throw away, break, abandon.
noun *money to pay for his keep:* maintenance, upkeep, sustenance, board (and lodging), food, livelihood.
■ **keep off** avoid, steer clear of, stay away from, not go near.

**keeper** noun curator, custodian, guardian, administrator, overseer, steward, caretaker, attendant.

**keeping** noun care, custody, charge, guardianship, possession, trust, protection.
■ **in keeping with** consistent with, in harmony with, in accord with, in agreement with, in line with, in character with, compatible with, appropriate to, befitting, suitable for.

**key** noun **1** *the key to the mystery:* answer, clue, solution, explanation, basis, foundation. **2** *the key to success:* means, way, route, path, passport, secret, formula.
adjective *a key figure:* crucial, central, essential, indispensable, pivotal, critical, dominant, vital, principal, prime, major, leading, main, important.
OPPOSITES peripheral.

**kick** verb *kick the ball:* boot, punt.
noun (informal) *I get a kick out of driving:* thrill, excitement, stimulation, tingle, frisson; informal buzz, high; N. Amer. informal charge.
■ **kick off** (informal) start, commence, begin, get going, get off the ground, get under way, open, start off, set in motion, launch, initiate, introduce, inaugurate. ■ **kick someone out** (informal) expel, eject, throw out, oust, evict, get rid of, dismiss, discharge; informal chuck out, send packing, boot out, sack, fire.

**kid** noun (informal) **child**, youngster, little one, baby, toddler, tot, infant, boy, girl, young person, minor, juvenile, adolescent, teenager, youth, stripling; Scottish bairn; informal kiddie, nipper, kiddiewink; Brit. informal sprog; N. Amer. informal rug rat; Austral./NZ ankle-biter; derogatory brat.

**kidnap** verb abduct, carry off, capture, seize, snatch, take hostage.

**kill** verb **1** murder, take the life of, assassinate, eliminate, terminate, dispatch, finish off, put to death, execute, slaughter, exterminate; informal bump off, do away with, do in, top, take out, blow away; N. Amer. informal rub out, waste; literary slay. **2** (informal) *Congress killed the bill:* veto, defeat, vote down, rule against, reject, throw out, overturn, put a stop to.

**killer** noun murderer, assassin, butcher, serial killer, gunman, terminator, executioner; informal hit man.

**killing** noun murder, assassination, homicide, manslaughter, execution, slaughter, massacre, butchery, bloodshed, extermination.

**kind**[1] noun *all kinds of gifts:* sort, type, variety, style, form, class, category, genre.

**kind**[2] adjective *a kind and caring person:* kindly, good-natured, kind-hearted, warm-hearted, caring, affectionate, loving, warm, considerate, obliging, compassionate, sympathetic, understanding, benevolent, benign; Brit. informal decent.
OPPOSITES unkind.

**kindly** adjective *a kindly old lady:* benevolent, kind, kind-hearted, warm-hearted, generous, good-natured, gentle, warm, compassionate, caring, loving, benign, well meaning, considerate.

OPPOSITES unkind, cruel.

**adverb** *he looked at her kindly:* nicely, warmly, affectionately, tenderly, lovingly, compassionately, considerately, obligingly, generously.
OPPOSITES unkindly, harshly.

**kindness** noun kindliness, affection, warmth, gentleness, concern, care, consideration, altruism, compassion, sympathy, benevolence, generosity.
OPPOSITES unkindness.

**king** noun ruler, sovereign, monarch, Crown, His Majesty, emperor, prince, potentate.

**kingdom** noun realm, domain, dominion, country, empire, land, territory, nation, (sovereign) state, province.

**kiss** verb 1 *he kissed her:* informal peck, smooch, canoodle, neck, pet; Brit. informal snog; N. Amer. informal buss. 2 *the ball just kissed the crossbar:* brush (against), caress, touch, stroke, skim.
**noun** informal peck, smack, smacker, smooch; Brit. informal snog; N. Amer. informal buss.

**kit** noun 1 *the dental kit for the hospital:* equipment, tools, implements, instruments, gadgets, utensils, appliances, gear, tackle, hardware, paraphernalia; informal things, stuff; Military accoutrements. 2 (Brit. informal) *their football kit:* clothes, clothing, garments, outfit, dress, costume, attire, garb; informal gear, get-up, rig-out. 3 *a tool kit:* set, selection, collection, pack.

■ **kit someone/something out** equip, fit (out/up), furnish, supply, provide, issue, dress, clothe, attire, rig out, deck out; informal fix up.

**knack** noun 1 *a knack for making money:* gift, talent, flair, genius, instinct, ability, capability, capacity, aptitude, bent, facility, trick; informal the hang of something. 2 *he has a knack of getting injured:* tendency, habit, liability, propensity.

**knickers** plural noun (Brit.) underpants, briefs; Brit. pants; informal panties, undies; Brit. informal knicks, smalls; dated drawers; historical bloomers.

**knife** noun blade, cutter.
**verb** *he was knifed in the back:* stab, hack, gash, slash, lacerate, cut, bayonet.

**knit** verb 1 *disparate regions began to knit together:* unite, unify, come together, bond, fuse, coalesce, merge, meld, blend. 2 *we expect broken bones to knit:* heal, mend, join, fuse. 3 *Marcus knitted his brows:* furrow, contract, gather, wrinkle.

**knob** noun lump, bump, protrusion, bulge, swelling, knot, boss.

**knock** verb 1 *he knocked on the door:* bang, tap, rap, thump, pound, hammer, beat, strike, hit. 2 *she knocked her knee on the table:* bump, bang, hit, strike, crack, injure, hurt, bruise; informal bash, whack. 3 *he knocked into an elderly man:* collide with, bump into, bang into, run into, crash into, smash into, plough into; N. Amer. impact; informal bash into.
**noun** 1 *a knock at the door:* tap, rap, rat-tat, knocking, bang, banging, pounding, hammering, thump, thud. 2 *the casing can withstand knocks:* bump, blow, bang, jolt, jar, shock, collision, crash, smash, impact.

■ **knock someone down** fell, floor, flatten, bring down, knock to the ground, knock over, run over/down. ■ **knock something down** demolish, pull down, tear down, destroy, raze (to the ground), level, flatten, bulldoze. ■ **knock someone out** knock unconscious, knock senseless, floor, prostrate; informal lay out, KO, fell.

**knot** noun *a knot of people:* cluster, group, band, huddle, bunch, circle, ring.
verb *a scarf knotted round her throat:* tie, fasten, secure, bind, do up.

**knotted** adjective tangled, matted, snarled, unkempt, tousled; informal mussed up.

**know** verb **1** *she doesn't know I'm here:* be aware, realize, be conscious. **2** *do you know the rules:* be familiar with, be conversant with, be acquainted with, be versed in, have mastered, have a grasp of, understand, comprehend; informal be clued up on. **3** *I don't know many people here:* be acquainted with, have met, be familiar with; Scottish ken.

**know-how** noun (informal) expertise, skill, proficiency, knowledge, understanding, mastery, technique; informal savvy.

**knowing** adjective significant, meaningful, expressive, suggestive, superior.

**knowledge** noun **1** *his knowledge of history:* understanding, comprehension, grasp, command, mastery; informal know-how. **2** *people anxious to display their knowledge:* learning, erudition, education, scholarship, schooling, wisdom. **3** *he slipped away without my knowledge:* awareness, consciousness, realization, cognition, apprehension, perception, appreciation. **4** *a knowledge of the countryside:* familiarity, acquaintance, conversance, intimacy.
OPPOSITES ignorance.

**knowledgeable** adjective **1** *a knowledgeable old man:* well informed, learned, well read, (well) educated, erudite, scholarly, cultured, cultivated, enlightened. **2** *he is knowledgeable about modern art:* conversant with, familiar with, well acquainted with, au fait with, up on, up to date with, abreast of; informal clued up on.
OPPOSITES ignorant.

**known** adjective *a known criminal:* recognized, well known, widely known, noted, celebrated, notable, notorious, acknowledged.

a
b
c
d
e
f
g
h
i
j
**k**
l
m
n
o
p
q
r
s
t
u
v
w
x
y
z

# How to use a thesaurus

In this brief guide, you can discover that it's easy to make a thesaurus work for you, to improve your writing and get better results.

## The Basics

Suppose you are writing a story and find that you are saying that somebody *said* this and then they *said* that, and you want to use a different word to *said*. Just look up the verb **say** in this book under S, as you would in a dictionary—there are letters down the edge of each page to guide you—and you will find this:

the word you have in mind

**say** verb 1 *he said her name:* speak, utter, voice, pronounce. **2** *'I must go,' she said:* declare, state, announce, remark, observe, mention, comment, note, add. **3** *they said a prayer:* recite, repeat, utter, deliver, perform. **4** *her watch said one twenty:* indicate, show, read.

words you can use instead

You can quickly see alternatives to make your writing more varied: *declare, state, announce,* and so on.

Read on to discover more about what is in a thesaurus.

# Contents

# Difference between a thesaurus and a dictionary

Although some people use a thesaurus to try to find out the meaning of a word, a thesaurus is not the same as a dictionary. A thesaurus provides alternative words with a similar meaning, or 'synonyms', whereas a dictionary tells you what a word means.

## Dictionaries

A dictionary is a record of words in the English language. It provides an account of each word and includes at least some of these features:

- the spelling of the entry word, or 'headword'
- its pronunciation
- its word class, or 'part of speech': for example, whether it is a noun, verb, or adjective
- its different meanings
- different forms of the word ('inflections') that do not follow a standard pattern, such as *caught* as the past tense of *catch*, or *leaves* as the plural of *leaf*
- the history and origin of the word ('etymology')
- any words formed from it ('derivatives', such as *leafy*, formed from *leaf*)
- phrases and idioms containing the headword, such as *turn over a new leaf* at the entry for *leaf*
- information on how the word is used, e.g. whether it is formal or informal

**leaf** noun (plural **leaves**) **1** a flat green part of a plant that is attached to a stem. **2** a single sheet of paper in a book. **3** gold or silver in the form of very thin sheet. **4** a hinged or detachable part of a table. •verb (**leaf through**) turn over pages or papers, reading them quickly or casually. ▫ **turn over a new leaf** start to behave in a better way.
■ **leafy** adjective.

## Thesauruses

The purpose of a thesaurus is to provide you with 'synonyms'—words that have a similar meaning and could be used instead of one that you have in mind. For example, the words *declare*, *state*, and *announce* are all synonyms for the word *say*.

Most thesauruses also include other features, such as 'antonyms'—words which mean the opposite.

Remember that a thesaurus contains entries for only selected words. Unlike a dictionary, a thesaurus does not set out to describe every word in the English language systematically: it contains only words which have synonyms. Therefore you will not find entries for certain words—typically names for specific things—such as *giraffe* or *computer*.

# What's in a thesaurus?

## Part of speech

The first piece of information given after the headword is the part of speech (or 'word class', as it is also known). Most words in a thesaurus are either nouns, verbs, adjectives, or adverbs. This is because those are the types of word most likely to have synonyms.

A **noun** is a word that names something. This could be a person (*woman, boy, Martin*), a thing (*building, tree, chair*), or an abstract concept such as an event, quality, or feeling (*birth, difficulty, happiness*). Some nouns, such as *clothes* or *earnings*, are always used in the plural; these are labelled **plural noun**.

A **verb** is a word that describes an action (*go, claim, put*) or a state (*be, live*) and is essential for forming a sentence.

An **adjective** is a word that describes a noun (*sweet, rich, green, technical*) and gives greater depth and interest to a sentence.

An **adverb** is a word that describes or 'modifies' a verb, such as *happily* or *obviously*.

Further parts of speech that you will come across occasionally in this thesaurus are:

A **preposition** is a word such as *after, in, to, on*, and *with*, which usually stands before a noun or pronoun and tells you how that noun relates to what has gone before.

A **conjunction** is a word such as *and, because, but, for, if, or*, and *when*, and is used to connect other words or parts of a sentence together.

An **exclamation** is a word, typically used on its own, expressing an emotion, such as *goodbye* or *sorry*.

Some words have more than one part of speech. For example, the word *place* can be either a noun (*a beautiful place*) or a verb (*place the tray in the oven*). If an entry has more than one part of speech, make sure you choose the right one for your needs.

## Senses

Many words have more than one meaning or 'sense'. Some entries are therefore divided into different senses. For example, the adjective *dry* is divided into three different senses:

> **dry** adjective **1** *the dry desert:* arid,
> parched, waterless, dehydrated,
> desiccated, withered, shrivelled,
> wizened. **2** *a dry debate:* dull,
> uninteresting, boring,
> unexciting, tedious, dreary,
> monotonous, unimaginative,
> sterile; informal deadly. **3** *a dry
> sense of humour:* wry, subtle,
> laconic, ironic, sardonic,
> sarcastic, cynical.
> OPPOSITES wet, moist,
> interesting, lively, broad.

*Dry* most commonly means 'not wet' or 'arid' (*a dry desert*) but it also has the other meanings 'dull' (*a dry debate*) and 'wry' (*a dry sense of humour*).

When you are looking at the different senses for a word, you can use both the examples and the synonyms to guide you to the meaning you are trying to express.

## Examples

This thesaurus includes many examples which show how the headword is used and guide you to the correct sense.

For instance, the adjective *fair* has five senses:

> **fair**[1] adjective **1** *the courts were generally fair:* just, equitable, honest, impartial, unbiased, unprejudiced, neutral, even-handed. **2** *fair weather:* fine, dry, bright, clear, sunny, cloudless. **3** *fair hair:* blond(e), yellow, golden, flaxen, light. **4** *fair skin:* pale, light, pink, white, creamy. **5** *a fair achievement:* reasonable, passable, tolerable, satisfactory, acceptable, respectable, decent, all right, good enough, pretty good.
> OPPOSITES unfair, inclement, dark, poor.

To find the right sense, first read the example sentences and phrases: *the courts were generally fair, fair weather, fair hair, fair skin, a fair achievement*. Decide which of these is closest to the idea you wish to express: are you looking for a word to describe the mark given to a piece of school work? Or are you describing someone's hair, or their complexion? Or the weather? When you have chosen the right sense, look at the selection of synonyms following it.

## Synonyms

In this thesaurus, the first synonyms given in each group are the commonest and nearest to the meaning of the headword. However, you may have to read the whole list to find the synonym which is best suited to your needs. If you are not sure whether a word is the one you want, you should check its meaning in a dictionary.

As well as thinking about meaning, you need to think about the style or tone when selecting a synonym. If you are writing an email to a friend you can be quite informal: you could describe a party as being *cool*, for example. But in an essay at school you need to use a more formal word, such as *marvellous* or *excellent*. If you wanted to use a more unusual word you could even try *sublime*—your thesaurus opens up all sorts of possibilities.

## Labels

Some words, like *good* and *bad*, can be used in any context. They are part of Standard English. But some words are only used in certain contexts; in this thesaurus they are labelled to show what the context is. There are two different types of label in this thesaurus: labels about level or style (register labels) and labels about where the word is used (geographical labels).

### Register labels

Register is the word used to describe the level of language—for example, whether it is *formal* or *informal*.

Standard English is the language that we use in the company of people we are not that familiar with, in a workplace, to teachers, or indeed in any other 'business' situation, from speaking to a shop assistant to booking a holiday. It is the most accepted and established use of the language.

'Formal' language is reserved for official uses. It is the language of reports and official letters and notices. It represents a more authoritative voice. Words in this category include *residence* or *dwelling* instead of *home*, and *deceased* instead of *dead*.

'Informal' language, on the other hand, is the language that you will use when you are with people that are close to you. When you are talking or writing to family and friends, you will automatically adopt this freer, chattier style. For example, the thesaurus entry for *very* shows that synonyms such as *extremely*, *decidedly*, and *highly* are Standard English, but that the alternatives *majorly* and *well* are informal, and so care must be taken to ensure they are used only in informal contexts.

> **very** adverb *that's very kind of you:* extremely, exceedingly, exceptionally, extraordinarily, tremendously, immensely, acutely, abundantly, singularly, decidedly, highly, remarkably, really; informal awfully, terribly,

*How to use a thesaurus*

majorly, seriously, mega, ultra;
Brit. informal ever so, well, dead,
jolly; N. Amer. informal real, mighty.
OPPOSITES slightly.

'Literary' words are used in poetry or other literature written in a high-sounding style; these include *slay*, meaning 'kill', and *wondrous*, meaning 'amazing'.

Even if you have spoken English all your life, you may not always realize which category a word belongs to, so it is important to check that language is appropriate for the occasion.

## Geographical labels

Most of the words included in the thesaurus are in use throughout the English-speaking world (although spellings may vary), but some are found only (or chiefly) in a particular region. These are labelled British (abbreviated to Brit.), **North American** (N. Amer.), **Australian** (Austral.), **New Zealand** (NZ), **Northern English** (N. English), or **Scottish**. Using these labels as guidance, you can either avoid using a word that your audience or readers may not understand, or you can consciously choose a labelled synonym if you want to use a word that is typical of a region of the world. Many of these are informal words, as can be seen from an entry such as *bad-tempered*:

> **bad-tempered** adjective
> irritable, irascible, tetchy, testy,
> grumpy, grouchy, crotchety, in a
> (bad) mood, cantankerous,
> curmudgeonly, ill-tempered, ill-
> humoured, peevish, cross,
> fractious, pettish, crabby; informal
> snappish, on a short fuse; Brit.
> informal shirty, stroppy, ratty; N.
> Amer. informal cranky, ornery;
> Austral./NZ informal snaky.
> OPPOSITES good-humoured,
> affable.

Other examples from North America include *garbage*, which is the standard word for 'rubbish', and *bill* in the sense of 'banknote', as well as the less well known *forehanded*, meaning 'thrifty', and *slate*, meaning 'to schedule or plan'.

Australian and New Zealand English give us words such as *shonky* (dishonest), *crook* (ill), *hophead* (drinker), and *ropeable* (angry), while from Scotland you will find *agley* (crooked), *couthy* (friendly), and *greet* (cry).

## Opposites

As well as synonyms, this thesaurus contains opposites (called 'antonyms'). Bad is the opposite of good, for example. You can use opposites to find the word you need. For example, if you are looking for a word that means 'not fancy', you can look up *fancy* and find that the opposite word listed is *plain*. *Plain* has its own entry in the thesaurus, and if you look it up you find many synonyms for *plain* listed: *simple*, *ordinary*, *unadorned*, and so on.

# When to use a thesaurus

So in what circumstances will you find a thesaurus useful, and how can it actually help you?

## Homework and essays

If you are writing an essay, story, or other piece of work, it is a good idea to have not only a dictionary but also a thesaurus to hand.

Writing often tests how broad our vocabulary is, and it is easy to find yourself using the same words over and over again. The thesaurus can show you alternatives, so that you do not constantly need to refer to, say, the *founder* of modern physics; you can choose other words such as *originator*, *creator*, *father*, *architect*, *engineer*, *pioneer*, and *inventor*. Beware, though, of using different words for the same person or thing just for the sake of it, because it may leave the reader feeling confused, as in this newspaper report, which uses the synonyms *actor* and *thespian*:

> Actor Gerry Bentham got more than he bargained for when he strode on to the stage on his birthday last week. The 35-year-old thespian found …

Creative writing can be improved by putting your thesaurus to use. If you are writing a story, the descriptive passages can be brought more alive by researching the correct descriptive word for any situation. You may, for example, think of the word *fussy*, but if you look at the wide range of synonyms supplied for *fussy*, you can pinpoint the particular type of fussiness:

> **fussy** adjective 1 *he's very fussy about what he eats:* particular, finicky, fastidious, hard to please, faddish; informal

> pernickety, choosy, picky; Brit.
> informal **faddy**; N. Amer. informal
> persnickety. **2** *a fussy bridal
> gown:* over-elaborate, ornate,
> fancy, busy, cluttered.

You might want to describe a startling colour, and the word *bright* comes to mind, but you want a more interesting word to capture how dazzling it is; a look under *bright* will give you the option of *vibrant*, as well as *vivid*, *brilliant*, and *intense*.

At other times you may have a word in mind but know that it is not right for the context. For example, you may be writing about sticking to a rule but know that *stick to* is too informal; in this case either *abide by* or *adhere to* would be a good choice as a more formal expression.

## Solving word puzzles

A thesaurus can be used to solve crosswords or other word puzzles.

In their simplest form, many crosswords give a synonym as the clue to the answer. If the solution does not immediately come to mind, then you can refer to your thesaurus to find a range of synonyms for the clue word.

> Clue: Lively (8).
>
> Under *lively* in the thesaurus, there are forty synonyms, of which seven have eight letters, but as soon as you know, say, two of the letters in the answer, such as _ P _ _ I _ _ _ , you can pick out *spirited* as the answer.

Many crosswords are more obscure, however, and involve a degree of lateral thinking. Then the thesaurus can provide the perfect stepping stones to lead you from one idea to another.

> Clue: Mail writing as an afterthought (10).
>
> You could solve this by looking up all three main words in a thesaurus: a synonym for *mail* is *post*; a synonym for *writing* is *script*; put those together to make a synonym of *afterthought*, and you get *postscript*—the answer.

Other features can help in word games. For example, many larger thesauruses include lists of nouns such as birds, aircraft parts, and equestrian sports. These are ideal for word-search squares, as well as being useful as prompts for crossword solutions.

## Expanding your vocabulary

The main purpose of a thesaurus is to help you to find a suitable synonym on a particular occasion, but it can also help you to build your vocabulary and improve your English language skills.

It is fun to try to follow a trail from one word to another; often you will trace a circle and come back to your original headword. On the other hand, you may discover how a slight shift in sense may take you further away from your original meaning.

For example, if you first look at the entry *inaccurate*, you could next look up its given synonym *imprecise*, leading you through *approximate* to *inexact* on then to *incorrect*, and returning once more to *inaccurate*. However, you could look up *inaccurate* and then select *wrong*, which could take you to *fallacious*, then *untrue*, leading to *fabricated* and then to *invented*, each taking you further away from your original word.

In fact there is no such thing as a true synonym—a word that means exactly the same as another. The richness of the English language gives each word a slightly different shade of meaning, and using a thesaurus allows you to express yourself more powerfully than ever before.

# Finally...

We hope that this brief guide to the thesaurus and its uses will help you to get the most from it. Remember that its main purpose is to give you alternative words to use (where they exist), and that it cannot replace a dictionary for finding out what a particular word means.

Take time to browse the pages of your thesaurus, and you will discover how easy it is to find your way around it. No doubt you will be drawn into the fascinating links and chains of words that it can weave. A thesaurus serves many practical purposes, but you can also have fun just dipping into your personal treasure trove of words.

a
b
c
d
e
f
g
h
i
j
k
l
m
n
o
p
q
r
s
t
u
v
w
x
y
z

**label** noun 1 *the price is clearly stated on the label:* tag, ticket, tab, sticker, marker, docket. 2 *a designer label:* brand (name), (trade) name, trademark, make, logo. 3 *the label the media came up with for me:* designation, description, tag, name, epithet, nickname, title.
verb 1 *label each jar with the date:* tag, ticket, mark, stamp. 2 *tests labelled him an underachiever:* categorize, classify, class, describe, designate, identify, mark, stamp, brand, call, name, term, dub.

**laborious** adjective 1 *a laborious job:* arduous, hard, heavy, difficult, strenuous, gruelling, punishing, exacting, tough, onerous, burdensome, back-breaking, trying, challenging. 2 *Doug's laborious style:* laboured, strained, forced, stiff, stilted, unnatural, artificial, overwrought, heavy, ponderous.
OPPOSITES easy, effortless.

**labour** noun 1 *manual labour:* work, toil, exertion, industry, drudgery, effort; informal slog, grind. 2 *the conflict between capital and labour:* workers, employees, working people, labourers, workforce, staff, labour force. 3 *a difficult labour:* childbirth, birth, delivery.
OPPOSITES rest, management.
verb 1 *a project on which he had laboured for many years:* work (hard), toil, slave (away), grind away, struggle, strive, exert oneself; informal slog away, plug away. 2 *Newcastle laboured to break down their defence:* strive, struggle, endeavour, work, try hard, make every effort, do one's best, do one's utmost, do all one can, give one's all, go all out, fight, exert oneself; informal bend/lean over backwards, pull out all the stops.

**laboured** adjective 1 *laboured breathing:* strained, difficult, forced, laborious. 2 *a rather laboured joke:* contrived, strained, forced, unconvincing, unnatural, artificial, overdone, ponderous, over-elaborate.
OPPOSITES natural, easy.

**labourer** noun workman, worker, working man, manual worker, unskilled worker, blue-collar worker, (hired) hand, roustabout, drudge, menial; Austral./NZ rouseabout.

**lace** verb 1 *he laced up his running shoes:* fasten, do up, tie up, secure, knot. 2 *tea laced with rum:* flavour, mix, blend, fortify, strengthen, season, spice (up), liven up, doctor, adulterate; informal spike.
OPPOSITES untie.

**lack** noun *a lack of cash:* absence, want, need, deficiency, dearth, shortage, shortfall, scarcity, paucity, scarceness.
OPPOSITES abundance.
verb *she lacks judgement:* be without, be in need of, be short of, be deficient in, be low on, be pressed for; informal be strapped for.
OPPOSITES have, possess.

**lad** noun (informal) 1 *a young lad:*

boy, schoolboy, youth, youngster, juvenile, stripling; informal **kid**, **nipper**; Scottish informal **laddie**; derogatory **brat**. **2** *a hard-working lad:* (young) man; informal **guy**, **fellow**, **geezer**; Brit. informal **chap**, **bloke**; N. Amer. informal **dude**, **hombre**.

**laden** adjective loaded, burdened, weighed down, overloaded, piled high, full, packed, stuffed, crammed; informal **chock-full**, **chock-a-block**.

**lady** noun **1** *several ladies were present:* woman, female, girl; Scottish & N. English **lass**, **lassie**; N. Amer. informal **dame**. **2** *lords and ladies:* noblewoman, duchess, countess, peeress, viscountess, baroness.

**laid-back** adjective (informal) relaxed, easy-going, free and easy, casual, nonchalant, unexcitable, blasé, cool, calm, unconcerned, leisurely, unhurried; informal **unflappable**.
OPPOSITES uptight.

**lake** noun pool, pond, tarn, reservoir, lagoon, waterhole, inland sea; Scottish **loch**; Anglo-Irish **lough**; N. Amer. **bayou**.

**lame** adjective **1** *the mare was lame:* limping, hobbling, crippled, disabled, incapacitated; informal **gammy**. **2** *a lame excuse:* feeble, weak, thin, flimsy, poor, unconvincing, implausible, unlikely.
OPPOSITES sound, convincing.

**lament** verb **1** *he was lamenting the death of his daughter:* mourn, grieve, sorrow, weep, cry. **2** *entrepreneurs lamented the red tape:* complain about, bewail, bemoan, deplore, be disappointed at.
OPPOSITES celebrate, welcome.

**land** noun **1** *the lookout sighted*

*land:* dry land, terra firma, coast, coastline, shore. **2** *Lyme Park has 1323 acres of land:* grounds, fields, open space, property, territory, acres, acreage, estate, lands, real estate. **3** *many people are leaving the land:* the countryside, the country, rural areas. **4** *Tunisia is a land of variety:* country, nation, state, realm, kingdom, province, region, area, domain.
verb **1** *Allied troops landed in France:* disembark, go ashore, debark, alight, get off. **2** *the ship landed at Le Havre:* berth, dock, moor, (drop) anchor, tie up, put in. **3** *their plane landed at Chicago:* touch down, make a landing, come in to land, come down. **4** (informal) *Nick landed the job of editor:* get, obtain, acquire, secure, gain, net, win, achieve, attain, bag, carry off; informal **swing**.
OPPOSITES embark, take off.

**landlady, landlord** noun **1** *the landlady had objected to the noise:* owner, proprietor, lessor, householder, landowner. **2** *the landlord of the pub:* licensee, innkeeper, owner, hotelier, restaurateur; Brit. **publican**.
OPPOSITES tenant.

**landmark** noun **1** *one of London's most famous landmarks:* feature, sight, monument, building. **2** *the ruling was hailed as a landmark:* turning point, milestone, watershed, critical point.

**landscape** noun scenery, country, countryside, topography, terrain, view, panorama.

**landslide** noun **1** *floods and landslides:* landslip, rockfall, mudslide, avalanche. **2** *the Labour landslide:* decisive victory, runaway triumph, overwhelming majority; informal whitewash.

**lane** noun country road, track, course, trail, street, alley, alleyway, passage.

**language** noun **1** *the structure of language:* speech, speaking, conversation, talking, talk, discourse, communication, words, writing, vocabulary, text. **2** *the English language:* tongue, mother tongue, native tongue, dialect; informal lingo. **3** *the booklet is written in simple, everyday language:* wording, phrasing, phraseology, style, vocabulary, terminology, expressions, turn of phrase, parlance; informal lingo.

**languish** verb **1** *the plants languished and died:* weaken, deteriorate, decline, go downhill, wither, droop, wilt, fade, waste away. **2** *the general is languishing in prison:* waste away, rot, be abandoned, be neglected, be forgotten, suffer, lie.
OPPOSITES thrive.

**lap**[1] verb **1** *waves lapped against the sea wall:* splash, wash, swish, slosh, break. **2** *the dog lapped water out of a puddle:* drink, lick up, sup, swallow, slurp, gulp.
■ **lap something up** relish, revel in, savour, delight in, wallow in, glory in, enjoy.

**lap**[2] noun *a race of eight laps:* circuit, leg, circle, revolution, round.
verb *she lapped the other runners:* overtake, outstrip, leave behind, pass, go past, catch up with.

**lapse** noun **1** *a lapse of concentration:* failure, slip, error, mistake, blunder, fault, omission; informal slip-up. **2** *his lapse into petty crime:* decline, fall, falling, slipping, deterioration, degeneration, backsliding, regression. **3** *a lapse of time:* interval, gap, pause, interlude, lull, hiatus, break.
verb **1** *the planning permission has lapsed:* expire, become void, become invalid, run out. **2** *do not let friendships lapse:* (come to an) end, cease, stop, terminate, pass, fade, wither, die. **3** *she lapsed into silence:* revert, relapse, drift, slide, slip, sink.

**lapsed** adjective **1** *a lapsed Catholic:* non-practising, backsliding, apostate. **2** *a lapsed season ticket:* expired, void, invalid, out of date.
OPPOSITES practising, valid.

**large** adjective big, great, sizeable, substantial, considerable, extensive, voluminous, vast, huge, immense, enormous, colossal, massive, heavy, mammoth, gigantic, giant, fat, stout, bulky.
OPPOSITES small.

**largely** adverb mostly, mainly, to a large/great extent, chiefly, predominantly, primarily, principally, for the most part, in the main, typically, commonly.

**lash** verb **1** *rain lashed the window panes:* beat against, dash against, pound, batter, strike, drum. **2** *the tiger lashed his tail:* swish, flick, twitch, whip. **3** *two boats were lashed together:* fasten, bind, tie (up), tether, hitch, knot, rope.
noun *he brought the lash down*

a
b
c
d
e
f
g
h
i
j
k
l
m
n
o
p
q
r
s
t
u
v
w
x
y
z

*upon the prisoner's back:* whip, scourge, flail, birch, cane; historical cat-o'-nine-tails, cat.

■ **lash out 1** *the president lashed out at the opposition:* criticize, attack, disparage, condemn, run down; informal lay into, dis; Brit. informal slag off, have a go at. **2** *Norman lashed out with a knife:* hit out at, strike, let fly at, take a swing at, set upon/about, turn on, round on, attack; informal lay into, pitch into.

**last¹** adjective **1** *Rembrandt's last years:* final, closing, concluding, end, terminal, later, latter. **2** *the last woman in the queue:* rearmost, hindmost, endmost, furthest (back), ultimate. **3** *last year:* previous, preceding, prior, former. **4** *the last edition:* latest, most recent.
OPPOSITES first, next.
adverb *the candidate coming last is eliminated:* at the end, at/in the rear, bringing up the rear, at the back.
OPPOSITES first.
■ **at last** finally, in the end, eventually, ultimately, at long last, after a long time, in time, in (the fullness of) time.

**last²** verb **1** *the hearing lasted for six days:* continue, go on, carry on, keep on/going, take. **2** *how long will he last as manager?* survive, endure, hold on/out, keep going, persevere, persist, stay, remain; informal stick it out, hang on, go the distance. **3** *the car is built to last:* endure, wear well, stand up, bear up; informal go the distance.
OPPOSITES end, wear out.

**lasting** adjective enduring, long-lasting, long-lived, abiding, continuing, long-term, permanent, durable, stable, secure, long-standing, eternal,

undying, everlasting, unending, never-ending.
OPPOSITES ephemeral.

**late** adjective **1** *the train was late:* behind schedule, tardy, overdue, delayed. **2** *her late husband:* dead, departed, lamented, passed on/away; formal deceased. **3** *some late news:* recent, fresh, new, up to date, latter-day, current.
OPPOSITES punctual, early, living, old.
adverb *she had arrived late:* behind schedule, belatedly, tardily, at the last minute.

**lately** adverb recently, not long ago, of late, latterly, in recent times.

**later** adjective *a later chapter:* subsequent, following, succeeding, future, upcoming, to come, ensuing, next.
OPPOSITES earlier, preceding.
adverb *later, the film rights were sold:* subsequently, eventually, then, next, later on, after this/that, afterwards, at a later date, in the future, in due course, by and by, in a while, in time; formal thereafter.

**latest** adjective most recent, newest, just out, up to the minute, state-of-the-art, current; informal in, with it, trendy, hip, hot, happening, cool.
OPPOSITES old.

**latitude** noun freedom, scope, leeway, (breathing) space, flexibility, liberty, independence, free rein, licence, slack.
OPPOSITES restriction.

**latter** adjective **1** *the latter half of the season:* later, closing, end, concluding, final. **2** *the latter option:* last-mentioned, second, last, final.

OPPOSITES earlier, former.

**laugh** verb *he started to laugh:* chuckle, chortle, guffaw, giggle, titter, snigger, roar, hoot with laughter, split one's sides; informal be in stitches, be rolling in the aisles, crease up, fall about, crack up; Brit. informal kill oneself.

noun **1** *he gave a short laugh:* chuckle, chortle, guffaw, giggle, titter, snigger, roar, hoot, shriek. **2** (informal) *I entered the contest for a laugh:* joke, prank, bit of fun, jest; informal lark, hoot, scream.

■ **laugh at** ridicule, mock, deride, scoff at, jeer at, sneer at, jibe at, make fun of, poke fun at; informal take the mickey out of; Austral./NZ informal poke mullock at. ■ **laugh something off** dismiss, make a joke of, make light of, shrug off, brush aside, scoff at; informal pooh-pooh.

**laughter** noun **1** *the laughter subsided:* laughing, chuckling, chortling, guffawing, giggling, tittering, sniggering. **2** *a source of laughter:* amusement, entertainment, humour, mirth, merriment, gaiety, hilarity, jollity, fun.

**launch** verb **1** *a chair was launched at him:* propel, throw, hurl, fling, pitch, lob, let fly, fire, shoot; informal chuck, heave, sling. **2** *the government launched a new campaign:* start, begin, initiate, put in place, set up, inaugurate, introduce; informal kick off.

**lavatory** noun toilet, WC, convenience, privy, latrine; Brit. cloakroom; N. Amer. washroom, bathroom, rest room, men's/ ladies' room, comfort station; informal little girls'/boys' room, smallest room; Brit. informal loo, bog, the Ladies, the Gents, khazi; N. Amer. informal can, john; Austral./NZ informal dunny.

**lavish** adjective **1** *a lavish apartment:* sumptuous, luxurious, gorgeous, costly, expensive, opulent, grand, splendid, rich, fancy; informal posh. **2** *he was lavish with his hospitality:* generous, liberal, bountiful, unstinting, unsparing, free, munificent, extravagant, prodigal. **3** *lavish praise:* extravagant, excessive, wasteful, prodigal, fulsome, effusive. **4** *lavish amounts of champagne:* abundant, copious, plentiful, liberal, prolific, generous; literary plenteous.
OPPOSITES meagre, mean, frugal.
verb *she lavished money on her children:* shower, heap, pour, deluge, throw at, squander, dissipate.
OPPOSITES begrudge, stint.

**law** noun **1** *the law:* legislation, constitution, rules, regulations, legal code. **2** *a new law:* regulation, statute, act, bill, decree, edict, rule, ruling, dictum, command, order, directive, dictate, diktat, fiat, by-law; N. Amer. formal ordinance. **3** *the laws of the game:* rule, regulation, principle, convention, instruction, guideline. **4** *a moral law:* principle, rule, precept, commandment, belief, creed, credo, maxim, tenet, doctrine, canon.

**lawyer** noun legal adviser, legal representative, solicitor, barrister, advocate, counsel, Queen's Counsel, QC; N. Amer. attorney, counselor(-at-law); informal brief, legal eagle.

**lay¹** verb **1** *Curtis laid the*

a
b
c
d
e
f
g
h
i
j
k
**l**
m
n
o
p
q
r
s
t
u
v
w
x
y
z

*newspaper on the table:* put (down), place, set (down), deposit, rest, position, shove; informal stick, dump, park, plonk; Brit. informal bung. **2** *I'd lay money on it:* bet, wager, gamble, stake. **3** *we laid plans for the next voyage:* devise, arrange, prepare, work out, hatch, design, plan, scheme, plot, conceive, put together, draw up, produce, develop, formulate; informal cook up.
■ **lay something down 1** *they laid down their weapons:* relinquish, surrender, give up, abandon. **2** *the ground rules have been laid down:* formulate, set down, draw up, frame, prescribe, ordain, dictate, decree, enact, pass, decide, determine. ■ **lay something in** stock up with/on, stockpile, store (up), amass, hoard, stow (away), put aside/away/by, garner, squirrel away; informal salt away, stash away. ■ **lay off** (informal) give up, stop, refrain from, abstain from, desist from, cut out; informal pack in, leave off, quit. ■ **lay someone off** make redundant, dismiss, let go, discharge, give notice to; informal sack, fire. ■ **lay something on** provide, supply, furnish, line up, organize, prepare, produce, make available; informal fix up. ■ **lay someone out** (informal) knock out/down, knock unconscious, fell, floor, flatten; informal KO, kayo; Brit. informal knock for six.

**lay²** adjective **1** *a lay preacher:* non-ordained, non-clerical. **2** *a lay audience:* non-expert, non-professional, non-specialist, non-technical, amateur, unqualified, untrained.

**layer** noun sheet, stratum, level, tier, seam, coat, coating, film,

covering, blanket, skin.

**layout** noun arrangement, design, plan, formation, format, configuration, composition, organization, geography, structure.

**laze** verb idle, relax, unwind, do nothing, loaf (around/about), lounge (around/about), loll (around/about), lie (around/about), take it easy; informal hang around/round, veg (out).

**lazy** adjective **1** *a lazy worker:* idle, indolent, slothful, bone idle, work-shy. **2** *a lazy stream:* slow, slow-moving, languid, leisurely, lethargic, sluggish.
OPPOSITES industrious, fast.

**lead** verb **1** *Michelle led them into the house:* guide, conduct, show (the way), usher, escort, steer, shepherd, accompany, see, take. **2** *he led us to believe they were lying:* cause, induce, prompt, move, persuade, drive, make. **3** *she led a coalition of radicals:* control, preside over, head, command, govern, run, manage, rule, be in charge of; informal head up. **4** *Rangers were leading at half-time:* be ahead, be winning, be (out) in front, be in the lead, be first. **5** *the champion was leading the field:* be ahead of, head, outrun, outstrip, outpace, leave behind, outdo, outclass, beat. **6** *I just want to lead a normal life:* live, have, spend, pass, enjoy.
OPPOSITES follow.

noun **1** *I was in the lead early on:* first place, winning position, vanguard. **2** *Newcastle built up a 3-0 lead:* margin, advantage, gap, edge, interval. **3** *sixth-formers should give a lead to younger pupils:* example, model, pattern,

standard, guidance, direction, role model. **4** *playing the lead:* leading role, star/starring role, title role, principal role. **5** *a dog on a lead:* leash, tether, rope, chain. **6** *detectives were following up a new lead:* clue, pointer, hint, tip, tip-off, suggestion, indication, sign.
**adjective** *the lead position:* leading, first, top, foremost, front, pole, head, chief, principal, premier.
■ **lead to** result in, cause, bring on/about, give rise to, create, produce, occasion, effect, generate, contribute to, promote, provoke, stir up, spark off.

**leader** noun chief, head, principal, commander, captain, controller, superior, chairman, chair, director, manager, superintendent, supervisor, overseer, master, mistress, prime minister, president, premier, governor, ruler, monarch, sovereign; informal boss, skipper, gaffer, guv'nor, number one.
OPPOSITES follower, supporter.

**leadership** noun **1** *the leadership of the Party:* control, rule, command, dominion, headship, directorship, premiership, chairmanship, governorship, captaincy. **2** *firm leadership:* guidance, direction, authority, management, supervision, government.

**leading** adjective main, chief, top, front, major, prime, principal, foremost, key, central, dominant, most powerful, most important, greatest, pre-eminent, star.
OPPOSITES subordinate, minor.

**leaf** noun *a folder of loose leaves:* page, sheet, folio.

**verb** *he leafed through the documents:* flick, flip, thumb, skim, browse, glance, riffle, scan, run one's eye over, peruse.

**leaflet** noun pamphlet, booklet, brochure, handbill, circular, flyer, handout; N. Amer. folder, dodger.

**league** noun **1** *a league of nations:* alliance, confederation, confederacy, federation, union, association, coalition, consortium, affiliation, cooperative, partnership, fellowship, syndicate. **2** *the store is not in the same league:* class, group, category, level, standard.
■ **in league** collaborating, cooperating, in alliance, allied, conspiring, hand in glove; informal in cahoots.

**leak** verb **1** *oil was leaking from the tanker:* seep, escape, ooze, drip, dribble, drain, run. **2** *civil servants leaking information:* disclose, divulge, reveal, make public, tell, expose, release, bring into the open.
noun **1** *check that there are no leaks in the bag:* hole, opening, puncture, perforation, gash, slit, break, crack, fissure, rupture, tear. **2** *a gas leak:* escape, leakage, discharge, seepage. **3** *leaks to the media:* disclosure, revelation, exposé.

**lean**[1] verb **1** *Polly leaned against the door:* rest, recline. **2** *trees leaning in the wind:* slant, incline, bend, tilt, slope, tip, list. **3** *he leans towards existentialist philosophy:* tend, incline, gravitate, have a preference for, have an affinity with. **4** *someone to lean on:* depend, rely, count, bank, trust in.

a
b
c
d
e
f
g
h
i
j
k
l
m
n
o
p
q
r
s
t
u
v
w
x
y
z

**lean²** adjective **1** *a tall, lean man:* slim, thin, slender, spare, spindly, wiry, lanky. **2** *a lean harvest:* meagre, sparse, poor, mean, inadequate, insufficient, paltry.
OPPOSITES fat, abundant.

**leaning** noun inclination, tendency, bent, propensity, penchant, preference, predisposition, predilection.

**leap** verb **1** *he leapt over the gate:* jump, vault, spring, bound, hop, clear. **2** *profits leapt by 55%:* rise, jump, soar, rocket, skyrocket, shoot up.
noun *a leap of 33%:* rise, surge, upsurge, upswing, upturn.

**learn** verb **1** *learn a foreign language:* acquire, grasp, master, take in, absorb, assimilate, digest, familiarize oneself with, be taught; informal get the hang of. **2** *she learnt the poem:* memorize, learn by heart, commit to memory, learn parrot-fashion, get off/down pat. **3** *he learned that the school would be closing:* discover, find out, become aware, be informed, hear, understand, gather; informal get wind of the fact.

**learned** adjective scholarly, erudite, knowledgeable, widely read, cultured, intellectual, academic, literary, bookish, highbrow; informal brainy.
OPPOSITES ignorant.

**learner** noun beginner, novice, starter, trainee, apprentice, pupil, student, fledgling.
OPPOSITES expert, veteran.

**learning** noun study, knowledge, education, schooling, tuition, teaching, scholarship, erudition, research, understanding, wisdom.
OPPOSITES ignorance.

**lease** verb **1** *the film crew leased a large hangar:* rent, hire, charter. **2** *they leased the mill to a reputable family:* rent (out), let (out), hire (out), charter (out), loan (out).

**leave¹** verb **1** *I left the hotel:* go away from, depart from, withdraw from, retire from, take oneself off from, take one's leave of, pull out of, quit, escape from, flee, abandon, desert, vacate; informal push off, shove off, clear out/off, split, make tracks. **2** *the next morning we left for Leicester:* set off, head, make, set sail, get going. **3** *he's left his wife:* abandon, desert, jilt, leave in the lurch, leave high and dry, throw over; informal dump, ditch, walk/run out on. **4** *he left his job in November:* resign from, retire from, step down from, withdraw from, pull out of, give up; informal quit, jack in. **5** *she left her handbag on a bus:* leave behind, forget, lose, mislay. **6** *I thought I'd leave it to the experts:* entrust, hand over, pass on, refer, delegate. **7** *he left her £100,000:* bequeath, will, endow, hand down.
OPPOSITES arrive.
■ **leave someone/something out 1** *Adam left out the address:* miss out, omit, overlook, forget, skip, miss. **2** *he was left out of the England squad:* exclude, omit, drop, pass over.

**leave²** noun **1** *the judge granted leave to appeal:* permission, consent, authorization, sanction, dispensation, approval, clearance, blessing, agreement, assent; informal the go-ahead, the green light. **2** *he was on leave:* holiday, vacation, break, furlough, sabbatical, leave of absence; informal vac.

**lecture** noun **1** *a lecture on children's literature:* speech, talk, address, discourse, presentation, oration. **2** *Dave got a severe lecture:* reprimand, scolding, rebuke, reproach; informal dressing-down, telling-off, talking-to, tongue-lashing.
verb **1** *he lectures on drugs:* talk, speak, discourse, hold forth, teach; informal spout, sound off. **2** *he was lectured by the headmaster:* reprimand, scold, rebuke, reproach, take to task; informal tell off, bawl out; Brit. informal tick off, carpet.
OPPOSITES praise.

**leeway** noun freedom, scope, latitude, space, room, liberty, flexibility, licence, free hand, free rein.

**left** adjective left-hand, sinistral; Nautical port.
OPPOSITES right, starboard.

**left-wing** adjective socialist, communist, leftist, Labour; informal Commie, lefty, red, pinko.
OPPOSITES right-wing, conservative.

**leg** noun *the first leg of a European tour:* part, stage, section, phase, stretch, lap.

**legacy** noun **1** *a legacy from a great aunt:* bequest, inheritance, endowment, gift, birthright, estate, heirloom. **2** *the legacy of the war:* consequence, effect, repercussion, aftermath, by-product, result.

**legal** adjective **1** *a legal tax-avoidance scheme:* lawful, legitimate, within the law, legalized, valid, permissible, permitted, allowable, allowed, above board, acceptable, constitutional; informal legit. **2** *the legal profession:* judicial,

juridical, forensic.
OPPOSITES illegal.

**legend** noun **1** *the Arthurian legends:* myth, saga, epic, folk tale, folk story, fable, lore, folklore, mythology, folk tradition. **2** *pop legends:* celebrity, star, superstar, icon, phenomenon, luminary, giant, hero; informal celeb, megastar. **3** *the wording of the legend:* caption, inscription, dedication, slogan, heading, title.

**legendary** adjective **1** *legendary kings:* fabled, heroic, traditional, fairy-tale, storybook, mythical, mythological. **2** *a legendary figure in the trade-union movement:* famous, celebrated, famed, renowned, acclaimed, illustrious, esteemed, honoured, exalted, venerable, distinguished, great, eminent.
OPPOSITES historical, insignificant.

**legion** noun horde, throng, multitude, crowd, mass, mob, gang, swarm, flock, herd, army.

**legislation** noun law, rules, rulings, regulations, acts, bills, statutes; N. Amer. formal ordinances.

**legitimate** adjective **1** *legitimate gambling:* legal, lawful, authorized, permitted, sanctioned, approved, licensed; informal legit. **2** *the legitimate heir:* rightful, lawful, genuine, authentic, real, true, proper. **3** *legitimate grounds for unease:* valid, sound, admissible, acceptable, well founded, justifiable, reasonable, sensible, just, fair, bona fide.
OPPOSITES illegal, invalid.

**leisure** noun free time, spare time, time off, rest, recreation, relaxation.

a b c d e f g h i j k l m n o p q r s t u v w x y z

a
b
c
d
e
f
g
h
i
j
k
**l**
m
n
o
p
q
r
s
t
u
v
w
x
y
z

OPPOSITES work.

**leisurely** adjective unhurried, relaxed, easy, gentle, sedate, comfortable, restful, undemanding, slow.
OPPOSITES hurried.

**lend** verb 1 *I'll lend you my towel:* loan, let someone use, advance; Brit. informal sub. 2 *these examples lend weight to his assertions:* add, impart, give, bestow, confer, provide, supply, furnish, contribute.
OPPOSITES borrow.

**length** noun 1 *the whole length of the valley:* extent, distance, span, reach, area, expanse, stretch, range, scope. 2 *a considerable length of time:* period, duration, stretch, span. 3 *a length of blue silk:* piece, strip.
■ at length 1 *he spoke at length:* for a long time, for ages, for hours, interminably, endlessly, ceaselessly, unendingly. 2 *his search led him, at length, to Seattle:* eventually, in time, finally, at (long) last, in the end, ultimately.

**lengthen** verb 1 *he lengthened his stride:* elongate, make longer, extend, expand, widen, broaden, enlarge. 2 *you'll need to lengthen the cooking time:* prolong, make longer, increase, extend, expand, protract, stretch out.
OPPOSITES shorten.

**lengthy** adjective (very) long, long-lasting, protracted, extended, long-drawn-out, prolonged, interminable, time-consuming, long-winded.
OPPOSITES short.

**lenient** adjective merciful, forgiving, forbearing, tolerant, charitable, humane, indulgent, magnanimous.
OPPOSITES severe.

**lessen** verb 1 *exercise lessens the risk of heart disease:* reduce, make less/smaller, minimize, decrease, attenuate, narrow, moderate. 2 *the pain began to lessen:* grow less, grow smaller, decrease, diminish, decline, subside, slacken, abate, fade, die down, let up, ease off, tail off, drop (off/away), dwindle, ebb, wane, recede.
OPPOSITES increase.

**lesser** adjective 1 *a lesser offence:* less important, minor, secondary, subsidiary, peripheral. 2 *you look down at us lesser mortals:* subordinate, minor, inferior, second-class, subservient, lowly, humble.
OPPOSITES greater, superior.

**lesson** noun 1 *a maths lesson:* class, session, seminar, tutorial, lecture, period. 2 *Stuart's accident should be a lesson to all parents:* warning, deterrent, caution, example, message, moral.

**let** verb 1 *let him sleep for now:* allow, permit, give permission to, give leave to, authorize, license, empower, enable, entitle. 2 *they've let their flat:* rent (out), let out, lease, hire (out).
OPPOSITES prevent, prohibit.
■ let someone down fail, disappoint, disillusion, abandon, desert, leave in the lurch. ■ let go release (one's hold on), loose one's hold on, relinquish. ■ let something off detonate, discharge, fire, set off, fire (off), launch. ■ let someone off 1 (informal) *I'll let you off this time:* pardon, forgive, acquit, absolve, exonerate, clear, vindicate; informal let someone off the

hook. **2** *he let me off work:* excuse from, exempt from, spare from. ■ **let something out 1** *I let out a cry of triumph:* utter, emit, give (vent to), produce, issue, express, voice, release. **2** *she let out that he'd given her a lift home:* reveal, make known, tell, disclose, mention, divulge, let slip, give away, let it be known, blurt out. ■ **let someone out** release, liberate, (set) free, let go, discharge, set/turn loose. ■ **let up** (informal) **1** *the rain has let up.* See **LESSEN** sense 2. **2** *you never let up, do you?* relax, ease up/off, slow down, pause, break (off), take a break, rest, stop.

**lethal** adjective fatal, deadly, mortal, terminal, life-threatening, murderous, poisonous, toxic, noxious, venomous, dangerous.
OPPOSITES harmless, safe.

**letter** noun **1** *capital letters:* character, sign, symbol, figure. **2** *she received a letter:* message, note, line, missive, dispatch, communication, correspondence, post, mail.

**level** adjective **1** *a smooth and level surface:* flat, smooth, even, uniform, plane, flush, horizontal. **2** *he kept his voice level:* steady, even, uniform, regular, constant. **3** *the scores were level:* equal, even, drawn, tied, all square, neck and neck, level pegging, on a par, evenly matched; informal even-stevens. **4** *his eyes were level with hers:* at the same height, on a level, in line.
OPPOSITES uneven, unsteady, unequal.
noun **1** *the post is at a senior level:* rank, position, degree, grade, stage, standard, class, group, set, classification. **2** *a high level of employment:* quantity, amount, extent, measure, degree, volume.
verb **1** *tilt the tin to level the mixture:* even off/out, flatten, smooth (out). **2** *bulldozers levelled the building:* raze (to the ground), demolish, flatten, bulldoze, destroy. **3** *Carl levelled the score:* equalize, equal, even (up), make level. **4** *he levelled his pistol at me:* aim, point, direct, train, focus, turn.
■ **on the level** (informal) genuine, straight, honest, above board, fair, true, sincere, straightforward; informal upfront; N. Amer. informal on the up and up.

**lever** noun *the lid can be removed with a lever:* handle, arm, switch, crowbar, bar, jemmy.
verb *he levered the door open:* prise, force, wrench; N. Amer. pry; informal jemmy.

**leverage** noun **1** *the long handles provide increased leverage:* force, purchase, grip, hold, anchorage. **2** *they have significant leverage in negotiations:* influence, power, authority, weight, sway, pull, control, say, advantage, pressure; informal clout, muscle, teeth.

**levy** verb impose, charge, exact, raise, collect.
noun tax, tariff, toll, excise, duty.

**liability** noun **1** *they have big liabilities:* obligations, debts, arrears, dues, commitments. **2** *he's become a bit of a liability:* hindrance, encumbrance, burden, handicap, nuisance, inconvenience, embarrassment, impediment, disadvantage,

millstone.
OPPOSITES asset.

**liable** adjective **1** *they are liable for negligence*: responsible, accountable, answerable, chargeable, blameworthy, at fault, culpable, guilty. **2** *my income is liable to fluctuate wildly*: likely, inclined, tending, apt, prone, given. **3** *areas liable to flooding*: exposed, prone, subject, susceptible, vulnerable, in danger of, at risk of.

**liaise** verb cooperate, collaborate, communicate, network, interface, link up.

**liaison** noun **1** *the branches work in close liaison*: cooperation, contact, association, connection, collaboration, communication, alliance, partnership. **2** *Dave was my White House liaison*: intermediary, mediator, middleman, contact, link, go-between. **3** *a secret liaison*: love affair, relationship, romance, attachment, fling.

**liar** noun fibber, deceiver, perjurer, dissembler, faker, hoaxer, impostor.

**libel** noun *she sued two newspapers for libel*: defamation (of character), character assassination, calumny, misrepresentation, scandalmongering, aspersions, malicious gossip, slur, smear; informal mud-slinging.
verb *she claimed the magazine had libelled her*: defame, malign, blacken someone's name, sully someone's reputation, smear, cast aspersions on, drag someone's name through the mud/mire, denigrate; N. Amer. slur.

**liberal** adjective **1** *the values of a liberal society*: tolerant, unprejudiced, broad-minded, open-minded, enlightened, permissive, free (and easy), easy-going, libertarian, indulgent, lenient. **2** *a liberal social agenda*: progressive, advanced, modern, forward-looking, forward-thinking, enlightened, reformist, radical; informal go-ahead. **3** *a liberal interpretation of divorce laws*: flexible, broad, loose, rough, free, non-literal. **4** *liberal coatings of paint*: abundant, copious, ample, plentiful, generous, lavish. **5** *they were liberal with their cash*: generous, open-handed, unsparing, unstinting, lavish, free, munificent.
OPPOSITES reactionary, strict, miserly.

**liberate** verb (set) free, release, let out, let go, set loose, save, rescue, emancipate, enfranchise.
OPPOSITES imprison, enslave.

**liberty** noun freedom, independence, immunity, self-determination, autonomy, emancipation, sovereignty, self-government, self-rule, self determination, civil liberties, human rights.
OPPOSITES constraint, slavery.
■ at liberty **1** *he was at liberty for three months*: free, loose, on the loose, at large, on the run, out. **2** *I am not at liberty to say*: free, able, entitled, permitted.

**licence** noun **1** *a driving licence*: permit, certificate, document, documentation, authorization, warrant, credentials, pass, papers. **2** *they manufacture footwear under licence*: franchise, consent, sanction, warrant, charter, concession. **3** *the army have too much* *licence:* freedom, liberty, free rein, latitude, independence, scope, carte blanche; informal a blank cheque. **4** *poetic licence:* disregard, inventiveness, invention, creativity, imagination, fancy, freedom.

**license** verb permit, allow, authorize, grant/give authority to, grant/give permission to, certify, empower, entitle, enable, sanction.
OPPOSITES ban.

**lid** noun cover, top, cap, covering.

**lie**[1] noun *it was a lie:* untruth, falsehood, fib, fabrication, deception, invention, (piece of) fiction, falsification, white lie; informal tall story, whopper; humorous terminological inexactitude.
OPPOSITES truth.
verb *he had lied to the police:* tell a lie, tell an untruth, fib, dissemble, tell a white lie, perjure oneself.

**lie**[2] verb **1** *he was lying on the bed:* recline, lie down/back, be recumbent, be prostrate, be supine, be prone, be stretched out, sprawl, rest, repose, lounge, loll. **2** *her handbag lay on the chair:* be, be situated, be positioned, be located, be placed, be found, be sited, be arranged, rest.
OPPOSITES stand.

**life** noun **1** *the joy of giving life to a child:* existence, being, living, animation, sentience, creation, viability. **2** *life on Earth:* living beings/creatures, human/animal/plant life, fauna, flora, the ecosystem, the biosphere, the ecosphere. **3** *an easy life:* way of life, lifestyle, situation, fate, lot. **4** *the last nine months of his life:* lifetime, lifespan, days, time

(on earth), existence. **5** *the life of a Parliament:* duration, lifetime, existence. **6** *he is full of life:* vitality, animation, liveliness, vivacity, verve, high spirits, exuberance, zest, enthusiasm, energy, vigour, dynamism, elan, gusto, bounce, spirit, fire. **7** *a life of Chopin:* biography, autobiography, life story/history, chronicle, account, memoirs, diary.
OPPOSITES death.

**lifestyle** noun way of life, life, situation, conduct, behaviour, ways, habits, mores.

**lifetime** noun lifespan, life, days, time (on earth), existence, career.

**lift** verb **1** *lift the pack on to your back:* raise, hoist, heave, haul up, heft, raise up/aloft, elevate, hold high, pick up, grab, take up, winch up, jack up; informal hump. **2** *the fog had lifted:* clear, rise, disperse, dissipate, disappear, vanish, dissolve. **3** *the ban has been lifted:* cancel, remove, withdraw, revoke, rescind, end, stop, terminate.
OPPOSITES drop, put down.
noun **1** *give me a lift up:* push, hand, heave, thrust, shove. **2** *he gave me a lift to the airport:* ride, run, drive. **3** *that goal will give his confidence a real lift:* boost, fillip, impetus, encouragement, spur, push; informal shot in the arm.
■ **lift off** take off, become airborne, be launched, take to the air, blast off.

**light**[1] noun **1** *the light of the candles:* illumination, brightness, shining, gleam, brilliance, radiance, glow, blaze, glare. **2** *there was a light on in the hall:* lamp, lantern, torch,

beacon, candle, bulb. **3** *we'll be driving in the light:* daylight, daytime, day, natural light, sunlight.
OPPOSITES darkness.
**adjective 1** *a light bedroom:* bright, well lit, sunny. **2** *light blue:* pale, pastel, delicate, subtle, insipid, faint.
OPPOSITES dark.

**light²** adjective **1** *it's light and compact:* lightweight, portable, underweight. **2** *a light cotton dress:* flimsy, lightweight, thin, floaty, gauzy, diaphanous. **3** *she is light on her feet:* nimble, agile, lithe, graceful, quick, sprightly. **4** *a light dinner:* small, modest, simple, insubstantial, quick. **5** *light duties:* easy, simple, undemanding, untaxing; informal cushy. **6** *light reading:* entertaining, lightweight, diverting, undemanding, middle-of-the-road, mainstream, frivolous, superficial, trivial. **7** *a light touch:* gentle, delicate, dainty, soft, faint, careful, sensitive, subtle.
OPPOSITES heavy.

**lighten¹** verb **1** *the sky was beginning to lighten:* become/grow/get lighter, brighten. **2** *the first touch of dawn lightened the sky:* brighten, make brighter, light up, illuminate. **3** *he used lemon juice to lighten his hair:* make lighter, whiten, bleach, blanch.
OPPOSITES darken.

**lighten²** verb **1** *lightening the burden of taxation:* reduce, lessen, decrease, diminish, ease, alleviate, relieve. **2** *an attempt to lighten her mood:* cheer (up), brighten, gladden, lift, boost, buoy (up), revive, restore,

revitalize.
OPPOSITES increase, depress.

**lightly** adverb **1** *Maisie kissed him lightly on the cheek:* softly, gently, faintly, delicately. **2** *season very lightly:* sparingly, sparsely, moderately, delicately, subtly. **3** *her views are not to be dismissed lightly:* carelessly, airily, readily, heedlessly, uncaringly, unthinkingly, thoughtlessly, flippantly.
OPPOSITES hard, heavily, seriously.

**lightweight** adjective **1** *a lightweight jacket:* thin, light, flimsy, insubstantial, summery. **2** *lightweight entertainment:* trivial, insubstantial, superficial, shallow, undemanding, frivolous.
OPPOSITES heavy, serious.

**like¹** verb **1** *I like him:* be fond of, have a soft spot for, think well/highly of, admire, respect, be attracted to, fancy, find attractive, be keen on, be taken with; informal rate. **2** *she likes gardening:* enjoy, have a taste for, have a liking for, be partial to, find/take pleasure in, be keen on, appreciate, love, adore, relish; informal have a thing about, be into, be mad about/for, be hooked on. **3** *feel free to say what you like:* choose, please, wish, want, see/think fit, care to, will.
OPPOSITES hate.

**like²** preposition **1** *you're just like a teacher:* similar to, the same as, identical to, akin to, resembling. **2** *the figure landed like a cat:* in the manner of, in the same way/manner as, in a similar way to. **3** *big cities, like Birmingham:* such as, for example, for instance, in particular, namely, viz.

**4** *Richard sounded mean, which isn't like him:* characteristic of, typical of, in character with.
OPPOSITES unlike.

**likelihood** noun probability, chance, prospect, possibility, odds, risk, threat, danger, hope, promise.

**likely** adjective **1** *it seemed likely that a scandal would break:* probable, (distinctly) possible, odds-on, plausible, imaginable; informal on the cards. **2** *a likely explanation:* plausible, reasonable, feasible, acceptable, believable, credible, tenable.
OPPOSITES improbable, unbelievable.

**liken** verb compare, equate, set beside.
OPPOSITES contrast.

**likeness** noun **1** *her likeness to Anne is quite uncanny:* resemblance, similarity, correspondence. **2** *a likeness of the president:* representation, image, depiction, portrayal, picture, drawing, sketch, painting, portrait, photograph, study.
OPPOSITES dissimilarity.

**likewise** adverb **1** *an ambush was out of the question, likewise poison:* also, equally, in addition, too, as well, to boot, besides, moreover, furthermore. **2** *encourage your family and friends to do likewise:* the same, similarly, correspondingly.
OPPOSITES differently.

**liking** noun fondness, love, affection, penchant, attachment, taste, passion, preference, partiality, predilection.
OPPOSITES dislike.

**limb** noun arm, leg, wing, appendage; archaic member.

**limelight** noun attention, interest, scrutiny, the public eye/gaze, the glare of publicity, prominence, the spotlight, fame, celebrity.
OPPOSITES obscurity.

**limit** noun **1** *the city limits:* boundary (line), border, frontier, edge, perimeter, margin. **2** *a limit of 4,500 supporters:* maximum, ceiling, upper limit.
verb *the pressure to limit costs:* restrict, curb, cap, (hold in) check, restrain, regulate, control, govern.

**limitation** noun **1** *a limitation on the number of newcomers:* restriction, curb, restraint, control, check. **2** *he is aware of his own limitations:* imperfection, flaw, defect, failing, shortcoming, weak point, deficiency, frailty, weakness.
OPPOSITES strength.

**limited** adjective restricted, finite, small, tight, slight, in short supply, short, meagre, scanty, sparse, inadequate, insufficient, paltry, poor, minimal.
OPPOSITES limitless, ample.

**limp**[1] verb *she limped out of the house:* hobble, hop, lurch, stagger, shuffle, shamble.

**limp**[2] adjective *a limp handshake:* soft, flaccid, loose, slack, lax, floppy, drooping, droopy, sagging.
OPPOSITES firm.

**line** noun **1** *he drew a line through the name:* stroke, dash, score, underline, underscore, slash, stripe, strip, band, belt; Brit. oblique. **2** *there were lines round her eyes:* wrinkle, furrow, crease, crinkle, crow's foot. **3** *the classic lines of the*

*Bentley:* contour, outline, configuration, shape, design, profile. **4** *the county line:* boundary, limit, border, frontier, touchline, margin, perimeter. **5** *the clothes line:* cord, rope, cable, wire, thread, string. **6** *a line of soldiers:* file, rank, column, string, train, procession, row, queue; Brit. informal crocodile. **7** *their line of flight:* course, route, track, path, trajectory.
**verb 1** *her face was lined with age:* furrow, wrinkle, crease. **2** *the driveway was lined by poplars:* border, edge, fringe, bound.
■ **in line 1** *standing in line for food:* in a queue, in a row, in a file. **2** *the adverts are in line with the editorial style:* in agreement, in accord, in accordance, in harmony, in step, in compliance. **3** *in line with the goal:* aligned, level, alongside, abreast, side by side. ■ **in line for** *a candidate for, in the running for, due for;* informal up for. ■ **line up** form a queue/line, queue up, fall in. ■ **line someone/something up** assemble, get together, organize, prepare, arrange, fix up, lay on, book, schedule, timetable.

**lined¹** adjective **1** *lined paper:* ruled, feint, striped, banded. **2** *his lined face:* wrinkled, wrinkly, furrowed, wizened.
OPPOSITES plain, smooth.

**lined²** adjective *lined curtains:* covered, backed, padded, insulated, sealed.

**line-up** noun **1** *a star-studded line-up:* cast, bill, programme. **2** *United's line-up:* team, squad, side, configuration.

**linger** verb **1** *the crowd lingered:*

wait (around), stand (around), remain, loiter; informal stick around, hang around/round. **2** *the infection can linger for years:* persist, continue, remain, stay, endure, carry on, last.
OPPOSITES vanish.

**lining** noun backing, facing, padding, insulation.

**link** noun **1** *the links between transport and the environment:* connection, relationship, association, linkage, tie-up. **2** *their links with the labour movement:* bond, tie, attachment, connection, association, affiliation.
**verb 1** *four boxes were linked together:* join, connect, fasten, attach, bind, secure, fix, tie, couple, yoke. **2** *the evidence linking him with the body:* associate, connect, relate, bracket.
OPPOSITES separate.

**lip** noun *the lip of the crater:* edge, rim, brim, border, verge, brink.

**liquid** noun *a vat of liquid:* fluid, moisture, liquor, solution, juice, sap.
OPPOSITES solid.
**adjective** *liquid fuels:* fluid, liquefied, melted, molten, thawed, dissolved.
OPPOSITES solid.

**liquor** noun **1** *alcoholic liquor:* alcohol, spirits, (alcoholic) drink; informal booze, the hard stuff, hooch, moonshine. **2** *strain the liquor into the sauce:* stock, broth, bouillon, juice, liquid.

**list¹** noun *a list of the world's wealthiest people:* catalogue, inventory, record, register, roll, file, index, directory, checklist.
**verb** *the accounts are listed*

*below:* record, register, enter, itemize, enumerate, catalogue, file, log, minute, categorize, inventory, classify, group, sort, rank, index.

**list²** verb *the boat listed to one side:* lean (over), tilt, tip, heel (over), pitch, incline, slant, slope, bank.

**listen** verb **1** *are you listening?* pay attention, be attentive, attend, concentrate, keep one's ears open, prick up one's ears; informal be all ears. **2** *policymakers should listen to popular opinion:* heed, take heed of, take notice/note of, bear in mind, take into consideration/account.

**literal** adjective strict, technical, concrete, original, true.
OPPOSITES figurative.

**literary** adjective **1** *literary works:* artistic, poetic, dramatic. **2** *her literary friends:* scholarly, intellectual, academic, bookish, erudite.

**literate** adjective (well) educated, well read, widely read, scholarly, learned, knowledgeable, cultured, cultivated, well informed.
OPPOSITES ignorant.

**literature** noun **1** *English literature:* writing, poetry, drama, prose. **2** *the literature on prototype theory:* publications, reports, studies, material. **3** *election literature:* documentation, material, publicity, blurb, propaganda, advertising; informal bumf.

**litigation** noun legal/judicial proceedings, legal action, lawsuit, legal dispute, legal case, prosecution, indictment.

**litter** noun **1** *never drop litter:* rubbish, refuse, junk, waste, debris; N. Amer. trash, garbage. **2** *the litter of glasses around*

*her:* clutter, jumble, muddle, mess, heap; informal shambles.
verb *clothes littered the floor:* cover, clutter up, pepper.

**little** adjective **1** *a little writing desk:* small, compact, miniature, tiny, toy, baby, undersized, dwarf, midget; Scottish wee; informal teeny-weeny; Brit. informal titchy, dinky; N. Amer. informal vest-pocket. **2** *a little man:* short, small, slight, petite, diminutive, tiny; Scottish wee; informal teeny-weeny, pint-sized. **3** *my little sister:* young, younger, baby. **4** *a little while:* brief, short, quick, hasty, cursory. **5** *a few little problems:* minor, unimportant, insignificant, trivial, trifling, petty, paltry, inconsequential.
OPPOSITES big, large, elder, major.

determiner *they have little political influence:* hardly any, not much, scant, limited, restricted, modest, little or no, minimal, negligible.
OPPOSITES considerable.

adverb **1** *he is little known as a teacher:* hardly, barely, scarcely, not much, only slightly. **2** *this disease is little seen nowadays:* rarely, seldom, infrequently, hardly (ever), scarcely ever, not much.
OPPOSITES well, often.

■ a little **1** *add a little water:* some, a bit of, a touch of, a dash of, a taste of, a spot of, a hint of, a dribble of, a splash of, a pinch of, a sprinkling of, a speck of; informal a smidgen of, a tad of. **2** *after a little, Oliver came in:* a short time, a while, a bit, an interval, a short period, a minute, a moment, a second, an instant; informal a sec, a mo, a jiffy. **3** *this reminds me a little*

a
b
c
d
e
f
g
h
i
j
k
**l**
m
n
o
p
q
r
s
t
u
v
w
x
y
z

*of the Adriatic:* slightly, somewhat, a little bit, quite, to some degree.

**live¹ verb 1** *the greatest mathematician who ever lived:* exist, be alive, be, have life, breathe, draw breath, walk the earth. **2** *I live in London:* reside, have one's home, lodge, inhabit, occupy, populate; Scottish stay. **3** *she had lived a difficult life:* experience, spend, pass, lead, have, go through, undergo. **4** *Freddy lived by scavenging:* survive, make a living, eke out a living, subsist, support oneself, sustain oneself, make ends meet, keep body and soul together.
OPPOSITES die, be dead.

**live² adjective 1** *live bait:* living, alive, conscious. **2** *a live rail:* electrified, charged, powered up, active, switched on. **3** *a live grenade:* unexploded, explosive, active, primed. **4** *a live issue:* topical, current, controversial, burning, pressing, important, relevant.
OPPOSITES dead, inanimate.

**livelihood noun** (source of) income, means of support, living, subsistence, bread and butter, job, work, employment, occupation.

**lively adjective 1** *a lively young woman:* energetic, active, animated, dynamic, full of life, outgoing, spirited, high-spirited, vivacious, enthusiastic, vibrant, buoyant, exuberant, effervescent, cheerful; informal full of beans. **2** *a lively bar:* busy, crowded, bustling, buzzing, vibrant, boisterous, jolly. **3** *a lively debate:* heated, vigorous, animated, spirited, enthusiastic, forceful. **4** *a lively portrait of the local community:* vivid, colourful, striking, graphic. **5** *he bowled at a lively pace:* brisk, quick, fast, rapid, swift, speedy, smart.
OPPOSITES quiet, dull, slow.

**livid adjective** (informal) very angry, enraged, furious, infuriated, irate, incensed, fuming, ranting, raving, seething, beside oneself, outraged; informal hopping mad, wild.

**living noun 1** *she cleaned floors for a living:* livelihood, (source of) income, means of support, subsistence, keep, daily bread, bread and butter, job, work, employment, occupation. **2** *healthy living:* way of life, lifestyle, life, conduct, behaviour, activities, habits.
**adjective 1** *living organisms:* alive, live, animate, sentient, breathing, existing. **2** *a living language:* current, contemporary, active.
OPPOSITES dead, extinct.

**load noun 1** *MacDowell's got a load to deliver:* cargo, freight, consignment, delivery, shipment, goods, pack, bundle, parcel. **2** *a heavy teaching load:* commitment, responsibility, duty, obligation, burden.
**verb 1** *we quickly loaded the van:* fill (up), pack, lade, charge, stock, stack. **2** *Larry loaded boxes into the jeep:* pack, stow, store, stack, bundle, place, deposit, put away. **3** *loading the committee with responsibilities:* burden, weigh down, saddle, charge, overburden, overwhelm, encumber, tax, strain, trouble, worry. **4** *he loaded a gun:* prime, charge, set up, prepare. **5** *load the cassette into the camcorder:* insert, put, place, slot, slide.

**loaded** adjective **1** *a loaded freight train:* full, filled, laden, packed, stuffed, crammed, brimming, stacked; informal chock-full, chock-a-block. **2** *a politically loaded word:* charged, emotive, sensitive, delicate.

**loaf** verb laze, lounge, loll, idle; informal hang around/round; Brit. informal hang about, mooch about/around; N. Amer. informal bum around.

**loan** noun credit, advance, mortgage, overdraft, Brit. informal sub.

**loath** adjective reluctant, unwilling, disinclined, averse, opposed, resistant.
OPPOSITES willing.

**loathe** verb hate, detest, abhor, not be able to bear/stand.
OPPOSITES love.

**loathing** noun hatred, hate, abhorrence, antipathy, dislike, hostility, animosity, malice, enmity, repugnance.

**loathsome** adjective hateful, detestable, abhorrent, repulsive, odious, repugnant, repellent, disgusting, revolting, sickening, abominable, despicable, contemptible, reprehensible, vile, horrible, nasty, obnoxious, gross, foul; informal horrid; literary noisome.

**lobby** noun **1** *the hotel lobby:* entrance (hall), hallway, hall, vestibule, foyer, reception area. **2** *the anti-hunt lobby:* pressure group, interest group, movement, campaign, crusade, faction, camp.
verb **1** *readers are urged to lobby their MPs:* approach, contact, importune, sway, petition, solicit, appeal to, pressurize. **2** *a group lobbying for better rail services:* campaign, crusade, press, push, ask, call, demand, promote, advocate, champion.

**local** adjective **1** *the local council:* community, district, neighbourhood, regional, town, municipal, provincial, village, parish. **2** *a local restaurant:* neighbourhood, nearby, near, at hand, close by, handy, convenient. **3** *a local infection:* confined, restricted, contained, localized.
OPPOSITES national, widespread.
noun *complaints from the locals:* local person, native, inhabitant, resident, parishioner.
OPPOSITES outsider.

**locate** verb **1** *spotter planes located the submarines:* find, pinpoint, track down, unearth, sniff out, smoke out, search out, uncover. **2** *a company located near Pittsburgh:* situate, site, position, place, base, put, build, establish, station.

**location** noun position, place, situation, site, locality, locale, spot, whereabouts, scene, setting, area, environment, venue, address.

**lock**[1] noun *the lock on the door:* bolt, catch, fastener, clasp, hasp, latch.
verb **1** *he locked the door:* bolt, fasten, secure, padlock, latch, chain. **2** *the police locked arms:* join, interlock, link, engage, combine, connect, couple. **3** *the wheels locked:* become stuck, stick, jam, seize. **4** *he locked her in an embrace:* clasp, clench, grasp, embrace, hug, squeeze.
OPPOSITES unlock, open, separate, divide.
■ **lock someone up** imprison, jail, incarcerate, intern, send to prison, put behind bars, put

under lock and key, cage, pen, coop up; informal send down, put away, put inside.

**lock²** noun *a lock of hair:* tuft, tress, curl, ringlet, hank, strand, wisp, coil.

**locker** noun cupboard, cabinet, chest, safe, box, case, coffer, storeroom.

**lodge** noun **1** *the porter's lodge:* gatehouse, cottage. **2** *a hunting lodge:* house, cottage, cabin, chalet. **3** *a Masonic lodge:* section, branch, wing, hall, clubhouse, meeting room; N. Amer. chapter.
verb **1** *William lodged at our house:* reside, board, stay, live, stop; N. Amer. room. **2** *the government lodged a protest:* submit, register, enter, put forward, advance, lay, present, tender, proffer, put on record, record, table, file. **3** *the money was lodged in a bank:* deposit, put, bank, stash, store, stow, put away. **4** *the bullet lodged in his back:* become embedded, get/become stuck, stick, catch, become caught, wedge.

**lodging** noun accommodation, rooms, chambers, living quarters, a roof over one's head, housing, shelter; informal digs; formal residence, dwelling.

**lofty** adjective **1** *a lofty tower:* tall, high. **2** *lofty ideals:* noble, exalted, high, high-minded, worthy, grand, fine, elevated. **3** *lofty disdain:* haughty, arrogant, disdainful, supercilious, condescending, scornful, contemptuous, self-important, conceited, snobbish; informal stuck-up, snooty; Brit. informal toffee-nosed.
OPPOSITES low, short, base, lowly, modest.

**log** noun *a log of phone calls:*
record, register, logbook, journal, diary, minutes, chronicle, record book, ledger, account, tally.
verb **1** *all complaints are logged:* register, record, note, write down, put in writing, enter, file. **2** *the pilot had logged 95 hours:* attain, achieve, chalk up, make, do, go, cover, clock up.

**logic** noun **1** *this case appears to defy all logic:* reason, judgement, rationality, wisdom, sense, good sense, common sense, sanity. **2** *the logic of their argument:* reasoning, line, rationale, argument.

**logical** adjective **1** *information displayed in a logical fashion:* reasoned, rational, sound, cogent, valid, coherent, clear, systematic, orderly, methodical, analytical, consistent. **2** *the logical outcome:* natural, reasonable, sensible, understandable, predictable, unsurprising, likely.
OPPOSITES illogical, unlikely.

**lone** adjective **1** *a lone police officer:* solitary, single, solo, unaccompanied, sole, isolated. **2** *a lone parent:* single, unmarried, separated, divorced, widowed.

**loneliness** noun **1** *his loneliness was unbearable:* isolation, friendlessness, abandonment, rejection; N. Amer. lonesomeness. **2** *the enforced loneliness of a prison cell:* solitariness, solitude, aloneness, separation, seclusion.
OPPOSITES popularity, company.

**lonely** adjective **1** *I felt very lonely:* isolated, alone, friendless, with no one to turn to, abandoned, rejected, unloved, unwanted; N. Amer. lonesome. **2** *a lonely road:*

deserted, uninhabited, desolate, solitary, isolated, remote, out of the way, secluded, in the back of beyond, godforsaken; informal in the middle of nowhere.
OPPOSITES popular, crowded.

**long**[1] adjective *a long silence:* lengthy, extended, prolonged, protracted, long-lasting, drawn-out, endless, lingering, interminable.
OPPOSITES short, brief.

**long**[2] verb *I longed for the holidays:* yearn, pine, ache, hanker for/after, hunger, thirst, itch, be eager, be desperate, crave, dream of; informal be dying.

**longing** noun yearning, craving, ache, burning, hunger, thirst, hankering; informal yen, itch.

**long-standing** adjective well established, long-established, time-honoured, traditional, abiding, enduring.
OPPOSITES new, recent.

**look** verb **1** *Mrs Wright looked at him:* glance, gaze, stare, gape, peer, peep, peek, watch, observe, view, regard, examine, inspect, eye, scan, scrutinize, survey, study, contemplate, take in, ogle; informal take a gander, rubberneck, get a load of; Brit. informal gawp; N. Amer. informal eyeball. **2** *they looked shocked:* seem (to be), appear (to be), come across/over as.
OPPOSITES ignore.
noun **1** *have a look at this report:* glance, examination, study, inspection, scrutiny, peep, peek, glimpse; informal eyeful, once-over, squint. **2** *the look on her face:* expression, mien. **3** *that rustic look:* appearance, air, aspect, manner, mien, demeanour, impression, effect,

ambience. **4** *this season's look:* fashion, style; informal thing.
■ **look after** take care of, care for, attend to, minister to, tend, mind, keep an eye on, keep safe, be responsible for, protect, nurse, babysit, childmind. ■ **look down on** disdain, scorn, look down one's nose at, sneer at, despise.
■ **look for** search for, hunt, try to find, seek, cast about/around/round for, try to track down, forage for. ■ **look forward to** await with pleasure, eagerly anticipate, lick one's lips over, be unable to wait for, count the days until. ■ **look into** investigate, enquire into, go into, probe, explore, follow up, research, study, examine; informal check out; N. Amer. informal scope out. ■ **look like** resemble, bear a resemblance to, look similar to, take after, remind one of, make one think of; informal be the (spitting) image of, be a dead ringer for. ■ **look out** beware, watch out, mind out, be on one's guard, be alert, be wary, be vigilant, be careful, take care, be cautious, pay attention, keep one's eyes open/peeled, keep an eye out, watch one's step. ■ **look something over** inspect, examine, scrutinize, cast an eye over, take stock of, vet, view, peruse, read through; informal give something a/the once-over; N. Amer. check out; N. Amer. informal eyeball. ■ **look up** improve, get better, pick up, come along/on, progress, make progress, make headway, perk up, rally, take a turn for the better. ■ **look someone up** (informal) visit, pay a visit to, call on, go to see, look in on; N. Amer. visit with, go see; informal drop in on. ■ **look up to** admire, have

a
b
c
d
e
f
g
h
i
j
k
**l**
m
n
o
p
q
r
s
t
u
v
w
x
y
z

a high opinion of, think highly of, hold in high regard, regard highly, respect, esteem, venerate, idolize.

**lookout** noun **1** *the lookout sighted sails:* watchman, watch, guard, sentry, sentinel, observer. **2** (Brit. informal) *that's your lookout:* problem, concern, business, affair, responsibility, worry; informal pigeon.
■ **be on the lookout** keep watch, keep an eye out, keep one's eyes peeled, be alert.

**loom** verb **1** *ghostly shapes loomed out of the fog:* emerge, appear, materialize, reveal itself. **2** *the church loomed above him:* soar, tower, rise, rear up, hang, overshadow. **3** *without reforms, disaster looms:* be imminent, be on the horizon, impend, threaten, brew, be just around the corner.

**loop** noun *a loop of rope:* coil, ring, circle, noose, spiral, curl, bend, curve, arc, twirl, whorl, twist, helix.
verb **1** *Dave looped rope around their hands:* coil, wind, twist, snake, spiral, curve, bend, turn. **2** *he looped the cables together:* fasten, tie, join, connect, knot, bind.

**loophole** noun flaw, discrepancy, inconsistency, ambiguity, omission, excuse; Brit. get-out.

**loose** adjective **1** *a loose floorboard:* not secure, unsecured, unattached, detached, wobbly, unsteady, dangling, free. **2** *she wore her hair loose:* untied, free, down. **3** *there's a wolf loose:* free, at large, at liberty, on the loose. **4** *a loose interpretation:* vague, imprecise, approximate, broad, general, rough, liberal. **5** *a loose jacket:* baggy, generously cut, slack, roomy, oversized, shapeless, sloppy.
OPPOSITES secure, literal, narrow, tight.
verb **1** *the hounds have been loosed:* free, let loose, release, untie, unchain, unfasten, unleash. **2** *the fingers loosed their hold:* relax, slacken, loosen.
OPPOSITES confine, tighten.

**loosen** verb **1** *you simply loosen two screws:* undo, slacken, unfasten, detach, release, disconnect. **2** *her fingers loosened:* slacken, become loose, let go, ease. **3** *Philip loosened his grip:* weaken, relax, slacken, loose.
OPPOSITES tighten.

**loot** noun *a bag full of loot:* booty, spoils, plunder, stolen goods, contraband, informal swag.
verb *troops looted the cathedral:* plunder, pillage, ransack, sack, rifle, rob, strip, gut.

**lord** noun **1** *lords and ladies:* noble, nobleman, peer, aristocrat. **2** *it is my duty to obey my lord's wishes:* master, ruler, leader, chief, superior, monarch, sovereign, king, emperor, prince, governor, commander.
OPPOSITES commoner, servant, inferior.

**lose** verb **1** *I've lost my watch:* mislay, misplace, be unable to find, lose track of. **2** *he lost his pursuers:* escape from, evade, elude, dodge, avoid, give someone the slip, shake off, throw off, leave behind, outdistance, outrun. **3** *you've lost your opportunity:* waste, squander, let pass, miss; informal pass up, blow. **4** *they always lose at football:* be defeated,

be/get beaten; informal come a cropper, go down.
OPPOSITES find, seize, win.

**loser** noun (informal) failure, underachiever, dead loss, write-off, has-been, informal also-ran, non-starter, no-hoper.
OPPOSITES success.

**loss** noun 1 *the loss of the papers*: mislaying, misplacement, destruction, theft. 2 *loss of earnings*: forfeiture, diminution, erosion, reduction, depletion. 3 *the loss of her husband*: death, demise, passing away, end. 4 *British losses in the war*: casualty, fatality, victim, dead. 5 *a loss of £15,000*: deficit, debit, debt.
OPPOSITES recovery, profit.
■ **at a loss** baffled, nonplussed, mystified, puzzled, perplexed, bewildered, confused, stumped, stuck; informal flummoxed, beaten.

**lost** adjective 1 *her lost keys*: missing, mislaid, misplaced, stolen. 2 *I think we're lost*: off course, going round in circles, adrift, at sea. 3 *a lost opportunity*: missed, wasted, squandered, gone by the board; informal down the drain. 4 *lost traditions*: bygone, past, former, old, vanished, forgotten, dead. 5 *lost species and habitats*: extinct, died out, defunct, vanished, gone, destroyed, wiped out, exterminated. 6 *lost in thought*: engrossed, absorbed, rapt, immersed, deep, intent, engaged, wrapped up.
OPPOSITES current, living, saved.

**lot** pronoun *a lot of money | lots of friends*: a large amount, a good/great deal, an abundance, a wealth, a profusion, plenty, many, a great many, a large

number, a considerable number; informal hundreds, loads, masses, heaps, piles, stacks, tons; Brit. informal a shedload, lashings.
OPPOSITES a little, a few.
adverb *I work in pastels a lot*: a great deal, a good deal, much, often, frequently, regularly.
OPPOSITES a little.
noun 1 (informal) *what do your lot think?* group, crowd, circle, crew; informal bunch, gang, mob. 2 *an auction lot*: item, article, batch, group, bundle, parcel. 3 *his lot in life*: fate, destiny, fortune, situation, circumstances, plight, predicament.

**lotion** noun ointment, cream, balm, rub, moisturizer, lubricant, embrocation.

**lottery** noun raffle, (prize) draw, sweepstake, sweep, tombola, lotto, pools.

**loud** adjective 1 *loud music*: noisy, blaring, booming, deafening, roaring, thunderous, ear-splitting, powerful, stentorian; Music forte, fortissimo. 2 *loud complaints*: vociferous, clamorous, insistent, vehement, emphatic. 3 *a loud T-shirt*: garish, gaudy, lurid, showy, ostentatious, vulgar, tasteless; informal flashy.
OPPOSITES quiet, gentle, sober, tasteful.

**loudly** adverb at high volume, at the top of one's voice, noisily, stridently, vociferously, shrilly.
OPPOSITES quietly.

**lounge** verb *lounging around*: laze, lie, loll, recline, relax, rest, take it easy, sprawl, slump, slouch, loaf, idle, do nothing.
noun *sitting in the lounge*: living room, sitting room, front room, drawing room.

a
b
c
d
e
f
g
h
i
j
k
**l**
m
n
o
p
q
r
s
t
u
v
w
x
y
z

**lout** noun hooligan, ruffian, thug, boor, oaf, rowdy; informal tough, bruiser; Brit. informal yob, yobbo.
OPPOSITES gentleman.

**love** noun 1 *a friendship that blossomed into love:* infatuation, adoration, attachment, devotion, fondness, tenderness, warmth, intimacy, passion, desire, lust, yearning, besottedness. 2 *her love of fashion:* liking, taste, passion, zeal, zest, enthusiasm, keenness, fondness, weakness, partiality, predilection, penchant. 3 *their love for their fellow human beings:* compassion, care, regard, concern, altruism, unselfishness, philanthropy, benevolence, humanity. 4 *he was her one true love:* beloved, loved one, dearest, darling, sweetheart, sweet, angel, honey.
OPPOSITES hatred.
verb 1 *she loves him dearly:* be in love with, be infatuated with, be smitten with, be besotted with, adore, idolize, worship, think the world of, be devoted to, dote on, care for, hold dear; informal be mad/crazy/nuts/wild/potty about, carry a torch for. 2 *Laura loved painting:* like, delight in, enjoy, have a passion for, take pleasure in, have a weakness for, be partial to, be taken with; informal have a thing about, be mad/crazy/nuts/wild/potty about, be hooked on.
OPPOSITES hate.

**love affair** noun relationship, affair, romance, liaison, fling, entanglement, involvement; Brit. informal carry-on.

**lovely** adjective 1 *a lovely young woman:* beautiful, pretty, attractive, good-looking, handsome, adorable, enchanting, gorgeous, alluring, ravishing, glamorous; Scottish & N. English bonny; informal tasty, stunning, drop-dead gorgeous; Brit. informal fit; N. Amer. informal cute, foxy. 2 *a lovely view:* scenic, picturesque, pleasing, magnificent, stunning, splendid. 3 (informal) *we had a lovely day:* delightful, very pleasant, very nice, marvellous, wonderful, sublime, superb; informal terrific, fabulous, heavenly, divine, amazing, glorious.
OPPOSITES ugly, horrible.

**lover** noun 1 *she had a secret lover:* boyfriend, girlfriend, beloved, sweetheart, mistress, partner; informal bit on the side, fancy man, fancy woman. 2 *a dog lover:* devotee, admirer, fan, enthusiast, aficionado; informal buff, nut, ...head.

**loving** adjective affectionate, fond, devoted, adoring, doting, caring, tender, warm, close, amorous, passionate.
OPPOSITES cold, cruel.

**low** adjective 1 *a low fence:* short, small, little, squat, stubby, stunted. 2 *low prices:* cheap, economical, moderate, reasonable, affordable, modest, bargain, bargain-basement, rock-bottom. 3 *supplies were low:* scarce, scant, meagre, sparse, few, little, reduced, depleted, diminished. 4 *low quality:* inferior, substandard, poor, low-grade, unsatisfactory. 5 *a low voice:* quiet, soft, faint, gentle, muted, subdued, muffled, hushed. 6 *a low note:* bass, low-pitched, deep, rumbling, booming, sonorous.

**7** *she was feeling low:* depressed, dejected, despondent, downhearted, downcast, down, miserable, dispirited, flat; informal fed up, down in the dumps, blue. OPPOSITES high, expensive, plentiful, superior, loud, cheerful, lively.

**lower¹** adjective **1** *the lower house of parliament:* subordinate, inferior, lesser, junior, minor, secondary, subsidiary, subservient. **2** *her lower lip:* bottom, bottommost, nether, under. **3** *a lower price:* cheaper, reduced, cut. OPPOSITES upper, higher, increased.

**lower²** verb **1** *she lowered the mask:* let down, take down, drop, let fall. **2** *lower your voice:* soften, modulate, quieten, hush, tone down, muffle, turn down. **3** *they are lowering their prices:* reduce, decrease, lessen, bring down, cut, slash. OPPOSITES raise, increase.

**lowly** adjective humble, low, low-ranking, common, ordinary, plain, modest, simple, obscure. OPPOSITES aristocratic, exalted.

**loyal** adjective faithful, true, devoted, constant, steadfast, staunch, dependable, reliable, trustworthy, trusty, patriotic. OPPOSITES disloyal.

**loyalty** noun allegiance, faithfulness, obedience, adherence, devotion, steadfastness, staunchness, dedication, commitment, patriotism. OPPOSITES disloyalty.

**lucid** adjective rational, sane, in possession of one's faculties, compos mentis, clear-headed, sober; informal all there. OPPOSITES confused.

**luck** noun **1** *with luck you'll make it:* good fortune, good luck, stroke of luck; informal lucky break. **2** *I wish you luck:* success, prosperity, good fortune, good luck. **3** *it is a matter of luck whether it hits or misses:* fortune, fate, serendipity, chance, accident, a twist of fate. OPPOSITES bad luck, misfortune.

**luckily** adverb fortunately, happily, providentially, by good fortune, as luck would have it, mercifully, thankfully. OPPOSITES unluckily.

**lucky** adjective **1** *the lucky winner:* fortunate, in luck, favoured, charmed, successful; Brit. informal jammy. **2** *a lucky escape:* providential, fortunate, timely, opportune, serendipitous, chance, fortuitous, accidental. OPPOSITES unlucky.

**lucrative** adjective profitable, gainful, remunerative, moneymaking, well paid, rewarding, worthwhile. OPPOSITES unprofitable.

**ludicrous** adjective absurd, ridiculous, farcical, laughable, risible, preposterous, mad, insane, idiotic, stupid, asinine, nonsensical; informal crazy. OPPOSITES sensible.

**luggage** noun baggage, bags, suitcases, cases.

**lukewarm** adjective **1** *lukewarm coffee:* tepid, warmish, at room temperature. **2** *a lukewarm response:* indifferent, cool, half-hearted, apathetic, unenthusiastic, tepid, offhand. OPPOSITES hot, cold, warm.

**lull** verb *the sound of the bells lulled us to sleep:* soothe, calm, hush, rock to sleep.

a b c d e f g h i j k l m n o p q r s t u v w x y z

OPPOSITES waken, arouse.

noun **1** *a lull in the fighting:* pause, respite, interval, break, suspension, breathing space; informal let-up, breather. **2** *the lull before the storm:* calm, stillness, quiet, tranquillity, peace, silence, hush.
OPPOSITES agitation, activity.

**lumber**[1] verb *elephants lumbered past:* trundle, stumble, lurch, shamble, shuffle, trudge, clump.

**lumber**[2] verb (Brit. informal) *she was lumbered with debt:* burden, saddle, encumber, land.
OPPOSITES free.

**lumbering** adjective clumsy, awkward, slow, blundering, bumbling, ponderous; informal clodhopping.
OPPOSITES nimble, agile.

**lump** noun **1** *a lump of coal:* chunk, hunk, piece, block, wedge, slab, ball, knob, clod. **2** *a lump on his head:* swelling, bump, bulge, protuberance, protrusion, growth, tumour.
verb *it is convenient to lump them together:* combine, put, group, bunch, throw.

**lunatic** noun *he drives like a lunatic:* maniac, madman, madwoman, fool, idiot; informal loony, nutcase; Brit. informal nutter; N. Amer. informal screwball.
adjective *a lunatic idea:* stupid, foolish, idiotic, absurd, ridiculous, ludicrous, preposterous; informal crazy, mad; Brit. informal barmy, daft.
OPPOSITES sensible.

**lunge** noun *Darren made a lunge at his attacker:* thrust, dive, rush, charge, grab.
verb *he lunged at Finn with a knife:* thrust, dive, spring, launch oneself, rush.

**lurch** verb **1** *he lurched into the kitchen:* stagger, stumble, sway, reel, roll, totter. **2** *the car lurched to the left:* swing, list, roll, pitch, veer, swerve.

**lure** verb *consumers are frequently lured into debt:* tempt, entice, attract, induce, coax, persuade, inveigle, seduce.
OPPOSITES deter, put off.
noun *the lure of the stage:* temptation, attraction, pull, draw, appeal, inducement, allure, fascination, interest, glamour.

**lurk** verb skulk, loiter, lie in wait, hide.

**lush** adjective **1** *lush vegetation:* profuse, rich, abundant, luxuriant, riotous, vigorous, dense, thick, rampant. **2** *a lush apartment:* luxurious, sumptuous, palatial, opulent, lavish, elaborate, extravagant, fancy; informal plush, posh, swanky; Brit. informal swish; N. Amer. informal swank.
OPPOSITES sparse, shrivelled, austere.

**lust** noun **1** *his lust for her:* desire, longing, passion, libido, sex drive, sexuality, lechery, lasciviousness; informal horniness; Brit. informal randiness. **2** *a lust for power:* greed, desire, craving, eagerness, longing, yearning, hunger, thirst, appetite, hankering.
OPPOSITES dread, aversion.
■ **lust after someone** *he lusted after his employer's wife:* desire, be consumed with desire for; informal fancy, have a thing about/for, drool over. ■ **lust for/after something** *she lusted after adventure:* crave, desire, want, long for, yearn for, dream of, hanker for/after, hunger for,

thirst for, ache for.

**luxurious** adjective opulent, sumptuous, grand, palatial, magnificent, extravagant, fancy; Brit. upmarket; informal plush, posh, classy, swanky; Brit. informal swish; N. Amer. informal swank.
OPPOSITES plain, basic.

**luxury** noun **1** *we'll live in luxury:* opulence, sumptuousness, grandeur, magnificence, splendour, affluence. **2** *a TV is his only luxury:* indulgence, extravagance, treat, extra, frill.
OPPOSITES simplicity, necessity.

**lying** noun *she was no good at lying:* dishonesty, fabrication, fibbing, perjury, untruthfulness, mendacity, misrepresentation, deceit, duplicity.
OPPOSITES honesty.
adjective *he was a lying womanizer:* dishonest, false, untruthful, mendacious, deceitful, duplicitous, double-dealing, two-faced.
OPPOSITES honest.

**lyrical** adjective **1** *a subtle, lyrical film:* expressive, emotional, deeply felt, personal, passionate. **2** *she was lyrical about her success:* enthusiastic, effusive, rapturous, ecstatic, euphoric.
OPPOSITES unenthusiastic.

# Mm

**machine** noun **1** device, appliance, apparatus, engine, gadget, mechanism. **2** *an efficient publicity machine:* organization, system, structure, machinery; informal set-up.

**machinery** noun **1** equipment, apparatus, plant, hardware, gear, gadgetry, technology. **2** *the machinery of local government:* workings, organization, system, structure, institution; informal set-up.

**macho** adjective manly, male, masculine, virile, red-blooded; informal butch, laddish.
OPPOSITES wimpish.

**mad** adjective **1** *he was killed by his mad brother:* insane, out of one's mind, deranged, demented, crazed, lunatic, unbalanced, unhinged; informal crazy, mental, off one's head, round the bend; Brit. informal barmy, crackers, barking (mad), potty, round the twist. **2** (informal) *I'm still mad at him:* angry, furious, infuriated, enraged, fuming, incensed, beside oneself; informal livid, spare; N. Amer. informal sore. **3** *some mad scheme:* foolish, insane, stupid, lunatic, idiotic, absurd, silly, asinine, wild; informal crazy, crackpot; Brit. informal daft. **4** (informal) *he's mad about jazz:* passionate, fanatical, ardent, fervent, devoted to, infatuated with, in love with; informal crazy, dotty, nuts, wild, hooked on; Brit. informal potty; N. Amer. informal nutso. **5** *it was a mad dash to get ready:* frenzied, frantic, frenetic, feverish, hysterical, wild, hectic, manic.
OPPOSITES sane, pleased,

a
b
c
d
e
f
g
h
i
j
k
l
**m**
n
o
p
q
r
s
t
u
v
w
x
y
z

sensible, indifferent, calm.

**madden** verb infuriate, exasperate, irritate, incense, anger, enrage, provoke, make someone see red; informal aggravate, make someone's blood boil; Brit. informal nark; N. Amer. informal tee off, tick off.
OPPOSITES calm.

**madly** adverb 1 *she was smiling madly:* insanely, wildly; informal crazily. 2 *it was fun, hurtling madly downhill:* furiously, hurriedly, speedily, energetically; informal like mad, like crazy. 3 (informal) *he loved her madly:* intensely, fervently, wildly, to distraction. 4 (informal) *his job isn't madly exciting:* very, tremendously, wildly, all that, hugely; informal awfully, terribly.
OPPOSITES sanely, slowly, slightly.

**madman, madwoman** noun lunatic, maniac, psychotic, psychopath; informal loony, nut, nutcase, head case; Brit. informal nutter; N. Amer. informal screwball.

**madness** noun 1 *today madness is called mental illness:* insanity, mental illness, dementia, derangement, lunacy, mania, psychosis. 2 *it would be madness to do otherwise:* folly, foolishness, idiocy, stupidity, insanity, lunacy. 3 *it's absolute madness in here:* bedlam, mayhem, chaos, pandemonium, uproar, turmoil, all hell broken loose; N. Amer. three-ring circus.
OPPOSITES sanity, sense.

**magazine** noun journal, periodical, supplement, colour supplement; informal glossy, mag, 'zine.

**magic** noun 1 *do you believe in magic?* sorcery, witchcraft, wizardry, necromancy,

enchantment, the supernatural, occultism, the occult, black magic, the black arts, voodoo. 2 *he does magic at children's parties:* conjuring (tricks), illusion, sleight of hand; formal prestidigitation. 3 *the magic of the stage:* allure, excitement, fascination, charm, glamour. 4 *the old Liverpool magic:* brilliance, skill, accomplishment, expertise, art, finesse, talent.

**magical** adjective 1 *magical powers:* supernatural, magic, mystical, other-worldly. 2 *the news had a magical effect:* extraordinary, remarkable, incredible, amazing, astonishing, astounding, staggering, miraculous. 3 *this magical island:* enchanting, entrancing, spellbinding, bewitching, fascinating, captivating, alluring, enthralling, charming, lovely, delightful, beautiful; informal heavenly, gorgeous.
OPPOSITES predictable, boring.

**magician** noun 1 sorcerer, sorceress, witch, wizard, warlock, enchanter, enchantress, necromancer. 2 conjuror, illusionist; formal prestidigitator.

**magnetic** adjective attractive, irresistible, seductive, charismatic, hypnotic, alluring, fascinating, captivating.
OPPOSITES repellent.

**magnificent** adjective 1 *a magnificent view:* splendid, spectacular, impressive, striking, glorious, superb, majestic, awe-inspiring, breathtaking. 2 *a magnificent apartment:* sumptuous, grand, impressive, imposing, monumental, palatial, opulent,

luxurious, lavish, rich, dazzling, beautiful; informal posh, classy; Brit. informal swish.
OPPOSITES uninspiring, modest, tawdry.

**magnify** verb enlarge, increase, augment, extend, expand, boost, enhance, maximize, amplify, intensify; informal blow up.
OPPOSITES reduce, minimize, understate.

**mail** noun 1 *the mail arrived:* post, letters, correspondence, email. 2 *we sent it by mail:* post, postal system, postal service, post office; informal snail mail; N. Amer. the mails.
verb *we mailed the parcels:* send, post, dispatch, forward, ship, email.

**maim** verb injure, wound, cripple, disable, incapacitate, mutilate, disfigure, mangle.

**main** adjective principal, chief, leading, foremost, most important, major, dominant, central, focal, key, prime, primary, first, fundamental, predominant, pre-eminent.
OPPOSITES subsidiary, minor.

**mainly** adverb mostly, for the most part, in the main, on the whole, largely, by and large, to a large extent, predominantly, chiefly, principally, primarily.

**maintain** verb 1 *they wanted to maintain peace:* preserve, conserve, keep, retain, keep going, prolong, perpetuate, sustain, carry on, continue. 2 *the council maintains the roads:* look after, service, care for, take care of. 3 *the costs of maintaining a family:* support, provide for, keep, sustain. 4 *he maintains that he is innocent:* insist, declare, assert, protest, affirm, profess, claim, contend, argue.
OPPOSITES break, discontinue, neglect, deny.

**maintenance** noun 1 *the maintenance of peace:* preservation, conservation, keeping, carrying on, prolongation, continuation. 2 *car maintenance:* servicing, service, repair(s), running repairs, care. 3 *the maintenance of his children:* support, keeping, upkeep, sustenance, nurture. 4 *absent fathers are forced to pay maintenance:* financial support, child support, alimony, upkeep.
OPPOSITES breakdown, discontinuation, neglect.

**majestic** adjective stately, dignified, distinguished, solemn, magnificent, grand, splendid, glorious, impressive, noble, awe-inspiring, monumental, palatial, imposing.
OPPOSITES modest, wretched.

**majesty** noun stateliness, dignity, solemnity, magnificence, pomp, grandeur, grandness, splendour, glory, impressiveness, nobility.
OPPOSITES modesty, wretchedness.

**major** adjective 1 *the major English poets:* greatest, best, finest, most important, chief, main, prime, principal, leading, foremost, outstanding, pre-eminent. 2 *a major factor:* crucial, vital, important, big, significant, considerable, weighty, serious, key, utmost, great, paramount, prime.
OPPOSITES minor, trivial.

**majority** noun 1 *the majority of cases:* most, bulk, mass, larger part/number, best/better part,

a
b
c
d
e
f
g
h
i
j
k
l
**m**
n
o
p
q
r
s
t
u
v
w
x
y
z

more than half, lion's share, (main) body, preponderance, predominance. **2** *a majority in the election:* (winning) margin, landslide, whitewash.
OPPOSITES minority.

**make** verb **1** *he makes models:* construct, build, assemble, put together, manufacture, produce, fabricate, create, form, fashion, model, improvise. **2** *she made me drink it:* force, compel, coerce, press, drive, pressurize, oblige, require; informal railroad, steamroller. **3** *don't make such a noise:* cause, create, produce, generate, effect. **4** *she made a little bow:* perform, execute, give, do, accomplish, achieve, bring off, carry out. **5** *they made him chairman:* appoint, designate, name, nominate, select, elect, vote in. **6** *he's made a lot of money:* acquire, obtain, gain, get, secure, win, earn. **7** *he made tea:* prepare, get ready, put together, concoct, cook, dish up, throw together, whip up, brew; informal fix.
OPPOSITES destroy, lose.
noun brand, marque, label.
■ **make for** contribute to, be conducive to, produce, promote, facilitate, foster.
■ **make it 1** *he never made it as a singer:* succeed, be a success, make good; informal make the grade, arrive. **2** *she's very ill—is she going to make it?* survive, pull through, get better, recover.
■ **make off** run away/off, take to one's heels, flee, take off, take flight, bolt; informal clear off/out, beat it, split, scram; Brit. informal scarper, do a runner; N. Amer. informal take a powder; Austral./NZ informal shoot through.
■ **make something out**

**1** *I could just make out a figure in the distance:* see, discern, distinguish, detect, observe, recognize. **2** *he couldn't make out what she was saying:* understand, grasp, follow, work out, make sense of, interpret, decipher, make head or tail of, catch. **3** *she made out that he was violent:* allege, claim, suggest, imply, hint, insinuate, indicate, intimate. ■ **make up 1** *let's kiss and make up:* be friends again, bury the hatchet, make peace, forgive and forget, shake hands, settle one's differences. **2** *she tried to make up for what she'd said:* atone, make amends, compensate.
■ **make something up 1** *exports make up 42% of earnings:* comprise, form, compose, constitute, account for. **2** *he made up an excuse:* invent, fabricate, concoct, think up; informal cook up. ■ **make up for** *job satisfaction can make up for low pay:* offset, counterbalance, counteract, compensate for, cancel out.

**maker** noun creator, manufacturer, constructor, builder, producer.

**makeshift** adjective temporary, provisional, stopgap, standby, rough and ready, improvised, ad hoc.
OPPOSITES permanent.

**make-up** noun **1** *she used too much make-up:* cosmetics; informal warpaint, slap. **2** *the cellular make-up of plants:* composition, constitution, structure, configuration, arrangement. **3** *jealousy isn't part of his make-up:* character, nature, temperament, personality, mentality, persona.

**makings** plural noun qualities,

characteristics, ingredients, potential, capacity, capability, stuff.

**male** adjective masculine, manly, virile, macho.
OPPOSITES female.

**malfunction** verb *the computer has malfunctioned:* crash, go wrong, break down, fail, stop working; informal conk out, go kaput; Brit. informal play up, pack up.

**malicious** adjective spiteful, malevolent, vindictive, vengeful, resentful, malign, nasty, hurtful, cruel.
OPPOSITES benevolent.

**maltreat** verb ill-treat, mistreat, abuse, ill-use, mishandle, persecute, molest.

**man** noun 1 *a handsome man:* male, adult male, gentleman, youth; informal guy, fellow, gent; Brit. informal bloke, chap, lad; N. Amer. informal dude, hombre. 2 *all men are mortal:* human being, human, person, mortal, individual, soul. 3 *the evolution of man:* the human race, the human species, Homo sapiens, humankind, humanity, human beings, humans, people, mankind.
verb 1 *the office is manned from 9 to 5:* staff, crew, occupy, people. 2 *firemen manned the pumps:* operate, work, use.

**manage** verb 1 *she manages a staff of 80:* be in charge of, run, head, direct, control, preside over, lead, govern, rule, command, supervise, oversee, administer; informal head up.
2 *how much work can you manage this week?* accomplish, achieve, carry out, perform, undertake, deal with, cope with, get through. 3 *will you be able to manage without him?*

cope, get along/on, make do, do all right, carry on, survive, get by, muddle through/along, make ends meet; informal make out, hack it.

**management** noun 1 *he's responsible for the management of the firm:* administration, running, managing, organization, direction, leadership, control, governance, rule, command, supervision, guidance, operation. 2 *workers are in dispute with the management:* managers, employers, directors, board, directorate, executive, administration; informal bosses.
OPPOSITES employees, workforce.

**manager** noun executive, head, supervisor, principal, director, superintendent, foreman, forewoman, overseer, organizer, administrator; informal boss, chief, governor; Brit. informal gaffer, guv'nor.

**mandate** noun 1 *he sought a mandate for his policies:* authority, approval, ratification, endorsement, sanction, authorization. 2 *a mandate from the UN:* instruction, directive, decree, command, order, injunction.

**mandatory** adjective obligatory, compulsory, binding, required, requisite, necessary.
OPPOSITES optional.

**mania** noun obsession, compulsion, fixation, fetish, fascination, preoccupation, passion, enthusiasm, desire, urge, craving, craze, fad, rage; informal thing.

**maniac** noun lunatic, madman, madwoman, psychopath; informal loony, nutcase, nut, head case, headbanger, sicko; Brit. informal nutter; N. Amer. informal screwball.

**manifest** verb display, show, exhibit, demonstrate, betray, present, reveal.
OPPOSITES hide.
adjective obvious, clear, plain, apparent, evident, patent, distinct, definite, blatant, overt, transparent, conspicuous, undisguised.
OPPOSITES secret.

**manifestation** noun 1 *the manifestation of anxiety:* display, demonstration, show, exhibition, presentation. 2 *manifestations of global warming:* sign, indication, evidence, symptom, testimony, proof, mark, reflection, example, instance.

**manipulate** verb 1 *he manipulated some levers:* operate, work, turn, pull, push, twist, slide. 2 *the government tried to manipulate the situation:* control, influence, use to one's advantage, exploit, twist.

**mankind** noun the human race, humankind, humanity, human beings, humans, Homo sapiens, people, man, men and women.

**manly** adjective virile, masculine, strong, all-male, red-blooded, muscular, muscly, strapping, well built, rugged, tough, powerful, brawny; informal hunky.
OPPOSITES effeminate.

**man-made** adjective artificial, synthetic, manufactured, imitation, ersatz, simulated, mock, fake.
OPPOSITES natural, real.

**manner** noun 1 *it was dealt with in a very efficient manner:* way, fashion, mode, means, method, system, style, approach, technique, procedure, process. 2 *her rather unfriendly manner:* behaviour, attitude, demeanour, air, aspect, bearing, conduct. 3 *the life and manners of Victorian society:* customs, habits, ways, practices, conventions, usages. 4 *you ought to teach him some manners:* etiquette, social graces, protocol, politeness, decorum, propriety, civility, Ps and Qs.

**mannerism** noun idiosyncrasy, quirk, oddity, foible, trait, peculiarity, habit, characteristic.

**manoeuvre** verb 1 *I manoeuvred the car into the space:* steer, guide, drive, negotiate, navigate, pilot, direct, manipulate, move, work. 2 *he manoeuvred things to suit himself:* manipulate, contrive, manage, engineer, fix, organize, arrange, orchestrate, choreograph, stage-manage; informal wangle.
noun 1 *a tricky parking manoeuvre:* operation, exercise, move, movement, action. 2 *diplomatic manoeuvres:* stratagem, tactic, gambit, ploy, trick, dodge, ruse, scheme, device, plot, machination, artifice, subterfuge, intrigue.

**mansion** noun country house, stately home, hall, manor house; informal palace, pile.
OPPOSITES hovel.

**manual** adjective 1 *manual work:* physical, labouring, blue-collar. 2 *a manual typewriter:* hand-operated, hand.
noun *a training manual:* handbook, instructions, guide, companion, ABC, guidebook; informal bible.

**manufacture** verb 1 *the company manufactures laser*

*printers:* make, produce, mass-produce, build, construct, assemble, put together, turn out. **2** *a story manufactured by the press:* make up, invent, fabricate, concoct, hatch, dream up, think up, contrive; informal cook up.
**noun** *the manufacture of aircraft engines:* production, making, manufacturing, mass production, construction, building, assembly.

**manufacturer** noun maker, producer, builder, constructor, industrialist.

**many** determiner & adjective numerous, a lot of, plenty of, countless, innumerable, scores of, untold, copious, abundant; informal lots of, umpteen, loads of, masses of, stacks of, heaps of, a slew of; Brit. informal a shedload of; Austral./NZ informal a swag of; literary myriad.
OPPOSITES few.

**map** noun plan, chart, A to Z, atlas.
**verb** *the region was mapped from the air:* chart, plot, draw, record.

**mar** verb **1** *an ugly bruise marred his features:* spoil, impair, disfigure, blemish, scar. **2** *the celebrations were marred by violence:* spoil, ruin, damage, wreck, taint, tarnish.
OPPOSITES enhance.

**march** verb **1** *the men marched past:* stride, walk, troop, step, pace, tread, slog, tramp, hike, trudge, parade, file. **2** *she marched in without even knocking:* stride, stalk, strut, flounce, storm, stomp, sweep.
**noun** **1** *a 20-mile march:* walk, trek, slog, route march, hike. **2** *police sought to ban the march:* parade, procession,

cortège, demonstration; informal demo. **3** *the march of technology:* progress, advance, development, evolution, passage.

**margin** noun **1** *the margin of the lake:* edge, side, verge, border, perimeter, brink, brim, rim, fringe, boundary, periphery, extremity. **2** *there's no margin for error:* leeway, latitude, scope, room, space, allowance. **3** *they won by a narrow margin:* gap, majority, amount.

**marginal** adjective **1** *the difference is marginal:* slight, small, tiny, minute, insignificant, minimal, negligible. **2** *a very marginal case:* borderline, disputable, questionable, doubtful.
OPPOSITES considerable, clear-cut.

**marine** adjective **1** *marine plants:* seawater, sea, saltwater, aquatic. **2** *a marine insurance company:* maritime, nautical, naval, seafaring, seagoing, ocean-going.

**mariner** noun sailor, seaman, seafarer.

**marital** adjective matrimonial, married, wedded, conjugal, nuptial, marriage, wedding.

**maritime** adjective naval, marine, nautical, seafaring, seagoing, sea, ocean-going.

**mark** noun **1** *a dirty mark:* blemish, streak, spot, fleck, blot, stain, smear, speck, smudge; informal splodge. **2** *a punctuation mark:* symbol, sign, character, accent, diacritic. **3** *the mark of a well-known bookseller:* logo, seal, stamp, symbol, emblem, device, insignia, badge, brand, trademark, monogram, hallmark. **4** *a mark of respect:*

a b c d e f g h i j k l m n o p q r s t u v w x y z

sign, token, symbol, indication, symptom, proof. **5** *the mark of a civilized society:* characteristic, feature, trait, attribute, quality, hallmark, indicator. **6** *he got a good mark for maths:* grade, grading, rating, score, percentage.
**verb 1** *be careful not to mark the paintwork:* discolour, stain, smear, smudge, streak, dirty; informal splodge. **2** *her possessions were clearly marked:* label, identify, flag, initial, name. **3** *I've marked the relevant passages:* indicate, label, tick, identify, highlight. **4** *a festival to mark the town's 200th anniversary:* celebrate, observe, recognize, acknowledge, keep, honour, commemorate, remember. **5** *these incidents marked a new phase:* represent, signify, indicate, herald. **6** *his style is marked by simplicity:* characterize, distinguish, identify, typify. **7** *I have a pile of essays to mark:* assess, evaluate, appraise, correct; N. Amer. grade.

**marked** adjective noticeable, pronounced, decided, distinct, striking, clear, unmistakable, obvious, conspicuous, notable.
OPPOSITES imperceptible.

**market** noun shopping centre, marketplace, mart, bazaar, souk, fair.
verb *the product was marketed worldwide:* sell, retail, merchandise, trade, advertise, promote.

**marriage** noun **1** *a proposal of marriage:* matrimony, wedlock. **2** *the marriage took place at St Margaret's:* wedding, wedding ceremony, nuptials, union, match. **3** *a marriage of jazz,*

*pop, and gospel:* union, fusion, mixture, mix, blend, amalgamation, combination, hybrid.
OPPOSITES divorce, separation.

**marry** verb **1** *the couple married last year:* get/be married, wed, be wed, become man and wife; informal tie the knot, walk down the aisle, get spliced, get hitched, say 'I do'. **2** *John wanted to marry her:* wed; informal make an honest woman of. **3** *the show marries poetry with art:* join, unite, combine, fuse, mix, blend, merge, amalgamate.
OPPOSITES divorce, separate.

**marsh** noun swamp, marshland, bog, swampland, morass, mire, quagmire, slough, fen.

**marshal** verb assemble, gather (together), collect, muster, call together, draw up, line up, array, organize, group, arrange, deploy, position, summon, round up.

**martial** adjective military, soldierly, army, warlike, fighting, militaristic; informal gung-ho.

**marvel** verb *she marvelled at their courage:* be amazed, be astonished, be in awe, wonder; informal be gobsmacked.
noun *a marvel of technology:* wonder, miracle, sensation, spectacle, phenomenon.

**marvellous** adjective excellent, splendid, wonderful, magnificent, superb, glorious, sublime, lovely, delightful; informal super, great, amazing, fantastic, terrific, tremendous; Brit. informal smashing, brilliant.
OPPOSITES commonplace, awful.

**masculine** adjective **1** *a masculine trait:* male, man's, men's, male-oriented. **2** *a*

powerfully masculine man: virile, macho, manly, all-male, muscular, muscly, strong, strapping, well built, rugged, robust, brawny, powerful, red-blooded, vigorous; informal hunky. 3 a rather masculine woman: mannish, unfeminine, unladylike; informal butch.
OPPOSITES feminine, effeminate.

**mask** noun a mask of respectability: pretence, semblance, veil, screen, front, facade, veneer, disguise, cover, cloak, camouflage.
verb poplar trees masked the factory: hide, conceal, disguise, cover up, obscure, screen, cloak, camouflage.

**mass** noun 1 a soggy mass of fallen leaves: pile, heap, accumulation, mess, mat, tangle. 2 a mass of cyclists: crowd, horde, throng, host, troop, army, herd, flock, swarm, mob, pack, flood, multitude. 3 the mass of the population: majority, greater part/number, best/better part, major part, bulk, main body.
adjective mass hysteria: widespread, general, extensive, large-scale, wholesale, universal, indiscriminate.
verb they began massing troops in the region: assemble, gather together, collect, rally.

**massacre** noun a cold-blooded massacre: slaughter, mass killing, mass murder, mass execution, ethnic cleansing, genocide, holocaust, annihilation, liquidation, extermination, carnage, butchery, bloodbath, bloodletting.
verb thousands were massacred: slaughter, butcher, murder, kill, annihilate, exterminate,

execute, liquidate, eliminate, mow down, cut to pieces.

**massage** noun rub, rub-down, kneading.
verb 1 he massaged her tired muscles: rub, knead, manipulate, pummel, work. 2 the statistics have been massaged: alter, tamper with, manipulate, doctor, falsify, juggle, fiddle with, tinker with, distort, rig; informal cook, fiddle.

**massive** adjective huge, enormous, vast, immense, mighty, great, colossal, tremendous, gigantic, mammoth, monumental, giant, mountainous; informal monster, whopping, astronomical; Brit. informal whacking, ginormous.
OPPOSITES tiny.

**master** noun 1 (historical) he acceded to his master's wishes: lord, ruler, sovereign, monarch. 2 a chess master: expert, genius, maestro, virtuoso, authority; informal ace, wizard, whizz, hotshot; Brit. informal dab hand; N. Amer. informal maven, crackerjack. 3 the geography master: teacher, schoolteacher, schoolmaster, tutor, instructor. 4 their spiritual master: guru, teacher, leader, guide, mentor.
OPPOSITES servant, amateur, pupil.
verb 1 I managed to master my fears: overcome, conquer, beat, quell, suppress, control, triumph over, subdue, vanquish, subjugate, curb, check, defeat, get the better of; informal lick. 2 it took ages to master the technique: learn, become proficient in, pick up, grasp, understand; informal get the hang of.
OPPOSITES succumb to.
adjective a master craftsman:

a
b
c
d
e
f
g
h
i
j
k
l
**m**
n
o
p
q
r
s
t
u
v
w
x
y
z

expert, adept, proficient, skilled, skilful, deft, dexterous, adroit, practised, experienced, masterly, accomplished; informal crack, ace; N. Amer. informal crackerjack.
OPPOSITES amateur.

**masterful** adjective
commanding, powerful, imposing, authoritative.
OPPOSITES weak.

**masterly** adjective expert, adept, skilful, skilled, adroit, proficient, deft, dexterous, accomplished, polished, consummate.
OPPOSITES inept.

**mastermind** noun *the mastermind behind the project:* genius, intellect, informal brain, brains.
verb *he masterminded the whole campaign:* plan, control, direct, be in charge of, run, conduct, organize, arrange, preside over, orchestrate, stage-manage, engineer, manage, coordinate.

**masterpiece** noun magnum opus, chef-d'œuvre, masterwork, pièce de résistance, tour de force, classic.

**mastery** noun 1 *her mastery of the language:* proficiency, ability, capability, knowledge, understanding, comprehension, command, grasp. 2 *man's mastery over nature:* control, domination, command, supremacy, superiority, power, authority, jurisdiction, dominion, sovereignty.

**mat** noun 1 *the hall mat:* rug, carpet, doormat. 2 *a thick mat of hair:* mass, tangle, mop, thatch, shock, mane.

**match** noun 1 *a football match:* contest, competition, game, tournament, tie, fixture, meet,

friendly, (local) derby, bout, fight. 2 *the vase was an exact match of hers:* lookalike, double, twin, duplicate, mate, companion, counterpart, pair, replica, copy; informal spitting image, dead ringer.
verb 1 *the curtains matched the duvet cover:* go with, coordinate with, complement, suit, set off. 2 *did their statements match?* correspond, tally, agree, match up, coincide, square. 3 *no one can match him at chess:* equal, compare with, be in the same league as, touch, rival, compete with; informal hold a candle to.

**matching** adjective
corresponding, equivalent, parallel, complementary, paired, twin, identical, alike.
OPPOSITES different, clashing.

**mate** noun 1 (Brit. informal) *he's gone out with his mates:* friend, companion, schoolmate, classmate, workmate; informal pal, chum; N. Amer. informal buddy, amigo, compadre. 2 *she's finally found her ideal mate:* partner, husband, wife, spouse, consort, lover; informal better half; Brit. informal other half. 3 *a plumber's mate:* assistant, helper, apprentice.
verb *pandas rarely mate in captivity:* breed, couple, pair.

**material** noun 1 *organic material:* matter, substance, stuff. 2 *the materials for a new building:* constituent, raw material, component, supplies. 3 *cleaning materials:* things, items, articles, stuff, supplies; Brit. informal gubbins. 4 *curtain material:* fabric, cloth, textiles. 5 *material for a magazine article:* information, data, facts, facts and figures, statistics, evidence, details, particulars, background, notes; informal info.

**adjective 1** *the material world*: physical, corporeal, tangible, mundane, worldly, earthly, secular, temporal, concrete, real. **2** *she was too fond of material pleasures*: sensual, physical, carnal, corporal, fleshly, bodily. **3** *information that could be material to the enquiry*: relevant, pertinent, applicable, germane, vital, essential, key.
OPPOSITES spiritual, aesthetic, irrelevant.

**maternal** adjective motherly, protective, caring, nurturing, maternalistic.

**matted** adjective tangled, knotted, tousled, dishevelled, uncombed, unkempt, ratty.

**matter** noun **1** *vegetable matter*: material, stuff, substance. **2** *a serious matter*: affair, business, situation, concern, incident, episode, subject, topic, issue, question, point at issue, case.
**verb** *it doesn't matter what you wear*: be important, make any difference, be of consequence, be relevant, count.

**matter-of-fact** adjective unemotional, practical, down-to-earth, sensible, realistic, unsentimental, pragmatic, businesslike, commonsensical, level-headed, hard-headed, no-nonsense, straightforward.

**mature** adjective **1** *a mature woman*: adult, grown, fully grown, in one's prime. **2** *he's very mature for his age*: grown-up, sensible, responsible, adult, level-headed. **3** *mature cheese*: ripe, mellow, rich, strong, flavoursome, full-bodied.
OPPOSITES immature.
**verb 1** *kittens mature when they are about a year old*: become fully grown, come of age, reach adulthood, reach maturity. **2** *he's matured since he left home*: grow up, blossom. **3** *leave the cheese to mature*: ripen, mellow, age. **4** *their friendship didn't have time to mature*: develop, grow, evolve, bloom, blossom, flourish, thrive.

**maturity** noun **1** *her progress from childhood to maturity*: adulthood, coming of age, manhood, womanhood. **2** *he displayed a maturity beyond his years*: responsibility, sense, level-headedness.

**maul** verb savage, attack, claw, scratch, lacerate, mangle, tear.

**maverick** noun individualist, nonconformist, free spirit, original, eccentric, rebel, dissenter, dissident.
OPPOSITES conformist.

**maximum** adjective *the maximum amount*: greatest, highest, biggest, largest, top, most, utmost.
OPPOSITES minimum.
**noun** *production levels are near their maximum*: upper limit, limit, utmost, greatest, most, peak, height, ceiling, top.
OPPOSITES minimum.

**maybe** adverb perhaps, possibly, for all one knows; N. English happen; literary perchance.

**mayhem** noun chaos, havoc, bedlam, pandemonium, uproar, turmoil, a riot, anarchy; informal a madhouse.

**maze** noun labyrinth, network, warren, web, tangle, confusion, jungle.

**meadow** noun field, paddock, pasture; literary lea.

a b c d e f g h i j k l **m** n o p q r s t u v w x y z

a
b
c
d
e
f
g
h
i
j
k
l
**m**
n
o
p
q
r
s
t
u
v
w
x
y
z

**mean**[1] verb 1 *flashing lights mean the road is blocked:* signify, denote, indicate, show, express, spell out, stand for, represent, symbolize, imply, suggest, intimate. 2 *she didn't mean to break it:* intend, aim, plan, have in mind, set out, want. 3 *this will mean war:* entail, involve, necessitate, lead to, result in, give rise to, bring about, cause, engender, produce.

**mean**[2] adjective 1 *he's too mean to leave a tip:* miserly, niggardly, parsimonious, penny-pinching, cheese-paring; informal tight-fisted, stingy, tight; N. Amer. informal cheap. 2 *a mean trick:* unkind, nasty, unpleasant, spiteful, malicious, unfair, shabby, despicable, contemptible, obnoxious, vile, loathsome, base, low; informal horrible, rotten.
OPPOSITES generous, kind.

**meaning** noun 1 *the meaning of his remark:* significance, sense, signification, import, gist, thrust, drift, implication, message. 2 *the word has several different meanings:* definition, sense, explanation, interpretation.

**meaningful** adjective 1 *a meaningful remark:* significant, relevant, important, telling. 2 *a meaningful relationship:* sincere, deep, serious, earnest, significant, important. 3 *a meaningful glance:* expressive, eloquent, pointed, pregnant, revealing, suggestive.
OPPOSITES inconsequential, insincere.

**meaningless** adjective unintelligible, incomprehensible, incoherent.

**means** plural noun 1 *the best means to achieve your goal:* method, way, manner, course, procedure. 2 *she doesn't have the means to support herself:* money, resources, capital, income, finance, funds, cash, the wherewithal, assets, wealth, riches, affluence, fortune.

**meanwhile, meantime** adverb 1 *meanwhile, I'll stay here:* for now, for the moment, for the present, for the time being, in the meanwhile, in the meantime, in the interim. 2 *cook for a further half hour; meanwhile, make the stuffing:* at the same time, simultaneously, concurrently.

**measure** verb quantify, gauge, size, count, weigh, evaluate, assess, determine, calculate, compute.
noun 1 *cost-cutting measures:* action, act, course of action, deed, procedure, step, expedient, initiative, programme. 2 *the Senate passed the measure:* statute, act, bill, law. 3 *use a measure to check the size:* ruler, tape measure, gauge, meter, scale, level. 4 *sales are the measure of the company's success:* yardstick, test, standard, barometer, touchstone, benchmark.

**measured** adjective 1 *his measured tread:* regular, steady, even, rhythmic, unfaltering, slow, dignified, stately, sedate, leisurely, unhurried. 2 *his measured tones:* thoughtful, careful, considered, deliberate, restrained.

**measurement** noun 1 *measurement of the effect is difficult:* quantification, evaluation, assessment, calculation, computation. 2 *all measurements are in metric* *units:* size, dimension, proportions, value, amount, quantity.

**mechanical** adjective 1 *a mechanical device:* mechanized, machine-driven, automated, automatic. 2 *a mechanical response:* automatic, knee-jerk, unthinking, instinctive, habitual, routine, unemotional, unfeeling.
OPPOSITES manual, thoughtful.

**mechanism** noun 1 *an electrical mechanism:* apparatus, machine, appliance, device, instrument, contraption, gadget; informal gizmo. 2 *the train's safety mechanism:* machinery, gear, system, equipment. 3 *a complaints mechanism:* procedure, process, system, method, means, medium, channel.

**mediate** verb 1 *Austria tried to mediate between the two sides:* arbitrate, conciliate, moderate, make peace, intervene, intercede, act as an intermediary, liaise. 2 *a tribunal was set up to mediate disputes:* resolve, settle, arbitrate in, umpire, reconcile, referee, mend, clear up; informal patch up.

**mediation** noun arbitration, conciliation, reconciliation, intervention, intercession, negotiation, shuttle diplomacy.

**mediator** noun arbitrator, arbiter, negotiator, conciliator, peacemaker, go-between, middleman, intermediary, moderator, honest broker, liaison officer, umpire, referee, adjudicator, judge.

**medicine** noun medication, drug, prescription, treatment, remedy, cure, nostrum, panacea, cure-all.

**mediocre** adjective average, ordinary, undistinguished, uninspired, indifferent, unexceptional, unexciting, unremarkable, run-of-the-mill, pedestrian, prosaic, lacklustre, forgettable, amateurish; informal so-so.
OPPOSITES excellent.

**meditate** verb contemplate, think, consider, ponder, muse, reflect, deliberate, ruminate, brood, mull over.

**medium** noun *a medium of expression:* means, method, avenue, channel, vehicle, organ, instrument, mechanism.
adjective *he is of medium build:* average, middling, medium-sized, middle-sized, moderate, normal, standard.

**meet** verb 1 *I met an old friend on the train:* encounter, come face to face with, run into, run across, come across/upon, chance on, happen on, stumble across; informal bump into. 2 *she first met Paul at a party:* get to know, be introduced to, make the acquaintance of. 3 *the committee met on Saturday:* assemble, gather, come together, get together, congregate, convene. 4 *the place where three roads meet:* converge, connect, touch, link up, intersect, cross, join.

**meeting** noun 1 *he stood up to address the meeting:* gathering, assembly, conference, congregation, convention, summit, rally; informal get-together. 2 *she demanded a meeting with the minister:* consultation, audience, interview. 3 *he intrigued her on their first meeting:* encounter, contact, appointment, assignation, rendezvous. 4 *the*

a
b
c
d
e
f
g
h
i
j
k
l
**m**
n
o
p
q
r
s
t
u
v
w
x
y
z

*meeting of land and sea:* convergence, coming together, confluence, conjunction, union, intersection, crossing. **5** *an athletics meeting:* event, tournament, meet, rally, competition, match, game, contest.

**melancholy** adjective *a melancholy mood:* sad, sorrowful, unhappy, gloomy, despondent, glum, miserable, morose; informal down in the dumps, blue.
OPPOSITES cheerful.
noun *a feeling of melancholy:* sadness, sorrow, unhappiness, depression, despondency, gloom, misery; informal the blues.
OPPOSITES happiness.

**mellow** adjective **1** *she loved the mellow tone of his voice:* sweet-sounding, dulcet, soft, smooth, warm, full, rich. **2** *a mellow wine:* full-bodied, mature, full-flavoured, rich, smooth. **3** *a mellow mood:* genial, affable, amiable, good-humoured, good-natured, pleasant, relaxed, easy-going.
OPPOSITES harsh, rough, irritable.

**melody** noun tune, air, strain, theme, song, refrain.

**melt** verb **1** *the snow was beginning to melt:* liquefy, thaw, defrost, soften, dissolve. **2** *his anger melted away:* vanish, disappear, fade, dissolve, evaporate.
OPPOSITES freeze, grow.

**member** noun subscriber, associate, supporter, fellow, representative.

**memoir** noun **1** *a touching memoir of her childhood:* account, history, record, chronicle, narrative, story, portrayal, depiction, portrait,

profile. **2** *he published his memoirs in 1955:* autobiography, life story, journal, diary.

**memorable** adjective unforgettable, indelible, catchy, haunting, momentous, significant, historic, notable, noteworthy, outstanding, arresting.

**memorial** noun **1** *the war memorial:* monument, cenotaph, mausoleum, statue, plaque, cairn, shrine. **2** *the festival is a memorial to his life's work:* tribute, testimonial, remembrance, memento.
adjective *a memorial service:* commemorative, remembrance.

**memorize** verb commit to memory, remember, learn (by heart), become word-perfect in.

**memory** noun **1** *happy memories of her childhood:* recollection, remembrance, reminiscence. **2** *the town built a statue in memory of him:* commemoration, remembrance, honour, tribute, recognition, respect.

**menace** noun **1** *an atmosphere full of menace:* threat, intimidation, malevolence, oppression. **2** *a menace to society:* danger, peril, risk, hazard, threat. **3** *that child is a menace:* nuisance, pest, troublemaker, mischief-maker; informal bad news.
verb **1** *the elephants are still menaced by poaching:* threaten, endanger, put at risk, jeopardize, imperil. **2** *a gang of skinheads menaced local residents:* intimidate, threaten, terrorize, frighten, scare, terrify.

**menacing** adjective

threatening, ominous, intimidating, frightening, forbidding, hostile, sinister, baleful.
OPPOSITES friendly.

**mend** verb repair, fix, restore, sew (up), stitch, darn, patch, renew, renovate, fill in; informal patch up.
OPPOSITES break.

**mental** adjective **1** *mental faculties:* intellectual, cerebral, rational, cognitive. **2** *a mental disorder:* psychiatric, psychological, behavioural.
OPPOSITES physical.

**mentality** noun way of thinking, mind set, mind, psychology, attitude, outlook, make-up.

**mentally** adverb psychologically, intellectually, in one's mind, in one's head, inwardly, internally.

**mention** verb **1** *don't mention the war:* allude to, refer to, touch on/upon, bring up, raise, broach. **2** *Jim mentioned that he'd met them before:* state, say, indicate, let someone know, disclose, divulge, reveal.
noun reference, allusion, comment, citation; informal namecheck, plug.

**mentor** noun adviser, counsellor, guide, guru, consultant, confidant(e), trainer, teacher, tutor, instructor.

**menu** noun bill of fare, tariff, carte du jour, set menu, table d'hôte.

**merchandise** noun goods, wares, stock, commodities, produce, products.

**merchant** noun trader, tradesman, dealer, wholesaler, broker, agent, seller, retailer, supplier, buyer, vendor, distributor.

**mercy** noun pity, compassion, leniency, clemency, charity, forgiveness, forbearance, kindness, sympathy, indulgence, tolerance, generosity, magnanimity.
OPPOSITES ruthlessness, cruelty.

**merely** adverb only, purely, solely, simply, just, but.

**merge** verb **1** *the company merged with a European firm:* join (together), join forces, amalgamate, unite, affiliate, team up. **2** *the two organizations were merged:* amalgamate, bring together, join, consolidate, conflate, unite, unify, combine, incorporate, integrate. **3** *the two colours merged:* mingle, blend, fuse, mix, intermix, intermingle, coalesce.
OPPOSITES separate.

**merger** noun amalgamation, combination, union, fusion, coalition, affiliation, unification, incorporation, consolidation, link-up, alliance.
OPPOSITES split.

**merit** noun **1** *composers of outstanding merit:* excellence, quality, calibre, worth, value, distinction, eminence. **2** *the merits of the scheme:* good point, strong point, advantage, benefit, value, asset, plus.
OPPOSITES inferiority, fault, disadvantage.
verb *the accusation did not merit a response:* deserve, warrant, justify, earn, rate, be worthy of, be entitled to, have a right to, have a claim to/on.

**merry** adjective cheerful, cheery, in high spirits, sunny, smiling, light-hearted, lively, carefree, joyful, joyous, jolly, convivial, festive, gleeful, happy,

a
b
c
d
e
f
g
h
i
j
k
l
**m**
n
o
p
q
r
s
t
u
v
w
x
y
z

laughing; informal chirpy.
OPPOSITES miserable.

**mesh** noun *wire mesh:* netting, net, grille, screen, lattice, gauze.
verb **1** *one gear meshes with the input gear:* engage, connect, lock, interlock. **2** *our ideas just do not mesh:* harmonize, fit together, match, dovetail, connect, interconnect.

**mess** noun **1** *please clear up the mess:* untidiness, disorder, disarray, clutter, muddle, chaos; informal shambles; Brit. informal tip. **2** *I've got to get out of this mess:* plight, predicament, tight spot, tight corner, difficulty, trouble, quandary, dilemma, problem, muddle, mix-up; informal jam, fix, pickle, hole.
■ **mess about/around** potter about, fiddle about/around, footle about/around, play about/around, fool about/ around, fidget, toy, trifle, tamper, tinker, interfere, meddle, monkey (about/ around); Brit. informal muck about/around. ■ **mess something up** dirty, clutter up, jumble, dishevel, rumple; N. Amer. informal muss up.

**message** noun **1** *are there any messages for me?* communication, news, note, memo, email, letter, missive, report, bulletin, communiqué, dispatch. **2** *the message of his teaching:* meaning, sense, import, idea, point, thrust, moral, gist, essence, implication.

**messenger** noun courier, postman, runner, dispatch rider, envoy, emissary, agent, go-between.

**messy** adjective **1** *messy clothes:* dirty, filthy, grubby, soiled, grimy, mucky, muddy, stained, smeared, smudged, dishevelled, scruffy, unkempt, rumpled, matted, tousled; informal yucky. **2** *a messy kitchen:* untidy, disordered, in a muddle, chaotic, confused, disorganized, in disarray, cluttered, in a jumble; informal like a bomb's hit it; Brit. informal shambolic. **3** *a messy legal battle:* complex, tangled, confused, convoluted, unpleasant, nasty, bitter, acrimonious.
OPPOSITES clean, tidy.

**metaphor** noun figure of speech, image, trope, analogy, comparison, symbol.

**method** noun **1** *they use very old-fashioned methods:* procedure, technique, system, practice, routine, modus operandi, process, strategy, tactic, approach. **2** *there's no method in his approach:* order, organization, structure, form, system, logic, planning, design, consistency.
OPPOSITES disorder.

**methodical** adjective orderly, well ordered, well organized, (well) planned, efficient, businesslike, systematic, structured, logical, disciplined, consistent, scientific.

**meticulous** adjective careful, conscientious, diligent, scrupulous, punctilious, painstaking, thorough, studious, rigorous, detailed, perfectionist, fastidious.
OPPOSITES careless.

**midday** noun noon, twelve noon, high noon, noonday.
OPPOSITES midnight.

**middle** noun **1** centre, midpoint, halfway point, dead centre, hub, eye, heart, core, kernel. **2** *he had a towel round his*

*middle:* midriff, waist, belly, stomach; informal tummy.
OPPOSITES edge.
adjective *the middle point:* central, mid, mean, medium, median, midway, halfway.

**might** noun strength, force, power, vigour, energy, brawn.

**mighty** adjective powerful, forceful, hard, heavy, violent, vigorous, hefty.
OPPOSITES feeble.

**migrant** noun *economic migrants:* immigrant, emigrant, nomad, itinerant, traveller, transient, wanderer, drifter.
adjective *migrant workers:* travelling, mobile, wandering, drifting, nomadic, itinerant, transient.

**migrate** verb 1 *rural populations migrated to towns:* relocate, resettle, move (house), emigrate, go abroad.
2 *wildebeest migrate across the Serengeti:* roam, wander, drift, rove, travel.

**mild** adjective 1 *a mild tone of voice:* gentle, tender, soft, sympathetic, peaceable, quiet, reasonable. 2 *a mild punishment:* lenient, light. 3 *he was eyeing her with mild interest:* slight, faint, vague. 4 *mild weather:* warm, balmy, temperate, clement. 5 *a mild curry:* bland, light, insipid.
OPPOSITES harsh, strong, cold, severe, hot.

**militant** adjective *militant workers:* hard-line, extreme, active, extremist, committed, zealous, fanatical, radical.
noun *a confrontation with militants:* activist, extremist, radical, zealot.

**military** adjective fighting, service, army, armed, defence, martial.
OPPOSITES civilian.
noun *the military took power:* (armed) forces, services, militia, army, navy, air force, marines.

**militate**
■ militate against work against, hinder, discourage, be prejudicial to, be detrimental to.

**milk** verb *milking rich clients:* exploit, take advantage of, suck dry; informal bleed, squeeze, fleece.

**mill** noun *a steel mill:* factory, plant, works, workshop, shop, foundry.
verb *the wheat is milled into flour:* grind, pulverize, powder, granulate, pound, crush, press.
■ mill around/about wander, drift, swarm, crowd, pack, fill.

**mimic** verb imitate, copy, impersonate, do an impression of, ape, caricature, parody; informal send up, take off.
noun impersonator, impressionist; informal copycat.

**mince** verb grind, chop up, cut up, dice, crumble; N. Amer. hash.

**mind** noun 1 *a good teacher must stretch pupils' minds:* brain, intelligence, intellect, brains, brainpower, wits, understanding, reasoning, judgement, sense, head; informal grey matter; N. Amer. informal smarts. 2 *he kept his mind on the job:* attention, thoughts, concentration. 3 *the tragedy affected her mind:* sanity, mental faculties, senses, wits, reason, reasoning, judgement. 4 *a great mind:* intellect, thinker, brain, scholar.
verb 1 *do you mind if I smoke?* object, care, be bothered, be

a
b
c
d
e
f
g
h
i
j
k
l
m
n
o
p
q
r
s
t
u
v
w
x
y
z

annoyed, be upset, take offence, disapprove, look askance; informal give/care a damn. **2** *mind the step!* be careful of, watch out for, look out for, beware of. **3** *mind you wipe your feet*: make sure, see, remember to, don't forget to. **4** *her husband was minding the baby*: look after, take care of, keep an eye on, attend to, care for.

**mine** noun **1** *a coal mine*: pit, colliery, excavation, quarry. **2** *a mine of information*: store, storehouse, reservoir, repository, gold mine, treasure house, treasury.
verb *the iron ore was mined from shallow pits*: quarry, excavate, dig, extract.

**mingle** verb **1** *fact and fiction are mingled*: mix, blend, intermingle, intermix, interweave, interlace, combine, merge, fuse, unite, join, amalgamate. **2** *guests mingled in the marquee*: socialize, circulate, associate, fraternize, get together; informal hobnob.
OPPOSITES separate.

**miniature** adjective small, mini, little, small-scale, baby, toy, pocket, diminutive; Scottish wee; N. Amer. vest-pocket.
OPPOSITES giant.

**minimal** adjective very little/small, minimum, the least (possible), nominal, token, negligible.
OPPOSITES maximum.

**minimize** verb **1** *the aim is to minimize costs*: keep down, keep to a minimum, reduce, decrease, cut (down), lessen, curtail, prune; informal slash. **2** *we should not minimize his contribution*: belittle, make light of, play down, underrate,

downplay, undervalue.
OPPOSITES maximize, exaggerate.

**minimum** noun *costs will be kept to the minimum*: lowest level, lower limit, rock bottom, least, lowest, slightest.
OPPOSITES maximum.
adjective *with the minimum effort*: minimal, least, smallest, least possible, slightest, lowest, minutest.
OPPOSITES maximum.

**minister** noun **1** *a government minister*: member of the government, member of the cabinet, secretary of state. **2** *a minister of religion*: clergyman, clergywoman, cleric, pastor, vicar, rector, priest, parson, curate; informal reverend, padre.
verb *doctors were ministering to the injured*: tend, care for, take care of, look after, nurse, treat, attend to, see to, help.

**ministry** noun **1** *the ministry for foreign affairs*: department, bureau, agency, office. **2** *he's training for the ministry*: the priesthood, holy orders, the cloth, the church.

**minor** adjective **1** *a minor problem*: slight, small, unimportant, insignificant, inconsequential, negligible, trivial, trifling, paltry, petty; N. Amer. nickel-and-dime; informal piffling. **2** *a minor poet*: little known, unknown, lesser, unimportant, insignificant, obscure; N. Amer. minor-league; informal small-time; N. Amer. informal two-bit.
OPPOSITES major, important.
noun *the accused was a minor*: child, infant, youth, adolescent, teenager, boy, girl; informal kid.
OPPOSITES adult.

**mint** verb coin, stamp, strike, cast, manufacture.

**minute**¹ noun 1 *it'll only take a minute:* moment, short time, little while, second, instant; informal sec, jiffy; Brit. informal tick, mo, two ticks. 2 *at that minute, Tony walked in a:* point (in time), moment, instant, second, juncture. 3 *their objection was noted in the minutes:* record(s), proceedings, log, notes, transcript, summary.

**minute**² adjective 1 *minute particles:* tiny, minuscule, microscopic, miniature; Scottish wee; informal teeny, teeny-weeny; Brit. informal titchy, tiddly. 2 *a minute chance of success:* negligible, slight, infinitesimal, minimal. 3 *in minute detail:* exhaustive, painstaking, meticulous, rigorous, thorough.
OPPOSITES huge.

**miracle** noun wonder, marvel, sensation, phenomenon.

**miraculous** adjective amazing, astounding, remarkable, extraordinary, incredible, unbelievable, sensational, phenomenal.

**mirror** noun 1 *a quick look in the mirror:* looking glass; Brit. glass. 2 *the Frenchman's life was a mirror of his own:* reflection, replica, copy, match, parallel.
verb *pop music mirrored the mood of desperation:* reflect, match, reproduce, imitate, copy, mimic, echo, parallel.

**misbehave** verb behave badly, be naughty, be disobedient, get up to mischief, get up to no good, be rude, informal carry on, act up.

**miscellaneous** adjective various, varied, different, assorted, mixed, sundry, diverse, disparate.

**mischief** noun 1 *the boys are always getting up to mischief:* naughtiness, bad behaviour, misbehaviour, misconduct, disobedience. 2 *the mischief in her eyes:* impishness, roguishness, glint, twinkle.

**miser** noun penny-pincher, Scrooge; informal skinflint, cheapskate; N. Amer. informal tightwad.
OPPOSITES spendthrift.

**miserable** adjective 1 *I'm too miserable to eat:* unhappy, sad, sorrowful, dejected, depressed, down, despondent, disconsolate, wretched, glum, forlorn; informal blue, down in the dumps. 2 *their miserable surroundings:* dreary, dismal, gloomy, drab, wretched, depressing, grim, cheerless, bleak, desolate.
OPPOSITES cheerful, lovely.

**misery** noun unhappiness, distress, wretchedness, suffering, anguish, anxiety, angst, torment, pain, grief, heartache, heartbreak, despair, despondency, dejection, depression, gloom, sorrow; informal the blues.
OPPOSITES contentment, pleasure.

**misfortune** noun problem, difficulty, setback, trouble, adversity, (stroke of) bad luck, misadventure, mishap, blow, failure, accident, disaster.

**misguided** adjective unwise, ill-advised, ill-judged, ill-considered, injudicious, imprudent, unsound, mistaken, misplaced.
OPPOSITES wise.

**mislay** verb lose, misplace, be unable to find.
OPPOSITES find.

**mislead** verb deceive, delude, take in, lie to, fool, hoodwink, misinform; informal lead up the garden path; N. Amer. informal give someone a bum steer.

**misleading** adjective deceptive, confusing, deceiving, equivocal, false.
OPPOSITES clear, honest, straightforward.

**miss** verb 1 *the shot missed her by inches:* go wide of, fall short of, pass, overshoot. 2 *I left early to miss the traffic:* avoid, beat, evade, escape, dodge, sidestep, elude, circumvent, bypass. 3 *she missed him when he was away:* pine for, yearn for, ache for, long for. 4 *she never missed a meeting:* fail to attend, be absent from, play truant from, cut, skip, omit; Brit. informal skive off.
OPPOSITES hit, catch, attend.
noun *one hit and three misses:* failure, omission, slip, error, mistake.
■ **miss someone/something out** leave out, exclude, miss (off), fail to mention, pass over, skip, omit, ignore.

**missing** adjective 1 *his wallet is missing:* lost, mislaid, misplaced, absent, gone (astray), unaccounted for. 2 *passion was missing from her life:* absent, lacking, gone, wanting.
OPPOSITES present.

**mission** noun 1 *a mercy mission to Romania:* assignment, commission, expedition, journey, trip, undertaking, operation, project. 2 *her mission in life:* vocation, calling, goal, aim, quest, purpose, function, task, job, labour, work, duty.

**missionary** noun evangelist, apostle, proselytizer, preacher.

**mist** noun haze, fog, smog, murk, cloud, vapour, steam, spray, condensation.

**mistake** noun *it was all a mistake:* error, fault, inaccuracy, omission, slip, blunder, miscalculation, misunderstanding, oversight, misinterpretation, gaffe, faux pas; informal slip-up, boo-boo, howler; Brit. informal boob, clanger; N. Amer. informal goof.
verb 1 *men are apt to mistake their own feelings:* misunderstand, misinterpret, get wrong, misconstrue, misread. 2 *children often mistake pills for sweets:* confuse with, mix up with, take for.
■ **make a mistake** make an error etc., go wrong, err, blunder, miscalculate.

**mistaken** adjective 1 *such a mistaken view:* inaccurate, wrong, erroneous, incorrect, off beam, false, fallacious, unfounded, misguided. 2 *you are mistaken there:* misinformed, wrong, in error, under a misapprehension, barking up the wrong tree.
OPPOSITES correct.

**mistimed** adjective ill-timed, badly timed, inopportune, inappropriate, untimely.
OPPOSITES opportune.

**mistrust** verb be suspicious of, be sceptical of, be wary of, be chary of, distrust, have doubts about, have misgivings about, have reservations about, suspect.

**misunderstand** verb misapprehend, misinterpret, misconstrue, misconceive, mistake, misread, be mistaken, get the wrong idea; informal get (hold of) the wrong end of the stick.

**misunderstanding** noun 1 *a*

# misuse → mock

*misunderstanding of juvenile crime:* misinterpretation, misreading, misapprehension, misconception, false impression. **2** *we have had some misunderstandings:* disagreement, difference (of opinion), dispute, falling-out, quarrel, argument, clash.

**misuse** verb *misusing public funds:* embezzle, misappropriate, abuse, waste, squander.
noun *a misuse of company assets:* embezzlement, fraud, squandering, waste.

**mix** verb **1** *mix all the ingredients together:* blend, mingle, combine, jumble, fuse, unite, join, amalgamate, incorporate, meld, homogenize; technical admix; literary commingle. **2** *she mixes with all sorts:* associate, socialize, keep company, consort, mingle, circulate; Brit. rub shoulders; N. Amer. rub elbows; informal hang out/around, hobnob.
OPPOSITES separate.
noun *a mix of ancient and modern:* mixture, blend, combination, compound, fusion, union, amalgamation, medley, selection, assortment, variety.

**mixed** adjective **1** *a mixed collection:* assorted, varied, variegated, miscellaneous, disparate, diverse, diversified, motley, sundry, jumbled, heterogeneous. **2** *mixed reactions:* ambivalent, equivocal, contradictory, conflicting, confused, muddled.
OPPOSITES homogeneous.

**mixture** noun **1** *the pudding mixture:* blend, mix, brew, combination, compound, composition, compound, alloy,

amalgam. **2** *a strange mixture of people:* assortment, miscellany, medley, blend, variety, mixed bag, mix, diversity, collection, selection, hotchpotch, ragbag; N. Amer. hodgepodge.

**mix-up** noun confusion, muddle, misunderstanding, mistake, error.

**moan** verb **1** *he moaned in agony:* groan, wail, whimper, sob, cry. **2** (informal) *you're always moaning about the weather:* complain, grouse, grumble, whine, carp; informal gripe, grouch, bellyache, bitch, beef, whinge.

**mob** noun *troops dispersed the mob:* crowd, horde, multitude, rabble, mass, throng, gathering, assembly.
verb *the Chancellor was mobbed:* surround, crowd round, besiege, jostle.

**mobile** adjective **1** *both patients are mobile:* able to move (around), able to walk, walking; informal up and about. **2** *a mobile library:* travelling, transportable, portable, movable, itinerant, peripatetic.
OPPOSITES immobilized, fixed.

**mobilize** verb **1** *the government mobilized the troops:* marshal, deploy, muster, rally, call up, assemble, mass, organize, prepare. **2** *mobilizing support for the party:* generate, arouse, awaken, excite, stimulate, stir up, encourage, inspire, whip up.

**mock** verb *the local children mocked the old people:* ridicule, jeer at, sneer at, deride, make fun of, laugh at, scoff at, tease, taunt; informal take the mickey out of; N. Amer. informal goof on, rag on; Austral./NZ informal chiack, sling off at.
adjective *mock leather:*

a b c d e f g h i j k l **m** n o p q r s t u v w x y z

**imitation**, artificial, man-made, simulated, synthetic, ersatz, fake, reproduction, false, counterfeit; informal pretend.
OPPOSITES genuine.

**mocking** adjective **sneering**, derisive, contemptuous, scornful, sardonic, ironic, sarcastic.

**mode** noun **1** *an informal mode of policing:* **manner**, way, means, method, system, style, approach. **2** *the camera is in manual mode:* **function**, position, operation, setting, option.

**model** noun **1** *a working model:* **replica**, copy, representation, mock-up, dummy, imitation, duplicate, reproduction, facsimile. **2** *the American model of airline deregulation:* **prototype**, archetype, type, version, mould, template, framework, pattern, design, blueprint. **3** *a top model:* **fashion model**, supermodel, mannequin; informal clothes horse.
adjective **1** *model trains:* **replica**, toy, miniature, dummy, imitation, duplicate, reproduction, facsimile. **2** *a model teacher:* **ideal**, perfect, exemplary, classic, flawless, faultless.

**moderate** adjective **1** *moderate success:* **average**, modest, medium, middling, tolerable, passable, adequate, fair; informal OK, so-so, bog-standard, fair-to-middling. **2** *moderate prices:* **reasonable**, acceptable, affordable, inexpensive, fair, modest. **3** *moderate views:* **middle-of-the-road**, non-extremist, liberal, pragmatic.
OPPOSITES great, unreasonable, extreme.

verb **1** *the wind has moderated:* **die down**, abate, let up, calm down, lessen, decrease, diminish, recede, weaken, subside. **2** *you can help her moderate her temper:* **curb**, control, check, temper, restrain, subdue, tame, lessen, decrease, lower, reduce, diminish, alleviate, allay, appease, ease, soothe, calm, tone down.
OPPOSITES increase.

**moderately** adverb **somewhat**, quite, fairly, reasonably, comparatively, relatively, to some extent, tolerably, adequately; informal pretty.

**modern** adjective **1** *modern times:* **present-day**, contemporary, present, current, twenty-first-century, latter-day, recent. **2** *her clothes are very modern:* **fashionable**, up to date, trendsetting, stylish, chic, à la mode, the latest, new, newest, newfangled, advanced; informal trendy, cool, in.
OPPOSITES past, old-fashioned.

**modest** adjective **1** *she was modest about her poetry:* **humble**, self-deprecating, self-effacing, unassuming, shy, diffident, reserved, coy. **2** *modest success:* **moderate**, fair, limited, tolerable, passable, adequate, satisfactory, acceptable, unexceptional. **3** *a modest house:* **small**, ordinary, simple, plain, humble, inexpensive, unostentatious, unpretentious. **4** *her modest dress:* **demure**, decent, seemly, decorous, proper.
OPPOSITES conceited, great, grand, indecent.

**modesty** noun **humility**, self-effacement, shyness, bashfulness, self-consciousness, reserve.

**modification** noun change, adjustment, alteration, adaptation, refinement, revision, amendment; informal tweak.

**modify** verb 1 *their economic policy has been modified:* change, alter, adjust, adapt, amend, revise, refine; informal tweak. 2 *he modified his more extreme views:* moderate, temper, soften, tone down, qualify.

**moist** adjective 1 *the air was moist:* damp, steamy, humid, muggy, clammy, dank, wet, soggy, sweaty, sticky. 2 *a moist fruitcake:* succulent, juicy, soft, tender.
OPPOSITES dry.

**moisten** verb dampen, wet, damp, water, humidify.

**moisture** noun wetness, wet, water, liquid, condensation, steam, vapour, dampness, damp, humidity.

**moment** noun 1 *he thought for a moment:* little while, short time, bit, minute, instant, (split) second; informal sec, jiffy; Brit. informal tick, mo, two ticks. 2 *just at that moment:* point (in time), stage, juncture, instant, time, hour, second, minute, day.

**momentary** adjective brief, short, short-lived, fleeting, passing.
OPPOSITES lengthy.

**momentous** adjective important, significant, historic, critical, crucial, decisive, pivotal, consequential, far-reaching; informal earth-shattering.
OPPOSITES insignificant.

**momentum** noun impetus, energy, force, power, strength, thrust, speed, velocity.

**monarch** noun sovereign, ruler, Crown, crowned head, potentate, king, queen, emperor, empress, prince, princess.

**monastery** noun monastic community, friary, abbey, priory, cloister.

**monetary** adjective financial, fiscal, pecuniary, money, cash, capital, economic, budgetary.

**money** noun cash, hard cash, means, wherewithal, funds, capital, finances, notes, coins, change, currency; informal dough, bread, loot; Brit. informal dosh, brass, lolly; N. Amer. informal dinero, mazuma.

**monitor** noun 1 *monitors covered all entrances:* detector, scanner, recorder, sensor, security camera, CCTV. 2 *UN monitors:* observer, watchdog, overseer, supervisor, scrutineer. 3 *a computer monitor:* screen, display, VDU.
verb *his movements were closely monitored:* observe, watch, track, keep an eye on, keep under surveillance, record, note, oversee; informal keep tabs on.

**monster** noun 1 *legendary sea monsters:* giant, mammoth, demon, dragon, colossus, leviathan, creature. 2 *her husband is a monster:* fiend, animal, beast, devil, demon, barbarian, savage, brute; informal swine.

**monstrous** adjective 1 *a monstrous creature:* grotesque, hideous, ugly, ghastly, gruesome, horrible, horrific, horrifying, grisly, disgusting, repulsive, dreadful, frightening, terrible, terrifying. 2 *monstrous acts of violence:* appalling, wicked, abominable, terrible, horrible, dreadful, vile,

a
b
c
d
e
f
g
h
i
j
k
l
**m**
n
o
p
q
r
s
t
u
v
w
x
y
z

outrageous, unspeakable, despicable, vicious, savage, barbaric, inhuman.
OPPOSITES lovely, kind.

**monument** noun memorial, statue, pillar, cairn, column, obelisk, cross, cenotaph, tomb, mausoleum, shrine.

**monumental** adjective 1 *a monumental task:* huge, enormous, gigantic, massive, colossal, mammoth, immense, tremendous, mighty, stupendous. 2 *his monumental career:* significant, important, majestic, memorable, noteworthy, momentous, defining, grand, awe-inspiring, heroic, epic.
OPPOSITES tiny, insignificant.

**mood** noun 1 *she's in a good mood:* frame of mind, state of mind, humour, temper. 2 *he's obviously in a mood:* bad mood, temper, bad temper, sulk, low spirits, the doldrums, the blues; Brit. informal paddy. 3 *the mood of the film:* atmosphere, feeling, spirit, ambience, aura, character, flavour, feel, tone.

**moody** adjective temperamental, emotional, volatile, capricious, sullen, sulky, morose, glum, depressed, dejected, despondent, doleful.
OPPOSITES cheerful.

**moon** noun satellite.
verb 1 *stop mooning about:* waste time, loaf, idle, mope; Brit. informal mooch; N. Amer. informal lollygag. 2 *he's mooning over her photograph:* mope, pine, brood, daydream.

**moor**¹ verb *a boat was moored to the quay:* tie (up), secure, make fast, berth, dock.

**moor**² noun *a walk on the moor:* upland, heath, moorland; Brit. fell, wold.

**mop** noun *her tousled mop of hair:* shock, mane, tangle, mass.
verb *a man was mopping the floor:* wash, clean, wipe, sponge.

**moral** adjective 1 *moral issues:* ethical. 2 *a very moral man:* good, virtuous, righteous, upright, upstanding, high-minded, principled, honourable, honest, just, noble. 3 *moral support:* psychological, emotional, mental.
OPPOSITES dishonourable, practical.
noun 1 *the moral of the story:* lesson, message, meaning, significance, import, point, teaching. 2 (**morals**) moral code, code of ethics, values, principles, standards, (sense of) morality, scruples.

**morale** noun confidence, self-confidence, self-esteem, spirit(s), team spirit, motivation.

**morality** noun 1 *the morality of nuclear weapons:* ethics, rights and wrongs, whys and wherefores. 2 *a sharp decline in morality:* virtue, good behaviour, righteousness, uprightness, morals, principles, honesty, integrity, propriety, honour, decency. 3 *Christian morality:* morals, standards, ethics, principles, mores.

**morbid** adjective ghoulish, macabre, unhealthy, gruesome, unwholesome; informal sick.
OPPOSITES wholesome.

**more** determiner *some more clothes:* extra, further, added, additional, supplementary, increased, new.
OPPOSITES less, fewer.

**moreover** adverb besides, furthermore, what's more, in addition, also, as well, too, to boot, additionally, on top of that, into the bargain.

**morning** noun **1** *I've got a meeting this morning:* before lunch(time), a.m.; literary morn; Nautical & N. Amer. forenoon. **2** *morning is on its way:* dawn, daybreak, sunrise, first light; N. Amer. sunup.

**mortal** adjective **1** *all men are mortal:* perishable, physical, bodily, corporeal, human, fleshly, earthly, impermanent, transient, ephemeral. **2** *a mortal blow:* deadly, fatal, lethal, death-dealing, murderous, terminal.
OPPOSITES eternal.
noun *we are mere mortals:* human (being), person, man, woman, earthling.

**mortuary** noun morgue, funeral parlour; Brit. chapel of rest.

**mostly** adverb **1** *the other passengers were mostly businessmen:* mainly, for the most part, on the whole, in the main, largely, chiefly, predominantly, principally, primarily. **2** *I mostly wear jeans:* usually, generally, in general, as a rule, ordinarily, normally, customarily, typically, most of the time, almost always.

**mother** noun informal ma; Brit. informal mum, mummy; N. Amer. informal mom, mommy; Brit. informal, dated mater.
verb *her colleagues mothered her:* look after, care for, take care of, nurse, protect, tend, raise, rear, pamper, coddle, cosset, fuss over.
OPPOSITES neglect.

**motherly** adjective maternal, maternalistic, protective, caring, loving, affectionate, nurturing.

**motif** noun **1** *a colourful tulip motif:* design, pattern, decoration, figure, shape, device, emblem. **2** *a recurring motif in Pinter's work:* theme, idea, concept, subject, topic, leitmotif.

**motion** noun **1** *a planet's motion around the sun:* movement, locomotion, progress, passage, transit, course, travel, orbit. **2** *a motion of the hand:* gesture, movement, signal, sign, indication, wave, nod, gesticulation. **3** *the motion was passed:* proposal, proposition, recommendation.
verb *he motioned her to sit down:* gesture, signal, direct, indicate, wave, beckon, nod.

**motivate** verb **1** *motivated by greed:* prompt, drive, move, inspire, stimulate, influence, activate, impel, propel, spur (on). **2** *the teacher must motivate the child:* inspire, stimulate, encourage, spur (on), excite, incentivize, fire (with enthusiasm).

**motivation** noun motive, motivating force, incentive, stimulus, stimulation, inspiration, inducement, incitement, spur.

**motive** noun reason, motivation, motivating force, rationale, grounds, cause, basis.

**motto** noun slogan, maxim, saying, proverb, aphorism, adage, saw, axiom, formula, catchphrase.

**mould** noun **1** *a clay mould:* cast, die, form, matrix, shape, template, pattern, frame. **2** *an actress in the traditional Hollywood mould:* pattern, form, type, style, tradition, school.
verb **1** *a figure moulded from clay:* shape, form, fashion,

a
b
c
d
e
f
g
h
i
j
k
l
**m**
n
o
p
q
r
s
t
u
v
w
x
y
z

model, work, construct, make, create, sculpt, cast. **2** *the ideas that mould US policy:* determine, direct, control, guide, influence, shape, form, fashion, make.

**mound** noun **1** *a mound of books:* heap, pile, stack, mountain. **2** *high on the mound:* hillock, hill, knoll, rise, hummock, hump; Scottish brae.

**mount** verb **1** *he mounted the stairs:* go up, ascend, climb (up), scale. **2** *they mounted their horses:* get on to, bestride, climb on to, leap on to, hop on to. **3** *the museum is mounting an exhibition:* put on, present, install, organize, stage, set up, prepare, launch, set in motion. **4** *their losses mounted rapidly:* increase, grow, rise, escalate, soar, spiral, shoot up, rocket, climb, accumulate, build up, multiply.
OPPOSITES descend, dismount, fall.
noun *a picture mount:* setting, backing, support, mounting, frame, stand.

**mountain** noun **1** *climb a mountain:* peak, summit; (**mountains**) range, massif, sierra; Scottish ben. **2** *a mountain of work:* lot; informal heap, pile, stack, slew, lots, loads, tons, masses.

**mourn** verb **1** *Isobel mourned her husband:* grieve for, sorrow over, lament for, weep for. **2** *he mourned the loss of the beautiful buildings:* deplore, bewail, bemoan, rue, regret.

**mourning** noun grief, grieving, sorrowing, lamentation.

**mouth** noun **1** lips, jaws, muzzle; informal trap, chops, kisser; Brit. informal gob; N. Amer. informal puss, bazoo. **2** *the mouth* *of the cave:* entrance, opening. **3** *the mouth of the river:* estuary, delta, firth, outlet, outfall.

**move** verb **1** *she moved to the door | don't move!* go, walk, step, proceed, progress, advance, budge, stir, shift, change position. **2** *he moved the chair closer to the fire:* carry, transfer, shift, push, pull, lift, slide. **3** *things were moving too fast:* go, progress, advance, develop, evolve, change, happen. **4** *he urged the council to move quickly:* act, take steps, do something, take measures; informal get moving. **5** *she's moved to Cambridge:* relocate, move house, move away/out, change address, go (away), decamp. **6** *I was deeply moved by the story:* affect, touch, impress, shake, upset, disturb. **7** *she was moved to find out more about it:* inspire, prompt, stimulate, motivate, provoke, influence, rouse, induce, incite. **8** *I move that we adjourn:* propose, submit, suggest, advocate, recommend, urge.
noun **1** *his eyes followed her every move:* movement, motion, action, gesture. **2** *his recent move to London:* relocation, change of house/address, transfer, posting. **3** *the latest move in the war against drugs:* initiative, step, action, measure, manoeuvre, tactic, stratagem. **4** *it's your move:* turn, go; informal shot.

**movement** noun **1** *Rachel made a sudden movement:* motion, move, gesture, sign, signal, action. **2** *the movement of supplies:* transportation, shifting, conveyance, moving, transfer. **3** *a political movement:* group, party, faction, wing, lobby, camp. **4** *a movement to declare war on poverty:* campaign, crusade, drive, push, initiative.

**movie** noun film, picture, feature film; informal flick.

**moving** adjective **1** in motion, operating, operational, working, on the move, active, movable, mobile. **2** *a moving book:* affecting, touching, poignant, heart-warming, heart-rending, emotional, inspiring, inspirational, stimulating, stirring.
OPPOSITES stationary, fixed.

**mow** verb cut, trim, crop, clip, shear.

**much** determiner *is there much food?* a lot of, a great/good deal of, a great/large amount of, plenty of, ample, abundant, plentiful; informal lots of, loads of, heaps of, masses of, tons of, stacks of.
OPPOSITES little.
adverb **1** *it didn't hurt much:* greatly, a great deal, a lot, considerably, appreciably.
**2** *does he come here much?* often, frequently, many times, regularly, habitually, routinely, usually, normally, commonly; informal a lot.
pronoun *he did much for our team:* a lot, a great/good deal, plenty; informal lots, loads, heaps, masses, tons.

**muck** noun **1** *I'll just clean off the muck:* dirt, grime, filth, mud, mess; Brit. informal gunge; N. Amer. informal guck. **2** *spreading muck on the fields:* dung, manure, excrement, droppings.

**mud** noun dirt, sludge, ooze, silt, clay, mire, soil.

**muddle** verb **1** *the papers have got muddled up:* confuse, mix up, jumble (up), disarrange,
disorganize, disorder, mess up.
**2** *it would only muddle you:* bewilder, confuse, bemuse, perplex, puzzle, baffle, nonplus, mystify.
noun mess, confusion, jumble, tangle, chaos, disorder, disarray, disorganization.

**muddy** adjective **1** *muddy ground:* marshy, boggy, swampy, waterlogged, squelchy, squishy, mucky, slimy, wet, soft. **2** *muddy boots:* dirty, filthy, mucky, grimy, soiled. **3** *muddy water:* murky, cloudy, turbid.
OPPOSITES clean, clear.

**muffle** verb **1** *everyone was muffled up in coats:* wrap (up), swathe, enfold, envelop, cloak. **2** *the sound of their footsteps was muffled:* deaden, dull, dampen, mute, soften, quieten, mask, stifle, smother.

**mug** noun *a china mug:* beaker, cup, tankard, glass, stein.
verb (informal) *he was mugged by youths:* assault, attack, set upon, beat up, rob; informal jump.

**multiple** adjective numerous, many, various, different, diverse, several, manifold.
OPPOSITES single.

**multiply** verb increase, grow, accumulate, proliferate, mount up, mushroom, snowball.
OPPOSITES decrease.

**mumble** verb mutter, murmur, talk under one's breath.

**mundane** adjective humdrum, dull, boring, tedious, monotonous, tiresome, unexciting, uninteresting, uneventful, unremarkable, routine, ordinary.
OPPOSITES extraordinary.

**municipal** adjective civic, civil, metropolitan, urban, city, town, borough, council.
OPPOSITES private, rural.

a
b
c
d
e
f
g
h
i
j
k
l
**m**
n
o
p
q
r
s
t
u
v
w
x
y
z

**murder** noun *a brutal murder:* killing, homicide, assassination, extermination, execution, slaughter, butchery, massacre, manslaughter; literary slaying. verb *someone tried to murder him:* kill, put/do to death, assassinate, execute, butcher, slaughter, massacre, wipe out; informal bump off; N. Amer. informal ice, waste; literary slay.

**murderer, murderess** noun killer, assassin, serial killer, butcher; informal hit man, hired gun.

**murderous** adjective homicidal, brutal, violent, savage, ferocious, fierce, vicious, bloodthirsty, barbarous, barbaric, fatal, lethal, deadly.

**murky** adjective 1 *a murky winter afternoon:* dark, gloomy, grey, leaden, dull, dim, overcast, cloudy, clouded, sunless, dismal, dreary, bleak. 2 *murky water:* dirty, muddy, cloudy, turbid.
OPPOSITES bright, clear.

**murmur** noun 1 *his voice was a murmur:* whisper, mutter, mumble. 2 *the murmur of bees:* hum, buzz, drone. verb *he heard them murmuring in the hall:* mutter, mumble, whisper, talk under one's breath.

**muscle** noun 1 *he had muscle but no brains:* strength, power, brawn; informal beef, beefiness. 2 *financial muscle:* influence, power, strength, might, force, forcefulness, weight; informal clout.
■ **muscle in** (informal) interfere, force one's way in, impose oneself, encroach; informal horn in.

**muscular** adjective strong, brawny, muscly, well built,

burly, strapping, sturdy, powerful, athletic; informal hunky, beefy.

**muse** verb ponder, consider, think over/about, mull over, reflect on, contemplate, turn over in one's mind, chew over.

**musical** adjective tuneful, melodic, melodious, harmonious, sweet-sounding.
OPPOSITES discordant.

**must** verb ought to, should, have (got) to, need to, be obliged to, be required to, be compelled to.

**muster** verb 1 *they mustered 50,000 troops:* assemble, mobilize, rally, raise, summon, gather, mass, call up, call to arms, recruit, conscript; US draft. 2 *reporters mustered outside her house:* congregate, assemble, gather (together), come together, collect, convene, mass, rally. 3 *she mustered her courage:* summon (up), screw up, call up, rally.

**mutation** noun 1 alteration, change, transformation, metamorphosis, transmutation. 2 *a genetic mutation:* mutant, freak (of nature), deviant, monstrosity, monster.

**mute** adjective 1 *Yasmin remained mute:* silent, speechless, dumb, unspeaking, tight-lipped, taciturn; informal mum. 2 *a mute appeal:* wordless, silent, dumb, unspoken.
OPPOSITES voluble, spoken.

**muted** adjective 1 *the muted hum of traffic:* muffled, faint, indistinct, quiet, soft, low, distant, faraway. 2 *muted tones:* subdued, pastel, delicate, subtle, understated, restrained.

**mutilate** verb 1 *the bodies had been mutilated:* mangle, maim, disfigure, dismember, slash, hack. **2** *the carved screen had been mutilated*: vandalize, damage, slash, hack, deface, violate, desecrate.

**mutiny** noun *a naval mutiny*: insurrection, rebellion, revolt, riot, uprising, insurgence, insubordination.
verb *the crew mutinied*: rise up, rebel, revolt, riot, strike.

**mutter** verb **1** *a group of men stood muttering*: talk under one's breath, murmur, mumble, whisper. **2** *residents muttered about the charge*: grumble, complain, grouse, carp, whine; informal moan, whinge.

**mutual** adjective reciprocal, reciprocated, requited, returned, common, joint, shared.

**mysterious** adjective
**1** *mysterious circumstances*: puzzling, strange, peculiar, curious, funny, odd, weird, bizarre, mystifying, inexplicable, baffling, perplexing. **2** *he was being very mysterious*: secretive, inscrutable, enigmatic, reticent, evasive, furtive, surreptitious. OPPOSITES straightforward.

**mystery** noun **1** *his death remains a mystery*: puzzle, enigma, conundrum, riddle, secret, paradox. **2** *her past is shrouded in mystery*: secrecy, obscurity, uncertainty, mystique.

**mystic, mystical** adjective spiritual, religious, transcendental, paranormal, other-worldly, supernatural, occult, metaphysical.

**myth** noun **1** *ancient Greek myths*: folk tale, folk story, legend, fable, saga, lore, folklore. **2** *the myths surrounding childbirth*: misconception, fallacy, old wives' tale, fairy story, fiction; informal cock and bull story.

# Nn

**nag** verb **1** *she's constantly nagging me*: harass, keep on at, go on at, badger, chivvy, hound, criticize, find fault with, moan at, grumble at, henpeck; informal hassle; N. Amer. informal ride. **2** *this has been nagging me for weeks*: trouble, worry, bother, plague, torment, niggle, prey on one's mind; informal bug.

**nail** noun *fastened with nails*: tack, pin, brad, clout, spike, staple.
verb *a board was nailed to the wall*: fasten, attach, fix, affix, secure, tack, hammer, pin.

**naive** adjective innocent, unsophisticated, artless, inexperienced, unworldly, trusting, gullible, credulous, immature, callow, raw, green; informal wet behind the ears. OPPOSITES worldly.

**naked** adjective nude, bare, in the nude, stark naked, having nothing on, stripped, unclothed, undressed; informal without a stitch on, in one's birthday suit, in the raw/buff, in the altogether, starkers; Brit. informal buck naked.

a
b
c
d
e
f
g
h
i
j
k
l
m
**n**
o
p
q
r
s
t
u
v
w
x
y
z

OPPOSITES clothed.

**name** noun *her name's Gemma:* title, honorific, designation, tag, epithet, label; informal moniker, handle.
verb **1** *they named the child Pamela:* call, dub, label, style, term, title, baptize, christen. **2** *he has named his successor:* nominate, designate, select, pick, decide on, choose.

**namely** adverb that is (to say), to be specific, specifically, viz., to wit, in other words.

**nap** noun sleep, catnap, siesta, doze, lie-down, rest; informal snooze, forty winks, shut-eye; Brit. informal kip.

**narcotic** noun *illegal narcotics:* drug, sedative, opiate, painkiller, analgesic, palliative.
adjective *a narcotic effect:* soporific, sedative, calming, sleep-inducing, opiate, painkilling, pain-relieving, analgesic, anodyne.

**narrate** verb tell, relate, recount, describe, chronicle, report, present.

**narrative** noun account, chronicle, history, description, record, report, story, tale.

**narrator** noun storyteller, relater, chronicler, commentator, presenter, author.
OPPOSITES listener, audience.

**narrow** adjective **1** *her narrow waist:* slender, slim, small, slight, spare, attenuated, tapering, thin, tiny. **2** *a narrow space:* confined, cramped, tight, restricted, limited, constricted, small, tiny. **3** *a narrow range of products:* limited, restricted, small, inadequate, insufficient, deficient.
OPPOSITES wide, broad.
verb *narrowing the gap between rich and poor:* become/make narrower, become/make smaller, taper, diminish, decrease, reduce, contract, shrink, constrict.
OPPOSITES widen.

**narrowly** adverb (only) just, barely, scarcely, hardly, by a hair's breadth; informal by a whisker.

**narrow-minded** adjective intolerant, illiberal, reactionary, conservative, parochial, provincial, insular, small-minded, petty, blinkered, inward-looking, narrow, hidebound, prejudiced, bigoted.
OPPOSITES tolerant.

**nasty** adjective **1** *a nasty smell:* unpleasant, disagreeable, disgusting, vile, foul, abominable, revolting, repulsive, repellent, obnoxious, unsavoury, noxious, foul-smelling, smelly, stinking, rank; informal ghastly, horrid, yucky; N. Amer. informal lousy. **2** *she can be really nasty:* unkind, unpleasant, unfriendly, disagreeable, rude, spiteful, malicious, mean, vicious, malevolent, hurtful. **3** *a nasty accident:* serious, dangerous, bad, awful, dreadful, terrible, severe, painful, ugly.
OPPOSITES nice, slight.

**nation** noun country, state, land, realm, people, race, tribe, clan.

**national** adjective **1** *national politics:* state, public, federal, governmental. **2** *a national strike:* nationwide, countrywide, state, general, widespread.
OPPOSITES local, international.
noun *a French national:* citizen, subject, native, resident, inhabitant, voter, passport holder.

**nationalism** noun patriotism, allegiance, xenophobia, chauvinism, jingoism.

**nationwide** adjective national, countrywide, state, general, widespread, extensive. OPPOSITES local.

**native** noun *a native of Sweden:* inhabitant, resident, local, citizen, national, countryman. OPPOSITES foreigner.
adjective 1 *the native population:* indigenous, original. 2 *native produce:* domestic, home-grown, home-made, local, indigenous. 3 *her native tongue:* mother, home, local, vernacular. OPPOSITES immigrant, imported.

**natural** adjective 1 *a natural occurrence:* normal, ordinary, everyday, usual, regular, common, commonplace, typical, routine, standard. 2 *natural products:* unprocessed, organic, pure, unrefined, additive-free, green, GM-free. 3 *Alex is a natural leader:* born, instinctive, congenital, pathological. 4 *his natural instincts:* innate, inborn, inherent, native, hereditary, inherited, inbred. 5 *she seemed very natural:* unaffected, spontaneous, uninhibited, relaxed, unselfconscious, genuine, open, artless, guileless, unpretentious. 6 *it was quite natural to think she admired him:* reasonable, logical, understandable, (only) to be expected, predictable. OPPOSITES abnormal, artificial, affected.

**naturally** adverb 1 *he's naturally shy:* by nature, by character, inherently, innately, congenitally, pathologically. 2 *try to act naturally:* normally, in a natural manner, spontaneously, genuinely, unpretentiously; informal natural. 3 *naturally, they wanted everything kept quiet:* of course, as might be expected, needless to say, obviously, clearly, it goes without saying. OPPOSITES self-consciously.

**nature** noun 1 *the beauty of nature:* the natural world, the environment, the universe, the cosmos, wildlife, the countryside, the land, the landscape. 2 *the very nature of such crimes:* essence, inherent features, character, complexion. 3 *nastiness was not in her nature:* character, personality, disposition, temperament, make-up, psyche. 4 *experiments of a similar nature:* kind, sort, type, variety, category, genre, order; N. Amer. stripe.

**naughty** adjective 1 *a naughty boy:* badly behaved, disobedient, bad, wayward, defiant, unruly, insubordinate, wilful, delinquent, undisciplined, disruptive, mischievous, impish. 2 *naughty jokes:* indecent, risqué, rude, racy, vulgar, dirty, filthy, smutty, crude, coarse. OPPOSITES well behaved, clean.

**nausea** noun sickness, biliousness, queasiness, vomiting, retching.

**nautical** adjective maritime, marine, naval, seafaring, boating, sailing.

**navigate** verb 1 *he navigated the yacht across the Atlantic:* steer, pilot, guide, direct, captain; informal skipper. 2 *I'll drive—you can navigate:* map-read, give directions.

**navy** noun fleet, flotilla, armada, squadron, task force.

a
b
c
d
e
f
g
h
i
j
k
l
m
**n**
o
p
q
r
s
t
u
v
w
x
y
z

**near** adjective 1 *the house is quite near:* close, nearby, (close/near) at hand, a stone's throw away, within reach, accessible, handy, convenient; informal within spitting distance. 2 *the final judgement is near:* imminent, in the offing, (close/near) at hand, (just) around the corner, on its way, coming, impending, looming.
OPPOSITES far, distant.

**nearby** adjective not far away/off, close at hand, close by, near, within reach, neighbouring, local, accessible, handy, convenient.
OPPOSITES faraway.

**nearly** adverb almost, just about, more or less, practically, virtually, all but, as good as, not far off, to all intents and purposes, not quite; informal pretty well.

**neat** adjective 1 *the bedroom was neat and clean:* tidy, orderly, well ordered, in (good) order, spick and span, uncluttered, straight, trim. 2 *he's very neat:* smart, spruce, dapper, trim, well groomed, well turned out; informal natty. 3 *her neat handwriting:* clear, regular, precise, elegant; informal easy to read. 4 *this neat little gadget:* compact, well designed, handy; Brit. informal dinky, nifty. 5 *his neat footwork:* skilful, deft, dexterous, adroit, adept, expert; informal nifty. 6 *a neat solution:* clever, ingenious, inventive, imaginative. 7 *neat gin:* undiluted, straight, unmixed; N. Amer. informal straight up.
OPPOSITES untidy.

**necessarily** adverb as a consequence, as a result, automatically, as a matter of course, certainly, incontrovertibly, inevitably, unavoidably, inescapably, of necessity.

**necessary** adjective 1 *planning permission is necessary:* obligatory, requisite, required, compulsory, mandatory, imperative, needed. 2 *a necessary consequence:* inevitable, unavoidable, inescapable, inexorable.

**necessity** noun 1 *the VCR is now regarded as a necessity:* essential, requisite, prerequisite, necessary, basic; informal must-have. 2 *political necessity forced him to resign:* force of circumstance, obligation, need, call, exigency.

**need** verb 1 *do you need money?* require, be in/have need of, want, be crying out for, be desperate for, demand, call for, necessitate, entail, involve, lack, be without, be short of. 2 *do I need to come?* have to, be meant to, be supposed to, be expected to.
noun 1 *there's no need to apologize:* necessity, requirement, call, demand. 2 *basic human needs:* requirement, necessity, want, requisite, prerequisite. 3 *my hour of need:* difficulty, trouble, distress, crisis, emergency, urgency, extremity.

**needed** adjective necessary, required, called for, wanted, desired, lacking.
OPPOSITES optional.

**needless** adjective unnecessary, unneeded, uncalled for, gratuitous, pointless, superfluous, redundant, excessive.
OPPOSITES necessary.

**needy** adjective poor, deprived, disadvantaged, underprivileged,

in need, needful, hard up, poverty-stricken, impoverished, destitute, penniless; informal broke, strapped (for cash); Brit. informal skint.
OPPOSITES wealthy.

**negative** adjective **1** *a negative reply:* opposing, opposed, contrary, anti-, dissenting, in the negative. **2** *stop being so negative:* pessimistic, defeatist, gloomy, cynical, fatalistic, dismissive, unenthusiastic, apathetic, unresponsive. **3** *a negative effect on the economy:* harmful, bad, adverse, damaging, detrimental, unfavourable, disadvantageous.
OPPOSITES positive, optimistic, favourable.

**neglect** verb **1** *she neglected the children:* fail to look after, leave alone, abandon. **2** *he's neglecting his work:* pay no attention to, let slide, not attend to, be remiss about, be lax about, leave undone. **3** *I neglected to inform her:* fail, omit, forget.
OPPOSITES cherish, heed, remember.
noun **1** *the place had an air of neglect:* disrepair, dilapidation, shabbiness, disuse, abandonment. **2** *her doctor was guilty of neglect:* negligence, dereliction (of duty), carelessness, laxity, slackness, irresponsibility.
OPPOSITES care.

**neglected** adjective **1** *neglected animals:* uncared for, abandoned, mistreated, maltreated. **2** *a neglected cottage:* derelict, dilapidated, tumbledown, ramshackle, untended. **3** *a neglected masterpiece:* disregarded, forgotten, overlooked, ignored,

unrecognized, unnoticed, unsung, underrated.
OPPOSITES cared for, maintained, well regarded.

**negligent** adjective neglectful, remiss, careless, lax, irresponsible, inattentive, thoughtless, unmindful, forgetful, slack, sloppy; N. Amer. derelict.
OPPOSITES dutiful.

**negligible** adjective trivial, trifling, insignificant, unimportant, minor, inconsequential, minimal, small, slight, infinitesimal; informal minuscule.
OPPOSITES significant.

**negotiate** verb **1** *she refused to negotiate:* discuss (terms), talk, consult, confer, debate, compromise, bargain, haggle. **2** *he negotiated a new contract:* arrange, broker, work out, thrash out, agree on. **3** *I negotiated the obstacles:* get round, get past, get over, clear, cross, surmount, overcome, deal with, cope with.

**negotiation** noun **1** *the negotiations resume next week:* discussion(s), talks, conference, debate, dialogue, consultation. **2** *the negotiation of a deal:* arrangement, brokering, settlement, conclusion, completion.

**negotiator** noun mediator, arbitrator, go-between, middleman, intermediary, representative, spokesperson, broker.

**neighbourhood** noun **1** *a quiet neighbourhood:* district, area, locality, locale, quarter, community; N. Amer. informal hood, nabe. **2** *in the neighbourhood of Canterbury:* vicinity, environs.

**neighbouring** adjective

a b c d e f g h i j k l m **n** o p q r s t u v w x y z

adjacent, adjoining, bordering, connecting, next-door, nearby.
OPPOSITES remote.

**neighbourly** adjective obliging, helpful, friendly, kind, considerate, amicable, sociable, hospitable, companionable, civil, cordial.
OPPOSITES unfriendly.

**nerve** noun 1 *the match will be a test of nerve*: confidence, assurance, courage, bravery, determination, will power, spirit, grit; informal guts; Brit. informal bottle; N. Amer. informal moxie. 2 *he had the nerve to chat her up*: audacity, cheek, effrontery, gall, temerity, presumption, impudence, impertinence, arrogance; informal face, front, brass neck, chutzpah. 3 (**nerves**) anxiety, tension, nervousness, stress, worry, cold feet, apprehension; informal butterflies (in one's stomach), collywobbles, jitters.

**nervous** adjective 1 *a nervous woman*: highly strung, anxious, edgy, nervy, tense, excitable, jumpy, neurotic. 2 *he was so nervous he couldn't eat*: anxious, worried, apprehensive, on edge, edgy, tense, stressed, agitated, uneasy, restless, worked up, keyed up, overwrought; informal jittery, twitchy, in a state, uptight, wired, in a flap; Brit. informal having kittens; N. Amer. informal squirrelly.
OPPOSITES relaxed, calm.

**nestle** verb snuggle, cuddle, huddle, nuzzle, settle, burrow.

**net**¹ noun *a dress of green net*: netting, mesh, tulle, fishnet, lace.
verb *they netted some big criminals*: catch, capture, trap, snare; informal nab, bag, collar, bust; Brit. informal nick.

**net**² adjective 1 *net earnings*: after tax, after deductions, take-home, clear, final; informal bottom line. 2 *the net result*: final, end, ultimate, closing, overall, actual, effective.
OPPOSITES gross.
verb *she netted £50,000*: earn, make, clear, take home, bring in, pocket, realize, be paid.

**network** noun 1 *a network of arteries*: web, lattice, net, matrix, mesh, criss-cross, grid. 2 *a network of lanes*: maze, labyrinth, warren, tangle.

**neurotic** adjective overanxious, oversensitive, nervous, tense, highly strung, paranoid, obsessive, fixated, hysterical, overwrought, irrational.
OPPOSITES stable, calm.

**neutral** adjective 1 *she's neutral on this issue*: impartial, unbiased, unprejudiced, objective, open-minded, non-partisan, even-handed, disinterested, dispassionate, detached. 2 *Switzerland remained neutral*: unaligned, non-aligned, unaffiliated, uninvolved. 3 *a neutral topic of conversation*: inoffensive, bland, unobjectionable, unexceptionable, anodyne, uncontroversial, safe, harmless, innocuous. 4 *a neutral background*: pale, light, colourless, indeterminate, drab, insipid, nondescript, dull.
OPPOSITES biased, partisan, provocative, colourful.

**new** adjective 1 *new technology*: recent, up to date, the latest, current, state-of-the-art, contemporary, advanced, cutting-edge, modern. 2 *is your boat new?* unused, brand new, pristine, fresh. 3 *new*

*neighbours moved in:* different, another, alternative, unfamiliar, unknown, strange. **4** *they had a new classroom built:* additional, extra, supplementary, further, another, fresh. **5** *I came back a new woman:* reinvigorated, restored, revived, improved, refreshed, regenerated.
OPPOSITES old, hackneyed, second-hand, present.

**newcomer** noun **1** *a newcomer to the village:* new arrival, immigrant, incomer, settler, stranger, outsider, foreigner, alien; informal new kid on the block; Austral. informal blow-in. **2** *photography tips for the newcomer:* beginner, novice, learner, trainee, apprentice, probationer; N. Amer. tenderfoot; informal rookie, newbie.

**newly** adverb recently, only just, lately, freshly, not long ago, a short time ago.

**news** noun report, story, account, announcement, press release, communication, communiqué, bulletin, intelligence, disclosure, revelation, gossip; informal scoop.

**next** adjective **1** *the next chapter:* following, succeeding, upcoming, to come. **2** *the next house in the street:* neighbouring, adjacent, adjoining, next-door, bordering, connected, closest, nearest.
OPPOSITES previous.
adverb *where shall we go next?* then, after, afterwards, after this/that, later, subsequently; formal thereafter.
OPPOSITES before.

**nice** adjective **1** *have a nice time:* enjoyable, pleasant, agreeable, good, satisfying, entertaining, amusing; informal lovely, great; N. Amer. informal neat. **2** *nice people:*

pleasant, likeable, agreeable, personable, congenial, amiable, affable, genial, friendly, charming, delightful, engaging, sympathetic. **3** *nice manners:* polite, courteous, civil, refined, polished, genteel, elegant. **4** *that's a rather nice distinction:* subtle, fine, delicate, precise, strict, close, careful, meticulous, scrupulous. **5** *it's a nice day:* fine, pleasant, agreeable, dry, sunny, warm, mild.
OPPOSITES unpleasant, nasty, rough.

**niche** noun **1** *a niche in the wall:* recess, alcove, nook, cranny, hollow, bay, cavity, cubbyhole, pigeonhole. **2** *he found his niche in life:* (ideal) position, slot, place, function, vocation, calling, métier, station, job, level.

**nick** noun *a slight nick in the blade:* cut, scratch, incision, notch, chip, dent, indentation. verb *I nicked the edge of the table:* cut, scratch, graze, chip, dent.

**nickname** noun pet name, diminutive, endearment, tag, label, sobriquet, epithet; informal moniker.

**night** noun night-time, (hours of) darkness, dark.
OPPOSITES day.

**nightly** adjective **1** *nightly raids:* every night, night after night. **2** *his nightly wanderings:* nocturnal, night-time.
adverb *a band plays there nightly:* every night, each night, night after night.

**nightmare** noun ordeal, trial, hell, misery, agony, torture, murder, purgatory, disaster; informal the pits.

**nil** noun nothing, none, nought,

zero; Tennis love; Cricket a duck.

**nimble** adjective **1** *he was nimble on his feet:* agile, sprightly, light, spry, quick, lithe, skilful, deft, dexterous, adroit; informal nippy. **2** *a nimble mind:* quick, alert, lively, astute, perceptive, penetrating, discerning, shrewd, sharp, intelligent, bright, smart, clever, brilliant; informal quick on the uptake.
OPPOSITES clumsy, dull.

**nip** verb & noun bite, nibble, peck, pinch, tweak.

**no** adverb absolutely not, definitely not, of course not, under no circumstances, not at all, negative, never; informal nope, no way, not a chance; Brit. informal no fear; archaic nay.
OPPOSITES yes.

**noble** adjective **1** *a noble family:* aristocratic, blue-blooded, high-born, titled. **2** *a noble cause:* worthy, righteous, virtuous, good, honourable, worthwhile. **3** *a noble pine forest:* magnificent, splendid, grand, stately, imposing, dignified, proud, striking, majestic.
OPPOSITES humble, base, unimpressive.
noun *Scottish nobles:* aristocrat, nobleman, noblewoman, lord, lady, peer (of the realm), peeress; informal aristo.
OPPOSITES commoner.

**nod** verb **1** *she nodded her head:* incline, bob, bow, dip. **2** *he nodded to me to start:* signal, gesture, gesticulate, motion, sign, indicate.
noun **1** *a nod of his head:* inclination, bob, bow, dip. **2** *she gave a nod to the manager:* signal, indication, sign, cue, gesture.

**noise** noun sound, din, hubbub, clamour, racket, uproar, tumult, commotion; informal hullabaloo; Brit. informal row.
OPPOSITES silence.

**noisy** adjective **1** *a noisy crowd:* rowdy, raucous, clamorous, boisterous, chattering, talkative, vociferous, shouting, screaming. **2** *noisy music:* loud, blaring, booming, deafening, thunderous, ear-splitting, piercing, strident, cacophonous.
OPPOSITES quiet, soft.

**nominal** adjective **1** *the nominal head of the campaign:* in name only, titular, formal, official, theoretical, supposed, ostensible, so-called. **2** *a nominal rent:* token, symbolic, minimal; Brit. peppercorn.
OPPOSITES real, considerable.

**nominate** verb **1** *any member may nominate a candidate:* propose, put forward, put up, submit, present, recommend, suggest. **2** *the President nominated her to the Supreme Court:* appoint, designate, assign, select, choose, decide on, promote.

**non-existent** adjective imaginary, imagined, unreal, fictional, fictitious, made up, invented, fanciful, mythical, illusory.
OPPOSITES real.

**nonsense** noun **1** *he was talking nonsense:* rubbish, gibberish, claptrap, garbage; informal baloney, tripe, drivel, gobbledegook, twaddle; Brit. informal cobblers, codswallop, double Dutch; Scottish & N. English informal havers; N. Amer. informal flapdoodle, bushwa, applesauce. **2** *she stands no nonsense:* mischief, messing about, misbehaviour, funny business; informal tomfoolery, monkey

business, shenanigans; Brit. informal monkey tricks, jiggery-pokery. **3** *the whole thing is a nonsense:* joke, farce, travesty, insanity, madness.
OPPOSITES sense, wisdom.

**non-stop** adjective *non-stop entertainment:* continuous, constant, continual, incessant, ceaseless, uninterrupted, perpetual, round-the-clock, unremitting, relentless, persistent.
OPPOSITES intermittent, occasional.
adverb *we worked non-stop:* continuously, continually, incessantly, ceaselessly, all the time, constantly, perpetually, round the clock, steadily, relentlessly, persistently; informal 24-7.
OPPOSITES intermittently, occasionally.

**noon** noun midday, twelve o'clock, twelve hundred hours, twelve noon, high noon, noonday.

**norm** noun **1** *norms of behaviour:* standard, convention, criterion, yardstick, benchmark, touchstone, rule, formula, pattern. **2** *such teams are now the norm:* normal, usual, the rule, standard, typical, average, par for the course, expected.

**normal** adjective **1** *they issue books in the normal way:* usual, standard, ordinary, customary, conventional, habitual, accustomed, typical, common, regular, routine, traditional. **2** *a normal couple:* ordinary, average, typical, run-of-the-mill, middle-of-the-road, common, conventional, mainstream; N. Amer. garden-variety; Brit. informal common or

garden, bog-standard. **3** *the man was not normal:* sane, in one's right mind, right in the head, of sound mind, compos mentis; informal all there.
OPPOSITES unusual, insane.

**normally** adverb **1** *she wanted to be able to walk normally:* naturally, conventionally, properly, like everyone else. **2** *normally we'd keep quiet about this:* usually, ordinarily, as a rule, generally, in general, mostly, for the most part, by and large, mainly, most of the time, on the whole, typically, traditionally.

**nose** noun **1** snout, muzzle, proboscis, trunk; informal beak, conk, schnozz, schnozzle, hooter. **2** *a nose for scandal:* instinct, feeling, sixth sense, intuition, insight, feel.
verb **1** *she's nosing into my business:* pry, enquire, poke about/around, interfere (in), meddle (in), be a busybody, stick/poke one's nose in; informal be nosy (about), snoop; Austral./NZ informal stickybeak. **2** *he nosed the car into the traffic:* ease, inch, edge, move, manoeuvre, steer, guide.

**nostalgia** noun reminiscence, remembrance, recollection, wistfulness, regret, sentimentality.

**nostalgic** adjective wistful, romantic, sentimental, emotional, homesick, regretful, dewy-eyed, maudlin.

**notable** adjective **1** *notable examples of workmanship:* noteworthy, remarkable, outstanding, important, significant, memorable, marked, striking, impressive. **2** *a notable author:* prominent, important, well known, famous,

a
b
c
d
e
f
g
h
i
j
k
l
m
n
o
p
q
r
s
t
u
v
w
x
y
z

famed, noted.
OPPOSITES unremarkable, unknown.

noun *movie stars and other notables:* celebrity, public figure, VIP, dignitary, luminary, star, superstar, big name; informal celeb, bigwig, megastar.
OPPOSITES nonentity.

**notably** adverb 1 *other countries, notably the USA:* in particular, particularly, especially, primarily, principally. 2 *these are notably short-lived birds:* remarkably, especially, exceptionally, singularly, particularly, peculiarly, distinctly, significantly, unusually, uncommonly, conspicuously.

**notch** noun nick, cut, incision, score, scratch, slit, snick, slot, groove.

**note** noun 1 *a note in her diary:* record, entry, reminder; informal memo. 2 *notes of the meeting:* minutes, record, details, report, account, transcript, summary. 3 *notes in the margins:* annotation, footnote, comment. 4 *he wrote me a note:* message, letter, line. 5 (Brit.) *a £20 note:* banknote; N. Amer. bill; US informal greenback. 6 *a note of hopelessness in her voice:* tone, hint, indication, sign, element, suggestion, sense.
verb 1 *we will note your suggestion:* bear in mind, be mindful of, consider, take notice of, register, record, enter. 2 *the letter noted the ministers' concern:* mention, refer to, touch on, indicate, point out, make known, state. 3 *note the date in your diary:* write down, put down, jot down, take down, enter, mark, record, register, pencil.

**notebook** noun notepad, exercise book, register, logbook, log, diary, journal, record; Brit. jotter, pocketbook.

**noted** adjective famous, famed, well known, renowned, prominent, notable, important, eminent, acclaimed, celebrated.
OPPOSITES unknown.

**nothing** noun 1 *there's nothing I can do:* not a thing, zero; N. English nowt; informal zilch, sweet FA, not a dicky bird; Brit. informal damn all, not a sausage; N. Amer. informal zip, nada, diddly-squat. 2 *the price fell to nothing:* zero, nought, nil, o; Tennis love; Cricket a duck.
OPPOSITES something.

**notice** noun 1 *nothing escaped his notice:* attention, observation, awareness, consciousness, perception, regard, consideration, scrutiny. 2 *a notice on the wall:* sign, announcement, advertisement, poster, bill, bulletin. 3 *we will give you notice of any changes:* notification, (advance) warning, news, word.
verb *I noticed that the door was open:* observe, note, see, discern, detect, spot; Brit. informal clock.
OPPOSITES overlook.

**noticeable** adjective obvious, evident, apparent, manifest, plain, clear, conspicuous, perceptible, discernible, detectable, observable, visible, appreciable.

**notify** verb inform, tell, advise, give (advance) warning, let someone know, alert, warn.

**notion** noun 1 *he had a notion that something was wrong:* idea, impression, (funny) feeling, (sneaking) suspicion, intuition, hunch, belief,

a b c d e f g h i j k l m n o p q r s t u v w x y z

opinion. **2** *Claire had no notion of what he meant:* understanding, idea, clue, inkling.

**notorious** adjective infamous, scandalous, disreputable.

**nought** noun nil, zero, nothing; Tennis love; Cricket a duck; informal zilch; Brit. informal not a sausage; N. Amer. informal zip, nada.

**nourish** verb **1** *patients must be well nourished:* feed, sustain, provide for, maintain. **2** *we nourish the talents of children:* encourage, promote, foster, nurture, cultivate, boost, strengthen, enrich.

**nourishing** adjective nutritious, wholesome, good for one, full of goodness, healthy, health-giving, beneficial.
OPPOSITES unhealthy.

**novel**[1] noun *a good novel:* story, tale, narrative, romance.

**novel**[2] adjective *a novel way of making money:* new, original, unusual, unconventional, unorthodox, different, fresh, imaginative, innovative.
OPPOSITES traditional.

**novelty** noun **1** *the novelty of our approach:* originality, newness, freshness, unconventionality, creativity, innovation, unfamiliarity, strangeness. **2** *we sell seasonal novelties:* knick-knack, trinket, bauble, toy, trifle, ornament; N. Amer. kickshaw.

**novice** noun beginner, learner, newcomer, fledgling, trainee, probationer, student, pupil, apprentice; informal rookie, newie; N. Amer. informal greenhorn.
OPPOSITES expert, veteran.

**now** adverb **1** *I'm busy now:* at the moment, at present, at this moment in time, at this time, currently; N. Amer. presently.

**2** *television is now the main source of news:* nowadays, these days, today, in this day and age. **3** *you must leave now:* at once, straight away, right away, this minute, this instant, immediately, instantly, directly; informal pronto, asap.

**nucleus** noun core, centre, heart, hub, middle, focal point, pivot, crux.

**nude** adjective naked, stark naked, bare, unclothed, undressed, stripped, with nothing on; informal without a stitch on, in one's birthday suit, in the raw/buff, in the altogether; Brit. informal starkers; N. Amer. informal buck naked.
OPPOSITES clothed.

**nudge** verb **1** *he nudged Ben:* prod, elbow, dig, poke, jab. **2** *the canoe nudged the bank:* touch, bump (against), push (against), run into. **3** *we nudged them towards a decision:* prompt, encourage, persuade, prod.
noun *Maggie gave him a nudge:* prod, dig (in the ribs), poke, jab, push.

**nuisance** noun annoyance, inconvenience, bore, bother, irritation, trial, burden, pest; informal pain (in the neck), hassle, bind, drag, headache.
OPPOSITES blessing.

**numb** adjective **1** *my fingers are numb:* dead, without sensation, without feeling, numbed, desensitized, frozen, anaesthetized. **2** *the news left me numb:* dazed, stunned, unfeeling, stupefied, paralysed, immobilized.
OPPOSITES sensitive.
verb **1** *the cold weather numbed his fingers:* deaden, desensitize, anaesthetize, immobilize,

freeze. **2** *the news updates
numb us:* daze, stun, dull,
stupefy, paralyse, immobilize.
OPPOSITES sensitize.

**number** noun **1** *a whole number:*
numeral, integer, figure, digit,
character. **2** *a large number of
complaints:* quantity, total,
aggregate, tally, quota. **3** *the
wedding of one of their number:*
group, crowd, circle, party,
band, crew, set, company;
informal gang. **4** *the band
performed another number:*
song, piece, tune, track, dance.
verb **1** *visitors numbered more
than two million:* add up to,
amount to, total, come to. **2** *he
numbers her among his friends:*
include, count, reckon, deem.

**numerous** adjective many, a
number of, a lot of, several,
plenty of, copious, an
abundance of, frequent; informal
umpteen.
OPPOSITES few.

**nurse** verb **1** *they nursed
smallpox patients:* care for, take
care of, look after, tend,

minister to. **2** *they nursed old
grievances:* harbour, foster,
bear, have, hold (on to), retain.

**nurture** verb **1** *she nurtured her
children into adulthood:* bring
up, care for, take care of, look
after, tend, rear, support. **2** *we
nurtured these plants:*
cultivate, grow, keep, tend,
raise. **3** *he nurtured my love of
art:* encourage, promote,
stimulate, develop, foster,
cultivate, boost, strengthen,
fuel.
OPPOSITES neglect, hinder.

**nut** noun **1** (informal) *some nut
arrived at the office:* maniac,
lunatic, madman, madwoman;
informal loony, nutcase, head
case; Brit. informal nutter; N. Amer.
informal screwball. **2** (informal) *a
movie nut:* enthusiast, fan,
devotee, aficionado; informal
freak, fanatic, addict, buff.

**nutritious** adjective nourishing,
wholesome, good for one, full
of goodness, healthy, health-
giving, beneficial.

# Oo

**oath** noun **1** *an oath of
allegiance:* vow, pledge,
promise, affirmation, word (of
honour), guarantee. **2** *a stream
of oaths:* swear word,
profanity, expletive, four-letter
word, dirty word, obscenity,
curse.

**obedient** adjective compliant,
biddable, acquiescent, good,
law-abiding, deferential,
governable, docile, submissive.
OPPOSITES rebellious.

**obey** verb **1** *I obeyed him:* do

what someone says, submit to,
defer to, do as one is told. **2** *he
refused to obey the order:* carry
out, perform, act on, execute,
discharge, implement. **3** *the
rules have to be obeyed:* comply
with, adhere to, observe, abide
by, act in accordance with,
conform to, respect, follow,
keep to, stick to.
OPPOSITES defy, ignore.

**object** noun **1** *wooden objects:*
thing, article, item, entity.
**2** *the object of criticism:* target,

butt, focus, recipient, victim.
**3** *his object was to resolve the crisis:* objective, aim, goal, target, purpose, end, plan, point, ambition, intention, idea.
**verb** *teachers objected to the scheme:* protest about, oppose, take exception to, take issue with, take a stand against, argue against, quarrel with, condemn, draw the line at, demur at, mind, complain about; informal kick up a fuss/ stink about.
OPPOSITES approve of, accept.

**objection** noun protest, protestation, complaint, opposition, demurral, counter-argument, disagreement, disapproval, dissent.

**objective** adjective **1** *try to be objective:* impartial, unbiased, unprejudiced, non-partisan, disinterested, neutral, uninvolved, even-handed, fair, dispassionate, detached.
**2** *objective knowledge:* factual, actual, real, empirical, verifiable.
OPPOSITES subjective, emotional.
**noun** *our objective is to make a profit:* aim, intention, purpose, target, goal, object, idea, plan.

**objectively** adverb impartially, without bias/prejudice, even-handedly, fairly, dispassionately, with an open mind, without fear or favour.

**obligation** noun **1** *his professional obligations:* commitment, duty, responsibility, function, task, job, charge, onus, liability, requirement, debt. **2** *a sense of obligation:* duty, compulsion, indebtedness, necessity, pressure, constraint.

**obligatory** adjective compulsory, mandatory, prescribed, required, statutory, enforced, binding, requisite, necessary, imperative.
OPPOSITES optional.

**oblige** verb **1** *we are obliged to accept the decision:* compel, force, require, bind, constrain. **2** *I'll be happy to oblige you:* do someone a favour, accommodate, help, assist, indulge, humour.

**obliged** adjective thankful, grateful, appreciative, beholden, indebted, in someone's debt.

**obliging** adjective helpful, accommodating, cooperative, agreeable, amenable, generous, kind; Brit. informal decent.
OPPOSITES unhelpful.

**obscene** adjective **1** *obscene literature:* pornographic, indecent, smutty, dirty, filthy, X-rated, explicit, lewd, rude, vulgar, coarse, scatological; informal blue, porn; euphemistic adult. **2** *an obscene amount:* scandalous, shocking, outrageous, immoral.
OPPOSITES clean, family.

**obscure** adjective **1** *his origins remain obscure:* unclear, uncertain, unknown, mysterious, hazy, vague, indeterminate. **2** *obscure references to Proust:* abstruse, oblique, opaque, cryptic, enigmatic, puzzling, perplexing, baffling, elliptical. **3** *an obscure Peruvian painter:* little known, unknown, unheard of, unsung, unrecognized, forgotten.
OPPOSITES clear, plain, famous.
**verb** **1** *clouds obscured the sun:* hide, conceal, cover, veil, shroud, screen, mask, cloak, block, obliterate, eclipse. **2** *recent events have obscured the issue:* confuse, complicate,

a
b
c
d
e
f
g
h
i
j
k
l
m
n
**o**
p
q
r
s
t
u
v
w
x
y
z

a b c d e f g h i j k l m n **o** p q r s t u v w x y z

obfuscate, cloud, blur, muddy.
OPPOSITES reveal, clarify.

**observation** noun 1 *detailed observation of their behaviour*: monitoring, watching, scrutiny, survey, surveillance, attention, study. 2 *his observations were correct*: remark, comment, opinion, impression, thought, reflection.

**observe** verb 1 *she observed that he was drunk*: notice, see, note, perceive, discern, spot. 2 *he had been observing her*: watch, look at, contemplate, view, survey, regard, keep an eye on, scrutinize, keep under surveillance, keep watch on, monitor; informal keep tabs on, keep a beady eye on. 3 *'You look tired,' she observed*: remark, comment, say, mention, declare, announce, state. 4 *they agreed to observe the ceasefire*: comply with, abide by, keep, obey, adhere to, heed, honour, fulfil, respect, follow, consent to, accept.

**observer** noun 1 *the casual observer*: spectator, onlooker, watcher, fly on the wall, viewer, witness. 2 *industry observers are worried*: commentator, reporter, monitor.

**obsessed** adjective fixated, possessed, consumed, infatuated, besotted; informal smitten, hung up; N. Amer. informal hipped.

**obsession** noun fixation, passion, mania, compulsion, preoccupation, infatuation, hobby horse, phobia, complex, neurosis; informal bee in one's bonnet, hang-up, thing.

**obsessive** adjective consuming, all-consuming, compulsive, controlling, fanatical, neurotic, excessive; informal pathological.

**obsolete** adjective out of date, outdated, outmoded, old-fashioned, passé, antiquated, antediluvian, anachronistic, archaic, ancient, fossilized, extinct, defunct; informal out of the ark; Brit. informal past its sell-by date.
OPPOSITES current, modern.

**obstacle** noun barrier, hurdle, stumbling block, obstruction, bar, block, impediment, hindrance, snag, catch, drawback, hitch, fly in the ointment, handicap, difficulty, problem, disadvantage; Brit. spanner in the works.
OPPOSITES advantage, aid.

**obstinate** adjective stubborn, pig-headed, unyielding, inflexible, unbending, intransigent, intractable, self-willed.
OPPOSITES compliant.

**obstruct** verb 1 *ensure that vents are not obstructed*: block (up), clog (up), occlude, cut off, bung up, choke, dam up. 2 *he was obstructing the traffic*: hold up, bring to a standstill, stop, halt, block. 3 *they may obstruct aid distribution*: impede, hinder, interfere with, hamper, block, interrupt, hold up, stand in the way of, frustrate, slow down, delay.
OPPOSITES clear, facilitate.

**obstruction** noun obstacle, barrier, stumbling block, impediment, hindrance, difficulty, check, restriction, blockage, stoppage, congestion, bottleneck, hold-up.

**obtain** verb get, acquire, come by, secure, procure, pick up, be given, gain, earn, achieve, attain; informal get hold of, lay one's hands on, land.
OPPOSITES lose.

**obtainable** adjective available, to be had, in circulation, on the market, on offer, in season, at one's disposal, accessible; informal up for grabs, on tap.

**obvious** adjective clear, plain, evident, apparent, manifest, conspicuous, pronounced, prominent, distinct, noticeable, perceptible, visible; informal sticking out a mile.
OPPOSITES imperceptible.

**obviously** adverb clearly, plainly, evidently, patently, visibly, discernibly, manifestly, noticeably, of course, naturally, needless to say, it goes without saying.
OPPOSITES perhaps.

**occasion** noun 1 *a previous occasion:* time, instance, juncture, point, moment, experience, case. 2 *a special occasion:* event, affair, function, celebration, party, get-together, gathering; informal do, bash.

**occasional** adjective infrequent, intermittent, irregular, periodic, sporadic, odd; N. Amer. sometime.
OPPOSITES regular, frequent.

**occasionally** adverb sometimes, from time to time, (every) now and then, (every) now and again, at times, every so often, (every) once in a while, on occasion, periodically.
OPPOSITES often.

**occult** adjective supernatural, magic, magical, satanic, mystical, unearthly, esoteric, psychic.
■ the occult the supernatural, magic, black magic, witchcraft, necromancy, the black arts, occultism.

**occupant** noun resident, inhabitant, owner, householder, tenant, leaseholder, lessee; Brit.

occupier, owner-occupier.

**occupation** noun 1 *his father's occupation:* job, profession, work, line of work, trade, employment, business, career, métier, calling. 2 *among her leisure occupations is birdwatching:* pastime, activity, leisure activity, hobby, pursuit, interest, entertainment, recreation. 3 *the Roman occupation of Britain:* conquest, capture, invasion, seizure, annexation, colonization, subjugation.

**occupied** adjective 1 *tasks which kept her occupied:* busy, working, at work, active; informal tied up, hard at it, on the go. 2 *the table was occupied:* in use, full, engaged, taken. 3 *only two flats are occupied:* inhabited, lived in.
OPPOSITES free, vacant.

**occupy** verb 1 *Carol occupied the basement flat:* live in, inhabit, lodge in, move into, people, populate, settle. 2 *he occupies a post at the Treasury:* hold, fill, have; informal hold down. 3 *something to occupy my mind:* engage, busy, distract, absorb, engross, hold, interest, involve, entertain. 4 *the region was occupied by Japan:* capture, seize, conquer, invade, colonize, annex, subjugate.

**occur** verb 1 *an accident occurred at 3.30:* happen, take place, come about; N. Amer. informal go down. 2 *the disease occurs in the tropics:* be found, be present, exist, appear, develop.
■ occur to enter someone's head/mind, cross someone's mind, come/spring to mind, strike someone, come to

someone, dawn on someone, suggest itself.

**occurrence** noun **1** *a rare occurrence:* event, incident, happening, phenomenon, circumstance. **2** *the occurrence of cancer:* existence, instance, appearance, frequency, incidence, rate, prevalence; Statistics distribution.

**odd** adjective **1** *an odd man:* strange, peculiar, queer, funny, bizarre, eccentric, unusual, weird, quirky, zany; informal wacky, off the wall. **2** *some odd things had happened:* unusual, strange, peculiar, funny, curious, weird, bizarre, queer, abnormal, puzzling, mystifying, baffling, unaccountable. **3** *he does odd jobs:* occasional, casual, irregular, isolated, sporadic, periodic, miscellaneous, various, varied, sundry. **4** *an odd shoe:* mismatched, unmatched, unpaired, single, lone, solitary, extra, leftover, spare. opposites normal, ordinary, regular.

**odds** plural noun likelihood, probability, chances.
■ **odds and ends** bits and pieces, bits and bobs, stuff, paraphernalia, things, sundries, bric-a-brac, knick-knacks, oddments; informal junk; Brit. informal odds and sods, clobber, gubbins.

**odour** noun smell, stench, stink, reek, aroma, bouquet, scent, perfume, fragrance; Brit. informal pong, whiff; N. Amer. informal funk.

**odyssey** noun journey, voyage, trip, trek, travels, quest, crusade, pilgrimage.

**off** adjective **1** *Kate's off today:* away, absent, not at work, off duty, on holiday, on leave, free;

N. Amer. on vacation. **2** *the game's off:* cancelled, postponed, called off. **3** *the fish was off:* rotten, bad, stale, mouldy, sour, rancid, turned, spoiled. opposites in, on, good.

**offence** noun **1** *he has committed an offence:* crime, illegal act, misdemeanour, breach of the law, felony, infringement, violation, wrongdoing, sin. **2** *I do not want to cause offence:* annoyance, resentment, indignation, displeasure, bad feeling, animosity.

**offend** verb **1** *I'm sorry if I offended him:* upset, give offence to, affront, hurt someone's feelings, insult, hurt, wound, slight. **2** *criminals who offend repeatedly:* break the law, commit a crime, do wrong.

**offender** noun wrongdoer, criminal, lawbreaker, crook, villain, miscreant, felon, delinquent, culprit, guilty party.

**offensive** adjective **1** *offensive remarks:* insulting, rude, derogatory, disrespectful, personal, hurtful, upsetting, wounding, abusive. **2** *an offensive smell:* unpleasant, disagreeable, nasty, distasteful, objectionable, off-putting, dreadful, frightful, obnoxious, abominable, disgusting, repulsive, repellent, vile, foul, sickening, nauseating; informal ghastly, horrible, horrid, gross; Brit. informal beastly. **3** *offensive operations:* hostile, attacking, aggressive, invading, incursive, combative, threatening, martial, warlike, belligerent, bellicose.
opposites complimentary, pleasant, defensive.

a b c d e f g h i j k l m n o p q r s t u v w x y z

noun *a military offensive:*
attack, assault, onslaught,
invasion, push, thrust, charge,
raid, incursion, blitz, campaign.

**offer** verb 1 *Frank offered a
suggestion:* put forward,
proffer, give, present, come up
with, suggest, propose,
advance, submit, tender. 2 *she
offered to help:* volunteer, step/
come forward, show willing.
3 *he offered $200:* bid, tender,
put in a bid/offer of.
OPPOSITES withdraw, refuse.
noun 1 *an offer of help:*
proposal, proposition,
suggestion, submission,
approach, overture. 2 *the
highest offer:* bid, tender,
bidding price.

**offering** noun contribution,
donation, gift, present,
sacrifice, tribute.

**office** noun 1 *we met at her
office:* place of work, place of
business, workplace, workroom.
2 *the company's Paris office:*
branch, division, section,
bureau, department. 3 *the office
of President:* post, position,
appointment, job, occupation,
role, situation, function.

**officer** noun official, office-
holder, committee member,
board member, functionary,
executive.

**official** adjective 1 *an official
enquiry:* authorized, approved,
validated, authenticated,
certified, accredited, endorsed,
sanctioned, licensed,
recognized, legitimate, legal,
lawful, valid, bona fide, proper;
informal kosher. 2 *an official
function:* ceremonial, formal,
solemn, bureaucratic.
OPPOSITES unauthorized,
informal.
noun *a union official:* officer,

office-holder, executive,
functionary, administrator,
bureaucrat, mandarin,
representative, agent; derogatory
apparatchik.

**offset** verb counteract, balance
(out), even out/up,
counterbalance, compensate
for, make up for, neutralize,
cancel (out).

**offspring** noun children, sons
and daughters, progeny,
youngsters, babies, infants,
brood, descendants, heirs,
successors; informal kids; Brit.
informal sprogs, brats.

**often** adverb frequently, many
times, on many/numerous
occasions, a lot, repeatedly,
again and again, regularly,
commonly, generally,
ordinarily; N. Amer. oftentimes.
OPPOSITES seldom.

**oily** adjective greasy, fatty,
buttery, rich.

**ointment** noun lotion, cream,
salve, liniment, embrocation,
rub, gel, balm, emollient,
unguent.

**old** adjective 1 *old people:* elderly,
aged, older, senior, venerable,
in one's dotage, long in the
tooth, ancient, decrepit,
doddery, senescent, senile;
informal getting on, past it, over
the hill. 2 *old clothes:* worn,
worn out, shabby, threadbare,
frayed, patched, tattered, moth-
eaten, ragged; informal tatty. 3 *old
cars:* antique, veteran, vintage,
classic. 4 *an old girlfriend:*
former, previous, earlier, past,
ex-, one-time, sometime,
erstwhile.
OPPOSITES young, new, modern
current.

**old-fashioned** adjective out of
date, outdated, dated, out of
fashion, outmoded,

a
b
c
d
e
f
g
h
i
j
k
l
m
n
o
p
q
r
s
t
u
v
w
x
y
z

unfashionable, passé, outworn, behind the times, archaic, obsolescent, obsolete; informal out of the ark; N. Amer. informal horse-and-buggy.
OPPOSITES modern.

**ominous** adjective threatening, menacing, baleful, forbidding, foreboding, fateful, sinister, black, dark, gloomy.
OPPOSITES promising.

**omission** noun 1 *the omission of certain news items:* exclusion, leaving out, deletion, elimination. 2 *I regret any omission on my part:* negligence, neglect, dereliction, oversight, lapse, failure.

**omit** verb 1 *they omitted his name from the list:* leave out, exclude, leave off, miss out, miss, cut, drop, skip. 2 *I omitted to mention this:* forget, neglect, fail.
OPPOSITES add, include, remember.

**once** adverb 1 *I only met him once:* on one occasion, one time. 2 *he didn't help once:* ever, at any time, on any occasion, at all. 3 *they were friends once:* formerly, previously, in the past, at one time, at one point, once upon a time, in days/times gone by, in the (good) old days, long ago.
OPPOSITES often, now.
conjunction *once she's gone:* as soon as, the moment, when, after.

■ **at once 1** *leave at once:* immediately, right away, right now, this moment/instant/ second/minute, straight away, instantly, directly, forthwith, without delay/hesitation, without further ado. 2 *they all arrived at once:* at the same

time, (all) together, simultaneously, as a group, in unison.

**one-sided** adjective 1 *a one-sided account:* biased, prejudiced, partisan, partial, slanted, distorted, unfair. 2 *a one-sided game:* unequal, uneven, unbalanced.
OPPOSITES impartial, equal.

**ongoing** adjective in progress, under way, going on, continuing, proceeding.

**onlooker** noun eyewitness, witness, observer, spectator, bystander; informal rubberneck.

**only** adverb 1 *only enough for two:* at most, at best, just, no more than, hardly, barely, scarcely. 2 *for your eyes only:* exclusively, solely, purely. 3 *you're only saying that:* merely, simply, just.
adjective *their only son:* sole, single, one (and only), solitary, lone, unique, exclusive.

**onset** noun start, beginning, commencement, arrival, appearance, inception, day one, outbreak.
OPPOSITES end.

**onslaught** noun attack, assault, offensive, advance, charge, blitz, bombardment, barrage.

**ooze** verb 1 *blood oozed from the wound:* seep, discharge, flow, exude, trickle, drip, dribble, drain, leak. 2 *positively oozing charm:* exude, gush, drip, emanate, radiate.

**open** adjective 1 *the door's open:* unlatched, unlocked, off the latch, ajar, gaping, yawning. 2 *a silk shirt, open at the neck:* unfastened, undone, unbuttoned, unzipped. 3 *an open packet:* opened, undone, unsealed, uncorked, unstoppered. 4 *open*

countryside | open spaces: unenclosed, rolling, sweeping, wide open, exposed, spacious, uncluttered. **5** *a map was open beside him:* spread out, unfolded, unfurled, unrolled, stretched out. **6** *the bank wasn't open:* open for business, open to the public, working, accessible. **7** *the position is still open:* available, vacant, free, unfilled; informal up for grabs. **8** *open to abuse:* vulnerable, subject, susceptible, liable, exposed. **9** *she was very open:* frank, candid, honest, forthcoming, communicative, forthright, direct, unreserved, plain-spoken, outspoken; informal upfront. **10** *open hostility:* overt, manifest, conspicuous, plain, undisguised, unconcealed, clear, naked, blatant, flagrant, barefaced, brazen. **11** *I'm open to suggestions:* receptive, amenable, willing to listen, responsive. **12** *what other options are open to us?* available, accessible, on hand, on offer. **13** *an open meeting:* public, general, unrestricted. OPPOSITES shut, fastened, enclosed, closed, filled, protected, reticent, suppressed, private.
verb **1** *she opened the front door:* unfasten, unlock, throw wide. **2** *Katherine opened the parcel:* unwrap, undo, untie. **3** *shall I open another bottle?* uncork, crack open. **4** *Adam opened the map:* spread out, unfold, unfurl, unroll, straighten out. **5** *we'll be opening next week:* start trading, set up shop. **6** *Bryan opened the meeting:* begin, start, commence, initiate, set in motion, get going, get under way, get off

the ground; informal kick off. **7** *the lounge opens on to a patio:* give access, lead. OPPOSITES close, shut, end.

**open-air** adjective outdoor, out-of-doors, outside, alfresco. OPPOSITES indoor.

**opening** noun **1** *an opening in the roof:* hole, gap, aperture, orifice, vent, crack, slit, chink. **2** *the opening of the session:* beginning, start, commencement, outset; informal kick-off. **3** *a gallery opening:* launch, inauguration, opening/first night, premiere.
adjective *her opening remarks:* first, initial, introductory, preliminary, maiden, inaugural. OPPOSITES final, closing.

**openly** adverb **1** *drugs were openly on sale:* publicly, blatantly, flagrantly, overtly. **2** *he spoke openly of his problems:* frankly, candidly, explicitly, honestly, sincerely, forthrightly, freely. OPPOSITES secretly, privately.

**open-minded** adjective unbiased, unprejudiced, neutral, objective, disinterested, tolerant, liberal, permissive, broad-minded. OPPOSITES prejudiced, narrow-minded.

**operate** verb **1** *he can operate the crane:* work, run, use, handle, control, manage, drive, steer, manoeuvre. **2** *the machine ceased to operate:* function, work, go, run. **3** *the way the law operates:* take effect, act, apply, work, function. **4** *we operated the mines until 1979:* direct, control, manage, run, be in control/charge of.

**operation** noun **1** *the sliders ensure smooth operation:*

a b c d e f g h i j k l m n o p q r s t u v w x y z

functioning, working, running, performance, action. **2** *the operation of the factory:* management, running, administration, supervision. **3** *a military operation:* action, exercise, undertaking, enterprise, manoeuvre, campaign. **4** *their mining operation:* business, enterprise, company, firm.

**operational** adjective running, up and running, working, functioning, operative, in operation, in use, in action, ready for use, in working order, serviceable, functional.

**operative** adjective **1** *the steam railway is operative:* running, up and running, working, functioning, operational, in operation, in use, in action, in effect. **2** *the operative word:* key, significant, relevant, crucial, critical.
OPPOSITES inoperative, invalid.
noun **1** *the operatives clean the machines:* machinist, operator, mechanic, engineer, worker, workman, (factory) hand. **2** *a CIA operative:* agent, secret/undercover agent, spy, mole, plant; N. Amer. informal spook.

**operator** noun **1** *a machine operator:* operative, mechanic, handler, driver, worker, engineer, machinist. **2** *a tour operator:* contractor, entrepreneur, promoter.

**opinion** noun belief, thought(s), idea, way of thinking, feeling, mind, view, point of view, assessment, estimation, judgement.

**opponent** noun **1** *his Republican opponent:* rival, adversary, competitor, enemy, antagonist, combatant, contender, challenger. **2** *an*

*opponent of the reforms:* critic, objector, dissenter.
OPPOSITES ally, supporter.

**opportunity** noun chance, time, occasion, moment, opening, option, window, possibility, scope, freedom; informal shot, break, look-in.

**oppose** verb be against, object to, be hostile to, disagree with, disapprove of, resist, take a stand against, put up a fight against, fight, counter, challenge; informal be anti.
OPPOSITES support.

**opposed**
■ opposed to against, dead set against, averse to, hostile to, antagonistic to, antipathetic to; informal anti. ■ as opposed to in contrast with, as against, as contrasted with, rather than, instead of.

**opposing** adjective **1** *opposing points of view:* conflicting, contrasting, opposite, incompatible, irreconcilable, contradictory, clashing, at variance, at odds, opposed. **2** *opposing sides:* rival, opposite, enemy, competing.
OPPOSITES similar, allied.

**opposite** adjective **1** *they sat opposite each other:* facing, face to face with, across from. **2** *the opposite page:* facing, opposing. **3** *opposite views:* conflicting, contrasting, incompatible, irreconcilable, contradictory, at variance, at odds, differing. **4** *opposite sides:* rival, opposing, competing, enemy.
OPPOSITES same, similar, allied.
noun *the opposite was true:* reverse, converse, antithesis, contrary.
OPPOSITES same.

**opposition** noun **1** *the proposal met with opposition:* resistance,

hostility, antagonism, antipathy, objection, dissent, disapproval. **2** *they beat the opposition:* opponent(s), opposing side, other side/team, competition, rival(s), adversary, adversaries.
OPPOSITES agreement, goodwill.

**oppress** verb persecute, tyrannize, crush, repress, subjugate, subdue, keep down.

**oppression** noun persecution, abuse, ill-treatment, tyranny, repression, suppression, subjection, subjugation, cruelty, brutality, injustice.
OPPOSITES freedom.

**oppressive** adjective **1** *an oppressive dictatorship:* harsh, cruel, brutal, repressive, tyrannical, despotic, ruthless, merciless, pitiless. **2** *it was overcast and oppressive:* muggy, close, heavy, hot, humid, sticky, airless, stuffy, stifling, sultry.
OPPOSITES kindly, fresh.

**opt** verb choose, select, pick, decide, elect.
■ **opt for** choose, select, pick (out), decide on, go for, settle on, plump for.

**optimistic** adjective **1** *she felt optimistic about the future:* positive, confident, hopeful, sanguine, bullish, buoyant; informal upbeat. **2** *the forecast is optimistic:* encouraging, promising, hopeful, reassuring, favourable.
OPPOSITES pessimistic, depressing.

**optimum** adjective best, most favourable, most advantageous, ideal, perfect, prime, optimal.

**option** noun choice, preference, alternative, selection, possibility.
OPPOSITES impossibility.

**optional** adjective voluntary,

non-compulsory, elective, discretionary.
OPPOSITES compulsory.

**opulent** adjective luxurious, sumptuous, palatial, lavishly appointed, rich, splendid, magnificent, grand, fancy; informal plush; Brit. informal swish; N. Amer. informal swank.
OPPOSITES spartan.

**oral** adjective spoken, verbal, unwritten, vocal, uttered.
OPPOSITES written.

**orbit** noun circuit, course, path, track, trajectory, rotation, revolution.
verb circle, go round, revolve round, travel round, circumnavigate.

**orchestra** noun ensemble, group; informal band, combo.

**orchestrate** verb **1** *the piece was orchestrated by Mozart:* arrange, adapt, score, set. **2** *orchestrating a protest campaign:* organize, arrange, plan, set up, mobilize, mount, stage, mastermind, coordinate, direct.

**ordain** verb **1** *the decision to ordain women:* confer holy orders on, admit to the priesthood, priest, appoint, anoint, consecrate. **2** *the path ordained by God:* determine, predestine, preordain, predetermine, prescribe, designate.

**ordeal** noun unpleasant experience, trial, hardship, suffering, nightmare, trauma, hell, torture, torment, agony.

**order** noun **1** *alphabetical order:* sequence, arrangement, organization, system, series, succession. **2** *some semblance of order:* tidiness, neatness, orderliness. **3** *the police managed to keep order:* peace,

a
b
c
d
e
f
g
h
i
j
k
l
m
n
o
p
q
r
s
t
u
v
w
x
y
z

control, law and order, calm.
**4** *his sense of order:*
orderliness, organization,
method, symmetry, uniformity,
regularity, routine. **5** *in good
order:* condition, state, repair,
shape; Brit. informal nick. **6** *I had
to obey his orders:* command,
instruction, directive, direction,
decree, edict, injunction. **7** *the
company has won the order:*
commission, request,
requisition. **8** *the lower orders
of society:* class, level, rank,
grade, caste. **9** *a religious order:*
community, brotherhood,
sisterhood. **10** *the Orange
Order:* organization,
association, society, fellowship,
fraternity, lodge, guild, league,
union, club.
OPPOSITES chaos.
**verb 1** *he ordered me to return:*
instruct, tell, command, direct,
charge, require, enjoin. **2** *he
ordered that their assets be
confiscated:* rule, ordain,
decree, direct. **3** *order your
tickets by phone:* request, apply
for, book, reserve. **4** *the
messages are ordered
chronologically:* organize,
arrange, sort out, lay out,
group, classify, categorize,
catalogue.
OPPOSITES forbid.

**orderly** adjective **1** *an orderly
desk:* neat, tidy, well ordered,
in order, trim, in apple-pie
order. **2** *the orderly
presentation of information:*
organized, efficient,
methodical, systematic,
coherent, structured, logical.
**3** *the crowd was orderly:* well
behaved, law-abiding,
disciplined, peaceful, peaceable,
non-violent.
OPPOSITES untidy, disorganized,
unruly.

**ordinary** adjective **1** *the ordinary
course of events:* usual, normal,
standard, typical, common,
customary, habitual, everyday,
regular, routine, day-to-day.
**2** *my life seemed very ordinary:*
average, normal, run-of-the-
mill, standard, typical, middle-
of-the-road, conventional,
unremarkable, unexceptional;
informal bog-standard; Brit. informal
common or garden; N. Amer.
informal ornery.
OPPOSITES unusual.

**organ** noun newspaper, paper,
journal, periodical, magazine,
voice, mouthpiece.

**organic** adjective **1** *organic
matter:* living, live, animate,
biological. **2** *organic vegetables:*
additive-free, chemical-free,
pesticide-free, bio-, natural. **3** *a
society is an organic whole:*
structured, organized,
coherent, integrated,
coordinated, ordered,
harmonious.

**organism** noun **1** *fish and other
organisms:* living thing, being,
creature, animal, plant, life
form. **2** *a complex political
organism:* structure, system,
organization, entity.

**organization** noun **1** *the
organization of conferences:*
planning, arrangement,
coordination, organizing,
running, management. **2** *the
overall organization of the book:*
structure, arrangement, plan,
pattern, order, form, format,
framework, composition. **3** *his
lack of organization:* efficiency,
order, orderliness, planning. **4** *a
large organization:* institution,
body, group, company, firm,
business, corporation, agency,
association, society; informal
outfit.

**organize** verb 1 *organize the information:* order, arrange, sort, assemble, marshal, put straight, group, classify, collate, categorize, catalogue. 2 *they organized a search party:* arrange, coordinate, sort out, put together, fix up, set up, lay on, orchestrate, see to, mobilize.
OPPOSITES muddle.

**orient, orientate** verb 1 *she found it hard to orient herself:* acclimatize, familiarize, adjust, accustom, find one's feet, get/ find one's bearings. 2 *oriented to the business community:* aim, direct, pitch, design, intend. 3 *the stones are oriented from north to south:* align, place, position, arrange.

**orientation** noun 1 *the orientation of the radar station:* positioning, location, position, situation, placement, alignment. 2 *broadly Marxist in orientation:* attitude, inclination. 3 *orientation courses:* induction, training, initiation, briefing.

**origin** noun 1 *the origins of life:* beginning, start, genesis, birth, dawning, dawn, emergence, creation, source, basis, cause, root(s). 2 *the origin of the word:* source, derivation, root(s), provenance, etymology; N. Amer. provenience. 3 *his Scottish origins:* descent, ancestry, parentage, pedigree, lineage, line (of descent), heritage, birth, extraction, family, roots.

**original** adjective 1 *the original inhabitants:* indigenous, native, first, earliest, early. 2 *an original Rembrandt:* authentic, genuine, actual, true, bona fide. 3 *a highly original film:* innovative, creative, imaginative, inventive, new, novel, fresh, unusual, unconventional, unorthodox, groundbreaking, pioneering, unique, distinctive.
noun *a copy of the original:* prototype, source, master.

**originally** adverb at first, in the beginning, to begin with, initially, in the first place, at the outset.

**originate** verb 1 *the disease originates from Africa:* arise, have its origin, begin, start, stem, spring, emerge, emanate. 2 *Bill originated the idea:* invent, create, devise, think up, dream up, conceive, formulate, form, develop, produce, mastermind, pioneer.

**ornament** noun 1 *cheap ornaments:* knick-knack, trinket, bauble; N. Amer. informal tchotchke, kickshaw. 2 *a dress with no ornament at all:* decoration, adornment, embellishment, ornamentation, trimming, accessories, frills.

**ornamental** adjective decorative, fancy, ornate, ornamented, for show.

**ornate** adjective elaborate, decorated, embellished, adorned, ornamented, fancy, fussy, ostentatious, showy; informal flashy.
OPPOSITES plain.

**orthodox** adjective 1 *orthodox views:* conventional, mainstream, conformist, established, traditional, traditionalist, prevalent, popular, conservative, received. 2 *an orthodox Hindu:* conservative, traditional, observant, devout, strict.
OPPOSITES unconventional, liberal.

a b c d e f g h i j k l m n o p q r s t u v w x y z

a
b
c
d
e
f
g
h
i
j
k
l
m
**o**
p
q
r
s
t
u
v
w
x
y
z

**other** adjective **1** *these homes use other fuels:* alternative, different, distinct, separate, various. **2** *are there any other questions?* more, further, additional, extra, fresh, new, added, supplementary.

**otherwise** adverb **1** *hurry up, otherwise we'll be late:* or (else), if not. **2** *she's exhausted, but otherwise she's fine:* in other respects, apart from that. **3** *he could not have acted otherwise:* in any other way, differently.

**oust** verb expel, drive out, force out, remove from office/power, eject, get rid of, depose, topple, unseat, overthrow, bring down, overturn, dismiss, dislodge.

**out** adjective & adverb **1** *she's out at the moment:* not here, not at home, not in, away, gone away, elsewhere. **2** *the secret was out:* revealed, (out) in the open, common/public knowledge. **3** *the roses are out:* in flower, flowering, in (full) bloom, blooming, in blossom, blossoming. **4** *the book should be out soon:* available, obtainable, to be had, in the shops, published, in print. **5** (informal) *grunge is out:* unfashionable, out of fashion, dated, outdated, passé; informal old hat. **6** *smoking is out:* forbidden, not permitted, not allowed, unacceptable; informal not on. **7** *he was slightly out in his calculations:* mistaken, inaccurate, incorrect, wrong, in error.
OPPOSITES in.
verb (informal) *it was not our intention to out him:* expose, unmask.

**outbreak** noun **1** *outbreaks of violence:* eruption, flare-up,

upsurge, rash, wave, spate, burst, flurry. **2** *the outbreak of war:* start, beginning, commencement, onset.

**outburst** noun eruption, explosion, flare-up, storm, outpouring, surge, fit.

**outcome** noun result, end result, net result, consequence, upshot, conclusion, end product; informal pay-off.

**outcry** noun protest, protestation, complaints, objections, furore, fuss, uproar, opposition, dissent; informal hullabaloo, ructions, stink.

**outdated** adjective old-fashioned, out of date, outmoded, out of fashion, unfashionable, dated, passé, old, behind the times; informal out, old hat, square; N. Amer. informal horse-and-buggy.
OPPOSITES modern.

**outdoor** adjective open-air, out-of-doors, outside, al fresco.
OPPOSITES indoor.

**outer** adjective **1** *the outer layer:* outside, outermost, outward, exterior, external, surface. **2** *the outer islands:* outlying, distant, remote, faraway, far-flung, furthest.
OPPOSITES inner.

**outfit** noun **1** *a new outfit:* costume, suit, uniform, ensemble, clothes, clothing, dress, garb; informal get-up; Brit. informal kit. **2** (informal) *a local manufacturing outfit:* organization, enterprise, company, firm, business, group, body, team; informal set-up.

**outgoing** adjective **1** *he's very outgoing:* extrovert, uninhibited, unreserved, demonstrative, affectionate, warm, sociable, convivial, lively, gregarious. **2** *the*

**outgoing president:** departing, retiring, leaving.
OPPOSITES introverted, incoming.

**outgoings** plural noun expenses, expenditure, spending, outlay, payments, costs, overheads.

**outing** noun trip, excursion, jaunt, expedition, day out, tour, drive, ride, run; informal spin.

**outlaw** noun *a band of outlaws:* fugitive, wanted criminal, bandit, robber.
verb *fox-hunting has been outlawed:* ban, bar, prohibit, forbid, make illegal, proscribe.
OPPOSITES permit.

**outlet** noun 1 *a central-heating outlet:* vent, way out, outfall, opening, channel, conduit, duct. 2 *an outlet for farm produce:* market, retail outlet, shop, store. 3 *an outlet for their energies:* means of expression, means of release, vent, avenue, channel.

**outline** noun 1 *the outline of the building:* silhouette, profile, shape, contours, form, lines. 2 *an outline of our proposal:* rough idea, thumbnail sketch, rundown, summary, synopsis, résumé, precis, main points, gist, bare bones.
verb *she outlined the plan briefly:* rough out, sketch out, draft, give a rough idea of, summarize, precis.

**outlook** noun 1 *a positive outlook:* point of view, viewpoint, way of thinking, perspective, attitude, standpoint, stance, frame of mind. 2 *a lovely open outlook:* view, vista, prospect, panorama. 3 *the outlook for the economy:* prospects, future, expectations, prognosis.

**out of date** adjective 1 *the design is out of date:* old-fashioned, outmoded, outdated, dated, old, passé, behind the times, obsolete, antiquated, anachronistic; informal old hat; N. Amer. informal horse-and-buggy, clunky. 2 *your ticket is out of date:* expired, lapsed, invalid, void. 3 *your information is out of date:* obsolete, no longer valid/relevant/true, incorrect, inaccurate.
OPPOSITES fashionable, valid, current.

**output** noun production, yield, product, productivity, work, result, processed data.

**outrage** noun 1 *public outrage:* indignation, fury, anger, rage, wrath. 2 *it is an outrage:* scandal, offence, insult, affront, disgrace, atrocity.
verb *his remarks outraged everyone:* enrage, infuriate, incense, anger, scandalize, offend, affront, shock.

**outrageous** adjective 1 *outrageous behaviour:* shocking, disgraceful, scandalous, atrocious, appalling, dreadful. 2 *an outrageous claim:* exaggerated, improbable, preposterous, ridiculous, unwarranted. 3 *outrageous clothes:* eye-catching, flamboyant, showy, gaudy, ostentatious; informal flashy.

**outright** adverb 1 *he rejected the proposal outright:* completely, entirely, wholly, totally, categorically, absolutely, utterly, flatly, unreservedly, out of hand. 2 *I told her outright:* explicitly, directly, frankly, candidly, bluntly, plainly, to someone's face; Brit. informal straight up. 3 *they were killed*

*outright*: instantly, instantaneously, immediately, at once, straight away, then and there, on the spot.
**adjective 1** *an outright lie*: complete, absolute, out-and-out, downright, utter, sheer, categorical. **2** *the outright winner*: definite, unequivocal, clear, unmistakable, overall.

**outset** noun start, starting point, beginning; informal the word go.
OPPOSITES end.

**outside** noun *the outside of the building*: exterior, outer/external surface, case, skin, shell, covering, facade.
**adjective 1** *outside lights*: exterior, external, outer, outdoor, out-of-doors. **2** *outside contractors*: independent, freelance, consultant, external.
**adverb** *shall we eat outside?*: outdoors, out of doors, alfresco.
OPPOSITES inside.

**outsider** noun stranger, visitor, non-member, foreigner, alien, interloper, immigrant, incomer, newcomer.

**outskirts** plural noun edges, fringes, suburbs, suburbia, periphery.

**outspoken** adjective forthright, direct, candid, frank, straightforward, open, straight from the shoulder, plain-spoken, blunt.

**outstanding** adjective **1** *an outstanding painter*: excellent, marvellous, magnificent, superb, fine, wonderful, superlative, exceptional; informal great, terrific, tremendous, super; Brit. informal brilliant; N. Amer. informal neat. **2** *how much work is still outstanding?* to be done, undone, unfinished,

incomplete, remaining, pending. **3** *outstanding debts*: unpaid, unsettled, owing, owed, to be paid, payable, due, overdue; N. Amer. delinquent.

**outward** adjective external, surface, superficial, seeming, apparent, ostensible.
OPPOSITES inward.

**outweigh** verb be greater than, exceed, be superior to, prevail over, override, supersede, offset, cancel out, more than make up for, outbalance, compensate for.

**ovation** noun applause, round of applause, cheers, bravos, acclaim, standing ovation; informal (big) hand.

**over** preposition **1** *there was cloud over the hills*: above, on top of, higher (up) than, atop, covering. **2** *he walked over the grass*: across, on. **3** *he has three people over him*: superior to, above, higher up than, in charge of, responsible for. **4** *over 2,000 people*: more than, above, in excess of, upwards of. **5** *an argument over money*: about, on the subject of, concerning, with reference to, regarding, relating to, in connection with.
OPPOSITES under.
**adverb 1** *a plane flew over*: overhead, past, by. **2** *the relationship is over*: at an end, finished, ended, no more, a thing of the past.

**overall** adjective *the overall cost*: total, all-inclusive, gross, final, inclusive, complete, entire.
**adverb** *overall, things are better*: generally (speaking), in general, altogether, all in all, on balance, on average, for the most part, in the main, on the whole, by and large.

**overcome** verb *he overcame his pain:* conquer, defeat, beat, prevail over, control, get/bring under control, master, get the better of; informal lick, best.
adjective *she was overcome with excitement:* overwhelmed, moved, affected, speechless.

**overdue** adjective **1** *the ship is overdue:* late, behind schedule, behind time, delayed. **2** *overdue payments:* unpaid, unsettled, owing, owed, payable, due, outstanding, undischarged; N. Amer. delinquent.
OPPOSITES early, punctual.

**overflow** verb *chemicals overflowed from the tank:* spill over, flow over, brim over, well over, flood.
noun *offices to accommodate the overflow:* surplus, excess, additional people/things, extra, remainder, overspill.

**overhaul** verb service, maintain, repair, mend, fix up, rebuild, renovate, recondition, refit, refurbish.

**overhead** adverb *the sky overhead:* above, high up, in the sky, on high, above one's head.
OPPOSITES below.
adjective *overhead lines:* aerial, elevated, raised, suspended, overhanging.
OPPOSITES surface, underground.

**overheads** plural noun running costs, operating costs, fixed costs, expenses.

**overlook** verb **1** *he overlooked the mistake:* fail to notice, fail to spot, miss. **2** *his work has been overlooked:* disregard, neglect, ignore, pass over, forget. **3** *she was willing to overlook his faults:* ignore, disregard, take no notice of, make allowances for, turn a blind eye to, excuse, pardon, forgive. **4** *the lounge overlooks the garden:* have a view of, look over/across, look on to, look out on/over.

**overpower** verb overwhelm, get the better of, overthrow, subdue, suppress, subjugate, repress, bring someone to their knees.

**overpowering** adjective **1** *overpowering grief:* overwhelming, oppressive, unbearable, unendurable, intolerable, shattering. **2** *an overpowering smell:* stifling, suffocating, strong, pungent, powerful, nauseating, offensive, acrid, fetid.

**overrate** verb overestimate, overvalue, think too much of.
OPPOSITES underestimate.

**override** verb **1** *the court overrode the decision:* disallow, overrule, countermand, veto, quash, overturn, overthrow, cancel, reverse, rescind, revoke, repeal. **2** *our interests should override all others:* outweigh, supersede, take precedence over, take priority over, be more important than, cancel out, outbalance.

**overrule** verb countermand, cancel, reverse, rescind, repeal, revoke, disallow, override, veto, quash, overturn, overthrow.

**overrun** verb invade, storm, occupy, swarm into, surge into, inundate, overwhelm.

**overshadow** verb outshine, eclipse, surpass, exceed, outclass, outstrip, outdo, upstage; informal be head and shoulders above.

**overt** adjective undisguised, unconcealed, plain (to see), clear, conspicuous, obvious, noticeable, manifest, patent,

a
b
c
d
e
f
g
h
i
j
k
l
m
n
**o**
p
q
r
s
t
u
v
w
x
y
z

open, blatant.
OPPOSITES covert.

**overtake** verb 1 *a green car overtook us:* pass, go past, pull ahead of. 2 *Goa overtook Ibiza as the favourite destination:* outstrip, surpass, overshadow, eclipse, outshine, outclass, exceed, top, cap. 3 *the calamity which overtook us:* befall, happen to, come upon, hit, strike, overwhelm, overcome.

**overthrow** verb *the regime was overthrown:* oust, remove, bring down, topple, depose, displace, unseat, defeat, conquer.
noun *the overthrow of capitalism:* ousting, removal, downfall, toppling, supplanting, displacement, unseating, defeat, fall, collapse, demise.

**overture** noun 1 *the overture to a long debate:* preliminary, prelude, introduction, lead-in, precursor, start, beginning. 2 *peace overtures:* opening move, approach, advances, feeler, signal.

**overturn** verb 1 *the boat overturned:* capsize, turn turtle, keel over, tip over, topple over. 2 *I overturned the stool:* upset, tip over, topple over, turn over, knock over, upend. 3 *the Senate may overturn this ruling:* cancel, reverse, rescind, repeal, revoke, countermand, disallow, override, overrule, veto, quash, overthrow.

**overweight** adjective fat, obese, stout, plump, portly, chubby, pot-bellied, flabby; informal tubby; Brit. informal podgy.
OPPOSITES underweight.

**overwhelm** verb 1 *Spain overwhelmed Russia in the hockey:* defeat heavily, trounce, rout, beat hollow, conquer, be victorious over, crush; informal thrash, lick, wipe the floor with. 2 *she was overwhelmed by a sense of tragedy:* overcome, move, stir, affect, touch, strike, dumbfound, shake, leave speechless; informal bowl over, knock sideways, floor; Brit. informal knock/hit for six.

**overwhelming** adjective 1 *an overwhelming number of people:* very large, enormous, immense, inordinate, massive, huge. 2 *an overwhelming desire to laugh:* very strong, powerful, uncontrollable, irrepressible, irresistible, overpowering, compelling.

**owe** verb be in debt (to), be indebted (to), be in arrears (to), be under an obligation (to).

**owing** adjective *the rent was owing:* unpaid, to be paid, payable, due, overdue, undischarged, owed, outstanding, in arrears; N. Amer. delinquent.
OPPOSITES paid.
■ **owing to** because of, as a result of, on account of, due to, as a consequence of, thanks to, in view of.

**own** adjective *he has his own reasons:* personal, individual, particular, private, personalized, unique.
verb *I own this house:* possess, keep, hold, be the owner of, have to one's name.

**owner** noun possessor, holder, proprietor, homeowner, freeholder, landlord, landlady.

**ownership** noun possession, freehold, proprietorship, proprietary rights, title.

# Pp

**pace** noun **1** *ten paces:* step. **2** *a slow, steady pace:* gait, stride, walk, march. **3** *a furious pace:* speed, rate, velocity, tempo.
verb *she paced up and down:* walk, stride, march, pound.

**pack** noun **1** *a pack of cigarettes:* packet, container, package, box, carton, parcel. **2** *a pack of wolves:* group, herd, troop. **3** *a pack of hooligans:* crowd, mob, group, band, party, set, gang, rabble, horde, throng, huddle, mass, assembly, gathering, host; informal crew, bunch.
verb **1** *she helped pack the car:* fill (up), put things in, load. **2** *they packed their belongings:* stow, put away, store, box up. **3** *the glasses were packed in straw:* wrap (up), package, parcel, swathe, swaddle, encase, envelop, bundle. **4** *shoppers packed the store:* throng, crowd, fill, cram, jam, squash into, squeeze into.

**package** noun **1** *the delivery of a package:* parcel, packet, box. **2** *a package of services:* collection, bundle, combination, range, complement, raft, platform.
verb *goods packaged in recyclable materials:* wrap, gift-wrap, pack, box, seal.

**packet** noun pack, carton, container, case, package.

**pact** noun agreement, treaty, entente, protocol, deal, settlement, armistice, truce.

**pad**[1] noun **1** *a pad over the eye:* dressing, pack, wad. **2** *making notes on a pad:* notebook, notepad, writing pad, jotter; N. Amer. scratch pad.

**pad**[2] verb *he padded along the landing:* creep, sneak, steal, tiptoe, pussyfoot.

**padded** adjective cushioned, insulated, lined, quilted, stuffed, lagged.

**padding** noun **1** *padding around the ankle:* wadding, cushioning, stuffing, packing, filling, lining. **2** *a concise style with no padding:* verbiage, wordiness; Brit. informal waffle.

**paddle**[1] noun *use the paddles to row ashore:* oar, scull.
verb *we paddled around the bay:* row, pull, scull.

**paddle**[2] verb *children were paddling in the water:* splash (about), dabble, wade.

**pagan** noun & adjective heathen, infidel, non-Christian.

**page**[1] noun folio, sheet, side, leaf.

**page**[2] noun **1** *a page in a hotel:* errand boy, messenger boy; N. Amer. bellboy, bellhop. **2** *a page at a wedding:* attendant, pageboy, train-bearer.
verb *could you please page Mr Johnson?* call (for), summon, send for.

**pageant** noun parade, procession, cavalcade, tableau, spectacle, extravaganza, show.

**pageantry** noun spectacle, display, ceremony, magnificence, pomp, splendour, grandeur, show; informal razzle-dazzle, razzmatazz.

**pain** noun **1** *she endured great pain:* suffering, agony, torture, torment, discomfort. **2** *a pain in the stomach:* ache, aching,

soreness, throbbing, sting, twinge, stab, pang, discomfort, irritation. **3** *the pain of losing a loved one:* sorrow, grief, heartache, heartbreak, sadness, unhappiness, distress, misery, despair, agony, torment, torture. **4** *he took great pains to hide his feelings:* care, effort, bother, trouble.
verb *it pained him to watch:* sadden, grieve, distress, trouble, perturb, oppress, cause anguish to.

**painful** adjective **1** *a painful arm:* sore, hurting, tender, aching, throbbing. **2** *a painful experience:* disagreeable, unpleasant, nasty, distressing, upsetting, traumatic, miserable, sad, heartbreaking, agonizing, harrowing.

**painfully** adverb distressingly, disturbingly, uncomfortably, unpleasantly, dreadfully.

**painstaking** adjective careful, meticulous, thorough, assiduous, attentive, conscientious, punctilious, scrupulous, rigorous.
OPPOSITES slapdash.

**paint** noun colouring, colour, tint, dye, stain, pigment.
verb **1** *I painted the ceiling:* colour, decorate, whitewash, emulsion, gloss, spray-paint, airbrush. **2** *painting slogans on a wall:* daub, smear, spray-paint, airbrush. **3** *Rembrandt painted his mother:* portray, picture, paint a picture/portrait of, depict, represent.

**painting** noun picture, illustration, portrayal, depiction, representation, image, artwork, canvas, oil, watercolour.

**pair** noun *a matching pair:* set, brace, couple, duo, two.

verb *a cardigan paired with a matching skirt:* match, put together, couple, combine.

**palace** noun castle, château, mansion, stately home, residence.

**pale** adjective **1** *she looked pale:* white, pallid, pasty, wan, colourless, anaemic, washed out, peaky, ashen, sickly; informal like death warmed up. **2** *pale colours:* light, pastel, muted, subtle, soft, faded, bleached, washed out. **3** *the pale light of morning:* dim, faint, weak, feeble.
OPPOSITES rosy-cheeked, dark.
verb *he paled at the news:* go/turn white, grow/turn pale, blanch, lose colour.

**pamper** verb spoil, indulge, overindulge, cosset, mollycoddle, coddle, baby, wait on someone hand and foot.

**pamphlet** noun brochure, leaflet, booklet, circular; N. Amer. mailer, folder.

**pan**[1] noun *a pan of water:* saucepan, pot, bowl, frying pan, skillet.

**pan**[2] verb *the camera panned to the building:* swing (round), sweep, move, turn.

**panel** noun **1** *a control panel:* console, instrument panel, dashboard, instruments, controls, dials, array. **2** *a panel of judges:* group, team, body, committee, board.

**panic** noun *a wave of panic:* alarm, anxiety, fear, fright, trepidation, dread, terror, hysteria, apprehension; informal flap, fluster, cold sweat; N. Amer. informal swivet.
OPPOSITES calm.
verb **1** *there's no need to panic:* be alarmed, be scared, be afraid, take fright, be

hysterical, lose one's nerve, get overwrought, get worked up; informal get in a flap, run around like a headless chicken; Brit. informal get the wind up, go into a flat spin, have kittens. **2** *talk of love panicked her:* frighten, alarm, scare, unnerve; Brit. informal put the wind up.
OPPOSITES stay calm, calm down.

**panorama** noun view, vista, prospect, scenery, landscape, seascape, cityscape, skyline.

**pant** verb breathe heavily, breathe hard, puff and blow, huff and puff, gasp, heave, wheeze.

**pants** plural noun **1** (Brit.) underpants, briefs, boxer shorts, boxers, knickers; N. Amer. shorts, undershorts; informal panties; N. Amer. dated step-ins. **2** (N. Amer.) trousers, slacks; Brit. informal trews, strides, kecks; Austral. informal daks.

**paper** noun **1** newspaper, journal, gazette, periodical, tabloid, broadsheet, daily, weekly; informal rag; N. Amer. informal tab. **2** *a three-hour paper:* exam, examination, test. **3** *he has written a paper on global warming:* essay, article, monograph, thesis, work, dissertation, treatise, study, report, analysis; N. Amer. theme. **4** *personal papers:* document, certificate, letter, file, deed, record, archive; (**papers**) paperwork, documentation. **5** *they asked us for our papers:* identification, identity card, ID, credentials.

**parable** noun allegory, moral tale, fable.

**parade** noun **1** *a victory parade:* procession, march, cavalcade, motorcade, spectacle, display, pageant, review, tattoo; Brit.

march past. **2** *she walked along the parade:* promenade, walkway, esplanade, mall; N. Amer. boardwalk; Brit. informal prom.
verb **1** *the teams paraded through the city:* march, process, file, troop. **2** *she paraded up and down:* strut, swagger, stride. **3** *he was keen to parade his knowledge:* display, exhibit, make a show of, flaunt, show (off), demonstrate.

**paradise** noun **1** heaven, the promised land, the Elysian Fields. **2** *a tropical paradise:* Utopia, Shangri-La, Eden, heaven, idyll. **3** *this is sheer paradise!* bliss, heaven, ecstasy, delight, joy, happiness, heaven on earth.
OPPOSITES hell.

**paradox** noun contradiction, self-contradiction, inconsistency, incongruity, conflict, enigma, puzzle, conundrum.

**paragraph** noun section, division, part, portion, segment, passage, clause.

**parallel** adjective **1** *parallel lines:* aligned, side by side, equidistant. **2** *parallel careers:* similar, analogous, comparable, corresponding, like, equivalent, matching.
OPPOSITES divergent, different.
noun **1** *an exact parallel:* counterpart, analogue, equivalent, match, twin, duplicate, mirror. **2** *there is an interesting parallel between these figures:* similarity, likeness, resemblance, analogy, correspondence, comparison, equivalence, symmetry.
OPPOSITES divergence, difference.

**paralyse** verb 1 *both of his legs were paralysed:* disable, cripple, immobilize, incapacitate; (**paralysed**) Medicine paraplegic, quadriplegic. 2 *the capital was paralysed by a strike:* bring to a standstill, immobilize, bring to a halt, freeze, cripple, disable.

**paralysis** noun 1 *the disease can cause paralysis:* immobility, powerlessness, incapacity; Medicine paraplegia, quadriplegia. 2 *complete paralysis of the ports:* shutdown, immobilization, stoppage, gridlock, standstill, blockage.

**paramount** adjective most important, supreme, chief, overriding, predominant, foremost, prime, primary, principal, main, key, central; informal number-one.

**paranoid** adjective suspicious, mistrustful, anxious, fearful, insecure, obsessive.

**paraphrase** verb reword, rephrase, express differently, rewrite, gloss.

**parasite** noun hanger-on, cadger, leech, passenger; informal sponger, scrounger, freeloader; N. Amer. informal mooch; Austral./NZ informal bludger.

**parcel** noun *a parcel of clothes:* package, packet, pack, bundle, box, case, bale.
verb *she parcelled up the papers:* pack (up), package, wrap (up), gift-wrap, tie up, bundle up.

**pardon** noun 1 *pardon for your sins:* forgiveness, absolution. 2 *he offered them a full pardon:* reprieve, amnesty, exoneration, release, acquittal, discharge.
verb 1 *I know she will pardon me:* forgive, absolve. 2 *they were subsequently pardoned:* exonerate, acquit, reprieve; informal let off.

OPPOSITES blame, punish.

**parish** noun 1 *the parish of Upton:* district, community. 2 *the vicar scandalized the parish:* parishioners, churchgoers, congregation, fold, flock, community.

**park** noun 1 public garden, recreation ground, playground, play area. 2 parkland, grassland, woodland, garden(s), lawns, grounds, estate.
verb 1 *he parked his car:* leave, position, stop, pull up. 2 (informal) *park your bag by the door:* put (down), place, deposit, leave, stick, shove, dump; informal plonk; Brit. informal bung.

**parliament** noun legislature, assembly, chamber, house, congress, senate, diet.

**parliamentary** adjective legislative, law-making, governmental, congressional, democratic, elected.

**parochial** adjective narrow-minded, small-minded, provincial, small-town, conservative; N. Amer. informal jerkwater.
OPPOSITES broad-minded.

**parody** noun 1 *a parody of the news:* satire, burlesque, lampoon, pastiche, caricature, imitation; informal spoof, take-off, send-up. 2 *a parody of the truth:* distortion, travesty, caricature, misrepresentation, perversion, corruption.

**parry** verb 1 *Sharpe parried the blow:* ward off, fend off, deflect, block. 2 *I parried her questions:* evade, sidestep, avoid, dodge, field.

**parson** noun priest, minister, clergyman, vicar, rector, cleric, chaplain, pastor, curate; informal reverend, padre; Austral. informal josser.

**part** noun **1** *a large part of their life:* piece, amount, portion, proportion, percentage, fraction; informal slice, chunk. **2** *car parts:* component, bit, constituent, element, module. **3** *body parts:* organ, limb, member. **4** *the third part of the book:* section, division, volume, chapter, act, scene, instalment. **5** *another part of the country:* district, neighbourhood, quarter, section, area, region. **6** *the part of Juliet:* role, character. **7** *he was jailed for his part in the affair:* involvement, role, function, hand, responsibility, capacity, participation, contribution; informal bit.
OPPOSITES whole.
verb **1** *the curtains parted:* separate, divide, split, move apart. **2** *we parted on bad terms:* leave each other, part company, say goodbye/farewell, say one's goodbyes/farewells, go one's separate ways, take one's leave.
OPPOSITES join, meet.
■ part with give away, give up, relinquish, forgo, surrender, hand over. ■ take part participate, join in, get involved, enter, play a part, play a role, be a participant, contribute, have a hand; informal get in on the act.

**partial** adjective **1** *a partial recovery:* incomplete, limited, qualified, imperfect, fragmentary, unfinished. **2** *a very partial view of the situation:* biased, prejudiced, partisan, one-sided, slanted, skewed, coloured, unbalanced.
OPPOSITES complete, unbiased.
■ be partial to like, love, enjoy, be fond of, be keen on, have a soft spot for, have a taste for,

have a penchant for.

**partially** adverb somewhat, to a limited extent, to a certain extent, partly, in part, up to a point, slightly.
OPPOSITES wholly.

**participant** noun participator, contributor, party, member, entrant, competitor, player, contestant, candidate.

**participate** verb take part, join, engage, get involved, share, play a part, play a role, contribute, partake, have a hand in.

**particle** noun (tiny) bit, (tiny) piece, speck, spot, fragment, sliver, splinter.

**particular** adjective **1** *a particular group of companies:* specific, certain, distinct, separate, definite, precise. **2** *an issue of particular importance:* special, exceptional, unusual, uncommon, notable, noteworthy, remarkable, unique. **3** *he was particular about what he ate:* fussy, fastidious, finicky, discriminating, selective; informal pernickety, choosy, picky; Brit. informal faddy.
OPPOSITES general, indiscriminate.
noun *the same in every particular:* detail, item, point, element, fact, circumstance, feature.

**particularly** adverb **1** *the acoustics are particularly good:* especially, specially, exceptionally, unusually, remarkably, outstandingly, uncommonly, uniquely. **2** *he particularly asked that I should help you:* specifically, explicitly, expressly, in particular, especially, specially.

**parting** noun *an emotional*

*parting:* farewell, leave-taking, goodbye, adieu, departure.

**partisan** noun guerrilla, freedom fighter, resistance fighter, underground fighter, irregular.
adjective biased, prejudiced, one-sided, discriminatory, partial, sectarian, factional.
OPPOSITES unbiased.

**partition** noun 1 *the partition of Palestine:* division, partitioning, separation, dividing up, splitting up, breaking up, break-up. 2 *room partitions:* screen, room divider, dividing wall, barrier, panel.
verb 1 *moves to partition Poland:* divide, separate, split up, break up. 2 *the hall was partitioned:* subdivide, divide (up), separate, section off, screen off.

**partly** adverb in part, partially, somewhat, a little, up to a point, in some measure, slightly, to some extent.
OPPOSITES wholly.

**partner** noun 1 *business partners:* colleague, associate, co-worker, fellow worker, collaborator, comrade, teammate; Austral./NZ informal offsider. 2 *his partner in crime:* accomplice, confederate, accessory, collaborator, fellow conspirator, helper; informal sidekick. 3 *your relationship with your partner:* spouse, husband, wife, lover, girlfriend, boyfriend, fiancé, fiancée, significant other, live-in lover, mate; Brit. informal other half.

**partnership** noun 1 *close partnership:* cooperation, association, collaboration, coalition, alliance, union, affiliation, connection. 2 *thriving partnerships:*

company, association, consortium, syndicate, firm, business, organization.

**party** noun 1 *150 people attended the party:* social gathering, function, get-together, celebration, reunion, festivity, reception, soirée, social; informal bash, do; Austral./NZ informal shivoo. 2 *a party of visitors:* group, company, body, gang, band, crowd, pack, contingent; informal bunch, crew, load. 3 *a left-wing party:* faction, group, bloc, camp, caucus, alliance.

**pass** verb 1 *the traffic passing through the village:* go, proceed, move, progress, make one's way, travel. 2 *a car passed him:* overtake, go past/by, pull ahead of, leave behind. 3 *time passed:* elapse, go by/past, advance, wear on, roll by, tick by. 4 *he passed the time reading:* occupy, spend, fill, use (up), employ, while away. 5 *pass the salt:* hand, let someone have, give, reach. 6 *her estate passed to her grandson:* be transferred, go, be left, be bequeathed, be handed down/on, be passed on; Law devolve. 7 *his death passed unnoticed:* happen, occur, take place. 8 *the storm passed:* come to an end, fade (away), blow over, run its course, die out/down, finish, end, cease. 9 *he passed the exam:* be successful in, succeed in, gain a pass in, get through; informal sail through, scrape through. 10 *the Senate passed the bill:* approve, vote for, accept, ratify, adopt, agree to, authorize, endorse, legalize, enact; informal OK.
OPPOSITES start, fail, reject.
noun *you must show your pass:* permit, warrant, authorization, licence.

■ **pass as/for** be mistaken for, be taken for, be accepted as.
■ **pass out** faint, lose consciousness, black out. ■ **pass something up** turn down, reject, refuse, decline, give up, forgo, let pass, miss (out on); informal give something a miss.

**passage** noun **1** *their passage through the country:* progress, transit, advance, journey, trip, voyage. **2** *the passage of time:* passing, advance, course, march. **3** *clearing a passage to the front door:* way, route, path. **4** *the passage to the kitchen:* corridor, hall, hallway. **5** *a passage between the buildings:* alley, alleyway, passageway, lane, path, footpath, track, thoroughfare; N. Amer. areaway. **6** *a passage from 'Macbeth':* extract, excerpt, quotation, quote.

**passenger** noun traveller, commuter, fare-payer, rider, fare.

**passing** adjective **1** *of passing interest:* fleeting, transient, transitory, ephemeral, brief, short-lived, temporary, momentary. **2** *a passing glance:* hasty, rapid, hurried, brief, quick, cursory, superficial, casual, perfunctory.
noun **1** *the passing of time:* passage, course, progress, advance. **2** *Jack's passing:* death, demise, passing away, end, loss.

**passion** noun **1** *the passion of activists:* enthusiasm, ardour, fervour, eagerness, zeal, vigour, fire, energy, spirit, fanaticism. **2** *he worked himself up into a passion:* rage, fit of anger, temper, tantrum, fury, frenzy; Brit. informal paddy. **3** *hot with passion:* love, desire, lust, ardour, lasciviousness,

lustfulness. **4** *his passion for football:* enthusiasm, love, mania, fascination, obsession, preoccupation, fanaticism, fixation, compulsion, appetite, addiction; informal thing.
OPPOSITES apathy, calm.

**passionate** adjective **1** *a passionate entreaty:* intense, impassioned, ardent, fervent, vehement, fiery, heated, emotional, heartfelt, excited. **2** *McGregor is passionate about sport:* very keen, very enthusiastic, addicted; informal mad, crazy, hooked; Austral./NZ informal shook. **3** *a passionate kiss:* amorous, ardent, hot-blooded, loving, sexy, sensual, erotic, lustful; informal steamy, hot, turned on.
OPPOSITES apathetic, cool.

**passive** adjective **1** *a passive role:* inactive, non-active, non-participative, uninvolved. **2** *passive victims:* submissive, acquiescent, unresisting, compliant, docile.
OPPOSITES active, resistant.

**past** adjective **1** *times past:* gone by, bygone, former, previous, old, of old, olden, long-ago. **2** *the past few months:* last, recent, preceding. **3** *a past chairman:* previous, former, foregoing, erstwhile, one-time, sometime, ex-.
OPPOSITES present, future.
noun *details of her past:* history, background, past life, life story.
preposition **1** *I drove past the cafe:* in front of, by. **2** *it's past 9 o'clock:* beyond, after, later than.
adverb *they hurried past:* along, by, on.

**paste** noun **1** *blend the ingredients to a paste:* purée, pulp, mush, spread, pâté.

2 *wallpaper paste:* adhesive, glue, gum; N. Amer. mucilage.
**verb** *a notice was pasted on the door:* stick, glue, gum, fix, affix.

**pastel** adjective pale, soft, light, delicate, muted.
OPPOSITES dark, bright.

**pastime** noun hobby, leisure activity, leisure pursuit, recreation, game, amusement, diversion, entertainment, interest.

**pastor** noun priest, minister, parson, clergyman, cleric, chaplain, vicar, rector, curate; informal reverend, padre; Austral. informal josser.

**pastoral** adjective 1 *a pastoral scene:* rural, country, rustic, agricultural, bucolic. 2 *his pastoral duties:* priestly, clerical, ecclesiastical, ministerial.
OPPOSITES urban, lay.

**pasture** noun grassland, grass, grazing, meadow, field; Austral./ NZ run.

**pat** verb & noun tap, clap, touch, stroke.

**patch** noun 1 *a reddish patch on her wrist:* blotch, mark, spot, smudge, smear, stain, streak, blemish; informal splodge. 2 *a patch of ground:* plot, area, piece, strip, tract, parcel, bed; Brit. allotment; N. Amer. lot. 3 (Brit. informal) *going through a difficult patch:* period, time, spell, phase, stretch.
**verb** *her jeans were neatly patched:* mend, repair, sew up, stitch up, cover, reinforce.

**patent** adjective 1 *patent nonsense:* obvious, clear, plain, evident, manifest, conspicuous, blatant, barefaced, flagrant. 2 *patent medicines:* proprietary, patented, licensed, branded.

**path** noun 1 *the path to the beach:* footpath, pathway, track, trail, bridle path, lane, cycle track; N. Amer. bikeway. 2 *journalists blocked his path:* route, way, course. 3 *the best path to follow:* course of action, route, road, avenue, line, approach, tack.

**pathetic** adjective 1 *a pathetic sight:* pitiful, moving, touching, poignant, plaintive, wretched. 2 (informal) *a pathetic excuse:* feeble, woeful, sorry, poor, pitiful, lamentable, deplorable, contemptible.
OPPOSITES funny, plausible, commendable.

**patience** noun 1 *she tried everyone's patience:* forbearance, tolerance, restraint, equanimity, understanding, indulgence. 2 *a task requiring patience:* perseverance, persistence, endurance, tenacity, application, staying power, doggedness.

**patient** adjective 1 *I must ask you to be patient:* forbearing, uncomplaining, tolerant, long-suffering, accommodating, understanding, indulgent. 2 *patient research:* persevering, persistent, tenacious, dogged, determined.
**noun** *a doctor's patient:* sick person, case, sufferer.

**patriotic** adjective nationalistic, loyalist, loyal, chauvinistic, jingoistic, flag-waving.
OPPOSITES traitorous.

**patrol** noun 1 *ships on patrol in the straits:* guard, watch, vigil. 2 *the patrol stopped a woman:* squad, detachment, party, force.
**verb** *a guard was patrolling the estate:* guard, keep watch on,

police, make the rounds of, stand guard (over), defend, safeguard.

**patron** noun **1** *a patron of the arts:* sponsor, backer, benefactor, contributor, subscriber, donor, philanthropist, promoter, friend, supporter. **2** *club patrons:* customer, client, consumer, user, visitor, guest; informal regular.

**patronage** noun **1** *arts patronage:* sponsorship, backing, funding, financing, assistance, support. **2** *thank you for your patronage:* custom, trade, business.

**patronize** verb **1** *don't patronize me!* talk down to, treat like a child. **2** *they patronized local tradesmen:* use, buy from, shop at, be a customer/client of, deal with, frequent, support.

**patronizing** adjective condescending, supercilious, superior, imperious, scornful; informal uppity, high and mighty.

**pattern** noun **1** *the pattern on the wallpaper:* design, decoration, motif, device, marking. **2** *working patterns:* system, order, arrangement, form, method, structure, scheme, plan, format. **3** *this set the pattern for a generation:* model, example, criterion, standard, norm, yardstick, touchstone, benchmark, blueprint.

**pause** noun *five minutes' pause:* break, interruption, lull, respite, breathing space, gap, interlude, adjournment, rest, wait, hesitation; informal let-up, breather.
verb *let's pause here:* stop, break off, take a break, adjourn, rest, wait, hesitate; informal take a breather.

**pave** verb surface, floor, cover, tile, flag.

**pavement** noun footpath, walkway; N. Amer. sidewalk.

**pay** verb **1** *I must pay him for his work:* reward, reimburse, recompense, remunerate. **2** *I paid £7 for a ticket:* spend, pay out; informal lay out, shell out, fork out, cough up; N. Amer. informal ante up, pony up. **3** *he paid his debts:* discharge, settle, pay off, clear. **4** *he made the buses pay:* be profitable, make money, make a profit. **5** *it may pay you to be early:* be advantageous to, benefit, be of advantage to, be beneficial to. **6** *he will pay for his mistakes:* suffer (the consequences), be punished, atone, pay the penalty/price.
noun *equal pay:* salary, wages, payment, earnings, remuneration, fee, reimbursement, income, revenue.
■ **pay someone back** get one's revenge on, get back at, get even with, settle the score. ■ **pay something back** repay, pay off, give back, return, reimburse, refund. ■ **pay something off** pay (in full), settle, discharge, clear, liquidate. ■ **pay off** (informal) meet with success, be successful, be effective, get results, work.

**payable** adjective due, owed, owing, outstanding, unpaid, overdue; N. Amer. delinquent.

**payment** noun **1** *discounts for early payment:* remittance, settlement, discharge, clearance. **2** *monthly payments:* instalment, premium. **3** *extra payment for good performance:*

salary, wages, pay, earnings, fees, remuneration, reimbursement, income.

**peace** noun **1** *peace at last!* quiet, silence, peace and quiet, hush, stillness, still. **2** *peace of mind:* serenity, peacefulness, tranquillity, calm, calmness, composure, ease, contentment. **3** *we pray for peace:* order, harmony, agreement. **4** *a lasting peace:* treaty, truce, ceasefire, armistice.
OPPOSITES noise, agitation, war.

**peaceful** adjective **1** *peaceful surroundings:* tranquil, calm, restful, quiet, still, relaxing. **2** *his peaceful mood:* serene, calm, tranquil, composed, placid, at ease, untroubled, unworried, content. **3** *peaceful relations:* harmonious, on good terms, amicable, friendly, cordial, non-violent.
OPPOSITES noisy, agitated, hostile.

**peak** noun **1** *the peaks of the mountains:* summit, top, crest, pinnacle, cap. **2** *the highest peak:* mountain, hill, height. **3** *the peak of his career:* height, high point, pinnacle, summit, top, climax, culmination, apex, zenith, acme.
verb *Labour support has peaked:* reach its height, climax, culminate.
adjective *at peak times:* maximum, greatest, busiest, highest.

**peculiar** adjective **1** *something peculiar happened:* strange, unusual, odd, funny, curious, bizarre, weird, eccentric, abnormal, unconventional, outlandish; informal wacky. **2** *customs peculiar to this area:* distinctive, exclusive, unique, characteristic, distinct,

individual, typical, special, personal.
OPPOSITES ordinary.

**pedantic** adjective finicky, fussy, fastidious, dogmatic, purist, hair-splitting, quibbling; informal nit-picking, pernickety.

**peddle** verb sell, hawk, tout, trade, deal in, traffic in.

**pedestrian** noun walker, person on foot.
OPPOSITES driver.
adjective dull, boring, tedious, monotonous, unremarkable, uninspired, unimaginative, unexciting, routine, commonplace, ordinary, everyday, run-of-the-mill, mundane, humdrum; informal bog-standard.
OPPOSITES exciting.

**pedigree** noun *a fine pedigree:* ancestry, lineage, line, descent, genealogy, extraction, parentage, bloodline.
adjective *a pedigree cat:* pure-bred, full-blooded, thoroughbred.

**peel** verb **1** *peel and core the fruit:* pare, skin, hull, shell. **2** *the wallpaper was peeling:* flake (off), come off, fall off.
noun *orange peel:* rind, skin, covering, zest.

**peep** verb *I peeped through the keyhole:* peek, look, sneak a look, glance; informal squint.
noun *I'll just take a peep:* peek, look, glance; informal squint.

**peer**[1] verb *he peered at the manuscript:* look closely, squint, gaze.

**peer**[2] noun **1** *hereditary peers:* aristocrat, lord, lady, noble, nobleman, noblewoman. **2** *his academic peers:* equal, fellow, contemporary.

**peg** noun *a tent peg:* pin, nail, dowel.

**verb 1** *the flysheet is pegged to the ground:* fix, pin, attach, fasten, secure. **2** *we decided to peg our prices:* set, hold, fix, freeze, keep down, hold down.

**pen**[1] **verb** *he penned a number of articles:* write, compose, draft, dash off, scribble.

**pen**[2] **noun** *a sheep pen:* enclosure, fold, pound, compound, stockade, sty, coop; N. Amer. corral.
**verb** *the hostages were penned up in a basement:* confine, coop, cage, shut, box, lock, trap, imprison, incarcerate.

**penalize verb 1** *if you break the rules you will be penalized:* punish, discipline. **2** *a new tax would penalize the poor:* handicap, disadvantage, discriminate against.
OPPOSITES reward, benefit.

**penalty noun** punishment, sanction, fine, forfeit, sentence.
OPPOSITES reward.

**pending adjective 1** *nine cases were still pending:* unresolved, undecided, unsettled, up in the air, ongoing, outstanding; informal on the back burner.
**2** *with a general election pending:* imminent, impending, about to happen, forthcoming, on the way, coming, approaching, looming, near, on the horizon, in the offing.
**preposition** *they were released on bail pending an appeal:* awaiting, until.

**penetrate verb 1** *the knife penetrated his lungs:* pierce, puncture, enter, perforate, stab, gore. **2** *they penetrated enemy lines:* infiltrate, slip through, enter. **3** *his words finally penetrated:* register, sink in, become clear, fall into place; informal click.

**penetrating adjective 1** *a penetrating wind:* cold, cutting, biting, keen, sharp, harsh, raw, freezing, chill, bitter. **2** *a penetrating voice:* shrill, strident, piercing, ear-splitting. **3** *her penetrating gaze:* intent, searching, piercing, probing, sharp, keen. **4** *a penetrating analysis:* perceptive, insightful, keen, sharp, intelligent, clever, smart, incisive, trenchant, astute.
OPPOSITES mild, soft, stupid.

**pension noun** old-age pension, retirement pension, superannuation, allowance, benefit, support, welfare.

**pensioner noun** retired person, old-age pensioner, OAP, senior citizen; N. Amer. senior, retiree.

**people plural noun 1** *crowds of people:* human beings, persons, individuals, humans, mortals, living souls, personages, {men, women, and children}; informal folk. **2** *the British people:* citizens, subjects, electors, voters, taxpayers, residents, inhabitants, public, citizenry, nation, population, populace. **3** *a man of the people:* the common people, the proletariat, the masses, the populace, the rank and file; derogatory the hoi polloi; informal, derogatory the proles, the plebs. **4** *her people don't live far away:* family, parents, relatives, relations, folk, kinsfolk, flesh and blood, nearest and dearest; informal folks. **5** (singular) *a proud people:* race, ethnic group, tribe, clan, nation.
**verb** *those who once peopled Newfoundland:* populate, settle (in), colonize, inhabit, live in, occupy.

**pepper verb 1** *stars peppered the*

*desert skies*: sprinkle, fleck, dot, spot, stipple. **2** *gunfire peppered the area*: bombard, pelt, shower, rain down on, strafe, rake, blitz.

**perceive** verb **1** *he perceived a tear in her eye*: see, discern, detect, catch sight of, spot, observe, notice. **2** *he was perceived as too negative*: regard, look on, view, consider, think of, judge, deem.

**perception** noun **1** *popular perceptions about old age*: impression, idea, conception, notion, thought, belief. **2** *he talks with great perception*: insight, perceptiveness, understanding, intelligence, intuition, incisiveness.

**perceptive** adjective insightful, discerning, sensitive, intuitive, observant, penetrating, intelligent, clever, canny, keen, sharp, astute, shrewd, quick, smart, acute; informal on the ball; N. Amer. informal heads-up.
OPPOSITES obtuse.

**perch** verb **1** *a swallow perched on the telegraph wire*: sit, rest, alight, settle, land, roost. **2** *she perched her glasses on her nose*: put, place, set, rest, balance.

**perennial** adjective lasting, enduring, abiding, long-lasting, long-lived, perpetual, continuing, continual, recurring.
OPPOSITES ephemeral.

**perfect** adjective **1** *a perfect wife*: ideal, model, faultless, flawless, consummate, exemplary, best, ultimate, copybook. **2** *in perfect condition*: flawless, mint, as good as new, pristine, immaculate, optimum, prime, peak; informal tip-top, A1. **3** *a perfect copy*: exact, precise,

accurate, faithful, true; Brit. informal spot on; N. Amer. informal on the money. **4** *the perfect Christmas present*: ideal, just right, appropriate, fitting, suitable, tailor-made, very; Brit. informal spot on, just the job. **5** *she felt a perfect idiot*: absolute, complete, total, real, out-and-out, thorough, downright, utter; Brit. informal right; Austral./NZ informal fair.
verb *he's perfecting his style*: improve, polish (up), hone, refine, brush up, fine-tune.

**perfection** noun the ideal, a paragon, the last word, the ultimate; informal the tops, the bee's knees.

**perfectly** adverb **1** *a perfectly cooked meal*: superbly, superlatively, excellently, flawlessly, faultlessly, to perfection, immaculately, exquisitely, consummately; N. Amer. to a fare-thee-well; informal like a dream, to a T. **2** *we understand each other perfectly*: absolutely, completely, altogether, entirely, wholly, totally, fully, in every respect.
OPPOSITES badly, partly.

**perform** verb **1** *duties to perform*: carry out, do, execute, discharge, conduct, implement; informal pull off. **2** *the car performs well*: function, work, operate, run, go, respond, behave, act. **3** *the play was performed in Britain*: stage, put on, present, mount, act, produce. **4** *the band performed live*: play, sing, appear.
OPPOSITES neglect.

**performance** noun **1** *the evening performance*: show, production, showing, presentation, staging, concert, recital; informal gig. **2** *their*

**performance** *was excellent:* rendition, interpretation, playing, acting. **3** *the performance of his duty:* carrying out, execution, discharge, completion, fulfilment. **4** *the performance of the processor:* functioning, working, operation, running, behaviour, response, economy.

**performer** noun actor, actress, artiste, artist, entertainer, trouper, player, musician, singer, dancer, comic, comedian, comedienne.

**perfume** noun **1** *a bottle of perfume:* scent, fragrance, eau de toilette, toilet water. **2** *the heady perfume of lilacs:* smell, scent, fragrance, aroma, bouquet.

**perhaps** adverb maybe, for all one knows, it could be, it may be, it's possible, possibly, conceivably; N. English happen.

**peril** noun danger, jeopardy, risk, hazard, menace, threat.
OPPOSITES safety.

**perimeter** noun boundary, border, limits, bounds, edge, margin, fringe(s), periphery.
OPPOSITES centre.

**period** noun **1** *a six-week period:* time, spell, interval, stretch, term, span, phase, bout; Brit. informal patch. **2** *the post-war period:* era, age, epoch, time, days, years.

**periodic** adjective regular, at fixed intervals, recurrent, recurring, repeated, cyclical, seasonal, occasional, intermittent, sporadic, odd.

**periodical** noun journal, magazine, newspaper, paper, review, digest, gazette, newsletter, organ; informal mag, glossy.

**peripheral** adjective secondary, subsidiary, incidental, tangential, marginal, minor, unimportant, ancillary.
OPPOSITES central.

**perish** verb **1** *millions of soldiers perished:* die, lose one's life, be killed, fall, be lost; informal buy it. **2** *the rubber had perished:* go bad, spoil, rot, decay, decompose.

**perk** noun fringe benefit, advantage, bonus, extra, plus; informal freebie.

**permanent** adjective
**1** *permanent brain damage:* lasting, enduring, indefinite, continuing, constant, irreparable, irreversible, lifelong, indelible, standing. **2** *a permanent job:* long-term, stable, secure.
OPPOSITES temporary.

**permanently** adverb **1** *the attack left her permanently disabled:* forever, for all time, for good, irreversibly, incurably, irreparably, indelibly; informal for keeps. **2** *I was permanently hungry:* continually, constantly, perpetually, always.

**permission** noun authorization, consent, leave, authority, sanction, licence, dispensation, assent, agreement, approval, blessing, clearance; informal the go-ahead, the green light, say-so.
OPPOSITES ban.

**permit** verb *other synthetic drugs would be permitted:* allow, let, authorize, sanction, grant, license, consent to, assent to; informal give the go-ahead to, give the green light to.
OPPOSITES ban.
noun *a work permit:* authorization, licence, pass,

a
b
c
d
e
f
g
h
i
j
k
l
m
n
o
**p**
q
r
s
t
u
v
w
x
y
z

ticket, warrant, passport, visa.

**perpetual** adjective **1** *a perpetual state of fear:* constant, permanent, uninterrupted, continuous, unremitting, unending, everlasting, eternal, unceasing, without end, persistent, lasting, abiding. **2** *perpetual nagging:* interminable, incessant, ceaseless, endless, relentless, unrelenting, persistent, continual, continuous, non-stop, never-ending, repeated, unremitting, round-the-clock, unabating; informal eternal.
OPPOSITES temporary, intermittent.

**perplexing** adjective puzzling, baffling, mystifying, mysterious, bewildering, confusing, disconcerting, worrying.

**persecute** verb **1** *they were persecuted for their beliefs:* oppress, abuse, victimize, ill-treat, mistreat, maltreat, torment, torture. **2** *she was persecuted by the press:* harass, hound, plague, badger, harry, intimidate, pick on, pester; informal hassle.

**persist** verb **1** *Corbett persisted with his questioning:* persevere, continue, carry on, go on, keep on, keep going, hammer away, keep at it; informal soldier on, plug away. **2** *if dry weather persists, water the lawn thoroughly:* continue, hold, carry on, last, keep on, remain, linger, stay, endure.
OPPOSITES give up, stop.

**persistence** noun perseverence, tenacity, determination, staying power, endurance, doggedness, stamina; informal stickability; N. Amer. informal stick-to-it-iveness.

**persistent** adjective **1** *a very*

*persistent man:* tenacious, determined, resolute, dogged, tireless, indefatigable, insistent, unrelenting. **2** *persistent rain:* constant, continuous, continuing, continual, non-stop, never-ending, steady, uninterrupted, unbroken, interminable, incessant, endless, unending, unrelenting. **3** *a persistent cough:* chronic, nagging, frequent, repeated, habitual.
OPPOSITES irresolute, intermittent.

**person** noun human being, individual, man, woman, human, being, living soul, mortal, creature; informal type, sort, beggar, cookie.
■ in person physically, in the flesh, personally, oneself.

**personal** adjective **1** *a highly personal style:* distinctive, characteristic, unique, individual, idiosyncratic. **2** *a personal appearance:* in person, in the flesh, actual, live, physical. **3** *his personal life:* private, intimate. **4** *personal remarks:* derogatory, disparaging, belittling, insulting, rude, disrespectful, offensive, pejorative.
OPPOSITES common, public, complimentary.

**personality** noun **1** *her cheerful personality:* character, nature, disposition, temperament, make-up, psyche. **2** *she had loads of personality:* charisma, magnetism, character, charm, presence. **3** *a famous personality:* celebrity, VIP, star, superstar, big name, somebody, leading light, luminary, notable; informal celeb.
OPPOSITES nobody.

**personally** adverb **1** *I'd like to*

*thank him personally:* in person, oneself. **2** *every pupil is known personally:* individually, specially. **3** *personally, I like it:* for my part, for myself, as far as I am concerned, subjectively.

**personnel** noun staff, employees, workforce, workers, labour force, manpower, human resources.

**perspective** noun outlook, view, viewpoint, point of view, standpoint, position, stand, stance, angle, slant, attitude.

**persuade** verb **1** *he persuaded her to go with him:* prevail on, talk into, coax, convince, get, induce, win over, bring round, influence, sway; informal sweet-talk. **2** *lack of money persuaded them to abandon the scheme:* cause, lead, move, dispose, incline.
OPPOSITES dissuade, deter.

**persuasion** noun **1** *Monica needed a lot of persuasion:* coaxing, urging, inducement, convincing, encouragement, enticement; informal sweet-talking. **2** *various religious persuasions:* group, grouping, sect, denomination, party, camp, side, faction, school of thought, belief, creed, faith.

**persuasive** adjective convincing, compelling, effective, telling, forceful, powerful, eloquent, impressive, sound, cogent, valid, strong, plausible, credible.
OPPOSITES unconvincing.

**pertinent** adjective relevant, to the point, apposite, appropriate, suitable, applicable, material, germane.
OPPOSITES irrelevant.

**perverse** adjective **1** *he is being deliberately perverse:* awkward, contrary, difficult,

unreasonable, uncooperative, unhelpful, obstructive, stubborn, obstinate; Brit. informal bloody-minded. **2** *a verdict that is manifestly perverse:* illogical, irrational, wrong-headed.
OPPOSITES accommodating, reasonable.

**pervert** verb *perverting the course of justice:* distort, warp, corrupt, subvert, twist, bend, abuse, divert.
noun *a nasty pervert:* deviant, degenerate; informal perv, dirty old man, sicko.

**perverted** adjective unnatural, deviant, warped, twisted, abnormal, unhealthy, depraved, perverse, aberrant, debased, degenerate; informal sick, kinky.

**pessimistic** adjective gloomy, negative, defeatist, downbeat, cynical, bleak, fatalistic, depressed.
OPPOSITES optimistic.

**pest** noun nuisance, annoyance, irritant, thorn in one's flesh/ side, trial, menace, trouble, problem, worry, bother; informal pain in the neck, headache.

**pester** verb badger, hound, harass, plague, annoy, bother, harry, worry; informal hassle, bug.

**pet** adjective **1** *a pet lamb:* tame, domesticated, companion; Brit. house-trained; N. Amer. housebroken. **2** *his pet theory:* favourite, favoured, cherished, particular, special, personal.
verb **1** *the cats came to be petted:* stroke, caress, fondle, pat, tickle. **2** *couples petting in their cars:* cuddle, embrace, caress, kiss; informal canoodle, neck, smooch; Brit. informal snog; N. Amer. informal make out.

**petition** noun *2,500 people have signed a petition:* appeal, round robin, letter, request, entreaty,

application, plea.
**verb** *the islanders petitioned the government to help them:* appeal to, request, ask, call on, entreat, beg, implore, plead with, apply to, press, urge.

**petty** adjective **1** *petty regulations:* trivial, trifling, minor, insignificant, inconsequential, footling; informal piffling. **2** *a petty form of revenge:* small-minded, mean, shabby, spiteful.
OPPOSITES important, magnanimous.

**phantom** noun ghost, apparition, spirit, spectre, wraith; informal spook.

**phase** noun **1** *the final phase of the campaign:* stage, period, chapter, episode, part, step. **2** *he's going through a difficult phase:* period, stage, time, spell; Brit. informal patch.
■ **phase something in** introduce (gradually), ease in. ■ **phase something out** withdraw (gradually), discontinue, stop using, run down, wind down.

**phenomenal** adjective remarkable, exceptional, extraordinary, marvellous, miraculous, wonderful, outstanding, unprecedented; informal fantastic, terrific, tremendous, stupendous.
OPPOSITES ordinary.

**phenomenon** noun **1** *a rare phenomenon:* occurrence, event, happening, fact, situation, circumstance, experience, case, incident, episode. **2** *a pop phenomenon:* marvel, sensation, wonder, prodigy.

**philosopher** noun thinker, theorist, theoretician, scholar, intellectual, sage.

**philosophical** adjective **1** *a*
*philosophical question:* theoretical, metaphysical. **2** *a philosophical mood:* thoughtful, reflective, pensive, meditative, contemplative, introspective. **3** *he was very philosophical about it:* stoical, self-possessed, serene, dispassionate, phlegmatic, long-suffering, resigned.

**philosophy** noun **1** *the philosophy of Aristotle:* thinking, thought, reasoning, logic. **2** *her political philosophy:* beliefs, credo, ideology, ideas, thinking, theories, doctrine, principles, views, outlook.

**phobia** noun fear, dread, horror, terror, aversion, antipathy, revulsion; informal hang-up.

**phone** noun *she spent hours on the phone:* telephone; Brit. informal blower.
**verb** *I'll phone you later:* call, telephone; Brit. ring, ring up, give someone a ring; informal call up, give someone a buzz; Brit. informal give someone a bell, give someone a tinkle, get on the blower to; N. Amer. informal get someone on the horn.

**phoney** (informal) adjective *a phoney address:* bogus, false, fake, fraudulent, counterfeit, forged, imitation, affected, insincere; informal pretend; Brit. informal cod.
OPPOSITES authentic.
**noun 1** *he's a phoney:* impostor, sham, fake, fraud, charlatan; informal con artist. **2** *the diamond's a phoney:* fake, imitation, counterfeit, forgery.

**photocopy** noun *a photocopy of the letter:* copy, duplicate, reproduction, facsimile; trademark Xerox, photostat.
**verb** *I photocopied the form:* copy, duplicate, xerox,

photostat, reproduce.

**photograph** noun *a colour photograph:* picture, photo, snap, snapshot, shot, print, still. verb *he was photographed in Paris:* take a picture/photo of, take someone's picture, snap, shoot, film.

**photographic** adjective 1 *a photographic record:* pictorial, graphic, in photographs. 2 *a photographic memory:* detailed, exact, precise, accurate, vivid.

**phrase** noun *an elegant phrase:* expression, construction, term, turn of phrase, idiom, saying. verb *how did you phrase the question?* express, put into words, put, word, formulate, couch, frame.

**physical** adjective 1 *physical pleasure:* bodily, corporeal, corporal, carnal, fleshly, non-spiritual. 2 *physical work:* manual, labouring, blue-collar. 3 *the physical universe:* material, concrete, tangible, palpable, solid, substantial, real, actual, visible.
OPPOSITES mental, spiritual.

**physician** noun doctor, medical practitioner, general practitioner, GP, clinician, specialist, consultant; informal doc, medic.

**pick** verb 1 *picking apples:* harvest, gather (in), collect, pluck. 2 *pick a time that suits you:* choose, select, single out, opt for, plump for, elect, decide on, settle on, fix on, name, nominate, identify. 3 *he tried to pick a fight:* provoke, start, cause, incite, instigate, prompt.
OPPOSITES reject, avoid.
noun *the pick of the crop:* best, finest, choice, choicest, cream, flower, crème de la crème, elite.
■ **pick on** bully, victimize, torment, persecute, taunt, tease; informal get at, needle.
■ **pick someone/something out** see, make out, distinguish, discern, spot, perceive, detect, notice, recognize, identify, catch sight of, glimpse. ■ **pick up** improve, recover, rally, bounce back, perk up, look up, take a turn for the better, turn the corner, be on the mend, make headway, make progress.
■ **pick someone/something up** 1 *he picked up the baby:* lift, take up, raise, hoist, scoop up, gather up, snatch up. 2 *I'll pick up the parcel on my way:* fetch, collect, call for. ■ **pick someone up** (informal) 1 *he was picked up by the police:* arrest, apprehend, detain, take into custody, seize; informal nab, run in; Brit. informal nick. 2 *he picked her up in a club:* meet; informal get off with, pull, cop off with. ■ **pick something up** 1 *we picked it up at a flea market:* find, discover, come across, stumble across, happen on, chance on, acquire, obtain, come by, get, buy, purchase; informal get hold of, get one's hands on. 2 *he picked up the story in the 1950s:* resume, take up, start again, recommence, continue, carry/go on with. 3 *she picked up a virus:* catch, contract, get, go/come down with. 4 *all the gossip he'd picked up:* hear, hear tell, get wind of, be told, learn, glean. 5 *we're picking up a distress signal:* receive, detect, get, hear.

**picket** noun 1 *forty pickets were arrested:* demonstrator, striker, protester. 2 *they decided to organize a picket:* demonstration, picket line, blockade, boycott, strike. verb *workers picketed the*

a
b
c
d
e
f
g
h
i
j
k
l
m
n
o
**p**
q
r
s
t
u
v
w
x
y
z

*factory:* demonstrate at, blockade, boycott.

**pickup** noun improvement, recovery, revival, upturn, upswing, rally, resurgence, renewal, turnaround.
OPPOSITES slump.

**picture** noun 1 *pictures in an art gallery:* painting, drawing, sketch, watercolour, print, canvas, portrait, illustration, depiction, likeness, representation, image. 2 *we were told not to take pictures:* photograph, photo, snap, snapshot, shot, frame, exposure, still, print. 3 *my picture of the ideal woman:* concept, idea, impression, (mental) image, vision, visualization, notion. 4 *the picture of health:* personification, embodiment, epitome, essence, quintessence, soul, model.
verb 1 *they were pictured playing in the snow:* depict, portray, show, represent, draw, sketch, photograph, paint. 2 *Anne still pictured Richard as he had been:* visualize, see (in one's mind's eye), imagine, remember.

**picturesque** adjective attractive, pretty, beautiful, lovely, scenic, charming, quaint, pleasing, delightful.
OPPOSITES ugly.

**piece** noun 1 *a piece of cheese:* bit, slice, chunk, segment, section, lump, hunk, wedge, slab, block, cake, bar, stick, length. 2 *the pieces of a clock:* component, part, bit, constituent, element, section, unit, module. 3 *a piece of furniture:* item, article, specimen. 4 *a piece of the profit:* share, portion, slice,

quota, part, percentage, amount, quantity, ration, fraction; Brit. informal whack. 5 *pieces from his collection:* work (of art), artwork, artefact, composition, opus. 6 *the reporter who wrote the piece:* article, item, story, report, essay, feature, review, column.

**pier** noun jetty, quay, wharf, dock, landing stage.

**pierce** verb penetrate, puncture, perforate, prick, spike, stab, drill, bore.

**piercing** adjective 1 *a piercing shriek:* shrill, ear-splitting, high-pitched, penetrating, strident. 2 *his piercing gaze:* searching, probing, penetrating, sharp, keen.

**pigment** noun colouring, colour, tint, dye, stain.

**pile**¹ noun 1 *a pile of stones:* heap, stack, mound, pyramid, mass, collection, accumulation, assemblage, stockpile, hoard. 2 (informal) *I've a pile of work to do:* lot, mountain, reams, abundance; informal load, heap, mass, slew, stack, ton; Brit. informal shedload; Austral./NZ informal swag.
verb 1 *he piled up the plates:* heap, stack. 2 *he piled his plate with salad:* load, heap, fill (up), stack, charge. 3 *we piled into the car:* crowd, clamber, pack, squeeze, scramble, struggle.
■ pile up accumulate, grow, mount up, build up, multiply, escalate, soar, spiral, rocket, increase.

**pile**² noun *a carpet with a short pile:* nap, fibres, threads.

**pile-up** noun crash, collision, smash, accident; Brit. RTA; N. Amer. wreck; Brit. informal shunt.

**pilgrim** noun traveller,

wayfarer, worshipper, devotee, believer; Islam haji, alhaji.

**pilgrimage** noun journey, expedition, mission, hajj, visit, trek, trip, odyssey.

**pill** noun tablet, capsule, pellet, lozenge, pastille.

**pillar** noun 1 *stone pillars*: column, post, support, upright, pier, pile, prop, stanchion, obelisk. 2 *a pillar of the community*: stalwart, mainstay, bastion, leading light, worthy, backbone, supporter, upholder, champion.

**pilot** noun 1 *a fighter pilot*: airman, airwoman, flyer, captain; informal skipper; N. Amer. informal jock; dated aviator. 2 *a harbour pilot*: navigator, helmsman, steersman, coxswain. 3 *a pilot for a TV series*: trial, sample, experiment.
adjective *a pilot project*: experimental, exploratory, trial, test, sample, preliminary.
verb *he piloted the jet to safety*: navigate, guide, manoeuvre, steer, control, direct, captain, fly, drive, sail; informal skipper.

**pin** noun 1 *fasten the hem with a pin*: tack, safety pin, nail, staple, fastener. 2 *a broken pin in the machine*: bolt, peg, rod, rivet, dowel. 3 *they wore name pins*: badge, brooch.
verb 1 *she pinned the brooch to her dress*: attach, fasten, affix, fix, join, secure, clip, nail. 2 *they pinned him to the ground*: hold, press, pinion.
■ **pin someone/something down** confine, trap, hem in, corner, close in, shut in, pen in. ■ **pin something on someone** blame for, hold responsible for, attribute to, ascribe to, lay something at someone's door;

informal stick on.

**pinch** verb 1 *he pinched my arm*: nip, tweak, squeeze, grasp. 2 *my new shoes pinch my toes*: hurt, squeeze, crush, cramp.
noun 1 *he gave her arm a pinch*: nip, tweak, squeeze. 2 *a pinch of salt*: bit, touch, dash, spot, trace, soupçon, speck, taste; informal smidgen, tad.

**pine** verb *she thinks I am pining away from love*: fade, waste away, weaken, decline, languish, wilt, sicken.
■ **pine for** long for, yearn for, ache for, sigh for, hunger for, thirst for, itch for, carry a torch for, miss, mourn.

**pink** adjective rose, rosy, rosé, pale red, salmon, coral, flushed, blushing.

**pinnacle** noun 1 *the pinnacle of his career*: height, peak, high point, top, apex, zenith, acme. 2 *pinnacles of rock*: peak, needle, crag, tor.
OPPOSITES low point.

**pinpoint** adjective *pinpoint accuracy*: precise, exact, strict, absolute, complete, scientific.
verb *the technology can pinpoint a cellphone's position*: identify, determine, distinguish, discover, find, locate, detect, track down, spot, diagnose, recognize, pin down, home in on.

**pioneer** noun 1 *the pioneers of the Wild West*: settler, colonist, colonizer, frontiersman, explorer. 2 *a pioneer of motoring*: developer, innovator, trailblazer, groundbreaker, founding father, architect, creator.
verb *he pioneered the sale of insurance*: introduce, develop, launch, instigate, initiate,

a b c d e f g h i j k l m n o p q r s t u v w x y z

spearhead, institute, establish, found.

**pious** adjective religious, devout, God-fearing, churchgoing, holy, godly, saintly, reverent, righteous.
OPPOSITES irreligious.

**pipe** noun *a central-heating pipe:* tube, conduit, hose, main, duct, line, channel, pipeline, drain.
verb **1** *the beer is piped into barrels:* feed, siphon, channel, run, convey. **2** *programmes piped in from London:* relay, feed, patch, transmit.

**pirate** noun *pirates boarded the ship:* raider, hijacker, marauder, freebooter; historical privateer; buccaneer.
verb *designers may pirate good ideas:* steal, copy, plagiarize, poach, appropriate, bootleg; informal crib, lift, rip off.

**pit** noun **1** *we dug a pit:* hole, trough, hollow, cavity, crater, pothole. **2** *pit closures:* coal mine, colliery, quarry, shaft.
verb *his skin had been pitted by acne:* mark, pockmark, pock, scar, dent, indent.

**pitch** noun **1** *a football pitch:* playing field, ground, sports field, stadium; Brit. park. **2** *her voice rose in pitch:* tone, key, modulation, frequency. **3** *the pitch of the roof:* gradient, slope, slant, angle, tilt, incline. **4** *at fever pitch:* level, intensity, point, degree, height, extent. **5** *his sales pitch:* patter, talk; informal spiel, line.
verb **1** *a kid pitched a snowball:* throw, toss, fling, hurl, cast, lob, flip; informal chuck, sling, heave, bung. **2** *he pitched overboard:* fall, tumble, topple, plunge, plummet. **3** *they pitched their tents:* put up, set

up, erect, raise. **4** *the boat pitched:* lurch, toss, plunge, roll, reel, sway, rock, list.

**pitfall** noun hazard, danger, risk, peril, difficulty, catch, snag, stumbling block, drawback.

**pity** noun **1** *a voice full of pity:* compassion, commiseration, condolence, sympathy, fellow feeling, understanding. **2** *it's a pity he never had children:* shame, misfortune, too bad; informal bummer.
OPPOSITES indifference, cruelty.
verb *they pitied me:* feel sorry for, feel for, sympathize with, empathize with, commiserate with, take pity on, be moved by, bleed for.

**place** noun **1** *an ideal place for dinner:* location, site, spot, setting, position, situation, area, region, locale, venue. **2** *foreign places:* country, state, area, region, town, city. **3** *a place of her own:* home, house, flat, apartment, accommodation, property, rooms, quarters; informal pad; Brit. informal gaff; formal residence, abode, dwelling. **4** *in your place, I'd agree:* situation, position, circumstances; informal shoes. **5** *a place was reserved for her:* seat, chair, space. **6** *I offered him a place in the company:* job, position, post, appointment, situation, employment. **7** *I know my place:* status, position, standing, rank, niche. **8** *it was not her place to sort it out:* responsibility, duty, job, task, role, function, concern, affair, charge.
verb **1** *books were placed on the table:* put (down), set (down), lay, deposit, position, plant, rest, stand, station, situate,

leave; informal stick, dump, bung, park, plonk, pop; N. Amer. informal plunk. **2** *the trust you placed in me:* put, lay, set, invest. **3** *a survey placed the company sixth:* rank, order, grade, class, classify, put. **4** *Joe couldn't quite place her:* identify, recognize, remember, put a name to, pin down, locate, pinpoint. **5** *we were placed with foster parents:* accommodate, house, home, allocate, assign.
■ in place of instead of, rather than, as a substitute for, as a replacement for, in exchange for, in lieu of, in someone's stead. ■ out of place **1** *he said something out of place:* inappropriate, unsuitable, unseemly, improper, untoward, out of keeping, unbecoming. **2** *she seemed out of place in a launderette:* incongruous, out of one's element, like a fish out of water, uncomfortable, uneasy. ■ take place happen, occur, come about, go on, transpire; N. Amer. informal go down. ■ take the place of replace, stand in for, substitute for, act for, fill in for, cover for, relieve.

**plague** noun **1** *they died in a plague:* pandemic, epidemic, disease, sickness; dated contagion; archaic pestilence. **2** *a plague of fleas:* infestation, invasion, swarm, epidemic.
verb **1** *he was plagued by poor health:* afflict, trouble, torment, beset, dog, curse, bedevil. **2** *he plagued her with questions:* pester, harass, badger, bother, torment, harry, hound, trouble, nag, molest; informal hassle, bug; N. English informal mither; N. Amer. informal devil.

**plain** adjective **1** *it was plain that something was wrong:* obvious,
clear, evident, apparent, manifest, unmistakable. **2** *plain English:* intelligible, comprehensible, understandable, clear, lucid, simple, straightforward, user-friendly. **3** *plain speaking:* candid, frank, outspoken, forthright, direct, honest, truthful, blunt, bald, unequivocal; informal upfront. **4** *a plain dress:* simple, ordinary, unadorned, homely, basic, modest, unsophisticated, restrained. **5** *a plain girl:* unattractive, unprepossessing, ugly, ordinary; N. Amer. homely; Brit. informal no oil painting. **6** *it was plain bad luck:* sheer, pure, downright, out-and-out.
OPPOSITES obscure, fancy, attractive, pretentious.
noun *the plains of North America:* grassland, flatland, prairie, savannah, steppe, tundra, pampas, veld, plateau.

**plan** noun **1** *a plan for raising money:* scheme, idea, proposal, proposition, project, programme, system, method, strategy, stratagem, formula, recipe. **2** *her plan was to break even:* intention, aim, idea, objective, object, goal, target, ambition. **3** *a plan of the new office:* map, diagram, chart, blueprint, drawing, sketch, impression; N. Amer. plat.
verb **1** *plan your route in advance:* organize, arrange, work out, outline, map out, prepare, formulate, frame, develop, devise. **2** *he plans to buy a house:* intend, aim, propose, mean, hope. **3** *I'm planning a new garden:* design, draw up a plan for, sketch out, map out; N. Amer. plat.

**plane**[1] noun *a higher plane of achievement:* level, degree,

standard, stratum, dimension.
verb *boats planed across the water:* skim, glide.

**plane**[2] noun *the plane took off:* aircraft, airliner, jet, flying machine; Brit. aeroplane; N. Amer. airplane, ship.

**plant** noun 1 *garden plants:* flower, vegetable, herb, shrub, bush, weed; (**plants**) vegetation, greenery, flora. 2 *a CIA plant:* spy, informant, informer, secret agent, mole, infiltrator, operative; N. Amer. informal spook. 3 *a chemical plant:* factory, works, facility, refinery, mill. 4 *investment in new plant:* machinery, machines, equipment, apparatus, appliances, gear.
verb 1 *plant the seeds:* sow, scatter. 2 *he planted his feet on the ground:* place, put, set, position, situate, settle; informal plonk. 3 *she planted the idea in his mind:* instil, implant, put, place, introduce, fix, establish, lodge.

**plaster** noun 1 *the plaster covering the bricks:* plasterwork, stucco. 2 *a statuette made of plaster:* plaster of Paris, gypsum. 3 *waterproof plasters:* sticking plaster, adhesive dressing; trademark Elastoplast, Band-Aid.
verb 1 *bread plastered with butter:* spread, smother, smear, cake, coat. 2 *his hair was plastered down with sweat:* flatten (down), smooth down, slick down.

**plastic** adjective 1 *at high temperatures the rocks become plastic:* soft, pliable, pliant, flexible, malleable, workable, mouldable; informal bendy. 2 *a plastic smile:* artificial, false, fake, bogus, insincere; informal

phoney, pretend.
OPPOSITES rigid, genuine.

**plate** noun 1 *a dinner plate:* dish, platter, salver; historical trencher; archaic charger. 2 *a plate of spaghetti:* plateful, helping, portion, serving. 3 *steel plates:* panel, sheet, slab. 4 *a brass plate on the door:* plaque, sign, tablet. 5 *the book has colour plates:* picture, print, illustration, photograph, photo.
verb *the roof was plated with steel:* cover, coat, overlay, laminate, veneer, armour, gild, chrome.

**plateau** noun upland, mesa, highland, tableland.

**platform** noun 1 *he made a speech from the platform:* stage, dais, rostrum, podium, stand. 2 *the Democratic Party's platform:* programme, manifesto, policies, principles, party line.

**plausible** adjective credible, believable, reasonable, likely, possible, conceivable, imaginable, convincing, persuasive.
OPPOSITES unlikely.

**play** verb 1 *the children played with toys:* amuse oneself, entertain oneself, enjoy oneself, have fun, relax, occupy oneself, frolic, romp; informal mess about/around. 2 *I used to play football:* take part in, participate in, be involved in, compete in, do. 3 *Liverpool play Oxford on Sunday:* compete against, take on, meet. 4 *he was to play Macbeth:* act the part of, take the role of, appear as, portray, perform.
noun 1 *work and play:* amusement, relaxation, recreation, diversion, leisure, enjoyment, pleasure, fun. 2 *a*

*Shakespeare play:* drama, theatrical work, piece, comedy, tragedy, production, performance. **3** *there was no play in the rope:* movement, slack, give.

■ **play something down** make light of, make little of, gloss over, downplay, understate, soft-pedal, diminish, trivialize.

■ **play up** (Brit. informal) **1** *the boys really did play up:* misbehave, be bad, be naughty. **2** *the boiler's playing up:* malfunction, not work, be defective, be faulty; informal be on the blink, act up. **3** *his leg was playing up:* be painful, hurt, ache, be sore; informal kill someone, give someone gyp.

**player** noun **1** *a tournament for young players:* participant, contestant, competitor, contender, sportsman, sportswoman. **2** *the players in the orchestra:* musician, performer, artist, virtuoso, instrumentalist. **3** *the players of the Royal Shakespeare Company:* actor, actress, performer, thespian, entertainer, artiste, trouper.

**playful** adjective **1** *a playful mood:* frisky, lively, full of fun, frolicsome, high-spirited, exuberant, mischievous, impish; informal full of beans. **2** *a playful remark:* light-hearted, jokey, teasing, humorous, jocular, facetious, frivolous, flippant.
OPPOSITES serious.

**plea** noun appeal, entreaty, supplication, petition, request, call.

**plead** verb *she pleaded ignorance:* claim, use as an excuse, assert, allege, argue.
■ **plead with** beg, implore, entreat, appeal to, ask.

**pleasant** adjective **1** *a pleasant evening:* enjoyable, pleasurable, nice, agreeable, entertaining, amusing, delightful, charming; informal lovely, great. **2** *the staff are pleasant:* friendly, charming, agreeable, amiable, nice, delightful, sweet, genial, cordial, good-natured, personable, hospitable, polite.
OPPOSITES unpleasant.

**please** verb **1** *he'd do anything to please her:* make happy, give pleasure to, make someone feel good, delight, charm, amuse, satisfy, gratify, humour, oblige. **2** *do as you please:* like, want, wish, desire, see fit, think fit, choose, will, prefer.
OPPOSITES annoy.

**pleased** adjective happy, glad, delighted, gratified, grateful, thankful, content, contented, satisfied, thrilled; informal over the moon, on cloud nine; Brit. informal chuffed; N. English informal made up; Austral. informal wrapped.
OPPOSITES unhappy.

**pleasing** adjective **1** *a pleasing result:* good, agreeable, pleasant, pleasurable, satisfying, gratifying, great. **2** *her pleasing manner:* friendly, amiable, pleasant, agreeable, affable, nice, genial, likeable, charming, engaging, delightful; informal lovely.
OPPOSITES poor, unfriendly.

**pleasure** noun **1** *she smiled with pleasure:* happiness, delight, joy, gladness, glee, satisfaction, gratification, contentment, enjoyment, amusement. **2** *his greatest pleasure in life:* joy, amusement, diversion, recreation, pastime, treat, thrill. **3** *don't mix business and pleasure:* enjoyment, fun,

entertainment, recreation,
leisure, relaxation.
OPPOSITES unhappiness, trial,
duty, work.

**pledge** noun *his election pledge:*
promise, vow, undertaking,
word, commitment, assurance,
oath, guarantee.
verb *he pledged to root out
corruption:* promise, vow,
undertake, swear, commit
oneself, declare, affirm.

**plentiful** adjective abundant,
copious, ample, profuse, rich,
lavish, generous, bountiful,
bumper, prolific; informal galore.
OPPOSITES scarce.

**plenty** pronoun *there are plenty
of books:* a lot of, many, a great
deal of, a plethora of, enough
and to spare, no lack of, a
wealth of; informal loads of,
heaps of, stacks of, masses of.
noun *times of plenty:* prosperity,
affluence, wealth, opulence,
comfort, luxury, abundance.

**plight** noun predicament,
difficult situation, dire straits,
trouble, difficulty, bind; informal
tight corner, tight spot, hole,
pickle, jam, fix.

**plod** verb trudge, walk heavily,
clump, stomp, tramp, lumber,
slog.
OPPOSITES stride, skip.

**plot** noun 1 *a plot to overthrow
him:* conspiracy, intrigue,
stratagem, plan. 2 *the plot of
her novel:* storyline, story,
scenario, action, thread,
narrative. 3 *a three-acre plot:*
piece of ground, patch, area,
tract, acreage; Brit. allotment; N.
Amer. lot, plat; N. Amer. & Austral./NZ
homesite.
verb 1 *he plotted their downfall:*
plan, scheme, arrange,
organize, contrive. 2 *his brother
was plotting against him:*

conspire, scheme, intrigue,
connive. 3 *the points were
plotted on a graph:* mark, chart,
map.

**plough** verb 1 *the fields were
ploughed:* till, furrow, harrow,
cultivate, work. 2 *the car
ploughed into a wall:* crash,
smash, career, plunge, bulldoze,
hurtle, cannon.

**ploy** noun ruse, tactic, move,
device, stratagem, scheme,
trick, gambit, plan, manoeuvre,
dodge, subterfuge; Brit. informal
wheeze.

**pluck** verb 1 *he plucked a thread
from his lapel:* remove, pick,
pull, extract. 2 *she plucked at
his T-shirt:* pull, tug, clutch,
snatch, grab, catch, tweak, jerk;
informal yank. 3 *she plucked the
guitar strings:* strum, pick,
thrum, twang.
noun *it took a lot of pluck:*
courage, bravery, nerve, daring,
spirit, grit; informal guts; Brit.
informal bottle; N. Amer. informal
moxie.

**plug** noun 1 *she pulled out the
plug:* stopper, bung, cork,
connector; N. Amer. stopple.
2 (informal) *a plug for his new
book:* advertisement,
promotion, commercial,
recommendation, mention,
good word; informal hype, push,
puff.
verb 1 *plug the holes:* stop, seal,
close, block, fill. 2 (informal) *she
plugged her new film:* publicize,
promote, advertise, mention,
bang the drum for, draw
attention to; informal hype, push.

**plumb** verb *an attempt to plumb
her psyche:* explore, probe,
delve into, search, examine,
investigate, fathom, penetrate,
understand.
adverb (informal) *it went plumb*

*through the screen:* right, exactly, precisely, directly, dead, straight; informal (slap) bang.

**plummet** verb **1** *the plane plummeted to the ground:* plunge, dive, drop, fall, hurtle. **2** *share prices plummeted:* fall steeply, plunge, tumble, drop rapidly, slump; informal crash, nosedive.
OPPOSITES soar.

**plump** adjective fat, chubby, rotund, ample, round, stout, portly, overweight; informal tubby, roly-poly, pudgy; Brit. informal podgy; N. Amer. informal zaftig, corn-fed.
OPPOSITES thin.

**plunder** verb **1** *they plundered the countryside:* pillage, loot, rob, raid, ransack, rifle, strip, sack. **2** *money plundered from pension funds:* steal, seize, thieve, pilfer, embezzle.
noun *huge quantities of plunder:* booty, loot, stolen goods, spoils, ill-gotten gains; informal swag.

**plunge** verb **1** *Joy plunged into the sea:* dive, jump, throw oneself. **2** *the aircraft plunged to the ground:* plummet, nosedive, drop, fall, tumble, descend. **3** *the car plunged down an alley:* charge, hurtle, career, plough, tear; N. Amer. informal barrel. **4** *oil prices plunged:* fall sharply, plummet, drop, tumble, slump; informal crash, nosedive. **5** *he plunged the dagger into her back:* thrust, stab, sink, stick, ram, drive, push, shove, force. **6** *plunge the pears into water:* immerse, submerge, dip, dunk. **7** *the room was plunged into darkness:* throw, cast.
OPPOSITES soar.
noun **1** *a plunge in the pool:* dive, jump, dip. **2** *a plunge in*

*profits:* fall, drop, slump; informal nosedive, crash.
OPPOSITES rise.

**plus** preposition *four novels plus various poems:* as well as, together with, along with, in addition to, and, added to, not to mention.
OPPOSITES minus.
noun *one of the pluses of the job:* advantage, good point, asset, pro, benefit, bonus, attraction; informal perk.
OPPOSITES disadvantage.

**plush** adjective (informal) luxurious, luxury, de luxe, sumptuous, opulent, magnificent, rich, expensive, fancy; Brit. upmarket; informal posh, classy; Brit. informal swish; N. Amer. informal swank.
OPPOSITES austere.

**ply** verb **1** *he plied a profitable trade:* engage in, carry on, pursue, conduct, practise. **2** *ferries ply between all lake resorts:* travel, shuttle, go back and forth. **3** *she plied me with scones:* provide, supply, shower. **4** *he plied her with questions:* bombard, assail, pester, plague, harass; informal hassle.

**poach** verb **1** *he's been poaching salmon:* hunt illegally, catch illegally, steal. **2** *workers were poached by other firms:* steal, appropriate, headhunt; informal nab, swipe; Brit. informal nick, pinch.

**pocket** noun **1** *a bag with two pockets:* pouch, compartment. **2** *pockets of resistance:* area, patch, region, cluster.
adjective *a pocket dictionary:* small, little, miniature, mini, compact, concise, abridged, portable, travel; N. Amer. vest-pocket.
verb **1** *he pocketed $4m for a*

a b c d e f g h i j k l m n o **p** q r s t u v w x y z

*few months' work:* acquire, obtain, gain, get, secure, win, make, earn. **2** *they were pocketing money supposed to be used for repairs:* steal, appropriate, purloin, misappropriate, embezzle.

**pod** noun shell, husk, hull, case; N. Amer. shuck.

**podium** noun platform, stage, dais, rostrum, stand.

**poem** noun verse, rhyme, lyric, piece of poetry.

**poetic** adjective expressive, figurative, symbolic, flowery, artistic, imaginative, creative.

**poetry** noun poems, verse, versification, rhyme.

**poignant** adjective touching, moving, sad, affecting, pitiful, pathetic, plaintive.

**point** noun **1** *the point of a needle:* tip, (sharp) end, extremity, prong, spike, tine, nib, barb. **2** *points of light:* pinpoint, dot, spot, speck. **3** *a meeting point:* place, position, location, site, spot. **4** *this point in her life:* time, stage, juncture, period, phase. **5** *the tension had reached such a high point:* level, degree, stage, pitch, extent. **6** *an important point:* detail, item, fact, thing, argument, consideration, factor, element, subject, issue, topic, question, matter. **7** *get to the point:* heart of the matter, essence, nub, core, crux; informal nitty-gritty. **8** *what's the point of this?* purpose, aim, object, objective, goal, intention, use, sense, value, advantage. **9** *he had his good points:* attribute, characteristic, feature, trait, quality, property, aspect, side. verb *she pointed the gun at him:* aim, direct, level, train.

■ **point something out** identify, show, draw attention to, indicate, specify, detail, mention. ■ **point to something** indicate, suggest, evidence, signal, signify, denote.

**pointed** adjective **1** *a pointed stick:* sharp, spiky, spiked, tapering, barbed; informal pointy. **2** *a pointed remark:* cutting, biting, incisive, acerbic, caustic, scathing, venomous, sarcastic; informal sarky; N. Amer. informal snarky.

**pointer** noun **1** *the pointer moved to 100rpm:* indicator, needle, arrow, hand. **2** *a pointer to the outcome of the election:* indication, indicator, clue, hint, sign, signal, evidence. **3** *I can give you a few pointers:* tip, hint, suggestion, guideline, recommendation.

**pointless** adjective senseless, futile, hopeless, unavailing, aimless, idle, worthless, valueless.
OPPOSITES valuable.

**poise** noun **1** *poise and good deportment:* grace, gracefulness, elegance, balance, control. **2** *in spite of the setback she retained her poise:* composure, equanimity, self-possession, aplomb, self-assurance, self-control, sangfroid, dignity; informal cool.

**poised** adjective **1** *she was poised on one foot:* balanced, suspended, motionless, hanging, hovering. **2** *he was poised for action:* prepared, ready, braced, geared up, all set, standing by.

**poison** noun toxin, venom.
verb **1** *her mother poisoned her:* give poison to, murder. **2** *the Amazon is being poisoned:* pollute, contaminate, taint, spoil. **3** *they poisoned his mind:*

twist, warp, corrupt.

**poisonous** adjective **1** *a poisonous snake:* venomous, deadly. **2** *a poisonous chemical:* toxic, noxious, deadly, fatal, lethal, mortal. **3** *a poisonous glance:* malicious, malevolent, hostile, spiteful, bitter, venomous, malign.
OPPOSITES harmless, non-toxic, benevolent.

**poke** verb **1** *she poked him in the ribs:* prod, jab, dig, elbow, nudge, shove, jolt, stab, stick. **2** *leave the cable poking out:* stick out, jut out, protrude, project, extend.
noun *Carrie gave him a poke:* prod, jab, dig, elbow, nudge.

**poky** adjective small, little, tiny, cramped, confined, restricted, boxy.
OPPOSITES spacious.

**pole** noun post, pillar, stanchion, stake, support, prop, stick, paling, staff.

**police** noun police force, police service, police officers, policemen, policewomen; Brit. constabulary; informal the cops, the fuzz, the law, the boys in blue; Brit. informal the (Old) Bill; N. Amer. informal the heat.
verb **1** *we must police the area:* guard, watch over, protect, defend, patrol. **2** *the regulations will be policed by the ministry:* enforce, regulate, oversee, supervise, monitor, observe, check.

**police officer** noun policeman, policewoman; Brit. constable; N. Amer. patrolman, trooper, roundsman; informal cop; Brit. informal rozzer; N. Amer. informal uniform.

**policy** noun plans, approach, code, system, guidelines, theory, line, position, stance.

**polish** verb **1** *I polished his shoes:* shine, wax, buff, rub up/down, gloss, burnish. **2** *polish up your essay:* perfect, refine, improve, hone, enhance, brush up, revise, edit, correct, rewrite, go over, touch up.
noun *his poetry has clarity and polish:* sophistication, refinement, urbanity, suaveness, elegance, style, grace, finesse; informal class.

**polished** adjective **1** *a polished table:* shiny, glossy, gleaming, lustrous, glassy, waxed, buffed, burnished. **2** *a polished performance:* expert, accomplished, masterly, skilful, adept, adroit, dexterous, consummate, superb, superlative.
OPPOSITES dull, inexpert.

**polite** adjective **1** *a very polite girl:* well mannered, civil, courteous, respectful, well behaved, well bred, gentlemanly, ladylike, genteel, gracious, tactful, diplomatic. **2** *polite society:* civilized, refined, cultured, sophisticated.
OPPOSITES rude, uncivilized.

**politic** adjective wise, prudent, sensible, judicious, expedient, advantageous, beneficial, profitable.
OPPOSITES unwise.

**political** adjective governmental, government, constitutional, ministerial, parliamentary, diplomatic, legislative, administrative.

**politician** noun legislator, Member of Parliament, MP, representative, minister, statesman, stateswoman, senator, congressman, congresswoman; informal politico.

**politics** noun **1** *a career in politics:* government, affairs of state, public affairs, diplomacy. **2** *he studies politics:* political science, civics. **3** *what are his politics?* political views, political leanings. **4** *office politics:* power struggles, machinations, manoeuvring, realpolitik.

**poll** noun **1** *the poll to elect a new leader:* vote, ballot, show of hands, referendum, plebiscite, election. **2** *a poll to investigate holiday choices:* survey, opinion poll, market research, census.
verb **1** *most of those polled supported him:* canvass, survey, ask, question, interview, ballot. **2** *she polled 119 votes:* get, gain, register, record, return.

**pollute** verb contaminate, taint, poison, foul, dirty, soil, infect.
OPPOSITES purify.

**pollution** noun contamination, impurity, dirt, filth, infection.

**pompous** adjective
self-important, overbearing, sententious, grandiose, affected, pretentious, puffed up, haughty, proud, conceited, supercilious, condescending, patronizing.
OPPOSITES modest.

**ponder** verb think about, contemplate, consider, review, reflect on, mull over, meditate on, muse on, dwell on.

**pool**¹ noun **1** *pools of water:* puddle, pond, lake. **2** *the hotel has a pool:* swimming pool, baths; Brit. swimming baths; N. Amer. natatorium.

**pool**² noun **1** *a pool of skilled labour:* supply, reserve(s), reservoir, fund, store, bank, stock, cache. **2** *a pool of money for emergencies:* fund, reserve, kitty, pot, bank, purse.
verb *they pooled their skills:*

combine, group, join, unite, merge, share.

**poor** adjective **1** *a poor family:* poverty-stricken, penniless, impoverished, impecunious, needy, destitute; Brit. on the breadline; informal hard up, strapped, on one's uppers. **2** *poor workmanship:* substandard, bad, deficient, defective, faulty, imperfect, inferior, unsatisfactory, shoddy, crude, inadequate, unacceptable; informal crummy, rubbishy, rotten; Brit. informal ropy, duff, rubbish, dodgy. **3** *a poor crop:* meagre, scanty, scant, paltry, reduced, modest, sparse, spare, deficient, insubstantial, skimpy, lean; informal measly, stingy. **4** *the poor thing:* unfortunate, unlucky, unhappy, hapless, wretched.
OPPOSITES rich, superior, abundant, lucky.

**poorly** adverb *the text is poorly written:* badly, imperfectly, incompetently, crudely, shoddily, inadequately.
adjective *she felt poorly:* ill, unwell, not very well, ailing, indisposed, out of sorts, under par, peaky; Brit. off colour; informal under the weather, rough; Brit. informal ropy, grotty; Scottish informal wabbit; Austral./NZ informal crook.

**pop** verb **1** *champagne corks popped:* go bang, go off, crack, snap, burst, explode. **2** *I'm just popping home:* go; informal tootle, whip; Brit. informal nip. **3** *pop a bag over the pot:* put, place, slip, throw, slide, stick, set, lay, position.
noun *the balloons burst with a pop:* bang, crack, snap, explosion, report.

**popular** adjective **1** *the*

*restaurant is very popular:* well liked, sought-after, in demand, commercial, marketable, fashionable, in vogue, all the rage, hot; informal in, cool, big. **2** *popular science books:* non-specialist, non-technical, amateur, lay person's, general, middle-of-the-road, accessible, simplified, understandable, mass-market. **3** *popular opinion:* widespread, general, common, current, prevailing, standard, ordinary, conventional.
OPPOSITES unpopular, specialist, restricted.

**population** noun inhabitants, residents, people, citizens, public, community, populace, society, natives, occupants.

**pornographic** adjective obscene, indecent, dirty, smutty, filthy, erotic, titillating, sexy, risqué, X-rated, adult.

**port** noun harbour, docks, marina, haven, seaport.

**portable** adjective transportable, movable, mobile, battery, wireless, lightweight, compact, handy, convenient.

**porter**[1] noun *a porter helped with the bags:* carrier, bearer; N. Amer. redcap, skycap.

**porter**[2] noun (Brit.) *the college porter:* doorman, doorkeeper, commissionaire, gatekeeper, concierge, security officer.

**portion** noun **1** *the upper portion of the chimney:* part, piece, bit, section, segment. **2** *her portion of the allowance:* share, slice, quota, ration, allocation, tranche; Brit. informal whack. **3** *a portion of cake:* helping, serving, plateful, slice, piece.

**portrait** noun **1** *a portrait of the King:* picture, likeness, painting, drawing, photograph, image. **2** *a vivid portrait of Italy:* description, portrayal, representation, depiction, impression, account, profile.

**portray** verb **1** *he always portrays Windermere in sunny weather:* paint, draw, sketch, picture, depict, represent, illustrate, render, show. **2** *the man portrayed by Waugh:* describe, depict, characterize, represent. **3** *he portrays her as a doormat:* represent, depict, characterize, describe, present. **4** *the actor portrays a spy:* play, act the part of, take the role of, represent, appear as.

**portrayal** noun **1** *her portrayal of adolescence:* description, representation, characterization, depiction, evocation. **2** *Brando's portrayal of Corleone:* performance as, representation, interpretation, rendering.

**pose** verb **1** *pollution poses a threat to health:* constitute, present, offer. **2** *the question posed earlier:* raise, ask, put, submit, advance, propose. **3** *the guys posing at the bar:* posture, attitudinize, put on airs; informal show off, ponce about.
noun **1** *a formal pose:* posture, position, stance, attitude. **2** *her pose of aggrieved innocence:* act, affectation, show, display, posture, expression.
■ **pose as** pretend to be, impersonate, pass oneself off as, masquerade as.

**posh** adjective **1** (informal) *a posh hotel:* smart, stylish, fancy, high-class, fashionable, chic, luxurious, luxury, exclusive; Brit. upmarket; informal classy, plush, flash; Brit. informal swish; N. Amer. informal swank, tony. **2** (Brit.

a
b
c
d
e
f
g
h
i
j
k
l
m
n
o
**p**
q
r
s
t
u
v
w
x
y
z

a
b
c
d
e
f
g
h
i
j
k
l
m
n
o
**p**
q
r
s
t
u
v
w
x
y
z

informal) *a posh accent:* **upper-class**, aristocratic.

**position** noun 1 *the aircraft's position:* **location**, place, situation, spot, site, locality, setting, area, whereabouts, bearings. 2 *a standing position:* **posture**, stance, attitude, pose. 3 *our financial position:* **situation**, state, condition, circumstances, predicament, plight. 4 *their position in society:* **status**, place, level, rank, standing, stature, prestige, reputation. 5 *a secretarial position:* **job**, post, situation, appointment, opening, vacancy, placement. 6 *the government's position on the matter:* **viewpoint**, opinion, outlook, attitude, stand, standpoint, stance, perspective, thinking, policy, feelings.
▸ verb *he positioned a chair between them:* **put**, place, locate, situate, set, site, stand, station, plant, stick; informal plonk, park.

**positive** adjective 1 *a positive response:* **affirmative**, favourable, good, enthusiastic, supportive, encouraging. 2 *say something positive:* **constructive**, useful, productive, helpful, worthwhile, beneficial. 3 *she seems a lot more positive:* **optimistic**, hopeful, confident, cheerful, sanguine, buoyant; informal upbeat. 4 *positive economic signs:* **favourable**, good, promising, encouraging, heartening, propitious, auspicious. 5 *positive proof:* **definite**, certain, reliable, concrete, tangible, clear-cut, explicit, firm, decisive, real, actual. 6 *I'm positive he's coming back:* **certain**, sure, convinced, confident, satisfied.

OPPOSITES negative, pessimistic, doubtful, unsure.

**positively** adverb 1 *I could not positively identify the voice:* **confidently**, definitely, firmly, categorically, with certainty, conclusively. 2 *he was positively livid:* **absolutely**, utterly, downright, simply, virtually; informal plain.

**possess** verb 1 *the only hat she possessed:* **own**, have (to one's name), be in possession of. 2 *he did not possess a sense of humour:* **have**, be blessed with, be endowed with, enjoy, boast. 3 *an evil force possessed him:* **take control of**, take over, bewitch, enchant, enslave.

**possession** noun 1 *the estate came into their possession:* **ownership**, control, hands, keeping, care, custody, charge. 2 *she packed her possessions:* **belongings**, things, property, worldly goods, personal effects, stuff, bits and pieces; informal gear, junk; Brit. informal clobber.

**possibility** noun 1 *a possibility that he might be alive:* **chance**, likelihood, probability, potentiality, hope, risk, hazard, danger, fear. 2 *buying a smaller house is one possibility:* **option**, alternative, choice, course of action, solution. 3 *the idea has distinct possibilities:* **potential**, promise, prospects.

**possible** adjective 1 *it's not possible to check the figures:* **feasible**, practicable, viable, attainable, achievable, workable; informal on, doable. 2 *a possible reason for his disappearance:* **likely**, plausible, imaginable, believable, potential, probable, credible. 3 *a possible future leader:* **potential**, prospective, likely,

probable.
OPPOSITES unlikely.

**possibly** adverb 1 *possibly he took her with him*: perhaps, maybe, it is possible. 2 *you can't possibly refuse*: conceivably, under any circumstances, by any means. 3 *could you possibly help me?* please, kindly, be so good as to.

**post**[1] noun *wooden posts*: pole, stake, upright, shaft, prop, support, picket, strut, pillar.
verb 1 *the notice posted on the wall*: affix, attach, fasten, display, pin up, put up, stick up. 2 *the group posted a net profit*: announce, report, make known, publish.

**post**[2] noun (Brit.) 1 *the winners will be notified by post*: mail; informal snail mail. 2 *did we get any post?* letters, correspondence, mail.
verb (Brit.) *post the order form today*: send (off), mail, put in the post/mail, get off.
■ **keep someone posted** keep informed, keep up to date, keep in the picture.

**post**[3] noun 1 *there were seventy candidates for the post*: job, position, appointment, situation, place, vacancy, opening. 2 *back to your posts*: assigned position, station, place, base.
verb 1 *he'd been posted to Berlin*: send, assign, dispatch. 2 *armed guards were posted*: put on duty, mount, station.

**poster** noun notice, placard, bill, sign, advertisement, playbill.

**postpone** verb put off, put back, delay, defer, hold over, reschedule, adjourn, shelve; informal put on ice, put on the back burner.
OPPOSITES bring forward.

**posture** noun 1 *a kneeling posture*: position, pose, attitude, stance. 2 *good posture*: bearing, carriage, stance, comportment; Brit. deportment. 3 *trade unions adopted a militant posture*: attitude, stance, standpoint, point of view, opinion, position.
verb *Keith postured, flexing his biceps*: pose, strike an attitude, strut.

**pot** noun 1 *a pot of soup*: pan, saucepan, casserole. 2 *Neolithic pots*: vessel, bowl, earthenware, pottery.

**potent** adjective 1 *a potent political force*: powerful, strong, mighty, formidable, influential, dominant. 2 *a potent argument*: forceful, convincing, cogent, compelling, persuasive, powerful, strong. 3 *a potent drug*: strong, powerful, effective; formal efficacious.
OPPOSITES weak.

**potential** adjective *a potential source of conflict*: possible, likely, prospective, future, probable.
noun *he has great potential*: possibilities, potentiality, prospects, promise, capability, capacity.

**potter** verb amble, wander, meander, stroll, saunter; informal mosey, tootle, toddle; N. Amer. informal putter.

**pottery** noun ceramics, crockery, earthenware, terracotta, stoneware, china, porcelain.

**pounce** verb jump, spring, leap, dive, lunge, swoop, attack.

**pound**[1] verb 1 *the two men pounded him with their fists*: beat, strike, hit, batter, thump, pummel, punch, rain blows on, belabour, hammer; informal bash, clobber, wallop. **2** *waves pounded the seafront:* beat against, crash against, batter, dash against, lash, buffet. **3** *gunships pounded the capital:* bombard, bomb, shell. **4** *pound the garlic to a paste:* crush, grind, pulverize, mash, pulp. **5** *I heard him pounding along the gangway:* stomp, stamp, clomp, clump, tramp, lumber. **6** *her heart was pounding:* throb, thump, thud, hammer, pulse, race.

**pound²** noun *a dog pound:* enclosure, compound, pen, yard, corral.

**pour** verb **1** *blood was pouring from his nose:* stream, flow, run, gush, course, jet, spurt, surge, spill. **2** *Amy poured wine into his glass:* tip, splash, spill, decant; informal slosh, slop. **3** *it was pouring:* rain heavily/hard, teem down, pelt down, tip down, rain cats and dogs; informal be chucking it down; Brit. informal bucket down; N. Amer. informal rain pitchforks. **4** *people poured off the train:* crowd, throng, swarm, stream, flood.

**poverty** noun **1** *abject poverty:* pennilessness, destitution, penury, impoverishment, neediness, hardship, impecuniousness. **2** *the poverty of choice:* scarcity, deficiency, dearth, shortage, paucity, absence, lack. **3** *the poverty of her imagination:* inferiority, mediocrity, sterility.
OPPOSITES wealth, abundance, fertility.

**powdery** adjective fine, dry, fine-grained, powder-like, dusty, chalky, floury, sandy, crumbly, friable.

**power** noun **1** *the power of*
speech: ability, capacity, capability, potential, faculty. **2** *the union has enormous power:* control, authority, influence, dominance, sway, leverage; informal clout, teeth; N. Amer. informal drag. **3** *the power to stop and search:* authority, right, authorization. **4** *a major European power:* state, country, nation. **5** *he hit the ball with as much power as he could:* strength, might, force, vigour, energy; Brit. informal welly. **6** *the power of his arguments:* forcefulness, powerfulness, strength, force, cogency, persuasiveness. **7** *the new engine has more power:* driving force, horsepower, acceleration, torque; informal oomph, poke. **8** *generating power from waste:* energy, electricity.
OPPOSITES inability, weakness.

**powerful** adjective **1** *powerful shoulders:* strong, muscular, muscly, sturdy, strapping, robust, brawny, burly, athletic, manly, well built, solid; informal beefy. **2** *a powerful drink:* intoxicating, hard, strong, stiff. **3** *a powerful blow:* violent, forceful, hard, mighty. **4** *he felt a powerful urge to kiss her:* intense, keen, fierce, strong, irresistible, overpowering, overwhelming. **5** *a powerful nation:* influential, strong, important, dominant, commanding, formidable. **6** *a powerful critique:* cogent, compelling, convincing, persuasive, forceful.
OPPOSITES weak, gentle.

**powerless** adjective impotent, helpless, ineffectual, ineffective, useless, defenceless, vulnerable.

**practicable** adjective realistic,

feasible, possible, viable, reasonable, sensible, workable, achievable; informal doable.

**practical** adjective **1** *practical experience:* empirical, hands-on, actual. **2** *there are no practical alternatives:* feasible, practicable, realistic, viable, workable, possible, reasonable, sensible; informal doable. **3** *practical clothes:* functional, sensible, utilitarian. **4** *try to be more practical:* realistic, sensible, down-to-earth, businesslike, commonsensical, hard-headed, no-nonsense; informal hard-nosed. **5** *a practical certainty:* virtual, effective, near.
OPPOSITES theoretical, impractical.

**practically** adverb **1** *the cinema was practically empty:* almost, very nearly, virtually, just about, all but, more or less, as good as, to all intents and purposes; informal pretty nearly, pretty well. **2** *'You can't afford it,' he pointed out practically:* realistically, sensibly, reasonably, rationally, matter-of-factly.

**practice** noun **1** *the practice of radiotherapy:* application, exercise, use, operation, implementation, execution. **2** *it is common practice:* custom, procedure, policy, convention, tradition. **3** *the team's final practice:* training, rehearsal, repetition, preparation, dummy run, run-through; informal dry run. **4** *the practice of medicine:* profession, career, business, work. **5** *a small legal practice:* business, firm, office, company; informal outfit.

**practise** verb **1** *he practised the songs every day:* rehearse, run

through, go over/through, work on/at, polish, perfect. **2** *the performers were practising:* train, rehearse, prepare, go through one's paces. **3** *we still practise these rituals today:* carry out, perform, observe. **4** *she practises medicine:* work at/in, pursue a career in.

**practised** adjective expert, experienced, seasoned, skilled, skilful, accomplished, proficient, talented, able, adept.

**pragmatic** adjective practical, matter of fact, sensible, down-to-earth, commonsensical, businesslike, hard-headed, no-nonsense; informal hard-nosed.
OPPOSITES impractical.

**praise** verb commend, applaud, pay tribute to, speak highly of, compliment, congratulate, sing the praises of, rave about.
OPPOSITES criticize.
noun approval, acclaim, admiration, approbation, plaudits, congratulations, commendation, accolade, compliment, a pat on the back, eulogy.
OPPOSITES criticism.

**preach** verb **1** *he preached to a large congregation:* give a sermon, sermonize, address, speak. **2** *preaching the gospel:* proclaim, teach, spread, propagate, expound. **3** *they preach toleration:* advocate, recommend, advise, urge, teach, counsel.

**precarious** adjective insecure, uncertain, unpredictable, risky, parlous, hazardous, dangerous, unsafe, unstable, unsteady, shaky; informal dicey, iffy; Brit. informal dodgy.
OPPOSITES safe.

**precaution** noun safeguard, preventive measure, safety

measure, insurance; informal backstop.

**precede** verb 1 *adverts preceded the film:* go/come before, lead up to, pave the way for, herald, introduce, usher in. 2 *Catherine preceded him into the studio:* go ahead of, go in front of, lead the way.
OPPOSITES follow.

**precedent** noun model, exemplar, example, pattern, paradigm, criterion, yardstick, standard.

**precinct** noun district, zone, sector, quarter, area.

**precious** adjective 1 *precious works of art:* valuable, costly, expensive, invaluable, priceless. 2 *her most precious possession:* valued, cherished, treasured, prized, favourite, dear, beloved, special. 3 *his precious manners:* affected, pretentious; informal la-di-da; Brit. informal poncey.

**precipitate** verb 1 *the incident precipitated a crisis:* bring about/on, cause, lead to, give rise to, instigate, trigger, spark off, touch off, provoke. 2 *they were precipitated down the mountain:* hurl, catapult, throw, plunge, launch, fling, propel.
adjective *their actions were precipitate:* hasty, overhasty, rash, hurried, rushed, impetuous, impulsive, precipitous, incautious, imprudent, injudicious, ill-advised, reckless.

**precipitous** adjective 1 *a precipitous drop:* steep, sheer, perpendicular, abrupt, sharp, vertical. 2 *his precipitous fall from power:* sudden, rapid, swift, abrupt, headlong, speedy, quick, fast.

**precise** adjective 1 *precise measurements:* exact, accurate, correct, specific, detailed, explicit, careful, meticulous, strict, rigorous. 2 *at that precise moment:* exact, particular, very, specific.
OPPOSITES inaccurate.

**precisely** adverb 1 *at 2 o'clock precisely:* exactly, sharp, on the dot, promptly, on the stroke of ...; informal bang (on); Brit. informal spot on; N. Amer. informal on the button. 2 *precisely the man I am looking for:* exactly, just, in all respects; informal to a T. 3 *fertilization can be timed precisely:* accurately, exactly. 4 *'So you knew?' 'Precisely.':* yes, exactly, absolutely, (that's) right, quite so.

**precision** noun exactness, accuracy, exactitude, correctness, care, meticulousness, scrupulousness, punctiliousness, rigour.

**predecessor** noun 1 *the Prime Minister's predecessor:* forerunner, precursor, antecedent. 2 *our Victorian predecessors:* ancestor, forefather, forebear, antecedent.
OPPOSITES successor, descendant.

**predicament** noun difficulty, mess, plight, quandary, muddle, dilemma; informal hole, fix, jam, pickle.

**predict** verb forecast, foretell, prophesy.

**predictable** adjective foreseeable, to be expected, anticipated, likely, foreseen, unsurprising, reliable; informal inevitable.
OPPOSITES unpredictable.

**prediction** noun forecast, prophecy, prognosis, prognostication.

**predominantly** adverb mainly, mostly, for the most part, chiefly, principally, primarily, in the main, on the whole, largely, by and large, typically, generally, usually.

**prefer** verb like better, would rather (have), would sooner (have), favour, be more partial to, choose, select, pick, opt for, go for, plump for.

**preferable** adjective better, best, more desirable, more suitable, advantageous, superior, preferred, recommended.

**preferably** adverb ideally, if possible, for preference, from choice.

**preference** noun 1 *her preference for gin:* liking, partiality, fondness, taste, inclination, leaning, bent, penchant, predisposition. 2 *preference was given to female applicants:* priority, favour, precedence, preferential treatment.

**pregnant** adjective 1 *she is pregnant:* expecting, expectant, carrying a child; informal in the family way, preggers. 2 *a pregnant pause:* meaningful, significant, suggestive, expressive, charged.

**prejudice** noun 1 *male prejudices about women:* preconceived idea, preconception. 2 *they are motivated by prejudice:* bigotry, bias, partiality, intolerance, discrimination, unfairness, inequality.
verb 1 *the article could prejudice the jury:* bias, influence, sway, predispose, make partial, colour. 2 *this could prejudice his chances:* damage, be detrimental to, be prejudicial to, injure, harm, hurt, spoil, impair, undermine, compromise.

**prejudiced** adjective biased, bigoted, discriminatory, partisan, intolerant, narrow-minded, unfair, unjust, inequitable, coloured.
OPPOSITES impartial.

**preliminary** adjective *at a preliminary stage:* preparatory, introductory, initial, opening, early, exploratory.
OPPOSITES final.
noun *he began without any preliminaries:* introduction, preamble, preface, opening remarks, formalities.

**prelude** noun preliminary, overture, opening, preparation, introduction, lead-in, precursor.

**premature** adjective 1 *his premature death:* untimely, too early, before time, unseasonable. 2 *such a step would be premature:* rash, overhasty, hasty, precipitate, impulsive, impetuous; informal previous.
OPPOSITES overdue.

**premier** adjective *Germany's premier rock band:* leading, foremost, chief, principal, head, top-ranking, top, prime, primary, first, highest, pre-eminent, senior, outstanding; N. Amer. ranking.
noun *the British premier:* head of government, prime minister, PM, president, chancellor.

**premiere** noun first performance, first night, opening night, debut.

**premise** noun proposition, assumption, hypothesis, thesis, presupposition, supposition, presumption, assertion.

**premises** plural noun building(s), property, site,

a b c d e f g h i j k l m n o **p** q r s t u v w x y z

office, establishment.

**premium** noun **1** *monthly premiums of £30:* (regular) payment, instalment. **2** *you must pay a premium for organic fruit:* surcharge, additional payment, extra.
■ **at a premium** scarce, in great demand, hard to come by, in short supply, thin on the ground.

**preoccupation** noun obsession, fixation, concern, passion, enthusiasm, hobby horse; informal bee in one's bonnet.

**preoccupied** adjective **1** *he's preoccupied with work:* obsessed, fixated, concerned, absorbed, engrossed, involved, wrapped up. **2** *she looked preoccupied:* lost in thought, deep in thought, oblivious, pensive, distracted.

**preparation** noun **1** *the preparation of a plan:* devising, putting together, drawing up, construction, composition, production, getting ready, development. **2** *preparations for the party:* arrangements, planning, plans, groundwork, provisions. **3** *a preparation to kill mites:* mixture, compound, concoction, solution, medicine, potion.

**prepare** verb **1** *I will prepare a report:* make/get ready, put together, draw up, produce, arrange, assemble, construct, compose, formulate. **2** *the meal is easy to prepare:* cook, make, get, put together, concoct; informal fix, rustle up; Brit. informal knock up. **3** *preparing for war:* get ready, make preparations, arrange things, make provision. **4** *athletes preparing for the Olympics:* train, get into shape,

practise, get ready, warm up, limber up. **5** *prepare yourself for a shock:* brace, ready, tense, steel, steady.

**prepared** adjective **1** *prepared for action:* ready, (all) set, equipped, primed, waiting, poised. **2** *I'm prepared to negotiate:* willing, ready, disposed, (favourably) inclined, of a mind, minded.

**prescribe** verb **1** *a doctor may prescribe antibiotics:* advise, recommend, advocate, suggest. **2** *rules prescribing your duty:* stipulate, lay down, dictate, order, direct, specify, determine.

**presence** noun **1** *the presence of an intruder:* existence. **2** *I requested the presence of a lawyer:* attendance, appearance. **3** *a woman of great presence:* aura, charisma, personality.
OPPOSITES absence.
■ **presence of mind** composure, self-possession, level-headedness, self-assurance, calmness, alertness, quick-wittedness; informal cool, unflappability.

**present**[1] adjective **1** *a doctor must be present:* in attendance, here, there, near, nearby, at hand, available. **2** *organic compounds are present:* in existence, detectable, occurring, here, there. **3** *the present economic climate:* current, present-day, existing, extant.
OPPOSITES absent.
noun *think about the present:* now, today, the present time, the here and now, modern times.
OPPOSITES past, future.
■ **at present** at the moment, just

now, right now, at the present time, currently, at this moment in time.

**present**[2] verb **1** *Eddy presented a cheque to the winner:* hand over, give (out), confer, bestow, award, grant, accord. **2** *the committee presented its report:* submit, set forth, put forward, offer, tender, table. **3** *may I present my wife?* introduce, make known, acquaint someone with. **4** *she presents a TV show:* host, introduce, compère; N. Amer. informal emcee. **5** *they present him as a criminal:* represent, describe, portray, depict.

**present**[3] noun *a birthday present:* gift, donation, offering, contribution, gratuity, tip, hand-out; informal prezzie.

**presentation** noun **1** *the presentation of his certificate:* awarding, presenting, giving, handing over, bestowal, granting. **2** *the presentation of food:* appearance, arrangement, packaging, layout. **3** *a sales presentation:* demonstration, talk, lecture, address, speech, show, exhibition, display, introduction, launch, launching, unveiling.

**presently** adverb **1** *I shall see you presently:* soon, shortly, quite soon, in a short time, in a little while, at any moment/minute/second, before long; N. Amer. momentarily; Brit. informal in a mo. **2** *he is presently abroad:* at present, currently, at the/this moment.

**preservation** noun **1** *wood preservation:* conservation, protection, care. **2** *the preservation of the status quo:* continuation, conservation, maintenance, upholding,

sustaining, perpetuation.

**preserve** verb **1** *oil preserves the wood:* conserve, protect, maintain, care for, look after. **2** *the wish to preserve the status quo:* continue (with), conserve, keep going, maintain, uphold, sustain, perpetuate, prolong. **3** *preserving him from harm:* guard, protect, keep, defend, safeguard, shelter, shield. OPPOSITES attack, abandon. noun **1** *the preserve of the rich:* domain, area, field, sphere, orbit, realm, province, territory; informal turf, bailiwick. **2** *a game preserve:* sanctuary, (game) reserve, reservation.

**preside**

■ **preside over** be in charge of, be responsible for, head, manage, administer, control, direct, chair, conduct, officiate at, lead, govern, rule, command, supervise, oversee; informal head up.

**press** verb **1** *press the paper down firmly:* push (down), press down, depress, hold down, force, thrust, squeeze, compress. **2** *his shirt was pressed:* iron. **3** *she pressed the child to her bosom:* clasp, hold close, hug, cuddle, squeeze, clutch, grasp, embrace. **4** *the crowd pressed round:* cluster, gather, converge, congregate, flock, swarm, crowd. **5** *the government pressed its claim:* plead, urge, advance, present, submit, put forward. **6** *they pressed him to agree:* urge, put pressure on, pressurize, force, push, coerce, dragoon, steamroller, browbeat; informal lean on, put the screws on, twist someone's arm, railroad, bulldoze. **7** *they pressed for a ban:* call, ask, clamour, push, campaign, demand.

**noun 1** *the freedom of the press:* the media, the newspapers, journalism, reporters; Brit. dated Fleet Street. **2** *the company had some bad press:* (press) reports, press coverage, press articles, press reviews.

**pressing** adjective **1** *a pressing problem:* urgent, critical, crucial, acute, desperate, serious, grave, life-and-death. **2** *a pressing engagement:* important, high-priority, critical, crucial, unavoidable.

**pressure** noun **1** *atmospheric pressure:* force, load, stress, thrust, compression, weight. **2** *there was pressure to conform:* persuasion, intimidation, coercion, compulsion, duress, harassment, nagging, badgering. **3** *she had a lot of pressure at work:* strain, stress, tension, trouble, difficulty, burden; informal hassle.
verb *they pressured him into resigning:* coerce, push, persuade, force, bulldoze, hound, nag, badger, browbeat, bully, intimidate, dragoon, twist someone's arm; informal railroad, lean on; N. Amer. informal hustle.

**pressurize** verb *he pressurized us into selling:* coerce, pressure, push, persuade, force, bulldoze, hound, nag, badger, browbeat, bully, bludgeon, intimidate, dragoon, twist someone's arm; informal railroad, lean on; N. Amer. informal hustle.

**prestige** noun status, standing, kudos, cachet, stature, reputation, repute, renown, honour, esteem, importance, prominence.

**prestigious** adjective reputable, distinguished, respected, high-status, esteemed, eminent, highly regarded, renowned, influential.
OPPOSITES disreputable, obscure.

**presumably** adverb I presume, I expect, I assume, I take it, I imagine, I dare say, doubtless, no doubt, apparently, probably.

**presume** verb **1** *I presume it was once an attic:* assume, suppose, surmise, imagine, take it, expect. **2** *I wouldn't presume to advise you:* dare, venture, have the effrontery, be so bold as, go so far as, take the liberty of.

**pretence** noun **1** *cease this pretence:* make-believe, acting, faking, play-acting, posturing, deception, trickery. **2** *he made a pretence of being concerned:* (false) show, semblance, affectation, (false) appearance, outward appearance, impression, guise, facade.
OPPOSITES honesty.

**pretend** verb **1** *they pretend to listen:* make as if, act like, affect, go through the motions, fake it. **2** *I'll pretend to be the dragon:* make believe, play at, act, impersonate.
adjective (informal) mock, fake, sham, simulated, artificial, false, pseudo; informal phoney.

**pretty** adjective *a pretty girl:* attractive, good-looking, nice-looking, personable, fetching, prepossessing, appealing, charming, delightful, cute; Scottish & N. English bonny.
OPPOSITES plain, ugly.
adverb (informal) *it's pretty cold:* quite, rather, somewhat, fairly.

**prevail** verb **1** *common sense will prevail:* win (out/through), triumph, be victorious, carry the day, come out on top, succeed, rule, reign.

**2** *the conditions that prevailed in the 1950s:* exist, be present, be the case, occur, be prevalent, be in force.

**prevailing** adjective current, existing, prevalent, usual, common, general, widespread.

**prevalent** adjective widespread, frequent, usual, common, current, popular, general.
OPPOSITES rare.

**prevent** verb stop, avert, nip in the bud, foil, inhibit, thwart, prohibit, forbid.
OPPOSITES allow.

**previous** adjective **1** *the previous five years:* preceding, foregoing, prior, past, last.
**2** *her previous boyfriend:* former, preceding, old, earlier, ex-, past, last, sometime, one-time, erstwhile. **3** (informal) *I was a bit previous:* overhasty, hasty, premature; informal ahead of oneself.
OPPOSITES next.

**previously** adverb formerly, earlier (on), before, hitherto, at one time, in the past.

**prey** noun **1** *the lions' prey:* quarry, kill. **2** *con men choose their prey carefully:* victim, target, dupe; informal sucker; Brit. informal mug.
OPPOSITES predator.

**price** noun **1** *the purchase price:* cost, charge, fee, fare, amount, sum; informal damage. **2** *the price of success:* consequence, result, cost, penalty, toll, sacrifice, downside, drawback, disadvantage, minus.

**priceless** adjective invaluable, beyond price, irreplaceable, expensive, costly.
OPPOSITES worthless, cheap.

**prick** verb *prick the potatoes:* pierce, puncture, stab, perforate, spike, penetrate, jab.

noun *a prick in the leg:* jab, sting, pinprick, stab, pinhole, wound.

**prickly** adjective spiky, spiked, thorny, barbed, spiny, bristly.

**pride** noun **1** *a source of pride:* self-esteem, dignity, honour, self-respect. **2** *pride in a job well done:* pleasure, joy, delight, gratification, fulfilment, satisfaction, sense of achievement. **3** *he refused out of pride:* arrogance, vanity, self-importance, hubris, conceitedness, egotism, snobbery.
OPPOSITES shame, humility.

**priest** noun clergyman, clergywoman, minister, cleric, pastor, vicar, rector, parson, churchman, churchwoman, father, curate; Scottish kirkman; N. Amer. dominie; informal reverend, padre.

**primarily** adverb **1** *he was primarily a singer:* first and foremost, firstly, essentially, in essence, fundamentally, principally, predominantly.
**2** *work is done primarily for large institutions:* mostly, for the most part, chiefly, mainly, in the main, on the whole, largely, principally, predominantly.

**primary** adjective main, chief, key, prime, central, principal, foremost, first, most important, predominant, paramount; informal number-one.
OPPOSITES secondary.

**prime**[1] adjective **1** *his prime reason for leaving:* main, chief, key, primary, central, principal, foremost, first, most important, paramount, major; informal number-one. **2** *prime agricultural land:* top-quality, top, best, first-class, superior, choice, select, finest; informal tip-top, A1.

OPPOSITES secondary, inferior.

noun *he is in his prime*: heyday, peak, pinnacle, high point/spot, zenith, flower, bloom, flush.

**prime²** verb *Lucy had primed him carefully*: brief, fill in, prepare, advise, instruct, coach, drill, train.

**primitive** adjective 1 *primitive times*: ancient, earliest, first, prehistoric, primordial, primeval. 2 *primitive tools*: crude, simple, rough (and ready), basic, rudimentary, makeshift.

OPPOSITES modern, sophisticated.

**prince** noun ruler, sovereign, monarch, crowned head.

**principal** adjective main, chief, primary, leading, foremost, first, most important, predominant, dominant, pre-eminent, highest, top; informal number-one.

OPPOSITES minor.

noun head teacher, headmaster, headmistress, head, dean, rector, master, mistress, chancellor, vice-chancellor, president, provost, warden; N. Amer. informal prexy.

**principally** adverb mainly, mostly, chiefly, for the most part, in the main, on the whole, largely, predominantly, primarily.

**principle** noun 1 *a basic principle of science*: truth, concept, idea, theory, fundamental, essential, precept, rule, law. 2 *the principle of laissez-faire*: doctrine, belief, creed, credo, code, ethic. 3 *a woman of principle*: morals, morality, ethics, ideals, standards, integrity, virtue,

probity, honour, decency, conscience, scruples.

■ in principle 1 *there is no reason, in principle, why not*: in theory, theoretically, on paper, ideally. 2 *he accepted the idea in principle*: in general, in essence, on the whole, in the main.

**print** verb 1 *when was the book printed?* publish, issue, release, circulate, run off, copy, reproduce. 2 *patterns were printed on the cloth*: imprint, impress, stamp, mark.

noun 1 *large print*: type, printing, letters, lettering, characters, typeface, font. 2 *a print of his left hand*: impression, handprint, fingerprint, footprint. 3 *sporting prints*: picture, engraving, etching, lithograph, woodcut. 4 *prints and negatives*: photograph, photo, snap, snapshot, picture, still, enlargement, copy, reproduction.

**prior** adjective earlier, previous, preceding, advance, pre-existing.

OPPOSITES subsequent.

■ prior to before, until, up to, previous to, preceding, earlier than, in advance of.

**priority** noun 1 *safety is our priority*: prime concern, main consideration. 2 *giving priority to education*: precedence, preference, pre-eminence, predominance, primacy. 3 *oncoming traffic has priority*: right of way, precedence, supremacy, seniority.

**prison** noun jail, penal institution; N. Amer. jailhouse, penitentiary, correctional facility; informal clink, slammer; Brit. informal nick; N. Amer. informal can, pen.

■ **in prison** behind bars; informal inside, doing time; Brit. informal doing porridge.

**prisoner** noun **1** *a prisoner serving a life sentence:* convict, detainee, inmate; informal jailbird, con; Brit. informal lag; N. Amer. informal yardbird. **2** *the army took many prisoners:* prisoner of war, POW, internee, captive, hostage.

**pristine** adjective immaculate, perfect, in mint condition, as new, spotless, unspoilt.
OPPOSITES dirty, spoilt.

**privacy** noun seclusion, solitude, isolation.

**private** adjective **1** *his private plane:* personal, own, special, exclusive. **2** *private talks:* confidential, secret, classified. **3** *private thoughts:* intimate, personal, secret, innermost, undisclosed, unspoken, unvoiced. **4** *a very private man:* reserved, introverted, self-contained, reticent, retiring, unsociable, withdrawn, solitary, reclusive. **5** *somewhere private to talk:* secluded, undisturbed, remote, isolated. **6** *in a private capacity:* unofficial, personal. **7** *private industry:* independent, non-state, privatized, commercial, private-enterprise.
OPPOSITES public, open, extrovert, busy, crowded, official, state, nationalized.
noun *a private in the army:* private soldier, trooper; Brit. sapper, gunner; US GI; Brit. informal Tommy, squaddie.

■ **in private** in secret, secretly, privately, behind closed doors, in camera.

**privilege** noun **1** *senior pupils have certain privileges:* advantage, benefit, prerogative, entitlement, right, concession, freedom, liberty. **2** *it was a privilege to meet her:* honour, pleasure.

**privileged** adjective **1** *a privileged background:* wealthy, rich, affluent, prosperous. **2** *I feel very lucky and privileged:* honoured, advantaged, favoured, valued, appreciated. **3** *privileged information:* confidential, private, secret, restricted, classified, not for publication, off the record, inside; informal hush-hush.
OPPOSITES underprivileged, disadvantaged, snubbed, public.

**prize** noun *an art prize:* award, reward, trophy, medal, cup, winnings, purse, honour.
adjective **1** *a prize bull:* champion, award-winning, top, best. **2** *a prize idiot:* utter, complete, total, absolute, real, perfect; Brit. informal right.
OPPOSITES second-rate.

**probability** noun **1** *the probability of winning:* likelihood, prospect, expectation, chance(s), odds. **2** *relegation is a distinct probability:* prospect, possibility.

**probable** adjective likely, odds-on, expected, anticipated, predictable; informal on the cards, a safe bet.
OPPOSITES improbable, unlikely.

**probably** adverb in all likelihood, in all probability, as likely as not, ten to one, the chances are, doubtless.

**probation** noun trial, trial period, test period, apprenticeship, training.

**probe** noun *a probe into city hall corruption:* investigation,

a b c d e f g h i j k l m n o **p** q r s t u v w x y z

enquiry, examination, inquest, study.

**verb 1** *their long beaks are suited to probing the ground:* prod, poke, dig into, delve into, explore, feel around in, examine. **2** *an enquiry probed the cause of the disaster:* investigate, enquire into, look into, go into, study, examine, explore.

**problem noun 1** *there's a problem:* difficulty, worry, complication, snag, hitch, drawback, stumbling block, obstacle, hiccup, setback, catch; informal dilemma, headache. **2** *I don't want to be a problem:* nuisance, bother; informal drag, pain. **3** *arithmetical problems:* puzzle, question, poser, riddle, conundrum; informal brain-teaser.

**problematic adjective** difficult, troublesome, tricky, awkward, controversial, ticklish, complicated, complex, knotty. OPPOSITES easy, straightforward.

**procedure noun** course of action, method, system, strategy, way, approach, formula, mechanism, technique, routine, drill, practice.

**proceed verb 1** *she was uncertain how to proceed:* begin, make a start, get going, move. **2** *he proceeded down the road:* go, make one's way, advance, move, progress, carry on, press on, push on. **3** *we should proceed with the talks:* go ahead, carry on, go on, continue, keep on, get on. OPPOSITES stop.

**proceedings plural noun 1** *the evening's proceedings:* events, activities, happenings, goings-on. **2** *the proceedings of the meeting:* report, transactions, minutes, account, story, record(s). **3** *legal proceedings:* legal action, litigation, lawsuit, case, prosecution.

**proceeds plural noun** profits, earnings, receipts, returns, takings, income, revenue, profit, yield; Sport gate (money); N. Amer. take.

**process noun 1** *investigation is a long process:* procedure, operation, action, activity, exercise, affair, business, job, task, undertaking. **2** *a new canning process:* method, system, technique, means, practice, way, approach.
**verb** *applications are processed rapidly:* deal with, attend to, see to, sort out, handle, take care of.

**procession noun** parade, march, march past, cavalcade, motorcade, cortège, column, file; Brit. informal crocodile.

**proclaim verb** declare, announce, pronounce, state, make known, give out, advertise, publish, broadcast, trumpet.

**prod verb 1** *Cassie prodded him in the chest:* poke, jab, stab, dig, nudge, elbow. **2** *the Department was prodded into action:* spur, stimulate, prompt, push, galvanize, persuade, urge, chivvy, remind.
**noun 1** *a sharp prod in the ribs:* poke, jab, stab, dig, nudge, elbow. **2** *he might need a prod to get him to come:* urging, stimulus, push, prompt, reminder, chivvying.

**prodigal adjective** wasteful, extravagant, spendthrift. OPPOSITES thrifty.

**prodigy noun** genius, mastermind, virtuoso,

wunderkind; informal whizz-kid, whizz.

OPPOSITES dunce, amateur.

**produce** verb 1 *the company produces furniture*: manufacture, make, construct, build, fabricate, put together, assemble, turn out, create, mass-produce. 2 *the vineyards produce excellent wines*: yield, grow, give, supply, provide, furnish, bear. 3 *she produced ten puppies*: give birth to, bear, deliver, bring forth, bring into the world. 4 *he produced five novels*: create, fashion, turn out, compose, write, pen, paint. 5 *she produced an ID card*: pull out, extract, fish out, present, offer, proffer, show. 6 *that will produce a reaction*: cause, bring about, give rise to, occasion, generate, lead to, result in, provoke, precipitate, spark off, trigger. 7 *James produced the play*: stage, put on, mount, present, exhibit.
noun *local produce*: food, foodstuff(s), products, crops, fruit and vegetables.

**producer** noun 1 *a car producer*: manufacturer, maker, builder, constructor. 2 *coffee producers*: grower, farmer. 3 *the producer of the show*: impresario, manager, administrator, promoter, director.

**product** noun 1 *household products*: artefact, commodity; (**products**) goods, ware(s), merchandise, produce. 2 *a product of experience*: result, consequence, outcome, effect, upshot.

**production** noun 1 *the production of cars*: manufacture, making, construction, building, fabrication, assembly, creation, mass production. 2 *the production of literary works*: creation, origination, fashioning, composition, writing. 3 *agricultural production*: output, yield, productivity. 4 *a theatre production*: performance, staging, presentation, show, piece, play.

**productive** adjective 1 *a productive artist*: prolific, inventive, creative. 2 *productive talks*: useful, constructive, profitable, fruitful, valuable, effective, worthwhile, helpful. 3 *productive land*: fertile, fruitful, rich, fecund.
OPPOSITES unproductive.

**productivity** noun efficiency, work rate, output, yield, production.

**profess** verb 1 *he professed his love*: declare, announce, proclaim, assert, state, affirm, maintain, protest. 2 *she professed to loathe publicity*: claim, pretend, purport, affect, make out.

**professed** adjective 1 *their professed independence*: claimed, supposed, ostensible, self-styled, apparent, pretended, purported. 2 *a professed Christian*: declared, self-acknowledged, self-confessed, confessed, sworn, confirmed.

**profession** noun career, occupation, calling, vocation, métier, line of work, job, business, trade, craft.

**professional** adjective 1 *professional occupations*: white-collar, non-manual, graduate, qualified, chartered. 2 *a professional cricketer*: paid, salaried. 3 *a very professional*

**job:** expert, accomplished, skilful, masterly, fine, polished, skilled, proficient, competent, able, businesslike, deft. **4** *not a professional way to behave:* appropriate, fitting, proper, honourable, ethical.
OPPOSITES manual, amateur, amateurish, inappropriate, unethical.

noun *she was a real professional:* expert, virtuoso, old hand, master, maestro, past master; informal pro, ace.
OPPOSITES amateur.

**profile** noun **1** *his handsome profile:* outline, silhouette, side view, contour, shape, form, lines. **2** *a profile of the organization:* description, account, study, portrait, rundown, sketch, outline.

**profit** noun **1** *the firm made a profit:* financial gain, return(s), yield, proceeds, earnings, winnings, surplus; informal pay dirt, bottom line. **2** *there was little profit in going on:* advantage, benefit, value, use, good; informal mileage.
OPPOSITES loss, disadvantage.

verb **1** *we will not profit from the deal:* make money, earn; informal rake it in, clean up, make a killing; N. Amer. informal make a fast buck. **2** *how will that profit us?* benefit, be advantageous to, be of use to, do someone good, help, be of service to, serve.
OPPOSITES lose, disadvantage.

**profitable** adjective **1** *a profitable company:* moneymaking, profit-making, paying, lucrative, commercial, successful, money-spinning, gainful. **2** *profitable study:* beneficial, useful, valuable, advantageous, productive, worthwhile, rewarding, fruitful, illuminating, informative, well spent.
OPPOSITES unprofitable, loss-making, fruitless, useless.

**profound** adjective **1** *profound relief:* heartfelt, intense, keen, extreme, acute, severe, sincere, earnest, deep, deep-seated, overpowering, overwhelming. **2** *a profound change:* far-reaching, radical, extensive, sweeping, exhaustive, thoroughgoing. **3** *a profound analysis:* wise, learned, intelligent, scholarly, discerning, penetrating, perceptive, astute, thoughtful, insightful.
OPPOSITES superficial, mild, slight.

**programme** noun **1** *our programme for the day:* schedule, agenda, calendar, timetable, order, line-up. **2** *the government's reform programme:* scheme, plan, package, strategy, initiative, proposal. **3** *a television programme:* broadcast, production, show, presentation, transmission, performance; informal prog. **4** *a programme of study:* course, syllabus, curriculum.

verb *they programmed the day well:* arrange, organize, schedule, plan, map out, timetable, line up; N. Amer. slate.

**progress** noun **1** *snow made progress difficult:* (forward) movement, advance, going, headway, passage. **2** *scientific progress:* development, advance, advancement, headway, step forward, improvement, growth.
OPPOSITES regression.

**verb 1** *they progressed slowly down the road:* go, make one's way, move, proceed, advance, go on, continue, make headway, work one's way. **2** *the school has progressed rapidly:* develop, make progress, advance, make headway, take steps forward, move on, get on, gain ground, improve, get better, come on, come along, make strides; informal be getting there.
OPPOSITES regress, lapse.
■ **in progress** under way, going on, ongoing, happening, occurring, taking place, proceeding, continuing.

**progression** noun **1** *progression to the next stage:* progress, advancement, movement, passage, development, evolution, growth. **2** *a progression of peaks on the graph:* succession, series, sequence, string, stream, chain, train, row, cycle.

**progressive** adjective
**1** *progressive deterioration:* continuing, continuous, ongoing, gradual, step-by-step, cumulative. **2** *progressive views:* modern, liberal, advanced, forward-thinking, enlightened, pioneering, reforming, reformist, radical; informal go-ahead.
OPPOSITES sporadic, conservative, reactionary.

**prohibit** verb **1** *state law prohibits gambling:* forbid, ban, bar, proscribe, make illegal, outlaw, disallow. **2** *a cash shortage prohibited the visit:* prevent, stop, rule out, preclude, make impossible.
OPPOSITES allow.

**prohibition** noun ban, bar, veto, embargo, boycott, injunction, moratorium.

**project** noun **1** *an engineering project:* scheme, plan, programme, enterprise, undertaking, venture, proposal, idea, concept. **2** *a history project:* assignment, piece of work, piece of research, task.
verb **1** *profits are projected to rise:* forecast, predict, expect, estimate, calculate, reckon. **2** *his projected book:* intend, plan, propose. **3** *balconies projected over the lake:* stick out, jut (out), protrude, extend, stand out, bulge out. **4** *the sun projected his shadow on the wall:* cast, throw, send, shed, shine.

**projection** noun **1** *a sales projection:* forecast, prediction, prognosis, expectation, estimate. **2** *tiny projections on the cliff face:* outcrop, outgrowth, overhang, ledge, shelf, prominence, protrusion, protuberance; informal sticky-out bit.

**proliferate** verb increase, grow, multiply, rocket, mushroom, snowball, burgeon, spread, expand, run riot.
OPPOSITES decrease, dwindle.

**prolific** adjective **1** *a prolific crop of tomatoes:* plentiful, abundant, bountiful, profuse, copious, luxuriant, rich, lush, fruitful. **2** *a prolific composer:* productive, fertile, creative, inventive.
OPPOSITES meagre, unproductive.

**prolong** verb lengthen, extend, drag out, draw out, protract, spin out, carry on, continue, keep up, perpetuate.
OPPOSITES shorten.

**prominence** noun **1** *his rise to prominence:* fame, celebrity, eminence, importance,

a b c d e f g h i j k l m n o p q r s t u v w x y z

distinction, greatness, prestige, stature, standing. **2** *the press gave prominence to the reports:* **wide coverage**, importance, precedence, weight, a high profile, top billing.

**prominent** adjective **1** *a prominent surgeon:* **important**, well known, leading, eminent, distinguished, notable, noteworthy, noted, illustrious, celebrated, famous, renowned; N. Amer. major-league.
**2** *prominent cheekbones:* **jutting (out)**, protruding, projecting, protuberant, standing out, sticking out, proud, bulging.
**3** *a prominent feature of the landscape:* **conspicuous**, noticeable, obvious, unmistakable, eye-catching, pronounced, salient, striking, dominant, obtrusive.
OPPOSITES unimportant, unknown, flat, inconspicuous.

**promise** noun **1** *you broke your promise:* **word (of honour)**, assurance, pledge, vow, guarantee, oath, bond, undertaking, agreement, commitment, contract. **2** *he shows promise:* **potential**, ability, talent, aptitude, possibility.
verb **1** *she promised to go:* **give one's word**, swear, pledge, vow, undertake, guarantee, warrant, contract, give an assurance, commit oneself. **2** *the skies promised sunshine:* **indicate**, lead one to expect, point to, be a sign of, give hope of, augur, herald, portend.

**promising** adjective **1** *a promising start:* **good**, encouraging, favourable, hopeful, auspicious, propitious, bright, rosy, heartening. **2** *a promising actor:* **with**

potential, gifted, talented, budding, up-and-coming, rising, coming, in the making.
OPPOSITES unfavourable, hopeless.

**promote** verb **1** *she's been promoted:* **upgrade**, give promotion to, elevate, advance, move up. **2** *an organization promoting justice:* **encourage**, further, advance, foster, develop, boost, stimulate, work for. **3** *she is promoting her new film:* **advertise**, publicize, give publicity to, beat/bang the drum for, market, merchandise; informal push, plug, hype; N. Amer. informal flack.
OPPOSITES demote, obstruct, play down.

**promotion** noun **1** *her promotion at work:* **upgrading**, preferment, elevation, advancement, step up (the ladder). **2** *the promotion of justice:* **encouragement**, furtherance, furthering, advancement, contribution to, fostering, boosting, stimulation; N. Amer. boosterism. **3** *the promotion for her new film:* **advertising**, marketing, publicity, campaign, propaganda; informal hard sell, plug, hype, puff.

**prompt** verb **1** *curiosity prompted him to look:* **induce**, make, move, motivate, lead, dispose, persuade, incline, encourage, stimulate, prod, impel, spur on, inspire. **2** *the statement prompted a hostile reaction:* **give rise to**, bring about, cause, occasion, result in, lead to, elicit, produce, precipitate, trigger, spark off, provoke. **3** *the actors needed prompting:* **remind**, cue, feed, help out, jog someone's

memory.
OPPOSITES deter, avoid.
**adjective** *a prompt reply:* quick, swift, rapid, speedy, fast, direct, immediate, instant, early, punctual, in good time, on time.
OPPOSITES slow, late.
**adverb** *at 3.30 prompt:* exactly, precisely, sharp, on the dot, dead, punctually; informal bang on; N. Amer. informal on the button, on the nose.

**promptly** adverb **1** *William arrived promptly at 7.30:* punctually, on time; informal on the dot, bang on; Brit. informal spot on; N. Amer. informal on the button, on the nose. **2** *I expect the matter to be dealt with promptly:* without delay, straight/right away, at once, immediately, now, as soon as possible, quickly, swiftly, rapidly, speedily, fast; informal pronto, asap.
OPPOSITES late, slowly.

**prone** adjective **1** *softwood is prone to rotting:* susceptible, vulnerable, subject, open, liable, given, predisposed, likely, disposed, inclined, apt. **2** *his prone body:* lying face down, on one's stomach/front, lying flat, lying down, horizontal, prostrate.
OPPOSITES resistant, immune, upright.

**pronounce** verb **1** *his name is difficult to pronounce:* say, enunciate, utter, voice, sound, vocalize, get one's tongue round. **2** *the doctor pronounced her fit for work:* declare, proclaim, judge, rule, decree.

**pronounced** adjective noticeable, marked, strong, conspicuous, striking, distinct, prominent, unmistakable, obvious.
OPPOSITES slight.

**proof** noun evidence, verification, corroboration, demonstration, authentication, confirmation, certification, documentation.
**adjective** resistant, immune, unaffected, impervious.

**prop** noun **1** *the roof is held up by props:* pole, post, support, upright, brace, buttress, stay, strut. **2** *a prop for the economy:* mainstay, pillar, anchor, support, cornerstone.
**verb** *he propped his bike against the wall:* lean, rest, stand, balance.
■ **prop something up 1** *this post is propping the wall up:* hold up, shore up, buttress, support, brace, underpin. **2** *they prop up loss-making industries:* subsidize, underwrite, fund, finance.

**propaganda** noun information, promotion, advertising, publicity, disinformation; informal hype.

**propel** verb **1** *a boat propelled by oars:* move, power, push, drive. **2** *the impact propelled him into the street:* throw, thrust, toss, fling, hurl, pitch, send, shoot.

**proper** adjective **1** *he's not a proper scientist:* real, genuine, actual, true, bona fide; informal kosher. **2** *the proper channels:* right, correct, accepted, conventional, established, official, regular, acceptable, appropriate. **3** *they were terribly proper:* formal, conventional, correct, orthodox, polite, punctilious, respectable.
OPPOSITES fake, inappropriate, wrong, unconventional.

**property** noun **1** *lost property:*

a
b
c
d
e
f
g
h
i
j
k
l
m
n
o
**p**
q
r
s
t
u
v
w
x
y
z

possessions, belongings, things, effects, stuff, goods; informal gear. **2** *private property:* building(s), premises, house(s), land; N. Amer. real estate. **3** *healing properties:* quality, attribute, characteristic, feature, power, trait, hallmark.

**prophecy** noun prediction, forecast, prognostication, prognosis, divination.

**prophesy** verb predict, foretell, forecast, foresee, prognosticate.

**prophet, prophetess** noun forecaster, seer, soothsayer, fortune teller, clairvoyant, oracle.

**proportion** noun **1** *a proportion of the land:* part, portion, amount, quantity, bit, piece, percentage, fraction, section, segment, share. **2** *the proportion of water to alcohol:* ratio, distribution, relative amount/number, relationship. **3** *a sense of proportion:* balance, symmetry, harmony, correspondence, correlation, agreement. **4** *men of huge proportions:* size, dimensions, magnitude, measurements, mass, volume, bulk, expanse, extent.

**proportional, proportionate** adjective corresponding, comparable, in proportion, pro rata, commensurate, equivalent, consistent.
OPPOSITES disproportionate.

**proposal** noun scheme, plan, idea, project, programme, motion, proposition, suggestion, submission.

**propose** verb **1** *he proposed a solution:* put forward, suggest, submit, advance, offer, present, move, come up with. **2** *do you propose to go?* intend, mean,

plan, have in mind, aim. **3** *he proposed to her!* ask someone to marry you, ask for someone's hand in marriage; informal pop the question.
OPPOSITES withdraw.

**proposition** noun **1** *a business proposition:* proposal, scheme, plan, project, idea, programme. **2** *doing it for real is a very different proposition:* task, job, undertaking, venture, activity, affair.

**proprietor, proprietress** noun owner, possessor, holder, householder, master, mistress, landowner, landlord, landlady, shopkeeper.

**prosecute** verb charge, take to court, take legal action against, sue, try, bring to trial, put on trial, put in the dock, indict; N. Amer. impeach.
OPPOSITES defend, let off.

**prospect** noun **1** *there is little prospect of success:* likelihood, hope, expectation, chance, odds, probability, possibility, promise, lookout, fear, danger. **2** *her job prospects:* possibilities, potential, expectations, outlook. **3** *a daunting prospect:* vision, thought, idea, task, undertaking.
verb *prospecting for oil:* search, look, explore, survey, scout, hunt, dowse.

**prospective** adjective potential, possible, probable, likely, future, eventual, -to-be, soon-to-be, in the making, intending, aspiring, would-be.

**prospectus** noun brochure, syllabus, curriculum, catalogue, programme, list, schedule.

**prosper** verb flourish, thrive, do well, bloom, blossom, burgeon, progress, do all right for oneself, get ahead, get on

(in the world), be successful; informal go places.
OPPOSITES fail, flounder.

**prosperity** noun success, affluence, wealth, ease, plenty.
OPPOSITES hardship, failure.

**prosperous** adjective thriving, flourishing, successful, strong, vigorous, profitable, lucrative, expanding, booming, burgeoning, affluent, wealthy, rich, moneyed, well off, well-to-do; informal in the money.
OPPOSITES ailing, poor.

**prostitute** noun whore, sex worker, call girl, rent boy; informal working girl; Brit. informal tom; N. Amer. informal hooker, hustler.
verb *they prostituted their art:* betray, sacrifice, sell, sell out, debase, degrade, demean, devalue, cheapen, lower, shame, misuse.

**protect** verb keep safe, keep from harm, guard, defend, shield, save, safeguard, preserve, cushion, insulate, shelter, screen, keep, look after.
OPPOSITES expose, neglect, attack, harm.

**protection** noun 1 *protection against frost:* defence, security, safeguard, safety, sanctuary, shelter, refuge, immunity, indemnity. 2 *the protection of the Church:* safe keeping, care, charge, umbrella, guardianship, support, aegis, patronage. 3 *a good protection against noise:* barrier, buffer, shield, screen, cushion, bulwark, armour, insulation.

**protective** adjective 1 *protective clothing:* special, safety, thick, heavy, insulated, ...-proof, ...-resistant. 2 *he felt protective towards her:* solicitous, caring, defensive, paternal, maternal, overprotective, possessive, jealous.

**protector** noun 1 *a protector of the environment:* defender, preserver, guardian, champion, patron, custodian. 2 *ear protectors:* guard, shield, buffer, cushion, pad, screen.

**protest** noun 1 *a storm of protest:* objection, complaint, challenge, dissent, demurral, remonstration, fuss, outcry. 2 *the women staged a protest:* demonstration, rally, vigil, sit-in, occupation, work-to-rule, stoppage, strike, walkout, mutiny, picket, boycott; informal demo.
OPPOSITES support, approval.
verb 1 *residents protested at the plans:* object, express opposition, dissent, take issue, take a stand, put up a fight, take exception, complain, express disapproval, disagree, make a fuss, speak out; informal kick up a fuss. 2 *he protested his innocence:* insist on, maintain, assert, affirm, announce, proclaim, declare, profess.
OPPOSITES acquiesce, support, deny.

**protocol** noun etiquette, convention, formalities, custom, the rules, procedure, ritual, decorum, the done thing.

**prototype** noun original, master, template, pattern, sample.

**protracted** adjective prolonged, extended, long-drawn-out, lengthy, long.
OPPOSITES short.

**proud** adjective 1 *the proud parents:* pleased, glad, happy, delighted, thrilled, satisfied, gratified. 2 *a proud day:*

pleasing, gratifying, satisfying, cheering, heart-warming, happy, glorious. **3** *he is too proud to admit to being in the wrong:* arrogant, conceited, vain, self-important, full of oneself, overbearing, bumptious, presumptuous, overweening, haughty, high and mighty; informal big-headed, too big for one's boots, stuck-up.
OPPOSITES ashamed, shameful, humble, modest.

**prove** verb **1** *that proves I'm right:* show (to be true), demonstrate (the truth of), provide proof, substantiate, verify, validate, authenticate. **2** *the rumour proved to be correct:* turn out, be found.
OPPOSITES disprove.

**proverb** noun saying, adage, saw, maxim, axiom, motto, aphorism, epigram.

**provide** verb **1** *we will provide funds:* supply, give, furnish, come up with, dispense, produce, yield, deliver, donate, contribute; informal fork out, lay out. **2** *he was provided with tools:* equip, furnish, issue, supply, fit out, rig out, kit out, arm, provision; informal fix up. **3** *the test may provide the answer:* offer, present, afford, give, add, bring, yield, impart, reveal.
OPPOSITES refuse, withhold, deprive, neglect.
■ **provide for** feed, nurture, nourish, support, maintain, keep, sustain.

**provided, providing** conjunction if, on condition that, provided that, presuming (that), assuming (that), as long as, with/on the understanding that.

**provider** noun supplier, donor, giver, contributor, source.

**province** noun **1** *a province of the Roman Empire:* territory, region, state, department, canton, area, district, sector, zone, division. **2** (**the provinces**) the regions, the rest of the country, rural areas/districts, the countryside; informal the sticks, the middle of nowhere; N. Amer. informal the boondocks. **3** *that's outside my province, I'm afraid:* domain, area, department, responsibility, sphere, world, realm, field, discipline, territory; informal bailiwick.

**provincial** adjective **1** *the provincial government:* regional, state, territorial, district, local, county. **2** *provincial areas:* rural, country, rustic, small-town, outlying, backwoods, backwater; informal one-horse. **3** *they're so dull and provincial:* unsophisticated, narrow-minded, parochial, small-town, suburban, insular, inward-looking; N. Amer. informal corn-fed.
OPPOSITES national, metropolitan, cosmopolitan, sophisticated, broad-minded.

**provision** noun **1** *the provision of weapons to guerrillas:* supply, giving, donation, equipping, furnishing, distribution. **2** *limited provision for young children:* facilities, services, amenities, resource(s), arrangements, means, funds, assistance. **3** (**provisions**) *provisions for the trip:* supplies, food and drink, stores, groceries, foodstuff(s), rations. **4** *the provisions of the Act:* term, requirement, specification, stipulation.

a b c d e f g h i j k l m n o p q r s t u v w x y z

**provisional** adjective interim, temporary, transitional, changeover, stopgap, short-term, fill-in, acting, working.
OPPOSITES permanent, definite.

**provocation** noun goading, prodding, incitement, pressure, harassment, teasing, taunting, torment; informal hassle, aggravation.

**provocative** adjective annoying, irritating, maddening, galling, insulting, offensive, inflammatory, incendiary; informal aggravating.
OPPOSITES soothing, calming.

**provoke** verb 1 *the plan has provoked outrage:* arouse, produce, evoke, cause, give rise to, excite, spark off, touch off, kindle, generate, engender, instigate, result in, lead to, bring on, precipitate, prompt, trigger. 2 *he was provoked into replying:* goad, spur, prick, sting, prod, incite, rouse, stimulate. 3 *he's dangerous if provoked:* annoy, anger, enrage, irritate, madden, nettle; Brit. rub up the wrong way; informal aggravate, rile, needle, get/put someone's back up; Brit. informal wind up.
OPPOSITES allay, deter, pacify, appease.

**prowess** noun skill, expertise, mastery, ability, capability, capacity, talent, aptitude, dexterity, proficiency, finesse; informal know-how.
OPPOSITES inability, ineptitude.

**prowl** verb steal, slink, skulk, sneak, stalk, creep; informal snoop.

**proxy** noun deputy, representative, substitute, delegate, agent, surrogate, stand-in, go-between.

**prudent** adjective 1 *it is prudent to obtain consent:* wise, sensible, politic, judicious, shrewd, advisable. 2 *a prudent approach to borrowing:* cautious, careful, provident, far-sighted, judicious, shrewd, circumspect, thrifty, economical.
OPPOSITES unwise, reckless, extravagant.

**prune** verb 1 *I pruned the roses:* cut back, trim, clip, shear, shorten, thin, shape. 2 *staff numbers have been pruned:* reduce, cut (back/down), pare (down), slim down, trim, downsize, axe, shrink; informal slash.
OPPOSITES increase.

**psychiatrist** noun psychotherapist, psychoanalyst, analyst; informal shrink.

**psychic** adjective 1 *psychic powers:* supernatural, paranormal, other-worldly, metaphysical, extrasensory, magic(al), mystic(al), occult. 2 *I'm not psychic:* clairvoyant, telepathic.
OPPOSITES normal.
noun *she is a psychic:* clairvoyant, fortune teller, medium, spiritualist, telepath, mind-reader.

**psychological** adjective 1 *his psychological state:* mental, emotional, inner, cognitive. 2 *her pain was psychological:* (all) in the mind, psychosomatic, emotional, subjective, subconscious, imaginary, irrational.
OPPOSITES physical.

**psychology** noun *the psychology of the road user:* mind, thought processes, way of thinking, mentality, psyche, attitude(s), make-up, character,

a b c d e f g h i j k l m n o **p** q r s t u v w x y z

temperament; informal what makes someone tick.

**pub** noun (Brit.) bar, inn, tavern, hostelry; Brit. public house; Austral./NZ hotel; informal watering hole; Brit. informal local, boozer; N. Amer. historical saloon.

**public** adjective 1 *public affairs:* state, national, government, constitutional, civic, civil, official, social, municipal, community, nationalized. 2 *by public demand:* popular, general, common, communal, collective, shared, joint, universal, widespread. 3 *a public figure:* prominent, well known, important, leading, eminent, distinguished, celebrated, household, famous; N. Amer. major-league. 4 *public places:* open (to the public), communal, available, free, unrestricted, community. 5 *the news became public:* known, published, publicized, open, obvious.
OPPOSITES private, obscure, unknown, restricted, secret.
noun 1 *the British public:* people, citizens, subjects, electors, electorate, voters, taxpayers, residents, inhabitants, citizenry, population, populace, community, society, country, nation, everyone. 2 *his adoring public:* audience, spectators, followers, following, fans, devotees, admirers.

**publication** noun 1 *the author of this publication:* book, volume, title, opus, tome, newspaper, paper, magazine, periodical, newsletter, bulletin, journal, report. 2 *the publication of her new book:* issuing, publishing, printing, distribution, spreading,

appearance.

**publicity** noun 1 *the blaze of publicity:* public attention/ interest, media attention/ interest, exposure, glare, limelight. 2 *publicity should boost sales:* promotion, advertising, propaganda, boost, push; informal hype, ballyhoo, puff, build-up, plug.

**publish** verb 1 *we publish novels:* issue, bring out, produce, print. 2 *he ought to publish his views:* make known, make public, publicize, announce, broadcast, issue, put out, distribute, spread, promulgate, disseminate, circulate, air.

**pudding** noun dessert, sweet, last course; Brit. informal afters, pud.

**puff** noun 1 *a puff of wind:* gust, blast, flurry, rush, draught, waft, breeze, breath. 2 *he took a puff at his cigar:* pull; informal drag, toke.
verb 1 *he walked fast, puffing a little:* breathe heavily, pant, blow, gasp. 2 *she puffed at her cigarette:* smoke, draw on, drag on, suck at/on, inhale; informal toke on.

**pull** verb 1 *he pulled the box towards him:* tug, haul, drag, draw, tow, heave, jerk, wrench; informal yank. 2 *she pulled a muscle:* strain, sprain, wrench, tear. 3 *race day pulled big crowds:* attract, draw, bring in, pull in, lure, seduce, entice, tempt.
OPPOSITES push, repel.
noun 1 *give the chain a pull:* tug, jerk, heave; informal yank. 2 *she took a pull at her beer:* gulp, draught, drink, swallow, mouthful, slug; informal swig. 3 *a pull on a cigarette:* puff; informal

drag, toke. **4** *the pull of the theatre*: attraction, draw, lure, magnetism, fascination, appeal, allure.
■ **pull something off** achieve, fulfil, succeed in, accomplish, bring off, carry off, clinch, fix.
■ **pull out** withdraw, resign, leave, retire, step down, bow out, back out, give up; informal quit. ■ **pull through** get better, get well again, improve, recover, rally, come through, recuperate.

**pulp** noun **1** *he ground it into a pulp*: mush, mash, paste, purée, slop, slush, mulch. **2** *the sweet pulp on cocoa seeds*: flesh, marrow, meat.
verb *pulp the gooseberries*: mash, purée, cream, crush, press, liquidize.

**pulse** noun **1** *the pulse in her neck*: heartbeat, heart rate. **2** *the pulse of the engine*: rhythm, beat, tempo, pounding, throbbing, thudding, drumming. **3** *pulses of ultrasound*: burst, blast, surge.
verb *music pulsed through the building*: throb, pulsate, vibrate, beat, pound, thud, thump, drum, reverberate, echo.

**pump** verb **1** *they pumped air down the tube*: force, drive, push, inject, suck, draw. **2** *she pumped up the tyre*: inflate, blow up, fill up, swell, enlarge, distend, expand, dilate, puff up. **3** *blood was pumping from his leg*: spurt, spout, squirt, jet, surge, spew, gush, stream, flow, pour, spill, well, cascade.

**punch**[1] verb *Jim punched him in the face*: hit, strike, thump, jab, smash; informal sock, slug, biff, bop; Brit. informal stick one on, slosh; N. Amer. informal boff, bust; Austral./NZ informal quilt.
noun *a punch on the nose*: blow, hit, knock, thump, box, jab, clip; informal sock, slug, biff, bop; N. Amer. informal boff, bust.

**punch**[2] verb *he punched her ticket*: perforate, puncture, pierce, prick, hole, spike, skewer.

**punctual** adjective on time, prompt, on schedule, in (good) time; informal on the dot.
OPPOSITES late.

**punctuate** verb break up, interrupt, intersperse, pepper, sprinkle, scatter.

**puncture** noun **1** *the tyre developed a puncture*: hole, perforation, rupture, cut, gash, slit, leak. **2** *my car has a puncture*: flat tyre; informal flat.
verb *he punctured the balloon*: prick, pierce, stab, rupture, perforate, cut, slit, deflate.

**punish** verb **1** *they punished their children*: discipline, penalize, correct, sentence, teach someone a lesson; informal come down on (like a ton of bricks), have someone's guts for garters; dated chastise. **2** *higher charges would punish the poor*: disadvantage, handicap, hurt, penalize.

**punishing** adjective arduous, demanding, taxing, strenuous, rigorous, stressful, trying, heavy, difficult, tough, exhausting, tiring, gruelling.
OPPOSITES easy.

**punishment** noun penalty, sanction, penance, discipline, forfeit, sentence.

**punitive** adjective penal, disciplinary, corrective, retributive, retaliatory.

**puny** adjective **1** *a puny boy*: small, weak, feeble, slight, undersized, stunted; informal

weedy. **2** *their puny efforts:* pitiful, pitiable, miserable, sorry, meagre, paltry; informal pathetic, measly.
OPPOSITES sturdy, substantial.

**pupil** noun **1** *former pupils of the school:* student, scholar, schoolchild, schoolboy, schoolgirl. **2** *the guru's pupils:* disciple, follower, student, protégé, apprentice, trainee, novice.
OPPOSITES teacher.

**puppet** noun **1** *a show with puppets:* marionette, glove puppet, finger puppet. **2** *a puppet of the government:* pawn, tool, instrument, cat's paw, poodle, mouthpiece, stooge.

**purchase** verb *we purchased new software:* buy, acquire, obtain, pick up, procure, pay for, invest in; informal get hold of, score.
OPPOSITES sell.
noun **1** *he's happy with his purchase:* acquisition, buy, investment, order, bargain, shopping, goods. **2** *he could get no purchase on the wall:* grip, grasp, hold, foothold, toehold, anchorage, support, traction, leverage.
OPPOSITES sale.

**pure** adjective **1** *pure gold:* unadulterated, undiluted, sterling, solid, 100%. **2** *the air is so pure:* clean, clear, fresh, sparkling, unpolluted, uncontaminated, untainted. **3** *pure in body and mind:* virtuous, moral, good, righteous, honourable, reputable, wholesome, clean, honest, upright, upstanding, exemplary, chaste, decent, worthy, noble; informal squeaky clean. **4** *three hours of pure*

*magic:* sheer, utter, absolute, out-and-out, complete, total, perfect.
OPPOSITES adulterated, polluted, immoral, practical.

**purely** adverb entirely, wholly, exclusively, solely, only, just, merely.

**purge** verb **1** *this purges the system of impurities:* cleanse, clear, purify, rid, empty, strip, scour. **2** *the founders were purged from the firm:* remove, get rid of, eliminate, clear out, sweep out, expel, eject, evict, dismiss, sack, oust, axe, depose, root out, weed out.
noun removal, elimination, expulsion, ejection, exclusion, eviction, dismissal, sacking, ousting.

**purify** verb clean, cleanse, refine, decontaminate, filter, clear, freshen, deodorize, sanitize, disinfect, sterilize.

**purity** noun **1** *the purity of our tap water:* cleanness, freshness, cleanliness, wholesomeness. **2** *they sought purity in a foul world:* virtue, morality, goodness, righteousness, piety, honour, honesty, integrity, decency, innocence.

**purpose** noun **1** *the purpose of his visit:* motive, motivation, grounds, occasion, reason, point, basis, justification. **2** *their purpose was to subvert the economy:* intention, aim, object, objective, goal, plan, ambition, aspiration. **3** *the original purpose of the porch:* function, role, use. **4** *they started with some purpose:* determination, resolution, resolve, enthusiasm, ambition, motivation, commitment, conviction, dedication; informal get-up-and-go.

■ **on purpose** deliberately, intentionally, purposely, wilfully, knowingly, consciously.

**purposeful** adjective determined, resolute, steadfast, single-minded, committed.
OPPOSITES aimless.

**purposely** adverb deliberately, intentionally, on purpose, wilfully, knowingly, consciously.

**purse** noun 1 *the money fell out of her purse:* wallet, money bag; N. Amer. change purse, billfold. 2 (N. Amer.) *a woman's purse:* handbag, shoulder bag, clutch bag; N. Amer. pocketbook. 3 *the fight will net him a $75,000 purse:* prize, reward, winnings, stake(s).
verb *he pursed his lips:* press together, compress, tighten, pucker, pout.

**pursue** verb 1 *I pursued him down the garden:* follow, run after, chase, hunt, stalk, track, trail, hound. 2 *pursue the goal of political union:* strive for, work towards, seek, search for, aim at/for, aspire to. 3 *she pursued a political career:* engage in, be occupied in, practise, follow, conduct, ply, take up, undertake, carry on, continue, take further, stick with/at.
OPPOSITES avoid, shun.

**pursuit** noun 1 *the pursuit of profit:* striving for, quest after/for, search for. 2 *a worthwhile pursuit:* activity, hobby, pastime, diversion, recreation, amusement, occupation.

**push** verb 1 *she tried to push him away:* shove, thrust, propel, send, drive, force, prod, poke, nudge, elbow, shoulder,

sweep, ram. 2 *she pushed her way into the flat:* force, shove, thrust, squeeze, jostle, elbow, shoulder, bundle, hustle, work, inch. 3 *he pushed the panic button:* press, depress, hold down, squeeze, operate, activate. 4 *don't push her to join in:* urge, press, pressure, pressurize, force, coerce, nag; informal lean on, twist someone's arm.
OPPOSITES pull.

noun 1 *I felt a push in the back:* shove, thrust, nudge, bump, jolt, prod, poke. 2 *the army's eastward push:* advance, drive, thrust, charge, attack, assault, onslaught, onrush, offensive.

**put** verb 1 *she put the parcel on a chair:* place, set, lay, deposit, position, leave, plant; informal stick, dump, park, plonk, pop; N. Amer. informal plunk. 2 *she put it bluntly:* express, word, phrase, frame, formulate, render, convey, state.

■ **put something across/over** communicate, convey, get across/over, explain, make clear, spell out. ■ **put someone off** deter, discourage, dissuade, daunt, unnerve, intimidate, scare off; informal turn off. ■ **put something off** postpone, defer, delay, put back, adjourn, hold over, reschedule, shelve; N. Amer. table; informal put on ice, put on the back burner. ■ **put someone out 1** *Maria was put out by the slur:* annoy, anger, irritate, offend, displease, irk, gall, upset; informal rile, miff. 2 *I don't want to put you out:* inconvenience, trouble, bother, impose on. ■ **put something out 1** *firemen put out the blaze:* extinguish, quench, douse, smother, blow out, snuff out.

a
b
c
d
e
f
g
h
i
j
k
l
m
n
o
**p**
**q**
r
s
t
u
v
w
x
y
z

**2** *he put out a press release:* issue, publish, release, bring out, circulate, publicize, post. ■ **put someone up 1** *we can put him up for a few days:* accommodate, house, lodge, give someone a roof over their head. **2** *they put up a candidate:* nominate, propose, put forward, recommend. ■ **put something up 1** *the building was put up 100 years ago:* build, construct, erect, raise. **2** *she put up a poster:* display, pin up, stick up, hang up, post. **3** *he put up most of the funding:* provide, supply, furnish, give, contribute, donate, pledge, pay; informal cough up, shell out;

N. Amer. informal ante up, pony up. ■ **put up with** tolerate, take, stand (for), accept, stomach, swallow, endure, bear; informal abide, lump it; Brit. informal stick, be doing with; formal brook.

**puzzle** verb *her decision puzzled me:* baffle, perplex, bewilder, confuse, bemuse, mystify, nonplus; informal stump, beat. noun *the poem has always been a puzzle:* enigma, mystery, paradox, conundrum, poser, riddle, problem.

**puzzling** adjective baffling, perplexing, bewildering, confusing, complicated, unclear, mysterious, enigmatic. OPPOSITES clear.

# Qq

**quaint** adjective **1** *a quaint town:* picturesque, charming, sweet, attractive, old-fashioned, old-world; Brit. twee; N. Amer. cunning. **2** *quaint customs:* unusual, curious, eccentric, quirky, bizarre, whimsical, unconventional; informal offbeat. OPPOSITES ugly, ordinary.

**quake** verb shake, tremble, quiver, shudder, sway, rock, wobble, move, heave, convulse.

**qualification** noun **1** *a teaching qualification:* certificate, diploma, degree, licence, document, warrant. **2** *I can't accept it without qualification:* modification, limitation, reservation, stipulation, alteration, amendment, revision, moderation, mitigation, condition, proviso, caveat.

**qualified** adjective **1** *a qualified*

*engineer:* certified, certificated, chartered, licensed, professional. **2** *qualified approval:* limited, conditional, restricted, contingent, circumscribed, guarded, equivocal, modified, adapted, amended, adjusted, moderated, reduced.
OPPOSITES unqualified, wholehearted.

**qualify** verb **1** *I qualify for free travel:* be eligible, meet the requirements, be entitled to, be permitted to. **2** *they qualify as refugees:* count, be considered, be designated, be eligible. **3** *she qualified as a solicitor:* be certified, be licensed, pass, graduate, succeed. **4** *the course qualified them to teach:* authorize, empower, allow, permit, license. **5** *they qualified their findings:* modify, limit, restrict, make conditional, moderate, temper, modulate, mitigate.

**quality** noun 1 *a poor quality of signal:* standard, grade, class, calibre, condition, character, nature, form, rank, value, level. **2** *work of such quality:* excellence, superiority, merit, worth, value, virtue, calibre, distinction. **3** *her good qualities:* feature, trait, attribute, characteristic, point, aspect, facet, side, property.

**quantity** noun amount, total, aggregate, sum, quota, mass, weight, volume, bulk.

**quarrel** noun *they had a quarrel:* argument, disagreement, squabble, fight, dispute, wrangle, clash, altercation, feud; informal tiff, slanging match, run-in; Brit. informal row, bust-up.
OPPOSITES agreement, harmony.
verb *don't quarrel over it:* argue, fight, disagree, fall out, differ, be at odds, bicker, squabble, cross swords; Brit. informal row.
OPPOSITES agree, get on.
■ **quarrel with** *you can't quarrel with the verdict:* fault, criticize, object to, oppose, take exception to, attack, take issue with, impugn, contradict, dispute, controvert; informal knock; formal gainsay.

**quarry** noun prey, victim, object, goal, target, kill, game, prize.

**quash** verb 1 *he may quash the sentence:* cancel, reverse, rescind, repeal, revoke, retract, countermand, withdraw, overturn, overrule. **2** *we want to quash these rumours:* stop, put an end to, stamp out, crush, put down, check, curb, nip in the bud, squash, suppress, stifle.

OPPOSITES validate, encourage, perpetuate.

**queen** noun monarch, sovereign, ruler, head of state, Crown, Her Majesty.

**queer** adjective odd, strange, unusual, funny, peculiar, curious, bizarre, weird, uncanny, freakish, eerie, unnatural, abnormal, anomalous; informal spooky.
OPPOSITES normal.

**query** noun 1 *we can answer any queries:* question, enquiry. **2** *there was a query as to who owned the hotel:* doubt, uncertainty, question (mark), reservation.
verb 1 *'Why do that?' queried Isobel:* ask, enquire, question; Brit. informal quiz. **2** *folk may query his credentials:* challenge, question, dispute, doubt, have suspicions about, distrust.
OPPOSITES accept, trust.

**quest** noun 1 *their quest for her killer:* search, hunt, pursuance of. **2** *Sir Galahad's quest:* expedition, journey, voyage, trek, travels, odyssey, adventure, exploration, search, crusade, mission, pilgrimage.

**question** noun 1 *please answer my question:* enquiry, query, interrogation. **2** *there is no question that he is ill:* doubt, dispute, argument, debate, uncertainty, reservation. **3** *the political questions of the day:* issue, matter, topic, business, problem, concern, debate, argument, dispute, controversy.
OPPOSITES answer, certainty.
verb 1 *the magistrate questions the suspect:* interrogate, cross-examine, cross-question, quiz, interview, debrief, examine; informal grill, pump. **2** *she questioned his motives:* query,

challenge, dispute, cast aspersions on, doubt, suspect.
■ **out of the question** impossible, impracticable, unfeasible, unworkable, inconceivable, unimaginable, unrealizable, unsuitable; informal not on.

**questionable** adjective
suspicious, suspect, dubious, irregular, odd, strange, murky, dark, unsavoury, disreputable; informal funny, fishy, shady, iffy; Brit. informal dodgy.
OPPOSITES honest.

**questionnaire** noun question sheet, survey form, opinion poll, test, quiz.

**queue** noun row, column, file, chain, string, procession, waiting list; N. Amer. line, wait list.

**quick** adjective **1** *a quick worker:* fast, swift, rapid, speedy, brisk, smart, lightning, whirlwind, whistle-stop, breakneck; informal nippy, zippy. **2** *a quick look:* hasty, hurried, cursory, perfunctory, desultory, superficial, brief. **3** *a quick end to the recession:* sudden, instantaneous, instant, immediate, abrupt, precipitate. **4** *she isn't as quick as the others:* intelligent, bright, clever, gifted, able, astute, sharp-witted, smart, alert, sharp, perceptive; informal brainy, on the ball.
OPPOSITES slow, long.

**quicken** verb **1** *she quickened her pace:* speed up, accelerate, step up, hasten, hurry (up). **2** *the film quickened his interest in nature:* stimulate, excite, arouse, rouse, stir up, activate, whet, inspire, kindle.

**quickly** adverb **1** *he walked quickly:* fast, swiftly, briskly,

rapidly, speedily, at full tilt, at a gallop, at the double, post-haste, hotfoot; informal like (greased) lightning, hell for leather, like blazes, like the wind; Brit. informal like the clappers, like billy-o; N. Amer. informal lickety-split. **2** *you'd better leave quickly:* immediately, directly, at once, straight away, right away, instantly, forthwith; N. Amer. momentarily; informal like a shot, asap, p.d.q., pronto. **3** *he quickly inspected it:* briefly, fleetingly, briskly, hastily, hurriedly, cursorily, perfunctorily, superficially, desultorily.

**quiet** adjective **1** *the whole pub went quiet:* silent, still, hushed, noiseless, soundless, mute, dumb, speechless. **2** *a quiet voice:* soft, low, muted, muffled, faint, hushed, whispered, suppressed. **3** *a quiet village:* peaceful, sleepy, tranquil, calm, still, restful.
OPPOSITES loud, busy.
noun *the quiet of the countryside:* silence, still, hush, restfulness, calm, tranquillity, serenity, peace.

**quietly** adverb **1** *she read quietly:* silently, noiselessly, soundlessly, inaudibly. **2** *he spoke quietly:* softly, faintly, in a low voice, in a whisper, in a murmur, under one's breath, in an undertone.
OPPOSITES out loud, loudly.

**quilt** noun duvet, cover(s); Brit. eiderdown; N. Amer. comforter, puff; Austral. trademark Doona.

**quirk** noun **1** *they all know his quirks:* idiosyncrasy, peculiarity, oddity, eccentricity, foible, whim, vagary, habit, characteristic, trait, fad. **2** *a quirk of fate:* chance, fluke, freak, anomaly, twist.

**quirky** adjective eccentric, idiosyncratic, unconventional, unorthodox, unusual, strange, bizarre, peculiar, zany; informal wacky, way-out, offbeat.
OPPOSITES conventional.

**quit** verb **1** *he quit the office at 12.30:* leave, vacate, exit, depart from. **2** (informal) *he quit his job:* resign from, leave, give up, hand in one's notice; informal chuck, pack in. **3** (informal) *quit living in the past:* give up, stop, discontinue, drop, abandon, abstain from; informal pack in, leave off.
OPPOSITES arrive at, continue, start.

**quite** adverb **1** *two quite different types:* completely, entirely, totally, wholly, absolutely, utterly, thoroughly, altogether. **2** *red hair was quite common:* fairly, rather, somewhat, relatively, comparatively, moderately, reasonably; informal pretty.
OPPOSITES slightly, not at all.

**quiz** noun competition, test of knowledge.
verb *a man was quizzed by police:* question, interrogate, cross-examine, cross-question, interview; informal grill, pump.

**quota** noun share, allocation, allowance, ration, portion, slice; Brit. informal whack.

**quotation** noun **1** *a quotation from Dryden:* extract, quote, citation, excerpt, passage; N. Amer. cite. **2** *a quotation for the work:* estimate, quote, price, tender, bid, costing.

**quote** verb **1** *he quoted from the book:* recite, repeat, reproduce, retell, echo. **2** *she quoted one case in which a girl died:* mention, cite, refer to, name, instance, allude to, point out.
noun. See **QUOTATION** senses 1, 2.

# Rr

**race**¹ noun **1** *Dave won the race:* contest, competition, event, fixture, heat, trial(s). **2** *the race for naval domination:* competition, rivalry, contention, quest.
verb **1** *he will race in the final:* compete, contend, run. **2** *Claire raced after him:* hurry, dash, rush, run, sprint, bolt, charge, shoot, hurtle, hare, fly, speed; informal tear, belt.

**race**² noun **1** *pupils of different races:* ethnic group, racial type, origin, stock, blood, tribe. **2** *a bloodthirsty race:* people, nation.

**racial** adjective ethnic, ethnological, race-related, cultural, national, tribal, genetic.

**rack** noun *the boots live on that rack:* frame, framework, stand, holder, trestle, support, shelf.
verb *he was racked with guilt:* torment, afflict, torture, agonize, harrow, plague, persecute, trouble, worry.

**racket** noun **1** noise, din, hubbub, clamour, uproar, tumult, commotion, rumpus; informal hullabaloo; Brit. informal row. **2** (informal) *a gold-smuggling racket:* fraud, swindle, sharp practice; informal game, scam, rip-off.

**radiate** verb 1 *stars radiate energy:* emit, give off, discharge, diffuse, scatter, shed, cast. 2 *light radiated from the hall:* shine, beam, emanate, pour. 3 *four spokes radiate from the hub:* fan out, spread out, branch out/off, extend, issue.

**radical** adjective 1 *radical reform:* thorough, complete, total, comprehensive, exhaustive, sweeping, far-reaching, wide-ranging, extensive, profound, major. 2 *radical differences between the two theories:* fundamental, basic, essential, quintessential, structural, deep-seated. 3 *a radical political movement:* revolutionary, progressive, reformist, revisionist, progressivist, extreme, fanatical, militant. OPPOSITES superficial, minor, conservative.

**rage** noun 1 *his rage is due to frustration:* fury, anger, wrath, outrage, indignation, temper, spleen, resentment, pique, annoyance, vexation, displeasure; informal grump, strop. 2 *the current rage for DIY:* craze, passion, fashion, taste, trend, vogue, fad, mania; informal thing.
verb *she raged silently:* be angry, be furious, be enraged, be incensed, seethe, be beside oneself, rave, storm, fume, spit; informal be livid, be wild, be steamed up.

**ragged** adjective 1 *ragged jeans:* tattered, torn, ripped, frayed, worn (out), threadbare, scruffy, shabby; informal tatty. 2 *a ragged coastline:* jagged, craggy, rugged, uneven, rough, irregular, indented. OPPOSITES new, smart, sound, smooth.

**raid** noun 1 *the raid on Dieppe:* attack, assault, descent, blitz, incursion, sortie, onslaught, storming. 2 *a raid on a shop:* robbery, burglary, hold-up, break-in, ram raid; informal smash-and-grab, stick-up; N. Amer. informal heist. 3 *a police raid:* swoop, search; N. Amer. informal bust, takedown.
verb 1 *they raided shipping in the harbour:* attack, assault, set upon, descend on, swoop on, storm. 2 *armed men raided the store:* rob, hold up, break into, plunder, steal from, pillage, loot, ransack; informal stick up. 3 *homes were raided by police:* search, swoop on; N. Amer. informal bust.

**raider** noun robber, burglar, thief, housebreaker, plunderer, pillager, looter, marauder, attacker, assailant, invader.

**railing** noun fence, fencing, rail(s), palisade, balustrade, banister.

**rainy** adjective wet, showery, drizzly, damp, inclement. OPPOSITES dry, fine.

**raise** verb 1 *he raised a hand:* lift (up), hold aloft, elevate, uplift, hoist, haul up, hitch up; Brit. informal hoick up. 2 *they raised prices:* increase, put up, push up, up, mark up, inflate; informal hike (up), jack up, bump up. 3 *he raised his voice:* amplify, louden, magnify, intensify, boost, lift, increase. 4 *how will you raise the money?* get, obtain, acquire, accumulate, amass, collect, fetch, net, make. 5 *he raised several objections:* bring up, air, present, table, propose, submit, advance,

suggest, put forward. **6** *the disaster raised doubts about safety:* give rise to, occasion, cause, produce, engender, elicit, create, result in, lead to, prompt. **7** *most parents raise their children well:* bring up, rear, nurture. **8** *he raised cattle:* breed, rear, nurture, keep, tend, farm, produce.
OPPOSITES lower, reduce, demolish.

**rake** verb **1** *he raked the leaves into a pile:* scrape, collect, gather. **2** *she raked the gravel:* smooth (out), level, even out, flatten, comb. **3** *I raked through my pockets:* rummage, search, hunt, sift, rifle.

**rally** verb **1** *the troops rallied and held their ground:* regroup, reassemble, re-form, reunite. **2** *share prices rallied:* recover, improve, get better, pick up, revive, bounce back, perk up, look up, turn a corner.
OPPOSITES disperse, slump.
noun **1** *a rally in support of the strike:* (mass) meeting, gathering, assembly, demonstration, (protest) march; informal demo. **2** *a rally in oil prices:* recovery, upturn, improvement, comeback, resurgence.
OPPOSITES slump.

**ram** verb **1** *he rammed his sword into its sheath:* force, thrust, plunge, stab, push, sink, dig, stick, cram, jam, stuff. **2** *a van rammed the car:* hit, strike, crash into, collide with, impact, smash into, butt.

**ramble** verb **1** *we rambled around the lanes:* walk, hike, tramp, trek, backpack. **2** *she does ramble on:* chatter, babble, prattle, blather, gabble, jabber, twitter, rattle; Brit. informal witter,

chunter, rabbit.

**ramp** noun slope, bank, incline, gradient, rise, drop.

**rampage** verb riot, run amok, go berserk, storm, charge, tear.
■ go on the rampage riot, go berserk, get out of control, run amok; N. Amer. informal go postal.

**rampant** adjective uncontrolled, unrestrained, unchecked, unbridled, out of control, out of hand, widespread, rife, spreading.
OPPOSITES controlled.

**random** adjective unsystematic, unmethodical, arbitrary, unplanned, chance, casual, indiscriminate, non-specific, haphazard, stray, erratic.
OPPOSITES systematic, deliberate.
■ at random unsystematically, arbitrarily, randomly, unmethodically, haphazardly.

**range** noun **1** *his range of vision:* extent, limit, reach, span, scope, compass, sweep, area, field, orbit, ambit, horizon, latitude. **2** *a range of mountains:* row, chain, sierra, ridge, massif. **3** *a range of foods:* assortment, variety, diversity, mixture, collection, array, selection, choice.
verb **1** *charges range from 1% to 5%:* vary, fluctuate, differ, extend, stretch, reach, go, run, cover. **2** *they ranged over the steppes:* roam, wander, travel, journey, rove, traverse, walk, hike, trek.

**rank**[1] noun **1** *he was elevated to ministerial rank:* position, level, grade, echelon, class, status, standing. **2** *a family of rank:* high standing, blue blood, high birth, nobility, aristocracy. **3** *a rank of riflemen:* row, line, file, column, string, train, procession.

**verb 1** *the plant is ranked as endangered:* classify, class, categorize, rate, grade, bracket, group, designate, list. **2** *tulips were ranked like guardsmen:* line up, align, order, arrange, dispose, set out, array, range.

**rank²** adjective **1** *rank vegetation:* abundant, lush, luxuriant, dense, profuse, vigorous, overgrown; informal jungly. **2** *a rank smell:* offensive, nasty, revolting, sickening, obnoxious, foul, fetid, high, rancid, putrid; Brit. informal pongy, humming. **3** *rank stupidity:* downright, utter, out-and-out, absolute, complete, sheer, blatant, arrant, thorough, unqualified.
OPPOSITES sparse, pleasant.

**ransom** noun pay-off, payment, sum, price.

**rant** verb shout, sound off, hold forth, go on, fulminate, spout, bluster; informal mouth off.

**rap** verb hit, knock, strike, smack, bang; informal whack, thwack, bash, wallop.

**rapid** adjective quick, fast, swift, speedy, express, brisk, lightning, meteoric, whirlwind, sudden, instantaneous, instant, immediate.
OPPOSITES slow.

**rare** adjective **1** *rare moments of privacy:* infrequent, scarce, sparse, few and far between, occasional, limited, odd, isolated, unaccustomed. **2** *rare stamps:* unusual, recherché, uncommon, thin on the ground, like gold dust, unfamiliar, atypical. **3** *a man of rare talent:* exceptional, outstanding, unparalleled, peerless, matchless, unique, unrivalled.
OPPOSITES common,

commonplace.

**rarely** adverb seldom, infrequently, hardly (ever), scarcely.
OPPOSITES often.

**raring** adjective eager, keen, enthusiastic, impatient, longing, desperate; informal dying, itching, gagging.

**rarity** noun **1** *the rarity of earthquakes in the UK:* infrequency, scarcity. **2** *this book is a rarity:* curiosity, oddity, collector's item, rare bird, wonder, nonpareil, one of a kind; Brit. informal one-off.

**rash¹** noun **1** *he broke out in a rash:* spots, eruption, nettlerash, hives. **2** *a rash of articles in the press:* series, succession, spate, wave, flood, deluge, torrent, outbreak, epidemic, flurry.

**rash²** adjective reckless, impulsive, impetuous, hasty, foolhardy, incautious, precipitate, careless, heedless, thoughtless, imprudent, foolish.
OPPOSITES prudent.

**rate** noun **1** *a fixed rate of interest:* percentage, ratio, proportion, scale, standard. **2** *an hourly rate of £30:* charge, price, cost, tariff, fare, fee, remuneration, payment. **3** *the rate of change:* speed, pace, tempo, velocity.
**verb 1** *they rated their ability at driving:* assess, evaluate, appraise, judge, weigh up, estimate, gauge. **2** *he rated only a brief mention:* merit, deserve, warrant, be worthy of.
■ **at any rate** in any case, anyhow, anyway, in any event, come what may.

**rather** adverb **1** *I'd rather you went:* sooner, by preference, by choice. **2** *it's rather complicated:* quite, a bit, a little, fairly, slightly, somewhat, relatively, comparatively; informal pretty. **3** *she seemed sad rather than angry:* more, as opposed to, instead of.

**ratify** verb confirm, approve, sanction, endorse, agree to, accept, uphold, authorize, formalize, sign.
OPPOSITES reject.

**rating** noun grade, classification, ranking, position, category, assessment, evaluation, mark, score.

**ratio** noun proportion, relationship, rate, percentage, fraction, correlation.

**ration** noun **1** *a daily ration of chocolate:* allowance, allocation, quota, share, portion, helping. **2** *the garrison ran out of rations:* supplies, provisions, food, stores.
verb *fuel supplies were rationed:* control, limit, restrict, conserve.

**rational** adjective logical, reasoned, sensible, reasonable, realistic, cogent, intelligent, shrewd, common-sense, sane, sound.
OPPOSITES irrational.

**rationale** noun reason(s), thinking, logic, grounds, sense.

**rattle** verb **1** *hailstones rattled against the window:* clatter, patter, clink, clunk. **2** *he rattled some coins:* jingle, jangle, clink, tinkle. **3** *the government was rattled by the strike:* unnerve, disconcert, disturb, fluster, shake, perturb, throw; informal faze.

**ravage** verb lay waste, devastate, ruin, destroy, wreak havoc on.

**rave** verb **1** *I raved and swore at them:* rant, rage, lose one's temper, storm, fume, shout; informal fly off the handle, hit the roof; Brit. informal go spare; N. Amer. informal flip one's wig. **2** *he raved about her talent:* enthuse, go into raptures, wax lyrical, rhapsodize, sing the praises of, acclaim, eulogize, extol; N. Amer. informal ballyhoo.
OPPOSITES criticize.

**raw** adjective **1** *raw carrot:* uncooked, fresh, natural. **2** *raw materials:* unprocessed, untreated, unrefined, crude, natural. **3** *raw recruits:* inexperienced, new, untrained, untried, untested, callow, green. **4** *his skin is raw:* sore, red, painful, tender, chafed.
OPPOSITES cooked, processed, experienced, sound.

**ray** noun beam, shaft, stream, streak, flash, glimmer, flicker, spark.

**reach** verb **1** *Travis reached out a hand:* extend, stretch, outstretch, thrust, stick, hold. **2** *she reached Helen's house:* arrive at, get to, come to, end up at. **3** *the temperature reached 94 degrees:* attain, get to, rise to, fall to, sink to, drop to; informal hit. **4** *the leaders reached an agreement:* achieve, work out, draw up, put together, negotiate, thrash out, hammer out. **5** *I have been trying to reach you all day:* contact, get in touch with, get through to, get, speak to; informal get hold of.
noun **1** *Bobby moved out of her reach:* grasp, range, stretch. **2** *small goals within your reach:* capabilities, capacity. **3** *beyond the reach of the law:* jurisdiction, authority, influence, power, scope, range,

compass, ambit.

**react** verb respond, act in response, reply, answer, behave.

**reaction** noun 1 *his reaction bewildered her:* response, answer, reply, rejoinder, retort, riposte; informal comeback. 2 *a reaction against modernism:* backlash, counteraction.

**reactionary** adjective *a reactionary policy:* right-wing, conservative, traditionalist, conventional.
OPPOSITES radical, progressive.
noun *an extreme reactionary:* right-winger, conservative, traditionalist.
OPPOSITES radical.

**read** verb 1 *he was reading the newspaper:* peruse, study, scrutinize, look through, pore over, run one's eye over, cast an eye over, leaf through, scan. 2 *he read the letter to me:* read out/aloud, recite, declaim. 3 *I can't read my writing:* understand, make out, make sense of, interpret, decipher.

**readily** adverb 1 *Durkin readily offered to drive:* willingly, unhesitatingly, ungrudgingly, gladly, happily, eagerly. 2 *the island is readily accessible:* easily, without difficulty.
OPPOSITES reluctantly, with difficulty.

**readiness** noun 1 *their readiness to accept change:* willingness, eagerness, keenness, enthusiasm. 2 *a state of readiness:* preparedness.
■ **in readiness** (at the) ready, available, on hand, accessible, handy.

**reading** noun 1 *a cursory reading of the page:* perusal, study, scanning, browse, look, glance, leaf. 2 *a man of wide reading:* learning, scholarship,

education, erudition. 3 *a poetry reading:* recital, recitation, performance. 4 *a Bible reading:* lesson, passage, excerpt. 5 *my reading of the situation:* interpretation, understanding, explanation, analysis, construction.

**ready** adjective 1 *are you ready?* prepared, all set, organized, primed; informal fit, psyched up, geared up. 2 *everything is ready:* completed, finished, prepared, organized, done, arranged, fixed. 3 *he's always ready to help:* willing, prepared, pleased, inclined, disposed, eager, keen, happy, glad; informal game. 4 *a ready supply of food:* (easily) available, accessible, handy, close/near at hand, to/ on hand, convenient, within reach, near, at one's fingertips. 5 *a ready answer:* prompt, quick, swift, speedy, fast, immediate, unhesitating, clever, sharp, astute, shrewd, keen, perceptive, discerning.
verb prepare, organize, gear up; informal psych up.

**real** adjective 1 *based on real events:* actual, true, non-fictional, factual, historical, material, physical, tangible, concrete. 2 *real gold:* genuine, authentic, bona fide; informal pukka, kosher. 3 *tears of real grief:* sincere, genuine, true, unfeigned, heartfelt. 4 *a real man:* proper, true; informal regular. 5 *you're a real idiot:* complete, utter, thorough, absolute, total, prize, perfect; Brit. informal right, proper.
OPPOSITES imaginary, imitation.

**realism** noun 1 *optimism tinged with realism:* pragmatism, practicality, common sense, level-headedness. 2 *a degree of*

*realism:* **authenticity**, accuracy, fidelity, verisimilitude, truthfulness.
OPPOSITES fancy, inauthenticity.

**realistic** adjective **1** *you've got to be realistic:* **practical**, pragmatic, matter-of-fact, down-to-earth, sensible, commonsensical, rational, level-headed; informal no-nonsense. **2** *a realistic aim:* **achievable**, attainable, feasible, practicable, reasonable, sensible, workable; informal doable. **3** *a realistic portrayal of war:* **authentic**, accurate, true to life, lifelike, truthful, faithful, natural, naturalistic.
OPPOSITES idealistic, impracticable, inauthentic.

**reality** noun **1** *distinguishing fantasy from reality:* **the real world**, real life, actuality, truth. **2** *the harsh realities of life:* **fact**, actuality, truth. **3** *the reality of the detail:* **authenticity**, verisimilitude, fidelity, truthfulness, accuracy.
OPPOSITES fantasy, inaccuracy.

**realization** noun **1** *a growing realization of the danger:* **awareness**, understanding, comprehension, consciousness, appreciation, recognition, discernment. **2** *the realization of our dreams:* **fulfilment**, achievement, accomplishment, attainment.

**realize** verb **1** *he suddenly realized what he meant:* **register**, perceive, understand, grasp, recognize; informal tumble to; Brit. informal twig. **2** *they realized their dream:* **fulfil**, achieve, accomplish, make happen, bring to fruition, bring about/off. **3** *the company realized significant profits:* **make**, clear, gain, earn, return, produce. **4** *the goods realized £30:* be sold for, fetch, go for, make, net.

**really** adverb **1** *he is really very wealthy:* **in (actual) fact**, actually, in reality, in truth. **2** *he really likes her:* **genuinely**, truly, certainly, honestly, undoubtedly, unquestionably.

**realm** noun **1** *peace in the realm:* **kingdom**, country, land, dominion, nation. **2** *the realm of academia:* **domain**, sphere, area, field, world, province, territory.

**reap** verb **1** *the corn was reaped:* **harvest**, cut, pick, gather, garner. **2** *reaping the benefits:* **receive**, obtain, get, derive, acquire, secure, realize.

**rear**[1] noun **1** *the rear of the building:* **back (part)**, hind part; Nautical stern. **2** *the rear of the queue:* **end**, tail (end), back (end).
OPPOSITES front, bow, head.
adjective *the rear bumper:* **back**, end, rearmost, hind, last.
OPPOSITES front.

**rear**[2] verb **1** *I was reared in Newcastle:* **bring up**, care for, look after, nurture; N. Amer. raise. **2** *he reared cattle:* **breed**, raise, keep. **3** *laboratory-reared plants:* **grow**, cultivate. **4** *houses reared up on either side:* **rise**, tower, soar, loom.

**reason** noun **1** *the main reason for his decision:* **cause**, ground(s), basis, rationale, motive, explanation, justification, defence, vindication, excuse. **2** *postmodern voices railing against reason:* **rationality**, logic, cognition. **3** *he was losing his reason:* **sanity**, mind, mental faculties, senses, wits; informal marbles.

verb *Scott reasoned that Annabel might be ill:* calculate, conclude, reckon, think, judge, deduce, infer, surmise; informal figure.

■ **reason something out** work out, think through, make sense of, get to the bottom of, puzzle out; informal figure out. ■ **reason with** talk round, bring round, persuade, prevail on, convince.

**reasonable** adjective **1** *a reasonable explanation:* sensible, rational, logical, fair, just, equitable, intelligent, wise, level-headed, practical, realistic, sound, valid, commonsensical, tenable, plausible, credible, believable. **2** *take all reasonable precautions:* practicable, sensible, appropriate, suitable. **3** *cars in reasonable condition:* fairly good, acceptable, satisfactory, average, adequate, fair, tolerable, passable; informal OK. **4** *reasonable prices:* inexpensive, affordable, moderate, low, cheap, budget, bargain.

**reassure** verb put someone's mind at rest, encourage, hearten, buoy up, cheer up, comfort, soothe.
OPPOSITES alarm.

**rebate** noun partial refund, partial repayment, discount, deduction, reduction.

**rebel** noun **1** *the rebels took control of the capital:* revolutionary, insurgent, insurrectionist, mutineer, guerrilla, terrorist, freedom fighter. **2** *the concept of the artist as a rebel:* nonconformist, dissenter, dissident, maverick.
OPPOSITES loyalist, conformist.
verb *the citizens rebelled:* revolt,

mutiny, riot, rise up, take up arms.
OPPOSITES comply.
adjective **1** *rebel troops:* rebellious, insurgent, revolutionary, mutinous. **2** *rebel MPs:* defiant, disobedient, insubordinate, subversive, rebellious, nonconformist, maverick.
OPPOSITES loyal, compliant.
■ **rebel against** defy, disobey, kick against, challenge, oppose, resist.

**rebellion** noun **1** *troops suppressed the rebellion:* revolt, uprising, insurrection, mutiny, revolution, insurgence. **2** *an act of rebellion:* defiance, disobedience, insubordination, subversion, resistance.
OPPOSITES compliance.

**rebellious** adjective **1** *rebellious troops:* rebel, insurgent, mutinous, revolutionary. **2** *a rebellious adolescent:* defiant, disobedient, insubordinate, unruly, mutinous, obstreperous, recalcitrant, intractable; Brit. informal bolshie.
OPPOSITES loyal, compliant.

**rebound** verb **1** *the ball rebounded:* bounce (back), spring back, ricochet, boomerang. **2** *Thomas's tactics rebounded on him:* backfire, boomerang.

**rebuff** verb *his offer was rebuffed:* reject, turn down, spurn, refuse, decline, snub, slight, dismiss, brush off.
OPPOSITES accept.
noun *for fear of a rebuff:* rejection, snub, slight, refusal, spurning; informal brush-off, kick in the teeth, slap in the face.
OPPOSITES acceptance.

**rebuke** verb *she never rebuked him:* reprimand, reproach,

scold, admonish; informal tell off; Brit. informal tick off; N. Amer. informal chew out.
OPPOSITES praise.
noun *a severe rebuke:* reprimand, reproach, scolding, admonition; informal telling-off; Brit. informal ticking-off.
OPPOSITES praise.

**recall** verb **1** *he recalled his student days:* remember, recollect, call to mind, think back on/to, reminisce about. **2** *their exploits recall the days of chivalry:* remind someone of, bring to mind, call up, conjure up, evoke. **3** *the ambassador was recalled:* call back, order home, withdraw.
OPPOSITES forget, post.
noun **1** *their recall of dreams:* recollection, remembrance, memory. **2** *the recall of the ambassador:* calling back, ordering home, withdrawal.

**recede** verb **1** *the waters receded:* retreat, go back/down/away, withdraw, ebb, subside, abate, return, retire. **2** *fears of violence have receded:* diminish, lessen, dwindle, fade, abate, subside.
OPPOSITES advance, grow.

**receipt** noun **1** *the receipt of a letter:* receiving, getting, obtaining, gaining. **2** *make sure you get a receipt:* proof of purchase, sales ticket, till receipt, acknowledgement.

**receive** verb **1** *Tony received an award:* be given, be presented with, be awarded, be sent, be told, hear, collect, get, obtain, gain, acquire, be paid. **2** *he received her suggestion with a lack of interest:* hear, listen to, respond to, react to. **3** *she received an injury:* experience, sustain, undergo, meet with,

suffer, bear.
OPPOSITES give, send, inflict.

**recent** adjective new, the latest, current, fresh, modern, late, contemporary, up to date, up to the minute.
OPPOSITES old.

**recently** adverb not long ago, a little while back, just now, newly, freshly, of late, lately, latterly.

**reception** noun **1** *a chilly reception:* response, reaction, treatment, welcome. **2** *a wedding reception:* party, function, social occasion, celebration, get-together, gathering, soirée; N. Amer. levee; informal do.

**recess** noun **1** *two recesses fitted with bookshelves:* alcove, bay, niche, nook, corner. **2** *the Christmas recess:* break, adjournment, interlude, interval, rest, holiday, vacation.

**recession** noun downturn, depression, slump, slowdown.
OPPOSITES boom.

**recipe** noun *a recipe for success:* formula, prescription, blueprint.

**recital** noun **1** *a piano recital:* performance, concert, rendering, recitation, reading. **2** *her recital of Adam's failures:* report, account, listing, catalogue, litany.

**recite** verb **1** *he began to recite the Koran:* quote, say, speak, read aloud, declaim, deliver, render. **2** *Sir John recited the facts:* recount, list, detail, reel off, relate, enumerate.

**reckless** adjective rash, careless, thoughtless, heedless, precipitate, impetuous, impulsive, irresponsible, foolhardy.
OPPOSITES cautious.

a
b
c
d
e
f
g
h
i
j
k
l
m
n
o
p
q
r
s
t
u
v
w
x
y
z

a
b
c
d
e
f
g
h
i
j
k
l
m
n
o
p
q
**r**
s
t
u
v
w
x
y
z

**reckon** verb 1 *the cost was reckoned at £60:* calculate, compute, work out, figure, count (up), add up, total; Brit. tot up. 2 *Anselm reckoned Hugh among his friends:* include, count, regard as, look on as. 3 *it was reckoned a failure:* regard as, consider, judge, think of as, deem, rate, gauge, count.
■ **reckon on/with** take into account, take into consideration, bargain for/on, anticipate, foresee, be prepared for, consider.

**reckoning** noun calculation, estimation, computation, working out, addition, count.

**reclaim** verb 1 *expenses can be reclaimed:* get back, claim back, recover, retrieve, recoup. 2 *Henrietta had reclaimed him from a life of vice:* save, rescue, redeem, salvage.

**recline** verb lie (down/back), lean back, relax, loll, lounge, sprawl, stretch out.

**recognition** noun 1 *there was no sign of recognition on his face:* identification, recollection, remembrance. 2 *his recognition of his lack of experience:* acknowledgement, acceptance, admission, confession. 3 *you deserve recognition for your work:* appreciation, gratitude, thanks, congratulations, credit, commendation, acclaim, acknowledgement.

**recognize** verb 1 *Hannah recognized him at once:* identify, place, know, put a name to, remember, recall, recollect; Scottish & N. English ken. 2 *they recognized Alan's ability:* acknowledge, accept, admit, concede, confess, realize. 3 *the Trust recognized their hard work:* pay tribute to, appreciate, be grateful for, acclaim, commend.

**recollect** verb remember, recall, call to mind, think of, think back to, reminisce about. OPPOSITES forget.

**recollection** noun memory, recall, remembrance, impression, reminiscence.

**recommend** verb 1 *his former employer recommended him:* advocate, endorse, commend, suggest, put forward, propose, nominate, put up, speak favourably of, put in a good word for, vouch for; informal plug. 2 *the committee recommended a cautious approach:* advise, counsel, urge, exhort, enjoin, prescribe, argue for, back, support. OPPOSITES advise against.

**recommendation** noun 1 *the adviser's recommendations:* advice, counsel, guidance, suggestion, proposal. 2 *a personal recommendation:* commendation, endorsement, good word, testimonial, tip; informal plug.

**reconsider** verb rethink, review, revise, re-evaluate, reassess, have second thoughts, change one's mind.

**reconstruct** verb 1 *the building had to be reconstructed:* rebuild, recreate, remake, restore, reassemble. 2 *reconstructing events:* recreate, piece together, re-enact.

**record** noun 1 *written records:* account, document, data, file, dossier, evidence, report, annals, archive, chronicle, minutes, transactions, transcript, certificate, deed, register, log.

**2** *listening to records:* album, vinyl; dated LP, single. **3** *a good attendance record:* previous conduct, previous performance, history, reputation. **4** *a new British record:* best performance, highest achievement, best time, fastest time.

**verb 1** *the doctor recorded her blood pressure:* write down, take down, note, jot down, put down on paper, document, enter, minute, register, log. **2** *the thermometer recorded a high temperature:* indicate, register, show, display. **3** *the recital was recorded live:* capture on film/tape/disk, film, photograph, tape, tape-record, video-record, videotape.

**recount** verb tell, relate, narrate, describe, report, relay, convey, communicate, impart.

**recover** verb **1** *he's recovering from a heart attack:* get better, improve, recuperate, convalesce, be on the mend, respond to treatment, heal, bounce back. **2** *later, shares recovered:* rally, improve, pick up, rebound, bounce back. **3** *the stolen material has been recovered:* retrieve, regain, get back, recoup, reclaim, repossess. **4** *gold coins recovered from a wreck:* salvage, save, rescue, retrieve. OPPOSITES deteriorate, lose.

**recovery** noun **1** *her recovery may be slow:* improvement, recuperation, convalescence, rally, mend. **2** *the recovery of stolen goods:* retrieval, repossession, reclamation. OPPOSITES relapse, loss.

**recreation** noun **1** *she cycles for recreation:* pleasure, leisure, relaxation, fun, enjoyment, entertainment, amusement. **2** *his favourite recreations:* pastime, hobby, leisure activity. OPPOSITES work.

**recruit** verb **1** *more soldiers were recruited:* enlist, call up, conscript; US draft. **2** *the king recruited an army:* muster, form, raise, mobilize. **3** *the company is recruiting staff:* hire, employ, take on, enrol, sign up, engage. OPPOSITES demobilize, disband, dismiss.

noun **1** *new recruits were enlisted:* conscript; US draftee; N. Amer. informal yardbird. **2** *top-quality recruits:* new member, newcomer, initiate, joiner, beginner, novice.

**recur** verb happen again, reoccur, repeat (itself), come back, return, reappear.

**recycle** verb reuse, reprocess, reclaim, recover, salvage.

**red** adjective **1** *a red dress:* scarlet, vermilion, ruby, cherry, cerise, cardinal, carmine, wine. **2** *he was red in the face:* flushed, blushing, pink, rosy, florid, ruddy. **3** *red hair:* auburn, Titian, chestnut, carroty, ginger.

**redeem** verb **1** *redeeming sinners:* save, deliver from sin, absolve. **2** *Billy redeemed his drums from the pawnbrokers:* retrieve, regain, recover, get back, reclaim, repossess, buy back. **3** *this voucher can be redeemed at any branch:* exchange, convert, trade in, cash in. OPPOSITES damn, pawn, buy.

**redemption** noun **1** *God's redemption of his people:* saving, freeing from sin, absolution. **2** *the redemption of their possessions:* retrieval,

recovery, reclamation, repossession, return. **3** *the redemption of vouchers:* exchange, conversion, trade-in, cashing in.
OPPOSITES condemnation, pawning, purchase.

**redress** verb **1** *we redressed the problem:* rectify, correct, right, compensate for, amend, remedy, make good. **2** *we aim to redress the balance:* even up, regulate, equalize.
noun *your best hope of redress:* compensation, reparation, restitution, recompense, repayment, amends.

**reduce** verb **1** *the aim to reduce pollution:* lessen, make smaller, lower, bring down, decrease, diminish, minimize, shrink, narrow, contract, shorten; informal chop. **2** *he reduced her to tears:* bring to, drive to.
OPPOSITES increase.

**reduction** noun **1** *a reduction in pollution:* lessening, lowering, decrease, diminution. **2** *a reduction in staff:* cut, cutback, axing, downsizing.

**redundancy** noun dismissal, sacking, lay-off, discharge, unemployment.

**redundant** adjective *redundant churches:* unnecessary, not required, unneeded, surplus (to requirements), superfluous.
OPPOSITES necessary.
■ **make someone redundant** dismiss, lay off, give someone their notice, discharge; informal sack, fire.

**reel** verb **1** *he reeled as the ship began to roll:* stagger, lurch, sway, rock, stumble, totter, wobble. **2** *the room reeled:* go round (and round), whirl, spin, revolve, swirl, twirl, turn, swim.

**refer** verb *the matter has been referred to my insurers:* pass, direct, hand on/over, send on, transfer, entrust, assign.
■ **refer to 1** *he referred to errors in the article:* mention, allude to, touch on, speak of/about, talk of/about, write about, comment on, point out, call attention to. **2** *these figures refer only to 2001:* apply to, relate to, pertain to, be relevant to, concern, be connected with. **3** *the constable referred to his notes:* consult, turn to, look at, have recourse to.

**referee** noun **1** *the referee blew his whistle:* umpire, judge, adjudicator; informal ref. **2** *include the names of two referees:* supporter, character witness, advocate.
verb *he refereed the game:* umpire, judge, adjudicate; informal ref.

**reference** noun **1** *a reference to his book:* mention, allusion, quotation, comment, remark. **2** *references are given in the bibliography:* source, citation, authority, credit. **3** *a glowing reference:* testimonial, recommendation, character reference, credentials.

**referendum** noun (popular) vote, ballot, poll, plebiscite.

**refine** verb **1** *refining our cereal foods:* purify, filter, distil, process, treat. **2** *helping students to refine their skills:* improve, perfect, polish (up), hone, fine-tune.

**refined** adjective **1** *refined sugar:* purified, processed, treated. **2** *a refined lady:* cultivated, cultured, polished, elegant, sophisticated, urbane, polite, gracious, well bred. **3** *a person of refined taste:* discriminating,

discerning, fastidious, exquisite, impeccable, fine.
OPPOSITES crude, coarse.

**reflect** verb **1** *the snow reflects light:* mirror, send back, throw back, echo. **2** *their expressions reflected their feelings:* indicate, show, display, demonstrate, be evidence of, reveal, betray. **3** *he reflected on his task:* think, consider, review, mull, contemplate, cogitate, meditate, muse, brood.

**reflection** noun **1** *her reflection in the mirror:* image, likeness. **2** *your hands are a reflection of your well-being:* indication, display, demonstration, manifestation, expression, evidence. **3** *after some reflection, he turned it down:* thought, consideration, contemplation, deliberation, pondering, meditation, musing.

**reform** verb **1** *a plan to reform the system:* improve, better, ameliorate, correct, rectify, restore, revise, refine, adapt, revamp, redesign, reconstruct, reorganize. **2** *after his marriage he reformed:* mend one's ways, change for the better, turn over a new leaf.
noun *the reform of the prison system:* improvement, amelioration, refinement, rectification, restoration, adaptation, revision, redesign, revamp, reconstruction, reorganization.

**refrain** verb abstain, desist, hold back, stop oneself, forbear, avoid; informal swear off.

**refresh** verb **1** *the cool air will refresh me:* reinvigorate, revitalize, revive, restore, perk up, brace, freshen, wake up; informal buck up. **2** *let me refresh*

*your memory:* jog, stimulate, prompt, prod.
OPPOSITES weary.

**refreshing** adjective **1** *a refreshing drink:* invigorating, revitalizing, reviving, bracing, fortifying, enlivening, stimulating. **2** *a refreshing change of direction:* welcome, stimulating, fresh, new, imaginative, innovative.
OPPOSITES wearying.

**refreshment** noun food and drink, snacks, titbits; informal nibbles.

**refuge** noun **1** *homeless people seeking refuge:* shelter, protection, safety, security, asylum, sanctuary. **2** *a refuge for mountain gorillas:* sanctuary, shelter, haven, sanctum, retreat, bolt-hole, hiding place.

**refugee** noun asylum seeker, fugitive, displaced person, exile, émigré.

**refund** verb **1** *we will refund your money:* repay, give back, return, pay back. **2** *they refunded the subscribers:* reimburse, compensate, recompense.
noun *a full refund:* repayment, reimbursement, compensation, rebate.

**refurbish** verb renovate, recondition, rehabilitate, revamp, overhaul, restore, redecorate, upgrade, refit; informal do up.

**refusal** noun **1** *we had one refusal to our invitation:* non-acceptance, no, rejection, rebuff, turndown; informal knock-back. **2** *the refusal of planning permission:* withholding, denial.
OPPOSITES acceptance, granting.

**refuse**[1] verb **1** *he refused the*

a b c d e f g h i j k l m n o p q r s t u v w x y z

*invitation:* decline, turn down, say no to, reject, spurn, rebuff; informal pass up. **2** *the Council refused planning permission:* withhold, deny.
OPPOSITES accept, grant.

**refuse²** noun *piles of refuse:* rubbish, waste, litter; N. Amer. garbage, trash; informal dreck, junk.

**regain** verb **1** *government troops regained the capital:* recover, get back, win back, recoup, retrieve, repossess, take back, retake, recapture, reconquer. **2** *they regained dry land:* return to, get back to, reach again, rejoin.

**regal** adjective **1** *a regal feast.* See SPLENDID sense 1. **2** *his regal forebears:* royal, kingly, queenly, princely, majestic.

**regard** verb **1** *we regard the results as encouraging:* consider, look on, view, see, think of, judge, deem, estimate, assess, reckon, rate. **2** *he regarded her coldly:* look at, contemplate, eye, gaze at, stare at, observe, view, study, scrutinize.
noun **1** *he has no regard for life:* consideration, care, concern, thought, notice, heed, attention. **2** *doctors are held in high regard:* esteem, respect, admiration, approval, honour, estimation. **3** *his steady regard:* (fixed) look, gaze, stare, observation, contemplation, study, scrutiny. **4** (**regards**) best wishes, greetings, respects, compliments, best, love.

**regarding** preposition concerning, as regards, with/in regard to, with respect to, with reference to, relating to, respecting, re, about, apropos, on the subject of, in connection

with, vis-à-vis.

**regardless** adverb anyway, anyhow, in any case, nevertheless, nonetheless, despite everything, even so, all the same, in any event, come what may.
■ **regardless of** irrespective of, without reference to, without consideration of, discounting, ignoring, notwithstanding, no matter.

**regime** noun **1** *regime change:* government, administration, leadership, authority, control, rule, command. **2** *a health regime:* system, arrangement, scheme, policy, method, course, plan, programme.

**region** noun district, province, territory, division, area, section, sector, zone, belt, quarter.

**regional** adjective **1** *regional variation:* geographical, territorial. **2** *a regional parliament:* local, provincial, district, parochial, zonal.
OPPOSITES national.

**register** noun **1** *the register of electors:* list, roll, roster, index, directory, catalogue, inventory. **2** *the parish register:* record, chronicle, log, ledger, archive, annals, files.
verb **1** *I wish to register a complaint:* record, enter, file, lodge, write down, submit, report, note, minute, log. **2** *I'd like to register for the course:* enrol, put one's name down, enlist, sign on/up, apply. **3** *the dial registered 100mph:* indicate, read, record, show. **4** *her face registered anger:* display, show, express, exhibit, betray, reveal.

**regret** verb **1** *they came to regret their decision:* be sorry about, feel contrite about, feel

remorse for, rue. **2** *regretting the passing of youth:* mourn, grieve for/over, weep over, sigh over, lament, sorrow for.
OPPOSITES welcome.
**noun 1** *both players expressed regret:* remorse, contrition, repentance, compunction.
**2** *they left with genuine regret:* sadness, sorrow, disappointment, unhappiness, grief.
OPPOSITES satisfaction.

**regular adjective 1** *plant them at regular intervals:* uniform, even, consistent, constant, unchanging, unvarying, fixed.
**2** *the subject of regular protests:* frequent, repeated, continual, recurrent, periodic, constant, perpetual, numerous. **3** *his regular route to work:* usual, normal, customary, habitual, routine, typical, accustomed, established.
OPPOSITES erratic, occasional, unusual.

**regulate verb 1** *the flow has been regulated:* control, adjust, manage, govern. **2** *a new act regulating businesses:* police, supervise, monitor, check (up on), be responsible for, control, manage, direct, govern.

**regulation noun 1** *EC regulations:* rule, order, directive, act, law, by-law, statute, dictate, decree. **2** *the regulation of blood sugar:* adjustment, control, management, balancing. **3** *the regulation of financial services:* policing, supervision, superintendence, monitoring, control, governance, management, responsibility for.

**rehearsal noun 1** practice, trial performance, read-through, run-through, drill, training,

coaching; informal dry run.

**rehearse verb 1** *I rehearsed the role:* prepare, practise, read through, run through/over, go over. **2** *he rehearsed the Vienna Philharmonic:* train, drill, prepare, coach. **3** *the document rehearsed all the arguments:* list, enumerate, itemize, detail, spell out, catalogue, recite, repeat, go over, run through; informal recap.

**reign verb 1** *Robert II reigned for nineteen years:* be king/queen, sit on the throne, wear the crown, be supreme, rule. **2** *chaos reigned:* prevail, exist, be present, be the case, occur, be rife, be rampant, be the order of the day.
**noun** *Henry's reign:* rule, sovereignty, monarchy, dominion.

**rein verb** *they reined back costs:* restrain, check, curb, constrain, hold back/in, keep under control, regulate, restrict, control, curtail, limit.
■ **free rein** freedom, a free hand, leeway, latitude, flexibility, liberty, independence, licence, room to manoeuvre, carte blanche.
■ **keep a tight rein on** regulate, discipline, regiment, keep in line.

**reinforce verb 1** *contractors reinforced the dam:* strengthen, fortify, bolster up, shore up, buttress, prop up, underpin, brace, support. **2** *reinforcing links between colleges and companies:* strengthen, fortify, cement, boost, deepen, enrich, enhance, intensify, improve. **3** *the need to reinforce NATO troops:* augment, increase, add to, supplement, boost, top up.

**reinforcement noun 1** *the*

a b c d e f g h i j k l m n o p q r s t u v w x y z

*reinforcement of our defences:* strengthening, fortification, bolstering, shoring up, buttressing, bracing.
**2** (**reinforcements**) additional troops, auxiliaries, reserves, support, backup, help.

**reinstate** verb restore, put back, bring back, reinstitute, reinstall, re-establish.

**reject** verb **1** *the miners rejected the offer:* turn down, refuse, decline, say no to, spurn.
**2** *Jamie rejected her:* rebuff, spurn, shun, snub, cast off/aside, discard, abandon, desert, turn one's back on.
OPPOSITES accept, welcome.
noun **1** *what a reject!* failure, loser, incompetent. **2** *it is only a reject:* second, discard, misshape, faulty item, cast-off.

**rejection** noun **1** *a rejection of the offer:* refusal, declining, turning down, dismissal, spurning. **2** *Madeleine's rejection of him:* repudiation, rebuff, spurning, abandonment, desertion; informal brush-off.
OPPOSITES agreement, acceptance, welcome.

**rejoice** verb be happy, be glad, be delighted, celebrate, make merry; informal be over the moon.
OPPOSITES mourn.
■ rejoice in delight in, enjoy, revel in, glory in, relish, savour.

**rejoin** verb return to, be reunited with, join again, reach again, regain.

**relate** verb *he related stories:* tell, recount, narrate, report, recite.
■ relate to **1** *mortality is related to unemployment levels:* connect with, associate with, link with, ally with, couple with. **2** *the charges relate to other offences:* apply to, concern, pertain to, have a bearing on, involve. **3** *she cannot relate to her father:* have a rapport with, get on (well) with, feel sympathy with, identify with, empathize with, understand; informal hit it off with.

**related** adjective connected, interconnected, associated, linked, allied, corresponding, analogous, parallel, comparable, equivalent.
OPPOSITES unrelated.

**relation** noun **1** *the relation between church and state:* connection, relationship, association, link, correlation, correspondence, parallel. **2** *are you a relation of his?* relative, member of the family, kinsman, kinswoman; (**relations**) family, kin, kith and kin, kindred. **3** (**relations**) *improving relations with India:* dealings, communication, relationship, connections, contact, interaction.

**relationship** noun **1** *the relationship between diet and diabetes:* connection, relation, association, link, correlation, correspondence, parallel.
**2** *their relationship to a common ancestor:* family ties/connections, blood relationship, kinship, affinity, common ancestry/lineage. **3** *the end of their relationship:* romance, affair, love affair, liaison, amour, fling.

**relative** adjective **1** *the relative importance of each factor:* comparative, respective, comparable. **2** *food required is relative to body weight:* proportionate, in proportion, commensurate, corresponding.

a
b
c
d
e
f
g
h
i
j
k
l
m
n
o
p
q
r
s
t
u
v
w
x
y
z

OPPOSITES disproportionate.

noun *he's a relative of mine:* relation, member of the family, kinsman, kinswoman; (**relatives**) family, kin, kith and kin, kindred.

**relax** verb 1 *relax after work:* rest, loosen up, ease up/off, slow down, de-stress, unbend, unwind, put one's feet up, take it easy; informal chill out; N. Amer. informal hang loose. 2 *a walk will relax you:* calm, unwind, rest, loosen up, make less tense, make less uptight, soothe. 3 *he relaxed his grip:* loosen, slacken, unclench, weaken, lessen. 4 *they relaxed the restrictions:* moderate, temper, ease, loosen, lighten, dilute, weaken, reduce, decrease; informal let up on.
OPPOSITES tense, tighten.

**relaxation** noun recreation, enjoyment, amusement, entertainment, fun, pleasure, leisure.
OPPOSITES activity, work.

**relay** noun *a live relay of the performance:* broadcast, transmission, showing, feed, patch.
verb *I'd relayed the messages:* pass on, hand on, transfer, repeat, communicate, send, transmit, circulate.

**release** verb 1 *all prisoners were released:* free, set free, let go/out, liberate, discharge. 2 *Burke released the animal:* untie, undo, loose, let go, unleash. 3 *police released the news yesterday:* make public, make known, issue, put out, publish, broadcast, circulate, launch.
OPPOSITES imprison, tie up, embargo.
noun 1 *the release of political prisoners:* freeing, liberation,

deliverance, freedom, liberty. 2 *the release of the news:* issuing, announcement, publication, broadcasting, circulation, launch.
OPPOSITES imprisonment, embargo.

**relegate** verb downgrade, demote, lower, put down, move down.
OPPOSITES upgrade, promote.

**relentless** adjective 1 *their relentless pursuit of quality:* persistent, unfaltering, unremitting, unflagging, untiring, unwavering, dogged, single-minded, tireless, indefatigable. 2 *a relentless taskmaster:* harsh, cruel, remorseless, merciless, pitiless, implacable, ruthless.

**relevant** adjective pertinent, applicable, apposite, material, apropos, to the point, germane.
OPPOSITES irrelevant.

**reliable** adjective dependable, trustworthy, good, safe, authentic, faithful, genuine, sound, true, loyal, unfailing.
OPPOSITES unreliable.

**reliance** noun 1 *reliance on the state:* dependence. 2 *reliance on his judgement:* trust, confidence, faith, belief, conviction.

**relic** noun artefact, historical object, antiquity, remnant, vestige, remains.

**relief** noun 1 *a bit of relief from work:* freedom, release, liberation, deliverance, comfort, respite, diversion. 2 *pain relief:* alleviation, relieving, palliation, soothing, easing, lessening. 3 *a little light relief:* respite, amusement, diversion, entertainment, jollity, recreation. 4 *bringing relief to the starving:* help, aid,

assistance, charity. **5** *his relief arrived to take over:* replacement, substitute, deputy, reserve, cover, stand-in, supply, locum, understudy.
OPPOSITES intensification.

**relieve** verb **1** *this helps relieve pain:* alleviate, mitigate, ease, counteract, dull, reduce. **2** *the helpers relieved us:* replace, take over from, stand in for, fill in for, substitute for, deputize for, cover for. **3** *this relieves the teacher of a heavy load:* free, release, exempt, excuse, absolve, let off.
OPPOSITES aggravate, inflict.

**religion** noun faith, belief, worship, creed, church, sect, denomination, cult.

**religious** adjective **1** *a religious person:* devout, pious, reverent, godly, God-fearing, churchgoing. **2** *religious beliefs:* spiritual, theological, scriptural, doctrinal, ecclesiastical, church, holy, divine, sacred. **3** *religious attention to detail:* scrupulous, conscientious, meticulous, punctilious, strict, rigorous.
OPPOSITES atheistic, secular, casual.

**relinquish** verb **1** *he relinquished control of the company:* renounce, give up/away, hand over, let go of. **2** *he relinquished his post:* leave, resign from, stand down from, bow out of, give up; informal quit, chuck.
OPPOSITES retain, continue.

**relish** noun **1** *he dug into his food with relish:* enjoyment, gusto, delight, pleasure, glee, appreciation, enthusiasm. **2** *a hot relish:* condiment, sauce, dressing.
OPPOSITES distaste.

verb **1** *he was relishing his moment of glory:* enjoy, delight in, love, adore, take pleasure in, rejoice in, appreciate, savour, revel in, luxuriate in, glory in. **2** *I don't relish the drive:* look forward to, fancy.
OPPOSITES dislike.

**reluctance** noun unwillingness, disinclination, hesitation, wavering, vacillation, doubts, second thoughts, misgivings.

**reluctant** adjective unwilling, disinclined, unenthusiastic, resistant, opposed, hesitant, loath.
OPPOSITES willing, eager.

**rely**
■ **rely on** depend on, count on, bank on, be confident of, be sure of, have faith in, trust in; informal swear by; N. Amer. informal figure on.

**remain** verb **1** *the problem will remain:* continue, endure, last, abide, carry on, persist, stay around, survive, live on. **2** *he remained in hospital:* stay, stay behind, stay put, wait behind, be left, hang on; informal hang around/round. **3** *union leaders remain sceptical:* continue to be, stay, keep.

**remainder** noun rest, balance, residue, others, remnant(s), leftovers, surplus, extra, excess.

**remains** plural noun **1** *the remains of her drink:* remainder, residue, rest, remnant(s), leftovers. **2** *Roman remains:* antiquities, relics, artefacts. **3** *the saint's remains:* corpse, body, carcass, bones.

**remark** verb *'You're quiet,' he remarked:* comment, say, observe, mention, reflect. noun *he made a few remarks:* comment, statement, utterance, observation, reflection.

**remarkable** adjective
extraordinary, exceptional, outstanding, notable, striking, memorable, unusual, conspicuous, momentous.
OPPOSITES ordinary.

**remedy** noun 1 *herbal remedies:* treatment, cure, medicine, medication, medicament, drug. 2 *a remedy for all kinds of problems:* solution, answer, cure, fix, antidote, resolution.
verb *remedying the situation:* put right, set right, rectify, solve, sort out, straighten out, resolve, correct, repair, mend, fix.

**remember** verb 1 *remembering happy times:* recall, call to mind, recollect, think of, reminisce about, look back on. 2 *can you remember all that?* memorize, retain, learn off by heart. 3 *you must remember she's only five:* bear in mind, be mindful of, take into account. 4 *remember to feed the cat:* be sure, be certain, mind that you, make sure that you. 5 *the nation remembered those who gave their lives:* commemorate, pay tribute to, honour, salute, pay homage to.
OPPOSITES forget.

**remembrance** noun 1 *an expression of remembrance:* recollection, reminiscence, recall. 2 *we sold poppies in remembrance:* commemoration, memory, recognition.

**remind** verb jog someone's memory, prompt.
■ remind someone of make someone think of, cause someone to remember, put someone in mind of, call to mind, evoke.

**reminiscent** adjective similar to, comparable with, evocative of, suggestive of, redolent of, that reminds one of.

**remnant** noun remains, remainder, leftovers, offcut, residue, rest.

**remorse** noun regret, guilt, contrition, repentance, shame.

**remote** adjective 1 *a remote village:* isolated, faraway, distant, out of the way, off the beaten track, secluded, lonely; N. Amer. in the backwoods; informal in the middle of nowhere. 2 *a remote possibility:* unlikely, improbable, doubtful, dubious, faint, slight, slim, small, slender. 3 *she seems very remote:* aloof, distant, detached, withdrawn, unforthcoming, unapproachable, unresponsive, unfriendly, unsociable, introspective, introverted; informal stand-offish.
OPPOSITES close, distinct, friendly.

**removal** noun 1 *the removal of church treasures:* taking away, moving, carrying away, transporting. 2 *his removal from office:* dismissal, ejection, expulsion, ousting; N. Amer. ouster; informal sacking, firing. 3 *the removal of customs barriers:* withdrawal, elimination, abolition, taking away. 4 *her removal to France:* move, transfer, relocation.
OPPOSITES installation, appointment, imposition.

**remove** verb 1 *she removed the lid:* take off, take away, take out, pull out, withdraw, detach, undo, unfasten, disconnect. 2 *he was removed from his post:* dismiss, discharge, get rid of, expel, oust, depose; informal sack,

a b c d e f g h i j k l m n o p q **r** s t u v w x y z

fire, kick out. **3** *tax relief was removed:* abolish, withdraw, eliminate, get rid of, do away with, stop, cut, axe.
OPPOSITES attach, insert, replace, appoint, impose.

**renaissance** noun revival, renewal, resurrection, reawakening, re-emergence, rebirth, reappearance, resurgence.

**render** verb **1** *her fury rendered her speechless:* make, cause to be/become, leave, turn. **2** *rendering assistance:* give, provide, supply, furnish, contribute. **3** *the characters are vividly rendered:* act, perform, play, depict, portray, interpret, represent, draw, paint, execute.

**renew** verb **1** *I renewed my search:* resume, return to, take up again, come back to, begin again, restart, recommence, continue (with), carry on (with). **2** *they renewed their vows:* reaffirm, repeat, reiterate, restate. **3** *something to renew her interest in life:* revive, regenerate, revitalize, reinvigorate, restore, resuscitate. **4** *the hotel was completely renewed:* renovate, restore, refurbish, revamp, remodel, modernize; informal do up; N. Amer. informal rehab.

**renounce** verb **1** *Edward renounced his claim to the throne:* give up, relinquish, abandon, surrender, waive, forego, desist from, keep off; informal say goodbye to. **2** *she renounced her family:* reject, repudiate, deny, abandon, wash one's hands of, turn one's back on, disown, spurn, shun.
OPPOSITES assert, continue, keep, accept.

**renovate** verb modernize,

restore, refurbish, revamp, recondition, rehabilitate, update, upgrade, refit; informal do up; N. Amer. informal rehab.

**renowned** adjective famous, well known, celebrated, famed, eminent, distinguished, acclaimed, illustrious, prominent, great, esteemed.
OPPOSITES unknown.

**rent** noun *I can't afford to pay the rent:* hire charge, rental.
verb **1** *she rented a car:* hire, lease, charter. **2** *why don't you rent it out?* let (out), lease (out), hire (out), charter (out).

**repair** verb **1** *the car was repaired:* mend, fix (up), put/set right, restore (to working order), darn; informal patch up. **2** *repairing relations with other countries:* put/set right, mend, fix, straighten out, improve; informal patch up. **3** *she sought to repair the wrong she had done:* rectify, make good, (put) right, correct, make up for, make amends for.
noun **1** *in need of repair:* restoration, fixing (up), mending, renovation. **2** *an invisible repair:* mend, darn, patch. **3** *in good repair:* condition, working order, state, shape, fettle; Brit. informal nick.

**repay** verb **1** *repaying customers who have been cheated:* reimburse, refund, pay back, recompense, compensate. **2** *the grants have to be repaid:* pay back, return, refund, reimburse. **3** *I'd like to repay her generosity:* reciprocate, return, requite, reward.

**repeal** verb *the Act was repealed:* cancel, abolish, reverse, rescind, revoke, annul, quash.
OPPOSITES enact.

**noun** *the repeal of the law:* cancellation, abolition, reversal, rescinding, annulment.

**repeat** verb 1 *she repeated her story:* say again, restate, reiterate, go/run through again, recapitulate; informal recap. 2 *children can repeat chunks of text:* recite, quote, parrot, regurgitate, echo; informal trot out. 3 *Steele was invited to repeat his work:* do again, redo, replicate, duplicate. 4 *the episodes were repeated:* rebroadcast, rerun, reshow.
noun 1 *a repeat of the previous year's final:* repetition, replication, duplicate. 2 *repeats of his TV show:* rerun, rebroadcast, reshowing, replay.

**repeatedly** adverb frequently, often, again and again, over and over (again), time and (time) again, many times, persistently, recurrently, constantly, continually, regularly; N. Amer. oftentimes.

**repel** verb 1 *the US repelled an Iraqi attack:* fight off, repulse, drive back, force back, beat back, hold off; Brit. see off. 2 *the sight of the food repelled me:* revolt, disgust, repulse, sicken, nauseate, turn someone's stomach; informal turn off; N. Amer. informal gross out.
OPPOSITES attract, delight.

**repertoire** noun collection, range, repertory, list, store, stock, repository, supply.

**repetition** noun 1 *the statistics bear repetition:* reiteration, restatement, retelling. 2 *a repetition of the scene in the kitchen:* recurrence, rerun, repeat. 3 *there is some repetition:* repetitiousness, repetitiveness, redundancy, tautology.

**repetitive, repetitious** adjective recurring, recurrent, repeated, unvaried, unchanging, routine, mechanical, automatic, monotonous, boring.
OPPOSITES unique, varied.

**replace** verb 1 *Adam replaced the receiver:* put back, return, restore. 2 *a new chairman came in to replace him:* take the place of, succeed, take over from, supersede, stand in for, substitute for, deputize for; informal step into someone's shoes/boots. 3 *she replaced the spoon with a fork:* substitute, exchange, change, swap.
OPPOSITES remove.

**replacement** noun 1 *we have to find a replacement:* substitute, stand-in, locum, understudy, relief, cover, successor. 2 *the wiring was in need of replacement:* renewal.

**replica** noun 1 *is it real or a replica?* copy, model, duplicate, reproduction, dummy, imitation, facsimile. 2 *a replica of her mother:* perfect likeness, double, lookalike, living image, twin, clone; informal spitting image, dead ringer.

**reply** verb *Rachel didn't reply:* respond, answer, write back, rejoin, retort, riposte, counter, come back.
noun *he waited for a reply:* answer, response, rejoinder, retort, riposte; informal comeback.

**report** verb 1 *the press reported the story:* communicate, announce, divulge, disclose, reveal, make public, publish, broadcast, proclaim, publicize. 2 *I reported him to the police:* inform on; informal shop, tell on,

a
b
c
d
e
f
g
h
i
j
k
l
m
n
o
p
q
**r**
s
t
u
v
w
x
y
z

squeal on, rat on; Brit. informal grass on. **3** *Juliet reported for duty:* present oneself, arrive, turn up; informal show up.
noun **1** *a full report on the meeting:* account, record, minutes, proceedings, transcript. **2** *reports of drug dealing:* news, information, word, intelligence. **3** *newspaper reports:* story, account, article, piece, item, column, feature, bulletin, dispatch. **4** (Brit.) *a school report:* assessment, evaluation, appraisal. **5** *reports of his imminent resignation:* rumour, whisper; informal buzz. **6** *the report of a gun:* bang, crack, explosion, boom.

**reporter** noun journalist, correspondent, newsman, newswoman, columnist; Brit. pressman; informal hack, stringer, journo; N. Amer. informal newsie.

**represent** verb **1** *a character representing a single quality:* stand for, symbolize, personify, epitomize, typify, embody, illustrate. **2** *Hathor is represented as a woman with cow's horns:* depict, portray, render, picture, delineate, show, illustrate. **3** *his solicitor represented him in court:* appear for, act for, speak on behalf of. **4** *the Queen was represented by Lord Lewin:* deputize for, substitute for, stand in for.

**representation** noun
**1** *Rossetti's representation of women:* portrayal, depiction, presentation, rendition.
**2** *representations of the human form:* likeness, painting, drawing, picture, illustration, sketch, image, model, figure, statue.

**representative** adjective **1** *a*
*representative sample:* typical, characteristic, illustrative. **2** *a female figure representative of Britain:* symbolic, emblematic.
OPPOSITES atypical.
noun **1** *a representative of the Royal Society:* spokesperson, spokesman, spokeswoman, agent, official, mouthpiece. **2** *a sales representative:* salesman, saleswoman, commercial traveller, agent, negotiator; informal rep; N. Amer. informal drummer. **3** *he acted as his father's representative:* deputy, substitute, stand-in, proxy, delegate, ambassador, emissary.

**repress** verb **1** *the rebellion was repressed:* suppress, quell, quash, subdue, put down, crush, extinguish, stamp out, defeat, contain. **2** *the peasants were repressed:* oppress, subjugate, keep down, tyrannize. **3** *these emotions may well be repressed:* restrain, hold back/in, suppress, keep in check, control, curb, stifle, bottle up; informal button up, keep the lid on.
OPPOSITES express.

**repression** noun **1** *the repression of the protests:* suppression, quashing, subduing, crushing, stamping out. **2** *political repression:* oppression, subjugation, suppression, tyranny, authoritarianism. **3** *the repression of sexual urges:* restraint, suppression, control, curbing, stifling, bottling up.

**reprieve** verb *she was reprieved:* pardon, spare, amnesty; informal let off (the hook).
noun *she was given a reprieve:* pardon, stay of execution, amnesty.

**reprimand** verb *he was publicly*

*reprimanded:* rebuke, reproach, scold, admonish; informal tell off; Brit. informal tick off; N. Amer. informal chew out.
OPPOSITES praise, pardon.
noun *a severe reprimand:* rebuke, reproach, scolding, admonition; informal telling-off; Brit. informal ticking-off.
OPPOSITES praise, pardon.

**reproduce** verb 1 *each artwork is reproduced in colour:* copy, duplicate, replicate, photocopy, xerox, photostat, print. 2 *this work has not been reproduced in other laboratories:* repeat, replicate, recreate, redo, simulate, imitate, emulate, mimic. 3 *some animals reproduce prolifically:* breed, procreate, propagate, multiply.

**reproduction** noun 1 *a reproduction of the original:* print, copy, reprint, duplicate, facsimile, photocopy; trademark Xerox. 2 *the process of reproduction:* breeding, procreation, multiplying, propagation.

**repulsive** adjective disgusting, revolting, foul, nasty, obnoxious, sickening, nauseating, stomach-churning.
OPPOSITES attractive.

**reputation** noun name, good name, character, repute, standing, stature, position, renown, esteem, prestige.

**request** noun 1 *requests for assistance:* appeal, entreaty, plea, petition, application, demand, call. 2 *Charlotte spoke, at Ursula's request:* bidding, entreaty, demand, insistence. 3 *indicate your requests on the form:* requirement, wish, desire, choice.
verb 1 *the government requested aid:* ask for, appeal for, call for,

seek, solicit, plead for, apply for, demand. 2 *I requested him to help:* ask, call on, beg, entreat, implore; literary beseech.

**require** verb 1 *the child required hospital treatment:* need. 2 *a situation requiring patience:* necessitate, demand, call for, involve, entail. 3 *unquestioning obedience is required:* demand, insist on, call for, ask for, expect. 4 *she was required to pay costs:* order, instruct, command, enjoin, oblige, compel, force. 5 *do you require anything else?* want, desire, lack, be short of.

**requirement** noun need, necessity, prerequisite, stipulation, demand, want, essential.

**rescue** verb 1 *an attempt to rescue the hostages:* save, free, set free, release, liberate, deliver. 2 *Boyd rescued his papers:* retrieve, recover, salvage.
noun *the rescue of ten crewmen:* saving, rescuing, release, freeing, liberation, deliverance.

**research** noun *medical research:* investigation, experimentation, testing, analysis, fact-finding, examination, scrutiny.
verb *the phenomenon has been widely researched:* investigate, study, enquire into, look into, probe, explore, analyse, examine, scrutinize.

**resemblance** noun similarity, likeness, similitude, correspondence, congruence, conformity, comparability, parallelism.
OPPOSITES dissimilarity.

**resemble** verb look like, be similar to, remind one of, take after, approximate to, smack of,

correspond to, echo, mirror, parallel.
OPPOSITES differ from.

**resent** verb begrudge, feel aggrieved at/about, feel bitter about, grudge, be resentful of, take exception to, object to, take amiss, take offence at.
OPPOSITES welcome.

**resentment** noun bitterness, indignation, irritation, pique, dissatisfaction, disgruntlement, discontentment, acrimony, rancour.

**reservation** noun 1 *grave reservations*: doubt, qualm, scruple; (**reservations**) misgivings, scepticism, unease, hesitation, objection. 2 *an Indian reservation*: reserve, enclave, sanctuary, territory, homeland.

**reserve** verb 1 *ask your newsagent to reserve you a copy*: put aside, set aside, keep (back), save, hold back, keep in reserve, earmark. 2 *he reserved a table*: book, order, arrange for, secure. 3 *all rights reserved*: retain, keep, hold. 4 *reserve your judgement until you know him better*: defer, postpone, put off, delay, withhold.
noun 1 *reserves of petrol*: stock, store, supply, stockpile, pool, hoard, cache. 2 *the army are calling up reserves*: reinforcements, extras, auxiliaries. 3 *a nature reserve*: national park, sanctuary, preserve, conservation area. 4 *his natural reserve*: shyness, diffidence, timidity, taciturnity, inhibition, reticence, detachment, distance, remoteness. 5 *she trusted him without reserve*: reservation, qualification, condition, limitation, hesitation, doubt.

adjective *a reserve goalkeeper*: substitute, stand-in, relief, replacement, fallback, spare, extra.

**reserved** adjective 1 *Sewell is rather reserved*: uncommunicative, reticent, unforthcoming, quiet, silent, taciturn, withdrawn, secretive, shy, retiring, diffident, timid, introverted; informal stand-offish. 2 *that table is reserved*: booked, taken, spoken for, prearranged.
OPPOSITES outgoing.

**reservoir** noun 1 *sailing on the reservoir*: lake, pool, pond, basin. 2 *an ink reservoir*: receptacle, container, holder, tank. 3 *the reservoir of managerial talent*: stock, store, stockpile, reserve(s), supply, bank, pool.

**residence** noun (formal) home, house, address, quarters, lodgings; informal pad; formal dwelling.

**resident** noun *the residents of New York City*: inhabitant, local, citizen, native, householder, homeowner, occupier, tenant.
adjective 1 *resident in the UK*: living, residing; formal dwelling. 2 *a resident nanny*: live-in.

**residue** noun remainder, rest, remnant(s), surplus, extra, excess, remains, leftovers.

**resign** verb 1 *the manager resigned*: leave, give notice, stand down, step down; informal quit. 2 *19 MPs resigned their seats*: give up, leave, vacate, stand down from; informal quit, pack in.
■ **resign oneself to** reconcile oneself to, come to terms with.

**resignation** noun 1 *his resignation from his post*: departure, leaving, standing down, stepping down; informal quitting. **2** *he accepted his fate with resignation:* patience, forbearance, stoicism, fortitude, fatalism, acceptance.

**resigned** adjective patient, long-suffering, uncomplaining, forbearing, stoical, philosophical, fatalistic.

**resist** verb **1** *built to resist cold winters:* withstand, be proof against, combat, weather, endure, be resistant to, keep out. **2** *they resisted his attempts to change things:* oppose, fight against, object to, defy, kick against; informal be anti. **3** *I resisted the urge to retort:* refrain from, abstain from, forbear from, desist from, not give in to, restrain oneself from.
OPPOSITES welcome, submit to.

**resistance** noun **1** *resistance to change:* opposition, hostility. **2** *a spirited resistance:* struggle, fight, battle, stand, opposition, defiance. **3** *the body's resistance to disease:* immunity from, defences against. **4** *the French resistance:* freedom fighters, underground, partisans.

**resistant** adjective **1** *resistant to water:* impervious, immune, invulnerable, proof, unaffected. **2** *resistant to change:* opposed, averse, hostile, inimical, against; informal anti.
OPPOSITES vulnerable, favourable.

**resolution** noun **1** *her resolution not to smoke:* intention, resolve, decision, intent, aim, plan, commitment, pledge, promise. **2** *the committee passed the resolution:* motion, proposal, proposition; N. Amer. resolve. **3** *she handled the work with resolution:*

determination, purpose, resolve, single-mindedness; informal guts. **4** *a satisfactory resolution of the problem:* solution, answer, end, settlement, conclusion.

**resolve** verb **1** *this matter cannot be resolved overnight:* settle, sort out, solve, fix, straighten out, deal with, put right, rectify; informal hammer out, thrash out. **2** *David resolved to wait:* determine, decide, make up one's mind. **3** *the committee resolved that the project should proceed:* vote, rule, decide formally, agree.
noun *he reaffirmed his resolve:* determination, purpose, resolution, single-mindedness; informal guts.

**resort** noun *strike action is our last resort:* option, alternative, choice, possibility, hope, measure, step, recourse, expedient.
■ *resort to* fall back on, have recourse to, turn to, make use of, use, avail oneself of.

**resound** verb echo, reverberate, ring, boom, thunder, rumble, resonate.

**resounding** adjective **1** *a resounding voice:* reverberating, resonating, echoing, ringing, sonorous, deep, rich. **2** *a resounding success:* enormous, huge, very great, tremendous, terrific, colossal, emphatic, outstanding, remarkable, phenomenal.

**resource** noun **1** *your tutor is there as a resource:* facility, amenity, aid, help, support. **2** *a person of resource:* initiative, resourcefulness, enterprise, ingenuity, inventiveness. **3** (**resources**) *use your resources efficiently:* assets, funds, wealth, money, capital, supplies, materials, stores, stocks, reserves.

**resourceful** adjective ingenious, enterprising, inventive, creative, clever, talented, able, capable.

**respect** noun 1 *the respect due to a great artist:* esteem, regard, high opinion, admiration, reverence, deference, honour. 2 *he spoke to her with respect:* due regard, politeness, courtesy, civility, deference. 3 (**respects**) *paying one's respects:* regards, compliments, greetings, best/ good wishes. 4 *the report was accurate in every respect:* aspect, regard, feature, way, sense, particular, point, detail.
OPPOSITES contempt.
verb 1 *he is highly respected for his industry:* esteem, admire, think highly of, have a high opinion of, look up to, revere, honour. 2 *they respected our privacy:* show consideration for, have regard for, observe, be mindful of, be heedful of. 3 *father respected her wishes:* abide by, comply with, follow, adhere to, conform to, act in accordance with, obey, observe, keep (to).
OPPOSITES despise, disregard, disobey.

**respectable** adjective 1 *a respectable middle-class background:* reputable, upright, honest, honourable, trustworthy, decent, good, well bred, clean-living. 2 *a respectable salary:* fairly good, decent, fair-sized, reasonable, moderately good, large, sizeable, considerable.
OPPOSITES disreputable, paltry.

**respectful** adjective deferential, reverent, dutiful, polite, well mannered, civil, courteous, gracious.
OPPOSITES rude.

**respective** adjective separate, personal, own, particular, individual, specific, special.

**respite** noun rest, break, breathing space, interval, lull, pause, time out, relief; informal breather, let-up.

**respond** verb 1 *they do not respond to questions:* answer, reply, write back, come back, rejoin, retort, riposte, counter. 2 *they were slow to respond:* react, reciprocate, retaliate.

**response** noun 1 *his response to the question:* answer, reply, rejoinder, retort, riposte; informal comeback. 2 *an angry response:* reaction, reply, retaliation; informal comeback.
OPPOSITES question.

**responsibility** noun 1 *it was his responsibility to find witnesses:* duty, task, function, job, role, business; Brit. informal pigeon. 2 *they denied responsibility for the attack:* blame, fault, guilt, culpability, liability. 3 *a sense of responsibility:* trustworthiness, (common) sense, maturity, reliability, dependability. 4 *managerial responsibility:* authority, control, power, leadership.
OPPOSITES irresponsibility.

**responsible** adjective 1 *who is responsible for prisons?* in charge of, in control of, at the helm of, accountable for, liable for. 2 *I am responsible for the mistake:* accountable, answerable, to blame, guilty, culpable, blameworthy, at fault, in the wrong. 3 *a responsible job:* important, powerful,

executive. **4** *a responsible tenant:* trustworthy, sensible, mature, reliable, dependable.
OPPOSITES irresponsible.

**responsive** adjective reactive, receptive, open to suggestions, amenable, flexible, forthcoming.
OPPOSITES unresponsive.

**rest**[1] verb **1** *he needed to rest:* relax, ease up/off, let up, slow down, have/take a break, unbend, unwind, take it easy, put one's feet up; informal take five, have/take a breather, chill out. **2** *his hands rested on the rail:* lie, be laid, repose, be placed, be positioned, be supported by. **3** *she rested her basket on the ground:* support, prop (up), lean, lay, set, stand, position, place, put.
noun **1** *get some rest:* relaxation, repose, leisure, respite, time off, breathing space; informal lie-down. **2** *a short rest from work:* holiday, vacation, break, breathing space, interval, interlude, intermission, time off/out; informal breather. **3** *she took the poker from its rest:* stand, base, holder, support, rack, frame, shelf. **4** *we came to rest 100 metres lower:* a standstill, a halt, a stop.

**rest**[2] noun *the rest of the board are appointees:* remainder, residue, balance, others, those left, remnant(s), surplus, excess.

**restful** adjective relaxing, quiet, calm, tranquil, soothing, peaceful, leisurely, undisturbed, untroubled.
OPPOSITES exciting.

**restless** adjective **1** *Maria was restless:* uneasy, ill at ease, fidgety, edgy, tense, worked up, nervous, nervy, agitated,

anxious; informal jumpy, jittery, twitchy, uptight. **2** *a restless night:* sleepless, wakeful, fitful, broken, disturbed, troubled, unsettled.

**restoration** noun **1** *the restoration of democracy:* reinstatement, reinstitution, re-establishment, reimposition, return. **2** *the restoration of derelict housing:* repair, fixing, mending, refurbishment, reconditioning, rehabilitation, rebuilding, reconstruction, renovation; N. Amer. informal rehab.

**restore** verb **1** *the aim to restore democracy:* reinstate, bring back, reinstitute, reimpose, reinstall, re-establish. **2** *he restored it to its rightful owner:* return, give back, hand back. **3** *the building has been restored:* repair, fix, mend, refurbish, recondition, rehabilitate, renovate; informal do up; N. Amer. informal rehab. **4** *a good sleep can restore you:* reinvigorate, revitalize, revive, refresh, energize, freshen.
OPPOSITES abolish, tire.

**restrain** verb **1** *Charles restrained his anger:* control, check, curb, suppress, contain, rein back/in; informal keep the lid on. **2** *she could barely restrain herself from swearing:* prevent, stop, keep, hold back.

**restrained** adjective **1** *Julie was quite restrained:* self-controlled, not given to excesses, sober, steady, unemotional, undemonstrative. **2** *restrained elegance:* muted, soft, discreet, subtle, quiet, unobtrusive, unostentatious, understated, tasteful.
OPPOSITES impetuous, ostentatious.

**restraint** noun **1** *a restraint on*

*their impulsiveness:* constraint, check, control, restriction, limitation, curtailment, rein, brake. **2** *the customary restraint of the police:* self-control, self-discipline, control, moderation, judiciousness. **3** *the room has been decorated with restraint:* subtlety, understatedness, taste, discretion, discrimination.
OPPOSITES impetuousness, ostentation.

**restrict** verb **1** *a busy job restricted his leisure activities:* limit, keep within bounds, regulate, control, moderate, cut down. **2** *the belt rather restricts movement:* hinder, interfere with, impede, hamper, obstruct, block, check, curb.

**restricted** adjective **1** *restricted space:* cramped, confined, constricted, small, narrow, tight. **2** *a restricted calorie intake:* limited, controlled, regulated, reduced. **3** *a restricted zone:* out of bounds, off limits, private, exclusive. **4** *restricted information:* secret, classified; informal hush-hush.
OPPOSITES generous, unlimited, public, open.

**restriction** noun **1** *there is no restriction on the number of places:* limitation, constraint, control, check, curb. **2** *the restriction of personal freedom:* reduction, limitation, diminution, curtailment. **3** *restriction of movement:* hindrance, impediment, slowing, reduction, limitation.

**result** noun *stress is the result of overwork:* consequence, outcome, upshot, sequel, effect, reaction, repercussion.
OPPOSITES cause.
verb *anger may result from an*

*argument:* follow, ensue, develop, stem, spring, arise, derive, proceed; (**result from**) be caused by, be brought about by, be produced by, originate in.
■ result in end in, culminate in, lead to, trigger, cause, bring about, occasion, effect, give rise to, produce.

**resume** verb restart, recommence, begin again, start again, reopen, renew, return to, continue with, carry on with.
OPPOSITES suspend, abandon.

**résumé** noun summary, precis, synopsis, abstract, outline, abridgement, overview.

**resumption** noun restart, recommencement, reopening, continuation, renewal, return, revival.

**resurgence** noun renewal, revival, renaissance, recovery, comeback, reawakening, resurrection, reappearance, re-emergence, resumption, continuation.

**resurrect** verb revive, restore, regenerate, revitalize, breathe new life into, reinvigorate, resuscitate, rejuvenate, re-establish, relaunch.

**retain** verb **1** *the government retained a share in the industries:* keep (possession of), keep hold of, hang on to. **2** *existing footpaths are to be retained:* maintain, keep, preserve, conserve.
OPPOSITES give up, abolish.

**retaliate** verb fight back, hit back, respond, react, reply, reciprocate, counter-attack, get back at someone, pay someone back; informal get one's own back.

**retaliation** noun revenge, vengeance, reprisal, retribution, repayment, response, reaction, reply, counter-attack.

# retard → revel

**retard** verb delay, slow down/up, hold back/up, postpone, detain, decelerate, hinder, impede, check.
OPPOSITES accelerate, bring forward.

**reticent** adjective uncommunicative, unforthcoming, unresponsive, tight-lipped, quiet, taciturn, silent, reserved.
OPPOSITES expansive.

**retire** verb **1** *he has retired:* give up work, stop work. **2** *Gillian retired to her office:* withdraw, go away, take oneself off, shut oneself away. **3** *everyone retired early:* go to bed, call it a day; informal turn in, hit the hay/sack.
OPPOSITES emerge, get up.

**retired** adjective *a retired teacher:* former, ex-, past, elderly.
noun (**the retired**) (old-age) pensioners, OAPs, senior citizens, the elderly; N. Amer. seniors.

**retort** verb *'Oh, sure,' she retorted:* answer, reply, respond, return, counter, riposte, retaliate.
noun *a sarcastic retort:* answer, reply, response, counter, rejoinder, riposte, retaliation; informal comeback.

**retreat** verb *the army retreated:* withdraw, retire, draw back, pull back/out, fall back, give way, give ground.
OPPOSITES advance.
noun **1** *the retreat of the army:* withdrawal, retirement, pullback, flight. **2** *her rural retreat:* refuge, haven, sanctuary, hideaway, hideout, hiding place; informal hidey-hole.

**retrieve** verb **1** *I retrieved our ball from their garden:* get back, bring back, recover, recapture, regain, recoup. **2** *they tried to retrieve the situation:* put/set right, rectify, remedy, restore, sort out, straighten out, resolve.

**return** verb **1** *he returned to London:* go back, come back, arrive back, come home. **2** *the symptoms returned:* recur, reoccur, repeat (itself), reappear. **3** *he returned the money:* give back, hand back, pay back, repay. **4** *Peter returned the book to the shelf:* restore, put back, replace, reinstall. **5** *the jury returned a verdict:* deliver, bring in, hand down.
OPPOSITES keep.
noun **1** *the return of hard times:* recurrence, reoccurrence, repeat, repetition, reappearance. **2** *I requested the return of my books:* giving back, handing back, replacement, restoration, reinstatement, restitution. **3** *a quick return on investments:* yield, profit, gain, revenue, interest, dividend.

**revamp** verb renovate, redecorate, refurbish, remodel, refashion, redesign, restyle; informal do up, give something a facelift, give something a makeover, vamp up; Brit. informal tart up.

**reveal** verb **1** *the police can't reveal his whereabouts:* disclose, make known, make public, broadcast, publicize, circulate, divulge, tell, let slip/drop, give away/out, blurt out, release, leak; informal let on. **2** *he revealed his new car:* show, display, exhibit, unveil, uncover.
OPPOSITES keep secret, hide.

**revel** verb *they revelled all night:*

a
b
c
d
e
f
g
h
i
j
k
l
m
n
o
p
q
**r**
s
t
u
v
w
x
y
z

a
b
c
d
e
f
g
h
i
j
k
l
m
n
o
p
q
**r**
s
t
u
v
w
x
y
z

celebrate, make merry; informal party, live it up, whoop it up, paint the town red.
noun *late-night revels:* celebration, festivity, jollification, merrymaking, party; informal rave, shindig, bash; Brit. informal rave-up; N. Amer. informal wingding, blast.
■ revel in enjoy, delight in, love, like, adore, take pleasure in, relish, lap up, savour; informal get a kick out of.

**revelation** noun 1 *revelations about his personal life:* disclosure, announcement, report, admission, confession. 2 *the revelation of a secret:* disclosure, divulging, letting slip/drop, giving away/out, leak, betrayal, publicizing.

**revenge** noun *she is seeking revenge:* retaliation, retribution, vengeance, reprisal, recrimination, an eye for an eye (and a tooth for a tooth), redress.
OPPOSITES forgiveness.
verb *he revenged his brother's murder:* avenge, exact retribution for, take reprisals for, get redress for, make someone pay for; informal get one's own back for.
OPPOSITES forgive.

**revenue** noun income, takings, receipts, proceeds, earnings, profit(s), gain, yield.
OPPOSITES expenditure.

**revere** verb respect, admire, think highly of, esteem, venerate, look up to, be in awe of.
OPPOSITES despise.

**reverse** verb 1 *the car reversed:* back, move back/backwards. 2 *reverse the bottle in the ice bucket:* turn upside down, turn over, upend, invert, turn back

to front. 3 *reverse your roles:* swap (round), change (round), exchange, switch (round), transpose. 4 *the umpire reversed the decision:* alter, change, overturn, overthrow, disallow, override, overrule, veto, revoke.
adjective *in reverse order:* backward(s), inverted, transposed, opposite.
noun 1 *the reverse is the case:* opposite, contrary, converse, inverse, antithesis. 2 *successes and reverses:* setback, reversal, upset, failure, misfortune, mishap, disaster, blow, disappointment, adversity, hardship, affliction, vicissitude, defeat. 3 *the reverse of the page:* other side, back, underside, wrong side.
OPPOSITES success, front.

**revert** verb return, go back, change back, default, relapse.

**review** noun 1 *the Council undertook a review:* analysis, evaluation, assessment, appraisal, examination, investigation, enquiry, probe, inspection, study. 2 *the rent is due for review:* reconsideration, reassessment, re-evaluation, reappraisal. 3 *book reviews:* criticism, critique, assessment, evaluation, commentary.
verb 1 *I reviewed the evidence:* survey, study, research, consider, analyse, examine, scrutinize, explore, look into, probe, investigate, inspect, assess, appraise; informal size up. 2 *the referee reviewed his decision:* reconsider, re-examine, reassess, re-evaluate, reappraise, rethink. 3 *she reviewed the play:* comment on, evaluate, assess, appraise, judge, criticize.

**reviewer** noun critic, commentator, judge.

**revise** verb 1 *she revised her opinion:* reconsider, review, re-examine, reassess, re-evaluate, reappraise, rethink, change, alter, modify. 2 *the editor revised the text:* amend, correct, alter, change, edit, rewrite, redraft, rephrase, rework. 3 (Brit.) *revise your lecture notes:* go over, reread, memorize, cram; informal bone up on; Brit. informal swot up (on), mug up (on).

**revision** noun 1 *a revision of the Prayer Book:* alteration, adaptation, editing, rewriting, redrafting, correction, updating. 2 *a major revision of the system:* reconsideration, review, re-examination, reassessment, re-evaluation, reappraisal, rethink, change, alteration, modification. 3 (Brit.) *he was doing some revision:* rereading, memorizing, cramming; Brit. informal swotting.

**revival** noun 1 *a revival in the economy:* improvement, rallying, picking up, turn for the better, upturn, upswing, resurgence. 2 *the revival of traditional crafts:* comeback, re-establishment, reintroduction, restoration, reappearance, resurrection.
OPPOSITES downturn, disappearance.

**revive** verb 1 *attempts to revive her failed:* resuscitate, bring round, bring back to consciousness. 2 *the man soon revived:* regain consciousness, come round, wake up. 3 *a cup of tea revived her:* reinvigorate, revitalize, refresh, energize, reanimate. 4 *reviving old traditions:* reintroduce, re-establish, restore, resurrect, bring back.

**revolt** verb 1 *the people revolted:* rebel, rise up, take to the streets, riot, mutiny. 2 *the smell revolted him:* disgust, sicken, nauseate, turn someone's stomach, put off, offend; informal turn off; N. Amer. informal gross out.
noun *an armed revolt:* rebellion, revolution, insurrection, mutiny, uprising, riot, insurgence, coup (d'état).

**revolting** adjective disgusting, sickening, nauseating, stomach-turning, repulsive, repugnant, hideous, nasty, foul, offensive; N. Amer. vomitous; informal ghastly, horrid, gross.
OPPOSITES attractive, pleasant.

**revolution** noun 1 *the French Revolution:* rebellion, revolt, insurrection, mutiny, rising, uprising, riot, insurgence, coup (d'état). 2 *a revolution in printing techniques:* dramatic change, sea change, metamorphosis, transformation, innovation, reorganization, restructuring; informal shake-up; N. Amer. informal shakedown. 3 *one revolution of a wheel:* (single) turn, rotation, circle, spin, orbit, circuit, lap.

**revolutionary** adjective 1 *revolutionary troops:* rebellious, rebel, insurgent, rioting, mutinous, renegade. 2 *a revolutionary kind of wheelchair:* new, novel, original, unusual, unconventional, unorthodox, newfangled, innovatory, modern, state-of-the-art, futuristic, pioneering.
noun *political revolutionaries:* rebel, insurgent, mutineer, insurrectionist, agitator.

a
b
c
d
e
f
g
h
i
j
k
l
m
n
o
p
q
**r**
s
t
u
v
w
x
y
z

a
b
c
d
e
f
g
h
i
j
k
l
m
n
o
p
q
**r**
s
t
u
v
w
x
y
z

**revolve** verb **1** *a fan revolved slowly:* go round, turn round, rotate, spin. **2** *the moon revolves around the earth:* circle, travel, orbit.

**reward** noun *a reward for long service:* award, honour, decoration, bonus, premium, bounty, present, gift, payment, recompense, prize; informal pay-off.
verb *they were well rewarded:* recompense, pay, remunerate. OPPOSITES punish.

**rewarding** adjective satisfying, gratifying, pleasing, fulfilling, enriching, illuminating, worthwhile, productive, fruitful.

**rhetoric** noun **1** *a form of rhetoric:* oratory, eloquence, command of language, way with words. **2** *empty rhetoric:* wordiness, verbosity, grandiloquence, bombast, pomposity, extravagant language, purple prose, turgidity; informal hot air.

**rhetorical** adjective **1** *rhetorical devices:* stylistic, oratorical, linguistic, verbal. **2** *rhetorical exchanges in parliament:* extravagant, grandiloquent, high-flown, bombastic, grandiose, pompous, pretentious, overblown, oratorical, turgid, flowery; informal highfalutin.

**rhyme** noun poem, verse, ode; (**rhymes**) poetry, doggerel.

**rhythm** noun **1** *the rhythm of the music:* beat, cadence, tempo, time, pulse, throb, swing. **2** *poetic features such as rhythm:* metre, measure, stress, accent, cadence. **3** *the rhythm of daily life:* pattern, flow, tempo.

**rich** adjective **1** *rich people:* wealthy, affluent, moneyed, well off, well-to-do, prosperous; informal loaded, well heeled, made of money. **2** *rich furnishings:* sumptuous, opulent, luxurious, lavish, gorgeous, splendid, magnificent, costly, expensive, fancy; informal plush; Brit. informal swish; N. Amer. informal swank. **3** *a garden rich in flowers:* well stocked, well provided, abounding, crammed, packed, teeming, bursting. **4** *a rich supply of restaurants:* plentiful, abundant, copious, ample, profuse, lavish, liberal, generous. **5** *rich soil:* fertile, productive, fruitful. **6** *a rich sauce:* creamy, fatty, heavy, full-flavoured. **7** *rich colours:* strong, deep, full, intense, vivid, brilliant.
OPPOSITES poor, cheap, light.

**riches** plural noun money, wealth, funds, cash, means, assets, capital, resources; informal bread, loot; Brit. informal dosh, brass, lolly, spondulicks; N. Amer. informal bucks; US informal greenbacks.

**richly** adverb **1** *richly furnished:* sumptuously, opulently, luxuriously, lavishly, gorgeously, splendidly, magnificently. **2** *the joy she richly deserves:* fully, amply, well, thoroughly, completely, wholly, totally, entirely, absolutely, utterly.
OPPOSITES meanly.

**rid** verb *the aim was to rid the town of malaria:* clear, free, purge, empty, strip.
■ **get rid of** dispose of, throw away/out, clear out, discard, scrap, dump, bin, jettison, expel, eliminate; informal chuck (away), ditch, junk; Brit. informal get shot of; N. Amer. informal trash.

**riddle** noun puzzle, conundrum, brain-teaser, problem, question, poser, enigma, mystery.

**ride** verb 1 *she can ride a horse:* sit on, mount, control, manage, handle. 2 *riding round the town:* travel, move, proceed, drive, cycle, trot, canter, gallop. noun *he took us for a ride:* trip, journey, drive, run, excursion, outing, jaunt, lift; informal spin.

**ridicule** noun *he was subjected to ridicule:* mockery, derision, laughter, scorn, scoffing, jeering.
OPPOSITES respect.
verb *his theory was ridiculed:* mock, deride, laugh at, heap scorn on, jeer at, make fun of, scoff at, satirize, caricature, parody.
OPPOSITES respect.

**ridiculous** adjective 1 *that looks ridiculous:* laughable, absurd, comical, funny, hilarious, risible, droll, amusing, farcical. 2 *a ridiculous suggestion:* foolish, silly, senseless, foolhardy, stupid, idiotic. 3 *a ridiculous exaggeration:* absurd, preposterous, ludicrous, laughable, risible, nonsensical, outrageous.
OPPOSITES sensible.

**rife** adjective widespread, general, common, universal, extensive, ubiquitous, endemic, inescapable.
OPPOSITES unknown.

**rifle** verb 1 *she rifled through her wardrobe:* rummage, search, hunt, forage. 2 *a thief rifled her home:* burgle, rob, steal from, loot, raid, plunder, ransack.

**rift** noun 1 *a deep rift in the ice:* crack, split, breach, fissure, fracture, cleft, crevice, opening. 2 *the rift between them:* breach, division, split, quarrel, disagreement, falling-out, row, conflict, feud; Brit. informal bust-up.

**rig**¹ verb 1 *the boats were rigged with a single sail:* equip, kit out, fit out, supply, furnish, provide, arm. 2 *I rigged myself out in black:* dress, clothe, attire, robe, garb, get up; informal doll up. 3 *he will rig up a shelter:* set up, erect, assemble, put together, whip up, improvise, contrive; Brit. informal knock up.

**rig**² verb *they rigged the election:* manipulate, engineer, distort, misrepresent, pervert, tamper with, falsify, fake; informal fix; Brit. informal fiddle.

**right** adjective 1 *it wouldn't be right to do that:* just, fair, proper, good, upright, righteous, virtuous, moral, ethical, honourable, honest, lawful, legal. 2 *the right answer:* correct, accurate, exact, precise, proper, valid, conventional, established, official, formal; Brit. informal spot on. 3 *the right person for the job:* suitable, appropriate, fitting, correct, proper, desirable, preferable, ideal. 4 *you've come at the right time:* opportune, advantageous, favourable, good, lucky, fortunate. 5 *on my right side:* right-hand; Nautical starboard.
OPPOSITES wrong, bad, left, port.
adverb 1 *she was right at the limit of her patience:* completely, fully, totally, absolutely, utterly, thoroughly, quite. 2 *right in the middle of the village:* exactly, precisely, directly, immediately, just, squarely, dead; informal (slap) bang, smack, plumb. 3 *I think I heard right:* correctly,

accurately, properly, precisely, perfectly. **4** *make sure you're treated right:* well, properly, justly, fairly, equitably, impartially, honourably, lawfully, legally. **5** *things will turn out right:* well, for the best, favourably, happily, advantageously, profitably, luckily, conveniently.
OPPOSITES wrong, badly.
**noun 1** *the difference between right and wrong:* goodness, righteousness, virtue, integrity, propriety, morality, truth, honesty, honour, justice, fairness, equity. **2** *you have the right to say no:* entitlement, prerogative, privilege, liberty, authority, power, licence, permission, dispensation, leave, due.
OPPOSITES wrong.
**verb** *we must right the situation:* remedy, rectify, retrieve, fix, resolve, sort out, settle, square, straighten out, correct, repair, mend, redress.
■ **right away** at once, straight away, (right) now, this (very) minute, this instant, immediately, instantly, directly, forthwith, without further ado, promptly, quickly, without delay, asap, as soon as possible; N. Amer. in short order; informal straight off, pronto.

**righteous** adjective good, virtuous, upright, upstanding, decent, ethical, principled, moral, honest, honourable, blameless.
OPPOSITES wicked.

**right-wing** adjective conservative, rightist, reactionary, traditionalist, conventional.
OPPOSITES left-wing.

**rigid** adjective **1** *a rigid container:* stiff, hard, firm, inflexible, unbending, unyielding. **2** *a rigid routine:* fixed, set, firm, inflexible, invariable, hard and fast, cast-iron. **3** *a rigid approach to funding:* strict, stringent, rigorous, inflexible, uncompromising, intransigent.
OPPOSITES flexible, lenient.

**rigorous** adjective **1** *rigorous attention to detail:* meticulous, conscientious, punctilious, careful, scrupulous, painstaking, exact, precise, accurate, particular, strict. **2** *the rigorous enforcement of rules:* strict, stringent, rigid, inflexible, draconian, intransigent, uncompromising. **3** *rigorous conditions:* harsh, severe, bleak, extreme, demanding.
OPPOSITES slapdash, lax, mild.

**rim** noun edge, brim, lip, border, side, margin, brink, boundary, perimeter, circumference, limits, periphery.

**ring**[1] noun **1** *a ring round the moon:* circle, band, halo, disc. **2** *the horses entered the ring:* arena, enclosure, circus, amphitheatre, bowl. **3** *a spy ring:* gang, syndicate, cartel, mob, band, circle, organization, association, society, alliance, league.
**verb** *police ringed the building:* surround, circle, encircle, enclose, hem in, confine, seal off.

**ring**[2] verb **1** *church bells rang:* chime, sound, peal, toll, clang, bong; literary knell. **2** *the room rang with laughter:* resound, reverberate, resonate, echo. **3** *I'll ring you tomorrow:* telephone, phone, call (up); informal give someone a buzz; Brit. informal give someone a bell, give someone a tinkle, get on the blower to.

**rinse** verb wash (out), clean, cleanse, bathe, dip, drench, splash, swill, sluice.

**riot** noun 1 *a riot in the capital:* disorder, disturbance, lawlesssness, upheaval, uproar, commotion. 2 *a riot of colour:* mass, sea, splash, show, profusion.
verb *the miners rioted:* (go on the) rampage, run wild, run amok, run riot, go berserk; informal raise hell.
■ run riot grow profusely, spread uncontrolled, burgeon, multiply, rocket.

**rip** verb 1 *he ripped the posters down:* tug, wrench, pull, snatch, tear, heave, drag, peel, pluck; informal yank. 2 *she ripped Leo's note into pieces:* tear, claw, hack, slit.

**ripe** adjective 1 *a ripe tomato:* mature, full grown. 2 *ripe for development:* ready, fit, suitable, right. 3 *the time is ripe for his return:* opportune, advantageous, favourable, auspicious, good, right.
OPPOSITES young, unsuitable, unfavourable.

**rise** verb 1 *the sun rose:* climb, come up, arise, ascend, mount, soar. 2 *the mountains rising above us:* loom, tower, soar. 3 *prices rose:* go up, increase, soar, shoot up, surge, leap, jump, rocket, escalate, spiral. 4 *living standards have risen:* improve, get better, advance. 5 *his voice rose:* get higher, grow, increase, become louder, swell, intensify. 6 *he rose from his chair:* stand up, get to one's feet, get up, jump up, leap up. 7 *he rises at dawn:* get up, stir, bestir oneself, be up and about;

informal surface.
OPPOSITES fall, sit down, go to bed.
noun 1 *a price rise:* increase, hike, leap, upsurge, upswing, climb. 2 *he got a rise of 4%:* raise, increase, hike, increment. 3 *a rise in standards:* improvement, advance. 4 *his rise to power:* progress, climb, promotion, elevation. 5 *we walked up the rise:* slope, incline, hill.

**risk** noun 1 *there is a certain amount of risk:* chance, uncertainty, unpredictability, instability, insecurity. 2 *the risk of fire:* possibility, chance, probability, likelihood, danger, peril, threat, menace, prospect.
OPPOSITES certainty, safety, impossibility.
verb *he risked his life to save them:* endanger, imperil, jeopardize, hazard, gamble (with), chance, put on the line.

**risky** adjective dangerous, hazardous, perilous, unsafe, insecure, precarious, touch-and-go, treacherous, uncertain, unpredictable; informal dicey; N. Amer. informal gnarly.

**rite** noun ceremony, ritual, ceremonial, custom, service, observance, liturgy, worship, office.

**ritual** noun *an elaborate civic ritual:* ceremony, rite, act, practice, custom, tradition, convention, formality, protocol.
adjective *a ritual burial:* ceremonial, prescribed, set, formal, traditional, conventional.

**rival** noun 1 *his rival for the nomination:* opponent, challenger, competitor, contender, adversary, antagonist, enemy. 2 *the tool*

*has no rival:* equal, match, peer, equivalent.
OPPOSITES ally.
**verb** *few countries can rival it for scenery:* match, compare with, compete with, vie with, equal, measure up to, touch; informal hold a candle to.
**adjective** *rival candidates:* competing, opposing.

**rivalry** noun competition, contention, opposition, conflict, feuding; informal keeping up with the Joneses.

**river** noun 1 stream, brook, watercourse, rivulet, tributary; Scottish & N. English burn; N. English beck; S. English bourn; N. Amer. & Austral./NZ creek. 2 *a river of molten lava:* stream, torrent, flood, deluge, cascade.

**riveting** adjective fascinating, gripping, engrossing, intriguing, absorbing, captivating, enthralling, compelling, spellbinding, mesmerizing; informal unputdownable.
OPPOSITES boring.

**road** noun 1 street, thoroughfare, roadway, highway, lane; Brit. motorway. 2 *on the road to recovery:* way, path, route, course.

**roam** verb wander, rove, ramble, drift, walk, traipse, range, travel, tramp, trek; Scottish & Irish stravaig; informal cruise, mosey.

**roar** noun 1 *the roars of the crowd:* shout, bellow, yell, cry, howl, clamour; informal holler. 2 *the roar of the sea:* boom, crash, rumble, roll, thunder.
**verb** 1 *'Get out!' roared Angus:* bellow, yell, shout, bawl, howl; informal holler. 2 *thunder roared:* boom, rumble, crash, roll, thunder.

**roaring** adjective *a roaring fire:* blazing, burning, flaming.

**rob** verb 1 *the gang robbed a bank:* burgle, steal from, hold up, break into, raid, loot, plunder, pillage; N. Amer. burglarize. 2 *he robbed an old woman:* steal from, hold up; informal mug. 3 *he was robbed of his savings:* cheat, swindle, defraud; informal do out of, con out of. 4 *defeat robbed him of his title:* deprive, strip, deny.

**robber** noun burglar, thief, housebreaker, mugger, shoplifter, raider, looter.

**robbery** noun *they were arrested for the robbery:* burglary, theft, stealing, housebreaking, shoplifting, embezzlement, fraud, hold-up, raid; informal mugging, smash-and-grab, stick-up; N. Amer. informal heist.

**robe** noun 1 *the women wore black robes:* cloak, kaftan, djellaba, wrap, mantle, cape; N. Amer. wrapper. 2 *ceremonial robes:* garb, regalia, costume, finery, vestments.

**robot** noun machine, automaton, android, golem; informal bot, droid.

**robust** adjective 1 *a robust man:* strong, vigorous, sturdy, tough, powerful, solid, rugged, hardy, strapping, healthy, (fighting) fit, hale and hearty. 2 *these knives are robust:* durable, resilient, tough, hard-wearing, long-lasting, sturdy, strong.
OPPOSITES frail, fragile.

**rock**¹ noun boulder, stone, pebble.

**rock**² verb 1 *the ship rocked on the water:* move to and fro, sway, see-saw, roll, pitch, plunge, toss, lurch. 2 *Wall Street was rocked by the news:* stun, shock, stagger, astonish, startle, surprise, shake, take aback, throw, unnerve, disconcert.

**rocky**[1] adjective *a rocky path:* stony, pebbly, shingly, rough, bumpy, craggy, mountainous.

**rocky**[2] adjective unsteady, shaky, unstable, wobbly, tottery, rickety.
OPPOSITES steady, stable.

**rod** noun bar, stick, pole, baton, staff, shaft, strut, rail, spoke.

**rogue** noun 1 *a rogue without ethics:* scoundrel, rascal, good-for-nothing, wretch, villain, criminal, lawbreaker; informal crook. 2 *your boy's a little rogue:* rascal, imp, devil, monkey; informal scamp, scallywag.

**role** noun 1 *a small role in the film:* part, character. 2 *his role as President:* capacity, position, function, job, post, office, duty, responsibility.

**roll** verb 1 *the bottle rolled down the table:* bowl, turn over and over, spin, rotate, wheel, trundle. 2 *tears rolled down her cheeks:* flow, run, course, stream, pour, trickle. 3 *he rolled his handkerchief into a ball:* wind, coil, fold, curl, twist. 4 *the ship began to roll:* rock, sway, reel, list, pitch, plunge, lurch, toss.
noun 1 *a roll of paper:* cylinder, tube, scroll, reel, spool. 2 *a roll of the dice:* throw, toss, turn, spin. 3 *the electoral roll:* list, register, directory, record, file, index, catalogue, inventory. 4 *a roll of thunder:* rumble, reverberation, echo, boom, clap, crack, roar.

**romance** noun 1 *he's had many romances:* love affair, relationship, liaison, courtship, attachment, amour. 2 *an author of romances:* story, tale, legend, fairy tale. 3 *the romance of the Far East:* mystery, glamour, excitement, exoticism, mystique, appeal, allure, charm.

**romantic** adjective 1 *he's so romantic:* loving, amorous, passionate, tender, affectionate; informal lovey-dovey. 2 *romantic songs:* sentimental, hearts-and-flowers, mawkish, sickly, saccharine, syrupy; informal slushy, mushy, sloppy, schmaltzy; Brit. informal soppy. 3 *a romantic setting:* idyllic, picturesque, fairy-tale, beautiful, lovely, charming, pretty. 4 *romantic notions of rural communities:* idealistic, unrealistic, fanciful, impractical, head-in-the-clouds, starry-eyed, utopian, fairy-tale.
OPPOSITES unsentimental, realistic.
noun *an incurable romantic:* idealist, sentimentalist, dreamer, fantasist.
OPPOSITES realist.

**romp** verb play, frolic, frisk, gambol, skip, prance, caper, cavort.

**room** noun 1 *there isn't much room:* space, headroom, legroom, area, expanse, extent. 2 *room for improvement:* scope, capacity, leeway, latitude, freedom.

**root** noun 1 *the root of the problem:* source, origin, cause, reason, basis, foundation, bottom, seat. 2 *(roots)* origins, beginnings, family, birth, heritage.
verb *he rooted around in the cupboard:* rummage, hunt, search, rifle, delve, forage, dig, nose, poke.
■ **root something out** eradicate, eliminate, weed out, destroy, wipe out, stamp out, abolish,

a
b
c
d
e
f
g
h
i
j
k
l
m
n
o
p
q
**r**
s
t
u
v
w
x
y
z

end, put a stop to.

**rope** noun cord, cable, line, hawser, string.

**rosy** adjective **1** *a rosy complexion:* pink, roseate, reddish, glowing, healthy, fresh, radiant, blooming, blushing, flushed, ruddy. **2** *his future looks rosy:* promising, optimistic, auspicious, hopeful, encouraging, favourable, bright, golden.
OPPOSITES pale, bleak.

**rot** verb **1** *the floorboards rotted:* decay, decompose, disintegrate, crumble, perish. **2** *the meat began to rot:* go bad, go off, spoil, moulder, putrefy, fester. **3** *poor neighbourhoods have been left to rot:* deteriorate, degenerate, decline, decay, go to seed, go downhill; informal go to pot, go to the dogs.
OPPOSITES improve.
noun *the leaves turned black with rot:* decay, decomposition, mould, mildew, blight, canker.

**rotate** verb **1** *the wheels rotate continually:* revolve, go round, turn (round), spin, gyrate, whirl, twirl, swivel, circle, pivot. **2** *many nurses rotate jobs:* alternate, take turns, change, switch, interchange, exchange, swap.

**rotation** noun **1** *the rotation of the wheels:* revolving, turning, spinning, gyration, circling. **2** *a rotation of the Earth:* turn, revolution, orbit, spin. **3** *each member is chair for six months in rotation:* sequence, succession, alternation, cycle.

**rotten** adjective **1** *rotten meat:* decaying, bad, off, decomposing, putrid, perished, rancid, festering, fetid. **2** *he's rotten to the core:* corrupt, unprincipled, dishonest,

dishonourable, unscrupulous, untrustworthy, immoral; informal crooked; Brit. informal bent.
OPPOSITES fresh, honourable.

**rough** adjective **1** *rough ground:* uneven, irregular, bumpy, stony, rocky, rugged, rutted, pitted. **2** *the terrier's rough coat:* coarse, bristly, scratchy, prickly, shaggy, hairy, bushy. **3** *rough skin:* dry, leathery, weather-beaten, chapped, calloused, scaly. **4** *his voice was rough:* gruff, hoarse, harsh, rasping, husky, throaty, gravelly. **5** *he gets rough when he's drunk:* violent, brutal, vicious, aggressive, belligerent, pugnacious, boisterous, rowdy, disorderly, unruly, riotous. **6** *a machine that can take rough handling:* careless, clumsy, inept, unskilful. **7** *rough manners:* boorish, loutish, oafish, brutish, coarse, crude, uncouth, vulgar, unrefined, unladylike, ungentlemanly, uncultured. **8** *rough seas:* turbulent, stormy, tempestuous, violent, heavy, choppy. **9** *a rough draft:* preliminary, hasty, quick, sketchy, cursory, basic, crude, rudimentary, raw, unpolished, incomplete, unfinished. **10** *a rough estimate:* approximate, inexact, imprecise, vague, estimated; N. Amer. informal ballpark.
OPPOSITES smooth, sleek, soft, dulcet, sweet, gentle, careful, refined, calm, exact.
noun *the artist's initial roughs:* sketch, draft, outline, mock-up.

**round** adjective *a round window:* circular, spherical, globular, cylindrical.
noun **1** *mould the dough into rounds:* ball, sphere, globe, orb, circle, disc, ring, hoop. **2** *a*

*policeman on his rounds:* circuit, beat, route, tour. **3** *the first round of the contest:* stage, level, heat, game, bout, contest. **4** *an endless round of parties:* succession, sequence, series, cycle.

**preposition 1** *the alleys round the station:* around, about, encircling, near, orbiting. **2** *casinos dotted round France:* throughout, all over.

**verb** *the ship rounded the point:* go round, travel round, skirt, circumnavigate, orbit.

■ **round something off** complete, finish off, crown, cap, top, conclude, close, end. ■ **round someone/something up** gather together, herd together, muster, marshal, rally, assemble, collect, group; N. Amer. corral.

**roundabout adjective 1** *a roundabout route:* circuitous, indirect, meandering, serpentine, tortuous. **2** *I asked in a roundabout sort of way:* indirect, oblique, circuitous, circumlocutory.
OPPOSITES direct.

**rouse verb 1** *he roused Ralph at dawn:* wake (up), awaken, arouse; Brit. informal knock up. **2** *she roused and looked around:* wake up, awake, come to, get up, rise, bestir oneself. **3** *he roused the crowd:* stir up, excite, galvanize, electrify, stimulate, inspire, inspirit, move, inflame, agitate, goad, provoke, prompt. **4** *he's got a temper when he's roused:* provoke, annoy, anger, infuriate, madden, incense, vex, irk; informal aggravate.
OPPOSITES calm, pacify, allay.

**rousing adjective** stirring, inspiring, exciting, stimulating, moving, electrifying, invigorating, energizing, exhilarating.

**rout noun** *the army's ignominious rout:* defeat, beating, retreat, flight; informal licking, hammering, thrashing, pasting, drubbing.
OPPOSITES victory.

**verb** *his army was routed:* defeat, beat, conquer, vanquish, crush, put to flight, drive off, scatter; informal lick, hammer, clobber, thrash; Brit. informal stuff.

**route noun** way, course, road, path, direction.

**routine noun 1** *his morning routine:* procedure, practice, pattern, drill, regime, programme, schedule, plan. **2** *a stand-up routine:* act, performance, number, turn, piece; informal spiel, patter.

**adjective 1** *a routine health check:* standard, regular, customary, normal, usual, ordinary, typical, everyday. **2** *a routine action movie:* boring, tedious, monotonous, humdrum, run-of-the-mill, pedestrian, predictable, hackneyed, unimaginative, unoriginal, banal, trite.
OPPOSITES unusual.

**row¹ noun 1** *rows of children:* line, column, file, queue, procession, chain, string, succession; informal crocodile. **2** *the middle row of seats:* tier, line, rank, bank.

■ **in a row** consecutively, in succession, running, straight; informal on the trot.

**row² (Brit. informal) noun 1** *have you two had a row?* argument, quarrel, squabble, fight, dispute; informal tiff, run-in, slanging match, spat; Brit. informal bust-up. **2** *I couldn't hear for the row:* din, noise, racket,

a
b
c
d
e
f
g
h
i
j
k
l
m
n
o
p
q
**r**
s
t
u
v
w
x
y
z

uproar, hubbub, rumpus; informal hullabaloo.

verb *they rowed about money:* argue, quarrel, squabble, bicker, fight, fall out, disagree, have words; informal scrap.

**royal** adjective regal, kingly, queenly, princely, sovereign.

**rub** verb 1 *Polly rubbed her arm:* massage, knead, stroke, pat. 2 *he rubbed sun lotion on her back:* apply, smear, spread, work in. 3 *my shoes rub painfully:* chafe, scrape, pinch.

noun 1 *she gave his back a rub:* massage, rub-down. 2 *I gave my shoes a rub:* polish, wipe, clean. ■ rub something down clean, sponge, wash. ■ rub something out erase, delete, remove, obliterate.

**rubbish** noun 1 *throw away that rubbish:* refuse, waste, litter, scrap, dross; N. Amer. garbage, trash; informal dreck, junk. 2 *she's talking rubbish:* nonsense, gibberish, claptrap, garbage; informal baloney, tripe, drivel, bilge, bunk, piffle, poppycock, twaddle, gobbledegook; Brit. informal codswallop, cobblers, tosh.

**rude** adjective 1 *a rude man:* ill-mannered, bad-mannered, impolite, discourteous, uncivil, impertinent, insolent, impudent, disparaging, abusive. 2 *rude jokes:* vulgar, coarse, smutty, dirty, filthy, crude, lewd, obscene, risqué; informal blue; Brit. informal near the knuckle. 3 *a rude awakening:* abrupt, sudden, sharp. OPPOSITES polite, clean, gentle.

**ruffle** verb 1 *he ruffled her hair:* disarrange, tousle, dishevel, rumple, mess up. 2 *don't let him ruffle you:* disconcert, unnerve,

fluster, agitate, upset, disturb, discomfit, put off, perturb, unsettle; informal faze, throw, get to. OPPOSITES smooth, calm.

**rugged** adjective 1 *the rugged path:* rough, uneven, bumpy, rocky, stony, pitted. 2 *a rugged vehicle:* robust, durable, sturdy, strong, tough, resilient. 3 *rugged manly types:* well built, burly, strong, muscular, muscly, brawny, strapping, tough, hardy, robust, sturdy, solid; informal hunky. 4 *his rugged features:* strong, craggy, rough-hewn, manly, masculine. OPPOSITES smooth, flimsy, weedy, delicate.

**ruin** noun 1 *the buildings were saved from ruin:* disintegration, decay, disrepair, dilapidation, destruction, demolition. 2 *the ruins of a church:* remains, remnants, fragments, rubble, debris, wreckage. 3 *electoral ruin for Labour:* downfall, collapse, defeat, undoing, failure. 4 *shopkeepers are facing ruin:* bankruptcy, insolvency, penury, poverty, destitution. OPPOSITES preservation, triumph, wealth.

verb 1 *don't ruin my plans:* spoil, wreck, blight, shatter, dash, torpedo, scotch, mess up, sabotage; informal screw up; Brit. informal scupper. 2 *the bank's collapse ruined them:* bankrupt, make insolvent, impoverish, pauperize, wipe out, break, cripple, bring someone to their knees. 3 *a country ruined by civil war:* destroy, devastate, lay waste, ravage, raze, demolish, wreck, wipe out, flatten. OPPOSITES save, rebuild.

**rule** noun 1 *health and safety rules:* regulation, directive, order, law, statute. 2 *church attendance on Sunday was the general rule:* procedure, practice, protocol, convention, norm, routine, custom, habit. 3 *moderation is the golden rule:* principle, precept, standard, axiom, truth, maxim. 4 *under British rule:* government, jurisdiction, command, power, dominion, control, administration, sovereignty, leadership.
verb 1 *El Salvador was ruled by Spain:* govern, preside over, control, lead, dominate, run, head, administer. 2 *Mary ruled for six years:* reign, be on the throne, be in power, govern. 3 *the judge ruled that they be set free:* decree, order, pronounce, judge, adjudge, ordain, decide, find. 4 *subversion ruled:* prevail, predominate, be the order of the day, reign supreme.
■ **as a rule** usually, in general, normally, ordinarily, customarily, for the most part, on the whole, by and large, in the main, mostly, commonly, typically. ■ **rule something out** exclude, eliminate, disregard, preclude, prohibit, prevent, disallow.

**ruler** noun leader, sovereign, monarch, potentate, king, queen, emperor, empress, prince, princess, crowned head, head of state, president, premier, governor.
OPPOSITES subject.

**ruling** noun *the judge's ruling:* judgement, decision, adjudication, finding, verdict, pronouncement, resolution, decree, injunction.
adjective 1 *Japan's ruling party:* governing, controlling, commanding, supreme. 2 *football was their ruling passion:* main, chief, principal, major, dominating, consuming; informal number-one.

**rumour** noun gossip, hearsay, talk, tittle-tattle, speculation, word, report, story, whisper; informal the grapevine, the word on the street, the buzz.

**run** verb 1 *she ran across the road:* sprint, race, dart, rush, dash, hasten, hurry, scurry, scamper, gallop, jog, trot; informal leg it. 2 *the robbers turned and ran:* flee, take flight, make off, take off, take to one's heels, bolt, make one's getaway, escape; informal beat it, clear off/out, scram; Brit. informal scarper. 3 *the road runs the length of the valley:* extend, stretch, reach, continue. 4 *water ran from the eaves:* flow, pour, stream, gush, flood, cascade, roll, course, spill, trickle, drip, dribble, leak. 5 *a bus runs to Sorrento:* travel, shuttle, go. 6 *he runs a transport company:* be in charge of, manage, direct, control, head, govern, supervise, superintend, oversee. 7 *it's expensive to run a car:* maintain, keep, own, possess, have, use, operate. 8 *he left the engine running:* operate, function, work, go. 9 *the lease runs for twenty years:* last, continue, survive.
noun 1 *his morning run:* jog, sprint, dash, gallop, trot. 2 *she did the school run:* route, journey, circuit, round, beat. 3 *a run in the car:* drive, ride, turn, trip, excursion, outing, jaunt; informal spin, tootle. 4 *an unbeaten run of victories:* series, succession, sequence, string, streak, spate. 5 *a chicken*

**run**: enclosure, pen, coop. **6** *a ski run*: slope, track, piste; N. Amer. trail.
■ **run someone down 1** *he was run down by joyriders*: run over, knock down/over, hit. **2** *she ran him down in front of other people*: criticize, denigrate, belittle, disparage, deprecate, find fault with; informal put down, knock, bad-mouth; Brit. informal rubbish, slag off. ■ **run into 1** *a car ran into his van*: collide with, hit, strike, crash into, smash into, plough into, ram. **2** *I ran into Hugo the other day*: meet (by chance), run across, chance on, stumble on, happen on; informal bump into. **3** *we ran into a problem*: experience, encounter, meet with, be faced with, be confronted with. ■ **run out 1** *supplies ran out*: be used up, dry up, be exhausted, be finished, peter out. **2** *her contract ran out*: expire, end, terminate, finish, lapse. ■ **run over 1** *the bathwater ran over*: overflow, spill over, brim over. **2** *the project ran over budget*: exceed, go over, overshoot, overreach. **3** *he quickly ran over the story*: review, repeat, run through, go over, reiterate, recapitulate, look over, read through; informal recap on. ■ **run someone over**. See **RUN SOMEONE DOWN** sense 1.

**rundown** noun summary, synopsis, precis, run-through, review, overview, briefing, sketch, outline; informal low-down, recap.

**run down** adjective **1** *a run-down area of London*: dilapidated, tumbledown, ramshackle, derelict, crumbling, neglected, uncared-for, slummy. **2** *she was feeling rather run down*: unwell, ill, poorly, unhealthy, peaky, tired, drained, exhausted, worn out, below par, washed out; Brit. off colour; informal under the weather; Brit. informal off; Austral./ NZ informal crook.

**runner** noun **1** athlete, sprinter, hurdler, racer, jogger. **2** *the bookmaker employed runners*: messenger, courier, errand boy; informal gofer.

**running** noun **1** *the running of the school*: administration, management, organization, coordination, orchestration, handling, direction, control, supervision. **2** *the smooth running of her department*: operation, working, function, performance.
adjective **1** *running water*: flowing, gushing, rushing, moving. **2** *a running argument*: ongoing, continuous, incessant, ceaseless, constant, perpetual. **3** *she was late two days running*: in succession, in a row, in sequence, consecutively, straight, together; informal on the trot.

**runny** adjective liquid, liquefied, fluid, melted, molten, watery, thin.
OPPOSITES solid, thick.

**rupture** noun & verb break, fracture, crack, burst, split, fissure, breach.

**rural** adjective country, rustic, bucolic, pastoral, agricultural, agrarian.
OPPOSITES urban.

**ruse** noun ploy, stratagem, tactic, scheme, trick, gambit, dodge, subterfuge, machination, wile; Brit. informal wheeze.

**rush** verb **1** *she rushed home*: hurry, dash, run, race, sprint, bolt, dart, gallop, career,

charge, shoot, hurtle, hare, fly, speed, zoom, scurry, scuttle, scamper, hasten; informal tear, belt, pelt, scoot, zip, whip; Brit. informal bomb. **2** *water rushed along gutters:* gush, pour, surge, stream, course, cascade. **3** *the tax was rushed through parliament:* push, hurry, hasten, speed, hustle, press, force. **4** *they rushed the cordon of troops:* attack, charge, storm.
**noun 1** *Tim made a rush for the exit:* dash, run, sprint, dart, bolt, charge, scramble. **2** *the lunchtime rush:* hustle and bustle, commotion, hubbub, hurly-burly, stir. **3** *a rush for tickets:* demand, clamour, call, request, run on. **4** *he was in no rush to leave:* hurry, haste, urgency. **5** *I made a sudden rush at him:* charge, onslaught, attack, assault.

**adjective** *a rush job:* urgent, high-priority, emergency, hurried, hasty, fast, quick, swift.
**rust verb** corrode, oxidize, tarnish.
**rustic adjective 1** *a rustic setting:* rural, country, pastoral, bucolic, agricultural, agrarian. **2** *rustic wooden tables:* plain, simple, homely, unsophisticated, rough, crude. OPPOSITES urban, ornate, sophisticated.
**noun** peasant, countryman, countrywoman, bumpkin, yokel, country cousin; N. Amer. informal hillbilly, hayseed, hick; Austral./NZ informal bushy.
**ruthless adjective** merciless, pitiless, cruel, heartless, hard-hearted, cold-hearted, cold-blooded, harsh, callous. OPPOSITES merciful.

# Ss

**sabotage noun** vandalism, wrecking, destruction, damage, obstruction, disruption; Brit. informal a spanner in the works.
**verb** vandalize, wreck, damage, destroy, incapacitate, obstruct, disrupt, spoil, ruin, undermine.
**sack noun** bag, pouch, pocket, pack.
**verb** (informal) dismiss, discharge, lay off, make redundant, let go, throw out; informal fire, give someone the sack; Brit. informal give someone their cards.
■ **the sack** (informal) dismissal, discharge, redundancy; informal the boot, the axe, the heave-ho, the push.
**sacred adjective 1** *a sacred place:*

holy, hallowed, blessed, consecrated, sanctified. **2** *sacred music:* religious, spiritual, devotional, church, ecclesiastical. OPPOSITES secular, profane.
**sacrifice noun 1** *the sacrifice of animals:* (ritual) slaughter, (votive) offering. **2** *the sacrifice of privileges:* surrender, giving up, abandonment, renunciation. **verb 1** *two goats were sacrificed:* offer up, slaughter. **2** *he sacrificed his principles:* give up, abandon, renounce, relinquish, betray. **3** *he sacrificed his life:* give (up), lay down, surrender, forfeit.
**sad adjective 1** *we felt sad:*

unhappy, sorrowful, depressed, downcast, miserable, down, despondent, wretched, glum, gloomy, doleful, melancholy, mournful, forlorn, heartbroken; informal blue, down in the mouth, down in the dumps. **2** *a sad story*: tragic, unhappy, miserable, wretched, sorry, pitiful, pathetic, heartbreaking, heart-rending. **3** *a sad state of affairs*: unfortunate, regrettable, sorry, deplorable, lamentable, pitiful, shameful, disgraceful.
OPPOSITES happy, cheerful, fortunate.

**sadden** verb depress, dispirit, deject, dishearten, grieve, discourage, upset, get down.

**saddle** verb burden, encumber, lumber, land, impose something on.

**sadness** noun unhappiness, sorrow, dejection, depression, misery, despondency, wretchedness, gloom, gloominess, melancholy.

**safe** adjective **1** *the jewels are safe in the bank*: secure, protected, out of harm's way. **2** *the children are all safe*: unharmed, unhurt, uninjured, unscathed, all right, fine, well, in one piece, out of danger. **3** *a safe place*: secure, sound, impregnable, invulnerable, secret. **4** *a safe driver*: cautious, circumspect, prudent, careful, unadventurous, conservative. **5** *the drug is safe*: harmless, innocuous, benign, non-toxic, non-poisonous.
OPPOSITES insecure, dangerous, reckless, harmful.

**safeguard** noun protection, defence, buffer, provision, security, cover, insurance.
verb protect, preserve, conserve,

save, secure, shield, guard, keep safe.
OPPOSITES jeopardize.

**safety** noun **1** *the safety of the residents*: welfare, well-being, protection, security. **2** *the safety of ferries*: security, soundness, dependability, reliability. **3** *the safety of the shore*: shelter, sanctuary, refuge.

**sag** verb **1** *he sagged back in his chair*: sink, slump, loll, flop, crumple. **2** *the floors all sag*: dip, droop, bulge, bag.

**saga** noun **1** *Icelandic sagas*: epic, legend, (folk) tale, romance, narrative, myth. **2** *the saga of how they met*: story, tale, yarn.

**sage** noun wise man/woman, philosopher, scholar, guru, prophet, mystic.

**sail** verb **1** *we sailed across the Atlantic*: voyage, travel, navigate, cruise. **2** *we sail tonight*: set sail, put to sea, leave, weigh anchor. **3** *who is sailing the ship?* steer, pilot, captain; informal skipper. **4** *clouds were sailing past*: glide, drift, float, flow, sweep, skim, coast, flit, scud.

**sailor** noun seaman, seafarer, mariner, yachtsman, yachtswoman, hand, merchant seaman.

**sake** noun **1** *for the sake of clarity*: purpose(s), reason(s). **2** *for her son's sake*: benefit, advantage, good, well-being, welfare.

**salary** noun pay, wages, earnings, payment, remuneration, fee(s), stipend, income.

**sale** noun **1** *the sale of firearms*: selling, dealing, trading. **2** *they make a sale every minute*: deal, transaction, bargain.

OPPOSITES purchase.

**salty** adjective salt, salted, saline, briny, brackish.

**salute** noun tribute, testimonial, homage, honour, celebration (of), acknowledgement (of).
verb pay tribute to, pay homage to, honour, celebrate, acknowledge, take one's hat off to.

**salvage** verb rescue, save, recover, retrieve, reclaim.

**salvation** noun 1 *praying for salvation:* redemption, deliverance. 2 *that man was her salvation:* lifeline, means of escape, saviour.
OPPOSITES damnation, ruin.

**same** adjective 1 *we stayed at the same hotel:* identical, selfsame, very same. 2 *they had the same symptoms:* matching, identical, alike, carbon-copy, twin, indistinguishable, interchangeable, corresponding, equivalent, parallel, like, comparable, similar.
OPPOSITES another, different, dissimilar, varying.
■ the same unchanging, unvarying, unvaried, consistent, uniform.

**sample** noun 1 *a sample of the fabric:* specimen, example, snippet, swatch, taste, taster. 2 *a representative sample:* cross section, selection.
verb *we sampled the food:* try (out), taste, test, put to the test, appraise, evaluate; informal check out.
adjective *a sample copy:* specimen, test, trial, pilot, dummy.

**sanction** noun 1 *trade sanctions:* penalty, punishment, deterrent, restriction, embargo, ban, prohibition, boycott. 2 *the scheme has the sanction of the court:* authorization, consent, leave, permission, authority, dispensation, assent, acquiescence, agreement, approval, endorsement, blessing; informal the thumbs up, the OK.
OPPOSITES reward, prohibition.
verb *the rally was sanctioned by the government:* authorize, permit, allow, endorse, approve, accept, back, support; informal OK.
OPPOSITES prohibit.

**sanctuary** noun 1 *the garden is our sanctuary:* refuge, haven, oasis, shelter, retreat, bolt-hole, hideaway. 2 *he was given sanctuary in the embassy:* safety, protection, shelter, immunity, asylum. 3 *a bird sanctuary:* reserve, park.

**sane** adjective 1 *he is presumed to be sane:* of sound mind, in one's right mind, compos mentis, lucid, rational, balanced, normal; informal all there. 2 *a sane suggestion:* sensible, practical, realistic, prudent, reasonable, rational, level-headed.
OPPOSITES mad, foolish.

**sap** noun *tree sap:* juice, secretion, fluid, liquid.
verb *illness sapped his energy:* erode, wear away/down, deplete, reduce, lessen, undermine, drain, bleed.

**satanic** adjective diabolical, fiendish, devilish, demonic, ungodly, hellish, infernal, wicked, evil, sinful.
OPPOSITES godly.

**satire** noun parody, burlesque, caricature, irony, lampoon, skit; informal spoof, take-off, send-up.

**satirical** adjective mocking, ironic, sardonic, critical, irreverent, disparaging, disrespectful.

**satisfaction** noun contentment, content, pleasure, gratification, fulfilment, enjoyment, happiness, pride.

**satisfactory** adjective adequate, all right, acceptable, good enough, sufficient, reasonable, competent, fair, decent, average, passable, fine, in order, up to scratch, up to the mark.
OPPOSITES unsatisfactory.

**satisfy** verb 1 *a chance to satisfy his lust:* fulfil, gratify, meet, fill, indulge, appease, assuage, quench, slake, satiate. 2 *she satisfied herself that it was an accident:* convince, assure, reassure. 3 *products which satisfy EC law:* comply with, meet, fulfil, answer, conform to, measure up to, come up to.
OPPOSITES frustrate.

**saturate** verb 1 *rain had saturated the ground:* soak, drench, waterlog. 2 *the company has saturated the market:* flood, glut, oversupply, overfill, overload.

**saturated** adjective 1 *his trousers were saturated:* soaked, soaking (wet), wet through, sopping (wet), sodden, dripping, wringing wet, drenched, soaked to the skin. 2 *the saturated pitch:* waterlogged, flooded, boggy, awash.
OPPOSITES dry.

**sauce** noun relish, condiment, ketchup, dip, dressing, jus, coulis, gravy.

**savage** adjective 1 *savage dogs:* ferocious, fierce, vicious, wild, feral. 2 *a savage assault:* vicious, brutal, cruel, sadistic, ferocious, fierce, violent. 3 *a savage attack on free trade:* fierce, blistering, scathing, searing, stinging, devastating, withering, virulent, vitriolic.
OPPOSITES tame, mild.
noun *she described her assailants as savages:* brute, beast, monster, barbarian, sadist, animal.
verb 1 *savaged by a dog:* maul, attack, lacerate, claw, bite. 2 *critics savaged the film:* criticize, attack, lambaste, condemn, denounce, pillory, revile; informal pan; Brit. informal slate; N. Amer. informal trash.

**save** verb 1 *the captain was saved by his crew:* rescue, set free, free, liberate, deliver. 2 *the house was saved from demolition:* preserve, keep, protect, safeguard, salvage, retrieve, reclaim, rescue. 3 *start saving old newspapers:* put/set aside, put by/to one side, keep, retain, store, hoard; informal squirrel away. 4 *asking her saved a lot of trouble:* prevent, avoid, forestall, spare, stop, obviate, avert.

**saving** noun 1 *a considerable saving in cost:* reduction, cut, decrease, economy. 2 (**savings**) nest egg, capital, assets, funds, resources, reserves.

**saviour** noun rescuer, liberator, deliverer, champion, protector, redeemer.

**savour** verb *she savoured every moment:* relish, enjoy, appreciate, delight in, revel in, luxuriate in.
noun *the subtle savour of wood smoke:* smell, aroma, fragrance, scent, perfume, bouquet, taste, flavour, tang, smack.

**say** verb 1 *he said her name:* speak, utter, voice, pronounce. 2 *'I must go,' she said:* declare, state, announce, remark,

observe, mention, comment, note, add. **3** *they said a prayer:* recite, repeat, utter, deliver, perform. **4** *her watch said one twenty:* indicate, show, read.
**noun** *don't I have any say in the matter?* influence, sway, weight, voice, input.

**saying noun** proverb, maxim, aphorism, axiom, expression, phrase, formula, slogan, catchphrase.

**scale noun 1** *opposite ends of the social scale:* hierarchy, ladder, ranking, pecking order, order, spectrum. **2** *the scale of the map:* ratio, proportion. **3** *the scale of the disaster:* extent, size, scope, magnitude, dimensions, range, breadth, degree.
**verb** *thieves scaled the fence:* climb, ascend, clamber up, scramble up, shin (up), mount; N. Amer. shinny (up).

**scan verb 1** *Adam scanned the horizon:* study, examine, scrutinize, inspect, survey, search, scour, sweep, watch. **2** *I scanned the papers:* glance through, look through, have a look at, run one's eye over, cast one's eye over, flick through, browse through.
**noun 1** *a quick scan through the report:* glance, look, flick, browse. **2** *a brain scan:* examination, screening.

**scandal noun 1** *a scandal that led him to resign:* affair, issue, incident, outrage, skeleton in the cupboard; informal ...-gate. **2** *it's a scandal:* disgrace, outrage, (crying) shame, sin. **3** *a name tarnished by scandal:* gossip, rumour(s), slander, libel, aspersions, muckraking; informal dirt.

**scant adjective** little, little or no,

minimal, limited, negligible, meagre, insufficient, inadequate.
OPPOSITES abundant, ample.

**scapegoat noun** whipping boy, Aunt Sally; informal fall guy; N. Amer. informal patsy.

**scar noun 1** *the scar on his arm:* mark, blemish, disfigurement, discoloration, pockmark, pit, lesion, stitches. **2** *psychological scars:* trauma, damage, injury.
**verb** *scarred for life:* disfigure, mark, blemish.

**scarce adjective 1** *food was scarce:* in short supply, scant, meagre, sparse, hard to come by. **2** *wading birds are now scarce:* rare, few and far between, thin on the ground.
OPPOSITES plentiful.

**scarcely adverb 1** *she could scarcely hear him:* hardly, barely, only just. **2** *I scarcely see her:* rarely, seldom, infrequently, not often, hardly ever; informal once in a blue moon. **3** *this could scarcely be an accident:* surely not, not, hardly.
OPPOSITES often.

**scare verb** *stop it, you're scaring me:* frighten, startle, alarm, terrify, unnerve, worry, intimidate, terrorize, cow; informal freak out; Brit. informal put the wind up; N. Amer. informal spook.
**noun** *you gave me a scare:* fright, shock, start, turn, jump.

**scared adjective** frightened, afraid, fearful, nervous, panicky, terrified; informal in a cold sweat; N. Amer. informal spooked.

**scary adjective** (informal) frightening, terrifying, hair-raising, spine-chilling, blood-curdling, eerie, sinister; informal

a b c d e f g h i j k l m n o p q r **s** t u v w x y z

creepy, spine-tingling, spooky.

**scatter** verb **1** *scatter the seeds evenly*: spread, sprinkle, distribute, strew, disseminate, sow. **2** *the crowd scattered*: disperse, break up, disband, separate, dissolve. **3** *the floor was scattered with books*: cover, dot, sprinkle, spot, pepper, litter.
OPPOSITES gather, assemble.

**scenario** noun **1** *Walt wrote scenarios for various studios*: plot, outline, storyline, framework, screenplay, script. **2** *consider every possible scenario*: situation, chain of events, course of events.

**scene** noun **1** *the scene of the accident*: location, site, place, position. **2** *the scene is London in the 1890s*: background, setting, context, milieu, backdrop. **3** *scenes of violence*: incident, event, episode, happening. **4** *an impressive mountain scene*: view, vista, outlook, panorama, landscape, scenery. **5** *she made a scene*: fuss, exhibition of oneself, performance, tantrum, commotion, disturbance, row; informal to-do; Brit. informal carry-on. **6** *the political scene*: arena, stage, sphere, world, milieu, realm. **7** *a scene from a movie*: clip, section, segment, part, sequence, extract.

**scenery** noun **1** *beautiful scenery*: landscape, countryside, country, terrain, setting, surroundings, environment. **2** *scenery and costumes*: set, setting, backdrop.

**scenic** adjective picturesque, pretty, attractive, beautiful, charming, impressive, striking, spectacular, breathtaking, panoramic.

**scent** noun **1** *the scent of freshly cut hay*: smell, fragrance, aroma, perfume, savour, odour. **2** *a bottle of scent*: perfume, fragrance, eau de toilette, eau de cologne. **3** *the hounds picked up the scent*: spoor, trail, track.
verb *sharks soon scent the blood*: smell, nose out, detect, pick up, sense.

**scented** adjective perfumed, fragranced, fragrant, sweet-smelling, aromatic.

**sceptic** noun cynic, doubter, unbeliever, doubting Thomas.

**sceptical** adjective dubious, doubtful, doubting, cynical, distrustful, suspicious, disbelieving, unconvinced.
OPPOSITES certain, convinced.

**scepticism** noun doubt, a pinch of salt, disbelief, cynicism, distrust, suspicion, incredulity.

**schedule** noun **1** *our production schedule*: plan, programme, timetable, scheme. **2** *I have a busy schedule*: timetable, agenda, diary, calendar, itinerary.
verb *a meeting has been scheduled*: arrange, organize, plan, programme, timetable, set up, line up; N. Amer. slate.

**scheme** noun **1** *fund-raising schemes*: plan, project, programme, strategy, stratagem, tactic; Brit. informal wheeze. **2** *his schemes and plots*: plot, intrigue, conspiracy, ruse, ploy, stratagem, manoeuvre, subterfuge, machinations; informal racket, scam.
verb *he schemed endlessly*: plot, conspire, intrigue, connive, manoeuvre, plan.

**scheming** adjective cunning, crafty, calculating, devious,

**scholar** noun academic, intellectual, learned person, man/woman of letters, authority, expert; informal egghead; N. Amer. informal pointyhead.

**scholarly** adjective learned, educated, erudite, academic, well read, intellectual, literary, highbrow.
OPPOSITES uneducated, illiterate.

**scholarship** noun 1 *a centre of scholarship*: learning, knowledge, erudition, education, academic study. 2 *a scholarship of £2,000*: grant, award, endowment; Brit. bursary.

**school** noun 1 *the village school*: college, academy, alma mater. 2 *the university's School of English*: department, faculty, division. 3 *the Columbia school of history*: tradition, approach, style, way of thinking, persuasion, creed, credo, doctrine, belief, opinion, point of view.
verb *he schooled her in horsemanship*: train, teach, tutor, coach, instruct, drill.

**science** noun *the science of criminology*: subject, discipline, field, branch of knowledge, body of knowledge, area of study.

**scientific** adjective 1 *scientific research*: technological, technical, evidence-based, empirical. 2 *a more scientific approach*: systematic, methodical, organized, ordered, rigorous, exact, precise, accurate, mathematical.

**scoff** verb sneer, jeer, laugh; (**scoff at**) mock, deride, ridicule, dismiss, belittle; informal poohpooh.

**scoop** noun *a measuring scoop*: spoon, ladle, dipper.
■ **scoop out** 1 hollow out, gouge out, dig, excavate. 2 remove, take out, spoon out, scrape out.
■ **scoop up** pick up, gather up, lift, take up, snatch up, grab.

**scope** noun 1 *the scope of the investigation*: extent, range, breadth, reach, sweep, span, area, sphere, realm, compass, orbit, ambit, terms of reference, remit. 2 *the scope for change is limited*: opportunity, freedom, latitude, leeway, capacity, room (to manoeuvre).

**scorch** verb 1 *trees were scorched by the fire*: burn, sear, singe, char, blacken, discolour. 2 *grass scorched by the sun*: dry up, parch, wither, shrivel.

**scorching** adjective hot, red-hot, blazing, flaming, fiery, burning, blistering, searing; informal boiling, baking, sizzling.
OPPOSITES freezing, mild.

**score** noun 1 *the final score was 4–3*: result, outcome, total, tally, count. 2 *an IQ score of 161*: rating, grade, mark, percentage.
verb 1 *he's scored 13 goals this season*: get, gain, chalk up, achieve, make, record, rack up, notch up; informal bag, knock up. 2 *the piece was scored for horn and strings*: arrange, set, adapt, orchestrate, write, compose. 3 *score the wood in criss-cross patterns*: scratch, cut, notch, incise, scrape, nick, gouge.
■ **score something out/through** cross out, strike out, delete, put a line through, obliterate.

**scorn** noun *the scorn in his voice*: contempt, derision, disdain, mockery, sneering.

conniving, wily, sly, tricky, artful.
OPPOSITES ingenuous, honest.

a
b
c
d
e
f
g
h
i
j
k
l
m
n
o
p
q
r
**s**
t
u
v
w
x
y
z

OPPOSITES admiration, respect.
verb 1 *critics scorned the talks:* deride, treat with contempt, mock, scoff at, sneer at, jeer at, laugh at. 2 *they scorned my offers of help:* spurn, rebuff, reject, ignore, shun, snub.
OPPOSITES admire, respect.

**scour**[1] verb *the saucepan needs scouring:* scrub, rub, clean, polish, buff, shine, burnish, grind, abrade.

**scour**[2] verb *Christine scoured the shops:* search, comb, hunt through, rummage through, look high and low in, ransack, turn upside-down.

**scout** noun 1 *scouts reported that the Romans were advancing:* lookout, outrider, spy. 2 *a lengthy scout round the area:* reconnaissance, reconnoitre, survey, exploration, search; informal recce; Brit. informal shufti.
verb 1 *I scouted around for some logs:* search, look, hunt, ferret around, root around. 2 *a patrol was sent to scout out the area:* reconnoitre, explore, inspect, investigate, spy out, survey, scan, study; informal check out, case.

**scramble** verb 1 *we scrambled over the boulders:* clamber, climb, crawl, claw one's way, scrabble, struggle; N. Amer. shinny. 2 *the speaker can scramble the words:* muddle, confuse, mix up, jumble (up), disarrange, disorganize, disorder, disturb, mess up.
noun 1 *a short scramble over the rocks:* clamber, climb. 2 *the scramble for a seat:* struggle, jostle, scrimmage, scuffle, tussle, free-for-all, jockeying, competition, race.

**scrap** noun 1 *a scrap of paper:* fragment, piece, bit, snippet,

shred, oddment, remnant. 2 *there wasn't a scrap of evidence:* bit, shred, speck, iota, particle, ounce, jot. 3 *the foxes ate all our scraps:* leftovers, crumbs, remains, remnants, residue. 4 *a sculpture made from scrap:* waste, rubbish, refuse, debris; N. Amer. garbage, trash; informal junk.
verb 1 *old computers are scrapped:* throw away, throw out, dispose of, get rid of, discard, dispense with, bin, decommission, break up, demolish; informal chuck (away/out), ditch, dump, junk; Brit. informal get shot of; N. Amer. informal trash. 2 *the scheme is to be scrapped:* abandon, drop, abolish, withdraw, do away with, put an end to, cancel, axe; informal ditch, dump, junk.
OPPOSITES keep, preserve.

**scrape** verb 1 *we scraped all the paint off the windows:* rub, scratch, scour, grind, sand, sandpaper, abrade, file. 2 *their boots scraped along the floor:* grate, creak, rasp, scratch. 3 *Ellen scraped her shins on the wall:* graze, scratch, scuff, rasp, skin, cut, lacerate, bark, chafe.
noun 1 *the scrape of her key in the lock:* grating, creaking, rasp, scratch. 2 *a long scrape on his shin:* graze, scratch, abrasion, cut, laceration, wound.

**scratch** verb 1 *the paintwork was scratched:* score, abrade, scrape, scuff. 2 *thorns scratched her skin:* graze, scrape, skin, cut, lacerate, bark, chafe.
noun 1 *a scratch on the paintwork:* score, mark, line, scrape. 2 *he had scratches on his cheek:* graze, scrape, abrasion, cut, laceration.
■ up to scratch good enough, up to the mark, up to standard, up

to par, satisfactory, acceptable, adequate, passable, sufficient, all right; informal OK.

**scream** verb & noun shriek, screech, yell, howl, bawl, yelp, squeal, wail, squawk.

**screen** noun 1 *he dressed behind the screen*: partition, divider, windbreak. 2 *a computer with a 15-inch screen*: display, monitor, visual display unit. 3 *a screen to keep out mosquitoes*: mesh, net, netting. 4 *the hedge acts as a screen against the wind*: buffer, protection, shield, shelter, guard.
verb 1 *the end of the hall had been screened off*: partition, divide, separate, curtain. 2 *the cottage was screened by the trees*: conceal, hide, veil, shield, shelter, shade, protect. 3 *all blood is screened for the virus*: check, test, examine, investigate, vet; informal check out. 4 *the programme is screened on Thursday*: show, broadcast, transmit, televise, put out, air.

**screw** noun 1 *four steel screws*: bolt, fastener. 2 *the ship's twin screws*: propeller, rotor.
verb 1 *he screwed the lid back on the jar*: tighten, turn, twist, wind. 2 *the bracket was screwed in place*: fasten, secure, fix, attach. 3 (informal) *she intended to screw more money out of them*: extort, force, extract, wrest, wring, squeeze; informal bleed.
■ screw something up
1 *Christina screwed up her face*: wrinkle, pucker, crumple, crease, furrow, contort, distort, twist. 2 (informal) *they'll screw up the whole thing*: wreck, ruin, destroy, damage, spoil, mess up; informal louse up, foul up; Brit. informal cock up.

**scribble** verb *he scribbled a note*: scrawl, scratch, dash off, jot (down), doodle, sketch.
noun *I can't read this scribble*: scrawl, squiggle(s), jottings, doodle, doodlings.

**script** noun 1 *her neat, tidy script*: handwriting, writing, hand. 2 *the script of the play*: text, screenplay, libretto, score, lines, dialogue, words.

**scrub** verb 1 *he scrubbed the kitchen floor*: brush, scour, rub, clean, cleanse, wash. 2 (informal) *the plans were scrubbed*: abandon, scrap, drop, cancel, call off, axe; informal ditch, dump, junk.

**scrutinize** verb examine, inspect, survey, study, look at, peruse, investigate, explore, probe, enquire into, go into, check.

**sculpture** noun carving, statue, statuette, figure, figurine, effigy, bust, head, model.

**sea** noun 1 ocean, waves; informal the drink; Brit. informal the briny; literary the deep. 2 *a sea of roofs*: expanse, stretch, area, tract, sweep, carpet, mass.
OPPOSITES land.
adjective *a sea story*: marine, ocean, oceanic, maritime, naval, nautical.
■ at sea confused, perplexed, puzzled, baffled, mystified, bemused, bewildered, nonplussed, dumbfounded, at a loss, lost; informal flummoxed, fazed.

**seal** noun *the seal round the bath*: sealant, adhesive, mastic, joint.
verb 1 *seal each bottle while hot*: stop up, seal up, cork, stopper, plug. 2 *they sealed the bargain*: clinch, secure, settle, conclude, complete, finalize, confirm.

a b c d e f g h i j k l m n o p q r **s** t u v w x y z

■ **seal something off** close off, shut off, cordon off, fence off, isolate.

**seam** noun 1 *the seam was coming undone*: join, stitching, joint. 2 *a seam of coal*: layer, stratum, vein, lode.

**seaman** noun sailor, seafarer, mariner, boatman, hand, merchant seaman.
OPPOSITES landlubber.

**sear** verb 1 *the heat of the blast seared his face*: scorch, burn, singe, char. 2 *sear the meat*: flash-fry, seal, brown.

**search** verb 1 *I searched for the key*: hunt, look, seek, forage, fish, look high and low, ferret, root, rummage. 2 *he searched the house*: look through, scour, go through, sift through, comb, turn upside down; Austral./NZ informal fossick through. 3 *the guards searched my face*: examine, inspect, check, frisk.
noun *we continued our search*: hunt, look, quest, examination, exploration.

**searching** adjective penetrating, piercing, probing, keen, shrewd, sharp, intent.

**seaside** noun coast, shore, seashore, beach, sand, sands.

**season** noun *the seasons of the year*: period, time, time of year, spell, term.
verb *a well seasoned dish*: flavour, add salt/pepper to, spice.

**seasoned** adjective experienced, practised, well versed, knowledgeable, established, veteran, hardened.
OPPOSITES inexperienced.

**seasoning** noun flavouring, salt and pepper, herbs, spices, condiments.

**seat** noun 1 *a wooden seat*: chair, bench, stool; (**seats**) seating.

2 *the seat of government*: headquarters, base, centre, nerve centre, hub, heart, location, site. 3 *the family's country seat*: residence, ancestral home, mansion.
verb 1 *they seated themselves round the table*: position, put, place, ensconce, install, settle. 2 *the hall seats 500*: have room for, contain, take, sit, hold, accommodate.

**second**[1] adjective 1 *the second day of the trial*: next, following, subsequent. 2 *a second pair of glasses*: additional, extra, alternative, another, spare, backup; N. Amer. alternate.
3 *second prize*: secondary, subordinate, subsidiary, lesser, inferior.
OPPOSITES first.
noun *Eva had been working as his second*: assistant, attendant, helper, aide, supporter, auxiliary, second in command, number two, deputy, understudy; informal sidekick.
verb *George seconded the motion*: support, vote for, back, approve, endorse.

**second**[2] noun *I'll be gone for a second*: moment, bit, little while, instant, flash; informal sec, jiffy; Brit. informal mo, tick.

**secondary** adjective 1 *a secondary issue*: less important, subordinate, lesser, minor, peripheral, incidental, subsidiary. 2 *secondary infections*: accompanying, attendant, concomitant, consequential, resulting, resultant.
OPPOSITES primary, main.

**second-hand** adjective 1 *second-hand clothes*: used, old, worn, pre-owned, nearly new, handed-down, hand-me-down, cast-off.

**2** *second-hand information:* indirect.
OPPOSITES new, direct.
**adverb** *I heard this second-hand:* indirectly; informal on the grapevine.
OPPOSITES directly.

**secondly adverb** furthermore, also, moreover, second, in the second place, next.

**secrecy noun** confidentiality, privacy, mystery, concealment, stealth.

**secret adjective 1** *a secret plan:* confidential, top secret, classified, undisclosed, unknown, private, under wraps; informal hush-hush. **2** *a secret drawer in the table:* hidden, concealed, disguised. **3** *a secret campaign:* clandestine, covert, undercover, underground, surreptitious, cloak-and-dagger; informal hush-hush. **4** *a secret code:* cryptic, mysterious, abstruse, recondite, arcane, esoteric.
OPPOSITES public, open.
**noun 1** *it's a secret:* confidential matter, confidence, skeleton in the cupboard. **2** *the secrets of the universe:* mystery, enigma. **3** *the secret of their success:* recipe, magic formula, blueprint, key, answer, solution.
■ **in secret** secretly, in private, behind closed doors, under cover, furtively, stealthily, on the quiet, covertly.

**secretive adjective** uncommunicative, secret, unforthcoming, playing one's cards close to one's chest, reticent, tight-lipped.
OPPOSITES open, communicative.

**secretly adverb** in secret, in private, privately, behind closed doors, under cover, furtively,
stealthily, on the quiet, covertly.

**sect noun** group, cult, denomination, order, splinter group, faction, camp.

**section noun 1** *the separate sections of the box:* part, bit, portion, segment, compartment, module. **2** *the last section of the questionnaire:* passage, subsection, chapter, subdivision, clause. **3** *the reference section of the library:* department, area, division.

**sector noun 1** *every sector of the industry:* part, branch, arm, division, area, department, field, sphere. **2** *the north-eastern sector of the town:* district, quarter, section, zone, region, area, belt.

**secular adjective** non-religious, lay, temporal, civil, worldly, earthly, profane.
OPPOSITES sacred, religious.

**secure adjective 1** *check that all bolts are secure:* fastened, fixed, secured, done up, closed, shut, locked. **2** *a place where children feel secure:* safe, protected, safe and sound, out of harm's way, in safe hands, invulnerable, at ease, unworried, relaxed, happy, confident. **3** *a secure future:* certain, assured, reliable, dependable, settled, fixed.
OPPOSITES loose, vulnerable, uncertain.
**verb 1** *secure the handle to the main body:* fix, attach, fasten, affix, connect, couple. **2** *the doors had been secured:* fasten, close, shut, lock, bolt, chain, seal. **3** *the division secured a major contract:* obtain, acquire, gain, get; informal land.

**security noun 1** *the security of our citizens:* safety, protection.

a
b
c
d
e
f
g
h
i
j
k
l
m
n
o
p
q
r
**s**
t
u
v
w
x
y
z

a
b
c
d
e
f
g
h
i
j
k
l
m
n
o
p
q
r
**s**
t
u
v
w
x
y
z

**2** *he could give her security:* peace of mind, stability, certainty. **3** *security at the court was tight:* safety measures, safeguards, surveillance, defence, protection, policing. **4** *additional security for your loan:* guarantee, collateral, surety, pledge, bond.
OPPOSITES insecurity.

**sediment** noun dregs, grounds, lees, residue, deposit, silt.

**seduce** verb **1** *customers are seduced by the advertising:* attract, allure, lure, tempt, entice, beguile, inveigle, manipulate. **2** *he tried to seduce her:* have one's (wicked) way with, take advantage of.

**seductive** adjective tempting, inviting, enticing, alluring, beguiling, attractive.

**see** verb **1** *he saw her in the street:* discern, spot, notice, catch sight of, glimpse, make out, pick out, spy; informal clap eyes on, clock; literary behold. **2** *I saw a programme about it:* watch, look at, view, catch. **3** *would you like to see the house?* inspect, view, look round, tour, survey, examine, scrutinize. **4** *I finally saw what she meant:* understand, grasp, comprehend, follow, realize, appreciate, recognize, work out, fathom; informal get, latch on to, tumble to, figure out; Brit. informal twig, suss (out). **5** *I must see what Victor is up to:* find out, discover, learn, ascertain, determine, establish. **6** *see that no harm comes to him:* ensure, make sure/certain, see to it, take care, mind. **7** *I see trouble ahead:* foresee, predict, forecast, prophesy, anticipate. **8** *later, I saw him in town:* encounter, meet, run into, come across, stumble across, happen on, chance on; informal bump into. **9** *you'd better see a doctor:* consult, confer with, talk to, have recourse to, call in, turn to. **10** *he's seeing someone else now:* go out with, date, take out, be involved with; informal go steady with; dated court.
■ **see to** attend to, deal with, see about, take care of, look after, sort out, organize, arrange.

**seed** noun pip, stone, kernel.

**seek** verb **1** *he is seeking work:* search for, try to find, look for, be after, hunt for. **2** *he sought help from a motorist:* ask for, request, solicit, call for, appeal for, apply for. **3** *we constantly seek to improve the service:* try, attempt, endeavour, strive, work, do one's best.

**seem** verb appear (to be), have the appearance/air of being, give the impression of being, look, sound, come across as, strike someone as.

**seep** verb ooze, trickle, exude, drip, dribble, flow, leak, drain, bleed, filter, percolate, soak.

**seethe** verb **1** *the water seethed with fish:* teem, swarm, boil, swirl, churn, surge, bubble, heave. **2** *I seethed at the injustice of it all:* be angry, be furious, be enraged, be incensed, be beside oneself, boil, rage, rant, fume; informal be livid, foam at the mouth.

**segment** noun piece, bit, section, part, portion, division, slice, wedge.

**segregate** verb separate, set apart, keep apart, isolate, quarantine, partition, divide, discriminate against.
OPPOSITES integrate.

**seize** verb **1** *she seized the microphone*: grab, grasp, snatch, take hold of. **2** *rebels seized the air base*: capture, take, overrun, occupy, conquer, take over. **3** *the drugs were seized by customs*: confiscate, impound, commandeer, requisition, appropriate, expropriate. **4** *terrorists seized his wife*: kidnap, abduct, take captive, take prisoner, take hostage; informal snatch.
OPPOSITES liberate, relinquish, release.

**seizure** noun **1** *Napoleon's seizure of Spain*: capture, takeover, annexation, invasion, occupation. **2** *the seizure of banned goods*: confiscation, appropriation, expropriation. **3** *the seizure of UN staff*: kidnap, abduction. **4** *the baby suffered a seizure*: convulsion, fit, spasm, paroxysm.
OPPOSITES liberation, release.

**seldom** adverb rarely, infrequently, hardly (ever), scarcely (ever); informal once in a blue moon.
OPPOSITES often.

**select** verb *select the correct tool for the job*: choose, pick (out), single out, sort out, take, adopt. adjective **1** *a small, select group*: choice, hand-picked, elite; informal top-flight. **2** *a very select area*: exclusive, privileged, wealthy; informal posh.
OPPOSITES inferior.

**selection** noun **1** *Jim made his selection*: choice, pick, option, preference. **2** *a wide selection of dishes*: range, array, diversity, variety, assortment, mixture. **3** *a selection of his poems*: anthology, assortment, collection, assemblage, miscellany, medley.

**selective** adjective discerning, discriminating, exacting, demanding, particular; informal choosy, picky.
OPPOSITES indiscriminate.

**selfish** adjective egocentric, egotistic, self-centred, self-absorbed, self-obsessed, wrapped up in oneself, mean, greedy; informal looking after number one.
OPPOSITES altruistic.

**sell** verb **1** *they are selling their house*: put up for sale, put on the market, auction (off), trade in. **2** *he sells cakes*: trade in, deal in, traffic in, peddle, retail, market.
OPPOSITES buy.

**seller** noun vendor, dealer, retailer, trader, merchant, agent, hawker, pedlar, purveyor, supplier, stockist.
OPPOSITES buyer.

**send** verb **1** *they sent a message to HQ*: dispatch, post, mail, consign, forward, transmit, convey, communicate, broadcast. **2** *the pump sent out a jet of petrol*: propel, project, eject, deliver, discharge, spout, fire, shoot, release, fling, cast. **3** *it's enough to send one mad*: make, drive, turn.
OPPOSITES receive.

■ **send someone down** (informal) send to prison, imprison, jail, incarcerate, lock up, confine, detain, intern; informal put away; Brit. informal bang up. ■ **send for** call, summon, ask for, request, order. ■ **send someone off** (Sport) order off, dismiss, show the red card; informal red-card, send for an early bath. ■ **send someone/ something up** (informal) satirize, ridicule, make fun of, parody, lampoon, mock, caricature,

a b c d e f g h i j k l m n o p q r s t u v w x y z

imitate, ape; informal take off, spoof, take the mickey out of.

**send-off** noun farewell, goodbye, adieu, leave-taking, funeral.
OPPOSITES welcome.

**senior** adjective 1 *senior school pupils*: older, elder. 2 *a senior officer*: superior, higher-ranking, more important; N. Amer. ranking.
OPPOSITES junior, subordinate.

**sensation** noun 1 *a sensation of heaviness*: feeling, sense, perception, impression. 2 *she caused a sensation*: commotion, stir, uproar, furore, scandal, impact; informal splash, to-do.

**sensational** adjective 1 *a sensational murder trial*: shocking, scandalous, appalling, fascinating, thrilling, interesting, dramatic, momentous, historic, newsworthy. 2 *sensational stories*: overdramatized, melodramatic, exaggerated, sensationalist, graphic, explicit, lurid; informal shock-horror, juicy. 3 (informal) *she looked sensational*: gorgeous, stunning, wonderful, superb, excellent, first-class; informal great, terrific, tremendous, fantastic, fabulous, out of this world; Brit. informal smashing.
OPPOSITES dull, understated, unremarkable.

**sense** noun 1 *the sense of touch*: feeling, faculty, awareness, sensation, recognition, perception. 2 *a sense of humour*: appreciation, awareness, understanding, comprehension. 3 *she had the sense to leave*: wisdom, common sense, wit, intelligence, judgement, reason, brain(s); informal gumption,

nous, horse sense, savvy; Brit. informal loaf, common; N. Amer. informal smarts. 4 *I can't see the sense in this*: purpose, point, use, value, advantage, benefit. 5 *different senses of the word*: meaning, definition, nuance, drift, gist, thrust, tenor, message.
OPPOSITES stupidity.
verb *she sensed their hostility*: detect, feel, observe, notice, recognize, pick up, be aware of, distinguish, make out; informal catch on to.

**senseless** adjective pointless, futile, useless, needless, meaningless, absurd, foolish, insane, stupid, idiotic, mindless, illogical.
OPPOSITES wise.

**sensible** adjective practical, realistic, responsible, reasonable, commonsensical, rational, logical, sound, no-nonsense, level-headed, down-to-earth, wise.
OPPOSITES foolish.

**sensitive** adjective 1 *she's sensitive to changes in temperature*: responsive to, reactive to, sensitized to, aware of, conscious of, susceptible to, affected by, vulnerable to. 2 *sensitive skin*: delicate, fragile, tender, sore. 3 *the matter needs sensitive handling*: tactful, careful, thoughtful, diplomatic, delicate, subtle, kid-glove. 4 *he's sensitive about his bald patch*: touchy, oversensitive, hypersensitive, easily offended, thin-skinned, defensive, paranoid, neurotic. 5 *a sensitive issue*: difficult, delicate, tricky, awkward, problematic, ticklish, controversial, emotive.
OPPOSITES impervious, resilient,

clumsy, thick-skinned, uncontroversial.

**sensitivity** noun **1** *the sensitivity of the skin:* responsiveness, sensitiveness, reactivity, susceptibility. **2** *the job calls for sensitivity:* tact, diplomacy, delicacy, subtlety, understanding. **3** *her sensitivity on the subject:* touchiness, oversensitivity, hypersensitivity, defensiveness. **4** *the sensitivity of the issue:* delicacy, trickiness, awkwardness, ticklishness.

**sensual** adjective **1** *sensual pleasure:* physical, carnal, bodily, fleshly, animal. **2** *a very sensual woman:* passionate, sexual, physical, tactile, hedonistic.
OPPOSITES spiritual, passionless.

**sensuous** adjective **1** *big sensuous canvases:* rich, sumptuous, luxurious. **2** *sensuous lips:* voluptuous, sexy, seductive, luscious, lush, ripe.

**sentence** noun **1** *the judge delivered his sentence:* judgement, ruling, decision, verdict. **2** *a long sentence:* punishment, prison term; informal time, stretch.
verb *they were sentenced to death:* condemn, doom, punish, convict.

**sentiment** noun **1** *the comments echo my own sentiments:* view, feeling, attitude, thought, opinion, belief. **2** *there's no room for sentiment:* sentimentality, emotion, softness; informal schmaltz, slush; Brit. informal soppiness; N. Amer. informal sappiness.

**sentimental** adjective **1** *she kept the vase for sentimental reasons:* nostalgic, emotional.

**2** *the film is too sentimental:* mawkish, overemotional, cloying, sickly, romantic; Brit. twee; informal slushy, schmaltzy, corny; Brit. informal soppy; N. Amer. informal sappy.
OPPOSITES practical, gritty.

**separate** adjective **1** *his personal life was separate from his job:* unconnected, unrelated, different, distinct, discrete, detached, divorced, disconnected, independent. **2** *the infirmary was separate from the school:* set apart, detached, cut off, segregated, isolated, free-standing, self-contained.
OPPOSITES linked, attached.
verb **1** *they separated the two youths:* split (up), break up, part, pull apart. **2** *the connectors can be separated:* disconnect, detach, disengage, uncouple, split. **3** *the wall that separated the two estates:* partition, divide, keep apart. **4** *the south aisle was separated off:* isolate, partition off, section off, close off, shut off, cordon off. **5** *they separated at the airport:* part (company), go their separate ways, split up, disperse, scatter. **6** *the road separated:* fork, divide, branch, diverge. **7** *her parents separated:* split up, break up, part, divorce.
OPPOSITES unite, join, link, meet, merge, marry.

**separately** adverb individually, one by one, one at a time, singly, severally, apart, independently, alone, by oneself, on one's own.

**separation** noun **1** *the separation of the two companies:* disconnection, splitting, division, breaking up.

a
b
c
d
e
f
g
h
i
j
k
l
m
n
o
p
q
r
**s**
t
u
v
w
x
y
z

**2** *her parents' separation:* break-up, split, estrangement, divorce; Brit. informal bust-up.

**sequel** noun continuation, further episode, follow-up.

**sequence** noun **1** *the sequence of events:* succession, order, course, series, chain, train, progression, chronology, pattern, flow. **2** *a sequence from his film:* excerpt, clip, extract, section.

**series** noun succession, sequence, string, chain, run, round, spate, wave, rash, course, cycle, row.

**serious** adjective **1** *a serious expression:* solemn, earnest, grave, sombre, unsmiling, stern, grim, humourless, stony. **2** *serious decisions:* important, significant, momentous, weighty, far-reaching. **3** *serious consideration:* careful, detailed, in-depth. **4** *a serious play:* intellectual, highbrow, heavyweight, deep, profound, literary, learned, scholarly; informal heavy. **5** *serious injuries:* severe, grave, bad, critical, acute, terrible, dire, dangerous. **6** *we're serious about equality:* sincere, earnest, genuine, wholehearted, committed, resolute, determined.
OPPOSITES light-hearted, trivial, superficial, lowbrow, minor, half-hearted.

**seriously** adverb **1** *Faye nodded seriously:* solemnly, earnestly, gravely, sombrely, sternly, grimly, humourlessly.
**2** *seriously injured:* severely, gravely, badly, critically, dangerously. **3** *seriously, I'm very pleased:* really, honestly, truthfully, truly, actually; Brit. informal straight up.

**sermon** noun address, homily,

talk, speech, lecture.

**servant** noun attendant, domestic, maid, housemaid, retainer, flunkey, minion, slave.

**serve** verb **1** *they served their masters faithfully:* work for, obey, do the bidding of. **2** *this job serves the community:* benefit, help, assist, aid, make a contribution to, do one's bit for. **3** *he served his apprenticeship in Scotland:* carry out, perform, do, fulfil, complete, discharge, spend. **4** *serve the soup hot:* present, offer, give out, distribute, dish up, provide, supply. **5** *she served another customer:* attend to, deal with, see to, assist, help, look after. **6** *a saucer serving as an ashtray:* act, function, work, perform. **7** *official forms will serve in most cases:* suffice, do, be good enough, be adequate, fit/fill the bill, suit.

**service** noun **1** *conditions of service:* work, employment, labour. **2** *he has done us a service:* favour, kindness, good turn, helping hand. **3** *the service was excellent:* waiting, serving, attendance, attention. **4** *products which give reliable service:* use, usage, functioning, operation. **5** *he took his car in for a service:* overhaul, check, maintenance. **6** *a marriage service:* ceremony, ritual, rite, liturgy. **7** *a range of local services:* amenity, facility, resource, utility. **8** *soldiers leaving the services:* (armed) forces, military, army, navy, air force.
verb *the appliances are serviced regularly:* overhaul, check, go over, maintain.

**session** noun **1** *a session of the committee:* meeting, sitting, assembly, conclave; N. Amer. & NZ caucus. **2** *this parliamentary session*: period, time, term, year.

**set¹** verb **1** *Beth set the bag on the table*: put (down), place, lay, deposit, position, settle, leave, stand, plant; informal stick, dump, park, plonk, pop. **2** *the fence is set in concrete*: fix, embed, insert, mount. **3** *a ring set with precious stones*: adorn, ornament, decorate, embellish. **4** *I'll set the table*: lay, prepare, arrange, fix. **5** *we set them some work*: assign, allocate, give, allot. **6** *they set a date for the election*: arrange, schedule, fix (on), settle on, determine, designate, name, specify. **7** *he set his watch*: adjust, regulate, synchronize, calibrate, put right, correct. **8** *the adhesive will set in an hour*: solidify, harden, stiffen, thicken, gel, cake, congeal, coagulate, clot. OPPOSITES melt.
■ **set off/out** set out, start out, sally forth, leave, depart, embark, set sail; informal hit the road. ■ **set something up 1** *a monument was set up*: erect, put up, construct, build. **2** *she set up her own business*: establish, start, begin, institute, found, create. **3** *set up a meeting*: arrange, organize, fix (up), schedule, timetable, line up.

**set²** noun **1** *a set of postcards*: series, collection, group, batch, arrangement, array, assortment, selection. **2** *the literary set*: group, circle, crowd, crew, band, fraternity, company, ring, camp, school, clique, faction; informal gang, bunch.

**set³** adjective **1** *a set routine*: fixed, established,

predetermined, hard and fast, unvarying, unchanging, invariable, rigid, inflexible, strict, settled. **2** *she had very set ideas*: inflexible, rigid, fixed, entrenched. **3** *I was all set for the evening*: ready, prepared, organized, equipped, primed; informal geared up, psyched up. OPPOSITES variable, flexible, unprepared.

**setback** noun problem, difficulty, hitch, complication, upset, blow; informal glitch, hiccup.
OPPOSITES breakthrough.

**setting** noun surroundings, position, situation, environment, background, backdrop, spot, place, location, locale, site, scene.

**settle** verb **1** *they settled the dispute*: resolve, sort out, clear up, end, fix, work out, iron out, set right, reconcile; informal patch up. **2** *she settled her affairs*: put in order, sort out, tidy up, arrange, organize, order, clear up. **3** *they settled on a date for the wedding*: decide on, set, fix, agree on, name, establish, arrange, choose, pick. **4** *she went to settle her bill*: pay, square, clear. **5** *he settled in London*: make one's home, set up home, take up residence, put down roots, establish oneself, live, move to. **6** *immigrants settled much of Australia*: colonize, occupy, populate. **7** *a brandy will settle your nerves*: calm, quieten, quiet, soothe, pacify, quell. **8** *a butterfly settled on the flower*: land, come to rest, alight, perch.
OPPOSITES stir up, take off.

**settlement** noun **1** *a pay settlement*: agreement, deal,

a
b
c
d
e
f
g
h
i
j
k
l
m
n
o
p
q
r
**s**
t
u
v
w
x
y
z

arrangement, resolution, understanding, pact. **2** *the settlement of the dispute:* **resolution**, settling, solution, reconciliation. **3** *a frontier settlement:* **community**, colony, outpost, encampment, post, village.

**settler** noun **colonist**, frontiersman, pioneer, immigrant, newcomer, incomer. OPPOSITES native.

**sever** verb **1** *the head was severed from the body:* **cut off**, chop off, detach, separate, amputate. **2** *a knife had severed the artery:* **cut (through)**, rupture, split, pierce. **3** *they severed diplomatic relations:* **break off**, discontinue, suspend, end, cease, dissolve. OPPOSITES join, maintain.

**several** adjective **some**, a number of, a few, various, assorted.

**severe** adjective **1** *severe injuries:* **acute**, very bad, serious, grave, critical, dangerous, life-threatening. **2** *severe storms:* **fierce**, violent, strong, powerful. **3** *a severe winter:* **harsh**, bitter, cold, freezing, icy, arctic. **4** *severe criticism:* **harsh**, scathing, sharp, strong, fierce, savage, devastating, withering. **5** *his severe expression:* **stern**, dour, grim, forbidding, disapproving, unsmiling, unfriendly, sombre, stony, cold, frosty. **6** *a severe style of architecture:* **plain**, simple, austere, unadorned, stark, clinical, uncluttered. OPPOSITES minor, gentle, mild, friendly, ornate.

**severely** adverb **1** *he was severely injured:* **badly**, seriously, critically. **2** *murderers should be treated more severely:*

harshly, strictly, sternly, rigorously. **3** *she looked severely at Harriet:* **sternly**, grimly, dourly, disapprovingly.

**sew** verb **stitch**, tack, seam, hem, embroider.

**sex** noun **1** *they talked about sex:* **sexual intercourse**, lovemaking, making love, the sex act, sexual relations, mating, copulation. **2** *adults of both sexes:* **gender**.

**sexual** adjective **1** *the sexual organs:* **reproductive**, genital, sex. **2** *sexual activity:* **carnal**, erotic.

**sexuality** noun **1** *she had a powerful sexuality:* **sensuality**, sexiness, seductiveness, eroticism, physicality, sexual appetite, passion, desire, lust. **2** *I'm open about my sexuality:* **sexual orientation**, sexual preference, leaning, persuasion.

**sexy** adjective **1** *she's so sexy:* **sexually attractive**, seductive, desirable, alluring; informal fanciable; Brit. informal fit; N. Amer. informal foxy. **2** *sexy videos:* **erotic**, sexually explicit, titillating, naughty, X-rated, rude, pornographic, crude; informal raunchy, steamy; euphemistic adult. **3** *they weren't feeling sexy:* **sexually aroused**, amorous, lustful, passionate; informal turned on; Brit. informal randy.

**shabby** adjective **1** *a shabby little bar:* **run down**, scruffy, dilapidated, squalid, sordid; informal crummy; Brit. informal grotty; N. Amer. informal shacky. **2** *a shabby grey coat:* **scruffy**, old, worn out, threadbare, ragged, frayed, tattered, battered, faded, moth-eaten; informal tatty; N. Amer. informal raggedy. **3** *her shabby treatment of Ben:* **mean**,

unkind, unfair, shameful, shoddy, unworthy, contemptible, despicable, discreditable; informal rotten.
OPPOSITES smart, decent.

**shack** noun hut, cabin, shanty, lean-to, shed, hovel; Scottish bothy.

**shade** noun 1 *they sat in the shade:* shadow, shelter, cover, cool. 2 *shades of blue:* colour, hue, tone, tint, tinge. 3 *shades of meaning:* nuance, gradation, degree, difference, variation, variety, nicety, subtlety, undertone, overtone. 4 *her skirt was a shade too short:* little, bit, trace, touch, modicum, tinge; informal tad, smidgen; (**a shade**) slightly, rather, somewhat. 5 *the window shade:* blind, curtain, screen, cover, covering, awning, canopy.
OPPOSITES light.
verb *vines shaded the garden:* cast a shadow over, shadow, shelter, cover, screen.

**shadow** noun 1 *he saw her shadow in the doorway:* silhouette, outline, shape, contour, profile. 2 *he emerged from the shadows:* shade, darkness, twilight, gloom.
verb *he is shadowing a suspect:* follow, trail, track, stalk, pursue; informal tail, keep tabs on.

**shady** adjective 1 *a shady garden:* shaded, shadowy, dim, dark, sheltered, leafy. 2 (informal) *shady deals:* suspicious, suspect, questionable, dubious, irregular, underhand; N. Amer. snide; informal fishy, murky; Brit. informal dodgy; Austral./NZ informal shonky.
OPPOSITES bright, honest.

**shaft** noun 1 *the shaft of a golf club:* pole, shank, stick, rod,

staff, handle, stem. 2 *shafts of sunlight:* ray, beam, gleam, streak. 3 *a ventilation shaft:* tunnel, passage, hole, bore, duct, well, flue, vent.

**shake** verb 1 *the building shook:* vibrate, tremble, quiver, quake, shiver, shudder, judder, wobble, rock, sway, convulse. 2 *she shook the bottle:* jiggle, agitate; informal wiggle, waggle. 3 *he shook his stick:* brandish, wave, flourish, swing, wield. 4 *what she saw shook her:* upset, distress, disturb, unsettle, disconcert, discompose, unnerve, throw off balance, agitate, fluster, shock, alarm, scare, worry; informal rattle.
OPPOSITES soothe.
noun 1 *camera shake:* judder, trembling, quivering, quake, tremor, shiver, shudder, wobble. 2 *he gave his coat a shake:* jiggle, joggle; informal waggle. 3 *a shake of his fist:* flourish, wave.

**shaky** adjective 1 *shaky legs:* unsteady, unstable, rickety, wobbly; Brit. informal wonky. 2 *I feel a bit shaky:* faint, dizzy, light-headed, giddy, weak, wobbly, in shock. 3 *the evidence is shaky:* unreliable, untrustworthy, questionable, dubious, doubtful, tenuous, suspect, flimsy, weak; informal iffy; Brit. informal dodgy.
OPPOSITES steady, stable, sound.

**shallow** adjective superficial, trivial, facile, insubstantial, lightweight, empty, trifling, surface, skin-deep, frivolous, foolish, silly.
OPPOSITES profound.

**sham** noun *it's all a sham:* pretence, fake, act, simulation, fraud, lie, counterfeit, humbug.
adjective *a sham marriage:* fake,

a
b
c
d
e
f
g
h
i
j
k
l
m
n
o
p
q
r
**s**
t
u
v
w
x
y
z

pretended, feigned, simulated, false, artificial, bogus, insincere, affected, make-believe; informal pretend, put-on, phoney.
OPPOSITES genuine.
verb *he's shamming:* pretend, fake, malinger; informal put it on; Brit. informal swing the lead.

**shambles** plural noun 1 *we have to sort out this shambles:* chaos, muddle, jumble, confusion, disorder, havoc. 2 *the room was a shambles:* mess, pigsty; informal disaster area; Brit. informal tip.

**shame** noun 1 *a sense of shame:* guilt, remorse, contrition. 2 *he brought shame on the family:* humiliation, embarrassment, indignity, mortification, disgrace, dishonour, discredit, ignominy, disrepute, infamy, scandal. 3 *it's a shame she never married:* pity, sad thing, bad luck; informal crime, sin.
OPPOSITES pride, honour.
verb 1 *you shamed your family:* disgrace, dishonour, discredit, blacken, drag through the mud. 2 *he was shamed in public:* humiliate, embarrass, humble, take down a peg or two, cut down to size; informal show up; N. Amer. informal make someone eat crow.
OPPOSITES honour.

**shameful** adjective 1 *shameful behaviour:* disgraceful, deplorable, despicable, contemptible, discreditable, reprehensible, unworthy, shabby, shocking, scandalous, outrageous, abominable, atrocious, appalling, inexcusable, unforgivable. 2 *a shameful secret:* embarrassing, mortifying, humiliating, ignominious.
OPPOSITES admirable.

**shape** noun 1 *the shape of the dining table:* form, appearance, configuration, structure, contours, lines, outline, silhouette, profile. 2 *a spirit in the shape of a fox:* guise, likeness, semblance, form, appearance, image. 3 *in good shape:* condition, health, trim, fettle, order; Brit. informal nick.
verb 1 *the metal is shaped into tools:* form, fashion, make, mould, model. 2 *attitudes shaped by his report:* determine, form, fashion, mould, develop, influence, affect.

**share** noun *her share of the profits:* portion, part, division, quota, allowance, ration, allocation; informal cut, slice; Brit. informal whack.
verb 1 *we share the bills:* split, divide, go halves on; informal go fifty-fifty on. 2 *they shared out the peanuts:* apportion, divide up, allocate, portion out, measure out, carve up; Brit. informal divvy up. 3 *we all share in the learning process:* participate, take part, play a part, be involved, have a hand.

**sharp** adjective 1 *a sharp knife:* keen, razor-edged, sharpened, well-honed. 2 *a sharp pain:* intense, acute, severe, agonizing, excruciating, stabbing, shooting, searing. 3 *a sharp taste:* tangy, piquant, acidic, acid, sour, tart, pungent. 4 *a sharp wind:* cold, chilly, icy, bitter, biting, brisk, keen, penetrating. 5 *sharp words:* harsh, bitter, cutting, spiteful, hurtful, cruel. 6 *a sharp photo:* clear, distinct, crisp, focused. 7 *a sharp increase:* sudden, abrupt, rapid, steep. 8 *she was sharp and witty:* astute, intelligent, bright, incisive,

keen, quick-witted, shrewd, canny, perceptive, smart, quick; informal on the ball, quick on the uptake; N. Amer. informal heads-up.
OPPOSITES blunt, mild, sweet, soft, kind, indistinct, gradual, slow, stupid.
adverb precisely, exactly, promptly, prompt, punctually; informal on the dot; N. Amer. informal on the button.
OPPOSITES roughly.

**sharpen** verb hone, whet, strop, grind, file.

**shatter** verb 1 *the glasses shattered:* smash, break, splinter, crack, fracture, fragment, disintegrate. 2 *the announcement shattered their hopes:* destroy, wreck, ruin, dash, crush, devastate, demolish, torpedo, scotch; informal do for, put paid to; Brit. informal scupper.

**shattered** adjective 1 *he was shattered by the reviews:* devastated, shocked, stunned, dazed, traumatized. 2 (informal) *I feel too shattered to move:* exhausted, tired, worn out, weary, fatigued, ready to drop; informal done in, all in, dead beat; Brit. informal knackered, whacked, zonked; N. Amer. informal pooped, tuckered out.
OPPOSITES thrilled, fresh.

**shave** verb 1 *he shaved his beard:* cut off, crop, trim, barber. 2 *shave off excess wood:* plane, pare, whittle, scrape.

**sheath** noun covering, cover, case, casing, sleeve, scabbard.

**shed**[1] noun *a shed in the garden:* hut, lean-to, outhouse, outbuilding, cabin, shack.

**shed**[2] verb 1 *the trees shed their leaves:* drop, scatter, spill. 2 *the caterpillar shed its skin:* throw off, cast off, discard, slough off,

moult. 3 *we shed our clothes:* take off, remove, discard, climb out of, slip out of; Brit. informal peel off. 4 *the moon shed a watery light:* cast, radiate, emit, give out.
OPPOSITES keep, put on.

**sheen** noun shine, lustre, gloss, patina, burnish, polish, shimmer.

**sheer** adjective 1 *the sheer audacity of the plan:* utter, complete, absolute, total, pure, downright, out-and-out. 2 *a sheer drop:* steep, abrupt, sharp, precipitous, vertical. 3 *a sheer dress:* thin, fine, gauzy, diaphanous, transparent, see-through, flimsy.
OPPOSITES gradual, thick.

**sheet** noun 1 *a sheet of ice:* layer, covering, blanket, coat, film, veneer, crust, skin, surface, stratum. 2 *a sheet of glass:* pane, panel, slab, plate, piece. 3 *a fresh sheet of paper:* page, leaf, piece. 4 *a sheet of water:* expanse, area, stretch, sweep.

**shell** noun 1 *peanut shells:* pod, hull, husk; N. Amer. shuck. 2 *the metal shell of the car:* body, case, casing, framework, hull, fuselage, hulk.
verb 1 *they were shelling peas:* pod, hull, husk; N. Amer. shuck. 2 *rebel artillery shelled the city:* bombard, fire on, attack, bomb, blitz.

**shelter** noun 1 *the trees provide shelter for animals:* protection, cover, shade, safety, security, refuge. 2 *a shelter for abandoned cats:* sanctuary, refuge, home, haven, safe house.
OPPOSITES exposure, danger.
verb 1 *the hut sheltered him from the sun:* protect, shield,

screen, cover, shade, defend, cushion, guard, insulate. **2** *the convoy sheltered in a bay:* take shelter, take refuge, take cover; informal hole up.
OPPOSITES expose.

**sheltered** adjective **1** *a sheltered stretch of water:* protected, tranquil, still, shady. **2** *a sheltered life:* protected, cloistered, insulated, privileged, secure, safe, quiet.

**shelve** verb postpone, put off, delay, defer, put back, reschedule, hold over/off, put to one side, suspend, stay, mothball; N. Amer. put over, table; informal put on ice, put on the back burner.
OPPOSITES execute, bring forward, revive.

**shepherd** verb usher, steer, herd, lead, take, escort, guide, conduct, marshal, walk.

**shield** noun *a shield against radiation:* protection, guard, defence, cover, screen, shelter. verb *he shielded his eyes:* protect, guard, defend, cover, screen, shade, shelter.
OPPOSITES expose.

**shift** verb **1** *he shifted some chairs:* move, transfer, transport, switch, relocate, reposition, rearrange. **2** *the cargo has shifted:* move, slide, slip, be displaced. **3** *the wind shifted:* veer, alter, change, turn. **4** (Brit.) *this brush really shifts the dirt:* get rid of, remove, get off, budge, lift.
OPPOSITES leave.
noun **1** *a shift in public opinion:* change, alteration, adjustment, variation, modification, revision, reversal, U-turn. **2** *they worked three shifts:* stint, stretch, spell.

**shimmer** verb *the sea shimmered in the sunset:* glint, glisten, twinkle, sparkle, flash, gleam, glow, glimmer, wink. noun *a shimmer of moonlight:* glint, twinkle, sparkle, flash, gleam, glow, glimmer, lustre, glitter.

**shine** verb **1** *the sun shone:* beam, gleam, radiate, glow, glint, glimmer, sparkle, twinkle, glitter, glisten, shimmer, flash. **2** *she shone her shoes:* polish, burnish, buff, rub up, brush, clean. **3** *they shone at university:* excel, stand out. noun *linseed oil restores the shine:* polish, gleam, gloss, lustre, sheen, patina.

**shiny** adjective glossy, bright, glassy, polished, gleaming, satiny, lustrous.
OPPOSITES matt.

**ship** noun boat, vessel, craft. verb *goods are shipped within 24 hours:* deliver, send, dispatch, transport, carry, distribute.

**shiver** verb *she was shivering with fear:* tremble, quiver, shake, shudder, quake. noun *she gave a shiver:* shudder, twitch, start.

**shock**[1] noun **1** *the news came as a shock:* blow, upset, surprise, revelation, bolt from the blue, rude awakening, eye-opener. **2** *you gave me a shock:* fright, scare, start; informal turn. **3** *suffering from shock:* trauma, collapse, breakdown, post-traumatic stress disorder. **4** *the first shock of the earthquake:* vibration, reverberation, shake, jolt, impact, blow. verb *the murder shocked the nation:* appal, horrify, outrage, scandalize, disgust, traumatize, distress, upset, disturb, stun, rock, shake.
OPPOSITES delight.

**shock²** noun *a shock of red hair:* **mass**, mane, mop, thatch, head, bush, tangle, cascade, halo.

**shocking** adjective **appalling**, horrifying, horrific, dreadful, awful, terrible, scandalous, outrageous, disgraceful, abominable, atrocious, disgusting, distressing, upsetting, disturbing, startling.

**shoot** verb **1** *they shot him in the street:* **gun down**, mow down, hit, wound, injure, shoot someone dead, kill. **2** *they shot at the police:* **fire**, open fire, snipe, let fly, bombard, shell. **3** *it can shoot bullets or grenades:* **discharge**, fire, launch, propel, release. **4** *a car shot past:* **race**, speed, flash, dash, rush, hurtle, streak, whizz, zoom, career, fly; informal belt, tear, zip, whip; Brit. informal bomb; N. Amer. informal hightail it, barrel. **5** *the film was shot in Tunisia:* **film**, photograph, take, make, record.
noun *new shoots:* **sprout**, bud, runner, tendril.

**shop** noun **store**, retail outlet, boutique, emporium, department store, supermarket, hypermarket, superstore, chain store; N. Amer. minimart.

**shore** noun **seashore**, beach, sand(s), shoreline, coast.

**short** adjective **1** *short people:* **small**, little, petite, tiny, diminutive, elfin; Scottish wee. **2** *a short report:* **concise**, brief, succinct, compact, pithy, abridged, abbreviated, condensed. **3** *a short visit:* **brief**, fleeting, lightning, quick, cursory. **4** *money is a bit short:* **scarce**, scant, meagre, sparse, insufficient, deficient, inadequate, lacking. **5** *he was rather short with her:* **curt**,

sharp, abrupt, blunt, brusque, terse, offhand.
OPPOSITES tall, long, plentiful, courteous.
adverb *she stopped short:* **abruptly**, suddenly, sharply, all of a sudden, unexpectedly, without warning.
■ **short of** deficient in, lacking, in need of, low on, short on, missing; informal strapped for, pushed for, minus.

**shortage** noun **scarcity**, dearth, poverty, insufficiency, deficiency, inadequacy, famine, lack, deficit, shortfall.
OPPOSITES abundance.

**shortcoming** noun **fault**, defect, flaw, imperfection, deficiency, limitation, failing, drawback, weakness, weak point.
OPPOSITES strength.

**shorten** verb **abbreviate**, abridge, condense, contract, compress, reduce, shrink, diminish, cut (down), trim, pare (down), prune, curtail, truncate.
OPPOSITES lengthen.

**shortly** adverb **soon**, presently, in a little while, at any moment, in a minute, in next to no time, before long, by and by; N. Amer. momentarily; informal anon, any time now, in a jiffy; Brit. informal in a mo.

**shot** noun **1** *a shot rang out:* **report**, crack, bang, blast; (shots) gunfire, firing. **2** *a winning shot:* **stroke**, hit, strike, kick, throw. **3** *Mike was an excellent shot:* **marksman**, markswoman, shooter. **4** *a shot of us on holiday:* **photograph**, photo, snap, snapshot, picture, print, slide, still.

**shoulder** verb **1** *I shouldered the responsibility:* **take on**

a
b
c
d
e
f
g
h
i
j
k
l
m
n
o
p
q
r
**s**
t
u
v
w
x
y
z

(oneself), undertake, accept, assume, bear, carry. **2** *another lad shouldered him aside:* push, shove, thrust, jostle, force, bulldoze, bundle.

**shout** verb *I heard a shout:* yell, cry (out), call (out), roar, howl, bellow, bawl, raise one's voice; informal holler.
OPPOSITES whisper.
noun *he shouted a warning:* yell, cry, call, roar, howl, bellow, bawl; informal holler.

**shove** verb **1** *she shoved him back:* push, thrust, propel, drive, force, ram, knock, elbow, shoulder. **2** *she shoved past him:* push (one's way), force one's way, barge (one's way), elbow (one's way), shoulder one's way.
noun *a hefty shove:* push, thrust, bump, jolt, barge.

**show** verb **1** *the stitches do not show:* be visible, be seen, be in view, be obvious. **2** *he wouldn't show the picture:* display, exhibit, put on show, put on display, put on view. **3** *Frank showed his frustration:* manifest, exhibit, display, reveal, convey, communicate, make known, express, make plain, make obvious, disclose, betray. **4** *I'll show you how to cook:* demonstrate, explain, describe, illustrate, teach, instruct. **5** *events show this to be true:* prove, demonstrate, confirm, substantiate, corroborate, verify, bear out. **6** *she showed them to their seats:* escort, accompany, take, conduct, lead, usher, guide, direct.
OPPOSITES conceal.
noun **1** *a spectacular show of bluebells:* display, array, sight, spectacle. **2** *the motor show:* exhibition, display, fair, festival, parade; N. Amer. exhibit. **3** *a TV show:* programme, broadcast, presentation, production, episode. **4** *she's only doing it for show:* appearance, display, image. **5** *Drew made a show of looking busy:* pretence, outward appearance, (false) front, guise, pose.
■ **show off** (informal) put on airs, put on an act, swank, strut, grandstand, posture, draw attention to oneself. ■ **show something off** display, show to advantage, exhibit, demonstrate, parade, draw attention to, flaunt. ■ **show up 1** *cancers show up on X-rays:* be visible, be obvious, be seen, be revealed, appear. **2** (informal) *only two waitresses showed up:* turn up, appear, arrive, come, get here/there, put in an appearance, materialize. ■ **show someone up** (informal) humiliate, embarrass, shame, put someone to shame, mortify. ■ **show something up** expose, reveal, make obvious, highlight, emphasize, draw attention to.

**showdown** noun confrontation, clash, face-off.

**shower** noun **1** *a shower of rain:* fall, drizzle, sprinkling. **2** *a shower of missiles:* volley, hail, salvo, barrage.
verb **1** *confetti showered down on us:* rain, fall, hail. **2** *she showered them with gifts:* deluge, flood, inundate, swamp, overwhelm, snow under.

**show-off** noun (informal) exhibitionist, extrovert, poser, poseur, swaggerer, self-publicist.

**showy** adjective ostentatious, flamboyant, gaudy, garish, brash, vulgar, loud, fancy,

ornate; informal flash, flashy.
OPPOSITES restrained.

**shred** noun 1 *her dress was torn to shreds:* tatter, ribbon, rag, fragment, sliver. 2 *not a shred of evidence:* scrap, bit, speck, particle, ounce, jot, crumb, fragment, grain, drop, trace.
verb *shredding vegetables:* grate, mince, grind.

**shrewd** adjective astute, sharp, smart, intelligent, clever, canny, perceptive; informal on the ball.
OPPOSITES stupid.

**shriek** verb & noun scream, screech, squeal, squawk, roar, howl, shout, yelp.

**shrink** verb 1 *the number of competitors shrank:* get smaller, contract, diminish, lessen, reduce, decrease, dwindle, decline, fall off. 2 *he doesn't shrink from naming names:* recoil, shy away, flinch, be averse, be afraid, hesitate.
OPPOSITES expand, increase.

**shrivel** verb wither, shrink, wilt, dry up, dehydrate, parch, frazzle.

**shroud** noun *a shroud of mist:* covering, cover, cloak, mantle, blanket, layer, cloud, veil, winding sheet.
verb *shrouded by cloud:* cover, envelop, veil, cloak, blanket, screen, conceal, hide, mask, obscure.

**shudder** verb *the ground shuddered:* shake, shiver, tremble, quiver, judder.
noun *the truck's shudders and jolts:* shake, shiver, tremor, trembling, quivering, vibration, judder.

**shuffle** verb 1 *they shuffled along the passage:* shamble, dodder, drag one's feet. 2 *she shuffled her feet:* scrape, drag, scuffle. 3 *he shuffled the cards:* mix (up), rearrange, jumble (up).

**shun** verb avoid, steer clear of, give a wide berth to, have nothing to do with; informal freeze out; Brit. informal send to Coventry.
OPPOSITES welcome.

**shut** verb *please shut the door:* close, pull to, push to, slam, fasten, put the lid on, lock, secure.
OPPOSITES open, unlock.
■ **shut down** cease activity, close (down), cease trading; informal fold. ■ **shut up** (informal) be quiet, keep quiet, stop talking, quieten down; informal shut it, shut your face/mouth/trap, belt up, give it a rest; Brit. informal shut your gob; N. Amer. informal save it. ■ **shut someone/something up** (informal) silence, quieten down, hush, gag, muzzle.

**shuttle** verb commute, run, ply, go/travel back and forth, ferry.

**shy** adjective bashful, diffident, timid, reserved, introverted, retiring, self-effacing, withdrawn.
OPPOSITES confident.
■ **shy away from** flinch, recoil, hang back, be loath, be reluctant, be unwilling, be disinclined, hesitate, baulk at.

**sick** adjective 1 *the children are sick:* ill, unwell, poorly, ailing, indisposed; informal laid up, under the weather; Austral./NZ informal crook. 2 *he was feeling sick:* nauseous, queasy, bilious, green about the gills. 3 *I'm sick of this music:* fed up, bored, tired, weary. 4 (informal) *a sick joke:* macabre, tasteless, ghoulish, morbid, black, gruesome, gallows, cruel.
OPPOSITES well.

■ **be sick** (Brit.) vomit, heave; informal puke, throw up; N. Amer. informal barf, upchuck.

**sicken** verb **1** *the stench sickened him:* nauseate, make sick, turn someone's stomach, disgust; N. Amer. informal gross out. **2** *she sickened and died:* fall ill, catch something.
OPPOSITES please, recover.

**sickening** adjective nauseating, stomach-turning, repulsive, revolting, disgusting, offensive, off-putting, distasteful, obscene, gruesome, grisly; N. Amer. vomitous; informal gross.

**sickness** noun **1** *she was absent through sickness:* illness, disease, ailment, infection, malady, infirmity; informal bug, virus; Brit. informal lurgy; Austral. informal wog. **2** *a wave of sickness:* nausea, biliousness, queasiness. **3** *sickness and diarrhoea:* nausea, vomiting, retching; informal throwing up, puking.

**side** noun **1** *the side of the road:* edge, border, verge, boundary, margin, fringe(s), flank, bank, perimeter, extremity, periphery, limit(s). **2** *the wrong side of the road:* half, part, carriageway, lane. **3** *the east side of the city:* district, quarter, area, region, part, neighbourhood, sector, zone. **4** *one side of the paper:* surface, face. **5** *his side of the argument:* point of view, viewpoint, perspective, opinion, standpoint, position, outlook, slant, angle. **6** *the losing side:* faction, camp, bloc, party. **7** *the players in their side:* team, squad, line-up.
OPPOSITES centre, end.
adjective **1** *elaborate side pieces:* lateral, wing, flanking. **2** *a side issue:* subordinate, secondary,

minor, peripheral, incidental, subsidiary.
OPPOSITES front, central.
■ **side with** support, take someone's part, stand by, back, be loyal to, defend, champion, ally oneself with.

**sideways** adverb **1** *I slid sideways:* to the side, laterally. **2** *the expansion slots are mounted sideways:* edgewise, edgeways, side first, end on. adjective **1** *sideways force:* lateral, sideward, on the side, side to side. **2** *a sideways look:* indirect, oblique, sidelong, surreptitious, furtive, covert, sly.

**sift** verb **1** *sift the flour into a large bowl:* sieve, strain, screen, filter. **2** *we sift out unsuitable applications:* separate out, filter out, sort out, weed out, get rid of, remove. **3** *sifting through the wreckage:* search, look, examine, inspect, scrutinize, pore over.

**sight** noun **1** *she has excellent sight:* eyesight, vision, eyes. **2** *her first sight of it:* view, glimpse, glance, look. **3** *historic sights:* landmark, place of interest, monument, spectacle, marvel, wonder.
verb *one of the helicopters sighted wreckage:* glimpse, catch sight of, see, spot, spy, make out, pick out, notice, observe.

**sign** noun **1** *a sign of affection:* indication, signal, symptom, pointer, suggestion, intimation, mark, manifestation, demonstration, token. **2** *a sign of things to come:* warning, omen, portent, threat, promise. **3** *signs saying 'danger':* notice, board, placard, signpost. **4** *the dancers were daubed with signs:*

a b c d e f g h i j k l m n o p q r s t u v w x y z

symbol, figure, emblem, device, logo, character.
**verb 1** *he signed the letter:* write one's name on, autograph, initial, countersign. **2** *the government signed the treaty:* endorse, validate, agree to, approve, ratify, adopt. **3** *he signed his name:* write, inscribe, pen.

**signal** noun **1** *a signal to stop:* gesture, sign, wave, cue, indication, warning, prompt, reminder. **2** *a clear signal that we're in trouble:* indication, sign, symptom, hint, pointer, clue, demonstration, evidence, proof.
**verb 1** *the driver signalled to her:* gesture, sign, indicate, motion, wave, beckon, nod. **2** *they signalled their displeasure:* indicate, show, express, communicate. **3** *his death signals the end of an era:* mark, signify, mean, be a sign of, be evidence of.

**significance** noun importance, import, consequence, seriousness, gravity, weight, magnitude.
OPPOSITES insignificance.

**significant** adjective **1** *a significant fact:* notable, noteworthy, remarkable, important, of consequence. **2** *a significant increase:* large, considerable, sizeable, appreciable, conspicuous, obvious, sudden. **3** *a significant look:* meaningful, expressive, eloquent, suggestive, knowing, telling.
OPPOSITES insignificant.

**signify** verb mean, denote, designate, represent, symbolize, stand for.

**silence** noun **1** *the silence of the night:* quietness, quiet, still, stillness, hush, tranquillity, peace. **2** *her silence was answer enough:* failure to speak, dumbness, reticence, taciturnity.
OPPOSITES sound, loquacity.
**verb 1** *he silenced her with a kiss:* quieten, quiet, hush. **2** *dissidents have been silenced:* gag, muzzle, censor.

**silent** adjective **1** *the forest was silent:* quiet, still, hushed, noiseless, soundless, inaudible. **2** *the right to remain silent:* speechless, quiet, unspeaking, dumb, mute, taciturn, uncommunicative, tight-lipped. **3** *silent thanks:* unspoken, wordless.
OPPOSITES audible, noisy, spoken.

**silhouette** noun *silhouettes of aircraft:* outline, contour(s), profile, form, shape.
**verb** *silhouetted against the window:* outline, define.

**silly** adjective **1** *don't be so silly:* foolish, stupid, scatterbrained, frivolous, inane, immature, childish, empty-headed; informal dotty, scatty. **2** *that was a silly thing to do:* unwise, imprudent, thoughtless, foolish, stupid, unintelligent, idiotic, rash, reckless, foolhardy, irresponsible; informal crazy, mad; Brit. informal daft. **3** *he would worry about silly things:* trivial, trifling, frivolous, petty, small, insignificant, unimportant; informal piffling.
OPPOSITES sensible, serious.

**similar** adjective **1** *you two are very similar:* alike, the same; informal much of a muchness. **2** *northern India and similar areas:* comparable, like, corresponding, equivalent.
OPPOSITES different, unlike.

■ **similar to** like, much the same as, comparable to.

**similarity** noun resemblance, likeness, comparability, correspondence, parallel, equivalence, uniformity.

**simmer** verb 1 *the soup was simmering on the stove:* boil gently, cook gently, bubble. 2 *she was simmering with resentment:* seethe, fume, smoulder.

■ **simmer down** calm down, cool off/down.

**simple** adjective 1 *it's really pretty simple:* straightforward, easy, uncomplicated, uninvolved, undemanding, elementary. 2 *simple language:* clear, plain, straightforward, unambiguous, understandable, comprehensible, accessible; informal user-friendly. 3 *a simple white blouse:* plain, unadorned, basic, unsophisticated, no-frills, classic, understated, uncluttered, restrained. 4 *simple country people:* unpretentious, unsophisticated, ordinary, unaffected, unassuming, natural, straightforward; N. Amer. cracker-barrel.
OPPOSITES difficult, complex, fancy, sophisticated.

**simplicity** noun 1 *the simplicity of the recipes is an advantage:* straightforwardness, ease. 2 *the simplicity of the language:* clarity, plainness, intelligibility, comprehensibility, accessibility. 3 *the building's simplicity:* austerity, plainness, spareness, clean lines. 4 *the simplicity of their lifestyle:* plainness, modesty, naturalness.
OPPOSITES difficulty, complexity, adornment, sophistication.

**simplify** verb make simpler, clarify, put into words of one syllable, streamline; informal dumb down.
OPPOSITES complicate.

**simply** adverb 1 *he always spoke simply and forcefully:* straightforwardly, directly, clearly, plainly, lucidly, unambiguously. 2 *she was dressed simply:* plainly, soberly, unfussily, classically. 3 *they lived simply:* modestly, plainly, quietly. 4 *they are welcomed simply because they are rich:* merely, just, purely, solely, only. 5 *she was simply delighted:* utterly, absolutely, completely, positively, just; informal plain.
OPPOSITES confusingly, elaborately.

**simulate** verb 1 *they simulated pleasure:* feign, pretend, fake, affect, put on. 2 *simulating conditions in space:* imitate, reproduce, replicate, duplicate, mimic.

**simultaneous** adjective concurrent, happening at the same time, contemporaneous, coinciding, coincident, synchronized.
OPPOSITES separate.

**simultaneously** adverb at the same time, at one and the same time, at once, concurrently, (all) together, in unison, in concert, in chorus.

**sin** noun 1 *a sin in the eyes of God:* wrong, act of wickedness, transgression, crime, offence, misdeed. 2 *the human capacity for sin:* wickedness, wrongdoing, evil, immorality, iniquity, vice, crime.
OPPOSITES virtue.
verb *I have sinned:* transgress, do wrong, misbehave, err, go astray.

**sincere** adjective **1** *our sincere gratitude:* heartfelt, wholehearted, profound, deep, true, honest. **2** *a sincere person:* honest, genuine, truthful, direct, frank, candid; informal straight, on the level; N. Amer. informal on the up and up.

**sincerely** adverb genuinely, honestly, really, truly, truthfully, wholeheartedly, earnestly.

**sincerity** noun genuineness, honesty, truthfulness, integrity, directness, openness, candour.

**sing** verb **1** *he began to sing:* chant, trill, intone, croon, chorus. **2** *the birds were singing:* trill, warble, chirp, chirrup, cheep.

**singe** verb scorch, burn, sear, char.

**singer** noun vocalist, songster, songstress, soloist, chorister, cantor.

**single** adjective **1** *a single red rose:* sole, one, lone, solitary, unaccompanied, alone. **2** *every single word:* individual, separate, distinct. **3** *is she single?* unmarried, unwed, unattached, free, a bachelor, a spinster.
OPPOSITES double, multiple, married.
■ **single someone/something out** select, pick out, choose, decide on, target, earmark, mark out, separate out, set apart.

**singly** adverb one by one, one at a time, one after the other, individually, separately.
OPPOSITES together.

**sinister** adjective **1** *there was a sinister undertone in his words:* menacing, threatening, ominous, forbidding, frightening, alarming, disturbing, dark. **2** *a sinister motive:* evil, wicked, criminal, nefarious, villainous, base, malicious; informal shady.
OPPOSITES unthreatening, innocent.

**sink** verb **1** *the coffin sank below the waves:* submerge, founder, go down, be engulfed, drop, fall, descend. **2** *they sank their ships:* scuttle; Brit. scupper. **3** *the sun was sinking:* set, go down. **4** *Loretta sank into an armchair:* lower oneself, flop, collapse, drop, slump; informal plonk oneself. **5** *sink the pots into the ground:* embed, insert, drive, plant.
OPPOSITES float, rise.

**sip** verb *she sipped her martini:* drink, taste, sample, nip.
noun *have a sip:* mouthful, swallow, drink, drop, dram, nip; informal swig.

**sit** verb **1** *you'd better sit down:* take a seat, be seated, perch, ensconce oneself, flop; informal take the load off one's feet; Brit. informal take a pew. **2** *she sat the package on the table:* put, place, set, lay, deposit, rest, stand; informal stick, park. **3** *the committee sits on Saturday:* be in session, meet, be convened. **4** *she sits on the tribunal:* serve on, have a seat on, be a member of.
OPPOSITES stand.

**site** noun *the site of the battle:* location, place, position, situation, locality, whereabouts.
verb *sited in an industrial area:* place, put, position, situate, locate.

**situation** noun **1** *their financial situation:* circumstances, state of affairs, state, condition. **2** *I'll fill you in on the situation:* the facts, how things stand, the lie of the land, what's going on;

size noun dimensions, measurements, proportions, magnitude, largeness, area, expanse, breadth, width, length, height, depth.
■ size someone/something up (informal) assess, appraise, get the measure of, judge, take stock of, evaluate; Brit. informal suss out.

sizeable adjective large, substantial, considerable, respectable, significant, goodly.
OPPOSITES small.

sizzle verb crackle, frizzle, sputter, hiss, spit.

sketch noun a sketch of the proposed design: drawing, outline, draft, diagram, design, plan; informal rough.
verb he sketched the garden: draw, make a drawing of, pencil, rough out, outline.

skilful adjective expert, accomplished, skilled, masterly, talented, deft, dexterous, handy; informal mean, crack, ace; N. Amer. informal crackerjack.
OPPOSITES incompetent.

skill noun expertise, accomplishment, skilfulness, mastery, talent, deftness, dexterity, prowess, competence, artistry.
OPPOSITES incompetence.

skim verb 1 skim off the fat: remove, scoop off, separate. 2 the boat skimmed over the water: glide, move lightly, slide, sail, skate. 3 she skimmed through the newspaper: glance, flick, flip, leaf, thumb, scan, run one's eye over.

skin noun 1 leopard skins: hide, pelt, fell, fleece. 2 a banana skin: peel, rind. 3 milk with a skin on it: film, layer, membrane, crust, covering, coating.
verb 1 skin the tomatoes: peel, pare. 2 he skinned his knee: graze, scrape, abrade, bark, rub raw, chafe.

skinny adjective thin, underweight, scrawny, bony, gaunt, emaciated, skeletal, wasted, pinched, spindly, gangly; informal anorexic.

skip verb 1 skipping down the path: caper, prance, trip, dance, bound, bounce, gambol. 2 we skipped the boring stuff: omit, leave out, miss out, dispense with, pass over, skim over, disregard; informal give something a miss.

skirt verb 1 he skirted the city: go round, walk round, circle. 2 the fields that skirt the park: border, edge, flank, line. 3 he carefully skirted round the subject: avoid, evade, sidestep, dodge, pass over, gloss over; informal duck; Austral./NZ informal duck-shove.

slab noun piece, block, hunk, chunk, lump, cake, tablet, brick, panel, plate, sheet.

slack adjective 1 the rope went slack: limp, loose. 2 slack skin: sagging, flabby, flaccid, loose, saggy. 3 business is slack: sluggish, slow, quiet, slow-moving, flat, depressed, stagnant. 4 slack procedure: lax, negligent, careless, slapdash, slipshod; informal sloppy.
OPPOSITES taut, firm, busy, strict.
verb (Brit. informal) no slacking! idle, shirk, be lazy, be indolent, waste time, lounge about; Brit. informal skive; N. Amer. informal goof off.

slam verb 1 he slammed the door:

**bang**, shut with a bang. **2** *the car slammed into a lamp post:* **crash**, smash, plough, run, bump, collide with, hit, strike, ram; N. Amer. impact.

**slant** verb **1** *the floor slanted:* **slope**, tilt, incline, be at an angle, tip, lean, dip, pitch, shelve, list, bank. **2** *their findings were slanted in our favour:* **bias**, distort, twist, skew, weight.
noun **1** *the slant of the roof:* **slope**, incline, tilt, gradient, pitch, angle, camber. **2** *a feminist slant:* **point of view**, viewpoint, standpoint, stance, angle, perspective, approach, view, attitude, position, bias.

**slap** verb *he slapped her hard:* **smack**, strike, hit, cuff, clip, spank; informal whack.
noun *a slap across the face:* **smack**, blow, cuff, clip, spank; informal whack.

**slash** verb **1** *her tyres had been slashed:* **cut**, gash, slit, lacerate, knife. **2** (informal) *the company slashed prices:* **reduce**, cut, lower, bring down, mark down.
noun *a slash across his temple:* **cut**, gash, slit, laceration, incision, wound.

**slaughter** verb **1** *the cattle were slaughtered:* **kill**, butcher, cull, put down. **2** *civilians are being slaughtered:* **massacre**, murder, butcher, kill, exterminate, wipe out, put to death, execute; literary slay.
noun *a scene of slaughter:* **massacre**, (mass) murder, (mass) killing, (mass) execution, extermination, carnage, bloodshed, bloodletting, bloodbath; literary slaying.

**slave** noun *the work was done by slaves:* **servant**, lackey; Brit.

informal skivvy, dogsbody; historical serf, vassal.
OPPOSITES freeman, master.
verb *we slaved away:* **toil**, labour, sweat, work like a Trojan/dog; informal kill oneself, sweat blood, slog away; Brit. informal graft; Austral./NZ informal bullock.

**slavery** noun **enslavement**, servitude, serfdom, bondage, captivity.
OPPOSITES freedom.

**sleazy** adjective **1** *sleazy politicians:* **corrupt**, immoral. **2** *a sleazy bar:* **squalid**, seedy, seamy, sordid, insalubrious.
OPPOSITES honest, reputable, upmarket.

**sleek** adjective **1** *his sleek dark hair:* **smooth**, glossy, shiny, shining, lustrous, silken, silky. **2** *the car's sleek lines:* **streamlined**, elegant, graceful.
OPPOSITES scruffy, crude.

**sleep** noun **nap**, doze, siesta, catnap; informal snooze, forty winks, shut-eye; Brit. informal kip; literary slumber.
OPPOSITES wakefulness.
verb *be asleep:* **doze**, take a siesta, take a nap, catnap; informal snooze, snatch forty winks, get some shut-eye; Brit. informal kip; N. Amer. informal catch some Zs; literary slumber.
OPPOSITES wake up.
■ **go to sleep** fall asleep, get to sleep; informal drop off, nod off, drift off, crash out, flake out; N. Amer. informal sack out.

**sleepy** adjective **1** *she felt very sleepy:* **drowsy**, tired, somnolent, heavy-eyed; informal dopey. **2** *a sleepy little village:* **quiet**, peaceful, tranquil, placid, slow-moving, dull, boring.
OPPOSITES awake, alert.

**slender** adjective **1** *her tall,*

*slender figure:* slim, lean, willowy, svelte, lissom, graceful, slight, thin, skinny.
**2** *slender evidence:* meagre, limited, slight, scanty, scant, sparse, flimsy, insubstantial.
**3** *the chances seemed slender:* faint, remote, tenuous, fragile, slim.
OPPOSITES plump, strong.

**slice** noun **1** *a slice of cake:* piece, portion, slab, wedge, rasher, sliver, wafer. **2** *a huge slice of public spending:* share, part, portion, tranche, percentage, proportion, allocation.
verb *slice the cheese thinly:* cut, carve, divide.

**slick** adjective **1** *a slick advertising campaign:* efficient, smooth, smooth-running, polished, well organized, well run, streamlined. **2** *a slick salesman:* glib, polished, assured, self-assured, smooth-talking, plausible; informal smarmy.
OPPOSITES incompetent, hesitant.
verb *his hair was slicked down:* smooth, plaster, sleek, grease, oil, gel.

**slide** verb glide, slip, slither, skim, skate, skid, slew.

**slight** adjective **1** *the chance of success is slight:* small, tiny, minute, negligible, insignificant, minimal, remote, slim, faint. **2** *Elizabeth's slight figure:* slim, slender, delicate, dainty, fragile.
OPPOSITES good, plump.
verb *he had been slighted:* insult, snub, rebuff, spurn, give someone the cold shoulder, cut (dead), scorn.
OPPOSITES respect.
noun *an unintended slight:* insult, affront, snub, rebuff;

informal put-down.
OPPOSITES compliment.

**slightly** adverb a little, a bit, somewhat, faintly, vaguely, a shade.
OPPOSITES very.

**slim** adjective **1** *tall and slim:* slender, lean, thin, willowy, sylphlike, svelte, lissom, trim. **2** *a slim silver bracelet:* narrow, slender. **3** *a slim chance:* slight, small, slender, faint, poor, remote.
OPPOSITES plump, wide, good.
verb *I'm trying to slim:* lose weight, get into shape; N. Amer. slenderize.
OPPOSITES put on weight.

**slimy** adjective slippery, slithery, greasy; informal slippy, gloopy.
OPPOSITES firm, grippy.

**sling** verb **1** *a hammock was slung between two trees:* hang, suspend, string, swing.
**2** (informal) *she slung her jacket on the sofa:* throw, toss, fling, hurl, cast, pitch, lob, flip; informal chuck, heave, bung.

**slip** verb **1** *she slipped on the ice:* slide, skid, slither, fall (over), lose one's balance, tumble.
**2** *the envelope slipped through Luke's fingers:* fall, drop, slide.
**3** *we slipped out by a back door:* creep, steal, sneak, slide, sidle, slope, slink, tiptoe. **4** *she slipped the map into her pocket:* put, tuck, shove; informal pop, stick, stuff.
noun **1** *a single slip could send them plummeting down:* false step, slide, skid, fall, tumble.
**2** *a careless slip:* mistake, error, blunder, gaffe, oversight, omission, lapse; informal slip-up, boo-boo, howler; Brit. informal boob, clanger, bloomer; N. Amer. informal goof, blooper.
■ **slip up** (informal) make a

mistake, blunder, get something wrong, make an error, err; informal make a boo-boo; Brit. informal boob, drop a clanger; N. Amer. informal goof up.

**slippery** adjective 1 *the roads are slippery:* slithery, greasy, oily, icy, glassy, smooth, slimy, wet; informal slippy. 2 *a slippery customer:* sneaky, sly, devious, crafty, cunning, tricky, evasive, scheming, unreliable, untrustworthy; N. Amer. snide; informal shady, shifty; Brit. informal dodgy; Austral./NZ informal shonky.

**slit** noun 1 *three diagonal slits:* cut, incision, split, slash, gash. 2 *a slit in the curtains:* opening, gap, chink, crack, aperture, slot.
verb *he threatened to slit her throat:* cut, slash, split open, slice open.

**slogan** noun catchphrase, catchline, motto, jingle; N. Amer. informal tag line.

**slope** noun *the slope of the roof:* tilt, pitch, slant, angle, gradient, incline, inclination, fall, camber; N. Amer. grade.
verb *the garden sloped down to a stream:* tilt, slant, incline, lean, drop/fall away, descend, shelve, camber, rise, ascend, climb.

**sloping** adjective slanting, leaning, inclined, angled, cambered, tilted.
OPPOSITES level.

**sloppy** adjective 1 *sloppy chicken curry:* runny, watery, liquid, mushy; informal gloopy. 2 *their defending was sloppy:* careless, slapdash, slipshod, untidy, slack, slovenly; informal slap-happy. 3 *sloppy letters:* sentimental, mawkish, romantic; informal slushy, schmaltzy; Brit. informal soppy;

N. Amer. informal cornball, sappy, hokey.

**slot** noun 1 *he slid a coin into the slot:* aperture, slit, crack, hole, opening. 2 *a mid-morning slot:* time, spot, period, niche, space; informal window.
verb *he slotted a cassette into the machine:* insert, slide, fit, put, place.

**slow** adjective 1 *their slow walk home:* unhurried, leisurely, steady, sedate, sluggish, plodding. 2 *a slow process:* lengthy, time-consuming, long-drawn-out, protracted, prolonged, gradual. 3 *he's a bit slow:* stupid, unintelligent, obtuse; informal dense, dim, thick, slow on the uptake, dumb, dopey; Brit. informal dozy.
OPPOSITES quick.
verb 1 *the traffic forced him to slow down:* reduce speed, go slower, decelerate, brake. 2 *this would slow down economic growth:* hold back/up, delay, retard, set back, check, curb.
OPPOSITES accelerate.

**slowly** adverb 1 *Rose walked off slowly:* unhurriedly, without hurrying, steadily, at a leisurely pace, at a snail's pace. 2 *her health is improving slowly:* gradually, bit by bit, little by little, slowly but surely, step by step.
OPPOSITES quickly.

**sluggish** adjective lethargic, listless, lacking in energy, lifeless, inactive, slow; N. Amer. logy.
OPPOSITES vigorous.

**slum** noun hovel; (**slums**) ghetto, shanty town.

**slump** verb 1 *he slumped into a chair:* sit heavily, flop, collapse, sink; informal plonk oneself. 2 *house prices slumped:* fall,

plummet, tumble, collapse, drop; informal crash, nosedive.
OPPOSITES rise, boom.
noun 1 *a slump in profits:* fall, drop, tumble, downturn, downswing, slide, decline, decrease; informal nosedive. 2 *an economic slump:* recession, decline, depression, slowdown.
OPPOSITES rise, boom.

**sly** adjective 1 *she's very sly:* cunning, crafty, clever, wily, artful, tricky, scheming, devious, underhand, sneaky. 2 *a sly grin:* roguish, mischievous, impish, playful, wicked, arch, knowing. 3 *she took a sly sip of water:* surreptitious, furtive, stealthy, covert.
OPPOSITES open, straightforward.

**smack** noun *she gave him a smack:* slap, blow, cuff, clip, spank; informal whack.
verb *he tried to smack her:* slap, strike, hit, cuff, clip, spank; informal whack.
adverb (informal) *smack in the middle:* exactly, precisely, straight, right, directly, squarely, dead, plumb; informal slap, bang; N. Amer. informal smack dab.

**small** adjective 1 *a small flat:* little, compact, tiny, miniature, mini, minute, toy, baby, poky, cramped; Scottish wee; informal tiddly; Brit. informal titchy; N. Amer. informal little-bitty. 2 *a very small man:* short, little, petite, diminutive, elfin, tiny; Scottish wee; informal teeny, pint-sized. 3 *a few small changes:* slight, minor, unimportant, trifling, trivial, inconsequential, negligible; informal minuscule, piffling.
OPPOSITES big, tall, major.

**smart** adjective 1 *you look very*

smart: well dressed, stylish, chic, fashionable, modish, elegant, dapper; N. Amer. trig; informal natty, snappy; N. Amer. informal fly. 2 *a smart restaurant:* fashionable, stylish, high-class, exclusive, chic, fancy; Brit. upmarket; N. Amer. high-toned; informal trendy, classy, swanky; Brit. informal swish; N. Amer. informal swank. 3 (informal) *he's very smart:* clever, bright, intelligent, quick-witted, shrewd, astute, perceptive; informal brainy, quick on the uptake. 4 *a smart pace:* brisk, quick, fast, rapid, lively, energetic, vigorous; informal cracking.
OPPOSITES untidy, downmarket, stupid, slow, gentle.
verb 1 *her eyes were smarting:* sting, burn, tingle, prickle, hurt. 2 *she smarted at the accusations:* feel hurt, feel upset, take offence, feel aggrieved, feel indignant, be put out.

**smash** verb 1 *he smashed a window:* break, shatter, splinter, crack; informal bust. 2 *she's smashed the car:* crash, wreck; Brit. write off; N. Amer. informal total. 3 *they smashed into a wall:* crash, smack, slam, plough, run, bump, hit, strike, ram, collide with; N. Amer. impact.
noun *a motorway smash:* crash, collision, accident; N. Amer. wreck; informal pile-up; Brit. informal shunt.

**smear** verb 1 *the table was smeared with grease:* streak, smudge, mark. 2 *smear the meat with olive oil:* cover, coat, grease. 3 *she smeared sunblock on her skin:* spread, rub, daub, slap, smother, plaster. 4 *they are trying to smear our* *reputation:* sully, tarnish, blacken, drag through the mud, damage, defame, malign, slander, libel; N. Amer. slur.

**noun 1** *smears of blood:* streak, smudge, daub, dab, spot, patch, blotch, mark; informal splodge. **2** *press smears about his closest aides:* accusation, lie, untruth, slur, slander, libel, defamation.

**smell noun** *the smell of the kitchen:* odour, aroma, fragrance, scent, perfume, bouquet, nose, stench, stink; Brit. informal pong.

**verb 1** *he smelled her perfume:* scent, get a sniff of, detect. **2** *the dogs smelled each other:* sniff, nose. **3** *the cellar smells:* stink, reek; Brit. informal pong.

**smelly adjective** foul-smelling, stinking, reeking, rank; informal stinky; Brit. informal pongy.

**smile verb** *he smiled at her:* beam, grin (from ear to ear), smirk, simper, leer.
OPPOSITES frown.
**noun** *the smile on her face:* beam, grin, smirk, simper, leer.

**smooth adjective 1** *the smooth flat rocks:* even, level, flat, glassy, glossy, silky, polished. **2** *a smooth sauce:* creamy, fine, velvety. **3** *a smooth sea:* calm, still, tranquil, undisturbed, unruffled, even, flat, like a millpond. **4** *smooth operation:* steady, regular, uninterrupted, unbroken, straightforward, easy, effortless, trouble-free. **5** *a smooth, confident man:* suave, urbane, sophisticated, polished, debonair, courteous, gracious, glib, slick; informal smarmy.
OPPOSITES uneven, rough, lumpy, irregular, gauche.
**verb 1** *she smoothed the soil:* flatten, level (out/off), even

out/off, press, roll, iron, plane. **2** *brokers smooth the passage of goods:* ease, facilitate, expedite, assist, aid.
OPPOSITES roughen, hinder.

**smother verb 1** *she tried to smother her baby:* suffocate, asphyxiate, stifle, choke. **2** *we smothered the flames:* extinguish, put out, snuff out, douse, stamp out. **3** *we smothered ourselves with suncream:* smear, daub, spread, cover. **4** *she smothered a sigh:* stifle, muffle, strangle, suppress, hold back, fight back, swallow, conceal.

**smug adjective** self-satisfied, conceited, complacent, superior, pleased with oneself.

**snack noun** light meal, sandwich, refreshments, nibbles, titbit(s); informal bite (to eat).

**snag noun** *we've met a snag:* complication, difficulty, catch, hitch, obstacle, pitfall, problem, setback, disadvantage, drawback.
**verb** *thorns snagged his sweater:* catch, hook, tear.

**snap verb 1** *the ruler snapped:* break, fracture, splinter, split, crack; informal bust. **2** *'Shut up!' Anna snapped:* bark, snarl, growl, retort. **3** *photographers snapped the royals:* photograph, picture, take, shoot, film, capture.
**noun 1** *she closed her purse with a snap:* click, crack, pop. **2** *holiday snaps:* photograph, picture, photo, shot, snapshot, print, slide.
■ **snap something up** buy eagerly, accept eagerly, jump at, take advantage of, grab, seize (on), pounce on.

**snare noun** *a fox caught in a*

*snare:* trap, gin, wire, net, noose.

**verb** *game birds were snared:* trap, catch, net, bag, ensnare, hook.

**snatch verb 1** *she snatched the microphone:* grab, seize, take hold of, take, pluck, grasp at, clutch at. **2** (informal) *someone snatched my bag:* steal, take, thieve; informal swipe, nab, lift; Brit. informal nick, pinch, whip.

**noun 1** *brief snatches of sleep:* period, spell, time, fit, bout, interval, stretch. **2** *a snatch of conversation:* fragment, snippet, bit, scrap, extract, excerpt, portion.

**sneak verb 1** *I sneaked out:* creep, slink, steal, slip, slide, sidle, tiptoe, pad. **2** *she sneaked a camera in:* smuggle, spirit, slip.

**adjective** *a sneak preview:* furtive, secret, stealthy, sly, surreptitious, clandestine, covert, private, quick, exclusive.

**sneaking adjective 1** *a sneaking admiration for him:* secret, private, hidden, concealed, unvoiced. **2** *a sneaking feeling:* niggling, nagging, lurking, insidious, lingering, persistent.

**sneaky adjective** sly, crafty, cunning, wily, scheming, devious, deceitful, underhand.
OPPOSITES honest.

**sneer noun 1** *a sneer on her face:* smirk, curled lip. **2** *the sneers of others:* jibe, jeer, taunt, insult; informal dig.

**verb 1** *he looked at me and sneered:* smirk, curl one's lip. **2** *it is easy to sneer at them:* scoff, laugh, scorn, disdain, mock, ridicule, deride; N. Amer. slur.

**sniff verb 1** *she sniffed and blew her nose:* inhale, snuffle. **2** *Tom*

*sniffed the fruit:* smell, scent, get a whiff of.

**noun 1** *she gave a loud sniff:* snuffle, snort. **2** *a sniff of fresh air:* smell, scent, whiff, lungful.
■ **sniff something out** (informal) detect, find, discover, bring to light, track down, dig up, root out, uncover, unearth.

**snigger verb & noun** giggle, titter, snicker, chortle, laugh, sneer, smirk.

**snobbish, snobby adjective** elitist, superior, supercilious, arrogant, condescending, pretentious, affected; informal snooty, high and mighty, la-di-da, stuck-up; Brit. informal toffee-nosed.

**snub verb** *sponsors find themselves snubbed by politicians:* rebuff, spurn, cold-shoulder, cut (dead), ignore, insult, slight; informal freeze out; N. Amer. informal stiff.

**noun** *a very public snub:* rebuff, slap in the face; informal brush-off, put-down.

**snug adjective 1** *our tents were snug:* cosy, comfortable, warm, sheltered, secure; informal comfy. **2** *a snug dress:* tight, skintight, close-fitting, figure-hugging.
OPPOSITES bleak, loose.

**soak verb 1** *soak the beans in water:* dip, immerse, steep, submerge, douse, marinate, souse. **2** *we got soaked outside:* drench, wet through, saturate, waterlog. **3** *the sweat soaked through his clothes:* permeate, penetrate, impregnate, percolate, seep, spread. **4** *use towels to soak up the water:* absorb, suck up, blot, mop up.

**soaking adjective** drenched, wet (through), soaked (through), sodden, soggy, waterlogged, saturated, sopping, dripping,

wringing.
OPPOSITES parched.

**soar** verb **1** *the bird soared into the air:* rise, ascend, climb. **2** *the gulls soared on the winds:* glide, plane, float, hover. **3** *the cost of living soared:* increase, escalate, shoot up, spiral; informal go through the roof, skyrocket.
OPPOSITES plummet.

**sob** verb weep, cry, snivel, whimper; Scottish greet; informal blubber; Brit. informal grizzle.

**sober** adjective **1** *the driver was clearly sober:* clear-headed, teetotal, abstinent, dry; informal on the wagon. **2** *a sober view of life:* serious, solemn, sensible, grave, sombre, level-headed, businesslike, down-to-earth. **3** *a sober suit:* sombre, subdued, severe, quiet, drab, plain.
OPPOSITES drunk, frivolous, sensational, flamboyant.

**so-called** adjective supposed, alleged, presumed, inappropriately named, ostensible, reputed, self-styled.

**sociable** adjective friendly, amicable, affable, companionable, gregarious, cordial, warm, genial.
OPPOSITES unfriendly.

**social** adjective **1** *a social problem:* communal, community, collective, group, general, popular, civil, public. **2** *a social club:* recreational, leisure, entertainment.
OPPOSITES individual, professional.
noun *the club has a social once a month:* party, gathering, function, get-together, celebration; informal do.

**society** noun **1** *a danger to society:* the community, the (general) public, the people, the population, civilization, humankind, mankind. **2** *an industrial society:* culture, community, civilization, nation, population. **3** *Lady Angela will help you enter society:* high society, polite society, the upper classes, the gentry, the elite, the smart set; informal the upper crust. **4** *a local history society:* club, association, group, circle, institute, guild, lodge, league, union, alliance. **5** *the society of others:* company, companionship, fellowship, friendship.

**sofa** noun settee, couch, divan, chaise longue, chesterfield.

**soft** adjective **1** *soft fruit:* mushy, squashy, pulpy, slushy, squelchy, squishy, doughy; informal gooey; Brit. informal squidgy. **2** *soft ground:* swampy, marshy, boggy, muddy, squelchy. **3** *a soft cushion:* squashy, spongy, supple, springy, elastic, resilient. **4** *soft fabric:* smooth, velvety, fleecy, downy, furry, silky. **5** *soft light:* dim, low, faint, subdued, muted. **6** *soft colours:* pale, pastel, muted, restrained, subdued, subtle. **7** *soft voices:* quiet, low, gentle, faint, muted, subdued, muffled, hushed, whispered. **8** *soft outlines:* blurred, vague, hazy, misty, foggy, nebulous, fuzzy, indistinct. **9** *soft words:* kind, gentle, sympathetic, soothing, tender, sensitive, affectionate, loving, warm, sweet, sentimental. **10** *she's too soft with her pupils:* lenient, easy-going, tolerant, forgiving, forbearing, indulgent, liberal, lax.
OPPOSITES hard, firm, rough, harsh, lurid, strident, sharp, strict.

a
b
c
d
e
f
g
h
i
j
k
l
m
n
o
p
q
r
**s**
t
u
v
w
x
y
z

**soften** verb *the compensation should soften the blow:* ease, alleviate, relieve, soothe, take the edge off, cushion, lessen, diminish, blunt, deaden.

**soil**[1] noun **1** *acid soil:* earth, dirt, clay, ground, loam. **2** *British soil:* territory, land, region, country, domain, dominion.

**soil**[2] verb *he soiled his tie:* dirty, stain, smear, smudge, spoil, foul.

**soldier** noun fighter, trooper, serviceman, servicewoman, warrior; US GI; Brit. informal squaddie.

**sole** adjective only, one, single, solitary, lone, unique, exclusive.

**solely** adverb only, simply, purely, just, merely, uniquely, exclusively, entirely, wholly, alone.

**solemn** adjective **1** *a solemn occasion:* dignified, ceremonial, stately, formal, majestic, imposing, splendid, magnificent, grand. **2** *he looked very solemn:* serious, grave, sober, sombre, unsmiling, stern, grim, dour, humourless. **3** *a solemn promise:* sincere, earnest, honest, genuine, firm, heartfelt, wholehearted, sworn.
OPPOSITES frivolous, light-hearted, insincere.

**solid** adjective **1** *the plaster was solid:* hard, rock-hard, rigid, firm, solidified, set, frozen. **2** *solid gold:* pure, unadulterated, genuine. **3** *solid houses:* well built, sound, substantial, strong, sturdy, durable. **4** *a solid argument:* well founded, valid, sound, logical, authoritative, convincing. **5** *solid support from their colleagues:* unanimous, united, consistent, undivided.
OPPOSITES liquid, alloyed, flimsy, untenable, half-hearted.

**solidarity** noun unanimity, unity, agreement, team spirit, accord, harmony, consensus; formal concord.

**solitary** adjective **1** *a solitary man:* lonely, unaccompanied, by oneself, on one's own, alone, friendless, unsociable, withdrawn, reclusive; N. Amer. lonesome. **2** *solitary farmsteads:* isolated, remote, lonely, out of the way, in the back of beyond, outlying, off the beaten track, secluded; N. Amer. in the backwoods. **3** *a solitary piece of evidence:* single, lone, sole, only, one, individual.
OPPOSITES sociable, accessible.

**solution** noun **1** *a solution to the problem:* answer, result, resolution, key, explanation. **2** *a solution of salt and water:* mixture, blend, compound.

**solve** verb answer, resolve, work out, puzzle out, fathom, decipher, decode, clear up, straighten out, get to the bottom of, unravel, explain; informal figure out, crack; Brit. informal suss out.

**sombre** adjective **1** *sombre clothes:* dark, drab, dull, dingy, restrained, subdued, sober, funereal. **2** *a sombre expression:* solemn, earnest, serious, grave, sober, unsmiling, stern, grim, dour, gloomy, sad, mournful, lugubrious.
OPPOSITES bright, cheerful.

**somehow** adverb one way or another, no matter how, by fair means or foul, by hook or by crook, come what may.

**sometimes** adverb occasionally, from time to time, now and then, every so often, once in a while, on occasion, at times, off and on.

**song** noun **air**, strain, ditty, chant, number, track, melody, tune.

**soon** adverb **shortly**, presently, in the near future, before long, in a little while, in a minute, in a moment; Brit. informal in a tick.

**sooner** adverb **1** *he should have done it sooner:* **earlier**, before now. **2** *I would sooner stay:* **rather**, preferably, given the choice.

**soothe** verb **1** *Rachel tried to soothe him:* **calm (down)**, pacify, comfort, hush, quiet, settle (down), appease, mollify; Brit. quieten (down). **2** *an anaesthetic to soothe the pain:* **ease**, alleviate, relieve, take the edge off, allay, lessen, reduce.
OPPOSITES agitate, aggravate.

**soothing** adjective **relaxing**, restful, calm, calming, tranquil, peaceful.

**sophisticated** adjective **1** *sophisticated technology:* **advanced**, state-of-the-art, the latest, up-to-the-minute, cutting-edge, trailblazing, complex. **2** *a sophisticated woman:* **worldly**, worldly-wise, experienced, cosmopolitan, urbane, cultured, cultivated, polished, refined.
OPPOSITES crude, naive.

**sophistication** noun **worldliness**, experience, urbanity, culture, polish, refinement, elegance, style, poise, finesse, savoir faire.

**sore** adjective **1** *a sore leg:* **painful**, hurting, hurt, aching, throbbing, smarting, stinging, inflamed, sensitive, tender, raw. **2** *(N. Amer. informal) they were sore at us:* **upset**, angry, annoyed, cross, disgruntled, dissatisfied,

irritated; informal aggravated, miffed, peeved; Brit. informal narked; N. Amer. informal ticked off.

**sorrow** noun **1** *he felt sorrow at her death:* **sadness**, unhappiness, misery, despondency, regret, despair, desolation, heartache, grief. **2** *the sorrows of life:* **trouble**, difficulty, problem, woe, affliction, trial, tribulation, misfortune.
OPPOSITES joy.

**sorry** adjective **1** *I was sorry to hear about his accident:* **sad**, moved, sorrowful, distressed. **2** *he felt sorry for her:* **full of pity**, sympathetic, compassionate, moved, concerned. **3** *I'm sorry I was rude:* **regretful**, apologetic, remorseful, contrite, repentant, rueful, penitent, guilty, shamefaced, ashamed.
OPPOSITES glad, unsympathetic, unrepentant.

**sort** noun *what sort of book is it?* **type**, kind, variety, class, category, style, form, genre, species, make, model.
verb **1** *they sorted the books alphabetically:* **classify**, class, group, organize, arrange, order. **2** *the problem was soon sorted out:* **resolve**, settle, solve, fix, work out, straighten out, deal with, put right, set right, rectify, iron out.

**soul** noun **1** *his soul cried out:* **spirit**, psyche, (inner) self. **2** *their music lacked soul:* **feeling**, emotion, passion, animation, intensity, warmth, energy, vitality, spirit.

**sound**[1] noun **1** *the sound of a car:* **noise**, din, racket, row, resonance, reverberation. **2** *she did not make a sound:* **utterance**, cry, word, noise, peep. **3** *the sound of the flute:* tone, timbre, call, song, voice. OPPOSITES silence.

**verb 1** *the buzzer sounded:* make a noise, resonate, resound, reverberate, go off, ring, chime, ping. **2** *drivers must sound their horns:* blow, blast, toot, ring, use, operate, activate, set off. **3** *it sounds a crazy idea:* appear, look (like), seem, give every indication of being.

**sound**[2] adjective **1** *your heart is sound:* healthy, in good condition/shape, fit, hale and hearty, in fine fettle, undamaged, unimpaired. **2** *a sound building:* well built, solid, substantial, strong, sturdy, durable, stable, intact. **3** *sound advice:* well founded, valid, reasonable, logical, weighty, authoritative, reliable. **4** *a sound judge of character:* reliable, dependable, fair, good. **5** *financially sound:* solvent, debt-free, in the black, in credit, creditworthy, secure. **6** *a sound sleep:* deep, undisturbed, uninterrupted, untroubled, peaceful. OPPOSITES unhealthy, unsound, unsafe, unreliable, insolvent.

**sour** adjective **1** *sour wine:* acid, acidic, tart, bitter, sharp, vinegary, pungent. **2** *sour milk:* bad, off, turned, curdled, rancid, high, fetid. **3** *a sour old man:* embittered, resentful, jaundiced, bitter, cross, crabby, crotchety, cantankerous; informal grouchy. OPPOSITES sweet, fresh, amiable.

**verb** *the dispute soured relations:* spoil, mar, damage, harm, impair, wreck, upset, poison, blight. OPPOSITES improve.

**source** noun **1** *the source of the river:* spring, origin. **2** *the source of the rumour:* origin, starting point, root, author, originator. **3** *historical sources:* reference, authority, informant, document.

**souvenir** noun memento, keepsake, reminder, memorial, trophy.

**sovereign** noun *the sovereign's prerogative:* ruler, monarch, potentate, overlord, king, queen, emperor, empress, prince, princess.

**adjective** *a sovereign state:* autonomous, independent, self-governing, self-determining, non-aligned, free.

**sovereignty** noun **1** *their sovereignty over the islands:* power, rule, supremacy, dominion, jurisdiction, ascendancy, domination, authority, control. **2** *full sovereignty was achieved in 1955:* autonomy, independence, self-government, self-rule, home rule, self-determination, freedom.

**sow** verb plant, scatter, disperse, strew, broadcast, seed.

**space** noun **1** *there was not enough space:* room, capacity, latitude, margin, leeway, play, elbow room, clearance. **2** *green spaces in London:* area, expanse, stretch, sweep, tract. **3** *a space between the timbers:* gap, interval, opening, aperture, cavity, niche. **4** *write your name in the appropriate space:* blank, gap, box, field. **5** *a space of seven years:* period, span, time, duration, stretch, course, interval, gap. **6** *the first woman in space:* outer space, deep space, the universe.

**verb** *the chairs were spaced*

*widely:* position, arrange, range, array, spread, lay out, set.

**spacious** adjective roomy, capacious, commodious, voluminous, sizeable, generous.
OPPOSITES cramped.

**span** noun 1 *a six-foot wing span:* extent, length, width, reach, stretch, spread, distance, range. 2 *the span of one week:* period, space, time, duration, course, interval.
verb 1 *an arch spanned the stream:* bridge, cross, traverse, pass over. 2 *his career spanned twenty years:* last, cover, extend, spread over.

**spare** adjective 1 *a spare set of keys:* extra, supplementary, additional, second, other, alternative, emergency, reserve, backup, relief, substitute; N. Amer. alternate. 2 *they sold off the spare land:* surplus, superfluous, excess, leftover, redundant, unnecessary, unwanted; informal going begging. 3 *your spare time:* free, leisure, own. 4 *her spare, elegant form:* slender, lean, willowy, svelte, lissom, thin, skinny, gaunt, lanky, spindly.
verb 1 *he couldn't spare any money:* afford, manage, part with, give, provide. 2 *they were spared by their captors:* pardon, let off, forgive, have mercy on, reprieve, release, free.

**sparing** adjective thrifty, economical, frugal, careful, prudent, cautious.
OPPOSITES lavish, extravagant.

**spark** noun *a spark of light:* flash, glint, twinkle, flicker, flare.
verb *the arrest sparked off riots:* cause, give rise to, occasion, bring about, start, precipitate,

prompt, trigger (off), provoke, stimulate, stir up.

**sparkle** verb & noun glitter, glint, glisten, twinkle, flicker, flash, shimmer.

**sparkling** adjective 1 *sparkling wine:* effervescent, fizzy, carbonated, aerated. 2 *a sparkling performance:* brilliant, dazzling, scintillating, exciting, exhilarating, stimulating, invigorating, vivacious, lively, vibrant.
OPPOSITES still, dull.

**spate** noun series, succession, run, cluster, string, rash, epidemic, outbreak, wave, flurry.

**speak** verb 1 *she refused to speak about it:* talk, converse, communicate, chat, have a word, gossip, commune, say anything/something. 2 *she spoke her words carefully:* say, utter, state, declare, voice, express, pronounce, articulate, enunciate, verbalize. 3 *the Minister spoke for two hours:* give a speech, talk, lecture, hold forth; informal spout, sound off.

**speaker** noun speech-maker, lecturer, talker, orator, spokesperson, spokesman/woman, reader, commentator, broadcaster, narrator.

**special** adjective 1 *a very special person:* exceptional, unusual, remarkable, outstanding, unique. 2 *our town's special character:* distinctive, distinct, individual, particular, specific, peculiar. 3 *a special occasion:* momentous, significant, memorable, important, historic. 4 *a special tool for cutting tiles:* specific, particular, purpose-built, tailor-made, custom-built.
OPPOSITES ordinary, general.

a
b
c
d
e
f
g
h
i
j
k
l
m
n
o
p
q
r
**s**
t
u
v
w
x
y
z

a
b
c
d
e
f
g
h
i
j
k
l
m
n
o
p
q
r
**s**
t
u
v
w
x
y
z

**specialist** noun expert, authority, pundit, professional, connoisseur, master, maestro; informal buff.
OPPOSITES amateur.

**speciality** noun 1 *his speciality was watercolours:* strength, strong point, forte, métier, strong suit, party piece, pièce de résistance; informal bag, thing. 2 *a speciality of the region:* delicacy.

**species** noun type, kind, sort, breed, strain, variety, class, classification, category.

**specific** adjective 1 *a specific purpose:* particular, specified, fixed, set, determined, distinct, definite. 2 *I gave specific instructions:* detailed, explicit, express, clear-cut, unequivocal, precise, exact.
OPPOSITES general, vague.

**specification** noun 1 *clear specification of objectives:* statement, identification, definition, description, setting out. 2 *a shelter built to their specifications:* instruction, guideline, parameter, stipulation, requirement, condition, order, detail.

**specify** verb state, name, identify, define, set out, itemize, detail, list, spell out, stipulate, lay down.

**specimen** noun sample, example, model, instance, illustration, demonstration.

**spectacle** noun 1 *his love of spectacle:* display, show, pageantry, performance, exhibition, pomp and circumstance, extravaganza, spectacular. 2 *they were rather an odd spectacle:* sight, vision, scene, prospect, picture.

**spectacular** adjective 1 *a spectacular view:* striking, picturesque, eye-catching, breathtaking, arresting, glorious; informal out of this world. 2 *a spectacular victory:* impressive, magnificent, splendid, dazzling, sensational, dramatic, outstanding, memorable, unforgettable.
OPPOSITES dull, unimpressive.

**spectator** noun watcher, viewer, observer, onlooker, bystander, witness.
OPPOSITES participant.

**spectre** noun ghost, phantom, apparition, spirit, wraith, presence; informal spook.

**speculate** verb 1 *they speculated about my private life:* conjecture, theorize, hypothesize, guess, surmise, wonder, muse. 2 *investors speculate on the stock market:* gamble, venture, wager, invest, play the market; Brit. informal punt.

**speculative** adjective 1 *any discussion is largely speculative:* conjectural, suppositional, theoretical, hypothetical, tentative, unproven, unfounded, groundless, unsubstantiated. 2 *a speculative investment:* risky, hazardous, unsafe, uncertain, unpredictable; informal chancy.

**speech** noun 1 *the power of speech:* speaking, talking, verbal expression, verbal communication. 2 *her speech was slurred:* diction, elocution, articulation, enunciation, pronunciation, delivery, words. 3 *an after-dinner speech:* talk, address, lecture, discourse, oration, presentation, sermon. 4 *in popular speech:* language, parlance, tongue, idiom, dialect, vernacular; informal lingo.

**speed** noun 1 *the speed of their*

*progress:* rate, pace, tempo, momentum, velocity; informal lick. **2** *the speed with which they responded:* rapidity, swiftness, promptness, briskness, haste, hurry.
OPPOSITES slowness.

**verb 1** *I sped home:* hurry, rush, dash, race, sprint, career, shoot, hurtle, hare, fly, zoom, hasten; informal tear, belt, pelt; Brit. informal bomb. **2** *a holiday will speed his recovery:* hasten, speed up, accelerate, advance, further, promote, boost, stimulate, aid, assist, facilitate.
OPPOSITES dawdle, slow, hinder.
■ **speed up** hurry up, accelerate, go faster, get a move on, put a spurt on, pick up speed; informal step on it.

**speedy** adjective fast, swift, quick, rapid, prompt, immediate, brisk, hasty, hurried, precipitate, rushed.
OPPOSITES slow.

**spell**[1] verb *the drought spelled disaster:* signal, signify, mean, amount to, add up to, constitute.
■ **spell something out** explain, make clear, clarify, specify, detail.

**spell**[2] noun **1** *the witch muttered a spell:* charm, incantation, formula, curse; N. Amer. hex; (**spells**) magic, sorcery, witchcraft. **2** *she surrendered to his spell:* influence, charm, magnetism, charisma, magic.
■ **put a spell on** bewitch, enchant, entrance, curse, jinx, witch; N. Amer. hex.

**spell**[3] noun **1** *a spell of dry weather:* period, time, interval, season, stretch, run; Brit. informal patch. **2** *a spell of dizziness:* bout, fit, attack.

**spend** verb **1** *she spent £185 on*

*shoes:* pay out, expend; informal blow, splurge. **2** *the morning was spent gardening:* pass, occupy, fill, take up, while away. **3** *I've spent hours on this essay:* put in, devote, waste, squander.

**sphere** noun **1** *a glass sphere:* globe, ball, orb, bubble. **2** *sphere of influence:* area, field, compass, orbit, range, scope, extent. **3** *the sphere of foreign affairs:* domain, realm, province, field, area, territory, arena, department.

**spice** noun **1** *the spices in curry powder:* seasoning, flavouring, condiment. **2** *the risk added spice to their affair:* excitement, interest, colour, piquancy, zest, and an edge.

**spicy** adjective hot, tangy, peppery, piquant, spiced, highly seasoned, pungent.
OPPOSITES bland.

**spike** noun prong, pin, barb, point, skewer, stake, spit.

**spill** verb **1** *Kevin spilled his drink:* knock over, tip over, upset, overturn. **2** *the bath water spilled on to the floor:* overflow, slop, slosh, splash, leak. **3** *students spilled out of the building:* stream, pour, surge, swarm, flood, throng, crowd.

**spin** verb **1** *the wheels are spinning:* revolve, rotate, turn, go round, whirl. **2** *she spun round to face him:* whirl, wheel, twirl, turn, swing, twist, swivel, pivot.
noun **1** *a spin of the wheel:* rotation, revolution, turn, whirl, twirl. **2** *a positive spin:* slant, angle, twist, bias. **3** *a spin in the car:* trip, jaunt, outing, excursion, journey,

a
b
c
d
e
f
g
h
i
j
k
l
m
n
o
p
q
r
**s**
t
u
v
w
x
y
z

drive, ride, run, turn; informal tootle.

**spine** noun **1** *he injured his spine:* backbone, spinal column, back. **2** *cactus spines:* needle, quill, bristle, barb, spike, prickle, thorn.

**spiral** adjective *a spiral column:* coiled, helical, curling, winding, twisting.
noun *a spiral of smoke:* coil, curl, twist, whorl, scroll, helix, corkscrew.
verb *smoke spiralled up:* coil, wind, swirl, twist, snake.

**spirit** noun **1** *body and spirit:* soul, psyche, inner self, inner man/woman, mind. **2** *a spirit haunts the island:* ghost, phantom, spectre, apparition, presence. **3** *in good spirits:* mood, frame/state of mind, humour, temper. **4** *team spirit:* morale, esprit de corps. **5** *the spirit of the age:* ethos, essence, atmosphere, mood, feeling, climate. **6** *they played with spirit:* enthusiasm, energy, verve, vigour, dynamism, dash, sparkle, exuberance, gusto; fervour, zeal, fire, passion; informal get-up-and-go. **7** *the spirit of the law:* real meaning, true meaning, essence, substance, idea.
OPPOSITES body, flesh.

**spirited** adjective lively, energetic, enthusiastic, vigorous, dynamic, passionate; informal feisty, gutsy; N. Amer. informal peppy.
OPPOSITES apathetic, lifeless.

**spiritual** adjective **1** *your spiritual self:* inner, mental, psychological, incorporeal, non-material. **2** *spiritual writings:* religious, sacred, divine, holy, devotional.
OPPOSITES physical, secular.

**spit** verb **1** *Cranston coughed and spat:* expectorate, hawk; Brit. informal gob. **2** *the fat began to spit:* sizzle, hiss, crackle, sputter.
noun *spit dribbled from his mouth:* spittle, saliva, sputum, slobber, dribble; Brit. informal gob.

**spite** noun *he said it out of spite:* malice, malevolence, ill will, vindictiveness, meanness, nastiness; informal bitchiness, cattiness.
OPPOSITES kindness.
verb *he did it to spite me:* upset, hurt, wound.
OPPOSITES please.
■ **in spite of** despite, notwithstanding, regardless of, in defiance of, in the face of.

**splash** verb **1** *splash your face with water:* sprinkle, spray, shower, wash, squirt, daub, wet. **2** *his boots were splashed with rain:* spatter, splatter, speck, smear, stain, mark. **3** *waves splashing on the beach:* wash, break, lap, pound. **4** *children splashed in the water:* paddle, wade, wallow.
noun **1** *a splash of rain:* spot, blob, smear, speck. **2** *a splash of lemonade:* drop, dash, bit, spot, soupçon, dribble; Scottish informal scoosh. **3** *a splash of colour:* patch, burst, streak.

**splendid** adjective **1** *splendid costumes:* magnificent, sumptuous, grand, imposing, superb, spectacular, resplendent, rich, lavish, ornate, gorgeous, glorious, dazzling, handsome, beautiful; informal plush; Brit. informal swish. **2** (informal) *a splendid holiday:* excellent, wonderful, marvellous, superb, glorious, lovely, delightful, first-class; informal super, great, amazing,

fantastic, terrific, tremendous; Brit. informal smashing, brilliant.
OPPOSITES simple, modest, awful.

**splendour** noun magnificence, sumptuousness, grandeur, resplendence, richness, glory, majesty.
OPPOSITES simplicity, modesty.

**splinter** noun *a splinter of wood:* sliver, chip, shard, fragment, shred; Scottish skelf.
verb *the glass splintered:* shatter, smash, break into smithereens, fracture, split, crack, disintegrate.

**split** verb **1** *the force split the wood:* break, cut, burst, snap, crack. **2** *the ice split under him:* break, fracture, rupture, burst, snap, crack, come apart, splinter. **3** *her dress was split:* tear, rip, slash, slit. **4** *they split the profit:* share, divide up, distribute, dole out, parcel out, carve up, slice up. **5** *the path split:* fork, divide, branch, diverge. **6** *the band split up last year:* break up, separate, part, part company, go their separate ways.
OPPOSITES mend, join, unite, pool, converge, get together.
noun **1** *a split in the rock face:* crack, fissure, cleft, crevice, break, fracture, breach. **2** *a split in the curtain:* rip, tear, cut, rent, slash, slit. **3** *a split in the Party:* division, rift, breach, schism, rupture, partition. **4** *the acrimonious split with his wife:* break-up, split-up, separation, parting, estrangement, rift.
OPPOSITES join, merger, marriage.

**spoil** verb **1** *smoking spoils your complexion:* damage, ruin, impair, blemish, disfigure, blight, deface, harm, destroy,

wreck. **2** *rain spoiled my plans:* ruin, wreck, upset, undo, mess up, sabotage, scotch, torpedo; informal muck up, screw up, do for; Brit. informal cock up, scupper.
**3** *his sisters spoil him:* overindulge, pamper, indulge, mollycoddle, cosset, wait on someone hand and foot.
**4** *stockpiled food may spoil:* go bad, go off, go rancid, turn, go sour, rot, perish.
OPPOSITES improve, enhance, further, neglect, be strict with, keep.

**spoken** adjective verbal, oral, vocal, unwritten, word-of-mouth.
OPPOSITES non-verbal, written.

**spokesperson, spokesman, spokeswoman** noun representative, voice, mouthpiece, agent, official; informal spin doctor.

**sponsor** noun backer, patron, promoter, benefactor, supporter, contributor.
verb finance, fund, subsidize, back, promote, support, contribute to; N. Amer. informal bankroll.

**spontaneous** adjective **1** *a spontaneous display of affection:* unplanned, unpremeditated, impulsive, impromptu, spur-of-the-moment, unprompted; informal off-the-cuff. **2** *a spontaneous kind of person:* natural, uninhibited, relaxed, unselfconscious, unaffected.
OPPOSITES planned, inhibited.

**sport** noun game, physical recreation.
verb *he was sporting a new tie:* wear, have on, dress in, show off, parade, flaunt.

**sporting** adjective sportsmanlike, generous,

considerate, fair; Brit. informal decent.
OPPOSITES dirty, unfair.

**sporty** adjective (informal) athletic, fit, active, energetic.
OPPOSITES unfit, lazy.

**spot** noun 1 *a grease spot:* mark, patch, dot, fleck, smudge, smear, stain, blotch, splash; informal splodge. 2 *a spot on his nose:* pimple, pustule, blackhead, boil; informal zit; Scottish informal plook; (**spots**) acne. 3 *a secluded spot:* place, site, position, situation, setting, location, venue.
verb *she spotted him:* see, notice, observe, detect, make out, recognize, identify, locate; Brit. informal clock.

**spotlight** noun attention, glare of publicity, limelight, public eye.

**spotted** adjective spotty, dotted, polka-dot, freckled, mottled.
OPPOSITES plain.

**spotty** adjective 1 *a spotty dress:* polka-dot, spotted, dotted. 2 (Brit.) *his spotty face:* pimply, pimpled, acned; Scottish informal plooky.

**spouse** noun partner, husband, wife, mate, consort; informal better half; Brit. informal other half.

**sprawl** verb stretch out, lounge, loll, slump, flop, slouch.

**spray** noun 1 *a spray of water:* shower, sprinkle, jet, squirt, mist, spume, foam, froth. 2 *a perfume spray:* aerosol, vaporizer, atomizer, sprinkler.
verb 1 *we sprayed water on the soil:* sprinkle, dribble, drizzle. 2 *spray the plants with weedkiller:* water, mist, soak, douse, drench. 3 *water sprayed into the air:* spout, jet, gush, spurt, shoot, squirt.

**spread** verb 1 *he spread the map out:* lay out, open out, unfurl, unroll, roll out, straighten out, fan out, stretch out, extend. 2 *the landscape spread out below:* extend, stretch, sprawl. 3 *papers were spread all over his desk:* scatter, strew, disperse, distribute. 4 *he's spreading rumours:* circulate, broadcast, put about, publicize, propagate, repeat. 5 *the disease spread rapidly:* travel, move, be borne, sweep, diffuse, reproduce, be passed on, be transmitted. 6 *she spread sun cream on her arms:* smear, daub, plaster, apply, rub.
OPPOSITES fold up, suppress.
noun 1 *the spread of learning:* expansion, proliferation, dissemination, diffusion, transmission, propagation. 2 *a spread of six feet:* span, width, extent, stretch, reach.

**spree** noun bout, orgy; informal binge, splurge.

**spring** verb 1 *the cat sprang off her lap:* leap, jump, bound, vault. 2 *the branch sprang back:* fly, whip, flick, whisk, kick, bounce. 3 *all art springs from feelings:* originate, derive, arise, stem, emanate, evolve.
noun *the mattress has lost its spring:* springiness, bounce, resilience, elasticity, flexibility, stretch, stretchiness, give.

**sprinkle** verb 1 *he sprinkled water on the cloth:* splash, trickle, drizzle, spray, shower, drip. 2 *sprinkle sesame seeds over the top:* scatter, strew. 3 *sprinkle the cake with icing sugar:* dredge, dust.

**sprint** verb run, race, rush, dash, bolt, fly, charge, shoot, speed; informal hotfoot it, leg it.
OPPOSITES walk.

**sprout** verb **1** *the seeds begin to sprout*: germinate, put/send out shoots, bud. **2** *parsley sprouted from the pot*: spring, come up, grow, develop, appear.

**spur** noun *the spur of competition*: stimulus, incentive, encouragement, inducement, impetus, motivation.
OPPOSITES disincentive.
verb *the thought spurred him into action*: stimulate, encourage, prompt, prod, impel, motivate, move, galvanize, inspire, drive.
OPPOSITES discourage.

**spurn** verb reject, rebuff, scorn, turn down, treat with contempt, disdain, look down one's nose at; informal turn one's nose up at.
OPPOSITES welcome, accept.

**spy** noun *a foreign spy*: agent, mole, plant; N. Amer. informal spook.
verb *she spied a coffee shop*: notice, observe, see, spot, sight, catch sight of, glimpse, make out, discern, detect.
■ **spy on** observe, keep under surveillance, eavesdrop on, watch, bug.

**spying** noun espionage, intelligence gathering, surveillance, infiltration.

**squabble** noun *there was a brief squabble*: quarrel, disagreement, row, argument, dispute, wrangle, clash, altercation; informal tiff, set-to, run-in, scrap, dust-up; Brit. informal barney, ding-dong; N. Amer. informal rhubarb.
verb *they squabbled over money*: quarrel, row, argue, bicker, disagree; informal scrap.

**squad** noun **1** *a maintenance squad*: team, crew, gang, force.

**2** *a squad of marines*: detachment, detail, unit, platoon, battery, troop, patrol, squadron, commando.

**squander** verb waste, throw away, misuse, fritter away, spend like water; informal blow, go through, splurge, pour down the drain.
OPPOSITES manage, make good use of, save.

**square** adjective *the sides were square at half-time*: level, even, drawn, equal, tied, level pegging; informal even-steven(s).
OPPOSITES uneven.
verb **1** *this does not square with the data*: agree, tally, be in agreement, be consistent, match up, correspond, fit.
**2** *Tom squared things with his boss*: resolve, sort out, settle, clear up, work out, iron out, straighten out, set right, rectify, remedy; informal patch up.

**squash** verb **1** *the fruit got squashed*: crush, squeeze, mash, pulp, flatten, compress, distort, pound, trample. **2** *she squashed her clothes inside the bag*: force, ram, thrust, push, cram, jam, stuff, pack, squeeze, wedge.

**squeeze** verb **1** *I squeezed the bottle*: compress, press, crush, squash, pinch, nip, grasp, grip, clutch. **2** *squeeze the juice from both oranges*: extract, press, force, express. **3** *Sally squeezed her feet into the sandals*: force, thrust, cram, ram, jam, stuff, pack, wedge, press, squash. **4** *we all squeezed into Steve's van*: crowd, crush, cram, pack, jam, squash, shove, push, force one's way.
noun **1** *he gave her hand a squeeze*: press, pinch, nip, grasp, grip, clutch, hug. **2** *it was*

a
b
c
d
e
f
g
h
i
j
k
l
m
n
o
p
q
r
**s**
t
u
v
w
x
y
z

*quite a squeeze:* crush, jam, squash, congestion.

**stab** verb *he stabbed him in the stomach:* knife, run through, skewer, spear, gore, spike, impale.
noun 1 *a stab of pain:* twinge, pang, throb, spasm, cramp, prick, flash, thrill. 2 (informal) *a stab at writing:* attempt, try; informal go, shot, crack, bash.

**stability** noun 1 *the stability of the equipment:* firmness, solidity, steadiness. 2 *his mental stability:* balance (of mind), (mental) health, sanity, reason. 3 *the stability of their relationship:* strength, durability, lasting nature, permanence.

**stable** adjective 1 *a stable vehicle:* firm, solid, steady, secure. 2 *a stable person:* well balanced, of sound mind, compos mentis, sane, normal, rational. 3 *a stable relationship:* secure, solid, strong, steady, firm, sure, steadfast, established, enduring, lasting.
OPPOSITES wobbly, unbalanced, rocky, changeable.

**stack** noun *a stack of boxes:* heap, pile, mound, mountain, pyramid, tower.
verb 1 *Leo was stacking plates:* heap (up), pile (up), assemble, put together, collect. 2 *they stacked the shelves:* load, fill (up), pack, charge, stuff, cram, stock.
OPPOSITES clear.

**staff** noun 1 *we'll take on new staff:* employees, workers, workforce, personnel, human resources, manpower, labour. 2 *a wooden staff:* stick, stave, pole, rod.
verb *the centre is staffed by teachers:* man, people, crew,

work, operate.

**stage** noun 1 *this stage of the development:* phase, period, juncture, step, point, level. 2 *the last stage of the race:* part, section, portion, stretch, leg, lap, circuit. 3 *a raised stage:* platform, dais, stand, rostrum, podium.

**stagger** verb 1 *he staggered to the door:* lurch, reel, sway, teeter, totter, stumble. 2 *I was absolutely staggered:* amaze, astound, astonish, surprise, stun, confound, daze, take aback; informal flabbergast; Brit. informal gobsmack.

**stain** verb 1 *her clothing was stained with blood:* discolour, soil, mark, spot, spatter, splatter, smear, splash, smudge. 2 *the wood was stained:* colour, tint, dye, pigment.
noun 1 *a mud stain:* mark, spot, blotch, smudge, smear. 2 *a stain on his character:* blemish, taint, blot, smear, dishonour.

**stake¹** noun *a stake in the ground:* post, pole, stick, spike, upright, support, cane.

**stake²** noun 1 *high stakes:* bet, wager, ante. 2 *a 40% stake in the business:* share, interest, ownership, involvement.
verb *he staked his week's pay:* bet, wager, lay, put on, gamble.

**stale** adjective 1 *stale food:* old, past its best, off, dry, hard, musty, rancid. 2 *stale air:* stuffy, musty, fusty, stagnant. 3 *stale beer:* flat, spoiled, off, insipid, tasteless. 4 *stale jokes:* overused, hackneyed, tired, worn out, overworked, threadbare, banal, clichéd; N. Amer. played out.
OPPOSITES fresh, original.

**stalk** verb 1 *he was stalking a deer:* trail, follow, shadow,

track, go after, hunt; informal tail.
**2** *she stalked out*: strut, stride, march, flounce, storm, stomp, sweep.

**stall** noun **1** *a market stall*: stand, table, counter, booth, kiosk. **2** *stalls for larger animals*: pen, coop, sty, corral, enclosure, compartment.
verb **1** *quit stalling*: delay, play for time, procrastinate, hedge, drag one's feet, filibuster, stonewall. **2** *stall him for a bit*: delay, divert, distract, hold off.

**stalwart** adjective staunch, loyal, faithful, committed, devoted, dedicated, dependable, reliable.
OPPOSITES disloyal, unfaithful, unreliable.

**stamina** noun endurance, staying power, energy, toughness, determination, tenacity, perseverance, grit.

**stammer** verb stutter, stumble over one's words, hesitate, falter, pause, splutter.

**stamp** verb **1** *he stamped on my toe*: trample, step, tread, tramp, crush, squash, flatten. **2** *John stamped off, muttering*: stomp, stump, clump. **3** *the name is stamped on the cover*: imprint, print, impress, punch, inscribe, emboss.
noun *the stamp of authority*: mark, hallmark, sign, seal, sure sign, smack, savour, air.
■ **stamp something out** put an end to, end, stop, crush, put down, curb, quell, suppress, extinguish, stifle, abolish, get rid of, eliminate, eradicate, destroy, wipe out.

**stance** noun **1** *a natural golfer's stance*: posture, body position, pose, attitude. **2** *a liberal stance*: attitude, opinion, standpoint, position, approach,

policy, line.

**stand** verb **1** *the men stood up*: rise, get to one's feet, get up, pick oneself up. **2** *today a house stands on the site*: be situated, be located, be positioned, be sited, have been built. **3** *he stood the vase on the shelf*: put, set, erect, place, position, prop, install, arrange; informal park.
**4** *my decision stands*: remain in force, remain in operation, hold, hold good, apply, be the case, exist. **5** *his heart could not stand the strain*: withstand, endure, bear, put up with, take, cope with, handle, sustain, resist, stand up to. **6** (informal) *I won't stand cheek*: put up with, endure, tolerate, accept, take, abide, stand for, support, countenance; formal brook.
OPPOSITES sit, lie down.
noun **1** *the party's stand on immigration*: attitude, stance, opinion, standpoint, position, approach, policy, line. **2** *a stand against tyranny*: opposition, resistance. **3** *a mirror on a stand*: base, support, platform, rest, plinth, tripod, rack, trivet. **4** *a newspaper stand*: stall, counter, booth, kiosk.
■ **stand by** wait, be prepared, be in (a state of) readiness, be ready for action, be on full alert, wait in the wings. ■ **stand by someone/something 1** *she stood by her husband*: remain/be loyal to, stick with/by, remain/be true to, stand up for, support, back up, defend, stick up for. **2** *the government must stand by its pledges*: abide by, keep (to), adhere to, hold to, stick to, observe, comply with.
■ **stand for** mean, be short for, represent, signify, denote, symbolize. ■ **stand in** deputize, act, substitute, fill in, take over,

cover, hold the fort, step into the breach, replace, relieve, take over from; informal sub, step into someone's shoes; N. Amer. pinch-hit. ■ **stand out** be noticeable, be visible, be obvious, be conspicuous, stick out, attract attention, catch the eye, leap out; informal stick/stand out a mile, stick/stand out like a sore thumb.

**standard** noun 1 *the standard of her work:* quality, level, calibre, merit, excellence. 2 *a safety standard:* guideline, norm, yardstick, benchmark, measure, criterion, guide. 3 *a standard to live by:* principle, ideal; (standards) code of behaviour, morals, ethics. 4 *the regiment's standard:* flag, banner, ensign, colour(s).
adjective 1 *the standard way of doing it:* normal, usual, typical, stock, common, ordinary, customary, conventional, established. 2 *the standard work on the subject:* definitive, classic, recognized, accepted.
OPPOSITES unusual, special.

**standing** noun 1 *his standing in the community:* status, ranking, position, reputation, stature. 2 *a person of some standing:* prestige, rank, eminence, seniority, repute, stature, esteem, importance, account.

**staple** adjective main, principal, chief, major, primary, leading, foremost, first, most important, predominant, dominant, basic, prime; informal number-one.

**star** noun 1 *the sky was full of stars:* celestial/heavenly body, sun. 2 *the stars of the film:* principal, leading lady/man, lead, hero, heroine. 3 *a star of the world of chess:* celebrity, superstar, famous name,

household name, leading light, VIP, personality, luminary; informal celeb, big shot, megastar.
OPPOSITES nobody.
adjective 1 *a star pupil:* outstanding, exceptional. 2 *the star attraction:* top, leading, greatest, foremost, major, pre-eminent.
OPPOSITES poor, minor.

**stare** verb gaze, gape, goggle, glare, ogle, peer; informal gawk; Brit. informal gawp.

**stark** adjective 1 *a stark silhouette:* sharp, crisp, distinct, clear, clear-cut. 2 *a stark landscape:* desolate, bare, barren, empty, bleak. 3 *a stark room:* austere, severe, plain, simple, bare, unadorned. 4 *stark terror:* sheer, utter, absolute, total, pure, downright, out-and-out, outright. 5 *the stark facts:* blunt, bald, bare, simple, plain, unvarnished, harsh, grim.
OPPOSITES fuzzy, indistinct, lush, ornate, disguised.
adverb *stark naked:* completely, totally, utterly, absolutely, entirely, wholly, fully, quite, altogether, thoroughly.

**start** verb 1 *the meeting starts at 7.45:* begin, commence, get under way, get going, go ahead; informal kick off. 2 *this was how her illness started:* come into being/existence, begin, commence, be born, arise, originate, develop. 3 *she started her own charity:* establish, set up, found, create, bring into being, institute, initiate, introduce, open, launch. 4 *you can start the machine:* activate, switch/turn on, start up, fire up, boot up. 5 *the machine started:* begin working, start up, get going,

spring into life. 6 *'Oh my!' she said, starting:* flinch, jerk, jump, twitch, wince.
OPPOSITES finish, stop, wind up, close down.
noun 1 *the start of the event:* beginning, commencement, inception. 2 *the start of her illness:* onset, emergence. 3 *a quarter of an hour's start:* lead, head start, advantage. 4 *she awoke with a start:* jerk, twitch, spasm, jump.
OPPOSITES end, finish.

**startle** verb surprise, frighten, scare, alarm, shock, give someone a fright, make someone jump.
OPPOSITES put at ease.

**starving** adjective hungry, undernourished, malnourished, starved, ravenous, famished.
OPPOSITES full.

**state**[1] noun 1 *the state of the economy:* condition, shape, position, predicament, plight. 2 *an autonomous state:* country, nation, land, kingdom, realm, power, republic. 3 *the country is divided into thirty-two states:* province, region, territory, canton, department, county, district; Brit. shire. 4 *the power of the state:* government, parliament, administration, regime, authorities.

**state**[2] verb express, voice, utter, put into words, declare, announce, make known, put across/over, communicate, air.

**stately** adjective dignified, majestic, ceremonious, courtly, imposing, solemn, regal, grand.
OPPOSITES undignified.

**statement** noun declaration, expression, affirmation, assertion, announcement, utterance, communication, bulletin, communiqué.

**station** noun 1 *a research station:* establishment, base, camp, post, depot, mission, site, facility, installation. 2 *a police station:* office, depot, base, headquarters; N. Amer. precinct, station house. 3 *a radio station:* channel, wavelength.
verb *the regiment was stationed at Woolwich:* base, post, establish, deploy, garrison.

**stationary** adjective static, parked, motionless, immobile, still, stock-still, at a standstill, at rest.
OPPOSITES moving, shifting.

**stature** noun 1 *small in stature:* height, size, build. 2 *an architect of international stature:* reputation, repute, standing, status, position, prestige, distinction, eminence, prominence, importance.

**status** noun 1 *the status of women:* standing, rank, position, level, place. 2 *wealth and status:* prestige, kudos, cachet, standing, stature, esteem, image, importance, authority, fame.

**staunch**[1] adjective *a staunch supporter:* stalwart, loyal, faithful, committed, devoted, dedicated, reliable.
OPPOSITES disloyal, unfaithful, unreliable.

**staunch**[2] verb *try to staunch the flow:* stem, stop, halt, check, curb; N. Amer. stanch.

**stay** verb 1 *he stayed where he was:* remain (behind), wait, linger, stick, be left, hold on, hang on; informal hang around; Brit. informal hang about. 2 *they won't stay hidden:* continue (to be), remain, keep, carry on being, go on being. 3 *our aunt is staying with us:* visit, stop (off/over), holiday, lodge;

N. Amer. vacation.

OPPOSITES leave, stop being.

**noun** *a stay at a hotel:* visit, stop, stopover, break, holiday; N. Amer. vacation.

**steady** adjective 1 *the ladder must be steady:* stable, firm, fixed, secure. 2 *keep the camera steady:* still, motionless, static, stationary. 3 *a steady gaze:* fixed, intent, unwavering, unfaltering. 4 *a steady income:* constant, regular, consistent, reliable. 5 *steady rain:* continuous, continual, unceasing, ceaseless, perpetual, unremitting, endless. 6 *a steady boyfriend:* regular, settled, firm, committed, long-term.

OPPOSITES unstable, loose, shaky, darting, fluctuating, sporadic, occasional.

**verb** 1 *he steadied the rifle:* stabilize, hold steady, brace, support, balance, rest. 2 *she needed to steady her nerves:* calm, soothe, quieten, compose, settle, subdue, quell.

**steal** verb 1 *burglars stole the TV:* take, thieve, help oneself to, pilfer, embezzle; informal swipe, lift, filch; Brit. informal nick, pinch, knock off; N. Amer. informal heist. 2 *his work was stolen by his tutor:* plagiarize, copy, pirate; informal rip off, lift, pinch, crib; Brit. informal nick. 3 *he stole out of the room:* creep, sneak, slink, slip, glide, tiptoe, slope.

**stealth** noun furtiveness, secretiveness, secrecy, surreptitiousness.

OPPOSITES openness.

**stealthy** adjective furtive, secretive, secret, surreptitious, sneaky, sly.

OPPOSITES open.

**steep** adjective 1 *steep cliffs:* sheer, precipitous, abrupt,

sharp, perpendicular, vertical. 2 *a steep increase:* sharp, sudden, dramatic.

OPPOSITES gentle, gradual, reasonable.

**steeped**
■ steeped in imbued with, filled with, permeated with, suffused with, soaked in, pervaded by.

**steer** verb guide, direct, manoeuvre, drive, pilot, navigate.

**stem**[1] noun *a plant stem:* stalk, shoot, trunk.
■ stem from come from, arise from, originate from, have its origins in, spring from, derive from.

**stem**[2] verb *they stemmed the flow of blood:* stop, staunch, halt, check, curb; N. Amer. stanch.

**step** noun 1 *Frank took a step forward:* pace, stride. 2 *she heard a step on the stairs:* footstep, footfall, tread. 3 *the top step:* stair, tread; (steps) stairs, staircase, flight of stairs. 4 *resigning is a very serious step:* action, act, course of action, measure, move, operation. 5 *a significant step towards a ceasefire:* advance, development, move, movement, breakthrough. 6 *the first step on the managerial ladder:* stage, level, grade, rank, degree, phase.

**verb** *she stepped forward:* walk, move, tread, pace, stride.
■ step down resign, stand down, give up one's post/job, bow out, abdicate; informal quit.
■ step in intervene, become involved, intercede. ■ step something up increase, intensify, strengthen, escalate, speed up, accelerate; informal crank up.

**stereotype** noun *the stereotype*

*of the woman as carer:*
conventional idea, standard
image, cliché, formula.
verb *bodybuilders are
stereotyped as 'muscleheads':*
typecast, pigeonhole,
conventionalize, categorize,
label, tag.

**sterile** adjective **1** *sterile desert:*
unproductive, infertile,
unfruitful, barren. **2** *sterile
conditions:* hygienic, clean,
pure, uncontaminated,
sterilized, disinfected, germ-
free, antiseptic.
OPPOSITES fertile, productive,
septic.

**stern** adjective **1** *a stern
expression:* unsmiling,
frowning, serious, severe,
forbidding, grim, unfriendly,
austere, dour. **2** *stern measures:*
strict, severe, stringent, harsh,
drastic, hard, tough, extreme,
draconian.
OPPOSITES genial, friendly,
lenient, lax.

**stick**¹ noun **1** *a fire made of
sticks:* branch, twig. **2** *he walks
with a stick:* walking stick,
cane, staff, crutch. **3** *the plants
need supporting on sticks:* post,
pole, cane, stake. **4** *he beat me
with a stick:* club, cudgel,
truncheon, baton, cane, switch,
rod; Brit. informal cosh.

**stick**² verb **1** *he stuck his fork
into the sausage:* thrust, push,
insert, jab, poke, dig, plunge.
**2** *the bristles stuck into his skin:*
pierce, penetrate, puncture,
prick, stab. **3** *the mug stuck to
the mat:* adhere, cling. **4** *stick
the stamp there:* attach, fasten,
affix, fix, paste, glue, gum, tape.
**5** *the wheels stuck fast:* jam, get
jammed, catch, get caught, get
trapped. **6** *that sticks in his
mind:* remain, stay, linger,

persist, continue, endure. **7** (Brit.
informal) *I can't stick it:* tolerate,
put up with, take, stand,
stomach, endure, bear; informal
abide.
■ **stick out 1** *his front teeth
stuck out:* protrude, jut (out),
project, stand out, extend, poke
out, bulge. **2** *they stuck out in
their new clothes:* be
conspicuous, be obvious, stand
out, attract attention, stand out;
informal stick out a mile. ■ **stick
to** abide by, keep, adhere to,
hold to, comply with, fulfil,
stand by. ■ **stick up for** support,
take someone's side, side with,
stand by, stand up for, defend.

**sticky** adjective **1** *sticky tape:*
adhesive, self-adhesive,
gummed. **2** *sticky clay:* tacky,
gluey, gummy, treacly,
glutinous; informal gooey. **3** *sticky
weather:* humid, muggy, close,
sultry, steamy, sweaty. **4** *a
sticky situation:* awkward,
difficult, tricky, ticklish,
delicate, embarrassing,
sensitive; informal hairy.
OPPOSITES dry, fresh, cool, easy.

**stiff** adjective **1** *stiff cardboard:*
rigid, hard, firm. **2** *a stiff paste:*
thick, firm, viscous, semi-solid.
**3** *I'm stiff all over:* aching, achy,
painful, arthritic. **4** *a rather
stiff manner:* formal, reserved,
wooden, forced, strained,
stilted; informal starchy, uptight.
**5** *a stiff fine:* harsh, severe,
heavy, stringent, drastic,
draconian; Brit. swingeing. **6** *stiff
resistance:* vigorous,
determined, strong, spirited,
resolute, tenacious, dogged,
stubborn. **7** *a stiff climb:*
difficult, hard, arduous, tough,
strenuous, laborious, exacting,
tiring, demanding. **8** *a stiff
breeze:* strong, fresh, brisk. **9** *a
stiff drink:* strong, potent,

alcoholic.
OPPOSITES flexible, limp, runny,
supple, relaxed, informal,
lenient, mild, half-hearted,
easy, gentle, weak.

**stifle** verb suppress, smother,
restrain, check, curb, silence,
hinder, hamper, impede,
prevent, inhibit.
OPPOSITES encourage, let out.

**still** adjective **1** *Polly lay still:*
motionless, unmoving, stock-
still, immobile, rooted to the
spot, transfixed, static,
stationary. **2** *a still night:* quiet,
silent, calm, peaceful, serene,
windless. **3** *the lake was still:*
calm, flat, smooth, like a
millpond.
OPPOSITES moving, active, noisy,
rough.
adverb **1** *he's still here:* even
now, yet. **2** *He's crazy. Still, he's
harmless:* nevertheless,
nonetheless, all the same, even
so, but, however, despite that,
in spite of that, for all that.
verb *he stilled the crowd:*
quieten, quiet, silence, hush,
calm, settle, pacify, subdue.
OPPOSITES stir up.

**stimulate** verb encourage,
prompt, motivate, trigger,
spark, spur on, galvanize, fire,
inspire, excite; N. Amer. light a
fire under.
OPPOSITES discourage.

**stimulating** adjective
thought-provoking,
interesting, inspiring,
inspirational, lively, exciting,
provocative.
OPPOSITES uninspiring, boring.

**stimulus** noun motivation,
encouragement, impetus,
prompt, spur, incentive,
inspiration.
OPPOSITES deterrent,
discouragement.

**sting** noun **1** *a bee sting:* prick,
wound, injury. **2** *this cream will
take the sting away:* pain,
pricking, smart, soreness, hurt,
irritation.
verb **1** *she was stung by a
scorpion:* prick, wound. **2** *the
smoke made her eyes sting:*
smart, burn, hurt, be irritated,
be sore. **3** *the criticism stung
her:* upset, wound, hurt, pain,
mortify.

**stink** verb *his clothes stank of
sweat:* reek, smell.
noun *the stink of sweat:* stench,
reek; Brit. informal pong; N. Amer.
informal funk.

**stint** noun spell, stretch, turn,
session, term, time, shift, tour
of duty.

**stipulate** verb specify, set out,
lay down, demand, require,
insist on.

**stir** verb **1** *stir the mixture well:*
mix, blend, beat, whip, whisk,
fold in; N. Amer. muddle. **2** *James
stirred in his sleep:* move,
change one's position, shift. **3** *a
breeze stirred the leaves:*
disturb, rustle, shake, move,
agitate. **4** *the war stirred him to
action:* spur, drive, rouse,
prompt, propel, motivate,
encourage, urge, impel,
provoke.
noun *the news caused a stir:*
commotion, disturbance, fuss,
excitement, sensation; informal
to-do, hoo-ha.

**stock** noun **1** *the shop doesn't
carry much stock:* merchandise,
goods, wares. **2** *a stock of fuel:*
store, supply, stockpile,
reserve, hoard, cache, bank.
**3** *farm stock:* animals,
livestock, beasts, flocks, herds.
**4** *his mother was of French
stock:* descent, ancestry,
origin(s), lineage, birth,

extraction, family, blood, pedigree.

**adjective** *the stock response:* **usual**, routine, predictable, set, standard, staple, customary, familiar, conventional, traditional, stereotyped, clichéd, hackneyed, unoriginal, formulaic.
OPPOSITES non-standard, original.

**verb** *we do not stock GM food:* **sell**, carry, keep (in stock), offer, supply, provide, furnish.

**stomach** noun **1** *a pain in my stomach:* **abdomen**, belly, gut, middle; informal tummy, insides. **2** *his fat stomach:* **paunch**, belly, beer belly, girth; informal pot, tummy, spare tyre, middle-aged spread; N. Amer. informal bay window. **3** *no stomach for a fight:* **appetite**, taste, inclination, desire, wish.
**verb** *they couldn't stomach it:* **tolerate**, put up with, take, stand, endure, bear; informal hack, abide; Brit. informal stick.

**stone** noun **1** *someone threw a stone:* **rock**, pebble, boulder. **2** *a precious stone:* **gem**, gemstone, jewel; informal rock, sparkler. **3** *a peach stone:* **kernel**, seed, pip, pit.

**stoop** verb *she stooped to pick up the pen:* **bend**, lean, crouch, bow, duck.
**noun** *a man with a stoop:* **hunch**, round shoulders.

**stop** verb **1** *we can't stop the decline:* **end**, halt, finish, terminate, wind up, discontinue, cut short, interrupt, nip in the bud, shut down. **2** *he stopped running:* **cease**, discontinue, desist from, break off, give up, abandon, cut out; informal quit, pack in; Brit. informal jack in. **3** *the car stopped:*

**pull up**, draw up, come to a stop/halt, come to rest, pull in/over. **4** *the music stopped:* **cease**, end, come to an and, halt, finish, draw to a close, be over, conclude. **5** *the police stopped her leaving:* **prevent**, obstruct, impede, block, bar, preclude, dissuade from.
OPPOSITES start, begin, continue, allow, encourage.
**noun 1** *all business came to a stop:* **halt**, end, finish, close, standstill. **2** *a brief stop in the town:* **break**, stopover, stop-off, stay, visit. **3** *the next stop is Oxford Street:* **stopping place**, station, halt.
OPPOSITES start, beginning, continuation.

**store** noun **1** *a store of food:* **stock**, supply, stockpile, hoard, cache, reserve, bank, pool. **2** *a grain store:* **storeroom**, storehouse, repository, stockroom, depot, warehouse. **3** *ship's stores:* **supplies**, provisions, stocks, food, rations, materials, equipment, hardware. **4** *a DIY store:* **shop**, (retail) outlet, boutique, department store, supermarket, hypermarket, superstore, megastore.
**verb** *rabbits don't store food:* **keep**, stockpile, lay in, set aside, put aside, put away/by, save, collect, accumulate, hoard; informal squirrel away.
OPPOSITES use, discard.

**storehouse** noun warehouse, depository, repository, store, storeroom, depot.

**storm** noun **1** *battered by a storm:* **tempest**, squall, gale, hurricane, tornado, cyclone, typhoon, thunderstorm, rainstorm, monsoon, hailstorm, snowstorm, blizzard. **2** *there*

a b c d e f g h i j k l m n o p q r **s** t u v w x y z

was a storm over his remarks:
uproar, outcry, fuss, furore,
rumpus, trouble; informal to-do,
hoo-ha, ructions, stink; Brit.
informal row.

verb 1 she stormed out: stride,
march, stomp, stamp, stalk,
flounce, fling. 2 police stormed
the building: attack, charge,
rush, swoop on.

**stormy** adjective **1** stormy
weather: blustery, squally,
windy, gusty, blowy, thundery,
wild, violent, rough, foul. **2** a
stormy debate: angry, heated,
fierce, furious, passionate,
acrimonious.
OPPOSITES calm, fine, peaceful.

**story** noun **1** an adventure story:
tale, narrative, account, history,
anecdote, saga; informal yarn.
**2** the novel has a good story:
plot, storyline, scenario. **3** the
story appeared in the papers:
news, report, item, article,
feature, piece. **4** there have
been a lot of stories going
round: rumour, whisper,
allegation, speculation, gossip;
Austral./NZ informal furphy.

**stout** adjective **1** a short stout
man: fat, plump, portly, rotund,
dumpy, corpulent; informal tubby;
Brit. informal podgy; N. Amer. informal
zaftig, corn-fed. **2** stout leather
shoes: strong, sturdy, solid,
robust, tough, durable, hard-
wearing. **3** stout resistance:
determined, vigorous, forceful,
spirited, committed, brave;
informal gutsy.
OPPOSITES thin, flimsy, feeble.

**straight** adjective **1** a long,
straight road: direct, linear,
unswerving, undeviating. **2** that
picture isn't straight: level,
even, in line, aligned, square,
vertical, upright, perpendicular,
horizontal. **3** we must get the

place straight: in order, tidy,
neat, shipshape, orderly,
organized, arranged, sorted out,
straightened out. **4** a straight
answer: honest, direct, frank,
candid, truthful, sincere,
forthright, straightforward,
plain-spoken, blunt,
unambiguous; informal upfront.
**5** straight brandy: neat,
undiluted, pure; N. Amer. informal
straight up.
OPPOSITES winding, crooked,
untidy, evasive.

adverb **1** he looked me straight in
the eyes: right, directly,
squarely, full; informal smack,
(slap) bang; N. Amer. informal
spang, smack dab. **2** she drove
straight home: directly, right.
**3** I told her straight: frankly,
directly, candidly, honestly,
forthrightly, plainly, point-
blank, bluntly, flatly; Brit. informal
straight up. **4** he can't think
straight: logically, rationally,
clearly, lucidly, coherently,
cogently.

■ straight away at once, right
away, (right) now, this/that
(very) minute, this/that
instant, immediately, instantly,
directly, forthwith, then and
there; N. Amer. in short order;
informal straight off, pronto;
N. Amer. informal lickety-split.

**straighten** verb **1** Rory
straightened his tie: put
straight, adjust, arrange,
rearrange, tidy. **2** we must
straighten things out with Viola:
put right, sort out, clear up,
settle, resolve, rectify, remedy;
informal patch up.

**straightforward** adjective
**1** the process was remarkably
straightforward:
uncomplicated, simple, plain
sailing. **2** a straightforward
man: honest, frank, candid,

open, truthful, sincere, on the level, forthright, plain-speaking, direct; informal upfront; N. Amer. informal on the up and up.
OPPOSITES complicated, devious.

**strain**[1] verb 1 *take care that you don't strain yourself:* overtax, overwork, overextend, overreach, overdo it, exhaust, wear out; informal knacker, knock oneself out. 2 *you have strained a muscle:* injure, damage, pull, wrench, twist, sprain. 3 *strain the mixture:* sieve, sift, filter, screen.
noun 1 *the rope snapped under the strain:* tension, tightness, tautness. 2 *muscle strain:* injury, sprain, wrench, twist. 3 *the strain of her job:* pressure, demands, burdens, stress; informal hassle. 4 *Melissa was showing signs of strain:* stress, (nervous) tension, exhaustion, fatigue, pressure, overwork.

**strain**[2] noun *a different strain of flu:* variety, kind, type, sort, breed, genus.

**strained** adjective 1 *relations were strained:* awkward, tense, uneasy, uncomfortable, edgy, difficult, troubled. 2 *a strained smile:* forced, unnatural, artificial, insincere, false, affected, put-on.
OPPOSITES friendly, genuine.

**strait** noun 1 channel, sound, narrows, stretch of water. 2 (**straits**) difficulty, trouble, crisis, mess, predicament, plight; informal hot water, jam, hole, fix, scrape.

**strand** noun thread, filament, fibre, length.

**stranded** adjective 1 *stranded on a desert island:* shipwrecked, wrecked, marooned, high and dry, grounded, aground,

beached. 2 *stranded in a strange city:* helpless, abandoned, lost, adrift.

**strange** adjective 1 *strange things have been happening:* unusual, odd, curious, peculiar, funny, bizarre, weird, uncanny, anomalous; informal fishy. 2 *visiting a strange house:* unfamiliar, unknown, new, novel.
OPPOSITES ordinary, familiar.

**stranger** noun newcomer, new arrival, visitor, guest, outsider, foreigner.

**strangle** verb throttle, choke, garrotte, asphyxiate.

**strap** noun *thick leather straps:* belt, tie, band, thong.
verb *a bag was strapped to the bicycle:* tie, lash, secure, fasten, bind, make fast, truss.

**strapping** adjective big, strong, well-built, brawny, burly, muscular; informal beefy.
OPPOSITES weedy.

**strategic** adjective planned, calculated, deliberate, tactical, judicious, prudent, shrewd.

**strategy** noun plan, grand design, game plan, policy, programme, scheme.

**stray** verb 1 *the gazelle had strayed from the herd:* wander off, get separated, get lost, drift away. 2 *we strayed from our original topic:* digress, deviate, wander, get sidetracked, go off at a tangent, get off the subject.
adjective 1 *a stray dog:* homeless, lost, abandoned, feral. 2 *a stray bullet:* random, chance, freak, unexpected.

**streak** noun 1 *a streak of light:* band, line, strip, stripe, vein, slash, ray, smear. 2 *a streak of self-destructiveness:* element, vein, strain, touch. 3 *a winning* *streak:* **period, spell, stretch, run**; Brit. informal **patch.**

**verb 1** *the sky was streaked with red:* **stripe, band, fleck, smear, mark. 2** *Miranda streaked across the road:* **race, speed, flash, shoot, dash, rush, hurtle, whizz, zoom, career, fly**; informal **belt, tear, zip, whip**; Brit. informal **bomb**; N. Amer. informal **barrel.**

**stream** noun **1** *a mountain stream:* **brook, rivulet, tributary**; Scottish & N. English **burn**; N. English **beck**; S. English **bourn**; N. Amer. & Austral./NZ **creek. 2** *a stream of boiling water:* **jet, flow, rush, gush, surge, torrent, flood, cascade. 3** *a steady stream of visitors:* **succession, series, string.**

**verb 1** *tears were streaming down her face:* **flow, pour, course, run, gush, surge, flood, cascade, spill. 2** *children streamed out of the classrooms:* **pour, surge, flood, swarm, pile, crowd.**

**streamlined** adjective **1** *streamlined cars:* **aerodynamic, smooth, sleek. 2** *a streamlined organization:* **efficient, smooth-running, well run, slick.**

**street** noun **road, thoroughfare, avenue, drive, boulevard, lane**; N. Amer. **highway.**

**strength** noun **1** *enormous physical strength:* **power, muscle, might, brawn, force. 2** *Oliver began to regain his strength:* **health, fitness, vigour, stamina. 3** *her great inner strength:* **fortitude, resilience, spirit, backbone, courage, bravery, pluck, grit**; informal **guts. 4** *the strength of the retaining wall:* **robustness, sturdiness, firmness, toughness, soundness, solidity, durability. 5** *political*

*strength:* **power, influence**; informal **clout. 6** *strength of feeling:* **intensity, vehemence, force, depth. 7** *the strength of their argument:* **force, weight, power, persuasiveness, soundness, cogency, validity. 8** *what are your strengths?* **strong point, advantage, asset, forte, aptitude, talent, skill, speciality. 9** *the strength of the army:* **size, extent, magnitude.**
OPPOSITES **weakness.**

**strengthen** verb **1** *calcium strengthens growing bones:* **make strong/stronger, build up, harden, toughen, fortify, stiffen, reinforce. 2** *the wind had strengthened:* **become strong/stronger, gain strength, intensify, pick up.**
OPPOSITES **weaken.**

**strenuous** adjective **1** *a strenuous climb:* **difficult, arduous, hard, tough, taxing, demanding, exacting, exhausting, tiring, gruelling, back-breaking**; Brit. informal **knackering. 2** *strenuous efforts:* **vigorous, energetic, forceful, strong, spirited, intense, determined, resolute, dogged.**
OPPOSITES **easy, half-hearted.**

**stress** noun **1** *he's under a lot of stress:* **strain, pressure, (nervous) tension, worry, anxiety, trouble, difficulty**; informal **hassle. 2** *laying greater stress on education:* **emphasis, importance, weight.**
**verb 1** *they stress the need for reform:* **emphasize, draw attention to, underline, underscore, point up, highlight. 2** *all the staff were stressed:* **overstretch, overtax, pressurize, pressure, worry, harass**; informal **hassle.**
OPPOSITES **play down.**

**stretch** verb 1 *this material stretches:* expand, give, be elastic, be stretchy. 2 *he stretched the elastic:* pull (out), draw out, extend, lengthen, elongate, expand. 3 *stretching the truth:* bend, strain, distort, exaggerate, embellish. 4 *she stretched out her arm:* reach out, hold out, extend, straighten (out). 5 *she stretched out on the sofa:* lie down, recline, lean back, sprawl, lounge, loll. 6 *the desert stretches for miles:* extend, spread, continue, go on.
OPPOSITES shorten, contract, fold up.

noun 1 *magnificent stretches of forest:* expanse, area, tract, belt, sweep, extent. 2 *a four-hour stretch:* period, time, spell, run, stint, session, shift.

**strict** adjective 1 *a strict interpretation of the law:* precise, exact, literal, faithful, accurate, careful, meticulous, rigorous. 2 *strict controls on spending:* stringent, rigorous, severe, harsh, hard, rigid, tough. 3 *strict parents:* stern, severe, harsh, uncompromising, authoritarian, firm. 4 *in strict confidence:* absolute, utter, complete, total.
OPPOSITES loose, liberal.

**stride** verb & noun step, pace, march.

**strife** noun conflict, friction, discord, disagreement, dissension, dispute, argument, quarrelling.
OPPOSITES peace.

**strike** verb 1 *the teacher struck Mary:* hit, slap, smack, thump, punch, beat, bang; informal clout, wallop, belt, whack, thwack, bash, clobber, bop, biff; Austral./ NZ informal quilt. 2 *the car struck a tree:* crash into, collide with, hit, run into, bump into, smash into; N. Amer. impact. 3 *a thought struck her:* occur to, come to (mind), dawn on one, hit, spring to mind, enter one's head. 4 *you strike me as intelligent:* seem to, appear to, give someone the impression of being. 5 *train drivers are to strike:* take industrial action, go on strike, down tools, walk out.

noun 1 *a 48-hour strike:* industrial action, walkout. 2 *a military strike:* attack, assault, bombing.

**striking** adjective 1 *a striking resemblance:* noticeable, obvious, conspicuous, marked, unmistakable, strong, remarkable. 2 *Kenya's striking landscape:* impressive, imposing, magnificent, spectacular, breathtaking, marvellous, wonderful, stunning, sensational, dramatic.
OPPOSITES unremarkable.

**string** noun 1 *a ball of string:* twine, cord, yarn, thread. 2 *a string of brewers:* chain, group, consortium. 3 *a string of convictions:* series, succession, chain, sequence, run, streak. 4 *a string of wagons:* queue, procession, line, file, column, convoy, train, cavalcade. 5 (**strings**) *a guaranteed loan with no strings:* conditions, qualifications, provisions, provisos, caveats, stipulations, riders, limitations, restrictions; informal catches.

verb *lights were strung across the promenade:* hang, suspend, sling, stretch, run, thread, loop, festoon.

**stringent** adjective strict, firm, rigid, rigorous, severe, harsh,

tough, tight, exacting, demanding.
OPPOSITES lax.

**strip**[1] verb **1** *he stripped and got into bed:* undress, strip off, take one's clothes off, disrobe. **2** *stripping the paint off the door:* peel, remove, scrape, clean. **3** *I stripped down the engine:* dismantle, disassemble, take to bits/pieces, take apart. **4** *the house had been stripped:* empty, clear, clean out, plunder, rob, burgle, loot, pillage, ransack, sack.
OPPOSITES dress, reassemble.

**strip**[2] noun *a strip of paper:* (narrow) piece, band, belt, ribbon, slip, shred, stretch.

**stroke** noun **1** *five hammer strokes:* blow, hit. **2** *light upward strokes:* movement, action, motion. **3** *broad brush strokes:* mark, line. **4** *he suffered a stroke:* thrombosis, seizure, apoplexy.
verb *she stroked the cat:* caress, fondle, pat, pet, touch, rub, massage, soothe.

**stroll** verb & noun walk, amble, wander, meander, ramble, promenade, saunter; informal mosey.

**strong** adjective **1** *a strong lad:* powerful, sturdy, robust, athletic, tough, rugged, lusty. **2** *she isn't very strong:* well, healthy, fit. **3** *a strong character:* forceful, determined, spirited, self-assertive, tough, formidable, strong-minded; informal gutsy, feisty. **4** *a strong fortress:* secure, well built, well fortified, well protected, solid. **5** *strong cotton bags:* durable, hard-wearing, heavy-duty, tough, sturdy, well made, long-lasting. **6** *a strong interest in*

*literature:* keen, passionate, fervent. **7** *strong feelings:* intense, forceful, passionate, ardent, fervent, deep-seated. **8** *strong arguments:* forceful, compelling, powerful, convincing, persuasive, sound, valid, cogent, well founded. **9** *a strong voice:* loud, powerful, forceful, resonant, sonorous, rich, deep, booming. **10** *strong language:* bad, foul, obscene, profane. **11** *a strong blue colour:* intense, deep, rich, bright, brilliant, vivid, vibrant. **12** *strong lights:* bright, brilliant, dazzling, glaring. **13** *strong coffee:* concentrated, undiluted. **14** *strong cheese:* highly flavoured, mature, ripe, piquant, tangy, spicy. **15** *strong drink:* alcoholic, intoxicating, hard, stiff.
OPPOSITES weak, gentle, mild.

**stronghold** noun **1** *the enemy stronghold:* fortress, fort, castle, citadel, garrison. **2** *a Tory stronghold:* bastion, centre, hotbed.

**structure** noun **1** *a vast Gothic structure:* building, edifice, construction, erection. **2** *the structure of local government:* construction, organization, system, arrangement, framework, form, formation, shape, composition, anatomy, make-up.
verb *the programme is structured around periods of study:* arrange, organize, design, shape, construct, build.

**struggle** verb **1** *they struggled to do better:* strive, try hard, endeavour, make every effort. **2** *James struggled with the raiders:* fight, battle, grapple, wrestle, scuffle. **3** *she struggled over the dunes:* scramble,

flounder, stumble, fight/battle one's way, labour.
**noun 1** *the struggle for justice:* striving, endeavour, campaign, battle, crusade, drive, push.
**2** *no signs of a struggle:* fight, scuffle, brawl, tussle, fracas; informal bust-up, ding-dong.
**3** *many perished in the struggle:* conflict, fight, battle, confrontation, clash, hostilities, fighting, war, warfare, campaign. **4** *a struggle within the leadership:* contest, competition, fight, clash, rivalry, friction, feuding, conflict.

**strut** verb swagger, prance, parade, stride, sweep; N. Amer. informal sashay.
OPPOSITES slink.

**stubborn** adjective **1** *you're too stubborn to admit it:* obstinate, headstrong, wilful, strong-willed, pig-headed, inflexible, uncompromising, unbending; informal stiff-necked. **2** *stubborn stains:* indelible, permanent, persistent, tenacious, resistant.
OPPOSITES compliant, removable.

**stuck** adjective **1** *a message was stuck to his screen:* fixed, fastened, attached, glued, pinned. **2** *the gate was stuck:* jammed, immovable. **3** *if you get stuck, leave a blank:* baffled, beaten, at a loss; informal stumped, bogged down, flummoxed, bamboozled.

**student** noun **1** *a university student:* undergraduate, postgraduate. **2** *a former student:* pupil, schoolchild, schoolboy, schoolgirl, scholar. **3** *a nursing student:* trainee, apprentice, probationer, novice, learner.

**studio** noun workshop, workroom, atelier.

**studious** adjective scholarly, academic, bookish, intellectual, erudite, learned, donnish; informal brainy.

**study** noun **1** *two years of study:* learning, education, schooling, scholarship, tuition, research.
**2** *a study of global warming:* investigation, enquiry, research, examination, analysis, review, survey. **3** *Bob was in the study:* office, workroom, studio.
verb **1** *Anne studied hard:* work, revise; informal swot, cram. **2** *he studied maths:* learn, read, be taught. **3** *Thomas studied ants:* investigate, research, look at, examine, analyse. **4** *she studied him thoughtfully:* scrutinize, examine, inspect, consider, regard, look at, observe, watch, survey; informal check out.

**stuff** noun **1** *suede is tough stuff:* material, substance, fabric, cloth. **2** *first-aid stuff:* items, articles, objects, goods; informal things, bits and pieces, odds and ends. **3** *all my stuff is in the suitcase:* belongings, possessions, effects, paraphernalia; informal gear, things, kit; Brit. informal clobber.
verb **1** *stuffing pillows:* fill, pack, pad, upholster. **2** *Robyn stuffed her clothes into a bag:* shove, thrust, push, ram, cram, squeeze, force, jam, pack, pile.

**stuffing** noun padding, wadding, filling, packing.

**stuffy** adjective **1** *a stuffy atmosphere:* airless, close, musty, stale. **2** *a stuffy young man:* staid, sedate, sober, priggish, strait-laced, conformist, conservative, old-fashioned; informal straight, starchy, fuddy-duddy.
OPPOSITES airy, clear, informal, modern.

a
b
c
d
e
f
g
h
i
j
k
l
m
n
o
p
q
r
s
t
u
v
w
x
y
z

**stumble** verb 1 *he stumbled and fell*: trip, lose one's balance, lose one's footing, slip. 2 *he stumbled back home*: stagger, totter, blunder, hobble.
■ **stumble across/on** find, chance on, happen on, light on, come across/upon, discover, unearth, uncover; informal dig up.

**stump** verb (informal) baffle, perplex, puzzle, confound, defeat, put at a loss; informal flummox, fox, throw, floor.

**stun** verb 1 *the force of the blow stunned him*: daze, stupefy, knock out, lay out. 2 *she was stunned by the news*: astound, amaze, astonish, dumbfound, stupefy, stagger, shock, take aback; informal flabbergast, knock sideways.

**stunning** adjective beautiful, lovely, glorious, wonderful, marvellous, magnificent, superb, sublime, spectacular, fine, delightful; informal fantastic, terrific, tremendous, sensational, heavenly, divine, gorgeous, fabulous, awesome.
OPPOSITES ordinary.

**stunt** noun feat, exploit, trick.

**stunted** adjective small, undersized, underdeveloped, diminutive.

**stupid** adjective 1 *he's really stupid*: unintelligent, dense, foolish, slow, idiotic, simple-minded; informal thick, dim, dumb, dopey, dozy; Brit. informal daft. 2 *a stupid idea*: foolish, silly, senseless, idiotic, ill-advised, ill-considered, unwise; informal crazy, half-baked, cockeyed, hare-brained; Brit. informal potty.
OPPOSITES intelligent, sensible.

**sturdy** adjective 1 *a sturdy lad*: strapping, well built, muscular, strong, hefty, brawny, powerful, solid, burly; informal beefy. 2 *sturdy boots*: robust, strong, well built, solid, stout, tough, durable, long-lasting, hard-wearing.
OPPOSITES feeble, flimsy.

**style** noun 1 *differing styles of management*: manner, way, technique, method, approach, system, form. 2 *dressing with style*: flair, elegance, taste, grace, poise, polish, sophistication, dash; informal class. 3 *Laura travelled in style*: comfort, luxury. 4 *modern styles*: fashion, trend, vogue.
verb *sportswear styled by Karl*: design, fashion, tailor, cut.

**stylish** adjective fashionable, modern, up to date, modish, smart, sophisticated, elegant, chic, dapper, dashing; informal trendy, natty; N. Amer. informal kicky, tony.
OPPOSITES unfashionable.

**subdue** verb conquer, defeat, vanquish, overcome, overwhelm, crush, beat, subjugate, suppress.

**subdued** adjective 1 *Lewis's subdued air*: sombre, downcast, sad, dejected, depressed, gloomy, despondent. 2 *subdued voices*: hushed, muted, quiet, low, soft, faint, muffled, indistinct. 3 *subdued lighting*: dim, muted, soft, low, mood.
OPPOSITES cheerful, loud, bright.

**subject** noun 1 *the subject of this chapter*: theme, subject matter, topic, issue, question, concern. 2 *popular university subjects*: branch of study, discipline, field. 3 *British subjects*: citizen, national, resident, taxpayer, voter.
verb *subjected to violence*: expose to, treat with, put through.

■ **subject to** conditional on, contingent on, dependent on.

**subjective** adjective personal, individual, emotional, biased, intuitive.
OPPOSITES objective.

**submerge** verb 1 *the U-boat submerged:* go under (water), dive, sink, plunge, blow its tanks. 2 *submerge the bowl in water:* immerse, plunge, sink. 3 *the farmland was submerged:* flood, deluge, swamp, overwhelm, inundate.
OPPOSITES surface, drain.

**submission** noun 1 *submission to authority:* yielding, capitulation, surrender, resignation, acceptance, consent, compliance, acquiescence, obedience, subjection, subservience, servility. 2 *a report for submission to the Board:* presentation, proffering, tendering, proposing. 3 *his original submission:* proposal, suggestion, proposition, entry, recommendation. 4 *the judge rejected his submission:* argument, assertion, contention, statement, claim, allegation.
OPPOSITES defiance, resistance.

**submit** verb 1 *she was forced to submit:* yield, give in/way, back down, cave in, capitulate, surrender. 2 *he refused to submit to their authority:* be governed by, abide by, comply with, accept, be subject to, agree to, consent to, conform to. 3 *we submitted an application:* put forward, present, offer, tender, propose, suggest, enter, put in, send in. 4 *they submitted that the judgement was incorrect:*

contend, assert, argue, state, claim.
OPPOSITES resist, withdraw.

**subordinate** adjective inferior, junior, lower-ranking, lower, supporting.
OPPOSITES superior, senior.
noun junior, assistant, second (in command), number two, deputy, aide, underling, minion.
OPPOSITES superior, senior.

**subscribe** verb *we subscribe to charity:* contribute, donate, give, pay.
■ **subscribe to** support, endorse, agree with, accept, go along with.

**subscription** noun membership fee, dues, annual payment, charge.

**subsequent** adjective following, ensuing, succeeding, later, future, coming, to come, next.
OPPOSITES previous.

**subsequently** adverb later (on), at a later date, afterwards, in due course, following this/that, eventually; formal thereafter.

**subside** verb 1 *wait until the storm subsides:* abate, let up, quieten down, calm, slacken (off), ease (up), relent, die down, diminish, decline. 2 *the flood has subsided:* recede, ebb, fall, go down, get lower. 3 *the house is gradually subsiding:* sink, settle, cave in, collapse, give way.
OPPOSITES intensify, rise.

**subsidiary** adjective *a subsidiary company:* subordinate, secondary, subservient, supplementary, peripheral, auxiliary.
OPPOSITES principal.
noun *the firm's Spanish*

a b c d e f g h i j k l m n o p q r **s** t u v w x y z

*subsidiary:* branch, division, subdivision, derivative, offshoot.
OPPOSITES headquarters, holding company.

**subsidize** verb finance, fund, support, contribute to, give money to, underwrite, sponsor; informal shell out for; N. Amer. informal bankroll.

**subsidy** noun finance, funding, backing, support, grant, sponsorship, allowance, contribution, handout.

**substance** noun 1 *organic substances:* material, compound, matter, stuff. 2 *none of the objections has any substance:* significance, importance, import, validity, foundation. 3 *the substance of the tale is very thin:* content, subject matter, theme, message, essence. 4 *men of substance:* wealth, fortune, riches, affluence, prosperity, money, means.

**substantial** adjective
1 *substantial progress had been made:* considerable, real, significant, important, major, valuable, useful. 2 *substantial damages:* sizeable, considerable, significant, large, ample, appreciable.
3 *substantial Victorian villas:* sturdy, solid, stout, strong, well built, durable, long-lasting, hard-wearing.
OPPOSITES little, meagre, flimsy.

**substitute** noun *substitutes for permanent employees:* replacement, deputy, relief, proxy, reserve, surrogate, cover, stand-in, understudy; informal sub.
adjective *a substitute teacher:* acting, replacement, deputy,

relief, reserve, surrogate, stand-in.
OPPOSITES permanent.
verb 1 *curd cheese can be substituted for yogurt:* exchange, swap, use instead of, use as an alternative to, use in place of, replace with. 2 *the Senate was empowered to substitute for the President:* deputize, stand in, cover.

**subtle** adjective 1 *subtle colours:* understated, muted, subdued, delicate, soft. 2 *subtle distinctions:* fine, nice. 3 *a subtle change:* gentle, slight, gradual.
OPPOSITES gaudy, crude, dramatic.

**subtlety** noun delicacy, understatedness, refinement, mutedness, softness.

**subversive** adjective *subversive literature:* disruptive, troublemaking, insurrectionary, seditious, dissident.
noun *suspected of being a subversive:* troublemaker, dissident, agitator, renegade.

**succeed** verb 1 *Darwin finally succeeded:* triumph, achieve success, be successful, do well, flourish, thrive; informal make it, make the grade. 2 *the plan succeeded:* be successful, turn out well, work (out), be effective; informal come off, pay off. 3 *he succeeded Gladstone as Prime Minister:* replace, take over from, follow, supersede.
OPPOSITES fail, precede.

**success** noun 1 *the success of the scheme:* favourable outcome, triumph. 2 *the trappings of success:* prosperity, affluence, wealth, riches, opulence. 3 *a box-office success:* triumph, best-seller, sell-out; informal hit, smash, winner.

OPPOSITES failure.

**successful** adjective 1 *a successful designer:* prosperous, affluent, wealthy, rich, famous, eminent, top, respected. 2 *successful companies:* flourishing, thriving, booming, buoyant, doing well, profitable, moneymaking, lucrative.

**succession** noun sequence, series, progression, chain, string, train, line, run.

**successive** adjective consecutive, in a row, sequential, in succession, running; informal on the trot.

**succumb** verb 1 *she finally succumbed to temptation:* yield, give in/way, submit, surrender, capitulate, cave in. 2 *he succumbed to the disease:* die from/of.
OPPOSITES resist.

**suck** verb 1 *they sucked orange juice through straws:* sip, sup, siphon, slurp, drink. 2 *Fran sucked in a deep breath:* draw, pull, breathe, gasp.

**sudden** adjective unexpected, unforeseen, immediate, instantaneous, instant, precipitous, abrupt, rapid, swift, quick.

**suddenly** adverb all of a sudden, all at once, abruptly, swiftly, unexpectedly, without warning, out of the blue.
OPPOSITES gradually.

**sue** verb take legal action (against), go to court, take to court.

**suffer** verb 1 *I hate to see him suffer:* hurt, ache, be in pain, be in distress, be upset, be miserable. 2 *he suffers from asthma:* be afflicted by, be affected by, be troubled with, have. 3 *England suffered a humiliating defeat:* undergo, experience, be subjected to, receive, endure, face. 4 *our reputation has suffered:* be impaired, be damaged, decline.

**suffering** noun hardship, distress, misery, adversity, pain, agony, anguish, trauma, torment, torture, hurt, affliction.
OPPOSITES pleasure, joy.

**sufficient** adjective & determiner enough, adequate, plenty of, ample.
OPPOSITES inadequate.

**suggest** verb 1 *Ruth suggested a holiday:* propose, put forward, recommend, advocate, advise. 2 *evidence suggests that voters are unhappy:* indicate, lead to the belief, demonstrate, show. 3 *what exactly are you suggesting?* hint, insinuate, imply, intimate.

**suggestion** noun 1 *some suggestions for tackling this problem:* proposal, proposition, recommendation, advice, counsel, hint, tip, clue, idea. 2 *the suggestion of a smirk:* hint, trace, touch, suspicion, ghost, semblance, shadow, glimmer. 3 *a suggestion that he knew about the plot:* insinuation, hint, implication.

**suggestive** adjective 1 *an odour suggestive of a brewery:* redolent, evocative, reminiscent, characteristic, indicative, typical. 2 *suggestive remarks:* indecent, indelicate, improper, unseemly, sexual, sexy, smutty, dirty.

**suit** noun 1 *a pinstriped suit:* outfit, ensemble. 2 *a medical malpractice suit:* legal action, lawsuit, (court) case, action, (legal/judicial) proceedings, litigation.
verb 1 *blue really suits you:* look

a
b
c
d
e
f
g
h
i
j
k
l
m
n
o
p
q
r
**s**
t
u
v
w
x
y
z

attractive on, look good on, become, flatter. **2** *savings schemes to suit all pockets:* be convenient for, be acceptable to, be suitable for, meet the requirements of; informal fit. **3** *recipes suited to students:* be appropriate, tailor, fashion, adjust, adapt, modify, fit, gear, design.

**suitable** adjective **1** *suitable employment:* acceptable, satisfactory, fitting; informal right up someone's street. **2** *a drama suitable for all ages:* appropriate, fitting, fit, acceptable, right. **3** *music suitable for a dinner party:* appropriate, suited, befitting, in keeping with. **4** *they treated him with suitable respect:* proper, seemly, decent, appropriate, fitting, correct, due.
OPPOSITES inappropriate.

**suite** noun apartment, flat, rooms.

**sum** noun **1** *a large sum of money:* amount, quantity, price, charge, fee, cost. **2** *the sum of two numbers:* total, sum total, grand total, tally. **3** *the sum of his wisdom:* entirety, totality, total, whole, beginning and end. **4** *we did sums at school:* calculation, problem; (**sums**) arithmetic, mathematics; Brit. informal maths; N. Amer. informal math.
OPPOSITES difference.

■ **sum someone/something up 1** *that just about sums him up:* evaluate, describe, encapsulate, summarize, put in a nutshell. **2** *he summed up his reasons:* summarize, make/give a summary of, precis, outline, recapitulate, review; informal recap.

**summarize** verb sum up, abridge, condense, outline, put in a nutshell.

**summary** noun *a summary of the findings:* synopsis, precis, résumé, abstract, outline, rundown, summing-up, overview.

**summit** noun **1** *the summit of Mont Blanc:* (mountain) top, peak, crest, crown, apex, tip, cap, hilltop. **2** *the next superpower summit:* meeting, conference, talk(s).
OPPOSITES base.

**summon** verb **1** *he was summoned to the Embassy:* send for, call for, request the presence of, ask, invite. **2** *they were summoned as witnesses:* summons, subpoena. **3** *he summoned the courage to move closer:* muster, gather, collect, rally, screw up.

**sumptuous** adjective lavish, luxurious, opulent, magnificent, resplendent, gorgeous, splendid; informal plush; Brit. informal swish.
OPPOSITES plain.

**sunny** adjective **1** *a sunny day:* bright, sunlit, clear, fine, cloudless. **2** *a sunny disposition:* cheerful, cheery, happy, bright, merry, joyful, bubbly, jolly.
OPPOSITES dull, miserable.

**sunrise** noun dawn, crack of dawn, daybreak, break of day, first light, early morning; N. Amer. sunup.

**sunset** noun nightfall, twilight, dusk, evening; N. Amer. sundown.

**superb** adjective **1** *a superb goal:* excellent, first-class, outstanding, marvellous, wonderful, splendid, admirable, fine, exceptional, glorious; informal great, fantastic, fabulous, terrific, super,

awesome, ace; Brit. informal brilliant, smashing. **2** *a superb house:* magnificent, splendid, grand, impressive, imposing, awe-inspiring, breathtaking, gorgeous, beautiful.
OPPOSITES poor, unimpressive.

**superficial** adjective
**1** *superficial burns:* surface, exterior, external, outer, slight. **2** *a superficial investigation:* cursory, perfunctory, casual, sketchy, desultory, token, slapdash, offhand, rushed, hasty, hurried. **3** *a superficial resemblance:* apparent, seeming, outward, ostensible, cosmetic, slight. **4** *a superficial person:* facile, shallow, flippant, empty-headed, trivial, frivolous, silly, inane.
OPPOSITES deep, thorough, strong, intelligent.

**superfluous** adjective surplus (to requirements), redundant, unneeded, unnecessary, excess, extra, (to) spare, remaining, unused, left over, waste.
OPPOSITES necessary.

**superior** adjective **1** *a superior officer:* senior, higher-level, higher-ranking, higher. **2** *the superior candidate:* better, worthier, finer, preferred. **3** *superior chocolate:* top-quality, choice, select, exclusive, prime, fine, excellent, best, choicest, finest. **4** *a superior smile:* condescending, supercilious, patronizing, haughty, disdainful; informal high and mighty.
OPPOSITES junior, inferior, modest.
noun *my immediate superior:* manager, chief, supervisor, senior, controller, foreman; informal boss.
OPPOSITES subordinate.

**superiority** noun supremacy, advantage, lead, dominance, primacy, ascendancy, eminence.

**supernatural** adjective
**1** *supernatural powers:* paranormal, psychic, magic, magical, occult, mystic, mystical. **2** *a supernatural being:* ghostly, phantom, spectral, other-worldly, unearthly.

**supersede** verb replace, take the place of, take over from, succeed, supplant.

**supervise** verb oversee, be in charge of, superintend, preside over, direct, manage, run, look after, be responsible for, govern, keep an eye on, observe, monitor, mind.

**supervisor** noun manager, director, overseer, controller, superintendent, governor, chief, head, foreman; informal boss; Brit. informal gaffer.

**supple** adjective **1** *her supple body:* lithe, lissom, willowy, flexible, agile, acrobatic, nimble. **2** *supple leather:* pliable, flexible, soft, bendy, workable, stretchy, springy.
OPPOSITES stiff, rigid.

**supplement** noun **1** *a dietary supplement:* extra, add-on, accessory, adjunct. **2** *a single room supplement:* surcharge, addition, increase. **3** *a supplement to the essay:* appendix, addendum, postscript, addition, coda. **4** *a special supplement with today's paper:* pull-out, insert.
verb *he supplemented his income by teaching:* add to, augment, increase, boost, swell, amplify, enlarge, top up.

**supply** verb **1** *they supplied money to the rebels:* give, contribute, provide, furnish,

a
b
c
d
e
f
g
h
i
j
k
l
m
n
o
p
q
r
**s**
t
u
v
w
x
y
z

a
b
c
d
e
f
g
h
i
j
k
l
m
n
o
p
q
r
**s**
t
u
v
w
x
y
z

donate, confer, dispense. **2** *the lake supplies the city with water:* provide, furnish, serve, endow, equip, arm. **3** *windmills supply their power needs:* satisfy, meet, fulfil, cater for.
**noun 1** *a limited supply of food:* stock, store, reserve, reservoir, stockpile, hoard, cache, fund, bank. **2** *the supply of alcoholic liquor:* provision, distribution, serving. **3** (**supplies**) provisions, stores, rations, food, necessities.

**support** verb **1** *a roof supported by pillars:* hold up, bear, carry, prop up, keep up, brace, shore up, underpin, buttress, reinforce. **2** *he struggled to support his family:* provide for, maintain, sustain, keep, take care of, look after. **3** *she supported him to the end:* stand by, defend, back, stand/stick up for. **4** *evidence to support the argument:* back up, substantiate, bear out, corroborate, confirm. **5** *the money supports charitable projects:* help, aid, assist, contribute to, back, subsidize, fund, finance; N. Amer. informal bankroll. **6** *a candidate supported by local people:* back, champion, favour, be in favour of, advocate, encourage, promote, endorse, espouse.
OPPOSITES neglect, contradict, oppose.
**noun 1** *bridge supports:* pillar, post, prop, upright, brace, buttress, foundation. **2** *I was lucky to have their support:* encouragement, friendship, backing, endorsement, help, assistance, comfort. **3** *thank you for your support:* contributions, backing, donations, money, subsidy, funding, funds, finance, capital.

OPPOSITES opposition.

**supporter** noun **1** *supporters of gun control:* advocate, backer, adherent, promoter, champion, defender, upholder, campaigner. **2** *the charity relies on its supporters:* contributor, donor, benefactor, sponsor, backer, patron, subscriber, well-wisher. **3** *the team's supporters:* fan, follower, enthusiast, devotee, admirer.

**supportive** adjective encouraging, caring, sympathetic, reassuring, understanding, concerned, helpful.

**suppose** verb **1** *I suppose he's used to it:* assume, presume, expect, dare say, take it, guess. **2** *suppose you had a spacecraft:* imagine, assume, (let's) say, hypothesize, theorize, speculate.

**supposed** adjective **1** *the supposed phenomena:* alleged, reputed, rumoured, claimed, purported. **2** *I'm supposed to meet him at 8.30:* meant, intended, expected, required, obliged.

**suppress** verb **1** *they will suppress any criticism:* subdue, repress, crush, quell, quash, squash, stamp out, put down, crack down on. **2** *she suppressed her irritation:* conceal, restrain, stifle, smother, check, curb, contain. **3** *the report was suppressed:* censor, keep secret, conceal, hide, hush up, gag, withhold, cover up, stifle.
OPPOSITES allow, encourage, reveal.

**supremacy** noun control, power, rule, sovereignty, dominance, superiority, predominance, primacy, dominion, authority, mastery, ascendancy.

**supreme** adjective **1** *the supreme commander:* highest, chief, head, top, foremost, principal, superior, premier, first, prime. **2** *a supreme achievement:* extraordinary, remarkable, phenomenal, exceptional, outstanding, incomparable, unparalleled. **3** *the supreme sacrifice:* ultimate, greatest, highest, extreme, final, last.
OPPOSITES subordinate, insignificant.

**sure** adjective **1** *I'm sure they knew:* certain, positive, convinced, confident, definite, satisfied, persuaded. **2** *someone was sure to find out:* bound, likely, destined, fated. **3** *a sure winner:* guaranteed, unfailing, infallible, unerring, certain, inevitable; informal sure-fire. **4** *a sure sign that he's worried:* reliable, dependable, trustworthy, certain, unambiguous.
OPPOSITES uncertain, unlikely.

**surface** noun **1** *the surface of the wall:* outside, exterior, top, side, finish. **2** *the surface of polite society:* outward appearance, facade, veneer.
OPPOSITES inside, interior.
verb **1** *a submarine surfaced:* come to the surface, come up, rise. **2** *the idea first surfaced in the sixties:* emerge, arise, appear, come to light, crop up, materialize, spring up.
OPPOSITES dive.

**surge** noun **1** *a surge of water:* gush, rush, outpouring, stream, flow. **2** *a surge in demand:* increase, rise, growth, upswing, upsurge, escalation, leap. **3** *a sudden surge of anger:* rush, storm, torrent, blaze, outburst, eruption.

verb **1** *the water surged into people's homes:* gush, rush, stream, flow, burst, pour, cascade, spill, sweep, roll. **2** *the Dow Jones index surged 47.63 points:* increase, rise, grow, leap.

**surpass** verb excel, exceed, transcend, outdo, outshine, outstrip, outclass, eclipse, improve on, top, trump, cap, beat, better, outperform.

**surplus** noun *food surpluses:* excess, surfeit, superfluity, oversupply, glut, remainder, residue, remains, leftovers.
OPPOSITES dearth.
adjective *surplus cash:* excess, leftover, unused, remaining, extra, additional, spare, superfluous, redundant, unwanted, unneeded, dispensable.
OPPOSITES insufficient.

**surprise** noun **1** *Kate looked at me in surprise:* astonishment, amazement, wonder, bewilderment, disbelief. **2** *the test came as a big surprise:* shock, bolt from the blue, bombshell, revelation, rude awakening, eye-opener.
verb **1** *I was so surprised that I dropped it:* astonish, amaze, startle, astound, stun, stagger, shock; informal bowl over, floor, flabbergast; Brit. informal knock for six. **2** *she surprised a burglar:* take by surprise, catch unawares, catch off guard, catch red-handed.

**surprising** adjective unexpected, unforeseen, astonishing, amazing, startling, astounding, staggering, incredible, extraordinary.

**surrender** verb **1** *the gunmen surrendered:* give up, give oneself up, give in, cave in,

a
b
c
d
e
f
g
h
i
j
k
l
m
n
o
p
q
r
**s**
t
u
v
w
x
y
z

capitulate, concede (defeat), submit, lay down one's arms/weapons. **2** *they surrendered power to the government:* give up, relinquish, renounce, cede, abdicate, forfeit, sacrifice, hand over, turn over, yield.
OPPOSITES resist, seize.
noun **1** *the surrender of the hijackers:* capitulation, submission, yielding. **2** *a surrender of power:* relinquishment, renunciation, abdication, resignation.

**surround** verb encircle, enclose, encompass, ring, hem in, confine, cut off, besiege, trap.

**surrounding** adjective neighbouring, enclosing, nearby, near, local, adjoining, adjacent.

**surroundings** plural noun environment, setting, background, backdrop, vicinity, locality, habitat.

**survey** verb **1** *he surveyed his work:* look at, look over, view, contemplate, regard, gaze at, stare at, eye, scrutinize, examine, inspect, scan, study; informal size up. **2** *they surveyed 4,000 drug users:* interview, question, canvass, poll, investigate, research, study. **3** *he was asked to survey the house:* inspect, assess, appraise, prospect.
noun **1** *a survey of the current literature:* study, review, overview, examination. **2** *a survey of sexual behaviour:* poll, investigation, enquiry, study, probe, questionnaire, census, research. **3** *a thorough survey of the property:* inspection, assessment, appraisal.

**survive** verb **1** *he survived by escaping through a hole:* remain alive, live, sustain oneself, pull through, hold out, make it. **2** *the theatre must survive:* continue, remain, persist, endure, live on, persevere, abide, go on, carry on. **3** *he was survived by his sons:* outlive, outlast.

**suspect** verb **1** *I suspected she'd made a mistake:* have a suspicion, have a feeling, feel, be inclined to think, fancy, reckon, guess, surmise, have a hunch, fear. **2** *he had no reason to suspect me:* doubt, distrust, mistrust, have misgivings about, have qualms about, be suspicious of.
adjective *a suspect package:* suspicious, dubious, doubtful, untrustworthy; informal fishy, funny; Brit. informal dodgy.

**suspend** verb **1** *the court case was suspended:* adjourn, interrupt, break off, cut short, discontinue; N. Amer. table. **2** *he was suspended from college:* exclude, debar, remove, expel, eject, rusticate. **3** *lights were suspended from the ceiling:* hang, sling, string, swing, dangle.

**suspense** noun tension, uncertainty, doubt, anticipation, excitement, anxiety, strain.

**suspicion** noun **1** *she had a suspicion that he didn't like her:* intuition, feeling, impression, inkling, hunch, fancy, notion, idea, theory, premonition; informal gut feeling. **2** *I confronted him with my suspicions:* misgiving, doubt, qualm, reservation, hesitation, question.
OPPOSITES trust.

**suspicious** adjective **1** *she gave him a suspicious look:* doubtful,

unsure, dubious, wary, sceptical, mistrustful. **2** *a suspicious character:* suspect, dubious, unsavoury, disreputable; informal shifty, shady; Brit. informal dodgy. **3** *in suspicious circumstances:* strange, odd, questionable, irregular, funny, doubtful, mysterious, murky; informal fishy; Brit. informal dodgy.
OPPOSITES trusting, honest, innocent.

**sustain** verb **1** *her memories sustained her:* comfort, help, assist, encourage, support, give strength to, buoy up. **2** *they were unable to sustain a coalition:* continue, carry on, keep up, keep alive, maintain, preserve. **3** *she had bread and cheese to sustain her:* nourish, feed, nurture, keep alive, keep going. **4** *she sustained slight injuries:* suffer, experience, undergo, receive. **5** *the allegation was not sustained:* confirm, corroborate, substantiate, bear out, prove, authenticate, back up, uphold.

**sustained** adjective continuous, ongoing, steady, continual, constant, prolonged, persistent, non-stop, perpetual, relentless.
OPPOSITES sporadic.

**swallow** verb eat, drink, gulp down, consume, devour, put away, quaff, slug; informal swig, swill, down; Brit. informal scoff.

**swamp** noun *he got stuck in the swamp:* marsh, bog, fen, quagmire.
verb **1** *the rain was swamping the boat:* flood, inundate, deluge, fill. **2** *he was swamped by media attention:* overwhelm, inundate, flood, deluge, engulf, snow under.

**swap** verb exchange, trade,

barter, switch, change, replace.

**swarm** noun **1** *a swarm of bees:* hive, flock. **2** *a swarm of reporters:* crowd, horde, mob, throng, mass, army, herd, pack.
verb *reporters were swarming all over the place:* flock, throng, surge, stream.

**swathe** verb wrap, envelop, bandage, cover, shroud, drape, wind, enfold.

**sway** verb **1** *the curtains swayed in the breeze:* swing, shake, undulate, move to and fro. **2** *she swayed on her feet:* stagger, wobble, rock, lurch, reel, roll. **3** *we are swayed by the media:* influence, affect, manipulate, bend, mould.
noun **1** *the sway of her hips:* swing, roll, shake, undulation. **2** *a province under the sway of the Franks:* power, rule, government, sovereignty, dominion, control, jurisdiction, authority.

**swear** verb **1** *they swore to protect each other:* promise, vow, pledge, give one's word, undertake, guarantee. **2** *she swore she would never go back:* insist, declare, proclaim, assert, maintain, emphasize, stress. **3** *Kate spilled her wine and swore:* curse, blaspheme, use bad language; informal cuss, eff and blind.

**swearing** noun bad language, strong language, cursing, blaspheming, obscenities, expletives, swear words; informal effing and blinding, four-letter words.

**sweat** noun *drenched with sweat:* perspiration.
verb **1** *she was sweating heavily:* perspire. **2** *I've sweated over this book:* work, labour, toil, slog, slave, work one's fingers

to the bone.

**sweep** verb 1 *she swept the floor:* brush, clean, scrub, mop, scour. 2 *he was swept out to sea:* carry, pull, drag, tow. 3 *riots swept the country:* engulf, overwhelm, flood, spread across. 4 *she swept down the stairs:* glide, sail, breeze, drift, race, speed, stride.
noun 1 *a sweep of his hand:* gesture, stroke, wave, movement. 2 *a long sweep of golden sand:* expanse, tract, stretch, extent. 3 *the broad sweep of our interests:* range, scope, compass, reach, spread, extent.

**sweeping** adjective 1 *sweeping changes:* extensive, wide-ranging, broad, comprehensive, far-reaching, thorough, radical. 2 *sweeping statements:* wholesale, blanket, general, unqualified, indiscriminate, oversimplified.
OPPOSITES limited, focused.

**sweet** adjective 1 *sweet biscuits:* sugary, sweetened, sugared, honeyed, sickly, cloying. 2 *the sweet scent of roses:* fragrant, aromatic, perfumed. 3 *her sweet voice:* musical, melodious, dulcet, tuneful, soft, harmonious, silvery. 4 *life was still sweet:* pleasant, agreeable, delightful, nice, satisfying, gratifying, good. 5 *she has a sweet nature:* likeable, appealing, engaging, amiable, pleasant, agreeable, kind, thoughtful, considerate, delightful, lovely. 6 *she looks sweet:* cute, lovable, adorable, endearing, charming.
OPPOSITES sour, savoury, harsh, disagreeable.
noun (Brit.) 1 *sweets for the children:* confectionery,

bonbon; N. Amer. candy; informal sweetie. 2 *a delicious sweet for the guests:* dessert, pudding; Brit. informal afters, pud.

**sweetheart** noun 1 *you look lovely, sweetheart:* darling, dear, dearest, love, beloved, sweet; informal honey, sweetie, sugar, baby, poppet. 2 *my high-school sweetheart:* lover, love, girlfriend, boyfriend, beloved; informal steady, flame.

**swell** verb 1 *her lip swelled up:* expand, bulge, distend, inflate, dilate, bloat, puff up, balloon, fatten, fill out. 2 *the population swelled:* grow, enlarge, increase, expand, rise, escalate, multiply, proliferate, snowball, mushroom.
OPPOSITES shrink, decrease.
noun *a heavy swell on the sea:* surge, wave, roll.

**swelling** noun bump, lump, bulge, protuberance, protrusion, distension.

**swift** adjective 1 *a swift decision:* prompt, rapid, quick, sudden, immediate, instant, abrupt, hasty, hurried. 2 *swift runners:* fast, rapid, quick, speedy, brisk, lively.
OPPOSITES slow, leisurely.

**swing** verb 1 *the sign swung in the wind:* sway, move back and forth, oscillate, wave, rock, swivel, pivot, turn, rotate. 2 *Helen swung the bottle:* brandish, wave, flourish, wield. 3 *the road swings round:* curve, bend, veer, turn, bear, wind, twist, deviate, slew. 4 *the needle swings to the right:* rotate, swivel, pivot, turn.
noun 1 *a swing of the pendulum:* oscillation, sway, wave. 2 *the swing to the Conservatives:* change, move, turnaround, turnabout, reversal. 3 *mood*

*swings:* fluctuation, change, shift, variation, oscillation.

**swirl** verb whirl, eddy, billow, spiral, twist, twirl, circulate, revolve, spin.

**switch** noun **1** *the switch on top of the telephone:* button, lever, control. **2** *a switch from direct to indirect taxation:* change, move, shift, transition, transformation, reversal, turnaround, U-turn, changeover, transfer, conversion.
verb **1** *he switched sides:* change, shift; informal chop and change. **2** *he managed to switch the envelopes:* exchange, swap, interchange, change round, rotate.

**swoop** verb **1** *pigeons swooped down after the grain:* dive, descend, pounce, plunge, pitch, nosedive. **2** *police swooped on the flat:* raid, descend on, pounce on, attack; N. Amer. informal bust.

**symbol** noun **1** *the lotus is the symbol of purity:* representation, token, sign, emblem, figure, image, metaphor, allegory. **2** *the chemical symbol for helium:* sign, character, mark, letter. **3** *the Red Cross symbol:* logo, emblem, badge, stamp, trademark, crest, insignia, coat of arms, seal, device, monogram, hallmark, motif.

**symmetrical** adjective regular, uniform, consistent, even, equal, balanced, proportional.

**sympathetic** adjective **1** *a sympathetic listener:* compassionate, caring, concerned, understanding, sensitive, supportive. **2** *the most sympathetic character in the book:* likeable, pleasant, agreeable, congenial.
OPPOSITES unsympathetic, unfeeling, unlikeable.

**sympathize** verb commiserate, show concern, offer condolences; (**sympathize with**) pity, feel sorry for, feel for, identify with, understand, relate to.

**sympathy** noun compassion, care, concern, commiseration, pity.
OPPOSITES indifference.

**symptom** noun indication, indicator, manifestation, sign, mark, feature, trait, clue, hint, warning, evidence, proof.

**synthetic** adjective artificial, fake, imitation, mock, simulated, man-made, manufactured; informal pretend.
OPPOSITES natural.

**system** noun **1** *a system of canals:* structure, organization, arrangement, complex, network; informal set-up. **2** *a system for regulating sales:* method, technique, procedure, means, way, scheme, plan, policy, programme, formula, routine. **3** (**the system**) the establishment, the administration, the authorities, the powers that be, bureaucracy, officialdom.

**systematic** adjective structured, methodical, organized, orderly, planned, regular, routine, standardized, standard, logical, coherent, consistent.
OPPOSITES unstructured, disorganized.

a
b
c
d
e
f
g
h
i
j
k
l
m
n
o
p
q
r
**s**
t
u
v
w
x
y
z

# Tt

**table** noun chart, diagram, figure, graphic, graph, plan, list.

**taboo** noun *the taboo against lying:* prohibition, proscription, veto, ban.
adjective *taboo language:* forbidden, prohibited, banned, proscribed, outlawed, off limits, unmentionable, unspeakable, unutterable; informal no go.
OPPOSITES acceptable.

**tack** noun *tacks held the carpet down:* pin, nail, staple, rivet.
verb *a photo tacked to the wall:* pin, nail, staple, fix, fasten, attach, secure.
■ **tack something on** add, append, attach, join on, tag on.

**tackle** noun 1 *fishing tackle:* gear, equipment, apparatus, kit, hardware; informal things, clobber. 2 *a tackle by the scrum half:* interception, challenge, block, attack.
verb 1 *we must tackle the problems:* deal with, take care of, attend to, see to, handle, manage, get to grips with, address, take on. 2 *he tackled an intruder:* confront, face up to, take on, challenge, attack, grab, struggle with, intercept, block, stop, bring down, floor, fell; informal have a go at.

**tactful** adjective diplomatic, discreet, considerate, sensitive, understanding, thoughtful, delicate, judicious, subtle.

**tactic** noun 1 *a tax-saving tactic:* scheme, plan, manoeuvre, method, trick, ploy. 2 (**tactics**) strategy, policy, campaign, game plan, planning, generalship, manoeuvres, logistics.

**tactical** adjective calculated, planned, strategic, prudent, politic, diplomatic, judicious, shrewd.

**tactless** adjective insensitive, inconsiderate, thoughtless, indelicate, undiplomatic, indiscreet, unsubtle, inept, gauche, blunt.

**tag** noun *a price tag:* label, ticket, badge, mark, tab, sticker, docket.
verb *bottles tagged with stickers:* label, mark, ticket, identify, flag, indicate.

**tail** noun *the tail of the queue:* rear, end, back, extremity, bottom.
OPPOSITES head, front, start.
verb (informal) *the detectives tailed him to his hide-out:* follow, shadow, stalk, trail, track, keep under surveillance.

**tailor** noun outfitter, couturier, costumier, dressmaker, fashion designer.
verb *services can be tailored to requirements:* customize, adapt, adjust, modify, change, convert, alter, mould, gear, fit, shape, tune.

**taint** verb 1 *the wilderness is tainted by pollution:* contaminate, pollute, adulterate, infect, blight, spoil, soil, ruin. 2 *fraudulent firms taint our reputation:* tarnish, sully, blacken, stain, blot, damage.
OPPOSITES clean, improve.

**take** verb 1 *she took his hand:* grasp, get hold of, grip, clasp,

clutch, grab. **2** *he took an envelope from his pocket:* remove, pull, draw, withdraw, extract, fish. **3** *a passage taken from my book:* extract, quote, cite, excerpt, derive, abstract, copy, cull. **4** *many prisoners were taken:* capture, seize, catch, arrest, apprehend, take into custody, carry off, abduct. **5** *someone's taken my car:* steal, remove, appropriate, make off with, pilfer, purloin; informal filch, swipe, snaffle; Brit. informal pinch, nick. **6** *take four from the total:* subtract, deduct, remove, discount; informal knock off, minus. **7** *all the seats had been taken:* occupy, use, utilize, fill, hold, reserve, engage; informal bag. **8** *he took notes:* write, note (down), jot (down), scribble, scrawl, record, register, document, minute. **9** *I took it back to London:* bring, carry, bear, transport, convey, move, transfer, shift, ferry; informal cart, tote. **10** *the priest took her home:* escort, accompany, help, assist, show, lead, guide, see, usher, convey. **11** *he took the train:* travel on/ by, journey on, go via, use. **12** *I can't take much more:* endure, bear, tolerate, stand, put up with, abide, stomach, accept, allow, countenance, support, shoulder; formal brook.
OPPOSITES give, free, add.
■ **take after** resemble, look like, remind one of. ■ **take something apart** dismantle, take to pieces, take apart, disassemble, break up. ■ **take someone in** deceive, delude, hoodwink, mislead, trick, dupe, fool, cheat, defraud, swindle; informal con. ■ **take something in** comprehend, understand, grasp, follow, absorb; informal get.

■ **take off 1** *the plane took off:* become airborne, take to the air, leave the ground, lift off, blast off. **2** *the idea really took off:* succeed, do well, become popular, catch on, prosper, flourish. ■ **take someone on 1** *there was no challenger to take him on:* compete against, oppose, challenge, confront, face. **2** *we took on extra staff:* engage, hire, employ, sign up. ■ **take something on** undertake, accept, assume, shoulder, acquire. ■ **take something over** assume control of, take charge of, take command of, seize, hijack, commandeer. ■ **take something up 1** *he took up abstract painting:* begin, start, commence, engage in, practise. **2** *the meetings took up all her time:* consume, fill, absorb, use, occupy. **3** *her cousin took up the story:* resume, recommence, restart, carry on, continue, pick up, return to. **4** *he took up their offer of a job:* accept, say yes to, agree to, adopt.

**takeover** noun buyout, purchase, acquisition, merger, amalgamation.

**tale** noun story, narrative, anecdote, account, history, legend, fable, myth, saga; informal yarn.

**talent** noun flair, aptitude, facility, gift, knack, technique, bent, ability, forte, genius, brilliance.

**talented** adjective gifted, skilful, accomplished, brilliant, expert, consummate, able; informal ace.
OPPOSITES untalented, inept.

**talk** verb **1** *I was talking to a friend:* speak, chat, chatter, gossip, jabber; informal yak; Brit. informal natter. **2** *they were able to talk in peace:* converse, communicate, speak, confer, consult, negotiate, parley; informal have a confab.

**noun 1** *he was bored with all this talk:* chatter, gossip, prattle, jabbering; informal yak; Brit. informal nattering. **2** *she needed a talk with Vi:* conversation, chat, discussion, tête-à-tête, heart-to-heart, dialogue; informal confab, gossip. **3** (**talks**) negotiations, discussions, conference, summit, meeting, consultation, dialogue. **4** *she gave a talk on her travels:* lecture, speech, address, discourse, oration, presentation, report, sermon.

**talkative** adjective chatty, garrulous, loquacious, voluble, communicative; informal mouthy.
OPPOSITES taciturn.

**tall** adjective **1** *a tall man:* big, large, huge, towering, gigantic, giant, leggy, gangling. **2** *tall buildings:* high, big, lofty, towering, sky-high. **3** *a tall tale:* unlikely, improbable, exaggerated, far-fetched, implausible, dubious, unbelievable, incredible, untrue; informal cock and bull. **4** *a tall order:* demanding, exacting, difficult, unreasonable, impossible.
OPPOSITES short, low, wide, credible, easy.

**tally** noun *a tally of the score:* running total, count, record, reckoning, register, account, roll.
**verb** *these statistics tally with government figures:* correspond, agree, accord, concur, coincide, match, fit, be consistent, conform, equate, parallel; informal square.
OPPOSITES disagree.

**tame** adjective **1** *a tame elephant:* domesticated, docile, broken,

trained, gentle, mild, pet. **2** *a tame affair:* unexciting, uninteresting, uninspiring, dull, bland, flat, pedestrian, humdrum, boring.
OPPOSITES wild, exciting.
**verb 1** *wild rabbits can be tamed:* domesticate, break, train, master, subdue. **2** *she learned to tame her emotions:* subdue, curb, control, calm, master, moderate, discipline, suppress, temper, bridle.

**tangible** adjective real, actual, physical, solid, palpable, material, substantial, concrete, visible, definite, perceptible, discernible.
OPPOSITES abstract, theoretical.

**tangle** verb *the wool got tangled up:* entangle, snarl, catch, entwine, twist, knot, mat, jumble.
**noun 1** *a tangle of branches:* snarl, mass, knot, mesh, mishmash. **2** *the defence got into an awful tangle:* muddle, jumble, mix-up, confusion, shambles.

**tantrum** noun fit of temper, fit of rage, outburst, pet, paroxysm, frenzy; informal paddy, wobbly; N. Amer. informal hissy fit.

**tap¹** noun *she turned the tap on:* valve, stopcock; N. Amer. faucet, spigot.
**verb 1** *their telephones were tapped:* bug, wiretap, monitor, overhear, eavesdrop on. **2** *the resources were to be tapped for our benefit:* draw on, exploit, milk, mine, use, utilize, turn to account.

**tap²** verb *she tapped on the door:* knock, rap, strike, beat, pat, drum.

**tape** noun **1** *a package tied with tape:* binding, ribbon, string, braid, band. **2** *they made a tape* *of the concert:* **(audio) cassette, (tape) recording,** video.

**verb 1** *a card was taped to the box:* bind, stick, fix, fasten, secure, attach. **2** *police taped his confession:* record, tape-record, video.

**target** noun **1** *their profit target:* objective, goal, aim, mark, end, plan, intention, aspiration, ambition. **2** *she was the target for abuse:* victim, butt, recipient, focus, object, subject.

**verb 1** *he was targeted by a gunman:* pick out, single out, earmark, fix on, attack, aim at, fire at. **2** *the product is targeted at a specific market:* aim, direct, level, intend, focus.

**tariff** noun **1** *import tariffs:* tax, duty, toll, excise, levy, charge, rate, fee. **2** *the bar tariff:* price list, menu.

**tarnish** verb **1** *gold does not tarnish easily:* discolour, rust, oxidize, corrode, stain, dull, blacken. **2** *it tarnished his reputation:* sully, blacken, stain, blemish, ruin, disgrace, mar, damage, harm.
OPPOSITES polish, enhance.

noun **1** *the tarnish on the candlesticks:* discoloration, oxidation, rust, verdigris. **2** *the tarnish on his reputation:* smear, stain, blemish, blot, taint, stigma.

**tart**[1] noun *a jam tart:* pastry, flan, quiche, tartlet, vol-au-vent, pie.

**tart**[2] (informal) verb **1** *she tarted herself up:* dress up, make up, smarten up; informal doll oneself up, titivate oneself. **2** *we must tart this place up a bit:* decorate, renovate, refurbish, redecorate, smarten up; informal do up, fix up.

**tart**[3] adjective **1** *a tart apple:* sour, sharp, acidic, zesty, tangy, piquant. **2** *a tart reply:* scathing, sharp, biting, cutting, sarcastic, acrimonious, nasty, rude, vicious, spiteful.
OPPOSITES sweet, kind.

**task** noun job, duty, chore, charge, assignment, detail, mission, engagement, occupation, undertaking, exercise.

**taste** noun **1** *a distinctive sharp taste:* flavour, savour, relish, tang, smack. **2** *a taste of brandy:* mouthful, drop, bit, sip, nip, touch, soupçon, dash. **3** *it's too sweet for my taste:* palate, appetite, stomach. **4** *a taste for adventure:* liking, love, fondness, fancy, desire, penchant, inclination. **5** *my first taste of prison:* experience, impression, exposure to, contact with, involvement with. **6** *the house was furnished with taste:* judgement, discrimination, discernment, refinement, elegance, grace, style. **7** *the photo was rejected on grounds of taste:* sensitivity, decorum, propriety, etiquette, nicety, discretion.
OPPOSITES dislike.

verb **1** *Adam tasted the wine:* sample, test, try, savour. **2** *he could taste blood:* perceive, discern, make out, distinguish. **3** *a beer that tasted of cashews:* have the flavour, savour, smack, be reminiscent.

**tasteful** adjective stylish, refined, cultured, elegant, smart, chic, exquisite.
OPPOSITES tasteless.

**tasty** adjective delicious, palatable, luscious, mouth-watering, delectable, appetizing, tempting; informal yummy, scrumptious, moreish.

OPPOSITES bland.

**taunt** noun *the taunts of his classmates:* jeer, gibe, sneer, insult, barb; informal dig, put-down; (**taunts**) teasing, provocation, goading, derision, mockery.
verb *she taunted him about his job:* jeer at, sneer at, scoff at, poke fun at, make fun of, get at, insult, tease, torment, ridicule, deride, mock; N. Amer. ride; informal rib, needle.

**tax** noun *they have to pay tax:* duty, excise, customs, dues, levy, tariff, toll, tithe, charge.
verb *his whining taxed her patience:* strain, stretch, overburden, overload, overwhelm, try, wear out, exhaust, sap, drain, weary, weaken.

**teach** verb educate, instruct, school, tutor, inform, coach, train, drill.

**teacher** noun educator, tutor, instructor, schoolteacher, master, mistress, schoolmarm, governess, coach, trainer, lecturer, professor, don, guide, mentor, guru.

**team** noun *the sales team:* group, squad, company, party, crew, troupe, band, side, line-up; informal bunch, gang.
verb *ankle boots teamed with jeans:* match, coordinate, complement, pair up.
■ team up join (forces), collaborate, work together, unite, combine, cooperate, link, ally, associate, club together.

**tear** verb 1 *your shirt's torn:* rip, split, slit, pull apart, pull to pieces, shred, rupture, sever. 2 *his flesh was torn:* lacerate, cut (open), gash, slash, scratch, hack, pierce, stab. 3 *Gina tore the book from his hands:* snatch, grab, seize, rip, wrench, wrest, pull, pluck; informal yank.
noun *a tear in her dress:* rip, hole, split, slash, slit, ladder, snag.

**tease** verb make fun of, laugh at, deride, mock, ridicule, guy, make a monkey (out) of, taunt, bait, goad, pick on; informal take the mickey out of, rag, have on, pull someone's leg; Brit. informal wind up.

**technical** adjective 1 *an important technical achievement:* practical, scientific, technological, high-tech. 2 *this might seem very technical:* specialist, specialized, scientific, complex, complicated, esoteric.

**technique** noun 1 *different techniques for solving the problem:* method, approach, procedure, system, way, means, strategy. 2 *I was impressed with his technique:* skill, ability, proficiency, expertise, artistry, craftsmanship, adroitness, deftness, dexterity.

**tedious** adjective boring, dull, monotonous, repetitive, unrelieved, unvaried, uneventful, lifeless, uninteresting, unexciting, uninspiring, lacklustre, dreary, soul-destroying; informal deadly; N. Amer. informal dullsville.
OPPOSITES exciting.

**teenager** noun adolescent, youth, young person, minor, juvenile; informal teen.

**telephone** noun *Sophie picked up the telephone:* phone, handset, receiver; informal blower; N. Amer. informal horn.
verb *he telephoned me:* phone, call, dial; Brit. ring (up); informal call up, give someone a buzz, get on the blower to; Brit. informal

give someone a bell, give someone a tinkle; N. Amer. informal get someone on the horn.

**television** noun TV; informal the small screen; Brit. informal telly, the box; N. Amer. informal the tube.

**tell** verb 1 *why didn't you tell me?* inform, notify, let know, make aware, acquaint with, advise, put in the picture, brief, fill in, alert, warn; informal clue in/up. 2 *she told the story slowly:* relate, recount, narrate, report, recite, describe, sketch. 3 *she told him to leave:* instruct, order, command, direct, charge, enjoin, call on, require. 4 *it was hard to tell what he said:* ascertain, determine, work out, make out, deduce, discern, perceive, see, identify, recognize, understand, comprehend; informal figure out; Brit. informal suss out. 5 *he couldn't tell one from the other:* distinguish, differentiate, discriminate. 6 *the strain began to tell on him:* take its toll, leave its mark, affect.

**telling** adjective revealing, significant, weighty, important, meaningful, influential, striking, potent, powerful, compelling.
OPPOSITES insignificant.

**temper** noun 1 *he walked out in a temper:* rage, fury, fit of pique, tantrum, bad mood, pet, sulk, huff; Brit. informal strop, paddy; N. Amer. informal hissy fit. 2 *a display of temper:* anger, fury, rage, annoyance, irritation, pique, petulance; Brit. informal stroppiness. 3 *she struggled to keep her temper:* composure, self-control, self-possession, calm, good humour; informal cool.
verb *their idealism is tempered with realism:* moderate, modify, modulate, mitigate, alleviate, reduce, weaken, lighten, soften.
■ **lose one's temper** get angry, fly into a rage, erupt; informal go mad, go bananas, have a fit, see red, fly off the handle, blow one's top, hit the roof, lose one's rag; Brit. informal go spare, throw a wobbly.

**temperamental** adjective volatile, excitable, emotional, unpredictable, hot-headed, quick-tempered, impatient, touchy, moody, sensitive, highly strung.
OPPOSITES placid.

**temple** noun house of God, shrine, sanctuary, church, cathedral, mosque, synagogue.

**temporarily** adverb 1 *they are temporarily abroad:* for the time being, for the moment, for now, for the present, provisionally, pro tem. 2 *he was temporarily blinded by the light:* briefly, for a short time, momentarily, fleetingly.
OPPOSITES permanently.

**temporary** adjective 1 *temporary accommodation:* provisional, short-term, interim, makeshift, stopgap, acting, fill-in, stand-in, caretaker. 2 *a temporary loss of self-control:* brief, short-lived, momentary, fleeting, passing, ephemeral.
OPPOSITES permanent, lasting.

**tempt** verb 1 *the manager tried to tempt me to stay:* entice, persuade, convince, inveigle, induce, cajole, coax, lure; informal sweet-talk. 2 *more customers are being tempted by credit:* attract, allure, appeal to, whet the appetite of, seduce.
OPPOSITES discourage, deter.

a b c d e f g h i j k l m n o p q r s **t** u v w x y z

a b c d e f g h i j k l m n o p q r s **t** u v w x y z

**temptation** noun **1** *Mary resisted the temptation to answer back:* desire, urge, itch, impulse, inclination. **2** *the temptations of London:* lure, enticement, attraction, draw, pull. **3** *the temptation of exotic travel:* allure, appeal, attraction, fascination.

**tempting** adjective enticing, alluring, attractive, appealing, inviting, seductive, beguiling, fascinating.
OPPOSITES off-putting, uninviting.

**tenant** noun occupant, resident, inhabitant, leaseholder, lessee, lodger; Brit. occupier.
OPPOSITES owner, freeholder.

**tend**[1] verb **1** *I tend to get very involved in my work:* be inclined, be apt, be disposed, be prone, be liable. **2** *younger voters tended towards the tabloid press:* incline, lean, gravitate, prefer, favour; N. Amer. trend.

**tend**[2] verb *she tended her cattle:* look after, take care of, minister to, attend to, see to, watch over, keep an eye on, mind, protect, guard.
OPPOSITES neglect.

**tendency** noun inclination, propensity, proclivity, proneness, aptness, likelihood, bent, leaning, liability.

**tender**[1] adjective **1** *a gentle, tender man:* caring, kind, kind-hearted, soft-hearted, compassionate, sympathetic, warm, gentle, mild, benevolent. **2** *a tender kiss:* affectionate, fond, loving, romantic, emotional; informal lovey-dovey. **3** *simmer until the meat is tender:* soft, succulent, juicy, melt-in-the-mouth. **4** *her ankle was swollen and tender:* sore, sensitive, inflamed, raw, painful, hurting, aching, throbbing. **5** *the tender age of fifteen:* young, youthful, impressionable, inexperienced; informal wet behind the ears.
OPPOSITES hard-hearted, callous, tough, ripe.

**tender**[2] verb *she tendered her resignation:* offer, proffer, present, put forward, propose, suggest, advance, submit, hand in.
noun *contractors were invited to submit tenders:* bid, offer, quotation, quote, estimate, price.

**tense** adjective **1** *tense muscles:* taut, tight, rigid, stretched, strained, stiff. **2** *Loretta was feeling tense:* anxious, nervous, on edge, edgy, strained, stressed, under pressure, ill at ease, uneasy, restless, worked up, keyed up, overwrought, jumpy, nervy; informal a bundle of nerves, jittery, twitchy, uptight. **3** *a tense moment:* nerve-racking, stressful, anxious, worrying, fraught, charged, strained, nail-biting.
OPPOSITES slack, relaxed, calm.
verb *Hebden tensed his muscles:* tighten, tauten, flex, contract, brace, stiffen.
OPPOSITES relax.

**tension** noun **1** *the tension of the rope:* tightness, tautness, rigidity, pull. **2** *the tension was unbearable:* strain, stress, anxiety, pressure, worry, nervousness, jumpiness, edginess, restlessness, suspense, uncertainty. **3** *months of tension between the military and the government:* strained relations, strain, ill feeling, friction, antagonism, antipathy, hostility.

**tentative** adjective **1** *tentative arrangements:* provisional, unconfirmed, preliminary, exploratory, experimental. **2** *he took a few tentative steps:* hesitant, uncertain, cautious, timid, hesitating, faltering, shaky, unsteady, halting.
OPPOSITES definite, confident.

**term** noun **1** *scientific terms:* word, expression, phrase, name, title, designation, label, description. **2** *the terms of the contract:* condition, stipulation, specification, provision, proviso, restriction, qualification. **3** *the President is elected for a four-year term:* period, length of time, spell, stint, duration, stretch, run, session.
verb *he has been termed the father of modern theology:* call, name, entitle, title, style, designate, describe as, dub, label, tag.

**terminal** adjective **1** *a terminal illness:* incurable, untreatable, inoperable, fatal, lethal, mortal, deadly. **2** *a terminal bonus may be payable:* final, last, concluding, closing, end.
OPPOSITES curable, initial.
noun **1** *a railway terminal:* station, last stop, end of the line, depot; Brit. terminus. **2** *a computer terminal:* workstation, VDU, visual display unit.

**terminate** verb **1** *treatment was terminated:* bring to an end, bring to a close, close, conclude, finish, stop, wind up, discontinue, cease, cut short, abort, end; informal pull the plug on. **2** *the pregnancy was terminated:* abort, end.
OPPOSITES begin, start, continue.

**terrain** noun land, ground, territory, topography, landscape, countryside, country.

**terrestrial** adjective earthly, worldly, mundane, earthbound.

**terrible** adjective **1** *a terrible crime:* dreadful, awful, appalling, horrific, horrible, horrendous, atrocious, monstrous, sickening, heinous, vile. **2** *he was in terrible pain:* severe, extreme, intense, excruciating, agonizing, unbearable. **3** *the film was terrible:* very bad, dreadful, awful, frightful, atrocious, poor; informal pathetic, pitiful, useless, lousy, appalling; Brit. informal chronic, rubbish, pants.
OPPOSITES minor, slight, excellent.

**terribly** adverb **1** *he played terribly:* very badly, atrociously, awfully, dreadfully, appallingly, execrably; informal abysmally, pitifully. **2** (informal) *I shall miss you terribly:* very much, greatly, a great deal, a lot; informal loads.

**terrific** adjective **1** *a terrific bang:* tremendous, huge, massive, gigantic, colossal, mighty, considerable; informal mega, whopping; Brit. informal ginormous. **2** (informal) *a terrific game of top-quality football:* marvellous, wonderful, sensational, outstanding, superb, excellent, first-rate, dazzling, out of this world, breathtaking; informal great, fantastic, fabulous, super, ace, wicked, awesome; Brit. informal brilliant.

**terrify** verb frighten, horrify, petrify, scare, strike terror into, paralyse, transfix.

**territory** noun **1** *British overseas territories:* region, area, enclave, country, state, land, dependency, colony, dominion. **2** *mountainous territory:* terrain, land, ground, countryside. **3** *the territory of biblical scholarship:* domain, province, department, field, preserve, sphere, arena, realm, world.

**terror** noun fear, dread, horror, fright, alarm, panic, shock.

**test** noun **1** *a series of scientific tests:* trial, experiment, check, examination, assessment, evaluation, appraisal, investigation. **2** *candidates must take a test:* exam, examination; N. Amer. quiz.
verb *a small-scale prototype was tested:* try out, trial, put through its paces, experiment with, check, examine, assess, evaluate, appraise, investigate, sample.

**testify** verb swear, attest, give evidence, state on oath, declare, assert, affirm.

**testimonial** noun reference, letter of recommendation, commendation.

**testimony** noun evidence, sworn statement, attestation, affidavit, statement, declaration, assertion.

**testing** adjective difficult, challenging, tough, hard, demanding, taxing, stressful.
OPPOSITES easy.

**text** noun **1** *a text which explores pain and grief:* book, work, textbook. **2** *the pictures relate well to the text:* words, content, body, wording, script, copy.

**textiles** plural noun fabrics, cloths, materials.

**texture** noun feel, touch, appearance, finish, surface, grain, consistency.

**thank** verb express one's

gratitude to, say thank you to, show one's appreciation to.

**thankful** adjective grateful, relieved, pleased, glad.

**thanks** plural noun *they expressed their thanks and wished her well:* gratitude, appreciation, acknowledgement, recognition, credit.
■ **thanks to** as a result of, owing to, due to, because of, through, on account of, by virtue of.

**thaw** verb melt, unfreeze, defrost, soften, liquefy.
OPPOSITES freeze.

**theatrical** adjective **1** *a theatrical career:* stage, dramatic, thespian, show-business; informal showbiz. **2** *Henry looked over his shoulder with theatrical caution:* exaggerated, ostentatious, stagy, showy, melodramatic, affected.

**theft** noun robbery, stealing, larceny, shoplifting, burglary, embezzlement, raid, hold-up; informal smash-and-grab; N. Amer. informal heist.

**theme** noun **1** *the theme of her speech:* subject, topic, argument, idea, thrust, thread, motif, keynote. **2** *the first violin takes up the theme:* melody, tune, air, motif, leitmotif.

**then** adverb **1** *I was living in Cairo then:* at that time, in those days, at that point (in time), at that moment, on that occasion. **2** *she won the first and then the second game:* next, after that, afterwards, subsequently; formal thereafter.

**theoretical** adjective hypothetical, speculative, academic, conjectural, suppositional, notional, unproven.
OPPOSITES actual, real, practical.

**theory** noun **1** *that confirms my theory:* hypothesis, thesis, conjecture, supposition, speculation, postulation, proposition, premise, opinion, view, belief, contention. **2** *modern economic theory:* principles, ideas, concepts, philosophy, ideology, thinking.

**therapeutic** adjective healing, curative, remedial, medicinal, restorative, health-giving. OPPOSITES harmful.

**therapist** noun psychologist, psychotherapist, analyst, psychoanalyst, psychiatrist, counsellor; informal shrink.

**therapy** noun **1** *complementary therapies:* treatment, remedy, cure. **2** *he's currently in therapy:* psychotherapy, psychoanalysis, counselling.

**therefore** adverb consequently, because of that, for that reason, that being the case, so, as a result, hence, accordingly.

**thesis** noun **1** *the central thesis of his lecture:* theory, contention, argument, proposal, proposition, premise, assumption, hypothesis. **2** *a doctoral thesis:* dissertation, essay, paper, treatise, composition, study; N. Amer. theme.

**thick** adjective **1** *thick stone walls:* broad, wide, deep, stout, bulky, hefty, chunky, solid, plump. **2** *the station was thick with people:* crowded, full, packed, teeming, seething, swarming, crawling, crammed, thronged, bursting at the seams, solid, overflowing; informal jam-packed, chock-a-block, stuffed; Austral./NZ informal chocker. **3** *the thick vegetation:* plentiful, abundant, profuse, luxuriant, bushy, rich, riotous, exuberant, rank, rampant, dense; informal jungly. **4** *a thick paste:* semi-solid, firm, stiff, heavy, viscous, gelatinous. **5** *thick fog:* dense, heavy, opaque, impenetrable, soupy, murky. OPPOSITES thin, slender, sparse.

**thicken** verb stiffen, condense, solidify, set, gel, congeal, clot, coagulate.

**thief** noun robber, burglar, housebreaker, shoplifter, pickpocket, mugger, kleptomaniac; informal crook.

**thieve** verb steal, take, purloin, help oneself to, snatch, pilfer, embezzle, misappropriate; informal rob, swipe, nab, lift; Brit. informal nick, pinch, knock off; N. Amer. informal heist.

**thin** adjective **1** *a thin white line:* narrow, fine, attenuated. **2** *a thin cotton nightdress:* lightweight, light, fine, delicate, flimsy, diaphanous, gossamer, sheer, filmy, transparent, see-through. **3** *a tall, thin woman:* slim, lean, slender, willowy, svelte, sylphlike, spare, slight, skinny, underweight, scrawny, scraggy, bony, gaunt, emaciated, skeletal, lanky, spindly, gangly; informal anorexic. **4** *thin soup:* watery, weak, runny, sloppy. OPPOSITES thick, broad, fat.
verb **1** *some paint must be thinned down:* dilute, water down, weaken. **2** *the crowds were beginning to thin out:* disperse, dissipate, scatter. OPPOSITES thicken, gather.

**thing** noun **1** *the room was full of strange things:* object, article, item, artefact, commodity; informal doodah, whatsit, whatchamacallit, thingummy, thingy; Brit. informal gubbins.

a
b
c
d
e
f
g
h
i
j
k
l
m
n
o
p
q
r
s
**t**
u
v
w
x
y
z

**2** (**things**) *I'll collect my things:* belongings, possessions, stuff, property, worldly goods, effects, paraphernalia, bits and pieces, luggage, baggage; informal gear, junk; Brit. informal clobber.
**3** (**things**) *his gardening things:* equipment, apparatus, gear, kit, tackle, stuff, implements, tools, utensils, accoutrements.

**think** verb **1** *I think he's gone home:* believe, be of the opinion, be of the view, be under the impression, expect, imagine, anticipate, suppose, guess, fancy; informal reckon, figure. **2** *his family was thought to be rich:* consider, judge, hold, reckon, deem, presume, estimate, regard as, view as.
**3** *Jack thought for a moment:* ponder, reflect, deliberate, consider, meditate, muse, brood.
**4** *she thought of all the visits she had made:* recall, remember, recollect, call to mind. **5** *I can't think how bad it must be:* imagine, picture, visualize, envisage.
■ **think something up** devise, dream up, come up with, invent, create, concoct, make up, hit on.

**thinker** noun intellectual, philosopher, scholar, sage, ideologist, theorist, intellect, mind; informal brain.

**thinking** adjective *a thinking man:* intelligent, sensible, reasonable, rational, logical, analytical, thoughtful.
OPPOSITES stupid, irrational.
noun *the thinking behind the campaign:* reasoning, idea(s), theory, thoughts, philosophy, beliefs, opinion(s), view(s).

**thirst** noun *his thirst for knowledge:* craving, desire,

longing, yearning, hunger, hankering, eagerness, lust, appetite; informal yen, itch.
■ **thirst for** crave, want, covet, desire, hunger for, lust after, hanker after, wish for, long for.

**thirsty** adjective longing for a drink, dry, dehydrated; informal parched, gasping.

**thorn** noun prickle, spike, barb, spine.

**thorough** adjective **1** *a thorough investigation:* rigorous, in-depth, exhaustive, minute, detailed, close, meticulous, methodical, careful, complete, comprehensive. **2** *he is slow but thorough:* meticulous, scrupulous, assiduous, conscientious, painstaking, punctilious, methodical, careful. **3** *the child is being a thorough nuisance:* utter, downright, absolute, complete, total, out-and-out, real, perfect, proper; Brit. informal right; Austral./NZ informal fair.
OPPOSITES superficial, cursory, careless.

**though** conjunction *though she smiled bravely, she looked tired:* although, even though, even if, despite the fact that, notwithstanding (the fact) that, for all that.
adverb *You can't always do that. You can try, though.* nevertheless, nonetheless, even so, however, be that as it may, for all that, despite that, having said that; informal still and all.

**thought** noun **1** *what are your thoughts on the matter?* idea, notion, opinion, view, impression, feeling, theory.
**2** *he gave up any thought of taking a degree:* hope, aspiration, ambition, dream, intention, idea, plan, design,

aim. **3** *it only took a moment's thought:* thinking, contemplation, musing, pondering, consideration, reflection, deliberation, meditation. **4** *have you no thought for others?* consideration, understanding, regard, sensitivity, compassion, sympathy, care, concern.

**thoughtful** adjective **1** *a thoughtful expression:* pensive, reflective, contemplative, musing, meditative, philosophical, preoccupied. **2** *how very thoughtful of you!* considerate, caring, attentive, understanding, sympathetic, solicitous, concerned, helpful, obliging, accommodating, kind, compassionate.
OPPOSITES vacant, inconsiderate.

**thrash** verb **1** *she thrashed him with a whip:* hit, beat, strike, batter, thump, hammer, pound; informal belt. **2** *he was thrashing around in pain:* flail, writhe, thresh, jerk, toss, twist, twitch.

**thread** noun **1** *a needle and thread:* cotton, yarn, filament, fibre. **2** *she lost the thread of the conversation:* train of thought, drift, direction, theme, tenor.
verb **1** *he threaded the rope through a pulley:* pass, string, work, ease, push, poke. **2** *she threaded her way through the tables:* weave, inch, squeeze, navigate, negotiate.

**threat** noun **1** *Maggie ignored his threats:* threatening remark, warning, ultimatum. **2** *a possible threat to aircraft:* danger, peril, hazard, menace, risk. **3** *the company faces the threat of liquidation:* possibility, chance, probability, likelihood, risk.

**threaten** verb **1** *how dare you threaten me?* menace, intimidate, browbeat, bully, terrorize. **2** *these events could threaten the stability of Europe:* endanger, jeopardize, imperil, put at risk. **3** *the grey skies threatened snow:* herald, bode, warn of, presage, foreshadow, indicate, point to, be a sign of, signal.

**threshold** noun **1** *the threshold of the church:* doorstep, entrance, entry, gate. **2** *on the threshold of a new era:* start, beginning, commencement, brink, verge, dawn, inception, day one, opening, debut. **3** *the human threshold of pain:* limit, minimum.

**thrifty** adjective frugal, economical, sparing, careful with money, provident, prudent, abstemious, parsimonious, penny-pinching.
OPPOSITES extravagant.

**thrill** noun *the thrill of jumping out of an aeroplane:* excitement, stimulation, pleasure, tingle; informal buzz, kick; N. Amer. informal charge.
OPPOSITES boredom.
verb **1** *his words thrilled her:* excite, stimulate, arouse, rouse, inspire, delight, exhilarate, intoxicate, stir, electrify, move; informal give someone a buzz, give someone a kick; N. Amer. informal give someone a charge. **2** *he thrilled at the sound of her voice:* feel excited, tingle; informal get a buzz out of, get a kick out of; N. Amer. informal get a charge out of.
OPPOSITES bore.

**thrilling** adjective exciting, stimulating, stirring, action-packed, rip-roaring, gripping, electrifying, riveting,

a
b
c
d
e
f
g
h
i
j
k
l
m
n
o
p
q
r
s
**t**
u
v
w
x
y
z

fascinating, dramatic, hair-raising.
OPPOSITES boring.

**thrive** verb flourish, prosper, burgeon, bloom, blossom, do well, advance, succeed, boom.
OPPOSITES decline, wither.

**thriving** adjective flourishing, prospering, growing, developing, blooming, healthy, successful, booming, profitable; informal going strong.
OPPOSITES declining.

**throb** verb *her arms and legs throbbed with tiredness:* pulsate, beat, pulse, palpitate, pound, thud, thump, drum, judder, vibrate, quiver.
noun *the throb of the ship's engines:* pulsation, beat, pulse, palpitation, pounding, thudding, thumping, drumming, juddering, vibration, quivering.

**throng** noun *throngs of people blocked her way:* crowd, horde, mass, army, herd, flock, drove, swarm, sea, troupe, pack; informal gaggle, bunch, gang.
verb **1** *the pavements were thronged with tourists:* fill, crowd, pack, cram, jam.
**2** *people thronged to see the play:* flock, stream, swarm, troop. **3** *visitors thronged round him:* crowd, cluster, mill, swarm, congregate, gather.

**throttle** verb choke, strangle, garrotte.

**through** preposition **1** *he got the job through an advertisement:* by means of, by way of, by dint of, via, using, thanks to, by virtue of, as a result of, as a consequence of, on account of, owing to. **2** *he worked through the night:* throughout, for the duration of, until/to the end of, all.

**throughout** preposition **1** *it had repercussions throughout Europe:* all over, in every part of, everywhere in. **2** *Rose had been very fit throughout her life:* all through, for the duration of, for the whole of, until the end of, all.

**throw** verb **1** hurl, toss, fling, pitch, cast, lob, launch, bowl; informal chuck, heave, sling, bung. **2** *he threw the door open:* push, thrust, fling, bang. **3** *a chandelier threw its light over the walls:* cast, send, give off, emit, radiate, project. **4** *his intervention threw me:* disconcert, unnerve, fluster, ruffle, put off, throw off balance, unsettle, confuse; informal rattle, faze.
noun lob, toss, pitch, bowl.
■ **throw something away/out** discard, dispose of, get rid of, scrap, dump, jettison; informal chuck (away/out), ditch, bin, junk; Brit. informal get shot of.
■ **throw someone out** expel, eject, evict, drive out, force out, oust, remove, get rid of, depose, topple, unseat, overthrow; informal boot out, kick out; Brit. informal turf out.

**thrust** verb **1** *a spear was thrust into the sack:* shove, push, force, plunge, stick, drive, ram. **2** *fame had been thrust on him:* force, foist, impose, inflict. **3** *he thrust his way past her:* push, shove, force, elbow, shoulder, barge.
noun **1** *a hard thrust:* shove, push, lunge, poke. **2** *a thrust by the Third Army:* advance, push, drive, attack, assault, onslaught, offensive. **3** *only one engine is producing thrust:* force, propulsion, power, impetus. **4** *the thrust of the speech:* gist, substance, drift,

message, import, tenor.

**thug** noun ruffian, hooligan, bully boy, hoodlum, gangster, villain; informal tough, bruiser, heavy; Brit. informal rough, bovver boy; N. Amer. informal hood, goon.

**thump** verb 1 *he thumped the policeman:* hit, punch, strike, smack; informal whack, wallop, bash, biff, bop, clobber; Brit. informal slosh; N. Amer. informal slug. 2 *her heart thumped with fright:* throb, pound, thud, hammer.
noun 1 *a thump in the eye:* blow, punch, box, cuff, smack; informal whack, wallop, bash, biff; Brit. informal slosh; N. Amer. informal boff, slug. 2 *she put the box down with a thump:* thud, clunk, clonk, crash, smack, bang.

**thunder** noun rumble, boom, roar, pounding, thud, crash, reverberation.
verb 1 *below me the surf thundered:* rumble, boom, roar, pound, thud, thump, bang. 2 *'Answer me!' he thundered:* shout, roar, bellow, bark, bawl.

**thus** adverb 1 *the studio handled production, thus cutting its costs:* consequently, so, therefore, accordingly, hence, as a result. 2 *legislation forbids such data being held thus:* like this/that, in this/that way, so, like so, as follows.

**thwart** verb foil, frustrate, forestall, stop, check, block, prevent, defeat, impede, obstruct, derail, snooker; informal put paid to, do for, stymie; Brit. informal scupper.
OPPOSITES help.

**ticket** noun 1 *a bus ticket:* pass, authorization, permit, token, coupon, voucher. 2 *a price ticket:* label, tag, sticker, tab, slip, docket.

**tickle** verb 1 stroke, pet, chuck. 2 *something tickled his imagination:* stimulate, interest, appeal to, arouse, excite. 3 *the idea tickled Lewis:* amuse, entertain, divert, please, delight.

**tide** noun 1 current, flow, stream, ebb. 2 *the tide of history:* course, movement, direction, trend, current, drift, run.

**tidy** adjective 1 *a tidy room:* neat, orderly, well ordered, well kept, in apple-pie order, uncluttered, straight. 2 *a very tidy person:* organized, neat, methodical, meticulous.
OPPOSITES messy, disorganized.
verb *I'd better tidy up the living room:* put in order, clear up, sort out, straighten (up), clean up, spruce up.
OPPOSITES mess up.

**tie** verb 1 *he tied the boat to the jetty:* bind, tie up, tether, hitch, strap, truss, fetter, rope, make fast, moor, lash. 2 *he bent to tie his shoelaces:* do up, lace, knot. 3 *women can feel tied by childcare responsibilities:* restrict, restrain, limit, tie down, constrain, cramp, hamper, handicap, hamstring, encumber, shackle. 4 *a pay deal tied to productivity:* link, connect, couple, relate, join, marry. 5 *they tied for second place:* draw, be equal, be even.
noun 1 *he tightened the ties of his robe:* lace, string, cord, fastening. 2 *family ties:* bond, connection, link, relationship, attachment, affiliation. 3 *pets can be a tremendous tie:* restriction, constraint, curb, limitation, restraint, hindrance, encumbrance, handicap, obligation, commitment. 4 *a tie*

a
b
c
d
e
f
g
h
i
j
k
l
m
n
o
p
q
r
s
**t**
u
v
w
x
y
z

*for first place:* draw, dead heat.

**tier** noun **1** *six tiers of seats:* row, rank, bank, line, layer, level. **2** *a tier of management:* grade, gradation, echelon, rung on the ladder.

**tight** adjective **1** *a tight grip:* firm, secure. **2** *the rope was pulled tight:* taut, rigid, stiff, tense, stretched, strained. **3** *tight jeans:* close-fitting, narrow, figure-hugging, skintight; *informal* sprayed on. **4** *a tight mass of fibres:* compact, compressed, dense, solid. **5** *a tight space:* small, tiny, narrow, limited, restricted, confined, cramped, constricted. **6** *a tight joint:* sealed, sound, impenetrable, impervious.
OPPOSITES slack, loose, roomy, leaky.

**tighten** verb **1** *he tightened his grip:* strengthen, harden. **2** *she tightened the rope:* stretch, tauten, strain, stiffen, tense.
OPPOSITES loosen, slacken, relax.

**tilt** verb *the ground seemed to tilt:* slope, tip, lean, list, bank, slant, incline, pitch, cant, angle.
noun *a tilt of some 45°:* slope, list, camber, gradient, bank, slant, incline, pitch, cant, bevel, angle.

**timber** noun **1** *houses built of timber:* wood; N. Amer. lumber. **2** *the timbers of wrecked ships:* beam, spar, plank, batten, lath, board, joist, rafter.

**time** noun **1** *the best time to leave:* moment, point (in time), occasion, instant, juncture, stage. **2** *he worked there for a time:* while, spell, stretch, stint, interval, period, length of time, duration, phase. **3** *the time of the dinosaurs:* era, age, epoch, period, years, days.
verb *the meeting is timed for*

*4 o'clock:* schedule, arrange, set, organize, fix, book, line up, timetable, plan; N. Amer. slate.
■ **all the time** constantly, the entire time, around the clock, day and night, {morning, noon, and night}, {day in, day out}, always, without a break, ceaselessly, endlessly, incessantly, perpetually, permanently, continuously, continually, eternally; *informal* 24-7. ■ **at times** occasionally, sometimes, from time to time, now and then, every so often, once in a while, on occasion, off and on, at intervals, periodically.

**timeless** adjective lasting, enduring, classic, ageless, permanent, perennial, abiding, unchanging, unvarying, never-changing, eternal, everlasting.
OPPOSITES ephemeral.

**timely** adjective opportune, well timed, convenient, appropriate, expedient, seasonable, propitious.
OPPOSITES ill-timed.

**timetable** noun schedule, programme, agenda, calendar, diary.
verb schedule, arrange, programme, organize, fix, time, line up; Brit. diarize; N. Amer. slate.

**timid** adjective fearful, afraid, faint-hearted, timorous, nervous, scared, frightened, shy, diffident.
OPPOSITES bold.

**tinge** verb **1** *white blossom tinged with pink:* tint, colour, stain, shade, wash. **2** *his optimism is tinged with realism:* influence, affect, touch, flavour, colour.
noun **1** *a blue tinge:* tint, colour, shade, tone, hue. **2** *a tinge of*

*cynicism:* trace, note, touch, suggestion, hint, flavour, element, streak, suspicion, soupçon.

**tinker** verb fiddle, play about, mess about, adjust, try to mend; Brit. informal muck about.

**tint** noun 1 *an apricot tint:* shade, colour, tone, hue, tinge, cast, flush, blush. 2 *a hair tint:* dye, colourant, colouring, wash. verb *she had her hair tinted:* dye, colour, tinge.

**tiny** adjective minute, minuscule, microscopic, very small, mini, diminutive, miniature, baby, toy, dwarf; Scottish wee; informal teeny, tiddly; Brit. informal titchy; N. Amer. informal little-bitty.
OPPOSITES huge.

**tip**[1] noun 1 *the tip of the spear:* point, end, extremity, head, spike, prong, nib. 2 *the tips of the mountains:* peak, top, summit, apex, crown, crest, pinnacle.
verb *mountains tipped with snow:* cap, top, crown, surmount.

**tip**[2] verb 1 *the boat tipped over:* overturn, turn over, topple (over), fall (over), keel over, capsize, roll over. 2 *a whale could tip over a small boat:* upset, overturn, topple over, turn over, push over, upend, capsize; informal roll. 3 *the car tipped to one side:* lean, tilt, list, slope, bank, slant, incline, pitch, cant. 4 *she tipped the water into the trough:* pour, empty, drain, dump, discharge, decant.
noun (Brit.) *rubbish must be taken to the tip:* dump, rubbish dump, landfill site.

**tip**[3] noun 1 *a generous tip:* gratuity, baksheesh, present, gift, reward. 2 *useful tips:* piece of advice, suggestion, word of advice, pointer, hint; informal wrinkle.

**tire** verb 1 *he began to tire:* get tired, weaken, flag, droop. 2 *the journey had tired him:* fatigue, tire out, exhaust, wear out, drain, weary; informal knock out, take it out of; Brit. informal knacker. 3 *they tired of his difficult behaviour:* weary, get tired, get fed up, get sick, get bored.

**tired** adjective 1 *tired from travelling:* exhausted, worn out, weary, fatigued, ready to drop, drained; informal all in, dead beat, shattered; Brit. informal knackered, whacked; N. Amer. informal pooped, tuckered out; Austral./NZ informal stonkered. 2 *are you tired of having him here?* fed up with, weary of, bored with/by, sick (and tired) of; informal up to here with. 3 *tired jokes:* hackneyed, overused, stale, clichéd, predictable, unimaginative, unoriginal, dull, boring; informal corny.
OPPOSITES energetic, lively, fresh.

**tiring** adjective exhausting, wearying, taxing, draining, hard, arduous, strenuous, onerous, gruelling; informal killing; Brit. informal knackering.

**title** noun 1 *the title of the article:* heading, label, inscription, caption, subheading, legend. 2 *the title of Duke of Marlborough:* name, designation, form of address, rank, office, position; informal moniker, handle. 3 *an Olympic title:* championship, crown, first place.

**toast** noun 1 *he raised his glass in a toast:* tribute, salutation. 2 *he was the toast of the West*

*End:* darling, favourite, pet, heroine, hero, talk; Brit. informal blue-eyed boy/girl.
**verb** *we toasted the couple with champagne:* drink (to) the health of, salute, honour, pay tribute to.

**together** adverb 1 *friends who work together:* with each other, in conjunction, jointly, in cooperation, in collaboration, in partnership, in combination, in league, side by side; informal in cahoots. **2** *they both spoke together:* simultaneously, at the same time, at once, concurrently, as a group, in unison, in chorus.
OPPOSITES separately, successively.
**adjective** (informal) *she looks a very together young woman:* level-headed, well adjusted, sensible, practical, realistic, mature, stable, full of common sense, well organized, efficient, methodical, self-confident, self-assured; informal unflappable.
OPPOSITES flighty, disorganized.

**toil** verb 1 *she toiled all night:* work, labour, slave, strive; informal slog, beaver; Brit. informal graft. **2** *she began to toil up the path:* struggle, drag oneself, trudge, slog, plod; N. Amer. informal schlep.
OPPOSITES rest, relax.
**noun** *a life of toil:* hard work, labour, exertion, slaving, drudgery, effort, {blood, sweat, and tears}; informal slog, elbow grease; Brit. informal graft.

**toilet** noun lavatory, WC, (public) convenience, cloakroom, powder room, latrine, privy, urinal; N. Amer. bathroom, washroom, rest room, men's/ladies' room, comfort station; Brit. informal loo,

the Ladies, the Gents; N. Amer. informal can, john; Austral./NZ informal dunny.

**token** noun 1 *a token of our appreciation:* symbol, sign, emblem, badge, representation, indication, mark, expression, demonstration. **2** *a book token:* voucher, coupon, note.
**adjective** *token resistance:* symbolic, nominal, perfunctory, slight, minimal, superficial, emblematic, indicative.

**tolerance** noun 1 *an attitude of tolerance towards people:* acceptance, open-mindedness, broad-mindedness, forbearance, patience, charity, understanding. **2** *the plant's tolerance of pollution:* endurance, resilience, resistance, immunity. **3** *a 1% maximum tolerance in measurement:* deviation, variation, play, inaccuracy, imprecision.

**tolerant** adjective open-minded, forbearing, broad-minded, liberal, unprejudiced, unbiased, patient, long-suffering, understanding, charitable, lenient, easy-going.
OPPOSITES intolerant, strict.

**tolerate** verb 1 *a regime unwilling to tolerate dissent:* allow, permit, condone, accept, swallow, countenance. **2** *he couldn't tolerate her moods any longer:* endure, put up with, bear, take, stand, support, stomach; informal abide; Brit. informal stick.

**toll**[1] noun 1 *a motorway toll:* charge, fee, payment, levy, tariff, tax. **2** *the toll of dead and injured:* number, count, tally, total, sum. **3** *the toll on the environment has been high:*

harm, damage, hurt, injury, detriment, adverse effect, cost, price, loss.

**toll**[2] verb *I heard the bell toll:* ring, sound, clang, chime, strike, peal.

**tomb** noun burial chamber, vault, crypt, catacomb, sepulchre, mausoleum, grave.

**tone** noun **1** *the tone of the tuba:* sound, timbre, voice, colour, tonality. **2** *the impatient tone of his letter:* mood, air, feel, flavour, note, attitude, character. **3** *a dialling tone:* note, signal, bleep. **4** *tones of lavender and rose:* shade, colour, hue, tint, tinge.
verb *the shirt toned well with her cream skirt:* harmonize, go, blend, coordinate, team, match, suit, complement.
■ **tone something down 1** *the colour needs to be toned down:* soften, lighten, mute, subdue. **2** *the papers refused to tone down their criticism:* moderate, modify, temper, soften, modulate.

**tonic** noun stimulant, boost, restorative, refresher, fillip; informal shot in the arm, pick-me-up, bracer.

**too** adverb **1** *invasion would be too risky:* excessively, overly, unduly, immoderately, inordinately, unreasonably, extremely, very. **2** *he was unhappy, too, you know:* also, as well, in addition, into the bargain, besides, furthermore, moreover.

**tool** noun implement, utensil, instrument, device, apparatus, gadget, appliance, machine, contrivance, contraption; informal gizmo.

**top** noun **1** *the top of the cliff:* summit, peak, pinnacle, crest, crown, brow, head, tip, apex. **2** *the top of the coffee jar:* lid, cap, cover. **3** *he was at the top of his profession:* height, peak, pinnacle, zenith, culmination, climax, prime.
OPPOSITES bottom, base.
adjective **1** *the top floor:* highest, topmost, uppermost. **2** *top scientists:* foremost, leading, principal, pre-eminent, greatest, best, finest, elite. **3** *the organization's top management:* chief, principal, main, leading, highest, ruling, commanding, most powerful, most important. **4** *a top hotel:* prime, premier, excellent, superior, choice, select, five-star, grade A, best, finest. **5** *at top speed:* maximum, greatest, utmost.
OPPOSITES bottom, lowest, minimum.
verb **1** *sales topped £1 billion:* exceed, surpass, go beyond, better, beat, outstrip, outdo, outshine, eclipse. **2** *their CD is currently topping the charts:* lead, head, be at the top of. **3** *mousse topped with cream:* cover, cap, coat, finish, garnish.
■ **top something up** fill, refill, refresh, freshen, replenish, recharge, resupply.

**topic** noun subject, theme, issue, matter, point, question, concern, argument, thesis.

**topical** adjective current, up to date, up to the minute, contemporary, recent, relevant, in the news.
OPPOSITES out of date.

**topple** verb **1** *she toppled off the chair:* fall, tumble, tip, overbalance, overturn, keel over, lose one's balance. **2** *protesters toppled a statue:* knock over, upset, push over,

a
b
c
d
e
f
g
h
i
j
k
l
m
n
o
p
q
r
s
**t**
u
v
w
x
y
z

tip over, upend. **3** *a plot to topple the government:* overthrow, oust, unseat, overturn, bring down, defeat, get rid of, dislodge, eject.

**torment** noun *emotional torment:* agony, suffering, torture, pain, anguish, misery, distress, trauma.
verb **1** *she was tormented by shame:* torture, afflict, rack, harrow, plague, haunt, distress, agonize. **2** *she began to torment the boys:* tease, taunt, bait, provoke, harass, bother, persecute; informal needle.

**torn** adjective **1** *a torn shirt:* ripped, rent, cut, slit, ragged, tattered. **2** *she was torn between the two options:* wavering, vacillating, irresolute, dithering, uncertain, unsure, undecided, in two minds.

**tornado** noun whirlwind, cyclone, typhoon, storm, hurricane; N. Amer. informal twister.

**torrent** noun **1** *a torrent of water:* flood, deluge, spate, cascade, rush. **2** *a torrent of abuse:* outburst, outpouring, stream, flood, volley, barrage, tide.
OPPOSITES trickle.

**torture** noun **1** *the torture of political prisoners:* abuse, ill-treatment, mistreatment, maltreatment, persecution, cruelty, atrocity. **2** *the torture of losing a loved one:* torment, agony, suffering, pain, anguish, misery, distress, heartbreak, trauma.
verb **1** *the forces routinely tortured suspects:* abuse, ill-treat, mistreat, maltreat, persecute. **2** *he was tortured by grief:* torment, rack, afflict,

harrow, plague, distress, trouble.

**toss** verb **1** *he tossed his tools into the boot:* throw, hurl, fling, sling, pitch, lob, launch; informal heave, chuck, bung. **2** *he tossed a coin:* flip, flick, spin. **3** *the ship tossed about on the waves:* pitch, lurch, rock, roll, plunge, reel, sway. **4** *toss the ingredients together:* mix, combine, stir, turn, shake.

**total** adjective **1** *the total cost:* entire, complete, whole, full, combined, aggregate, gross, overall. **2** *a total disaster:* utter, complete, absolute, thorough, perfect, downright, out-and-out, outright, sheer, unmitigated.
OPPOSITES partial, net.
noun *a total of £16:* sum, aggregate, whole, entirety, totality.
verb **1** *the prize money totalled £33,050:* add up to, amount to, come to, run to, make. **2** *he totalled up his score:* add, count, reckon, tot up, compute, work out.

**totally** adverb completely, entirely, wholly, thoroughly, fully, utterly, absolutely, perfectly, unreservedly, unconditionally, downright, one hundred per cent.
OPPOSITES partly.

**touch** verb **1** *his feet touched the floor:* contact, meet, brush, graze, come up against, be in contact with, border, abut. **2** *he touched her cheek:* feel, pat, tap, stroke, fondle, caress, pet, handle. **3** *sales touched twenty grand:* reach, attain, come to, make, rise to, soar to, sink to, plummet to; informal hit.
**4** *nobody can touch him when he's on form:* compare with, be

on a par with, equal, match, rival, measure up to, better, beat; informal hold a candle to.
**5** *you're not supposed to touch the computer:* handle, hold, pick up, move, use, meddle with, play about with, fiddle with, interfere with, tamper with, disturb. **6** *Lisa felt touched by her kindness:* affect, move, stir.
noun **1** *her touch on his shoulder:* tap, pat, contact, stroke, caress. **2** *his political touch:* skill, expertise, dexterity, deftness, adroitness, adeptness, ability, talent, flair, facility, proficiency, knack. **3** *there was a touch of bitterness in her voice:* trace, bit, suggestion, suspicion, hint, scintilla, tinge, dash, taste, spot, drop, dab, soupçon. **4** *the gas lights are a nice touch:* detail, feature, point, element, addition. **5** *have you been in touch with him?* contact, communication, correspondence.
■ **touch on/upon** refer to, mention, comment on, remark on, bring up, raise, broach, allude to, cover, deal with.

**touching** adjective moving, affecting, heart-warming, emotional, emotive, poignant, sad, tear-jerking.

**tough** adjective **1** *tough leather:* durable, strong, resilient, sturdy, rugged, solid, stout, robust, hard-wearing, long-lasting, heavy-duty, well built, made to last. **2** *he'll survive— he's pretty tough:* robust, resilient, strong, hardy, rugged, fit; informal hard. **3** *tough sentencing for offenders:* strict, stern, severe, stringent, rigorous, hard, firm, hard-hitting, uncompromising. **4** *the training was pretty tough:*
difficult, hard, strenuous, onerous, gruelling, exacting, arduous, demanding, taxing, tiring, exhausting, punishing.
**5** *tough questions:* difficult, hard, knotty, thorny, tricky.
OPPOSITES weak, lenient, light, easy.
noun *a gang of toughs:* ruffian, thug, hoodlum, hooligan, bully boy; Brit. rough; informal heavy, bruiser; Brit. informal yob.

**tour** noun **1** *a three-day walking tour:* trip, excursion, journey, expedition, jaunt, outing, trek, safari. **2** *a tour of the factory:* visit, inspection, walkabout.
verb **1** *this hotel is well placed for touring Devon:* travel round, explore, holiday in; informal do. **2** *the Prince toured a local factory:* visit, inspect, go round, walk round.

**tourist** noun holidaymaker, traveller, sightseer, visitor, backpacker, globetrotter, tripper; N. Amer. vacationer.
OPPOSITES local.

**tournament** noun competition, contest, championship, meeting, event.

**tow** verb pull, haul, drag, draw, tug, lug.

**towards** preposition **1** *they were driving towards her flat:* in the direction of, to, on the way to, on the road to. **2** *towards evening dark clouds gathered:* just before, shortly before, near, around, approaching, getting on for. **3** *her attitude towards politics:* with regard to, regarding, in/with regard to, in relation to, concerning, about, apropos.

**tower** verb *snow-capped peaks towered over the valley:* soar, rise, rear, overshadow, overhang, hang over, dominate.

a
b
c
d
e
f
g
h
i
j
k
l
m
n
o
p
q
r
s
**t**
u
v
w
x
y
z

**toxic** adjective poisonous, dangerous, harmful, injurious, noxious, pernicious, deadly, lethal.
OPPOSITES harmless.

**toy** noun *playing with their toys:* plaything, game.
adjective *a toy gun:* model, imitation, replica, miniature.
■ **toy with 1** *I was toying with the idea:* think about, consider, flirt with, entertain the possibility of; informal kick around. **2** *Adam toyed with his glasses:* fiddle with, play with, fidget with, twiddle, finger.

**trace** verb **1** *police hope to trace the owner:* track down, find, discover, detect, unearth, turn up, hunt down, ferret out, run to ground. **2** *she traced a pattern in the sand:* draw, outline, mark.
noun **1** *no trace had been found of the missing plane:* sign, mark, indication, evidence, clue, vestige, remains, remnant. **2** *a trace of bitterness crept into her voice:* bit, touch, hint, suggestion, suspicion, shadow, dash, tinge; informal smidgen, tad.

**track** noun **1** *a gravel track:* path, footpath, lane, trail, route. **2** *the final lap of the track:* course, racecourse, racetrack, velodrome; Brit. circuit. **3** *he found the tracks of a fox:* traces, marks, prints, footprints, trail, spoor. **4** *the railway tracks:* rail, line. **5** *the album's title track:* song, recording, number, piece.
verb *he tracked a bear for 40 km:* follow, trail, pursue, shadow, stalk; informal tail.
■ **track someone/something down** discover, find, detect, hunt down, unearth, uncover, turn up, dig up, ferret out, run to ground.

**trade** noun **1** *the trade in stolen cattle:* dealing, buying and selling, commerce, traffic, business. **2** *the glazier's trade:* occupation, work, craft, job, career, profession, business, line (of work), métier.
verb **1** *he made his fortune trading in diamonds:* deal, do business, bargain, negotiate, traffic, buy and sell. **2** *the business is trading at a loss:* operate, run, do business, deal. **3** *I traded the old machine for a newer model:* swap, exchange, barter, part-exchange.

**trader** noun dealer, merchant, buyer, seller, vendor, purveyor, supplier, trafficker.

**tradition** noun custom, practice, convention, ritual, observance, way, usage, habit, institution, unwritten law; formal praxis.

**traditional** adjective customary, long-established, time-honoured, classic, wonted, accustomed, standard, regular, normal, conventional, habitual, ritual, age-old, folk.

**traffic** noun **1** *the increased use of railways for goods traffic:* transport, freight, shipping. **2** *the traffic in stolen art:* trade, dealing, commerce, business, buying and selling.
verb *he confessed to trafficking in ivory:* trade, deal, do business, buy and sell.

**tragedy** noun disaster, calamity, catastrophe, cataclysm, misfortune, adversity.

**tragic** adjective **1** *a tragic accident:* disastrous, calamitous, catastrophic, cataclysmic, devastating, terrible, dreadful, awful, appalling, horrendous, fatal. **2** *a*

*tragic tale:* sad, unhappy, pathetic, moving, distressing, painful, harrowing, heart-rending, sorry.
OPPOSITES fortunate, happy.

**trail** noun 1 *a trail of clues:* series, string, chain, succession, sequence. 2 *wolves on the trail of their prey:* track, spoor, path, scent, traces, marks, signs, prints, footprints. 3 *the plane's vapour trail:* wake, tail, stream. 4 *nature trails:* path, way, footpath, track, route.
verb 1 *her robe trailed along the ground:* drag, sweep, be drawn, dangle. 2 *the roses trailed over the banks:* hang, droop, fall, spill, cascade. 3 *Sharpe suspected they were trailing him:* follow, pursue, track, shadow, stalk, hunt; informal tail. 4 *the defending champions were trailing 10–5:* lose, be down, be behind, lag behind.
OPPOSITES lead.

**train** verb 1 *an engineer trained in remote-sensing techniques:* instruct, teach, coach, tutor, school, educate, prime, drill, ground. 2 *she's training to be a hairdresser:* study, learn, prepare, take instruction. 3 *with the Olympics in mind, athletes are training hard:* exercise, work out, get into shape, practise. 4 *she trained the gun on him:* aim, point, direct, level, focus.
noun *a bizarre train of events:* chain, string, series, sequence, succession, set, course.

**trainer** noun coach, instructor, teacher, tutor, handler.

**trait** noun characteristic, attribute, feature, quality, habit, mannerism, idiosyncrasy, peculiarity.

**traitor** noun betrayer, back-stabber, double-crosser, renegade, Judas, quisling, fifth columnist, turncoat, defector; informal snake in the grass.

**tramp** verb 1 *men were tramping through the shrubbery:* trudge, plod, stamp, trample, lumber; informal traipse. 2 *he spent ten days tramping through the jungle:* trek, walk, hike, slog, march, roam, ramble, rove; informal traipse; N. Amer. informal schlep.
noun 1 *a dirty old tramp:* vagrant, vagabond, homeless person, down-and-out, traveller, drifter; N. Amer. hobo; N. Amer. informal bum. 2 *the tramp of boots:* tread, step, footstep, footfall. 3 *a tramp round York:* trek, walk, hike, slog, march, roam, ramble; N. Amer. informal schlep.

**trample** verb tread, stamp, walk, squash, crush, flatten.

**trance** noun daze, stupor, hypnotic state, dream, reverie.

**tranquil** adjective 1 *a tranquil village:* peaceful, calm, restful, quiet, still, relaxing, undisturbed. 2 *Martha smiled, perfectly tranquil:* calm, serene, relaxed, unruffled, unperturbed, unflustered, untroubled, composed; informal unflappable.
OPPOSITES busy, excitable.

**transaction** noun deal, bargain, agreement, undertaking, arrangement, negotiation, settlement.

**transfer** verb move, take, bring, shift, convey, remove, carry, transport, relocate.

**transform** verb change, alter, convert, revolutionize, overhaul, reconstruct, rebuild, reorganize, rearrange, rework.

**transition** noun change,

a
b
c
d
e
f
g
h
i
j
k
l
m
n
o
p
q
r
s
**t**
u
v
w
x
y
z

passage, move, transformation, conversion, metamorphosis, alteration, changeover, shift, switch.

**transitional** adjective **1** *a transitional period*: intermediate, interim, changeover, changing, fluid, unsettled. **2** *the transitional government*: interim, temporary, provisional, pro tem, acting, caretaker.

**translate** verb interpret, convert, render, put, change, express, decipher, reword, decode, gloss, explain.

**translation** noun interpretation, rendition, conversion, change, alteration, adaptation.

**transmission** noun **1** *the transmission of knowledge*: transfer, communication, passing on, conveyance, dissemination, spread, circulation, relaying. **2** *the transmission of the film*: broadcasting, airing, televising. **3** *a live transmission*: broadcast, programme, show.

**transmit** verb **1** *the use of computers to transmit information*: transfer, communicate, pass on, hand on, convey, impart, channel, carry, relay, dispatch, disseminate, spread, circulate. **2** *the programme will be transmitted on Sunday*: broadcast, send out, air, televise.

**transparent** adjective **1** *transparent blue water*: clear, translucent, limpid. **2** *fine transparent fabrics*: see-through, sheer, filmy, gauzy, diaphanous. **3** *a transparent attempt to buy votes*: obvious, blatant, unambiguous, unequivocal,

clear, plain, apparent, unmistakable, manifest, conspicuous, patent.
OPPOSITES opaque, obscure.

**transplant** verb **1** *these ideas were transplanted to America*: transfer, move, remove, shift, relocate, take, replant. **2** *kidneys are frequently transplanted*: transfer, implant, graft.

**transport** verb *the blocks were transported by lorry*: convey, carry, take, transfer, move, shift, send, deliver, bear, ship, ferry; informal cart.
noun *the transport of crude oil*: conveyance, carriage, delivery, shipping, freight, shipment, haulage.

**trap** noun **1** *an animal caught in a trap*: snare, net, mesh, gin; N. Amer. deadfall. **2** *the question was set as a trap*: trick, ploy, ruse, deception, subterfuge; informal set-up.
verb **1** *police trapped the men*: snare, entrap, capture, catch, ambush. **2** *a rat trapped in a barn*: confine, cut off, corner, shut in, pen in, hem in, imprison. **3** *I hoped to trap him into an admission*: trick, dupe, deceive, fool, hoodwink.

**trash** noun **1** (N. Amer.) *the entrance was blocked with trash*: rubbish, refuse, waste, litter, junk; N. Amer. garbage. **2** (informal) *they read trash*: rubbish, nonsense, trivia, pulp fiction, pap; N. Amer. garbage; informal drivel.

**trauma** noun **1** *the trauma of divorce*: shock, upheaval, distress, stress, strain, pain, anguish, suffering, upset, ordeal. **2** *trauma to the liver*: injury, damage, wound.

**traumatic** adjective disturbing,

shocking, distressing, upsetting, painful, agonizing, hurtful, stressful, devastating, harrowing.
OPPOSITES comforting.

**travel** verb journey, tour, take a trip, voyage, go sightseeing, globetrot, backpack, trek.
noun (**travels**) travelling, journeys, expeditions, trips, tours, excursions, voyages, treks, wanderings, jaunts.

**traveller** noun tourist, tripper, holidaymaker, sightseer, globetrotter, backpacker, passenger, commuter; N. Amer. vacationer.

**tread** verb 1 *he trod purposefully down the hall:* walk, step, stride, pace, march, tramp, plod, stomp, trudge. 2 *the snow had been trodden down by the horses:* crush, flatten, press down, squash, trample on, stamp on.
noun *we heard his heavy tread on the stairs:* step, footstep, footfall, tramp.

**treason** noun treachery, disloyalty, betrayal, sedition, subversion, mutiny, rebellion.
OPPOSITES allegiance, loyalty.

**treasure** noun 1 *a casket of treasure:* riches, valuables, jewels, gems, gold, silver, precious metals, money, cash, wealth, fortune. 2 *art treasures:* masterpiece, gem, pearl, jewel.
verb *I treasure the photographs:* cherish, hold dear, prize, set great store by, value greatly.

**treasury** noun storehouse, repository, treasure house, exchequer, fund, mine, bank, coffers, purse.

**treat** verb 1 *Charlotte treated him badly:* behave towards, act towards, use, deal with, handle. 2 *police are treating the fires as*

*arson:* regard, consider, view, look on, put down as. 3 *the book treats its subject with insight:* deal with, tackle, handle, discuss, explore, investigate. 4 *she was treated in hospital:* tend, nurse, attend to, give medical attention to. 5 *a cream used to treat sunburn:* cure, heal, remedy. 6 *he treated her to lunch:* buy, take out for, stand, give, pay for, entertain, wine and dine; informal foot the bill for. 7 *delegates were treated to dance performances:* entertain with/to, regale with, fête with, amuse with.
noun 1 *a birthday treat:* celebration, entertainment, amusement, surprise. 2 *I bought you some chocolate as a treat:* present, gift, titbit, delicacy, luxury, indulgence, extravagance; informal goody. 3 *it was a real treat to see them:* pleasure, delight, thrill, joy.

**treatment** noun 1 *the company's treatment of its workers:* behaviour towards, conduct towards, handling of, dealings with. 2 *she's responding well to treatment:* medical care, therapy, nursing, medication, drugs. 3 *her treatment of the topic:* discussion, handling, investigation, exploration, consideration, study, analysis.

**treaty** noun agreement, settlement, pact, deal, entente, concordat, accord, protocol, compact, convention; formal concord.

**trek** noun journey, trip, expedition, safari, hike, march, tramp, walk.

**tremble** verb 1 *Joe's hands were trembling:* shake, quiver, twitch. 2 *the entire building*

a
b
c
d
e
f
g
h
i
j
k
l
m
n
o
p
q
r
s
t
u
v
w
x
y
z

a
b
c
d
e
f
g
h
i
j
k
l
m
n
o
p
q
r
s
**t**
u
v
w
x
y
z

*trembled:* shudder, shake, judder, vibrate, wobble, rock, move, sway.

**tremendous** adjective
**1** *tremendous sums of money:* huge, enormous, immense, colossal, massive, prodigious, stupendous; informal whopping, astronomical; Brit. informal ginormous. **2** *a tremendous result:* excellent, first-class, outstanding, marvellous, wonderful, splendid, admirable; informal great, fantastic, fabulous, terrific, super, awesome, ace; Brit. informal brilliant, smashing.
OPPOSITES tiny, poor.

**trench** noun ditch, channel, trough, excavation, furrow, rut, conduit.

**trend** noun **1** *an upward trend in unemployment:* tendency, movement, drift, swing, shift, course, current, direction, inclination, leaning. **2** *the latest trend in music:* fashion, vogue, style, mode, craze, mania, rage; informal fad, thing.

**trespass** verb intrude, encroach, invade, enter without permission.

**trial** noun **1** *a county court trial:* case, lawsuit, hearing, tribunal, litigation, proceedings. **2** *the drug is undergoing clinical trials:* test, experiment, pilot study, examination, check, assessment, audition, evaluation, appraisal; informal dry run. **3** *trials and tribulations:* trouble, affliction, ordeal, tribulation, difficulty, problem, misfortune, mishap, misadventure.

**tribe** noun ethnic group, people, family, clan, race, dynasty, house, nation.

**tribunal** noun court, board, panel, committee.

**tribute** noun accolade, praise, commendation, salute, testimonial, homage, congratulations, compliments, plaudits.
OPPOSITES criticism, condemnation.

**trick** noun **1** *a mean trick:* stratagem, ploy, ruse, scheme, device, manoeuvre, dodge, subterfuge, swindle, fraud; informal con, set-up, scam, sting. **2** *he's playing a trick on us:* practical joke, prank; informal leg-pull, spoof, put-on. **3** *it was probably a trick of the light:* illusion, figment of the imagination, mirage. **4** *the tricks of the trade:* knack, skill, technique, secret, art.
verb *tricked by villains:* deceive, delude, hoodwink, mislead, take in, dupe, fool, cheat, defraud, swindle; informal con, diddle, take for a ride, shaft, do; N. Amer. informal sucker.

**trickle** verb *blood was trickling from two cuts:* dribble, drip, ooze, leak, seep, spill.
OPPOSITES pour, gush.
noun *trickles of water:* dribble, drip, thin stream, rivulet.

**tricky** adjective **1** *a tricky situation:* difficult, awkward, problematic, delicate, ticklish, sensitive; informal sticky. **2** *a tricky politician:* cunning, crafty, wily, devious, sly, scheming, calculating, deceitful.
OPPOSITES straightforward, honest.

**trifle** noun triviality, thing of no consequence, bagatelle, inessential, nothing, technicality; (**trifles**) trivia, minutiae.

**trifling** adjective trivial,

unimportant, insignificant, inconsequential, petty, minor, of little/no account, footling, incidental; informal piffling.
OPPOSITES important.

**trigger** verb start, set off, initiate, spark (off), activate, touch off, provoke, precipitate, prompt, stir up, cause, give rise to, lead to, set in motion, bring about.

**trim** verb 1 *his hair had been trimmed:* cut, crop, bob, shorten, clip, snip, shear, dock, lop off, prune, shave, pare.
2 *gloves trimmed with fake fur:* decorate, adorn, ornament, embellish, edge, border, fringe.
noun 1 *white curtains with a blue trim:* decoration, ornamentation, adornment, embellishment, border, edging, piping, fringe, frill. 2 *hair in need of a trim:* haircut, cut, clip, snip.
adjective 1 *a very trim garden:* neat, tidy, orderly, uncluttered, well kept, well maintained, immaculate, spick and span, spruce, dapper. 2 *her trim figure:* slim, slender, lean, sleek, willowy.
OPPOSITES untidy, messy.
■ in trim fit, in good health, in fine fettle, slim, in shape.

**trimming** noun 1 *a black dress with lace trimming:* decoration, ornamentation, adornment, borders, edging, piping, fringes, frills. 2 (**trimmings**) accompaniments, extras, frills, accessories, accoutrements, trappings, paraphernalia, garnish.

**trio** noun threesome, three, triumvirate, triad, troika, trinity, trilogy.

**trip** verb 1 *he tripped on the stones:* stumble, lose one's

footing, catch one's foot, slip, fall (down), tumble. 2 *they tripped up the steps:* skip, dance, prance, bound, spring, scamper.
noun 1 *a trip to Paris:* excursion, outing, jaunt, holiday, break, visit, tour, journey, expedition, voyage, drive, run; informal spin. 2 *trips cause many accidents:* stumble, slip, fall, misstep.

**triple** adjective 1 *a triple alliance:* threefold, tripartite, three-way.
2 *triple the going rate:* three times, treble.

**triumph** noun 1 *Napoleon's triumphs:* victory, win, conquest, success, achievement.
2 *his eyes shone with triumph:* jubilation, exultation, elation, delight, joy, happiness, glee, pride, satisfaction.
OPPOSITES defeat, disappointment.
verb *he triumphed in the Grand Prix:* win, succeed, come first, be victorious, carry the day, prevail.
OPPOSITES lose.
■ triumph over defeat, beat, conquer, trounce, vanquish, overcome, overpower, overwhelm, get the better of; informal lick.

**triumphant** adjective 1 *the triumphant team:* victorious, successful, winning, conquering. 2 *a triumphant expression:* jubilant, exultant, celebratory, elated, joyful, delighted, gleeful, proud, cock-a-hoop.
OPPOSITES unsuccessful, defeated, despondent.

**trivial** adjective unimportant, insignificant, inconsequential, minor, of no account, of no importance, petty, trifling,

footling, negligible; informal piffling.
OPPOSITES important, significant.

**troop** noun 1 *a troop of musicians:* group, party, band, gang, body, company, troupe, crowd, squad, unit. 2 (**troops**) soldiers, armed forces, soldiery, servicemen, servicewomen.
verb *we trooped out of the hall:* walk, march, file, flock, crowd, throng, stream, swarm.

**trophy** noun 1 *a swimming trophy:* cup, medal, prize, award. 2 *trophies from his travels:* souvenir, memento, keepsake, spoils, booty.

**tropical** adjective hot, sweltering, humid, sultry, steamy, sticky, oppressive, stifling.
OPPOSITES cold.

**trot** verb run, jog, scuttle, scurry, bustle, scamper.

**trouble** noun 1 *you've caused enough trouble:* difficulty, problems, bother, inconvenience, worry, anxiety, distress, stress, agitation, harassment, unpleasantness; informal hassle. 2 *she poured out all her troubles:* problem, misfortune, difficulty, trial, tribulation, woe, grief, heartache, misery, affliction, suffering. 3 *he's gone to a lot of trouble:* bother, inconvenience, fuss, effort, exertion, work, labour. 4 *I wouldn't want to be a trouble to her:* nuisance, bother, inconvenience, irritation, problem, trial, pest; informal headache, pain, drag. 5 *you're too gullible, that's your trouble:* shortcoming, weakness, failing, fault. 6 *he had heart trouble:* disease, illness, sickness, ailment, complaint, problem, disorder,

disability. 7 *the crash was due to engine trouble:* malfunction, failure, breakdown. 8 *a match marred by crowd trouble:* disturbance, disorder, unrest, fighting, scuffles, breach of the peace.
verb 1 *this matter had been troubling her for some time:* worry, bother, concern, disturb, upset, agitate, distress, perturb, annoy, nag, prey on someone's mind; informal bug. 2 *he was troubled by ill health:* afflict, burden, suffer from, be cursed with. 3 *there is nothing you need trouble about:* worry, upset oneself, fret, be anxious, be concerned. 4 *I'm sorry to trouble you:* inconvenience, bother, impose on, disturb, put out, disoblige; informal hassle.

**troublesome** adjective 1 *a troublesome problem:* annoying, irritating, exasperating, maddening, infuriating, bothersome, tiresome, nagging, difficult, awkward; N. Amer. informal pesky. 2 *a troublesome child:* difficult, awkward, uncooperative, rebellious, unmanageable, unruly, obstreperous, disruptive, disobedient, naughty, recalcitrant.
OPPOSITES simple, cooperative.

**truce** noun ceasefire, armistice, cessation, peace.

**true** adjective 1 *what I say is true:* correct, accurate, right, verifiable, the case, so. 2 *true craftsmanship:* genuine, authentic, real, actual, bona fide, proper. 3 *true repentance:* sincere, genuine, real, unfeigned, heartfelt. 4 *a true friend:* loyal, faithful, constant, devoted, trustworthy, reliable, dependable. 5 *a true reflection*

*of life:* accurate, faithful, telling it like it is, realistic, factual, lifelike.
OPPOSITES untrue, false, disloyal, inaccurate.

**truly** adverb 1 *tell me truly what you want:* truthfully, honestly, frankly, candidly, openly. 2 *I'm truly grateful:* sincerely, genuinely, really, indeed, heartily, profoundly. 3 *a truly dreadful song:* really, absolutely, simply, utterly, totally, perfectly, thoroughly, completely. 4 *this is truly a miracle:* without (a) doubt, unquestionably, certainly, surely, definitely, undeniably, really, actually, in fact.

**trumpet** verb proclaim, announce, declare, noise abroad, shout from the rooftops.
OPPOSITES keep quiet about.

**trunk** noun 1 *the trunk of a tree:* stem, bole, stock, stalk. 2 *his powerful trunk:* torso, body. 3 *an elephant's trunk:* proboscis, nose, snout. 4 *an enormous tin trunk:* chest, box, crate, coffer, case, portmanteau.

**trust** noun *good relationships are built on trust:* confidence, belief, faith, certainty, assurance, conviction, credence, reliance.
OPPOSITES distrust, mistrust, doubt.
verb 1 *I should never have trusted her:* have faith in, have (every) confidence in, believe in, pin one's hopes/faith on. 2 *he can be trusted to carry out an impartial investigation:* rely on, depend on, bank on, count on, be sure of. 3 *I trust we shall meet again:* hope, expect, take it, assume, presume. 4 *they won't trust their money to*

*strangers:* entrust, consign, commit, give, hand over, turn over, assign.
OPPOSITES distrust, mistrust, doubt.

**trusting** adjective trustful, unsuspecting, unquestioning, naive, innocent, childlike, ingenuous, wide-eyed, credulous, gullible, easily taken in.
OPPOSITES distrustful, suspicious.

**trustworthy** adjective reliable, dependable, honest, as good as one's word, above suspicion; informal on the level.
OPPOSITES unreliable.

**truth** noun 1 *he doubted the truth of her statement:* accuracy, correctness, authenticity, veracity, verity. 2 *truth is stranger than fiction:* fact(s), reality, real life, actuality.
OPPOSITES lies, fiction, falsehood.

**truthful** adjective true, accurate, correct, factual, faithful, reliable.
OPPOSITES deceitful, untrue.

**try** verb 1 *try to help him:* attempt, endeavour, make an effort, strive, do one's best, do one's utmost, aim; informal have a go, go all out. 2 *try it and see what you think:* test, sample, taste, inspect, investigate, examine, appraise, evaluate, assess; informal check out. 3 *Mary tried everyone's patience:* tax, strain, test, stretch, sap, drain, exhaust, wear out.
noun *I'll have one last try:* attempt, effort, endeavour; informal go, shot, crack, stab, bash.

**trying** adjective 1 *a trying day:* stressful, taxing, demanding,

a
b
c
d
e
f
g
h
i
j
k
l
m
n
o
p
q
r
s
**t**
u
v
w
x
y
z

difficult, challenging, pressured, frustrating, fraught; informal hellish. **2** *Steve was very trying:* annoying, irritating, exasperating, maddening, infuriating, tiresome, troublesome.
OPPOSITES easy, accommodating.

**tuck** verb push, insert, slip, thrust, stuff, stick, cram; informal pop.

**tug** verb **1** *Ben tugged at her sleeve:* pull, pluck, tweak, twitch, jerk, catch hold of; informal yank. **2** *she tugged him towards the door:* drag, pull, lug, draw, haul, heave, tow, trail.

**tuition** noun instruction, teaching, coaching, tutoring, tutelage, lessons, education, schooling, training.

**tumble** verb **1** *he tumbled over:* fall (over/down), topple over, lose one's balance, take a spill, trip (up), stumble. **2** *oil prices tumbled:* plummet, plunge, dive, nosedive, drop, slump, slide; informal crash.
OPPOSITES rise.

**tumour** noun cancer, growth, lump, malignancy; Medicine carcinoma, sarcoma.

**tune** noun *she hummed a tune:* melody, air, strain, theme, song, jingle, ditty.
verb *a body clock tuned to the tides:* attune, adapt, adjust, regulate.

**tunnel** noun underground passage, underpass, subway, shaft, burrow, hole, warren, labyrinth.
verb dig, burrow, mine, bore, drill.

**turbulent** adjective tempestuous, stormy, unstable, unsettled, tumultuous, chaotic, anarchic, lawless.
OPPOSITES peaceful.

**turmoil** noun confusion, upheaval, turbulence, tumult, disorder, disturbance, ferment, chaos, mayhem.
OPPOSITES peace, order.

**turn** verb **1** *the wheels were still turning:* go round, revolve, rotate, spin, roll, circle, wheel, whirl, gyrate, swivel, pivot. **2** *I turned and headed back:* change direction, change course, make a U-turn, turn about/round, wheel round. **3** *the path turned to right and left:* bend, curve, wind, twist, meander, snake, zigzag. **4** *Emma turned red:* become, go, grow, get. **5** *the milk had turned:* (go) sour, go off, curdle, become rancid, go bad, spoil.
noun **1** *a turn of the wheel:* rotation, revolution, spin, whirl, gyration, swivel. **2** *a turn to the left:* change of direction, veer, divergence. **3** *we're approaching the turn:* bend, corner, junction, twist, dog-leg; Brit. hairpin bend. **4** *you'll get your turn:* opportunity, chance, say, stint, time, try; informal go, shot, stab, crack. **5** *she did me some good turns:* service, deed, act, favour, kindness, disservice, wrong.
■ **turn someone/something down 1** *his novel was turned down:* reject, spurn, rebuff, refuse, decline. **2** *Pete turned the sound down:* reduce, lower, decrease, lessen, mute. ■ **turn into** become, develop into, turn out to be, be transformed into, change into. ■ **turn something into something** convert, change, transform, make, adapt, modify. ■ **turn something off/out** switch off, shut off, put off, extinguish, deactivate; informal kill, cut. ■ **turn something on**

switch on, put on, start up, activate, trip. ■ **turn out 1** *a huge crowd turned out:* come, be present, attend, appear, turn up, arrive, assemble, gather; informal show up. **2** *it turned out that she had been abroad:* transpire, emerge, come to light, become apparent. **3** *things didn't turn out well:* happen, occur, come about, develop, work out, come out, end up; informal pan out. ■ **turn up 1** *the documents turned up:* be found, be discovered, be located, reappear. **2** *the police turned up:* arrive, appear, present oneself; informal show (up). **3** *something better will turn up:* present itself, occur, happen, crop up. ■ **turn something up 1** *she turned up the volume:* increase, raise, amplify, intensify. **2** *they turned up lots of information:* discover, uncover, unearth, find, dig up, expose.

**turning** noun junction, turn-off, side road, exit; N. Amer. turnout.

**turning point** noun watershed, critical moment, decisive moment, moment of truth, crossroads, crisis.

**turnout** noun **1** *the lecture attracted a good turnout:* **attendance**, audience, house, congregation, crowd, gate, gathering. **2** *his turnout was very elegant:* **outfit**, clothing, dress, garb, attire, ensemble; informal get-up.

**turnover** noun **1** *a turnover of £2 million:* **gross revenue**, income, yield, sales. **2** *staff turnover:* **replacement**, change, movement.

**tutor** noun *a history tutor:* **teacher**, instructor, coach,

educator, lecturer, trainer, mentor.
verb *he was tutored at home:* **teach**, instruct, educate, school, coach, train, drill.

**twilight** noun **1** *we arrived at twilight:* **dusk**, sunset, sundown, nightfall, evening, close of day. **2** *it was scarcely visible in the twilight:* **half-light**, semi-darkness, gloom.
OPPOSITES dawn.

**twin** noun *a sitting room that was the twin of her own:* **duplicate**, double, carbon copy, likeness, mirror image, replica, lookalike, clone, match, pair; informal spitting image, dead ringer.
adjective **1** *the twin towers of the stadium:* **matching**, identical, paired. **2** *the twin aims of conservation and recreation:* **twofold**, double, dual, related, linked, connected, parallel, complementary.
verb *the company twinned its brewing with distilling:* **combine**, join, link, couple, pair.

**twinkle** verb & noun glitter, sparkle, shine, glimmer, shimmer, glint, gleam, glisten, flicker, flash, wink.

**twist** verb **1** *the impact twisted the chassis:* **crumple**, crush, buckle, mangle, warp, deform, distort, contort. **2** *he twisted round in his seat:* **turn**, swivel, spin, pivot, rotate, revolve, twiddle. **3** *I twisted my ankle:* **sprain**, wrench, turn, rick, crick. **4** *she twisted her hair round her finger:* **wind**, twirl, coil, curl, wrap. **5** *the wires were twisted together:* **intertwine**, interlace, weave, plait, braid, coil, wind. **6** *the*

a b c d e f g h i j k l m n o p q r s t u v w x y z

a
b
c
d
e
f
g
h
i
j
k
l
m
n
o
p
q
r
s
**t**
**u**
v
w
x
y
z

*road twisted and turned:* wind, bend, curve, turn, meander, weave, zigzag, snake.

noun **1** *the twist of a dial:* turn, twirl, spin. **2** *the twists of the road:* bend, curve, turn, zigzag, dog-leg. **3** *the twists of the plot:* convolution, complication, complexity, intricacy, surprise, revelation.

**twitch** verb **1** *he twitched and then lay still:* jerk, convulse, have a spasm, quiver, tremble, shiver, shudder. **2** *he twitched the note out of my hand:* snatch, tweak, pluck, pull, tug; informal yank.

noun **1** *a twitch of her lips:* spasm, convulsion, quiver, tremor, shiver, shudder, tic. **2** *he gave a twitch at his moustache:* pull, tug, tweak; informal yank.

**tycoon** noun magnate, mogul, businessman, captain of industry, industrialist, financier, entrepreneur; informal, derogatory fat cat.

**type** noun **1** *six types of coffee:* kind, sort, variety, class, category, set, genre, species, order, breed. **2** *italic type:* print, typeface, characters, lettering, font; Brit. fount.

**typical** adjective **1** *a typical example of art deco:* representative, characteristic, classic, quintessential, archetypal. **2** *a fairly typical day:* normal, average, ordinary, standard, regular, routine, run-of-the-mill, conventional, unremarkable; informal bog-standard.
OPPOSITES unusual, exceptional.

**tyranny** noun despotism, absolute power, autocracy, dictatorship, totalitarianism, fascism, oppression, repression, subjugation, enslavement.

# Uu

**ubiquitous** adjective everywhere, omnipresent, all over the place, all-pervasive, universal, worldwide, global.
OPPOSITES rare.

**ugly** adjective **1** unattractive, unsightly, ill-favoured, hideous, plain, unprepossessing, horrible, ghastly, repellent; N. Amer. homely; Brit. informal no oil painting. **2** *things got pretty ugly:* unpleasant, nasty, disagreeable, alarming, charged, dangerous, perilous, threatening, menacing, hostile, ominous, sinister.
OPPOSITES beautiful, pleasant.

**ultimate** adjective **1** *the ultimate collapse of the Empire:* eventual, final, concluding, terminal, end. **2** *ultimate truths:* fundamental, basic, primary, elementary, absolute, central, crucial, essential, pivotal. **3** *the ultimate gift for cat lovers:* best, ideal, greatest, supreme, quintessential.

**ultimately** adverb **1** *the cost will ultimately fall on us:* eventually, in the end, in the long run, at length, finally, in time, one day. **2** *two ultimately contradictory reasons:* fundamentally, basically, primarily, essentially, at heart, deep down.

**umpire** noun referee, judge, line judge, linesman, touch judge, adjudicator, arbitrator, moderator; informal ref.

**unable** adjective incapable, powerless, impotent, inadequate, incompetent, unqualified, unfit.

**unanimous** adjective 1 *doctors were unanimous about the effects:* in agreement, of one mind, in accord, united, undivided. 2 *a unanimous vote:* uniform, consistent, united.
OPPOSITES split.

**unarmed** adjective defenceless, unprotected, unguarded.
OPPOSITES armed.

**unaware** adjective ignorant, oblivious, unconscious, unwitting, unsuspecting, uninformed, unenlightened, innocent; informal in the dark.
OPPOSITES aware.

**unbelievable** adjective incredible, inconceivable, unthinkable, unimaginable, unconvincing, far-fetched, implausible, improbable; informal hard to swallow.
OPPOSITES believable.

**unborn** adjective expected, embryonic, fetal, in utero.

**unbroken** adjective 1 *the last unbroken window:* undamaged, unharmed, unscathed, untouched, sound, intact, whole. 2 *an unbroken chain of victories:* uninterrupted, continuous, endless, constant, unremitting, ongoing. 3 *his record is still unbroken:* unbeaten, undefeated, unsurpassed, unrivalled, unmatched, supreme.

**uncanny** adjective 1 *the silence was uncanny:* eerie, unnatural, unearthly, other-worldly, ghostly, strange, abnormal,
weird; informal creepy, spooky. 2 *an uncanny resemblance:* striking, remarkable, extraordinary, exceptional, incredible.

**uncertain** adjective 1 *the effects are uncertain:* unknown, debatable, open to question, in doubt, unsure, in the balance, up in the air, unpredictable, unforeseeable; informal iffy. 2 *Ed was uncertain about the decision:* unsure, doubtful, dubious, undecided, irresolute, hesitant, vacillating, vague, unclear, ambivalent, in two minds.
OPPOSITES certain, predictable, sure.

**unclear** adjective uncertain, unsure, unsettled, up in the air, in doubt, ambiguous, equivocal, indefinite, vague, mysterious, obscure, hazy, nebulous.
OPPOSITES clear, evident.

**uncomfortable** adjective 1 *an uncomfortable chair:* painful, awkward, lumpy, confining, cramped. 2 *I felt uncomfortable in her presence:* uneasy, awkward, nervous, tense, edgy, restless, embarrassed, anxious; informal rattled, twitchy.
OPPOSITES comfortable, relaxed.

**uncommon** adjective unusual, abnormal, rare, atypical, exceptional, unconventional, unfamiliar, strange, extraordinary, peculiar, scarce, few and far between, isolated, infrequent.
OPPOSITES common.

**unconditional** adjective unquestioning, unqualified, unreserved, unlimited, unrestricted, wholehearted, complete, total, entire, full, absolute, unequivocal.

**unconscious** adjective 1 *she*

a
b
c
d
e
f
g
h
i
j
k
l
m
n
o
p
q
r
s
t
u
v
w
x
y
z

a
b
c
d
e
f
g
h
i
j
k
l
m
n
o
p
q
r
s
t
**u**
v
w
x
y
z

*made sure he was unconscious:* knocked out, senseless, comatose, inert; informal out cold, out for the count. **2** *an unconscious desire:* subconscious, instinctive, involuntary, uncontrolled, subliminal; informal gut. **3** *blissfully unconscious of these problems:* unaware of, oblivious to, insensible to, impervious to, unaffected by.
OPPOSITES conscious, voluntary, aware.

**uncouth** adjective uncivilized, uncultured, rough, coarse, crude, loutish, boorish, rude, discourteous, disrespectful, bad-mannered, ill-bred.
OPPOSITES civilized.

**uncover** verb **1** *she uncovered the sandwiches:* expose, reveal, lay bare, bare, unwrap, unveil, strip. **2** *they uncovered a plot:* discover, detect, come across, stumble on, chance on, find, turn up, unearth, dig up.

**under** preposition **1** *they hid under a bush:* below, beneath, underneath. **2** *the rent is under £250:* less than, lower than, below. **3** *branch managers are under the retail director:* subordinate to, answerable to, responsible to, subject to, junior to, inferior to.
OPPOSITES above, over.

**undercover** adjective secret, covert, clandestine, underground, surreptitious, furtive, cloak-and-dagger, stealthy; informal hush-hush.
OPPOSITES overt.

**underestimate** verb underrate, undervalue, miscalculate, misjudge, do an injustice to.
OPPOSITES overestimate.

**undergo** verb experience, go

through, submit to, face, be subjected to, receive, endure, brave, bear, withstand, weather.

**underground** adjective **1** *an underground car park:* subterranean, buried, sunken, basement. **2** *underground organizations:* secret, clandestine, surreptitious, covert, undercover, closet, cloak-and-dagger, resistance, subversive.
noun **1** *he took the underground:* metro; N. Amer. subway; Brit. informal tube. **2** *information from the French underground:* resistance, partisans, guerrillas, freedom fighters.

**underline** verb **1** *she underlined a phrase:* underscore, mark, pick out, emphasize, highlight. **2** *the programme underlines the benefits of exercise:* emphasize, stress, highlight, accentuate, accent, focus on, spotlight.

**underlying** adjective fundamental, basic, primary, central, essential, principal, elementary, initial.

**undermine** verb weaken, diminish, reduce, impair, mar, spoil, ruin, damage, sap, shake, threaten, subvert, compromise, sabotage.
OPPOSITES strengthen, support.

**understand** verb **1** *he couldn't understand anything we said:* comprehend, grasp, take in, see, apprehend, follow, make sense of, fathom; informal work out, figure out, make head or tail of, get; Brit. informal twig, suss. **2** *she understood how hard he'd worked:* know, realize, recognize, acknowledge, appreciate, be aware of, be conscious of. **3** *I understand that you wish to go:* believe, gather, take it, hear (tell), notice, see, learn.

**understandable** adjective
**1** *make it understandable to the layman:* comprehensible, intelligible, clear, plain, unambiguous, transparent, straightforward, explicit, coherent. **2** *an understandable desire:* unsurprising, expected, predictable, inevitable, reasonable, acceptable, logical, rational, normal, natural, justifiable, excusable, pardonable, forgivable.
OPPOSITES incomprehensible, surprising, illogical, abnormal, unforgivable.

**understanding** noun **1** *test your understanding of the language:* comprehension, grasp, mastery, appreciation, knowledge, awareness, skill, expertise, proficiency; informal know-how. **2** *a young man of brilliant understanding:* intellect, intelligence, brainpower, judgement, insight, intuition, acumen, sagacity, wisdom; informal nous. **3** *it was my understanding that this was free:* belief, perception, view, conviction, feeling, opinion, intuition, impression. **4** *he treated me with understanding:* sympathy, compassion, pity, feeling, concern, consideration, kindness, sensitivity, decency, goodwill. **5** *we had a tacit understanding:* agreement, arrangement, deal, bargain, settlement, pledge, pact.
OPPOSITES ignorance, indifference.
adjective *an understanding friend:* sympathetic, compassionate, sensitive, considerate, kind, thoughtful, tolerant, patient, forbearing, lenient, forgiving.

**understate** verb play down, underrate, underplay, trivialize, minimize, diminish, downgrade, brush aside, gloss over.
OPPOSITES exaggerate.

**undertake** verb **1** *we undertook a survey of the site:* set about, embark on, go about, engage in, take on, be responsible for, get down to, get to grips with, tackle, attempt; informal have a go at. **2** *the Minister undertook to attend:* promise, pledge, vow, give one's word, swear, guarantee, contract, give an assurance, commit oneself.

**undertaker** noun funeral director; N. Amer. mortician.

**undertaking** noun **1** *a risky undertaking:* enterprise, venture, project, campaign, scheme, plan, operation, endeavour, effort, task. **2** *sign this undertaking to comply with the rules:* promise, pledge, agreement, oath, covenant, vow, commitment, guarantee, assurance.

**underwater** adjective submerged, sunken, undersea, submarine.

**underwear** noun underclothes, undergarments, underthings, lingerie; informal undies; Brit. informal smalls.

**underwrite** verb sponsor, support, back, insure, indemnify, subsidize, pay for, finance, fund; N. Amer. informal bankroll.

**undesirable** adjective unpleasant, disagreeable, nasty, unwelcome, unwanted, unfortunate.
OPPOSITES pleasant.

**undo** verb **1** *he undid his shirt:* unfasten, unbutton, unhook, untie, unlace, unlock, unbolt,

a
b
c
d
e
f
g
h
i
j
k
l
m
n
o
p
q
r
s
t
u
v
w
x
y
z

loosen, detach, free, open.
**2** *they will undo a decision by the lords:* cancel, reverse, overrule, overturn, repeal, rescind, countermand, revoke, annul, invalidate, negate. **3** *she undid much of the good work:* ruin, undermine, overturn, scotch, sabotage, spoil, impair, mar, destroy, wreck; informal blow; Brit. informal scupper.
OPPOSITES fasten, ratify, enhance.

**undoubtedly** adverb doubtless, indubitably, unquestionably, indisputably, undeniably, incontrovertibly, without (a) doubt, clearly.

**unearth** verb **1** *workmen unearthed an artillery shell:* dig up, excavate, exhume, disinter, root out. **2** *I unearthed an interesting fact:* discover, uncover, find, come across, hit on, bring to light, expose, turn up.

**uneasy** adjective **1** *the doctor made him feel uneasy:* worried, anxious, troubled, disturbed, nervous, nervy, tense, edgy, apprehensive, fearful, uncomfortable, unsettled; informal jittery. **2** *an uneasy peace:* tense, awkward, strained, fraught, precarious, unstable, insecure.
OPPOSITES calm, stable.

**unemployed** adjective jobless, out of work, unwaged, redundant, laid off, on benefit; Brit. signing on; N. Amer. on welfare; Brit. informal on the dole, resting.

**uneven** adjective **1** *uneven ground:* bumpy, rough, lumpy, stony, rocky, rutted. **2** *uneven teeth:* irregular, crooked, lopsided, askew, asymmetrical. **3** *uneven quality:* inconsistent,

variable, fluctuating, irregular, erratic, patchy.
OPPOSITES flat, regular.

**unfair** adjective **1** *the trial was unfair:* unjust, prejudiced, biased, discriminatory, one-sided, unequal, uneven, unbalanced, partisan. **2** *his comments were unfair:* undeserved, unmerited, unreasonable, unjustified; Brit. informal out of order. **3** *unfair play:* unsporting, dirty, underhand, dishonourable, dishonest.
OPPOSITES fair, just, justified.

**unfasten** verb undo, open, disconnect, remove, untie, unbutton, unzip, loosen, free, unlock, unbolt.

**unfit** adjective **1** *the film is unfit for children:* unsuitable, inappropriate, not designed. **2** *unfit for duty:* incapable of, not up to, not equal to, unequipped, inadequate; informal not cut out for. **3** *I am unfit:* unhealthy, out of condition/ shape.
OPPOSITES fit, suitable, capable, healthy.

**unfold** verb **1** *May unfolded the map:* open out, spread out, flatten, straighten out, unroll. **2** *I watched the events unfold:* develop, evolve, happen, take place, occur.
OPPOSITES fold up.

**unfortunate** adjective **1** *unfortunate people:* unlucky, hapless, wretched, forlorn, poor, pitiful; informal down on one's luck. **2** *an unfortunate start to our holiday:* unwelcome, disadvantageous, unfavourable, unlucky, adverse, unpromising, inauspicious. **3** *an unfortunate remark:* regrettable, inappropriate,

unsuitable, tactless, injudicious.
OPPOSITES fortunate, lucky,
auspicious, well-chosen.

**ungainly** adjective awkward,
clumsy, graceless, inelegant,
gawky, gauche, uncoordinated.
OPPOSITES graceful.

**unhappy** adjective 1 *why are
you looking so unhappy?* sad,
miserable, sorrowful, dejected,
despondent, disconsolate,
morose, heartbroken, down,
dispirited, downhearted,
depressed, melancholy,
mournful, gloomy, glum; informal
down in the mouth, fed up,
blue. 2 *I was unhappy with the
service:* dissatisfied, displeased,
discontented, disappointed,
disgruntled. 3 *an unhappy
coincidence:* unfortunate,
unlucky, ill-starred, ill-fated,
doomed; informal jinxed.
OPPOSITES happy, pleased,
cheerful, lucky.

**unhealthy** adjective 1 *an
unhealthy lifestyle:* harmful,
detrimental, destructive,
injurious, damaging, noxious,
poisonous. 2 *he's pretty
unhealthy:* sick, poorly, ill,
unwell, unfit, ailing, weak,
frail, infirm, washed out, run
down. 3 *an unhealthy obsession:*
abnormal, morbid, macabre,
twisted, unwholesome, warped,
depraved, unnatural; informal
sick.

**uniform** adjective 1 *a uniform
temperature:* constant,
consistent, steady, invariable,
unchanging, stable, static,
regular, fixed, even. 2 *pieces of
uniform size:* identical,
matching, similar, equal, same,
like, consistent.
OPPOSITES variable.
noun *a soldier in uniform:*
costume, outfit, suit, ensemble,

livery, regalia; informal get-up,
rig, gear.

**unify** verb unite, combine, bring
together, join, merge, fuse,
amalgamate, coalesce,
consolidate.
OPPOSITES separate.

**uninteresting** adjective boring,
dull, unexciting, tiresome,
tedious, dreary, lifeless,
humdrum, colourless, bland,
insipid, banal, dry.
OPPOSITES interesting, exciting.

**union** noun 1 *the union of art
and nature:* unification,
joining, merger, fusion,
amalgamation, coalition,
combination, synthesis, blend.
2 *a trade union:* association,
league, guild, confederation,
federation.
OPPOSITES separation, parting.

**unique** adjective 1 *each town has
its unique quality:* distinctive,
individual, special, particular,
specific, idiosyncratic, single,
sole, lone, unrepeated, solitary,
exclusive; informal one-off. 2 *a
unique insight into history:*
remarkable, special, notable,
unequalled, unparalleled,
unmatched, unsurpassed,
incomparable.
OPPOSITES common.

**unit** noun 1 *the family is the
fundamental unit of society:*
component, element,
constituent, subdivision. 2 *a
unit of currency:* quantity,
measure, denomination. 3 *a
guerrilla unit:* group,
detachment, contingent,
division, cell, faction,
department, office, branch.

**unite** verb 1 *uniting the nation:*
unify, join, link, connect,
combine, amalgamate, fuse,
weld, bond, bring together.
2 *environmentalists and*

*activists united:* join together, join forces, combine, band together, ally, cooperate, collaborate, work together, team up. **3** *he sought to unite comfort with elegance:* merge, mix, blend, mingle, combine. OPPOSITES divide.

**unity** noun **1** *European unity:* union, unification, integration, amalgamation, coalition, federation, confederation. **2** *unity between opposing factions:* harmony, accord, cooperation, collaboration, agreement, consensus, solidarity. **3** *the organic unity of the universe:* oneness, singleness, wholeness, uniformity, homogeneity. OPPOSITES division, discord.

**universal** adjective general, common, widespread, ubiquitous, comprehensive, global, worldwide, international.

**universally** adverb always, without exception, by everyone, in all cases, everywhere, worldwide, globally, internationally, commonly, generally.

**universe** noun cosmos, macrocosm, space, infinity, nature, all existence.

**unkind** adjective **1** *everyone was being unkind to him:* unpleasant, disagreeable, nasty, mean, cruel, vicious, spiteful, malicious, callous, unsympathetic; informal bitchy. **2** *unkind weather:* inclement, intemperate, rough, severe, filthy.

**unknown** adjective **1** *the outcome was unknown:* undisclosed, unrevealed, secret, undetermined, undecided. **2** *unknown country:* unexplored, uncharted, unmapped, undiscovered. **3** *persons unknown:* unidentified, unnamed, anonymous. **4** *firearms were unknown to the Indians:* unfamiliar, unheard of, new, novel, strange. **5** *unknown artists:* obscure, unheard of, unsung, minor, undistinguished. OPPOSITES known, familiar.

**unlike** preposition **1** *England is totally unlike Jamaica:* different from, dissimilar to. **2** *unlike Lyn, Chris was a bit of a radical:* in contrast to, as opposed to. OPPOSITES similar to.

**unlikely** adjective improbable, doubtful, dubious, questionable, unconvincing, implausible, far-fetched, unrealistic, incredible, unbelievable, inconceivable. OPPOSITES probable, believable.

**unload** verb **1** *we unloaded the van:* unpack, empty. **2** *they unloaded the cases from the lorry:* remove, offload, discharge, dump. OPPOSITES load.

**unlucky** adjective **1** *the unlucky victim:* unfortunate, hapless, ill-fated. **2** *an unlucky number:* unfavourable, inauspicious, unpropitious, ominous, jinxed. OPPOSITES fortunate, favourable.

**unnatural** adjective **1** *the life of a battery hen is completely unnatural:* abnormal, unusual, uncommon, extraordinary, strange, unorthodox, exceptional, irregular, untypical. **2** *an unnatural colour:* artificial, man-made, synthetic, manufactured. **3** *her voice sounded unnatural:* affected, artificial, stilted,

forced, false, fake, insincere; informal put on, phoney.
OPPOSITES normal, genuine.

**unnecessary** adjective
unneeded, inessential, not required, uncalled for, unwarranted, dispensable, optional, extraneous, expendable, redundant.
OPPOSITES necessary.

**unpleasant** adjective 1 *a very unpleasant situation:* disagreeable, irksome, distressing, nasty, horrible, terrible, awful, dreadful, invidious, objectionable. 2 *an unpleasant man:* unlikeable, unlovable, disagreeable, unfriendly, rude, impolite, obnoxious, nasty, spiteful, mean, insufferable, objectionable, unbearable, annoying, irritating. 3 *an unpleasant taste:* unappetizing, unpalatable, unsavoury, unappealing, disgusting, revolting, nauseating, sickening.
OPPOSITES agreeable, likeable.

**unpopular** adjective disliked, friendless, unloved, unwelcome, avoided, ignored, rejected, shunned, out of favour.

**unravel** verb 1 *he unravelled the strands:* untangle, disentangle, separate out, unwind, untwist. 2 *detectives are trying to unravel the mystery:* solve, resolve, clear up, puzzle out, get to the bottom of, explain, clarify; informal figure out.
OPPOSITES entangle.

**unreal** adjective imaginary, fictitious, pretend, make-believe, made-up, dreamed-up, mock, false, illusory, mythical, fanciful, hypothetical, theoretical; informal phoney.

**unrest** noun disturbance, trouble, turmoil, disruption, disorder, chaos, anarchy, dissatisfaction, dissent, strife, agitation, protest, rebellion, uprising, rioting.
OPPOSITES peace, contentment.

**unsafe** adjective 1 *the building was unsafe:* dangerous, risky, hazardous, high-risk, treacherous, insecure, unsound, harmful, injurious, toxic. 2 *the verdict was unsafe:* unreliable, insecure, unsound, questionable, doubtful, dubious, suspect; informal iffy; Brit. informal dodgy.
OPPOSITES safe, harmless, secure.

**unsatisfactory** adjective disappointing, displeasing, inadequate, unacceptable, poor, bad, substandard, weak, mediocre, not up to par, defective, deficient; informal leaving a lot to be desired.

**unscrupulous** adjective dishonest, deceitful, devious, underhand, unethical, immoral, shameless, exploitative, corrupt, unprincipled, dishonourable, disreputable; informal crooked, shady.

**unsettle** verb disturb, disconcert, unnerve, upset, disquiet, perturb, alarm, dismay, trouble, bother, agitate, fluster, ruffle, shake (up), throw; informal rattle, faze.

**unsightly** adjective unattractive, ugly, unprepossessing, hideous, horrible, repulsive, revolting, offensive, grotesque.
OPPOSITES attractive.

**unsociable** adjective unfriendly, uncongenial, unneighbourly, unapproachable, introverted,

OPPOSITES real.

a
b
c
d
e
f
g
h
i
j
k
l
m
n
o
p
q
r
s
t
**u**
v
w
x
y
z

reserved, withdrawn, retiring, aloof, distant, remote, detached; informal stand-offish. OPPOSITES sociable, friendly.

**unstable** adjective **1** *icebergs are notoriously unstable:* unsteady, rocky, wobbly, rickety, shaky, unsafe, insecure, precarious. **2** *unstable coffee prices:* changeable, volatile, variable, fluctuating, irregular, unpredictable, erratic. **3** *he was mentally unstable:* unbalanced, of unsound mind, mentally ill, deranged, demented, disturbed, unhinged. OPPOSITES stable, steady, firm.

**unsuccessful** adjective **1** *an unsuccessful attempt:* failed, abortive, ineffective, fruitless, profitless, unproductive, vain, futile. **2** *an unsuccessful business:* unprofitable, loss-making. **3** *an unsuccessful candidate:* failed, losing, beaten, unlucky.

**unsuitable** adjective **1** *an unsuitable product:* inappropriate, ill-suited, inapposite, unacceptable, unfitting, incompatible, out of place, out of keeping. **2** *an unsuitable moment:* inopportune, badly timed, unfortunate, difficult, infelicitous. OPPOSITES appropriate, opportune.

**unsure** adjective **1** *she felt very unsure:* unconfident, unassertive, insecure, hesitant, diffident, anxious, apprehensive. **2** *Sally was unsure what to do:* undecided, uncertain, irresolute, dithering, in two minds, in a quandary. **3** *some teachers are unsure about the proposed strike:* dubious, doubtful, sceptical,

uncertain, unconvinced. OPPOSITES confident.

**untangle** verb disentangle, unravel, unsnarl, straighten out, untwist, unknot, sort out. OPPOSITES tangle.

**unthinkable** adjective unimaginable, inconceivable, unbelievable, incredible, implausible, out of the question, impossible, unconscionable, unreasonable.

**untidy** adjective **1** *untidy hair:* scruffy, tousled, dishevelled, unkempt, messy, rumpled, bedraggled, uncombed, tangled, matted. **2** *the room was untidy:* disordered, messy, disorganized, cluttered, in chaos, haywire, in disarray; informal higgledy-piggledy. OPPOSITES tidy, neat, orderly.

**untoward** adjective unexpected, unforeseen, surprising, unusual, inappropriate, inconvenient, unwelcome, unfavourable, adverse, unfortunate, infelicitous.

**untrue** adjective false, invented, made up, fabricated, concocted, trumped up, erroneous, wrong, incorrect, inaccurate. OPPOSITES true, correct.

**unusual** adjective **1** *an unusual sight:* uncommon, abnormal, atypical, unexpected, surprising, unfamiliar, different, strange, odd, curious, extraordinary, unorthodox, unconventional, peculiar; informal weird, offbeat. **2** *a man of unusual talent:* remarkable, extraordinary, exceptional, particular, outstanding, notable, noteworthy, distinctive, striking, significant, special, unique, unparalleled, prodigious. OPPOSITES common.

**unwarranted** adjective **1** *the criticism is unwarranted:* unjustified, indefensible, inexcusable, unforgivable, unpardonable, uncalled for, unnecessary, unjust, groundless. **2** *an unwarranted invasion of privacy:* unauthorized, unsanctioned, unapproved, uncertified, unlicensed, illegal, unlawful, illicit, illegitimate, criminal, actionable.
OPPOSITES justified.

**unwieldy** adjective awkward, unmanageable, unmanoeuvrable, cumbersome, clumsy, massive, heavy, hefty, bulky.

**unwilling** adjective **1** *unwilling conscripts:* reluctant, unenthusiastic, hesitant, resistant, grudging, involuntary, forced. **2** *he was unwilling to take on responsibility:* disinclined, reluctant, averse, loath; (**be unwilling to do something**) baulk at, demur at, shy away from, flinch from, shrink from, not have the heart to, have qualms about, have misgivings about, have reservations about.
OPPOSITES willing, keen.

**upbeat** adjective (informal) cheerful, optimistic, cheery, positive, confident, hopeful, bullish, buoyant.
OPPOSITES pessimistic, negative.

**upbringing** noun childhood, early life, formative years, teaching, instruction, rearing.

**update** verb **1** *security measures are continually updated:* modernize, upgrade, improve, overhaul. **2** *I'll update him on developments:* brief, bring up to date, inform, fill in, tell, notify, keep posted; informal clue in, put in the picture, bring/keep up to speed.

**upgrade** verb improve, modernize, update, reform.
OPPOSITES downgrade.

**upheaval** noun disturbance, disruption, trouble, turbulence, disorder, confusion, turmoil.

**uphill** adjective **1** *an uphill path:* upward, rising, ascending, climbing. **2** *an uphill job:* difficult, hard, tough, demanding, arduous, taxing, exacting, stiff, gruelling, onerous.
OPPOSITES downhill.

**uphold** verb **1** *the court upheld his claim:* confirm, endorse, sustain, approve, support, back (up). **2** *they've a tradition to uphold:* maintain, sustain, continue, preserve, protect, keep, hold to, keep alive, keep going.
OPPOSITES overturn, oppose.

**upkeep** noun **1** *the upkeep of the road:* maintenance, repair(s), servicing, care, preservation, conservation, running. **2** *the child's upkeep:* (financial) support, maintenance, keep, subsistence, care.

**uplifting** adjective inspiring, stirring, inspirational, rousing, moving, touching, affecting, cheering, heartening, encouraging.

**upper** adjective **1** *the upper floor:* higher, superior, top. **2** *the upper echelons of the party:* senior, superior, higher-level, higher-ranking, top.
OPPOSITES lower.

**upper-class** adjective aristocratic, noble, patrician, titled, blue-blooded, high-born, elite; Brit. county; informal upper-crust, top-drawer; Brit. informal posh.

a
b
c
d
e
f
g
h
i
j
k
l
m
n
o
p
q
r
s
t
**u**
v
w
x
y
z

a
b
c
d
e
f
g
h
i
j
k
l
m
n
o
p
q
r
s
t
**u**
v
w
x
y
z

**upright** adjective **1** *an upright position:* vertical, perpendicular, plumb, straight (up), erect, on end, on one's feet. **2** *an upright member of the community:* honest, honourable, upstanding, respectable, high-minded, law-abiding, worthy, righteous, decent, good, virtuous, principled.
OPPOSITES flat, horizontal, dishonourable.

**uprising** noun rebellion, revolt, insurrection, mutiny, revolution, insurgence, rioting, coup.

**uproar** noun **1** *the uproar in the kitchen continued:* commotion, disturbance, rumpus, disorder, confusion, chaos, tumult, mayhem, pandemonium, bedlam, noise, din, clamour, hubbub, racket; informal hullabaloo; Brit. informal row.
**2** *there was an uproar when he was dismissed:* outcry, furore, fuss, commotion, hue and cry, rumpus; informal hullabaloo, stink, ructions; Brit. informal row.
OPPOSITES calm.

**upset** verb **1** *the accusation upset her:* distress, trouble, perturb, dismay, sadden, grieve, disturb, unsettle, disconcert, disquiet, worry, bother, agitate, fluster, throw, ruffle, unnerve, shake. **2** *he upset the soup:* knock over, overturn, upend, tip over, topple, spill. **3** *the dam will upset the ecological balance:* disrupt, interfere with, disturb, throw into confusion, mess up.
OPPOSITES calm, reassure.
noun **1** *a legal dispute will cause upset:* distress, trouble, dismay, disquiet, worry, bother, agitation, hurt, grief. **2** *a*

*stomach upset:* disorder, complaint, ailment, illness, sickness; informal bug; Brit. informal lurgy.
OPPOSITES reassurance.
adjective **1** *I was upset by the news:* distressed, troubled, perturbed, dismayed, disturbed, unsettled, disconcerted, worried, bothered, anxious, agitated, flustered, ruffled, unnerved, shaken, saddened, grieved; informal cut up, choked; Brit. informal gutted. **2** *an upset stomach:* disturbed, unsettled, queasy, bad, poorly; informal gippy.
OPPOSITES unperturbed, calm.

**upside down** adjective **1** *an upside-down canoe:* upturned, upended, wrong side up, overturned, inverted, capsized. **2** *they left the flat upside down:* in disarray, in disorder, jumbled up, in a muddle, untidy, disorganized, in chaos, in confusion; informal higgledy-piggledy.

**up to date** adjective **1** *up-to-date equipment:* modern, contemporary, the latest, state-of-the-art, new, up-to-the-minute, advanced. **2** *the newsletter will keep you up to date:* informed, up to speed, in the picture, in touch, au fait, conversant, familiar, knowledgeable, acquainted.
OPPOSITES out of date, old-fashioned.

**urban** adjective town, city, municipal, metropolitan, built-up, inner-city, suburban.
OPPOSITES rural.

**urge** verb **1** *she urged him to try:* encourage, exhort, press, entreat, implore, call on, appeal to, beg, plead with. **2** *I urge caution in interpreting these*

*results:* advise, counsel, advocate, recommend.
**noun** *his urge to travel:* desire, wish, need, compulsion, longing, yearning, hankering, craving, hunger, thirst; informal yen, itch.

**urgent adjective** pressing, acute, dire, desperate, critical, serious, grave, intense, crying, burning, compelling, extreme, high-priority, life-and-death.

**usage noun 1** *energy usage:* consumption, use. **2** *the usage of equipment:* use, utilization, operation, manipulation, running, handling. **3** *English usage:* language, expression, phraseology, parlance, idiom.

**use verb 1** *she used her key to open the door:* utilize, employ, avail oneself of, work, operate, wield, ply, apply, put into service. **2** *the court will use its discretion:* exercise, employ, bring into play, practise, apply. **3** *she was using me:* take advantage of, exploit, manipulate, take liberties with, impose on, abuse, capitalize on, profit from, trade on, milk; informal cash in on, walk all over. **4** *we have used up our funds:* consume, get/go through, exhaust, deplete, expend, spend.
**noun 1** *the use of such weapons:* utilization, application, employment, operation, manipulation. **2** *his use of other people for his own ends:* exploitation, manipulation, abuse. **3** *what is the use of that?* advantage, benefit, good, point, object, purpose, sense, reason, service, utility, help, gain, avail, profit, value, worth.

**used adjective** *a used car:* second-hand, pre-owned,

nearly new, old, worn, hand-me-down, cast-off.
OPPOSITES new.
■ **used to** accustomed to, no stranger to, familiar with, at home with, in the habit of, experienced in, versed in, conversant with, acquainted with.

**useful adjective 1** *a useful tool:* functional, practical, handy, convenient, utilitarian, serviceable, of service; informal nifty. **2** *a useful experience:* beneficial, advantageous, helpful, worthwhile, profitable, rewarding, productive, constructive, valuable, fruitful.
OPPOSITES useless, disadvantageous.

**useless adjective 1** *it was useless to try:* futile, pointless, to no avail, vain, to no purpose, unavailing, hopeless, ineffectual, fruitless, unprofitable, unproductive. **2** (informal) *he was useless at his job:* incompetent, inept, ineffective, incapable, inadequate, hopeless, bad; informal a dead loss.
OPPOSITES useful, beneficial, competent.

**usher verb** *she ushered him to a seat:* escort, accompany, take, show, see, lead, conduct, guide.
**noun** *ushers showed them to their seats:* guide, attendant, escort.

**usual adjective** normal, customary, accustomed, wonted, habitual, routine, regular, standard, typical, established, set, stock, conventional, traditional, expected, familiar.
OPPOSITES unusual, exceptional.

**usually adverb** normally,

generally, habitually, customarily, routinely, typically, ordinarily, commonly, as a rule, in general, more often than not, mainly, mostly.

**utensil** noun implement, tool, instrument, device, apparatus, gadget, appliance, contrivance, contraption; informal gizmo.

**utility** noun usefulness, use, benefit, value, advantage, help, practicality, effectiveness, service.

**utilize** verb use, employ, avail oneself of, press into service,

bring into play, deploy, draw on, exploit.

**utmost** adjective greatest, highest, maximum, most, extreme, supreme, paramount.

**utter**[1] adjective *that's utter nonsense:* complete, total, absolute, thorough, perfect, downright, out-and-out, outright, sheer, arrant, positive, prize, pure, unmitigated.

**utter**[2] verb say, speak, voice, mouth, express, articulate, pronounce, enunciate, emit, let out, give, produce.

# Vv

**vacancy** noun opening, position, post, job, opportunity.

**vacant** adjective 1 *a vacant house:* empty, unoccupied, not in use, free, unfilled, uninhabited, untenanted. 2 *a vacant look:* blank, expressionless, unresponsive, emotionless, impassive, vacuous, empty, glazed.
OPPOSITES full, occupied, expressive.

**vacate** verb 1 *he was forced to vacate the premises:* leave, move out of, evacuate, quit, depart from. 2 *he will be vacating his post next year:* resign from, leave, stand down from, give up, bow out of, relinquish, retire from; informal quit.
OPPOSITES occupy, take up.

**vacation** noun holiday, trip, tour, break, leave, time off, recess.

**vagrant** noun tramp, drifter, down-and-out, beggar,

itinerant, wanderer, nomad, traveller; N. Amer. hobo; N. Amer. informal bum.

**vague** adjective 1 *a vague shape:* indistinct, indefinite, indeterminate, unclear, ill-defined, hazy, fuzzy, misty, blurry, out of focus, shadowy, obscure. 2 *a vague description:* imprecise, rough, approximate, inexact, non-specific, ambiguous, hazy, uncertain. 3 *she was so vague in life:* absent-minded, forgetful, dreamy, abstracted; informal scatty, not with it.
OPPOSITES clear, precise, certain, sharp.

**vain** adjective 1 *their flattery made him vain:* conceited, proud, arrogant, boastful, cocky, immodest; informal big-headed. 2 *a vain attempt:* futile, useless, pointless, ineffective, fruitless, unproductive, unsuccessful, failed, abortive.
OPPOSITES modest, successful.

■ **in vain** unsuccessfully, to no avail, to no purpose, fruitlessly.

**valid** adjective **1** *a valid criticism:* well founded, sound, reasonable, rational, logical, justifiable, defensible, cogent, credible, forceful. **2** *a valid contract:* legally binding, lawful, official, in force, in effect.
OPPOSITES invalid.

**valley** noun dale, vale, hollow, gully, gorge, ravine, canyon, rift; Brit. combe; Scottish glen.

**valuable** adjective **1** *a valuable watch:* precious, costly, high-priced, expensive, dear, priceless. **2** *a valuable contribution:* useful, helpful, beneficial, invaluable, productive, worthwhile, worthy, important.
OPPOSITES cheap, worthless, useless.

**valuables** plural noun precious items, costly items, prized possessions, treasures.

**value** noun **1** *houses exceeding £250,000 in value:* price, cost, worth, market price. **2** *the value of adequate preparation:* worth, usefulness, advantage, benefit, gain, profit, good, help. **3** (**values**) principles, ethics, morals, standards, code of behaviour.
verb **1** *his estate was valued at £45,000:* evaluate, assess, estimate, appraise, price. **2** *she valued his opinion:* think highly of, have a high opinion of, rate highly, esteem, set great store by, respect.
OPPOSITES despise.

**vanish** verb **1** *he vanished into the darkness:* disappear, be lost to sight, become invisible, recede from view. **2** *all hope vanished:* fade (away), evaporate, melt away, end, cease to exist, pass away, die out.
OPPOSITES appear, materialize.

**vanity** noun conceit, self-love, self-admiration, egotism, pride, arrogance, boastfulness, cockiness, swagger; informal big-headedness.
OPPOSITES modesty.

**variable** adjective changeable, shifting, fluctuating, irregular, inconstant, inconsistent, fluid, unstable; informal up and down.
OPPOSITES constant.

**variant** noun *variants of the same idea:* variation, form, alternative, version, adaptation, alteration, modification.
adjective *a variant spelling:* alternative, other, different, divergent.

**variation** noun **1** *regional variations in farming:* difference, dissimilarity, disparity, contrast, discrepancy, imbalance. **2** *opening times are subject to variation:* change, alteration, modification. **3** *there was very little variation from the pattern:* deviation, variance, divergence, departure, fluctuation.

**varied** adjective diverse, assorted, miscellaneous, mixed, sundry, wide-ranging, disparate, motley.
OPPOSITES similar, unchanging.

**variety** noun **1** *the lack of variety in the curriculum:* diversity, variation, diversification, change, difference. **2** *a wide variety of flowers:* assortment, miscellany, range, array, collection, selection, mixture, medley. **3** *fifty varieties of pasta:* sort, kind, type, class, category, style, form, make,

a
b
c
d
e
f
g
h
i
j
k
l
m
n
o
p
q
r
s
t
u
**v**
w
x
y
z

a
b
c
d
e
f
g
h
i
j
k
l
m
n
o
p
q
r
s
t
u
**v**
w
x
y
z

model, brand, strain, breed.
OPPOSITES uniformity.

**various** adjective diverse, different, differing, varied, assorted, mixed, sundry, miscellaneous, disparate, motley.
OPPOSITES similar.

**vary** verb **1** *estimates of the cost vary:* differ, be dissimilar, disagree. **2** *rates of interest vary over time:* fluctuate, rise and fall, go up and down, change, alter, shift, swing. **3** *the diaphragm is used for varying the aperture:* modify, change, alter, adjust, regulate, control, set.

**vast** adjective huge, extensive, broad, wide, boundless, enormous, immense, great, massive, colossal, gigantic, mammoth, giant, mountainous; informal mega, whopping; Brit. informal ginormous.
OPPOSITES tiny.

**vault**[1] noun **1** *the vault under the church:* cellar, basement, crypt, undercroft, catacomb, burial chamber. **2** *valuables stored in the vault:* strongroom, safe deposit.

**vault**[2] verb *he vaulted over the gate:* jump, leap, spring, bound, clear.

**veer** verb turn, swerve, swing, weave, wheel, change direction, change course, deviate.

**vehicle** noun **1** *a stolen vehicle:* means of transport, conveyance. **2** *a vehicle for the communication of ideas:* channel, medium, means, agent, instrument, mechanism, organ, apparatus.

**veil** noun *a thin veil of cloud:* covering, screen, curtain, mantle, cloak, mask, blanket, shroud, canopy, cloud, pall.

verb *the peak was veiled in mist:* cover, surround, swathe, enfold, envelop, conceal, hide, obscure, screen, shield, cloak, blanket, shroud.

**vein** noun **1** *veins of quartz:* layer, seam, lode, stratum, deposit. **2** *he closes his article in a humorous vein:* mood, humour, attitude, tone, spirit, character, feel, flavour, quality, atmosphere, manner, way, style.

**velocity** noun speed, pace, rate, tempo, rapidity.

**vengeance** noun revenge, retribution, retaliation, requital, reprisal, an eye for an eye.
OPPOSITES forgiveness.

**venomous** adjective poisonous, toxic, dangerous, deadly, lethal, fatal.
OPPOSITES harmless.

**vent** noun *an air vent:* outlet, inlet, opening, aperture, hole, gap, orifice, space, duct, flue, shaft, well, passage, airway.
verb *the crowd vented their fury:* let out, release, pour out, utter, express, air, voice.

**venture** noun *a business venture:* enterprise, undertaking, project, scheme, operation, endeavour, speculation.
verb **1** *we ventured across the moor:* set out, go, travel, journey. **2** *may I venture an opinion?* put forward, advance, proffer, offer, air, suggest, volunteer, submit, propose. **3** *I ventured to invite her:* dare, be so bold as, presume, have the audacity, have the nerve, take the liberty of.

**verbal** adjective oral, spoken, word-of-mouth, stated, said, unwritten.

**verdict** noun judgement,

adjudication, decision, finding, ruling, sentence.

**verge** noun 1 *the verge of the lake:* edge, border, margin, side, brink, rim, lip, fringe, boundary, perimeter. 2 *I was on the verge of tears:* brink, threshold, edge, point.
■ **verge on** approach, border on, be close/near to, resemble, be tantamount to, tend towards, approximate to.

**verify** verb confirm, prove, substantiate, corroborate, back up, bear out, justify, support, uphold, testify to, validate, authenticate.
OPPOSITES refute.

**versatile** adjective 1 *a versatile player:* adaptable, flexible, all-round, multitalented, resourceful. 2 *a versatile device:* adjustable, adaptable, multi-purpose, all-purpose.

**verse** noun 1 *Elizabethan verse:* poetry, lyrics. 2 *a verse he'd composed:* poem, lyric, rhyme, ditty, lay. 3 *a poem with sixty verses:* stanza.
OPPOSITES prose.

**version** noun 1 *his version of events:* account, report, statement, description, record, story, rendering, interpretation, explanation, understanding, reading, impression, side. 2 *the English version will be published next year:* edition, translation, impression. 3 *they have replaced coal-burning fires with gas versions:* type, sort, kind, form, equivalent, variety, variant, design, model, style.

**vertical** adjective upright, erect, perpendicular, plumb, on end, standing.
OPPOSITES flat, horizontal.

**very** adverb *that's very kind of you:* extremely, exceedingly,

exceptionally, extraordinarily, tremendously, immensely, acutely, abundantly, singularly, decidedly, highly, remarkably, really; informal awfully, terribly, majorly, seriously, mega, ultra; Brit. informal ever so, well, dead, jolly; N. Amer. informal real, mighty.
OPPOSITES slightly.
adjective 1 *those were his very words:* exact, actual, precise. 2 *the very thought of food made her feel ill:* mere, simple, pure, sheer.

**vessel** noun 1 *a fishing vessel:* boat, ship, craft. 2 *a cooking vessel:* container, receptacle, basin, bowl, pan, pot, jug.

**vestige** noun remnant, fragment, relic, echo, trace, mark, legacy, reminder.

**vet** verb check up on, screen, investigate, examine, scrutinize, inspect, look over, assess, evaluate, appraise; informal check out.

**veteran** noun *a veteran of many political campaigns:* old hand, past master, doyen, doyenne; informal old-timer; N. Amer. informal vet.
OPPOSITES novice.
adjective *a veteran diplomat:* long-serving, seasoned, old, hardened, practised, experienced; informal battle-scarred.

**veto** noun *parliament's right of veto:* rejection, dismissal, prohibition, proscription, embargo, ban.
OPPOSITES approval.
verb *the president vetoed the bill:* reject, turn down, throw out, dismiss, prohibit, forbid, proscribe, disallow, embargo, ban; informal kill.
OPPOSITES approve.

**viable** adjective feasible,

a
b
c
d
e
f
g
h
i
j
k
l
m
n
o
p
q
r
s
t
u

**v**

w
x
y
z

workable, practicable, practical, realistic, achievable, attainable; informal doable.
OPPOSITES impracticable.

**vibrant** adjective **1** *a vibrant performance:* spirited, lively, energetic, vigorous, storming, dynamic, passionate, fiery; informal feisty. **2** *vibrant colours:* vivid, bright, striking, brilliant, glowing, strong, rich.
OPPOSITES lifeless, pale.

**vibrate** verb shake, tremble, shiver, quiver, shudder, throb, pulsate.

**vice** noun **1** *youngsters may be driven to vice:* immorality, wrongdoing, wickedness, evil, iniquity, villainy, corruption, misconduct, sin, depravity. **2** *smoking is my only vice:* fault, failing, flaw, defect, shortcoming, weakness, deficiency, foible, frailty.
OPPOSITES virtue.

**vicious** adjective **1** *a vicious killer:* brutal, ferocious, savage, violent, ruthless, merciless, heartless, callous, cruel, cold-blooded, inhuman, barbaric, bloodthirsty. **2** *a vicious hate campaign:* malicious, spiteful, vindictive, cruel, bitter, acrimonious, hostile, nasty; informal catty.
OPPOSITES gentle, kindly.

**victim** noun sufferer, injured party, casualty, fatality, loss, survivor.

**victorious** adjective triumphant, conquering, vanquishing, winning, champion, successful.
OPPOSITES unsuccessful, losing.

**victory** noun success, triumph, conquest, win, coup; informal walkover.
OPPOSITES defeat, loss.

**vie** verb compete, contend,

struggle, fight, battle, jockey.

**view** noun **1** *the view from her flat:* outlook, prospect, panorama, vista, scene, scenery, landscape. **2** *we agree with this view:* opinion, viewpoint, belief, judgement, thinking, notion, idea, conviction, persuasion, attitude, feeling, sentiment. **3** *the church came into view:* sight, perspective, vision, visibility.
verb **1** *they viewed the landscape:* look at, observe, eye, gaze at, contemplate, regard, scan, survey, inspect, scrutinize; informal check out; N. Amer. informal eyeball. **2** *the law was viewed as a last resort:* consider, regard, look on, see, perceive, judge, deem, reckon.

**viewer** noun watcher, spectator, onlooker, observer; (**viewers**) audience, crowd.

**vigilant** adjective watchful, observant, attentive, alert, eagle-eyed, on the lookout, on one's guard; informal beady-eyed.
OPPOSITES inattentive.

**vigorous** adjective **1** *the child was vigorous:* robust, healthy, hale and hearty, strong, sturdy, fit, hardy, tough, energetic, lively, active. **2** *a vigorous defence:* strenuous, powerful, forceful, spirited, determined, aggressive, passionate; informal punchy, feisty.
OPPOSITES weak, feeble.

**vigorously** adverb strenuously, strongly, powerfully, forcefully, energetically, heartily, all out, fiercely, hard; informal like mad; Brit. informal like billy-o.

**vigour** noun health, strength, robustness, energy, life, vitality, spirit, passion, determination, dynamism, drive; informal oomph, get-up-and-go.

# vile → virtue

OPPOSITES lethargy.

**vile** adjective foul, nasty, unpleasant, bad, horrid, repulsive, disgusting, hateful, nauseating; informal gross.
OPPOSITES pleasant.

**villain** noun criminal, lawbreaker, offender, felon, miscreant, wrongdoer, rogue, scoundrel, reprobate; informal crook, baddy.

**vindicate** verb 1 *he was vindicated by the jury:* acquit, clear, absolve, exonerate; informal let off. 2 *our concerns were vindicated:* justify, warrant, substantiate, confirm, corroborate, prove, defend, support, back, endorse.
OPPOSITES incriminate.

**vintage** adjective 1 *vintage French wine:* high-quality, quality, choice, select, superior. 2 *vintage motor vehicles:* classic, ageless, timeless, old, antique, heritage, historic.

**violate** verb 1 *this violates human rights:* contravene, breach, infringe, break, transgress, disobey, defy, flout, disregard, ignore. 2 *the tomb was violated:* desecrate, profane, defile, degrade, debase, damage, vandalize, deface, destroy.
OPPOSITES respect.

**violation** noun 1 *a traffic violation:* contravention, breach, infringement, transgression, defiance, flouting, disregard. 2 *the violation of the relics:* desecration, defilement, damage, vandalism, destruction.

**violence** noun 1 *police violence:* brutality, savagery, cruelty, barbarity. 2 *the violence of the blow:* force, power, strength,

might. 3 *the violence of his passion:* intensity, severity, strength, force, vehemence, power, ferocity, fury.

**violent** adjective 1 *a violent alcoholic:* brutal, vicious, savage, rough, aggressive, threatening, fierce, ferocious. 2 *a violent blow:* powerful, forceful, hard, sharp, smart, strong, vigorous, mighty, hefty. 3 *violent jealousy:* intense, extreme, strong, powerful, unbridled, uncontrollable, ungovernable, consuming, passionate.
OPPOSITES gentle, weak, mild.

**virgin** adjective 1 *virgin forest:* untouched, unspoilt, untainted, pristine, spotless, unpolluted, undefiled, perfect, intact, unexplored, uncharted. 2 *virgin girls:* chaste, celibate, abstinent, pure, uncorrupted, undefiled, innocent, immaculate.

**virtual** adjective effective, near (enough), essential, practical, to all intents and purposes, in all but name, implied, unacknowledged.

**virtually** adverb effectively, all but, more or less, practically, almost, nearly, close to, verging on, just about, as good as, essentially, to all intents and purposes.

**virtue** noun 1 *the simple virtue of peasant life:* goodness, righteousness, morality, integrity, dignity, rectitude, honour. 2 *promptness was not one of his virtues:* good point, good quality, strong point, asset, forte, attribute, strength, talent. 3 *I can see no virtue in this:* merit, advantage, benefit, usefulness, strength.
OPPOSITES vice, failing,

a
b
c
d
e
f
g
h
i
j
k
l
m
n
o
p
q
r
s
t
u
**v**
w
x
y
z

disadvantage.

**visible** adjective observable, perceptible, noticeable, detectable, discernible, in sight, in view, on display, evident, apparent, manifest, plain.
OPPOSITES invisible.

**vision** noun 1 *her vision was blurred:* eyesight, sight, observation, eyes, view, perspective. 2 *visions of the ancestral pilgrims:* apparition, spectre, phantom, ghost, wraith, manifestation, hallucination, illusion, mirage; informal spook. 3 *visions of a better future:* dream, reverie, plan, hope, fantasy, delusion. 4 *his speech lacked vision:* imagination, creativity, inventiveness, innovation, inspiration, intuition, perception, insight.

**visit** verb 1 *I visited my uncle:* call on, go to see, look in on, stay with, holiday with, stop by, drop by; informal pop in on, drop in on, look up. 2 *Alex was visiting America:* stay in, stop over in, spend time in, holiday in, vacation in, tour, explore, see; informal do.
noun 1 *she paid a visit to her mum:* (social) call. 2 *a visit to the museum:* trip, tour of, look round, stopover, stay, holiday, break, vacation.

**visitor** noun 1 *I am expecting a visitor:* guest, caller, company. 2 *the monument attracts many visitors:* tourist, traveller, holidaymaker, tripper, vacationer, sightseer, pilgrim, foreigner, stranger.

**vista** noun view, scene, prospect, panorama, sight, scenery, landscape.

**visual** adjective 1 *visual defects:* optical, ocular, eye, vision,

sight. 2 *a visual indication that the alarm works:* visible, observable, perceptible, discernible.
OPPOSITES acoustic.

**visualize** verb envisage, conjure up, picture, call to mind, see, imagine, dream up.

**vital** adjective 1 *it is vital that action is taken:* essential, critical, crucial, indispensable, all-important, imperative, mandatory, high-priority. 2 *he is young and vital:* lively, energetic, active, sprightly, spirited, vivacious, exuberant, dynamic, vigorous; informal full of beans.
OPPOSITES unimportant, listless.

**vitality** noun life, energy, spirit, vivacity, exuberance, dynamism, vigour, passion, drive; informal get-up-and-go.

**vivid** adjective 1 *a vivid blue:* bright, colourful, brilliant, radiant, vibrant, strong, bold, deep, intense, rich, warm. 2 *a vivid account:* graphic, realistic, lifelike, faithful, authentic, striking, evocative, arresting, colourful, dramatic, memorable, powerful, stirring, moving, haunting.
OPPOSITES dull, vague.

**vocal** adjective 1 *vocal sounds:* spoken, said, voiced, uttered, articulated, oral. 2 *a vocal critic:* vociferous, outspoken, forthright, plain-spoken, blunt, frank, candid, passionate, vehement, vigorous.

**vocation** noun calling, life's work, mission, purpose, profession, occupation, career, job, employment, trade, craft, line (of work).

**vogue** noun fashion, trend, fad, fancy, craze, rage, enthusiasm, passion.

**voice** noun **1** *the voice of the people:* opinion, view, feeling, wish, desire, vote. **2** *a powerful voice for conservation:* mouthpiece, representative, spokesperson, agent, vehicle. verb *they voiced their opposition:* express, communicate, declare, state, vent, utter, say, speak, articulate; informal come out with.

**void** noun *the void of space:* vacuum, emptiness, nothingness, blankness, (empty) space, gap, cavity, chasm, gulf.
verb *the contract was voided:* invalidate, annul, nullify, negate, quash, cancel, countermand, repeal, revoke, rescind, retract, withdraw, reverse.
OPPOSITES validate, fill.
adjective **1** *vast void spaces:* empty, vacant, blank, bare, clear, free. **2** *the election was void:* invalid, null, ineffective, worthless.
OPPOSITES full, valid.

**volatile** adjective **1** *a volatile personality:* unpredictable, temperamental, capricious, fickle, impulsive, emotional, excitable, turbulent, erratic, unstable. **2** *the atmosphere is too volatile for an election:* tense, strained, fraught, uneasy, uncomfortable, charged, explosive, inflammatory, turbulent.
OPPOSITES stable, calm.

**volley** noun barrage, cannonade, battery, bombardment, salvo, burst, storm, hail, shower, deluge, torrent.

**volume** noun **1** *a volume from the library:* book, publication, tome, work, title. **2** *a syringe of known volume:* capacity, mass, bulk, extent, size, dimensions. **3** *a huge volume of water:* quantity, amount, mass, bulk, measure. **4** *she turned the volume down:* loudness, sound, amplification.

**voluntarily** adverb of one's own free will, of one's own volition, by choice, by preference, spontaneously, willingly, readily, freely.
OPPOSITES compulsorily.

**voluntary** adjective **1** *attendance is voluntary:* optional, discretionary, elective, non-compulsory. **2** *voluntary work:* unpaid, unsalaried, for free, without charge, for nothing, honorary.
OPPOSITES compulsory, paid.

**volunteer** verb **1** *I volunteered my services:* offer, tender, proffer, put forward, put up, venture. **2** *he volunteered as a driver:* offer one's services, present oneself, make oneself available, come forward.
OPPOSITES withdraw, refuse.

**vomit** verb **1** *he needed to vomit:* be sick, spew, fetch up, heave, retch, gag; informal throw up, puke; N. Amer. informal barf. **2** *I vomited my breakfast:* bring up, regurgitate, spew up; informal throw up, puke up; Brit. informal sick up.
noun *a coat stained with vomit:* sick; informal puke, spew; N. Amer. informal barf.

**vote** noun **1** *a rigged vote:* ballot, poll, election, referendum, plebiscite, show of hands. **2** *in 1918 women got the vote:* suffrage, franchise, voting rights, voice, say.
verb *I vote we have one more game:* suggest, propose,

recommend, advocate, move, submit.

**voucher** noun coupon, token, ticket, pass, chit, slip, stub, docket; Brit. informal chitty.

**vow** noun *a vow of silence:* promise, pledge, oath, bond, covenant, commitment, word (of honour).
verb *I vowed to do better:* promise, pledge, swear, undertake, make a commitment, give one's word, guarantee.

**voyage** noun journey, trip, cruise, passage, sail, crossing, expedition.

**vulgar** adjective 1 *a vulgar joke:* rude, crude, dirty, filthy, smutty, naughty, indecent, obscene, coarse, risqué; informal blue. 2 *the decor was lavish but vulgar:* tasteless, crass, tawdry, ostentatious, flamboyant, showy, gaudy, garish; informal flash, tacky. 3 *it was vulgar for a woman to whistle:* impolite, ill-mannered, boorish, uncouth, unsophisticated, unrefined.
OPPOSITES clean, tasteful, decent.

**vulnerable** adjective 1 *a vulnerable city:* in danger, in peril, in jeopardy, at risk, unprotected, undefended, unguarded, open to attack, exposed. 2 *he is vulnerable to criticism:* exposed, open, liable, prone, prey, susceptible, subject.
OPPOSITES invulnerable, safe.

# Ww

**waddle** verb toddle, totter, wobble, shuffle.

**wade** verb 1 *they waded in the water:* paddle, wallow, splash; informal splosh. 2 *I had to wade through some hefty documents:* plough, plod, trawl, labour, toil.

**wag** verb 1 *the dog's tail wagged:* swing, swish, switch, sway, shake; informal waggle. 2 *he wagged his stick at them:* shake, wave, wiggle, flourish, brandish.

**wage** noun *the workers' wages:* pay, salary, stipend, fee, remuneration, income, earnings.
verb *they waged war on the guerrillas:* engage in, carry on, conduct, execute, pursue, prosecute, proceed with.

**wail** noun & verb howl, cry, bawl, moan, groan, yowl, whine, lament.

**wait** verb 1 *we'll wait in the airport:* stay (put), remain, rest, stop, halt, pause, linger, loiter; informal stick around. 2 *she had to wait until her bags arrived:* stand by, hold back, bide one's time, mark time, kill time, waste time, kick one's heels, twiddle one's thumbs; informal hold on, hang around, sit tight. 3 *that job will have to wait:* be postponed, be delayed, be put off, be deferred; informal be put on the back burner, be put on ice.
noun *a long wait:* delay, hold-up, interval, interlude, pause, break, suspension, stoppage, halt, interruption, lull, gap.

**waiter, waitress** noun server,

steward, stewardess, attendant, butler, servant; N. Amer. waitperson.

**waive** verb **1** *he waived his right to a hearing:* give up, abandon, renounce, relinquish, surrender, sacrifice, turn down. **2** *the manager waived the rules:* disregard, ignore, overlook, set aside, forgo.

**wake**¹ verb **1** *at 4.30 a.m. Mark woke up:* awake, waken, stir, come to, come round. **2** *she woke her husband:* rouse, waken.
OPPOSITES go to sleep, send to sleep.
noun vigil, watch, funeral.
■ **wake up** to realize, become aware of, become conscious of.

**wake**² noun *the cruiser's wake:* backwash, slipstream, trail, path, track.
■ **in the wake of** in the aftermath of, after, subsequent to, following, as a result of, as a consequence of, on account of, because of.

**walk** verb **1** *they walked along the road:* stroll, saunter, amble, trudge, plod, hike, tramp, trek, march, stride, troop, wander, ramble, promenade, traipse; informal mosey, hoof it. **2** *he walked her home:* accompany, escort, guide, show, see, take.
noun **1** *country walks:* ramble, hike, tramp, march, stroll, promenade, constitutional, turn. **2** *her elegant walk:* gait, step, stride, tread. **3** *the riverside walk:* path, pathway, footpath, track, walkway, promenade, footway, pavement, trail, towpath.

**walker** noun rambler, hiker, trekker, stroller, pedestrian.

**wallet** noun purse, case, pouch, holder; N. Amer. billfold, pocketbook.

**wander** verb **1** *I wandered around the estate:* stroll, amble, saunter, walk, potter, ramble, meander, roam, range, drift; Scottish & Irish stravaig; informal traipse, mosey. **2** *we are wandering from the point:* stray, depart, diverge, deviate, digress, drift, get sidetracked.

**wane** verb decline, diminish, decrease, dwindle, shrink, tail off, ebb, fade, lessen, peter out, fall off, recede, slump, weaken, wither, evaporate, die out.
OPPOSITES wax, grow.

**want** verb desire, wish for, hope for, fancy, care for, like, long for, yearn for, crave, hanker after, hunger for, thirst for, cry out for, covet; informal have a yen for, be dying for.
noun **1** *his want of vigilance:* lack, absence, non-existence, dearth, deficiency, inadequacy, insufficiency, paucity, shortage, scarcity. **2** *a time of want:* need, austerity, privation, deprivation, poverty, destitution. **3** *her wants would be taken care of:* wish, desire, demand, longing, fancy, craving, need, requirement; informal yen.

**wanting** adjective deficient, inadequate, lacking, insufficient, imperfect, flawed, unsound, substandard, inferior, second-rate.
OPPOSITES sufficient.

**wanton** adjective deliberate, wilful, malicious, gratuitous, unprovoked, motiveless, arbitrary, unjustifiable, senseless.
OPPOSITES justifiable.

**war** noun **1** *the Napoleonic wars:* conflict, warfare, combat, fighting, action, bloodshed,

a
b
c
d
e
f
g
h
i
j
k
l
m
n
o
p
q
r
s
t
u
v
**w**
x
y
z

struggle, fight, campaign, hostilities, jihad, crusade. **2** *the war against drugs:* campaign, crusade, battle, fight, struggle.
OPPOSITES peace.

verb *rival Emperors warred against each other:* fight, battle, combat, wage war, take up arms, feud, quarrel, struggle, contend, wrangle, cross swords.

**ward** noun **1** *the surgical ward:* room, department, unit, area. **2** *the most marginal ward in Westminster:* district, constituency, division, quarter, zone, parish. **3** *the boy is my ward:* dependant, charge, protégé.

**warden** noun **1** *the flats have a resident warden:* superintendent, caretaker, porter, steward, custodian, watchman, concierge, doorman, commissionaire. **2** *a game warden:* ranger, keeper, guardian, protector. **3** *he was handcuffed to a warden:* prison officer, guard, jailer, warder, keeper; informal screw. **4** (Brit.) *the college warden:* principal, head, governor, master, mistress, rector, provost, dean, president, director, chancellor.

**warehouse** noun storeroom, depot, depository, stockroom, magazine, granary; informal lock-up.

**wares** plural noun goods, merchandise, products, produce, stock, commodities.

**warfare** noun fighting, war, combat, conflict, action, hostilities.

**warm** adjective **1** *a warm kitchen:* hot, cosy, snug. **2** *a warm day:* balmy, summery, sultry, hot, mild, temperate. **3** *warm water:* tepid, lukewarm. **4** *a warm sweater:* thick, chunky, thermal, winter, woolly. **5** *a warm welcome:* friendly, cordial, amiable, genial, kind, pleasant, fond, welcoming, hospitable, hearty.
OPPOSITES cold, chilly, light, hostile.

verb *warm the soup in that pan:* heat (up), reheat.
OPPOSITES chill.

**warmth** noun **1** *the warmth of the fire:* heat, cosiness, snugness. **2** *the warmth of their welcome:* friendliness, amiability, geniality, cordiality, kindness, tenderness, fondness.

**warn** verb **1** *David warned her that it was too late:* inform, notify, tell, alert, apprise, make someone aware, remind; informal tip off. **2** *police are warning galleries to be alert:* advise, exhort, urge, counsel, caution.

**warning** noun **1** *the earthquake came without warning:* (advance) notice, alert, hint, signal, sign, alarm bells; informal a tip-off. **2** *a health warning:* caution, notification, information, exhortation, advice. **3** *a warning of things to come:* omen, premonition, foreboding, prophecy, prediction, forecast, token, portent, signal, sign. **4** *his sentence is a warning to other drunk drivers:* example, deterrent, lesson, caution, message, moral. **5** *a written warning:* reprimand, caution, remonstrance, admonition, censure; informal dressing-down, talking-to, telling-off.

**warp** verb **1** *timber which is too dry will warp:* buckle, twist, bend, distort, deform, curve, bow, contort. **2** *he warped the mind of her child:* corrupt, twist, pervert, deprave.

OPPOSITES straighten.

**warrant** noun 1 *a warrant for his arrest:* authorization, order, writ, mandate, licence, permit, summons. **2** *a travel warrant:* voucher, chit, slip, ticket, coupon, pass.
verb 1 *the charges warranted a severe sentence:* justify, deserve, vindicate, call for, sanction, permit, authorize, excuse, account for, legitimize, support, license, merit, qualify for, rate. **2** *we warrant that the texts do not infringe copyright:* guarantee, promise, affirm, swear, vouch, vow, pledge, undertake, declare, testify.

**warranty** noun guarantee, assurance, promise, commitment, undertaking, pledge, agreement, covenant.

**warrior** noun fighter, soldier, serviceman, combatant.

**wary** adjective 1 *he was trained to be wary:* cautious, careful, circumspect, on one's guard, chary, alert, on the lookout, attentive, heedful, watchful, vigilant, observant. **2** *we are wary of strangers:* suspicious, chary, leery, careful, distrustful.
OPPOSITES inattentive, trustful.

**wash** verb 1 *he washed in the bath:* clean oneself, bathe, shower. **2** *she washed her hands:* clean, cleanse, scrub, wipe, shampoo, lather, sluice, swill, douse, swab, disinfect. **3** *she washed off the blood:* remove, expunge, eradicate, sponge off, scrub off, wipe off, rinse off. **4** *the women were washing clothes:* launder, clean, rinse. **5** *waves washed against the hull:* splash, lap, dash, break, beat, surge, ripple, roll. **6** *the wreckage was washed downriver:* sweep, carry,

convey, transport, deposit.
OPPOSITES dirty.
noun 1 *that shirt should go in the wash:* laundry, washing. **2** *the wash of a motor boat:* backwash, wake, trail, path.
■ **wash something away** erode, abrade, wear away, eat away, undermine.

**waste** verb 1 *he doesn't like to waste money:* squander, misspend, misuse, fritter away, throw away, lavish, dissipate; informal blow, splurge. **2** *kids are wasting away in the streets:* grow weak, grow thin, shrink, wilt, fade, flag, deteriorate. **3** *the disease wasted his legs:* emaciate, atrophy, wither, shrivel, shrink, weaken.
OPPOSITES conserve, thrive.
adjective 1 *waste material:* unwanted, excess, superfluous, left over, scrap, unusable, unprofitable. **2** *waste ground:* uncultivated, barren, desert, arid, bare, desolate.
noun 1 *a waste of money:* misuse, misapplication, abuse, extravagance, lavishness. **2** *household waste:* rubbish, refuse, litter, debris, junk, sewage, effluent; N. Amer. garbage, trash. **3** (**wastes**) desert, wasteland, wilderness, emptiness, wilds.

**wasteful** adjective prodigal, profligate, uneconomical, extravagant, lavish, excessive, imprudent, improvident, spendthrift.
OPPOSITES frugal.

**watch** verb 1 *she watched him as he spoke:* observe, view, look at, eye, gaze at, peer at, contemplate, inspect, scrutinize, scan; informal check out, get a load of, recce, eyeball. **2** *he was being watched*

a
b
c
d
e
f
g
h
i
j
k
l
m
n
o
p
q
r
s
t
u
v
**w**
x
y
z

*by the police:* spy on, keep in sight, keep under surveillance, track, monitor, tail; informal keep tabs on, stake out. **3** *we stayed to watch the boat:* guard, mind, protect, look after, keep an eye on, take care of, shield, defend. OPPOSITES ignore, neglect.
noun **1** *Bill looked at his watch:* wristwatch, timepiece, chronometer. **2** *we kept watch on the yacht:* guard, vigil, lookout, an eye, observation, surveillance.

**watchdog** noun ombudsman, monitor, scrutineer, inspector, supervisor.

**water** verb **1** *water the plants:* sprinkle, moisten, dampen, wet, spray, splash. **2** *my mouth watered:* moisten, become wet, salivate.
■ **water something down 1** *staff had watered down the drinks:* dilute, thin (out), weaken, adulterate. **2** *the proposals were watered down:* tone down, temper, mitigate, moderate, soften, tame.

**waterfall** noun falls, cascade, cataract, rapids.

**wave** verb **1** *he waved his flag:* flap, wag, shake, swish, swing, brandish, flourish, wield. **2** *the grass waved in the breeze:* ripple, flutter, undulate, stir, flap, sway, shake, quiver. **3** *the waiter waved them closer:* gesture, signal, beckon, motion.
noun **1** *she gave him a friendly wave:* signal, sign, motion, gesture. **2** *he surfs the big waves:* breaker, roller, comber, boomer, ripple; (**waves**) swell, surf. **3** *a wave of emigration:* rush, flow, surge, flood, stream, tide, deluge, spate. **4** *a wave of self-pity:* surge, rush, stab, upsurge, sudden feeling.

**waver** verb **1** *the candlelight wavered in the draught:* flicker, quiver. **2** *his voice wavered:* falter, wobble, tremble, quaver. **3** *he wavered between the choices:* hesitate, dither, be irresolute, be undecided, vacillate, blow hot and cold; Brit. haver, hum and haw; informal shilly-shally, sit on the fence.

**way** noun **1** *a way of reducing the damage:* method, process, procedure, technique, system, plan, strategy, scheme, means, mechanism, approach. **2** *she kissed him in her brisk way:* manner, style, fashion, mode. **3** *I've changed my ways:* practice, wont, habit, custom, convention, routine, trait, attribute, peculiarity, idiosyncrasy, conduct, behaviour, manner, style. **4** *which way leads home?* route, course, direction, track, path, access, gate, exit, entrance, door. **5** *a short way downstream:* distance, length, stretch, journey. **6** *April is a long way away:* time, stretch, term, span, duration. **7** *a car coming the other way:* direction, bearing, course, orientation, line, tack. **8** *in some ways, he may be better off:* respect, regard, aspect, facet, sense, detail, point, particular. **9** *the country is in a bad way:* state, condition, situation, circumstances, position, predicament, plight; informal shape.
■ **give way 1** *the government gave way and passed the bill:* yield, back down, surrender, concede defeat, give in, submit; informal throw in the towel/sponge, cave in. **2** *the door gave way:* collapse, give, cave in, fall in, come apart, crumble.

**weak** adjective **1** *they are too weak to move:* feeble, frail, delicate, fragile, infirm, debilitated, decrepit, exhausted; informal weedy. **2** *bats have weak eyes:* inadequate, poor, feeble, defective, faulty, deficient, imperfect, substandard. **3** *a weak excuse:* unconvincing, tenuous, implausible, unsatisfactory, poor, inadequate, feeble, flimsy, lame, hollow; informal pathetic. **4** *a weak bridge:* fragile, frail, rickety, insubstantial, wobbly, unstable, ramshackle, jerry-built, shoddy. **5** *I was too weak to be a rebel:* spineless, craven, cowardly, timid, irresolute, indecisive, ineffectual, meek, tame, soft, faint-hearted; informal yellow, gutless. **6** *a weak light:* dim, pale, wan, faint, feeble, muted. **7** *a weak voice:* indistinct, muffled, muted, hushed, faint, low. **8** *weak coffee:* watery, dilute, watered down, thin.
OPPOSITES strong, powerful, convincing, solid, resolute, bright, loud.

**weaken** verb **1** *the virus weakened him:* enfeeble, debilitate, incapacitate, sap, tire, exhaust. **2** *our morale weakened:* decrease, dwindle, diminish, wane, ebb, subside, peter out, fizzle out, tail off, decline, falter. **3** *the move weakened her authority:* impair, undermine, compromise, lessen.
OPPOSITES strengthen, bolster.

**weakness** noun **1** *with old age came weakness:* frailty, feebleness, fragility, delicacy, debility, incapacity, decrepitude; informal weediness. **2** *he has worked on his weaknesses:* fault, flaw, defect, deficiency, failing, shortcoming, imperfection, Achilles heel. **3** *a weakness for champagne:* fondness, liking, partiality, love, penchant, predilection, inclination, taste. **4** *the President was accused of weakness:* timidity, cravenness, cowardliness, indecision, irresolution, ineffectuality, ineffectiveness, impotence. **5** *the weakness of this argument:* inadequacy, implausibility, poverty, untenability, transparency, flimsiness, hollowness.

**wealth** noun **1** *a gentleman of wealth:* affluence, prosperity, riches, means, fortune, money, cash, capital, treasure, finance; informal wherewithal, dough, bread. **2** *a wealth of information:* abundance, profusion, plethora, mine, store; informal lot, load, mountain, stack, ton; Brit. informal shedload.
OPPOSITES poverty, dearth.

**wealthy** adjective rich, affluent, moneyed, well off, well-to-do, prosperous; informal well heeled, rolling in it, made of money, loaded, flush.
OPPOSITES poor.

**wear** verb **1** *he wore a suit:* dress in, be clothed in, have on, sport. **2** *Barbara wore a smile:* bear, have (on one's face), show, display, exhibit, give, put on, assume. **3** *the bricks have been worn down:* erode, abrade, rub away, grind away, wash away, crumble (away), eat away (at). **4** *the tyres are wearing well:* last, endure, hold up, bear up.
noun **1** *you won't get much wear out of that:* use, service, value; informal mileage. **2** *evening wear:*

clothes, garments, dress, attire, garb, wardrobe; informal get-up, gear, togs; Brit. informal kit, clobber. **3** *the varnish will withstand wear*: damage, friction, abrasion, erosion.
■ **wear off** *the novelty soon wore off*: fade, diminish, lessen, dwindle, decrease, wane, peter out, fizzle out, pall, disappear, vanish. ■ **wear out** deteriorate, become worn, fray, become threadbare, go into holes.
■ **wear someone out** tire out, fatigue, weary, exhaust, drain, sap, enervate; informal whack, poop, shatter, do in; Brit. informal knacker.

**wearing** adjective tiring, exhausting, wearying, fatiguing, enervating, draining, sapping, demanding, exacting, taxing, gruelling, punishing.

**weary** adjective **1** *he was weary after cycling*: tired, worn out, exhausted, fatigued, sapped, spent, drained; informal done in, ready to drop, bushed, shattered; Brit. informal knackered, whacked; N. Amer. informal pooped. **2** *a weary journey*: tiring, exhausting, fatiguing, enervating, draining, sapping, demanding, taxing, arduous, gruelling.
OPPOSITES fresh, keen, refreshing.

**weather** noun *what's the weather like?*: conditions, climate, elements, forecast, outlook.
verb *we weathered the recession*: survive, come through, ride out, pull through, withstand, endure, rise above; informal stick out.

**weave**[1] verb **1** *flowers were woven into their hair*: entwine, lace, twist, knit, braid, plait.

**2** *he weaves colourful plots*: invent, make up, fabricate, construct, create, spin.

**weave**[2] verb *he had to weave his way through the crowds*: thread, wind, wend, dodge, zigzag.

**web** noun **1** *a spider's web*: mesh, net, lattice, lacework, gauze, gossamer. **2** *a web of friendships*: network, nexus, complex, tangle, chain.

**wedded** adjective **1** *wedded bliss*: married, matrimonial, marital, conjugal, nuptial. **2** *he is wedded to his work*: dedicated, devoted, attached, fixated.

**wedding** noun marriage (service), nuptials, union.

**wedge** noun **1** *the door was secured by a wedge*: chock, stop. **2** *a wedge of cheese*: triangle, segment, slice, section, chunk, lump, slab, hunk, block, piece.
verb *she wedged her case between two bags*: squeeze, cram, jam, ram, force, push, shove; informal stuff, bung.

**weep** verb cry, shed tears, sob, snivel, whimper, wail, bawl, keen; Scottish greet; informal boohoo, blub.
OPPOSITES rejoice.

**weigh** verb **1** *she weighs the vegetables*: put on the scales. **2** *he weighed 118 kg*: tip the scales at. **3** *he has to weigh up the possibilities*: consider, contemplate, think about, mull over, chew over, reflect on, ruminate about, muse on, assess, examine, review, explore, take stock of. **4** *they need to weigh benefit against risk*: balance, evaluate, compare, juxtapose, contrast.

**weight** noun **1** *the weight of the book*: mass, heaviness, load, burden. **2** *his recommendation*

*will carry great weight:*
influence, force, leverage, sway,
pull, power, authority; informal
clout. **3** *a weight off her mind:*
burden, load, millstone,
trouble, worry. **4** *the weight of
the evidence is against him:*
most, bulk, majority,
preponderance, body, lion's
share.

**weird** adjective **1** *weird
apparitions:* uncanny, eerie,
unnatural, supernatural,
unearthly, other-worldly,
ghostly, mysterious, strange,
abnormal, unusual; informal
creepy, spooky, freaky. **2** *a
weird sense of humour:* bizarre,
odd, curious, strange, quirky,
outlandish, eccentric,
unconventional, unorthodox,
idiosyncratic, surreal, crazy,
absurd, grotesque, peculiar;
informal wacky, freaky; N. Amer.
informal wacko.
OPPOSITES normal, conventional.

**welcome** noun *a welcome from
the vicar:* greeting, salutation,
reception, hospitality, the red
carpet.
verb **1** *welcome your guests in
their own language:* greet,
salute, receive, meet, usher in.
**2** *we welcomed their decision:*
be pleased by, be glad about,
approve of, applaud, appreciate,
embrace.
OPPOSITES resent, object to.
adjective *welcome news:*
pleasing, agreeable,
encouraging, gratifying,
heartening, promising,
favourable, pleasant.
OPPOSITES unwelcome.

**weld** verb fuse, bond, stick, join,
attach, seal, splice, melt, solder.

**welfare** noun **1** *the welfare of
children:* well-being, health,
comfort, security, safety,

protection, success, interest,
good. **2** *we cannot claim
welfare:* social security, benefit,
public assistance, pension,
credit, support, sick pay,
unemployment benefit; Brit.
informal the dole.

**well¹** adverb **1** *please behave
well:* satisfactorily, nicely,
correctly, properly, fittingly,
suitably, appropriately. **2** *they
get on well together:* amicably,
agreeably, pleasantly, nicely,
happily, harmoniously, amiably,
peaceably; informal famously. **3** *he
plays the piano well:* skilfully,
ably, competently, proficiently,
adeptly, deftly, expertly,
excellently. **4** *treat your
employees well:* decently, fairly,
kindly, generously. **5** *mix the
ingredients well:* thoroughly,
completely, effectively,
rigorously, carefully. **6** *I know
her quite well:* intimately,
thoroughly, deeply, profoundly,
personally. **7** *they studied the
car market well:* carefully,
closely, attentively, rigorously,
in depth, exhaustively, in
detail, meticulously,
scrupulously, methodically,
comprehensively, fully,
extensively. **8** *they speak well of
him:* admiringly, highly,
approvingly, favourably,
appreciatively, warmly,
enthusiastically, glowingly.
**9** *she lives well:* comfortably, in
luxury, prosperously. **10** *you
may well be right:* quite
possibly, conceivably, probably.
**11** *he is well over forty:*
considerably, very much, a
great deal, substantially, easily,
comfortably, significantly.
**12** *she could well afford it:*
easily, comfortably, readily,
effortlessly.
OPPOSITES badly, negligently,

a
b
c
d
e
f
g
h
i
j
k
l
m
n
o
p
q
r
s
t
u
v
**w**
x
y
z

disparagingly, barely.

**adjective 1** *she was completely well again:* healthy, fine, fit, robust, strong, vigorous, blooming, thriving, in fine fettle; informal in the pink. **2** *all is not well:* satisfactory, all right, fine, in order, as it should be, acceptable; informal OK, hunky-dory.
OPPOSITES poorly, unsatisfactory.
■ **as well** too, also, in addition, into the bargain, besides, furthermore, moreover, to boot.
■ **as well as** together with, along with, besides, plus, and, with, on top of, not to mention.

**well²** noun *she drew water from the well:* borehole, spring, waterhole, shaft.
**verb** *tears welled from her eyes:* flow, spill, stream, gush, roll, cascade, flood, spout, burst, issue.

**wet** adjective **1** *wet clothes:* damp, moist, soaked, drenched, saturated, sopping, dripping, soggy, waterlogged, squelchy. **2** *it was cold and wet:* rainy, pouring, teeming, showery, drizzly. **3** *the paint is still wet:* sticky, tacky.
OPPOSITES dry, fine.
**verb** *wet the clothes before ironing them:* dampen, moisten, sprinkle, spray, splash, soak, saturate, flood, douse, drench.
OPPOSITES dry.

**wharf** noun quay, pier, dock, berth, landing, jetty, harbour, dockyard.

**wheel** verb **1** *she wheeled the trolley away:* push, trundle, roll. **2** *the flock of doves wheeled round:* turn, go round, circle, orbit.

**whereabouts** noun location, position, site, situation, spot, point, home, address,
neighbourhood.

**while** noun *we chatted for a while:* time, spell, stretch, stint, span, interval, period; Brit. informal patch.
**verb** *tennis helped to while away the time:* pass, spend, occupy, use up, kill.

**whim** noun impulse, urge, notion, fancy, caprice, vagary, inclination.

**whine** verb **1** *a child was whining:* wail, whimper, cry, mewl, moan, howl, yowl. **2** *the lift began to whine:* hum, drone, beep. **3** *he's always whining about something:* complain, grouse, grouch, grumble, moan, carp; informal gripe, bellyache, whinge.

**whip** noun *he used a whip on his dogs:* lash, scourge, strap, belt.
**verb 1** *he whipped the boy:* flog, lash, scourge, strap, belt, thrash, beat. **2** *then whip the cream:* whisk, beat. **3** *he whipped his listeners into a frenzy:* rouse, stir up, excite, galvanize, electrify, stimulate, inspire, fire up, inflame, provoke.

**whirl** verb **1** *leaves whirled in the wind:* rotate, circle, wheel, turn, revolve, orbit, spin, twirl. **2** *they whirled past:* hurry, race, dash, rush, run, sprint, bolt, career, charge, shoot, hurtle, hare, fly, speed; informal tear, belt; Brit. informal bomb. **3** *his mind was whirling:* spin, reel, swim.
**noun 1** *a whirl of dust:* swirl, flurry, eddy. **2** *the mad social whirl:* hurly-burly, activity, round, bustle, rush, flurry. **3** *Laura's mind was in a whirl:* spin, daze, muddle, jumble, confusion; informal dither.

**whisk** verb **1** *the cable car will*

# whisper → widespread

*whisk you to the top:* speed, hurry, rush, sweep, hurtle, shoot. **2** *she whisked the cloth away:* pull, snatch, pluck, tug, jerk; informal whip, yank. **3** *whisk the egg yolks:* whip, beat, mix.
noun *an egg whisk:* beater, mixer, blender.

**whisper** verb *Alison whispered in his ear:* murmur, mutter, mumble, speak softly, breathe.
OPPOSITES shout.
noun **1** *she spoke in a whisper:* murmur, mutter, mumble, low voice, undertone. **2** *I heard a whisper that he's left town:* rumour, story, report, gossip, speculation, suggestion, hint; informal buzz.
OPPOSITES shout.

**white** adjective *her face went white:* pale, pallid, wan, ashen, chalky, pasty, peaky, washed out, ghostly, deathly.

**whole** adjective **1** *the whole report:* entire, complete, full, unabridged, uncut. **2** *the eggs emerge whole:* intact, in one piece, unbroken, undamaged, flawless, unmarked, perfect.
OPPOSITES incomplete.
noun **1** *a single whole:* entity, unit, body, ensemble. **2** *the whole of the year:* all, every part, the lot, the sum.
■ on the whole overall, all in all, all things considered, for the most part, in the main, in general, by and large, normally, usually, almost always, typically, ordinarily.

**wholehearted** adjective unqualified, unreserved, unconditional, complete, full, total, absolute.
OPPOSITES half-hearted.

**wholesale** adverb *the images were removed wholesale:* extensively, on a large scale, comprehensively, indiscriminately, without exception.
OPPOSITES selectively.
adjective *wholesale destruction:* extensive, widespread, large-scale, wide-ranging, comprehensive, total, mass, indiscriminate.
OPPOSITES partial.

**wholly** adverb completely, totally, absolutely, entirely, fully, thoroughly, utterly, downright, in every respect; informal one hundred per cent.

**wicked** adjective **1** *wicked deeds:* evil, sinful, immoral, wrong, bad, iniquitous, corrupt, base, vile, villainous, criminal, nefarious; informal crooked. **2** *a wicked sense of humour:* mischievous, playful, naughty, impish, roguish, puckish, cheeky.
OPPOSITES virtuous.

**wide** adjective **1** *a wide river:* broad, extensive, spacious, vast, spread out. **2** *a wide range of opinion:* comprehensive, ample, broad, extensive, large, exhaustive, all-inclusive. **3** *his shot was wide:* off target, off the mark, inaccurate.
OPPOSITES narrow.
adverb **1** *he opened his eyes wide:* fully, to the fullest/furthest extent, as far/much as possible. **2** *he shot wide:* off target, wide of the mark/target, inaccurately.

**widen** verb broaden, open up/out, expand, extend, enlarge.

**widespread** adjective general, extensive, universal, common, global, worldwide, omnipresent, ubiquitous, across the board, predominant, prevalent, rife, broad.
OPPOSITES limited.

a b c d e f g h i j k l m n o p q r s t u v **w** x y z

a

b **width** noun breadth, thickness, span, diameter, girth.

**wield** verb 1 *he was wielding a sword:* brandish, flourish, wave, swing, use, employ, handle. 2 *he has wielded power since 1972:* exercise, exert, hold, maintain, command, control.

**wife** noun spouse, partner, mate, consort, bride; informal better half, missus; Brit. informal other half.

**wild** adjective 1 *wild animals:* untamed, undomesticated, feral, fierce, ferocious, savage. 2 *wild flowers:* uncultivated, native, indigenous. 3 *wild hill country:* uninhabited, unpopulated, uncultivated, rugged, rough, inhospitable, desolate, barren. 4 *a wild night:* stormy, squally, tempestuous, turbulent, boisterous. 5 *wild behaviour:* uncontrolled, unrestrained, undisciplined, unruly, rowdy, disorderly, riotous. 6 *Bill's wild schemes:* foolish, ridiculous, ludicrous, stupid, foolhardy, idiotic, madcap, absurd, silly, impractical, impracticable, unworkable; informal crazy, crackpot. 7 *a wild guess:* random, arbitrary, haphazard, uninformed. OPPOSITES tame, cultivated, calm, disciplined.

**wilderness** noun 1 *the Siberian wilderness:* wilds, wastes, desert. 2 *a litter-strewn wilderness:* wasteland.

**wilful** adjective 1 *wilful destruction:* deliberate, intentional, premeditated, planned, conscious. 2 *a wilful child:* headstrong, strong-willed, obstinate, stubborn, pig-headed, recalcitrant, uncooperative; Brit. informal bloody-minded, bolshie. OPPOSITES accidental, amenable.

**will** noun 1 *the will to succeed:* determination, strength of character, resolve, single-mindedness, drive, commitment, dedication, doggedness, tenacity, staying power. 2 *they stayed against their will:* desire, wish, preference, inclination, intention. 3 *God's will:* wish, desire, decision, choice, decree, command.
verb 1 *do what you will:* want, wish, please, see fit, think fit/best, like, choose, prefer. 2 *God willed it:* decree, order, ordain, command.

**willing** adjective 1 *I'm willing to give it a try:* ready, prepared, disposed, inclined, minded, happy, glad, pleased, agreeable, amenable; informal game. 2 *willing help:* readily given, ungrudging. OPPOSITES reluctant.

**willingly** adverb voluntarily, of one's own free will, of one's own accord, readily, without reluctance, ungrudgingly, cheerfully, happily, gladly, with pleasure. OPPOSITES reluctantly.

**willingness** noun readiness, inclination, will, wish, desire. OPPOSITES reluctance.

**wilt** verb 1 *the roses had begun to wilt:* droop, sag, become limp, flop. 2 *we were wilting in the heat:* languish, flag, droop, become listless. OPPOSITES flourish.

**win** verb 1 *Steve won the race:* come first in, take first prize in, triumph in, be successful in. 2 *she was determined to win:* come first, be victorious, carry/

win the day, come out on top, succeed, triumph, prevail. **3** *he won a cash prize:* earn, gain, secure, collect, pick up, walk away/off with, carry off; informal land, net, bag, scoop.
OPPOSITES lose.
noun *a 3–0 win:* victory, triumph, conquest.
OPPOSITES defeat.

**wince** verb grimace, pull a face, flinch, blench, start.

**wind**¹ noun **1** *the trees were swaying in the wind:* breeze, current of air, gale, hurricane, gust, draught; informal blow; literary zephyr. **2** *Jez got his wind back:* breath; informal puff.

**wind**² verb **1** *the road winds up the mountain:* twist (and turn), bend, curve, loop, zigzag, weave, snake. **2** *he wound a towel around his waist:* wrap, furl, entwine, lace. **3** *Anne wound the wool into a ball:* coil, roll, twist, twine.
■ **wind something up 1** *Richard wound up the meeting:* conclude, bring to an end/close, terminate; informal wrap up. **2** *the company has been wound up:* close (down), dissolve, put into liquidation.

**windfall** noun bonanza, jackpot, pennies from heaven, godsend.

**windy** adjective breezy, blowy, fresh, blustery, gusty, wild, stormy, squally.
OPPOSITES still.

**wing** noun **1** *the east wing of the house:* part, section, side, annexe, extension. **2** *the radical wing of the party:* faction, camp, caucus, arm, branch, group, section, set.
verb **1** *a seagull winged its way over the sea:* fly, glide, soar. **2** *she was shot at and winged:* wound, graze, hit.

**wink** verb **1** *he winked an eye at her:* blink, flutter, bat. **2** *the diamond winked in the moonlight:* sparkle, twinkle, flash, glitter, gleam, shine, scintillate.

**winner** noun victor, champion, conqueror, vanquisher, medallist; informal champ, top dog.
OPPOSITES loser.

**winning** adjective **1** *the winning team:* victorious, successful, triumphant, undefeated, conquering, first, top. **2** *a winning smile:* engaging, charming, appealing, endearing, sweet, cute, winsome, attractive, prepossessing, fetching, disarming, captivating.

**winnings** plural noun prize money, gains, booty, spoils, proceeds, profits, takings, purse.

**wipe** verb **1** *Beth wiped the table:* rub, mop, sponge, swab, clean, dry, polish. **2** *he wiped the marks off the window:* rub off, clean off, remove, erase, efface.

**wisdom** noun **1** *we questioned the wisdom of the decision:* understanding, intelligence, sagacity, sense, common sense, shrewdness, astuteness, judgement, prudence, circumspection, logic, rationale, soundness, advisability. **2** *the wisdom of the East:* knowledge, learning, erudition, scholarship, philosophy, lore.
OPPOSITES folly.

**wise** adjective *a wise old man:* sage, sagacious, intelligent, clever, learned, knowledgeable, enlightened, astute, smart, shrewd, sharp-witted, canny, knowing, sensible, prudent, discerning, perceptive.

OPPOSITES foolish.

**wish** verb 1 *they can do as they wish:* want, desire, feel inclined, feel like, care, choose, please, think fit. 2 *I wish you to send them a message:* want, desire, require.
noun 1 *his wish to own a Mercedes:* desire, longing, yearning, whim, craving, hunger, hope, aspiration, aim, ambition, dream; informal hankering, yen. 2 *her parents' wishes:* request, requirement, bidding, instruction, direction, demand, order, command, want, desire, will.
■ wish for desire, want, hope for, covet, dream of, long for, yearn for, crave, hunger for, aspire to, set one's heart on, seek, fancy, hanker after; informal have a yen for.

**wit** noun 1 *he needed all his wits to escape:* intelligence, shrewdness, astuteness, cleverness, canniness, sense, judgement, acumen, insight, brains, mind; informal nous. 2 *my sparkling wit:* wittiness, humour, drollery, repartee, badinage, banter, wordplay, jokes, witticisms, quips, puns. 3 *she's such a wit:* comedian, humorist, comic, joker; informal wag.

**witch** noun 1 *the witch cast a spell:* sorceress, enchantress, hex, Wiccan. 2 (informal) *she's a right old witch:* hag, crone, harpy, harridan, she-devil; informal battleaxe.

**witchcraft** noun sorcery, (black) magic, wizardry, spells, incantations, necromancy, Wicca.

**withdraw** verb 1 *she withdrew her hand from his:* remove, extract, pull out, take out, take back. 2 *the ban on advertising was withdrawn:* abolish, cancel, lift, set aside, end, stop, remove, reverse, revoke, rescind, repeal, annul. 3 *she withdrew the allegation:* retract, take back, go back on, recant, repudiate, renounce, back down, climb down, backtrack, back-pedal, do a U-turn, eat one's words. 4 *the troops withdrew from the city:* retreat, pull out of, evacuate, quit, leave. 5 *his partner withdrew from the project:* pull out of, back out of, bow out of. 6 *they withdrew to their rooms:* retire, retreat, adjourn, decamp, leave, depart, absent oneself; formal repair.
OPPOSITES insert, introduce, deposit, enter.

**withdrawal** noun 1 *the withdrawal of subsidies:* removal, abolition, cancellation, discontinuation, termination, elimination. 2 *the withdrawal of the troops:* departure, pull-out, exit, exodus, evacuation, retreat.

**wither** verb 1 *the flowers withered in the sun:* shrivel (up), dry up, wilt, droop, go limp, fade, perish. 2 *the muscles in his leg withered:* waste (away), shrivel (up), shrink, atrophy. 3 *her confidence withered:* diminish, dwindle, shrink, lessen, fade, wane, evaporate, disappear.
OPPOSITES thrive, grow.

**withering** adjective scornful, contemptuous, scathing, stinging, devastating, humiliating, mortifying.
OPPOSITES admiring.

**withhold** verb 1 *he withheld the information:* hold back, keep back, refuse to give, retain,

hold on to, hide, conceal, keep secret; informal sit on. **2** *she could not withhold her tears*: suppress, repress, hold back, fight back, choke back, control, check, restrain, contain.
OPPOSITES release.

**withstand** verb resist, weather, survive, endure, cope with, stand, tolerate, bear, defy, brave, hold out against.

**witness** noun *witnesses claimed that he started the fight*: observer, onlooker, eyewitness, spectator, viewer, watcher, bystander, passer-by.
verb **1** *who witnessed the incident?* see, observe, watch, view, notice, spot, be present at, attend. **2** *the will is correctly witnessed*: countersign, sign, endorse, validate.

**witty** adjective humorous, amusing, droll, funny, comic, jocular, sparkling, scintillating, entertaining, clever, quick-witted.

**wizard** noun **1** *the wizard cast a spell*: sorcerer, warlock, magus, (black) magician, enchanter. **2** *a financial wizard*: genius, expert, master, virtuoso, maestro, marvel; informal hotshot, whizz-kid; Brit. informal dab hand; N. Amer. informal maven.

**wobble** verb **1** *the table wobbled*: rock, teeter, jiggle, sway, see-saw, shake. **2** *he wobbled across to the door*: teeter, totter, stagger, lurch. **3** *her voice wobbled*: tremble, shake, quiver, quaver, waver.

**wobbly** adjective **1** *a wobbly table*: unsteady, unstable, shaky, rocky, rickety, unsafe, precarious; informal wonky. **2** *her legs were a bit wobbly*: shaky, quivery, weak, unsteady; informal like jelly.

OPPOSITES stable.

**woe** noun **1** *a tale of woe*: misery, sorrow, distress, sadness, unhappiness, heartache, heartbreak, despair, adversity, misfortune, disaster, suffering, hardship. **2** *financial woes*: trouble, difficulty, problem, trial, tribulation, misfortune, setback, reverse.
OPPOSITES joy.

**woman** noun lady, female; Scottish & N. English lass; Irish colleen; informal chick; N. Amer. informal sister, dame, broad; Austral./NZ informal sheila; literary damsel.

**womanly** adjective **1** *womanly virtues*: feminine, female. **2** *her womanly figure*: voluptuous, curvaceous, shapely, ample, buxom, full-figured; informal curvy, busty.
OPPOSITES manly, boyish.

**wonder** noun **1** *she was speechless with wonder*: awe, admiration, fascination, surprise, astonishment, amazement. **2** *the wonders of nature*: marvel, miracle, phenomenon, sensation, spectacle, beauty, curiosity.
verb **1** *I wondered what was on her mind*: ponder, think about, meditate on, reflect on, muse on, speculate about, conjecture, be curious about. **2** *people wondered at such bravery*: marvel, be amazed, be astonished, stand in awe, be dumbfounded; informal be flabbergasted.

**wonderful** adjective marvellous, magnificent, superb, glorious, sublime, lovely, delightful; informal super, great, fantastic, terrific, tremendous, sensational, fabulous, awesome, magic,

a
b
c
d
e
f
g
h
i
j
k
l
m
n
o
p
q
r
s
t
u
v
**w**
x
y
z

wicked; Brit. informal smashing, brilliant; N. Amer. informal peachy, dandy, neat; Austral./NZ informal beaut, bonzer.

**woo** verb 1 *Richard wooed Joan:* pay court to, pursue, chase (after); dated court, romance, seek the hand of. 2 *the party wooed voters with promises:* seek, pursue, curry favour with, try to win, try to attract, try to cultivate. 3 *an attempt to woo him out of retirement:* entice, tempt, coax, persuade, wheedle, seduce; informal sweet-talk.

**wood** noun 1 *polished wood:* timber, planks, logs; N. Amer. lumber. 2 *a walk through the woods:* forest, woodland, trees, copse, coppice, grove; Brit. spinney.

**wooded** adjective forested, afforested, tree-covered; literary sylvan.

**wooden** adjective 1 *a wooden door:* wood, timber. 2 *wooden acting:* stilted, stiff, unnatural, awkward, flat, stodgy, lifeless, soulless. 3 *her face was wooden:* expressionless, impassive, poker-faced, emotionless, blank, vacant, unresponsive.

**wool** noun fleece, hair, coat.

**word** noun 1 *the Italian word for 'ham':* term, name, expression, designation. 2 *his words were meant kindly:* remark, comment, observation, statement, utterance. 3 *I've got three weeks to learn my words:* script, lines, lyrics, libretto. 4 *I give you my word:* promise, assurance, guarantee, undertaking, pledge, vow, oath, bond. 5 *I want a word with you:* talk, conversation, chat, tête-à-tête, heart-to-heart, one-to-one, discussion; informal confab.

6 *there's no word from the hospital:* news, information, communication, intelligence, message, report, communiqué, dispatch, bulletin.
verb *the question was carefully worded:* phrase, express, put, couch, frame, formulate, style.

**wording** noun phrasing, phraseology, language, words, expression, terminology.

**wordy** adjective long-winded, verbose, lengthy, rambling, garrulous, voluble; informal windy; Brit. informal waffly.
OPPOSITES succinct.

**work** noun 1 *a day's work in the fields:* labour, toil, slog, drudgery, exertion, effort; informal grind, sweat; Brit. informal graft. 2 *I'm looking for work:* employment, job, post, position, situation, occupation, profession, career, vocation, calling. 3 *haven't you got any work?* tasks, jobs, duties, assignments, projects, chores. 4 *works of literature:* composition, piece, creation, opus. 5 *this is the work of a radical faction:* handiwork, doing, act, deed. 6 *a lifetime spent doing good works:* deeds, acts, actions, turns. 7 *the complete works of Shakespeare:* writings, oeuvre, canon, output. 8 *a car works:* factory, plant, mill, workshop, facility. 9 *the works of a clock:* mechanism, machinery, workings, parts, movement, action; informal insides.
OPPOSITES leisure, pleasure.
verb 1 *staff worked late into the night:* labour, toil, exert oneself, slave (away); informal slog (away), beaver away; Brit. informal graft. 2 *he worked in education for years:* be

employed, have a job, earn one's living, do business. **3** *farmers worked the land:* cultivate, farm, till, plough. **4** *his car was working perfectly:* function, go, run, operate; informal behave. **5** *how do I work this machine?* operate, use, handle, control, manipulate, run. **6** *their ploy worked:* succeed, turn out well, go as planned, get results, be effective; informal come off, pay off, do the trick. **7** *blusher can work miracles:* achieve, accomplish, bring about, produce, perform. **8** *he worked the crowd into a frenzy:* stir (up), excite, drive, move, rouse, fire, galvanize; whip up, agitate. **9** *work the mixture into a paste:* knead, squeeze, form; mix, stir, blend. **10** *he worked the blade into the padlock:* manipulate, manoeuvre, guide, squeeze, edge. **11** *he worked his way through the crowd:* manoeuvre, make, thread, wind, weave, wend, elbow.
OPPOSITES rest, fail.

■ **work something out 1** *work out what you can afford:* calculate, compute, reckon up, determine. **2** *I'm trying to work out what she meant:* understand, comprehend, puzzle out, sort out, make sense of, get to the bottom of, make head or tail of, unravel, decipher, decode; informal figure out; Brit. informal suss out. **3** *they worked out a plan:* devise, formulate, draw up, put together, develop, construct, arrange, organize, contrive, concoct; hammer out, negotiate.

**worker** noun employee, member of staff, workman, labourer, hand, operator, operative, agent, wage-earner, breadwinner, proletarian.

**workshop** noun **1** *an ideal set of tools for a workshop:* workroom, studio, factory, works, plant, industrial unit. **2** *a workshop on combating stress:* study group, discussion group, seminar, forum, class.

**world** noun **1** *he travelled the world:* earth, globe, planet, sphere. **2** *the academic world:* sphere, society, circle, arena, milieu, province, domain, preserve, realm, field. **3** (**the world**) *the world would hear of her achievements:* everyone, people, mankind, humankind, humanity, the public, all and sundry.

**worldly** adjective **1** *worldly pursuits:* earthly, terrestrial, temporal, mundane, mortal, human, material, physical. **2** *a worldly man:* sophisticated, experienced, worldly-wise, knowledgeable, knowing, enlightened, mature, seasoned, cosmopolitan, urbane, cultured.
OPPOSITES spiritual, naive.

**worldwide** adjective global, international, intercontinental, universal, ubiquitous.
OPPOSITES local.

**worn** adjective shabby, worn out, threadbare, in tatters, falling to pieces, ragged, frayed, moth-eaten, scruffy, having seen better days.
OPPOSITES new, smart.

**worried** adjective anxious, troubled, bothered, concerned, uneasy, fretful, agitated, nervous, edgy, tense, apprehensive, fearful, afraid, frightened; Brit. informal in a stew, in a flap.
OPPOSITES carefree.

**worry** verb **1** *she worries about*

a
b
c
d
e
f
g
h
i
j
k
l
m
n
o
p
q
r
s
t
u
v
**w**
x
y
z

*his health:* be anxious, be concerned, fret, agonize, brood, panic, lose sleep, get worked up; informal get in a flap, get in a state. **2** *is something worrying you?* trouble, bother, make anxious, disturb, distress, upset, concern, unsettle, perturb, scare, prey on someone's mind; informal bug, get to.
noun **1** *I'm beside myself with worry:* anxiety, distress, concern, unease, disquiet, nerves, agitation, edginess, tension, apprehension, fear, misgiving; informal butterflies. **2** *the rats are a worry:* problem, cause for concern, nuisance, pest, trial, trouble, bane, bugbear; informal pain, headache, hassle.
OPPOSITES peace of mind.

**worsen** verb **1** *insomnia can worsen a patient's distress:* aggravate, add to, intensify, increase, compound, magnify, heighten, inflame, exacerbate. **2** *the recession worsened:* deteriorate, degenerate, decline; informal go downhill.
OPPOSITES improve.

**worship** noun **1** *the worship of saints:* reverence, veneration, adoration, glorification, exaltation, devotion, praise, thanksgiving, homage, honour. **2** *morning worship:* service, rite, prayer, praise, devotion, observance.
verb **1** *they worship pagan gods:* revere, pray to, pay homage to, honour, adore, venerate, praise, glorify, exalt. **2** *he absolutely worshipped her:* love, cherish, treasure, hold dear, esteem, adulate, idolize, deify, hero-worship, lionize; informal put on a pedestal.
OPPOSITES mock, despise, shun.

**worth** noun **1** *evidence of the rug's worth:* value, price, cost, valuation, estimate. **2** *the intrinsic worth of education:* benefit, good, advantage, use, value, virtue, desirability, sense.

**worthless** adjective **1** *the item was worthless:* valueless. **2** *a mountain of worthless information:* useless, pointless, meaningless, senseless, inconsequential, ineffective, ineffectual, fruitless, unproductive, unavailing, valueless. **3** *his worthless son:* good-for-nothing, ne'er-do-well, useless, despicable, contemptible, degenerate; informal no-good, lousy.
OPPOSITES valuable, useful, worthy.

**worthwhile** adjective valuable, useful, of service, beneficial, rewarding, advantageous, positive, helpful, profitable, gainful, fruitful, productive, constructive, effective.

**worthy** adjective *a worthy citizen:* good, righteous, virtuous, moral, ethical, upright, respectable, upstanding, high-minded, principled, reputable, decent.
OPPOSITES disreputable.
noun *local worthies:* dignitary, personage, grandee, VIP, notable, pillar of society, luminary, leading light; informal bigwig.
OPPOSITES nobody.

**would-be** adjective aspiring, budding, promising, prospective, potential, hopeful, keen, eager, ambitious; informal wannabe.

**wound** noun **1** *a chest wound:* injury, cut, gash, laceration, graze, scratch, abrasion,

# wrap → wrinkle

puncture, lesion; Medicine trauma. **2** *the wounds inflicted by the media:* insult, blow, slight, offence, affront, hurt, damage, injury.
**verb 1** *he was critically wounded:* injure, hurt, harm, lacerate, cut, graze, gash, stab, slash, wing. **2** *her words had wounded him:* hurt, insult, slight, offend, affront, distress, grieve, pain, sting.

**wrap verb 1** *she wrapped herself in a towel:* enclose, enfold, envelop, encase, cover, fold, wind, swathe, bundle, swaddle. **2** *I wrapped the vase carefully:* pack, package, parcel up, bundle (up), gift-wrap.
**noun** *he put a wrap round her:* shawl, stole, cloak, cape, mantle, scarf.

**wrath noun** anger, rage, temper, fury, outrage, spleen, resentment, (high) dudgeon, indignation.
OPPOSITES happiness.

**wreath noun** garland, circlet, chaplet, crown, festoon, lei, ring, loop, circle.

**wreathe verb 1** *a pulpit wreathed in holly:* festoon, garland, drape, cover, deck, decorate, ornament, adorn. **2** *blue smoke wreathed upwards:* spiral, coil, loop, wind, curl, twist, snake.

**wreck noun 1** *salvage teams landed on the wreck:* shipwreck, sunken ship, hull. **2** *the wreck of a stolen car:* wreckage, debris, ruins, remains, burnt-out shell.
**verb 1** *he had wrecked her car:* destroy, break, demolish, crash, smash up, write off; N. Amer. informal trash, total. **2** *the crisis wrecked his plans:* ruin, spoil, disrupt, undo, put a stop to, frustrate, blight, crush, dash, destroy, scotch, shatter, devastate, sabotage; informal mess up, screw up, put paid to, stymie; Brit. informal scupper.

**wrench noun 1** *she felt a wrench on her shoulders:* tug, pull, jerk, jolt, heave; informal yank. **2** *hold the piston with a wrench:* spanner. **3** *leaving was an immense wrench:* blow, ache, trauma, pang.
**verb 1** *he wrenched the gun from her:* tug, pull, jerk, wrest, heave, twist, force, prise; N. Amer. pry; informal yank. **2** *she wrenched her ankle:* sprain, twist, turn, strain, rick, crick.

**wrestle verb** grapple, fight, struggle, scuffle, tussle, brawl; informal scrap.

**wretched adjective 1** *I felt so wretched without you:* miserable, unhappy, sad, heartbroken, grief-stricken, distressed, desolate, devastated, disconsolate, downcast, dejected, depressed, melancholy, forlorn. **2** *wretched living conditions:* harsh, hard, grim, difficult, poor, pitiful, piteous, pathetic, tragic, miserable, bleak, cheerless, hopeless, sorry, sordid; informal crummy.
OPPOSITES cheerful, comfortable.

**wriggle verb** *she tried to hug him but he wriggled:* squirm, writhe, wiggle, thresh, flounder, flail, twitch, twist and turn, snake, worm.
■ **wriggle out of** avoid, shirk, dodge, evade, sidestep; escape; informal duck.

**wrinkle noun** *fine wrinkles around her mouth:* crease, fold, pucker, line, crinkle, furrow, ridge, groove; informal crow's feet.

a b c d e f g h i j k l m n o p q r s t u v **w** x y z

a
b
c
d
e
f
g
h
i
j
k
l
m
n
o
p
q
r
s
t
u
v

**verb** *his coat tails wrinkled up:* crease, pucker, gather, crinkle, crumple, rumple, ruck up, scrunch up.

**write** verb **1** *he wrote her name in the book:* put in writing, put down, jot down, note (down), take down, record, inscribe, sign, scribble, scrawl, pen, pencil. **2** *I wrote a poem:* compose, draft, think up, formulate, compile, pen, dash off, produce. **3** *he promised to write:* correspond, communicate, get in touch, keep in contact; informal drop someone a line.

**writer** noun author, wordsmith; informal scribbler, scribe, pen-pusher, hack.

**writing** noun **1** *I can't read his writing:* handwriting, hand, script, calligraphy, lettering, print, printing; informal scribble, scrawl. **2** *this fear did not show in her writing:* written work, compositions, books, publications, papers, articles, essays, oeuvre.

**wrong** adjective **1** *the wrong answer:* incorrect, mistaken, erroneous, inaccurate, inexact, imprecise; informal off beam, out. **2** *he knew he had said the wrong thing:* inappropriate, unsuitable, ill-advised, ill-considered, ill-judged, unwise, infelicitous; informal out of order. **3** *I've done nothing wrong:* bad,

dishonest, illegal, unlawful, illicit, criminal, corrupt, unethical, immoral, wicked, sinful, iniquitous, nefarious, reprehensible; informal crooked. **4** *there's something wrong with the engine:* amiss, awry, out of order, not right, faulty, defective.
OPPOSITES right, correct, appropriate, legal.
**adverb** *she guessed wrong:* incorrectly, wrongly, inaccurately, erroneously, mistakenly.
**noun 1** *the difference between right and wrong:* immorality, sin, wickedness, evil, illegality, unlawfulness, crime, corruption, villainy, dishonesty, injustice, misconduct, transgression. **2** *an attempt to make up for past wrongs:* misdeed, offence, injury, crime, transgression, sin, injustice, outrage, atrocity.
OPPOSITES right.
**verb** *she was determined to forget the man who had wronged her:* mistreat, ill-use, ill-treat, do an injustice to, abuse, harm, hurt, injure.

**wrongdoer** noun offender, lawbreaker, criminal, felon, delinquent, villain, culprit, evil-doer, sinner, transgressor, malefactor, miscreant, rogue, scoundrel; informal crook, wrong 'un.

# Xx

w
x
y
z

**xenophobic** adjective jingoistic, chauvinistic, flag-waving, nationalistic, isolationist, prejudiced, bigoted, intolerant.

# Yy

**yank** verb & noun (informal) jerk, pull, tug, wrench.

**yarn** noun thread, cotton, wool, fibre, filament.

**yawning** adjective gaping, wide, cavernous, deep, huge, vast.

**yearly** adjective annual.
adverb annually, once a year, per annum, each/every year.

**yearn** verb long, pine, crave, desire, want, wish, hanker, covet, hunger, thirst, ache; informal itch.

**yell** verb *he yelled in agony:* shout, cry out, howl, wail, scream, shriek, screech, yelp, squeal, roar, bawl.
noun *a yell of rage:* shout, cry, howl, scream, shriek, screech, yelp, squeal, roar.

**yellow** adjective golden, gold, blonde, fair, flaxen.

**yes** adverb certainly, very well, of course, by all means, sure, all right, absolutely, indeed, affirmative, agreed, roger; Scottish & N. English: aye; Nautical aye aye; informal yeah, yep, uh-huh, okay, OK; Brit. informal righto, righty-ho; N. Amer. informal surely.
OPPOSITES no.

**yet** adverb 1 *he hasn't made up his mind yet:* so far, as yet, up to now, up till now. 2 *don't celebrate just yet:* (right) now, at this time, already, so soon. 3 *he did nothing, yet he seemed happy:* nevertheless, nonetheless, even so, but, however, still, notwithstanding, despite that, in spite of that, for all that, all the same, just the same, at the same time.

4 *yet more advice:* even, still.

**yield** verb 1 *such projects yield poor returns:* produce, bear, give, provide, afford, return, bring in, earn, realize, generate, deliver, pay out. 2 *Duke was forced to yield:* surrender, capitulate, submit, admit defeat, back down, give in.
OPPOSITES withhold, resist.
noun *we expected a higher yield:* profit, gain, return, dividend, earnings.
■ **yield to** give in to, give way to, submit to, comply with, agree to, consent to, go along with, grant, permit, allow; informal cave in to; formal accede to.

**yob, yobbo** noun (Brit. informal) lout, thug, hooligan, tearaway, vandal, ruffian, troublemaker; Austral. larrikin; informal tough, bruiser; Brit. informal lager lout; Scottish informal ned.

**young** adjective 1 *young people:* youthful, juvenile, junior, adolescent, teenage. 2 *she's very young for her age:* immature, childish, inexperienced, naive, green. 3 *a young industry:* fledgling, developing, budding, in its infancy, emerging.
OPPOSITES old, mature.
noun 1 *a robin feeding its young:* offspring, progeny, family, babies, litter, brood. 2 *the young don't care nowadays:* young people, children, boys and girls, youngsters, youth, the younger generation, juveniles, minors; informal kids.
OPPOSITES old.

a b c d e f g h i j k l m n o p q r s t u v w x **y** z

**youngster** noun child, teenager, adolescent, youth, juvenile, minor, junior, boy, girl; Scottish & N. English lass, lassie; informal lad, kid, whippersnapper, teen.

**youth** noun 1 *he was a fine athlete in his youth:* early years, teens, teenage years, adolescence, boyhood, girlhood, childhood, minority. 2 *local youths:* young man, boy, juvenile, teenager, adolescent, junior, minor; informal lad, kid. 3 *the youth of the nation:* young people, young, younger generation, next generation; informal kids.
OPPOSITES adulthood, old age, elderly.

**youthful** adjective young, boyish, girlish, fresh-faced, young-looking, spry, sprightly, vigorous, active.
OPPOSITES elderly.

# Zz

**zany** adjective eccentric, odd, unconventional, bizarre, weird, mad, crazy, comic, madcap, quirky, idiosyncratic; informal wacky, oddball, off the wall; Brit. informal daft; N. Amer. informal kooky, wacko.
OPPOSITES conventional, sensible.

**zeal** noun enthusiasm, passion, ardour, fervour, fire, devotion, gusto, vigour, energy.
OPPOSITES apathy.

**zero** noun 1 *the answer is zero:* nought, nothing, nil, o. 2 *there was absolutely zero I could do about it:* nothing (at all), nil, none; N. English nowt; informal zilch, not a dicky bird; Brit. informal damn all, not a sausage; N. Amer. informal zip, nada.

**zigzag** verb twist, meander, snake, wind, weave, swerve.

**zone** noun area, sector, section, belt, stretch, region, territory, district, quarter, neighbourhood.

**zoom** verb (informal) *he zoomed off:* hurry, rush, dash, race, speed, sprint, career, shoot, hurtle, hare, fly; informal tear, belt; Brit. informal bomb.